"How Can You Say That"

she cried, her voice thick with her tears. "I don't understand why you *hate* me. . . ."

"I don't hate you," he denied quickly, without thinking. When the words had been spoken, he knew at once that they were true. He didn't hate her, but whatever it was that he felt was as strong as hate at times. It brought out his most intense emotions. "I don't hate you," he said again, more deliberately. "It's just that you get under my skin more than anyone I've ever known."

CAROLE HALSTON
lives with her husband Monty, a professional seaman, on the north shore of Lake Pontchartrain, in Mandeville, Louisiana, thirty minutes from downtown New Orleans, ten minutes from the racquet club where they play tennis, and three minutes from the marina where their 31′ cruising sloop *Autumn Wind* is berthed.

Dear Reader:

Romance readers have been enthusiastic about Silhouette Special Editions for years. And that's not by accident: Special Editions were the first of their kind and continue to feature realistic stories with heightened romantic tension.

The longer stories, sophisticated style, greater sensual detail and variety that made Special Editions popular are the same elements that will make you want to read book after book.

We hope that you enjoy this Special Edition today, and will enjoy many more.

The Editors at Silhouette Books

CAROLE HALSTON
A Common Heritage

Silhouette Special Edition

Published by Silhouette Books New York

America's Publisher of Contemporary Romance

 SILHOUETTE BOOKS

Copyright © 1985 by Carole Halston
Cover artwork copyright © 1985 Roger Kastel

Distributed by Pocket Books

All rights reserved, including the right to reproduce
this book or portions thereof in any form whatsoever.
For information address Silhouette Books

ISBN: 0-373-09000-5

First Silhouette Books printing January, 1985

10 9 8 7 6 5 4 3 2 1

All of the characters in this book are fictitious. Any resemblance to actual persons, living or dead, is purely coincidental.

Map by Ray Lundgren

SILHOUETTE, SILHOUETTE SPECIAL EDITION and
colophon are registered trademarks

America's Publisher of Contemporary Romance

Printed in the U.S.A.

Books by Carole Halston

Silhouette Romance

Silhouette Special Edition

Special thanks to Hildegard and Nils; Solbritt and Gerard, our Swedish friends who welcomed us into their homes and spared no trouble in showing us their beautiful country.

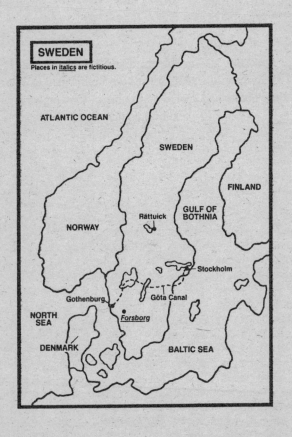

SWEDEN

Places in _italics_ are fictitious.

ATLANTIC OCEAN

SWEDEN

FINLAND

GULF OF BOTHNIA

NORWAY

Rättuick

Stockholm

Gothenburg

Göta Canal

NORTH SEA

Forsborg

DENMARK

BALTIC SEA

Chapter One

Richard Maxwell—"Max" to his employees, friends, and clients—paused at the open archway of one of the showrooms in his successful interior decorating establishment. He regarded the lone occupant of the room with mild surprise, but bit back the instinctive greeting that came to his lips. When he spoke, the words and tone were blandly tactful.

"Why, B.G., you're back. I didn't expect you until the end of the week. I know how a funeral can turn into a family reunion, with relatives converging from far and wide."

Like most people, Max found it extremely awkward to be in the presence of a bereaved person. He never knew quite what to say. One didn't want to be too cheerful and appear callous, but on the other hand, one didn't want to be morbid, either, and become mired in emotion. In this particular instance, he was at a disadvantage because he didn't know if B.G. had been close to her grandmother or not.

To Max's utter surprise, the young woman he had addressed, who was standing at a glass-topped table and flipping through some samples of silkscreen wallpaper that had arrived in her absence, now looked around at him with sharp irritation. He was taken aback first because the expression was one he had seen so seldom on her features and secondly because her reaction seemed so inappropriate to the occasion. What had there been in his words to irritate her?

"*I* had farther to go than anyone else in the family," she replied crossly. "And I swear, you'd think I was some kind of *traitor* because I moved out of the county. As far as my family is concerned, living in Minneapolis is as farfetched as living in *Timbuktu!*"

Max raised his eyebrows a fraction, momentarily at a loss for words in the face of B.G.'s unexpected bad temper, and surprised at her personal revelation itself. He knew that grief can manifest itself in many guises, including anger. While uncertain of exactly what he should do or say next, he was nonetheless definitely curious.

B.G. Jensen had come to *Maxwell's* six years ago when she was twenty, having opted to drop out of college after two years and learn the interior decorating business the hard way. She had begun as a lowly staff assistant, uncomplainingly running errands for the decorators Max employed, and worked herself up until now she was building a solid reputation as one of his best interior decorators. During the six years in Max's employ, she had mentioned virtually nothing of her family background.

One look at her was enough to establish her Scandinavian blood. Her hair was that blond color infused with sunlight, the kind that doesn't come in a bottle, despite the advertising claims to the contrary. Her eyes were the deep fathomless blue of the sky on a brilliant autumn day. Her complexion was the kind that tanned more gold than brown and with little inducement. Privately Max had always thought that B.G. would be a natural for those slick magazine ads featuring the outdoors type of girl. He could quite easily visualize her attired in a bright red ski outfit, poised at the top of a ski slope with the grandeur of the Alps in the background.

All he knew about her family background was that she had grown up in a rural farming area of Minnesota that was heavily settled by Swedish immigrants. Somehow Max had gotten the impression that B.G. probably didn't go home often to visit her family. Once or twice a year, usually following a major holiday like Christmas or Easter, she would come to work bearing homemade cheeses, rich bottled preserves, and loaves of crusty bread, all of which were greedily snatched up by her co-workers and by Max himself.

Feeling himself in the need right now for some safe, neutral subject, Max seized upon the homemade goods that B.G.'s mother presumably lavished upon her when she returned home for a visit.

"You didn't happen to bring back a supply of that fantastic homemade cheese, did you?" he inquired a trifle too heartily, taking several steps into the room. "If you did, I want to get my name in early before those scavengers I call employees make off with everything."

"Of course, I brought some back with me!" The underlying shrillness of the retort brought strange prickles to Max's neckline. "Also enough jam and jelly and bread to put ten pounds on half the population of Minneapol—*is*—" B.G.'s voice cracked on the last syllable. She swallowed hard at the pain in her throat. As though realizing intuitively that she needed all her strength to master the onslaught of emotion threatening her, she felt behind her for the chrome arms of a black leather director's chair and sank down abruptly. With one hand balled up into a fist and pressed to the corner of her trembling mouth, she continued in a ragged, indistinct voice.

"Max, would you tell me why people make such a fuss over people dying? Especially old people, like my grandmother. She was *old*, Max, I tell you! She had a long, full life." B.G. dropped the clenched fist to her lap and eyed Max defiantly, as though she expected him to make some argument. He said nothing, since he was quite at a loss as to what to say.

"And what's more," B.G. was continuing, the vehemence in her tone gaining strength, "she lived her life exactly the way she wanted to! That's what everyone should do—don't you agree?—live their lives the way *they* want to live them!"

Max was certain now that B.G. was genuinely distressed over her grandmother's death. Apparently the anger she was displaying was her own peculiar way of expressing her grief.

Placing a chair just like hers close to her, Max sat down and leaned a little sideways so that he could place his arm around B.G.'s shoulders, which she held so rigidly that he could feel the tension in her body. The situation clearly called for some sympathetic understanding on his part, and he was prepared to give the effort his best, ill-equipped as he felt for the task.

"Look, honey, there's nothing wrong in feeling rotten when a member of your family passes away," he pointed out soothingly. "Even if the person *is* elderly and has had a good life."

Max's words had a more drastic effect than he could possibly have anticipated. The shoulders beneath his arm slumped forward and then began heaving with great convulsive sobs. Max pulled her against his chest, patted her back tenderly, and generally felt inadequate as he murmured soothing words.

"There, now. There. You just go ahead and cry it out."

It was the first time Max had ever held B.G. in his arms, and though the thought had occurred to him more than once, these were certainly not the circumstances he would have chosen. In his early fifties, divorced, attractive, with hair graying at the temples and a body kept carefully trim, Max led an active social life, more often than not squiring female companions whose age was closer to B.G.'s than to his own.

His better judgment had always kept him from trying to date B.G. For one thing, he knew that it was better in almost all instances to keep business separate from pleasure. B.G. was a damned good decorator and an asset to his firm. Max didn't want to risk losing her. But aside from that pragmatic bit of wisdom, Max, cynic that he was, also didn't want to risk hurting B.G., and he suspected that she was softer and more vulnerable than she appeared.

He was just beginning to feel somewhat less awkward in his role of comforter when her sobs lessened and then stopped. She pulled away from him and sat up straight, wiping at tear-drenched cheeks with the palms of her hands.

"I'm awfully sorry, Max, for breaking down on you like that," she apologized wanly, making little hiccuping sounds between words. Max was amazed at the fatherly urge that made him want to take her back into his arms and reassure her that everything would be all right.

"Any time," he declared with a show of heartiness intended to dissipate the gloom. He didn't know whether he should assume that the worst was over and leave her to the privacy of her grief or stay there and encourage her to talk. Before he could decide what to do, the choice was taken out of his hands.

"Max, remember when you interviewed me for this job six years ago and you asked me what B.G. stood for?" B.G. asked sadly.

"Sure, I remember," Max replied promptly, trying not to sound bewildered by her unexpected question. "What was the answer you gave me? Betty Grable, as I recall. It was the same thing as telling me to mind my own business." His jocular tone was designed to draw a smile from her, but there wasn't a flicker of response to his lightness. She was looking straight ahead with her chin slightly lifted and her profile to Max.

"My real name is Birgitta. I was named after my grandmother, the same one who just died. She could never understand why I didn't like the name *Birgitta*. I tried to tell her it was nothing personal, that I simply didn't want to be named a Swedish name. But she couldn't . . . *wouldn't* understand—"

Max watched the cords in her throat tighten visibly and shut off her voice as she swallowed hard. For the life of him, he couldn't think of a thing to say that wouldn't sound impossibly banal, and yet he wished with all his heart and soul that he could think of *something* to say or do that would defuse the situation. He could sense the storm clouds of emotion building up in her again, and he dreaded the next eruption.

"Why would that be so hard for anyone to understand?" B.G. was continuing, her voice growing more strident and raising prickles along Max's neck again. "I'm an *American,* Max—not a Swede. I wanted a name that sounded American, not Swedish!"

"How on earth did you come up with B.G.?" Max put in hastily, half rising from his chair and yanking it around at an angle to hers so that they weren't sitting so close and side by side. He'd begun to feel like a priest in a confessional, and it wasn't a feeling he liked.

"A girlfriend and I thought it up. It was during the summer before we both started at the big county high school. The name stuck. In no time at all, I really felt like B.G.—not Birgitta. To this day, I just don't *feel* like a Birgitta, Max!" She turned her head to meet his gaze, her eyes begging him to understand. "I never wanted to hurt my grandmother *or* my parents, Max. I *swear* I didn't!" She swallowed hard and continued in a voice barely audible. "How could I explain to them that I didn't want to be a . . . *dumb Swede?*"

Max shifted uneasily in his chair. He knew how cruel people of any age—but especially adolescents—could be in setting up arbitrary standards of acceptance. It varied from one region of the United States to another, but there was usually some ethnic group to serve as the scapegoat of jokes. Chicago had its "Polacks," Michigan its "Hollanders," and Minnesota its "dumb Swedes."

"I know, of course, that I *did* hurt them," B.G. was continuing reflectively. "And not just by changing my name. I made it all too clear that I didn't approve of them. I believed then—and I believe now—that people who come to this country and become American citizens should want to be Americans, in every sense of the word. They should adopt American ways and speak the American language, instead of forming tight little foreign communities. After all, if it had really been so good back home, they would have *stayed* there!" she concluded grimly.

Max raised his eyebrows and whistled softly, fleetingly glad that *he* hadn't had to face this very opinionated young woman's censure.

"You *told* your parents and your grandparents all that?"

B.G.'s eyes did battle with Max's gaze for a long moment. Then without warning her mood changed swiftly again, and she turned imploring as she continued in what seemed an effort to convince him that she had been right in her youthful outspokenness with her family.

"Max, my father was only fourteen when he came to this country with his parents in the 1930s. My mother was twelve when she came over with her parents at about the same time. They both were young enough to change, to become a part of the society they were moving into. But would you believe that they *still* speak Swedish better than they speak English? Now I ask you, isn't that incredible?"

Max smoothed his impeccably combed hair with a restless hand and searched for a tactful way to phrase the obvious question: Wasn't all this water under the bridge at this stage in B.G.'s life? Why was she agonizing over the past? He supposed that her grandmother's death had caused old guilts to resurface, but he honestly lacked the nerve to suggest that B.G.'s turbulent emotions centered around just that—guilt.

"It's just so unfair, Max." The defiance had drained away once again, leaving her sad and defenseless. "Maybe I was too harsh in the way I said things when I was younger. But I never meant to hurt anybody. All I ever wanted was to live my own life as *I* wanted to live it, as a one-hundred-percent American. It would have been impossible for me to do that and please my parents, too. They would have had me marry a nice local Swedish boy and be a good dairy farmer's wife, just like my grandmother was. Just like my mother still is. Every time I go home they act as though I'd betrayed them . . . and it hurts."

The last words were barely audible. After they were

uttered, B.G. seemed to sink into a weary trance, looking inward. Max waited a long minute and then decided that he had to get to the bottom of whatever it was that had triggered her self-reprisal.

"What happened when you went home to your grandmother's funeral, B.G.? Did the whole family ostracize you or what?"

B.G. came back to the present and regarded him steadily, her lips pressed firmly together to control the occasional tremors.

"I'll tell you what happened, Max. My grandmother left her most prized possession in the world, a collection of antique porcelain plates that were made in Sweden, to her old friend back in the village she came from. And what's more, she especially asked that *I* be the one to take them personally."

Max failed to detect anything really upsetting in what B.G. had just told him unless she had wanted the plates herself, for sentimental reasons or because of the monetary value of the collection.

"Perhaps it is asking a bit much of you to go to that kind of expense," he suggested in a conciliatory tone, "but you may enjoy the trip. After you carry out your grandmother's request, you can always do some sightseeing on your own. Frankly, I'm a little envious."

"I don't have to go to any expense," B.G. corrected him tonelessly. "My grandmother left the money to pay for the trip."

Mentally Max threw up his hands at this news.

"That's great, then. You get an all-expense paid trip to Sweden out of the deal. Say, while you're there, maybe you'll get to Stockholm and do some scouting for *Maxwell's,* eh? You know how crazy some of our clients are about contemporary Scandinavian design."

Max knew that he sounded a trifle too enthusiastic, but surely there hadn't been anything in what he said to bring on another bout of tears! Much to his bafflement and chagrin, B.G. began crying again. This time she didn't sob or make any sounds of weeping. The huge tears just welled up in her eyes, spilled over, and coursed down her cheeks while he watched helplessly.

"My grandmother always told me those plates would be mine after she was gone," B.G. whispered in a tone of utter misery. "Because I was her namesake. You don't know how it hurt, Max, when I found out she was giving them to someone not even in the family." B.G. blinked hard and swallowed, but the tears wouldn't stop flowing. "I guess I can't blame her," she said thickly. "It's not that I mind someone else having the plates instead of me. I just wish she hadn't died without *understanding*. Her name was right for her. It just wasn't right for *me*. I still loved her—"

Max winced at the break in B.G.'s voice. He squirmed uncomfortably in his chair, filled with a sense of helplessness as he realized that there was nothing he could do or say to lessen her anguish. Nervously he watched as she squeezed her eyes tightly shut in the effort to turn off the wellspring of tears. After perhaps a minute, she opened her eyes again and sat up straight, incredibly composed and even strong following the storm of emotion.

An invincible young woman, Max found himself thinking with something like awe.

"I'll go to Sweden and do what my grandmother asked me to do," B.G. declared with grim dignity. "I'll take the collection that should have been mine to my grandmother's old friend, and I'll see something of Sweden while I'm there. But it will just be visiting a foreign country, as far as I'm concerned.

Sweden was my grandmother's country, not mine. I'll come back the same person I am now, B.G. Jensen, *American.*''

Max was altogether inclined to believe her. Even if he hadn't been, he would have kept his opinion to himself.

Chapter Two

$\mathcal{N}$ils Heidenstam accepted the cup of strong black coffee his grandmother had just poured for him and settled back into an armchair in her large but homey living room. He made a concerted effort to relax and attend to her conversation, but somehow the words failed to penetrate his consciousness. He had too much on his mind these days, and, besides, he was simply biding his time until he could turn the talk to himself and his plans for the future. Before the evening was over, he hoped to be able to unburden himself to his grandmother, in spite of deep reservations. Time was growing short. He had been all too well aware of that fact lately, as his father's health continued to deteriorate.

"You do remember hearing me mention her, don't you, Nils?" Solbritt Heidenstam prompted, glancing up from the task of pouring her own cup of coffee and noticing the distracted expression on her grandson's face. "My old friend, Birgitta Johannson," she added patiently when it was clear that Nils hadn't been hearing a word she was saying. "Birgitta left Forsborg and went to America with her husband and daughter in 1933. They settled in the northern part of the United States, where they already had relatives living—in Minnesota."

Nils nodded and sipped his coffee, burning his lips in the process. It was damned hard to appear even mildly interested in some old friend of his grandmother's when he was faced with the most crucial decision of his life, knowing that the choice he leaned toward was likely to wound her deeply. He had always wanted to please her as well as his parents, but he had himself and his own interests to consider, too.

"Birgitta and I were the closest of friends," Solbritt was continuing in a saddened voice. "It nearly killed us to have to part. At first we wrote often to each other, but then as the years passed and we both were so busy with our own lives and our families, we wrote letters mostly at holidays. That's the time people stop and think of old friends, isn't it?"

Judging from his grandmother's manner of narration and her expression, Nils guessed that this old friend of hers must have died recently. Losing one's friends was one of the unpleasant realities of living to be Solbritt's age. With a little inward sigh, he relinquished most of his hope for having that heart-to-heart discussion with his grandmother that night.

"I am going to miss Birgitta now that she has passed on," Solbritt declared softly, confirming Nils's intuition. "But it will be simply wonderful to be able to welcome her granddaughter to Forsborg."

Nils began to pay full attention.

"The granddaughter of your old friend Birgitta, who emigrated to America, is coming *here*—to Forsborg?"

Solbritt seemed not to take note of the obvious surprise in his voice. She answered the question as though he had calmly asked for information.

"Yes, she is bringing me a legacy her grandmother wanted me to have. The granddaughter's name is also Birgitta, but she calls herself some strange American nickname that I cannot manage to remember. It caused deep hurt to my poor friend Birgitta that her namesake did not choose to be known by her given name."

Nils had spent the major portion of his thirty-two years in the United States and been educated there. His father handled the New York office of the Heidenstam Fabrik, which exported much of its fine cabinetry to the United States. Nils was well aware that Americans were extremely fond of nicknames. Nine times out of ten, a Thomas would be addressed Tom, and a Peter would be Pete, while such was not the usual practice in Sweden.

"Most Americans have nicknames," he explained to his grandmother, trying with little success to muster some semblance of interest in her conversation. Idly he wondered how one could shorten a name like Birgitta into a suitably American nickname. In English *Birgitta* would be translated *Bridget*.

"What is the nickname your friend's granddaughter calls herself?" he asked, more in the spirit of cooperation than out of any genuine interest. He was glad that he had made the inquiry when he saw how inordinately pleased Solbritt looked. She must have been able to see how bored he was with talk of her now-deceased friend.

"I can't remember what it is except that it isn't a name at all—just initials." Solbritt slapped at the air in a very characteristic gesture to dismiss such silliness as changing one's name. "It seems that this girl did not want a Swedish name. Much to the disappointment of my friend Birgitta and this girl's mother and father, as well, she has always scorned Swedish ways and criticized her parents and her grandparents for not wanting to change. Even though the circumstances made it better for them to emigrate from Sweden to the United States to make a good living, they still had Swedish blood in their veins. Apparently this girl could not accept that truth.'' Solbritt's stern voice and solemn expression disapproved such an attitude.

Nils gave his head a slight shake as he leaned forward and set his coffee cup on the table.

''And this girl who doesn't want to be called her Swedish name and doesn't want to be reminded of her Swedish background is coming to Sweden to visit *you* here in Forsborg?'' he asked ironically. ''You don't by chance have some thought of showing this Swedish-American girl how wrong her attitude is?''

Solbritt looked slightly flustered, making Nils suspect that he had hit upon the truth.

''I wrote a letter to Birgitta some months ago, after she had already become very ill, and gave her my promise that if this girl would come to visit me in Sweden, I would do my best to make her come to appreciate the country of her grandmother's birth. Then perhaps she would learn to be proud of the Swedish blood in her veins.'' The admission carried such a ringing undertone of certainty that Nils could tell that his grandmother had every confidence she would be able to accomplish what she had promised her old friend who was far away on American soil at the time.

''I hope you won't be disappointed if this girl isn't at all impressed with Sweden,'' he warned, rising and pacing restlessly over to the fireplace, where he wheeled around and faced Solbritt, hands thrust deep in his pockets. His voice was sharper than he had meant it to be, but he felt that he should do whatever he could to protect her from being hurt. ''Keep in mind what a huge country the United States is. Americans are used to thinking of themselves as the biggest and the best country in the modern world. Sweden is smaller than most of their states and has only eight million people.''

Solbritt had listened very attentively to her grandson's words of caution, but appeared not in the least discouraged. Her blue eyes, so like his, swept proudly over his tall, athletic form. *So handsome, my grandson,* her face plainly said.

"You are right, of course. Sweden is a small country," she agreed in a conciliatory tone, as though she were humoring him. "It is a wonderful country, though. Its people are strong and honest and hardworking. It is a country with much beauty and character to recommend it. I often think what a shame it is that some Swedish people live and grow old and die without ever seeing much of their own country and coming to know it."

Nils wondered what there was in his grandmother's beaming smile to raise the stir of uneasiness inside him. He didn't have long to wait before he knew.

"You, for example, my grandson," she continued fondly. "You have lived more of your life in the United States than in Sweden, even though you are a Swedish citizen, Swedish born. You have traveled to many countries in Europe and visited most of the great cities in those countries. Yet have you not actually seen very little of Sweden?"

"I am beginning to see what this conversation is all about," Nils said slowly, comprehension finally dawning. "I would venture to guess that you have planned a travel holiday for your visitor from America, and you want to include *me* in those plans as well." The expression on Solbritt's face was confirmation enough for Nils that he had guessed correctly. He pulled both hands out of his pockets and held them palms out toward his grandmother. "No, I am *not* interested," he declared with soft emphasis. "Count me out!"

Solbritt's features took on a downcast expression as she absorbed his refusal. Her subdued voice accepted it as final.

"I have been looking forward to your visit for some weeks now," she pointed out sadly. "And you arrived only late yesterday. Your visits to Forsborg have been very important to me since your parents had to take you away to America when you were a small boy."

Nils's gaze sharpened.

"When is this American girl from Minnesota due to arrive in Sweden, anyway? You make it sound as though I won't have any time with you unless I agree to come along on this trip you have planned."

Solbritt became very busy loading the coffee cups on the tray that already held the china coffeepot and matching sugar bowl and cream pitcher.

"Her flight arrives in Gothenburg tomorrow."

"Tomorrow!" Nils ejaculated, reproof mingling with his surprise. "You could have given me a little more advance warning," he scolded sternly.

Solbritt met his gaze apologetically.

"I was afraid that you would postpone your visit." She hesitated, studying the capable hands folded in her lap. "Perhaps in this one instance, you will humor your old grandmother and help make this visitor from America feel welcome in Sweden? It would mean so much to me. There will come a time when you will not be bothered by such requests . . ." Solbritt let her voice drift off.

Nils shook his head helplessly, half-irritated and half-amused by her blatant manipulation. At seventy-four she was a vigorous, healthy woman. When the weather permitted, she still rode her bicycle down to the factory, where she helped out in the office. Hardly a day went by that she didn't go for a walk, and except for the aid of a cleaning woman once a week, she did her own cooking and housecleaning. Clearly she was making a play on Nils's sympathies by referring to her advancing age, but the fact remained that she *was* getting older and the time *would* come when he would not have the joy of her good-natured company. He knew that he would not be able to deny her this favor, however unappealing it might be. If she weren't so important to him, he wouldn't be so worried about the discussion he needed to have with her.

"I suppose you want me to drive you to the airport tomorrow to meet her." The grudging observation brought a bright smile to Solbritt's face, but she didn't reply until she had grasped the tray and stood up.

"Perhaps it would be better if you went alone to meet her." Solbritt managed to sound as though she were just offering this suggestion for his consideration, but Nils knew better. He would put money on the likelihood that she had everything worked out to her satisfaction. "It is quite a long, tiring drive for me," Solbritt continued reflectively. "I could stay here and have everything ready when you and Birgitta arrive. Then the three of us could sit right down and have some nice homemade cake and cookies and coffee. What do you think?"

"That definitely sounds like a good plan," Nils declared with heavy irony. "Let *me* meet this Minnesota farmgirl in Gothenburg tomorrow and have the pleasure of her company for the hour-and-a-half drive back here to Forsborg. We can probably talk about milking cows or raising chickens or something equally fascinating."

Anyone observing the scene would have sworn that Nils's sarcasm was lost on Solbritt, who with a guileless smile murmured a few words and took the tray from the room. Out in the kitchen, though, the smile broadened into a gleeful grin. Opening a cabinet drawer, Solbritt took out several snapshots and studied each of them in turn. Then with a little guttural sound in the back of her throat, she returned the snapshots to the drawer and proceeded to put her kitchen in immaculate order, her movements practiced and efficient.

Alone in the living room, Nils stood with one elbow propped on the mantel, his expression glum and discouraged. If his grandmother disapproved so strongly of an American-born girl's rebellion against her Swedish heritage, what would she think of what Nils was seriously thinking of doing? He was afraid she would be devastated. And no matter how many times he told himself that he had to live his own life and look after his own future and happiness, he abhorred the thought of hurting those closest to him, Solbritt in particular, because she was older and therefore somehow more vulnerable. His parents had always seemed more pragmatic in their outlook on life, more resilient.

Expelling his breath in an audible sigh that was part groan, Nils rubbed one palm across his brow, thinking grimly of the days ahead when he would have to play host to this visiting American girl from Minnesota. The burden on his mind would make it doubly hard for him to be sociable. His mental image of the visitor did nothing to lighten his spirits, either. She was probably robust and stolid and totally unimaginative, perhaps sullen and dogmatic, too, given what he had been told about her anti-Swedish sentiments and her apparent insensitivity to the feelings of her parents and grandparents.

No, Nils definitely did *not* look forward to the next week or two. But during that time, he would make up his mind about his future and he would have an honest talk with Solbritt.

After these two promises to himself, Nils felt better.

Chapter Three

B.G. had had every intention of following the well-known advice to travelers making transatlantic flights: Don't eat or drink too much and get plenty of sleep. She knew that upon her arrival in Sweden, the time would be six hours ahead of the time in New York, making her first day in Sweden an interminably long one.

It soon became apparent to her, though, once the jumbo plane was in the air and had gained its assigned altitude, that someone had forgotten to inform the airline of this cautionary advice. The attendants seemed bent upon keeping the three hundred passengers so busy eating, drinking, watching movies, and listening to stereo music that they would have neither the time nor the opportunity to sleep.

After everything had finally quieted down—the movie had ended and the last surge of movement up and down the aisles had died away—B.G. was at last able to drift into a sleep deeper than a doze. Then without warning, all the lights in the cabin flashed on, and the pilot, who sounded like a Texan, was announcing something over the intercom. Blinking irritably and yawning, B.G. sat upright and peered at her watch. They should be landing in about an hour. The attendants were serving still another meal!

Gathering up her handbag and the small piece of hand luggage stowed under the seat in front of her, she made her way down the aisle to the washrooms at the rear of the cabin. After brushing her teeth, washing her face, combing her hair, and restoring her makeup, she felt less like a refugee fleeing a wartorn country.

Her reflection in the small mirror over the wash basin made her congratulate herself on a good choice in traveling attire. Back in Minneapolis, the red suit had seemed almost too assertive, but now she found that she needed the demand its brightness made upon her spirits. One simply couldn't shuffle one's feet tiredly or slump one's shoulders when wearing such a color, especially not when arriving in a foreign country and being met by a total stranger. She had toned down the suit with a chastely ruffled white blouse. Thanks to modern wrinkle-resistant fabrics, she didn't even look as if she had slept—or, more aptly, *tried* to sleep—in her clothes.

Back in her seat, B.G. sipped a glass of orange juice and tried to prepare herself mentally for what she might encounter in Gothenburg when her plane landed. Her grandmother's old friend, Solbritt Heidenstam, had written that B.G. would be met at the airport by a grandson, Nils Heidenstam, leading B.G. to conclude that her grandmother's friend was probably not in good health and unable to come to the airport herself. B.G. had her fingers crossed that she wasn't getting herself into a situation where she had to sit by a sickbed and put up with the ramblings of a senile old woman, one who would speak only Swedish.

Since she had decided to comply with her grandmother's dying request and make this trip to Sweden, B.G. had been telling herself that she really should practice her Swedish. She should try to start thinking Swedish again, but the time had slid by and she hadn't practiced. Now that she was about to land on Swedish soil, she was feeling a little panicky and had to tell herself that surely the language would come back to her when she needed it. After all, Swedish had been spoken as the primary language in her home until she was sixteen and started high school.

At that time—the same time that she changed her name from Birgitta to B.G.—she had enlisted the aid of her younger brother and sister and embarked on a campaign to force everyone in the family to speak English. Their children would do better in school if they spoke English at home, she had told her parents.

Looking back now, B.G. had to blush at her bullying techniques with her parents and siblings. She had been so self-righteous and sure of herself! But there was no denying that her own personal rebellion had been good for her parents as well as her brother and sister. Her parents had learned to speak much better English, even though they still tended to lapse into Swedish with each other.

As the plane began its descent, she wished that she hadn't abandoned her parents' native language so thoroughly. Probably she was going to need it when she greeted the grandson of her grandmother's old friend. *Nils Heidenstam.* The very name summoned the image of a big-boned, burly, awkward man. He would probably have donned an ill-fitting suit for the occasion and would look vaguely uncomfortable in it the way her father and uncles had always looked on Sundays when dressed in their Sunday best for church services.

This picture was still clear in B.G.'s mind when the jet had landed and she had passed through customs and entered the terminal proper. Standing in the area where international arrivals are met by family and friends, she looked around for the man conjured up by her prosaic expectations. Her gaze faltered in its search as it touched upon a tall, athletic man whose blond-haired good looks would have caught any woman's eye. Something about his sea blue eyes and strong craggy features made B.G. think of storybook pictures she had seen in grammar school of the daring Vikings. Instead of rude clothing made from the skins of animals, though, he wore expensive, well-cut tan slacks, a short-sleeved shirt open at the neck, and worn but polished brown leather loafers that hadn't come from a bargain store. His eyes searched the crowd of passengers for the person he had come to meet.

Even as B.G. tore her gaze away from the handsome man she guessed to be in his early thirties, she felt a pang of regret that he wasn't there to meet *her* instead of some other lucky female. Why, she asked herself petulantly, couldn't life just *once* turn out like a romance novel?

Nils didn't see a single lone female who fit the description his imagination supplied for a farmgirl from Minnesota. He couldn't be lucky enough to have this Birgitta Jensen turn out to be that strikingly pretty blonde in the red suit. She looked more New York than Minnesota. Yet, she *was* waiting for someone to meet her, and her coloring was definitely Scandinavian. Nils decided that it wouldn't hurt anything to approach her and have a few words.

B.G. was so busy looking around that she didn't notice Nils Heidenstam coming toward her. She was getting more panicky every second and irritable, as well. Here she was in a strange country with nobody to meet her. If this Nils Heidenstam didn't show up, what the devil was she going to do?

"Where is that *dumb Swede* anyway?" she muttered

louder than she realized, using the term with an irony that only a Swedish-American from Minnesota could fully appreciate.

Nils caught the low words. Suddenly there wasn't a doubt in his mind that this impatient young woman in the red suit was his grandmother's visitor. Her tone of voice and the remark itself reinforced his reservations about the whole notion of this visit. Apparently she had brought along to Sweden all her anti-Swedish biases.

"Birgitta Jensen?" he inquired crisply, resisting the urge to present himself at once as the "dumb Swede" she was expecting to meet her.

B.G. turned abruptly toward the sound of the male voice and saw to her utter amazement that the good-looking Viking was addressing her! It took a second or two for her to relate the unfamiliar *Birgitta* to herself, since she hadn't thought of herself as Birgitta in so many years. In her own mind, she was B.G.

"*You* aren't Nils Heidenstam!" she blurted and then promptly grew even more horribly flustered as she searched her blank mind for an appropriate Swedish phrase of greeting. His coldly detached air did nothing to help restore her vanished poise.

"*Goddag,*" she managed finally, thrusting out her right hand. "*Angenamt.*"

Nils understood the error of her assumption at once. She obviously thought that he did not speak English! Perhaps it was an instinctive urge to retaliate for the "dumb Swede" attitude that made him reply to her awkward greeting in Swedish rather than English.

"*Goddag,*" he said formally, offering his hand as any Swede would do under the circumstances. "I'm very pleased to meet you, also," he continued in Swedish. "Welcome to Sweden. I hope you had a good flight."

Once he had initiated the charade, Nils experienced some second thoughts, but it was too late then, and he thought Birgitta Jensen was only getting what she deserved. Anyone who took the trouble to do the most elementary research about modern Sweden would know that every Swedish child is taught English in school from an early age. This young woman evidently hadn't cared enough to find out anything about the country she was visiting.

B.G. blundered along in Swedish, almost wishing that Nils Heidenstam had been the dull, uninspired man of her expectations instead of this really extraordinarily good-looking man who was nothing at all like any Swedish man she had ever known in Minnesota. His manners were smooth; his voice was low and assured. It was like opening the door to a blind date, prepared for the worst, and finding on your doorstep a guy who looked like your favorite movie idol! Carrying on conversation in Swedish was proving to be far more grueling than she had expected, perhaps because she wanted too much to make a favorable impression upon him after having behaved like a simpleton that first minute or two after he approached her. She found herself bogged down in awkward explanations almost at once.

"Please call me B.G. rather than Birgitta," she requested as Nils escorted her out of the terminal.

"*B.G.*," Nils repeated, his curious tone genuine. Last night he had wondered what kind of nickname she had been able to make out of Birgitta. *B.G.* He'd never known a woman who called herself initials like that, but somehow the nickname suited her. A sense of pure devilment made him ask a question whose answer he already knew from his grandmother.

"And why is it you do not wish to be called *Birgitta?*"

"*Oh, boy!*" B.G. muttered under her breath, glimpsing the complications at once. How did one explain to a handsome Viking that one did not want a Swedish name?

Reasons that seemed so plausible back home in Minnesota did not translate easily into Swedish, especially not on Swedish soil. She found herself weakly falling back upon an explanation that quite unbeknownst to her, Nils had given his grandmother just the previous night.

"All Americans have names other than their given names."

In the parking lot, Nils led B.G. to a low-slung, sporty Saab turbo. While he was busy placing her luggage in the trunk, B.G. gazed around the parking lot, feeling oddly like she had wandered onto the premises of a giant Volvo dealership.

"Goodness! I've never seen so many Volvos in my *life!*" she said aloud to herself in English. Talking to herself in such a manner was a habit she was quickly falling into in Nils's presence, since she knew he was unable to understand her.

As Nils straightened up and slammed the trunk lid closed, he wished that he hadn't perpetrated this silly myth that he couldn't speak English. Once they had reached his grandmother's home in Forsborg, the truth would come out in a matter of time. Solbritt spoke very little English herself. Beyond the simplest conversation between herself and her guest, Nils would probably be called upon to translate.

But how was he to explain to B.G. Jensen his pretense without making her embarrassed and angry? Nils pondered that difficult question as he maneuvered the car out of the parking lot and onto the highway. B.G. was intent on her first glimpses of Sweden.

"This all looks very modern and urbanized," she commented to herself in English after several minutes. Feeling Nils's gaze on her, she turned and flashed him an apologetic smile before painstakingly translating the observation into Swedish, stopping in the middle to mutter aloud, "*Modern, modern,* what's *modern* in Swedish?"

It required all of Nils's self-control not to supply the word for her. "Gothenburg is the second largest city in Sweden," he told her, speaking slowly and distinctly for her benefit. "It is an important industrial city with many shipyards. Very modern, as you say."

B.G.'s mind performed some strange acrobatics at the mention of shipyards. She wondered if this modern-day Viking designed ships. Wouldn't that be a suitable profession for the descendent of the great sea-going pirates? she thought whimsically.

"What kind of work is it that you do?" she asked him.

The question evidently surprised Nils, judging from the quick glance he shot over at her. Then, to her mystification, he frowned and became moody.

"I work for the Heidenstam factory," he replied almost curtly. When she didn't speak, he glanced sideways at her again, noting her expression as she waited for him to explain further. "You are not familiar with the cabinets we build," he stated matter-of-factly.

B.G. shook her head apologetically.

"My great-grandfather began the Heidenstam Fabrik in 1905." Nils spoke slowly, keeping the explanation simple. "We built most of the basic kinds of household furniture at first, but now our factory builds only cabinets. We export them to the United States and to other countries as well, besides selling them here in Sweden."

B.G.'s mouth suddenly dropped open.

"Oh, my God! You're *that* Heidenstam!" she gasped out in amazement. "I had no idea!" In Swedish, she told Nils, "Yes, I am familiar with your fabrik's cabinets, after all."

For the first time she made a connection between his

surname and the famous Heidenstam cabinetry. She was well aware of its reputation for quality construction and design as well as its high price. It enjoyed great popularity with those who were fond of contemporary Scandinavian design and who could afford it.

The discovery of Nils's identity gave B.G. food for further thought and took away the impetus for conversation, while she pondered the fact that the Heidenstams must be fabulously wealthy. It was curious to her now that her plain, hard-working grandmother had kept up a correspondence with Solbritt Heidenstam all those years, considering the social gap between their stations in life. B.G.'s grandparents had owned a prosperous dairy farm, but by no stretch of the imagination were they wealthy. Would Solbritt Heidenstam live in a fine mansion? Would she expect deference from her old friend's granddaughter?

Pondering these questions, B.G. saw her grandmother's bequest in a totally different light. How could a woman who presumably had everything she wanted appreciate the collection of odd old porcelain plates B.G.'s grandmother had so treasured? B.G. wasn't actually arriving with the plates in hand, but they should be arriving in Forsborg within days, having been entrusted to a shipping company that specialized in transporting fragile commodities. Once they had been unpacked, B.G. resolved now to take her leave and spend the remainder of her time in Sweden on her own, sightseeing and doing that scouting for *Maxwell's* that Max had jokingly suggested.

Nils wondered what his passenger was thinking about. Her hands gripped the navy leather handbag on her knees, and her mouth was set in a firm line. One minute she had been making every effort to be sociable, and then without warning she had lapsed into this rather grim introspection. Actually, the silence suited him fine. He had many things to think about, none of them very cheerful. That afternoon he would call his mother in New York and get a report on his father's health. Nils was almost certain of what the news would be. His father would still be driving himself, against all the advice of his physicians.

Before flying over to Sweden two days ago, Nils had met with Dr. Paulsen. "He's killing himself, Nils," the heart specialist had pronounced sternly. "He needs to retire. You know that for your father there can be no semiretirement. If he doesn't start to take care of himself soon, he will die a young man. Your father is only fifty-six, but he has driven and abused his body too many years."

Nils understood not only what Dr. Paulsen was saying about his father, but what he was assuming about Nils, that the son would step into the father's shoes when the father retired. The physician was a good friend of Nils's parents and had good reason to make such an assumption, because everyone did. There was no doubt in Nils's mind that he could take over his father's position. Hadn't he been groomed for it since birth? To be born a Heidenstam was to live and breathe the Heidenstam Fabrik, and Nils probably had a better knowledge of the total operation of the family business than anyone else had. If his ability had been in doubt, maybe his decision now would be easier. He had to choose between what everyone expected of him and what would certainly cause shock and dismay, between the sure thing of making a long-term commitment to the family business and the gamble of striking out into a venture that wasn't guaranteed to be a success at all but offered a challenge and an opportunity to shape his own future. . . .

"Why, this is Forsborg, where you live. How pretty!"

The words from his passenger, spoken in English,

roused Nils back to the present. The past hour he had been so deeply sunken into thought that he had forgotten her presence. Her reaction to the little Swedish village had seemed to be free of condescension. She was looking eagerly out of her window, taking note of the components that made up the immaculate overall impression. Without correcting her erroneous assumption that he resided in Forsborg, Nils looked at the village and saw it as it must appear to her.

The houses, each one neatly painted, were small with steep-pitched clay tile roofs. Each house had a small garden with well-tended flower beds and shrubbery. This time of the year, early August, the blossoms were at their most brilliant, as though reveling in their heyday before the advent of winter. Nils could identify few flowers by name, but he could point out the popular geraniums and marigolds. The name of the vine that ran rampant on garden trellises and white picket fences escaped him right now, but he especially liked its rich purple trumpet flowers.

"It's *exactly* the way a storybook village would look!" B.G. pronounced softly to herself, quite charmed by Forsborg. It was so small and compact and cheerful. The people that she glimpsed coming and going about their daily business looked calm and contented. But where did Solbritt Heidenstam live? she wondered. There weren't any large, imposing houses so far. A mansion would be sorely out of place and a wrong note in this delightful village.

Before she could ask if his grandmother lived on the outskirts of the village, Nils was pulling into the driveway of a two-story brick house painted austere white. B.G. saw that actually the house was rather large, but it didn't stand out as such because the architecture was plain with no ornamentation such as a portico.

The car had no more than come to a halt when the

front door of the house swung open and out came a
vigorous woman who looked not a day older than
sixty-five. She wore a sleeveless vee-necked summer
dress that revealed sun-browned arms and neck. On her
face was a broad smile of welcome. B.G. just barely had
time to reflect that *surely* this woman wasn't her grandmother's old friend before she stepped out of the car and
found herself enclosed in a hearty embrace.

"Welcome to Sweden! Come! You must be very tired
from your long journey! I have a little refreshment all
prepared!"

B.G. was able to understand every word of this
boisterous greeting spoken in Swedish. Still finding it
impossible to believe that the woman leading her up the
walk to the open door was actually Solbritt Heidenstam,
her grandmother's contemporary and a very rich
woman, she managed a polite, appropriate reply in
Swedish. For some reason, the Swedish words came
easier to her now than they had earlier with Nils
Heidenstam, who was left behind to see to B.G.'s
luggage.

"The weather is so *nice!* I thought we would sit
outside," Solbritt declared cheerfully, leading B.G.
straight through the house so that she had only a quick
impression of rooms with comfortable, traditional furnishings, nothing pretentious or grand.

The rear grounds of the house were quite large and
encircled by a high brick wall, painted white like the
house. Whoever was responsible for the gardening
obviously was no novice. B.G. had never seen so many
gorgeous roses of different colors and varieties.

"Your roses are beautiful," she complimented sincerely, and then realizing that she had unthinkingly
lapsed into English, translated the words into Swedish.

Solbritt beamed her pleasure.

"My husband was quite fond of roses," she ex-

plained. "He planted most of these himself and loved
working in the garden. Now that he is gone, I try to keep
it as he would have liked. But, *please*, do take a chair,"
she urged, gesturing toward a large round table surrounded by chairs with gaily printed cushions. The table
was placed in full sunshine, a tilted umbrella on a stand a
short distance away handy to provide shade should it be
wanted.

"Tack," B.G. replied, using the Swedish term for
"thank you." She took a step toward the table and then
paused to ask if she could be of some help to her hostess,
whose open manner encouraged informality.

Solbritt's face flooded with such horror that B.G. had
to discipline herself to keep from smiling. "But *no!*"
The older woman refused in her typically emphatic
manner. "There is nothing to *do!* You sit."

While her hostess went back into the house, B.G.
selected a chair and sat down, noting with appreciation
the deep blue of the tablecloth that harmonized with the
fabric of the chair cushions. The table had been set with
soft blue china and shining stainless steel. An exquisite
crystal vase held a bouquet of roses B.G. couldn't resist
leaning forward to smell.

Solbritt returned in an amazingly short time with a
large tray and a heart-felt apology for leaving her guest
alone so long. "We will not wait for Nils. You are
probably very hungry," she announced, taking her seat
and serving B.G. a cup of strong black coffee from a
blue china pot that matched the cups and plates.

B.G. sipped the coffee gratefully, feeling the fatigue
steal through her now that she was seated and relaxed. At
her hostess's urging she helped herself to a cookie and a
piece of cake from an amply loaded platter. When she bit
into the cookie, it was deliciously flavored with almond
and brought back memories.

"These are very delicious. My grandmother made

cookies like these," she commented a little nostalgical-
ly, wondering even as she spoke if Solbritt Heidenstam
had a cook to do her baking. So far B.G. hadn't
glimpsed a servant.

"I made them only this morning," Solbritt informed
her, pleased at the compliment. "They are best when
they are fresh. Please have another."

B.G. did as she was bade, hearing the ring of a
telephone just as she reached for a second cookie. A
moment later she heard Nils speaking to the caller. He
must have had time to take her luggage to her room and
would be joining them as soon as he finished his
conversation.

"Your grandson, Nils, does he live with you in your
home?" she inquired in Swedish that was coming to her
more easily now.

"Nej!" Solbritt slapped the air playfully, banishing
the notion that her grandson lived with her. "He only
visits me—" She broke off as the person about whom
she was talking appeared in the open back door and ran
lightly down the steps.

"That was Ollie on the telephone just now," he told
his grandmother in rapid Swedish. "He has to go to
Stockholm early in the morning. I must go over to the
fabrik now and meet with him. I should be back in time
for dinner tonight." Almost without hesitation, Nils
turned to B.G. and said in easy, unaccented English,
"I'm sorry I can't join you and my grandmother for
coffee, but I have an appointment with our production
manager at the factory."

Once the first few words were out, the incredulous
expression on B.G.'s face made Nils aware of his slip. In
his hurry he'd forgotten that he wasn't supposed to be
able to speak English. He'd gone to the airport that
morning with the notion firmly fixed in his mind that he
was meeting an American girl who would prefer to speak

English even if she had some knowledge of Swedish. Oh, well, the damage was done, and she would have found out eventually. Right now he didn't have the time or the inclination to stop and try to think up a diplomatic explanation.

"He speaks English," B.G. muttered aloud, looking after Nils's back as he made his rapid exit. "Your grandson speaks English," she said to Solbritt in Swedish, aware that the older woman was puzzled about what had just transpired between her guest and her grandson.

"*Ja!*" Solbritt agreed heartily. "Nils speaks very good English. No doubt he has told you already that he moved to America with his parents when he was a small child. He attended American schools." Solbritt sighed and looked almost pensive. "Sometimes I think Nils is more American than Swedish. Every year of his life he has spent some time with me here in Forsborg, but it was not enough."

B.G. paid little attention to that last remark, which she might have found puzzling if she hadn't been consumed by such a powerful thirst for vengeance. The *nerve* of Nils Heidenstam to pretend he didn't speak English and make a fool of her as he had done! What fun he must have had listening to her falter and search for Swedish words to express the simplest thoughts, talking to herself in English he well understood the whole time! What she couldn't understand was *why* he had done it. Why would he play such a shabby trick on a complete stranger? Whatever his reasons, she intended to let him know in fullest detail what a low opinion she held of him.

It required no little effort for B.G. to push the matter to the back of her mind and carry on conversation with Solbritt, who obviously was not aware of her grandson's mean little charade. The older woman was so likable and frankly delighted to have B.G. as her house guest that B.G. forgot how reluctant a visitor she actually was.

"We will make a trip together, you and Nils and I," Solbritt announced happily after she had reminisced at some length about her friendship with B.G.'s grandmother. "The first part is a boat passage that all Swedes long to make someday. We will travel from Gothenburg to Stockholm on the Göta Canal. It was built a hundred years ago and connects the west coast with the east coast, passing right through the heartland of Sweden—my much beloved country and the country of your grandmother, too, even though she had to leave it."

Inwardly B.G. sighed as she listened. She really should clarify matters with Solbritt at once and make it plain that she felt no emotional or sentimental allegiance whatever to Sweden. Solbritt should realize that B.G. was American through and through. If the older woman were planning this trip solely as entertainment, then that was fine. Any intention to make B.G. more Swedish was doomed to failure. But somehow she couldn't bring herself to interrupt her kind hostess with truths that might hurt her feelings.

B.G. also wished that Solbritt wouldn't call her Birgitta, but she didn't have the courage to ask the old woman to refer to her as B.G. After all, the visit to Sweden would be relatively brief, and it wouldn't actually do any harm for a nice old Swedish lady to call B.G. by the Swedish name she had cast off. And B.G. had already had some practice at trying to express in Swedish the reason she had changed her name. She was discouraged at the prospect of making another attempt.

"After we arrive in Stockholm," Solbritt was continuing, "we will stay there for several days at least so that you can see it. Many people call Stockholm the Venice of the North because it is so beautiful and, like Venice, built on water. Actually the city is a cluster of islands, you know."

B.G. had to admit that she hadn't known.

"From Stockholm we will travel north to Dalarna," Solbritt went on, the pride on her face deepening into a kind of reverence. "This is the part of Sweden that even Swedes regard as the 'most Swedish.' Many of the people live much as they lived a century ago. Their handicrafts have become famous all over Sweden and even all over the world. Dalarna is also very beautiful with lakes and green forests—" Seeing the yawn that B.G. was doing her best to stifle, Solbritt broke off with an exclamation. "But listen to me ramble on when you are exhausted from your journey!" She rose briskly from the table. "We will talk of travel plans later and of many other things, too. Now I will take you to your room so that you can rest."

B.G. didn't argue with her hostess. The idea of resting in her room had powerful appeal, since she had managed to sleep only an hour or two on the flight and not very restfully at that. Climbing the wooden stairs behind Solbritt, she felt her feet dragging tiredly.

"You are so youthful, Fru Heidenstam," she remarked admiringly, noting the springiness in the older woman's steps.

"God has blessed me with good health," Solbritt declared. "But like every other human being, I grow older each day and will not live forever." There was nothing of the morbid in the comment. She was merely stating a fact. "Here is the room you will have as your own while you visit."

Solbritt fussed a bit, reassuring herself that the room was in perfect order. She smoothed the already smooth bedspread and touched the beautifully embroidered scarf on the top of a chest of drawers.

"If you need anything, you will let me know at once," she commanded kindly. "The bathroom is across the hall and next to it is the *toalett*. We do not have so many bathrooms in a house as you have in the United

States.'' She was neither criticizing nor apologizing, merely giving information. ''Now I will leave you alone so that you can rest.''

For a moment B.G. thought that her hostess would leave the room without any further word or gesture, but instead she came over to B.G. and gave her a brief, hearty hug.

''I am so glad you have come,'' she declared sincerely and left.

B.G. stood as she was a long moment, still feeling the strength of the other woman's arms around her shoulders and strongly aware of the warm goodness of her outgoing personality. She had turned out to be nothing at all like B.G. had expected. But then *nothing* was turning out to be what she thought it would be. *Certainly Nils Heidenstam had come as a surprise.*

Thoughts of the man who had met her at the airport made B.G. tense as she slowly undressed and hung her clothes on fragrant padded hangers she found in the closet. Again she found herself posing the vexing questions that she couldn't answer for herself. Why had Nils played that dirty trick on her today, pretending that he couldn't speak English? Had he disliked her on sight, or was he just an innately cruel person who enjoyed making fun of foreign visitors to his country? It had been such an inhospitable thing to do, so unexpected from the grandson of Solbritt Heidenstam, the very essence of hospitality.

Forcing her thoughts away from Nils, B.G. looked around the bedroom, reflecting that it was not what she would expect in the guest bedroom of a rich woman. And surely Solbritt must be rich. The furniture in the room was good furniture, but it was serviceable, not luxurious—designed to be used, not to impress. Little personal touches in the room made it homey, hand-embroidered scarves and small framed photographs on the top of the chest of drawers, a single rose in a bud vase on the bedside table. Later B.G. would inspect the photographs more closely, but not now. Now she would climb into that inviting bed and sleep.

When she pulled back the bedspread, she wasn't surprised to find underneath it a soft down comforter enclosed in a pocket of smooth sheets. Beneath the comforter she knew that she would not find the usual top sheet; she would simply slip beneath the comforter itself. B.G. had grown up sleeping under such bedding, popular in all the Scandinavian countries.

Now, as she climbed into bed and pulled the downy softness of the cover up to her chin, she had a sense of homecoming that she would be hard put to explain, since she was in a foreign country in a stranger's house. In her personal life she had little tolerance for things "Swedish," and she had come to Sweden with reservations. Yet as she drifted off to sleep, she felt very much at home.

Chapter Four

$\mathcal{B}$.G. awoke, refreshed. For a few seconds longer, she lay snuggled under the soft comforter, listening to the sounds of the house and sniffing a delicious aroma of food that awakened pangs of hunger. Someone was downstairs in the kitchen preparing dinner, either Solbritt Heidenstam or an as yet unseen servant.

Getting up, B.G. slipped on a pretty quilted robe and went across the hall in search of the bathroom. The door directly opposite hers led into a sizable room equipped with a huge old-fashioned tub, a washbowl on a stout ceramic pedestal, and a bidet. But no toilet! After a moment of befuddlement, Solbritt's words came back to her. The *toalett* was next door to the bathroom.

B.G. took the time to splash water on her face before she tried the room next to the bathroom and found it to be smaller and equipped with a toilet and another washbowl identical to the first one.

When she had returned to her bedroom, she dressed for the evening, choosing, after some deliberation, a simple blue dress with long graceful sleeves and wide cuffs, the skirt softly gathered. After experimenting with several arrangements of her hair, she decided to let it hang free around her shoulders. It wasn't until she was applying her makeup that she admitted a little sheepishly to herself that she was taking considerable pains with her appearance, and she wasn't doing it to impress Solbritt Heidenstam.

Nils had said he would be back for dinner. She might be furious at him and determined to reduce him to shreds at the first opportunity, but she wanted to look fantastic while she did it! No amount of resentment for his treatment of her could change the fact that he was a devastatingly attractive man.

Downstairs she found Solbritt in the dining room giving the final touches to a lovely table. It was draped in ecru lace and set with ornate, old-fashioned china that reminded B.G. of her grandmother's Rörstrand plate collection. A bowl of fresh-cut flowers sat in the center of the table flanked by two porcelain candelabra that matched the china pattern. Each candelabra held three white tapers and reminded B.G. vaguely of plump Neptune's tridents.

"How pretty!" she praised. "But you didn't have to go to so much trouble!"

"No *trouble!*" Solbritt denied, slapping the air with one hand, but looking pleased nevertheless.

At that moment Nils walked into the room, wearing the same clothes he had worn earlier. B.G. assumed that he was just now returning from his appointment at the factory. His eyes went quickly but thoroughly over B.G., making her glad she had made an effort to look her best.

"*Hej,*" he said casually to both women, using the informal Swedish greeting similar to the American "hi." His eyebrows elevated as he noted the dining room table. "I see Grandmother's got out the good china in your honor," he remarked dryly to B.G. in English. Then he slipped back into Swedish as he told his grandmother, "It will take me only a minute or two to change clothes. Then I will return and make the drinks."

Solbritt beamed proudly at him. *You'd think he had done or said something clever*, B.G. thought sarcastically to herself.

"Well, hurry up!" the older woman ordered fondly. "Birgitta and I will be waiting for you in the living room. We are very thirsty!"

"And did you have a nice rest?" Solbritt inquired as Nils left the dining room. She sounded as though the answer were actually of real concern to her.

"*Ja*," B.G. assured her. "I felt as though I were in my own bed at home."

Solbritt looked inordinately pleased and then asked her guest one question after another about her family as she ushered B.G. into the living room, where little bowls of salted nuts and a silver tray of canapes were arranged on the low coffee table. At Solbritt's urging, B.G. sampled the nuts but avoided the canapes, which were crackers spread with an apricot-colored substance that looked like fish eggs.

"Swedish caviar," Solbritt announced, gesturing toward the silver tray. "Very special. You will try it?"

B.G. wasn't fond of expensive Russian caviar and didn't expect to find the Swedish equivalent any better, but she tried to conceal her reluctance as she reached for one of the crackers, politeness requiring her to sample the delicacy served for her special benefit.

"Don't be surprised if you don't like it."

This warning from Nils, who was just entering the room, made her pause in mid-action with her hand over the tray. Feeling the eyes of both Solbritt and Nils trained on her, each with a different kind of expectancy, she was stirred with sharp irritation. For Solbritt's sake, she felt almost *obligated* to like the damned canape, and if she *didn't* like it, she hated to give Nils the satisfaction of having accurately predicted her taste!

"It's a little salty for my taste," she admitted honestly, when she had taken a cracker, bit into it with some determination, chewed, and swallowed. In truth, she thought the Swedish caviar was *awful* and had to force herself to finish the cracker. "I've never cared for Russian caviar either," she added for Solbritt's benefit.

Nils took one of the crackers from the platter and consumed it with evident relish.

"It's an acquired Swedish taste," he observed with ever so slight an emphasis on *Swedish.*

B.G.'s eyes flew to his to verify her suspicion that there had been a subtle undertone of needling in his words. His blue eyes were bland as they met hers for the space of a second or two before he took another cracker and ate it.

"What would you like to drink this evening?" he asked his grandmother politely.

"Martini, I think," Solbritt replied after pursing her lips and giving the matter some thought.

Nils inclined his head and then turned to B.G.

"And you, Birgitta? What would you like to drink?" Before she could give him her preference or remind him that she preferred to be called B.G., he was continuing smoothly, "The drink my grandmother has requested is not your American martini, which is made with gin. This one is actually sweet vermouth and is a popular European aperitif."

B.G. sucked in her breath at the faint condescension in his tone. She *hadn't* known the difference before he explained it, but he needn't have spoken to her as though she were some kind of backwoods yokel!

"I'll have the same as your grandmother," she said stiffly. "Martini."

"Whatever you like." Nils inclined his head in a polite gesture and then excused himself before leaving the room.

Solbritt had sat quietly through the brief exchange. B.G. glanced over at her now to see if she had been aware of the currents flowing between her grandson and her house guest, but evidently she had not. She smiled benignly at B.G. and urged her to help herself to the bowls of salted nuts.

Out in the kitchen, Nils vented some of his pent-up frustration on the ice he clinked, one cube at a time, into his grandmother's Orrefors crystal glasses. He felt as though he could crush nails with his teeth. That afternoon he had called New York and verified what he suspected to be the state of his father's health: It hadn't improved and wasn't likely to.

"Nils, I'm so *worried* about him!" his mother had told him. "And so *angry* at him, too! Is he trying to kill himself?" Nils understood all too well her despair and her exasperation.

And now tonight he had to spend the evening playing social games when he needed desperately to talk to his grandmother alone. Any day his father could have a total collapse and have to be hospitalized. Nils didn't want to spring this whole matter upon his grandmother in a time of emergency. It wouldn't be fair to her or to himself.

When Nils re-entered the living room, B.G. noted with interest the reddish brown color of her drink and Solbritt's. A tentative sip told her that this European martini had a pleasantly sweet taste. It was easy to guess that the pale liquid in Nils's glass was Scotch, poured with a generous hand.

He sat next to her on the sofa, sprawling back in a

decidedly male pose with the ankle of his left leg resting
on his right knee. B.G. was keenly aware of long,
muscular legs encased in dark blue trousers. The cream
vee-necked pullover he had changed into fit loosely and
yet managed to emphasize the power of his shoulders
and chest and arms. Through conscious effort, she
managed not to look directly at him after a cursory first
inspection, but her peripheral vision allowed her to note
that the fingers balancing his Scotch glass on his right
thigh were long and capable and strong. Deep inside her
she felt a stirring of excitement that was sheer primitive
female response to his unstudied maleness.

The feeling didn't go away during a two-sided conversation between herself and Solbritt about the Heidenstam
Fabrik, with B.G. asking questions and Solbritt answering them while Nils sat there quietly, absorbed in his
own thoughts. His abstraction irritated B.G. There she
was, finely attuned to the slightest movement of his
long, masculine frame, while he seemed entirely impervious to her presence. She added this grievance to her
already strong resentment for the dirty trick he had
played on her earlier in the day.

In the spirit of retaliation, she pointedly ignored Nils
all through the evening meal, addressing her questions
and remarks to Solbritt. Nils was well aware that he was
getting the cold shoulder from his grandmother's guest
and knew the reason for it. She was no doubt angry
about his pretense that he couldn't speak English, and he
had needled her a bit before dinner. Somehow he didn't
feel apologetic for either offense. In his present unsettled
state of mind, he found a kind of tight-jawed pleasure in
being at odds with this girl from Minnesota. It was a
feeling he didn't analyze, and only deference to his
grandmother kept him from antagonizing B.G. further.

Astonishingly, Solbritt seemed to notice nothing
amiss. She urged generous helpings of succulent roasted

meat upon B.G., explaining that they were having elk, a Swedish delicacy. Accompanying the main dish were small boiled potatoes sprinkled with chopped fresh dill. As B.G. helped herself to several of the potatoes, she looked around for what she found to be absent from the table, butter. It galled her that Nils took note of her search and apparently read her mind.

"Swedish people don't drench their potatoes in butter," he observed in English.

B.G. didn't favor him with so much as a barbed glance. As though he hadn't spoken at all, she picked up her fork and proceeded to eat, discovering that animosity toward him hadn't diminished her appetite. She was very hungry, and the food tasted delicious, even with him watching her and baiting her at every opportunity. She took a small second helping of meat and another potato, not realizing that there would be dessert, too, a rich cherry cobbler served with creamy vanilla ice cream.

"Please, you must let me help you clean up," B.G. begged Solbritt after the meal was over. "I need the exercise after all that food I ate!"

"Nej! Nej!" Solbritt declined the offer emphatically. "You can have exercise later, after we have coffee in the living room. Then you and Nils can take a little promenade around the village."

B.G.'s instinctive reaction was to retort that she wanted no part of a "promenade" with Nils, but then the notion took hold and she could hardly wait. It was just the opportunity she had been waiting for to get Nils Heidenstam alone and tell him how despicable he was!

"But you will want to join us, surely," Nils spoke up, addressing the words to his grandmother in a soft voice that brought B.G. quickly back to the present. She looked at him and then at his grandmother, aware of unspoken communication between them.

"Not tonight," Solbritt insisted firmly, ignoring the

ironic glint in her grandson's eyes and training her gaze on B.G. as though *she* had spoken rather than Nils. "I would not be able to walk as fast or as far as you and Nils. You would have to turn back too soon, before you had had a chance to stretch your legs."

B.G. did not voice her skepticism, but not for a moment did she believe that Solbritt would be unable to keep up with the two younger people in an after-dinner stroll or that she would tire before they would. Surely Solbritt must have her own reasons for not wanting to go. For a fleeting second or two, B.G. wondered if there were some kind of matchmaking involved, but then she quickly discounted the suspicion. Surely not! After all, B.G. would be in Sweden a short time and then be gone, never to return.

Whatever Solbritt's reason for not joining them in a walk, B.G. was glad. As she drank her tiny cup of strong coffee in the living room and managed to hold up her end of the conversation, she was busy trying out in her mind various withering comments she might later direct at Nils to express her contempt for his ungracious treatment of her. He had fallen silent again, seemingly deeply engrossed in his own thoughts. It gave her grim pleasure to conjecture that he might be experiencing some acute pangs of discomfort at the prospect of facing B.G. without the shield of his grandmother's presence. Any second she expected him to make some attempt to postpone the inevitable confrontation that would surely occur once they were alone. With him the effort was sure not to be clumsy. B.G. looked forward to countering it in such a way that he would be unable to wriggle out of accompanying her on the suggested walk.

When Nils reached over to place his empty coffee cup on the table in front of the sofa, where he sat next to B.G., she steeled herself expectantly.

"Shall we take that little promenade my grandmother

has suggested?'' he inquired in a voice that was studiously polite but still managed to convey the resigned determination to be done with a necessary and somewhat tedious chore.

B.G. was so surprised, having expected a suggestion of a different kind, and so affronted by his attitude, that she almost blurted out the first words that came to mind. What satisfaction it would have given her to inform him that under *no* circumstances was she desperate enough to inflict upon herself the unpleasantness of his company! But Solbritt was rising from her chair, all smiles, seemingly unaware of anything amiss in her grandson's offer. B.G. had to hold her tongue and be polite. Then it occurred to her that Nils might have hoped that she would be egged into a refusal that would serve his purpose all too well! What a wily character the man was! She was glad that she had not given him the pleasure of manipulating her.

"I'm ready if you are." B.G. managed to sound agreeable and even produced a smile when she felt like grinding her teeth. You have no idea just how ready I am for you, Nils Heidenstam, she told him mentally.

Solbritt ushered them out of the house after insisting that B.G. wrap a soft white crocheted shawl around her shoulders to protect her from the night chill. B.G. was sure that in her present state of mind she had enough emotional steam to keep her warm, but she took the shawl without argument, and once outside she found that it felt good.

In spite of the hour, full darkness had not yet fallen, and the softness of the twilight seemed to accentuate the air of tranquility that lay over the small village. As she walked beside Nils in the direction that he took without consulting her, B.G. felt herself falling under the spell of the collective harmony and contentment of those who lived in the quiet houses. She was struck by the odd thought that the resentment she bore her companion and his apparent dislike of her, whatever the cause, were the only negative forces abroad. It seemed a shame that such was the case.

Why doesn't he like me? she found herself wondering with as much regret as puzzlement. And suddenly it seemed more important to learn the answer to that question than to satisfy her need for revenge. If she could find out what it was about her that annoyed him, maybe she could set things right between them and start all over again. She couldn't help thinking how nice it would be to have Nils like her and want her company.

"And have you enjoyed your first day in Sweden?"

His inquiry intruded into her hopeful thoughts with all the abrasiveness of a fingernail being scraped across a chalkboard. B.G. stiffened at the polite indifference that said clearly he couldn't care less whether she had enjoyed her day or not. Instantly she felt her sense of injury returning and abandoned any notion of being friends with him. She was able to check the flood of accusations and recriminations that came to her lips only because she knew instinctively that he would be pleased at such a loss of control.

"I might have enjoyed it much more if my present companion had been more hospitable," she replied cuttingly. "Do you always try to make visitors to your country feel foolish—or is there something special about me that brought on the impulse to pretend that you couldn't speak English when you speak it every bit as well as *I* do!"

"I apologize for that silly charade this afternoon at the airport and then on the ride to Forsborg," Nils said politely, without one note of real contrition. "We turn right here."

It seemed to the incensed B.G. that his already brisk

pace increased as they set off down an unpaved but obviously often-walked lane that led away from the village into wooded countryside. At first she tried to keep up with him, while she also struggled to contain her rising indignation.

"But why did you *do* it? Pretend that you didn't speak English?" Her questions came out in gasps due to her shortness of breath. Suddenly she had had more than enough of trying to match either his stride or his control. "And would you *mind* not walking so damned *fast!*" she exploded in exasperation. "Where are you *going* anyway?"

Nils slowed his pace at once.

"Sorry," he said readily, not sorry at all. "You should have spoken up sooner. I didn't realize I was walking too fast for you. As for where we're headed, this road leads back to the lake. My grandmother and I usually come this way. If you'd prefer another direction, we can turn back."

"Damn it! I don't *care* where we walk!" B.G. sputtered angrily, wishing that she could do *something* to shake that infuriating calm of his. She felt like picking up a club and hitting him over the head with it. The satisfaction that he obviously got from her frustration was simply more than she could stand. Stopping short in her tracks, she grabbed his arm to make him stop, too, which he did without any resistance.

"What's wrong with you?" she demanded furiously, shaking his arm. "Why do you act like this toward me? What is there about me that makes you dislike me so much?"

The grip of her fingers on his arm sent a thrill of sensation through Nils even though the fabric of his pullover separated his bare flesh from hers. He was aware of the light fragrance of her perfume, warmed seductively by the pulsing aliveness of her soft woman's body, whose shape invited the touch of his hands. The male response in his loins was as quick and involuntary as it was unwanted. He fought her physical attraction at the same time that he fought the powerful pull of her personality as she demanded explanations from him that he was unable to give.

Nils didn't know precisely why he had to make B.G. his adversary, but his instincts told him that he had to keep her at a safe distance. The way she was approaching the animosity between them confirmed what he had already learned about her from his grandmother: For B.G., there were only cut and dried questions with clear-cut answers. For her, issues would be divided into black and white. She was the kind of person who could discard the name her family had given her with no regard for anyone else's feelings. She wouldn't be capable of comprehending the complexity of the decision Nils was having to make at this time.

He knew that it was irrational of him to resent her because she saw life so simply when everything was so damnably complicated for him. A sense of fairness told him that she couldn't help her psychological makeup and wasn't responsible for any of the conditions of his life, but still he had to follow his deepest survival instincts in dealing with her. It would never do for him to open himself up to her.

Nils loosened the grip of B.G.'s fingers on his arm and took her elbow in a courtly but impersonal gesture as he started them walking once more, this time at a leisurely pace.

"I don't know what made you conclude that I dislike you," he denied politely. "Certainly I don't know you well enough to either like or dislike you."

B.G. heaved a small, weary sigh.

"Do you know me well enough to explain why you didn't speak English to me right away when it must have been all too evident that I was having a difficult time speaking Swedish?" She was just as determined now to talk openly as he was to maintain his phony show of politeness.

Nils recalled the "dumb Swede" comment he had overheard her utter at the airport.

"In my defense, I can only say that I was acting according to your obvious expectations," he answered shortly.

Remembering just how far Nils had been from fitting her expectations of the man who would meet her, B.G. didn't say anything for several moments. She certainly had no intention of telling him her fleeting whimsy that he filled the bill for a modern-day Viking and that she had wished he were meeting her. Forcing her mind back to their first encounter, she mentally winced as she recalled the way she had stumbled around trying to greet Nils when he approached her.

"You mean because I spoke to you in Swedish," she said, thinking aloud. "Well, don't you think it was perfectly natural for someone to expect a Swedish person to speak Swedish?" It was impossible not to sound reproachful when she still considered his actions inexcusable.

"Not if that 'someone' had taken the time and trouble to find out a little information about Sweden," Nils rejoined curtly and then instantly regretted his tone, since he was determined to maintain his distance from her and couldn't do that if he engaged in an emotional argument. "Anyone who knows anything at all about this country," he continued in a slightly bored voice, "would expect most of its citizens, particularly the younger ones, to have some command of the English language. Every Swedish child begins studying English at the age of nine and speaks it fluently by the time his or her basic education is completed."

B.G. nibbled on her bottom lip, knowing he had made a good point. She *hadn't* taken the trouble to read about Sweden, but then she really hadn't wanted to come to Sweden at all. For all her usual pride in her candor and forthrightness, she didn't mention this last fact to Nils.

"You have to realize that my expectations of what Swedish people would be like were based to a great extent on my experience of the Swedish immigrants who settled the area in which I grew up," she explained earnestly. "My grandparents—even my parents—knew little English when they came to the United States from this country." She paused, trying to read his reaction to her cautious efforts at conciliation. "Your grandmother doesn't speak English, does she?"

"She speaks a little." There was some concession in his reply, but he changed the subject by calling her attention to their whereabouts. "Here we are at Forsborg's lake. It's quite the center of recreational activities year round. In the summer there's swimming, fishing, boating, picnicking. Over there, beyond those trees, is a camping area. Quite a few people come from surrounding areas to camp here for weeks or even all summer. Then in the winter when the lake is frozen over, there's ice skating. As you can see, it's lighted back here." He pointed upward at a street lamp mounted in the branches of a tree.

They were walking along the edge of the lake, which B.G. could see was quite large. A now familiar sense of frustration welled inside her as she noted the attitude implicit in Nils's tone, if not in his actual words. He clearly did not expect her to be impressed with Forsborg's lake, and he wanted her to know that her opinion mattered not at all to him.

"I'm sure it's very pretty . . . in the daytime, I mean," she added lamely, aware of how banal the comment had sounded. "We have a lake at home, too. It's probably a lot like this one."

Their steps slowed as they neared a long pier that extended some distance out into the water. Nils still held her elbow in that impersonal clasp. In the falling darkness B.G. was intensely aware of his touch and of his nearness. It was difficult for her to think of anything to say because she was distracted by the yearning to have him touch her in a different way, the way a man touches a woman he wants. How could she feel this strong attraction to a man who disliked her and antagonized her at every opportunity? No sooner had she asked herself that baffling question than Nils was making another of his subtly needling remarks.

"I'm sure your lake in Minnesota is larger than this one. Everything in the United States is larger than it is in Sweden."

His insinuation that B.G.'s attitude toward everything she saw in Sweden would be condescending was like the proverbial straw that broke the camel's back. She had suddenly reached the limit of insolence she would tolerate from this man. It made her all the madder that she had been trying to make friends with him and even wishing deep down inside for something more than friendship.

Stopping short, she jerked her elbow free of his light grasp.

"You're a real horse's behind, do you know that?" Her angry voice sounded terribly loud in the stillness of the woods beside the lake. With arms akimbo in an aggressive stance, B.G. glared at him. It was almost fully dark now, the lamps in the trees casting a sallow, insubstantial light. "For your information," she continued angrily, "I don't know if my lake at home is bigger than this lake! And I definitely don't give a damn one way or the other! If your whole point is to try to make me out to be the boastful American, then go right ahead! Be my guest! There's nothing I'm prouder of than being an American, and nothing *you* can do or say will change that. I'm just glad *my* grandparents had the good sense—''

In the middle of that last sentence, B.G. realized that she was going too far, even in anger. As the words stuck in her throat, suddenly she knew that she had accomplished her purpose, to shake him out of that impervious calm and force his animosity out into the open. But as she stood there, momentarily frozen into speechlessness, it occurred to her that she may have unleashed a violence in him that he might turn on her! What is he going to do? she wondered in panic, fighting the urge to cower and back away.

As Nils reached for her, he didn't really know what he intended to do, probably just grab her shoulders and shake her senseless. The moment his hands made contact with her stiffly defiant form, he knew that he had to bring her to submission. The urge was a dark and primitive one he had never known before, a need that couldn't be denied in the heat of his rage. Sliding his arms around her, he crushed her hard against him and took advantage of her shock to assault her lips with a brutal kiss that made them part in a gasp that only made her further vulnerable.

Victorious at the easily won entry, he sent his tongue boldly into her mouth, found hers and conquered it arrogantly. The pounding of her fists on his shoulders, the whimpering sounds coming from her throat, and the futile twisting motions of her body against his only increased his excitement, and he ground his mouth harder against hers, bruising the softness. His hands reached down and sank without any gentleness into the firm swell of her buttocks and jerked her upward and against him so that her body was fitted hard to his groin.

The contact brought a low groan to his throat, followed by the sudden realization that he was more aroused than he had ever been before in his life. Dear God, what was he *doing?* Nils had never launched this kind of attack on a woman, never kissed a woman with such utter brutality. And to think that he'd actually turned himself on while he was behaving like an animal! Self-disgust gradually spread through him, and he could feel himself coming to his senses.

B.G. was aware that something had changed. Her assailant was lessening the pressure of his mouth against hers. His hands were relaxing the steel grip on her buttocks that welded her hips to his own and pressed her against the thrust of his aroused masculinity. It was B.G.'s opportunity to strengthen her resistance and extricate herself from his embrace.

Instead she stopped fighting altogether. Her fists came unclenched and her palms explored the muscular breadth of his shoulders. Rather than twisting her head aside and avoiding a continuation of his kiss, she softened her lips and let them cling to his, opposing his growing reluctance and luring him into a different kind of kiss, one that did not have punishment and retaliation as its aim.

Still there was nothing tender about the meeting of their lips, the battle of their tongues, the exploration of their hands, all far too intimate and demanding for the first embrace of virtual strangers. Nils had rushed them past the tentative stage of a new relationship and exploded in both of them a passion he hadn't wanted and temporarily couldn't control. Too late he realized that his punishment had backfired on him. He hadn't expected to want to devour this woman in his arms, to want to touch every inch of her and make love to her until they were too weak to move. But he wanted all of that.

In a kind of panic at what was happening to him, he pulled his lips away from hers and forced her head against his chest, knowing even as he did so that she would be able to hear and feel the thunderous beat of his heart.

"I think you're more Swedish than you admit," he said recklessly. The comment didn't make a hell of a lot of sense, and he knew it, but he was desperate, reaching out blindly for a weapon, any weapon, to push her back a safe distance.

B.G. struggled to clear her head. She couldn't see what being Swedish or *not* being Swedish had to do with the way she felt in Nils's arms, but even in her sensual fog, she perceived the remark to be a taunt. Without pulling back from him a single inch, she spoke the first words that came to mind and knew almost instantly that she had hit a target.

"Maybe you're more American than you admit."

Nils went straight as a ramrod and put her out of his arms.

"Not if being American means being insensitive to people who love you," he said cuttingly, throwing discretion to the winds.

B.G. shivered and folded her arms across her chest before she remembered the shawl and saw that it lay on the grass in a snowy white heap. Picking it up, she wrapped it around her shoulders. With the heat of passion draining quickly from her body, she felt suddenly very cold.

"And just what is *that* supposed to mean?"

Nils had already seen the trap he had set for himself. He would have to betray his grandmother's confidence and tell about those letters B.G.'s grandmother had written from Minnesota. There was no getting around it, unfortunately.

"I'm talking about such things as refusing to be called your grandmother's name when you were well aware that her feelings were being deeply hurt," he said coldly.

B.G. sucked her breath in sharply, making an audible little hissing sound.

"How do *you* know—" she began indignantly and then broke off, the answer being all too obvious. "I see," she said in an ominously quiet tone. "My grandmother wrote *your* grandmother letters, telling her things about me—and your grandmother in turn told *you* how I had disappointed everyone back in Minnesota by not wanting to be a Swede, but an American. So that's why you took an instant dislike to me, Nils."

She paused to let him speak, but Nils was silent, letting her believe that she had pinpointed the cause for his animosity. Her voice had a bitter edge when she continued.

"I wouldn't be surprised if this whole trip to Sweden hadn't been cooked up between my grandmother and yours, a kind of last-ditch effort to bring out the latent Swede in me. I'm not sure what *your* part in the whole scheme was, but—"

"Take my word for it. I had nothing to do with your coming to Sweden," Nils put in curtly. He was calling himself every kind of an ass for having opened up his big mouth and betrayed his grandmother. Somehow he had to patch things up so that she wouldn't suffer the consequences of his rashness.

"I'll take your word for it!" B.G. snapped back. "Your attitude has made it clear that I'm not welcome! But in spite of your deplorable manners and the fact that I might have been lured to Sweden under false pretenses, I have no intention of having my trip spoiled because you don't like me or approve of me. I happen to like your grandmother, and I believe she genuinely likes me. Once she accepts the fact that she can't make me a Swede, she and I are going to have a great visit—*without* your interference!''

Nils eased out a very quiet sigh of relief.

''My grandmother does like you,'' he said sincerely. ''And I hope you'll accept my apology for the way I've acted. You're right. I haven't been very hospitable. It's no excuse, but I have a lot on my mind right now. It wasn't your fault, I realize, but the timing of your visit couldn't have been worse for me. Now, I think we'd better be getting back,'' he suggested tersely, before she could ask any questions about whatever was weighing on his mind.

They walked along in silence. B.G. noticed that every now and then Nils would realize that he had stepped up the pace and would slow down again for her benefit. She was suddenly so tired that her feet seemed weighted down with lead, and her fatigue was mental as well as physical. It seemed that so much had happened since her arrival in Gothenburg earlier that day. There had been too much to absorb, too much to try to understand and cope with.

If she hadn't been so weary, she might have tried to initiate a conversation that would lead to what was bothering Nils and why this was such a bad time for her to visit Sweden. Perhaps if she knew those things, his boorishness toward her might seem more excusable. Even without knowing them, she harbored surprisingly little anger toward him. She'd gotten it all out of her system back there at the lake.

He was a complex man, Nils Heidenstam, a man with depths and secrets. In spite of her spirited declaration a few minutes earlier that she intended to enjoy her visit with his grandmother without his interference, B.G. knew she'd be more than a little disappointed if she arose the next morning and learned that he had gone away and wouldn't return for the duration of her stay. Nils had tricked her, insulted her, even assaulted her physically, but the prospect of spending more time in his company made her look forward to her Swedish visit with a new anticipation.

Chapter Five

The next morning B.G. slept late. She awoke with vague memories of dreams about her arrival and first day in Sweden. The dreams had been confused and illogical, as dreams usually are, but she did know that Nils Heidenstam had figured largely in them and that they hadn't been entirely unpleasant or she wouldn't be facing the day with such eagerness.

A glance toward the window confirmed that the sun was shining brilliantly. Not wanting to waste any more time lying abed, she got up, dressed, and went downstairs.

Solbritt was out in the garden at the rear of the house, occupied in some gardening task that she abandoned the moment she heard B.G.'s cheery greeting from the steps. Drawing off dirt-stained cotton gloves, she threw them down on the flower bed and headed at once for the house.

"*God morgon!*" she called out heartily.

B.G. watched her approach and marveled again that the energetic woman was actually a contemporary of her grandmother's and must be past seventy. This morning Solbritt wore a floral-printed red blouse, a blue denim skirt, and wooden-soled clogs. Even with the deep lines in her tanned face and the evidence of sagging in the skin exposed by the neck of her blouse, she still looked no older than sixty or sixty-five, at most. The one sign of vanity that B.G. noted with some curiosity was the coloring and styling of Solbritt's hair. It was quite obviously tinted the reddish blond color and was worn in curls too girlish for her.

"And did you sleep well?" Solbritt was inquiring solicitously in her lilting Swedish. B.G. felt herself once again wrapped in the friendliness and warmth of the older woman's personality as Solbritt hustled her into the house and set out a bountiful Scandinavian breakfast.

There were several kinds of bread, none having come out of a plastic wrapper except the *knäckebröd,* or "hard bread" that an American would liken to a rye crisp cracker. A large wedge of cheese was served on a wooden board with the typical Swedish cheese slicer. In addition to the cheese, there was sliced ham, liver pâté, crispy sliced sweet pickles, butter, and several home-made preserves, including tangy marmalade.

Smiling to herself, B.G. spread a slice of hard bread with butter, topped it with slivers of cheese, and then spread liver pâté on top of the cheese before adding a couple of pickle slices. It amused her to reflect that the typical American would take one look at the food on the table and call the meal lunch, not breakfast. But having grown up in a Swedish stronghold in Minnesota, B.G. was prepared.

"Are you positive you would not like a boiled egg?" Solbritt asked for the third time. "It would be no trouble to prepare. There is cereal, too, if you would like that and cultured milk to pour over it as well as sweet milk.''

"No, thank you!'' B.G. refused laughingly. ''There is more than enough food here.'' She bit into her open sandwich and chewed with enjoyment.

Satisfied that she had provided amply for her guest, Solbritt joined B.G. at the dining room table while she ate. Before long she had volunteered the answer to a question B.G. hadn't worked around to asking yet.

"Nils had to go to Jönköping today. He will be back in time to join us for the evening meal.''

B.G. was busy building herself another open sandwich, this time choosing a different variety of ingredients, opting for wheat bread spread with butter and wild cranberry jam.

"What kind of work does Nils do for the Heidenstam Fabrik?'' she asked offhandedly and then settled back to listen to the answer to that and many other questions she didn't have to ask, since Nils and the family business were obviously favorite topics of conversation with Solbritt.

Nils was a kind of liaison person between the Heidenstam factory in Forsborg and branches of the business in other countries. His father headed the New York office, while another of Solbritt's sons was in charge of London and still another of the Paris office. B.G.'s head was soon full of names and relationships, but the one thing that was clear to her was that the Heidenstam Fabrik was a family concern. It seemed that every uncle, nephew, cousin, and grandchild was involved in it in some way.

"Nils knows everything about the business,'' Solbritt boasted proudly. ''He even knows most of the workers in the factory by their family names.'' Her face clouded over for a moment and became almost sad. Then she shrugged off whatever reflection had dampened her mood. "The times change," she declared philosophically. "They cannot always remain the same."

B.G. might have followed up on the observation, but she wanted to glean more specific information about Nils and didn't want to risk getting bogged down in reminiscences about the "good old days" at the Heidenstam factory.

"Does Nils have brothers and sisters who also visit you here in Forsborg?" she asked craftily.

"*Nej*. Nils is an only child. That is a circumstance that can cause some difficulty, can it not?"

Before B.G. could respond to the question, which seemed to be a rhetorical one anyway, Solbritt went on to talk about her son Lars, who was Nils's father. From her description of him, he seemed to be one of those men known in the United States as a "workaholic," driving himself and working long hours to the detriment of his health. He suffered from stomach ulcers and a heart condition, but continued to smoke cigarettes, drink alcohol, and maintain a hectic schedule.

"Nils worries about his father. It is only natural," Solbritt said regretfully.

"Nils does seem to have something on his mind," B.G. ventured in what she tried to make a neutral tone, but the attempt to get information from Nils's grandmother about what was bothering him wasn't at all successful.

"Yes, I have noticed that Nils is worried," Solbritt said thoughtfully. "Perhaps our little trip will take his mind off his problems," she said, brightening, and before B.G. had a chance to say anything else, Solbritt had begun to discuss the first leg of the trip, the passage on the Göta Canal.

B.G. was reluctant to leave the subject of Nils, but she

had found the conversation over breakfast enlightening. Perhaps he was deeply concerned about his father's health, more concerned than even Solbritt realized. Some new diagnosis may have been made recently. Perhaps Nils had come to Forsborg to tell his grandmother some grave news. Maybe that was what he had meant when he had said that B.G.'s visit was ill-timed.

Whatever it was that currently preyed on Nils's mind and caused the moodiness B.G. had already observed, she would no doubt find out about it during her stay. Although she had known Nils Heidenstam for only a short time and he had treated her deplorably during that time, she hoped that nothing serious was wrong.

The remainder of the day passed most pleasantly. Solbritt took her on a walking tour of the village and introduced her to countless people along the way. It was quite evident to B.G. that her hostess and guide enjoyed a position of respect and prestige, yet there was nothing of the *grande dame* in her manner and certainly not a hint of servility in the townspeople, whose handshakes were strong and greetings hearty. One or two older people recalled B.G.'s grandmother.

Several times B.G. had the opportunity to voice her own strong American sentiments and let Solbritt know in a polite, but firm, way that B.G. was in Sweden strictly as a tourist, not as a Swedish-American discovering her "roots." One chance came when Solbritt mentioned that there was a "boat trip" planned for the following day, Sunday.

"You will see the beautiful west coast of Sweden!" the older woman promised. "And then after we take the Göta Canal from Gothenburg to Stockholm, you will see the Stockholm archipelago. It is different from this coast but also very beautiful! You will see for yourself that, although it is small, Sweden is a wonderful country."

Listening to the older woman's fervent praise of her beloved country, B.G. decided to keep her peace and not risk hurting Solbritt's feelings. What harm would it do anyone for Solbritt to show off her country? No more harm than it would do B.G. to answer to *Birgitta* for a couple of weeks.

Late in the day B.G. found herself looking forward to the evening ahead and knew the reason for her anticipation. She couldn't wait to see how Nils would react to her after their encounter the previous night. Would he be polite and aloof as he had been after their return from the walk to the lake? Or, now that she had forced his antagonism out into the open, would he be friendlier?

After a long, delightful soak in the gigantic bathtub, B.G. took her time choosing an outfit and doing her hair and makeup, only to learn when she went downstairs that Nils wouldn't be joining them after all. He had telephoned his grandmother and explained that he would be detained. B.G. had difficulty concealing her disappointment and could only hope that Solbritt wouldn't notice.

"Perhaps Nils will be able to join us for coffee or a drink later," the older woman suggested in a placating voice that suggested she *had* noticed and did not disapprove.

But Nils did not join them that night, and B.G. went up to bed with a strong sense of anticlimax and a renewed resentment of Nils Heidenstam that she would have been hard put to justify even to herself. No matter how many times she told herself that he might have had a legitimate reason for staying away the entire evening, she knew that he had stayed away out of sheer perversity. Somehow he had known that she was dying to see how he would behave toward her, and he had wanted to prolong her suspense!

B.G.'s indignation became mingled with mortification when she remembered that Solbritt had been aware of her young guest's disappointment in Nils's absence. What if the indulgent grandmother passed that information along to the insufferable grandson? B.G. could just imagine how pleased Nils would be to think he had ruined her evening. He might even construe her reported eagerness to see him again as reason to think she was panting for an encore of his brutish assault last evening! This train of thought led to a grim resolution to give Nils Heidenstam the deep freeze on the boating trip the next day. B.G. would ignore him and talk only to Solbritt.

B.G. had some difficulty falling asleep, and she found herself reviewing everything that had happened to her since her arrival at the Gothenburg airport, including the conversation with Solbritt about Nils that morning at breakfast. It infuriated her now to recall how sympathetic she had felt toward him after learning of his father's bad health. In the future she would not excuse Nils for inexcusable behavior no matter what problems weighed on his mind. After all, everybody had problems and there was no excuse for making innocent bystanders—like herself—suffer.

Sentiments like these soothed B.G.'s mind until she was at last able to drift off to sleep. One of her last waking reflections was the hope that Nils didn't make some excuse to bypass the boating trip tomorrow. It would be very frustrating not to have the opportunity to show him how indifferent she was to his presence.

The following morning Nils was the first person B.G. encountered when she went downstairs. He was having breakfast in the dining room and reading the Sunday paper at the same time. After a polite greeting, he kept on reading.

Solbritt must have heard the voices in the dining room because she came bustling out of the kitchen, all smiles and morning cheer, urging B.G. to sit down and then demanding to know if she had slept well.

"I've never slept better in my life." B.G. made the assurance with a little too much emphasis, as though to impress upon the man engrossed in his newspaper that his absence the previous evening had not interfered in the least with her slumber.

"It's a *wonderful* day for a boat trip!" Solbritt declared happily, casting a pleased glance toward the broad casement window. "Isn't it, Nils?"

Nils laid to one side the section of newspaper he had been reading, responding with reluctance to his grandmother's query. He, too, glanced toward the window, acknowledging the brilliance of the day.

"It should be a good day for sunbathing, anyway," he commented with a shrug. "According to the weather forecast, we're not likely to have much wind, though."

B.G. thought about the remark for a moment, trying to make some sense of it. "Isn't that good?" she ventured, concluding that surely wind would make for rough boating conditions.

Nils lifted one eyebrow in a quizzical expression and met her eyes directly for the first time since she'd sat down.

"A calm day is hardly good for sailing."

"*Sailing,*" B.G. echoed.

Before she could say more, Solbritt created a small distraction, exclaiming something about eggs and scurrying back toward the kitchen. Nils looked after his grandmother with slightly narrowed eyes and then concentrated on refilling his coffee cup from the china pot sitting on the table.

"Didn't my grandmother mention that you are invited to go sailing with me and two other couples today?"

B.G. couldn't fail to notice his lack of enthusiasm. Obviously, the invitation hadn't been his idea. Had

Solbritt pressured him into taking B.G. sailing the same way she'd pressured him into the after-dinner promenade the first evening?

"She said something about a boating trip, but I had no idea it was a *sailing* trip. Isn't she coming along, too?"

Solbritt swept into the room bearing a tray with three boiled eggs perched atop china egg cups. She had overheard at least the final part of B.G.'s faintly apologetic reply.

"Sailing is not for an old woman like me," she asserted vigorously, setting an egg in front of B.G. and then another in front of Nils before she placed the last one at her place and sat down. "The sea motion always made me seasick, even when I was much younger." She took up a tiny spoon and tapped busily at the top of her boiled egg.

"You wouldn't have to worry about any sea motion today," Nils pointed out as he lifted the top off his egg with a few deft motions, but Solbritt ignored him.

B.G. caught the teasing undertone in his voice and found herself disarmed once again by the way Nils spoke to his grandmother. His gentle irony said he wasn't fooled in the least by her machinations, but he would tolerate almost anything from her because he loved her. For B.G. it was terribly unflattering, though, to be one of those things he would simply "tolerate." She didn't want Nils to be forced into taking her sailing.

As she ate her breakfast, B.G. pondered what to do. She could refuse outright to go sailing with Nils, saying that she would prefer to spend the day with Solbritt, or she could make up some excuse to avoid going along. The plain truth was that she really *did* want to go, if only because she had never sailed before. Still, B.G.'s pride insisted that she give Nils the chance to escape what seemed to be just an onerous chore to him.

Her chance to talk to him alone came when breakfast

was nearly over and the doorbell rang. Nils started at once to get up, but Solbritt motioned him to stay seated.

"I will see who is there. It is probably Nils Bjornsen wanting to know if he can sell me firewood for the winter."

Nils watched his grandmother make her bustling exit and then turned to B.G. with an expression she thought was bordering on friendliness.

"*Nils* must be the most common name in Sweden," he said dryly.

"Like *John* is in the United States," she said quickly, gathering her nerve before plunging into what she had to say. "Look, Nils, I can see that you're being pressured into playing host for me. I'm sorry, because it's none of my doing. I won't go along on this sailing trip today if you would rather that I didn't."

Nils's expression said clearly that he halfway admired her for her blunt, direct approach and yet he was irritated by it, too. As soon as her words were out, B.G. realized that she had phrased her willingness to let him off the hook in such a way that he couldn't accept without being totally ungracious. No doubt he thought that she had expressed herself that way deliberately, when actually she hadn't.

"Of course, you'll go," he said immediately, discounting her offer. "The whole trip was planned for your benefit."

His brusque words brought such chagrin to B.G.'s features that Nils had to feel a little sympathetic. After all, she was speaking the truth when she said it wasn't her fault that Solbritt had manipulated him into taking her out sailing with his friends.

"You really must come along," he said in a kinder voice. "The other four people will be terribly disappointed if you don't. They're looking forward to meeting you, and I feel certain you'll like them."

B.G. was still undecided. It was silly of her, but she had hoped he would say that *he* wanted her to come along now that he knew he had a choice.

Seeing that her indecision was real and that she might refuse to go along with the day's plan, Nils thought about what it would be like to drive into Gothenburg by himself and go sailing with the others without her. Surprisingly, the idea wasn't terribly appealing and, undoubtedly, Solbritt would be upset. Nils couldn't bring himself to plead with her, but at least he could tell her the truth.

"In all likelihood, I'd be going sailing today whether you were here or not. Knowing that, my grandmother simply suggested that it would be nice for me to arrange a sailing trip for her visitor from America." Nils good-naturedly mocked his grandmother's sing-song cadences, even though he was speaking English. "And she was right. I think you will enjoy seeing the western coast of Sweden and meeting some 'typical' young Swedish people. I just resent being placed in a position of not being able to say no. So, knowing all that, will you reconsider and come along?"

B.G. nodded her willingness even before she spoke. The invitation wasn't even close to what she had hoped for, but Nils did sound as though he meant it.

"I would like to come along. Mainly because I've never been sailing before and it sounds like fun. But from now on, I'd much rather you didn't do *anything* for my benefit that you don't want to do." She paused deliberately for emphasis. "Is that agreed?"

"Agreed." Nils spoke without hesitation, knowing full well that the pact was impossible to keep. Good Lord, did she really think life was so simple that one could do only those things one chose to do? If only *he* could see the world in such simplistic terms! At least he had smoothed over her ruffled feelings for the time being. In the future he would have to be more careful to hide his true feelings. B.G. had a much keener perception than he would have expected from a farmgirl from Minnesota.

The first half of the ride from Forsborg to Gothenburg was fun for B.G. and yet unsettling, through no fault of Nils's. He was more relaxed and friendly than he had allowed himself to be in her presence before, without those lapses into moodiness she had come to expect. Given the casual nature of the conversation and the absence of innuendo in his contributions, she was able to let down her guard, only to discover a new enemy to her equanimity: herself. She found herself constantly appraising her companion's physical attributes and relating them to sensual memories and fantasies.

At first they talked at some length about sailing. Nils told her that his interest had begun when he was a young boy and had learned to sail his first sailboat, a Sunfish. B.G. listened with genuine interest, made appropriate remarks, and asked a question now and then, all the while seeing in her mind a Nils dressed in skin garments and holding a sword and shield aloft, while his crewmen guided a marauding longboat to shore. Her first thought upon seeing him at the airport had been that he looked like a descendent of the fierce sea-going Vikings, with his fair coloring and superb physique. Now it turned out that he had been an avid sailor nearly his whole life. How fitting that seemed.

"Do you own the boat we're sailing on today?" B.G. cleared her throat and tried to clear her mind of distracting images.

"I own it in partnership with Per and Gunnar, the other two guys who will be along today. It's an arrangement that suits me perfectly, since I wouldn't get enough use out of a sailboat here in Sweden to make owning one worthwhile. This way I have someone else to see to maintenance and keep an eye on it.''

His deep voice fell pleasantly on her ears. She watched his hands as they clasped the wheel with a casual air of command. Then without warning, and for no reason, as far as B.G. was able to determine, he ran his right palm lightly along his right thigh, calling her attention to sinewy muscles covered by soft brown corduroy. She felt with disruptive immediacy the rough strength of his hands when they had settled into the soft flesh of her buttocks two nights before by the Forsborg lake. She stirred restlessly in her seat and breathed out in relief when his hand returned to the wheel.

''Who else will be along today?''

She glanced at his profile. His bone structure was strong under a covering of smooth tanned skin. Blond hair was ruffled by a breeze from the open sunroof and the partially lowered window on his side.

''Per's wife, Eva, and Silvia, the girl Gunnar has been dating for a long time. I think they probably live together by now.''

Nils turned his head and met B.G.'s gaze, letting her take note again of the vivid contrast between the blue of his eyes and the golden brown of his skin. *He's almost too good-looking,* she told herself to combat the spread of pleasure. Every time she permitted herself to drop her gaze to the clean, firm shape of his mouth, she experienced the same sense of wonder. Had that mouth really ravaged hers the way she remembered?

''Do they all live in Gothenburg?''

She forced herself to look forward rather than at him, running her tongue surreptitiously over lips that tingled. She couldn't remember ever having reacted so *physically* to a man's presence. She could swear that the interior of the car had magically shrunk since that other time she had ridden in it with Nils. His long-limbed frame seemed to be taking up more than his rightful half of the front, crowding her against the door.

"They do now," Nils was answering. "Per is from Forsborg originally. I've known him as long as I can remember, and I met Gunnar through him."

A glance told Nils that B.G.'s attention was firmly riveted on the road ahead. He took the opportunity to let his eyes rove over her appreciatively. She was definitely good to look at, slim and nicely rounded in the right places, not at all what he had expected of a Swedish-American farmgirl from Minnesota. From the way she sat in her bucket seat, though, straight-shouldered and erect, he wondered if she might be nervous about the prospect of spending the day with strangers.

"I feel certain you'll like them. They're good people."

"I'm sure I'll like them," she answered mechanically, knowing the precise second when he turned his attention back to the road. It was unnerving to be so closely attuned to a man that you could *feel* his gaze slide over you.

"What kind of work do you do in Minnesota?" Nils had thought it might relax her to talk about herself, but she seemed to go even more tense.

"I'm an interior decorator."

B.G. waited for the inevitable question. She'd known he would ask her sooner or later whether she had ever used Heidenstam cabinets. All she could do was tell him the truth. No law said she had to use Swedish imports just because her parents were Swedish immigrants.

"An interior decorator," Nils mused, surprised and curious about the faint defensiveness of her tone. It seemed a remarkable coincidence, too, that both of them were actually in the same general line of business, furnishing interiors.

B.G. bristled a little at his surprise because she thought she had caught a tinge of amusement in his tone.

"What did you think I did—milked cows on my father's farm?" she countered defensively, still waiting for him to ask her.

"No, I didn't think that, not after I'd seen you, anyway. It's just coincidental, don't you think? I'm in the business of building furniture and you put it into buildings." Nils's words were no more than out when he had a quick intuition that he verified with a sideways glance at her profile. Now he knew why she was acting so prickly. She didn't want to admit that she *hadn't* put his furniture into buildings!

"How did you happen to get into interior decorating?" Nils made sure his tone conveyed nothing but interest.

B.G. seized on the question with relief. She sketched in her background, explaining that she had first become interested in home decorating when she was in high school and had taken the usual home economics courses that were all but requisite for girls in rural Minnesota. Then she'd gone on to college and majored in interior decorating for two years, but found herself to be impatient with the academic pace and structure.

"I had to take courses I wasn't interested in, and some of the ones that sounded so great in the catalog turned out to be a total waste of time. I decided I'd learn a lot more if I got a job with a good decorating firm and worked my way up from the bottom. Kind of the apprenticeship idea, I guess. So that's what I did."

"You decided all this completely on your own?"

There was something strange in Nils's voice that B.G. couldn't really analyze, so she just ignored it for the time being.

"Uh huh. My college advisor did everything she

could to talk me out of dropping out of school, but I wouldn't listen. And everything's worked out great. I admit I was lucky to get on at *Maxwell's,* since it's one of the most respected decorating firms in Minneapolis, but I have to give myself some credit, too. I put up with a lot that first year when I was nothing but a glorified errand girl. You wouldn't believe what some of the decorators had me do. But I learned a lot.''

"Then the next year they started giving me little projects to handle, which they were actually responsible for and got the credit for doing. Little by little, I've worked myself up until now I have some good clients who swear by me. They recommend me to their friends and so on. *You* must know how the decorating business works.''

B.G. realized that she had gotten quite carried away in talking about her job, which she thoroughly enjoyed.

"I'd say you like your job,'' Nils commented after a pause. He was trying not to sound as envious as he felt. She made her pursuance of the right career sound like a straight path between *A* and *Z* with no obstacles and no detours. Nils just couldn't imagine that kind of certainty.

"I *do* like my job,'' B.G. confirmed emphatically. "More than that, I *love* my work. If I didn't enjoy it, I'd quit tomorrow and do something else. Life is too short to waste time working at the wrong job.''

Something twisted in Nils's guts. *She doesn't have any idea what she's talking about,* he told himself. *Don't go resenting her when she has no way of understanding a more complicated set of circumstances than her own.* Still, the tight-jawed feeling was back, the latent aggression that made him want to attack her and shake her foundations.

"Scandinavian furnishings and design must be very popular in that part of the United States,'' he suggested with deliberate casualness. "There *is* a large concentration of Swedish and Norwegian immigrants in Minnesota, Wisconsin, and Michigan, isn't there?"

B.G. was taken off guard. Her eyes widened in dismay as she snapped her head around to stare at him. For the first time since their open talk at breakfast, the silky needling was back in his voice. But *why?* She couldn't think of a thing she had said that could have offended him, unless . . . She took her courage in hand and admitted what he must have guessed.

"Contemporary Scandinavian *is* quite popular, but I lean more toward a traditional look and feel right now." She bit her lower lip and darted a glance over toward Nils, which told her nothing of what he was thinking. "It's a little embarrassing to admit to you, but I've never used the Heidenstam cabinetry, for example." *There. She'd said it.* Now he could pick her apart and expose all the reasons she avoided things Scandinavian in her work. Somehow she was beginning to see for herself how silly her bias was.

"Haven't you?" Nils replied, without any surprise or indeed without any emotion at all. After that, he had nothing more to say about interior decorating or any other subject. He had slipped away from her into one of those thoughtful silences that shut her out totally and discouraged any efforts at initiating further conversation.

Between the time the conversation died and they arrived at the marina in Gothenburg, B.G. had far more time than she needed to go back over the exchange between them and try to figure out when and why the change had come over him. *What had she said?* For the life of her, she couldn't figure out anything that could have upset him other than her admission that she didn't like contemporary Scandinavian design and hadn't used his company's product. But when she admitted that she hadn't, he had seemed so totally unconcerned.

The whole thing was too puzzling for her to figure out. Nils Heidenstam was an enigma, a man with two completely different sides, like a coin all minted gold on one side and dark and indecipherable on the other. If she weren't so dazzled by the golden side, maybe she wouldn't have this compulsive need to penetrate the obscurity of that dark side of his personality.

Chapter Six

The whole matter was crowded out of her mind as soon as they had arrived at the marina. B.G. was too busy registering impressions.

The marina itself was quite large and filled with sailboats of every size, color, and description. Groups of casually dressed people, men, women, and children, headed along the docks carrying canvas totebags and coolers. Some were already aboard their boats and busy preparing to get underway or untying mooring lines and motoring out. The whole atmosphere was leisurely and relaxed with undercurrents of excited anticipation. There was much friendly calling back and forth between neighboring boats.

"Watch your step," Nils cautioned when they had turned off a main pier with protective railings on each side onto one without the railings and with boats on either side.

It was an unnecessary warning, since B.G. had never

walked quite so consciously before, unless it had been the first time she had worn high heels. She was putting one foot in front of the other as though she were on a catwalk, aware that she seemed to be the only person wearing sandals. Everyone else wore some sort of canvas sneakers or leather moccasins like those Nils wore. She was positively awed by his surefootedness as he strode along, paying no attention to where he stepped.

For all her sense of being in a totally unfamiliar world, she was excited to be doing something she'd never done before. Intuitively she trusted Nils to tell her what to do and to watch out for her safety. He was so obviously in his element.

"Looks like the others are here," he announced, pointing up ahead toward the right. "*Sea Gull*'s the one with the tall skinny guy taking the blue sail cover off the main. That's Per. Gunnar's sitting in the cockpit drinking a beer already. That's typical!" Nils called out as they came abreast of the large white-hulled sailboat.

"I'll say it's typical," shouted back the man sprawled in the cockpit. "You always manage to time your arrival perfectly. The work is all done. You can come aboard now."

While Nils grasped the stay at the bow and stepped onto the boat, B.G. had time to reflect that the exchange had taken place in English.

"Here. Give me your bag so that you have both hands free," he instructed her.

For just a moment she contemplated the distance between the dock and the tapering front of the boat, experiencing her first misgivings about this business of going sailing. Still, she kept them to herself as she handed her bag to Nils and tried to bolster her nerve for following his example.

"Wait," he ordered, setting the bag down behind him

and kneeling on the deck to grasp a mooring line and pull the boat right up to the edge of the dock. "Okay, now you can step aboard."

B.G. grabbed onto the same stout length of wire he had used, the one running from the top of the mast and fastened to the deck. When she had stepped to the deck of the boat, she let out her breath, realizing just at that time that she had been holding it. As she followed Nils back to the cockpit, mentally she was thanking him for having made the process of getting aboard the boat easy for her. Then she felt the movement under her feet as the boat responded to their weight, and she forgot everything else in the strangeness of walking on movement.

Per had finished his task on the cabin top, and both he and Gunnar were awaiting them in the cockpit. Two women came out from inside the boat, having been alerted to the arrival of the latecomers and quite obviously eager to meet Nils's guest. For several minutes good-natured greetings and insults flew back and forth. B.G. knew at once that she was among good friends who were completely at ease with one another. She felt remarkably at ease herself when Nils introduced her to each one of them, referring to her as B.G. with no inflection to suggest that the name was unusual.

Her first overall impression of the other four people was that they were healthy and attractive in an ordinary kind of way. Per was indeed very tall and thin and possessed of a nervous energy entirely lacking in the relaxed Gunnar, who was of average height and build and attired in old, faded navy swimming trunks and a tee-shirt. Eva, the wife of Per, was also tall and thin, like him, but was some months pregnant, a fact she had made no effort to conceal, since she wore a form-hugging shorts and pullover outfit, rather than a maternity top. Silvia was small and wiry and handled her body with the poised control of a ballet dancer or gymnast. Of all the company present, B.G. and Nils were the ones strikingly Scandinavian in their looks.

"Would you like to come down below?" Eva invited B.G. in English. "I will show you where you can put your bag."

B.G. followed her down a steep ladder with five steps and then moved out of the way as Silvia popped down after them.

"Isn't this *nice!*" B.G. commented admiringly, looking around her at the long open compartment in which they stood, a combination kitchen and sitting area, although she supposed *galley* was the appropriate word for a boat kitchen. The wood paneling on the walls had a soft luster, like the rubbed finish on fine furniture. The light fixtures were brass and gleamed. "It's just like a miniature efficiency apartment, isn't it?"

Both of the women hooted delightedly and then made a great show of hushing B.G.

"Don't let those men out there hear you say such a thing!" Silvia warned threatrically. "Remember that there is never to be a comparison between a house and a sailing vessel. *Never!* A boat is always far superior!"

"Thanks for telling me," B.G. whispered, grinning back at them conspiratorially and thinking to herself that she couldn't believe she was this relaxed with people she had just met—foreigners—in spite of the fact that they spoke English amazingly well. Now, more than before, she could appreciate Nils's reaction to her assumption that he wouldn't speak English when he picked her up at the airport. He was so right. She *had* been ignorant. Perhaps she had even deserved to have him play that trick on her.

"You did bring along a bathing suit?" Silvia wanted to know after the brief guided tour of the boat interior was completed and B.G. had been told how to operate the marine toilet.

"I wore it underneath my clothes," B.G. answered, glancing down at her white pleated shorts and bright blue tank top. Her feet were now bare, since at the suggestion of the other women, she had removed the sandals, which they had explained would not be as safe as bare feet.

"We are wearing our bathing suits, also," Silvia told B.G. approvingly. "As the sun gets hotter, one can start to remove the outer clothes. Today, since we have so little wind, it will become hot very soon, I think."

The engine of the boat leaped to life, bringing noise and vibration. Shortly thereafter, there were the footsteps of the men as they moved about on deck. B.G. accompanied the two women outside, glad when it became clear that no one expected her to do anything but sit safely in the cockpit and watch all the activity involved in getting underway.

Once they had motored out of the marina and all the fuss of raising sails was over, B.G. found herself quite relaxed and thoroughly pleased with her first sail, despite the fact that the others obviously found it disappointing that the wind was light and actually apologized to her as though they were somehow responsible. She thought it was delightful! With the engine turned off, she could hear the water against the hull making little gurgling, lapping sounds. The sea gulls called back and forth to one another in their forlorn tones, not worried in the least about the presence of humans in their habitat.

"This is *beautiful!*" she exclaimed, falling immediately under the spell of the bleak beauty of her surroundings as they passed between rocky islands with little vegetation. Some had cheerful little settlements, the pastel frame houses clinging to the rocky hillsides with a kind of stoic determination; others had no inhabitants save for wild creatures.

B.G. went into raptures when someone handed her the binoculars and directed her gaze toward a whole herd of fat, speckled gray seals sunning themselves on a little group of rocky islands. Minutes later she spotted a flock of wild swans floating gracefully on the surface of the blue sea, performing some instinctive, totally effortless ballet. It was only when she couldn't see the swans any longer that she reluctantly lowered the binoculars, realizing that she had been quite selfish in keeping them so long. She should let someone else have a chance to use them.

As she looked at her companions in the cockpit, B.G. opened her mouth to comment on how warm the sun had grown. The words stuck in her throat. While she had been totally preoccupied with gazing at the wild seals and swans, the sun growing hotter all the time, Eva and Silvia had shed most of their clothes. To her shock, the two women were leaning back, faces uplifted to the sun's rays, with their whole upper torsos *bare!* Eva still wore the aqua shorts, whose elastic waistband expanded to accommodate the gentle swell of her stomach, but Silvia had removed her bright red shorts and wore nothing but a scrap of a bikini bottom tied at either hip.

B.G. was unable at first to keep herself from staring, but fortunately no one seemed to be paying her any attention, no one, that is, except Nils. When she glanced over at him, she saw that he had been watching her reaction. Indignation spurted up inside her as she realized that he had known quite well that this was going to happen and had been looking forward to her shock and embarrassment. Yes, *embarrassment,* she was forced to admit. Even in college when the girls in the dormitory had paraded freely in the minimum of clothing, there had always been that vestige of female modesty that called for a towel on the trek from the shower down the hall to the room. B.G. wouldn't walk around bare-breasted in front of her best female friends.

"Maybe you'd like to take off a few clothes, too,"

Nils suggested, standing up and making his way over to the opening that led down inside the boat. He paused on the ladder and looked inquiringly at her, as though she might want to accompany him to remove her clothes.

B.G. glared at him and then averted her gaze, trying to look elsewhere, but not at the bare upper torsos of Eva and Silvia, who so far seemed oblivious to her regard. Without standing up, she took off the white shorts and then pulled the blue tank top over her head, revealing a blue and white striped bikini that was anything but prudish, yet made her feel overdressed.

Nils had disappeared down into the boat. When he appeared in the opening again, the upper part of his body was magnificently bare and smoothly tanned.

"Would you like me to put your things down below while I'm here?" he offered with excessive politeness.

B.G. sucked in her breath at the deliberateness with which he let his eyes linger on her breasts, commenting wordlessly on the fact that they were partially concealed behind blue and white striped triangles. It infuriated her that he could annoy her so effectively without even speaking a word! Especially when no one else seemed even to be aware of his mocking innuendo.

Nils had made the offer to her, but suddenly he was pelted by tee-shirts and shorts as Per and Gunnar unceremoniously stripped down to their swimming trunks and Eva and Silvia came out of their sunbathing trances long enough to toss their discarded clothing at Nils, too. He complained good-naturedly but went down inside the boat again to deposit the pile of clothes. B.G. was grateful for the chance to compose herself and summon her defenses.

"Hey, who wants a beer while I'm down here?" Nils called out and was heralded by a loud chorus of *"I do!"* By the time he had handed up bottles of beer to everyone, including B.G., she had regained her poise and was ready to counter questions and teasing about her American modesty. No one, however, made any open reference to the fact that she alone of the women chose not to take off her bikini top. If the modern young Swedes were curious as to her reasons, they were also too polite to show that they had noticed. Only Nils Heidenstam feels it is his *duty* to make me uncomfortable! B.G. told herself with fierce indignation.

Eva got up and, taking a cushion with her, made her way up to the foredeck where she was soon joined by the loose-limbed Per. Gunnar and Silvia apparently found the cockpit confining, too, because they stretched out on top of the cabin, lying side by side with their faces turned toward each other to facilitate desultory, private conversation. B.G. found herself alone in the cockpit with Nils, who was given no choice other than to handle the wheel.

At first she sat quite erect, staring off into the distance, determined to ignore him, but the need to put him in his place grew stronger and stronger as she felt his amusement wafting over to her in waves. She could also feel him staring at her.

"You are one of the *rudest* men I have ever met, do you know that?" She kept her voice low. To compensate for lack of volume, she enunciated each syllable of every word for emphasis.

When he didn't answer, she found that she *had* to look at him. He was watching her, waiting, a smile hovering at the corner of his mouth.

"What have I said to offend you?" he inquired innocently, lifting broad tanned shoulders in a travesty of the helpless shrug. With slow deliberation he let his gaze drift over her slender form, stopping to linger on each rounded breast, thrust forward by the rigid cast of her spine.

"You know!" she hissed back accusingly. "It's not so

much *what* you say or do—but *how* you do it. I want you just to leave me alone from now on. And *stop staring.*"

Making a great show of obeying her command, he shifted his gaze away from her, at the same time altering his position so that he leaned more to his left with his right foot resting up on the cockpit seat. The blatantly male stance heightened B.G.'s already keen awareness of his tall smoothly muscled frame in closely fitted blue nylon swim trunks whose color uncannily matched the blue stripes in her bikini. Even in her anger, she was unable to blot out the impact of his masculinity.

"Would you like to hear what I was thinking?" he inquired in a low tone, still keeping his gaze averted.

B.G. found it impossible to say no. The silence lengthened between them while he waited for her answer.

"What?" she said shortly.

"I was thinking how smart you American women are. It's much more provocative, you know, to tease a man by covering up a little of your breasts than to show all of them. I'm sitting here right this minute thinking how I would like to slip those straps off your shoulders and little by little lower those triangles of material . . ."

B.G. was silent, mesmerized against her will by the sheer eroticism of his tone as well as his words. Nils turned his head slowly toward her and met her eyes with his own. The electricity between them made her heart stop beating and then begin again with a rapid, irregular beat. When Nils's eyes dropped to her breasts, his regard was as unsettling as though he were actually uncovering her breasts in the way he had described. B.G. could feel her nipples hardening into sensitive, tingling peaks. Quickly she folded her arms across her chest so that he would not be able to see the way he was affecting her.

"I resent your insinuation that I wear my bathing suit top to stimulate any man, *especially* you," she said with stiff dignity. "In the United States, as you're probably already well aware, I could be arrested for indecent exposure if I appeared in a public place without it."

Nils had caught a quick glimpse of those hardened nipples before she crossed her arms. Whether she intended him to be or not, he *was* stimulated, by her and by the provocative conversation he had initiated.

"No one's going to arrest you here," he pointed out.

B.G. hugged her chest a little tighter and glared at him.

"You see. There you go again," she said accusingly. "You'll do or say anything to embarrass me or make me feel ill at ease. You know damned well I wouldn't take my top off in front . . . in front of—*everybody*."

"You're not ashamed of your body, are you?" Nils countered quickly.

"*No*." She uncrossed her arms and dropped her hands in her lap, eyeing him defiantly. "I'm not ashamed of my body, and I'm not going to be pressured into doing something I'm not comfortable with. Just call it a difference between your culture and mine."

"The modern Swedish woman definitely *has* discarded some of the moral hypocrisies of her ancestors," he agreed smoothly, "while the American woman has been perhaps a little less open and honest in her rebellion. Wouldn't you agree?"

"No, I would *not* agree," she replied in a strangled voice and didn't say more because she didn't trust herself to speak. If there was anything B.G. prided herself upon being, it was "open" and "honest." Nils was so clever with words that he could always manage to maneuver her right into a verbal corner. B.G. was plainly no match for him in the art of argument. He was not only better with words, but he knew her country as well as he knew his own and capitalized upon her own lack of information about modern Sweden, which she had so wrongly come here thinking of as a "backward" country in relationship to the United States.

Every time B.G. got into one of these verbal exchanges with Nils, he always seemed to have an instinct for piercing her defenses. She had the uncomfortable intuition that he *knew* all too well that his taunt about American women being less honest than Swedish women made her want to yank off not just her bathing suit top, but the bottom as well! Yet she *couldn't*. Truthfully, she did possess deep inhibitions about public nudity, as ingrained as those her mother and her grandmother would have felt about wearing the skimpy bikini B.G. wore today.

"Sweden is not what you expected it to be, is it?"

Nils's voice broke into her resentful reflections, posing a statement more than a question. He didn't seem to be taunting her now.

B.G. gave her head a brief negative shake.

"Not at all what I expected," she admitted with grudging honesty, determined to prove to him from now on in everything she said and did that she *was* honest, no matter what opinion he held of American women in general. "I guess I *should* have read up on Sweden before I came here, as you've already pointed out."

"You expected it to be a country of people like the Swedish immigrants you grew up with," he guessed shrewdly.

She nodded.

Nils was vaguely ashamed of himself. A few minutes before B.G. had been spontaneous and unself-conscious, enjoying herself thoroughly, and he had banished her high spirits. What he didn't understand about himself was why he had these elemental urges to grapple with her independent spirit and bring her to submission. After he had succeeded, he only felt apologetic and wished that he could make amends. Had he inherited more savagery from his Viking ancestors than he had ever suspected before now? Always in the past he had considered himself a fairly generous, considerate person. Why did this American offspring of Swedish immigrants irk him to the point that he would do or say almost anything to undermine her self-esteem and her irritating certainty about things? Was it because she was seemingly so free of self-questioning and moral ambivalence? Whatever the cause, Nils was coming to learn that no sooner had he made B.G. feel rotten about herself than he wanted to build her back up again.

"Underneath the surface, Swedish people haven't changed that much," he said thoughtfully. "Times have changed, and Sweden is undeniably a modern, progressive country in its social policies, but the values of the people are much the same as the values of those who emigrated to America. There's the belief in hard work and thriftiness and strong family ties."

B.G. wasn't about to let him take pity on her with the offering of this slick concession. If she was wrong, then she was wrong.

"If what you say is true, then your grandmother would be more like mine was," she pointed out skeptically. "My grandmother would be shocked at the sight of my bikini, but something tells me Fru Heidenstam wouldn't bat an eyelash if she had come along today and saw Eva and Silvia sunbathing topless."

Nils's face softened at her comparison.

"You're right," he mused fondly. "She probably wouldn't. But my grandmother is a very remarkable woman, if I do say so myself."

"I agree."

Their shared admiration of Solbritt Heidenstam brought them to a rather uncomfortable impasse. Nils had no intention of softening toward B.G. and welcoming her into his inner thoughts and emotions, neither of which he would expect her to be capable of understanding, not with her oversimplified view of the world. B.G. had learned the hard way not to let her guard down with Nils during those times when he seemed friendly, because he could launch another vicious attack when she least suspected it. She simply couldn't figure him out. He was complex and moody and entirely too shrewd in guessing her thoughts and targeting her weaknesses.

Nils and B.G. were both relieved when Per shouted from up on the foredeck that he was hungry. It was the reminder that they all must have been waiting for that lunch was overdue.

They anchored the boat near a small, uninhabited island. After a brief discussion, they decided to wait until they got to the island of Marstrand, their destination, before taking a swim. They wanted to walk around Marstrand with B.G. and show it to her without being rushed. From the discussion, B.G. gathered that Marstrand was a place they all considered special.

The lunch menu came as something of a surprise, but she made no comment when Eva and Silvia, having donned their swimsuit tops, served hot dogs with chips that looked like a not wholly successful attempt to imitate the American potato chip. Squeezing mustard from a metal tube, B.G. avoided Nils's eyes, irritably aware that he was probably reading her every reaction, as usual, and finding her amusing.

"Anything 'American' is very popular in Sweden," Nils commented to the world at large. "One of the most popular television programs is 'Dallas.'"

B.G. couldn't read any mockery in his tone, but she ignored him, nevertheless, and concentrated on finding out more about her companions, starting with inquiries about the kind of work they did. Per was an engineer with a large shipbuilding company in Gothenburg that now concentrated largely on constructing huge drilling platforms for the oil industry. Gunnar was a dentist. Eva and Silvia were both social workers. Eva was currently working in an administrative office, and Silvia worked with old people.

"What do you actually do?" B.G. asked the latter, mainly because Silvia was such a vivacious young woman that the job she had chosen came as a surprise.

Silvia was eager to talk about her work, making it apparent that she considered it worthwhile and rewarding. Before she explained in detail her own job, she outlined for B.G. the overall government attitude toward care of the aged. They were not to be forced into convalescent homes unless it was absolutely necessary that they have constant care. As long as an elderly person was able to live in his or her own home or government-subsidized apartment, he or she had that option.

"We provide someone to go to the old person's home and do housework and cooking whenever such aid is required," Silvia explained. "If an elderly person is unable to provide his own transportation, we arrange for a driver-companion. It is good for a person to be able to go shopping for himself or herself. An older person needs a sense of independence and dignity. I am trained in health care and make home visits to care for those in my district who are not ill enough to be hospitalized or placed in a nursing home."

B.G. was quite honestly impressed. If such a comprehensive plan for care of the aged existed in the United States, she did not know about it. Last winter there had been those horror stories about old people in cities freezing to death when their heat was turned off because they couldn't afford to pay their fuel bills.

"Do you know about the Swedish 'cradle to grave' philosophy?" Gunnar spoke up, noting her expression.

"No," she admitted. Involuntarily her gaze flew to Nils, but he wasn't looking at her or even seeming to be paying a great deal of attention to the conversation.

"Very simply, a citizen of Sweden is guaranteed the necessary things of life from the time that he or she is born until death. A Swedish person will have dental and health care, food to eat, and a home to live in, whether he is able to earn enough money to pay for them or not. The government promises that all will have enough rather than just a few having more than they need."

Silvia spoke up at this point, illustrating Gunnar's general explanation with a specific example.

"Eva, for example, will have the best hospital care available when it is time for her to deliver her baby. Her child will be born into the world with the assurance that it will have the opportunity for good health and a good education. Swedish children and young people do not have to pay to go to school."

"We have free public education in the United States, too," B.G. was glad to be able to put in.

The others, excepting Nils, all looked surprised.

"But we were under the impression that in the United States, you must pay to attend a university," Gunnar demurred politely.

"Well, you do," B.G. conceded, a little puzzled as she looked from one to the other and noted their expressions. "You don't mean that *college* is free in Sweden, too?"

They all nodded and then Per elaborated.

"It is to the advantage of the whole society that the citizens of a country be educated," he explained. "Of course, not everyone is qualified to go to a university. One must pass the required exams at each point in the process of schooling. But since there are so many different kinds of work that one can be trained to perform, everyone is certain to be able to find something to work at in order to earn a living.''

In theory, what he said made perfect sense, but B.G. knew that there had to be a catch. Before she could speak up and ask how the Swedish government *paid* for all these wonderful services that the people got free, Nils finally entered the conversation, surprising B.G. with his outspokenness.

''The perfect society comes with a high price tag,'' he observed dryly and couldn't say more at once because he was suddenly the target of outcries and gibes from his Swedish friends.

''Let us hear the loud voice of the capitalist!'' Gunnar sang out jeeringly.

Nils was coolly unaffected, and B.G. thought privately that he would probably hold his own quite effectively against the other four. It was a new experience for her to watch him in action when *she* wasn't his opponent.

''As my friends here will admit, Swedish taxes are exorbitantly high.'' Nils directed his words to her. ''And while no one would think of arguing with the philosophy of every person having a good, healthy life, it doesn't work that simply, I'm afraid. Once there is a guarantee of a high standard of living, there is a danger that the incentive for personal accomplishment can be undermined.'' Nils shrugged. ''Why should a person work for what he's going to be given, anyway?''

''The incentive is taken away from the capitalist to make a huge fortune, you mean!'' Per countered goodnaturedly. ''The capitalist wants to keep all his money for himself.'' Per turned to B.G., shaking his head. ''I'm surprised Nils hasn't defected to the United States long ago. His sympathies are far more American than Swedish.''

B.G. hardly had time to reflect to herself that this

wasn't a new debate among these friends before Nils was replying to Per.

"Mark my words, before long Sweden is going to feel the loss of that capitalistic talent that is fleeing this country," he said grimly. "It might be good in theory to distribute the wealth among all the people, but there must be incentive for capital investment. Just remember that someone has to head the factories and tell the workers what to do, my good socialistic friend."

B.G. was amazed at their frankness with one another. No one seemed to get angry at this open exchange. Her mind was awhirl with new ideas she had picked up from the conversation. Had she inadvertently come up with a key to Nils's moodiness? Perhaps he was having to decide how he fit into the modern Swedish economy. Was he thinking of taking his capitalistic expertise elsewhere? That thought was quickly discounted when she considered how old the Heidenstam operation was, with generation after generation of Heidenstams holding the reins of management.

"I have had enough of this debate," Silvia declared cheerfully. "Whenever this subject comes up, we all jump on poor Nils. If we were factory owners, we would perhaps see things more from the eyes of a factory owner ourselves. Besides, it is time to be on our way."

Everyone agreed that they should be getting underway again. For the time that it took to take up the anchor and set sail, there was no further conversation. B.G. could tell that she wasn't needed to help. Contentedly, she sat in the cockpit and watched, still mulling over what she'd learned.

Once they were under sail again, everyone returned to the cockpit.

"Eva, tell us about your house," Silvia requested before anyone could take up the matter of high Swedish taxes again. "Have you had the architect's plan approved? Has the application for a government loan been submitted yet?"

B.G.'s ears pricked up at "government loan."

"Does the Swedish government lend people money to build houses?" she asked after Eva had replied ruefully that their house plan had *not* been approved and, thus, they had not begun their application for a loan.

She had to listen attentively to the answers that came at her all at once. All of her companions seemed to want to be the one to fill her in, all except Nils, that is, who looked on with a faintly ironic detachment. B.G. managed to glean the assurance that the government did lend money to young married people who wanted to build a home, and the rates were very low.

"That's great." B.G. was aware of the tinge of skepticism in her voice and hoped that she did not come across as the critical American. "What kind of change do you have to make in your plans?" she hurriedly asked Eva. "Who decides that they're not okay the way they are, anyway?"

Eva shrugged philosophically.

"The house we want to build is too large for the neighborhood," she explained. "We have to make it smaller." Before she could answer B.G.'s second question, Per took over.

"Anyone who builds a house in Sweden must have the plans approved by a government building commission, whether there is a request for a government loan or not," he explained. "A house must conform to all the other houses in the general area. For example, if you are building a house in a neighborhood where all the houses are two stories high, then your house must also be two stories high. If all the houses are very small and built of wood, then your house must be small and built of wood." He offered the explanation in the most matter-of-fact manner, with no suggestion of apology or criticism. Apparently he considered the regulations entirely reasonable.

B.G. didn't want to hurt anyone's feelings, but everything inside her rejected the notion of such strict governmental control.

"You're saying that the national government tells you what you can or cannot build on a piece of property that you have paid for and own?" she asked unbelievingly. "Are you in favor of that?"

It was obvious from their expressions that the four young Swedes had never thought *not* to be in favor of the practice.

"It's for the benefit of everyone concerned," Per pointed out. "In the United States, are you allowed to build whatever you wish, with no regard to the surroundings?"

"We have zoning," B.G. conceded. "In certain areas you could build only a house for a single family to live in, not a commercial building or an apartment building. There are rules about how far you can build from property boundaries and that kind of thing, but each city or town makes up its own rules, the national government doesn't!" She really hadn't intended to sound quite so fervent, but she frankly found the notion of such heavy-handed government supervision repugnant.

B.G. had to overcome a strong urge to turn to Nils and ask him what *he* thought about the subject. He hadn't volunteered any comment, apparently content to listen and watch from the outskirts of the conversation. Before she could draw him in, her attention, like everyone else's, was diverted to their surroundings. The sailboat was approaching a narrow opening between steep rocks and up ahead was a broad harbor and the island of Marstrand, looking like a picture postcard with its colorful houses and old stone battlements crowning the highest hill.

B.G. once again was pleased to have her tentative offer of help refused. While all the preparations were made for docking, she observed the activity and mulled over her own thoughts. Today was turning out to be quite an education for her. She was learning a considerable amount about Sweden and its modern young adults, if Per, Eva, Gunnar, and Silvia were at all typical, as she thought they were. Seeing Nils among them and listening to his dissenting voice, she realized that he *wasn't* typical. He didn't fit into the same mold as the others.

Where did he fit?

The answer to that question held far more than casual interest for B.G.

Chapter Seven

There was ample docking space at Marstrand, most of it already filled with sailboats of every description, many of them bearing the flags of neighboring countries. When they had *Sea Gull* securely tied at the bow, with an anchor off the stern, B.G.'s companions took her ashore and filled her in on the little island resort town while they strolled along the wide cobblestone quay.

Marstrand had first been popularized as a summering place by the Swedish King, Oskar II, who had reigned at the turn of the century. He had chosen the island as his preferred summer retreat on the Swedish western coast. Today it looked much as it must have looked when he came there each summer, with several rambling old hotels along the waterfront and a restful atmosphere. B.G. looked around her and loved the quaint little town, trying at first to figure out what was really odd about it. There wasn't a single automobile in sight! she finally realized. No noise, no fumes, no hurry.

Facing the quay was a row of wooden buildings, steep

and narrow, neatly painted and housing several little gift shops and ordinary places of business such as a pharmacy, a grocery store, and a bank. Along the edge of the quay were fruit and vegetable stands, a public bath house, and an ice cream kiosk doing a typically brisk summer business with swimsuit-clad patrons of every age.

"All Swedish people *love* ice cream!" Silvia told her and then promptly demanded that everyone wait for her while she purchased some sort of chocolate-covered ice cream bar on a stick.

They climbed a steep road and made their way up to the fortress of Carlsten at the top of the hill. After paying a few *krona* to enter the premises, they made a casual tour of the fortress, skirting a crowd that followed a guide around and listened raptly to his lengthy narratives. B.G.'s companions sketched in the essential information for her: Built in the seventeenth century, the fortress had been used during the two successive centuries as a prison. There were a few legendary anecdotes about colorful prisoners that she found entertaining, but she thought the main attraction of Carlsten was its marvelous view from the ramparts at the top. They could see the little town nestled on the shore and the blue sea studded with other rocky islands in the distance.

"See that little cove down there." Silvia pointed. "That's where we will go to swim." She grabbed Gunnar's hand and pulled him along with her as they made their exit from the fortress grounds and entered a path leading down to the sea.

With those two plunging on ahead and Eva and Per taking their time and lagging behind, B.G. found herself paired off with Nils for the first time since going ashore.

"I like your friends very much," she told him sincerely.

"Good. I was fairly certain that you would. They're

nice people and fun to be around.'' He sounded genuinely pleased.

After that, B.G. was quiet for several seconds, not sure of how to proceed with the matter on her mind. It was pleasant walking along with Nils in his companionable mood, and she didn't want to get him on edge again with some poorly phrased question or comment.

"You're not really a whole lot *like* them, are you?" she asked tentatively when curiosity prevailed over prudence.

The rather faltering observation jerked Nils to full attentiveness, even though he didn't alter his pace or allow his face to show any change of expression. The last hour he had been drifting along, thinking his own thoughts, thanks to the eagerness of his friends to play the role of guide. He saw immediately where B.G. was headed and had no intention of satisfying her curiosity about him and how he differed from the others.

"Is that a nice way of saying you *don't* like me?" he shot back.

Mentally B.G. had been pursuing a straight path, intending to let one question lead to another. Nils's reply wasn't among any of those she had anticipated. It diverted her and made her appreciate once again the quickness of his mind.

"That's not what I meant at all,'' she denied laughingly.

"Am I to conclude, then, that you *do* like me, in spite of some of our clashes of temperament?'' Nils kept his tone light and playful, intimating that serious discussions would be out of place on such a carefree occasion.

B.G. couldn't answer the question in the spirit in which it had been asked.

"I don't know whether I like you or not,'' she said bluntly, after a moment of mulling it over.

Nils threw back his head and laughed. For a few

seconds he felt incredibly young and free of cumbersome decisions.

"I suspect the best way to find out what's on your mind, B.G., is just to *ask* you," he observed, chuckling.

If he had asked her what she was thinking just then, she would have been embarrassed to tell him. I *do* like you when you laugh like that, she would have had to admit. Nils was an extraordinarily handsome man even when he was hostile to her, but when his blue eyes ignited with amusement and his wide smile flashed even white teeth, she found him irresistibly appealing.

Not wanting to risk saying or doing anything to darken his present lighthearted mood, she decided to abandon for the time being her efforts to clarify the difference she perceived between him and the other Swedes.

"You're right. I *am* pretty straightforward, sometimes to a fault," she admitted cheerfully. "There have been many times when I would have been far better off *not* saying what was on my mind."

The path had brought them lower into denser vegetation. Striding along beside Nils in the sun-dappled shade, B.G. found herself, at his prompting, telling him about some of those instances when her honesty had gotten her into hot water, particularly with clients who pressed her for her opinion of their choices.

Then they emerged into the open again and clambered over great rounded boulders, arriving at the designated swimming place. Silvia and Gunnar were already in the water, which was tantalizingly clear but so icy cold that it literally took B.G.'s breath away when she plunged in.

"Like swimming in Lake Michigan," she sputtered, coming out almost immediately, shivering and covered with chill-bumps. The sun-warmed rock felt wonderful to the soles of her feet. Deciding that she much preferred basking in the sun to swimming, she took her beach towel and climbed up to a spot that would allow her to watch the others or just gaze out at sea, if she chose. A little hump of rock served nicely as a pillow. Before long, she was so totally relaxed that she felt herself dozing off.

Cold drops of icy water pelting her warm skin brought her awake with a gasp, and she opened her eyes to see Nils standing over her.

"That was a dirty trick," she protested weakly, feeling the full impact of his maleness in her half-waking state. He looked far more primitive now that he was wet, his fair hair darkened and sleek against his skull and forehead, drops of water clinging to his skin. The snug-fitting blue swimsuit was more noticeably revealing of aggressive maleness, especially with her lying below him and looking up.

B.G. felt a strong surge of response that Nils was able to read in her startled eyes and her softly parted lips. For a long moment he bent over her, the currents of sexuality coursing between them.

"I thought it was a kinder way of getting your attention than *this*."

He dropped down next to her and pressed his cold, wet body along the warm length of hers. B.G. squealed and hurriedly scooted over, giving him half of the beach towel. Her drowsiness had totally vanished, and Nils hadn't startled her enough to make her heart pound as forcefully as it was doing, jolting her with each muffled thud.

"It's dangerous to disturb a sleeping person that way!" she declared breathlessly. "You should feel the way my heart is beating!" It was the kind of remark one doesn't intend to be taken literally. She pressed the palm of her right hand over her heart.

"Here. Let me feel," he replied, all exaggerated concern. He reached over and pushed her hand aside, replacing it with his own. "Hmm. You're right," he mused in a low, thoughtful tone. "Your heart is beating unusually fast." Cupping his hand slightly to gather up the gently flattened contours of her breast, he kneaded slowly. "I don't think this is helping," he commented after a full minute of this ministration. Relaxing his hold, he rubbed his palm across the hard peak.

B.G. could barely suppress a little moan of mingled pleasure and pain. Rolling her head sideways, she let her gaze intersect with his and found that his eyes were intensely blue between tawny lashes.

"No, you're not helping at all," she murmured and then sucked in her breath as she felt his hand move lower and span her waist before sliding down to her lower abdomen. His fingertips ran teasingly under the edge of her bikini bottom.

"Mmm. I wonder what *would* help?" he murmured in a low voice that affected her almost as much as his caresses. He raised up on his elbow and watched his hand explore the sensitive territory so near the most intimate part of her which had begun to ache with the possibility that any second he might venture more boldly.

B.G.'s eyes were off on a sensual journey of their own, frankly delighting in his male beauty. How she wanted to touch those broad smooth shoulders she'd been looking at for hours and *feel* the golden brown color. It was so tempting to think of sliding her hands across his chest and down to his flat, muscled stomach and see him suck in *his* breath. With him touching her, she wanted badly to do all those things and to have his hands move over her whole body and keep setting fire to her, but most of all, she was dying for Nils to kiss her. When he looked up at her face, she let her gaze melt into his and then drop to the cleanly sensual mouth.

"Kiss me," she murmured.

Before she had even spoken, Nils had felt as though his head were being pulled downward in response to her urgent desire for him to kiss her. She might have been tugging at him with her hands, so little choice did she leave him. Up until this moment, he had felt himself completely in control, pleasurably stimulated by her female response to his teasing foreplay, but aware the whole time that they weren't going to make love there on that rock, in the open where someone could see them. It annoyed Nils that B.G. was coming on so strong, no doubt depending on him to be able to stop before they had gone too far. Aside from that, he didn't like giving in to the sexual power she was exerting over him. When his head was some eight inches above hers, he stopped.

"Kiss me," B.G. said again, a little petulant, disappointed, filled with even greater yearning to feel his lips on hers again.

"First, there's something else I want to do. Something I've wanted to do all day," Nils said softly, resisting the appeal in her eyes.

B.G.'s brain sent out an alarm, but she was unable to resist when his fingers slipped lightly beneath the straps on her shoulders and pushed them with excruciating slowness down her arms. Little by little the cups of her bikini top were lowered and her breasts exposed. He took so much time that B.G. could easily have stopped him. When her dazed mind began to clear a little of its sensual fog, she realized that he *intended* for her to stop him. He was playing some game she didn't understand except that it involved manipulation. For the first time, she also became aware that their location was far from private, and for that reason alone, she should stop him. Still, she didn't, and her reasons were more complex than simply wanting him to see her breasts.

"Hurry," she whispered when he had dawdled so long she couldn't bear it any more.

Nils went still. Slowly he raised his eyes to her face to let her see the sharp resentment.

"Do you really want me to undress you, to make love to you—here in the open?"

"Why did you start it, then? I don't understand you. I will *never* understand you. I don't even know why I *try*." With her accusing eyes holding his, she started pulling her straps back up on her shoulders.

Nils's face hardened with determination and his hands closed over hers. Using his superior strength, he jerked the straps all the way down to her wrists and held her with her arms pinned on either side of her. Then he dropped his gaze to view his plunder.

B.G. was so furious that she thought she might just explode. She followed her most powerful instinct, to escape. Twisting and arching her back, all to no avail, she muttered angrily, "Let me *go*, you big *bully!* Let me *go!*" He held her easily, his face tense with a strange exhilaration that made her come to her senses. She was only performing for his macho pleasure. With a little whimper of frustration, she went limp.

Feeling the resistance leave her, Nils frowned. He looked from the defiance in her face down to her bare breasts, noting again the contrast between pure white and golden skin. The small patches of pale ivory were perfect to offset the delicate shell pink aureoles surrounding the slightly darker beige tips, little hard buds that would have tempted any man to taste them. For a moment Nils closed out everything but the sensual contemplation of that treat.

B.G. felt him release her wrists from that hurtful grip and watched him as he brought his hands up to her breasts at the same time that he lowered his head. A strange lethargy gripped her and kept her from stopping him, even though she knew she *should* stop him. It was too late, though, when she felt the warmth of his hands encircling and cupping her breasts, gathering the sensitive flesh into higher mounds. Then his mouth had opened upon the more fortunate one, and B.G. forgot everything in the flood of stimulation that surged through her with the contact of moist, hot lips and tongue intent on savoring and devouring her.

With a moan of total pleasure, she arched her back and felt him open his mouth wider and enlarge the territory of warm suction while his tongue worried the stiff peak in circular rhythm. The erotic stimulation was almost more than she could stand without some outlet. Lifting her hands to his shoulders, she caressed the smooth breadth of them restlessly, as she had wanted to do earlier.

When he narrowed his attentions to the wildly tingling tip of her breast, first sucking hard and then without warning nipping sharply with his teeth, B.G. groaned his name aloud and wrapped her arms around his shoulders, pulling him to her.

Nils raised his head slowly and took his hands away from her breasts seemingly with the greatest reluctance. He reached up and took her arms from around his shoulders and braced himself over her, a palm on either side of her hips. His eyes were intense with his passion as he looked down at her, probing her face.

B.G. made no effort to hide her arousal from him. She would still have liked for him to kiss her and wouldn't have resisted, even though this wasn't the time or the place to make love. In truth, she was as disappointed as she was admiring when she saw the struggle for control he was undergoing and gradually winning. It mattered a great deal to her that he wanted her as much as she wanted him. This was probably the one time in their relationship so far that she could be sure he wasn't playing some kind of manipulatory game.

More than anything else, the soft complacency in the little smile curving B.G.'s lips helped Nils to regain his control. It was so obvious to him that she was congratulating herself on the successful exercise of her feminine powers, even when she had to be aware of the impropriety of time and place. To give himself time to think as well as time to quiet the ache in his loins and discipline his body, Nils absorbed himself in the task of restoring B.G.'s bikini top to its rightful place.

When he had tugged the straps back up on her shoulders and the blue-and-white-striped cups were covering the tantalizing creaminess of those soft patches of flesh not usually exposed to the sun's rays, he was to some degree recovered, but still vulnerable enough that he sat with his long legs bent and his arms loosely encircling his knees.

"This puts a whole new complexion on things," he mused, deliberately giving the impression that he was exploring possibilities and finding them to his liking. "I'm not nearly so sorry now that my grandmother roped me into her plans for showing you Sweden." He paused while she sat up, too. "We'll have to be discreet, though. She isn't *that* modern."

His meaning was crystal clear to B.G. He thought that she would gladly become involved with him in a meaningless, casual affair, thereby alleviating his boredom for the duration of the time he was forced into her company. Or *did* he think that? One way or the other, she was feeling degraded for having responded to him so easily and passionately.

"I'm not that modern either," she retorted grimly. "In spite of what just happened, I have no intention of sleeping with you."

Nils was finally confident enough to relax his protec-

tive stance. He leaned back indolently, bracing himself
with one long arm and sprawled a little to one side so
that he was able to meet her indignant gaze head on.

"You don't expect me to believe that you didn't want
me to make love to you just now, as much as I wanted it
myself?"

The amused derision in his voice was enough to make
B.G. wish with all her heart that she could honestly deny
the truth in his words. But she couldn't. They both knew
it.

"I do expect you to believe that I have no intention of
going to bed with you. I don't even *like* you!" This last
was added as much for her own benefit as his. The pain
she felt intermingled with her anger *had* to be hurt pride
if she didn't like him. It couldn't be anything else. She
needed to believe that her response to him had been all
physical.

His smile was maddening.

"You *have* made up your mind on that point, then?"

The softly spoken gibe triggered an instant recall in
B.G.'s mind of those several minutes on the walk down
from the fortress to the sea when she had tentatively set
about discovering the difference between Nils and the
other Swedes. She saw now that he had cleverly sidetracked her with his teasing and his pretense of friendliness.

"I'd have to be a masochist to like somebody like
you," she retorted with as much coolness as she could
manage. Her next words were in the nature of a blind
stab, which she delivered with the hope that she could
hurt him. "You might be able to outthink and outtalk me
and your friends down there any day in the week, but at
least *we* all know who and what we are. I'm not so sure
you can say that about yourself."

The words were hardly out before B.G. was wishing

that she could retract them, since she was not by nature a vicious person. Nils looked like a man with a knife twisting in his vitals.

"I'm sorry," she said swiftly. "I really shouldn't have said that. I don't know what I'm talking about."

The apology on her face was too akin to pity for Nils's liking. It was bad enough for her to penetrate his defenses and hit a live nerve. He sure as hell didn't want to be patronized.

"Save your apology," he advised curtly. "It's true that I don't view the world as simplistically as you and my good Swedish friends down there, but don't put yourself in the same category with Eva and Silvia. They're not afraid to feel and act like normal women with adult appetites. But you've bought the whole American romance myth, haven't you, *Birgitta?*" The subtle emphasis on her Swedish name made it a taunt. "You can't just admit that you have a strong sexual attraction to a man and want to go to bed with him. No, you want flowers and poems telling you that you're someone 'special,' don't you, even if it's all a lie?"

The mocking words were like sharp pellets hitting B.G., hurting and leaving little marks, but they didn't penetrate deeply enough to achieve their intended effect, to make her lose her temper and engage in a word-slinging match she wouldn't have a chance of winning. For the first time in a head-on confrontation with Nils, her mind remained in control of her emotions. She knew that she had hit close to some truth just now in her blind criticism of his character, and he was retaliating, not only to inflict pain but also to lead her away from that truth, shifting the emphasis from himself to *her*. For reasons not totally clear to her, she did not take advantage of her insight and direct another battery of hurtful words at him.

"You're right, in a way," she admitted proudly. "I *do* have to feel that a relationship with a man is 'special'— and that I'm special to him. I'm not so sure that attitude is restricted to American women, though. I wouldn't even be surprised if Eva and Silvia don't feel the same way."

Her honesty didn't serve Nils's purpose one bit. He had wanted to keep the antagonism flaring between them. It was safer by far to fight with her than to risk the complexities of a deeper relationship. Not even to himself would he want to admit that B.G. might already have become "special" to him, not just someone he wanted to take to bed. Nils had complications enough in his life right now without becoming emotionally involved with a flag-waving American girl with hangups about her Swedish heritage.

He couldn't see a single advantage in continuing the conversation, and yet to break it off at that point seemed a concession of some kind. Fortunately, Per and Eva chose that moment to appear down on the lower rocks and shout out reminders of the time to everybody. They were soon joined by Gunnar and Silvia, who reluctantly agreed to the necessity of getting back to the boat and beginning the homeward sail. The interruption couldn't have been better timed as far as Nils was concerned.

On the walk to the harbor, he made sure they all didn't pair off as they had earlier. "I recently received a wedding invitation from Karl and Helena," he remarked to his Swedish friends. "Are they really going to go through with the marriage this time?"

After that, he simply had to make an appropriate comment now and then and pretend to be listening while one and then another of his four friends took up the account of the latest happenings in the stormy relationship of the couple he had mentioned. There was also the necessity of telling B.G. all the background information about the people she hadn't met. Nils was able to walk along and think his own thoughts without any danger of having B.G. probe his mind and invade his privacy.

Tomorrow he was obligated to embark on the Göta Canal trip with her and Solbritt. There was no way he could wriggle out of it without severely disappointing his grandmother. During those three days from Gothenburg to Stockholm, Nils resolved that he would be on his most careful behavior with B.G. and avoid a reoccurrence of what had happened between them today. Then when they arrived in Stockholm, he would produce a handy excuse not to continue the sightseeing trip. Even though this was officially holiday time for him, he could fly back to New York and check personally on his father. The time didn't seem right for talking with his grandmother, anyway.

B.G. wasn't paying close attention to the talk about Karl and Helena, either, though they certainly sounded entertaining enough to be characters in a situation comedy. She was keenly aware of Nils's preoccupation and knew that he wasn't listening to the conversation he had deliberately initiated. *What is he thinking about?* she couldn't help wondering, even though she had no desire to be either curious or concerned about Nils. Was he thinking about what had happened between him and herself back at the rocky cove? Was he recalling all the turbulent sensations as well as the hot exchange of words?

Her instincts told her he was pondering something of deeper importance to him. The knowledge that he was carrying around some heavy mental burden made it necessary for her to nurture her resentment in order to counteract the sympathy that he didn't deserve from her. She found herself wishing that she wasn't so sensitive to his moods. It was all his fault for crashing through those barriers that separate a man and a woman before they become physically intimate.

On the sail back to Gothenburg, the wind was blowing harder so that sailing suddenly wasn't a leisurely kind of progress conducive to sunbathing and conversation. B.G. forgot about everything else for the first thirty minutes except hanging on for dear life. The boat heeled over sharply, and she no sooner got herself adjusted to one tack than Nils was rapping out new orders and there was pulling on lines and flapping of sails and they were heeling the *other* way.

No one except her seemed concerned about how close they came to other sailboats, and in time she relaxed, too, trusting Nils to guide them safely through the narrow straits between islands. Once she had stopped holding her breath every few minutes and tensing her body for an imminent collision that never came, she discovered to her amazement that the accelerated pace was highly exhilarating. She had the greatest difficulty in keeping her eyes away from Nils, who was too engrossed in his task of helmsman to notice her.

He had changed back into the brown corduroy trousers and knit shirt, but they failed to hide the sinewy strength she had already felt for herself on two occasions. He looked fit and vital and utterly capable. In spite of the alertness in every movement and the concentration evident in the abbreviated instructions to loosen this line and tighten that one, B.G. could see that all the tension had ebbed from his body.

He isn't thinking about anything now. The utter certainty with which she made that reflection amazed her and annoyed her more than a little. Why did she have to be so tuned in to his moods when he didn't even know *she* was alive? B.G. tore her gaze away from the man at the wheel and worked at building up her sense of indignation by reviewing, one by one, every insulting remark Nils had made to her in the last three days, every brutish show of force. By the time she had finished, she was able to assure herself that she would be happy if she *never* had to see Nils Heidenstam again after today. He would quickly become nothing more than an unpleasant memory.

For the remainder of the sail, she put all her efforts into fighting the magnetic attraction that drew her eyes toward him. Her success was only partial, with her sense of satisfaction being undermined by regret for what she was denying herself, but later, on the drive back to Forsborg when the two of them were alone again, she was glad that she had shored up her mental defenses against him.

Nils was excessively polite, guiding the conversation with skill and apparently with the determination that it would never falter and never be allowed to dip beneath a consideration of surface topics. First, they talked at length about sailing again, this time from the vantage point of her first-hand experience of what it was all about. Nils told her far more technical information than she wanted or needed to know. Next, they went over each of their sailing companions in depth with Nils filling in background information and coming up to the present with details about occupation and interests.

B.G. knew that she was being put through the conversational paces. All she had to do—or was being *allowed* to do—was ask the obvious questions he intended her to ask and make the obvious comments to his answers. Gradually a sense of obstinacy grew along with a little ache of disappointment she actually should not have been feeling, since she didn't like Nils and didn't ever want to see him again after that day. When he started an informative description of the Göta Canal trip they would begin the next day, she decided she had tolerated all the phony politeness she could stomach. Grimly, she waited for the next break in the smooth flow of words.

"Part of the charm of the trip is the mode of transportation itself," Nils was saying. "Speed is not the object, although when these boats were new, they were considered quite fast." He paused, waiting for her to ask how fast the boats did travel.

"You're expecting to find it very boring, aren't you? Today I could tell you liked sailing fast much better than sailing slow."

A silence followed her recalcitrant remarks. She waited, knowing that he was having to quell his irritation.

"You'll have to search far to find a confirmed sailor who prefers light winds," he said finally. "Actually a great many sailboats do make this Göta Canal trip, although it involves motoring in the canal itself. At certain places, I'm told, the going is so narrow that leaves and twigs from the trees growing along the banks drop onto the decks of the canal boats."

His words were as lacking in true interest as those of a professional tour guide. Yet B.G. thought that she could detect both irritation and wariness. He had no inkling of what she would say next.

"Why are you going along on this trip?" She was genuinely curious, not just bent upon annoying him. "Is it because you think it's unsafe for two women to travel without a man? Are you worried about your grandmother's safety? I'm sure you couldn't care less whether *I'm* safe or not," she added with a trace of sarcasm.

"Why are *you* so bent upon proving what is commonly thought about Americans abroad: that they have abominable manners?" he rejoined curtly, provoked at last into abandoning the polite mask. "To answer your impertinent questions, I am accompanying my grand-

mother on this trip at her request, not out of any concern
for her safety *or* yours. Sweden has some of the lowest
crime statistics you'll find anywhere in the world. It is
perfectly safe for two women to travel without a man to
protect them. Any other presumptuous questions you
would like to ask?''

He glared over at her, daring her to utter another
word, and then lapsed into stony silence. B.G. mulled
over his explosive response to her prodding, smarting a
little under his bluntness and yet honest enough to admit
that she had pushed him. So she had ''abominable
manners,'' had she? At the risk of providing further
evidence that the accusation was true, she *had* to say
more. Her pride demanded it.

''I am sure,'' she said in a lofty tone,''that Fru
Heidenstam had the best intentions when she 'invited'
you to go along with us. She probably wrongly assumed
that you and I would find each other's company pleasant.
That not being the case, she will no doubt not object if
you had some legitimate reason not to come along.''
There. B.G. thought that the suggestion was well-
phrased, even if she did have to say so herself.

Nils shot a murderous glance over at her.

''I hardly think it's your place to advise me what to
do. If you're worried about any more 'unwanted' advances on my part, let me assure you there will be
none.''

B.G. stiffened at the insolent insult in his slight
emphasis on *unwanted*.

''If there are any advances, I can assure you they will
be unwanted!'' she snapped back.

''To be sure,'' he taunted in a soft, maddening tone.
''I noticed how hard you fought me today. 'Kiss me,
Nils!''' he mocked. ''You were ready for me to make
love to you right there on that rock, in full sight of

anybody who cared to watch. Rather inconsistent behavior for a woman who won't take off her bathing suit top in front of other people, don't you think?''

B.G. wouldn't have been half so incensed if what he said hadn't been true. The sound that rose from her throat was pure, incoherent rage. She had to clench her fists in her lap to keep from attacking him, an act that might have gotten them both killed, since he was driving along at the maximum speed.

"I don't know *when* I've ever *detested* a man as much as I detest *you!*" she sputtered, frustrated that words were so incapable of providing an adequate release.

"So it has progressed from dislike to something stronger." His amusement was deliberately intended to fuel her anger.

Since she couldn't attack him physically and she couldn't best him with words, B.G.'s position was intolerable. Turning her face toward the side window, she let the tears of fury well under her eyelids and roll down her cheeks. *God, how she hated him!* How was she going to endure days in his company? How was she going to be able to impress upon him just how indifferent she was to his presence? To soothe her own hurt pride, B.G. imagined scene after scene where Nils made some overture and she reduced him to shreds.

Nils felt his hands tighten on the wheel as B.G.'s tears threatened to undermine his hardness. He reminded himself that he couldn't afford to soften toward her. He must fight her every second, keep her in the role of antagonist, or she would be coming at him again, probing into him and making those sweeping judgments of hers. He didn't want to hear what she thought he should do or what he should be. She wasn't capable of understanding how he dreaded the thought of disappointing the people who loved him.

Perhaps she was right, though, in suggesting that he

make some excuse and not accompany her and his grandmother on the Göta Canal trip tomorrow. The most obvious reason he could give was, sadly, a real one: his feeling of urgency about his father's health. At any time, day or night, Nils knew that the telephone could ring with news of a physical collapse. Nils thought that he had a good idea of how Damocles must have felt with that sword suspended over his head by a mere thread.

Once the worst was known, Nils's time of decision making would have come to an end. He would have to act, and whatever he did, it would be a long time before he could afford the leisure to visit his grandmother again in Forsborg. Either he would be tied to the New York office on a permanent basis, taking over his father's duties, or he would be embarking on a whole different venture. . . .

No, Nils couldn't give up this time with Solbritt, this last opportunity either of them would have to pretend that things were the same. He would go along on the Göta Canal trip, which was, he knew, something very special to Swedes, a kind of symbolic pilgrimage through the heartland of Sweden. The canal boats were quite small, too small for privacy for himself and B.G. Solbritt would be there with them, serving as a buffer to keep them from tearing at each other.

With his passion momentarily forgotten and his anger cooled, Nils surveyed the next three days with confidence. He shouldn't have any difficulty restraining himself and keeping at a distance the young woman who sat quiet and defeated beside him.

Chapter Eight

$\mathcal{B}$.G. had never been on any kind of cruise before. She boarded the *Wilhelm Tham* the next morning with barely suppressed excitement, refusing to have her fun dampened by Nils's coolness. After their knock-down-dragout verbal battle the day before, he was addressing her with frigid politeness and only when necessary. She had made up her mind at breakfast just to ignore him completely and enjoy herself on this latest adventure.

She thought the canal boat was adorable and said so, knowing even as she did that Nils was pained by the unnautical observation. The *Wilhelm Tham* was a miniature ship with three levels, all glossy varnish and paint and gleaming brass. The level onto which they stepped from the gangplank was, oddly enough, called the shelter deck, when it seemed more like the main deck to her. The level actually called the main deck was lower and accessible by a broad shallow stairway near the entrance of the dining room.

The top level was the bridge deck, so named because

the "bridge," or steering station, was located up there at the bow, an area restricted to official personnel, according to signs on the doors on either side of the boat. The preferred cabins were those six up on this top level, where there wasn't so much traffic as there would be on the shelter deck with passengers coming and going to the dining room and the lounge.

B.G., Solbritt, and Nils occupied the three cabins on the port, or left, side of the bridge deck. B.G. inspected hers, which turned out to be the one in the middle, with disbelief that so tiny a cell could indeed hold a full-length berth and a washstand. There was just barely enough room for one person to stand while he or she dressed or undressed. Obviously one spent all of one's waking time out on deck, she decided cheerfully, noting with relief that at least she had a window overlooking the deck that ran along in front of the cabins, connecting the bridge up forward with a large open deck across the stern of the boat.

She wasn't overjoyed at knowing that she would have to share the *toalett* located on the other side of Nils's cabin with the occupants of the other five cabins on this level, but there was no sense in making a fuss over what could not be avoided. She knew from hearing friends talk of their travels in Europe that communal bathrooms in hostels and *pensions* were not uncommon. At least she had her private washbowl and hot water.

By the time B.G. had explored the boat from stem to stern on all three levels and then rejoined Solbritt and Nils up on the bridge deck outside their cabins, she was no longer able to ignore what everyone else around her had already begun lamenting: the weather. The morning sky was gray and heavily overcast. A chilly breeze cut right through her navy slacks and buff pullover sweater. She would need to put on the jacket of her red traveling suit, which was styled like a blazer and thus versatile.

"I hope the sun will come out soon."

B.G. directed this remark to Solbritt in Swedish, keeping her tone cheerfully optimistic for the older woman's benefit. Solbritt had settled herself in a deck chair next to the rail. With her shoulders slightly hunched under a lined black raincoat, a headscarf covering her reddish gold hair, and a woolen lap robe tucked around her legs, she looked older than B.G. had ever seen her look.

"The sun isn't coming out today at all. We'll be lucky if it doesn't start to rain."

This terse prediction came from Nils, who was standing facing the rail, looking outward, his hands in his trouser pockets. B.G. noted somewhat resentfully that he was the only passenger she had seen on the entire boat who was perfectly attired for the kind of weather he forecast. His maroon hooded jacket was obviously water-repellent and would also serve well to block out the wind that was piercing right to her bones already. His jacket was just the sort of thing that a sailing enthusiast would own and know to bring along. Nils's preparedness was a source of distinct irritation for her.

"You don't have to sound so pleased about it," she said crisply, in English. "Besides, you don't know for sure what the weather will turn out to be. Even a forecaster can be wrong," she continued argumentatively.

"Not in Sweden." His clipped reply was also in English.

Solbritt intervened to explain to B.G. that a front was moving in from the west, following a very typical pattern, and they could only hope that it passed through quickly and didn't linger for days. She sounded so apologetic, as though she were personally responsible, that B.G. instantly regretted her peevishness with Nils. It wasn't the weather that made her grumpy. It was *him*.

He didn't have to act as if he were so all-fired *sure* of everything.

After hastening to assure Solbritt that a little damp, windy weather wouldn't hurt anybody, least of all herself, B.G. ignored a sound from Nils that sounded like a muffled grunt and slipped into her cabin to don the red jacket. When she came out on deck again, the older woman was alone, but B.G. would have died before she made any inquiry about Nils's whereabouts. She settled herself in a deck chair facing Solbritt, but before ten minutes had passed, she was so chilled that she had to get up and go back into her cabin to get a lap robe, too.

The first hour of their journey wouldn't have been of much interest to B.G. even if the sun had been shining. As the *Wilhelm Tham* got underway and traveled through the heart of Gothenburg along the busy Göta River, there was nothing to see on either bank but evidences of the city's industrial development, great cranes and ware-houses and shipping docks. Then, by the time they were leaving the city behind and were passing through more sparsely settled country, Nils's dire weather prediction came true. A misting rain began to fall, made all the more uncomfortable by a gusty wind that made it impossible to remain on the side deck.

"We will have to move!" B.G. gasped, stating the obvious, as she and Solbritt hurriedly arose from their deck chairs and backed away from the rail until they were up against the bulkhead.

Where the hell has Nils gone? she wondered irritably, as though he were somehow to blame for this miserable day, since he had predicted it, and should be here now to see to things. Almost as though she had conjured his presence with the thought, he appeared and snapped out instructions for them to go aft to the larger deck across the stern. He would bring them their chairs there.

B.G. had to suppress the instant rebellion that awoke

inside her at his peremptory manner. When he cautioned Solbritt to walk carefully on the damp deck, B.G. thought he had deliberately not included her in the warning. No doubt he hoped that *she* would conveniently slip over the side and out of his life.

Nils placed their chairs near the center of the stern deck. After B.G. and Solbritt had settled down under their lap robes once again, Nils directed several comments to his grandmother that revealed to B.G. where he had been. He had had to wait in a line outside the dining salon down on the shelter deck in order to make arrangements for their meals. Since the dining salon was small, there would be two seatings for each meal. One had to choose either the early or the later seating for all three meals.

"I chose the early time," Nils explained to his grandmother. "I thought that you would prefer it, since you arise early in the morning. However, I can go back and request the later time, if you prefer that instead."

Solbritt at once consulted B.G. to learn her wishes on the matter. Meeting the coolness of Nils's gaze, B.G. had to conquer an unworthy urge to say that she would prefer the later seating, just to put him to the trouble of making the change.

"The early time will suit me as well," she told Solbritt graciously. Shivering, she thought that today she would gladly go to the early lunch seating, just to get into a warm room.

"My poor child!" Solbritt exclaimed sorrowfully, having noticed the shiver. "This is all my doing. I had so hoped we would have good weather."

"Birgitta must have known when she came to Sweden that the weather is unpredictable in August," Nils put in unsympathetically and then turned and paced away before B.G. could answer. Nils knew damned well she hadn't researched the weather conditions in Sweden any more than she had researched social customs and educational requirements. What he was really saying was that she deserved to suffer a little for her ignorance! What made her irritation even stronger was the wish that she *had* brought along some warmer clothes.

By the time Nils had returned a few minutes later and stood nearby, B.G. had admonished herself for letting him get to her and resolved to tolerate the grandson's rudeness for the sake of his kind grandmother, who amazingly showed no sign that she was aware of the hostility between the two. It isn't fair, B.G. told herself firmly, to make Solbritt feel worse about the situation than she already did. But then when Nils walked off again, right in the middle of B.G.'s answer to a question from Solbritt about the weather in Minnesota this time of year, B.G. was afraid she might explode with resentment. He might as well have come right out and said he was bored with her conversation!

On Nils's next return, she was ready for him. "Why don't you sit down?" she gritted out in slow, restrained English. "You are making me *nervous*."

"I can't sit down," he muttered tersely.

When he left again, almost immediately, he didn't come back until it was time for the first midday seating. During the interim B.G. had mulled over the note of desperation in his admission of his restlessness and become a little more sympathetic. On the way down to the dining salon, she resolved to keep her temper and remain cheerful through the meal, no matter what he said or did.

Under different circumstances, she might have found the small dining salon crowded and stuffy, but after a morning out on deck in the chill dampness, she frankly luxuriated in the contrasting warmth and coziness. After helping herself to generous portions from the sumptuous smorgasbord laid out on the buffet table, she took her place at the table assigned them back in the corner on the starboard side and released a sigh of pure contentment. Large windows gave her a wonderful view of the pastoral countryside they were passing through at their stately pace.

"I think I might just stay here for the rest of the day," she murmured in an aside to Nils when he took the chair next to her. She would have sworn there was a flash of sympathetic response on his face, but he said nothing, and she had to remind herself that they weren't friends.

B.G. turned her attention to her smoked salmon, tender fresh shrimp, and the several varieties of pickled herring she had chosen from the tempting array of cold foods. If she managed to eat all of that, she didn't think she would have much room for the hot course that would follow.

The mood of the dining salon grew increasingly festive as the young waitresses moved from table to table serving wine and beer and whatever other beverages the diners requested. When a waitress arrived at their table to ask what they would like to drink with their meal, Solbritt spoke up at once.

"Nils, you will choose a bottle of wine for us," she commanded, beaming a smile at him as though he shared her expansive good will.

B.G. took the opportunity to watch him obliquely as he glanced at the listing of wines and then made a quick choice, either not caring enough to deliberate or not needing to. When the white German wine was served, she was forced to decide that it had been the latter.

"It's very good," she said generously. "I don't like a wine that's so dry it puckers your mouth."

"My grandmother prefers a fruity wine," he replied

repressively, but after that he did relax noticeably and join in the conversation.

B.G. found herself enjoying the congenial atmosphere of the salon with all the high-spirited conversation and laughter creating a considerable din. She also felt herself melting under the easy charm Nils could seemingly turn on with no effort, when he chose. Admittedly, most of his attention was concentrated on Solbritt. B.G. wondered fleetingly what it would be like to have him smile at *her* with open, indulgent affection the way he smiled at his grandmother.

Don't be stupid, she admonished herself sharply. *He won't ever smile at you like that. He doesn't like you or approve of you.* After that, she found her good spirits fast fading and told herself it was just because the meal was almost over and they would soon have to go out on deck again and brave the chill.

They were among the last to leave the dining room. As they made their exit, they had to squeeze through the cluster of passengers just outside the door who were impatiently awaiting their turn at food and warmth. B.G. envied them as she followed Solbritt up the steps of the steep, narrow companionway leading to the bridge deck. There was little improvement in the weather. While it wasn't actually pouring rain, the blustery wind carried a fine mist that soaked right through ordinary clothes, like those she wore. B.G. definitely did not look forward to the long afternoon ahead, but she didn't realize until they had reached the bridge deck that she would have to get through it without Solbritt's cheerful company.

"I shall go to my cabin and take a little rest," the older woman announced somewhat apologetically. "Nils, you will keep Birgitta company for an hour or two." Before her grandson could reply to this good-natured order, Solbritt was marching away to her cabin.

B.G. wandered over to stand in front of her deck chair, which was still in the same place under the fixed canopy that provided some protection from the elements. Her woolen lap robe was folded neatly across the chair, reserving it for her, but she stood with her arms folded across her breasts and her shoulders hunched against the chill. Glumly she gazed out at the passing countryside, seeing little charm in the golden grain fields, red barns, and white farmhouses, not when she couldn't remember the last time she had felt this uncomfortable and this bored.

"That's okay," she told Nils grudgingly when he had sauntered over with obvious reluctance and stood next to her. He was taking his grandmother's instructions seriously and meant to keep B.G. company against his own inclinations. "You don't have to stay with me. I'll be fine by myself."

The words were faintly self-pitying, lacking conviction, because she honestly didn't look forward to being by herself under these miserable circumstances, and a survey of the other passengers hadn't shown her anyone whose company was preferable to Nils's, even if he were unwilling. She'd almost rather trade insults with him than risk having some older lady or gentleman latch onto her for the afternoon. It seemed that older, retired people were the ones who took this canal boat trip, judging from the present group of passengers.

"We'll be arriving soon at the locks in Trollhätten. If you like, we can get off the boat and walk ahead while it goes through the locks," Nils suggested, ignoring the issue of whether he wanted to keep her company or not.

B.G. shivered, feeling the dampness and cold seeping right through her and penetrating her bones.

"That's fine for you," she retorted grumpily, eyeing his waterproof jacket with envy. "I'm not exactly properly dressed for a hike along the banks. In this mist, I'd be soaking wet in ten minutes.''

She regretted the waspishness of her tone when Nils turned around without a word and walked off, evidently having construed her words as a definite refusal and feeling relieved of his obligations. The afternoon ahead stretched forth, endless and boring. B.G. considered her alternatives and found them unappealing. She could stay where she was and suffer. She could go down to the lounge on the shelter deck and no doubt find it jammed with people whiling away the hours writing letters, playing cards, or talking. Earlier that day when she had been exploring the boat and had stepped inside the lounge, she had found the air thick with cigar and cigarette smoke and stepped out again quickly, trying not to breathe in the poison. As a last resort she could follow Solbritt's example and retire to her tiny cabin to nap or read.

Unable to make up her mind, B.G. just stood there for long minutes, cold and miserable. When Nils reappeared, carrying a bright yellow rain slicker with a drawstring hood, she was frankly delighted to see him and noted the garment he carried with both surprise and curiosity.

''You came back,'' she murmured gratefully. ''Where did you get that?''

''From one of the girls on the crew. Here, put it on.''

B.G. didn't argue. It wasn't a time to be fastidious about wearing a stranger's jacket or to worry about her appearance. Once she had slipped on the hip-length jacket and drawn the hood up over her head, she felt warmer and more cheerful almost immediately. The boost in her spirits was due largely to the realization that Nils had gone to some trouble to get the rain jacket for her, presumably so that she would now be able to get off the boat with him when they reached the series of locks at Trollhätten. Perhaps he was just being nice to her for the sake of his grandmother. Perhaps he might feel sorry for her, too. Or maybe, just *maybe*, he might want her company when he escaped the confinement of the canal boat and walked along the banks in the drizzle.

At their approach to the first lock, B.G. stood with Nils down on the shelter deck along with a cluster of other passengers eager to get ashore. She found herself quite fascinated by the sight of a small orange ship in full view above the closed gates of the lock. Gradually the ship lowered and then the gates opened to allow its exit and the *Wilhelm Tham*'s entry. When the gates closed behind the canal boat, they were surrounded by steep dank walls at first, but their ascent was steady as water poured into the closed compartment. B.G. found the whole process so interesting that Nils had to grab her arm and prompt her to leap ashore when the shelter deck had risen to the level of the bank.

"We'll be going to higher levels at each series of locks until we reach Lake Vänern," he explained, still holding her arm as they walked along. "After crossing it, we'll have to descend again."

B.G. took in her surroundings with pleasure, not at all mindful of the weather now. It was great to be walking along, free of the boat's confinement, with Nils acting not exactly friendly, but not antagonistic either. The lockkeeper's house was a delight, small and neatly painted and with a yardful of blooming flowers.

"It looks like the house the Three Bears might have lived in," she remarked whimsically before it had occurred to her that he might not understand the allusion to a popular children's story that every American would surely know. "Do you know that story?" she added.

Nils glanced over, alerted to the tentative quality in

her voice, and had to steel himself against her appealing loveliness. A tress of damp golden hair had escaped the hood and fluttered against her wind-reddened cheek. The shy friendliness in her blue eyes and the hesitancy of her smile tempted him to put aside all his firm resolutions about not getting involved with her.

"I know about the story," he said briefly, resisting the urge to stop and push the errant tress of hair back under the yellow hood. If he hadn't been keeping himself under such iron constraint, he would have teased her about looking like a grown-up Goldilocks herself.

His distant reply came as no surprise, but B.G. still had to stifle a wave of disappointment that he wouldn't loosen up and have fun with her. What would be the harm in their being friends, for a little while at least? To conceal her emotion, she stopped to turn around and look back at the canal boat, watching it as it rose steadily into view, now in the second lock. Her vision was affected by a spitting rain that started up suddenly and pelted her in the face.

"It's a good thing you talked somebody out of this rain jacket!" she gasped out cheerfully, starting to walk along beside him again. Instinctively, she hunched forward and edged a little closer to him. Nils threw his arm protectively across her shoulders and pulled her over to stand in the lee of a small shed that housed lock machinery.

Standing with her body pressed along his and her face turned into his shoulder, B.G. had to fight a rising tide of exhilaration at his closeness. *You idiot! What's wrong with you?* she scolded herself severely, disturbed by the fact that this man could insult her, ignore her, make her feel demeaned when she responded to him, and yet all he had to do was take her into his arms and she melted. At this very moment, she couldn't keep herself from thinking about what it would be like to tilt back her head, look up into his face, and have him kiss her with the cold rain drops on her cheeks. To combat the disruptive sensations that rippled through her at the thought, she turned her head aside so that the words wouldn't be muffled into his jacket, and talked nonstop.

"I really do feel bad for Fru Heidenstam that the weather has turned so bad. It was kind of her to go to the trouble and expense of arranging this trip for my benefit." The arm around her shoulders tightened, distracting her so that she hardly even knew what she was saying as she babbled on. "I hope the rain will stop soon, and the sun will come out, for her sake. In spite of the weather, though, it's easy to see that this part of Sweden *is* beautiful and very prosperous looking. The rolling grain fields, the white farmhouses, the big red barns. There's a feeling of space and yet a smallness. It's an awful lot like the part of Minnesota where I grew up. . . ."

She paused, struck with a thought.

"Maybe *that's* the whole point of what I'm supposed to see on this trip," she continued reflectively, then lost her train of thought when Nils shifted his weight suddenly and made her conscious of the hard length of his thigh against hers. It had stopped raining, although the air was still saturated with the mist. They wouldn't have to stand there any more. The realization brought as much regret as relief.

"You don't think this trip is solely for *your* benefit?" Nils was asking so angrily that she tilted back her head and stared at him.

"What do you mean?" she murmured in puzzlement, noting the hard set of his mouth and the cynicism in his blue eyes. Despite her puzzlement and her curiosity, she was nonetheless still affected by his closeness and would gladly have put off an answer to feel his mouth against hers instead. It was ridiculous for her to want that, but she did.

Nils saw the tell-tale distraction in her eyes and had to fight the soft message it and her parted lips communicated to him. He spoke too quickly and opened himself up to still more questions.

"I mean that this trip is meant for *my* benefit as well as yours. Take my word for it."

B.G. pulled back a few inches, and Nils's arm dropped from around her shoulders, but they still stood very close together.

"I have no idea what you're talking about." She gave her head a little shake. *"How* is this trip for your benefit? You were born in this country, weren't you? You know all about it. You're a Swedish citizen."

The time was right for Nils to throw up a protective smokescreen and give her some answer that would satisfy her curiosity without revealing the truth. Instead, he found himself doing the last thing he had ever intended to do when he boarded the *Wilhelm Tham* that morning, determined to keep her at a distance: blurting out what weighed on his mind.

"Sure, I was born in this country. I'm a Swedish citizen now, but I won't be if I decide to become an American citizen instead."

B.G.'s mouth dropped open in sheer astonishment.

"You are actually thinking of becoming an American citizen?" she demanded incredulously. "But *why?* Your father lives in New York and works for your family business, and *he* isn't an American citizen, is he? Lots of citizens of other countries live in the United States. You could do the same as your father, couldn't you?"

Nils leaned his head back against the side of the small building and closed his eyes wearily. He hadn't meant to tell her any of this, and he knew damned well he would be sorry, but, *God*, what a relief it was to say it all out loud to somebody.

"Sure, I can do the same as my father," he agreed tiredly. Before he went on to deliver his next bombshell, he opened his eyes so that he could watch her face. "I'm not sure I *want* to follow in my father's footsteps, though. I'm not even sure at this point that I want to remain a part of the Heidenstam Fabrik. I have an offer to go into partnership with the owner of a furniture factory in Massachusetts. It's a whole new venture with some different ideas about building furniture that's affordable for middle-income people and yet high quality. It would be a big gamble—" Nils broke off, the brief flare of animation in his face dying out. "If I should decide to take the offer, I would be committing myself to working and living in the United States, since the market would be primarily there. There would be no reason for me to remain a Swedish citizen, no reason for me to come back here to Sweden so often after my grandmother . . . is gone."

B.G. was having difficulty believing her ears. Could Nils really be thinking of terminating his connection with the Heidenstam business? From what she had gleaned from Solbritt, he was more than competent at his work. He knew every phase of the operation. *And he was a Heidenstam!* That very fact seemed a kind of inescapable responsibility.

"Your cabinets are known all over the world," she said vaguely, the words sounding like a protest. She gave her head another little shake and then frowned. "I still don't see what this has to do with the trip we're taking with your grandmother."

Her surprise and the faint disapproval that Nils read into her first comment irked him far more than was reasonable. He was all too well aware that if he broke with the family business, he would encounter the same reaction for some time.

"What if the Heidenstam product *is* known world-wide?" he replied curtly. "Is that any reason to assume that I just want to fall into line and do what has always been expected of me: take my father's place? Why can't I decide for myself what I want to do with my life? Just because I was born a Heidenstam, does that necessarily mean that I have no more choice than some prince in a royal family?" He glared at B.G. as though daring her to speak up. She gazed back at him, her wide eyes reflecting that same surprise that so irritated him.

"I should think you'd be able to figure out for yourself what all that has to do with this trip," he continued contemptuously. "You see how patriotic my grandmother is, and she may be getting older, but she is a long way from dumb or feeble-minded. Don't you think she would sense that something is wrong? Don't you think she *knows* I'm not as loyal to Sweden as she would like?" He paused in his harsh tirade, thoughtful. "I don't think she really suspects, though," he said to himself. "If she *did,* she would be too upset to hide her feelings—"

His introspection had allowed B.G. to recover somewhat from her initial amazement. She hastened to assure him that he was wrong in assuming that *she,* B.G., disapproved of the decision he was leaning toward.

"Nils, you have every right to decide what you want to do with your life," she asserted strongly. "If you want to go into business in the United States or *wherever,* that's certainly your prerogative. We all want to please people, our parents and other members of our family especially, but we have to do what makes *us* happy. We can't live our lives for other people." B.G. was especially emphatic toward the last because she believed her words so completely and also because she sensed that Nils's greatest reservation sprang out of the reluctance to hurt his family, especially Solbritt. Quite to her puzzlement and chagrin, Nils was looking more angry than ever.

"Easy as one, two, three," he grated out harshly between clenched teeth. "Just live your own life the way *you* want to live it and don't worry about anybody else, not the people who love you and have given you everything." He shook his head from side to side, his lips pulled back so that she could see his strong, even white teeth gritted together. "That's about the way I *knew* you would react. After all, that's been your whole credo, hasn't it? 'I'll do what I damn well please, and to hell with my family's feelings.' Well, I'm afraid I'm not built that way. Apparently, it's easy for you to be callous and indifferent to the pain you cause to those who love you. Do you have any sense of guilt at all, for example, when you think of the heartache you caused your grandmother over the ridiculous matter of a name?"

B.G. backed away a half-step, stricken to the point that she had to fight the tears that threatened her. His words, spoken in a voice of deepest contempt, had sunk into a rawness that hadn't healed since her grandmother's death. She *did* feel guilt and wished, now that it was too late, that she *had* been more gentle and considerate in the past, without sacrificing the principle that she had the right to live her own life.

"*Yes,* I feel guilty! But at least I am and always was honest with my family. That's more than *you* can say. I don't believe all this business of not wanting to *hurt* people either. You just don't have *guts* enough to decide one way or the other what to do—"

Whatever else she might have said was swallowed by a gasp as Nils reached out and grabbed her by the upper arms and shook her so hard that she couldn't breathe. For a second or two, he was beside himself with a murderous rage. He wasn't going to let her get by with talking to him like that, with making those sweeping pronouncements of hers.

When he had vented the worst of his anger and realized that he might actually hurt her, Nils stopped shaking her and then found that he couldn't let go, since she had crumpled and started crying. If he hadn't held on to her, she would have slumped right down to the wet ground. The brief triumph he experienced in having crushed her defiant spirit was quickly gone, and he immediately felt like the lowest kind of beast, sorry as hell he had been so brutal and used his superior strength.

"Damn it, I didn't mean to hurt you. . . . Don't do that! Don't cry—" he muttered, bringing her close to him and then reluctantly sliding his arms around her limp, sobbing form and drawing her head against his chest.

"You're so *mean*," she gulped out, her voice thick with her tears. "I don't understand why you *hate* me. . . ."

"I don't hate you," he denied quickly, without thinking. When the words had been spoken, he knew at once that they were true. He didn't hate her, but whatever it was that he felt was as strong as hate at times. It brought out this latent violence in him. "I don't hate you," he said again, more deliberately. "It's just that you get under my skin more than anyone I've ever known. I'm sorry I hurt you. I'm sorry for some of the things I said. I was out of line."

Nils's mind was working quickly now. He was sorry for more than hurting her feelings or shaking her up. He was damned sorry he had opened his big mouth and told her all this. It wasn't a matter of being worried about her discretion. He didn't think she would blab to Solbritt. He just deeply regretted having opened himself up to her.

A glance over toward the locks told him that the *Wilhelm Tham* had caught up with them now and was moving ahead into the next lock. They would be visible to anyone out on deck who cared to look, but what the hell did he care about the curious regard of some elderly strangers? What he did care about was getting B.G. composed and smoothing over the situation in the ten minutes he figured was remaining before they would have to start walking again in order to catch up with the canal boat when it reached the last lock.

"Are you okay?" he asked gruffly, cupping the side of her face and gently forcing her to look at him. Her eyes were red from crying and her mouth soft and vulnerable, like a heartbroken child's. "Think you can forgive me?" he cajoled lightly.

B.G. lifted her shoulders in a disconsolate shrug.

"What does it matter if I forgive you? You'll only do the same thing again, won't you?" she asked in a dull voice. "You seem determined to hurt me."

Nils framed her face with both hands and bent to place a gentle kiss on her lips, since he couldn't bring himself to speak the glib reassurance that came instantly to mind. She had spoken the truth. It was more than likely that they would find themselves in another encounter where he felt compelled to conquer her independent spirit. When that happened, he wasn't sure he wouldn't resort to cruelty to bring her to submission. The realization was deeply disturbing, since he wasn't a violent person.

"I'll try not to hurt you again," he promised, uneasy with himself. He kissed her again, this time more lingeringly.

B.G. was having doubts about herself, too. She could feel herself melting under his gentleness, and her hands had a will of their own as they slipped up around his neck. It was unthinkable that she would want him to hold her after what had just transpired between them, when she still quivered inside with injury. But she did want that. It bothered her that his attraction for her grew with every violent confrontation. How could she feel so much for a man bent upon hurting her?

Nils felt the surrender in her body as it leaned against his. Even as he took light tastes of her lips, he told himself he wouldn't initiate anything sexual. He just needed to restore her to normalcy before they hurried to catch the boat. The very next moment he was kissing her harder, with hunger, and her mouth was parting to admit his tongue. His arousal came so quickly that he had no chance to fend it off, and he found himself sliding his hands down to her rounded buttocks, sinking into the firmness and then lifting her hips against his aroused body.

"God—I want you," he heard himself murmuring as he broke the kiss off and sucked in a deep breath to calm himself. The raw need in his voice was like cold water being doused on his head, shocking him and awakening his dormant judgment.

B.G. wanted with all her heart to answer that she wanted him, too, but some deep reservation kept her from saying it. When Nils spoke again, saying what she fully expected but in the wrong voice, she was grateful that she had heeded that self-protective instinct.

"Will you sleep with me in my stateroom tonight? It's what we both want."

His hand pressed her head against his chest. She couldn't see his face to read his expression.

"I don't see how you can say no. It's your philosophy to do whatever makes you happy. You know sleeping with me would make you happy."

B.G. pushed away from him, hating the swift change that had occurred between the honest urgency of his kiss and the proposition he was making so sure she would recognize as that and nothing more. *He doesn't want me to make love with him.* That fact was inescapably clear. He had deliberately pressed his suit in such a way as to insure her refusal. Why, when she knew he *did* want her?

"No, I won't sleep with you, Nils." The emphasis was for herself as much as for him. "I can't go to bed with a man I don't trust, and I don't trust you. You're not honest with me. You say one thing and mean something else."

The flash of resentment in his face confirmed that he *had* wanted her to turn him down, but he *hadn't* meant for her to see through him as she had.

"We'd better go on ahead," he said briefly. "The canal boat is about to come up to the last lock now."

As B.G. half ran beside Nils in order to keep up with his long stride, she pondered the fact that he apparently had kept up with the progress of the *Wilhelm Tham* the whole time they had stood in the lee of the little building, while she had been enclosed in a world separate from everything and everybody else, a world with just herself and Nils. For the first time since meeting him, she felt a stirring of fear as she acknowledged the power he held over her.

That first night by the lake in Forsborg, he had forced her to kiss him, and her resistance had been a token one. She had had to combat not just his superior strength, but also the yearning that he awoke inside her, and she had lost the battle. Just now when she had stated her refusal to sleep with him, there had been the inner recognition that her decision would stand only if he *wanted* it so. Should Nils decide that he really wanted to make love to her, he would have his way, despite the fact that she had been speaking the truth when she said she couldn't trust him. Given these facts and the further intuition that once she made love to him, she would be dangerously vulnerable, B.G. had every reason to be grateful that Nils had kept her at arm's length. She should thank her lucky star and ignore the gnawing dissatisfaction inside her.

Maybe after a while it would go away.

Chapter Nine

$\mathcal{B}$y late afternoon the strong, gusting winds had increased to such a velocity that it was announced over the loudspeaker that the *Wilhelm Tham* would dock at Vänersborg rather than make the crossing over Lake Vänern during the night, according to the travel itinerary. The weather would make such a passage hazardous. B.G. knew that the *Wilhelm*'s crew member making the announcement was too diplomatic to mention the truth: The real risk of continuing on schedule was the prospect of a boatload of seasick passengers, most of them quite old.

Several of the more hardy types disembarked at Vänersborg and hiked into town, wearing their raincoats and boots to protect them from the recurrent rainshowers. B.G. would have agreed to such an unappealing outing herself if only Nils would have suggested it, but he didn't. She had to fight to control the restlessness that grew steadily along with the feeling of

being confined. The effort to appear cheerful, for
Solbritt's sake, was wearing. It was a relief when the
time grew near for dinner. Thank heaven they had
chosen the first seating, even though six-thirty was much
earlier than B.G. was accustomed to having dinner.

She went to her cabin at five-thirty and made a lengthy
procedure of getting dressed in the cramped space. A
shower would have been welcome, but the only showers
on the boat were down two levels, on the main deck.
B.G. had located them earlier in the day. She couldn't
quite bring herself to don a bathrobe and trek down to
them. Therefore, a sponge bath would have to do, and at
least she did have her own private washbowl and hot
water.

To boost her dragging spirits, she chose the most
festive dress she had packed to take to Sweden, a misty
green that looked and felt like silk, but was actually one
of those miracle blends that didn't wrinkle. The dress
was not only practical in that respect, but definitely sexy,
with straps made up of several tiny ropes intertwined and
a front overlapping neckline guaranteed to tantalize
almost any male with the possibility that it might come
unlapped, since there was no visible button or fastening.
Fortunately the dress had a jacket to provide some
protection to bare arms and shoulders on the walk from
her cabin down to the dining salon, which was toasty
warm.

A few minutes before six-thirty, she was still putting
the finishing touches to her eye makeup when a tap
sounded at her cabin door.

"Are you ready to go down, Birgitta?" The slightly
forced quality in Solbritt's cheerful inquiry made B.G.
glad that she was going to all this trouble.

She opened the door a crack to reply that she wasn't
quite ready and would meet them downstairs in the

salon. They were not to wait for her. At the time she
hadn't the least intention of making a special entrance,
but when she walked into the dining salon minutes later,
most of the other passengers were already seated at the
white-draped tables. A quick glance verified that almost
everyone else had also changed for dinner. The men
wore dark suits and the women nice dresses and jewelry.
Much to her surprise, there was a kind of general and
pleased recognition of her presence, and the men rose
from their chairs in the most courtly manner and waited
while she made her way back to her table.

Their unexpected gallantry and the admiration in their
faces warmed her through and through, even though they
were old enough to be her father or in some instances her
grandfather. With no intention of playing the coquette,
B.G. thanked them with the smile that came naturally to
her lips.

It became a little forced when she got to her table,
where Nils also was standing and holding out her chair.
He let his gaze intersect only briefly with hers and then
he looked away, the polite cynicism on his face telling
her plainly that he thought she had deliberately staged
her entrance. It irritated her that he could dampen her
high spirits without uttering a single word.

"Don't you look *pretty*, Birgitta!" Solbritt was exclaiming in a proud voice, noticing nothing amiss in her
grandson's manner. "Don't you think that is a pretty
dress, Nils?" she prompted.

"Birgitta is wearing a very pretty dress," he said
obligingly in stilted Swedish.

B.G. managed to keep the smile firmly in place as she
sat down next to him. "It pleases me very much that you
like my dress, Nils," she replied just as stiffly.

The jacket was designed not to conceal the provocative criss-crossed front of the dress. Nils was unable to

keep from glancing down at the place where the material of the dress overlapped to form a vee, showing just a hint of cleavage and the shadowy hollow between her breasts. He resented her for wearing that damned dress. She had to know it was cunningly designed to drive a man crazy at the thought of slipping his hand inside the front and capturing a firm round breast underneath. Since there wasn't another male on this boat among the passengers even remotely close to her age, she must have worn the dress to torment *him*.

Nils waited for his opportunity to retaliate. When their waitress came to pour the dinner wine he had chosen, Solbritt asked the young college-age girl if the weather frequently interfered with the schedule of the canal boats. While she was listening to the reply, Nils leaned over and spoke to B.G. in an undertone.

"I'm thinking that perhaps you've changed your mind since this afternoon." The insinuation in his tone brought a quick mixture of surprise and suspicion to her eyes. Nils deliberately dropped his gaze to the front of her dress and then murmured, "My offer to share my cabin with you still stands. By now, you must realize there isn't much else in the way of entertainment on this little tub."

The waitress had concluded her answer and was moving away. With Solbritt transferring her attention back to them again, B.G. had to conceal the hot indignation flooding through her and bite back a sarcastic retort. It helped her to realize that she was reacting on cue, just as he had intended.

"No, thank you, Nils, I have a good book to read tonight," she managed to get out in what she hoped was a maddeningly sweet tone and then explained to Solbritt that Nils had been kind enough to inquire whether B.G. had brought along some reading material.

"I often prefer reading a book to spending time doing less worthwhile things," she added.

Solbritt expressed admiration at that attitude, but cautioned that one so young as B.G. should also take out the time to enjoy life. Nils quickly added his agreement to his grandmother's sentiment, pleased at the murderous glance B.G. flung him while she searched for a polite reply with a hidden sting.

Throughout the meal, the dinner conversation followed the same kind of pattern, with the three of them discussing seemingly innocuous subjects and B.G. and Nils sparring with each other, keeping Solbritt as the shield between them. If she was aware of the undercurrents, which became all but tangible when the talk centered on the trip ashore at Trollhätten, she gave no visible sign.

"I do hope that Nils told you all about the building of the locks and showed you the old ones, which are no longer in use. I had wanted to see them myself, but it was more important to rest up for the evening." Solbritt was intent upon her plate when she made the latter, apologetic remark.

"Don't worry," Nils soothed. "I made every effort to entertain Birgitta while you were resting in your cabin this afternoon. She seemed to find our promenade along the banks so interesting that we had to hurry to get back on the boat."

"Nils told me many things this afternoon while we were walking, but not much about the building of the locks," B.G. came back quickly. "I'm afraid we got sidetracked and didn't have time to look at the old locks. Now I wish we had not wasted so much time."

"Yes, I agree. Our time could have been much better spent." With that rather terse concurrence, Nils changed the subject, even at the risk of having her think she had bested him in innuendo. It didn't seem to matter what they talked about. Every subject offered openings for jabs and counterattacks.

Following dinner, Nils took the two women back up to the bridge deck and settled them in the most sheltered place he could find. B.G. had to wrap her woolen lap robe around her shoulders like a cape, since her thin dress and jacket were no protection from the damp chill.

After determining that she and Solbritt would both prefer sherry as an after-dinner drink, he went away for about five minutes and returned with a tray bearing three liqueur glasses and a bottle of Amontillado. The canal boat stocked a varied selection of liquor to sell to its passengers, but there was no conventional bar to dispense drinks by the glass. One had to purchase a bottle, Nils had learned. Under the circumstances, he thought it just as well. He expected the night to be a long one.

Solbritt finished her sherry in short time and then took both of her companions by surprise when she announced that she had an invitation to play cards down in the lounge.

"If the two of you do not mind, I will go now," she declared, standing up. "I am not in the least sleepy after my long rest this afternoon," she added almost apologetically.

B.G. hastened to assure the older woman that she certainly did not mind, and Nils added his reassurances. After Solbritt had taken her somewhat self-conscious leave, it occurred to B.G. that no suggestion had been made that either she or Nils might be interested in a card game, too. Evidently Solbritt had assumed a lack of interest, in B.G.'s own case an accurate assumption.

With the buffer of the older woman's presence removed, the atmosphere between Nils and B.G. was uncomfortably strained. Now that there was no need to mask their animosity behind politeness, neither of them could think of anything to say. Nils sat in morose silence and consumed several small glasses of sherry while B.G. sipped on her second one. With each passing minute the cold and dampness seeped deeper into her bones, making her more miserable and restless. She knew that she couldn't bear to sit there much longer and suffer, but it was difficult to stir herself out of her lethargy when she considered the limited alternatives: She could go to her cabin and read, or she could go to her cabin and sleep. She didn't feel like doing either.

"I don't know when I've been so cold," she grumbled, shivering under her makeshift cape.

The remark was intended as a preamble to announcing her intention to retire, but before she could say anything more, Nils was standing up, the querulous sound of her voice apparently having nudged him to action.

"I've been colder lots of times, but it's silly for us to sit out here tonight. If you're ready to go to your cabin and read that good book you mentioned at dinner, I think I'll go to bed." His words held no hint of challenge or invitation. They were merely a statement of intention arising out of a restlessness that matched what she felt.

"That's a good idea," B.G. agreed briskly, standing up. It irritated her that *he* had been the one to suggest that they retire to their cabins. "Good night," she flung over her shoulder as she strode off, getting some satisfaction at least out of leaving him standing there.

A few minutes later when she was brushing her teeth, she heard his cabin door opening and closing and knew that he was just beyond the bulkhead behind her. Stifling the thought of his nearness, she continued her nightly ritual, taking as much time as possible cleaning her face and applying a night cream.

When she was finished, there was nothing remaining

to do but climb into her bunk, which had been neatly made up for her earlier, apparently while she was at dinner. Fortunately, she really had brought along a novel, but as she opened it up to where she had left off on the flight over, about midway through the first chapter, she felt a decided lack of interest.

Forty-five minutes later she was only five or six pages further along; she kept having to read pages over and still couldn't have passed the simplest quiz on what she had read so far. With a sigh of frustration, B.G. put the book down while she plumped up the pillows behind her back rather savagely and then sat back and listened for a minute or two.

The wind couldn't actually be said to be howling outside, but it was making its presence and velocity known. Now and then the *Wilhelm Tham* moved and bumped gently against something, she supposed against the wharf to which it was tied. Occasionally she heard a voice and the opening and closing of doors as passengers returned to their cabins. A glance at her watch told her that it was only a little after ten, but she thought that by eleven o'clock most of the passengers would be in their bunks and asleep.

Even Nils was probably asleep by now, she conjectured glumly, feeling very much alone in the world as she picked up her book again and began to plod through some more pages. This force-fed reading brought back memories of college.

Promptly at eleven o'clock she heard the quiet sounds of Solbritt's return to her cabin. Knowing that the three of them were now sealed in their tiny cells, all in a row on this side of the boat up on the bridge deck, didn't make B.G. feel cozy and secure; it made her feel claustrophobic. She knew that her mind was only reacting to a restrictive situation in which she had nowhere to go and nothing to do to relieve herself of this pent-up restlessness.

Finally, there was no recourse but to admit the hopelessness of trying to concentrate on the novel. The characters seemed flat and uninteresting even though the novel was a bestseller. B.G. closed the book without marking her place and turned out the reading light located very conveniently on the wall by her head.

Once she had snuggled down underneath the blankets, she told herself how nice it was to be protected and warm with the wind gusting outside and the night air saturated with that damp chill she had endured all day. Hopefully she waited for her mind to relax and become pleasantly fuzzy. No such luck. Her head might have been equipped with tiny wheels, all connected by tiny belts that made the wheels turn faster and faster and faster, producing images and voices with distinct clearness.

There was no particular order to her thoughts. She recalled scenes and conversations from her childhood and youth, some with her grandmother and her parents. Mixed in were more recent happenings, her arrival in Gothenburg, her first encounter with Nils when he had been dispatched to the airport to meet her. She went over conversations with him during the past four days, relived those times when they would confront each other head on and end up in each other's arms, violence fusing with passion and need.

"Stop thinking!" she finally murmured aloud, aching with frustration. Throwing back the bed covers, she sat up on the side of the bunk and shivered with the impact of the chilly air.

Wearily she switched on the light long enough to check her watch and find out that it was a little after midnight. Only about six hours remained before she would need to be getting up, and here she was not even close to falling asleep. It seemed to B.G. that in every one of those few instances when she had suffered from insomnia, there was always the feeling of *needing* to get her sleep. Knowing that she would have to be up and dressed and armed for the day by seven o'clock made her frantic. If she didn't get her rest, how in the world would she be able to cope with Nils.

"You can just skip breakfast and sleep late if you want to," she told herself soothingly and got up to slip on her quilted robe before she paid a visit to the *toalett* on the other side of Nils's cabin.

She was very quiet opening and closing the sturdy mahogany doors of her cabin and the *toalett;* the latter compartment was delightfully warmed by a small wall radiator. When she switched out the light and made her exit, again closing the door quietly behind her, she might have been the only person awake in the entire world. There wasn't a sound of another human moving about on the boat, just misty darkness beyond the rail and the relentless wind coming from some apparently eternal wellspring.

Drawing her robe more tightly around her and folding her arms across her chest, B.G. gave in to the impulse to delay her return to her own cabin. She wasn't dressed warmly enough to stay out on deck long, but there was an odd exhilaration in her utter aloneness. Making almost no noise with her soft slippers, she drifted back toward the stern, noting that someone had cleared the broad stern deck of the deck chairs, folding and stacking them out of the way.

At the furthest point aft, she leaned against the rail near the flagstaff that held the Swedish flag during the day. Swedish people apparently were quite fond of their flag, she mused, remembering how many of the sailboats she had seen the day before had flown the blue flag with its yellow **X**. It was a cheerful, simple design but called up no feeling at all in her the way the stars and stripes of the American flag did. B.G. was one of those Americans who couldn't stand through the worst rendition of "The Star-Spangled Banner" without getting choked up.

She was smiling to herself at the admission when a movement some yards behind her caught her attention and told her that she was no longer alone. With a little spurt of fright that was more the result of being taken unawares than real fear for her safety, she turned to see who it was and wasn't surprised when Nils loomed up close to her, wearing a dark robe belted at the waist. He had slippers on his feet, but even in the semidarkness she could see that his legs were bare.

"You can't sleep either." Her statement of the obvious was faintly pleased, as though she liked his having insomnia, too. "I've been reading," she added unconvincingly.

Nils came to lean against the rail near her.

"Is your book as good as you claimed?"

The query definitely held no interest, but evidently Nils felt that he had to say something. B.G. thought that he was as ill at ease as she was. They were both strongly conscious of being there together without any of the usual protections, without their day faces or day clothes, without Solbritt.

"It's hard to say. I couldn't concentrate on it very well," she admitted candidly.

He made no reply and the silence that stretched out between them became too awkward for B.G. to endure.

"I *hate* having insomnia, don't you?" she complained, hugging herself and giving into a convulsive shiver that took her by surprise, since she wasn't aware of feeling cold.

Nils made a movement toward her, lifting the arm

nearest her as though he meant to put it around her. Quickly he checked himself and put the arm back down on the rail.

"You're going to catch a cold standing out here dressed like that," he stated with a curious lack of either the disapproval or the concern that usually prompts such a remark.

"I know. I guess I'd better go back to my cabin."

Neither of them moved.

"I have the rest of that bottle of sherry in my cabin," he said a moment later.

B.G. felt the shiver coming on this time and managed to subdue it. She guessed that she must be cold and thought of returning to her cabin and getting back into her bunk again. Instantly she rejected the idea and let her mind consider the only other alternative, since staying out here on deck was out of the question. She could go to Nils's cabin with him, if that mention of the bottle of sherry was actually an invitation. His cabin was no larger than her own. His bunk would be mussed and tumbled, too, showing the imprint of his body where he had lain, trying to sleep. It would be inescapably intimate in his cabin at this time of the night with the rest of the world asleep. Yes, *too* intimate.

"Maybe some sherry *would* help me sleep," she heard herself saying.

Nils said nothing more as he straightened and turned away from the rail, with no noticeable reluctance or eagerness. B.G. knew, though, as she moved silently along the deck with him toward his cabin, that he was gripped with the same tension that she felt. She wondered if he saw them as approaching a new threshold, beyond which lay unknown territory.

Nils opened the door to his cabin and entered first to turn on the light over the washstand and straighten the rumpled bedcovers on his bunk. B.G. sat at one end, feeling ridiculously prim and shy, while he rinsed out the small stemmed glass he had apparently brought with him to his cabin and poured it full of sherry for her. She took the glass and waited while Nils poured himself a generous portion of sherry in the glass tumbler he emptied of toothbrush and tube of toothpaste.

"To sleep," he said, raising the glass in a toast and then dropping down at the opposite end of the bunk.

"To sleep."

B.G. took a sip of her sherry and felt its warmth slide down her throat. It was impossible not to be amused at the way she and Nils were behaving, like two people who hadn't already torn through several layers of privacy in the short time they'd known each other.

"Why weren't *you* able to sleep?" she asked, the tinge of humor in her voice inviting him to smile with her and be friends.

"Ladies first." Nils settled with indolent ease back against the bulkhead.

B.G. looked at him over the rim of her sherry glass while she took a sip to postpone her reply. His dark robe was perfectly modest, its proportions ample on his long frame, but she could tell that he wasn't wearing pajamas —bare legs and exposed tan skin at the vee neck made that plain. Was he wearing anything? Memory flashed the way he had looked the day before in those brief blue trunks and made her keenly aware of being with him here in his small cabin with both of them in night clothes. She was sure that she looked anything but sexy in the quilted robe that buttoned from neck to ankle. Her hair must look awful, too, uncombed and tumbled about her face.

"I'm not sure why I couldn't sleep," she started out evasively, looking away from him but finding little on which to fix her attention in the small room. "Probably because all of this is such a new experience for me.'' She took another drink of sherry and found she had finished the glass. Whether the sherry would help her sleep remained to be seen, but it certainly had warmed her up and eased her tenseness. She waited while Nils reached to the washstand for the bottle and refilled her glass, then continued, a little more recklessly.

"So much has happened in a few short days. Nothing has turned out the way I expected since I came here." She glanced over at him, seeing that contrary to his posture, he wasn't relaxed at all. "Fru Heidenstam doesn't seem like a person of my grandmother's generation. She not only looks and acts younger; she *thinks* younger. As you already know, Sweden is not what I expected it to be at all." She hesitated, shifting her body a little and working her courage up to say, *You aren't like anybody I've ever known before anywhere.*

Nils downed the remainder of the sherry in his tumbler and set it on the washstand beside the bottle.

"Don't you think the reason we're having trouble sleeping is that we started something this afternoon at Trollhätten that needs to be finished?" he asked casually. "A little uncomplicated sex would be better than a whole bottle of sleeping pills." He didn't move from his end of the bunk.

B.G. eyed him steadily, making no effort to hide the mixture of emotions she was feeling: renewed disappointment in him, scorn for herself that she had tried yet again to get close to him, and bafflement as she tried to figure out what made him tick. In one sense, he was right. Sex was an unfinished issue between them, but then so was everything else, all those equally important elements in a relationship between a man and a woman, like trust and sharing and open giving. Nils obviously wanted no part of real intimacy. She wasn't even convinced that he wanted the "uncomplicated sex" he had mentioned. Certainly he hadn't made a move toward her.

"You're probably right," she said softly, letting her eyes issue a direct challenge.

His gaze locked with hers and didn't waver as he slowly straightened from his lounging position and slid unhurriedly across the space separating them on the bunk.

"If you had admitted that yesterday at Marstrand, we'd both have saved ourselves a lot of tossing and turning," he said very deliberately as his hand reached for the top button of her robe and undid it.

"I guess I just don't have your experience with situations like this," B.G. countered bitterly, sitting there stiff-shouldered and resentful, leaving him little alternative but to finish unbuttoning her robe, which he did more rapidly, his face set in a determined expression.

They were engaged in yet another duel of wills that neither one was about to lose. When Nils had undone her robe all the way down the front, he pushed it off her shoulders, only to discover that the nightgown underneath it was a different prospect altogether: a pale blue and cream confection whose almost transparent silky material and lace insets made a mockery of the ladylike design. Gathers at the high bodice provided fullness for her firm, rounded breasts, which drew his attention immediately.

Aware of his reluctance to continue the contest that might backfire on him, B.G. pressed her advantage, reaching around behind her to tug the robe free of her arms. She watched his face as he noted the way her movements lifted her breasts and strained them outward to him, more temptation than any man—or, apparently, Nils, anyway—could withstand. He lifted both hands to her breasts as though he might capture the alluring roundness. Instead he only traced his fingertips around the perimeters and then grazed his knuckles across the hard peaks.

Her involuntary response to his touch made their situation a draw, with the outcome uncertain. It was B.G.'s turn to make a move.

"Kiss me, Nils," she demanded in a tone calculated to arouse his obstinacy. To irritate him even further, she tilted her head slightly backward in a classic siren pose she had seen actresses in old movies employ. He had gone completely still; his hands dropped somewhere out of her sight, and not touching her. After a long suspenseful moment, B.G. was ready to chalk up a final winning score. In her confidence, she indulged herself and brought her hands up to his face, lightly touching the strong bone structure before combing her fingertips through his hair, golden in the artificial light. The individual strands were soft, like silk threads. B.G. found herself quite engrossed in what she was doing and feeling.

Nils didn't find it easy to ignore her touch or to resist the invitation of her softly parted lips, moistened so deliberately and yet maddeningly with the pink tip of her tongue. If she wanted to play sex games with him, he would play sex games. Reaching up for her hands, he took them in his own and held them easily captive while he leaned forward, bypassing the proffered lips and grazing his mouth along her cheek to her ear. Aware that she had tensed with the uncertainty of what he intended to do, he took his time, letting his mouth hover at her ear and his breath warm the sensitive orifice before he used the tip of his tongue. When she gasped and made a little sound, he knew the moment was right. Bringing her hands down to the tie at his waist, he settled them there firmly and then took his hands away.

It was his turn now to bask in the confidence of having

the situation well in hand. He left her ear and slid his mouth lower, down to the curve of her neck, where he immersed himself in her wonderful fragrance and enjoyed the silky texture of her skin. It took some discipline to make his hands stay idle, but he wasn't so foolhardy as to start caressing her, or he would become more aroused than he already was.

B.G. felt the warmth of his breath against the vulnerable curve of her neck, kindling a heat that intensified as it traveled away from the source and spread all through her body, awakening a powerful need in every part of her to be touched. She wanted his hands all over her. She wanted to grasp his head and stop the delicious torment so that he could kiss her on the mouth. How she *yearned* for him to kiss her. But the woolen material of his dark robe beneath her hands was a reminder that Nils didn't really want to make love to her; he wanted to defeat her in a silly game of wills—with no worthwhile prize, as far as she could determine.

"I don't think this should go on, Nils." She paused, aware that his mouth had lifted a fraction from her neck, not too far, though, because she could still feel the seductive heat of his breath. "You don't really mean to follow through—and neither do I." She added the last to take out the element of challenge. Nils lifted his head now and looked at her distrustfully, plainly thinking that she was making some tricky move. "There can be no 'uncomplicated' sex with us, Nils," she said honestly and should have left the matter there instead of adding what probably rankled more than anything else. "Besides, you don't really want to make love to me."

Nils knew that every word she had spoken held some truth. He knew that he should let her get up and walk out. It would be the safest conclusion to a totally unsatisfactory situation. Knowing all that, he still couldn't stomach letting her have the final word. That urge was powerful inside him to dominate her, subdue her, bring her to his feet.

He picked up her hands, which had dropped away from the waist of his robe and lay in her lap, and brought them forcibly back to the loosely knotted tie. "I dare you to open this robe and tell me *I* don't intend to go through with this," he challenged, and then felt the surge of stimulation heighten at the sound of his own words. God, more than anything now he wanted her *not* to back down!

B.G. sucked in her breath as she stared back at Nils, feeling herself dangerously poised on the brink of some precipice. She wanted to take him up on the challenge simply because it *was* a challenge: He brought out a combativeness in her that made it difficult to back down on anything. More than that, though, her heart was running away with her and every nerve in her body was blazingly alive at the possibility of doing what he dared her to do. She wanted to undo the tie of the robe, let the folds open and look at his naked, aroused man's body. She wanted to touch him with her hands and know him intimately. *He* wanted that, too. She could see the stark desire there in his face and his eyes, along with the fear that she would take them over the precipice into an intimacy they had both intuitively avoided up until now.

"No," B.G. said, shaking her head at first slowly and then harder. "No, not like this. I don't want it to be like this."

As she got up from the bunk and put on her robe, she was shaking violently and not from cold. A strange kind of urgency had seized her, and she just knew that she had to get out of his cabin at once, before she wept, before she screamed at him, before she begged him to make love to her but not to hurt her even more than he had already, before she acted upon any of the dozens of clashing emotional impulses.

Nils sat there and watched her as she struggled to don her robe, making no offer to help. When she left his cabin without pausing to utter another word, he made no effort to stop her. B.G. was too full of her own conflict to sense what he was thinking or feeling.

Chapter Ten

The next morning the wind had lessened enough to allow the passage of the *Wilhelm Tham* across Lake Vänern, but the day promised to be raw and overcast, not the kind that encourages one to sit out on deck. At breakfast passengers were informed of an optional side trip provided by the canal boat company, which had encountered the problem of inclement weather many times and wanted to do whatever it could to keep them happy.

After breakfast a tour bus would be parked out on the wharf. Anyone interested in visiting historic Läckö Castle and the Rörstrand porcelain factory at Lidköping was encouraged to board the bus and meet up with the canal boat in the afternoon after it had crossed Lake Vänern.

B.G., who felt as raw inside as the weather she could see through the plate glass windows of the dining salon, voted yes in favor of the land trip without a second's hesitation. After only twenty-four hours, she felt as though she'd been aboard the *Wilhelm Tham* much longer than that. Anything would be preferable to another day like yesterday.

Solbritt also wanted to take the side trip. "You will have the opportunity to visit the same factory that made your grandmother's plates," she pointed out brightly, bringing up the subject she hadn't mentioned since B.G.'s arrival that first day.

"I hope nothing's happened to my grandmother's collection," B.G. reflected worriedly, her brow furrowed with irritation at this reminder that the plates had not followed her to Forsborg as promptly as the shipping company had promised.

A silent Nils didn't bother to vote once the two women had opted for the bus tour. Neither of the day's choices held any appeal for him. Yesterday's restlessness had grown to almost unendurable proportions. He simply hoped somehow to get through the next two days. Once having arrived in Stockholm, he would settle his grandmother and B.G. comfortably in one of the best hotels, make whatever arrangements needed to be made for excursions beyond Stockholm, and then leave them on their own. It had been sheer folly for him to agree to come along in his present state of mind. He was definitely not fit company for anyone, and now this thing between himself and B.G. had added a whole new complication he definitely did not need or want. Fortunately for him, Stockholm wasn't New York City. He could leave his grandmother and her guest with the assurance that they would be safe in Sweden's most populated city.

This calm plan for escape provided Nils with only transitory relief. The day of sightseeing was sheer hell, partly because after the previous night, the awareness between him and B.G. had intensified to such an extent that they both had difficulty pretending it wasn't there.

The need to challenge and antagonize her was stronger than ever, as well. Meanwhile, the usually perceptive Solbritt gave no indication that she noticed anything amiss. Nils had to conclude that his grandmother simply didn't want to notice. She added her own layers of torment by casting him continuously in the role of fellow proud Swede showing a stranger his country. It was "Nils, tell Birgitta about" first one thing and then another. He complied half-heartedly, thinking all the while of her disbelief and sense of betrayal if he told her the truth: Despite strong family ties to Sweden, his patriotism was not nearly so complete nor so irrevocable as was her own.

B.G., in that unerring way of hers, had hit upon a sensitive truth in Marstrand when she accused him of not knowing *what* he was, Swede or American. He guessed that he really didn't know for sure. He'd been straddling some line between being one or the other his whole life, spending most of his time in the States and yet a Swedish citizen by birthright. He could continue the same course if he took his place permanently in the Heidenstam operation and probably never have to face up to precisely who and what he was. The moment he rebelled and stepped out on his own, though, he would have to come to terms with himself.

B.G. rode next to Solbritt on the bus ride to Läckö Castle, with Nils sitting across the aisle from them. She glanced over at him from time to time and saw that he wasn't even looking out of the huge expanses of glass at the passing countryside. His head was tilted back against the headrest, and his eyes were closed, but she knew that he wasn't asleep. He was buried in his thoughts, now no longer a mystery to her. After yesterday's startling revelations at Trollhättan, she knew that he was thinking about the momentous decisions he had to make about his future.

With all her heart she wished she were free to speak openly to him, question him, learn more of his deepest feelings. There was no chance of that, though, not with the unsuspecting Solbritt on one side, urging B.G. every few minutes to observe this or that out of the window. B.G. didn't feel her best after last night's brief, fitful sleep, and it took all her willpower to force herself to chat with Solbritt and feign interest in the scenery, while Nils's anxiety penetrated her mind and heightened her inner tension. As the day wore on, she was eerily aware of feeling like two persons, outwardly the interested and impressionable visitor Solbritt wanted her to be and inwardly the person who had learned too much not to listen to each exchange between Nils and his grandmother with special insight.

"Nils can tell you everything about Läckö Castle. He has studied Swedish history and knows it well, even though he did not attend Swedish schools," the older woman asserted proudly as the three of them strolled up the gentle incline of the hill with the old castle in full view ahead of them.

"There is sure to be a guide," Nils demurred. "Besides, I am sure that Birgitta is not interested in a lot of dry historical facts."

B.G. wished that she could speak up at once and say that he was right, but then she might have hurt Solbritt's feelings. She had to hold her tongue and conceal her sympathy for Nils as he sketched in a brief history of the castle, its white walls looking like stucco from this distance and its circular towers capped with conical black roofs.

When they had reached the castle and passed through an outer courtyard into an inner one, they dutifully took note of the two blackened bronze statues of former owners occupying niches high up in the wall facing the entrance to the courtyard. Then they entered the castle

with the rest of the passengers from the *Wilhelm Tham*
and were herded along from room to room, up and down
flights of worn stone stairs. B.G. paid scant attention to
the tour guide's information, delivered entirely in Swedish. Nils had been correct in guessing that she wasn't a
history buff, fascinated by dates and historical facts.
Mainly she liked to look around and gather her own
impressions. From the decorator's point of view, she
noted how plain and primitive the structure of the
building was and appreciated the diamond-paned windows, many of which were swung open to afford a
beautiful view of blue lake water.

"A long way from the Royal Palace in Madrid," Nils
murmured in her ear when they had paused in some
noblewoman's bedchamber with a small, quaint old bed
and a closet that the noblewoman reportedly had used to
store chocolates, for which she had a passion.

"I wouldn't know. I've never been to Madrid," she
whispered back.

When the female guide had concluded the information
on that chamber and led the group on to the next one,
Nils hung back. B.G. obeyed an urge to linger with him.
His comments would be a lot more interesting to her than
the dry lecture delivered by the guide.

"Is this typical of the castles in Sweden?" she asked
him. His faintly ironic smile suggested that neither of
them was deeply interested in Swedish castles, but he
humored her with an answer nonetheless.

B.G. could hear the voice of the guide droning on in
the next room and regretted the necessity of having to
move on and catch up with the group. With Nils in this
mood, she was aware of him as an interesting, cosmopolitan man who had traveled widely and could comment
out of personal experience on places she had only read
about. He awoke in her the recognition that her world up
until now had been a small one, her travel confined to

several northern states. To have voiced her thoughts
would have sounded inane, so she said something else
instead.

"I can see that you really do know your Swedish
history, and the nice thing about you is that you don't tell
everything you know!" She made a little motion with
her head toward the next room.

Nils saw the shy friendliness in her eyes, heard the
tentative invitation in her voice to let bygones be
bygones, and cursed himself for not avoiding being alone
with her when he knew damned well it was getting
harder all the time to fight her.

"On the contrary," he disagreed, motioning for her to
precede him. "I've told you everything I know about
Swedish castles. Now you are as well informed as I
am."

After that Nils made sure there was no opportunity for
further private exchanges between them. He managed
not to stand too close to her, and he didn't hang back
when the group was trooping on to the next chamber.
B.G. was stung by his rebuff, and yet she couldn't
prevent herself from listening through Nils's ears and
viewing the whole experience through his eyes. He must
be noticing Solbritt's almost reverent attention to every
dry detail recited by the guide. He must be absorbing
those appreciative murmurs uttered not just by her but by
the whole company of Swedes, who outnumbered the
foreigners in the group. It was like a patriotic litany.
Such strong feeling was surprising in a people generally
considered stoic and unemotional.

It was a relief to her when they finally made their exit
from the castle and walked down the sloping grounds to
a modern building that housed a gift shop and a
restaurant. Upstairs was an open loft dining area furnished with tables and chairs. There several of the
waitresses from the *Wilhelm Tham* served a cold lunch

that had been packed and brought along on the bus. While B.G. munched her sandwich and sipped her strong hot coffee, she deliberately kept Solbritt occupied with busy chatter so that Nils could be left to the privacy of his own thoughts.

Afterward, the passengers made their way back to the bus in the parking lot. Next they would go on to the Rörstrand porcelain factory at Lidköping. There was conversation about the ''seconds'' shop where one could purchase items at a bargain price. Solbritt might have been intending to purchase a whole set of Rörstrand china, judging from her interest in this conversation. When she boarded the bus, she sat next to a stout Swedish man who was traveling alone and had visited the porcelain factory some years prior.

A somewhat surprised B.G. found herself without a seating companion and didn't know until Nils sat next to her whether he would do so or not. For the first five minutes or so, she looked out the window and debated with herself. *Mind your own business*, the prudent part of her advised. *He won't welcome any advice from you.* The urge to speak her thoughts proved to be too strong to be quelled by words of wisdom.

Turning her head abruptly, she saw that Nils, in the aisle seat, was gazing out of the window, too. ''Why don't you tell her?'' B.G. said in a low tone, without any preamble. Before he could recover from his surprise, she plunged on. ''She's really a great person. And she loves you more than anybody else in the world, it seems. Don't you think she would want what was best for you? Don't you think she would accept whatever you decided to do?''

Nils was so unprepared that at first he could only stare at her as the words tumbled out of her mouth. Then he immediately became incensed at her presumptuousness. Who was she to tell him what to do? The very person

whose ill-timed arrival had prevented him from coming
to an understanding with his grandmother! What infuriated him most was B.G.'s tone and manner. You'd think
that either he hadn't thought of telling his grandmother
or else he lacked the courage! And the implication was
there that B.G. in his place wouldn't have hesitated if the
decision had been hers. *She* would have known precisely
what decision to make and would have blurted it out at
once to Solbritt. But, then, hadn't she been barging right
through the sensitive feelings of those who loved her all
her life?

"I am quite aware of my grandmother's deep affection," he said in a low voice that trembled with fury. "I
don't need you to tell me she loves me and wants what is
best for me. I'll thank you kindly to let me take care of
my own life and the relationships with members of my
family! Frankly, I think you're the *last* person to give
advice about dealing with other people's feelings." He
kept his gaze locked with hers a long moment to
communicate the enormity of his contempt and then he
stared straight ahead, his profile like stone.

B.G. smarted at that indirect reference to the hurt she
had caused her grandmother, but she wasn't as deeply
offended by Nils's words and his tone as he had meant
her to be. She knew that he was reacting this way out of
frustration. He wanted to be open with Solbritt, but
something was holding him back, and B.G. just didn't
think that something was lack of courage. It was certainly lack of wisdom along with deep concern that made her
open her mouth and speak her mind again, at the risk of
provoking Nils to violence.

"Nils, I think you haven't said anything to her so far
because you haven't been able to make up your mind.
It's *you* that you're not certain of, not her."

Nils was certain of only one thing at that moment: He
wanted to *throttle* her! He had never known such an

infuriating woman in his whole life! There was no way to shut her up. Unable to trust himself to speak, he glared at her, threatening murder at the very least if she uttered another word, and then not only averted his gaze, but shifted his whole body toward the aisle to emphasize that further conversation was taboo.

B.G. waited several long minutes to let his anger cool.

"I don't understand," she murmured very carefully to the side of his head, "why you're so unwilling to talk to me about it. Don't you think it would do you good to speak your thoughts out loud to someone instead of keeping everything locked up inside you?"

"Oh, *God,*" Nils groaned, closing his eyes and dropping his head until his chin rested against his chest. "What did I ever do to deserve—" He slowly raised his head again and turned it so that she could view the menace in his face and eyes. B.G. stood her ground without any show of defiance that might egg him on to violence. "There is no way *you* could possibly ever understand my position," he said cuttingly. "Your first words were probably the pledge of allegiance to the American flag."

She stiffened a little under his contempt, but experienced none of the anger he was deliberately trying to provoke.

"Why don't you give me a chance?" she asked reasonably. "Maybe I'll surprise you. Maybe I *will* understand. A week ago I wouldn't have, but now I think I might. Probably my strongest impression of Sweden so far is how much Swedish people love their country. Their patriotism is more obvious than an American's." She paused, interested in the observation that had just popped out. "Americans are more prone to be outspoken in their criticisms of their government—maybe that's the difference," she went on thoughtfully. "Deep down we *are* patriotic, though. It must have been difficult for you, being born in one country and being taught attitudes of loyalty to that country and most of the time living in another country, where you had to absorb its attitudes and customs, too. Perhaps you feel as though you belong to *both* Sweden and the United States.'' This last suggestion was fortunately a very tentative one and did not offend Nils. B.G. was suddenly deeply thoughtful and then sad. ''For the first time, I can imagine just a little of what my grandparents must have felt when they left Sweden. It must have been hard to leave the country where all their roots were and go off to a new country that offered opportunity but was strange and different.'' She blinked at the sudden tears. ''You know, Nils, I'm so glad now that I came to Sweden. I'm deeply grateful to my grandmother—and to yours, too—for making this trip possible.''

Nils had been observing her narrowly, assuring himself that she was being completely candid with him and yet still reluctant to open himself up to her as she had opened herself to him. This broadmindedness and newfound insight into other people's feelings could just be a passing mood. She could go back to making pronouncements at any moment.

''It's not easy to think of changing one's citizenship,'' he admitted cautiously and then worked up his courage to add, ''There's a sense of betrayal.'' He broke the eye contact between them and glanced past her out at the countryside, noting with one part of his mind that the front had passed. Weak sunshine was struggling to assert itself. ''In my case, there would be no great effort to achieve assimilation, since, as you have pointed out, I'm something of a hybrid already. I can get along easily in either Sweden or the United States—in other countries in Europe, too, for that matter.''

B.G. had been listening carefully, aware that his formal phraseology was a kind of defense and admiring the way he handled the English language, actually with greater mastery than most of the Americans she knew, certainly better than *she* handled it. The United States would be the more fortunate to have Nils as a citizen. He had much to offer. She kept these thoughts to herself, which was the best thing she could have done at that particular moment. Her silence encouraged Nils to continue.

"It's a selfish decision I have to make—what is best for *me*. That's the difficult part, since by birthright I am offered so much, a chance to take my place in a very successful business run by generations of Heidenstams before me."

"If you don't continue in the family business, it makes you look ungrateful," B.G. put in.

Nils nodded agreement, but after that, he was silent, as regretful for lapsing into openness as he was momentarily relieved at the outlet of talking about the difficulties of the decision he had to make.

B.G. didn't want to leave the subject there, but she lacked the nerve to press him any further at that time. For the rest of the drive to Lidköping, she thought about what he had told her and about those discoveries she had made for herself since coming to Sweden. It seemed to her that her insight into human feelings had been incredibly expanded in a few short days.

Was it this new sensitivity to other people's feelings that made her unduly anxious on Nils's behalf? You'd have thought the decision he had to make affected her personally, when actually she had to face the truth that after her return to the United States, she would probably never see or hear from Nils again. With his good looks, sophistication, background, and connections, he would hardly be looking B.G. up in Minneapolis, no matter what he decided to do. He hadn't even seriously tried to get her into bed. This sound good sense put such a damper on her mood that she stared glumly out of the window, not at all buoyed by the sunshine, which heralded a change in the weather.

A tour through the Rörstrand porcelain works in Lidköping revealed gleaming stainless steel machinery being operated by women as well as men, of varying ages, in clean, well-lighted conditions. The factory workers looked competent and cheerful, not at all bothered by the close scrutiny of strangers. Like everyone else in Sweden, B.G. learned, they received five weeks of paid holiday each year, regardless of the number of years employment. The elderly guide who took the group from the *Wilhelm Tham* through the factory, a retired employee himself, explained almost apologetically that the Rörstrand factory did not shut down for a month in the summer. Employees had to stagger their holiday time.

Reading the expression of amazement on B.G.'s countenance and misinterpreting it for disapproval, the guide hastened to add that it simply was not feasible to shut off the huge brick ovens and then bring them back up to the incredibly high temperatures necessary to make porcelain. B.G. nodded her head solemnly the way all the Swedes in the group were doing to reassure the guide that she indeed understood the reasons. When the group was trooping along after him toward the next location where he would stop again and carefully explain a step in the process of making porcelain, she looked around for Nils and found him just behind her. He met her questioning gaze with a faintly amused expression, and she thought that he had probably been reading her mind again.

"Does the Heidenstam Fabrik close down for a whole month in the summer?" she queried in a low voice.

He nodded. "July," he said briefly.

"That's absolutely incredible!" B.G. breathed. "And

every single Swedish worker gets *five weeks'* paid vacation, even someone who's just started to work that year?''

Nils nodded again. "Right you are. By edict of the Swedish government."

They were strolling along very slowly in the wake of the others. "I just cannot imagine a factory closing down so that all the employees can take a vacation!" B.G. mused wonderingly.

"You probably can't imagine having to get government permission to install a new, more efficient machine either," Nils put in crisply.

"Does your factory have to do that?"

"If it means laying off a worker, we definitely do. Any changes of that kind are best timed to coincide with the retirement of older employees." He expelled a small sigh. "Oh, I'm not saying that the close supervision of government is all bad. Swedish workers have a great deal more job security than do American workers in general, but all the regulations and red tape play hell with running a factory at maximum efficiency."

B.G. slowed her steps even more, reluctant to catch up with the others. This exchange with Nils was much more interesting to her than was the procedure of making porcelain. His remarks provided some insights into his dissatisfaction with his present position as a part of the Heidenstam family business.

"It hasn't always been like this in Sweden, has it?" She noted with satisfaction that the tour group was moving on again.

Nils shook his head.

"No, but I look for things to get much worse for the factory owner. He'll have less and less to say about how he runs his own business. I was serious last Sunday when I warned Gunnar and Per about the flight of capitalistic talent from Sweden. Right now there are whole colonies of Swedes on the sun coast of Spain, for example. They saw the light early and withdrew their capital in time. Now it isn't even easy for a Swedish investor to divest himself of his ownership and have anything left when it's all said and done.''

"No wonder you're thinking of going into business for yourself in the United States,'' B.G. ventured, keeping her voice carefully neutral. She knew from experience that she could raise Nils's hackles in a second by expressing an opinion of some kind.

"It's not just the prospect of making money that attracts me,'' Nils pointed out quickly. "Certainly I have never lacked for anything I needed and not much that I even wanted badly. Maybe if I had grown up less fortunate, I would be willing now just to step into place in the Heidenstam operation and plod along, day by day, year by year, doing what the government tells me to do.'' The dissatisfaction in Nils's voice was enough in itself to express his impatience with such restriction. "But somehow I'm just not happy at the thought of running the factory built by my great-grandfather and expanded by his sons and their sons. I'd stay with the family business if I thought there were any chance I could put into it my own ideas, improve it and make it even better. But I seriously doubt there's any chance of that. If I stay, I'm afraid I will end up a very frustrated man.''

B.G.'s earlier discretion deserted her.

"Don't stay, Nils! You really shouldn't!'' she blurted out in her concern for his future. At once she realized her mistake in speaking her deepest feelings. Nils's face took on that closed expression that told her to mind her own business. "Er, that is, it sounds to me like you would be very dissatisfied if you did stay,'' she continued lamely in a futile attempt to repair the damage.

"I appreciate your concern,'' Nils said coolly, clearly

not appreciating her having given him her advice. "It looks as though we've fallen behind our group and have missed several steps in the process of making porcelain." He promptly increased his pace.

B.G. had to hurry to keep up with him.

"Nils, I apologize! I don't know *why* I can't keep my big mouth shut when I know how much my speaking my mind irritates you. I only meant—"

"I don't want to hear what you meant," he cut in sharply with a silencing glare.

They had caught up with the others now and stood on the outer fringes of the group. Nils ignored B.G.'s presence beside him, his attention grimly fixed upon the guide and his explanation about glazing the porcelain cup he held aloft in his hand. B.G. had no choice other than to stand there, emotions churning.

Why couldn't she ever keep her opinions to herself when she knew damned well that he always reacted this same way when she volunteered her point of view? At the same time, why did he always grow so hostile when she voiced her gut reactions? Surely everyone had some opinion on most matters! Nils didn't expect her to be as blank as a sheet of paper, did he? Vacillating between being angry at herself and angry at Nils, B.G. decided that she was going to broach this matter directly the next time she and Nils were alone. She would ask him point blank why her opinion on anything provoked and annoyed him to such an extent.

Such an opportunity did not present itself for the remainder of the afternoon. When the tour of the factory had been concluded, the passengers from the *Wilhelm Tham* were free to take advantage of several options. They could browse through the large showroom in an adjoining building, where all the Rörstrand products currently available were beautifully displayed. Further along in the complex of brick buildings was also a museum, a coffee shop, and a wholesale shop, where "seconds" could be purchased.

Since the majority of the tour group headed straight for the showroom, Solbritt, B.G., and Nils decided to go first to the museum. B.G., as usual, took little interest in the detailed historical data printed on cards next to porcelain items inside glass cases until she happened upon some of the patterns in her grandmother's collection. Suddenly she found herself reading the information with a new kind of interest, feeling strange all the while as she was able to put those odd old plates of her grandmother's into a larger historical framework.

She was able to guess that the collection probably did have some monetary value, but that realization was not responsible for the sense of regret that grew inside her as she thought of how the plates would never belong to her now, as she had grown up thinking that they would. For the first time, they had value, sentimental value, though, not monetary. If they had been hers, she would have displayed them someday in a home of her own. She would have designed a room especially for them.

But the plates would never be hers, she reminded herself, and had to combat the pang of sadness with the reflection that at least they would belong to Solbritt, who would take care of them and value them because they had been the possession of her dear friend Birgitta. But what would happen to the plates after Solbritt was gone? Who would value them then? Who would know how much they had meant to an old farm woman in Minnesota? Caught up in these somber questions, B.G. wandered along in front of the glass-fronted cases, so seemingly intent upon their contents that a casual observer would have guessed she was a serious collector.

"I think that Birgitta is thinking about her grandmother, my old friend," Solbritt confided to Nils in an undertone. "Do you see how sad she looks?"

Nils had sauntered through the small museum with little interest and stood waiting near a display of large modernistic pottery that was more to his taste than the fussily ornate porcelain in the glass cases. Most of that looked pretty much like what he'd grown up with in his grandmother's house. Solbritt's remark about B.G. made him look over at B.G. and note that she did indeed appear quite dejected about something.

"Why should this place remind her of her grandmother?" he asked skeptically, disconcerted by the surge of protectiveness that made him want to ease that sadness from B.G.'s face and bring the jaunty squareness back to her shoulders.

"Sometimes I think you do not listen when I am speaking to you," Solbritt scolded mildly. "Don't you remember that when I told you Birgitta would be coming to Forsborg to visit, I also mentioned her grandmother's Rörstrand plates?"

Nils didn't remember, but he did recall that he hadn't paid close attention to much that Solbritt had told him that evening. He had been so preoccupied with his own problems.

"Now I remember that you said something at breakfast this morning about B.G.'s being able to see where her grandmother's plates were made. I just thought you meant a set of china." It struck Nils as very strange that an old farm woman who had emigrated to America would have been a collector of fancy porcelain plates. Solbritt's next words eased his puzzlement on that point.

"My old friend, Birgitta, inherited some pieces from her grandmother, and she loved them very much. Then when she was moving to America, all the women in the family wanted to give her something to remember them by—something to remember Sweden by, too. It couldn't be anything too large, and yet it had to be something special. Well, almost everyone has odd pieces of china in the china cabinet, pieces that are old and once belonged to a grandmother or great-grandmother. Birgitta told me in her letters that when she was so lonely for Sweden that she thought she would die, she got out her Rörstrand plates from the cabinet and carefully washed and dried each one. The stories painted on each piece and the memory of the one who had given it to her provided great comfort.''

''B.G. knows what you have just told me, I suppose,'' Nils suggested gently, his eyes on the golden-haired young woman with the downcast features.

''Oh, yes,'' Solbritt affirmed, not quibbling with his use of the nickname she found so strange and did not use herself. ''We talked of it the first day she arrived. I think that now she is sad to think that she will not ever see her grandmother's plates again.'' The sharp inquiry on Nils's face made Solbritt shake her head and make disapproving sounds. ''You should listen when I talk to you, my grandson. I told you at the same time that I announced Birgitta's visit that she was to bring *me* her grandmother's Rörstrand plates, which my friend wanted me to have. As it turned out, Birgitta did not bring the plates but had them sent. They were to have arrived before we left on our trip.''

''I see.''

Nils was able to assimilate this information very quickly, and he wasn't at all approving of what he had just learned. Judging from what Solbritt had already told him about B.G.'s conflict with her grandmother, it sounded to him as though B.G. hadn't inherited the Rörstrand as a kind of punishment. He felt a flare of anger at the deceased woman he had never known. It was pretty rotten of her to deal a blow her granddaughter would have to live with the rest of her life. To think of B.G. as vulnerable was a new feeling for Nils, one that would take some getting used to.

"Why don't you let her take the porcelain back home with her?" he asked a little brusquely, nodding his head in B.G.'s direction. "Your old friend would never know the difference now, and by rights the porcelain *should* belong to B.G., even if she didn't like the name *Birgitta*." He paused before adding, "I was never too crazy about being called *Nils,* but it wouldn't have occurred to me to change my own name."

Solbritt said nothing, but she looked so enormously pleased with Nils's suggestion and its implied defense of B.G. that he wished he had kept his thoughts to himself. A suspicion that had come fleetingly to him several times now bloomed stronger: Solbritt had some matchmaking ideas about her grandson and her old friend's granddaughter. She had quite blatantly managed to see that the two of them were thrown together as much as possible.

"Do whatever you think best," Nils said dismissively. "It's really none of my affair." He wanted to close the subject once and for all and kill any romantic hopes he had unwittingly kindled. The feeling of sympathy for B.G. persisted, however, and he wished that there were some way he could make up to her the injustice of being denied her rightful inheritance.

B.G.'s mood underwent a change as she joined Nils and Solbritt and took note of the ultramodern pottery display. "I like this!" she exclaimed and then continued, thinking aloud. "While I'm here, I should talk to someone and get some prices to take back with me. Some of our clients at *Maxwell's* are sure to be interested in designs like these. We may even be able to buy directly from the factory. What do you think, Nils?"

As her eyes met his, B.G. saw the flicker of surprise and understood it: Just days ago she had admitted her strong bias against modern Scandinavian design; that bias had been the reason she gave for not having used the Heidenstam cabinetry. Now she was showing enthusiasm for Rörstrand pottery. B.G. thought quickly and decided that if Nils made some needling remark, she would point out that she hadn't said *her* clients would be interested; she had merely said *Maxwell's* clients.

"I doubt that you will be able to buy directly from Rörstrand," Nils replied evenly. "Most factories protect their retail outlets. I know we do. It's only fair, if you think about it. Why should a store go to the expense of stocking costly inventory if a buyer can go straight to the factory? Here, for example, the shop open to visitors sells only defective merchandise. If you want to buy a set of Rörstrand china, you'll have to go to a retail store."

He proved to be right. The sales consultant who responded courteously to B.G.'s introduction of herself and invited B.G. into her office gave her a thick folder full of brochures and information, including a list of the retail outlets in the United States where a customer could purchase Rörstrand available in the store or order the desired item.

By the time B.G. rejoined Nils and Solbritt, meeting them in the coffee shop as prearranged, it was time to board the tour bus and make the trip to Siötorp, where they were to meet up with the canal boat. This time Solbritt and B.G. sat together on the bus, giving B.G. no opportunity to talk in private with Nils. Solbritt, for once, seemed little inclined toward conversation, and B.G. was grateful for the chance to sit and think. Like every day so far in Sweden, this had been a full one. There had been some revealing exchanges with Nils. There had been some new insights into herself, too.

And the evening yet remained. . . .

Chapter Eleven

The passengers on the *Wilhelm Tham* were in high spirits that evening. Perhaps the change in weather was responsible. The front had passed through, leaving the forecast for the days ahead optimistic. Mellow rays of afternoon sunlight warmed and cheered those who lingered on deck while the passengers for the first seating dined. The late sunset cast its spell on every single person. It was magnificent as sunsets are apt to be when they flame scarlet and gold upon a body of water, even a narrow ribbon of water like the Göta Canal threading its way through the fallow grain fields of the heart of Sweden.

The pent-up restlessness inside B.G. had gone away, leaving in its place a pleasurable level of excitement and suspense. B.G. was aware of the world as full of wonderful possibilities. She was young and attractive in the eyes of a man who made her feel intensely alive and feminine. Some subtle change had occurred between her and Nils. She didn't know when or why it had happened or even precisely the nature of the change, but whenever her eyes would meet his, something in his made her heart beat faster. Nils's whole manner toward her was different.

Except for those few times when B.G. had pushed him over the brink of violence, Nils had always been the well-bred gentleman, even when it was patently clear that he despised being in her presence. Tonight there was something different about the way he held her chair for her when she sat down at the dinner table, about the way he refilled her wineglass, about the way he touched her in the performance of a routine courtesy.

Many times during the past days, B.G. had noted almost with jealousy Nils's tender indulgence toward his grandmother, whom he would obviously protect with his very life. While there was definitely a difference in the way he spoke to the two of them tonight, a difference in the way he smiled at them, B.G. was no longer an outsider foisted upon Nils by Solbritt. In some mysterious and utterly heart-warming way, it seemed to B.G. that she had eased her way inside the charmed circle of those women Nils made it his business to look after.

B.G. definitely considered herself a modern woman, independent and self-sufficient. She had never minded the rather casual manners of the men she dated at home nor did she yearn for some big, strong man to come along and take care of her. She could take care of herself. Still, she found herself reveling in Nils's courtliness, even if it did suggest, ever so subtly, that man was the stronger of the species and entrusted with the protection of certain special women.

After dinner, the three of them took a stroll around the boat, enjoying the serenity of twilight and exchanging friendly conversation with other passengers. One was the large, hearty man Solbritt had sat beside during one leg of the bus trip that day. He obviously admired B.G.'s

Scandinavian good looks and was eager to tell her about an experience from his youth, since he knew that she was from the United States but of Swedish descent. He had emigrated to America when he was a young man, going to Chicago where he had relatives. He had stayed there for several years, working for two uncles who had their own small construction business. Finally he had gotten so lonely for Sweden that he had come back and had lived in Sweden ever since. Now that he was retired, he intended to visit all those parts of Sweden he had never seen before.

"I am glad that I went to America," he declared sincerely, in his deep, booming voice. "It is a great country, a country with many opportunities, but it was not my home." He touched a large hand to his breast in an eloquent gesture. "If I had never left Sweden, perhaps I would not love it so much."

B.G. felt tears smart her eyes. Before she could think of anything to say, Solbritt was speaking up and reminding Mr. Swenson of the card game that had been arranged earlier that day. Nils was silent as he and B.G. climbed back up to the bridge deck. By unspoken consent, they walked back to the stern, to the same spot where they had stood together in the late hours the previous night.

"Do you think the same thing that happened to Mr. Swenson might happen to you, Nils?" B.G. ventured timidly, aching with the need to share whatever he was thinking and feeling, but fearful of antagonizing him as she had done often with ill-timed questions and statements of opinion.

The glance he cast her was impatient.

"There's a lot of difference between Mr. Swenson's situation fifty years ago and mine today. America isn't a strange land to me, after all. I know it as well as I know Sweden." He paused and added, "Better, actually."

"I really understand the way Mr. Swenson must have felt," B.G. mused, wisely deciding not to risk questioning him any further. "I can imagine what it must have been like for him, living in a country that wasn't home." She let her breath out in a little sigh. "I suppose my grandparents, both sets of them, must have felt the same way he did when they moved to Minnesota. Yet they stayed. I'm glad they did, but . . ." She pondered her thoughts before continuing. "It's strange to think that I could so easily have felt this same deep tie to Sweden instead of to the United States, if circumstances had been different. Isn't it weird, Nils, to think of how you could have been a different person?"

After lingering over the horizon and taking its time, night had suddenly fallen with a rush. The canopied deck area behind them was lighted sufficiently for the safety of the passengers, but where B.G. and Nils stood, by the railing at the furthest point aft, it was dark enough that B.G. couldn't read Nils's expression. She sensed, though, that something in her words had struck him wrong.

"Do you really think that you would have been a different person, B.G.?" Nils asked cuttingly. "Isn't it precisely your point that you *wouldn't* have been? Had you been born in Sweden, you'd be as passionately loyal to Sweden as you are to the United States. No matter what, you would stay here and defend your country to the last breath, wouldn't you? *You* would never defect and become a citizen of another country."

All day B.G. had worked at curbing her tongue in order not to irritate or offend Nils. His unexpected attack upon her hurt all the more because she knew that it was so completely unjustified. She hadn't meant to imply a criticism of him. He was being unfair after she had made every effort to understand him and his current difficult situation.

"What difference does it make whether I would or I *wouldn't!* I'm one person and you're another! Does that make either one of us right or wrong, for heaven's sake! I don't see why you always have to try to put me down and make me feel bad about myself!" B.G. turned her back on him angrily. She hadn't intended to speak quite so sharply or to sound so self-righteous. The old hostility was pulsing between them as strong as it had those other times when they had lashed out at each other, but now it was complicated with new feelings that made B.G. struggle to overcome her pride and anger.

"Nils, why do you always do this to us, just when we're beginning to get along?" Regret and puzzlement canceled out the aggrieved tone in her voice. "You know me so well that all you have to do is push a few buttons, and I'm too mad to think. But, why do you do it? I just don't understand you." She closed her eyes, tense and miserable. How could the world be so bright and full of promise one moment and so dead and empty the next?

"I don't know myself why I do it, B.G." There was grudging apology in Nils's voice along with self-disgust. The admission only deepened B.G.'s unhappiness. The touch of his hands on her shoulders came without any warning, communicating a message unrelated to the harsh exchange. She immediately wanted to succumb to the sensory magic and ignore the words, but she didn't dare until he continued, in a different voice that destroyed all her resistance.

"If I don't fight with you tonight, B.G., I won't be able to resist doing this." His hands squeezed her shoulders briefly and then slid down her arms. B.G. let out a sound between a sigh and a moan as Nils hugged her back against him in a tight embrace. She shivered at the warmth of his lips and the heat of his breath against her neck as he nuzzled his face beneath her hair.

"Nils, I *hate* fighting with you," B.G. murmured,

twisting around in his arms so that he held her facing him. Her arms slid up around his neck, undermining her protest. "You always hurt me—"

His mouth came down to smother the rest of her words. The harsh lessons B.G. had already learned at his hands failed to keep her from kissing him back with soft, eager lips that parted without resistance when his tongue came questing for deep, sweet intimacy. Their passion quickly welled, this time not to be denied. What was going to happen between them tonight was as inevitable as the steady progress of the canal boat through the old central artery of the small land to which they both had ties.

When their kisses had left them both short of breath, Nils was the one to speak the obvious: "We can't stay here." B.G. acquiesced as he took her arms from around his neck, clasped her hand in his, and led her forward in the direction of his cabin. She said nothing until she had stepped inside the small compartment and he had followed, closing the door behind him. The two of them took up most of the standing space. Before Nils could take her into his arms again and dispel all reason, B.G. said quickly, "Nils, I'm afraid." Her voice begged him for reassurance, yet even as she spoke, B.G. knew that he had only to touch her to overcome her reservations about what she was on the threshold of doing.

She blinked as he reached past her and turned on the light over the washbowl. For what seemed an interminable time, they looked at each other, not speaking, close but not touching.

"We can stop," he said finally. "Do you want to stop?"

"You know I don't," she breathed and moved into his arms, feeling that some hurdle was being passed, for better or worse. She had seen in Nils's eyes, along with his desire, an uncertainty that matched her own. That had given her the courage or the foolhardiness to plunge ahead.

For Nils there was no holding back now. His kisses and caresses were urgent, inflaming her need. "I want you so much, honey," he told her over and over, unable to keep the words inside. "God, I want you. You drive me out of my mind. I've never wanted a woman like this before."

He took off her clothes with her help, the sight of her bare flesh inciting his passion and intensifying his need to possess her. "You're beautiful," he told her as he kissed each pink-tipped breast and then worked his way lower, kissing her stomach, her hips, her thighs, the triangle of golden hair between her legs.

"Please, Nils, take off your clothes," she begged him softly, weak with her arousal. She sank back on the bed and lay watching him as he stripped off his clothes quickly, baring his tall, strong body completely. This time there was no skimpy, clinging swimsuit, no robe knotted at the waist.

"You're beautiful, too," she told him softly, smiling and holding out her arms.

They lay facing each other on the narrow bunk. Nils slid his hand lightly over the curves of her breast and then traced the graceful line of waist, hip, and thigh. "You're beautiful," he said again. "I love to look at you. You know, I wanted to make love to you from the first, even before I knew who you were. That day I went to the airport to meet this Birgitta Jensen, I was expecting some dowdy female, and there you were, looking sexy in that red suit." He kissed her on the lips, holding down his hunger with an effort. "Touch me," he ordered her softly, taking her hand and directing her unmistakably.

When she closed her hand around his throbbing hardness, Nils sucked in his breath and then he raised up

on his elbow and began kissing her with such deep
hunger that B.G. couldn't breathe. Before long, her
lungs were bursting and her heart pounding out of
control in her chest.

"Nils," she gasped.

As though she had given him some signal, he moved
on top of her and found that her legs were parted. She
guided him to her velvet warmth, where he paused for a
split second. Then he thrust inside her at the same
moment that she lifted her hips to meet him. They spoke
each other's name aloud in a kind of agony and joy.

B.G. offered more pleasure than Nils could enjoy, and
her abandoned response increased his mounting frenzy.

B.G. was much in the same state. Every inch of her
body wanted to be touched and stroked and kissed. The
ache that Nils filled when he entered her grew more
intolerable by the second as he moved inside her,
deliberately controlling the rhythm of his thrusts despite
the temptation of her own abandoned movements underneath him. He refused to hurry. She ran her hands over
his shoulders and back and down to the straining muscles
in his buttocks, feeling them harden with each surge. His
name came from her lips in a kind of desperate plea and
was lost in his mouth, but finally he heeded the message
and held back nothing. The increased tempo led to total
devastation of mind and senses.

B.G. lay in his arms for long minutes, gradually
coming back to reality. At first she was simply awed by
what had happened. For the first time she comprehended
the actuality of two people coming together as one.
Before it had always seemed just a romantic myth. But
what now? That question brought back her earlier fear.

"We shouldn't have done this, Nils," she whispered,
hoping that he would tell her that she was wrong or that
she was being silly, overreacting. But he said nothing.

"I don't want to fall in love with you, Nils. It wouldn't ever work out for us, would it? We disagree on too many things."

Nils pushed away from her a little, enough so that he could see her face and still hold her loosely in his arms.

"I can't get seriously involved with anyone right now, B.G." he said somberly. "My life is too complicated to allow me to make promises or commitments."

"I know." B.G. coughed as though the strangled quality of her voice were due to some throat obstruction. Nils had been as gentle as possible in telling her that he didn't care for her, but verification of the truth she already knew had been like a shard of glass piercing her chest. Who was she kidding anyway? It was a little late in the day to start worrying about falling in love with Nils. That had happened sometime before she gave herself to him tonight.

Nils let out a heavy sigh. "B.G., I'm sorry—" he began and then broke off when B.G. sat up abruptly.

"Why should you be sorry?" she broke in quickly, knowing that she couldn't bear to have him apologize for what had happened. "It wasn't your idea any more than it was mine. Besides, there's no harm done, is there? It was only . . . *sex* . . ." The lie stuck in her throat.

"You know that's not true," he said quietly, behind her. Nils wanted more than anything to touch her. He had to clench his hands into fists to restrain himself. "Or at least it's not true for me," he added. "I've never had anything like this happen to me before, and I've had my share of casual sex."

B.G. wondered if she was supposed to feel better because making love to her had been out of the ordinary. *Big Deal!* she felt like yelling at him. The fact remained that he did not want to be "involved" with her, which meant he was interested in nothing but a transitory affair.

She knew that that was out of the question for her. She was going to have a hard enough time getting over Nils, as things were.

"Well, whatever it was," she said in a tight, strained voice, getting up from the bunk while she talked, "I don't want it to happen again. I'm *not* used to casual sex, and I don't want to be hurt. Will you give me your word?" She picked up a filmy bit of red nylon and lace—her bikini panties—and stepped into them, intensely aware that his eyes followed her every move.

"I had no intention of having this happen *this* time," he replied a little shortly. He raised up on his elbows, aware of the sharp stirring of desire in his loins as she leaned over to pick up her bra. Instead of making promises about not touching her again, he wanted to pull her down on the bunk with him right now, caress her soft, rounded breasts, taste the delicate pink peaks, arouse her passion again and make love to her. "We arrive in Stockholm tomorrow evening. I can leave the two of you on your own there. I could make some excuse to return to Forsborg or to New York." Considering the fact that Nils had been planning to do this all along, he sounded less than enthusiastic.

"No!" The response was instinctive and revealed far too much. B.G. carefully fitted the lacy half-cups of her bra around her breasts and took her time fastening the front closure. "Your grandmother would be terribly disappointed," she added. "I wouldn't like to be responsible for depriving her of your company, when it means so much to her." Those reasons were perfectly true. There was no cause for B.G. to feel dishonest just because she didn't admit that she couldn't bear the thought of continuing her Swedish visit without Nils along. If he left them now, she'd never see him again.

"We can both control ourselves if we try." These words were slightly muffled, since B.G. was pulling her slip over her head. When her head was free, she glanced over at Nils to see his reaction and also to take in his nude length. When her eyes noted the unmistakable proof of his arousal, they flew back to his face.

"What do you want me to say?" he snapped out impatiently. "I *am* controlling myself, but I can't promise for how long if you don't finish getting your clothes on and get out of here." He didn't add what he was thinking, that it would be far more difficult now to control his passion than it had been before they made love.

B.G. pressed her lips together indignantly, but she finished dressing hurriedly. Her heart was pounding and her body had turned traitor to her mind. The knowledge that Nils wanted her again, and she *could* stay, if she chose, weakened her conviction. At the door she stopped and leaned against it.

"It isn't going to be easy, is it?" God, how she wanted to stay! She would, if he would ask her!

"B.G., would you get the hell *out* of here!" he ordered savagely.

She heard the movement behind her as he sat up on the edge of the bunk. Not daring to look back at him, she opened the door and slipped out, in flight from him, in flight from herself.

We can control ourselves if we try. How assertively she had spoken those words to Nils. They mocked her through an interminable night and the next day, which fortunately was in marked contrast to the first two days of the canal boat trip. The sun beamed down its golden warmth, encouraging all the passengers to sit out on deck and observe the scenery, which changed as they entered the St. Anna archipelago on the eastern coast.

The canal boat now threaded its way through islands green with rich verdure, markedly different from the gray rocky islands she had seen on the western coast the day she had sailed with Nils and his friends to Marstrand. On these more lush islands were homes, some with piers and boats tied up to them, some perched up among the trees in the hills, but none with stoic little settlements like those she had fallen in love with on the bleak west coast.

"Beautiful," she said aloud with everyone else, but the sentiment was empty. She couldn't respond to the scenery when all she could think about was what had happened between her and Nils the night before. Every time her eyes would collide with his, she suspected that *he* might be thinking of the same thing. It was either a blessing or the worst kind of hardship that Solbritt was there, making it necessary for the two of them to carry on as if nothing had happened between them.

Innumerable times B.G. decided somewhat desperately that Nils was probably right in suggesting that he should leave her and Solbritt on their own in Stockholm, but every instinct inside her cried out against the notion. She was truly living a dilemma, unable to bear Nils's presence and equally unable to bear the thought of his absence. To be close to him meant wanting intimacy, needing to touch him and to fathom each nuance of his mood, but his departure signaled a permanent separation too painful to contemplate.

Rather surprisingly for a young woman not used to analyzing her thoughts and feelings, B.G. was able to see the irony of her situation. All her life she had been dissociating herself from things Swedish. Here she had come to Sweden, purely out of a sense of obligation, and fallen in love with a Swedish man. It was the last thing she would have believed possible.

The *Wilhelm Tham* docked in Stockholm later than the itinerary had indicated because of the night's layover in Vänersborg. The passengers had already dined aboard the ship. Taxis were lined up and waiting when B.G.

walked down the gangplank behind Solbritt. The boat crew had gone ashore first and deposited all the luggage.

In the taxi B.G. found herself between Solbritt and Nils. She was so strongly conscious of his nearness that her first impressions of Stockholm were a blur: tall buildings, bridges, street lamps casting light on black water. Like every other taxi driver she had ever encountered, this one seemed in a great hurry. Several times she was thrown slightly off balance so that her body made contact with Nils's. Each time it took all her willpower to pull away, when she wanted to lean against him and absorb the strength and hardness of his masculine frame.

They had rooms at the Diplomat Hotel on Strandvagen, where Solbritt and Nils customarily stayed when they were in Stockholm. As she got out of the taxi in front of the canopied entrance, B.G. glanced up at the multistoried building and saw that it had a solid Victorian elegance. An ornate brass and iron grillwork elevator took them up to the tenth floor, where their rooms overlooked one of the many waterways in Stockholm.

Solbritt insisted that Nils open B.G.'s room first. Always the concerned hostess, Solbritt wanted to be sure that B.G. was satisfied with her accommodations, which, after the cramped quarters of the *Wilhelm Tham,* seemed enormous and luxurious. After she had passed through a large foyer, B.G. stood just inside the combination bedroom and sitting room, glancing around at gleaming white-painted paneling, high ceilings, and floor-to-ceiling velvet draperies along the outside wall. Her murmured words of admiration were sincere.

Having established that B.G. approved of her lodgings, Solbritt announced that she was tired and intended to go to bed early that night. However, she thought it was a good idea for B.G. and Nils to go out somewhere for a drink where they could dance to live music.

"I'm sure B.G. is tired, too," Nils put in firmly,

leaving B.G. little choice other than to agree. Shortly thereafter, the porter arrived with all their bags, and B.G. found herself alone. For a minute or two, she stood perfectly still in the middle of the room, straining to hear some sound from beyond that wall behind her long dressing table and console television set. But the walls of the old hotel were too solid. Nils would be there tonight, sleeping in an oversized bed like her own, but she wouldn't be able to hear him moving around.

B.G. made an impatient sound, irritated at herself for the way she was acting and irritated at Nils for keeping his word and staying his distance from her. Needing to do something to combat her restlessness and general sense of dissatisfaction with the state of things, she unpacked, finding in the process a small refrigerator built into one of the large closets in the entryway. It was stocked with fruit juices, soft drinks, a bottle of wine and several bottles of beer. The first thought to pop into her head was that Nils must have a refrigerator like this one in his room, too, with like contents. Would he tempt her with an invitation to share a bottle of wine?

Banishing the thought, B.G. ran a tubful of hot water and soaked in the giant tub for almost an hour, going over in her mind all the facts about her relationship with Nils. She found it necessary to repeat out loud, several times, "He *told* you he doesn't want to be 'involved' with you."

When she had finally gotten out of the tub and dried herself, B.G. dressed in her nightgown and robe and took her hairbrush with her back into the bedroom, where she snapped on the tv set before settling down into a velvet-upholstered armchair to brush her hair and try to watch the action on the screen. Some Grade Z American movie about knights and chivalry was in progress. When it was over, she turned out the lights and went to bed. Nils had been right after all. She *was* tired. She hadn't rested well a single night on the *Wilhelm Tham*. And this bed felt wonderfully comfortable. The sheets and pillow slip were smooth and ironed and fragrant with the scent of soap.

B.G. slept, but even in her sleep she wasn't free from her emotional entanglement with Nils. The next morning it seemed that she had dreamt of him the entire night. In scene after scene, he would kiss her, caress her with his hands, arouse her to a fever-pitch of desire and then draw back and say, "I'm sorry, but I don't want to get *involved* with you, B.G." Each time it happened she would get furious with herself and him and vow that he would not touch her again, but she was drawn to him so inexorably that all he had to do was reach for her and she came to him.

Finally, in desperation she cried out to him, forgetful of her pride, "Nils, you just *have* to love me! I won't be able to *stand* it if you don't!" But Nils just looked at her with an apologetic expression and gradually faded away. "Nils, *please!* Don't do this to me! Come back!" she begged, lunging for him, desperate, imploring. But he was always just out of her reach.

The dream was so vivid that when she awoke she was left with strong feelings of frustration, shame, and anger at Nils. How dare he tease and torment her that way! If he didn't care for her, he should have the decency to leave her alone! B.G. had to remind herself that it had all been a dream and Nils *was* leaving her alone. Last night he had quickly rejected Solbritt's suggestion that he take B.G. out somewhere for a drink.

Deeply disturbed with herself for her loss of control over her present situation, B.G. got out of bed, went to the window and opened the heavy velvet draperies. Bright sunlight spilled in through the filmy white inner curtains. She opened them, too, and stood at the window looking out at a spectacular view. Stockholm was a city

built on water, just as Solbritt had said. The Venice of
the North. This morning it was a busy, bustling city with
an unceasing stream of traffic on the street below and on
the waterways. Down on the cobblestone quay beyond
the street were old-fashioned boats that lent a picturesque
element to the scene.

B.G. took in a deep breath. "If I can fall *in* love, I can
fall *out* of love!" she announced to the bright, modern
city outside and felt immediately better as she elaborated
upon the declaration in her mind. A woman must have
some conscious control over loving a man. Surely falling
in love wasn't like contracting a terminal disease. Since
loving Nils promised only unhappiness and disappointment, B.G. would simply exorcise him from her deepest
affections. It would be as simple as that.

Feeling immensely better, she dressed in kelly green
slacks and a lemon yellow blouse and went down to
breakfast. Last night no plans had been made for
Solbritt, Nils, and herself to meet for breakfast. In her
present emancipated mood, that suited her just fine.

As she made her exit from the elevator, she turned
right to enter the hotel dining room, which came as such
a surprise to her that she paused in the entrance looking
around. The dining room was furnished to create the
effect of a garden room, with white-painted tables and
matching bentwood cafe chairs with cushions the green
of spring leaves. There was an abundance of real leaves
on the many live plants in the room, which this morning
were bathed in bright sunlight that streamed through the
windows across the front.

It was a cheery scene and one that complemented her
appearance perfectly. B.G. looked like a ray of sunshine
herself with her bright golden hair and her wholesome
blond good looks. Several people looked up at her and
then looked again, but she was only faintly aware of the
admiring glances. She had spotted Nils sitting alone at a

table for two near the window. He folded his newspaper, laid it aside and watched her approach, half rising from his chair when she had reached his table. The instinctive male approval in his blue eyes warmed her.

"Good morning," she greeted lightly with a smile.

"Good morning. I don't have to ask if you slept well. I can tell by looking." His tone made the words more of a compliment than they were on the surface.

B.G. hesitated before sitting opposite him, her glance touching upon the one remaining chair.

"Sit down," Nils invited. "My grandmother has already had breakfast. She was leaving the dining room just as I got here."

B.G. sat down, knowing that she shouldn't be feeling this upward surge of the spirits just because Nils was there, seemingly waiting for her to join him for breakfast. After all, he might have eaten already and just stayed to linger over a cup of coffee.

"Have you eaten yet?"

"Not yet." He glanced at his watch meaningfully. "You had ten more minutes, and I was going to give up on you."

"What are we waiting for, then?" she inquired buoyantly, pushing back her chair. When Nils was friendly like this toward her, how on earth was she expected to be immune to his charm?

They walked to the opposite end of the dining room, where several stations were set up buffet style. Hotel guests could help themselves to fruit juice, coffee or tea at one station. At another were wicker platters of Danish pastries and a selection of sliced breads with butter and jellies and jams. A round two-tiered table was filled with huge bowls of dry cereal with pitchers of sweet and cultured milk, platters of cold cuts and cheese, pickles, sliced tomatoes, and marinated herring. There was also a big bowl of steaming hot soft-boiled eggs.

B.G. began with a glass of tomato juice and a cup of black coffee. Having already passed the first-cup-of-coffee stage, Nils chose a first course of cereal topped with thick cultured milk and also a boiled egg.

"We're on our own today," he announced casually between bites. "My grandmother has gone off to visit one of her old friends who lives in the suburbs of Stockholm."

"Oh." This information came as a surprise to B.G. She had assumed that the three of them would be together today. It was necessary for her to adjust to the idea of spending the day alone with Nils, the man she had decided some minutes ago to fall out of love with.

Nils put down his spoon and looked directly at her.

"I hope you don't mind."

"Mind? Why should I mind?" B.G. replied quickly, meeting his gaze only fleetingly and then looking out of the window. "Actually, I can't wait to get started seeing Stockholm," she said brightly and then made a wry face to make light of what she felt she *had* to say. "Looks like Fru Heidenstam has done it again, doesn't it? Gone off and stuck you with the job of looking after me."

Her high spirits flagged quickly during the brief pause, and she had to fix a smile on her face as she turned back to him.

Nils met her gaze directly, but he wasn't altogether unguarded as he answered.

"I don't mind in the least. Although I've been to Stockholm many times, there are any number of places on the sightseeing lists that I haven't seen. So I won't just be showing you around, but seeing things for myself."

"Good. I won't feel bad, then." B.G. had to force the hearty note. Her appetite had gone, but she excused herself and went to get some food, taking her time in making her selections. Nils couldn't have been nicer just now in reassuring her that he didn't mind taking her around the city. It was ridiculous of her to feel this odd letdown because he hadn't been more personal. Falling out of love with Nils didn't seem nearly so easy when she was in his presence.

The day was crammed with sightseeing and bitter-sweet with torment and pleasure as the physical attraction between them flamed up every time they would happen to touch and sometimes when they would just look at each other. B.G. had to fight constantly against falling even more deeply in love with him. It didn't help matters that he was not only the perfect guide, but seemed to be having a great time himself.

They walked miles, going first from the Diplomat to the old section of the city, the Gamla Sta'n, where they browsed in antique shops and saw Sweden's narrowest alley, in actuality just an incredibly steep flight of stone steps. B.G. surprised Nils by wanting to see the Crown Jewels and the Official Apartments in the Royal Palace. He teased her by claiming that Americans were more fascinated by the trappings of royalty than anyone else. Then as if to prove his point, when they happened to be on hand to witness the changing of the guard in the huge central courtyard of the palace, B.G. was as excited as any child.

When Nils sensed that she had reached her surfeit of the usual sightseeing, he gave her a view of the shopping pleasures of Stockholm. They browsed through the glamorous NK department store and looked at Orrefors crystal and Rörstrand porcelain. When Nils informed her that one of the best bargains in Stockholm was fur coats, her eyes gleamed, and they spent several hours thereafter in boutiques, where B.G. indulged herself in trying on dozens of gorgeous fur coats.

"Enough!" she finally whispered and then held her breath when she saw in Nils's face that he wanted to kiss her, right there in front of the saleslady who had been standing by patiently.

That night they dined with Solbritt at one of Stockholm's most highly recommended restaurants. It was late when they returned to the hotel. B.G. didn't mind when Nils once again sidestepped Solbritt's less-than-subtle suggestion that the two younger people continue enjoying the evening without her. B.G. was pleasantly exhausted. It had been a wonderful day, and she knew she would be spending the following day with Nils, too. Solbritt had begged off from accompanying them. Two of her friends in the Stockholm area were taking her shopping and then to lunch.

The next morning B.G. and Nils set out on foot again, crossing the street in front of the hotel to the quay and turning left, toward Djurgarden, which had once been the royal game park but was now open to the public, offering a variety of entertainment with an amusement park, several museums, and numerous restaurants, in addition to many wooded acres for walking and bicycling.

It was a glorious day, the kind that made one glad to be alive. B.G. smiled to herself as she noticed the way Nils would walk faster and faster and then slow down, obviously for her benefit.

"Remember the first time we walked together?" she mused, seeing humor now in what hadn't been funny then at all. "I got so mad at you because you took off practically at a run, and I couldn't keep up. I didn't realize at the time what brisk walkers most Swedish people are."

"God, that seems like a long time ago now, doesn't it?"

His voice was so serious and yet so distracted that B.G. glanced over quickly at him, wondering what he was thinking. They were passing along by old wooden vessels tied to the quay, identified by Nils the previous day as Baltic traders. Some were being restored by crews of young workmen in jeans and tee-shirts. There was the whir of sanders and the whine of various power tools. B.G. summoned up her courage.

"Nils, have you made up your mind yet—about what you intend to do?" she asked hesitantly.

"Yes," he said briefly and then did not elaborate during a silence that was filled with tension for B.G. as she debated questioning him further. Surely he must know that his decision mattered a great deal to her. It hurt that he didn't volunteer to take her into his confidence. When he brought her attention to a brick building over to their right, on the other side of the waterway separating them from Djurgarden, she decided to follow his lead and drop the whole matter of the future. She would take what the day offered. It might be cowardice, but she didn't want to hear what she would consider a wrong decision for Nils: that he *hadn't* decided to take that offer in the United States and become an American citizen.

"That's the Nordic Museum. If you like, we can look through it on our way in," Nils suggested.

"I like the outside of it. All the towers and turrets and green copper roofs."

Nils flashed her a knowing grin, catching her hand up in his.

"Don't worry. I am aware of your general feelings toward museums. We won't stop to read all the signs and cards."

B.G. was suddenly as unreasoningly happy as she had ever been in her life, all because the man she loved had observed her closely enough to detect an attitude she hadn't voiced and referred to it in such a manner as to suggest that it only added to her uniqueness.

"In *that* case!" she rejoined gaily.

Inside the museum, Nils dropped her hand, but frequently when they would pause side by side looking at a display, he would rest his arm casually around her shoulders. As they moved on, his hand would fall lightly to the small of her back, not to guide her, it seemed, but because he simply wanted to touch her. Afterward B.G. would look back upon that day and wonder if the museums had really been so special or whether the circumstances had made them seem so.

After they had emerged from the Nordic Museum and were strolling along beneath huge shade trees, Nils casually took her hand again.

"Would you mind if we took out time to see the *Wasa?*" he asked almost apologetically. "I've been meaning to see it for years and just haven't ever gotten around to it."

"Of course, I don't mind," B.G. declared at once, and then giggled. "What *is* the *Wasa* anyway?"

Then they both were laughing, actually for no good reason other than the sheer delight of being in each other's company and having a whole day to spend however they chose. Nils explained that the *Wasa* was a seventeenth century warship that had sunk in the Stockholm harbor on its maiden voyage out and stayed there on the bottom for centuries until it was raised in 1961, remarkably intact, and brought to its present site, where restoration work was still in progress.

In the *Wasa* museum, Nils offered to bypass the film chronicling the history of the old warship, but B.G. insisted that they see it, since she suspected Nils was only being nice. During the guided tour later, she paid little attention to the historical facts relayed by their tour guide. She was enjoying Nils's total absorption. As he gazed at the rough, dark planks of the huge old hull, so close to them up on the high railed walkway that they could almost reach out and touch it, he seemed to have slipped back in time. B.G. was careful not to breathe a sigh or in any way appear restless.

"I really enjoyed that," she told him when they were leaving the *Wasa* museum grounds. "It's hard to believe that a ship made of wood could stay on the bottom for over three hundred years and still remain intact, isn't it?"

"Yes, it is." Nils took her hand and placed it inside the crook of his elbow. "I'm glad you weren't bored." He sounded pleased.

They had lunch in the open courtyard of one of the many restaurants in Djurgarden and then spent the afternoon in the unique open-air museum, Skansen, which B.G. found so diverse and so different from anything she had ever seen before that the name *museum* seemed a misnomer. They wandered through a Swedish village from the era before electricity and such conveniences, the buildings having been brought to the site. They watched a potter at work, a silversmith, a glass blower.

In one section of Skansen was a zoo. When they emerged from it, they happened upon a colorful folkdance exhibition and then wandered along at random until they came to an open-air concert with Dixieland Jazz New Orleans style.

"How strange," B.G. murmured in surprise, not having expected to hear jazz in Sweden.

"Jazz is very popular in Sweden," Nils explained. "All American music is. Would you like to sit down for a while?"

B.G. did want to sit down. She was tired of walking by now, but she was also quite thirsty. Nils saw her glance up toward a restaurant at the top of the hill and read her mind.

"We can hear the music from up there. Let's go get a beer."

The view from the large terrace in front of the restaurant was breathtaking. Stockholm was spread out before them with its gleaming waterways and graceful buildings. It was late enough that the sun had begun to take on a mellow quality. As B.G. sipped her Swedish beer with the strains of jazz in the background, she felt happy and yet poignantly sad, too, that moments like these could never last.

"I love Stockholm," she said with a sigh. "I don't see how any city could be more beautiful than this. Everywhere you look there's another view that makes you catch your breath. There's hardly ever a feeling of being locked in."

When Nils didn't reply at once, B.G. looked questioningly at him.

"Do you think you would like to live in Stockholm?" he asked unexpectedly, taking her completely off guard so that she didn't even hesitate before replying.

"Why, no. Not *permanently*." Some tension in the air made her vaguely nervous as she elaborated. "Before this trip, I wouldn't have believed I would ever consider living outside the United States even temporarily. I can see now that it could be interesting to live in a city like Stockholm. But I don't think I could ever think of living anywhere outside my country, no matter *how* interesting or beautiful it was, for ever and ever." B.G.'s voice was reluctant toward the last as she felt a gulf between herself and Nils open up and widen. She wouldn't voluntarily do or say anything to destroy the harmony they had felt with each other all day, but she had to be honest with him.

"I'm not surprised." Nils's reply was distant. "What would you do, then, if you fell in love with a man who wasn't an American citizen and couldn't guarantee you a permanent home in the United States?"

"You mean somebody like you?" B.G. breathed nervously, her eyes searching his.

Nils shrugged as if to say that she could use him for an example, if she wanted. B.G. searched her mind desperately for some escape and found none.

"I guess I couldn't afford to do that," she said unhappily, her shoulders slumping. "There's not just me to consider, but any children I might have. I would definitely want them to grow up in the United States. . . ." She shook her head at the unavoidable problems she would face in entering a marriage with a man who wouldn't share her citizenship.

Nils was staring off into the distance, his jaw set in a grim line. "Aren't you saying that your feelings for your country are stronger than any relationship you could have with a man?"

"Nils!" she blurted protestingly. "Please—that's not fair! *Why* do you have to spoil things—"

"I just want to get it straight the way things are," he replied stiffly.

B.G.'s heart was a lump of lead in her breast. She knew with a sickening certainty that Nils must have decided to stay with the Heidenstam Fabrik. He must have chosen to remain a Swedish citizen. His questions just now were posed to verify the truth of what he had already told her the night they made love on the *Wilhelm Tham:* He couldn't afford to get emotionally involved with her, not when her patriotic commitment to her country was so strong. She didn't know herself at the moment whether she could marry a man—even Nils— who wasn't American.

B.G. didn't trust herself to ask Nils point blank what he had decided. She knew that she wouldn't be able to keep from speaking her mind and awakening all the old animosities between them. Whatever Nils had decided to do with his future, it was quite obvious that he did not want her opinion of his choice, one way or the other. Surely he would have shared his plans if he had had any thoughts of sharing that future with her.

"Are you ready to go?" Nils asked, breaking into her troubled thoughts.

"I'm ready," she said tiredly, feeling much older than her twenty-six years as she got up from the table. When Nils stated that they would take a taxi back to the hotel, she didn't argue.

Chapter Twelve

The taxi ride back to the hotel was quiet and strained. B.G. waited by the elevator while Nils climbed the half flight of stairs to the lobby and got their room keys at the reception desk. When he returned, he had a telex message in his hand and looked like a man who has been expecting bad news and has finally received it.

"From my mother," he explained briefly, seeing the alarm flash across B.G.'s countenance. "She wants me to cut my holiday short and return to New York on Monday so that I can be there for a family conference with Dr. Paulsen on Tuesday. He's my father's doctor and also a close family friend." Nils gestured for B.G. to enter the elevator ahead of him and then followed her inside. "My father must be worse. Dr. Paulsen and Mother must be hoping that we can talk some sense into him if we all gang up on him at one time."

"Do you think you'll be able to reason with him?" B.G. asked sympathetically. She had forgotten everything else now but the worry Nils faced.

"I wish I could say yes with any confidence," he said grimly. "I don't really expect my father to pay any more attention to the three of us now than he has before." He glanced down at the crumpled telex message and spoke slowly, obviously talking mainly to himself. "It's time for me to get some matters set straight anyway." There was steely determination in his voice. B.G. knew intuitively that what Nils intended to get "straight" with his father had something to do with Nils's future in the Heidenstam family business.

After Nils, with his automatic courtesy, had unlocked her door and handed her the key, he went not to his own room, but to Solbritt's. As B.G. closed her door behind her and leaned on it a long moment, she held in her mind the image of him standing outside his grandmother's door, grim and resolute and yet deeply concerned. She knew that he would dread having to tell his grandmother news that would bring her worry and heartache.

In a strange way, B.G. felt the same way she imagined Nils must have felt when he got the telex message summoning him to New York, where he must face up to reality. In the back of her mind, she had been dreading the time when she must part from Nils, with no hope of a future meeting. Now that time was here. Along with the heaviness and the ache of loss was a certain terrible relief.

She expected dinner that night to be a somber affair, but, surprisingly, it was not. Nils and Solbritt both apparently had adjusted rapidly to his change in plans, and neither showed any inclination to dwell upon the reason for his sudden departure, though they both must have been worried about Lars Heidenstam. Nils had that relaxed air of a man who has been freed of indecision and can temporarily fix his attention upon the present. Solbritt entertained them briefly with several amusing anecdotes about her day of shopping with her two old friends and then demanded to know what B.G. and Nils had done that day.

B.G.'s recitation was a little self-conscious, since that conversation at the restaurant in Skansen was still fresh on her mind. She could feel Nils's eyes on her and suspected that he was thinking about it, too.

"And what will you do tomorrow?" Solbritt wanted to know in her lilting cadences.

Before B.G. could ask if Solbritt didn't intend to join them, Nils answered, directing his words to B.G. "I've arranged for tickets on the boat out to Sandhamn. It's about a three-hour trip each way with a couple of hours for lunch and swimming on the island. The hotel could have a picnic lunch ready for us in the morning." He paused, waiting for her reply.

B.G. was so taken aback at the element of uncertainty in his eyes and his voice that she couldn't answer at once. Surely Nils must know that she didn't care what they did tomorrow as long as she was with him. Their time was so short now.

"We can do something else," Nils was continuing. "I thought you'd probably had enough of walking and sightseeing and might enjoy a leisurely day in the sun. It looks like good weather tomorrow."

"You're right. I am tired of sightseeing," B.G. concurred softly, hindered by Solbritt's presence from saying more. The circumstances compelled her to turn to the older woman and ask if she didn't want to join them on the boat excursion. After all, Nils had only two days left and he would be leaving Stockholm. B.G. knew how much these visits from her grandson meant to Solbritt.

"I have already been to Sandhamn on several occasions in the past," Solbritt demurred at once. "Unlike my grandson, I am not in the least fond of boat rides."

She paused, glancing fondly from B.G. to Nils, and then divulged her real reason. "You two will want to spend the time alone with each other."

B.G.'s eyes flew to Nils. She expected him to tell his grandmother that her presence was not unwanted, but he said nothing, exchanging with Solbritt one of those unspoken communications. His silence was confirmation that he did want to spend the following day alone with B.G. That realization brought joy even though it did nothing to relieve the heaviness of reality. Nils would be leaving in two days, and he had made no commitment to her—nor was there much hope for any with the circumstances being what they were.

They lingered over dinner and afterward moved to the restaurant lounge for another after-dinner drink. B.G. sensed an unwillingness in Solbritt for the evening to end and appreciated all the more the older woman's unselfishness in giving B.G. and Nils the next day together. It was after midnight when they returned to the hotel. Outside her room Solbritt hugged and kissed B.G. and then Nils before bidding them good-night and going inside, leaving the two of them there together.

B.G.'s heart was pounding erratically in her breast as she walked beside Nils down the hallway to her room. One second she was sure that Nils would finally take her into his arms. The next second she was terrified that he wouldn't. With such a short time remaining, how could she not offer him all the warmth and joy of her body that she yearned to give him?

The suspense was unbearable as they stopped outside her door, and Nils fixed his total attention upon inserting the old-fashioned key into the lock of the huge, solid door. She could feel his tension and indecision and knew that he was reminding himself of the promise she had demanded of him, the promise not to make love to her again. The harsh click of the lock mechanism echoed loudly along the spacious hallway. Nils pushed the door open and looked at her.

B.G. breathed out his name and made the slightest movement toward him. His arms closed around her instantly, drawing her into a paradise of rugged masculine strength.

"You feel so good," Nils whispered into her hair, nuzzling his face into the pale silkiness. One hand roamed urgently over her back and shoulders and then downward to the curve of her hips and the rounded swell of her buttocks.

"I know, I know," B.G. whispered back, clinging hard to him.

"I've thought about holding you like this every single night in this damned hotel." The gruff emphasis in Nils's voice made it sound as though they had been staying in the hotel for an eternity.

"Me, too," B.G. mumbled against his chest. She leaned back her head and found that she didn't have to voice her deep need for him to kiss her. His head was already lowering and his lips were covering hers hungrily. She tightened her arms around his neck, sheer joy giving rise to little whimpering sounds in her throat. Whatever the risks, B.G. held back nothing from him. Her lips parted eagerly to welcome his tongue. The sweet merger failed to satisfy either of them, though; it only intensified the ache of need and made them strain closer together, trying to become a part of each other.

When his mouth tore away from hers, she moaned a protest that quickly became a sigh of pleasure when he pushed his face beneath the hair falling to her shoulder and found the curve of her neck. His kisses brought shivers of delight. His hands were moving over her aroused body, cupping and squeezing her breasts, stroking her back and hips and buttocks. B.G. was aflame with sensation that cried out for some verbal expression, but all she could manage was one syllable, his name.

"Nils—"

What she had meant to communicate was not transmitted because he apparently construed her utterance as a protest. The exquisite rain of kisses on the curve of her neck ceased. His arms tightened in a painful embrace that squeezed the breath from her lungs.

"I know what you're trying to say," he muttered harshly. "I shouldn't be doing this—you asked me to promise—" One hand clamped around her head and forced it against his chest. She could feel the wild thunder of his heartbeat and tried to tilt her head back so that she could look up at him, convince him that he had misunderstood.

"Nils—"

But he wouldn't give her a chance to tell him he was wrong. He was taking her by the shoulders, turning her toward the door and then propelling her through it before her dazed mind could even comprehend what his intentions were. The door slammed shut, leaving her on one side and him on the other. B.G. put out a hand dazedly and braced herself against the wall to keep from falling. Faintly she heard the sound of the elevator doors opening and closing and knew that her efforts to telephone Nils in his room would be futile.

There was no opportunity to talk to Nils privately at breakfast, since Solbritt was there. B.G. tried her best to act as though everything were normal, and bided her time. At least there had been no change in their plans for the day. She and Nils were still taking the excursion boat to Sandhamn, and Solbritt was staying behind at the hotel.

They walked the short distance from the Diplomat to Nybroviken, where the boat boarded its passengers and departed. As soon as they had crossed the street in front of the hotel and were striding along the quay, B.G. tried to bring up the subject of the previous night.

"Nils, about last night—" she began and had to pause for breath. He had taken off at a virtual gallop, the picnic hamper prepared by the hotel in one hand. "We're not late, are we?" she put in a trifle irritably.

Nils stopped, his expression apologetic.

"I've done it again, haven't I? Forgotten that your legs are a little shorter than mine." He started walking again, more slowly. It was obvious to her that he wanted to say more. She waited tensely, fearing that she wouldn't want to hear whatever it was.

"B.G., I'd like to ask a big favor of you." The wistfulness in his voice came as a surprise and something of a relief. "Could we *not* talk about last night or anything else that's happened since that first day when I picked you up at the airport in Gothenburg? Could we pretend that there's just today? I especially don't even want to think about the day after tomorrow when I'll be boarding that plane for New York. Is that asking too much?"

B.G. let her glance intersect with his. The yearning in his face and tone touched something deep inside her. Suddenly she, too, wanted to take this golden, sunshiny day and isolate it in time, protect it from both the past and the future.

"No, Nils," she told him softly. "It's not asking too much at all."

He picked up her hand and carried it to his lips and then he held it clasped warmly in his as they strode along.

The pact seemed to relax Nils and let free an adventurous spirit B.G. hadn't seen before. A large crowd gathered to board the *Stromma Kanal,* the local Swedes far outnumbering tourists. It was a perfect day for such an outing, the sky a clear blue and the sun already hot at nine o'clock. There were groups of adolescents, husbands and wives, whole families including grandparents, aunts and uncles, and children of all ages.

Since there were no seat reservations, everyone hurried aboard when the signal was given, eager to get the best seats up on the open sundeck. Nils was able to hold his own in the scramble. He jumped aboard, pulling B.G. after him. With his general knowledge of the layout of boats, he unerringly took the most direct route to the sundeck and claimed choice seats for them. B.G. hadn't felt so young and carefree since her teenaged days of hayrides.

Looking around her as the other passengers claimed their seats, she noticed that nearly everyone had brought along picnic containers. Hardly had the boat cleared the dock when the eating began. In no time at all the air was full of the aroma of home-baked bread and pastries. After that, it seemed to her that the consumption of food never ceased during the three-hour cruise through the Stockholm archipelago to Sandhamn.

"It's like magic," she murmured in Nils's ear when they had been underway for about an hour. "How do they manage to get so much food in a limited container?" She didn't really care one way or the other. It was just sheer pleasure to lean her head close to his and revel in the intimacy they shared in the midst of the laughing, joking crowd.

"I always wondered the same thing about the food hampers my grandmother would pack when I was a kid visiting her and we would go off for the day with my grandfather and a whole gang of aunts and uncles and cousins. There always seemed a limitless supply of great things to eat."

Their faces were very close together as he made this smiling reply. Neither of them was even remotely aware that they still were the object of admiring looks from time to time. Their fellow passengers couldn't resist glancing discreetly over at the striking young couple who epitomized the most attractive Scandinavian attributes. He was tall and strong with a hint of something in his blue eyes and his rugged features to suggest that daredevil courage of his Viking ancestors. The girl was slim and supple with a wholesome comeliness. With their heads bent together, as they frequently were, the sun turning their blond hair to pale spun gold, Nils and B.G. brought pleasure to those who looked their way.

The three-hour journey seemed much shorter than that. The cruise boat threaded its way among the wooded islands, stopping at some to take on and discharge passengers. As it neared Sandhamn, the number of sailing yachts increased, adding to the idyllic beauty of the scene. Sandhamn, Nils told her, was the location of the royal yacht club.

"Hungry?" he inquired when they had disembarked at their destination and were hiking along a well-marked path to a public bathing spot.

"Starving!" she replied and then added a few minutes later, "Did you say this was a fifteen-minute walk? Seems like we've already been walking that long."

"It's a fifteen-minute 'Swedish' walk," he corrected teasingly.

"I just hope that's a 'Swedish' lunch basket you're carrying," B.G. grumbled. "By the time we get there, I'll be able to eat my share and yours, too."

The path through a thickly wooded pine forest climbed up a sandy bluff and then emerged suddenly into the open. They found themselves looking down upon the bathing cove, which was circled by tiers of granite boulders. The clear blue sea down below sparkled brilliantly in the bright sunlight, but B.G. noticed that most of the bathers were children, a clue that the water would probably be icy cold, as it had been at Marstrand.

She didn't speak the thought aloud, since to mention Marstrand would be a violation of her pact with Nils. The day so far had been too wonderful to risk spoiling.

Nils found a level spot between boulders with a sparse carpet of grass, where they could overlook the beach and yet be some distance from the other picnickers. Trying hard to banish a mental comparison between this spot and another location high up among rocks, on another day when there hadn't been this harmony between them, B.G. busied herself getting the hotel bath sheet out of her totebag. She had brought it along to serve as a picnic blanket. After she had spread it out, she looked up and saw that Nils had stripped down to the blue bathing suit she remembered well. He stood there tall and powerful and male, looking down at her.

"Going in for a swim?" he challenged, his eyes communicating a different kind of message.

"The water's probably cold. Maybe I'll just wade around in the edges." B.G. heard the breathless quality in her voice. She was conscious of his eyes on her as she slipped out of her summer slacks and blouse to reveal the blue-and-white striped bikini she wore underneath, the blue the same color of his suit. For a long moment they stood immobile, looking into each other's eyes, remembering, reliving the passion and the animosity, the exhilaration and the hurt of another golden day.

That sail to Marstrand might seem like an eon ago, but it had only been the previous Saturday. Precisely a week had passed, during which time B.G. had learned what was weighing on Nils's mind and somehow in the process fallen in love with him. The pretence that there was no past or future was impossible for both of them as Nils held out his hand and said, "Ready?" B.G. thought the expression in his eyes might have been saying, *Trust me*.

B.G. put her hand in his and let him lead her down

through the boulders to the sandy beach. When they neared the water, he began to run, pulling her along with him. When they hit the icy water she squealed and jerked back.

"No! It's too cold!" she gasped when he looked around questioningly. "No, Nils, *don't!*" she begged when she saw the demon of inspiration gleaming in his eyes.

After a moment's hesitation when he considered picking her up and dumping her into the cold sea, he turned and plunged face forward and swam outward with powerful, rhythmic strokes. B.G. splashed in the shallows, watching him move away from her, his head wet and sleek, his bathing suit a dab of brilliant color. She almost regretted her cowardice and wished that she could have been moving alongside of him.

By the time he had turned and started back to shore, she had walked several steps from the edge of the water and stood with her feet burrowed in the warm sand. A sense of expectancy grew inside her as he came nearer and nearer and then stood up to walk through the shallows. He looked primitive and powerfully male, just as he had that day at Marstrand, the water coursing off his arms and legs, the brief blue suit plastered to his lower torso. There was passion in his face, just as there had been that day, but there was something more now, something that made B.G.'s heart want to burst with joy.

She held her breath as he reached her, his arms sliding around her to lift her and hold her against his cold, wet body and let her heat warm him. B.G. wound her arms tight around his neck and pressed her lips to his. The contact was like gasoline flung upon the embers of the passion they had stifled the night before.

Nils finally broke off the kiss, his breath coming and going so fast that his voice sounded harsh as he made an attempt at humor.

"The swim didn't help much, I'm afraid. I still want you as much as ever."

"I want you, too, Nils," B.G. told him unhesitatingly and then broke the pact. "I wanted you to make love to me last night."

He hugged her closer, burying his face into her neck, and then set her down, expelling a long, audible sigh. "Let's go see what's in that lunch basket, shall we?"

Hand in hand they climbed back up to their spot among the boulders and sat close beside each other on the makeshift beach blanket, their backs against sun-warmed granite.

"Still hungry?" Nils inquired ruefully and then planted a brief, hard kiss on her lips, acknowledging the hunger they both felt that couldn't be sated with food.

"Starving," B.G. said dreamily.

The lunch was good, but she was sure that tuna out of the can and a package of crackers would have tasted like the food of the gods under these same glorious conditions. She was cheating, she knew, to feel this wonderful sense of optimism for the future when she had promised to concentrate only upon the day itself. After they had finished eating the thick sandwiches, they finished the bottle of wine. B.G. was leaning against Nils and his arm was around her shoulders. She looked down upon the people on the beach and saw them through a haze of happiness.

"Nils," she said, turning her head so that her lips were temptingly close to his. "Is it okay to talk about tonight?"

The husky temptation in her voice and the open invitation in her eyes had the same effect upon Nils as an intimate caress. Passion flared in his face.

"It's definitely okay," he said softly, the arm around her shoulder tightening. His free hand cupped the side of her face as he took quick tastes of her lips. When she kissed him back and then twisted around toward him and clasped his head to hold his mouth against hers for a longer, deeper kiss, he lowered her until she was lying on her back.

With his mouth moving hungrily on hers and his tongue finding hers, sweet and passionately willing, Nils caressed the smooth, warm skin left bare by her bikini. When he slid his hand down the length of her thigh and then moved it to the inside and stroked upward, B.G. moved restlessly and moaned his name aloud. The ache of need he aroused in her demanded a satisfaction he couldn't give her there, in that place and time.

With a low groan, Nils stopped abruptly and fell back on the ground next to her. "This is pure torture." His voice showed the strain of control. "It's all I can do not to make love to you right here and to hell with anybody who cares to watch." He expelled an uneven breath and then turned on his side toward B.G., his arm cradling her loosely.

"Maybe we could find somewhere . . . *private*," B.G. suggested tentatively, reaching her hand up to caress the hard plane of his cheek.

Nils chuckled and tightened the arm lying across her.

"If we go off into the woods, we'll probably end up missing the boat back to Stockholm and be stranded here. As a matter of fact—" He held up his arm and looked at his watch. "We'd better think about packing up and getting back to the village pretty soon."

He sat up and smiled down at her bemused face. B.G. was finding the idea of being stranded on the island with Nils deeply appealing.

Some hours later she would wonder if a sixth sense hadn't been working, warning her that they should stay on Sandhamn and not return to Stockholm, where bad news awaited them. That moment Nils had been dreading for so long had finally arrived: His father had suffered a serious heart attack and was in critical condition.

Even as her heart went out to Nils and Solbritt, B.G. couldn't help a deep, personal anguish, selfish as it might be. If only she and Nils had had this one night together, they might have come to some understanding about their relationship. After today, she was sure that his feelings for her went much beyond physical attraction, but neither of them had actually spoken the word *love* to each other. All she could do was lend her support to both him and Solbritt now in this time of fear and worry and let the future take care of itself.

"You must go to your mother at once, Nils," Solbritt told her grandson as he put a protective arm around her shoulders, obviously not wholly believing her show of inner strength. "She is very frightened that he will die. You are the only person who can comfort her and make her hope."

"I'll take the first flight out," Nils replied grimly and started toward the telephone in his grandmother's suite.

"I asked the manager of the hotel to check on flights for you," Solbritt told him before he could pick up the receiver. "You must talk to him yourself and see what he has learned."

After the telephone exchange between Nils and the hotel manager, Nils hung up the phone and glanced at his watch. "I have an hour and a half to pack and get to the airport," he said briefly. "There isn't a direct flight, but I can fly to Heathrow and from there to New York." He glanced over toward B.G., who had been standing by, feeling horribly helpless. His eyes sent a message of apology for this intervention of fate. Mutely he held out his hand to her, and she went with him, without a word.

"I *knew* this was going to happen," Nils said as soon as they were out in the hallway and beyond Solbritt's hearing. Only then did B.G. realize how much control Nils had been exerting over his emotions. Intermingled with deep concern were anger and frustration.

B.G. had to fight against the impulse to utter all those hollow reassurances that people are wont to fall back upon at such times. She wanted to tell Nils that everything would be all right; but nobody knew what would await him in New York. By the time he got there, his father might not even be alive.

Inside his room, a mate to hers next door, Nils took B.G. into his arms and held her tight against him. She could feel his tension and sense his desperation.

"Nils, don't give up hope," she implored him softly. "Your father may recover. Wait until you get there and see for yourself."

His arms tightened, but he seemed unable to trust himself to speak. Gradually he relaxed, perhaps taking some comfort in her words.

"I'm so sorry this happened," he said finally, with a kind of resigned weariness. "It's going to make everything twice as hard. But I have only myself to blame." Gently he released her and stepped back, holding her lightly by the shoulders and regarding her deeply concerned expression. "Hey, don't look so worried," he chided, giving her a little shake. "This is a rotten thing to happen in the middle of your trip, but I'm glad you're here. It makes it easier for me to go off and leave my grandmother, knowing she'll have you to look after her."

B.G. had such a big lump in her throat that she couldn't speak right away. She just nodded her head hard to indicate that she would be there for Solbritt if the older woman needed her. Right now B.G. was awfully afraid that she was going to need a lot of emotional support herself.

"I guess I should go and let you pack," she said finally, fighting the onslaught of tears that she knew was a kind of nervous reaction to the tension.

Nils pulled her gently toward him and kissed her on the lips. "Whatever happens, today was a very special day," he said softly. He squeezed her shoulders and then let his hands drop away.

B.G. made her exit fast in order to get to her own room before the tears started falling. The words Nils had spoken had been alarmingly like a benediction, bringing as much painful uncertainty as hope and joy. "Whatever happens," he had said, still promising her nothing. Today *had* been a "very special day," but there was tomorrow and the next day and the next to consider. She couldn't content herself with wonderful memories.

B.G.'s final parting with Nils was no more satisfactory than that exchange with him in his room. She had showered and changed to clothes that would be appropriate for dinner later and then waited in her room, hoping that Nils would knock on the door any minute and say good-bye in private. When her telephone rang, it was Solbritt, asking B.G. to come down to her suite.

Nils was there, somber in jacket and tie for traveling. B.G. could sense as soon as she entered the room that he and his grandmother had been having a private talk. Knowing that her feelings were petty, she nonetheless experienced a pang of jealousy that Nils hadn't shared his last minutes before departure with *her*.

There was really nothing for any of them to say. It was one of those times when human beings feel particularly powerless and can only utter the obvious expressions of hope that all will turn out well.

"Well, my taxi's waiting," Nils said briskly. "You two take care of each other. I'll get news to you as soon as I can." He kissed Solbritt on the cheek, B.G. on the mouth, and was gone.

As soon as the door closed behind him, Solbritt crumbled. B.G. had no time to think about herself as she led the older woman over to the bed and tried to comfort her. It came to her in a flash of insight that Nils had known his grandmother was more deeply affected by the grave illness of her son in New York than she had shown. B.G. was heartened by the knowledge that Nils felt better about leaving his grandmother, knowing that B.G. would be with her.

Solbritt proved to be resilient, however, and had quite recovered by dinner. She seemed to be willing to continue their travel itinerary without Nils, explaining that all the arrangements had been made for a rental car. They could drive up to Lake Siljan the next day and spend several days visiting the small hamlets that were the centers for handicrafts for which Sweden was known, in particular the Dalarna wooden horse and the Nittsjo pottery.

B.G. hesitated, knowing what her own inclinations were but wanting to decide whatever would be best for Solbritt. Perhaps continuing their travels would take her mind off her son's illness, but she might be putting on a good front and be wishing deep inside that she could return home.

"Perhaps we could go back to Forsborg and visit some interesting places nearby," she suggested, as though weighing the idea. When she saw the enormous relief on Solbritt's face, she continued in a more definite tone. "Yes, I think I would prefer that. I would like to visit the fabrik before I return home. Also, I am concerned about the delivery of my grandmother's plates."

Solbritt nodded her head emphatically.

"We shall return to Forsborg tomorrow," she declared. Her face softened as she added, "My good friend Birgitta was blessed to have a wonderful granddaughter like you. I am glad that you came to visit me. I was right.

You are perfect for my Nils. Something here''—she touched a hand to her breast—''told me that you would be.''

B.G. was too astonished to speak. Solbritt's smile was a trifle conciliatory as she continued.

''It was no accident, my child, that you came to Forsborg at the same time that Nils was arriving for his visit. Your grandmother had sent me pictures of her grandchildren through the years. You were such a pretty little girl—so 'Swedish' in your looks, the spirit and courage there in your eyes. I cannot tell you the exact moment when it first occurred to me that you would be a good wife for my wonderful grandson, who had grown up in America.''

B.G. was shaking her head disbelievingly from side to side. What Solbritt was telling her sounded like a totally implausible movie plot.

''But how did you *know*—'' she blurted and then stopped, turning pink with embarrassment as she realized that she was admitting to the success of Solbritt's plot, at least insofar as B.G. was concerned. She had fallen in love with Nils, just as his grandmother had hoped.

Solbritt's lined old face lit up with pleasure and tenderness, but she tactfully made no comment about B.G.'s admission.

''Of course, I could do nothing but bring the two of you together.'' She shrugged philosophically. ''It was either meant to be or it was not.''

''But why would you want Nils to choose *me* for his wife? With our different backgrounds—I'm an American citizen and Nils is Swedish—how could you think that we were suited?'' B.G. asked confusedly. ''Did you and my grandmother just say to each other years ago that it would be nice for two of your grandchildren to marry?''

Solbritt shook her head, her expression growing sad.

"Birgitta and I never expressed such thoughts. She did not know of the hope I harbored in my breast. I did confide to her, though, the fear that Nils might make a terrible mistake and marry someone who did not share his Swedish heritage. It was such a great possibility, since he grew up in the United States and spends a great deal of time there. Don't you see that you are perfect for Nils? American and yet Swedish, too—just like he is."

The last comment made B.G. catch her breath. "You know, don't you?" she murmured. "You've known all along. And he has so dreaded telling you."

Solbritt looked wise.

"If you're asking me whether I always expected my grandson would someday want to build his future in the United States, the answer is *yes*. He will not be content merely to follow in the footsteps of his father and his grandfather." She paused, looking inward. "Who is to say? Perhaps things would have been different if he had grown up here in Sweden. Still, he must do whatever is best for him. Wherever he chooses to live and work, he is a Heidenstam with Swedish blood in his veins, just as *you* have Swedish blood in *your* veins, my child."

Just days earlier B.G. would have protested Solbritt's words, but not now. This trip had brought about a drastic change in her thinking. Being of Swedish descent had become something she was proud of. She couldn't have said when she started feeling that way, perhaps it was when she came to understand the courage it had taken her grandparents to leave their country and seek a better life.

"Why didn't you tell Nils you didn't object to his becoming an American citizen?" B.G. was gently accusing. She knew how much anguish Nils had needlessly suffered, not wanting to hurt his grandmother.

"But I do object," Solbritt corrected her somewhat sternly. "It hurts inside to think that my wonderful grandson will give his talents and his loyalty to a country other than Sweden. That does not change my love for him, however. He must make the choices necessary for his own happiness, and he must make them for himself. It is not for me or anyone else to make those decisions easier or more difficult.'' Solbritt sighed and suddenly looked terribly tired. "Now I shall be a poor hostess and retire to bed early. Tomorrow will be another day.''

B.G. had too much to think about to even consider going to sleep until far into the night. Those final remarks had made an especially deep impression. Solbritt loved her grandson too much to influence him one way or the other in the momentous decision she knew intuitively that he would have to make. That kind of restraint took remarkable strength of character. B.G. thought of how she had been making snap decisions all her life and was impatient of anyone of an unlike temperament, who weighed the costs more carefully— someone like Nils. If he had given her the slightest opening, she would have tried to tell *him* what he should do. She suspected that he had sensed that and, for that reason, *hadn't* shared his mental conflict with her except on those few occasions when his torment would cause him to open up, and then he would regret that he had done so.

Yesterday on the walk to Djurgarden, Nils had said he had made up his mind about whether he would stay with the Heidenstam Fabrik. Yet he hadn't told her that decision then or even tonight, before he left. Why? Because he thought she wouldn't approve and would try to change his mind? That was the only answer that made sense, and it suggested that Solbritt had been wrong in reading her grandson's character. Perhaps loyalty to his family had won out—over the allure of his own business venture, over his reservations about Swedish economic policies, over a future with B.G.

But the more B.G. thought about a life without Nils, the more she was convinced that she could compromise. If he took over his father's office, he would be living in New York. Marrying him wouldn't be like marrying a foreigner who would take her away to live in some far-off land. Nils was Swedish *and* American—just as Solbritt had said. *And so was B.G.*

Chapter Thirteen

The plate collection had arrived safely during their absence. Not a single piece was damaged. B.G. wasn't prepared for the depth of her emotion as she helped Solbritt carefully unpack each piece. She fought not to break down into tears.

"Don't be so sad, Birgitta," Solbritt told her gently. "These plates belong to *you*, not to me. You will have them to remind you of your grandmother and then to hand down to your own daughter. That is the way my old friend Birgitta intended it to be."

B.G. was afraid to believe what she was hearing. "But—but she left them to *you*. How could they be mine? . . ." The half-hearted protest was suffused with hope. She wanted her grandmother's plates very much.

"Your grandmother's greatest wish as she grew older was to have you come to Sweden. She was so sure that such a visit would be important to you the rest of your life. I wanted you to come, too, for reasons I have already confided to you. Birgitta and I had to think of some mission you would carry out after her death. You see, my child, she died knowing that you loved her deeply and would carry out her wish, whether it pleased you or not." Solbritt hesitated and added hopefully, "You are not angry at us for misleading you?"

B.G. shook her head helplessly. "How can I be angry? You've been simply wonderful to me, and my grandmother was right. This trip has been terribly important for me. It's just that I can't believe . . ." Would there be no end of surprises from this nice old Swedish woman, who had seemed so straightforward and uncomplicated?

There was no direct word from Nils during the following days. His mother was the one to call Solbritt and relay the sober reports on Lars Heidenstam's condition, which remained stable but still critical. Much to B.G.'s surprise, during one of these telephone calls from New York, Anna Heidenstam asked to speak to *her!* The voice that came over the line had only the slightest lilting cadence to suggest her nationality, and the tone was warm and friendly.

"Nils has told me much about you. I am sorry that your visit to Sweden was spoiled by the illness of my husband."

"Please don't be sorry . . . after all, it was nobody's *fault.* . . ." B.G. was aware that she sounded flustered. Her mind was a turmoil of all the questions she would like to ask and couldn't. Exactly *what* had Nils told his mother about her? Had he taken over his father's office permanently? Had there even been an opportunity for him to discuss with his mother his plans for the future?

Afterward, she couldn't decide whether she should be encouraged that Nils's mother had wanted to speak to her. There was no solid basis for the hope that Nils might have told his mother that he cared for B.G. Certainly there was nothing in Anna Heidenstam's voice to indicate that she thought she was speaking to her future daughter-in-law.

When Friday arrived and it was time for her to board her return flight to the United States, B.G. marveled at the paradoxical nature of time. It seemed that she had just arrived in Sweden, but it also seemed that she had been there forever. Whether her visit had been brief or interminable, she was returning to Minneapolis a changed person, even if she did look much the same.

In leaving Forsborg and Solbritt behind, B.G. felt that she was moving farther away from Nils when actually she was moving closer. Minneapolis wasn't that far from New York, just a short plane flight, just the matter of dialing a few numbers and hearing a voice at the other end of the telephone line.

Her first week home B.G. raced to the telephone every time it rang, her heart pounding with hope that Nils was calling. When she returned from work in the afternoons, her hands would tremble with eagerness as she thumbed through her mail searching for some personal missive that wasn't there. When another week passed, and Nils did not get in touch with her, her disappointment was heavily tinged with hurt and the beginnings of anger. Surely Nils couldn't be *that* busy that he couldn't afford a few minutes to call her?

When the phone rang on an evening of the third week after her return to Minneapolis, she answered without any heightened expectation and was taken totally unawares.

"Hello, B.G. This is Nils Heidenstam," came the familiar male voice over the line.

"*Nils!*—" Adrenaline poured into her body, bringing her alive. *Nils was calling her, finally!* "Nils, how *are* you? How's your father? Where are you calling from?"

"I'm calling from New York. I'm fine, and my father is doing much better. He's at home now. How are you?"

Nils's reply was so easy and friendly that it might have been yesterday they'd parted, not three weeks ago. The warmth in his voice was nearly B.G.'s undoing. She wanted to blurt out the truth, that she'd been miserable —thinking about him constantly and wishing with all her heart for some personal contact.

"I'm fine . . . just fine," she managed to get out unconvincingly.

"Do you plan to be home this weekend? I—"

"Yes, I'll be home," B.G. put in eagerly, her heart pounding with excitement. *Nils was going to come to Minneapolis to see her!*

There was a slight pause.

"I have a package from my grandmother to deliver to you. *Your* grandmother's porcelain plates. It seems that they belong to you after all. My grandmother said you would explain."

"Oh." B.G. felt much of her elation fading away. Nils hadn't just called because he wanted to hear her voice. He wasn't planning a trip to Minneapolis just to see her. He was being the dutiful grandson and carrying out his well-meaning grandmother's instructions.

"B.G., are you still there? Is it okay for me to come to Minneapolis this weekend?"

"Of course, I'm still here. Of course, it's okay." She tried not to sound disappointed.

"Good. My flight on Saturday is scheduled to arrive a little past 1:00 P.M. I'll take a taxi from the airport."

After she had hung up the phone, B.G. felt the conflicting tides of emotion rolling over her. She'd actually talked to Nils, heard his voice, and yet she knew nothing more than she had known before. He would be in her apartment this weekend. She would see him, touch him, but would it be only another parting? All her certainty that he cared for her was fast eroding. In three weeks time he hadn't called or written, when he could have done either. It didn't take much time just to get across the message, "I'm thinking of you. You *matter*." Would he have called tonight and made arrangements to come this weekend if Solbritt hadn't assigned him the mission of delivering her grandmother's plates?

Whatever Nils's reasons for coming to Minneapolis, by Saturday B.G. was in a state of nerves. She spent the whole morning deciding what to wear. She didn't want to look as if she'd gone all out dressing up for him, and yet she wanted to look her best. Finally, she settled upon white designer jeans and a tailored red silk shirt.

When the doorbell sent musical chimes through her apartment at a quarter of two, B.G. jumped as though the sonorous notes were bullets ricocheting from wall to wall. Taking a deep breath to calm herself and hoping that she would appear more composed than she felt, she went to open the door to Nils.

At the first sight of him, she forgot everything in the rush of pure exhilaration. It no longer mattered *why* he was there. The single important fact of her existence was simply that he *was* there, taller than she remembered, even more masculine and handsome, his blue eyes sweeping over her admiringly, bringing every inch of her glowingly alive.

"Nils! I'm so glad to see you!" The smile on her lips was totally natural now and welcoming. The light in her eyes told him the depth of her sincerity. B.G. didn't have time to finish opening up her arms to him before she felt herself being swooped up in a tight embrace and lifted off the floor. Nils was speaking her name aloud with a groaning urgency, telling her how beautiful she looked, how wonderful it was to see her and feel her in his arms again.

B.G. nestled against him, her arms tight around his neck. It was pure heaven being so close to him.

"I've missed you so much," she breathed, the words coming from deep inside her.

"I've missed you, too."

Nils lowered her so that her feet touched the floor again and pulled back a little so that he could see her. His eyes moved over her hungrily, taking in the spun gold hair, the blue eyes full of life and determination and something else now that thrilled him, the mouth so softly vulnerable that he could hardly resist kissing her.

"It seems like years instead of weeks since I left you in Stockholm," he said wonderingly.

His words brought back reality. B.G. sighed, not wanting to risk losing this wonderful glow but knowing that they had to talk.

"Nils, why didn't you call me or write a note at least or . . . *something?* I was beginning to think I'd never hear from you or see you again." Underneath the pleading was a hint of accusation.

Nils indulged himself a moment longer, letting his gaze move over her again and linger upon her lips. B.G. found herself holding her breath as he wrestled with the temptation to postpone explanations and kiss her instead. She lamented his willpower when he loosened his embrace with evident reluctance and then released her.

"I guess we do have to talk, don't we?" He turned to shut the door, which still stood ajar. B.G. remembered the plate collection he had promised to bring.

"Where's the box?" she asked in puzzlement. "My grandmother's plates—I thought you said you were bringing them."

Nils gave the door a little push. It closed with a quiet click.

"I didn't bring them after all. I hope you don't mind."

"You didn't bring them!" There was more delight

than surprise in the exclamation. B.G. could understand the reason for Nils's puzzlement. It had sounded as though she was glad that he hadn't delivered the collection.

"I'm glad you're not annoyed," he said slowly. "I thought you might be. I *will* see that they are delivered to you safely, of course."

B.G. took his arm and pulled him toward the living room.

"If you didn't bring my grandmother's collection, Nils, that must mean you came just to see *me!*" she declared buoyantly, a broad smile on her face.

"Of course, I came to see you." The comment held faint irritation. Nils didn't like being rushed into things, and B.G. was as impatient here in her own domain as she had been in Sweden. Nils glanced around her living room and saw that the accent colors were vivid and assertive, just like her personality. But not overwhelming, he conceded. If B.G. had been the demure, passive type who would surround herself with pastels and old lace, Nils knew that he wouldn't be here today.

"I like your decorating scheme," he complimented with an irony of which only he was aware.

"Do you really?" The note of uncertainty was genuine. Nils's opinion about *anything* mattered greatly to B.G. "I'm glad."

She led Nils over to a huge white sofa with red and blue throw pillows and sat next to him. "Now tell me *everything*," she begged eagerly. "How is your father? Have you taken over his office? What did you decide to *do*, anyway? You never told me—"

"*Wait*—" Nils stopped the barrage of questions by touching the fingers of one hand to her lips and then slowly taking them away. "Wait just a moment," he ordered softly, warning her with his eyes. "Let me tell you in my own way."

B.G. stared back at him, as hurt as she was annoyed.

"I've been waiting three whole weeks," she muttered righteously. "More than that, actually." She clamped her lips shut.

Nils had to smile at the picture of defiance that she presented, and then both of them were laughing. He had to contend once again with the powerful urge to dispense with words and kiss her, but he knew that he wouldn't be able to stop there.

"First, about my father. He's a lucky man. He will recover from this heart attack and be able to live a fairly normal life with certain restrictions. It took something like this to bring him to his senses. He and I have come to an understanding. I have taken over his office—"

"Oh, *Nils*—" B.G. blurted out. "I was so hoping you'd decided . . ." Her face reflected the deep dismay in her voice, which waned into nothing as she found the words in her mind too painful to speak. Nils had decided to remain with the family business. That meant he would also retain his Swedish citizenship and *not* become a U.S. citizen. B.G. was sick with disappointment even if she wasn't surprised.

Nils frowned, opened his mouth to speak, and then closed it, evidently having decided to say nothing. His stony silence left B.G. no choice but to blunder on. She wished with all her heart that she hadn't interrupted him.

"I'm sorry," she apologized miserably. "I shouldn't have said that—I shouldn't have said *anything*. It's wrong of me to be so biased. Sweden is a wonderful country. You have every reason to be proud of being a Swedish citizen. It's just that I think you have an awful lot to offer to *any* country, and I *was* hoping . . ." Again she couldn't finish. Every word she had spoken was true, but it was what she hadn't said that was really at the heart of her despair.

"What exactly were you hoping, B.G.?" Nils prompted.

B.G. tried to swallow the enormous lump in her throat, encouraged that Nils didn't look or sound angry. "Well, that you would become an American citizen, of course."

"And if I don't, is that really so important to you? Would it change what we feel for each other?"

B.G.'s heart lurched and then pounded wildly with hope. He had said "what *we* feel for each other"!

"I don't know *what* you feel for me, Nils. You've never told me. You said you didn't want to make any promises." B.G. spoke quickly, saying what was in her heart while she had the courage.

Nils had to smile at the accusation blended with hope and uncertainty in her voice. "You never told me what you feel for me, either, B.G.," he reminded. "You just said you *didn't* want to fall in love with me, remember? Right after we had made love that night on the canal boat, and I was still bowled over by what had happened."

"You *were?*—bowled over, I mean?" she said wonderingly and then got a faraway expression as she thought back. "I did tell you that, didn't I? But I was just afraid!" The accusing note was back. "I wanted you to tell me—oh, Nils, surely you must have known I was already in love with you, or I wouldn't have gone with you to your cabin! And you'd hardly said a kind word to me up until then!"

The light in Nils's eyes was amused and tender, but he held himself firmly in check.

"Even if I had realized what you felt for me and been able to identify what I felt for you, B.G., I still wouldn't have offered any commitment or made any promises. You had made it all too clear from the outset that I had the wrong kind of citizenship papers. I have my pride, you know."

B.G. met his eyes questioningly. He had said *"have my pride,"* present tense, which meant that it was up to her now to risk hers.

"I love you, Nils, no matter what kind of citizenship papers you have. I've been totally miserable since you left Stockholm, not knowing whether you'd want to see me again."

"Does that mean that if we continue our relationship and become even more involved with each other, you will consider marrying me, even though I am not an American citizen?" he asked gravely.

B.G. nodded, not stopping to reflect.

"Yes. I'd decided that even before I left Sweden."

Nils took her into his arms and hugged her close. "I needed to hear you say that," he said in a voice roughened with emotion.

B.G. caught the hint of apology and wondered at the reason for it, but she was more interested in his next words.

"I love you, B.G. I've thought about you every single day."

"You have?" she mumbled against his chest. "Why didn't you call me, then?"

"I needed time to work out some things in my life. I wanted to be on solid ground when I saw you again, or I knew I wouldn't stand a chance. Also, I wanted to give you some time. After you got back home, my attraction for you might just have turned out to be a holiday romance."

It was the first part that caught B.G.'s attention. She pushed back from him so that she could look into his face.

"What do you mean you had to be on 'solid ground'

or you wouldn't 'stand a chance'? I don't understand,"
she said, puzzled.

Nils met her gaze unwaveringly.

"I mean that you are a very strong person and inclined
to express your opinion, whether it is wanted or not," he
said gently, to take the bite out of the truth. "If I had
called you from New York, for example, and just
mentioned some business problem, I haven't a doubt that
you would know instantly what *you* would do and not
hesitate to tell me. Your total lack of ambivalence about
anything is a trait I sometimes envy and frequently find
most irritating."

B.G. was offended at his perception of her decisive-
ness as a possible flaw in her character.

"I don't mean to sound critical, Nils," she began and
then broke off when he burst out laughing. Working the
words in between sheepish giggles, she went ahead and
finished the thought, "You tend to . . . care too much
. . . about what's best . . . for *other* people."

"Is that so?" Nils sounded distracted because he had
lost interest in conversation now. The hunger for her had
been gnawing away inside him for several hellishly long
weeks now, and he wanted to kiss her and touch her.
Framing her face with his hands, he slowly lowered his
head.

"You *taste* so good," he murmured, expelling his
breath in what ended up being part sigh and part groan.
Then he kissed her again, this time as though he would
never stop until they had devoured each other. His hands
caressed her shoulders and back, sliding over the warm
silk covering her pliable softness.

"Let's take this off," he muttered, taking his lips
away from hers long enough to locate the top button of
her shirt and then kissing her again while his fingers
struggled on their own until B.G. helped.

When the blouse was removed, Nils cupped her

breasts in his hands and squeezed them before his fingers began to work at the front clasp of her bra. Reluctantly he broke off the kiss and gave the clasp his full attention.

"Why do you wear this thing? It's sexy as hell, but—" The clasp separated and he was able to lift the lacy half-cups away to reveal rounded, pink-tipped breasts. "I've dreamed about doing this," Nils murmured in a low voice that brought the peaks to hard points even before his mouth had reached one of them.

B.G. complied willingly when Nils pushed her backward on the pillows of the sofa. She lay beneath him, giving herself up to the warm tide of sensation that grew rapidly more intense as he kissed her breasts, his hands already unsnapping her jeans and sliding down the zipper. When he encountered problems getting the tight jeans down past her hips, he had to turn his full attention once again to undressing her. "These damned things look great, but they're hard to get off," he grumbled and joined B.G. in her laughter.

"I don't know what you expected," she said, giggling. "I could hardly greet you at the door in my nightie after all this time!"

"Sounds like a great idea to me." Nils tossed the jeans aside and eased his fingers under the waistband of bikini panties that were pure provocation and little else. "Next time just wear these," he suggested in that voice that made B.G. feel the most desirable of all women. Then he had taken off the scanty lace garment and was caressing her hips and thighs and kissing all the secret parts of her with an intimacy that drove her wild with pleasure and made her want something more: that deep, elemental coupling of his body with hers.

"Nils, please! Hurry!" she begged and then watched him with open desire in her eyes while he got up from the sofa and stripped off his clothes. When he was naked, she held her arms out to him.

"I love your body, Nils. I love *you*," she told him joyously and then felt him enter her. After that she didn't know what she said. There was incredible warmth and closeness and then a sensory explosion that took them into a realm of experience where time had no meaning.

"Making love with you is *incredible*," she murmured some time afterward when they lay nestled close together.

Nils mumbled something that was obviously agreement. After that there was silence for several more minutes while they reveled in that closeness that results from the deepest satisfaction.

"B.G."

Something vaguely hesitant and apologetic elicited her attention but failed to alarm her.

"Hmmmmm?" she murmured contentedly.

"I haven't been honest with you."

"Haven't you?" she replied, still complacent.

"No. I let you think earlier that I had decided to stay with the Heidenstam Fabrik, when actually I haven't decided that at all."

That brought B.G.'s head up. She searched his face and saw that he was serious.

"But why didn't you tell me?" she demanded delightedly.

"You didn't give me a chance to tell you. I started to explain that I've agreed to run my father's office for up to six months, until he can take over again along with the assistant I'm training. After that I will be going into the partnership I told you about, and I'll no longer be an employee of the Heidenstam Fabrik."

"*Nils!* Does that also mean you'll be applying for American citizenship?" B.G. leaned over him with an eagerly inquiring face and planted a kiss on his lips when he nodded.

"I'm so happy!" she exclaimed. "I love you either

way, but this makes everything even better! And from now on I promise never to interrupt when you're trying to tell me something!"

Nils smile was frankly skeptical.

"My father and mother were great about the whole thing. As it turns out, they weren't at all surprised. *Nobody* was—"

"I know your grandmother wasn't," B.G. broke in excitedly, forgetting her resolution of a moment ago. "She told me in Stockholm after you had left that she'd known for years that you were as American as you were Swedish. Oh, I've done it again, haven't I?" B.G. wailed apologetically. "I've broken in! Please continue."

"I was about to say that I finally had that talk with my grandmother right before I left the hotel to catch my flight back to New York. She told me essentially the same thing that she apparently told you. So everything has worked out much better than I ever expected."

"Nils, I am truly happy for you! Happy for *us!*" she added, feeling bold. "If we do get more involved with each other, to use your expression, and decide in the future to get married, this makes things just perfect! Our children will be born full-fledged Americans, won't they?" She sighed with her sense of the rightness of things and lay down next to Nils again.

"B.G., there's one thing I want to make absolutely clear." The gravity in Nils's voice brought B.G. back up so that she could see his face and meet his serious blue eyes.

"What's that, Nils?"

"I'm proud of being born a Swede and make no apologies for my background. I want any children of mine to be proud of their Swedish heritage. I want them to know something of Swedish history and have some familiarity with the Swedish language so that when they

go to Sweden to visit their cousins and aunts and
uncles—and, most important, my grandmother—they'll
be able to communicate as 'insiders,' so to speak, the
way *you* were able to do."

B.G. was relieved that it wasn't anything serious after
all.

"I couldn't agree with you more, Nils. I want
our—er, my—children to know my family and appreciate their experience as immigrants the way I can now. I
never did understand before I went to Sweden. Maybe
you could help me practice my Swedish. Then when I
meet your parents, I can be more fluent."

Nils grinned broadly, but the expression in his eyes
was tender.

"My parents would speak Swedish to humor you, but
they're every bit as comfortable speaking English. In
fact, they have an authentic New York accent after living
there all these years." He reached up and drew her down
beside him, cradling her head on his chest.

For a long while they lay contentedly, basking in their
harmony.

"Nils." B.G. broke the silence.

"Hmmm." Nils wasn't as unguarded as he managed
to sound. He knew that there wasn't any guessing what
B.G. might have on her mind now. She would probably
always have the capacity to surprise him. Life with her
would not be dull.

"Nils, I was just thinking about what you said earlier,
about the possibility of the two of us getting more
involved with each other and deciding eventually to get
married. Well, how long do you suppose that will take?
I'm already pretty involved with you." B.G. felt Nils's
chest move and heard a strangled sound in his throat. If
she hadn't been speaking with such perfect seriousness,
she might have suspected that he was chuckling. He
certainly was taking his time about answering.

"I am pretty involved with you, too, B.G., but we've actually known each other a week. It won't hurt for us to get to know each other better before we discuss something as serious as marriage. You'll want to come to New York and meet my parents. I want to visit your parents on their farm and meet your relatives. We have all the time in the world."

"Oh."

B.G. was silent for a whole minute. Nils waited.

"Well, maybe we could decide right now whether I should meet your parents first or you should meet mine," she suggested briskly, as though the conversation hadn't suffered the lag. "I could come to New York next weekend, and then the following weekend you could fly back here and we could drive in my car to my parents' farm—" B.G. stopped when Nils made the strangled sound again, and she knew definitely that it *was* a chuckle. "I don't know what's so funny," she said huffily. "I know already that I want to marry you. I could be pregnant right this minute, you know."

It was Nils's turn to raise up and subject her to a close scrutiny. "Are you serious?"

"I am," she replied with dignity. "Since I am not involved with anyone else, I'm not on the pill and I haven't taken any precautions."

Nils's expression was indulgent as he looked down at her and then bent to drop a kiss on her pouting lips.

"If you really think you could be pregnant, maybe we had better speed things up a bit," he said thoughtfully, and then laughed aloud when B.G.'s expression brightened immediately.

"I hope my grandmother knew what she was getting me into when she picked you out for my bride," he managed to get out between chuckles.

B.G.'s eyes widened with amazement.

"You know about *that*, too?"

"Oh, yes. That was quite an enlightening talk we had in her hotel room in Stockholm."

"No wonder you barely said a word to me. I remember how jealous I was when your grandmother called me down to her room and I saw that the two of you had been having a private talk. You left almost immediately."

"I had a plane to catch, and there was really nothing I could say at that time anyway."

"I'm glad all that's over," B.G. said softly, pulling his head down to hers for a kiss that quickly deepened and rekindled their desire for each other. This time there were no obstacles like the necessity of removing clothing.

"I really might be pregnant now," B.G. teased much later.

"Okay, okay, my parents next weekend," Nils said good-humoredly. He was having his own reservations now about waiting. New York and Minneapolis were seeming farther and farther apart.

Now that B.G. had her way, she was suddenly filled with anxiety that Nils's parents wouldn't approve of her. She'd have to find out everything she could about them from Nils. And there was the matter of deciding what clothes to pack. New York was a very sophisticated city, not easy-going like Minneapolis.

"Before we go any further, there's one thing I want to get straight." This rather grim declaration from Nils brought her back to the present. It wasn't until his next words that she realized he was actually kidding her. "Are you sure you want to take on a name like Heidenstam? Think about it now. How more Swedish can you get than *Birgitta*—"

B.G. clamped her hand over his mouth. "Stop teasing me!" she ordered with pretended fierceness. "I may have changed my attitude about a lot of things, but not about my name. I am *not* Birgitta and never will be. I am B.G."

She felt his mouth trying to grin underneath her hand and took her hand away.

"So you are," Nils said softly. "B.G. Heidenstam. You're not likely to run into anyone else with that name."

B.G. was flattered at his subtle implication that a person as unique as she should have an uncommon name. She was also confident enough to do a little teasing of her own.

"Have you ever considered changing *your* name?" she inquired with a thoughtful little frown. "How about something truly American, like Smith?"

Nils retaliated at once with a kiss that brought her to submission and left both of them short of breath. "Or Jones," she gasped when she was able to speak, loving his brand of punishment.

Silhouette Special Edition. Romances
for the woman who expects a little
more out of love.

If you enjoyed this book, and you're ready for more great romance

...get 4 romance novels FREE when you become a Silhouette Special Edition home subscriber.

Act now and we'll send you four exciting Silhouette Special Edition romance novels. They're our gift to introduce you to our convenient home subscription service. Every month, we'll send you six new passion-filled Special Edition books. Look them over for 15 days. If you keep them, pay just $11.70 for all six. Or return them at no charge.

We'll mail your books to you two full months *before they are available anywhere else.* Plus, with every shipment, you'll receive the Silhouette Books Newsletter absolutely free. *And with Silhouette Special Edition there are never any shipping or handling charges.*

Mail the coupon today to get your four free books—and more romance than you ever bargained for.

Silhouette Special Edition is a service mark and a registered trademark
of Simon & Schuster, Inc.

⸺ MAIL COUPON TODAY ⸺

Silhouette Special Edition°
120 Brighton Road, P.O. Box 5020, Clifton, N. J. 07015

☐ Yes, please send me FREE and without obligation, 4 exciting Silhouette Special Edition romance novels. Unless you hear from me after I receive my 4 FREE BOOKS, please send me 6 new books to preview each month. I understand that you will bill me just $1.95 each for a total of $11.70—with no additional shipping, handling or other charges. **There is no minimum number of books that I must buy, and I can cancel anytime I wish.** The first 4 books are mine to keep, even if I never take a single additional book.

BSSLR4

☐ Mrs. ☐ Miss ☐ Ms. ☐ Mr.

Name	(please print)
Address	Apt. No.
City	State	Zip

Signature (If under 18. parent or guardian must sign.)

This offer, limited to one per customer, expires June 30, 1985. Terms and prices subject to change. Your enrollment is subject to acceptance by Simon & Schuster Enterprises.

Enjoy romance and passion, larger-than-life...

Now, thrill to 4 Silhouette Intimate Moments novels (a $9.00 value)— ABSOLUTELY FREE!

If you want more passionate sensual romance, then Silhouette Intimate Moments novels are for you!

In every 256-page book, you'll find romance that's electrifying...involving...and intense. And now, these larger-than-life romances can come into your home every month!

4 FREE books as your introduction.

Act now and we'll send you four thrilling Silhouette Intimate Moments novels. They're our gift to introduce you to our convenient home subscription service. Every month, we'll send you four new Silhouette Intimate Moments books. Look them over for 15 days. If you keep them, pay just $9.00 for all four. Or return them at no charge.

We'll mail your books to you *as soon as they are published.* Plus, with every shipment, you'll receive the Silhouette Books Newsletter absolutely free. *And Silhouette Intimate Moments is delivered free.*

Mail the coupon today and start receiving Silhouette Intimate Moments. Romance novels for women...not girls.

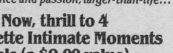

Silhouette Intimate Moments

Silhouette Intimate Moments™
120 Brighton Road, P.O. Box 5020, Clifton, NJ 07015

☐ YES! Please send me FREE and without obligation, 4 exciting Silhouette Intimate Moments romance novels. Unless you hear from me after I receive my 4 FREE books, please send 4 new Silhouette Intimate Moments novels to preview each month. I understand that you will bill me $2.25 each for a total of $9.00—with no additional shipping, handling or other charges. **There is no minimum number of books to buy and I may cancel anytime I wish.** The first 4 books are mine to keep, even if I never take a single additional book.

☐ Mrs. ☐ Miss ☐ Ms. ☐ Mr.   BMDL24

Name	(please print)

Address	Apt. #

City	State	Zip

Area Code	Telephone Number

Signature (if under 18, parent or guardian must sign)

This offer, limited to one per household, expires June 30, 1985. Terms and prices subject to change. Your enrollment is subject to acceptance by Simon & Schuster Enterprises.

Silhouette Intimate Moments is a service mark and trademark of Simon & Schuster, Inc.

If you've enjoyed this book,
mail this coupon and get 4 thrilling

Silhouette Desire®

novels FREE (a $7.80 value)

If you've enjoyed this Silhouette Desire novel, you'll love the 4 <u>FREE</u> books waiting for you! They're yours as our gift to introduce you to our home subscription service.

**Get Silhouette Desire novels
before they're available anywhere else.**

Through our home subscription service, you can get Silhouette Desire romance novels regularly—delivered right to your door! Your books will be *shipped to you two months before they're available anywhere else*—so you'll never miss a new title. Each month we'll send you 6 new books to look over for 15 days, without obligation. If not delighted, simply return them and owe nothing. Or keep them and pay only $1.95 each. There's no charge for postage or handling. And there's no obligation to buy anything at any time. You'll also receive a subscription to the Silhouette Books Newsletter *absolutely free!*

So don't wait. To receive your four FREE books, fill out and mail the coupon below *today!*

SILHOUETTE DESIRE and colophon are registered trademarks and a service mark of Simon & Schuster, Inc.

Silhouette Desire,® 120 Brighton Road, P.O. Box 5020, Clifton, NJ 07015

Yes, please send me FREE and without obligation, 4 exciting Silhouette Desire books. Unless you hear from me after I receive them, send me 6 new Silhouette Desire books to preview each month before they're available anywhere else. I understand that you will bill me just $1.95 each for a total of $11.70—with no additional shipping, handling or other hidden charges. **There is no minimum number of books that I must buy, and I can cancel anytime I wish.** The first 4 books are mine to keep, even if I never take a single additional book.

☐ Mrs. ☐ Miss ☐ Ms. ☐ Mr.   BDDLR4

Name	*(please print)*	
Address		Apt. #
City	State	Zip
( )		
Area Code	Telephone Number	

Signature (If under 18, parent or guardian must sign.)

This offer, limited to one per household, expires June 30, 1985. Prices and terms subject to change. Your enrollment subject to acceptance by Simon & Schuster Enterprises.

READERS' COMMENTS ON SILHOUETTE ROMANCES:

"I would like to congratulate you on the most wonderful books I've had the pleasure of reading. They are a tremendous joy to those of us who have yet to meet the man of our dreams. From reading your books I quite truly believe that he will some-day appear before me like a prince!"

—L.L.*, Hollandale, MS

"Your books are great, wholesome fiction, always with an upbeat, happy ending. Thank you."

—M.D., Massena, NY

"My boyfriend always teases me about Silhouette Books. He asks me, how's my love life and natu-rally I say terrific, but I tell him that there is always room for a little more romance from Sil-houette."

—F.N., Ontario, Canada

"I would like to sincerely express my gratitude to you and your staff for bringing the pleasure of your publications to my attention. Your books are well written, mature and very contemporary."

—D.D., Staten Island, NY

*names available on request

VAMPIRE VS. VAMPIRE

I tried to stand, but Cosgrove merely kicked me in the solar plexus, knocking me across the roof. I crashed into a pile of damp newspapers and splintering lumber and lay there trying hard to catch my wind.

"What kind of loads does it take?" he asked again.

"The bullet tips aren't metal. They're wooden."

"Ah, the twenty-first-century adaptation on the old stake-through-the-heart bit." He fondled the gun some more. "So this is the infamous Fixer gun I've always heard about. Interesting. Does it usually take just one bullet?"

"Depends on the individual."

"And just how many shots do you think it would take to kill you right now?"

"Way I'm feeling? You could probably do the job with a damned toothpick."

Cosgrove laughed and lowered the gun. "You haven't fed in a while have you?"

"Nope."

Cosgrove straightened and tilted his head back, licking his lips, tasting the night air as if it were some sweet nectar of the gods. "He was delicious, you know. Your friend, I mean. Absolutely exquisite." He leaned closer, reducing the distance between us so subtly that I could barely even sense it.

"Would you like a taste?" He pierced his forefinger. Crimson flowed from it, beading first on the pad, then dribbling down the length of his finger. "Taste him, taste your friend. It's customary, of course, your last meal and all. . . ."

Books by Jon F. Merz

THE FIXER

THE INVOKER*

Published by Pinnacle Books

*coming soon

(Please visit http://www.zrem.com
for more information.)

THE FIXER

Jon F. Merz

PINNACLE BOOKS
Kensington Publishing Corp.
http://kensingtonbooks.com

PINNACLE BOOKS are published by

Kensington Publishing Corp.
850 Third Avenue
New York, NY 10022

Copyright © 2002 by Jon F. Merz

All rights reserved. No part of this book may be reproduced
in any form or by any means without the prior written consent of the Publisher, excepting brief quotes used in reviews.

If you purchased this book without a cover, you should be
aware that this book is stolen property. It was reported as
"unsold and destroyed" to the Publisher and neither the
Author nor the Publisher has received any payment for this
"stripped book."

All Kensington Titles, Imprints, and Distributed Lines are
available at special quantity discounts for bulk purchases for
sales promotions, premiums, fund-raising, educational or in-
stitutional use. Special book excerpts or customized print-
ings can also be created to fit specific needs. For details,
write or phone the office of the Kensington special sales
manager: Kensington Publishing Corp., 850 Third Avenue,
New York, NY 10022, attn: Special Sales Department.
Phone: 1-800-221-2647.

Pinnacle and the P logo Reg. U.S. Pat. & TM Off.

First Printing: May 2002
10 9 8 7 6 5 4 3 2 1

Printed in the United States of America

For my father,
George Frederick Merz,
1944–1993

Dreams never end. . . .

ACKNOWLEDGMENTS

I owe a tremendous debt of gratitude to some very important people who were instrumental in the creation and publication of this novel.

First, thanks to my agents, Irene Kraas and Lisa Fitzgerald, for their passion and determination to help new authors break into both print and celluloid, respectively. To my editor, John Scognamiglio, for lighting the path with his friendship, patience, and wisdom.

Thanks to Mark Davis, Ken Savage, and Paul Etherington at the best martial arts school in the world—the Boston Martial Arts Center—for their friendship, knowledge, and guidance. Things I've been fortunate to learn from them have saved my life on more than one occasion, and that's not something I'll ever forget. And special thanks to Masaaki Hatsumi, Soke of the Bujinkan Dojo, for his amazing ability to teach the essence of real martial arts—humbling and inspiring simultaneously.

Thanks to Chris Holy, Steve Frederick, Leslie Irish Evans, Lori Heiberg, Bren O'Connor, Dolores D'Annolfo, and Gigi Dane—incredible writers from the Zoetrope Web site—for their cheers and twisted humor in the trenches. To my good friend Ken Hodgdon, fellow "Corporate America" survivor, and my self-described biggest fan. Thanks to my family for all their love and support—especially

Kat, the best first reader any author could ever hope to have.

But most especially thanks to my incredible wife Joyce. Without her unswerving belief in me, her wonderful smile, and musical laughter when the road looked bleak, this book would never have been written and my life would be far different from the great adventure it has become with her by my side. My love and thanks to you forever.

One

I sat like I always did: my back to the wall, keeping a good field of fire. That kind of instinctual discipline has kept me alive a long time. Usually, it's the only thing that does.

Neither of us spoke while our polyester-clad waiter slid bowls of steaming soup and a plate of appetizers onto our table. A quick bow and he was gone. Finally, McKinley cleared his throat, coughed up some phlegm, and dropped three words.

"Cosgrove's in town."

Jack Dempsey might as well have shot his trademark uppercut into my solar plexus. Keeping the mouthful of hot and sour soup where it belonged took a lot of effort. I chased it down with a gulp of ice water and a healthy intake of O2. "Well . . . That's just about the worst goddamned news you could spring on me."

McKinley's yellow-toothed grin slithered across his face. He always saved it for particularly nasty stuff. I'd swear he enjoyed seeing me suffer. "It's the little things that give me the most pleasure, Lawson. I knew your reaction would be worth coming out in this miserable rain for."

I wiped my mouth. "You really know how to ruin a good meal."

"Yeah, it's a gift." He waved his chopsticks. "We think he touched down yesterday."

"So why tell me? You want me to be his fucking tour guide or something?"

"Not exactly."

I sucked down another piece of slippery tofu. "Glad to hear it. Only trip I'd ever give that bastard would be a one-way ticket to hell."

"You don't have to be so sarcastic."

"This isn't sarcasm. This is me pissed off."

"You're overreacting. It's just Cosgrove."

I frowned. "What are you guys—poker buddies now?"

McKinley speared a pan-fried dumpling with one of his plastic chopsticks, the kind with the faded characters running down the side, and shrugged. "Maybe my viewpoint's a bit more objective. After all, he's not gunning for me."

"You know, you're a lot of things, but guardian angel ain't one of them."

Soy sauce dribbled down five miles of his chin. "Hey, I'm just a middleman. 'Life preserver' wasn't in the job description."

"Be like clutching a cinder block in an ocean if it was." I shook my head. "You're off the diet again, aren't you?"

He stopped chewing. "Give me a break, will you? We can't all look like we were built by the local bricklayers union."

"Taking care of myself goes with the job. You know that."

"Yeah, I know that. So what. I like to eat. Fuck

off, will ya? At least I'm not obsessing over some
two-bit psycho job."

I leaned closer to him. "I don't appreciate being
dragged out on a crappy night like this. And I
don't like being told I'm overreacting by an out-
of-shape has-been who hasn't seen the business end
of a field assignment in a decade."

He pulled away, gulped, and reached for another
victim. "Yeah, well, maybe I just don't consider Cosgrove to be all that dangerous. Maybe I just think
he's a pushover. A 'has-been,' to use your phrase."

"Maybe you weren't on the receiving end of his
last little killing spree here in town. Cosgrove is a
dangerous bastard. For you to tell me otherwise is
just plain stupid."

McKinley nodded. "I suppose I *should* bow to
your extensive, if not obsessive, knowledge of the
subject."

"Call it what you want. I know him. You don't."
I looked around the darkened interior of the restaurant. Located a quarter mile outside of Kenmore Square, they served the best Chinese food in
Boston here. As usual, the place was packed, but
McKinley and I had privacy, courtesy of the hostess
who always gets an extra twenty bucks to keep a
table for me at the back of the restaurant. Our
only neighbors were stoic characters painted on the
walls depicting scenes from the Ming Dynasty. Outside, the percolating drizzle we'd arrived with thirty
minutes ago exploded into a cold November downpour.

I faced him again. "So where's he holing up?"

McKinley yawned. "Guy like Cosgrove has more
rocks to crawl under than a miner."

"Jesus, I could have stayed home and played this

twenty-questions bullshit over the phone. Are you going to tell me where he is or do I have to walk out on a good dinner? I'm not in the mood for games."

"He's here."

I jumped out of my chair, instantly feeling a surge of adrenaline flood my bloodstream. I searched for Cosgrove's face in the crowd. McKinley laughed.

"Whoa, cowboy. I mean he's in town. In Boston."

I sucked in a lungful of air; waning adrenaline always left me queasy. It'd be a shame to puke a good meal. "How do you know?"

McKinley eyed me as he reached into the inside pocket of his muted plaid sport coat and withdrew a long manila envelope folded in half. "Everything OK? You seem a little jumpy."

"Now who's being sarcastic?" I frowned and took the envelope from him. "I'm fine." But I wasn't. I cursed Cosgrove silently for making me act like some goddamned amateur.

A single photograph spilled out of the envelope and landed next to the tarnished silver teapot. Even in the shadows I could easily make out the corpse on the gurney.

"Looks like the Boston City Hospital morgue."

"You should know; you've been there enough."

"Enough to know how easy it is to slip a body into the incinerator. Real convenient way to head off some uncomfortable questions."

McKinley's voice wafted over the scent of sizzling rice soup being served a few tables away. "ME made the time of death around two in the morning."

"Right after last call." I frowned. "That's his MO, all right." I looked up. "What else?"

He pointed at the picture. "They took that upon receipt of the corpse. Look at the skin color."

I looked closer at the corpse. White: like somebody had used a correcting pen on every inch of flesh.

"No fluids," said McKinley. "Absolutely drained. The sick bastard bled him dry."

I looked up. " 'Bastard'? Christ, a minute ago you were telling me what a pushover Cosgrove is. Now he's a bad boy? Damn, you flip-flop like a cheap whore." I passed the photo back to him.

McKinley looked at the picture. "Well, yes, but obviously I—we—can't condone *this* kind of behavior, Lawson."

"You seem surprised. Admit it, you know the guy's a certifiable maniac. He's a freak. And he's never been content with just killing his victims. He's gotta make a statement. Stand out like some damned insane artist. One of these days he'll probably mail me an ear."

I scooped some white rice onto my plate and quickly hid it under a pile of beef, brown sauce, and red peppers. "That makes him easy to track, thanks to the trail of dead bodies. But it also makes him more dangerous."

McKinley used one of his chopsticks to pick a piece of pork out of his teeth. "Well, Christmas comes early for you this year, whether I agree with your assessment or not." He replaced the envelope in his jacket. "Carte blanche on how you want to do it; they passed the termination order down this afternoon."

"All right. First things first: I'll need a fresh mug

shot. Chances are good he doesn't look a thing like he used to."

"A hundred percent good, in fact," said McKinley. "Rumor is he vacationed in Switzerland, got himself a new face. Problem is we don't have a photo."

I put my chopsticks down. "You're sending me out *blind?*"

"So it's not an easy mark, you'll improvise."

"Cosgrove and easy aren't even distant cousins. You're handing me a grenade with no pin."

"You've handled worse assignments before," said McKinley. "Remember Tokyo last year?"

"The only thing I remember about that operation is how much miso soup I ate. Stuff was like intestinal drain cleaner."

McKinley grinned. "Well, there's no miso soup on this assignment. Your orders are simple and clear. The Council wants him gone. Get rid of him. This time for good."

"There wouldn't be a *this time* if the Council had seen things my way before; if they'd listened, instead of dismissing me like some naive agent fresh out of training."

McKinley frowned. "What do you want me to say? They fucked up? Well, they probably did. But then again, hindsight's twenty-twenty. I'm sure you've got a lot of decisions you regret making."

"Only one stands out right now: having dinner with you tonight."

"You'd rather find out by having him show up at your house? I'm doing you a favor here."

"By giving me a sanction with no picture?" I shook my head. "That's some favor."

"Look, you want to stop your bitching and start

doing something about it or what? Honestly, I'd have bet good money you'd be all over this assignment."

I hated it. But I didn't have to like it. Or McKinley for that matter. A job was a job. And Cosgrove just happened to be another one. I wondered how long I'd be able to convince myself that's all it was.

The odds weren't good.

I looked at McKinley. "Guess I'll have to 'beat the grass and surprise the snake.'"

He stopped chewing. "That another one of your infamous Japanese philosophies?" He shook his head. "Don't know why you bother remembering that mumbo jumbo kung fu stuff."

"Maybe if you had some appreciation for things other than what you can stuff down your gullet, you'd learn something. It happens to be a Zen saying and a sword fighting strategy. I'll use it to find Cosgrove. Hopefully."

"Yeah? Enlighten me, o mighty Zen master. How you gonna use that to get your boy?"

"Cosgrove loves nightclubs. They're his hunting grounds. I hate nightclubs. Cosgrove knows that. But I'll do what he doesn't expect: I'll make them my hunting grounds too."

"Whatever," said McKinley. "Just so long as you get him."

"I don't really have a choice, do I? Sooner or later he's going to finish his business here in town and, according to you, come looking for me." I sighed and reached for another piece of beef. "You're right. With our past he can't afford to leave me alone. He's got to assume we know he's here. And that I'll be hunting him."

"You want backup?"

"You don't have any backup to give."

"I could pull some strings. Get someone transferred over temporarily if you think you can't handle him alone. If he's too much for you."

"Gee, thanks for the vote of confidence." I frowned. "I don't want a partner. I work better alone." I took a sip of tea. "Besides, I know Cosgrove better than anyone else. I'll handle it. My way. Just make damned sure the Council doesn't jerk me back in. If I get a bead on him this time, he goes down. Like it or not."

"Trust me, Lawson. You can stuff him and mount him on a wall for all we care," said McKinley, harpooning the final dumpling.

"If only it was that easy," I mumbled. "Killing him will be hard enough."

Midnight found me skirting puddles from the earlier downpour as I crossed the bridge at Brookline Avenue, over the traffic surging along the Massachusetts Turnpike. The night had blossomed into a crisp, clear sky with tendrils of rain clouds slinking to the north. My heated breath stained the air in front of my face as I dodged another pool of grimy water.

I love the darkness.

Most people are afraid of what they can't see. To me, the shadows hold the excitement, the risk, and even the danger I need in my life. I suppose I'd have to feel that way, given my occupation.

Cosgrove.

The last time he came to my theater of operations, he killed fifty people. Of course, the cops had no clue. They never did. And the Feds? Well, if you knew how they operated, it was no mystery why they were as clueless as the local doughnut jockeys.

Back then, I told the Council Cosgrove needed to be eliminated. He brought too much attention on an area of this world most people don't realize exists. An area most people think is reserved for old books and Stephen King novels. An area most people don't want to believe in because it tosses their reality the proverbial bird in a bad way.

The Council didn't believe me. Not enough evidence, they said, dismissing the dozens of bodies Cosgrove littered the streets and alleys with. They told me to leave Cosgrove alone.

I disobeyed the order.

Not a smart move on my part. The Council acts as a government of sorts for us. They hand down the laws of our society. I work for them with McKinley operating as my Control. Albeit a crappy one. But even the respect I had for the Council didn't stop me from defying them.

I tried to take Cosgrove out. I almost succeeded.

And I almost died.

Almost.

In this game, "almost" means about as much as two minus two.

Cosgrove vanished without a trace. I got a verbal warning for failure to follow orders.

That's called getting off lucky. On both counts.

Ahead of me, Landsdowne Street—Boston's nightclub Mecca—beckoned. And on a Friday night, it was packed with all sorts of people out to enjoy a night on the town. Most of them didn't realize how much danger was passing them by. Like the sharks that swam all around people at the beach. Just because you couldn't see them didn't mean they weren't there. It didn't mean they weren't just as deadly.

Especially when they were hungry.

Cosgrove may as well have been a poster child for Ethiopian famine.

His hunger for death was rivaled only by his lust for blood. In the time I'd spent trying to track him down and waste his ass on a permanent basis, I'd learned a little something about him.

What made him different was an infusion of bad blood into his family line. His grandfather, lazy bastard that he was, chose targets of convenience rather than maintaining the dignity of the hunt. He lounged around insane asylums and morgues, anyplace where the dregs of society congregated—where there were easy pickings.

Cosgrove's dad said Grandpop did it so no one would ever miss them. So they wouldn't know what had killed them. Cosgrove's father didn't want to believe the truth that Grandpop was just a miserable excuse for a hunter.

The mixture of blood he took in infected genes that were subsequently passed down to Cosgrove's father and Cosgrove himself. Cosgrove's father killed himself shortly after I paid him a visit to discuss his son's aberrant behavior.

Odd thing, that.

But the infectious mix of lunacy swirling about Cosgrove's bloodstream mutated and caused Cosgrove to kill with the same kind of zest a fourteen-year-old boy has when he discovers how to jerk off. I'd seen Cosgrove's death lust firsthand. His behavior, at least according to McKinley and the Council, could no longer be tolerated.

God knew I'd been tolerating longer than most.

I made my way past the sausage vendors peddling thick pieces of bloated meat by-products, sizzling over the blue flame of Sterno, to drunken night-clubbers. I walked past the homeless veteran with the old Campbell's soup can held outstretched in front of him looking for salvation in the guise of another quarter. And eventually past the lines of limousines double- and triple-parked in front of vel-vet cordons corralling long lines of supposedly beautiful people before herding them into the clubs.

I saw Simbik before he noticed me sidling through the five college girls attempting to bullshit him with fake IDs. The son of a wealthy Turkish importer, who lived on a huge estate outside of Istanbul, Simbik didn't have to work for anyone. He could have spent his life mooching off dear ol' dad. He didn't. I respected that. Rumor was the big lug had a soft spot for animals and was putting himself through veterinary school.

"Simbik."

He smiled immediately. "Who you pestering to-night, Lawson?"

I moved past the girls, who frowned and walked farther down the street to try conning another doorman. I scanned the area again. "Just out for a walk."

Simbik smiled. "Sure, and I'm just standing here farting for my health." He shook his head. "I got a better chance of seeing Istanbul and Athens be-come sister cities, fuhgeddaboutit." He glanced up the street as more patrons arrived. "Who you look-ing for?"

For a recent immigrant to the States, Simbik's accent was thoroughly Brooklyn. He once told me he'd worked in a pizza joint in Bensonhurst before moving up to Boston. He learned part of his English drowning in tomato sauce, cheese, and dough. He learned the other half wading through guys named Guido, Vinny, and Sal with his fists and an occasional head butt. At six feet two inches and a shade under two hundred and a quarter, the few foes Simbik couldn't handle could be counted on the fingers of one hand.

I watched him examine some more IDs and wave through another group of clubgoers before responding. Simbik knew very little about me. But he knew some.

"Man named Cosgrove."

"Friend of yours?"

I looked at him, and he broke into a toothy grin. Simbik knew if I was looking for someone, they definitely weren't a candidate for sainthood.

"So what's your boy look like?"

I looked farther down the street. "Don't know."

Simbik cocked one of his bushy eyebrows. "Great job you got, Lawson. If I wasn't so happy being a doorman here, rejecting little kids with bogus IDs and all, I might threaten to come aboard."

"What can I tell you—cosmetic surgery makes my life a bitch. No one's got a recent photo of him."

He nodded. "Figures." He adjusted the radio earpiece he wore. "So how you gonna do it?"

"He's got a certain style. I'll watch for it."

"Hey, man, Landsdowne's a short street, but it's got eight clubs, thousands of people, and only four hours to check them all out. You ain't got that many eyes, my friend."

"Simbik, I'm a professional. I use cunning, experience, and a lot of good detailed information."

His left eyebrow arched higher on his forehead.

I shrugged. "All right, so you're the only friend I've got down here. Your place is as good as any to start with, y'know?"

"Yeah." Simbik lit an unfiltered cigarette and took a long drag, expelling a thin stream of smoke into the night air. "Always knew my number would come up someday."

"Mind if I check it out?"

"Hey, *bana gore hava hos.*"

"Thanks." I started inside, but Simbik stopped me.

"Lawson."

I looked at him.

He blew more smoke into the night air. "You sure he'll be inside?"

"Not really."

"You find him in there, what happens?"

"I kill him."

He regarded me for a moment. "Can you whack him quietly? I got a job here and all."

"Simbik, if I find this guy in your club, I'll kill him any damned way I can. You'll thank me for it a million times and then buy me all the Bombay Sapphire I can drink."

"He's that bad, huh?"

"No." I shook my head. "He's even worse." I ducked under the blue velvet curtain and vanished into the shadowy recesses of the club.

Into the unknown.

Two

Inside, I felt the pulsing rhythm of amplified dance music rocket into my eardrums. Blue lasers and flashing lights pierced the darkness before being swallowed up again by the shadows. The dark kept me safe. If Cosgrove caught sight of me, he'd either try to escape or kill me.

Not knowing what Cosgrove looked like put me at a real disadvantage. Spend the kind of money Cosgrove had and you could put a new face on an elephant, call it a mouse, and no one would know any better.

Christ, he could look like anybody now.

Fortunately, the only thing more demanding than his blood lust was Cosgrove's vanity. Any changes to his appearance would have to make him look more attractive. He'd be a good-looking guy, probably with a couple of women around him. Cosgrove loved flaunting himself.

He hadn't always been like that. Time was, Cosgrove's looks ranked right down there with the kind of road rash you'd find at a motorcycle-accident scene. But a huge trust fund and family money enabled him to get the wrongs righted and come out looking like some *GQ* model, albeit a deranged one.

By comparison, my short, bristly, permanently graying hair poked straight out of my scalp at odd angles, accentuating my large forehead and reasonably strong jawline, which hadn't yet succumbed to age. McKinley once called me a walking military recruitment poster.

Maybe I could use some time in Switzerland.

I stopped at the first bar, leaned into the Naugahyde padding, and ordered a Bombay Sapphire with tonic from a guy with far too much metal lancing his skin. I slid a $10 bill on the counter, then turned to sip the drink and watch the crowd.

In Simbik's club there was only one VIP area. It overlooked the dance floor from an upper balcony wrapped in padded maroon couches. I felt sure Cosgrove would be sitting up there, surveying potential victims like he was on some kind of sick shopping spree.

"Is that a gin and tonic?"

Brunette. Too much makeup. In my peripheral vision I could see her holding her drink up next to mine in some kind of vain attempt at playing match game. "Good choice," she said.

I took another sip and continued watching the floor. "What kind of gin did you order?"

The look on her face told me she had no idea. "Try Bombay Sapphire next time," I said, and moved into the crowd.

That would count as my contribution to human society tonight. A little education for the masses on what constituted a damned fine drink. And if I took Cosgrove out, that'd be my angel's wings for sure. I might just make this a banner night.

I took the steps to the upper balcony slowly, using the black metal rail to cover my approach. Cosgrove would be sitting near an exit. A pompous bastard maybe, but he wasn't entirely stupid.

Unfortunately, he knew I always worked alone. The price of being the best at what I do.

Sometimes being good really sucked.

A club security guard barred my way; apparently, I wasn't wearing this season's appropriate Gucci fashion apparel. I smiled. "Simbik sent me."

He nodded and let me pass.

At the top of the stairs, I paused, scanning the recessed shadows for any signs Cosgrove might be there. Even with the onslaught of the steady musical rampage, I could hear the juicy sounds of several people swapping spit and Southern Hemisphere body fluids. So much for safe sex. It was only a matter of time before humans wiped themselves out. Even with AIDS killing thousands of people, they still wouldn't listen. I wouldn't even care, but continued epidemic levels of a killer disease threatened the food chain. And that meant my existence might even come into question.

I zeroed in on the recessed circular couch to my right. A man being wooed by two women—a possible threesome—reclined against the back wall. Lucky bastard.

I walked over and stood in front of him. He was about six-one and weighed maybe two hundred pounds. That was about right for Cosgrove. And it gave him about a twenty-pound advantage over yours truly.

I'm usually much more subtle. I wouldn't normally dream of making an approach this way. Unfortunately, McKinley having sent me out without even a vague idea of what Cosgrove looked like complicated things to the point where subtlety lost out to a frontal attack.

I cleared my throat.

Whoever he was, he wasn't happy with my sudden appearance.

"What the fuck do you want?"

I took a sip of my drink, felt the delicate flavoring of juniper and licorice as it coursed down my throat. I smiled.

"Mav kola an gurok."

It was the only greeting I knew in the old language. I wasn't quite sure what I hoped to gain by saying it. Maybe lull Cosgrove into replying, which would have been a dead giveaway.

I didn't get my wish.

"Fucking immigrants," said the man in front of me. He stood and tried to shove me away. I pivoted and, using his momentum, sent him sprawling down the stairs with me close on his heels.

I caught up with him just as he came to rest at the base of the steps. I tugged down the collar on his shirt and examined the base of his clavicle for the birthmark that would identify him as Cosgrove. The birthmark was the one guarantee I had that Cosgrove could never erase. Even with all the Swiss doctors working on it. It branded us all, the mark of my race. A tattoo of sorts that was as much a means of identification as it was a stigma.

Nothing.

Shit.

I looked up in time to see three bouncers closing in on me. One of them grabbed me around the upper right arm and another went for the same grip on my left. But they hadn't moved in unison, giving me valuable seconds to elbow the one on my right and drive him off. He floundered but came right back. This time I drove my elbow into his diaphragm and he backed off. But there were two more.

The second one flew in for a tackle around my waist and I dropped both elbows onto the top of his back, driving him down into my bent knees. He slid off, out cold.

The third one hesitated, having seen me deal with his two much bigger coworkers with apparent ease. Instead of trying to deal with me alone, he reached for his radio.

Time to go.

I sprinted for the fire exit near the back of the club on the ground floor. As I ran, one of the patrons raised his champagne flute in my direction. A shock of brown hair topping a set of piercing blue eyes. Prominent cheekbones narrowing to a fine nib at the chin. He smiled in the darkness, catching one of the blue lasers across his gleaming perfectly capped teeth. And four elongated incisors.

Cosgrove.

I stopped short—already reaching for my pistol— but at that moment I caught another flying tackle around the waist that sent both me and my attacker into the alleyway behind the club, toppling over trash cans, beer bottles, and garbage. Amid the smell of dank urine and week-old garbage, I knew instantly who had rushed me out of the club.

"Simbik!"

He got to his feet. *"Allah karetsin,* Lawson! You trying to get me fired? People saw us talking, man. You can't pull this kind of shit here. Even for you, I gotta draw the line."

I brushed myself off. "I would have handled it much quieter if the big lug upstairs hadn't tried to prove himself."

"Your mistake, your problem," said Simbik. "Aren't you supposed to be a professional, man? Shit, I know fourteen-year-olds who woulda pulled a hit cleaner than that."

"I told you I didn't know what my mark looked like. I had to be sure."

"So you go hassling everyone else? Forget about it, man. You can do better than that."

I started for the door. "All right, all right, it won't happen again—"

Simbik's hand on my chest stopped me. "Hold it, paesano."

"What's the problem?" I pulled his hand off me.

"You know I can't let you back in there."

"You have to. Cosgrove's in there."

"You mean the guy you're after?"

"Yeah."

Simbik frowned. "If he's in there, why'd you go after the other guy?"

"I didn't know he was in there at that point. I just saw him as you graciously escorted me out."

"It's dark in there, man. Maybe you just thought it was him. The shadows and lighting can really mess with your vision. Trust me. I go home with a headache at least twice a week."

"I saw him. You have to believe me."

Simbik sighed. "Yeah, yeah, I do." He frowned. "But I can't let you back in. I'm sorry."

I knew it was no good arguing. If history taught me anything, it was that Turks stuck to their decisions. Especially Turks named Simbik. I wasn't getting back inside.

"OK, but watch that guy. He's the one by the door at the exit here. He's dangerous."

"Yeah, I heard you the first time." Simbik turned back to the club door. "Be good, Lawson."

I watched him knock on the door and then disappear into the club. Back into the pulsating darkness. And the danger within.

Three

I'm not crazy about setbacks. They disrupt the flow of things and I'm a big fan of flow. So when Simbik put his foot down and forbade me reentrance to the club, I hoofed it around to the front and flagged a cab down. I slid into the backseat and handed the driver a $50 bill through the supposedly bullet-resistant Plexiglas.

"Where to?"

"Nowhere. How much wait time does a fifty buy me?"

"Make it a C note and you get 'bout an hour. 'Less of course a hot blonde offers me sex. That case, you're history."

"Fair enough." I slid another bill through.

He took the two fifties, turned the meter off, and picked up the paper next to him on the seat.

I leaned back against the vinyl and sighed. Always did hate surveillance. It was mind-numbing boredom, plain and simple. Let me tell you, it wasn't like Hollywood out here in reality. Joe Blow Detective did not roll up on a stakeout, have a burger and a cola, and only wait five minutes before his mark came out.

What a laugh. Even for me, caffeine ran through

my system like water through an open hand. And the wait was always, repeat, always long.

My watch read 1:05 A.M. An hour would just cover the mass exodus from the clubs. When Cosgrove would make his move.

Pangs of hunger gnawed at my insides. Despite the meal McKinley and I shared earlier. Despite the candy bar I'd had on the way down here . . .

I was hungry.

But business came first. I could always eat later. In this town, if you knew where to look, you could always find something to eat. Even if you had to hit an all-night convenience store.

I could see myself in the cabbie's rearview mirror. What a sight. The years were really starting to take their toll. Oh, not that *you* could tell, but I could. Stay around this damnable planet long enough and things began to take root on your face. The small crow's-feet clawed at my eyes. Even a second chin was trying to gain a beachhead. I might actually start looking middle-aged soon.

Youth was always a prize for me. For us. We all needed it. We all desired it. Those born into the society craved it like some young teenager on a first-time heroin high. Second only to the life force a mother could give, the need for youth was paramount.

It wasn't all about vanity. Never had been, despite what'd been written. Youth held the keys to our power. Our magnetism. Our success as a people.

It didn't come easily, though, especially nowadays. Everyone was into liposuction, plastic surgery, and whatever else they could do to try to keep the unstoppable assault of time from happening.

It made it real hard to find someone genuine.

Someone you could borrow from.

Well, that's what I called it. It was a lot more politically correct to say "borrow" as opposed to "suck the blood of."

We were, after all, scarcely noticed by human society. We blinked in and out of your lives as easily as you drew a breath. We were the darkness on the edge of your peripheral vision, the flash of light speeding past you. We were apex predators; we were invisible.

Except when nut jobs like Cosgrove came into town and threatened our anonymity by draining their victims of every ounce of precious fluid.

We didn't require all that much to sustain ourselves. And we didn't always go for the neck. A bad hangnail would do in a pinch. It was a lot less romantic to be sure, but it got the job done with little notice. It was a lot harder trying to explain bite marks on the neck; although with the S/M crowd, it was easier than it once was. But easier only if you were into the kink of that whole scene.

I'm not.

Maybe I was old-fashioned sexually, but the things that turned me on were beautiful women in nice lingerie. Especially thigh-highs. And two were always better than one. But that was it. I was not into seeing how much metal I could spear through my body or how much candle wax I could scald my skin with. And don't even mention animals. Christ.

So for a supposed prude like me, the hunting could get scarce sometimes. But I always made do.

Even if I didn't particularly care for it. Yeah, you heard me right. I wasn't really into the whole process. I didn't have a choice, of course. But it was like when you were a little kid and had to eat your vegetables. You didn't want to, but you did anyway. Had to grow up big and strong after all.

It's funny how time flies when you're thinking about something else. My hundred bucks ran out just as the first wave of drunken clubgoers tumbled out the doors, spilling onto the damp asphalt like so much candy from a piñata.

I gave the cab up to two guys who would probably need a crowbar to pry themselves apart within an hour and headed across the street, wading into the frenzied, albeit sluggish, mass.

The sirens interrupted my concentration. Two cop cars and an ambulance were trying to part the sea of limousines and taxis clogging Landsdowne Street. They eventually succeeded, and as they drew near, I knew Cosgrove'd already struck. I was too late.

I whirled around, frantically scanning the crowd for him. I knew he'd stay around. Cosgrove was a huge fan of his work. And if he'd spotted me, in fact, he'd do it just for spite. But he was nowhere that I could see.

The ambulance stopped and the paramedics dragged a gurney into the club. No defibrillator unit. It was like they already knew it was no use trying to revive what couldn't be brought back. Five minutes later they reemerged with a sheet-covered body.

It was then that I caught a snippet of conversation among the security crew of the club. And what I heard made me approach the paramedics and stop them.

I drew the sheet back.

Simbik's vacant eyes stared at me from beyond the curtain of death.

Then . . . laughter.

I turned. Across the street. Cosgrove. He laughed so softly no one else heard him. No one but me. He smiled and waved me on.

Then he ran.

I chased him down the rain-slicked, darkened streets. We ran past the office-supply store. Past one side of Fenway Park, where the Red Sox played baseball, sometimes badly. Our feet made no noise as we skirted broken beer bottles, used condoms, and an odd syringe. Cosgrove seemed to skip away from me with ease, but he always stayed just close enough to tease me. I hated him all the more for that. After all, he'd just fed and the vital energy coursing through his system made him stronger than me at the time.

But he'd killed a friend of mine and I was hoping my wrath would sustain me even when the last drop of Simbik's vitality was burned in the furnace of Cosgrove's dementia.

We spilled onto Brookline Avenue, down near the old Sears building that was vacant pending renovation and some new construction. They wanted to turn it into another useless shopping mall.

Cosgrove turned and smiled at me through the darkness; then he streaked toward the battered hulk of the building, leaped, and crashed through a window two stories up.

I didn't follow.

One of Cosgrove's specialties was ambushes. He was a downright sneaky bastard, and before I'd known any better, I had had the pleasure of firsthand experience. I don't like repeating mistakes; I made my entrance on the ground level.

It was dark outside.

Inside the building was an absolute abyss, a dank black hole void of light, and, thanks to Cosgrove, it was absolutely awash in unspeakable evil.

And sound.

Primarily high-pitched squeaks.

I've never liked rats. And at that moment I was in the giant Port Authority of ratdom.

They squealed and squeaked as I waded through their numbers. Sweat ran down every inch of my body as they searched for exposed bits of skin to nibble. Their coarse skin brushed against me as they swirled in undulating waves of mammalian pestilence against my jeans. One of them got caught in the cuff of my jeans and tried to run up my leg but failed and tumbled back out into his brethren.

It was all I could do not to retch and pass out.

I finally made it to the stairs, shaking and kicking off the last of my furry passengers. It took me a minute of solid heaving to catch my breath. Finally, I climbed the steps. Slowly.

A voice dripped down from high above.

"If memory serves me correctly, Lawson, you hate rats. You must be in agony right now."

The bastard wasn't far off the mark, but I shoved on. I was determined to finish that business there, that night. If not to spare any more innocent lives, then only to avenge Simbik. He may not have ever realized what I was, or maybe he did, but he was a friend all the same. Now he was dead. Murdered at the hands of a man I should have killed a long time ago. If I hadn't failed back then, Simbik would still be alive.

I stopped on the fifth floor. The stairs went no higher. In the darkness my vision let me see as clearly as a cat, but nothing stirred amid the old pipes and exposed girders. Paper littered the ground, covering mounds of dead roaches. A stale pile of human excrement still tickled the air, testimony to the vagabonds who used this building.

But no Cosgrove.

I scoured the entire floor and only on my second go-round did I notice the door that read ROOF. Without hesitating, I opened it and went up.

At the top an open door creaked as the night breezes caused it to sway back and forth. I timed my arrival to when the door was at its greatest aperture and stepped onto the roof.

Boston's skyline sparkled all around me and the neon CITGO sign in Kenmore Square burned like a sun in the darkness, casting shadows even in the blackness of night.

Cosgrove was there.

And he chose not to hide.

"Age is slowing you down, Lawson."

He stood at the edge of the roof, draped in expensive black silks that rippled like muscles in the breezes swirling around us. I felt like a peasant in my jeans and turtleneck compared to the luxury of the finery Cosgrove bathed his body in.

He turned, facing the city. "Time was, you would have followed me through that second-floor window without a moment's hesitation. Now you amble up steps like a man with no more spirit."

"Time was, I believed in the Tooth Fairy and Santa Claus too. Look where those got me." I looked around. "Last time I followed you head-on, I almost lost my life."

He laughed. "You speak like a human, always have. You're a vampire. Seems to me you've always had a problem accepting that. You even have human friends."

" 'Had' might be a better word for it, thanks to you."

He turned then, and he seemed somewhat surprised by that last remark. Then it dawned on him. "My, my, he was your friend. . . . How utterly delicious! You must be awfully sore with me right now, eh?"

"Actually, I'm just here because I enjoy the profound pleasure of your company."

He let that pass and smiled, teeth gleaming in the night air. "Admit it, Lawson, you want to kill me so bad every ounce of your being is obsessed by it."

"You're just another job, Cosgrove."

"Rubbish! I've never been just a job to you. You might be able to carry that cavalier attitude off with some of your other sanctions. But this is me." He smiled again. "And we do go so far back. Our delicious history still inspires me to this day."

"You're wrong. You're just another termination handed down by the Council."

"To hell with the Council! Nothing but a pathetic group of weaklings. They've kept our people hidden like rats, always in the shadows, feeding off the scraps of this world. We are a noble race. We're entitled to more. If they were strong, we would rule this world on our terms instead of merely existing in the background! We would own the planet!"

"And there'd be no Balance and chaos would erupt." I sighed. "We'd be destroyed."

"Not if it were handled properly. By the right man."

"And, of course, that'd be you, right?"

He nodded, casting his arms out as though about to hug the world. "Yes. I am the chosen one. It's true. I know exactly what to do." He cocked his head to one side. "Do you know what it's like to be born a messiah but have no way of realizing your potential? It's like you can see everything that needs to be done, but these silly laws—these pathetic anachronisms—keep you from accomplishing anything. And your dreams, your hopes for the people you've been chosen to lead, they shrivel up and crumple like so much dust in the wind."

"Sounds tragic."

"It's gut-wrenching. Believe me. I know." He shook his head. "And you know what the worst part is?"

"I'm sure you'll tell me."

"The worst part is knowing that you're right. That your cause is like a holy crusade to right the wrongs, to reverse the injustices wrought by so much arrogance. And yet, everywhere you turn, you're accused of being insane, off your rocker, a nut job. You're persecuted for your ambition." He looked at me. "Even hunted."

"You're right." It was time to end this.

"Of course I am. You know, Lawson, I could use a man like you in my organization. Old times aside, seriously. You're strong. Hardened. A pretty decent fighter. Not as good as me of course, but decent all the same. You'd be a big help. What do you say? Join the cause. Help me lead our people into the light. Take them to their rightful rule."

"Never been a real big fan of Megalomania Incorporated, Cosgrove."

He frowned. "Such a bloody snob, you are. Do you remember how you and the rest of those sorry sods at school used to tease me, Lawson? Do you remember those days? Did it feel good to feel so powerful?"

"We were just kids, Cosgrove. Besides, you eventually got your revenge."

"And so sweet it was." He smiled. "Sure you won't join me?"

I reached behind my right hip. "I've already got a job."

Simbik must have been good stock because his life force gave Cosgrove some amazing energy. He moved so fast even I didn't see it.

But I felt it.

Especially when he landed on me from above, driving his feet down into my stomach as he crashed down. My wind rushed out of me, knocking me senseless.

Cosgrove rolled off and laughed. "Now, what is this little toy you were going to use on me?"

I reached behind, but it was gone. He'd fleeced my weapon off me and now he was standing two meters away fiddling with it.

"A gun, is it? An ordinary gun?" He shook his head and he reminded me of one of my old grammar-school teachers. "Really, Lawson, as if this trifling piece of human machinery could dispatch me."

"It's been modified." I looked around, searching the roof for cover but there was little except for some old pipes, lumber, and a mass of old newspapers.

"Really? How so?" He turned the gun over in his hands until it pointed at me. "Explain it to me."

"The rounds are different." If I could get him to examine the magazine, it might just buy me enough time.

Cosgrove was enjoying himself. He thumbed the hammer back on the gun. "And what makes this ammunition so special?"

I tried to stand, but he merely kicked me in the solar plexus, knocking me across the roof like I'd been some pesky mosquito. I crashed into a pile of damp newspapers and splintering lumber and lay there, trying hard to catch my wind. I gasped and retched.

"What kind of loads does it take?" he said again.

I grimaced, feeling some measure of control come back over my breathing. "The bullet tips aren't metal. They're wooden."

"Ah, the twenty-first-century adaptation on the old stake-through-the-heart bit." He fondled the gun some more. "So this is the infamous Fixer gun I've always heard about. Interesting. Does it usually just take one bullet?"

"Depends on the individual."

He sighted down the barrel and I knew he had the damned thing locked onto my heart. "And just how many shots do you think it would take to kill you right now?"

"Way I'm feeling? You could probably do the job with a damned toothpick."

Cosgrove laughed and lowered the gun. "Ah, Lawson, you always were a card. You haven't fed in a while, have you?"

"Nope."

Cosgrove straightened and tilted his head back, licking his lips, tasting the night air as if it were some sweet nectar of the gods. "He was delicious, you know. Your friend, I mean. Absolutely exquisite. Did you know he must have had some Carpathian in his blood?"

"Turkish. He was Turkish."

Cosgrove nodded. "Close enough." He leaned closer, drawing down the distance between us so subtly I could barely even sense it. His voice became a mere whisper, or was he inside my head?

"Would you like a taste?"

"What?"

He pierced his forefinger. Crimson flowed from it, beading first on the pad, then dribbling down the length of his finger. "Taste him, taste your friend. It's customary, of course, your last meal and all."

Watching the blood made my mouth drown in saliva. I was starving for it. My energy was shot. Cosgrove knew this. Enjoyed this.

Slowly, I reached for his hand.

He held it aloft, watching and allowing the precious blood to pool before gravity began to exert itself on the first drop.

And in that instant I lashed out with a kick to his other hand, sending the pistol clattering off the edge of the roof. I followed by tackling Cosgrove and kneeing him sharply in the groin. We might have been vampires, but we weren't undead. We still felt pain. And Cosgrove grunted audibly as I slammed my knee into him a second and third time.

But he recovered fast and was on his feet even as I mounted another attack. He sidestepped my punch and used my momentum to send me hurtling against the rooftop again. I crashed and came to a stop. Totally spent.

Cosgrove licked his finger. "You ungrateful bastard. I would have let you die honorably."

"Get it over with Cosgrove. I'm not in the mood for your damned orations."

"Death is such an easy release, Lawson. Trust me; I've sent enough people there. It's quick. Too quick. And far too painless for the likes of you." He shook his head. "But now . . . Now I think I'll leave you alive for a little while more. I imagine it will annoy you to no end to have me hunting in your neighborhood."

"You annoy me just being alive."

"I'm sure." Cosgrove smiled. "Tell me, are you a sporting soul?"

My wind was coming back. "What the hell does that mean?"

"Well, let's make it interesting, shall we? Let's see how good a Fixer you truly are. Let's see if you can catch me. And, dare I say it, kill me?"

Laughing, he stood over me and looked down at his finger. "So nice," he murmured as he squeezed his finger, causing the blood to pool once again.

I watched him turn his finger slowly, and in the darkness I saw a single drop of blood fall, cross the infinity of night, then hit my lips like salvation from a god. My tongue shot out instinctively, licking the globule off my lips. Even as the first coppery taste crossed my tongue, my whole body trembled with desire. Saliva flooded my mouth. I needed more. So much more.

"I'll enjoy this immensely, Lawson. Good night."

Then he was gone.

The challenge had been issued. The gauntlet dropped.

And, even as I lay starving.

Famished.

Ravenous.

I knew I had no choice but to accept.

Four

McKinley's mood was as low as the limbo pole at a midget fiesta. "What do you mean, you missed?"

I cradled the telephone with my shoulder while I took another sip of juice from my private reserve. Well, I preferred to call it juice. You can call it blood if you're that kind of sick bastard who likes to imagine how wonderful it is to find nourishment in the life force of human beings. Me, it was difficult enough just keeping it down. After close to 135 years, I was still wrestling with this whole thing.

My energy was waxing again, which was good. Damned good, in fact. God knows I was a spent unit on that roof. I took another sip and cleared my throat. "Just what I said." I took a long drag. "I almost died up there, you know."

There was a pause and I knew McKinley would be doing his usual rip-a-tuft-of-hair-out-of-his-head-whenever-the-news-was-bad routine. I gave him the moment.

"Did he say anything?"

That brought me up short. So much for my Control being concerned about my health. "Yeah, we talked about the price of pork-belly futures. What the hell do you mean, did he say anything?"

"It's just that with Cosgrove, you know it's always something. He's always on the soapbox."

"Soapbox? When'd you get to be such an expert on his behavioral patterns?"

"I've been listening to you for the past six years, haven't I?"

"I been bitching that much?"

"Like a sorority house on a communal rag."

I sighed. "The only thing I got out of him was that he was going to enjoy pissing me off to no end while he leaves a trail of shriveled bodies around town. That and his usual take-over-the-world routine. Same old Cosgrove. Same old psychopathic bastard." I put the bottle down. "Damn it, McKinley, I warned the Council this would happen."

"Yeah, you did. But you also missed when they gave you the OK to hit him."

"Sue me. It won't happen again."

McKinley sighed. "I assume you'll be hunting him full-time?"

Jesus Christ. "Of course I am. What do you think I'm gonna kick back and forget I nearly died on some shitty rooftop?" I sighed. "I won't miss again."

"Good, keep me informed."

The phone went dead before I could throw another witty insult down the line. That was fine with me. I needed some sleep.

I recorked the wine bottle. Just looking at it, you'd never guess the contents. If anyone asked, I told them I preferred my red wine chilled. I slid it back into my fridge and washed the glass so it wouldn't dry with the stains in it. You never knew when company might come over. Besides, dried

bloodstains on glassware is a bitch to get clean.
And paper cups are out. Bloody cups draw all sorts
of four-legged nocturnal scavengers. If my trash
gets strewn across the street courtesy of a ravenous
raccoon family, I'll have a lot of explaining to do
to the neighbors.

Bedtime.

Now, I should explain that as far as being what
I am, I am required to get an inordinate amount
of sleep. You can, however, forget that sunlight
stuff. It just isn't so. Might have been once, I never
checked. But you show me one species that absolutely has to remain hidden from the sun, and I'll
show you that same species extinct within two generations. Unless they happen to live five miles under the ocean.

We've adapted, you see. Sunlight, while not the
most comfortable thing (you could liken it to the
experience a lot of albinos have), can nevertheless
be tolerated.

Personally, I work better at night.

Luckily for me, so did Cosgrove.

Christ, if he was a nine-to-fiver, I sure as hell
wouldn't be getting to him today.

I crawled into bed and clucked twice for my cats.
Like attracts like. Both of my girls were hunters.
Pure and true. I got them at the local shelter since
I could never bring myself to pay for a pet when
there were lots of great animals out there that
needed a home before they got euthanatized.

Mimi arrived first. She looked like Chewbacca on
a bad hair day, and I was sure she had some coon
cat a short way back up the family line. She was
big, but she carried it well. And best of all, she was
silent.

Phoebe came second, announcing herself with her characteristic chirp. A silver tabby with two pounds of extra weight swaying beneath her every time she walked, she was smaller than Mimi, but a helluva lot noisier. It was like no one had ever taught her how to land quietly. Listening to Phoebe jump down from something was like listening to a bag of bricks fall off a building.

Mimi tried in vain to claim my pillow, gave up after five minutes of using her head to ram into my skull, and settled down by my feet whereupon she engaged in aerobic-style self-cleansing. Phoebe, the tunnel rat, immediately dove under the covers, where she would remain for most of the day until I woke up.

One hundred and thirty-five years isn't old for a vampire. Compared to some of the others in Boston, I was just getting my feet under me. To me, it felt like I was approaching middle age. You think you've got it tough when you start noticing those good looks you had in college deserting you like rats on the *Titanic*? Try being a vampire sometime. It sucks.

Simply put, we've always been around. Like I said earlier about the whole shark thing: just because you can't see 'em doesn't mean they aren't there. Same thing goes for us. And especially since we'd adapted to the sunlight thing, you noticed us even less than before.

Oh, sure, there were the luminaries. We had that Vlad the Impaler guy. Man, what a freak. I mean, I needed juice to survive on, but let's do it in moderation, shall we? Old Vlad there was reminiscent of a Roman orgy the way he drank it down. You know the way some of you look at *really* obese people and shake your heads? That's the way I looked at folks like Vlad.

So we've always been a part of your society inasmuch as we're here. But we're separate from you. You could liken it to Orthodox Jews. Together but separate.

It's a homogenous society. It has to be. Our survival depends absolutely upon it. No interbreeding with humans. Too many things go awry and you get weird offspring that usually have to be exterminated. Besides, for the most part vampire semen and mortal female eggs don't get along and vice versa.

Sex is OK, just not impregnation. Sex is allowed because it helps us secure sustenance.

Love, though—that's strictly forbidden. Taboo. The ultimate sin in the vampire community. Needless to say, I've never had a problem adhering to that one.

So my folks were both vampires as well.

It was a strange thing for a kid to grow up with.

Different schools and everything.

Don't even get me started on my prom. Good God. It was like *Carrie* meets the bar mitzvah boys. One part bloodbath, one part coming of age, ten parts shit awful.

Somewhere down the line, between when you first start teething—that was when we hit puberty and the fangs come on out—and graduation, you visit with the Council. They're a group of older vampires who govern our society. Locally and internationally. Most of us as kids considered them a bunch of old fogies. No one had really ever paid much mind to them before our initial meeting.

They determined what part we'd play in the society. Some of us hold down ordinary jobs, some school the children, some are historians and monastics, and a few . . . very few, in fact . . . end up like yours truly.

At my meeting with the Council, I was led down a long hallway, then was brought in to face them, put through a weird set of tests that judged my reaction time, probed my responses to various stimuli, and was asked a bizarre set of questions. Mostly, they were about the history of the vampiric world and what the old values meant to me. I answered them honestly, saying that while I felt they were important, they sometimes seemed a little trivial.

When they were done with the questions, they brought out a series of objects and asked me to pick the one that I liked the best. On a simple tray with a bright crimson cloth were placed a small statue of a bull, a tiny silver dagger, a gold necklace, and a set of scales. I thought the scales looked kind of cool, so I chose them.

It brought a smile to their faces. It also garnered me my profession. The scales were the symbol of my new role.

We're called Fixers. Mainly because it's our job to make sure the Balance, the delicate, tenuous coexistence between the vampires and the humans, remains unbroken. Undetected. And if it gets thrown out of whack, we make it right.

Or we try to make it right. Having a royal ass like Cosgrove around tends to make things a little difficult.

Regardless, I'm a Fixer. Guess it sounds a little more humane than vampire hit man.

I've been working for thirty-five years now. Ever since I hit my centennial, which might be equivalent to your college graduation. That's when we go out into the real world and make something of ourselves. As subtly as possible, of course.

Thirty-five years is enough time, in my humble opinion, to suggest that humans have a helluva lot of problems, not including the Cosgrove situation. Between the constant murders, road rage, terrorism, and even the apocalyptic repercussions disco music will eventually cause, it amazes me sometimes.

Suffice it to say, and in case you haven't guessed by now, I'm a bit of a cynic.

Most folks think I'm a cop.

Except I don't have a weight problem from eating too many doughnuts. Yeah, I know it's a stereotype. But come with me over to the Dunkin' Donuts outside of Porter Square, and I'll show you exactly how stereotypes get started. Christ, it's got to be the safest place in America, what with all those cop cruisers and ambulances parked outside.

Mimi finished her calisthenics and began snoring. It seemed like a good idea, so I followed suit. After all, if I was going to kill Cosgrove, I'd need all the strength I could get.

Five

Monday morning dawned gray. The sky looked bloated with puffy clouds filled with the kind of cold spitting rain that makes November notorious. I watched the rain streak my bedroom windows in lazy downward rivulets and sighed. Definitely not the kind of morning I like to get out of bed.

But I had to.

Because before I resumed my hunt for Cosgrove, I had some other business to tend to. Personal business.

Showered and shaved, I went to my closet and took a long glance at the shirts and suits hanging there. Myself, I don't like the garb of corporate America. Suits are too confining for my taste and fighting in them is a royal pain in the ass. Still, there are times when I need them to blend in and do my work. And because of that, I chose my outfit with conservative care. Twenty minutes later found me dressed in a charcoal gray suit, white shirt, and navy tie with small polka dots maneuvering my way down South Huntington Avenue and onto Huntington Avenue proper.

The Eastern Orthodox church sat down near the bottom of Mission Hill, close to Northeastern University and the Wentworth Institute of Technology. Its architecture stood out from the sleek modern and decidedly American lines of the buildings nearby. A domed roof hinted vaguely toward Islamic influences and the heavy wooden doors seemed carved from giant redwoods. The sheer weight of its appearance was reinforced by the manicured green playing field nearby, almost as if city planners hadn't wanted to build anything else too close for fear of causing a sinkhole.

I was surprised the service was being held in this church instead of a mosque. I supposed Simbik's family was one of the few holdovers from the Eastern Orthodox influence of Turkey.

Inside the darkened church, the scent of myrrh and frankincense cloaked the air like a mist. I breathed in, feeling a little light-headed, and at the same time, the spiritual significance of this holy place washed over me.

Conservative thinkers tend to argue that as vampires we are at opposite ends of the religious spectrum from humans. As such, we can be dispatched with crosses, holy water, and the like.

That's not really the case.

Sure, some of the really twisted folks in the past may have fallen under those weapons, but by and large, vampires tend toward a very spiritual belief system. And it's not one focused on Satanism either. We're very much into leading a community-centered existence that benefits everyone, including the humans we coexist with. But we have our legends. We have our ancient superstitions. I'm not really big on them, but others, like an old friend of mine, make a hobby out of studying them, learning the old ways, and passing them down to the young kids. Me? I flunked ancient vampire history in school.

That said, crosses and churches don't really bother me at all. And I can gargle or chug as much holy water as I want to without any ill effects. To kill me, you've got to stake my heart and then cut my head off. That's it.

I sat in one of the back pews and watched the service. An Eastern Orthodox priest spoke in deep, resonating tones, his voice finding every niche within the confines of the church. The focus of his sermon, a brown mahogany coffin draped in a beautiful tapestry woven rich with burgundy and yellow silken hues, sat nearby.

Inside, Simbik's deflated body rested eternally more.

As I said before, I don't have many friends.

And even fewer are humans.

Simbik was an exception.

We understood each other on levels you can't easily fathom. He may never have known I was a vampire. He may never have cared what I was. But he always seemed to know there was something different about me. Just as I knew he was different himself.

Perhaps that's what drew us together.

I'd only ever seen Simbik's parents once before when they flew into Boston to surprise Simbik at work. I think they respected Simbik as much as I did for trying to forge his own path in life without relying on their wealth to sustain him. Their pride was obvious.

They must have flown in yesterday.

Simbik's father knelt with his head down. Every ounce of bodily control seemed exerted on not showing any emotion. At his left side Simbik's mother wept in controlled sobs that would not dishonor her son. Turks are an extremely proud people.

But there was someone else here too. To the left of Simbik's mother.

A woman.

I never recalled Simbik telling me he'd had a sister. So who was she? It was tough to see much about her beyond the confines of the lightweight black lace veil she wore on her head, draped slightly to conceal her eyes.

But even from this distance, I could sense her presence.

Japanese call it *"hara,"* the physical point about two inches below your navel. But on a much higher level, it refers to the presence of your being—physically, mentally, and spiritually—the total of them combined to make you what you are. People with a strong *hara* could walk into a room and everyone would feel the presence. Westerners try to brush it off as just having a strong personality, but as usual, they fall far short of its full ramifications.

This woman's *hara* was more than strong. It was almost tangible.

It was at that precise moment she straightened slightly and turned her head back in my direction.

Have you ever been caught looking at someone and when they pick it up and catch you, you feel as sheepish as a schoolboy looking at his first girl?

Well, that's precisely how I felt at that moment.

But I didn't look away. Instead, I inclined my head vaguely out of respect. When I brought it back up, she was still staring.

It was, no doubt, her eyes that made the impact.

Dark and luminous, they looked like the polished chestnuts I used to collect as a kid. She'd been crying too. I could tell even from my distance. But it was something else within her eyes that piqued my interest. An inner strength seemed to radiate out from her. Almost a predatorial presence.

She was a hunter.

And a good one at that.

But human.

She held my gaze, which isn't easy to do. It goes back to that whole magnetism thing that helps me secure my sustenance. I can pretty much talk a nun out of her underwear if I want to.

This woman, whoever she was, didn't flinch at all.

And all the while she held my gaze, I could feel her probing and searching me out. Was I friend or foe? Was I responsible for Simbik's death? Was I a threat to the sanctity of this funeral?

All of this rolled through my head in the space of a few seconds and then stopped just as fast as she resumed her position by turning around toward the front of the church once again.

It was only then I noticed I'd stopped breathing.

With the service concluded, I moved out of the pew toward the front of the church and stood in front of Simbik's casket. I placed a hand solemnly on the polished mahogany and closed my eyes, wishing him a final farewell.

"You're Lawson."

The words interrupted my silent homage and quickened my pulse. I opened my eyes and turned to see her standing before me. She didn't look Turkish at all.

Asian.

I must have frowned, because she smiled slightly. "Simbik told me about you. He didn't mention many people. You must have been good friends."

I paused, still looking at her. "We . . . understood each other, I think."

She nodded. "Simbik didn't have many friends to speak of."

"Good ones are harder to find than most people realize."

"Indeed." She was searching with her eyes again.

I looked down at the casket and shook my head. "I'll miss him."

"As will I."

I looked up. "Forgive me, miss, but what gives you that right?"

She began walking away from the casket toward the exit. "Let's leave this to the attendants now, shall we?"

I followed, and only after we'd exited the church, standing under the overhang still sheltered from the rain, did she turn around, take a deep breath, and offer me her hand.

"Talya."

"Sister or cousin?" I shook her hand, surprised at the flexible strength it seemed to contain.

She smiled and it was radiant despite her obvious grief. "Neither. His fiancée."

Fiancée? I'd never known Simbik to even have a girlfriend. Aside from an occasional warm body in his bed, he led a solitary existence. "I'm sorry; I had no idea."

She shrugged. "It wasn't really something he would have publicized." She sighed. "Honestly, it wasn't exactly a mad love affair."

I decided not to ask. "But you're not Turkish."

"No."

"Asian," I said. "But not from the Far East." I looked at her cheekbones. "Mongolian, possibly from the Kirgiz Steppes—"

"Not bad."

"I'm close," I said. "But not entirely."

"Not entirely. My mother was from Oskemen. In Kazakhstan. My father was Chinese."

"Kazakhstan, at the end of the old Silk Road. You grew up among some incredible mountain vistas, eh?"

She seemed surprised. "The Altai Mountains, yes. Not many people are familiar with that part of the world."

"It's remote," I said. "Some would say desolate. Lonely." I shrugged. "I prefer raw."

"Yes. Raw describes the land well. You've been?"

"My life has provided me with plenty of opportunities to travel. I was there once. A long time ago."

"We might have met."

"Possibly. But I'm afraid my business kept me from enjoying the region's hospitality for long."

"There's always tomorrow, then. Another day."

I smiled. "Your English is superb. No discernible trace of an accent—any accent, for that matter."

"I was . . . well schooled."

I nodded. "And you sure got here quickly. Kazakhstan is quite a ways away. Probably take you at least twenty-four hours of travel time to get here."

She turned, facing toward Huntington Avenue. "I was nearby. New York, actually. I caught the shuttle up this morning."

Something in the tone of her voice made me wonder exactly what she'd been doing in New

York. Hunting? It was possible, given the way she carried herself. It wasn't too obvious, but more subtle than anything else. And it was that subtlety that made me think she might be a professional. I just couldn't prove it.

Yet.

The rain increased as the pallbearers filed past us, ushering Simbik's coffin into the black hearse at the foot of the steps. In a few minutes it would be laid to rest in a nearby cemetery.

"Are you going to the burial site?"

I shook my head. "Cemeteries depress me. I've said too many good-byes before. Simbik's memory is strong with me. I'll grieve in my own way."

It was then she narrowed her eyes and focused another laser-intense gaze on me. It took her a few seconds of standing there, one foot on a higher step than the other. Rain pelted her gray coat, sliding south before slipping off to the cement below. Then she took a small breath and expelled it all at once.

"You know who killed him."

Her intuition must have been incredible—judging by the way she seemed to trust it. I was shocked, to say the least. And that takes a lot.

For some reason, unknown even to me, I answered.

"Yes."

She came closer. And suddenly seemed a lot more dangerous. Gone was the fact that she was Simbik's grieving betrothed. Gone was the proper and attractive woman I'd noticed in the front pew of the church.

In its place stood someone who operated on a

much more primal level. Talya had switched modes and become the predator I knew she truly was.

A wiser man would have been scared.

But wisdom's never been one of my strengths.

I was intrigued.

"Who did this?" It was more of a hiss than a question. She reminded me of a panther.

Trust me when I tell you that for her to have this kind of effect on a vampire—on a Fixer of all things—she must have been something unlike I'd ever known before.

I broke her stare and took a breath, tasted the rain and frowned. November rain never tasted like the freshness of a summer shower. November rain was a placeholder before the snows settled in. November rain held all the death that winter ushered in with it.

"Cosgrove," I said after a moment of introspection. "His name is Cosgrove."

She looked at me. Hell, she hadn't stopped looking at me. Her gaze seemed unshakable.

"Why Simbik?"

I looked at her. "There's no particular reason. He chose Simbik the way you or I choose the air we breathe. Maybe with even less thought than that."

"Killed for no reason?" She shook her head. "Makes no sense."

"Sense doesn't figure into Cosgrove's way of thinking. He kills for his own selfish reasons alone."

"Dead men kill no longer." She turned and hurried down the steps to the black limousine behind the hearse.

"Wait!" I called after her. She stopped, turned, and frowned. Waiting.

"It's not that easy."

"Why?"

I bit down on my inner lip. "He's not exactly an easy mark."

She smiled, but it looked like an empty, vacant smile with no joy in it. "I've heard that before."

"Not like this you haven't. Cosgrove is dangerous. Trust me."

"Why?"

I once knew a girl named Mary who asked "Why?" until she sounded like a broken record. But she was just plain dumb. Talya asked "Why?" with the kind of steadfast confidence usually reserved for people who don't let too many things get in their way.

"Because of Simbik. Because I know Cosgrove." I looked again at the sky. It seemed a lot darker all of a sudden. I looked back at her, weighing the options and deciding in a second. "Because I'm hunting him too."

She nodded. "So we'll hunt him down together."

I shook my head. "Not a chance."

She smiled. "You think maybe I couldn't hold up my end?"

Not against a vampire she couldn't. "It's not that simple."

She frowned again. "Nothing is as difficult as it seems. Why should this be any different?"

"You wouldn't believe me if I told you."

She hesitated. Then another smile. This one curious. "Try me."

So I did.

Six

If surprise was an almost forgotten aspect in my
life, I was making up for lost time today. Contrary
to what I expected, Talya wasn't the least bit
shocked when I told her about Cosgrove's true vo-
cation. In retrospect, I guess I hadn't really expected her to be shocked. She seemed too switched
on to allow that to happen.

Still, I would have thought telling a human about
the existence of vampires wouldn't normally be received with such nonchalance. Talya was rapidly re-
tooling my definition of "normal." Especially when
she skipped the burial to talk to me further.

I revealed it while she drank a cup of black coffee at the Beanery while I sipped some tea. I kept
my own history out of it, of course.

She stayed quiet while I hit the highlights of Cosgrove's illustrious and decidedly bloody career,
seemingly absorbing everything that came out of
my mouth. When I'd finished, she took another sip
of her coffee, put the mug down, wiped her mouth
on the coarse brown napkin, and looked at me.

"How did you find out?"

"I've been hunting him for a while. I know his
style. His preferences." I shrugged. "You can al-

most crawl inside the mind of the killer, isn't that what they say?"

She nodded, but seemed detached momentarily. "I've heard that, yes."

"Well, as much as it disgusts me to crawl around such filth, I've done it. I know him. Well. I wish to hell I didn't."

"You do what you have to, apparently. Makes sense if you are hunting him."

"I am."

"Information is the most valuable of all commodities, Lawson. With the right knowledge, governments can be toppled. A man can be reduced to a mere shell of his former stature. Even driven to suicide." She nodded. "Your information about this Cosgrove is valuable as well. We will use it to kill him."

Something about the way she said it sent a small shiver up my spine. I'd never met someone who could remain so detached about killing, except my fellow Fixers. I cleared my throat. Suddenly, I needed some verbal space to breathe. "Talya's an interesting name. Is it Kazakh?"

"Short for Natalya, actually," she said. "It's fairly common in Russia."

"Gotcha." I watched her stare into the ebony coffee and cleared my throat. "So. Want to tell me exactly what you do for work?"

She looked up, squinting. "What do you mean?"

"What do I mean? Hell, back on the church steps, you told me you'd kill Cosgrove. There was no indecision there. And it wasn't simple revenge naïveté." I took another sip of tea and looked out the window at Huntington Avenue. A bus zoomed by, vomiting dirty sludge out of puddles onto the rain-slicked sidewalk. I watched the water drift back toward the street. "The signs are too obvious."

"Signs?"

I nodded. "Maybe not to anyone else. Maybe not to the people you pass every day on the street. But to me . . ." I let it go and fixed her with a solid stare. "You're a pro."

She said nothing, but just looked at me. Piercing eyes that drew me in.

I broke the stare again. "Who do you work for?"

"No one."

I shook my head. "That's bullshit and you know it."

"I owe allegiance only to myself."

I took another sip of tea, realizing it finally. "A freelancer."

She inclined her head. I sat back, marveling at the woman before me. Like I said before, I've been around for a while. Long enough to learn all about the world of human covert operations. I've read it all, seen a lot of stuff firsthand, heard even more through the grapevine. But never had I ever come into contact with an actual human freelance assassin. Let alone as good a one as I presumed Talya would turn out to be.

Damned if I wasn't having my world tilted on its fucking side today. The revelation that Talya was what she was threw me for a loop. As a general rule of thumb, I don't have much respect for humans. Like I said, she was rapidly becoming an exception to that rule.

"How long have you been solo?"

"Long enough to know my way around."

"You wouldn't have survived without proper

schooling. You must have had formal training somewhere."

She shrugged. "I was employed once, by the Russians."

"KGB?"

"Yes. I was an illegal."

I nodded. The KGB had run illegals—their deep undercover agents—and penetrated them into the West. Some of them had gathered intelligence; others had orchestrated whole networks; a few select illegals had engaged in wet work.

Assassination.

I had no doubts what line of work Talya had been in and said as much. She nodded.

"I aspired to it."

"You wanted to kill?"

Talya smiled. "There was a sense of prestige associated with it. I don't know if you have read about the Soviet intelligence apparatus?"

"Some."

"Then you'd know that the two primary gathering organs were the KGB and the GRU."

"Soviet Military Intelligence." The *Glavnoe Razvedovatel'noe Upravlenie.*

"Yes." She took a sip of coffee. "The GRU prided itself on never having killed anyone. Their tactics were designed to keep them forever hidden. With the KGB, it was the exact opposite end of the spectrum. We used whatever tactics we could to get what we needed. We tortured, blackmailed, bought and stole our way into the biggest secrets of the West. And when all else failed . . . if someone crossed us . . . we killed."

"You operated alone?"

She shrugged. "Depended on the assignment.

But the pride of killing for your country helps take the sting out of what you actually do. I saw it as doing my national duty."

Something about that sounded vaguely familiar. I smiled. The irony of life could kill you if it didn't make you laugh first.

She smiled with me. "I saw a movie over here once back in the early 1980s. One of the characters said to another that 'professional assassination is the highest form of public service.' I took that to heart in my work."

"Interesting quote. What about after the Berlin Wall came down?"

"I went freelance after glasnost. I worked globally."

"Forgive me for asking, but what did Simbik think of your profession?"

She smiled. "He never knew. As I said, my mother was from Kazakhstan and my father was Chinese. If you know the region, you understand the borders are quite close."

"Yes."

"My father was the local Chinese commander for troops based at Karamay. Every so often, they would stage a lightning raid across the border."

"Chinese incursions into the Soviet Union?"

She nodded. "Don't seem so shocked. It happened on both sides with a degree of regularity." She took a sip of coffee. "My father was a Chinese platoon leader. He raped my mother." She shrugged. "I was the result."

I was speechless. Being the child of a rape victim isn't the kind of thing most folks would share with you. Talya didn't seem fazed by it.

"I've made peace with the fact that I was a bastard child, Lawson. If that's what you're thinking."

"It was."

She smiled. "You're honest. That's good." She took another sip of her coffee. "I could have handled it the way people nowadays do. I could wail and moan about being a victim. I could cry myself to sleep every night of my life. Doesn't change a damned thing. You can't change the past no matter how hard you try, you know?"

My tea tasted cold and my stomach ached. "Yeah, I know something about that."

"So it came down to either living in the pain or forging ahead with my life. I chose the latter. And I've almost never looked back."

"Almost never?"

"I looked back once. Let's leave it at that."

"So how did you meet Simbik?"

She smiled as if granting me the right to change the subject. "I met him once when I was fifteen, on a state-sponsored school trip to Istanbul. He saved my life."

"He did?"

She tilted her head, remembering. "One of those crazy bus drivers, you know? I was lagging behind in my school group, distracted by the sights, and never saw the silly thing bearing down on me."

"And Simbik did."

She nodded. "Yanked me out of the way. When my mother found out, she wrote to Simbik's family and promised me to him as his wife."

"Pretty old-fashioned, wouldn't you say?" I motioned for the waitress to refill my tea.

She smiled. "My mother was like that. She so wanted her only daughter to have a proper marriage and a decent family. I think she felt like she'd somehow gypped me of that by not having a father."

"Wasn't her fault."

"Of course not," she said. "But a lot of rape victims somehow get convinced it is their fault. It's not, but something happens during the trauma."

"And you went along with the arrangement?"

"When I was younger, I thought it was cool to have a potential husband already. Took a lot of stress out of puberty, you know? Simbik was a charming young man. He sent me pictures and letters regularly. In later life, once I started working for the government, it became a convenient cover for me. I used it."

I took another sip of tea, found it a little bitter and added two more sugar packets. "Did you love him?"

She smiled, almost remembering. "Once, I think I did. But I think we both knew somehow that it wouldn't work. It couldn't work. People nowadays don't follow through on arranged marriages unless they're part of some religious cult. As I said, I saw him once when I was fifteen, a few times after that." She paused. "Then today at the funeral."

"That's a long span of time."

She shrugged. "Today gave me a chance to talk things over with Simbik's family. As soon as I find Simbik's killer, I can concentrate on my job again."

"Interesting line of work you've got for yourself."

"You're one to talk." She gestured to the waitress for another cup of coffee. "Seems to me that we're cut from the same stone."

Not bloody likely. If she knew what stone I'd

been cut from, she probably would have run. No, check that. She'd probably try to waste me.

Instead, I just smiled. She smiled too. And we sat there smiling at each other like a couple of fools until a fresh cup of steaming blend arrived, breaking our toothpaste commercial.

She took a sip, seemed totally unfazed by the obvious hot contents, and licked her lips slightly. I found it vaguely appealing.

Talya looked at me. "So what do we do about this man Cosgrove?"

" 'We'?" I shook my head. "There's no 'we' in this equation, Talya. This isn't the sort of thing you just pick up like some secondhand recipe out of a magazine. Leave it to me. I'll kill him."

Her eyes crinkled at the edges. "Should I be naive and suggest we contact a priest?"

I smiled again. "Not much good in that. Things are a helluva lot different than the legends you grew up with."

"What makes you such an expert?"

"I've been tracking Cosgrove a long time. I know what will kill him. And it won't be silly superstitions. He can wear crosses with ease, drinks holy water like it's a fine wine, and he eats garlic like a wetback Dago fresh off the boat from Sicily." I sipped my tea. "Make no mistake: Cosgrove is a vicious bastard who can only be killed by ramming a stake into his heart and then hacking his head off. That's it."

She said nothing for a long time. Then she nodded. Slowly.

"Then that's exactly what we'll do."

"Anyone ever tell you you're stubborn?"

"No."

"No?"

"Usually, they just call me a bitch and be done with it. An ambitious, powerful woman is assumed to be menstruating. Silly, isn't it? Equating drive and discipline with an unavoidable monthly biological function. Men are movers and shakers; women are bitches."

"Listen, I don't want to break up this feminist bent you seem to be on, but I don't work with partners. It's no slight on your abilities. I'm sure you can hold your own. But hunting Cosgrove is different from anything you've ever done before."

"Lawson," she said, "I have killed a great many people in my years. Diplomats, spies, assassins, drug kingpins, terrorists, and others. I have seen my life flash before my eyes more times than I care to remember. And I have come across a great many foes who were far stronger than I have ever been. But I beat them all. And I will beat Cosgrove as well. He will pay for killing Simbik."

I finished my tea and set the cup down on the stained napkin. "If you say so, Talya." I fished a tenner out of my pocket and laid it across the bill. "But believe me when I tell you this is a whole new world you are stepping into. Your world of conventions does not apply in it. And if you go in thinking it does and that you're the exception, you will die. It's that simple."

"Then if I die, I will at least take him with me."

I stood up, but she grabbed my hand. "See you on the hunt, Lawson."

"We'll see."

"I'm at the Four Seasons." She cocked one of her eyebrows. "When you change your mind . . ."

Her tone told me she was finished listening to

any reason I might have been able to dredge up. Whether Cosgrove was a vampire or not, Talya was going to kill him. And in her mind, that was enough.

I only hoped it was enough for me too.

Seven

I left Talya sitting at the table and wound my way back to my car parked in the underground garage. I checked my watch—4:00 P.M. About eight o'clock would be a perfect time to go hunting. That's when Cosgrove would emerge on his nocturnal foray again. He was, after all, something of a traditionalist. While he might be able to stand the sun, he liked the night much more. As we all did.

I found myself amused and intrigued simultaneously with the thought of having a partner in the unlikely guise of a human assassin. Even if I'd wanted her along for the ride, there was no way I could justify it. I work alone.

I kill alone.

Part of me wanted to call McKinley and tell him. Hell, it'd be good for a laugh. But I couldn't do that. Interacting with Talya, let alone telling her about the existence of vampires, was verboten.

Made me wonder why I'd even done it.

I'd always loved women. I enjoyed impressing them. I needed to impress them. Part of me felt crushed when they weren't interested in me. Jealousy was something I should have conquered a long time ago. But we all have our faults. And right now, mine was that I wanted to impress Talya.

Somehow I knew that it would take a helluva lot to impress a woman like her. She'd probably seen a ton of stuff I hadn't. And that was saying something.

So maybe if I killed Cosgrove first, that would impress her. Especially since I'd just built the freak up. Or had I? I adjusted the rearview mirror and checked my reflection.

I grinned. *Lawson, you are one desperately lonely dude.*

It was a standing joke with myself. I'd get the hots for some woman and then find ways to get under her skin. I'd think about her nonstop. Total infatuation. Then, of course, I'd never follow through because of who I was and what I was.

In the end it didn't seem like such a joke after all.

I sighed. Monday night. Things would be a little different tonight with the nightclub scene around Boston. Clubs usually perked between Wednesday and Saturday nights. Sunday nights were when most clubs marketed themselves to the gay community. Mondays and Tuesdays were therefore the slim nights. Most of the clubs were closed. Cosgrove would have his field of prospects narrowed down to the bars and pubs. Cosgrove would hunt, but he wouldn't necessarily like it the way he did when he was in a nightclub.

Truth was, even though I'd denied it back on that godforsaken rooftop, Cosgrove would never be just another assignment. Like he said, we went way back. Back before either of us knew what we'd be doing at this point in our lives.

Hell, he'd grown up down the street from me.

If I'd ever had the kind of foresight my parents used to suggest I develop, I would have known back then things would eventually come to this point.

I met Cosgrove on a clear, sunny summer day when his family moved in, freshly transplanted from London. Resettled into a new community of vampires. Sounds like Suburbia meets Bloodbath Avenue, doesn't it? Still happens that way too.

I was eight. Pretty tall for my age, with a mop of shock black hair that was forever too long. I had been watching the movers unloading horse-drawn carriages all day long, heaving heavy travel trunks into the house with bangs and scrapes that produced a lot of yelling from Cosgrove's mother.

He had emerged after the movers finished. As he came out onto the front porch, I watched him. He stopped and simply stared at me. Neither of us had said anything. Finally, I'd wandered over, and stuck out a grimy hand and introduced myself.

His handshake was like holding a wriggling ball of earthworms. His voice dripped like sap in the fall. Needless to say, I wasn't too keen on him.

The remainder of the summer consisted of me trying to avoid contact with him. It wasn't difficult. Cosgrove gave new meaning to the term "loner." He never went down to the swimming hole, never made friends with any of the other children, kept to himself, and seemed to spend an eternity on his front porch reading big books with black leather covers and spines in an assortment of foreign languages.

The other kids dismissed him as weird.

I suspected something else.

When school started, things came to a head early

on. Cosgrove had established himself fairly easily as the self-appointed leader of the outcasts in class. He thought that gave him rule over everyone. My friends and I didn't agree, and since Cosgrove lived on my street, it was decided that I would teach him a lesson.

School fights in the 1870s were pretty basic tackle-and-punch affairs. I gave Cosgrove a fairly decent working over and then left him bleeding on the field near school.

I wish that was the whole story.

It never is, though. Cosgrove stopped trying to overtly assert himself, but he was always up to something. In class small spitballs would find their way into my hair. Tiny tacks on my chair after recess. A dead bug in my lunch sack. I could never pin it on him, but I knew.

As we grew older, my thoughts were less of him and more of girls. There was one in particular. Her name was Robin. An unusual name for that time, but she was an unusual girl.

I loved her.

A blaring honk jerked me back to reality and cut the memory of Robin short. I hauled my black VW Jetta to the right down Newbury Street and then turned right onto Massachusetts Avenue and drove another block before wheeling the car onto Beacon Street for a quick trip into Kenmore Square and beyond into Allston.

The Jetta handled well. I could have easily afforded a Mercedes or other finely tuned car, but that would have made me more conspicuous. I chose the Jetta because it was German and handled as well as some other cars at twice the price. Plus, I'd been seeing the damned things everywhere lately. That made it a lot easier to blend in. And I'm real big on blending in.

When I went through Fixer training, my instructors had hammered home the importance of not sticking out. It's just another fact of our society. We've got a whole fifth column of sorts to make sure things flow smoothly for us. Vampires work in every arm of the government, able to obtain Social Security cards and picture identifications; hell, we even pay taxes. I imagine that would really make old Bram Stoker jump into an epileptic seizure if he knew how easily we melded with human society.

After all, it's our survival at stake, so why wouldn't we?

One of the other things that I learned during training was the importance of continued discipline in training myself. I had to maintain a degree of readiness and strength that would aid me in my job. If I failed to ever be able to carry out my responsibilities, it would most likely result in my own death.

Therefore, I kept myself in superb condition.

That meant a lot of exercise. And martial arts.

You probably think it's hysterically funny for a vampire to need martial arts. Well, let me tell you something: when you're trying to take out a nut job like Cosgrove, you'll want all the advantage you can get. Especially since the nut jobs frequently are as adept as Fixers.

So, in this case, I chose to borrow from the humans and study martial arts. No, not those pitiful sport-oriented arts where you see folks sweeping the floor with their hair as they do insanely stupid high kicks that expose their groin to attack. No, I needed something developed for combat. Something designed to impart as much damage on an opponent with minimal effort. Something natural.

So I chose ninjutsu.

Again you're probably shaking your head at the thought of a vampire cloaked out like a Hollywood ninja in a black mask and sword strapped across my back.

Not so.

This was the real deal. The ninjutsu I studied was authentic stuff handed down for almost a thousand years. Hell, it was older than I was. It actually comforted me in some small way to know I was dwarfed by it in terms of age.

I'd been studying for eleven years now and had a second-degree black belt. The school I attended was owned by a man whom I respected infinitely. He put his heart and soul into learning the art as well as he could. He passed everything on to his students and made sure we all knew how to protect ourselves. He was definitely not into churning out black belts like a copy machine. People in this school knew how to protect themselves.

Still, I always enjoyed the thought of what they'd do if they knew what I truly was.

When I got to the dojo in Allston, the class was already in session. I spent the next hour working on a dizzying array of knife-defense techniques and it felt great to be able to lose myself so totally in the exercises.

But it was all over far too quickly. And outside, the afternoon had slowly drawn down the shades of night. Once again ushering in Cosgrove's hunt.

I drove back to Jamaica Plain and the old white Victorian I owned near Jamaica Pond. Ditching the gray charcoal suit into a pile in the corner of my bedroom, I showered quickly, soaping off the sheen of sweat I'd accumulated during the martial arts class. Back in my bedroom, I stood in front of my closet again. The choice was simple this time. I dressed in a black turtleneck, dark slacks, and a dark blazer, definitely more my flavor of clothing. I strapped my piece just behind my right hip where its outline would be hardest to discern.

Another facet of my training.

Constant discipline and attention to the smallest details ensured success.

I left a fresh bowl of water for Mimi and Phoebe. I'd feed them later. One quick motion to grab my keys, wallet, and pistol and to flatten the tuft of hair that kept sticking out of the back of my head; then I headed back out into the darkness.

Boston's a gorgeous city at night. Sure, New York has a great skyline that speaks volumes about the millions of people clustered there, but Boston's skyline has a pride all its own. I crested Mission Hill and paused to look at the sweeping expanse of lights that jousted with the darkness. Twinkling yellows and whites looked like a star field superimposed on the city.

Down past Northeastern University, I passed Symphony Hall and made a mental note to get concert tickets for the upcoming season. They'd be playing a lot of Vivaldi. I'm a big fan. Well, next to Gustav Holst. But they'd done his series last year.

I turned left onto Dartmouth and then right onto Boylston, following it past the giant teddy bear sitting outside the FAO Schwarz. A block farther down Boylston and I slid the car to a stop in front of the Four Seasons. It's a damned nice hotel.

Newer than the Ritz-Carlton, but they both suck in a lot of money.

Damn.

I rested my hands on the steering wheel and took a deep breath. I was doing it again.

I sighed. Women cause my otherwise airtight discipline to slip like a shoddy knot tied by a lazy Boy Scout.

I left the keys with the valet and wandered inside to the piano bar. To the left side there was a deep velvet couch with a small table in front of it. It gave me a clear view of the entrance to the bar and also the street outside.

I was nursing a Bombay Sapphire and tonic when Talya came in. I hadn't realized until then that I wasn't even sure I wanted her to see me. I'd just kind of planned on having a drink, maybe shadowing her once she went to hunt Cosgrove. You know, keep an eye on her. And all of a sudden, here she was, looking like my being there was the most natural thing in the world.

I don't know what disturbed me more, my lack of discipline or the fact that she seemed undisturbed by it.

The girl knew how to dress, that's for sure. Dark slacks that outlined muscular legs, a white blouse that showed an ample amount of bosom, and a blazer under which I was certain she packed a certain high degree of heat.

She stopped by the bar and ordered a vodka, straight, in an iced glass. I watched the bartender take a bottle out of the freezer and pour some out. She must have tipped him special for that.

Talya hefted the drink, winked at me, and wandered over. We were just casual acquaintances meeting in a bar, not a pair of top-notch killers waiting to stake an evil vampire.

She slid herself onto the couch next to me, took a sip of the vodka, and exhaled. "Nice to see you again, Lawson."

"Christ, if I hadn't know you worked for the Russians before . . ."

She smiled. "What, you've never known a woman who knew the proper way to drink vodka?"

"Maybe." I shrugged. "We going to swap love stories of old now?"

"Not a chance. I could go through mine in five minutes. We've got work to do and I don't want to bore you to sleep."

"That ever happen to you before?"

Talya smiled. "What do you think?"

Hell no. But I didn't say anything. I just sat and watched her.

She took a long sip, then put her drink down on the glass tabletop. "Before we get started, I need some information from you."

"Just because I'm here doesn't mean we're working together, you know."

"Doesn't it?"

"No."

"Then why *are* you here?"

I took a long haul on my drink and rested it back on the table, scanning the room. "Checking up on you, I guess."

She smirked. "I'm touched. You needn't worry about me."

"So you say."

"Well, even if you still claim that we're not working together, I still need some more information."

"About what?"

"Cosgrove."

"What about him?"

"You have a photograph?"

"No. The last photo we had went obsolete courtesy of some plastic surgeons in Geneva."

She nodded. "Describe him to me, then."

I did. She sat there and absorbed it all; when I finished, she polished off her drink. "I need to get going."

I nodded. "Fair enough. Say, you know the club scene in Boston is fairly limited on Mondays and Tuesdays."

"I know."

"You know?"

She ran her fingers along the rim of her glass and sighed. "Lawson, I did some homework today. I do have some experience in this type of thing, you know."

"Sorry." I finished the drink and set it back down. "I'm not even used to the prospect of working with anyone. I always operate alone."

"Speaking of which," she said, "who exactly do you work for?"

"What do you mean?"

"Well, you know all about my past—"

"Not all."

"Enough," she continued. "I don't know a damned thing about you. Aside from the fact that we're similar. But different."

"That's probably enough."

"Not for me."

I studied her. Strange bedfellows doth destiny make. Who'd have thought when I rolled out of bed this morning that I'd be sharing a drink and God knows what else with a human woman who had all the appearances of a true professional and was a damned sight better-looking than I could have imagined ever finding in an assassin? Sure as hell not me.

"I work for a group called the Council."

"Private or government?"

I smiled. "Yes."

She frowned. "Lawson, you're as much of an enigma as the man we're hunting. Maybe sometime soon you'll share some more of your secrets with me."

"I don't know about that. You already know far too much."

She laughed. "So you say." She checked her watch. "It's time I got started. Any later and I might miss him, no? I want to finish this tonight if possible."

"That may not fit in with Cosgrove's plan."

"The hell with his plan. After tonight it won't even matter anymore."

I hoped she was right. Check that, I prayed to every god I'd ever heard of that she was right.

Eight

History was something I never did particularly well in during my school years. Actually, I never did well in any of my subjects since I spent my time more interested in girls than anything else. But I managed to absorb a few facts along the way.

My race evolved out of the same line as modern humans. I know it's strange for the traditionalists to accept the idea that vampires aren't the undead but rather a living, evolving race just like yours. Seems weird, doesn't it? It weirds me out too, and I'm one of them.

Most of the elder historians believe we began a separate evolutionary trail from Homo sapiens between twenty-five thousand and fourteen thousand years ago, during the height of the last ice age. But we were so much alike at first that for a while we probably coexisted.

Humans at that time were the first hunter-gatherers, often preferring to attack feared predators as a means of acquiring the powers they believed the animals possessed. A hunter back then might eat the predator, drink its blood, and wear the pelts as a way of trying to gain its power.

We did much the same thing.

But we hunted humans.

We were nomadic by nature. We left no paintings on cave walls for anyone to speculate on thousands of years later. And our skeletons have largely confounded most of modern science. Sure, archaeologists find similarly sized skulls as humans, but with elongated incisors; they fail to conclude a separate evolving race. They chalk it up as an oddity that this "tribe" might have all shared this tooth abnormality.

But it was us.

Gradually, as time moved on, we grew into a larger body of people. We chose remote areas to settle. Usually in mountainous regions. Places like the Himalayas, the Andes, the Carpathians, and even the Canadian Rockies became home to our kind. Small villages grew out of the first settlements. Later we began to spread. Wherever we could settle in reasonable anonymity without attracting suspicion.

It was tough. We were hunted to extinction in several countries.

Elsewhere we flourished.

In the Himalayas, they called us the *yidam*. We weren't seen as evil. In fact, some of the monks even thought of us as enlightened.

With the onset of the industrial revolution and a rapidly shrinking world, communities of vampires reached out and established loose networks with each other. We became ingrained in every human city and town around the world. But our population growth is much slower than humans'. We might have two children to every ten humans. It's nature's way of keeping things in check. Like sharks that have one pup at a time. Too many predators ruin the food chain.

And we were predators.

Sure, you could romanticize it, but the fact remained that we needed human blood to survive. The ingestion of the life force is what sustains us. We can eat human food, but our metabolic process demands human blood. It's within the blood that the human life-force energy rests. Oxygenated blood crackles with electric energy. The Chinese call it *chi;* the Japanese call it *ki*.

We call it food.

It's not pretty, but it is necessary.

The result of borrowing life-force energy evolved us into a much stronger race. We're pretty much invulnerable to the usual causes of death. Fully nourished, we'd be a pain to put down.

But puncturing the heart with wood upsets our ability to keep blood and the vital life force flowing. Doesn't sound logical, I know, but for some basic elemental reason, wood can kill us once it pierces our heart. It's a theory I heard was based on the Five Elemental theory of Asian philosophy. Expanding energy characteristics of wood break up the concentrated stability of life-force energy. And as long as we're decapitated immediately afterward, regeneration is impossible.

We age as well and, yes, even die from it. Our typical life span can be hundreds of years. Think it sounds cool? It's probably the most boring existence imaginable.

Unless you're a Fixer.

In that case life can be pretty exciting. That is, if you like tracking down scumbags, getting shot at, and leading one of the loneliest lifestyles you never had the displeasure of living.

Talya left the Four Seasons and walked farther up Boylston Street, making no attempts to move discreetly. I shadowed her from a block back, knowing she knew I was there. Watching her move reminded me more of one of my own than a human. She was as much a predator this night as I was.

I kind of liked it.

The Alley, as it's known, was packed with bars that attracted postcollege kids who were now entering the corporate upward river swim. Like so many salmon unsure of why they do what they do—but they do it nonetheless—these young office kids packed the bars and pubs surrounding the financial district with mindless devotion. It's a kind of useless existence that has always baffled me. Humans seem curiously attached to doing what society thinks they should do, even if it's something they don't want to do in the first place.

Strange.

Most everyone else in the world on a Monday night was home trying to forget about their least favorite day of the week. But the young professionals were out in force. The former frat boys, still trying to pull off their glory-days appearances when they had full heads of hair, were mostly stocky. Their previously proud muscles had quickly accumulated fat when forced to reside inside tightly quartered cubicles for up to twelve hours every day.

The girls were much the same, finally realizing that precious youth, while still a resident in their life, was nevertheless anxiously looking to move to a better neighborhood. This realization and the omnipresent biological societal clock were stomping loud enough that even on a Monday night there'd be a lot of balding, paunchy guys heading home with a lot of marriage-seeking gals.

Except one.

She'd be dead before the night was over.

Another victim of Cosgrove's hell-bent streak.

Unless Talya and I had any say in the matter. Well, more so Talya. I had to be honest with myself. I wasn't exactly crazy about taking Cosgrove on again so soon after my last fiasco on Saturday night. I'm not a big fan of repeating mistakes over and over again.

I'm much more into successes.

But I didn't really have much of a choice. It's what I do, you know? I guess I was as locked into my job as these youngsters swirling around me were. So much for my enlightened existence.

Whatever tonight brought my way, I was going to be ready for it even if facing Cosgrove made my stomach hurt and my sphincter pucker like a nervous virgin in prison. After all, I'd fed before I met Talya and that would keep me going at least until I could get home and have another swig of juice.

Talya disappeared inside the club without so much as a lingering glance from the bouncer. I waited five minutes and then headed for the door. I had my piece on my hip, but the overzealous bouncer didn't notice it. Either he was too lazy to spot it, or he was too interested in frisking my crotch. I think I'd prefer option number one. But that's just me.

Inside, Talya slipped as easily as I did through the masses of people. She moved like a shark, but I suspected had she wanted to, she could have easily attracted anyone in the room. The ability to turn a magnetic personality on and off again at a whim is a pretty potent weapon. And I had no doubt it was one of many tools in Talya's arsenal.

She grabbed a seat by the main bar and gestured the bartender over. I saw him put a vodka in front of her and what looked like a gin and tonic in front of the empty seat next to her. I sighed and wandered over. I couldn't refuse the drink. That would be rude.

"It's Bombay Sapphire," she said without turning around. "Unless my sense of smell is off, that was what you were drinking at the Four Seasons, right?"

"Yeah." I tasted the drink. "Thanks."

"Ready to work together yet?"

"No."

She shook her head. "Why is it that women are called 'stubborn' and men are called 'determined'? If you ask me, they're two sides of the same coin."

I ignored that comment. "So what's your plan?"

She looked at me like I had two heads. "Didn't we discuss this already?"

"Did we?"

"We're going to kill him." She smiled. "Sorry, I forgot. *I'm* going to kill him."

I shook my head. "Yeah, I got that part. How are you planning to do it?"

She smiled at me. "How do *you* usually do it?"

OK, so she knew I was a professional as well. Damned if she didn't seem to know more about me than I was comfortable with. "I'd just walk around and look for him."

"You're hunting him too."

"Yes."

"So why don't you go ahead and do that."

It wasn't even vaguely a question, which disturbed me to no end. Like I said before, I am not used to attractive and highly capable women being a part of the equation that is my life.

You might think this whole thing ridiculous, but you've got to appreciate what I go through. Sexually speaking, I can get it whenever I want to, but sex is usually just a part of securing my sustenance. Sure, I can enjoy it and I can make it absolutely spectacular for any woman I want. Multiple orgasms, the whole bit. And we're not talking about those pathetic triples that so many women seem to think are so awesome after six hours of sweaty grinding. No, I'm talking about you have three before my pants even come off. I'm talking about long oral devotion. Hell, I bring a thermos and sandwiches and camp out. I enjoy pleasing women. Makes them a lot more eager to please me. And that means I get a lot more energy from whatever precious juice I can get out of them, whether it's a playful love bite or what have you. So I'm good. I have to be good.

But Talya was something else again.

So instead of questioning it, I stood there looking silly for a moment.

Talya waved the bartender over and ordered another drink without looking at me. "I'll be fine. Go hunt him down, Lawson."

Sometimes I think this whole vampire thing is really overrated. With Talya around, I wasn't even feeling like I still had control.

Now *that* was weird.

She was right, though. I was supposed to be hunting him.

I left her at the bar and started to make my way

around the place. Get a feel for it. I hadn't been here before since I usually try to avoid these joints altogether.

It was large for a bar. One main polished mahogany bar ran down the left side for about a hundred feet, stocked with simple wooden stools. On the opposite side there were the kind of high-backed booths the beautiful people liked to lounge in as they ordered their Cristal champagne in crystal flutes. They were packed.

I moved upstairs to the second floor where a small dance floor had been erected surrounded by more tables and more chairs and many more people. Guys watched girls dance from the safety of the seating area, not willing to venture onto the floor and risk exposing their inability to move in time to the beat.

Lights flickered in time to the music and spinning globes of crystal and light strobed the atmosphere into a dizzying array of light and sound.

It was entirely too chaotic and cramped to have made hunting easy for Cosgrove.

An arm reached out from the crowd and grabbed my hand. It was attached to a young woman sporting a black miniskirt and a buzz that would have made a homeless drunk proud.

"Dance with me!"

I maneuvered away, freeing myself from her tenuous grasp and headed back downstairs. If Cosgrove was here, it wouldn't be on this floor.

Back downstairs was even more crowded than when I'd left it five minutes earlier. So much for the fire code. They seemed intent on stocking as many people in here as they could. And to think this wasn't even the busiest night of the week. Amazing.

I took another sip of my drink as I meandered past the booths again. The other night Cosgrove had been sitting in one with his back to the wall while watching everything in the club happen around him.

Watching the many people he could reach out, stroke, and then pluck from life, raping them for their precious fluids. Just the thought of it brought back a fresh image of Simbik on the gurney.

That was quickly replaced by a need, an unquenchable thirst, for revenge. I wanted the man who had killed my friend.

And we are a vengeful people, let me tell you.

Even I, as a professional Fixer, fell victim to the desire for revenge. Especially when the victim had been one of my friends.

So even though facing Cosgrove made my stomach ache, I knew I'd do whatever it took to gain justice.

I moved around a gaggle of giggling girls putting far too much effort into flirting with a paunchy Euro-type and headed back to the bar.

I could just make out Talya over the tops of about twenty heads. Even from this distance she was a good-looking woman. Check that, she was gorgeous.

And currently laughing.

Talking.

Nodding.

She sat next to a man at the bar. Apparently, the idea of saving my seat hadn't occurred to her.

Frustrated that the immense crowd made it dif-

ficult to move, I frowned and then got a better
look at Talya and her companion.

I stopped breathing at roughly the same second
my sphincter shriveled up and my testicles headed
north to my throat.

Cosgrove.

Nine

There is a technical term for what I experienced when I saw Cosgrove chatting Talya up. Well, it's technical in my book. It's called the "jaw-drop-mouth-holy-shit" reaction. Because that's exactly what I did.

Cosgrove had his back to me and Talya obviously hadn't caught sight of me trying to push my way through the crowd. That gave me a moment to clear my head and try to put sense to what I was seeing.

Several theories popped into my head at once: The first was that Talya had no idea she was talking to Cosgrove and was using him as a convenient shield while she scanned the room for any suspicious goings-on. The second theory was that she knew exactly who she was talking to and was baiting him along until I got back so we could take him out together, thus enjoying a better chance of success. And the third was that she knew it was Cosgrove and wasn't the least bit concerned about it.

And that concerned me.

As I said before, I've danced in the covert-operations circles a few times before. Conspiracies are nothing new to me. Hell, if I was honest with myself, and I tend to be unless I'm looking in a mirror, my whole role in life was based upon maintaining a very successful conspiracy. As a Fixer, I preserved the Balance, never letting humans know there was such a race as vampires among them. Never letting that fact become exposed.

But if Talya was in league with Cosgrove, that meant something extremely bad was afoot. And just like failures, I'm not a big fan of "afoot."

I grabbed a seat close to the end of the bar and flashed a little magnetic energy at a short-haired blonde who immediately launched into how she worked in human resources (didn't they all?) at some huge mutual-fund conglomerate down the street. That's all it took. While she played "let me fascinate you with my pitiful existence," I feigned enough interest to keep her tongue moving and used her to study Talya and Cosgrove at the other end of the bar.

Have I mentioned anything about my Fixer training? Probably wasn't enough time before, but let me digress here and spend a moment describing a few things I went through in order to become the Fixer that I am today.

The instructors harped on the ability to be able to communicate in as many ways as possible. Then they reversed it and told us the more ways we knew how to communicate, the more methods of surveillance we'd have at our disposal. And one of the most effective means of eavesdropping on someone else's conversation was to practice the art of lipreading.

We practiced for months. It was not an easy discipline. Sure, there were the textbook cases we started with. Perfectly articulated speakers who made the right shapes at the right times with their lips and tongues. We practiced with them until we got every word being said from across the room. Then we were sent out to practice in the big wide world.

Talk about a reality check.

Nobody spoke as carefully as our test subjects did. We found that out quick. And when you added in the sprinkling of idiomatic speech, accents, second languages, and a myriad of other verbal booby traps, it got pretty difficult.

But we mastered it.

We had to.

So while Marijane, the pixie personnel recruiter with mosquito bites for breasts, chewed my ear off about loving a man with a strong chest, I watched Talya's lips move for ten minutes.

The prognosis was not good.

I speak roughly fifty languages, and maybe twelve other very esoteric dialects. And I speak them well.

Talya was speaking a language I didn't recognize.

Is there such a language as Kazakhstani? I didn't know. But whatever language it was, it was fairly obvious that Cosgrove spoke it too. Fluently.

That fact alone did not warm my heart.

And I was faced with more possibilities. Maybe Talya had somehow been planted on me by Cosgrove. Why? Perhaps to watch my movements. Perhaps to try to turn me to Cosgrove's side. Whatever mumbo jumbo he'd been spewing on the rooftop, it was obvious I hadn't put much faith in it. After all, it was Cosgrove, and that freak had always been a hell-bound, glory-seeking bastard. And besides, I was pretty well near dead at that point anyway. All in all, I think I could forgive myself. But this new revelation put a different spin on things.

And it raised new questions about Talya.

Number one might be what the hell she was doing communicating with a vampire? Was she one herself? I didn't think so, but there was the unnerving fact that she emanated a hunter's presence. Her background was an acceptable explanation for that. Or at least it had been.

If she was a vampire, how the hell could she have gotten that close to Simbik's family? And if she wasn't, how could she reconcile being in league with the killer of her fiancé?

My head swam with confusion. This was definitely getting out of hand and I was truly worried. Even without confirming my suspicions about Talya being in league with Cosgrove, things looked pretty dim.

I watched them talk for another ten minutes, still unable to decipher any of what Talya said. She seemed to grow anxious and began waving her hands around. Then Cosgrove eased himself out of the seat and disappeared out the front door of the bar, leaving Talya alone with her drink.

And me confused as hell.

I took the pixie's number and slid it into my pocket. I'd file her under the "divorced, easy lay" section of my phone book. Women with no self-esteem come in handy sometimes, and as ruthless as that sounds, when you're in my line of work, you need all the assets you can get.

Talya looked up as I approached. I hadn't quite decided on a course of action, but I did want to take a wait-and-see approach and watch what developed.

She smiled at me. "Any luck?"

"No. I didn't see him. You?"

She shook her head, closing her eyes just enough that I couldn't make out any fluctuation of her pupils that might have indicated lying. Not that I really needed to see that at this point.

"Nothing happened down here, that's for sure."

I said nothing. I just watched her. It was an old trick I'd learned in an interrogation course I took once. Don't say anything and people will feel compelled to fill in the void of silence. Often they give away some valuable information.

Apparently, Talya had taken the same course because she just kept looking at me. After about two minutes of this, she smiled. "So are we partners now?"

Too many doubts about what I was wading into filled my head. Partnering with Talya might not have been kosher from an objective viewpoint, but I needed to keep an eye on her. And this recent turn of events mandated a close watch even more.

If I'd been feeling particularly sure of myself, I might have put a gun to her head and demanded she tell me what the hell was going on. But I wanted some background on her first before I confronted her. I could be making a big deal out of nothing.

I usually do when there's a woman involved.

So I shrugged. "I suppose it makes better sense to stick together than go it alone. At least this way we can watch each other's backs."

She smiled again. "Exactly."

I checked my watch. It was already climbing toward 2:00 A.M.

Whatever had transpired, it seemed fairly certain that Cosgrove wasn't going to be killing anyone around here tonight. There was a chance he was still full from his meal of Simbik the other night. Or he'd killed before he'd come to see Talya.

"Doesn't look like much is happening."

"I wouldn't say that," said Talya.

"No?"

"You just made a wise decision about us becoming partners. I'd say that was important."

I mustered a small grin, but I had more questions than answers, a gnawing headache, and a feeling that before I figured out what the hell was going on, it was going to get a helluva lot worse.

And to think, people used to call me an optimist.

Ten

Outside the bar, Talya leaned in close to me. "So what now?"

I eased back off her. "It's late."

She smiled. "It's never too late, Lawson."

I should mention that vampires have an acute sense of smell. Our olfactory sense is one of the most heightened things we possess. So it was fairly easy to discern that Talya was horny. Pheromones leaped off of her like a lemming convention being held at high tide.

And she did little to hide it. "Why don't you take me home?"

Yeah, right. Not while I was still trying to figure out whose side she was playing on. Seeing her with Cosgrove had really fucked me up, not to put too fine a point on it. I needed some background on Talya, and to get it, I'd have to let McKinley know what was going on.

"Not tonight, sweetheart. I've got work to do."

"But you said yourself it was late. What more can you do tonight?" She snuggled herself against me and I was instantly aware of her curves and the warmth they contained. I wish I could say I wasn't tempted. I wish I could say that she wasn't extremely attractive. I wish I could.

But I couldn't.

However, given that I have an extremely ingrained sense of duty, and given that she happened to be my now-dead friend's fiancée (or was it ex-fiancée?), I did manage to find the self-discipline to pull myself away from her.

"Your hotel's as far as I go. That's where we say our good-nights."

She pouted the entire two blocks back down Boylston Street, but it wouldn't do any good. If Talya was dirty, her attempts to bed me could just be an ambush. I didn't feel like walking into one.

It also didn't help matters that the entire way back to the hotel, my other senses screamed at me. We were being watched. I presumed it was Cosgrove. But, in truth, it could have been anyone. Whoever they were, they knew their business. I couldn't pick anyone up, and since the streets were nearly deserted, it meant they were a lot better at their trade craft than I was comfortable with.

Across the street from us, the Boston Public Gardens stretched out; jagged tree trunks devoid of leaves yawned their shadowy limbs, expanding the realm of ebony that occupied the park. An entire surveillance team could set up shop behind the tree trunks and I'd never see it.

The sensation of being observed only made me want to drop Talya off as soon as possible and get home. I needed to know who she was, what she was doing, and who might be connected to her.

If she'd just hopped in from New York and hadn't been careful enough, she could have a kill team following her, just waiting for the right moment to waste her. Talented pros like Talya accumulated enemies the way a politician accumulates scandal and corruption. The kill team might be entirely unconnected to what I was working on right now, but I wasn't naive enough to think they'd spare me. Guilt by association meant they'd try to kill me just the same.

And that was the good news.

The bad news was if she was dirty, and Cosgrove was waiting for me, there was no telling how well I'd fare against the two of them. And if Cosgrove had more troops to call upon, odds weren't good on my getting home to feed Mimi and Phoebe. They'd be pissed.

We got back to the Four Seasons and went through the revolving door past the sleepy doorman in the long overcoat. Talya turned to me in the lobby.

"You sure you won't come up?"

I tried to smile, but I don't think it came out too well. "I don't think so."

"Don't you like me?"

Now there was a question I didn't have an answer to. At least, not yet. I grinned. "I like you just fine. I'm tired and need to get home. My cats get jealous if I stay out too late."

She smiled. "You don't strike me as being a slave to pussy."

"Think of it more as a healthy respect."

"You sure you won't come up?"

"Positive."

Her shoulders drooped, but she seemed to accept my excuse. "Tomorrow?"

"I'll call you in the morning. We'll strategize then. All right?"

She leaned in, lips already puckering. "Russians customarily kiss when they say good-bye."

I left her standing there. "Sleep well, Talya."

As I left, the doorman, who had come awake during our brief exchange, winked at me. "Nice."

Guess he'd seen his share of whipped guys come through and I was the exception. If only he knew how much of an exception I really was.

I picked up my car from the valet and drove home to Jamaica Plain via Somerville. Which, if you know Boston, makes absolutely no sense at all.

Unless, of course, you know all about taking people to the cleaners. That's how you lose a surveillance team.

Even if Cosgrove was following me, by the time I got through my circuitous drive home, he wouldn't have been behind me. When I went through Fixer training, losing tails was something we practiced in Moscow. Probably the toughest place during the height of the Cold War to practice trying to lose people. During those years, the KGB routinely assigned an average of six rookie gumshoes to every tourist who came through the city. Most of the time, the tourist merely smiled and accepted it.

For us, it was different.

We used to have to get them to notice us, most usually achieved by snapping pictures of the KGB building on Dzherzhinsky Square and then losing them across the city. Without getting caught.

I favored the old GUM department store for its huge selection of big coats and fur hats. You could duck into old stairwells or back storage rooms and easily lose the surveillance team. It was tough, though. Getting caught would have exposed us all, so the pressure was really on. But we all passed.

So this drive home was really no chore at all. Just added an extra forty-five minutes on my commute time.

I rolled up to my house at half past three and was greeted by incessant chirping coming from Mimi and Phoebe, who hadn't been fed since last night. I fixed them dinner and then sat down in the study to phone McKinley.

He answered on the sixth ring.

"Yeah?"

Asleep too. McKinley liked to keep daytime hours. "It's Lawson."

He yawned into the phone. "Yeah, I figured there'd only be one wretched bastard who'd forsake common courtesy and interrupt a decent sleep. Did you get him?"

"Not yet."

"Lawson, what the hell are you calling me for then?"

Some people. "Your sparkling personality. I need information."

"About?"

"I don't have many details. Female, I think she's human—"

"You think?"

"Christ, McKinley, I didn't get a chance to verify it."

"All right. What else?"

"Name's Talya."

"Talya what?"

"I only got Talya."

"Anything else?"

I could hear him writing this down, which was a

good sign. McKinley kept great notes. "She's a pro."

"You want information on a hooker?"

"A pro. A hitter. For crying out loud, McKinley, wake up!"

"Sorry. OK, Talya, possibly human, assassin. Anything else?"

"I need to know where she's been recently. Said she came in from New York this morning on the shuttle. Can you trace it?"

"See what I can do." He paused. "Lawson."

"Yeah?"

"What's so special about this broad?"

I frowned. "I don't know yet."

"She connected to this thing?"

"You know the guy Cosgrove took out on Saturday, Simbik?"

"Friend of yours, yeah, what about him?"

"Talya says she was his fiancée."

"You don't believe her?"

"I'm not sure. I've got reason to believe she might be holding back on me. That's where you come in."

"Gotcha. Twelve hours."

"I'll call you tonight."

I made myself a cup of hot chocolate and promptly burned my tongue trying to drink it too fast. Outside the night was starting to bleed reds and oranges. Dawn was coming. A new day approached and I was no closer to getting Cosgrove than I had been before. Add to that mix the whole Talya thing and I was gearing up for some decidedly bad shit.

I flipped the television on in time to see some

washed-up actress hawking new careers in computer repair, gunsmithing, and accounting.

Crunching numbers all day suddenly didn't seem so bad.

Eleven

It took McKinley just over his estimated twelve hours to gather all the necessary information. I'd just finished another grueling workout when the phone rang. Sweat dribbled off me as I grabbed for the receiver.

"Yeah?"

"It's me. Where the hell'd you find this chick?"

"A chat room on the Internet, McKinley. Where do you think? She was at Simbik's funeral." I mopped my brow. "Why? What'd you find out?"

There was a pause and I could hear McKinley shuffling what sounded like fax papers. "Lots. First, and most importantly, she's not one of us."

Was that good news or not? I had no answer for it myself. The fact that Talya wasn't a vampire could be good news, but it could also signal some kind of alliance between humans and vampires. An alliance Cosgrove could be trying to forge. And that was bad. Definitely bad.

"What else?"

"Definitely a professional. Top-notch murdering madam. History includes time with the KGB. She tell you that?"

"She drinks iced vodka."

"Just because she drank vodka you thought she was former KGB?"

"You ever known a woman who could put down three iced vodkas with no adverse effects?"

"No."

"Trust me, then, will you?" I paused. "So what'd you find out?"

"Did a number of 'black bag' ops for them in the early and mideighties. All successful. Had one of the best records for any international operative. She went freelance after communism flunked out. Had assignments all over the world. She's been employed by everyone from the Mossad to the Cali Cartel."

"Not very discriminating about her work, is she?"

"Doesn't seem to be," said McKinley. "But she's top-drawer stuff. Her KGB file came via a friend of mine down in Virginia. She did training with Spetznaz Alpha Groups. Did some time in Afghanistan and Lebanon. She's good. Hell, she's excellent."

"Top percentile?"

"And then some. Here check this out," he offered. "OK, Kabul in 1980, the local brigade commander is having trouble with a sect of very badass mujahideen fighters."

"So?"

"So the brigade commander keeps losing men and vehicles to these lightning raids. He's straight-out trying to find them and kill them. Can't do it. So he calls Moscow and asks for help. They send this Talya chick."

"And?"

"She disappears into the countryside alone for two weeks. You ever been to Afghanistan?"

"No."

"Place makes Newark, New Jersey, look like a goddamned rest home for the rich and famous. It sucks. Dry and inhospitable shit, Lawson. Anyway, your girl goes out there for two weeks, tracks this band of freedom fighters down, and eliminates every one of them."

"How many?"

"Fourteen. Including two sixteen-year-old boys."

"Damn."

"Damn? Shit, Lawson, this kind of info rates more on the fuck-me-very-much scale. This is one nasty woman."

"I assumed as much from the way she carries herself."

"She a player in this?"

I frowned and took a sip of juice. "Seems to be. But I'm not sure how the hell she fits into it. She claimed to want to kill Cosgrove. I took her out hunting last night—"

"You did what?"

"McKinley, she's got no clue about me. Relax."

"It's your funeral if she does, Lawson. Might be your funeral anyway, given her history. What happened?"

"We split up at one point. Basic recon of the place. I came back downstairs and saw her getting awfully friendly with Cosgrove."

"Shit. She see you?"

"Of course not."

"How friendly was she getting?"

"Laughing and carrying on like old-buddies-friendly. It didn't leave a very warm spot in my stomach."

"I'll bet. Did she know it was Cosgrove?"

"I think so."

"That's not good."

"No shit."

Another pause. McKinley shuffled more papers. "How do you want to play it?"

"I'm not sure yet." And I wasn't. Too many things seemed to be hurling themselves at me. Too much, too quick. "Any fresh kills?"

"Police reports only got down some gangland stuff. Nothing attributable to our boy."

"He'll strike again soon. He has to." I paused. "Say, McKinley, you have anything on Talya's birthplace?"

"Yeah, right here. File says she was born in what is now Kazakhstan. Central steppes–type area, couple of mountain ranges. Area borders China to the east."

"What language do they speak there?"

"Language? I don't know. Why?"

"Well, last night when I was watching her talk to Cosgrove, they were speaking a language I didn't recognize."

He laughed. "Hell, Lawson, you only speak fifty languages. Could be one you don't know."

"This was different. Even if I can't speak it, I can at least recognize most of them. This one was new to me."

"Maybe some type of regional dialect?"

"I was thinking, yeah."

McKinley sighed. "I can check. That will definitely take some time. But I'll look into it. In the meantime, got any theories about this?"

"Not really. I'm wishing I paid more attention to Cosgrove the other night on the roof."

"Can't be helped now. But you think this Talya woman is mixed up with it? Whatever it is?"

"She's either in it all the way or Cosgrove is using her for some reason."

"Not out of character for him to do that, is it?"

"No, it's not. But she's different. He's only ever used fools before. Talya is different."

"So you keep saying, Lawson. What about if neither of them knows who the other one is?"

"You mean they just happened to be talking in a strange, obscure language by sheer coincidence?"

"You never know."

"You know as well as I do, McKinley, that we can't afford the luxury of believing in coincidences. There's something going on; I know it. I'm just not sure about Talya."

There was a pause on the line. "Lawson . . . You're not too close to this broad, are you?"

I smiled. McKinley could be a dope, but he could be a good guy too. "Like you've got anyone else who can handle this?"

He chuckled. "No, but you know what I mean."

"I know what you mean. I'll stay cool."

"You do that. I'll check out that information for you and call you back later." The phone went dead again and I sat there taking small sips of juice, pondering. After five minutes of getting absolutely nothing worthwhile, I gave up and took a steaming shower.

Basically, what it came down to was simple: until I could figure out exactly how Talya fit into this whole mess, I had to make sure she suspected nothing was amiss. That was the only way I'd be able to observe things as they needed to be. And then maybe I'd be able to get some more out of this. Maybe.

I called her after my shower.

"Where have you been? I was worried."

I'll bet she was. "Asleep. It was a late night. I needed some rest. Time to think."

"About blowing off what could have been an amazing night of passion?"

"Not really. Look, Talya, don't take this the wrong way, but if we're going to work together on this thing, I can't be sleeping with you. You're Simbik's fiancée, for crying out loud!"

"Ex-fiancée, Lawson. He's dead now."

"Whatever. Fact remains, you were still a part of my friend's life and I'm certainly not ready to discount that so quickly."

"You don't find me attractive?"

"That's not it and you know it. You're a professional. I'm a professional. We have to stay objective about this."

"If you say so."

"I do." I just wished I meant it.

"Fine." She may have agreed, but her tonality told me she was pissed. Well, she didn't have to like me. I just needed to keep her around for now. Until I figured this all out.

"Are we on for tonight?"

"Yes. Same time, OK?"

"All right."

I hung up the phone and leaned back into the couch as Mimi jumped up, looking for some affection. I stroked her fur and she responded by kneading her claws into my jeans.

The first time I'd hunted Cosgrove it had been

because he'd left fifty bodies littering the streets of Boston. This was my town, after all. That's how it worked. Fixers were assigned a Control and a city to watch. We were the enforcers. We maintained the Balance. We made sure the locals obeyed the laws of the hunt.

What laws?

Well, there were a couple of minor ones that were so ingrained in us all we usually never had any infractions. We were only allowed to hunt at night. That one, I suppose, was a carryover from that superstitious crap about us being deathly afraid of sunlight. In truth, as I mentioned before, we could exist easily in sunlight. But we were only to hunt at night. It helped maintain the Balance, I suppose. No one really understood all of the rules—we just obeyed them. They'd been handed down from the Council, and everyone obeyed the Council.

Well, everyone except Cosgrove.

By far, the absolute cardinal sin was to borrow more juice than could be replenished by the lender. In short, if you killed a human, and exposed the community, you were in deep doo-doo.

It meant a termination order got passed down.

And yours truly would get a phone call from McKinley.

Then the offender would get a visit from me.

Simple.

Effective.

It worked.

Until Cosgrove came calling.

His first act of infamy, which really should have resulted in a global hunt for the bastard, was when he was observed killing a human in Amsterdam by a Fixer stationed there. He tried to take Cosgrove out, and was entirely justified in doing so, given that he'd witnessed the crime.

Unfortunately, he wasn't successful.

Cosgrove left him impaled on a church steeple. It took a frantic cleanup crew and the local Control two hours to get him off unnoticed before the locals started freaking out. And in Amsterdam, you knew it had to be bad to freak out the locals.

But that was Cosgrove.

I warned the Council upon his arrival that he would do the same things he'd been doing across the globe. They told me to leave him alone. Like I said earlier, family counts a sickening amount in this community.

Fifty dead humans later, I took it upon myself to hunt him down. Truthfully, I wanted it finished. After the history Cosgrove and I had, it would be a far better world if he was dead and gone. We covered the outcome of my first endeavor earlier.

Mimi chirped some form of appreciation and went wandering off to beat Phoebe up. I stared out the windows and watched the sun begin its lazy descent in the west. Nighttime was right around the corner.

Time to go to work.

Twelve

I entered Fixer training on a warm spring day in 1963. The camp, as the twenty of us called it, was a five-hundred-acre facility located in the Northeast Kingdom of Vermont. If you're not familiar with the territory, it's remote to say the least. Towns are few and far between, and back in the early 1960s, even more so. People up there kept to themselves and no one ever bothered us. Plus, the surrounding towns were primarily other vampire villages. They acted as a buffer zone.

Just past our centennials, the twenty of us were all brimming with unbridled enthusiasm and also feeling like a bunch of wild, young studs. On the ride up to Vermont from my home, I'd talked to several recruits who felt that being a Fixer was a prestigious career. They were proud of their destiny.

I was confused.

I didn't know what to expect. In everyday vampire society, Fixers aren't normally even discussed. I'd heard about them only in passing. And while it had always been in high regard, there had also been a degree of fear attributed to them as well. After all, they were the guardians of our society. A sort of police force with absolute jurisdiction and the ability to punish if the situation demanded it.

Off the rickety old yellow school bus, we were met by a small-framed man named Garza. He stood all of five feet tall and about the same width. But his voice boomed out a welcome I'd never forget.

"Welcome, ladies. You are all now officially my bitches and I will bend you over and fuck you anytime I damn well please."

Any murmurings vanished as soon as the words echoed across the camp.

If we'd had any women in the group, they might have been offended. But back then, the only Fixers were men. Even today, the profession is largely male. There are exceptions, however. And most of them are damned good exceptions.

But being men, instead of being offended, we were terrified.

Garza looked like he could do it too, if only on sheer confidence. He wasn't the kind of guy you dicked around with.

But by and large, it was all talk. Garza was our equivalent of a drill instructor. For six weeks he ran us ragged through a battery of physical endurance and strength tests. We started out with five-mile runs, added forty-pound rucksacks packed with sharp-edged rocks, and then drew out the runs to ten and fifteen miles.

I hated the running with a passion that survives to this day. It's so damned boring. Of course, that didn't mean a thing. I didn't have to like it. I just had to do it.

And do it, I did.

The obstacle courses followed and beefed up the stakes. For the first time we competed against each other. Natural rivalries developed, crested, and waned under the duress of the training.

And when it became apparent that we were forming a more cohesive unit, Garza introduced us to hand-to-hand combat.

Designed to be quick, dirty, and ultimately practical for our roles, the system was drawn from ancient styles of wrestling and bare-knuckle fighting. Brutal stuff that we practiced with little padding. Garza's philosophy was that we'd never appreciate its effectiveness unless we experienced it firsthand.

We did.

The sand ring, as Garza called it, was an eight-foot-diameter circle bounded by a bluff of densely packed sand. Inside the ring the sand was loose, soft to some extent, but unforgiving. A sudden misstep could mean broken bones. And even if we weren't working on the beach, our footwork had to be absolutely certain at all times. The sand would teach us.

The first time I stepped into the ring was against a taller, heavier recruit named Samuelson. Flush with Scandinavian blood, his blond hair and rugged physique gave him the look of a Norse god.

Garza had smiled, blown his whistle, and then stepped back.

Samuelson was on me so fast I hadn't even had time to lower my hips to improve my balance the way Garza had taught us. Samuelson knocked me off my feet and landed on top of me.

I blocked his punches and jabbed him in the floating ribs, rolled him off me, and scrambled to my feet again.

He lashed out with a kick that caught me square in the pit of my stomach. I fell, retching.

Garza called a halt and then leaned down by my face.

"You gonna give up that easy, boy? A man in this ring means to kill you dead and you're gonna let a little kick take you out of the fight? Better work through that shit and keep your damned self going. This ain't no Sunday-school picnic we're talking about here. It's life and death, and not just yours at that. You fuck up and fail, it could mean the lives of everyone in our society. You hear me?"

I nodded. And God knows I heard him. I worked harder than ever before to master the techniques he'd shown us. The next time I met Samuelson in the ring, things were different. I took him down in three seconds.

But if Garza had been happy with my results, he didn't let it show. It wasn't his way. He was there to mold us into the rawest of materials suitable for further training.

Six weeks after we started, Garza disappeared.

James replaced him.

About the same size as Garza, James looked like a miniature Jack Nicholson, complete with the sneer. He didn't yell. He didn't have to. The sight of him scared us all so much we were absolutely silent whenever he was around, which was all the time.

James's attitude toward our training was different from Garza's. Garza had been in charge of getting us into excellent physical condition. James was in charge of pushing us past the limits we thought we couldn't surpass.

Our first immersion into this new training came in the form of two weeks where we had a total of four hours of sleep and very limited quantities of juice. Energy levels absolutely sapped, we ran the obstacle courses again, fought each other in the sand ring, marched infinite hikes, and recited old nursery rhymes until we were blabbering fools.

But we survived.

We had to.

James forged a new spirit within us. We wouldn't quit. No matter how tired we were, no matter how hungry, no matter our state, we wouldn't give up.

"Give in to the littlest desire and the rest of your discipline will come crumbling down all around you. Then you won't be Fixers anymore. You'll be dead. Preservation of the Balance is the one thing you must at all times keep in your head. Protect it until you die. Never give up."

We didn't.

And after another six weeks of physical and mental torture at the hands of James, he disappeared too.

In his place stood "the Buffalo."

We never knew his real name. But he was our first glimpse of a real Fixer. Drawn from active service from wherever he'd been stationed out in the real world, the Buffalo would serve as our primary trainer for the remainder of our stay at the camp.

He would introduce us to the real arts of being a Fixer.

Compared to Garza and James, the Buffalo was soft-spoken and almost unobtrusive. You wouldn't look twice at him if you walked past him on the street.

Which is exactly what made him so utterly effective.

"You've all proven yourselves as capable, strong men. Naturally, you feel good about that, as well you should." He smiled. "Now I want you to forget it."

He continued. "Drawing attention to yourself will get you killed. It will expose the nature of our society. It is the antithesis of your role as a Fixer.

"You will be the living definition of low profile. Discreet, mild mannered, completely gray. Everything you do must not stand out. You must pass through the ranks of humans and vampires alike as if a ghost. Your success as Fixers depends on it."

Only when the situation demanded it were we permitted to display the skills and prowess we'd worked so hard to gain. Only then could we set the scales of justice right, to protect the Balance and ensure the continued success of our people. But then it was right back to our low profile.

The Buffalo taught us how to dress and walk so we never aroused interest. We worked at blending in until we could disappear in the midst of a crowd.

We went on international field trips to practice. Exotic cities like Moscow, Madrid, London, Paris, Rome, and Berlin became our playgrounds. The stakes were always high on these outings, as high as they'd be once we graduated. Any mistakes meant exposure. And exposure couldn't happen since it would mean the end of our society.

We started out with small exercises designed to allow us to improve our skill with a controllable amount of risk. Gradually, we got better. The exercises continued. The risk mounted.

And we got better.

The training progressed.

It was after dusk when I parked the Jetta in the Transportation Building just past Stuart Street. I figured if Cosgrove was still keeping tabs on me, the last thing I wanted to do was stick to the routine of having the valets at the Four Seasons always parking my car.

I walked over past the Park Plaza Building and along the rear of the hotel. This part of the city, despite attempts to prove otherwise, could still be dangerous at night. A cool breeze blew and in a few weeks the first snows of the winter would loom over Boston. This would be a bad winter.

I passed a couple hurrying along toward the theater district, mumbling about being late. I smiled.

That was when they hit me.

There were two of them and they came out of the shadows easily, as if they belonged in them. Their movements were practiced, flowing. They'd done this before.

If it was supposed to look like a mugging, it lost every flavor of it as soon as I watched their attack unfold. Whoever they were, their goal was obvious: to put me away. These were killers.

Unfortunately, I wasn't subscribing to the idea of going without a fight.

The first one moved fast, and I barely had time to glimpse the blade he'd concealed in the palm of his right hand before it was out and lunging straight in at my chest. A killing thrust by the look of it. Plunge the blade into the subaortic cavity and wrench it back and forth a couple of times. Bloody and dead within twenty seconds.

Even if it wouldn't have killed *me*, it still would have caused a loss of blood. I'm not real happy about losing any blood.

As he came in, his energy committed, I pivoted back on my front heel, allowing his attack to go past me. I got a feel on his knife hand and then found his wrist. I pivoted again, bringing the wrist back into a painful lock, and at the height of the takedown, I kicked his throat, making him gag uncontrollably as I sent him flying sans knife into the shrub-lined brick wall.

Thug number two took a look at number one's inert form and decided running was a more pressing engagement. I stooped over thug number one and rifled his wallet, looking for identification, but I didn't find any.

I did find a neat roll of $100 bills, though.

And a picture of me.

Friends, there are times when life suddenly looks real gloomy. This was definitely one of those times.

I'd been set up for a hit.

And while these clowns had had no clue that they'd never be able to successfully complete it, someone had set me up regardless.

The bills were fresh. They still smelled like ink and the serial numbers were all in order.

The picture drew my attention more, though. Since I don't photograph all that well, and since I had no idea where they would have gotten it, it became priority number one.

I know some of you out there who are still feverishly clinging to the old stereotypes will no doubt be cursing silently about vampires not being able to be photographed. Sorry to spoil your fun, but that's another myth. Sure, you could pass it off in the olden days, but try having a driver's license, passport, or any other form of identification with no picture on it. Hell, try going out without being able to see if the part in your hair was straight or not.

Of course we can be photographed. And yes, we cast reflections and shadows.

The presence of this photograph made my stomach hurt, however. As with any covert operative, I tended to shy away from having too many pictures available. The less I existed on film, the better.

But this was a recent photograph. Grainy. In black and white. And when I examined it under the glow of a streetlight, it became apparent where it was from. It was a video still from a security camera.

I had another hunch that when I walked the remaining block to visit Miss Talya, the background in the picture would match the background in the front lobby of the Four Seasons Hotel.

Have I mentioned how I don't believe in coincidences?

And have I mentioned my sudden pressing need to have a long-overdue sit-down talk with my new best buddy, Talya?

Well, consider them both mentioned.

As far as I was concerned, it was time to stop observing and trying to be Mr. Subtle. I wanted answers.

I picked up the knife from the ground, intending to drop it down the nearest sewer drain. Instead, my breathing stopped.

The blade wasn't steel. In fact, the entire knife was carved from a single piece of wood and painted to look like a real blade. If they'd stabbed me, I would have died.

Staked.

I don't scare that easily. Sure, Cosgrove freaks me out. But by and large, I'm not that given to the willies.

This, however, scared the piss out of me. A kill team had been set loose on me. And what bugged me the most was that it didn't feel at all like Cosgrove's style.

I used the remainder of the walk to Talya's hotel to slow down my heart rate. The doorman gave me a wink and I stopped long enough at the front desk to find out what room Talya was in before I made my way up in the elevators.

Out of professional habit, I stopped one floor below hers and took the stairs up. The fire door opened with a small squeak, but my footsteps were hushed by the thick carpeting on the hallway floor.

A single camera monitored the hallway, so I tried to walk as casually as possible. Outside her room I paused for a minute, listening.

Nothing.

I would have preferred to kick the door in, but you never knew who could be on the other side.

I stood just off the door and knocked, half expecting a blast of buckshot to splinter the door. But none came. In fact, no one answered the door.

I knocked again.

Still nothing.

The door was locked from inside and the door had an electronic card reader on it. The kind where you slip the card in and the little light goes from red to green and then grants you access.

Not too easy to jimmy.

But above the door was a key lock.

And those are easy to pick. Even for someone like myself who's not too skilled in picking locks.

It took me thirty seconds to get in, and I was sure if anyone was awake downstairs at the security console, it would be maybe two minutes before I had an unwelcome welcoming party.

Inside the room there was light from a table lamp in the corner. A magazine had been left open on the table. A small carryall in black nylon sat in the corner of the otherwise empty room. The bed was neatly arranged. It hadn't been slept in by the look of it.

I moved to the bureau and opened the drawers. There were only a few articles of clothing, mostly composed of the variety of bikini panties that I like so much. I like a woman who knows how to dress in her underwear.

I came up with an envelope of money in the nightstand. More hundreds. And guess what? The numbers continued the sequence I'd gotten off the thug downstairs.

"Looking for something?"

I wheeled around and found myself staring at Talya's naked body. Water dripped off all the right protrusions and found its way to the floor. Her hair was slicked back, eyes bright but narrowed. She glistened like a lithe predator and seemed totally comfortable with the fact that she was completely nude. I watched rivulets of water work their way south, converging at the thin Mohawk of pubic hair running ever farther into her deepest regions.

If she hadn't been leveling a 9mm pistol on me, I might actually have enjoyed the sight.

"You don't need that," I said.

"No?" She gestured toward the bed. "Move back slow. This thing's been modified and the trigger has a hair pull on it."

I made a show of holding my hands up. "Put it away, Talya."

"Not yet, Mr. Lawson. Not until we have a chance to talk."

That was rich. "Well, what should we talk about? The weather?"

"How about my almost getting offed by two thugs a few minutes ago in the Public Gardens?"

"What?"

"You heard me. They even had a picture of me. A security photo by the looks of it. You wouldn't know anything about that, would you?"

"Why the hell would I have someone kill you, Talya? It makes no sense."

"Might be exactly the reason why you would."

I smiled. "Mind if I show you something?"

She frowned. "Nothing funny, Lawson. I'll shoot you if I think I have to."

I reached into my pocket and brought out the photo of myself. "I just found that on some of my own would-be attackers downstairs." I tossed the picture onto her bed. "They tried to hit me as I came in."

She glanced down at it. "So what?"

I took out the roll of $100 bills. "Something else." I tossed the roll onto the photograph. "Seems someone paid for their services out of the envelope full of hundreds you keep in your nightstand."

Her face showed distress and the gun wavered. "What?" She turned to the nightstand, still keeping the gun on me with one hand as she rifled through the envelope. I leaned back and admired her rear assets.

She stood up. "I had five thousand dollars in here. A thousand's gone."

I pointed at the bed. "That would be it."

She frowned again and lowered the gun. "What the hell is going on?"

I shrugged. "Seems fairly obvious. We're being set up to be killed."

"But—"

"But nothing, Talya. That's it. Someone got access to the security cameras downstairs, to your room, and then went about hiring some young guns to waste us."

"But they were so untalented. I mean streetwise, yeah, but not professionals." She suddenly seemed aware of the fact that she had no clothes on and began dressing. I watched her bra encompass the fullness of her breasts, watched as she slid on the high-cut bikini panties. She pulled a turtleneck on first and then black stretch pants. I cleared my throat.

"Well, they knew where to stab with a knife, which is a cut above most. They might easily have succeeded against people with less training than us."

"But what was the point?"

I made a calculated decision, which in my books means I took a wild guess. I hoped it would prove to be the right one. Sometimes you just had to jump blind.

"Talya, when we were in the bar last night—"

"What about it?"

"Remember I went to look upstairs for Cosgrove."

"I remember. I stayed down at the bar."

I nodded. "I came back down and saw you talking to someone. A man. He was sitting next to you."

She shifted then and looked away. "Oh, yeah . . . What about him?"

I started to say it; started to explain that it had
been Cosgrove sitting with her, talking to her;
started to want to ask her all about their conversation and the language they were speaking. I started
to.

But I didn't complete it.

Because at that moment the entire room shook,
rumbled, and exploded, shattering my reality into
a million pieces of combustible hell.

Thirteen

There's nothing quite like being in the middle of an explosion to make you appreciate the sensation of pain. There's that real special moment when you feel the concussion wave smack you every which way, followed by the intense flash of heat and fire. If you're really lucky, you'll have the added bonus of some fragmentation. You could liken it to acupuncture done at Mach 5 and come away with a rough idea of what it feels like to be pierced through with a million shards of burning metal.

Fun stuff.

Really.

I got it all and more, it seemed. And when I woke up in the hospital bed, McKinley was looming over me, frowning.

"Jesus."

I tried to smile. "It's Lawson, you prick. How soon you forget."

"I see your sense of humor survived the explosion. That's always a good sign."

I took a deep inhale of air and grimaced. There's always been something about hospitals that makes me edgy. I don't know whether it's the sterile smell of antiseptic, the white and pale green color scheme most of them employ to calm down patients, or just the overall environment. If nurses still dressed in short little uniforms, I might like them a lot more. But they don't, so hospitals never make my list of cool places to hang out.

"Get me out of here."

McKinley shook his head. "No can do."

I tried lifting myself out of the bed. "McKinley, get me out of here. You know what could happen—"

He held up his hand. "Relax, Lawson, you're all set in that regard. Your doctor's one of us."

Thank God for that. All I needed was some eager young intern discovering I didn't exactly function like your everyday living human being. Hell, I'd have to off myself if that happened.

I slumped back against the pillows. "What the hell happened?"

"You mean besides the obvious? Someone had packed that little hotel room you were in with enough explosives to send you to the damned moon, Lawson. What the hell were you doing there?"

"What about the girl?"

McKinley frowned. "What girl?"

"Talya."

"Talya? You mean the one you wanted me to check out for you?" He shrugged. "When we got to the room, you were the only one in the rubble."

That wasn't possible. She'd been right near me. I tried getting out of bed again. McKinley held me back down. "Lawson, you're not going anywhere yet."

I slid back down, suddenly aware of the waves of

pain rippling through my body. "Ugh. What's my diagnosis?"

"Severe fragmentary damage. Doc's already pulled about fifty little metal souvenirs out of your body. You lost a lot of blood, which is actually good news for you since you get a couple of pints to chow down on. Don't binge now, you hear?"

I smiled. "When can I get the hell out of here?"

"They just took another set of X rays a short time ago. Once they figure out if you're clean, you can go. The doc will get you out hopefully tonight." He sighed.

"What else, McKinley?"

He looked away. "Cosgrove struck again last night."

I looked at the clock on the nightstand. I'd been out for over twelve hours. That was a long time for a human. For a vampire, given our increased ability to handle damage, it was a bad sign. If I'd been a mortal, that blast would have finished me.

It would have finished Talya, I realized.

"Talya was in there with me."

McKinley nodded. "We know it was her room, but believe me when I tell you, Lawson, there was no one else in that room but for you. There would have been remains, burned clothing, bones—hell, anything. Instead, all they found was your busted-up body."

"All right. Did Cosgrove hit another nightclub?"

McKinley frowned. "No."

"What's the matter?"

"Lawson." He sighed. "Cosgrove got one of our own."

"What? One of us? Who? And why? That doesn't make any sense."

"We'll talk later. You need to rest."

"The hell. Tell me what happened."

McKinley looked at the door and then back at me. "It was an Elder, Lawson. He got an Elder. We don't know why. We don't have any clues whatsoever. But he got him good. They found him inside his apartment when he didn't report for work today. Cosgrove left his guts draped all over the house and his head on a bedpost."

"Jesus."

McKinley leaned closer. "I want you at the apartment where he got wasted. Try to find out why Cosgrove would have bothered with an Elder."

"OK." I gestured to my bed. "You wanna wheel me over there?"

He grinned. "When you're released, Lawson. You can't do anything for the poor bastard now anyway. We'll talk tomorrow. Let me know what you find out."

I grabbed his arm. "I want a guard."

He pulled back and frowned. "What?"

"You heard me. Put someone on the door. Someone good. There's some serious shit going on, McKinley. There's no way I'm going to lay here like some clay pigeon waiting for whoever put me here to show up and finish the damned job."

"What kind of serious shit?"

I clued him in on the failed attack with the wooden blade.

McKinley frowned. "C'mon, Lawson, that could have just been for show. For the robbery."

"I know what a goddamned robbery looks like and I know a hit team when I see it." I took a breath. "And now Cosgrove hits an Elder? There's more going on than his simple psychotic episodes."

"More?"

"I'm not sure how it all comes together yet."

He flattened the wrinkles in his shirt. "You're serious."

I nodded. "Damn straight."

He sighed. "OK, OK, I'll call up a reserve. Got anybody in mind—?"

"No goddamned reserves, McKinley. Get me someone active."

"Active? Lawson, you know what kind of waves that's gonna cause?"

"I don't care. You get me someone I can trust my life with."

"Hey, buddy, you forget you aren't exactly due to win any popularity contests in the service? You don't have many friends out there. And even if you did, trust is an almost obsolete commodity nowadays. You got anybody in mind?"

I thought for a second. "Get me Zero."

"Zero? You kidding? He hasn't seen any action in years. He's a Control like me. You said you wanted an active agent."

"Zero's the best. And he's a former active agent. I want him here. ASAP."

McKinley sighed again. "OK, I'll ring him up. Jesus, this is getting to be a royal pain in my ass. Just try not to die in the meantime, OK? Try to get some sleep."

Easier said than done. How the hell could I sleep when somewhere out there Cosgrove was stalking another victim, and God knew what else. And then there was the whole matter about Talya. How the hell did she survive that blast? McKinley said she wasn't one of us. She was human. I didn't know too many humans who could survive being on ground zero with a huge packet of plastic explosive suddenly detonating close by. No way.

Too many questions. No answers.

And, man, did my body hurt.

It took Zero two hours to get there. I spent the entire time jumping at every creak and squeak in my immediate area. But when he hauled his six-two 220-pound frame through the door, I suddenly felt a lot better.

He stopped short when he saw the bandages. "Anyone tell the museum their Egyptian mummy had a run-in with a ketchup truck?"

"Nice to see you too, Zero."

He came over to the bed and grabbed my hand and shook it. "Been a long time, Lawson."

"Too long, Zero. Too long. Where you been?"

"Came as soon as I got the call from McKinley. Traffic was a bitch. They're doing construction outside of Hartford. It was stop and go the entire way."

"They're always doing construction in Connecticut."

"Tell me something I don't know. It's the official state hobby, I think."

"Ought to put a requisition in for a chopper."

Zero grinned. "Sure, we could paint it black and call it *Fang One* or something else original."

It was good to have him here with me. Zero oversaw Fixer operations in Connecticut. He was based in Hartford, and while McKinley had been right when he'd said Zero hadn't seen any action in a long time, there was still nobody else I would have wanted guarding my back during my temporary disability.

Zero and I went way back. He was my first partner when I graduated from Fixer training. Back then, they paired rookies with veterans. Zero'd been a Fixer longer than most.

He met me at Heathrow Airport where I'd just finished a transatlantic flight from Boston. I'd had no idea who to look out for, but my orders were simple enough: go to the concession stand, order a coffee, and wait.

Have I mentioned how much I hate coffee?

Well, this being my first real assignment, I wasn't about to let a simple dislike of ground beans stop me. I ordered the coffee black and then waited by a table with two chairs.

Zero waited a half-hour before approaching me.

He came up on me so quickly and quietly that it scared the hell out of me. He dropped into the chair opposite me and grinned.

"You're Lawson."

"Yes."

He nodded. "You were told to order coffee."

"I did."

He nodded. "But you didn't drink it, did you?"

I had attempted two or three halfhearted sips and told Zero as much. He chuckled.

"There will be times, my young friend, when you must drink down the worst concoctions you can imagine, all in the name of the Balance. And you know what? You'll drink them as if they were the sweetest-tasting nectar ever to grace your lips, and you'll do it because by the time I'm through with you, you'll be more of a professional than whatever walked out of the camp." He sat back. "After all, we're tied to the hip, you and I. My survival is now as much in your hands as yours is in mine." He smiled. "So don't fuck it up."

I'd mumbled an apology which he dismissed. He gestured over to the other side of the food area. "Do you see those two men in hats? With the dark suits?"

I looked and saw them. "Yes."

"The one on the right is Yuri Vasilev, a local KGB bloodhound. The man he is with is Hans Junger of the East German Stasi. They are both very skilled."

"What do they have to do with us?"

Zero took a sip of my coffee and then replaced it on the table. "Everything, Lawson. They have everything to do with us. We are alike in many, many ways. And even if they are human and we are vampires, there are similarities that go beyond mere flesh and blood."

"So I'm supposed to learn from them as well?"

Zero shrugged. "Perhaps. They are, after all, professionals. And you are an untested, green Fixer."

"But what can they teach me?"

Zero smiled, finished my coffee in a gulp, and gestured for me to follow him as we rose from the table. "For one thing, my young friend, they can teach you how to blend in better. They've been watching you since you arrived."

"Watching me?"

"Heathrow is a major way-point for intelligence agents from all over the world. You've just de-planed from an American carrier, ordered a coffee, and not taken many sips from it. To top it off, you've been sitting in the middle of a concession area for thirty minutes without a book or a newspaper, looking around the terminal like a lost puppy. Being the professionals that they are, although in truth it didn't take much, they picked you out as a potential newly active intelligence agent in the area."

I felt sick.

Zero kept talking. "Right now our pictures are being taken by the man next to the flower kiosk wearing the muted plaid sport coat. Within two hours those pictures will be developed and on their way back to Berlin or Moscow where they will be compared to a huge database of all known Western operatives."

"But we won't match anyone."

"No, we won't." Zero laughed again. "Which means, in all probability, they'll believe we are new agents and thus open a new file for us."

"God, I'm sorry."

"Don't be, Lawson. It happens to everyone." He sat back, watching me. "A lot different from the camp and those field exercises, isn't it?"

"Yes. Yes, it is."

And it was. But Zero took me under his wing until I wasn't a greenhorn any longer. We saw a lot of shit in Europe and in the Middle East where there had been some attempts to split from the Council and establish another organization independent of Council control.

Naturally, that hadn't sat too well with the powers that be. Zero and I were dispatched to put the leader down. We walked straight into an ambush and almost died in the process. If it hadn't been for Zero, I would have never lasted a second. But he brought me through it in spades.

He'd retired from fieldwork a long while back, choosing to run ops the way McKinley did in Boston. He'd had a long service record, so the Council granted his request. And while he may have been out of action, he still looked exactly the same way I remembered him: in great shape and able to kick mucho ass.

And that was what I wanted.

With Zero watching over me, I could at least get some sleep.

He looked me over again and prodded one of my bandaged legs. "For crying out loud, Lawson, didn't I teach you anything about hotel rooms?"

"You said they were nifty places to get laid in."

"I also said they were prime ambush sites, you knucklehead."

I smiled. "Must have missed that lesson."

"No shit." He picked up my chart and spent five minutes examining it. "Doctor one of ours?"

I nodded. "So says McKinley."

"Good. At least I won't have to bother with curious doctors and nurses." He pulled a chair up to the bed. "You want to tell me what the hell happened?"

I filled him in as best as I was able, which, in truth, wasn't much. He said nothing for a while, just frowned. Then he walked to the window.

"Get some sleep, Lawson. We'll talk when you wake up."

So I did.

Fourteen

I woke up in the back of Zero's black Chevy Tahoe as we cruised down Beacon Street toward Kenmore Square. I sat up and rubbed my head. It still ached like the bastard child of a whiskey, vodka, sake, and beer orgy.

"Welcome back, friend."

He smiled in the darkness and I clapped him on the shoulder. "Everything OK?"

He nodded. "Doc says they got most of that crap out of you. Most of it. He couldn't be completely certain. You're in no danger, of course, but you'll probably be able to tell when it's gonna rain in the future. That and metal detectors might be a problem for you."

"Damn, I was hoping for X-ray vision."

"Ingrate. He said everything else checked out. He also advised that you stay away from hotels for a while."

"Everybody's a goddamn comedian."

Zero chuckled. "That's it, shoot the messenger."

I watched Commonwealth Avenue zip past us. "Where we going?"

"Buddy of mine runs a bar in Allston. We need to have a drink and a long talk."

I checked myself over while he drove. My clothes had been replaced, thank God, courtesy of McKinley, who knew my sizes. Aside from my pounding head, I felt pretty achy, but all things considered, things seemed to be working all right. Probably wouldn't be back up to full operational capacity for a day or two. But it was better being out of that hospital than in it.

Zero parked just off Harvard Avenue and we threaded our way through the Wednesday-night crowds until he pulled me into a little recessed bar, just off the main thoroughfare.

"He keeps the joint understated. Doesn't really like catering to the college crowds."

"Make a fortune if he did."

Zero shrugged. "Never been real interested in making money." He yanked open the heavy wooden door and we went inside.

It was a dark, musty, old-world bar that brought you right back to a different time. A faint smell of peat hung in the air, and off in the corner I could see bright flames jumping inside a stone hearth. Smoke hung heavy in the room from a hundred cigars, pipes, and cigarettes. As we entered, heads turned, checking us over. The noise level dropped momentarily, but picked up as soon as we passed the nonverbal inspection.

Zero led the way to the bar, a thick plank of oaken timber polished to a bright sheen by the arms of thousands of patrons over the years. From out of the gloom, a short, squat man appeared. Judging by the girth of his forearms, the thickness of his neck, and the barrel-shaped chest, I knew his past included time in the navy, most likely in the SEALs.

He chuckled as he came up to us. "Well, well, well."

Zero grinned. "How are you, my friend?"

He leaned in toward Zero and grasped his hand, pumping it three times before letting him go. "I'm well, you ungrateful son of a bitch." His eyes narrowed. "I haven't seen or heard from you in years. You coulda been dead, man."

"You know the work. You know the hours."

The man nodded. "Got three divorces to prove it too." He leaned in closer. "What brings you back?"

Zero inclined his head. "Business, always the business."

The man tossed his thumb over his shoulder. "Gotcha. Grab a table in back. I'll bring some drinks."

We wove our way through the crowd and found our way to the rear of the bar. Several roughly hewn wooden tables stood on massive legs. Zero pulled a chair out and eased himself into it. I slid into the chair opposite.

The bartender appeared and with him came two bowls of what looked like beef stew and two ceramic steins of a dark, frothy German beer. I took a sip and found it was Dortmunder.

"Difficult beer to get here in the States."

Zero took a long haul on his and smiled. "Difficult, yes. But not impossible." He pointed at the bowl. "Eat some food, Lawson."

It smelled delicious and I could see the huge chunks of potatoes and carrots floating amid the sea of thick sauce and beef. I took a small spoonful, but could manage very little. My head hurt too much.

We sat there for another five minutes, drinking and allowing our eyes to become accustomed to the darkness of the bar. When Zero had something to say, it was best to just let him get to it when he felt the time was right. Prodding him never accomplished anything. He was always careful. Calculating.

It took ten minutes before he cleared his throat and got a fresh stein of beer, then turned to me.

"You're after Cosgrove."

I nodded. "Got the termination order this time. It's official."

He nodded. "You think so, huh?"

"What's that supposed to mean?"

He frowned and took another drag. "Lawson, if I asked you what the most important aspect of our job is, what would you say?"

"The Balance. Maintaining the Balance. Any new recruit would tell you that."

"Exactly. Our whole reason for being Fixers, our sole purpose if you will, is to ensure the preservation of the Balance. If we fail, if the world of humans discovers our existence, if the secret leaks out . . . then we'll be destroyed. Despite all our power, despite our advantages, we would be destroyed. We have our limitations after all."

"Agreed."

He took another long drag on his beer and belched. "What if I told you that some of the members of our community felt that maintaining our secrecy was no longer necessary?"

"I'd say you needed to get out of Connecticut more often."

"Even still," said Zero, "there are some who feel

just that way. In fact, there are some who want to form a partnership with humans."

"A partnership? This isn't a corporate merger. Don't be ridiculous."

"I wish I was. But I'm not." He leaned closer to me. "I have heard rumors, only rumors, but persistent rumors from all corners of our community. An alliance is being formed. Slowly, cautiously, to be sure, but an alliance nonetheless. And Cosgrove is the man forging the path."

"Well, I can see Cosgrove being that insane, sure, but why? What does he get out of it?"

"What he's always wanted, I would guess," said Zero. "Rule over the vampires. A virtual dictatorship. The good scenario is this: in exchange for the supposed safety of the vampire community, he would most likely allow experimentation on us. Study. The humans would be beside themselves with curiosity to study us, find out what makes us tick. How we exist. After all, we represent another branch in human evolution. One of the proverbial missing links, as it were. We'd be potential guinea pigs."

"Jesus."

"Not only that, but the humans would allow access to some of the blood supply. It would ensure our cessation of the hunt; it would enamor the vampires to Cosgrove. He'd be seen as a savior."

"What about the hunt? What about the old ways?"

Zero sighed. "There are some who see them as an anachronism, Lawson. Some want the hunt to stop altogether. Given the pace of technology, many feel having to hunt for blood is more an insult than a necessary skill. They see humans able to buy whatever they need at a grocery store and want the same. The hunt represents a time many want to forget. They're in favor of a more peaceful existence. A coexistence, as it were."

"But our very nature demands the hunt," I said. "You can't just stop thousands of years of heritage and tradition."

"You can if you're Cosgrove. Believe me, Lawson, he means to do it. The signs are all there." He paused again.

"What's the bad scenario?"

"If what I think is happening truly is, the humans Cosgrove is allying himself with aren't the leaders of the free world."

"What do you mean?"

"I mean, I would expect Cosgrove to form alliances with others like him. Psychotics, terrorists, criminals. They would understand each other. And the benefits they'd reap from each other would aid their own causes proportionally. With the aid of the vampires, criminals could become even more ferocious in their ways. Can you imagine a new brand of global vampiric terrorism? And again, in exchange for the aid of the vampires, we'd get access to untold amounts of blood. Just what we need to survive. And Cosgrove would emerge victorious. The Council would be disbanded. The old guardians of the ways would be unceremoniously killed. And as for us Fixers, well, we'd be seen as public enemy number one. Cosgrove would waste no time hunting us down. If he had access to the files, he could unleash his human allies on our heels. We'd have no safety anywhere and go from saviors to the refuse of our society."

My mouth was dry, and even several gulps of good German beer did little to restore its moisture.

"But humans could only frustrate us. We'd be more than a match for them if they chose to engage us in combat."

Zero looked away and then back at me. "Cosgrove would use the humans to herd us into a trap. Then he'd use other Fixers, Lawson. Some of the disenchanted Fixers who don't work anymore. There are plenty. Plenty who feel a kinship with Cosgrove's demented ways. Plenty enough to be a very viable threat. Especially if Cosgrove grants them invulnerability to the crackdown."

"What about the Council? Have you gone to them?"

Zero shook his head. "No, for several reasons. First, while the Council is vital to our society, they are slow to see the dangers we see. You've had first-hand experience with that when you tried to kill Cosgrove before."

I nodded.

"And second," said Zero, "I don't know how far up this conspiracy goes. And if we're to move to stop it, to maintain the Balance and do our job, we must do so in absolute secrecy. I have doubts as to who can be trusted and who may be under Cosgrove's spell. Every step we make must be cautious, and yet we cannot afford to wait any longer."

"What do you want me to do?"

"Your job has been to hunt down Cosgrove. That's what you will do. Find him. Kill him. It's essential."

"There was a woman with me in the hotel room yesterday."

"Who?"

"Name's Talya."

Zero squinted in the darkness. "Still using the present tense. I take it she's alive?"

I shrugged. "Don't know. According to McKinley, they never recovered another body. Just me."

"So she's alive."

"Damned if I know how," I said. "I barely escaped with my life. But she's human. She should have died in that room."

"She got a background?"

"Professional. Freelance assassin. Cosgrove killed her fiancée. She's sworn vengeance. I thought if I offered to help I could keep better tabs on her. Hell, she might even come in handy. Now she's gone."

Zero frowned. "Give me some time. I'll see if I can locate her. I still have some pretty decent contacts around here."

"There's something else."

He watched me and I had trouble even saying it. "Last night—while I was out of commission—Cosgrove took out an Elder."

Zero frowned. "Why would he do that?"

"I don't know. According to McKinley, they found his intestines strewn across his apartment and his head on a bedpost. That mean anything to you?"

"Just that Cosgrove's got a pretty strange sense of interior decorating. Can you get some details about this?"

"Yeah, McKinley wants me to check it out anyway. I'm going over tomorrow. You want me to look for anything in particular?"

"The Elder's name and age. But on your own,

see if you can dig up exactly what he was charged with safeguarding."

"On my own? What's that supposed to mean?"

Zero frowned again. "It means involve outside sources as little as possible. Even your Control. Like I said before, we don't know how far up this thing might go. We don't want to alert anyone we don't need to."

"All right. I'll see what I can do."

He stood up. "Finish your beer and wait fifteen minutes before you leave. I'll be in touch soon."

I watched him disappear in the gloomy darkness as easily as a shadow. There was a strong gust of cool air as the door opened and Zero exited. But the cold air died quickly under the curtain of smoke still hanging in the bar.

And there in the subdued interior, I stared into my beer stein and felt very much alone in a very dangerous world.

Fifteen

I left the bar after twenty minutes of beer swilling and found a pay phone a block farther down, close to the Dunkin' Donuts. On a vague whim I phoned the Four Seasons and asked for Talya's room. There was a minute of silence on the phone before the operator told me the room number no longer existed. I asked for Talya. The operator told me there was nobody registered under that name.

If Talya had gone to ground and effectively disappeared, it didn't really surprise me. I guess a part of me had actually hoped against hope that she wasn't bad. That she was really a player on the right side of the fence. But because she had gone under, because she'd vanished, I was left with no choice but to accept the fact that she was probably in league with Cosgrove.

That meant I technically no longer had just one target to eliminate. Talya had become a liability and a potential threat to the Balance. After all, she knew Cosgrove was a vampire. Hell, I'd told her as much. Not that she probably hadn't already known. She could have been playing me for a while, who knew?

What I did know was that she was now a threat

case and had to be eliminated as soon as possible, preferably after I had eliminated my primary objective, Cosgrove. Still, beggars couldn't be choosers, and if Talya showed herself as a target of opportunity, I'd waste her and then track down Cosgrove. Really made no difference to me. It was just part of the job.

Or at least that was the idea I was trying hard to sell myself on. It would have been nice to honestly believe Talya hadn't affected me at all during our brief interaction. It would have been.

Of course it wasn't.

On a purely physical level, Talya had aroused a desire in me I hadn't experienced for a human woman before. Sure, I could bed down with them whenever I wanted. I just had to turn the charm on and that was it. But I hadn't turned any charm on with Talya and she'd responded regardless. Of course, she could have been playing me, but maybe there was something more to it.

Or maybe I just hoped there was.

Truth be told, I never exactly felt as though I'd ever had much of a handle on women. Whether they were vampires or humans. Hell, they confused me.

On the professional level I respected her immensely. Usually, I want the chance to see somebody in action before I pass judgment on their skill level. I want to see how they react under pressure before they get any ounce of respect from me.

Are they a shooter? Or do they just talk a big game?

It's a common sentiment among professionals like myself. Doesn't matter whether you're vampire or not. Seasoned combat veterans are the same way.

They keep quiet about what they can do, because talking will get you killed. And it's always the blabbermouths who turn out to be the worst under fire.

But for some reason I hadn't needed to see Talya under duress to know that she'd respond accordingly, with grace and ease that only comes from years of being in the field.

Even knowing about her background hadn't affected my evaluation. Sure, the dossier McKinley had dug up on her dovetailed nicely with what I sensed, but there was something more.

Experience can't be bought, no matter how badly you want to believe it. And Talya had experience written all over her face. It was in her walk, that calculated, even flow as she glided over the sidewalk. It was instinctive. It wasn't something she tried to put on. She just had it naturally.

You don't find that very often these days.

And frankly, it pissed me off to no end she was in league with a psycho like Cosgrove. Now, I know the rules as well as the next guy, but it would have been nice, even if just for a moment, to think of her as something more than just a convenient fuck.

Well, it would have been.

Reality sucked sometimes.

My reality sucked pretty bad right now. It would have been nice to crawl home, feed my cats, and get about eighty hours of sleep to cure my headache. It would have been.

Instead, I took a mud-slicked yellow cab back downtown. Wednesday nights meant a lot more people out cruising the bar scene and nightclubs. Landsdowne came alive on Friday and Saturdays, but Wednesdays belonged to the theater district's clubs. Smaller and more intimate than Landsdowne

Street's, they nevertheless sucked in their share of eager sexual conquistadors and the maidens they sought.

I got out of the cab by the Wang Center and took a quarter from my pocket, tossed it in the air, checked the result, and set off for the club.

What, you think it's odd I chose to use a coin to make a decision? Maybe you thought I had some kind of superhoming sense I'd be able to detect Cosgrove with, eh? I wish. Doesn't work that way, though. And sometimes, just like any good detective will tell you, you just make a guess, close your eyes, and pray it's right.

I usually did everything but pray, since I was under no illusions that the gods didn't have any more important things to tend to than a silly vampire hit man.

The Roxy sat across the street from the Wang Center and I skirted three shiny white limousines and a red cab to get to the door. The doorman at this establishment took one look at my jeans and frowned.

"Got a dress code here, buddy."

I smiled. It was apparently time for what I affectionately refer to as the "Jedi mind trick."

"Yeah, I didn't have time to change your mind that's not really important with me."

The bouncer got a thousand-yard stare on his face, his skin color blushed slightly, and his pupils dilated. Then he nodded, moved aside, and mumbled something incoherent.

No, it wasn't some kind of cool vampire mind control. It was a science known as design human engineering that we'd been required to study as Fixers. Back when I took the course, it had been categorized as neurolinguistic programming. Whatever you wanted to call it, the damned stuff worked like a charm.

Inside, it was romping. A trio of well-proportioned women hung back by the door and checked me over as I threaded my way past them. I smiled at the ugliest one and that set them all chattering and giggling.

The darkness of the club made it easy to move around unnoticed. I swung back by the dance floor, checking out the red velour seating area that bordered it more than the gyrating and twisting bodies occupying the cramped parquet dance floor.

It must have been Euro night here. I saw more kids with OPEC written on their faces than anything even faintly resembling WASP. And if the number of yellow BMWs parked out front had anything to do with the current population of this club, I was definitely on the mark.

Cosgrove would stand out easily in a crowd like this, but he'd be watching as he always did, from an advantageous position. I didn't know the Roxy that well, which put me in a bad situation. The only way to figure out the best area would be to move around the entire club and spot from various angles.

Which, naturally, would expose me.

My choices were limited, though, so I did just that. I started at the closest bar and wound counterclockwise. If Zero had been with me, we could have cut the pie and covered the distance a lot sooner.

"Cutting the pie" is a term used by special operations when they take a room down. They divide it up into sections just like a pie. Each man on the team has an assigned section and that's it. Every-thing in that field of fire is his. It allows a hostage-rescue team to take control of a room in an extremely short amount of time. In my case it would allow Zero and I to comb the room for Cosgrove, simultaneously knowing we had each other's backs.

But Zero wasn't with me on this.

And so I did it the old-fashioned and much more dangerous way. It meant a lot more risk because if Talya was working with Cosgrove, I felt sure she'd be poking around somewhere. Maybe they were even waiting for me.

It'd be simple enough to take me out then.

Even in the darkened confines of this club.

A perfect ambush.

Cosgrove would prefer a big show, being the ego-maniac, but Talya would be inclined to keep it sub-tle. She'd stay true to her professionalism.

I wondered if Cosgrove had told her what I was. Maybe she'd known from the start of this whole thing.

I felt behind my right hip and felt a surge of re-assurance as my hand brushed against the pistol. The wooden-tipped bullets it held could kill a hu-man just as easily as Cosgrove. The loads were de-signed to blossom on impact, spraying and splintering the wooden heads all across a tremendous cavity caused by the impact.

Worked well for all types of enemies.

Hadn't used it on any werewolves yet, though.

The swirling lights of the dance floor forced me to move slower than I would have liked. I didn't want to stay fixed in any position long enough for Cosgrove or Talya to see me. If I kept moving, slow and with a lot of flow, chances were good I could get close without them seeing me.

But the strobe effects of the dance-floor lights made pinpointing anyone difficult, so I had to move slowly, edging my way around the perimeter—checking, moving, checking, moving.

It was when I was three-quarters of the way around the club that I heard the voice tickling my right ear. The low, husky drawl startling, but unmistakable—even over the roar of the throbbing dance music.

Talya's voice.

Sixteen

"Nice to see you again, Lawson"

I started to turn around, but the sharp prod in my back, unmistakably a gun barrel, stopped me.

"Uh-uh-uh, not so fast, lover. I wouldn't want to have to kill you before we get a chance to talk this out."

I felt her fleece my gun off me and then she steered me over to the left. "Back of the club, head for that empty booth. Move and keep very, very still."

I knew any number of techniques that technically would have allowed me to disarm Talya and kill her, but I chose not to employ them for several reasons.

First, while I knew I could get out of the way, I wanted to make sure I could get far enough so that Talya wouldn't be able to fill me full of holes. I didn't want to lose any more blood, and since we were in cramped quarters, maneuvering would have been problematical.

Second, she was a pro and would have anticipated my strategies. Therefore, by my doing something, I would be playing right into her countermoves. Who knew what kind of contingency plans she'd arranged for? Not good.

And most important, I had questions of my own I wanted to ask. Maybe I'd even get some answers. Maybe Cosgrove was waiting for me at the back of the club. Even though on my first pass, I hadn't seen him.

So curiosity kept me from trying anything. And we reached the booth uneventfully.

No one joined us. No one sat nearby.

No Cosgrove.

Talya gestured. "Take a seat, Lawson."

I did. "Why is it lately every time I run into you, you seem to feel leveling a gun on me is necessary?"

She frowned. "Given what's happened, recent events seem to dictate it out of necessity."

"Necessity?"

"My survival."

I watched another couple collapse into a booth ten feet away and proceed to engage in fully clothed sex. I turned my attention back to Talya. "Last time I saw you, your hotel room exploded. I don't suppose you'd care to tell me how the hell you survived when everything else, including me, got blown to shit?"

She sniffed. "I might ask you the same question. Unless, of course, I'm talking to a dead man right now."

"No, I'm alive. No idea how I came through it, but I did." I shrugged. "Just lucky."

It was as feeble as a fifteen-year-old's claim that he reads *Playboy* for the articles, but it was all I had.

She didn't buy it.

"Give me a break, Lawson. You're a professional just like me and you know damned well there's no such thing as luck." She leaned closer. "You should have died in that room."

"Maybe I've got a guardian angel."

"Maybe you're lying to me."

I shifted slowly. "Well, what about you? How'd you come through it without a scratch?"

"I have the gun, Lawson. You first."

I cleared my throat. "Why don't I finish what I was going to talk to you about before the explosion interrupted us?"

She scanned the area. "All right."

I shifted again. "I believe we were discussing your companion whom I saw you speaking with when I came back downstairs the other night."

"What about him?"

"Do you know who you were talking to?"

She shrugged. "Said his name was Robert. Why?"

"And the language you were speaking?"

She frowned and I could almost hear the gears grinding in her head. She'd remember to ask, I was sure, how the hell I could have overheard their conversation. "He guessed my nationality."

"He spoke Russian?" That was bullshit. They hadn't been speaking Russian and I knew it.

She shook her head. "No. He used a Kazakh dialect that my mother taught me to speak. It's very rare."

"Imagine the chances of someone knowing that, huh?"

She nodded. "Almost nonexistent."

"Unless you've had a lot of time to travel and learn languages," I said.

"What are you driving at, Lawson?"

"The man you were speaking to. Robert. Whatever he told you was a lie. Whatever you discussed. All of it was nothing but a lie."

"How can you be so sure? How did you overhear us?"

I ignored the second question and concentrated on the first. "I can be so sure because the man you were having such a great conversation with was the man we are hunting. Cosgrove."

She looked like she'd been hit with a tractor trailer and that was the moment I'd been waiting for. While her attention was focused inside, I grabbed the pistol and pointed it at her under the table.

"Now we play things my way, Talya."

I'd taken her weapon away so quickly it had clearly startled her. She obviously wasn't used to dealing with someone like me. And that was just fine.

I reached over and took my pistol back from the waistband of her slacks.

She recovered quickly, and I gave her credit for that. "How was I supposed to know it was Cosgrove? He didn't exactly ask to suck my blood and I didn't see any fangs."

"You wouldn't. They're retractable. And the only way to tell would be the birthmark at the base of his neck."

"He's got a birthmark?"

"All vampires do. It's a symbol of the race."

"What's it look like?"

"Just a blob of discolored skin. Down by the clavicle."

She nodded—absorbing, it seemed. "So now what?"

"Now you tell me how you got out of that hotel room without being blown to hell."

She looked down. "It was a shaped charge."

That got my attention. "Say what? Are you telling me you rigged the room to explode?"

She nodded. "I had to—"

"Are you fucking crazy? You could have killed me!" Well, not really, but it was important to make her still think I was as human as she was.

"Like I said, Lawson, it was shaped. I rigged it so the explosion would only impair you, not kill you."

"Really. All those delightful little pieces of fragmentation were designed to just impair me? You know how many splinters they dug out of me?"

"It wasn't supposed to be a frag explosion. My contact here in town made a mistake."

"No shit. Maybe I'll pay your contact a visit and give him a sample of his own medicine."

"That's not necessary."

"You weren't on the receiving end, Talya."

She looked at me. "It's not necessary because I already killed him. I do not tolerate mistakes like that."

That brought me up short. Talya didn't dick around. "Well, I still can't believe you blew up your hotel room."

She shrugged. "You think it makes no sense, and truthfully, if I was in your shoes, I'd agree with you. But you don't know the whole picture."

"Really. Well, suppose you goddamn well enlighten me."

Talya sighed. "I was scared."

"Bullshit, Talya. Don't try that feminine crap

with me. You don't strike me as the easily intimi-
dated type."

"I was scared, Lawson, because of the attempted
hit. You were the only person who could have
known where I was staying. You were the only one
who could have arranged a hit like that."

"So you rigged the room. Throw me off the
scent, make me think you were dead?" I smiled.
"You caused a loss of balance."

"What?"

"It's from an old book by Musashi on
swordsmanship. When you can start by making the
enemy think you are slow, or in this case—dead,
then you can attack strongly, thus keeping them
off balance."

"I guess that's what I wanted."

"But it wasn't me, Talya!"

She nodded. "I realized that too late. As soon as
you came into the room, I triggered the timer. I
couldn't have stopped it in time."

"So kill me; then your problems would have
been over."

"I told you, it wasn't supposed to kill you."

"Impair me? I find it hard to believe you'd spare
me but not the guy who made the bomb."

She smiled. "Maybe I like you, Lawson."

"Wonderful. So you get me out of the picture,
one way or another—"

"And I would have been able to kill Cosgrove
on my own."

I shook my head. "Not likely."

"I could do it, Lawson."

I really had to laugh. I mean, I had a lot of respect for this woman, but she was off her fucking

rocker. "Are you nuts? You wanted to take Cosgrove out by yourself?"

"Yes."

"And that small fact that he happens to be, well, you know, a goddamned vampire, that doesn't really make you think twice about confronting him?"

"No." She looked up at me and even in the darkness I could see the moisture in her eyes. It was the first time I'd seen her express emotion, I realized. The first time she'd shown remorse over Simbik's death. "I mean to kill him, Lawson. For what he did to my fiancé. I have to. Even if I was no longer in love with him, he was one of the few people I cherished in my life. And now it's my obligation." She looked away. "Mine alone."

I leaned back in the booth and watched the couple furiously grinding into each other. Judging by the extremely quick up-and-down motion, the guy couldn't have been hung much larger than my big toe.

I looked back at Talya and saw her vulnerability. A single tear had wound its way down her cheek and I understood just how much incredible self-control she must have been using to keep herself in check this entire time. The tear was testament to that fact.

"Talya," I said, sliding over closer to her.

She looked at me again, trying to will the moisture out of her eyes, draw it back in, suck back the visible turmoil. Just when I thought she'd succeeded, it came out in a torrent and she slumped into me, her chest heaving, my jacket muffling her sobs.

I held her close, feeling her warmth, smelling

her vague perfume, inhaling her essence, and tasting her delicious aroma. My mouth watered.

"Talya," I said again.

She sniffed and brought herself under control. She sat up, wiping away her face. "I'm sorry. I don't usually do that."

"I can tell."

She tried to smile. "Guess I needed that."

"I'd say so."

"Thank you, Lawson. You don't have to be so understanding."

"Yeah, I know. Women who try to blow me up, they're a real weakness of mine."

She laughed again, stronger this time. "You're a good man."

I shook my head. "You only say that because you don't know me. You'd change your mind in a hurry if you knew."

She moved closer to me. "I don't think so."

I cleared my throat. "There's still that business of the hit teams who tried to take us out just before the explosion. They'd been paid off from that wad of cash in your room. Got any explanations for that?"

"None at all, except to say someone must have broken into my room earlier. Maybe while I showered. Perhaps the night before when we were out."

"Well, I had an easy enough time getting in there myself, so I suppose that's possible."

"No place is ever secure," she said. "That fact has always unnerved me."

"I guess we can't go searching for evidence now anyway."

"Why no—" She stopped short, realizing her room had been reduced to splinters. "Sorry."

"Forget it. We've got more important things to think about."

She moved closer again. "I agree."

"Easy there. What makes you so sure I wouldn't blow you up in a heartbeat? I've got quite a vengeful streak in me."

"Is that so?"

"You have no idea. Trust me."

She smiled and moved even closer. "I do."

"Yeah?"

She grinned. "Uh-huh." Her lips came even closer. Full, pouty, expanding, widening; opening her mouth—

Metal jammed under my chin.

A gun barrel.

Her pistol.

Too late I realized she'd fleeced that damned thing back off me when she was crying on my shoulder.

She laughed and brought it down, then returned it to its holster under her armpit. "Now we're even." She grinned.

I had to smile too. She was quite a woman.

"Talya."

"Yes?"

"We're going to kill Cosgrove."

"I know."

"Together. You can't handle it alone."

She looked at me.

Then nodded.

Seventeen

I put a call in to McKinley the next morning. He sounded frazzled as usual. I asked what was going on and he sighed.

"Place is in a fucking uproar over the death of that Elder. I've got the Council screaming at me for results. I just got off the phone with them and I've got a pounding headache that feels like someone's ripping my brains apart."

"Who was the Elder, by the way? You promised me a better rundown on that whole thing. I'd like some info before I head over."

"Yeah, yeah, I did." I heard some papers being rummaged through. "Lessee . . . His name was Nyudar. He was a thousand years old."

"Jesus." That was a long time even for us. "How'd he manage that?"

"Elders, Lawson. You know how it is."

"Actually, I don't. Explain it to me."

"Elders are born into their professions just like Fixers. But they age even slower than the rest of us."

"How the hell do they do that?"

"Shit, I dunno. Magic, maybe."

"Magic? Give me a break."

"Hey, you can't tell me you haven't seen some stuff that defies description, pal. I know you too well for that. Our race is an old one. Who knows what these old fogies have locked in their skulls."

"Well, one thing's for sure. All the magic in the world didn't stop Cosgrove from ripping that poor guy apart."

"Can't imagine why. Nyudar was just a librarian, for crying out loud. Kept some old journals and stuff nobody's interested in nowadays."

"What kind of journals?"

"Dunno. I heard it was something to do with ancient customs. The old language. Stuff like that."

"Yeah, that is weird."

McKinley cleared his throat. "So what's the news, Lawson? You back in play or what? Please tell me you are. God knows I can't take much more badgering from the Council."

"Well, hang in there, McKinley. I'm back on the job. I'll be heading over in a few. I'll let you know if I find anything."

"You do that."

"What's the address?"

"South End. Down behind Copley Place." He gave me the address and sighed. "I'll be popping pills, trying to get this headache under control. Don't wait too long to call in."

"You getting worried about me?"

"Hell no. Just want to be able to give the Council some news is all."

"And here I thought you were getting all sentimental on me."

Zero called as soon as I hung up the phone. He wanted a meeting.

"Take the long way," he said before ringing off.

That told me to take extra precautions and ensure I didn't have anyone following me. I always took precautions anyway, especially after the other night.

But today I took extra care.

I'd left Talya last night at the Charles Hotel in Harvard Square. The concierge is an acquaintance of mine who understands the word "discreet." He got Talya squared away with a nice room on the third floor with a window overlooking an interior courtyard.

Talya had looked at it and smiled. "It's perfect, Lawson."

And it was.

Three floors off the ground, it was high enough that breaking in by climbing was tough, but not so high that she couldn't jump out and live if she had no other choice.

You might think it a little crazy to live life this way, but this is how professionals the world over think when it comes to their safety. It's a serious business we're in.

And while I may not have to focus on that aspect as much as my human contemporaries, I could still appreciate the idea of adhering to such principles.

I triple-backed on myself to make sure I was clean. I still had no idea how Cosgrove was getting around the city or even where he might be holing up. I had to assume he knew where I lived, even if he hadn't yet attacked me there. If I didn't assume the worst, he'd get me when I least suspected it. So I suspected everything.

Zero arranged to meet me at a small diner just outside of Kendall Square in Cambridge, close to the old candy factory situated by the Massachusetts Institute of Technology. According to Zero, they made the best turkey clubs in the city.

After biting into the sandwich, I had to agree with him. Plenty of mayonnaise, bacon not too crisp, ample lettuce, and plenty of cheese. I hated tomatoes, so I got mine without, which caused Zero to frown.

"Still can't eat 'em, huh?"

"You know I can't."

He smiled. "They're good for you, Lawson."

"I did my time when I was a kid. Couldn't get enough of them. Then suddenly it disappeared. Now I like cucumbers."

He shrugged and bit into his sandwich again. We waited until the lunchtime crowd had thinned out. The cramped little joint only had so many tables. Inside, the paint flicked off the walls in places, and pies and cakes still sat under the glass trays like you always see in old films. A real mom-and-pop-and-all-our-sons team from Greece ran the place and they gave you a lot of food for your buck. It was the kind of place I liked to eat in. Everyone was welcome.

And they didn't take shit from the Yuppies who came in pretending to be important. That was refreshing. If there was one thing that annoyed the holy bejesus out of me, it was young executives who thought the world started and stopped with them. They'd grown up cloistered and groomed in colleges designed to churn out corporate-business types who really contributed nothing to society. And somewhere along the line, someone had inserted a huge ego and a lot of attitude into an otherwise insecure shell. The result was a rude aberration with no sense of decency.

Ah, well, that was the twenty-first century for you.

Personally, I had been looking forward to the new millennium. I think I had some notion that there would be this huge overnight change. And yet somehow I doubted myself simultaneously.

Maybe just a small apocalypse, then. You know, take out some of those awful drivers who stay locked in second gear afraid to put a little gas into the engine. I clung to a belief that more traffic accidents were caused by timid drivers than those who knew how to drive well. Now if I could just get funding for the study . . .

We munched chocolate chip cookies for dessert and polished off our sodas before lapsing into conversation. Zero kept a full mug of coffee in front of him as incentive for the staff to leave us alone.

"Any luck so far?"

"McKinley says the Elder who was killed was named Nyudar. Some sort of librarian in charge of keeping journals."

"What kind of journals?"

"McKinley didn't know too much, just said they had old customs in them. Stuff to do with the old language."

"You asked McKinley?"

"Calm down. He volunteered the information."

Zero sighed. "Why kill an Elder? It doesn't make much sense. If he's trying to forge an alliance with the humans, why would he need the aid of an Elder? It doesn't make sense."

"Nothing Cosgrove does makes sense."

"That may seem true on the surface, Lawson, but there's always a pattern that flows out of even the darkest pools. There's something there we're not seeing. There has to be." He reached for his coffee. "What about the man himself? Any luck?"

I shook my head. "None. I have no idea where Cosgrove is shacking up. He's limited himself so far to nocturnal forays, but he can still skip around during the day. I can't find the bastard anywhere. Luckily, he didn't kill last night."

Zero nodded. "I know." He reached inside his leather jacket and brought out a manila folder. "Here's the dossier on your friend Talya. She's definitely not one of us, at least as far as the DIA is concerned."

"You took the DIA's assessment over Langley?"

Zero smiled. "You know as well as I do that the CIA hasn't had credible human intelligence since they went overly dependent on their satellites. The DIA still runs HUMINT networks keyed to the former Soviet Union." He pointed to the folder. "Give it a read."

I did. It seemed that McKinley may have had access to the same information Zero had just given me. Talya had been a KGB illegal in charge of wet work before she went freelance after the fall of communism. There were recent photos—well, recent in intelligence terms, which meant anything taken this decade—a list of her previous employers, and some biographical information. Seemed she'd been telling me the truth about being Simbik's fiancée. He was listed in her file.

I closed it and handed it back to Zero. "I see you're still maintaining your networks as well."

He took a sip of coffee. "A good thing I do too, Lawson."

"Why's that?"

"Because this thing, this conspiracy, goes deeper than I originally thought. Remember the other night when I told you I didn't want to go to the Council just yet?"

"Yeah." Personally, I felt we should. I didn't mention it to Zero, though.

"Good thing I didn't. I would have been killed trying to get there."

"By whom?"

"The old Fixers we talked about. Cosgrove's enforcers. His private termination squad."

I frowned. "So they exist."

"Yes, but I was wrong about something important."

"What's that?"

"When I mentioned the possibility that Cosgrove would use old Fixers, I thought he would use those of our kind who had retired from active service. That he'd use the old vets." He leaned forward. "I was wrong."

It dawned on me. "Jesus, he's using active Fixers."

Zero nodded. "It's one reason he's here in Boston. We still have to figure out the Elder connection."

That made sense. "Well, he did try to recruit me—"

"No, Lawson, not you, although I'm sure he'd love to have you come aboard and help him raise hell. But it's not you he's interested in getting to."

"Who, then?"

"McKinley."

"McKinley?" I shook my head. "Can't be, Zero. He's my Control; he wouldn't go over to Cosgrove. Hell, he gave me the termination order himself."

"Exactly," said Zero. "What better way to conceal the fact that he's becoming Cosgrove's chief operations man than by maintaining his role of your Control. Even if we went to the Council now with this, they'd never believe it. McKinley's got a great service record. He passed the termination order to you without incident and told you to go get your man. Hell, he even went so far as to call me up to protect your ass while you were in the hospital. He didn't have to do that. He could have killed you himself while you were out."

My stomach plunged toward my bowels; it felt like a kick in the balls. "Good God."

"You see the logic now?"

"I guess. It's a little tough picturing McKinley as a traitor, though."

Zero took a sip of coffee. "Even if it doesn't seem like the kind of thing you'd do if you were switching sides, Lawson, it's damned sound. It works. And it works well. It's no wonder you haven't gotten close to Cosgrove since that first night. McKinley's been keeping him abreast of your progress every step of the way. He's always just out of reach for you."

"But I saw him talking with Talya that night in the bar."

"A calculated move on his part."

"Calculated? What for?"

Zero shrugged. "Probably designed to make you mistrust her. If you figured she was part of his game plan, you might have killed her yourself."

"Get her out of the way in other words."

"Why not?" said Zero. "Did you tell McKinley about Talya?"

"After our first meeting."

"Makes perfect sense then. McKinley tells Cosgrove about Talya, about what an obvious professional she is. Cosgrove's no fool. He understands revenge better than most and would figure Talya to be another threat to his plans. If he can make you waste her, thinking she's with him, not only would it remove the threat, but it would also solidify McKinley's position. There'd be no way you'd think he was dirty."

It disgusted me to have fallen for Cosgrove's deceit so easily. And to think that McKinley was involved in it as well left me sick. But it vanished quickly enough. Rage filled the void.

"Who else?"

Zero looked up from his mug. "Who else?"

"Who else is involved?"

Zero shrugged. "Not sure yet. I only just got confirmation about McKinley from one of my sources. I double-checked the information on my own and it's legit."

"Who's your source?"

Zero looked at me like I'd just asked him to translate the Rosetta stone into Chinese. "What kind of question is that, Lawson? You know damned well I can't tell you. You know networks are never disclosed. Makes compromising them too easy."

"Like I'd tell."

Zero frowned again. "I'm not questioning your loyalty, Lawson. Hell, you know that's never been an issue. But even if you think you could hold out under duress, there's no telling what kind of shit they'd put you through if they thought you had information they needed. And everyone has a breaking point. Everyone."

"Fair enough."

"All right, so let's look at Cosgrove's other possible recruits." Zero glanced around the diner. "You and McKinley head operations here in Boston. There's no one else here to really figure into the plans. You've got Xavier in Portland, who controls the Maine and New Hampshire communities. And Dieter runs Vermont. I've got Connecticut and Rhode Island. There's always Gustafson and O'Reilly in New York, but I think Cosgrove is after the Northeast first; then he'll expand. After all, the Council is here."

It was true. The seat of power for the vampire community was the Council and they held court here in Boston. The Council liked to reside in old cities. And Boston was one of the oldest in the country.

"So you think he'll try to get the others into his scheme?"

"Probably use McKinley as his go-to man. Everyone knows what a nut Cosgrove is. It might make better sense to use McKinley as the initial contact. Once Cosgrove has solidified his alliances with the various Controls, he'll move against the Council. Kill them, usurp their power, and take over the rest of the country. From there it would only be a matter of time before he had the rule of the international vampire communities. You know they take their cues from us here."

I sighed. "You're sure about McKinley?"

"Absolutely."

"It's just that if he's mixed up in this, why would he feed me information about the Elder? He honestly sounded as confused as I was."

"He might well be. I'm sure Cosgrove wouldn't

reveal all the aspects of his plan, even to his co-horts. McKinley might honestly have no clue why Cosgrove is doing it. It helps make him look even less suspect."

Damn. I'd worked with McKinley for a long time. But I'd worked with Zero even longer and I trusted Zero with my life. I had to make a decision; right or wrong, I had to make one.

I shrugged my coat on. Zero looked up. "Got an idea?"

"Yeah. If McKinley's been keeping Cosgrove aware of my movements, maybe it's time to throw some disinformation out there and see if we can't trip them up."

Zero slid some cash on the tabletop. "Not too much, Lawson. Remember, I'm not ready to move yet. I need to call in some additional resources to make sure we can take them down if we need to. Wait for my signal."

"You've got additional resources?"

Zero smiled. "I hope so, Lawson. We're going to need them."

"So what do I do in the meantime? Sit tight?"

Zero smiled. "Hell no. If you can get Cosgrove, by all means do so. But be careful with McKinley. If he gets wind that you're onto the scheme, he may decide to kill you himself. And right now you're the only active Fixer I've got. I need you alive."

"Good to know. I'm heading over to that Elder's apartment. You want to tag along?"

"You don't need me."

"Actually, I could use your insight. This old-school stuff is much more up your alley than it is mine."

He grinned. "Yeah. OK."

I looked at him and wondered if he was enjoying the bit of adrenaline the situation had pumped into his blood. "Nice to be back walking that thin line again, Zero?"

"The hell," said Zero. "I'd rather prop my feet up after a long day and read a good book. This stuff is for you young pups. I'm far too old to be traipsing about like some greenhorn on his first time out."

"Luxury of choice isn't something we've ever had, though."

Zero smiled. "Well, we could always just walk away."

Fat chance of that. "If it was only that easy." Being a Fixer made you respect the Balance even more than most of your average everyday vampires. To us, the Balance represented the sanctity of our lives. It became our reason for existing. It was our Bushido. Protecting it became instinctive. Zero and I would rather die than walk away. He knew it. I knew it.

And unfortunately, Cosgrove and McKinley knew it too.

Eighteen

The South End is home to the kind of brownstones young professionals dream of owning one day. Old and stately, in as diverse a neighborhood as you can find in Boston. Zero and I wound our way down behind Copley Place and searched the streets for parking.

"Every sign says 'Resident Permit Parking Only,' " said Zero. "Don't they believe in meters?"

"Not in this part of town. Everyone here is keen on keeping outsiders away. You should see the double- and triple-parking that goes on down here on weekends."

I steered the Jetta into a squeeze between a Ford Explorer and a Lexus. Zero got out and looked around.

"This OK?"

"No signs anywhere. Maybe we got lucky."

Zero coughed. "Luck. Indeed."

Number 44 looked like someone had spent some serious bucks trying to turn back time. Fresh mortar had been spooned into cracks between the reddish bricks and a fresh coat of black paint had been slapped on the heavy wooden door. The wrought iron fence bordering the brownstone hadn't yet been repainted, and by the look of it, the house was a good hundred years old.

I pushed into the front hall and got hit with a whiff of musty mothballs.

Zero sniffed. "Could be sawdust too. After all, the cleanup crew would have had to use something for the blood."

The front-door key was under the mat and we let ourselves in. The inside looked like an abattoir, although the blood was much darker now, having dried since Cosgrove's visit.

Zero exhaled. "Jesus, what a mess."

The inside of the apartment had been completely trashed. Bookshelves were turned over, books with ancient scripts running down the spines had been tossed about, and pieces of parchment littered the hardwood floors.

"Looks like someone was looking for something pretty damned hard."

Zero nodded. "Yes. And by the look of it, I don't know if they were successful."

"That good news or bad news?"

"First we have to figure out what they were looking for, then we'll know the answer to that question."

He stooped down and picked up one of the books. "Do you know what this is?"

"Looks like the ancient script of our people."

"Taluk," said Zero. "Very rare."

"What's it a book of?"

"I think this one is a book of ancient recipes. There are numbers and measurements here."

"Y'know, you never told me you could read the old language."

He shrugged. "I read some of it. It's a hobby of

mine. Call me a cultural idealist; I cling to some of the old ways. I don't think they should be abandoned in favor of a more leisurely existence."

"Can you figure out what all these books are?"

"Maybe. Might take a while."

I checked my watch and saw I had some time before I had to meet with Talya again. "So let's get to work."

It was easier said than done, of course. Even with Zero's modest expertise, it took us the better part of the afternoon to sort through the various tomes and journals littering the floors and try to come up with a theory.

A bad one.

"It makes sense," said Zero. "I should have known the alliance was only part of it."

"So tell me already."

Zero pointed to a stack of black leather-bound books. "The Kavnora is missing."

Even to a low-watt history buff like me, that meant something. The Kavnora was an ancient text reputed to hold the secrets to vampire mysticism. The instructions for performing ancient ceremonies and even alleged magic were contained within its pages.

"So what's he doing with it, then?"

Zero shrugged. "I don't know. We'd need another copy of the book to try to narrow it down. There are all sorts of nasty things someone like Cosgrove would love to try out written inside."

"So where do we get one?" There were very few copies of the Kavnora available since the knowledge contained within was so powerful. Ordinary vampires were never permitted to read an unabridged copy, just carefully edited ones.

"Another Elder," said Zero. "They'd have a copy."

"I don't know of anyone else in the area, do you?"

Zero grinned. "Well, yeah, actually I do."

Zero and I split up.

"I'll call you within twenty-four hours," he said, and then hopped into a taxi and slid back into the stream of traffic. In seconds he vanished. I stood there for another minute, looking at nothing in particular, before getting into the Jetta.

It had been a long time since I'd been out in the cold. And without Zero around, I truly was operating alone. No safety nets. No one I could call who could cover my six.

In the human intelligence game, they call such operatives NOCs, which stands for nonofficial cover. They are the deep-cover agents chiefly responsible for producing grade A, top-of-the-line human intelligence. If they get caught doing their job, they are in a world of hurt. Imprisonment, torture, even death.

The reality of my current predicament seemed much the same way for me.

First, my Control was a traitor, and that meant he'd hang me out to dry without a moment's concern if he thought I was a threat. Therefore, the goal was to make him think that I was not, while simultaneously trying to see if I couldn't track Cosgrove down and kill him.

Second, I still had to rationalize this situation with Talya. As much as I felt we'd arrived at some understanding, a part of me still refused to completely trust her. At this point, I had no way of knowing whether paranoia or instinct was responsible for the lack of trust.

That said, there was no one else I could place any degree of trust in—minute as it might be—except Talya. Talk about being between a rock and a hard place.

So while Zero headed off to locate the other Elder whom he knew lived close by, I headed back to Talya.

I drove to Harvard Square under assault of one of the windiest November rains I had seen in a long time. Seemed to me that each year the rains came earlier and windier. October was such a beautiful month. The trees exploded with the vivid red and orange hues of autumn, the days still mild and the nights cool. Usually, the night skies crackled crisp and airy, filled with stars. And since I had been born in October, I happened to place a little extra admiration upon it.

But God, did I hate November.

Even the radio did little to buoy my drooping spirit. I flipped the channel over to my favorite station, 101.7 WFNX, and listened as the DJ cranked tunes from the 1980s. In comparison to today's gloom-and-doom total-lack-of-any-discernible-melody songs, music from the 1980s really had it going on. At least in my opinion.

Massachusetts Avenue slowed to a crawl by Central Square, but what else was new? Heading toward Harvard Square, the road went from three lanes down to two, down to one and a half. What a damned mess. Some poor excuse for a civil engineer was probably laughing all the way to the bank.

And me? I had conspiracy problems to deal with.

In the crapshoot of life, I seemed to have gotten some loaded dice.

I banked left and continued farther down Massachusetts Avenue, past the Out of Town Newsstand and then circled around and down JFK Street. At the end I swung around and into the Charles Hotel's garage, finding a spot on the second level down.

I took the stairs to the courtyard, walked into the lobby and into the bar, checking to see if anyone followed me in.

No one did.

I used the phone at the concierge station to ring Talya's room. She answered on the first ring.

"It's me."

"You want to come up?"

That was a loaded question. I'd found myself thinking back to the hotel room when she'd leveled the gun on me while standing there completely nude. She had a terrific body. Sculpted but wonderfully curved. She hadn't succumbed to the ridiculous notion that being beautiful meant you had to weigh less than the lettuce leaf most models ate for breakfast. She had some extra meat on her around the hips and thighs, sturdy muscle that made her more voluptuous.

So yeah, I wanted to go up to her room. And yeah, I wanted to ravage the hell out of her. Maybe even have some juice. Just a little. Strangely enough, I think I wanted the sex more.

That's why I said no.

She sounded disappointed. "I'll be right down."

I went back into the bar, ordered some orange juice, and sat down to wait. She slipped into the bar a few minutes later, wearing her trademark outfit of a turtleneck and stretch pants. If all women knew how to dress like Talya, my world would be a happier place. Just seeing her in a turtleneck really carbonated my hormones. And then, of course, I thought of her in the turtleneck and just a pair of string-bikini panties.

I took a long sip of orange juice.

She looked at me funny. "You OK?"

"Fine," I said, setting my juice back down on the glass tabletop. I watched a little condensation bleed through the paper napkin and soak onto the glass. "Sleep well?"

"Could have been better." She shrugged. "But someone didn't want to turn down my sheets."

It wasn't that I didn't want to. I just wouldn't. But instead of making a snappy comeback, I simply nodded.

She frowned. "Any news today?"

Plenty. But I couldn't tell her any of it. "Not really."

She leaned back in her seat. "You know, there's something that's been bothering me about this whole hunting thing."

"Yeah?"

She nodded. "Yeah. You never explained exactly why it is that you're hunting him."

"Just a job."

"I've heard that line before, Lawson. Usually, it means about as much as nothing."

I smiled. "Well, it really is my job."

"Really. And what made him one of your targets?"

"You know the kind of killer he is. I told you the last time he came to town he left a trail of bodies behind. My employers do not wish a repeat of the past."

"So who are your employers?"

I finished my juice and wished I had another. "A group that calls themselves the Council."

Talya grinned. "Sounds like you work for La Cosa Nostra."

"Not really, although there might be some vague similarities."

She glanced around the bar. I'd noticed she did it very nonchalantly, but all the while she was keeping track of who'd entered, where they'd sat, and who'd left. Extremely professional.

"And at what point did you realize that Cosgrove was a vampire?"

"Friend of mine was the medical examiner last time Cosgrove came through. I got a look at the bodies before anyone else."

"So what's the body look like? I mean, they're undead, right?"

I shook my head. "No, they're living. Like I said before, this isn't the stuff of legends and yet it is. But things are different. Vampires evolved parallel to humans. The ingestion of blood affected their metabolic process and enabled them to live longer and have heightened senses and abilities. Their physical makeup is more able to endure extreme punishment, but wooden splinters in the heart kill them easily."

"I take it that revelation didn't make the papers."

I looked at her. "Talya, what do you think would have happened if word had leaked to the media about a vampire killing fifty people?"

She laughed, which was good. "We probably wouldn't be sitting here talking right now."

"No shit. But you could always visit me in my padded cell."

"Mmm, yes, I could."

I'd meant it as a joke. Talya read some sexual innuendo into it. She seemed distracted for a moment and then refocused on me.

"Was it difficult selling your employers on the concept that Cosgrove was a vampire?"

I shifted in my seat, listening to the leather squeak and whine underneath me. "Not really. It's a very old organization; my employers, they're rather used to some oddities in life."

"Sounds interesting. Sounds a helluva lot more fascinating than any of the dreary assignments I've had lately."

I didn't know about that. One of her most recent assignments had been to assassinate the leader of a drug cartel operating out of Mexico. According to the dossier Zero had shown me, she must have lain in wait for four days in order to get close enough to take him out. Gee, what a boring life she had led.

"It has its ups and downs."

She leaned forward. "Have you ever killed any other vampires?"

I was becoming uncomfortable with this line of questioning. And discussing killing others of my kind doesn't really thrill me. When I told her it was a job I did, I meant it. It was a job. I didn't particularly relish the thought of killing one of my own. But the Balance had to be maintained at all cost. And if that meant I had to put down someone, then so be it. But I wasn't about to sit here

in a bar in Harvard Square and recall any glory
stories, acting like I was proud of them. I did my
job and I did it well. And the community stayed
safer because of it. That was it.

"Cosgrove will be the first," I lied.

She sat back. "And yet . . . You don't seem particularly fazed by it. It's almost as if you're accustomed to the idea that there are vampires."

"Look who's talking! When I told you about Cosgrove, you didn't even flinch—"

"But I'm from an area of the world where su-
perstition and reality overlap. My region is known
for its wild legends. We've got it all: vampires, werewolves, ghosts, and goblins. I'm immune to being
shocked by any of it."

"I highly doubt you grew up accustomed to the
idea of vampires being around you."

She shrugged. "You'd be surprised, Lawson.
We're talking about a very remote area of the
world. Old parts of the world. I grew up on the
land bridge that joins Asia and Europe. Growing
up, I heard some amazing stories. Who's to say
where myth stops and reality begins? It's a blurred
line, believe me." She twisted a lock of her hair
around a finger. "And when I got out into the big
wide world, the more I worked, the more I saw
things ordinary people would deem as bizarre. For
me, they became commonplace."

"Like what?"

"Well, of course, not vampires or ghouls. But
enough times I encountered strange things, like
precognition, heightened awareness, and so on.
Spiritual residue from kills. Even bizarre dreams."
She leaned forward again. "I'm not one of those
skeptical types who tries to discount everything only

because I'm too scared to accept the possibility that something might be real."

"You're a believer."

She smiled. "Call it whatever you want. Doesn't matter to me."

"You're proud of your convictions, apparently."

She smiled even more. "Lawson, you seem disturbed by all this. Is everything all right?"

"Fine," I said, but I didn't mean it. Even if Talya thought she was immune to her reality being forever skewed, I strongly doubted she'd come through our mission without being affected.

Cosgrove seemed to almost be more of a novelty to her right now rather than the vicious bastard I knew him to be. If she took that attitude when it came down to the wire, Cosgrove would kill her without a second thought. And that meant she might not be entirely reliable for backup duty. After all, it would be my ass on the line if she couldn't back me properly.

But I had little choice. With Zero temporarily out of sight, I had to place my safety into Talya's hands.

And, for better or for worse, we were about to step into the line of fire.

Nineteen

Talya stayed silent as we drove back toward Boston. In truth, we didn't have much to discuss, and besides, I've always liked the quiet. I hated being around people who always felt the need to stuff useless conversation into otherwise beautiful periods of silence.

Quiet introspection can have a profound effect on the problems of life. I bet myself five bucks that Talya's thoughts centered on Cosgrove and how to best play the coming battle. I hoped she'd be able to come up with some better ideas than I'd had recently.

She seemed strangely content to keep right on staring out the window as we drove. In some ways she almost reminded me of myself.

And that scared the hell out of me.

We broke out of traffic just in time to hit the bridge spanning the Charles River at Massachusetts Avenue. We cruised down past Marlborough Street and turned right onto Beacon Street. I timed the light perfectly and we sailed easily down toward Kenmore Square.

Throngs of college students clogged crosswalks like too much cholesterol in your arteries, filling the square to its capacity. Lights from nearby stores cast their shadows across the sidewalks and streets. I tried to remember the last time I'd felt as carefree as most of the students milling around us. I couldn't. But part of me doubted I ever had been.

"Where are we heading?"

She'd broken her silence, apparently finished strategizing for the time being. I wondered if her failure to kill Cosgrove thus far discouraged her.

Professionals tend to be patient people. They have to be. Their survival depends on them not making any stupid mistakes due to being overzealous. They're cautious.

But they're also driven.

And when time begins crawling by and results still have yet to surface, it becomes frustrating. I suspected our lack of progress frustrated Talya to no end. It certainly frustrated me. But then again, frustration and I are old pals. I'm used to it.

I rolled the window down a crack to let some air in. "Club farther up Commonwealth Avenue. Calls itself M Eighty. Home to the Euro crowd on Thursday nights."

"What's a Euro crowd?" she asked half interested, but I decided to humor her by giving her a lot of detail.

"You know, the foreign nationals who come over to Boston to go to school. Mom and Dad give 'em a huge expense account, buy them garish-colored luxury cars, and tell them to sow their oats before they come back and assume their roles as heirs to the family fortune."

Talya smiled. "I've never known anyone who used the word 'garish' in a sentence before, Lawson."

"Stick around, you might learn something."

"I'll bet." She looked out the window again. "You joking about the expense-account thing?"

"Not at all. I read an article about some Joe on Newbury Street who handles the kids' accounts for their moms and dads, you know, to give them peace of mind. After all, if Junior blows through a hundred Gs in a month, that's not good."

"A hundred thousand dollars? In one month?"

I shrugged. "Well, that may be overstating it slightly, but the truth is they have a lot of money. These kids buy bottles of Cristal champagne for their friends at these clubs. I remember Simbik—"

I stopped short. Damn. "Talya, I'm sorry—"

Her face fell slightly, but she composed herself. "No, don't stop. Go on. It makes me happy to know you shared some good times together."

I cleared my throat. "It doesn't really matter."

She touched my arm. "Yes, it does."

I looked at her long enough to see she was serious, and then continued. "Well, Simbik used to say the most popular drink at his club wasn't beer, it was champagne. He said the volume they had to buy just to keep the kids wet was absurd. There's tons of money to be made in the nightclub business, take my word for it. It's just a matter of knowing how to attract the rich kids and keep them coming back."

"Is that why Boston has such a limited nightlife?"

I shook my head. "No. Boston has a shitty nightlife because we've got Puritanical laws still on the books. Damned things date back to the 1600s and no one's bothered to change 'em." I chuckled. "Cambridge is even worse. Everything over there has to shut by one in the morning. You get an extra hour in Boston."

"Amazing," said Talya. "And yet everywhere else is open twenty-four hours a day."

"Price we pay for having a beautiful city."

She went back to staring out the window.

I eased the Jetta into a spot close to the McDonald's farther up Commonwealth Avenue. I turned in the seat.

"Give me your gun."

Talya's eyebrows shot off her forehead. "Excuse me?"

"What kind of loads are you using?"

"Standard nine millimeter. I think the brand is Federal."

"Planning on shooting Cosgrove with those?"

The look on her face softened as she realized the bullets wouldn't harm him. "All right, but you still aren't getting my piece." She smiled. "Give me the ammunition."

I sighed and dropped the bullets into her outstretched hand. She fingered them and examined the tips.

"Wood?"

"Yeah. They splinter on impact causing massive damage."

"I thought the old legends didn't apply. Now you're giving me a stake to put in his heart."

"Something about the physiological makeup makes them vulnerable to wood. Don't ask me to explain. I can't. All I know is it works."

She kept her eyes on me, ejected the magazine from her gun, and thumbed the old rounds out into her lap. Faster than I would have thought possible, she reloaded the magazine with the wood-tipped bullets and slid the magazine back into the pistol butt.

"You're quick," I said.

She jacked the slide, chambering a round. "And now I'm deadly to vampires. Shall we get going?"

I nodded and suggested we walk. Talya eased herself out of the car.

"What time do you have Lawson?"

I checked the dashboard of the Jetta. I never carry a watch because the damned things jump off my wrist with alarming frequency. I'd swear they were committing suicide rather than sit still on me.

"Going on ten o'clock."

She frowned. "Aren't we a bit early?"

"Yep, and that's exactly the reason why I think we'll find him tonight. We get here early enough, get a good vantage point, and try to beat him to the punch."

"You mean bite."

I looked back at her in the darkness and her smile radiated an almost tangible warmth. A breeze swept up her hair and tossed it around before she reached up with her hand and regained control over it.

"Yeah," I said thickly. "That too."

She nodded. "We'd better get inside then."

"Hold on a second." I pulled out my cell phone and dialed McKinley's number. He answered on the second ring.

"Lawson? That you?"

"You always answer the phone that professionally? I could have been important. I could have been a Council member."

"Up yours, you bastard. Where the hell have you been? I've been trying to reach you all day."

I'll bet. "Out and about, of course. Remember, I'm supposed to be doing my job."

"Yeah, but you're also supposed to be checking in with me. What if Cosgrove got to you first and I had no idea of where you were, I couldn't send any help."

As if he would have. "Yeah, well, I'm checking in now. Got any fresh news for me?"

"None. What'd you find out at the Elder's place? Anything that'd give us a clue as to why he hit him?"

"Place was a mess. Guy had a ton of books in the old language, but it's all scribble to me. Did me no good being there."

He grunted on the other end of the line. "Where are you?"

"In the Alley, by Tremont."

"Weren't you there the other night?"

"Monday, yeah. But you know how deserted the bars are on a Monday night. We figured we'd have a better shot at him if we checked them out again."

"What's this 'we' shit, Lawson?"

"Got Talya with me."

McKinley paused. "Jesus, Lawson, you think that's a good idea? What if you have to take Cosgrove out in front of her? How the hell you going to explain that one?"

"I'm not worried about it."

"I am."

"Worry about your Elders. This is not an issue."

"It could well be if the Council got wind of it. They'd shit themselves silly knowing you let a human work with you on a termination."

"The Council doesn't care about how I get results, McKinley. As long as I get them. So they don't have to know how I do my job, right?"

Another grunt. "I'm trusting you on this, Lawson."

"Yeah. Sometimes all we have is trust."

He paused. "Keep me informed."

"Will do." I hung up the phone and caught Talya giving me a curious look. "What?"

Her eyes narrowed. "Don't trust your Control?"

I shrugged, remembering Zero's words from earlier. "Let's just say I don't believe in showing my cards all the time."

"From what I've seen, you never really do anyway."

"What the hell's that supposed to mean?"

She didn't answer. "Come on, let's go find Cosgrove."

I followed after her. Damned if I'd ever be able to figure out women, human or vampire.

The place was thick with Europeans, just like I'd told Talya. I caught snippets of at least a half-dozen different languages ranging from Farsi, spoken only by Iranian aristocrats, to a Cairo dialect of Arabic, to gutter Russian straight out Georgia laced with enough Mafia references to make anyone with more than a first-grade education steer clear. An interesting and eclectic mix of folks, to be sure. All of them young, and all of them rich.

Talya and I threaded our way through the crowds, not even garnering so much as a disapproving glance from the Gucci- and Prada-conscious club denizens. If you didn't wear your money, you didn't even exist.

That worked in our favor and gave us a degree of anonymity. If they didn't see us, they couldn't remember us later.

Despite the early hour by club standards, the dance-floor divas jammed the parquet floor while the music pulsed. I'd assumed finding a good vantage point would not be a problem due to the time. I quickly reminded myself why assuming things usually lands me in a world of pain.

Talya came through, though. She'd been on point and led me toward the rear of the club about twenty feet from the emergency exit. A VIP area closed off with velvet ropes barred our path, but she simply smiled at the security man standing guard and he let us through. She slumped into the booth and I followed.

"Well?"

I grinned. "Looks good. We should be able to see him if he comes in here tonight."

"You think he will?"

I shrugged. "Who knows? There's only so many places he can go." Plus, I was hoping if McKinley tipped him off as to our whereabouts, he'd come down to the opposite end of the city and do his hunting here. But I wasn't ready to tell Talya that. "You know it's always a crapshoot."

She nodded. "The luxury of having good intelligence."

"Right." I laughed in spite of my growing apprehension. "When was the last time you had good intel prior to a hit?"

"Right around the last time I won the lottery," she said. "Never."

"You've got as much luck as I do."

She nodded. "Yeah, but you make do. I was

sprawled in a muddy field in the middle of Northern Ireland—County Armagh I think it was—covered in leaves, dirt, manure, and lots of rain, for almost a week one time before my target showed up. And I still had to pull myself together to take him out." She looked at me. "Ever done that?"

"Covered myself in cow dung? Nope. I'm a pro at getting myself into all sorts of other shit, though." I paused and checked the surroundings. "But I can understand the incredible discipline you must have had to summon to keep your wits about you while you waited." I inclined my head. "Damned admirable."

"I stayed in the shower for two hours when I came out. Sure makes you appreciate the little things everyone else takes for granted."

"Like a loofah?"

She chuckled. "Especially the loofah." She looked around the club and smiled again.

"What's so funny?"

She shrugged. "Just this. Could you imagine the reactions of every other person on this planet if they listened to our conversations? Here we are discussing the merits of discipline when it comes to assassinating people. Good Lord, what kind of times are we living in?"

"Strange times, Talya. Trust me."

"Exactly. And here we are hunting a vampire in the middle of a cosmopolitan town like Boston. You'd think vampires would be the last thing to exist here."

"Yet they do."

"Indeed. I wonder how."

I watched the front door of the club. "What do you mean?"

"Don't you wonder about it, Lawson? Aren't you curious? How do they exist? Do they grow old and die like everyone else? Now that I know they really exist, I'm bursting with questions."

And I didn't want to answer any of them. "Remember what you said a few days back? It's just a job I do. I'm not really interested in Cosgrove's life story. I just want to put him down with minimal fuss and no muss."

She narrowed her eyes. "Almost as if you didn't want to discuss the subject, Lawson."

"Cosgrove killed your fiancé. My friend. And roughly fifty other people. I want him dead. That's it, end of story."

"If only it was as simple as that."

I looked at her. "It's not?"

"Of course not. We're dealing with a vampire. It's an extraordinary thing, don't you see that?"

"This from the woman who told me she'd grown up with these legends surrounding her all her life. And now all of a sudden you're awestruck by the whole damned thing? That's strange."

She frowned. "Well, fine. Be that way. Maybe I'll just save my questions for Cosgrove when he shows up."

"Don't imagine he'll much feel like answering them by the time I plug his heart full of wood," I said.

"Maybe you could just wound him first."

I looked at her incredulously, but she only smiled.

"I'm kidding, Lawson. Just kidding."

Was she? Hell, I didn't even know anymore. I couldn't be mad with her for being curious. Anyone in her position, even with her background, would have felt the same way. After all, it's not every day you find out that vampires really do exist. It's akin to discovering that Roswell really did happen or that the CIA really wasted JFK. Kind of a reality-shattering event.

Maybe in some weird way, I was partially jealous. After all, she knew Cosgrove was a vampire and as much as she wanted revenge for his killing Simbik, she also wanted to understand the creature he was. And here I was sitting next to her in some vacuous club with people swirling all around us, her perfume teasing my nostrils, intimately aware of her body heat and desirous of her. And she was more into Cosgrove.

Damn, so much for being some kind of enlightened guru. Hell, I was still a prisoner to the kind of jealousy you could find in any junior high school.

I watched her watch the crowd. Everything she did had a degree of artfulness to it. Not that your ordinary run-of-the-mill Joe Blow could tell, but I could. One of the benefits of working in the same field.

Talya scanned the crowd with an amazing degree of detachment, never focusing on one thing, but simultaneously absorbing, processing, and sifting everything and everyone in the room. Each time she passed her eyes over the room, she did so in a different manner. You'd never guess she was so actively surveying the club searching for her—our—target.

Her skill mesmerized me. Her beauty haunted me. Her very presence made me feel like a fourteen-year-old boy.

And in that realization I knew I was in a lot of trouble.

I explained before about the rules governing interaction between my kind and humans. Sex was OK; love was not.

Was I falling in love with her? I didn't know. I wasn't exactly an expert on the emotion. I could count the times I'd fallen in love with one finger.

Sure, I'd had sex a lot of times.

But love? Me? You had to be joking. I was, after all, a vampire.

Oh, sure, it was possible. I mean, vampires hook up all the time with each other. It's how we keep producing our species. But I'd never met a vampire who did it for me.

After all, the prospects of sex were kind of bleak. You did the deed and shared each other's blood as a symbolic gesture of what had transpired. It was a really disturbing vision the first time I'd learned about the ritual of vampiric procreation.

Swore me off kids forever.

Never thought I'd have a problem either. I was a Fixer. Not the kind of job that allows for intimate relationships. Hell, the first few years I was active in the field I didn't even have so much as a home, I was on the road all the time.

I wondered if Talya had ever been in love.

And immediately realized things were worse than I thought.

"Lawson?"

I snapped back to reality. Talya grinned.

"Everything OK?"

I nodded. "Yeah, sure. Fine. Just doing some thinking is all."

She nodded. "Seemed to be deep in thought there. You sure you're all right?"

"Yeah." I scanned the club. "See anything?"

She nodded. "Yes. Judging by what I've seen, approximately sixty-five percent of the club will be getting some sex tonight."

"That it?"

She flashed me a healthy smile. "Well, Lawson, the night's not over yet." She leaned closer to me. "The percentage could increase . . . even by two."

I snapped my eyes away, aware of the pounding in my chest and the rising heat in my face. So much for professional demeanor. I cleared my throat and looked back at her.

"You're something else, Talya."

But she'd ceased looking at me. Her eyes focused beyond me, staring, narrowing, becoming acutely attuned to her environment. Even her body had shifted slightly, almost imperceptibly. She'd become more animalistic in the space of less than three seconds. I'd seen the look before.

On myself.

Talya had shifted to her combat mode, and as I turned in my seat, I saw why.

Cosgrove was in the club.

Twenty

I'd seen shadows disturb more things in their path than Cosgrove did as he entered. He didn't so much walk as ooze his way through the crowds. It felt eerie just watching him move inside and begin his stalk. I thought about sharks I'd seen, and the resemblance to their movements seemed uncanny.

Talya didn't take her eyes off him. "How do you want to play this?"

I brought my piece out, feeling the cold metal on one side and the warmth of the side that had lain next to my body. It felt good knowing I had a magazine full of death-dealing Cosgrove rounds.

Talya seemed as primed as I was to take this thing head-on and get it over with.

"Straight up," I said. "Give me two minutes to get into position. Then we'll hit him. Fast and hard. Got it?"

She nodded, scarcely moving her lips. "Go."

I slid out of the booth and back into the shadows. I had to make sure I stayed in his blind spot as much as possible. It would be OK if he spotted Talya. He might chalk it up to coincidence and maybe even try to take her out.

But he couldn't see me. If he did, the game would be over and I'd be left holding a heaving bag of shit. Cosgrove would run if he sensed anything remotely like an ambush.

I stayed in the dark recesses of the club, watching the lights dance off Cosgrove as he cut across the floor. His head seemed fixed in place, and he never swiveled it from one side to the other. His peripheral vision seemed to just absorb everything.

He drew abreast of me, and for just a second I thought he might actually turn and stare at me through the darkness, but he only just kept moving.

And a minute later I was safely in his blind spot.

Now it was my turn to go on the offensive.

I could see Talya sitting in the booth. She was smiling, but I thought it was just to draw Cosgrove in like a beacon in the night. If he wanted what he thought was an easy target, he'd move on her straightaway. After all, in his mind he'd already laid the groundwork the other night at the bar. And here was Talya, all alone, and already smiling at him.

A tempting target, to be sure.

I resisted the urge to just draw my gun and start pumping rounds into him from across the club. It was so tempting, the thought of going off half-cocked with no fire discipline, like some heroin-laced-gang-banger. Tempting because I suddenly realized how damned scared I was of another encounter with him. I wanted this finished as quickly as possible.

But to kill him I had to get close. The wooden rounds weren't much good beyond a dozen meters. That meant I had to close on him, get the muzzle up near his heart and then plug him.

Not exactly an easy thing to do to someone like Cosgrove.

Adrenaline poured into my bloodstream. My stomach ached. If I didn't kill Cosgrove soon, I'd become permanently constipated.

I took a deep breath and kept threading my way through the crowd. Closer to Cosgrove.

He noticed Talya, and although his back was mostly to me, I thought I saw a slight change in his body language. It almost took on a jaunty air. His confidence must have jumped when he'd seen her.

Sure enough, he moved over to the booth. She stood and shook his hand like an old friend and gestured for him to sit. Wisely, her position demanded he have his back to the outside when he sat down. I saw him hesitate as if recognizing the area of vulnerability he had moved into, but after a second he simply sat down and leaned forward speaking with her.

I physically had to move a couple out of my way, which didn't go over too well with the boy, who had far too much gel in his hair and far too much cologne on. It must have given him an extra dose of attitude as well, but I simply fixed a look on him and he thought better of it. Probably the smartest kid in Boston at that moment.

Talya smiled and laughed right along with Cosgrove. She kept her eyes on him all the time, never once betraying my position with a quick glance that Cosgrove surely would have picked up.

I kept moving.

At a dozen feet I slid the pistol out of my jacket pocket and thumbed the safety to the off position. I had a round in the chamber already, set to fire.

Two more seconds.

"What the fuck—"

A voice to my right.

I felt the hands—club security showed up.

They saw my gun.

I pivoted, sliding out of the security man's grasp, but the commotion and screams had already started.

Someone yelled, "Gun!"

Cosgrove whirled around, saw me heading for him—I was trying to level the pistol on him, aware that Talya was trying to hold him down.

He jerked out of her grasp.

I fired twice . . .

. . . bad shots that ricocheted off the ceiling and hit some lights, sending a shower of glass toward the floor.

Cosgrove leaped across two booths and made for the door.

By now, the security staff was in full crisis mode and converging on me at full speed. Talya was scrambling, trying to get after Cosgrove. She pulled her gun out as she went.

"Don't go after him!"

Another security guard tried to tackle me, but I moved and he slid into another couple entangled on the floor. I ran for Talya, chasing her as much as Cosgrove. If she went after him alone, he'd kill her.

I burst through the side emergency door and had two options. Right would bring me down behind the club into the dark shadows. Left would bring me onto Commonwealth Avenue.

Two shots exploding to my right made my decision for me and I eased down the alley.

My skin prickled.

I dived ahead.

Tucked.

Rolled.

Came up in a defensive stance with the gun in front of me.

I caught a silhouette against the night sky. Cosgrove was on the roof.

"Lawson!" he hissed.

I shot two more rounds at him, but he ducked back and away.

At the end of the alley, a pile of overflowing garbage cans sat neatly stacked by the roof. I used them, scrambling to get to the top, and finally managing to do so.

I didn't like what I saw.

Talya's body lay in a crumpled heap near the middle. She wasn't moving. Her gun lay ten feet away, useless.

And Cosgrove stood perched on the lip of the roof some thirty feet away like a predatory hawk waiting for his prey.

Simply smiling.

I leveled the gun on him. She wasn't moving. Why wasn't Talya moving?

Then I saw the blood.

It made a small droplet trail across the roof. I could smell the copper. But it smelled slightly different from human blood.

Cosgrove's blood.

I'd winged him with one of my rounds. Too bad it wasn't his heart or he'd be dead now. Still, he'd be smarting from the wound and it would need some medical attention, especially if one of the splinters had lodged under the skin or internally.

I kept the pistol on him and moved closer, but he didn't seem particularly concerned.

In fact, he began chuckling. "Two choices, Lawson. Save her or kill me. What will it be?"

Save her? What had he done—but it came to me before I'd even finished the thought. Cosgrove had taken a lot of her blood. Almost too much. And right now she'd be hovering right near the brink of death. She needed an infusion. More to the point, she needed another vampire's blood to survive. The antibodies in my blood would help her system fight off what Cosgrove had done to her.

But it had to be done quickly.

Unless I chose to just kill Cosgrove and be done with it.

But I knew, just as that son of a bitch knew, that I wouldn't do that. There was no way I was going to allow him to kill Simbik's fiancée as well. I'd injured him and he needed an escape. Threatening Talya's life would grant him that reprieve.

I lowered the pistol. "Another time, Cosgrove."

"Sooner than you think, Lawson." Then he leaped from the roof, vanishing from sight.

I knelt in front of Talya and felt for her pulse. Thin and waning. Definitely bad. I felt a vague heartbeat, but her entire circulatory system was in limbo.

I didn't hesitate. I stripped my jacket off and rolled up my sleeves. One fingernail on a vampire is always longer than the others for just this very instance. I slit the veins on my left wrist with it and held the bleeding over Talya's mouth. I watched as it dripped steadily into her mouth, staining her lips, her tongue.

It hurt like hell.

Her tongue came to life, as if realizing the blood flowing into her would prove her salvation, and fluttered against the open wounds of my wrist, seeking and suckling more of my essence.

I had to be careful. If I gave too much, it would hurt me. If I gave too little, she'd still die.

Her eyes opened slightly. She looked up at me, kneeling there on the dark roof. And a realization seemed to be in her eyes. Did she know what I was—did she know a vampire was saving her life?

Maybe she'd have decided that she really had been outclassed. Unlike every other person she might have killed, Cosgrove simply didn't register on the normal scale. Look what he'd done in the space of just a few short minutes. He'd evaded our ambush, escaped from the club, brought her down with no discernible effort, and drained her of a ton of blood.

Not the kind of evening most people would recall fondly. And Talya, least of all. But professionals are like that. They spend so much time training for what they have to do, that when they come up against someone or something better than they are, it hurts their pride.

Hell, Cosgrove outclassed me and I was a goddamned vampire. Pride—hell, mine was shot.

Time to stop the infusion. I could tell from my own pulse that if she took in too much more, I'd either pass out and die or else need to find a blood bank with a "Don't Ask, Don't Tell" withdrawal policy.

I withdrew my arm. Talya whimpered slightly, licking her lips to get the last bits of my blood.

"Lawson."

Her voice croaked out in a hoarse whisper. I'd

expected it to sound like that; after all, she'd just drunk blood. It coats the vocal cords like velvet.

I leaned close. "I'm here."

"Did you—did we—"

I shook my head. "No, he got away."

She frowned. "My fault."

"No."

"Shouldn't have gone after him."

I tried to quiet her down. "You need to rest now."

"—tried to shoot him."

I noticed the shell casings. She'd missed. And Cosgrove had disarmed her easily.

"Yeah, I think you wounded him."

She smiled. "No. You . . . did that."

"It doesn't matter."

"Should have listened to you."

"It can't be helped, Talya. Now, be quiet. Let your strength come back." I held my arm up to my lips and coated the wound with a hefty dose of my saliva, which has enormous coagulating qualities. The wound's bleeding would slow first and then stop.

Talya tried to lift herself off the roof, but I pushed her back down. "Not yet. You're still too weak. Wait a few more minutes."

"Where—"

"Roof of the club."

"What happened?"

"Cosgrove took you down and then he took a lot of your blood."

I thought she was going to puke then, but she fought it back, choking down the sour bile that must have risen in her throat. "God."

"You'll be OK now."

"You . . . saved me?"

"Well, it was either that or lose another friend."

"How?"

"A little trick I picked up a few years ago."

She smiled. "My hero."

Despite the evening's events, I smiled too. "You bet." I bent close to her ear and whispered a hypnotic command I hoped would erase the memory of the transfusion.

She spaced out for a moment, then sighed. "What about Cosgrove?"

I shrugged. "He'll be around. We'll get him another time."

And looking out into the night, I wished I felt more confident about it than it sounded. I had two strikes against me, and if Zero's theory about the depth of the conspiracy panned out, there were already two outs in this ninth inning.

Twenty-one

I smuggled Talya back to the hotel and got her into bed. She'd be out for a good twelve hours. Having your body ravaged by a nut job like Cosgrove meant a lot of rest. He'd damn near killed her.

And in the process I wondered what he'd done to me.

From the cushiony armchair in the corner of the room, I watched her sleep under the simple pale blue covers of the bed. A single floor lamp sat beside me, casting vague yellow hues across the room, illuminating one side of her face.

Only just managing to jaundice the deathly white pallor.

But that came with the territory.

In the movies, if you get bitten by a vampire you become one. Sometimes it takes three bites, but usually it's one. As usual, Hollywood hasn't got a clue.

The process of vampirical metamorphosis, as we call it, takes a great deal of time and effort. It's messy. It's invasive. It's a pain in the ass. The paperwork alone would drive anyone nuts.

Granted, what Cosgrove had done to Talya constituted the first step, that of bleeding the intended vampire of most of their human blood. The next step involved a commingling of human and vampire blood to see if they accepted each other. Kind of like a marriage blood test, except we didn't test for rubella.

If the blood types could coexist, the next step involved an apprenticeship of sorts where the petitioner attended history courses, severed all contact with former human friends and family, adopted the vampire lifestyle, and got fed a steady diet of blood. At first the blood would be 25 percent vampire and 75 percent human; then gradually the percentages would change. Until finally, the apprentice would consume 100 percent vampire blood for a period of seven days. Thereafter the percentages reversed until it was 100 percent human blood.

I'm not a scientific type, so don't ask me to get into the exact chemical compositions, white and red cell counts, and all that jazz. I'm just telling you what I read.

It happens, needless to say, about as often as an Independent gets elected as president of the United States.

Talya made no noise as she rested. And even in her depleted state, she maintained a quiet discipline while she slept. Almost as if she could spring up at any time and go immediately on a job. I wondered how many times she'd done just that.

Her history books would need rewriting after tonight. She'd had an encounter with one of the most highly developed killing machines on the planet. And she'd survived.

OK, so I'd helped. But it would be her constitution that bore out her survival, not mine. In the morning she'd feel like the victim of a hit-and-run accident with twelve tractor trailers. Sick but alive. And that's what counted.

The radio station whispered soft music into the room while I watched her. Vivaldi's the *Four Seasons*. Winter. *Non allegro molto.*

Haunting stuff.

With each pull on the strings, I watched Talya more intently than before. What was it about her that drew me in so much? What was it about her that made my mind generate excuses for a forbidden relationship between a human and a vampire?

Vivaldi must have known about love. His music spoke of it in every movement. With every note of music that drifted out of the speakers and fell into my ears, passion preceded it.

Talya.

She tugged on my heart with an unconscious effort that both excited and scared me.

My stomach ached.

Desire seemed to well up from deep inside and overflow almost at once, causing incredible fluctuations between my pulse and the adrenaline rising like the tide in my blood.

I'd been in love once before.

Only once.

Seem strange? You try being a Fixer. You try being all over the world, out to maintain the Balance, out to make sure no one causes ripples that can't be explained. Try doing all that and still have enough time to figure out the wacky ebbs and swells of your own heart.

Right.

There's no way you could.

No way I could either, for that matter. And yet, strangely, now I wanted to.

Robin. My mind drew her image up as easily as if I'd seen her twenty minutes ago. Her radiant smile, voluptuous breasts, and extraordinary curves had possessed my mind from the moment I'd laid eyes on her.

High school. A breezy September morning in my freshman year. The sun had danced through the yawning branches of the linden trees as she walked toward all of us in the schoolyard. My heart jumped into my mouth, my breath stopped, and my stomach hurt like no other pain I'd ever felt before.

She'd had that effect on a lot of people.

Including Cosgrove.

We'd pretty much been enemies for a few years now. Stronger and bigger, I could beat him up with no discernible effort.

But Cosgrove's cunning made him a formidable enemy. Never content to battle me in the open, he'd planned his battles with meticulous care, always ensuring the environment right before launching an attack.

Back then, they'd been the kind of schoolyard stunts that kids pulled all the time on one another. I'd be framed for cheating, passing notes, or calling someone names. I hadn't, of course, but Cosgrove had made it look so perfectly convincing that I ended up taking the blame.

I usually settled it by beating the snot out of him.

Robin's appearance at school changed everything.

In the space of a few weeks, Cosgrove and I had a new focus: we both fell in love with Robin.

And again, while I had the good looks, Cosgrove had the brains and finesse. The result was that Robin dated us both for a time. But gradually, she began enjoying her time with me more. I couldn't have been more pleased. More happy. We made plans, the kind of young naive plans kids make when they think the world will stop for them, provided they only have the courage to love each other.

We'd be married.

Children.

Everything . . . perfect.

Cosgrove made sure it never happened.

That night.

That cold, windy, rain-soaked November night during my senior year, I returned home after visiting relatives out of state. Robin and I had plans to meet at midnight by the brook that cut across the town line. A small cabin sat concealed in the forest by the brook that served as our rendezvous point. I'd lost count of how many times we'd passed hours locked in passionate embraces, feeling the warmth of each other's skin grow hotter with each nuzzle, with each tender kiss. That night it would be especially nice, making love and listening to the rain's pitter-patter on the rooftop.

Soaked to the bone and freezing, I arrived at the cabin. No light came from within, so I suspected I'd gotten there first. Anxious to start a small fire so she wouldn't be cold, and to get out of my own frigid clothes, I opened the door.

Inside the cabin the smell knocked me back off my feet.

Blood.

A fucking slaughterhouse.

Desperate, I found a small dry stick just inside and lit it with a match. Adrenaline already pumping, I lifted my makeshift torch and saw what Cosgrove had left me.

Robin.

The inside walls oozed with coagulating blood. Her body—her beautiful, nubile body—hung suspended from the timber rafters, dripping the remnants of her fluids to the damp floor.

In the center of our tiny oasis, staked to the floor, was her heart.

I heaved, slumped to the floor, slipped in my own vomit, and wailed—sputtering, sobbing, and gasping as my world, my love, my life, disintegrated into infinite grief.

By the time I returned home with Robin's corpse, Cosgrove had vanished.

And the Council, the very same Council who had sworn to uphold the laws of the Balance, the laws of our society, had written it off as a juvenile bout of temporary insanity.

Maybe my destiny as a Fixer had been set long before my birth. I believed for a long time, and maybe even to this day, that it fully realized itself that night in the woods.

The rage—the sheer rage, the erupting emotions, the insanity of my thoughts—and the notions and desires I wanted to wreak upon the world, upon everyone, absorbed every ounce of my being. I wanted them to feel my loss, my pain, my agonizing dismay over a lost love.

My emotional apocalypse.

It took almost a full year to even come to terms with it.

It took even longer to hide it away, deep inside where it couldn't be seen by anyone else.

But it was there.

And I still intended to make Cosgrove pay for what he'd stolen from me.

Talya shifted in the yellow light, snapping me out of the memories. I realized I was sucking in gulps of air and calmed down. And while I watched her in the yellow twilight of the room, while shadows played long across the expanse of my heart's longing, Robin's face danced across hers. Morphing, intermingling, changing, vanishing, and reappearing again and again while my eyes struggled to keep time with the changes.

Robin's death happened a long time ago. And yet it felt as recent as yesterday. When I let it.

Talya.

Tonight I'd made a choice to save her life.

I could have let her die.

I could have taken Cosgrove out.

Perfect range. I'd made longer shots.

One shot, two at the most. It would have been over.

But Talya would have been over too.

Any other Fixer wouldn't have given it another thought. They would have wasted Cosgrove. They would have let Talya die there, alone, depleted. Written off as just another casualty in the struggle to maintain the all-important Balance. It's a sacred duty after all; the Balance must come first. That's what they hammered into us constantly at the academy. Always, the Balance.

But something happened up there.

I think it scared me so much, the thought of losing her on that black pitch roof, the thought of losing another Robin, that I responded without even giving it any consideration.

I'd played it off as her being another one of Cosgrove's victims. As her being Simbik's fiancée. As her being someone I respected. An ally I needed. A resource I could trust.

That's how I'd comforted myself with my decision.

That's how I'd excused letting Cosgrove flee into the night, free for the time being to take another life from the city, while his plans for domination continued.

Lies.

All lies.

Funny what you'll tell yourself when the truth's too frightening to admit.

But I was beginning to think maybe something else made me do what I did.

Robin's face swam past me again and settled over Talya's. But only for an instant.

Then it was Talya again.

All Talya.

And in that moment, there in the hotel room, while she slept, I realized my world had just become a lot more complicated than it had ever been before.

And I felt powerless to stop it.

Twenty-two

Talya felt like shit the next morning. Having most of your blood drained and then receiving a vampiric infusion isn't the kind of thing your system can rebound from easily. So she hurt. Bad. Fever, dry heaves, chills, the works. Her body struggled to regain control over something that resembled a detox done at Mach 5.

With the worst over by midday, I made an excuse and headed home. With promises to call her soon, I left her recuperating in a hot bath.

At home Mimi greeted me at the top of the steps. Her stern look seemed to ask: Where the hell have you been? And didn't you know it was long past dinnertime? Phoebe led the way to the food dish, muttering the entire time. But they both clammed up once I'd gotten some food into the ceramic bowls. I changed their water and then put a call into McKinley. He answered immediately.

"Lawson, where in God's name have you been?"

"What's the problem?"

"Problem? There's no problem. Why should there be a problem? I mean, it's not like I'm your Control. It's not like I even have a vested interest in your safety and well-being." He paused. "The problem is I haven't been able to find you, Lawson. I didn't even know if you were still alive."

Interesting. "Why wouldn't I be alive?"

McKinley paused. "Well, you are hunting Cosgrove—"

"And?"

Another pause. "Police report came over the wire about a disturbance last night at a club called M Eighty. Thought it might be you."

"I told you I was down at the Alley last night."

"Yeah, but—"

"But you think I was at M Eighty." I sighed audibly into the phone. "You think I'm lying."

"What? No, it's not that at all—"

I smiled. "Well, you're right."

"I am?"

"I was."

"Was what?"

"At M Eighty. The disturbance, the ruckus, that was me. Cosgrove showed up. I almost got him too."

"Almost?"

"Obviously, I didn't."

"Oh. You'll be trying again tonight, I assume."

Funny how he didn't seem too disappointed. "Not tonight."

"Why not?"

"Tonight's my seafood-cooking class over in Brookline."

"Seafood cooking?"

"I'd sure hate to miss it."

This time McKinley paused a while longer. "Lawson, you hate seafood."

"Yeah. I also hate stupid questions. Of course I'm going to try again tonight. It's my job, damn it."

"Well, keep me informed, would you?"

"You sound like a fucking broken record."

I hung up the phone. Of course McKinley knew I'd been at M Eighty because Cosgrove probably gave him a boatload of shit for letting him walk into an almost perfect ambush.

What a shame.

I wanted to talk to Zero, but I couldn't take the risk of using my home phone. It pays to assume the absolute worst and I always did. If McKinley thought I had a clue about the conspiracy, he probably had my phone tapped.

That meant no direct telephoning to Zero. I had to use a pay phone somewhere across town to be sure it was reasonably secure. Of course, that meant Zero also had to get to a pay phone because his phone could have also been tapped. I could have called his cell phone, but I had no idea of knowing if he'd receive it or be out of range. I'd have to wait for him to contact me.

I checked my watch and saw that nearly two hours had passed since I'd left Talya. I already missed her. I shook my head. Since when had I become some damned silly old romantic fool? I found the whole situation utterly unsettling.

Mimi finished her meal and came wandering over, licking her chops. She sat down, looked up at me, and chirped once to be picked up. Phoebe began trying to dig up the tile floor and bury the food dish under it. She never succeeded, but it never stopped her from trying. I respected her tenacity.

Mimi snuggled close and I caught a whiff of the fish dinner and promptly put her back down. Her breath stunk.

I called Talya. She picked up on the fourth ring.
"Everything OK?"

"It was. I was resting."

"Sorry, I didn't—"

"Don't worry about it, Lawson. I understand
you're concerned about me. Thank you."

"We don't have to go out tonight, Talya. You
could take a night off."

"That's not an option, Lawson. You know that."

"Yeah, but I thought I'd give it a shot anyway."

"Pick me up at eleven o'clock. I'm going to get
some sleep now."

The phone went dead and I replaced the receiver. I wasn't really tired yet, despite not having
slept much last night. I went downstairs to the cellar and started working combinations on the heavy
bag.

My small dark cellar had low ceilings and walls
made from the old granite blocks the foundation
had been built on. Old coal dust still littered the
corners, a souvenir from when they'd burned coal
instead of oil for heat. I'd positioned a small workout room toward the front of the house, a woodworking shop near the back, and my old worn
leather heavy bag centered in between.

The duct tape wrapped around the middle was
starting to wear thin, with strands of silvery string
coming off like gossamer threads. Knuckle inden-
tations pockmarked the bag from the repeated
beatings I'd inflicted upon it.

I started slow on the bag, feeling it give and creak
on the supporting chains as I threw jabs into it. I
switched to a jab-cross combination and got into a
rhythm. I did high-low-low-high-middle-middle and
back again. Every time I sent one of my hands thud-

ding into the bag, I saw Cosgrove's face teasing and taunting me. I punched the bag a lot harder.

Thirty minutes passed in a breath and left me covered with sweat. Good warm-up. I walked to the weight bench and threw up three hundred pounds for two reps after I'd pyramided up from one hundred. My pecs felt stretched taut by the time I finished doing three sets of flyes.

I switched to biceps and cranked out some alternating dumbbell curls while thinking about how to get McKinley and Cosgrove in one room and finish them both off. I couldn't figure it, so I leaned back and did some lying-down triceps extensions; then when my arms felt ready to cave in and let the weight crash down on the bridge of my nose, I thought about Talya again.

I dropped the bar and walked back upstairs. I took a sixteen-ounce glass out of the cabinet and filled it up with some chilled juice. I sucked it down in three gulps. It hit fast and I felt great, restored, and refreshed. But a nap would make things even better, so I wandered upstairs with Mimi and Phoebe swirling around my feet as we went.

My bedroom faces out onto the street and I drew the blinds shut to close out as much light as possible. I crawled into bed and waited for Mimi to join me on my aching chest and Phoebe to nudge herself under the covers.

It took me twenty seconds to fall asleep.

My phone rang at exactly three o'clock. Once.

It rang again two minutes later. Twice.

I sat up in bed, dislodging Mimi and Phoebe simultaneously from either side of my pillow. Back in the early 1980s, Zero and I worked a couple of tough track-down cases for the Council over in London. The local Control had developed an unnatural taste for the blood of young blond boys. When Zero and I touched down, he'd already killed three.

Unfortunately, word of our imminent arrival reached him before our plane and he went to ground. Disappeared. And while he played ghost, he dispatched several hit teams to try to kill Zero and me. That meant we'd had to watch our backs constantly. Communications became compromised.

So we developed a code.

And eventually, we killed the Control.

I sat still in bed. If it was Zero attempting to contact me, he'd call again in two minutes and let it ring once again.

He did.

I showered, dressed quickly, and drove down Centre Street to the Dunkin' Donuts. The corner pay phone sloped at an odd angle, its sidewalls dented and covered in multicolored graffiti. Even the receiver looked like combat-zone surplus. Jutting out of the tar and cement sidewalk, it looked close to death. That's exactly why I felt reasonably safe about using it. I slid some coins into the slot, heard the telltale beeps, and dialed Zero's cell phone number.

"Bring back some memories, did I?"

I smiled. "You bet."

"Where are you?"

"Pay phone. Seems safe. You?"

"Mobile. But close. I need to see you. Visited your dad lately?"

"No."

"Might be a good time to."

Message received, I hung up, got back into the Jetta, and drove down South Street toward Forest Hills. Under the bridge I turned left and shot up parallel to the overpass, then stayed right just after the rotary turning into Forest Hills Cemetery.

Vampires are buried alongside mortals. We change the birth and death dates, though, to make it look normal.

I'd forgotten the inherent natural beauty of this park. Linden and maple trees reflected the expanse of autumn's color palette, frosted in red, yellow, and orange hues. By the main building I threaded through the old iron portcullis and wound my way down to Rosedale Path. On my right, scores of Canadian geese paused on the smooth pond waters before continuing south for the winter.

I rolled past the innumerable Chinese grave sites found in this section of the cemetery and found my way to the solitary headstone bearing my family name, just under the small Japanese red maple tree at the curve in the road.

It always felt good to come here and visit. It was something I hadn't done in a long time.

Humans might find it bizarre that a vampire visits his dead father. Well, no one lives forever; even vampires die. My dad lived to the ripe young age of 290. That's not a long time for a vampire. And I always felt cheated by his death, that he hadn't seen me graduate from Fixer training, that he hadn't seen some of my personal triumphs in life.

It was the standard kind of hang-up anyone would feel about a deceased parent. We always want them to be proud of us, to love us for our successes and our failures with equanimity. I often wondered if my father was proud of me. I wasn't the easiest kid to raise when I was younger. And some of the things I'd developed an interest in no doubt made him wonder who the hell his son was turning into.

But in that desire to seek his love and approval, I realized a long time ago he was aware of what I did now. That even if he was technically dead, he was still with me. Around me. And I gave thanks for that on many occasions when things got pretty hairy for me.

Nowadays I looked forward to visiting his grave site. It was more of a homecoming or a visit for me. I sat with him, talked to him, and generally felt good about being there.

After all, I was proud of the man I'd become.

And most of the credit belonged to him.

As his only son, I felt he'd poured a lot of himself into me. He taught me what it meant to be a man. To strive. To succeed. And even accept failure, but only as something to learn from and a means to excel even more.

But most of all, he taught me to live my life with no regrets. To seize what I had been presented with and run with it as far as I possibly could. To learn.

And so much more.

I didn't know it back then. Hell, it always seemed so much like punishment for not being able to live up to his ideals. He told me what he showed me was stuff I needed to know, stuff that would help me later in life. I did it, learned it—all grudgingly—longing more times than not to be off playing with my friends whose own fathers cared less about them and never spent the time that my father did making certain I grew into a man.

It wasn't a sudden stark revelation that brought

me to this understanding, but more of a gentle, nudging realization. By the time I graduated Fixer training and spent a few years abroad, often under the gun and in some bad situations, I instinctively realized that I was who I was, due to his direct influence throughout my life.

It felt good.

For a long time growing up, I'd wanted to be someone else. I'd wanted a different life, imagining, fantasizing about some heroic ideal that belonged more in fairy-tale books than on the pages of my real life. But with the realization came a sense of pride about who I really was, about the man I'd grown into.

It felt really good.

I knelt in front of the headstone, tracing the outline of my father's name in the carved granite face. I had no sadness left in me for his passing. Only happy memories and an undying sense of gratitude.

I heard Zero's car slow to a stop and corkscrewed around to face him. He came walking over without saying a word, placed a small bouquet of carnations on top of the headstone, and stood with his head bent forward for a moment. Zero's respect for the dead knew no limits.

He looked up. "Let's walk."

We moved away from the plot and crunched leaves underfoot that the grounds crew hadn't swept up yet.

"It's worse than I thought."

Exactly what I didn't want to hear. "What'd the Elder say?"

"I'll get to that in a second. McKinley's already buttoned up New Hampshire, Maine, and Vermont."

"Jesus." I stopped. "We're all that's left?"

Zero nodded. "I knew it wasn't good, but by God I didn't think they'd move so damned fast."

"But what's he sold them on? The idea that if the humans know about us it'll be a better world?"

We walked farther along the path as a breeze swept over us, rustling more leaves and twigs.

Zero shook his head. "I don't think it's that grand. Cosgrove doesn't try to appeal to anyone's philosophical outlook. He sticks with what works: greed, ego, power."

I nodded. "In other words, a share in the new government."

"I think so."

"Who can we count on?"

Zero stopped. "I was hoping you could tell me."

"You know anyone out of the service who'd come back?"

"There's a problem if we try. If Cosgrove has passed word that he's looking for help, if we try to recruit, it might send back alarms to McKinley and Cosgrove."

"But we can't take them out alone."

"Well, we could, but it'll be tough."

"Nothing's ever easy."

"It's going to get a whole lot worse too, according to my friend."

"So what's the deal with the missing Kavnora?"

"Apparently," said Zero, snapping a twig underfoot, "along with a lot of other old ceremonies, the book also outlines the proper method for the resurrection of the Sargoth."

"The what?"

"You never paid attention in history class, did you?"

"Girls occupied my time during school."

Zero sighed. "The Sargoth and the Jarog are the two polar extremes of vampire deities. They were brothers, like the human Cain and Abel. One guess what the Sargoth is like."

"Not the Avon lady, huh?"

"Not even close. And according to the Elder, a successful resurrection of the Sargoth would enable the summoner to reap untold power. That sound like something Cosgrove might be interested in?"

I nodded. "What now, then? He summons this Sargoth and we all die?"

"Not that easy, thankfully. The Kavnora only lists the necessary items for the ceremony, not the ceremony itself. That has to be pieced together once all the items are assembled."

"So Cosgrove's on a scavenger hunt."

"That's one way of putting it, yes."

"Where does he find these items?"

"They're safeguarded by a small cadre of vampires Loyalists."

"Loyalists?"

Zero paused. "Humans."

"What the hell are you talking about?"

"Calm down, Lawson. It makes perfect sense, doesn't it? Give the items to humans who are loyal to us. No one would ever suspect it."

"But that means the Balance has been compromised. Humans knowing about us endangers our society."

"We're talking about five people, not a community."

"Still, the temptation to talk, to whisper about us, must be overwhelming."

"Who'd believe them? Five people insisting vampires exist? I don't think that would get much air-time on the national news, do you?"

"It's still risky. How are they going to protect themselves if Cosgrove shows up?"

"About as well as that other Elder did, I guess," said Zero. "Look, the system isn't perfect; I certainly didn't have a hand in creating it. But we've got to work with what we've got. And right now we've got a desperate Cosgrove out hunting for the pieces of this puzzle. If he finds out about the human Loyalists, he'll kill them, get the keys, and unlock a very, very bad Pandora's box."

"Wonderful. So now not only do we have to hunt down Cosgrove, but we've also got to protect these Loyalists."

"Looks that way."

"Do you at least have the addresses of these people?"

Zero frowned. "That's going to be tough."

"Jesus, you don't even know where they are?"

"It's a cutout system, Lawson. The address of one Loyalist is stored at the Council here in town. That Loyalist has the contact information for the other Loyalist in line and so on."

"Nifty."

"I'm just letting you know what we're up against here."

"Yeah, I know it. I'm just sick of chasing this bastard all over the city. I had another damned run in with him last night."

"What happened?"

I filled him in. He looked at me funny. I frowned. "What?"

"You like this girl?"

"Talya? She's a real pro. She's got my respect, I

mean, for a human." I started walking again. Zero
fell in beside me.

"You know you can't."

"Can't what?"

He grabbed my arm. "Come on, Lawson, we've
known each other too damned long for this. You
know as well as I do that you're nuts about her.
Jesus, I can smell it on you."

I sighed. "Yeah. Damn it, I know. I wish to hell
I didn't."

"Hey, I'm not passing judgment on you, Lawson.
Take her to bed. Do what you've got to do to get
her out of your system. I know it's not easy, but
it's also forbidden."

"Yeah." What the hell could I say to him? We
passed the next few moments in silence. Zero
watched a red-tailed hawk swoop low over an un-
developed field and pluck a mouse out of it for
lunch, then cleared his throat.

"I've been there, pal. I know what it's like."

I looked at him. "When?"

He smiled. "Remember Cairo?"

"How could I forget? Two weeks of hunting that
damned fool Nadi down. It seemed like I had sand
in my crap for weeks."

"Remember the hotel we stayed at?"

"Yeah." It suddenly dawned on me. "Wait a minute; you mean the waitress in the café downstairs?
What was her name?"

"Wajiah."

I chuckled. "Sure enough." I looked at him. "Really?"

He shrugged. "I've always had a thing for Middle
Eastern women."

"You and my father both." I shook my head. "I've never seen it."

"Once again I will say your father was obviously a man of refined taste. My respect for him has grown by leaps and bounds."

"I'll bet. Finish the story, Romeo."

"Well, we were done in Cairo; you flew back to the States for some rest. I stayed behind to clean things up."

"Right, I remember you saying something about making sure everything was buttoned up."

"Yeah, well, I lied."

"Yeah?"

"I married her, Lawson."

My jaw dropped. "What?"

"It's true. I was smitten; I couldn't live without her. I asked her to marry me and she agreed. We did it in secret. She lived with me in Bonn for the two years I was stationed there."

I didn't want to ask, but I had to. "What happened?"

He turned away. "It's not like I could go on with it forever, Lawson. We're a small community, after all; word spreads."

"But you could have written her off as a maid or a servant or something right?"

Zero shook his head. "No. They knew." He shrugged. "But more important, she knew."

"Knew what?"

"What I was, Lawson. I hadn't told her I was a vampire."

"Damn."

"She left me. Broke my heart, but she left me. The Council placed me on administrative leave pending an investigation. Luckily, she'd left prior to the hearing. It saved my life. That and my record. They suspended me for a time and then brought me back to the States where I could be watched closer. I haven't strayed since."

"But—"

"No buts, Lawson. It won't work. Forget whatever you're trying to come up with; it can't happen. And we've got more important things to concentrate on, like killing Cosgrove and making sure this conspiracy doesn't come to pass. That's where your head has to be. You read me?"

I didn't like it, but I had to accept it. At least for right now. We'd see what the future held when the future came to pass.

"Yeah, I read you."

He nodded. "Good, now let's see what we can do to make sure Cosgrove's dreams never become a reality."

Twenty-three

Disrupting Cosgrove's plans meant that we had to get the addresses of the Loyalists and safeguard them before Cosgrove could use his unique and permanent charm on them.

Unfortunately, the fact that the address for the first Loyalist was stored at the Council's chambers on Beacon Hill did nothing to make me feel confident. After all, we couldn't just go waltzing in and ask for it. We had no way of knowing who was on our side. And technically, we probably weren't even supposed to know about the whole cutout system. I wondered aloud about the Elder Zero had gotten the information from.

"Interesting case, that one," he said as I drove us down Boylston Street, passing the FAO Schwarz toy store's giant bronze teddy bear out front. "Been around for a long time."

"His age make him special?"

"No, the fact that he's a soaked-through sponge of a drunk and still manages to help preserve our heritage."

I swerved to miss a bicycle messenger. "A drunk? You sure about his information—couldn't he just be feeding us anything for the price of a drink?"

"Not likely. He and I go way back."

"How far back?"

Zero smiled. "Let's just say I could have easily ended up exactly like him."

"Drunk or an Elder?"

"Yes."

Zero wasn't the only person in my life who answered questions like that and I have enough sense now to let it lie. I steered around Boston Common and headed for the garage. Zero checked his watch.

"Almost five. They ought to be leaving soon. That will leave the butler."

"Have you ever been inside this place?"

"Once. A long time ago. It's not that difficult."

Somehow the thought of breaking into the most respected institution of vampire society did not impress me as being easy. And given that Zero and I were about to break a few of the very laws we protected didn't make me feel any better. Sure, maybe it was old hat for Zero—hell, he'd married a human. But I was still a lawful citizen. Or at least for another ten minutes.

We mounted the steps leading upstairs from the Boston Common garage and hoofed across the buzz-cut lawns toward the nearest entrance. Beacon Street sloped up toward the State House's gold dome, but our destination rested a few doors south of it. Darkness peppered the Common with pockets of shadows not compromised by the antimugger sodium lights that sprouted like metallic trees. We stayed close to the darker patches.

Zero checked his watch again. "Ready?"

"You sure they won't be there?"

He paused. "No. But we don't really have a choice."

"And we can't just ask for it?"

"Let me put it this way: If Cosgrove knows the address is here, he'll be coming for it very soon. If he doesn't know it's here, and we tip our hand by showing up and asking for it, someone on the inside will let him know, we lose our surprise, and we'll probably be dead by morning."

"Great options. I can't decide which I hate more."

Zero led the way around to the back of the stately brownstone bordered by a high wrought iron fence that looked like six-foot spears jutting out of the ground. Away from the traffic on Beacon Street, silence blanketed the rear of the building, amplifying the noises of the stray animals working the night.

Zero pointed to the second-floor window and I nodded. We'd go up to get in. The principle of penetrating the building was one based on the simple fact that people usually never secured what they thought would be too much trouble to break into. Who would climb up to the second floor using the drainpipe Zero had located to access what looked like a small bathroom window?

Obviously, only two fools like us.

But the principle held sound as Zero checked the window for alarms. He shook his head and eased it open, gesturing me inside.

The window was a tight fit for me, and as I finally got myself in, I saw Zero struggling to haul his huge frame through it. He finally succeeded, but his face was damp with sweat and strain by the time he finished.

I cupped my hand over his ear and whispered to him. "Where to?"

He pointed down. That made me nervous. The Council chambers were located in the bowels of the building, far away from sunlight, which many of them still did not embrace.

I pushed the bathroom door open and peeked outside. A long, dimly lit corridor stretched on either side, bathed in deep navy carpet which fortunately looked plush. At least it would muffle any noise we might make.

Zero crept ahead of me, pausing at intervals to listen and try to feel the air ahead of us.

Finally, after ten minutes of creeping, we'd reached the ground floor, which was dark, and a new corridor with maroon carpet. We headed down it and toward a doorway at the end.

A small liquid-crystal display blinked as we approached and I swore silently. The entrance to the chamber was obviously alarmed.

Zero peered close to the display and examined the box from all angles without touching it. Finally, while my heart hammered in my chest and I watched for the Council's butler, he reached into his jacket and brought out a small box that looked similar to the one on the doorway.

He flipped it open and held it close to the alarm system. He glanced back over his shoulder, smiled through the darkness, and shrugged. Then he flipped the switch.

The effect was instantaneous. The alarm shut off and the door clicked open. Zero's shoulders slumped as he exhaled in a rush; caught himself and quietly opened the door.

A rush of cool air enveloped us as we stole downstairs. Despite the darkness, we could make out the details of the spiraling staircase and the room it led down to. I detest breaking my neck walking down dark staircases.

At the bottom we paused, listened, and then looked around the room. Six high-backed leather chairs sat like a crescent moon before a fireplace with small glowing embers almost out of life.

Zero moved immediately to the mantel and motioned me over, pointing at the carved wooden outline of a symbol I'd seen only a few times before. It was a letter in the old language and was in the exact center of the mantel.

"This is it." Zero pressed inward and a small doorway instantly opened to one side of the room. We walked over and entered.

Inside, it looked more like an office, with a large mahogany desk and several chairs. Zero walked behind the desk and began rifling through the drawers. Two minutes later he held up his hand and showed me a slip of paper.

"Thank God. Can we go now?"

He nodded and we backtracked through the rooms and up the stairs. At the top we paused and listened again. It seemed safe, so I went ahead and beckoned to Zero once I reached the corner.

That's when the lights came on.

Twenty-four

"Going somewhere, lads?"

The butler. Withered and tired-looking, he was nevertheless holding a shotgun in his hands. I couldn't tell what kind of loads it might have taken. But he answered my questions soon enough.

"You boys managed to get past that alarm system with no dramas, so I'm assuming you're part of the family. That said, you ought to know this lady's got enough wood in her to put you both into a world of hurt."

Zero came up behind me. "Slow down, Arthur."

"Who's that, then?" He squinted into the light. "That you Zero?"

"Who else would be able to smell that horrible breath a mile away?"

Arthur, the butler, chuckled. "It's me rotten gums." He lowered the shotgun just a bit, still ready to bring it to bear, though. "What are ya doing here?"

"It's an urgent matter, Arthur."

"It'd have to be, sneaking around here, wouldn't it? But ya'd better explain yourselves all the same." He stepped back and waved us into the main foyer.

Zero led the way and I trailed behind him. Despite appearances, Arthur seemed well capable of bringing that shotgun back up in a hurry, and Zero shot me a look that told me not to try to disarm him.

"So what gives, Zero? What's so urgent ya can't ring up an old chum and ask for his help?"

"Didn't want to get you into trouble, Arthur. Better that way, believe me."

"Yeah? Since when did we care about a spot of bother anyway? This is me, remember?"

Zero smiled as if remembering an old movie. "I remember, Arthur. I would have loved to involve you. But I couldn't."

"Well, ya have now." He frowned. "It'd be 'bout that Cosgrove character, wouldn't it?"

"How'd you hear about that?" I asked.

Arthur fixed me with a quick stare and shot a look at Zero. "That dumb question just an act or are we really training the stupid ones these days?"

"Hey . . ."

Arthur looked back at me. "You listen to me, sonny. I'm the butler around here and I do a bleeding good job of it, no complaints from the Council at all. And more important than serving as best I know how, I also keep these gummed-up, miserable pieces of cauliflower open for tidbits and whatnot. I hear stuff. And I'm not so far gone I can't piece it together, understand?"

"Yeah."

"Right." He nodded at Zero. "Spill it, you old cracker."

"It's about the Balance, Arthur. We initially thought Cosgrove was trying to form an alliance with the humans, and he may well still be doing that."

"But?"

"But there's something else."

Arthur nodded. "The Elder."

"Yeah. He's trying an ancient ritual it looks like. And to do that, he needs the pieces of the ceremony puzzle. He'll be looking to figure out where they're all kept."

"He won't be able to, though, will he? It's not . . ." He glanced in my direction. "General knowledge."

"It's OK, Arthur. He knows about the Loyalists."

"But Cosgrove—he can't have figured it out, can he?"

"He can," I said.

"What makes you such an expert, then?" asked Arthur.

"I've been tracking him for years. We go way back. And he's damned smart. He'll figure it out eventually. He might even come calling here."

"You've been on him for years, have you? And you haven't gotten him yet? I'm not impressed, Fixer."

"It's not for a lack of trying, Arthur," said Zero. "Lawson here was kept in check by the Council."

Arthur sighed. "I'm too old for this, Zero. I told you I was so happy doing next to nothing except waiting for these bones to rot away into the night."

"Like I said, Arthur, I didn't want to involve you."

"Yeah. Yeah, I know it all."

"You're not going to tell them, are you? We're not sure how far up the conspiracy goes yet."

"You're not implying—"

"Yes. Yes, we are," I said.

"Bollocks." Arthur sighed again. "All right. It's

against my judgment, but then I've never really been a decent sort at that anyhow. Get yourselves out of here the way ya came in. Just make sure you shut that damned window when ya leave."

Zero shook his hand. "Thanks, Arthur."

"Sod off, you old wanker. But take care just the same."

"And you too, old friend."

Zero pulled me toward the staircase and I followed him upstairs. When we were in the bathroom, I nudged him.

"What was that all about? Who was that guy?"

"Can't you figure it out? He was a Fixer. But he got tired of the killing. Some say he lost his cool. But I've known him a long time. He just got tired is all. He needed a break from it. Hell, he needed to get out of it. So the Council hired him as their butler and caretaker of this place. It's crap work, but it suits him fine. We're lucky it was him we ran into and not someone else."

I nodded. "Now what?"

Zero patted his pocket. "We've got the information. Let's go check it out."

Weston lies west of Boston by about ten miles. Not far on a good day, but traffic along Route 9 can tie things up trying to get to Route 128. Especially during rush hour. And since rush hour has now become rush-three-hour due to corporate America insisting people give up normal lives in favor of their employers, Zero and I got bogged down.

Finally exiting 128 north, he directed me to a small side road that wound down through Weston's outskirts. We passed the Case Estates, a tract of land belonging to Harvard University, and Zero asked me to slow down.

"We're almost there."

The clock on my dashboard read 8:30 P.M. Darkness had long since bled all over this suburb, masking shadows with infinite hidden possibilities. Streetlights seemed a forgotten concern out here.

"Kill your lights."

Normally, this would have been impossible since Jettas don't allow their lights to ever turn off. But I'd tinkered with my electrical system, so Zero's request was no problem.

I coasted the last few feet before pulling over to the gravel roadside. Stones crunched beneath the treads, popping and shearing against one another.

Zero pointed. "There."

It looked like a fairly nice house. Two floors, easy. Probably four or five bedrooms, two baths, maybe a sun roof over the back porch. Real estate ran expensive in Weston, but if this was the Loyalist house, they were probably receiving a fairly decent allowance from the Council. A little money always helps ensure trust.

Shrubs ran along the front walk, at about waist height. They'd help mask our approach.

Beside me, Zero was automatically checking his piece while never taking his eyes off the house. He was theorizing how it would probably look inside. If we'd had time, we might have even scared up the house plans filed at Weston's city hall.

But there was no more time.

"How you wanna do it?"

Zero placed his gun back in its holster temporarily. "We have to hit it hard. If he's in there, you can bet they won't be alive much longer."

"And if he's not?"

"Have them send the bill to the Council," said Zero. He nodded up. "Interior?"

"Never goes on when the doors open."

"All right. I'll take the front. You can have the back."

I pulled my door release and we oozed into the sea of inky darkness.

Cold night air immediately tried to nip at every exposed piece of skin. I felt my pores slam shut; stinging sensations ran along my jawline.

Zero crept along the hedge farther ahead of me. Our area of vulnerability right now was being along the roadside. I didn't think Weston's finest would take very well to two armed and very proficient vampire hit men sneaking along a shrubbery. We needed to get inside the house.

I found a small cut-through in the bushes, tapped Zero on the heel, and gestured. He nodded, held up his hand showing five fingers.

Five minutes.

Light poured from a few windows on the first floor, but I kept my eyes averted. I had to be careful not to trip over the several dozen toys littering the yard. So they had children.

That would complicate things.

Taking a house down is fairly manageable if you can control everyone in the shortest possible time. Two adults faced with guns will usually accept their situation. Children panic. That makes the adults nervous and unpredictable.

Naturally, we had no intention of hurting anyone but Cosgrove, but we still had to use shock to get inside and make sure the house was under control as fast as possible.

At the back of the house, wooden steps led up to the back door. A screen door before a heavy wooden door. Oak by the look and feel of it. Probably a dead bolt on the other side.

If I'd been Zero, I would have quietly picked it. But picking locks was one of those things I sucked at. Like fixing cars. Or bowling.

I'd have to take the door down. Or go in through a window.

The closest one was two feet to the left of the door, leading into the kitchen. It was dark inside, and as luck would have it, the window itself was unlocked. I eased the screen up and then got the window up just as smoothly. Modern windows don't make much noise, thankfully.

I'd been counting down since I'd left Zero and knew I had about thirty seconds before he went through the front door. I'd wait a second more and then move in from the rear.

The reasoning was simple. If we went in simultaneously, accurate though we were, we might mistake each other for an enemy. And I certainly didn't want a slug from Zero's piece embedding itself in my heart. Talk about ruining your day.

My heartbeat began accelerating, and it was during these times I always worried the most. Vampires have acute hearing. And a hammering heart makes a sound many vampires can hear. It's an unfortunate by-product of adrenaline and fear.

But there wasn't much you could do about it either. I didn't know any Fixer who was able to go through hell and back without getting worried. No matter how skilled, no matter how experienced, you still got the willies.

When it came, the bang jolted me. By the sound of it, Zero had kicked in the front door. I crashed through the swinging kitchen door and headed down a small hallway that led to the front of the house. I had my pistol in what experts refer to as a "low-ready" position, with the barrel dipped just below the horizon. It allowed a rapid target acquisition by bringing the rear sights up and then aligning the target on the front sights. Sight-acquire-fire. It worked and it was fast.

My breathing was short. Sporadic. It was always tough to keep from going tunnel-visioned in the tight confines of a home. Walls filled with framed photographs suddenly loomed closer. And you had to keep moving.

I got to a doorway and dropped to one knee, then poked my head around the corner. . . .

Nothing.

"Living room—clear!"

I could hear Zero shout the same thing from the room bordering the room I was in. We linked up and he frowned.

"Where the hell is everybody?"

"Upstairs?"

He nodded and we moved to the main staircase together.

Stairways are tough to move up without exposing yourself to unfriendly fire from above. The method we used was to go up the stairs backs to each other. Zero headed up facing front, his gun ready to take anything ahead of us; I went up backward, aiming high above us at any position where fire could rain down on us from above.

It's tough moving in concert unless you've practiced it. Zero and I had.

Still, by the time we finally cleared the stairs and rested a moment on the landing, we were out of breath. I sucked a gulp of oxygen down.

Then I stopped.

Zero had too.

The air up here was tinged with the smell of copper—the smell of blood. Death.

Zero was up and moving down the hall, but I could tell from his body language he wasn't expecting to find Cosgrove here. I wasn't expecting to find anyone alive here either.

They were in the master bedroom, which must have been quite nice only a few hours ago. But the walls were literally dripping with blood now. The bodies of the man, wife, and two small children were torn apart, utterly dismembered.

I knelt by what must have been one of the children. A small tuft of blond hair sat still, an oasis amid the sea of sticky, coagulating blood.

"Even the kids." I shook my head. "Jesus Christ, Zero. Even the goddamned kids."

Zero was searching the room for anything he could use to cover the bodies. "We'll have to call in a cleanup team. There's no way we can leave them like this."

He was right. There'd be too many questions. But I wasn't so sure that the Council would be the best resource right now. "They'd want to know how we found out. That could make things uncomfortable for Arthur."

Zero nodded. "What do you think?"

I surveyed the scene, grimacing, feeling the already painful ball in my throat grow larger. Words didn't want to come out of my mouth. "Fire," I said finally.

"Yeah" was the best Zero could manage.

We did a rudimentary search for the address of the next Loyalist family, but we both knew there'd be nothing to find. Cosgrove was a thorough bastard and he certainly would have unearthed all the information he needed prior to killing the family.

Instead, we concentrated on preparing the house for the coming inferno. A liberal application of household cleaners and old newspapers situated at key points of the house would ensure a rapid acceleration of fire. We spent some time in the bedroom last, dousing the bodies with a small can of lighter fluid that Zero had found under the kitchen sink.

"This is no way for someone to die."

"Especially Loyalists," said Zero. "They knew the risks and did it anyway." He looked at me. "Lawson, when this is all over, gather the remains and see to it they're buried properly, yeah?"

"Where you going?"

"Nowhere, but if anything comes up, you know, take care of it, OK?"

I frowned, trying to remember if Zero had ever witnessed any of Cosgrove's handiwork before. I couldn't recall, so if this was the first time, it was a helluva shock, even for someone with Zero's experience.

Zero knelt down a few feet away from the bodies, struck a single match, and watched the flame lick its way to the bloodied bodies. In an instant the crackling of fire encased the four corpses. Zero and I ducked out of the room and back down to the kitchen. The fire would rage undetected for only a few minutes. We had to get out of there before it was noticed.

We got back to the car without incident and headed back to Boston. In the dim green light cast by my dashboard, I turned to Zero.

"Now what?"

"You've got to kill him, Lawson."

"And you?"

"I've got to figure out how far this damned thing has gone. Try to find someone we can trust. Because after seeing what I saw tonight, it's pretty obvious we're going to need some help. A lot of help."

Twenty-five

I got back to the Charles Hotel at 10:30 P.M. and parked in the garage. Upstairs, I slumped into a high-backed chair by the front door of the bar, ordered a Bombay Sapphire, and tossed it down my gullet, feeling the warmth hit seconds later. Outside, the rapidly increasing November rain only added to my gloomy mood.

Gloomy because of Cosgrove's reappearance in my life with his damned conspiracy, his damned ceremonies, and his goddamned dementia.

And gloomy because of all the things missing from my risk-laden life, I wanted love the most. Talya's love. Angry because of everything I could have longed for, I wanted the most forbidden of all. And disgusted because obsessions like this were so typical of my personality, and as many times as I thought I'd learned my lesson, I never really changed.

Hell, I could trace it back to childhood. I'd become obsessed with wanting to fly. Not being able to change myself into a bat like the legends said really pissed me off. But I hadn't let reality intrude on my fantasy. The large oak tree that grew in back of my house had seemed a stable enough platform from which to experiment with flight. So I climbed up. High. And once at the top, I simply spread my arms and jumped.

Reality came crashing back into my life about the same time my head made contact with the ground. But I never stopped obsessing about other things. Things like Robin. My career. And now Talya.

Of course, I'd never stopped obsessing about Cosgrove.

I drained my drink.

The waitress put another one in front of me.

I started to say thank you when a voice cut me off.

"Bad news?"

Talya. Behind me. She'd had the waitress bring me a refill. I hadn't even noticed. I turned in my seat and caught her smiling at me. Shit. Talk about a pro.

"No. Not bad news. Just wanted one before I called you." I checked my watch. "It's not eleven yet."

She nodded. "I figured you'd be down here. I wasn't doing anything, so I thought I'd join you." She cocked an eyebrow. "That OK?"

"Yeah, sure." I took another healthy drag on the fresh glass.

"Slow down, Lawson. It could be a long night."

"It's already been a long night," I muttered. "That's the problem."

She frowned. "Don't turn into a grumpy drunk on me. I hate men who can't handle their drinks."

I slid the drink back onto the table. "Won't affect me, anyway."

"Why? Did you take the same course on how to drink alcohol without getting drunk that I did?"

"Something like that." I wished I had. I wished I was just another ordinary human sitting at a bar, slowly getting drunk. Pickling my brain cells. I wasn't. Alcohol didn't affect our blood the same way it did humans. I'd have to drink three bottles of straight gin to even get a buzz.

She smiled. "A man of mystery." She leaned closer. "I like that."

"Really." I couldn't help myself. Despite the shit I'd seen tonight, Talya had a way of making me feel OK. She was so damned attractive. I drained the drink and looked at her. "How are you feeling?"

She shrugged. "Like someone shredded my insides with a chain saw."

I toasted her with another sip. "Colorful. You'll be a poet yet."

"Nothing I haven't experienced before. Granted, the method was a little different."

" 'Different'—that's a good term for it."

She rubbed her neck. "I couldn't find the puncture marks, Lawson. Why?"

"They heal very fast." I finished my drink and wanted another. "They have to. Vampires can't afford to have victims walking around in public with gaping holes in their necks, or anywhere else for that matter. It'd start a panic."

Talya frowned. " 'Anywhere else'?"

"Yeah." Where was that waitress? "They can draw from anywhere. Neck, arm, chest, back, wherever's convenient."

She sat back in her chair. "How do you know so much about them, Lawson?"

"My job. I did some research. The rest is field experience."

"But you said you've never killed a vampire before."

Damn her memory. "Yeah, but I've chased them before."

"Cosgrove?"

"Yep."

"How many times?"

I looked out the window, remembering. In the darkness I saw scores of bodies float past in the blink of an eye. Then Robin. Then nothing but November night. "Once . . . twice . . . Hell, I've been chasing him my whole life."

"That long?"

"Isn't it obvious?"

"I suppose it might be if I knew why."

"Let's just say he and I have a lot more history than I'm comfortable sharing right now."

She paused. "And you never got him before. How come? You don't strike me as someone easily dissuaded from a goal."

"He almost got me." The waitress mercifully reappeared with another drink. I took another long drag and sighed. "I was out alone. Out in the cold. No backup. No support net. No Control." I shrugged. "You've been there."

"Yes, but not when I was chasing a vampire for heaven's sake."

I nodded. "Well, it all comes down to this. Everything has a beginning. It's time to write the ending. I'll get him this time. I have to."

She put her hand on top of mine. *"We'll* get him, Lawson. Together."

"Stealing my lines now, Talya?"

"They're good lines, Lawson. Spoken by a brave man."

"Spoken by a fool, more likely. If I had any sense at all, I'd run away from all of this shit."

"But you won't."

"I won't. I can't."

She leaned closer again. "Courage isn't the absence of fear, Lawson. It's acting in spite of the fear. You are brave."

That's what she thought. I finished my third drink and slid a $20 onto the table. I looked at Talya and then got to my feet. "Ready?"

"For anything." She stood. "Where to?"

"Club outside of Central Square. I think Cosgrove may just feel like hitting it tonight."

"Why?"

"Because it's in Cambridge and he hasn't hunted this side of the river yet, as far as I know. Also, Friday is their 'Goth Night.' He'll blend in easily. Hell, he could kill on the damned dance floor and nobody would even notice."

"Goth? You mean those dreary-looking wanna-be corpses?"

I smiled. "Think black clothing, albino pale skin, and nocturnally obsessive."

She looked down at her clothes. "These OK?"

She wore another ribbed turtleneck, this one charcoal gray, and another pair of black spandex pants. The leather boots complimented her feet, but I noticed the thick sole could take some abuse, not to mention give it out.

"Yeah, you'll have no problems."

She grabbed my hand. "Then let's go. I'm kind of anxious to see Cosgrove again. He and I have a score to settle."

"Still got the ammo I gave you?"

"Yes. Minus the two poor shots I made."

"Chalk it up to first-time jitters."

"Bullshit, Lawson. I—we—can't afford first-time jitters. I'm not some green rookie who needs to be let down easy. I missed. It's that simple. I don't miss often. And you can bet I won't miss again." That said, she turned and left the bar. I watched her walk for a moment and then trailed after her.

The drive to Manray took just under ten minutes due to the traffic on Massachusetts Avenue. I parked in a garage on a side street and we walked down together. Talya looped her arm through mine. I stopped short.

She cocked her head. "I figure we should look like a couple, Lawson. Good cover."

My ass. I smirked just the same, though. We continued down to the club entrance. Since it was still early, we got right in, past the doormen who showed a passing interest in me and a heavy interest in Talya. Hell, she was a knockout. A deadly knockout at that.

Inside, dim lights illuminated little pockets of space devoid of people. The clubgoers stayed in the darkness. Here the atmosphere wafted far different from any of the other clubs we'd staked out so far. This was the place to come if you hated the mainstream. And at least fifty people here were better poster children for vampires than me. I smirked at the irony and guided Talya to the left. We entered the main dance-floor room.

Larger than I would have expected from the outside, a square parquet dance floor sat bordered on all sides by long couches draped in red and purple velvets. Bars at both ends, staffed by pale-faced denizens, served a lot of strangely colored drinks tonight.

Gridlocked, shadowy packets of gyrating couples, triples, and foursomes packed the dance floor. Manray catered to alternative lifestyles more than any other club in the area. Straights, homosexuals, transvestites, hermaphrodites, and everyone in between congregated here, unabashed in what they liked to do.

I respected the freedom they enjoyed. Hell, I was jealous. At least they could love who they wanted.

I couldn't.

A wisp of a woman floated past me. She couldn't have weighed more than sixty pounds soaking wet. Talya looked at me and frowned.

"Do they eat?"

I shook my head. "Now, now, I believe the politically correct term is 'calorically challenged.' "

She laughed. "That's good."

I guided her to the left side of the room and sat her down next to a pair of purple lipsticked women locked in a passionate embrace. I've always loved two women kissing. It's a beautiful thing in my book.

Talya smiled. "See something you like, Lawson?"

They broke apart at that moment and I got a good look at them both. Ugh. Not exactly contestants for a beauty contest.

"Guess not," I said.

She looked and sat back. "You're right."

I looked at her, visualizing instantly, and tried to stop. But not before an image of Talya, myself, and another hot woman locked in a sweaty threesome floated through my mind and caused a surge of blood flow to other extremities. Damn, now I couldn't get a drink.

"Aren't you going to get me a drink, Lawson?"

I cleared my throat and purged my mind. "Sure thing. What do you want?"

She looked me up and down in answer before finally smiling. "The usual, of course. Vodka, straight over ice. Stolichnaya if they have it."

"Done." I walked back to the bar and ordered our drinks. The total came out to just under eight bucks and I left a tenner on the bar. I always believed that if the help was good, you tipped well. After all, in my profession you never knew who you might need help from in the future. And if they knew you tipped well, they just might be willing to give some.

Talya's feet moved in time to the slow beat of the music when I got back, which vaguely concerned me. We were here to hunt for Cosgrove, not dance. But just as quickly as I was concerned, I also knew Talya wouldn't let her inclinations violate her professionalism. She'd been far too well trained for that.

She took her drink and fondled it for a second before taking a long sip. She brought it way from her lips and sighed. "It always reminds me of Russia when I drink vodka."

"Does it?"

She nodded. "When I was growing up, my mother would always let us have some on holidays. It was a special treat."

I took a drag of my own drink. "What got you into the KGB?"

She shrugged. "What *didn't* get me into the KGB might be a better question." She took another swig and continued. "In Russia, in my youth, everywhere you went there were signs urging you to join. You could join anywhere. At the train station, the post office, everywhere. It seemed silly for me to consider anything else."

"That's it?"

She got a faraway look in her eyes. "My family was murdered when I was fifteen. I wanted vengeance."

"Who killed them?"

"Bandits that roamed the steppes. We weren't as modernized as other states were. Despite the KGB presence, despite the army base twenty miles from my home, despite being in the Soviet Union, we were still very much on our own."

"You were spared?"

"I was not at home when it happened. But it made my decision to enter the KGB an elementary one. I saw the KGB as the way to extract my revenge on them."

Jesus, she'd had a hard life. The bastard child of a rape victim and then the rest of her family murdered. I shook my head. "Did you get it?"

She shrugged. "In time. It took me a while to find them, in between the short spans of leave during my training and eventual work. But . . . yes."

I didn't doubt her. Why should I? She'd already shown her competence on several levels I couldn't even describe. Instead, I nodded.

"Sometimes revenge is the only thing that makes the hurt go away."

"Like now," she said.

I nodded and held up my drink. "For Simbik."

She clinked her glass against mine and we drank

long and deep. I finished my drink then and rested the empty glass on the table in front of me.

Talya rested hers there a moment later. "While we're on the subject, what made you do what you do?"

I shrugged. "I took a test. The results directed me into it."

"Destiny, huh?" She smiled. "No romantic notions of James Bond? No fantasy images of saving the world from dangerous hordes of your nation's enemies?" She smiled. "That seems strange to me."

It was. The Council had chosen me to become a Fixer, not the other way around. I hadn't aspired to anything after Robin's death, except becoming Cosgrove's executioner. Freedom of choice wasn't really an option for those of us born into the Profession. We were preordained somehow, sometime long before we saw the moment of our birth. Somewhere else, outside in the cosmos, our existence was decreed. The Council's responsibility lay with channeling us into the training and from there into our roles as saviors for the vampire community. No romance. No patriotism to speak of. Just an innate understanding of our purpose. An obsession for the Balance.

Simple, to be sure.

But also pure and total duty to a cause.

The closest thing it compared to was the feudal Japanese samurai commitment to Bushido, the way of the warrior. A code so strict, it demanded absolute loyalty to the warrior's lord. Just as we obeyed the laws of the Balance.

That's what I'd become, a vampire samurai.

It didn't help that I studied martial arts.

Talya looked at me funny.

"What?"

She shook her head. "You just got that weird look in your eyes again. Like you were a million miles away. Remembering something. Something you'd tucked away a long time ago."

She was far too perceptive for my comfort, and yet simultaneously, I think it drew me closer to her even more. "Just memories. Faraway memories."

"Do they comfort you as much as they haunt you?"

I sighed. "Yeah."

She nodded. "Me too, Lawson. Me too."

Above us, the music changed again, mixed into a slower beat that resonated heavy synth strings over a thudding bass line. It reminded me of a pulse. The pulse of life.

And of death.

The only absolute certainty in life.

A certainty I was a part of. Whether I liked it or not.

Twenty-six

Just after midnight my beeper went off. In the dim light the orange glow of the small screen seemed to cast an unnatural light over my hand. I read the number. Zero's.

"Gotta make a phone call," I said. "Be right back."

Talya nodded and kept watching the floor for Cosgrove. I had my doubts about whether he'd come in tonight. The clubs in Cambridge only stayed open until 1:00 A.M.

Downstairs by the coat check, I found the pay phone and punched in Zero's number. He answered on the first ring.

"Where are you?"

I told him. "What's up?"

"They're moving on you, Lawson."

"What?" I moved my hand to my right hip and rested it on my gun.

"McKinley contacted Cosgrove tonight and told him where you were."

"Impossible. I've watched my ass for days now. How?"

"Maybe they put a tracer on your car, maybe a surveillance team, I don't know."

"What about the Loyalists? What about the pieces of the ceremony?"

"Cosgrove must have already had the necessary information. He must have already killed the other Loyalists and gotten what he needed."

"Which means he can piece it all together."

"Yes. We've got nothing to go on except for the fact that you're now seen as a threat and they're going to take you out."

"But how?"

"I've been shadowing McKinley. He called Cosgrove from a parking lot in Chestnut Hill. I used a parabolic mike to pick up the conversation. You want to hear the tape?"

"Not necessary. Are you still with him?"

"Negative. He shook me. I don't know where the hell they are now, either of them. Are you alone?"

"No, Talya's with me. Upstairs."

"Stay put. I'm on my way."

I hung up the phone and watched the empty hallway. Shadows danced and flickered as I made my way down it. To my left, grunts and heavy breathing crowded the bathroom area. The dark steps drew me up faster than I'd descended. At the top the waves of intense music struck me as I emerged on the first floor again.

This late in the evening, the only illumination came from candles scattered about the club at strange positions. They flickered and made everything seem alive. Oozing. Mutating.

In the main room my hair stood on end and I got goose bumps. Something was wrong. I looked for Talya. She'd disappeared.

Then I heard the laughter invade my head.

"Lawson."

I pivoted and saw him. Decked out in all his splendor, complete with a damned collared cape, he looked like Bela Lugosi, for crying out loud. But even in the ridiculous attire, he was absolutely lethal.

And never more so, because he had Talya in his arms.

They had all the appearances of a bawdy couple slowly grinding in time to the music. But he was holding her hostage. I saw the one long nail of his pinkie finger resting over her carotid artery. If I moved on him, he'd slice her open and she'd die.

"Does she mean so much to you, Lawson? Does she mean so much that you'd not kill me for fear of losing her?"

His voice floated through even the loudest music. Our hearing gave us the ability to do that.

I said nothing.

He smiled. "I'll take your silence as a yes. Especially considering you saved her the other night rather than kill me. Which reminds me . . ." He tossed something at me with his left hand. It bounced on the floor and came to rest at my feet. "Have the souvenir you shot me with the other night. It took me two hours to dig the bloody thing out of my right leg."

I picked up the hunk of wood. It hadn't exploded on impact. Defective. I sighed and pocketed it.

"Let her go, Cosgrove. This doesn't concern her."

"Doesn't it? I did kill her fiancé after all."

McKinley, that bastard, had told him all about her background. "She doesn't know what she's dealing with."

"Whether or not that's true, which I doubt considering she was shooting wooden bullets at me the other night, she still means to kill me, given the chance. I should save myself the effort and execute her anyway. Self-defense and all, you know."

"Don't."

He smiled and kept them moving in time to the music. The bastard was hypnotizing Talya. "Why not? You don't actually love her, do you, Lawson? Tsk, tsk, that's not allowed you know."

"Neither is plotting to overthrow the Council. Or whatever other crazy shit you have planned."

"Touché." He looked down at Talya. "She is pretty, Lawson. In a way she reminds me of Robin." He looked at me with that insufferable grin. "Does she remind you of Robin too?"

"Fuck you, Cosgrove. Leave her out of this. I'm the one you want."

"Maybe not. Maybe I'll just take this pretty thing."

"Leave her alone."

Cosgrove laughed. "Do you think about Robin anymore? Did I ever tell you what it felt like to cut her heart out, Lawson? How her warm blood sprayed and coated my hands while I worked. It was delicious. Absolutely delicious."

I needed to break his train of thought. Rage swelled inside me, and if he kept talking about Robin, I might make a huge mistake. "I know about McKinley."

That surprised him. He stopped moving for a second, and Talya murmured something. He recovered and started his hypnotic dance again. "So what?"

"The conspiracy, Cosgrove. I know about it all.

You're using McKinley and the others in New England to take down the Council. You'll assume the role of leader of the vampire nation and begin a relationship with the humans."

"Well, so you know. So what?"

"I know about the Elder you killed as well. About the ceremony you're trying to piece together."

"Pieced together, Lawson. I found out all about the Loyalists a long time ago. I've known where to look from the start. And the puzzle pieces are together quite nicely. I'm just tying up loose ends now."

"Loose ends like killing her?"

He winked. "Well, I haven't quite decided yet. Perhaps I'll just take her with me."

"I can't let you do that." I hoped I sounded a lot tougher than I felt.

He kept laughing. "You're hardly in a position to demand anything, Lawson. After all, I have your girlfriend's life in my hands. You won't do anything right now."

"Don't be too sure."

"But I am. You didn't kill me when you had the chance the other night. Instead, you saved her. You saved her with your own blood, Lawson. I'd say that's a pretty telling event, wouldn't you?"

"Maybe I've reconsidered."

"I don't think so. If you had, you would have pulled your little gun and blown me away already." He shook his head. "No, you won't try anything here. Not while I have her."

Something still wasn't right. If Zero was correct, why was Cosgrove baiting me like this? Why hadn't he simply ambushed me and killed me outright?

The answer hit me at the exact same time my

body took over and jerked me across the room by eight feet. I heard-saw-felt the presence behind me and responded.

Another vampire.

He was moving fast on me, already mounting a second attack by the time I had realized what was happening. Cosgrove had played the diversion. The obvious diversion. He'd focused me on Talya and I'd almost allowed myself to be sucked in. While I was dealing with him, the assassin had been getting in position.

Jesus, I'd almost bought it.

He swarmed over me, tossed me off my feet, and we landed in the recessed shadows, grunting and spilling into chairs. He tried to get his knee into my groin, but I checked it.

His hands concerned me. He was holding a pistol just like mine in his left, desperately trying to get a bead on my heart.

Just like mine? Christ, this guy is another Fixer!

Time was on my side. If I could keep him checked long enough for the club's security to come charging us, I'd be OK long enough to get us on equal terms again. I brought my right elbow into his solar plexus hard and heard him grunt audibly.

His left hand was still gripping the pistol, though. I needed to get control of it before he could shoot me.

He brought his head down sharply at mine and I moved just enough to take a grazing blow by my left eye. Damn, that hurt. My vision blurred from tears, and in that second he managed to get the barrel of the gun closer to my shoulder.

Too close.

I used another elbow to stun him and smother his left arm, hugging it into my body, muffling his chance of using the pistol.

His knee came up again, this time targeting my stomach. I couldn't cover it and he landed a hard strike that made me feel like I was going to lose control of my bowels and bladder. He'd struck a vital point. My head swam in pain and my arms felt weak.

He rammed another knee strike into me. This was not good. If I took another one, I wouldn't be able to hold on to his arm and he'd get the shot off that he needed.

The bouncers showed up then, just in time, yanking him off me, but then the traitor shot one of them.

Someone yelled, "Gun!" and they scattered, leaving me dazed on the floor while the Fixer righted himself on his feet and then took aim at me. I watched as the pistol leveled off, giving him the bead he needed.

Another second and I wouldn't even matter anymore.

The shot, when it came, wasn't from his gun. It came from behind him. But the effect was instantaneous. The Fixer's chest blossomed bright red, cascading crimson down his shirt, and his arms dropped, taking the gun off my heart.

He dropped to the floor.

I scrambled over to him, grabbing him by the collar. "Who are you?" I got no response and shook him again. "Answer me!" No use. I took the gun off him and checked him over. Dead. I looked up in time to see Zero charging through the fleeing crowds.

"Is he dead?"

I nodded. "He used a goddamned Fixer, Zero. Who is he?"

Zero peered close. "Not a Fixer. A Control. Xavier. Runs New Hampshire."

"Not anymore he doesn't."

Zero helped me to my feet. "Lucky for you, I was nearby. He almost had you, Lawson. Where's Cosgrove?"

I turned. "Dance floor with—"

But I knew even as I turned. The dance floor was deserted. And even as I heard the first sirens over the relentless music, even as Zero pulled me along to the rear exit of the club, I realized Cosgrove had Talya.

And all the cards.

Twenty-seven

Zero rushed us out of the club and onto the side street, losing us in a crowd of panicked clubgoers. We bolted down the side street, finally pausing to catch our breath by the next intersection. Blue lights bounced off the buildings from the Cambridge cop cars rushing to the scene. In the distance even more sirens echoed through the night.

"Close," said Zero. "Too damned close."

"That's one I owe you, buddy."

He grinned in spite of our situation. "Yeah, I'll add it to your tab. At least we got one of the bastards."

"But Cosgrove—" I stopped. Paused.

Zero frowned. "I know, Lawson. He's got your girl. And as much as I can't condone it, I understand. We'll get her back. Even if you two never have the relationship you want . . . We'll get her back."

"How? We have no idea where he's hiding out."

Zero sighed. "It's time we went on the offensive, Lawson."

"How?"

"Could be time to pay your buddy McKinley a visit."

"Where, at home?"

"Yes."

"What if they're expecting us?"

Zero shrugged. "We're pretty much out of alternatives. If Cosgrove's pieced together the ceremony ritual and has everything he needs, time is scarce. We have to find out where he's holing up. And unless you've got another idea . . ."

I didn't and Zero knew that. Neither of us was crazy about possibly walking into an ambush.

"We don't have a choice, Lawson."

I shrugged. Sometimes you had to play the hand you were dealt. And since I wasn't palming any aces, the choice seemed clear. "Let's go."

We took my car back into Boston. McKinley's office sat in the Back Bay in a brownstone on Marlborough Street. The rest of the neighborhood, tucked away for the night in their million-dollar homes, looked like a carbon copy of McKinley's office. Stately brownstones, each sinking a few inches every year into the soggy landfill that had been used to build up this section of the city so many years ago. Not that it ever seemed to stop young professionals from desiring one of the prized homes.

I parked the Jetta behind a silver Lexus, the chosen car of rich people who can't drive, and killed the lights, scanning the area. After two minutes Zero and I wandered across the street toward McKinley's office.

The wrought iron fence screeched, penetrating the night like an angry crow in the woods. Zero just kept moving toward the door, and I followed. The best thing to do was get inside as fast as possible and not worry about people peeking out. If you acted like you had something to hide, they'd pick up on it. Act like you owned the place and no one would care.

Besides, I felt sure that McKinley had burned the midnight oil at this place a few times. Enough for his neighbors to conclude that it wasn't too unusual for people to be coming and going at strange hours.

Zero paused in front of the door and frowned. I came up behind him. "What's the problem?"

He pointed inside the vestibule. "Alarm."

Shit. You know, there were times when I definitely wished that vampires had all the cool superhero abilities everyone always made us out to have. Sure would have come in handy here tonight. Hell, I could have transformed into a gaseous state and simply drifted through the keyhole.

Instead, two very real vampires were being held up by a security system costing $100.

Fortunately for me, Zero had an uncanny talent for disarming these things. It was one of his many specialties, one that he was always trying to impress on me, but I hadn't ever picked it up like he had. I came from the school of "just break the damned door down and get in and out fast" rather than the subtle school of burglary Zero had mastered.

He focused on the sensor just inside the door and I knew he would figure out its pattern. It might have been computerized and supposedly random, but Zero's mind could figure it out and then use it to disarm the system. Don't ask me how; I don't know. But while he did that, I busied myself with watching the street for signs that we'd aroused suspicions.

After five minutes of standing in the concealing

darkness, Zero tapped me on the shoulder and motioned to the open door. Like I said, the guy was amazing.

He shut the door behind us and we moved inside. Lucky for us, we didn't need flashlights, since we had better night vision than humans. More rods in our eyes, like cats. It came in handy.

Vampires developed their extraordinary night vision way back in our early years as a race. We had to hunt at night and take our prey by surprise if possible. That necessitated the ability to see in the dark, move quietly, and seem almost invisible. Legends sprang up about us having supernatural abilities. And while our regenerative capacity was indeed tremendous, the other skills simply evolved due to the needs of our race.

The office was three rooms and a study. It seemed more laid out like a small apartment and I wondered if perhaps McKinley hadn't been using this as a romp pad for some of his nocturnal prowling with the mistresses he always liked to keep.

We entered the red carpeted foyer and wandered into the study. Bookcases lined the walls filled with the kinds of self-substantiating tomes most supposedly enlightened people like to keep and point out to visitors as signs that they were really cultured. McKinley had crap on the Roman Empire, Norse mythology, and a wide assortment of self-help books. And since I knew for a fact that McKinley didn't have a damned clue about who Nero was, or whether Thor was anything more than an old comic book, I figured the self-help books must have been another part of his ruse. Maybe it helped him get laid. Maybe he played the part of a caring psychologist to all those lonely ladies.

I had to admit, though, that seeing *Your Past Lives and You* on the bookshelf of a vampire made me grin. McKinley was always good for a laugh, even if it was at his expense.

Zero focused on the rolltop desk in the corner of the room, an old mahogany number that had more than a few dents in the wood. There was a seventeen-inch computer monitor on it and he switched it on. The pale blue luminescence of the screen filled the room, sending several shadows scurrying to the corners in search of more ebon realms.

Windows came up on the screen. Figures that McKinley used a PC. I preferred Macintosh myself. But then again, I'd always been something of an antiestablishment guy.

Zero clicked his way through the files with appalling rapidity. He found a personal file and opened it. There were a lot of graphics files, most in the form of JPEGs and GIFs, meaning McKinley liked to surf the Internet and download pictures. I was guessing they weren't business related.

Zero looked at me. "Shall we?"

I nodded. He clicked one of them.

Jesus.

McKinley was apparently into a lot more than I'd ever given him credit for.

"This might just help explain how Cosgrove got to him," said Zero.

"Blackmail?"

"Yeah, maybe that. And, of course, the promise of a lot more of this kind of sick deranged crap if they were successful."

The picture on the screen said it all. McKinley was a pedophile. I'm not about to describe the garbage filling the screen, simply because I categorize pedophiles under the same category I reserve for terrorists and that is "absolute scum." If I had my way and I wasn't in the role I'd been given, I'd probably be out hunting these sick fucks and exterminating them just on basis of belief alone. You might think it extreme, but both terrorist and child molesters prey on innocence.

I don't dig that.

Period. End of statement.

Zero clicked the picture away and we kept searching files.

It was buried under a subfile titled "research." God knows what McKinley was researching aside from a cheaper way to get to Bangkok so he could fulfill his sick thrills.

Zero opened the file. Text splashed across the screen. A lot of it. Lists of names and locations. I looked at Zero.

"Any of these make any sense to you?"

He nodded. "See there," he said, pointing. "Xavier's name. Location. And this is interesting." He paused.

"What?"

He drew a finger down the front of the screen. "Look at this. It looks like a numbered account."

I looked at Zero. "Money?"

He shook his head. "No, that doesn't make any sense at all."

Of course it didn't. Vampires don't really care all that much about money. All of us could have as much or as little as we wanted by virtue of our contacts within the government. Most of us chose to live comfortably. We knew the more flamboyant you were, the greater risk of exposure. Besides, we never really wanted for anything material.

So what was the deal with the numbered accounts? "If they're not transferring money into those accounts, then maybe it's not a bank account."

Zero looked up. "What, then?"

I shook my head. "I don't know. Could be anything really."

"No," said Zero. "It really can't be anything per se. It's got to be something. And we need to find out exactly what it is."

"We also need to find Cosgrove before he kills Talya."

Zero nodded. "You're right. This'll have to wait." He slid a new diskette into the drive and copied the files. "We can examine these later."

"You think it's in another file maybe?"

"We can look, but the question we have to ask ourselves is whether or not McKinley would keep Cosgrove's location on his computer."

"He's got everything else here. Hell, the stuff wasn't even encrypted."

Zero smiled. "Not that that's anything unusual."

He was right of course. Once we'd bypassed the alarm system and broken into the apartment, it had been smooth sailing. It was typical of so many people who thought that security ended with some flimsy alarm system. Bring along a talented pro like Zero and myself and that gets shot to shit awful quickly. And McKinley had left his Pandora's box wide open.

That's when we heard the noise from somewhere around us.

Zero clicked off the screen, plunging the room

back into darkness. We stayed absolutely still, listening. Our eyes adjusted back to their night-vision ability in only thirty seconds.

We heard it again.

Rhythmic.

And mumbled voices.

Zero motioned me to follow him and we moved closer to the bookshelves. We made no noise as we crept closer. The volume of noise grew.

Zero leaned close to my ear. "Must be a secret room."

I nodded.

Zero ran his hands over the shelves, found nothing, and then began scanning the book spines. It took him thirty seconds. He pointed it out to me. A pictorial guide to Roman bathhouses. Figured.

I drew my pistol as Zero stood off to the side and prepared to pull the spine back. He looked at me.

I nodded.

He pulled.

That section of the bookcase slid away to reveal a twelve-by-twelve room with maroon walls. In the middle of the room was a bed.

And on the bed lay a rail-thin boy who couldn't have been much older than sixteen.

And lying on the boy was McKinley, apparently defying several laws of gravity by not crushing the poor kid trapped beneath him.

He grunted.

Funny, though, how he stopped when he saw me standing there holding a gun on him and Zero leaning against the doorway.

"Shit."

"Seems to me you already found some, McKinley," said Zero. "Get off him."

McKinley frowned. "As always, Zero, your timing is impeccable."

I shook my head. "What, are we interrupting you?"

"Just a bit."

He drew on a smoking jacket and gestured to the boy. "Get dressed. Go home."

Zero frowned. "You're a real sick bastard, McKinley."

"Being gay isn't sick, Zero."

"No, it's not. But being a pedophile is."

McKinley shook his head. "He's eighteen."

"Maybe he is. I doubt it, though," I said. "Besides, we just saw enough of your Internet downloads to know most of them weren't legal. I'm willing to bet if we search Sonny there, we won't find a registered voter card in his wallet."

McKinley sighed. "What is it that I can do for you two, exactly?"

Zero guided him out into the study and sat him down in one of the chairs. The boy exited without looking at us. Probably a pro. Boston's prostitution rings had migrated off the streets and into more discreet escort services nowadays. McKinley probably had the number on speed dial.

"What you can do for us," said Zero, "is tell us exactly where Cosgrove is."

"What makes you think I know that?"

"We don't have time for this, I'm afraid." Zero looked at me. "Shoot him."

I pulled the hammer back on my pistol and leveled it on McKinley.

McKinley's eyes bulged. "You wouldn't."

Zero smiled. "Five seconds and you'll find out."

"This is crazy."

"One."

McKinley looked at me. "Lawson, I saved your life—"

"Two."

"I could have killed you."

"Three."

"I told him not to involve you."

"Four."

I squinted through one eye for effect.

McKinley squirmed. "All right!"

I eased the hammer down. "Tell him."

"That won't be necessary."

Zero looked at me and I looked at him because neither of us had spoken. At once we whirled around.

Cosgrove stood in the doorway. He held a pistol identical to mine. A Fixer gun. Designed to kill vampires. And right now it was aimed at Zero and me.

"Thank you so very much for disabling McKinley's alarm system, Zero. And you were kind enough to leave it off so I could enter unannounced." He looked at me. "Put your gun down slowly, Lawson. I really don't want to have to shoot you just yet."

I slid the pistol onto the small table next to me.

Cosgrove smiled at McKinley. "I told you to expect them."

"I thought you said you and Xavier could handle him."

"Apparently, Xavier failed," said Cosgrove. "And while we were trying to deal with Lawson, you felt perfectly content to indulge in a tryst, is that it?"

McKinley said nothing.

"Charming little fellow you found yourself, McKinley." Cosgrove smiled. "Such a shame I had to break his neck."

McKinley blanched. "You didn't."

"I'd bloody well do the same to you if it wasn't for the fact that you're needed, you stupid fool. Get dressed. We're all going for a ride."

Zero looked at me and I looked at him.

Cosgrove just laughed as if reading our minds. "Soon, gentlemen, very soon. But first we'll have a bit of fun."

Twenty-eight

We waited for McKinley to pull some clothes on. Cosgrove smiled at me.

"Dying to know, aren't you?"

"Know what?"

"As if," said Cosgrove. "You want to know what I've done with your little lovely. What's her name? Talya, isn't it?"

"Yes."

He hefted the gun. "Personally, I've never really cared for firearms. I'd never even touched a gun before that night a week back on the roof with you and your little toy. I'm much more of a hands-on chap. You know, I'll use something I can really get a good grip on. Get right up to my elbows in the muck of death. No long-range killing for me. Removes you from the spiritual cleansing that goes along with it."

"Only cleansing that needs to be done around here is for you," said Zero.

Cosgrove turned around and placed the muzzle of the pistol against Zero's heart. Zero never blinked.

"I should shoot you right now and be done with it."

"Why don't you?" said Zero. "I've been ready to die for years."

Cosgrove wiggled his eyebrows. "My secret. You'll find out soon enough anyway, I expect."

I sighed.

Cosgrove turned back to face me. "Sorry, Lawson, am I boring you?"

"Absolutely."

He laughed. "I admire your blunt attitude. At least a bloke knows exactly where he stands with you." He fondled the gun again. "She's safe, Lawson."

"Pardon me if I don't embrace that statement as truth."

"Understandable." Cosgrove nodded. "And mind you, before this is over, she might not be safe."

"Why is that?"

"I suppose that depends on you, really. But again I can't say that much now or the surprise won't be effective. And I do love surprises."

McKinley reappeared in the doorway, dressed in jeans and a sweater under his jacket.

Cosgrove smiled again. "All freshened up, McKinley? Lathered enough hemorrhoid cream on your arse so it isn't smarting on the drive over?"

McKinley frowned. "Comments like that aren't necessary."

"Tsk. I've hurt your feelings, have I? Tough toodles. We have work to do." Cosgrove tossed him the gun. "Right, you keep an eye on these two, then. You're a better shot than I am."

Cosgrove motioned for us to walk ahead of him. "Let's go."

Outside, Marlborough Street looked hopelessly

vacant. No chance of rescue from some silly fool out walking their black Labrador well after midnight. Not even someone sleepwalking. And not a chance of having a cop car roll past when you needed it. Zero and I were in the shit.

We could have tried to make a move, no doubt about it, but I figured Zero knew as I did that our best chance now was to go along and see what Cosgrove had planned for us. Then we could sort the mess out on the go.

Cosgrove's car was a black Lexus and it fit in perfectly with the surrounding neighborhood. It also probably meant he drove like hell.

"Zero drives," said Cosgrove, tossing him the keys. "And don't forget McKinley's got the gun on Lawson at all times."

Zero caught the keys.

A brief squelch in the night air as the alarm was deactivated and the doors unlocked. I slid in the backseat next to McKinley. Cosgrove rode up front with Zero.

Zero started the engine and turned the lights on. The interior was a cream leather that squealed absurdly when you moved against it. Cosgrove obviously enjoyed surrounding himself with luxury.

"Take us back into Kenmore Square, Zero. Then head out on Beacon Street."

Zero said nothing but wheeled the car in the appropriate direction. I knew he'd be trying to figure out a game plan so once we arrived, we'd have a chance to turn the tables. I was doing the same thing.

Unfortunately, there's not a lot of planning you can do in these situations. You have no idea where you're going, what the odds are, what the opposition has planned for you, and what kind of environment you'll be raising hell in. All of that lack of knowledge spells disaster for trying to plan an escape and counterattack. Usually, the best you can do is simply conserve your strength, try to stay aware and calm, and hope for the best. That way, when the opportunity to jump presents itself, you'll see it and be able to take full advantage of it.

After all, you only get one shot at this kind of stuff. There's no second place. Coming in second means you're dead. Or with Cosgrove—worse.

Cosgrove turned around to look at me. "So Lawson, come on and tell me all about your relationship with the scrumptious Talya. What's she like? Good in the sack or what?"

"We never slept together."

"No? Pity that. My advice to you would be to always take advantage of such an opportunity. After all, you never know when it might get snatched away from you, pardon the pun."

"I'll keep that in mind."

"You do that." Cosgrove looked at McKinley. "I don't imagine the Council would be too pleased if they learned one of their prize Fixers was in love with a human."

McKinley shook his head. "No, they certainly wouldn't."

Cosgrove chuckled. "Mind you, they probably wouldn't be too thrilled with discovering one of their Controls was a raging pedophile as well, though, eh?"

McKinley said nothing. Cosgrove kept chuckling as he turned back around.

We followed Beacon Street out past Coolidge Corner and down toward Cleveland Circle. Even at this hour there were tons of Boston College students cloistering around the small eateries and pizzerias that stayed open late. The cold of the night air only seemed to heighten the effects of whatever alcohol or narcotic haze they'd induced on themselves.

I wondered why Zero hadn't mentioned to Cosgrove that we knew about his plan to resurrect the Sargoth. But it might have been too risky. Cosgrove's ego might have been the only thing keeping us alive at that moment. Spoiling his surprise might have lethal consequences.

"Around the reservoir, Zero. It's coming up on your left."

Left? There was nothing there but an old water-treatment plant for the reservoir across the way. It hadn't been used in a long time and I realized it would be a great place to hide out. Cosgrove wouldn't have risked purchasing a home in the area, even under a pseudonym.

I caught Zero's eye in the rearview mirror and I managed a brief nod. It was all we had to say to each other. We'd been in trouble enough times before to understand how we worked. If I'd had to pick anyone to go into battle with, it would be Zero. And he knew it.

"Turn here."

Zero wheeled the car into the gravel-lined circular driveway in front of the plant, crunching white stones together underneath the tires. Even from the closing distance, I could make out some lights on inside.

"I thought this place was deserted," I said.

Cosgrove nodded. "It was until the Brookline DPW decided to reconsider using it."

"What made them do that?"

"Well, I had some influence in that area. And if you're thinking the police will notice the lights and come knocking, you needn't. They know to expect it."

Zero sighed. "Well, as long as no one crashes the party."

Cosgrove laughed again. "No worries, Zero. We'll be left alone. We can have as much fun as we want and no one will tell us to hush up."

"That's good," said Zero. "Because when we kill you and McKinley, there won't be any nosy neighbors asking what the horrible racket was all about."

Cosgrove looked at him and his smile slipped for just a second. But he brought it back quickly. "I do so enjoy listening to your pathetic threats, Zero. You have such a sense of humor."

"You can bet I'll be laughing when I kill you," said Zero as he wheeled us up to the front of the plant.

Cosgrove nodded. "Park here."

Zero slid the car into park and waited.

Cosgrove led the way. "Out, gentlemen. We're here and I want to introduce you to the greatest project ever conceived by a vampirical genius such as myself."

Zero raised his hand.

Cosgrove stopped talking and looked at him. "What is it?"

"It's just that if you're going to keep spewing this bullshit, would you mind awfully if I went home and got my hip boots? I've got a feeling I'm going to need them."

Cosgrove brought his face closer to Zero's, which was difficult considering Zero stood four inches taller than he did. "I shall enjoy watching you suffer, Zero. And believe me, you will suffer." He turned to McKinley. "Let me get things started properly. Bring them inside in five minutes."

Then he spun on one heel like some flamboyant Gestapo worshiper and vanished behind the heavy oaken door.

Zero looked at McKinley. "It's not too late, you know. Let us go and we'll put in a good word for you with the Council. Help us take him down."

McKinley smirked. "You have no idea how insignificant the Council is about to become, Zero."

I frowned. "So why not enlighten us?"

"And spoil Cosgrove's fun? Not a chance. He's already upset with me as it is. Considering what he's got planned for you two, there's no way I'm going to risk incurring his wrath any more than I have so far."

"It's that bad, is it?"

McKinley nodded. "Surprised the hell out of me, that's for sure."

"Really," said Zero. "Well, I can't wait to see it."

McKinley checked his watch. "You'll want to change your mind once we get inside." He looked up. "It's time, boys. Time to go see what this is all about."

He gestured with the gun. Zero and I walked toward the door. I was hoping this would work out, that we'd hatch some daring escape. But we couldn't. Not yet. Not until we got a chance to take them all down once and for all.

I only hoped it wouldn't be too late once we did.

Twenty-nine

The massive door slid open on oiled hinges like a giant gaping maw. We passed under the oaken door frame and felt it close, swallowing us whole as we moved inside the treatment plant.

Ahead, darkness loomed, pierced just vaguely by scattered forty-watt lightbulbs doing little to keep away the ravenous ebony interior. Shadows shifted as we walked across the old linoleum floor toward another large door at the end of the long corridor.

McKinley chuckled. "Won't be long now, boys."

From farther within the plant, I could make out clinks and clanks of old pipes and gears expanding and contracting in response to varying temperatures. It was easy to imagine this place as a bustling hive of activity in years past.

Now it was tangibly tainted with unspeakable evil.

Cosgrove's evil.

I've known folks who thought evil could be easily classified as one kind of attribute, simply the opposite of good. But that's just so much bullshit as far as I'm concerned. Evil has within it varying degrees of wretchedness that range from vaguely nasty to downright hellish. It's like any other kind of personality trait. It's as equally tough to try to classify discipline solely as one type of aspect of the self. Some people have a narcissistic discipline that borders on the vain, while others possess an innate form of it that drives them to unparalleled heights of success within their lives.

But folks nowadays simply find it easier to lump all of these things into a simple definition that spans the length of a few words in the most recent edition of their favorite dictionary. So we have to come up with other words to describe vain discipline or slightly evil.

I could come up with some very interesting words to describe Cosgrove's evil. But I prefer to just let it stand that he was a sick fuck.

McKinley reached the metallic door first and opened it. Even from where I stood I could sense what was beyond it. I could hear the strange chanting, the old language being spoken in strange tongues. Cosgrove had obviously figured out the ceremonial procedures for raising the Sargoth. I just hoped he hadn't finished it yet.

God knew how deep Cosgrove must have had to dig to unearth the kind of evil emanating from within the bowels of the treatment facility, but it sounded positively awful.

Zero stopped moving. "What the hell is he doing?"

McKinley laughed again. "You'll find out soon enough."

"The hell," said Zero. "He's invoking the Sargoth. I'm not going in there."

McKinley stopped short. "How do you know?"

"I'm not as stupid as you are, McKinley. I know what that creature's capable of. Do you?"

McKinley frowned. "I know enough."

"You don't know shit," said Zero. "If you did, there's no way you would have signed on to be a part of this stupid plan."

"Cosgrove assures me there will be no problems controlling him."

"You can't control the Sargoth, McKinley. It won't bow to the desires of a mere vampire."

"You don't know that. Cosgrove has the ability to control him. He told me."

"You believe everything everyone tells you?"

"I believe Cosgrove."

"What did it cost?" I asked.

McKinley turned to me. "What's that?"

"What did it cost to get you to sell us out, to betray the entire basis of our society? How much did Cosgrove give you to become the bottom-dwelling scumbag traitor that you are right now?"

"Isn't it obvious?"

"If it was, I wouldn't have wasted any breath asking it, you idiot."

McKinley grinned. "I get to kill the members of the Council."

"What kind of ax do you have to grind?"

McKinley turned away. "It's time for you two to see Cosgrove."

"I knew he wouldn't spill it," said Zero. "He's too much of a coward."

"I'm not a coward!" McKinley spun around, sending a gooey string of spittle flying into the air that Zero barely avoided. "You don't have the right to know what the Council did to me."

"Must have something to do with his posterior predilection," said Zero.

McKinley looked confused. I smirked.

"That word may not exist in his vocabulary."

Zero nodded. "Just goes to show you that they'll let anybody become a Control."

"Well, they let you, Zero. That probably means character doesn't count anymore."

"You can't call me into question, McKinley. My honor has never been suspect."

"If honor means marrying a human and hoping to get away with it, then I'd rather be a traitor."

If Zero was surprised by McKinley's revelation, he didn't let it show, although I suspected that he had just finalized plans to kill McKinley in his mind.

When Zero didn't say anything, McKinley smiled. "I thought that might make you a little less hostile. Didn't think anyone knew about your little indiscretion, did you? Well, I saw your file."

"Surprised you could read it," I said.

"Enough of this idle bullshit," said McKinley. "Boys, your time is at hand. Let's not keep Cosgrove waiting any longer."

We entered an inferno. Seriously, Cosgrove must have had the damned thermostat cranked to about a hundred degrees. Steam and condensation filled the room making it difficult to see, and I wondered whether this little soiree wasn't going to set off some temperature alarms at some meter somewhere out in Brookline.

And then his sick voice bled through the haze like a slimy snake oozing and coating everything like a viscous scum.

"Welcome, Lawson and Zero. Are you ready to witness my grand plan?"

Zero, who was never much on ceremony, cleared his throat. "It'll never work, Cosgrove."

"What's that, Zero?"

"Invoking the Sargoth. You won't be able to control him, no matter how much that twisted ego of yours insists otherwise. He's too powerful. You open that portal and he'll take over everything you've worked so hard to set up."

"Ridiculous."

The voice seemed closer, but it was still impossible to tell. I was sweating buckets in the damned heat. It was painfully oppressive.

"The Sargoth," Cosgrove continued, "is happy to help me bring his dreams to life."

"Did he tell you that? Or did you just dream it up to help convince Xavier, McKinley, and the other naive bastards that you were worth backing?"

Cosgrove's hand materialized and slapped Zero across the face. Zero reeled back, bringing his hand up and away from his face. I could make out a line of blood on the back of his hand.

"Fool," said Cosgrove. "You will see the glory of the Sargoth. Don't you understand? We are the true masters of this planet. Not the humans. Human beings have never been the rightful inheritors. It is we who were born into the night. It is we who should rule. And rule we shall. Once I finish invoking the Sargoth, once the possession has occurred, then the Council will fall, helped along to their graves by McKinley here. Then I will rule supreme."

Jesus, he was really baked this time. I wondered if the temperature had something to do with the increased tempo of Cosgrove's dementia.

"Lawson, you're being awfully quiet."

I tried taking a breath. "Me? I'm spellbound by your orations, Cosgrove. Besides, it's not polite to interrupt."

He paused, seeming to absorb this. "What do you think of my plans? Are you ready to join my team yet? I could use another team member now that Xavier seems to have met an untimely end."

"Oh, I'd say his demise was right on schedule, Cosgrove."

Cosgrove smiled. "Indeed."

"He died real nice," said Zero.

Cosgrove ignored him, still focused on me. "I'd imagine," he said, "that you're curious as to what I've done with your lovely partner, hmm?"

Of course I was. "Yes."

"Always so bloody honest." Cosgrove drew closer. "Really, Lawson, falling in love with a human. Not the sort of behavior fitting of the Fixers, is it? You've disgraced your profession."

Like he was the poster boy for upstanding vampires everywhere. I said nothing.

"You know, if you work for me, it won't be a problem." He smiled. "You can fall in love with as many mortals as you wish."

Fat chance. "Cosgrove, if I work for you, there won't be any mortals left to fall in love with."

"Not true, Lawson. Not true at all. Of course, some of them will have to go, certainly. That's only natural. We'll have to thin the herd, so to speak, make sure they don't ever regain power. But not your beloved. You see, I have great plans for your Talya. Great plans indeed. She figures prominently into the destiny of this miserable little planet, in fact. Did you know that?"

My stomach knotted up. "How so?"

Cosgrove smiled and waved his hands. As if on cue, the steam and haze cleared. I looked up and saw Talya strapped to a large circular hunk of wood. Engraved on the surface were symbols that I assumed were Taluk. I searched Talya's eyes for any sign of life, but she must have been in a trance still.

"You're a real bastard, Cosgrove."

"Names won't get you anywhere but dead."

"Let her go."

He grinned. "Ah, well, I cannot. You see, I'm about to go through rather a spot of bother invoking the Sargoth. And once invoked, it needs a host. A host body."

He didn't mean—

"And your Talya will be perfect."

Thirty

There wasn't really much left to say.

After all, Cosgrove had told me explicitly what he planned to do with Talya. That left me with the fact that Zero and I were fast becoming an expendable quantity.

And so, even as Cosgrove's words registered, I was already moving, already aware that Zero had initiated as well. There was that old bond between us, that old spirit that had kept us alive for so long.

I feinted left while Zero moved immediately on McKinley. It seemed like we were moving in slow motion, even though in reality we'd be moving as fast as our surging adrenaline allowed us.

Cosgrove seemed unfazed at first as Zero deflected McKinley's gun hand and went immediately into his disarm and takedown. I moved closer to Cosgrove, who stood ten feet from me.

He regarded me in the instant of a blink and then almost imperceptibly shrugged. It was as if our bid for freedom had merely accelerated his schedule. That disturbed me.

But he'd closed the distance down between us too fast for that concern to accumulate any dust. His hands shot out in front of him as he went for double strikes to my rib cage, possibly seeking to use the ribs to impale my heart. It wouldn't kill me, but it would put me down for the count. And long enough for him to find a piece of wood to kill me with properly.

I sidestepped, letting the energy go past, and then punched the back of his arm hard behind the elbow, hearing a large snap. I'd fractured his bone, but Cosgrove simply ignored the pain and wheeled, jamming his leg into my solar plexus. I grunted, wind rushing out of me, and crashed into the ground.

In my periphery I could see Zero wrestling with McKinley. Damned if these old guys didn't get stronger with age.

I rolled and came up just as Cosgrove zoomed in again, launching another attack with his feet. I recognized the kicking style as belonging to savate, a French art that combined boxing and kicking techniques. By the way Cosgrove moved, he was quite good. And since I hadn't seen this before, it surprised me.

I circled to the inside, dropping and rolling with my shoulder into the knee of his supporting leg. He crashed down as I went over and brought my foot down hard onto his jaw as I rolled over.

He grunted and then tried catching my ankle in a lock. I twisted, broke his hold, and rolled free again, searching for purchase on the hard cement floor; finding it, I got back on my feet.

Cosgrove's face was bloody. He smiled through it. "This is a first; Lawson, you've actually drawn blood on me."

I said nothing, just kept circling. Zero and McKinley were grunting on the floor twenty feet away. From the looks of it, Zero was gaining the upper hand.

I feinted to the left and then went right as Cosgrove reacted to the feint. I got in behind him, then entered and drove an elbow hard into his back by his spine. Cosgrove arched his back forward and grunted again, cursing me in the old language. That was a good sign. I'd hurt him bad.

He wheeled away and threw a back kick that caught me square in the chest, stopping my advance. My wind came in short spurts. It felt like an anvil was crushing my lungs. I heaved fire.

Retched.

Cosgrove closed again and flailed at my face with his fingernails, trying to gouge my eyes. I locked my arms over his, pulled them down fast. That brought Cosgrove's face in and I used my head to smash his face again. Another sickening crunch told me his nose would need a lot of work. I tasted copper and knew Cosgrove was losing a lot of blood. I shot my arms into his neck, trying to crush his larynx, but the blood made them slip off as Cosgrove sank down and punched at my groin.

I caught sight of it just in time to bring my knee up to ward it off, then dropped my elbows straight down on his head. He grunted again and vomited blood.

That's when the gun went off.

In the close confines of the plant, it echoed and made me wince from the explosive report. I wheeled around and saw Zero straddling McKinley's chest, the gun leveled point-blank at McKinley's heart, the barrel still smoking from the single gunshot.

McKinley was dead.

Zero looked at me.

I turned around.

Cosgrove was gone.

"Jesus."

Zero climbed off McKinley's inert form and motioned to Talya. "Get her down."

I found the rope and lowered the makeshift altar to the floor. "Where do you think he's gone?"

"Only place he can go, farther into the plant."

"Shit." I looked at Talya. "What's wrong with her?"

Zero frowned as we undid Talya's restraints. "Judging by the look in her eyes, Cosgrove has pumped her full of drugs or used more hypnosis."

"Great."

"Sounded like you hurt him pretty bad back there."

"I think so, yeah."

Zero nodded. "He's here somewhere. He can't have gotten far."

I pointed at the ground. "We can follow the blood."

"How bad do you think you hurt him?"

"Don't know. I'd guess fairly well. He's losing a lot of juice."

"In that case we don't have much time."

"What do you mean?"

"He knows we'll free Talya. That means if he still wants to invoke the Sargoth, he's got to find another host body."

"He doesn't have time to find another host now. It's too late."

Zero shook his head. "Not so. Cosgrove's crazy enough to do the last thing we'd ever expect: he'll use himself as the host."

"We'd better find him then—"

Zero stopped me. "No way, get Talya out of here. We can't risk taking her along unless she can fight for herself. I'll handle him."

I shook my head. "Cosgrove's my fight, Zero."

"If you don't get Talya out of here, Cosgrove might find a way to get her again. Take her back to the hotel. I'll find Cosgrove and meet up with you later."

"But—"

"But nothing. According to my research, if we don't get Cosgrove now, he'll become even more powerful than before. We can't afford to have him unleash the Sargoth. Besides, you said it yourself, you hurt him bad. I'll finish it." He smiled. "You remember when I told you about my affair?"

"Yeah."

"Well, I neglected to mention one important thing."

"What's that?"

"I've always wished I chased Wajiah and tried to make it work." He shrugged. "But I didn't. I chose my path." He looked at me and placed a hand on my shoulder. "You understand what I'm saying, Lawson?"

My throat ached, but I managed to nod. "Yeah."

"Then go. I'll catch up with you later." He turned and hurried down the hallway, vanishing quickly into the deep shadows of beyond.

I watched him go. "Be careful, my friend."

But he was already too busy stealing down the hallway to respond.

Thirty-one

The ride back to the Charles Hotel in Harvard Square seemed to take forever, but I got us there within twenty minutes and managed to get Talya to her room unnoticed by the majority of the hotel's guests.

She still looked drugged, and I knew Cosgrove must have worked some powerful hypnotism on her. Our magnetism gives us incredible command over human psyches, even over hardened spirits like Talya.

I got some water from the bathroom sink and put it beside her bed, then laid her back against the pale blue plush pillows. Her breathing remained deep, her eyes partially closed, fluttering vaguely in the dim light of the room. Every few seconds her breasts would rise on the gentle intake of another breath.

She looked gorgeous.

I leaned over her and inhaled the scent of her perfume, feeling it tickle the heightened olfactory senses I'd been blessed with. Then I began a slow cycle of timing my inhalations and exhalations to hers, first pacing her breathing and then eventually leading it back to the degree of normalcy I needed in order to bring her out of Cosgrove's spell.

After thirty minutes she began stirring a bit more.

After forty minutes she opened her eyes and asked for a drink.

I gave her the water and refilled the glass three times before she paused and shook the remaining vestiges off with a deep sigh.

"What the hell happened?"

I gave her the short version, stopping just prior to Zero's aid. The less she knew, the better.

She frowned. "Hypnotized?"

I nodded. "Another one of the abilities vampires have. Surely you remember the old movies where the count can manipulate his victims?"

She broke into a half smile. "Yes. I do."

"Well, that one happens to be true."

She ran a hand through her hair. "Nice to know." She stopped and looked at me half squinting. "How did you break it?"

I said nothing, then cleared my throat. "I saw some self-help guru a few weeks back on the tube. Either that or you must have just come out of it is all."

She shook her head. "And you knew I'd be thirsty when I came down."

"Seemed logical you might be thirsty."

She frowned, pointing. "What is that?"

I looked down and saw the collar of my shirt had come undone, exposing my mark. A small patch of skin darker than the surrounding area.

"Just a birthmark," I said, closing it with one hand.

"Would that be the same kind of birthmark that Cosgrove has?"

I tried to smile, but it was coming undone. I knew it. Talya knew it.

She kept the heat on. "You know, Lawson, we had a philosophy in the KGB: if it looks like a fox, talks like a fox, and walks like a fox, then it must be a fox."

"I didn't know that was peculiar to the KGB only."

"Everyone else borrowed it from us."

She leaned closer to me.

I cleared my throat. "So what's your point?"

She kissed me then, with her lips pressed fully into mine, enabling a perfect seal with our mouths. I tasted her tongue as it wrestled with mine, not seeking domination but only equal footing. Our juices swirled, rising in tidal fluctuations, urged on by an increasing insistence fueled by primal instinct.

Talya broke only long enough to say, "I don't care what you are, Lawson. I only know that I want you with every ounce of my soul."

And that was it.

A better Fixer might have been able to resist her, but I succumbed blissfully to the intimate desires swelling within me. We tore into each other, shedding clothes in a frenetic lust. I slid down between the juncture of her legs, allowing my mouth to engulf her mound entirely while my tongue probed, pushed, and lapped at her moistness, suckling her to her first raging orgasm. Her hips ground into my face while she rode my face, bucking in time to my tongue's eager quest. She came twice more before yanking me up, seeking my engorgement and thrusting herself upward meeting my initial entrance.

She cried out, leaning back, uttering guttural grunts in her native tongue as she arched her back, giving me more depth to fill before bringing her body closer to mine, pressing her nipples into my chest, writhing in time to my upward assaults.

Sweat tumbled off our bodies like raging rivers after a winter thaw, filling muscular crevices and valleys, winding and slip-sliding all the way south to meet a surging ocean of our juices.

I felt her body tensing again, heard her breathing growing shallow, and knew she'd be coming again. Her groin was hot liquid fire that engulfed every inch of me, pleading for ultimate release.

Her muscles contracted and I felt like the trapped prey of a boa constrictor. She cried out, moaning, grunting, begging just as my own heat began rising, then suddenly erupting into her—tripping and falling—plunging over the edge of this very steep cliff, looking down and embracing absolute all-encompassing, ecstatic . . . death.

My heart ticked over with a jolt at the sound of the telephone by the bedside table. I pulled myself free of Talya's entangled body and reached for it.

"Yeah?"

"You sound sleepy. I'm not disturbing anything naughty?"

If I'd been asleep when I reached for the phone, the voice on the other end brought me fully awake. "You never did have the common decency to die."

"Tsk, tsk, what kind of greeting is that for old friends like us?"

"We're not old friends, Cosgrove. I want you dead."

"Seems to be a prevailing sentiment lately. Although, unfortunately I have been disappointing people in that regard."

"Well, you can add me to your list. I'm disappointed as hell you're not dead yet."

"Yes, I gathered as much."

"And since it seems you're not calling me from beyond the grave—"

"Not yet, despite attempts to the contrary."

"What the hell does that mean?"

"It means, for one thing, Lawson, that your old friend Zero did not succeed in tracking me down and killing me."

Shit. "Where is he?"

"I really don't know." There was a pause. "Well, that's actually not quite true. I do know where his body is. As for his mind and soul, I can't really say."

"What did you do to him, scumbag?"

"Goodness, it's not me, Lawson. After all, he did insist on trying to stop me and I had little choice but to use him the best way I knew how: as the Sargoth's host body." He chuckled. "I must say it's a tad better than the feminine form of your beloved. The Sargoth appreciated the degree of fitness Zero impressed on himself."

I didn't want to speak, but I forced the words from my mouth. "What . . . do you want?"

"Want? I believe you know exactly what I want, Lawson. I want the Council abolished. I want all the Fixers dead. I want to rule the vampires. I want the world to be mine. And it will be too, now that I have successfully risen the Sargoth."

Anger loosened my tongue. "So basically what any other psychotic megalomaniac wants. How touching."

"Yes, isn't it?" He paused. "There is just one trifling matter to be resolved before my dreams become a reality, however."

"Me."

"Naturally, I don't imagine you'd still be interested in a job offer?"

"You know better than to ask that."

"Naturally. Of course you're not. You are a Fixer, after all. What is it they say about you all? Born to the cause? No real idea why you are what you are, but you are it nonetheless. Pitiful existence, really. I mean, the rest of us enjoy a certain degree of autonomy over ourselves, some of us more than others of course, but you and the rest of your antiquated brethren—well, I'd imagine it's a bit of a mind fuck and all, wouldn't you agree? You're a Fixer. Just because. How utterly inglorious."

"It's not about glory."

"Of course it's not. How silly of me to imply so. No, yours is the noblest of callings. Protectors of the masses. Beholders of the traditions. Saviors of the souls. A truly divine calling." He chuckled into the phone.

"Get on with it, Cosgrove."

"Very well. If you won't join me, you leave me no alternative. You'll have to be killed. The Sargoth will kill you."

"What's the matter, can't do it yourself?"

"Of course I could, Lawson. You've never given me much of a challenge. But the Sargoth needs to get used to his new body. And a little combat is just the ticket for success, I think."

"Glad I can help."

"I give you the option to choose the place and time. I know very well that you won't stop trying to kill me. Unfortunately, you're just troubling enough that I need you disposed of prior to wreaking my personal destiny upon this planet. Therefore, I propose we meet and settle our affairs once and for all."

As much as I didn't want to play into his hand, there wasn't much I could do. I had no one to call upon, save for Talya. I had no one I could trust. The Council would take too long to act. If I was going to finish this, it would be up to me, and me alone.

I gripped the phone. "Midnight."

"You cushy old romantic. Where?"

"Top of the old Sears Building in the Fenway."

"Weren't we just there the other night?"

"Yes."

"I like your sense of attempted irony, Lawson. In fact, I might just choose that as my fondest memory of you. You know, after you're dead and all. I'll see you at midnight."

The phone went dead before I could utter any tough-sounding one-liners. In truth, I didn't think I had any left to give.

Thirty-two

I left Talya asleep at the hotel and drove home to Jamaica Plain to prepare for my meeting with Cosgrove. In truth, there was nothing I would have preferred better than to have Talya with me, but she didn't need to be a part of this any longer. Cosgrove was my fight, not hers. I'd told that to Zero but hadn't backed it up by being there instead of him. Now in all likelihood he was probably dead.

Talya would disagree with my sentiment. But the truth was he hadn't only killed Simbik. He'd betrayed the cause and the Council, resurrected some unholy evil, and destroyed one of my oldest friends.

Plus, he still owed a back balance and a helluva lot of interest for killing Robin so many years ago.

For her alone, I was determined to see that he paid the ultimate price. Everything was extra. But it was a big extra.

There would be no quarter given tonight.

By the time we finished, one of us would be dead.

Death isn't something you can prepare for as much as people like to think they can. You can do all the fighting and mental conditioning you think

you can, but it still won't ready you for the first
time you see someone dead at your own hands.
When they slide from your grasp, their lifeless body
slipping to the ground, the last vestiges of life force
spilling out of them as fast as their blood.

Sure, you get over it, but the images stay with
you forever.

And when you think about it later, your own mor-
tality comes crashing back at you like some steroid-
driven linebacker on the football field and knocks
the hell out of your pleasant little picture of supposed reality.

It hurts.

It jars you awake.

Makes you think.

But even then, even when you know you can die
as easily as anyone else, whether you're a vampire
or not, even then there are times when you can't
avoid the possibility.

I'd faced death many times before.

And you know what? It never got any easier.

Maybe you can convince yourself dying gloriously
is a great way to go out. It's a different matter when
all of sudden you look down and see a fatal wound,
and then you know; you know in that split second
that you're a goner.

Glorious, my ass.

In my business there's only one kind of death . . .
and that's downright fucking scary.

But scary doesn't mean you can avoid it.

Sometimes you just had to run headfirst into it
and hope to hell you came through it all right.

Life's a bitch, ain't she?

I set out a couple of cans of cat food for Mimi
and Phoebe and then mailed a letter to one of my

neighbors. It was a worst-case-scenario-type thing
that she'd receive in two days. I enclosed a key with
it so she could get into the house. She'd expressed
affection for my cats and I couldn't think of anyone
else better suited to care for them if I was no
longer around.

Mimi sensed it first; she was always more in tune
with my mood. She ignored the food and brushed
up against my leg, chirping for a hug. I stooped
down and picked her up, bringing her close to my
face. She butted her head against my face and began purring. I hugged her close and then did the
same to Phoebe. I loved them dearly; for years
they'd been my only companions.

Downstairs in the basement, I opened the heavy
wooden trunk one of my ancestors had brought
over from Germany when the family had first come
over to the United States. It was handmade and
had always been used to house personal effects and
special items. Archaic symbols were etched in the
wood, inlaid with black mahogany and rosewood.
It was a beautiful piece, filled with the sweat and
tears of excellent craftsmanship. I'd never been
able to match the woodworking talent my ancestors
had, but that didn't stop me from trying.

I removed the long coarse cloth from inside the
trunk and slowly slid it off the curved length of
wood it covered. Even in the darkness I could see
the gleaming luster of the oiled lignum vitae, the
hardest wood known to man.

It was a *bokken*, a wooden sword hand made by
one of the most well-known weaponsmiths in Japan.
Exquisitely carved, masterfully balanced, and perfectly honed, it was as dangerous a killing weapon

as if it had been hand forged out of folded, layered steel.

And to Cosgrove, it would be even deadlier.

The tip could easily stab through flesh. I looked forward to piercing his heart with it.

Next to the *bokken*, I removed a smaller package. This one contained a hand-braided *tanto* blade over ten inches in length. The *tanto* was another gift from the weaponsmith. He'd crafted them for me in exchange for helping him with some unresolved monetary issues concerning the local Yakuza gang. Normally, getting involved with the Japanese Mafia isn't a favorite pastime of mine and I certainly hadn't meant to intercede, but sometimes destiny has a way of injecting you into the flow of life for some reason. And so I'd intervened and saved his life. While he acknowledged his *giri*, or obligation, to me would never be repaid, he hoped these two gifts would at least help me in my work.

I don't know, perhaps he sensed something about me. Regardless, I'd never had cause to use them before, but I was damned glad I had them now.

I'd bring the gun of course, and plenty of ammunition. But this fight was going to get dirty. Cosgrove was nothing if not dirty. Anyone who killed unarmed children wasn't going to abide by any rules or battlefield honor. And for that, I wanted something special. The *bokken* and the *tanto* would help me equalize the playing field.

Upstairs, the phone rang.

Something told me it was probably Talya searching all over town for me. And while I'd never given her my phone number, I knew she could get it if necessary.

She'd be pissed and I couldn't blame her. But this was something else entirely. As a mortal she didn't belong in this game. This was my responsibility alone. The stakes were simply too high.

Especially since I loved her.

My watch beeped and I checked the time. It was going on 4:00 P.M. In a little over eight hours, the battle would be joined. Hopefully, in nine hours I'd still be alive.

I needed information.

Like I said before, ancient history wasn't my gig in school, so anything not directly related to my own here and now I generally ignored. Having to face and possible battle the preeminent face of evil in vampire tradition changed matters.

If I was going to win—hell, if I was going to survive—I needed information.

I found Zero's Chevy Tahoe back over in the parking garage by Manray. Sliding underneath the truck with my bag of tools I'd brought from home, I found the alarm wire and cut it before using a slim jim to open the door.

Sliding into the driver's seat, I felt weird. I inhaled and caught a whiff of Zero's deodorant and suddenly it almost felt like he was still there.

But he wasn't.

On the passenger-side I found a zipped small duffel bag. Inside, I found a lot of racing papers, testifying to Zero's love for the ponies, but no books about dealing with the Sargoth.

I sat still in the driver's seat, trying to drum up anything that could help me. That's when I noticed the tape sitting in the dashboard player.

It was a homemade tape labeled COUNTRY HITS. I smiled and pushed it into the player. Zero hated country music.

I waited for the first minute of twangy guitar playing to ride out and was rewarded when Zero's voice came over the speakers.

"If you're listening to this, odds aren't good that I survived. Hopefully, you were able to get into my truck without setting off the alarm.

"You'll have to take Cosgrove out yourself, Lawson. Don't go to the Council. At a time like this, they'd be more likely to try to negotiate rather than fight back. And we both know all too well that negotiation with Cosgrove, or anyone like him, will never work.

"We've spent the last week or so trying to figure out exactly how Cosgrove hopes to ally himself with the humans. That and his damned quest to resurrect the Sargoth. If he succeeds at that, the game may well be over—not only for our society as we know it, but also for the humans.

"There aren't many like us, Lawson. I think you know that by now. Fixers, by and large, care only about the vampires, but we know it goes beyond that sometimes. Our protection, our devotion to the Balance, impacts the humans as well. And they fall, whether anyone else has the guts to admit it or not, under our protection.

"I'm betting that if indeed Cosgrove is crazy enough to try to invoke the Sargoth, he'll need a host body. The Sargoth can't exist on this plane without a material body. It can be human or vampire, but if it's human, once the Sargoth takes possession, the body becomes vampire and can never be returned to human.

"He'd prefer a vampire host, though. The Sargoth is much more powerful residing in a vampire body. That said, I am at a loss as to how you would go about destroying him. It may not even be possible, considering the awesome power inherent within the Sargoth.

"You'll have to find a way, Lawson. There must be one. The universe wouldn't allow the creation of such a power without a means to also destroy it.

"I told you I knew of another Elder here in the Boston area. I wasn't lying, but he's not what I'd call an active Elder. He has a bit of a checkered past.

"You must find the Elder known as Wirek. He lives on Beacon Hill, close to the Council chambers, above the store on the corner. He is perhaps the only trustworthy soul you can turn to now. Although he is a bit eccentric. And a drunk. But he is still the only person who has studied the ancient texts. Only he will know how to deal with the Sargoth.

"Whatever the outcome of your meeting with Wirek, take care when you go after Cosgrove. Do whatever you must do and never hesitate. There'll be time for sentiment later. Just get the job done.

"It's been a real honor working with you all these years. Now do me one last favor and finish what we started."

The tape clicked off, leaving me alone in the darkened interior. I removed the tape and sat there alone.

Barely breathing.

Thirty-three

Getting information from a drunken Elder didn't buoy my spirits any, but beggars can't be choosers, and right now I was looking like a skid row veteran.

I found the building easily enough. Just like Zero said, it sat above a small convenience store. I bought a few supplies before finding the small doorway around the corner. The name below the doorbell read WIREK. Evidently, he wasn't shy. Taking a quick breath, I pressed the buzzer.

It took him ten seconds to reply. "Yeah?"

"My name's Lawson. Zero sent me."

"Who the hell is Zero?"

Great. Amnesia too. I didn't have time to debate this. "Open the door and let me come up."

"No way. You might be one of those crazy teenagers down the block trying to get my Social Security check."

"I'm not here to rob you. I need your help." I paused. "I've got a gift for you."

"Yeah? What kind of gift?"

"A bottle of tequila."

There was a pause. "One worm or two?"

"Dos gusanos, amigo."

Another pause, and then the door latch clicked

open. I stepped inside, breathing in the heavy, musty air. Rickety wooden steps led up, winding as they went. I caught a whiff of dank urine, old mothballs, and a faint scent of alcohol. Wirek lived in a real palace.

A door opened somewhere above me. "You there?"

"Yeah, just dodging some trash down here."

"Hurry up with that tequila, damn it."

Wirek, when I finally crested the stairs, looked old. Check that, the guy looked ancient. Skin hung from his face like heavy drapes in a funeral parlor. His forehead was freckled and what little hair he had left poked out of his scalp at strange angles. He wore a stained, pockmarked gray sweatshirt emblazoned with RUNS WITH SCISSORS across the chest. He stretched out a bony hand and I went to shake it.

He frowned. "Gimme the damned bottle."

"Nice to meet you too." I handed him the tequila.

Wirek cradled it like he'd just spent twenty-four hours in labor delivering the silly thing. After a moment he looked at me. "You said Zero sent you?"

"Apparently, only as a last resort."

He chuckled. "Sonny, if you come to me, it *is* a last resort. Come inside."

He turned and wandered back into the apartment, already unscrewing the cap on the tequila.

I ducked inside the doorway and shuddered. Clutter filled every inch of space. Papers littered the floor and huge shelves of books lined the walls. A chandelier with burned-out bulbs hung over what must have once been a dining-room table but had long since become something of a desk. Over in the corner sat an orange plaid recliner with the footrest up and a remote control on the armrest. I noticed a porn tape nearby. An overwhelming stench of bad booze hung in the air. Glancing about the room, I could see the empty glass-bottle remains of a recent drinking binge.

Wirek freed the tequila and took a long drag. He belched once and looked at me. "Want some?"

"No." I pointed at the porno. "Not interrupting something, am I?"

He chuckled. "Nah, I finished a few minutes ago." He leaned closer. "Ain't ya glad I didn't shake your hand now?" He took another sip.

"Thrilled. I need some information."

He sighed and wandered back to his chair, easing himself down bone by bone. "You young ones, always in a rush these days. No time for socializing." He took another swig and looked me over. "Fixer, huh?"

"How'd you know?"

He frowned again. "You know how old I am? Eight hundred years old. You know how much I've seen in my lifetime? Enough for fifty lifetimes. You know how many Fixers I've seen? Too many. I know a Fixer when I see one." He shrugged. "Besides, you've got the look."

"What look?"

"Oh, that look of impending doom and disaster so common to anyone in the profession." He grinned. "Seen it a million times."

"Well, I've got good cause to look this way."

He laughed again. "If only you knew how many times I've heard *that.*"

I sighed. "Look, Wirek, I don't mean to be rude—"

"Too late."

"But there's some serious shit going on and I need your help. Obviously, if I could handle this on my own, I wouldn't be bothering you."

"But you can't. Yeah, yeah, I know." He helped himself to another swig and then wiped his mouth on his shirtsleeve. "So what is it this time?"

"A conspiracy."

Wirek frowned. "You don't need me to help with a conspiracy. If you're worth your salt, you oughta be able to handle a measly conspiracy."

"If it was just that, you're right—I could. But it's not. It's what the conspiracy hopes to accomplish."

Wirek looked up. "So what is it?"

"The resurrection of the Sargoth."

Wirek stopped smiling. "What did you just say?"

"You heard me."

"The Sargoth?"

"That's what I said."

Wirek put the tequila down. "We don't have much time."

"I was saying."

He leaped out of the armchair and strode over to one of the bookcases. "Tell me what's going on."

"Someone is trying to invoke him. Bring him onto this plane."

"Has he already done so?"

I nodded. "I'm pretty sure he has."

Wirek hauled a huge book off the shelf and slapped it down on the table. Dust flew from the leather-encased tome. I saw lettering that resembled the symbols I'd seen on Cosgrove's altar.

"That's Taluk, right?"

"I don't give out gold stars, kid." But he nodded anyway. "This is the tome of the ancients. There are very few copies left. I translated this version myself sometime ago." He flipped open the pages and began rifling through them.

"Who is the host?"

I shrugged. "I don't know."

"Human or vampire?"

I heard Zero's voice again in my mind. Saw him disappearing after Cosgrove at the plant, and felt a pain in my chest. "At this point, most likely vampire."

"Damn." Wirek kept turning pages and then abruptly stopped. "Here." He paused for a minute, reading the ancient scribble, and finally looked up. "You can't kill the Sargoth."

"But Zero said—"

"He couldn't have known. Once the Sargoth is invoked and resides in a vampire host body, it cannot be killed. If it was in a human body, possibly it could. But not a vampire."

I leaned back into the wall. "Then it's over."

Wirek shook his head. "Hang on, don't give up so easily." He frowned. "You this easily thwarted when you're out Fixing?"

"It's been a long fucking week."

"Hmph. Youth. No staying power." He pointed into the book. "See this?"

"I can't read Taluk."

Wirek frowned. "Of course you can't. Someday you should learn. This is the history of your people, you know." He leaned back into the book. "According to this, the Sargoth can be banished from this plane. You can send him back where he came from."

"Yeah? How so?"

Wirek chewed his lip. "You won't like it. I've known you for all of five minutes and I already know you won't like it."

"I don't have to like it. I just have to do it."

"Yeah." Wirek's teeth found a small piece of skin and tore it off his lip. Blood oozed out of the cut. "You'll have to destroy the host body."

My heart pounded. Zero. Wirek nodded.

"I take it you know the host."

"I think it's Zero."

Wirek sighed. "No one said the job would be easy all those years ago, did they, sonny?"

"No."

He put a hand on my shoulder. "You'll have to do it, you know? If the Sargoth is unleashed, there's no telling what kind of damage it would do to the society."

"It would be the end of our society. The man summoning him is bent on destroying the Council and assuming leadership himself."

"Figures." Wirek found the tequila bottle again and had himself another drag. "Powermongers always want more than they can handle. Bastards."

"There's no other way, is there?"

Wirek shook his head. "I wish there was. But there isn't."

By the time I got down to the Fenway and parked the Jetta, it was already creeping toward ten o'clock. I wanted to be in position first and be able to dominate the scene as opposed to walk into an unknown variable. In Cosgrove's case, unknown variable meant one of his specialty ambushes. Not the best way to start things off.

The November winds blasted through the thick black cotton fatigues I wore over my lug-soled boots. I'd washed the fatigues enough so that the cotton was now soft and made no noise when I brushed against it. I'd strapped the pistol under my armpit in a shoulder holster while I carried the *tanto* in one of my pockets and kept the *bokken* close to my side. No one seemed to notice another guy dressed in black walking the streets by abandoned office buildings. And the police only cruised the residential areas, so they wouldn't bother me.

Of course, if anybody thought about messing around with me, I felt certain that notion would be a short-lived one. Given what must have been a look of fierce and grim determination on my face, danger would do well to avoid me tonight.

I rounded the corner by D'Angelo's, crossed Brookline Avenue, and ducked into the shadowy recesses of the building. A knot in my stomach tightened as the woozy déjà vu swept over me, reminding me that I almost lost my life here a week ago.

Homecomings always thrilled me.

I once had a friend who insisted that everything in life was like a giant wheel. Stay around long enough and you'd see the same things come right back again. It made sense. Hell, even bell-bottom jeans had made an unfortunate attempt to reclaim their fifteen minutes of fame.

Maybe that's why I chose this place for what I hoped would be our final battle. Tonight was about waging war on my terms, not Cosgrove's. I had a grocery list of vendettas and plenty of Karmic coupons.

I cut across part of the parking lot and made my way over to the side door. The lock was already broken and I crept inside within a minute. I sprinted to the stairs, avoiding the sea of rats as much as I could. I'd remembered to tuck my pants into my boots so I didn't have to relive the unique terror of having one of those furry bastards crawl up my leg.

At the top of the stairs, I paused, catching my breath. The door before me gave easily and I stepped onto the roof.

Howling winds whipped at my face, roared in my ears, and made goose bumps leap off my skin. I glanced around quickly.

Empty.

Relief, a temporary sensation lately, laid its hand across my shoulder. Part of me had expected Cosgrove to set up an ambush. Apparently, he was going to play this one straight. Or at least as straight as was possible for someone like him.

I'd play it straight too.

I'd do whatever it took to send that bastard straight to hell.

Wirek's words came back to my mind. I was heartbroken about having to possibly kill Zero. Even trying to rationalize it as just his physical body wasn't working too well. In all likelihood Zero was already dead. Having the Sargoth take over your body presumably killed you. Zero's soul had already departed for the other side.

I hoped to hell he'd be watching me, trying to help me sort this whole mess out.

I thought about Talya. I thought about last night,

about how wonderful it felt to be in her arms, to feel the pulse of her body as we made love. It was a tragically long-overdue sensation.

I was willing to bet she was mighty pissed off right now.

I checked the black army watch strapped to my wrist and saw the two hands growing closer together.

Eleven o'clock.

One hour to go.

Thirty-four

Where sixty minutes went in such a short time, I'll never know. But despite there being nothing apparently different, as subtly as the wind drew another long, cold breath across that rooftop, something changed.

Cosgrove.

I don't know which part of me sensed him first. And honestly, spending too much time trying to figure it out would have most likely meant my death.

Breezes tossed broken bottles, crushed bits of paper, and rusty nails around the roof, making sounds difficult to pinpoint. I eased back toward one edge, keeping the *bokken* down against my leg, hopefully out of sight. I needed every advantage I could get.

In the blink of an eye, he was there. On the roof with me. More wind scared up the billowy length of his black overcoat, flapping it and spreading it like giant ironic wings behind his dark form. In the darkness his smile flashed like a beacon of light.

"Lawson."

It was more of a hiss than a voice. Never had I

felt such evil, even from him. It oozed from every pore, bled outward from his tainted aura, and contaminated everything around him. He was obviously enjoying the moment.

"You haven't brought your lover tonight?"

"Better she's not involved any longer," I said.

Cosgrove grunted. "I'll hunt her down anyway. Just out of spite."

His callous regard for her angered me. I gripped the *bokken* a little more tightly, almost feeling the oiled wood conform to the shape of my hand. Something about it lent me strength, perhaps the aged wood itself had been imbued with some ancient Shinto spirit.

"I imagine she'll be as easy to put down as she was before."

"She might surprise you, Cosgrove. She's certainly surprised me."

He chuckled. "That doesn't take much, Lawson."

I noticed the flesh-colored bandage on his face, the vague nasal twang to his voice. "How's your nose, Cosgrove? Still hurt?"

He grinned. "My nose, Lawson, has been redone so many times it no longer even feels like a part of my flesh. You caused me some pain, true, but once I've dealt with you and your lady, I'll simply have it fixed again."

"How about I do it for you instead? My services are free."

He laughed. "A card to the end. I'll treasure the memory of your humor long after you're dead."

It had felt good to sling a barb or two across the roof at him. I did it more to work out the butterflies hopping around my intestines than anything else. But nothing lasts forever and I wanted to get this over with as fast as possible. "Let's do this, Cosgrove."

He smiled again. "Of course." He shrugged. "Although, I would have thought you'd be curious to know what I've done with your old friend."

Zero. Damn. "Where is he?"

Cosgrove's smile grew even larger. "Why, Lawson, he's here of course."

He stepped away and Zero loomed behind him.

But it wasn't Zero any longer. His eyes stared at me across the expanse of the roof, empty and void. Where once his spirit had rested, now something else, the Sargoth, occupied it.

I'd mourn Zero's loss later. I couldn't afford to get emotional now. I needed to finish this.

"Naturally, Lawson, I'll be only too glad to fight with you, provided you're able to best the Sargoth, first."

There was no expression on Zero's face as he moved across the roof slowly. Each step seemed to make my apprehension grow even more. I'd never relished the idea of fighting Zero when he was Zero. Now that he was the embodiment of the most evil specter in vampire mythology, I was even less thrilled. I wondered briefly how the Sargoth would find operating in someone else's body.

But I'd learn soon enough.

Zero and I had never sparred before, so I had no idea what to expect from him. But anyway, it really wasn't Zero anymore. I felt certain the Sargoth had his own style of combat. One that would most likely be old and unforgiving.

When he launched the attack, I hardly had a chance to get out of the way. One second he was ambling over and the next he was rushing toward me with his hands outstretched, seeking my head, neck, and who knew what else.

I jerked to the side, avoided his attack, and brought the *bokken* up sharply against his rib cage. I heard a satisfying crack as several ribs shattered. I moved again and followed up by bringing the *bokken* down on his head—hard. Another dull thwack told me I'd fractured his skull. He sank to the rooftop and slumped to one side.

I turned my attention to Cosgrove, who strangely seemed totally unfazed by my countering of the Sargoth's initial attack.

My mistake, letting my attention be diverted. I found out why a second later when the Sargoth attacked me from behind and knocked me flat. I lost hold of the *bokken*, which went skittering across the roof toward one edge. Wind rushed out of my lungs as Zero's body landed squarely on top of me.

I wriggled around, getting my back against the rooftop, and fought off the first of ten rapid-fire punches aimed at my head. Ground fighting was a bitch, but if I kept moving, I stood a better chance rather than just bunching up and hoping for the best. In my case it'd mean death.

Two punches got through and bounced off my ears, making them ring. I grabbed a handful of flesh around Zero's rib cage and twisted and yanked.

It should have produced some kind of effect.

It should have made the Sargoth leap a bit and allow me room to get out of the situation.

It should have.

It didn't.

Cosgrove's voice floated across the rooftop, laden with glee. "In case you haven't already surmised,

Lawson, when the Sargoth takes possession of a host body, it does not invade the host's neurology. It therefore feels no pain. Your martial skills will unfortunately prove very ineffective against him."

Great.

I shifted again, trying to get my hips out from where he straddled me. I punched up, and as he shifted to block it, I squiggled out a bit more.

That move cost me. Three punches crashed into my diaphragm. I sucked in liquid fire.

But I had managed to get some more room, so I did it again. It brought the same response, but I finally managed to get to my feet.

The Sargoth looked up, seemed vaguely amused, and slowly got to his feet.

I put a front stomp kick into the side of his right knee, hoping to shatter the knee joint. If it couldn't walk, I reasoned, it couldn't get me.

Fat chance.

The kick was good, and I cracked the knee joint, but the Sargoth obviously paid no heed to it since he continued walking toward me.

"Structural damage does little as well," called Cosgrove. He was obviously enjoying his role as commentator.

I backed up, abruptly aware that I was getting far too close to the edge. The Sargoth loomed closer, spreading his arms as if to engulf me. I was sure it would mean a helluva lot of pain, so I backed up even more until I could go no farther without toppling headlong off the roof.

It sensed this. The Sargoth smiled.

And came closer.

My foot rolled off a rusted nail, almost causing me to stumble. I righted myself just as the Sargoth drew down the distance between us to almost nothing.

Then . . .

A single crack pierced the darkness, halting the Sargoth's approach. The front of his shirt blossomed bright crimson and the Sargoth looked down, amazed and confused, stumbling and falling. . . .

Dead.

Who?

A vortex of wind ripped the rooftop apart, sending papers, trash, and everything else into the air. It hurt to see, but Zero's body lifted off the roof ten feet, exploded into a bright rush of blue light, and then vanished, leaving intense silence. It looked like something out of the *Highlander,* a movie I'd seen a few years back.

But I'd caught a glimpse of someone in the flash of light. A lone figure silhouetted against a nearby rooftop with a long sniper rifle.

Talya?

"Well, it looks as though I may have underestimated your ability to take care of the Sargoth," said Cosgrove as he calmly removed his cape. "No bother. I'll simply invoke him again once I kill you. Shouldn't be too difficult to find another host body." He looked up, smiling. "My kudos to you on supplying your lover with the requisite wooden bullets needed to kill Zero's body."

I was still breathing hard. "Wasn't my doing."

"No?"

"No idea who that was."

Cosgrove smiled. "No matter. I'll find out soon enough."

He moved then, rushing at me almost as fast as

the Sargoth had. I tried sidestepping again, but my ribs ached badly and delayed my pivot just enough that Cosgrove caught me with a solid punch to my jaw.

Stars bounced around my skull. Damn, that hurt like hell.

He tried following up with a kick to my groin, but I deflected it by bringing my knee up. I used the moment to head butt him hard off the corner of his eyebrow. He grunted and fell back away, giving me a second.

If I'd been in better shape, I could have launched an attack, but I needed the space to catch my breath. Still, the blow to his eye must have stung him badly since he seemed a bit dizzy.

I faked a jab to his head, which he went to block, and then slammed a front kick to his left hip socket, knocking him back and down. I tried following up with another kick to his knee, but Cosgrove scrambled away, tossing a cloud of dirt at my face.

I ducked, catching just a bit in my left eye. Grit made blinking a bitch. Tears rolled down my face as I tried to clear my vision.

He came at me again, launching a kick into my stomach that propelled me back across the roof, falling and tumbling like a soda can toward the edge.

I scrambled, flailed, dragging myself to a stop, feeling bits of gravel bite into my palms.

He was on me then, kneeing, punching, grasping, spitting, trying his damnedest to wound me enough that he could then stake my heart with a sharpened piece of timber from the roof.

We rolled back toward the edge and then away

from it. I grunted loud when we rolled over something long and thin. I realized it was the *bokken* that the Sargoth had knocked away from me earlier. It hurt like hell when I rolled over it with my spine.

Cosgrove kept us moving and now I tried to use one of my hands to find the *bokken,* to try to get it in between us so I could slam it into him.

No good. Cosgrove kept the momentum moving away from the *bokken,* and his punches demanded my attention.

He spit in my face and nailed my left eye again. My vision blurred once more and I brought my knee into his groin hard, catching him full in the sac. He grunted, moaned, and rolled off me.

I wiped the sputum from my eye and went after him, catching him twice more with kicks to his thigh and midsection. He fell back to the rooftop and rolled backward into the shadows.

I turned slightly and was at last able to make out the outline of the *bokken* lying a short distance away.

If I could just get it—

The click made me stop.

"You've been practicing, I see."

I turned around, edging myself just a little bit closer to the *bokken.* Cosgrove was holding a pistol very much like the one I carried. I felt for my holster and frowned. In the grappling Cosgrove had fleeced the damned thing off me. If I made it through this alive, I was really going to have to improve my weapon-retention skills.

Now he was aiming my gun at me.

I sucked wind. "After all this you'll use that pussy gun on me, Cosgrove?"

He seemed to be breathing hard too. "Why not?

Dead is dead, Lawson. I must admit that I am getting very tired. Tired of your continued presence on this planet. Seems to me it's about time for you to join your recently departed friends. Leave me to my destined greatness."

"You've never been a warrior, Cosgrove. You've never been one to appreciate the rules of the hunt, the traditions of our community. The only thing you've ever obsessed about is your own personal gain."

"If you think talking to me is going to save your life, Lawson, I'm afraid you're wasting your time. I'm quite determined to pull this trigger and make all my Lawson problems go away forever." He smiled and I noticed his teeth were bloody. Good. That meant I'd hurt him. "Now stand still and let me make this nice and quick for you."

I shifted slightly. "Nice and quick? You're getting merciful now, Cosgrove?"

"Not merciful, Lawson. Just tired of you."

"I'll take that as a compliment." I moved a little farther to the right.

"Take it as whatever you wish. Now stand still."

In the darkness I heard the hammer being pulled back, could almost see his finger tightening on the trigger, his tendons flexing to take up the slack, almost feel the spring inside the gun tightening, then beginning to release.

I vaulted sideways just as the first of two shots rang out. I hit the rooftop hard, real hard, but rolled over my right shoulder and let my hands search the darkness for the *bokken*. I grasped it, continued rolling, aware that Cosgrove had his attention focused on the rooftop where the sniper bullet had originated from earlier.

With no time to waste, I came up, moving and breathing hard and fast, covering the space between Cosgrove and me, tearing it down to nothing just as he started to realize I was behind him and coming fast.

He turned.

I dropped.

Roared with every ounce of intention.

Straightened,

And plunged the *bokken* deep into his chest beneath his xyphoid process, rammed it home—heard the cartilage crack-give-relinquish the bloated prize within his chest.

Cosgrove gagged violently, coughed, and slumped backward, taking the *bokken* with him. It jutted obscenely out of his chest.

He looked down, amazed, and then looked up, trying to bring my pistol up and shoot me again.

I dived toward him, rolled, and came out of the roll with my foot slamming the pommel of the *bokken* into him even deeper, feeling his spine give as the wood went through his back. Cosgrove fell back to the rooftop and lay still.

I squatted on the roof, breathing hard. Saliva flooded my mouth, dripped and drooled out of me while my heart hammered in my chest. I felt nauseous. Hell, I wanted to vomit my soul.

The bulge in my cargo pocket was still there and I took out the *tanto*. It wasn't even bent from the constant rolling. Damned if it wasn't one of the finest pieces I'd ever owned.

I limped over to Cosgrove's form. He was still breathing, but shallow. His pupils were dilating fully. He was close to death.

Even still, I took my pistol out of his hands and

tucked it back into my shoulder holster. He tried to grin.

"Lawson."

I frowned. "You're finished, Cosgrove."

He grunted and some red foam trickled out of his mouth. "You haven't won, Lawson. This isn't over."

"No?" I nodded toward the *bokken* still jutting out of his chest cavity. "You're an optimistic soul, Cosgrove. I'd say you're as good as dead."

". . . I'll be back."

I shook my head. "I don't think so, Cosgrove. Not this time. Not ever again."

"I've made a deal with the Devil, Lawson. You can't kill me."

I lifted him up from the rooftop and brought my face close to his, smelling his bloody breath. "Oh, yes, I can. For your crimes against the Council. For your crimes against the community. For your crimes against humanity. For everything you've done in the name of evil." My voice was a hiss now. My eyes felt hot. "But especially for what you did to Robin, for the pain you've caused this world, our people. For everything, Cosgrove, you are sentenced to death."

His eyes grew wide then when he saw the *tanto* blade catch a glint from a nearby light and reflect into his dilated eyes.

With my last ounce of strength, I let his head go and simultaneously swung the length of the blade down and through his neck, decapitating him with one stroke of the finely honed steel.

A column of blood heaved out of him, spraying off the side of the rooftop. His head rolled to the rooftop, eyes open, and now entirely vacant. A final gasp of air escaped his lips, like a last sighing breath.

And it was over.

I wiped the *tanto* off on his cloak and replaced it in its sheath. It took me a few minutes to gather my breath, to calm the adrenaline that had been flooding my system, to come back down from the combat mode I'd been in.

I grabbed Cosgrove's head by a scruff of hair and stood looking out at the city. I scanned the nearby rooftops but couldn't see anything.

Talya was gone. If she'd ever been there to begin with.

Looking out over the city, everything seemed still. The winds had died down. The chill had thawed. Even the night seemed a little lighter.

Those of us who belong to the profession believe in the Balance as being more than just the line between humans and vampires. It's the scheme of universal justice, the laws of totality ruling that every act of evil will someday answer to an act of good.

Maybe tonight, the Balance had been restored.

It sure seemed like it.

Maybe.

Or maybe it was just that I was tired as hell.

I raised Cosgrove's head in silent salute. To Zero, Simbik, Robin, and to the last vestiges of my haunted, imperfect past. Beneath me, above me, and all around me, the city slept.

And suddenly, that seemed like a very good idea.

Epilogue

The next day dawned a lot brighter than I would have preferred, given the fact that I could easily have slept for another twelve hours. Unfortunately, cleaning up the mess of Cosgrove's insidious plot meant an unexpected trip to see the Council. Normally, Fixers never actually went before the Council since our respective Controls usually acted as intermediaries. But since McKinley had come to a rather sudden death and I was sans a handler, I went in person.

The brownstone on Beacon Hill seemed as old as the city itself. A heavy wrought iron fence barred outsiders, and a pair of gargoyles loomed over the main entrance, glaring at me as I paused to ring the bell.

It took three minutes for Arthur, who looked desperate for some plastic surgery in daylight, to answer the door and show me inside.

"I heard," he said by way of greeting.

I sighed. "Couldn't be helped. Believe me, I tried to find another way."

"I know it. We'll miss him, his old friends, we will."

"Yeah." But I felt like I'd miss him more than anyone else.

Arthur laid a hand on my shoulder. "You did your best, aye?"

"I did."

"Then that's as much an honor as he could have hoped for. You understand that, right, Lawson?"

Maybe I did. It still hurt like hell. I looked at him. "I need to see them."

He nodded at the bag I carried. "Can I take that for you?"

"No. Thanks. I'll hold on to it."

He gestured ahead of me down the corridor. "You know the way. I'll introduce you."

We walked down a mahogany-paneled hallway, passing painted portraits of former Council members who had since passed on. The thick red carpet underfoot muffled our footsteps as we continued on. I came to the conclusion that the interior of the house was a lot larger than it seemed from the outside.

Arthur paused outside of a heavy oak door and nodded. "Good luck."

I waited until he'd disappeared again down the hall and then grasped the doorknob, turned it, and swung it open.

A wall of heat from a crackling fireplace enveloped me as I stepped inside and let my eyes grow accustomed to the dimly lit interior.

There were six of them in total. All older than me by hundreds of years. Four men and two women sitting in the thick, worn high-backed leather chairs in a half circle. We stared at each other for a moment and finally one of them, older than the others, spoke.

"Lawson." He seemed unsure of my presence.

I nodded. "McKinley is dead."

"How?"

"Part of a conspiracy to destabilize the Council, to disrupt the fabric of our community, and threaten the Balance itself."

"What proof have you?"

Probably a lifetime of scars. "If you search his home on Marlborough Street, you'll find coded files on his computer showing distributions and account numbers."

"Money?" He laughed. "Absurd. McKinley would have no want of money."

"Children."

He stopped. "What did you say?"

"The distributions were sex slaves. McKinley's taste ran to the obscene. He was a pedophile, a predator, and took his bribe from Cosgrove in the form of children he could corrupt."

"How do you know this?"

"We interrupted one of his trysts."

"You mentioned Cosgrove. I take it he was involved."

I sighed. "Cosgrove was the instigator of this whole affair. I told you a long time ago that he was dangerous. You chose not to listen to me. Scores of humans have perished as a result."

"Humans do not interest us."

"Bullshit."

That got their attention. I continued. "You know as well as I do that we need humans. We'd be extinct without them in a generation. Cosgrove's flagrant disregard for the Balance, for the laws that govern us, almost resulted in our deaths."

"Perhaps."

"Perhaps nothing. You were his first target. With you out of the way, he intended to set himself up as dictator. He'd recruited Controls from all over the Northeast to help him."

"Who?"

"Xavier. McKinley. Possibly others. I can't be sure." The heat made me sweat. "Both of them are dead. As is Zero."

"Zero was involved too?"

"Zero is the one you should all be thankful for. He discovered the conspiracy, confided in me, and together we defeated the traitors. Cosgrove, however, had more up his sleeve than just a simple conspiracy of betrayal. He invoked the Sargoth and used Zero's body as the host."

The were murmurs in the room. The old one shushed them and turned back to me. "The Sargoth? You're joking. That's nothing but a legend."

"Then I fought a legend last night."

One of the women spoke up. "If that's true, you'd be dead."

"The host body was destroyed. According to the ancient texts, it had to be that way. The Sargoth was banished back to wherever he came from. He couldn't exist on this plane without a live host body."

"Indeed. And what of Cosgrove?"

"I killed him."

The old one smiled. "So after all this time, you finally succeeded."

I frowned. "Seems to me you'd be happy for that fact."

He shrugged. "All of this matters little over time."

I shifted the bag at my side. "I've done my duty."

"So you have." He paused and looked at the others. "There are other matters to discuss, however. It has come to our attention that you have committed some crimes yourself."

"What the hell does that mean?"

He looked at me. "The human woman named Talya. You are in love with her. The laws, our laws, state that is forbidden."

"I don't think that's an issue anymore."

"No?"

"I left her before I killed Cosgrove. She's likely so upset she'll never want to see me again."

"That doesn't change the fact that you loved her."

"No," I said, "it doesn't. But like you said. All of this matters little over time."

"Some things matter more than others."

I took a deep breath. "Are you telling me that the massive conspiracy I helped crush, the evil I dispatched back to wherever it came from, the deaths of several associates I considered friends, and the very destiny of our community doesn't matter as much as me falling in love with a human?"

"We didn't say that."

"Sure sounds to me like you just did."

"May I remind you, Lawson, that you are before the Council?"

"Remind me all you want. Right now I'm the only goddamned Fixer you've got operational in this sector who wasn't ready to see you all killed. Do you understand that? The only one. Seems to me you can overlook my small transgression and focus instead on the bigger picture."

"We'll take that into consideration."

"You do that. In the meantime I need a new

Control. And try to make sure he's not a god-damned traitor this time. I also want a few weeks of leave."

"Why on earth for?"

"Recuperation. I need a rest. Fighting the Sargoth and Cosgrove isn't exactly a prescription for healthy living. I'll be home if you need me. You know the number." I turned to leave.

"Lawson."

I turned back around. "What?"

"Your actions with a human woman won't be tolerated again."

No shit. But to be honest, the way I was feeling, I didn't even care. I hefted the bag at my side. "Here." I lobbed the sack and watched as it tumbled through the air, landed in front of them, and spilled Cosgrove's grayish-hued blood-encrusted head out onto the floor. Several of the Council members blanched and turned away.

I smirked. "You can do more with this than I can. Have fun cleaning up. I'm going home to sleep."

Outside, the typical November weariness had chased the sun away and replaced its warmth with wisps of gray indecision. I pulled the collar up on my leather jacket, turned left on Beacon Street, and continued down toward Charles, where the noontime lunch rush seemed in full swing.

At the Starbucks coffee shop, I caught a glimpse in the window, felt the hair on the back of my neck stand up, and eased off down Beacon toward the Hampshire House. I crossed over into the Public

Gardens and meandered through the winding asphalt pathways.

She caught up with me near the rose beds, long since wilted and hidden underground until the spring warmth woke them again.

I sat down on the bench as she approached.

I smiled.

She didn't.

She sat and kept a good six feet away from me. We were just two strangers on the bench. Even now, despite everything, she was professional to the end.

"You tried to fuck me, Lawson." It came out in a hiss. Spitting venom never sounded so hateful.

"I did fuck you, Talya."

"I'm not talking about the sex; I'm talking about screwing me out of my vengeance."

I kept looking straight ahead. "I did what I thought was necessary to protect your safety."

"You almost got yourself killed."

"Goes with the territory, hon."

"You make it sound so heroic. So noble." She snorted in derision. "Spare me that sentiment. I've heard it before."

"It's my job."

"It's more than a job to you, Lawson. I know *that* much about you."

"You know more about me than you're willing to admit, Talya. You said so yourself."

"Did I?"

"As I recall, you whispered that you didn't care what I was."

She fell silent for just a moment. "Would you have told me?"

I didn't know and told her as much. "But for

what it's worth, I knew you'd eventually realize it anyway."

"The man I killed on the roof. He was your friend Zero, wasn't he?"

I shook my head. "Not when you killed him. His body had been taken from him. Used as a conveyance for a powerful spirit entity. Zero was dead long before you killed his physical body."

"I wondered if you'd kill me for it. Do you know that?"

"For killing Zero? You did him a favor. Hell, you did me a favor." I shook my head. "Besides, I couldn't kill you, Talya. I love you too much for that."

Even without looking at her, I could feel her gaze on me, intense, probing.

"What did you say?"

"I said what you thought I said." I turned, looking at her for the first time. "I mean it."

She looked away. "I don't know what to say, Lawson."

"Say what you feel."

"I can't deny I feel love for you. It's more powerful than anything I've ever felt in my lifetime. It's so tangible that it makes my heart yearn for you completely." She shook her head. "But you left me, Lawson. You left me, knowing how badly I needed to kill Cosgrove. You betrayed me."

"I saved your life, Talya."

"I saved *your* life, Lawson."

I nodded. "Yes, you did. And I'm eternally grateful for that. But if you'd been on that rooftop with me, you would have perished. And you would have died without fulfilling your need for revenge. You'd have died empty. Alone."

"Maybe, but I would have tried—"

"You did try, and you did help kill Cosgrove. I certainly couldn't have done what needed to be done without your help. Your timing was superb. It gave me the opening I needed."

She searched the surrounding area with her eyes. "How long have you lived, Lawson?"

"Over a hundred years."

"And how much longer will you live?"

I smirked. "Don't know. In this line of work, you can never tell."

"Forget the goddamned line of work, Lawson. Tell me how long your kind lives."

"About four or five hundred years. On a good day."

"And how many other human women have you loved like me already in your lifetime, Lawson? How many other women have you watched grow old and die while you aged at a mere trifle in comparison?"

"None."

She seemed surprised. "None?"

"Love for a human is forbidden in our society. Sex is acceptable. Love is not. We're prohibited from entering into a courtship with humans."

"But you told me you loved me."

"I do."

"But it's forbidden."

"Yes, it is. And I don't care."

She looked at me again and I smiled at her. Emotions seemed to dance over her face with no regard to rhythm and order.

"What's the penalty for loving me, Lawson?"

I shrugged. "Depends, actually. It can range from a suspension to a termination order. With my record I could get a suspension and the relationship would have to end. But with my attitude they'd probably save themselves a lot of trouble and just order my death." I hesitated. "And yours."

She nodded. "I expected as much."

"But I don't care, Talya. They can hunt us to the ends of the earth. I—"

"Lawson. Stop." She shook her head. "Listen to yourself. You're talking like a naive fool. We're both too professional for this sentiment. You know as well as I do that if they want us badly enough, they'll find us no matter where we go. And I don't like running. I never have. I'd much rather meet them head-on and deal with it that way."

"They'd send more like me. Probably better. We'd die."

"Yes," she said, "we would."

I sighed.

Talya cleared her throat. "Which is why we can't go on with this."

I turned to her. "What do you mean?"

"Lawson, you know what I mean. This whole 'us' thing has to end. Here. Now. I can't have it on my conscience. I can't ask you to sacrifice your job, your life, your everything just for me." She grinned. "Hell, we haven't even really discussed the fact that you are a vampire, for God's sake. I can tell you that has messed me up something fierce."

"So what now?"

"Now nothing," said Talya. "Like I said, we end this. I want you out of my life. Forever."

"But—"

"But nothing, Lawson." She stood up and turned toward me. "Give me a hug and be done with it."

My heart ached. She looked so absolutely stunning in her long overcoat, her hair swept back off her face and tied in a neat bun. Her eyes even seemed moist. I knew it was tearing her up. Hell, it was killing me.

But I hugged her anyway, felt her arms close around my waist, inhaled her perfume, tried to hold on to the scent forever, leaned in and kissed her cold moist cheeks.

"I love you."

She pulled out of my embrace, turned away, then walked off. I watched her exit the park by the wrought iron gateway leading toward Newbury Street. In seconds she'd been swallowed up by the crowds.

I wanted to chase after her so badly.

Wanted to catch her.

Wanted.

I stayed solidly locked to the sidewalk. Unable to move. My heart pounded in my chest so hard it hurt like hell. I wanted to heave my guts all over the sidewalk.

But I didn't.

After five minutes I began breathing again, aware of the moist heat I felt in my eyes.

Two minutes later I could walk again.

But I didn't follow her.

I walked back to the Boston Common garage and descended the stairs until I reached the lower level. It was just as cold down here as it was outside. And in my heart I felt the coldest of all.

The Jetta warmed up quickly enough and I eased out of the space, turned left, and wound my way up toward the cashier booth.

The kid inside looked almost nineteen. I tried to remember how I looked when I was nineteen, and how the world had looked when I was that young. I decided it was far too long ago and rolled down the window.

I felt in my jacket for the parking stub and came out with a folded piece of paper instead. I opened it.

I'm assuming that whoever you work for has us under surveillance. The words I spoke were for their benefit alone. If you feel about me as I do you, I know we'll find a way to be together, regardless of the danger.

All my love—T.

Professional to the end. Somehow she'd known. I marveled at her skill.

"Sir?"

I snapped back to reality and looked at the parking attendant. "Yeah?"

"Your ticket?"

"Oh, yeah. Sorry."

He eyed me as I reached into my wallet and pulled out a $20 bill. "Everything OK, sir?"

I handed him the money, waved off the change, and slipped the Jetta into drive. "Everything is perfect, my friend. Absolutely perfect."

And for the first time in my life, it actually was.

Please turn the page for a sneak peek of

Jon F. Merz's next novel

THE INVOKER

Coming from Pinnacle Books in October 2002!

Killing is never easy.

Between the preparation time, tracking your target, and making sure things go like they're supposed to—it gets complicated.

In the end pulling the trigger is actually the easiest part.

For some.

Lying underneath the battered rusting hulk of an abandoned Buick sedan on crumbling cinder blocks wasn't the kind of activity I normally prefer for a Saturday night. Especially since the freezing rain made the ground underneath me soggy and home to all sorts of creepy crawlies that enjoyed the warmth bleeding out of my body and into the ground.

But a job's a job.

My name's Lawson.

I'm a Fixer by trade. I serve and protect the community. But mostly I help maintain the Balance. It's a noble profession and those of us born into it would never really feel at ease doing anything else. But there were days when I'd give anything to know the monotony of an accountant who stared at numbers all day long.

Right now was one of those times.

Lightning flashed overhead, briefly illuminating my surroundings. Damn. I could be seen if the lightning lit up the area at the wrong time.

And I definitely did not want to be seen.

Otherwise I wouldn't have been under that damned car.

But cover and concealment in this deserted auto-wreckage yard was scarce. I could either hide inside a compacted car or under one. And since trying to get out of a car is harder than rolling out from under it, I chose the latter.

But I didn't like it.

I shifted and instantly regretted the move. My crotch lay in a fresh pool of water that quickly soaked through the tough denim of my jeans. The cold helped shrink my balls farther into my tight scrotal sac, making me feel more like a castrato gunslinger than the professional killer I am. It would take a generous serving of Bombay Sapphire and tonic as well as a hot bath to help me relax after this escapade.

The air shifted, blowing in sideways from the east, and I caught a scent I hadn't detected before. Cologne. Cheap. Like the million department-store samples that flutter out of my credit card envelopes every month.

I heard the squishing sound of water and mud under shoes.

The footsteps sounded like rotten tomatoes being mashed together. But they seemed hesitant. They didn't sound purposeful.

But it didn't really matter how they sounded.

My job remained the same.

And it wouldn't be long before I finished it.

That was good. I didn't like soaking in the fetid rainwater and melting ice any longer than was absolutely necessary.

The footsteps approached as a thunderclap exploded in the night air. I held my breath and waited for another bolt of lightning.

But nothing happened.

I exhaled just as the shoes drew abreast of the car. I could see the soles and what looked like handmade leather uppers. Even in the dark I could see loose threads dangling from the cuffs on his suit pants. The hemline needed adjusting too.

Strange.

I wondered briefly if maybe this wasn't my target. But I shrugged that off. According to my information, there were only two people in this junkyard tonight: my target and his executioner.

The smell of the cheap cologne was killing me. I tried to mentally analyze it—to break down its individual components so it wouldn't bother me so much. I got as far as the ethyl alcohol before I realized I was going to sneeze.

There are a few techniques you can normally employ when sneezing isn't appropriate. The first involves sticking your tongue to the roof of your mouth right behind your front teeth. I did that.

It didn't work.

The next best option is to rub the spot under your nose and press in with a finger. It's an old pressure point a Japanese martial arts master once showed me.

I'm sure that would have worked fine, if both my hands had been free. They weren't. In one hand I held my modified pistol. In the other hand I had my small black bag that contained some other items I might have needed tonight.

Hands unavailable, I steeled myself for the sudden explosion of air. I tried to stifle it and did a good job. But as the air rushed out, I tensed my body, which then caused me to jerk upward suddenly and hit the steel, aluminum, and plastic undercarriage of the Buick with the back of my head.

And since bone and metals do not make fond friends or even remote acquaintances, I saw stars.

Shit, that hurt.

My eyes closed briefly with tears before I realized the shoes had shifted.

Double shit.

I'd been heard.

Calmly, I thumbed the safety off the pistol and waited. Most folks don't think to look above or below their line of sight, so if I stayed cool, he might not see me.

The shoes moved around the car. I could visualize him checking the area, searching the heaps of rusted mufflers and hubcaps, looking for the source of the sound. I watched as the shoes started to take a few steps away. Seemingly satisfied, he turned and came walking back toward me and the car.

Which, of course, was the exact moment Mr. Lightning decided to put in his overdue appearance and illuminate the entire area—including the Buick, the cinder blocks, and yours truly.

The shoes stopped.

Past experience has taught me it's better to go on the offensive at times like this than to wait. I've debated that idea in the past and usually come away with some bad scars because of it.

Not tonight.

I rolled out and got a bead on him center mass even as the shocked expression began to register on his face and he started to back away.

I squeezed off a single round—watched as it caught him square in the chest, lifting him off his feet and pitching him back over. He crashed to the ground, kicking up mud, icy water, and sludge before rolling a short distance away.

I got up—my gun at low-ready position—and walked over, squishing all the way like I was slogging through chest-high mounds of wet pasta.

He was breathing, but just barely. Dark blood soaked his shirt, diluted by the icy rain pelting him from above, turning it a softer shade of frothy pink. The shocked expression still clouded his face, almost as if he couldn't believe what was happening.

I knelt down. "The Council sent me."

He tried to speak. It came out as a stutter of gurgling consonants. "F-f-fixer?"

I nodded. His eyes grew wider. I'd seen the look before. Technically, most of my kind don't think Fixers exist. They think we're just legends told by parents to kids to get them to behave.

But we're real enough. We work in the shadows. Our accomplishments go unnoticed by all but a select few.

Unfortunately for this guy, tonight was the time he found out we really did exist.

I frisked him, looking for his gun. I came up empty. "Narcotics trafficking is bad business for humans to be in. It's even worse for a vampire."

He grimaced, feeling the agony of the wooden splinters in his heart, which came courtesy of the wood-tipped rounds my pistol packed. In the night air he drew his head back, trying to inhale a raspy breath. His canines lengthened, fully exposed. That happened only during feeding or when a vampire was close to death.

"You could have exposed the community. You threatened the Balance." I leaned closer. "You know the penalty for any of those violations is death."

He frowned, but it looked more like an upside-down grin. "They . . . They told you that?"

"The drugs? Yeah. I wouldn't be here otherwise." He only had a few minutes left.

"Lies . . . all of it . . . lies . . ."

I'd heard that before. Claims of innocence come with the job. Even when you've put them down, some of the most hardened criminals will deny they did anything wrong. They go off to the afterlife convinced of their own innocence.

"Whatever you say, pal." Time to end the repartee. I started to stand.

But he grabbed my hand, clutching it, and squeezed. Hard.

I started to pull away, started to break his grasp. He wouldn't let go. He still had some strength in him.

He pulled me closer, until his mouth was just a few inches away from my ear. I could hear the rasping of fluid in his lungs as he breathed in short gasps of dwindling air. And he managed to cough out two words.

"My son."

I frowned. "What about him?"

He closed his eyes, tears running out of them now dripping off his wet face to the ground beneath him where his blood ran crimson tinged with silt and grime. "You . . . must . . . protect him."

His head lolled back and to the side then as his hand went limp in mine. As it opened, a small photograph rolled out and fluttered toward the rain-slicked ground.

I scooped it up, wiping the bloody mud off it. Lightning flashed again and I peered closer. The picture showed a small boy. His son, no doubt.

But protection? What the hell was that about? The mission had been a simple termination order. Punishment for crimes committed. There had been no mention of protection.

None whatsoever.

And that's precisely what worried me even as the rain increased and pounded against my back. I looked up, feeling the cold pour down my face, coat my lips, and bleed into my mouth.

I swished around a mouthful and spat it back toward the ground.

Why was nothing ever as easy as I wanted it to be?

BOOK YOUR PLACE ON OUR WEBSITE AND MAKE THE READING CONNECTION!

We've created a customized website just for our very special readers, where you can get the inside scoop on everything that's going on with Zebra, Pinnacle and Kensington books.

When you come online, you'll have the exciting opportunity to:

- View covers of upcoming books
- Read sample chapters
- Learn about our future publishing schedule (listed by publication month *and author*)
- Find out when your favorite authors will be visiting a city near you
- Search for and order backlist books from our online catalog
- Check out author bios and background information
- Send e-mail to your favorite authors
- Meet the Kensington staff online
- Join us in weekly chats with authors, readers and other guests
- Get writing guidelines
- AND MUCH MORE!

**Visit our website at
http://www.kensingtonbooks.com**

Feel the Seduction of
Pinnacle Horror

__The Vampire Memoirs
  by Mara McCunniff   0-7860-1124-6 $5.99US/$7.99CAN
  & Traci Briery

__The Stake
  by Richard Laymon   0-7860-1095-9 $5.99US/$7.99CAN

__Blood of My Blood: The Vampire Legacy
  by Karen E. Taylor   0-7860-1153-X $5.99US/$7.99CAN

Call toll free **1-888-345-BOOK** to order by phone or use this coupon
to order by mail.
Name_____
Address_____
City_____ State_____ Zip_____
Please send me the books that I checked above.
I am enclosing $_____
Plus postage and handling* $_____
Sales tax (in NY, TN, and DC) $_____
Total amount enclosed $_____
*Add $2.50 for the first book and $.50 for each additional book.
Send check or money order (no cash or CODs) to: **Kensington Publishing
Corp., Dept. C.O., 850 Third Avenue, 16th Floor, New York, NY 10022**
Prices and numbers subject to change without notice.
All orders subject to availability.
Visit our website at **www.kensingtonbooks.com**.

Scare Up One of These Pinnacle Horrors

__Haunted
by Tamara Thorne   0-7860-1090-8 $5.99US/$7.99CAN

__Thirst
by Michael Cecilione   0-7860-1091-6 $5.99US/$7.99CAN

__The Haunting
by Ruby Jean Jensen   0-7860-1095-9 $5.99US/$7.99CAN

__The Summoning
by Bentley Little   0-7860-1480-6 $6.99US/$8.99CAN

Call toll free **1-888-345-BOOK** to order by phone or use this coupon to order by mail.

Name_____

Address_____

City_____ State_____ Zip_____

Please send me the books that I checked above.

I am enclosing	$_____
Plus postage and handling*	$_____
Sales tax (in NY, TN, and DC)	$_____
Total amount enclosed	$_____

*Add $2.50 for the first book and $.50 for each additional book.
Send check or money order (no cash or CODs) to: **Kensington Publishing Corp., Dept. C.O., 850 Third Avenue, 16th Floor, New York, NY 10022**
Prices and numbers subject to change without notice.
All orders subject to availability.
Visit our website at **www.kensingtonbooks.com**.

AUSTRALIA

ANTHOLLOPE

Selected from:

A Common Reader
175 Tompkins Avenue
Pleasantville, New York 10570
(914) 747-3388

· Gloucester

H, INC. · New York

First Published 1873

Copyright © in this edition 1987
Alan Sutton Publishing Limited

This edition first published in Great Britain 1987
   Alan Sutton Publishing Limited
   30 Brunswick Road
   Gloucester GL1 1JJ

British Library Cataloguing in Publication Data

Trollope, Anthony
   Australia.
   1. Australia—Description and
   travel—1851–1900
   I. Title
   919.4′.0431   DU102

ISBN 0–86299–358–X

This edition first published in the U.S.A. 1987
   Hippocrene Books, Inc.
   171 Madison Avenue
   New York, N.Y. 10016

ISBN 0–87052–435–6

Cover picture: detail from Sydney Harbour *by George Rowe.*
By courtesy of the Warrnambool Art Gallery, Warrnambool,
Victoria, Australia.
Photograph: Cheltenham Museum and Art Gallery.

Typesetting and origination by
Alan Sutton Publishing Limited.
Photoset Bembo 9/10
Printed in Great Britain
by The Guernsey Press Company Limited,
Guernsey, Channel Islands.

CONTENTS

QUEENSLAND

SOUTH AUSTRALIA

WESTERN AUSTRALIA

BIOGRAPHICAL NOTE

In his *Autobiography*, Trollope explains how he spent the early years of his life 'in a world altogether outside the world of my material life.' In this world nothing impossibly fantastic happened, but stories developed in a serial way over months and even years. Although nothing was written down, these imaginings obviously provided the foundation for Trollope's later prolific creativity.

The reasons for this mental need to escape from the real world are not difficult to find. For the first twenty-seven years of his life Trollope was unhappy and unsuccessful. He was born on 24 April 1815, the fourth of six children born to Thomas and Fanny Trollope. Thomas was a qualified barrister, but had the wrong personality to make a success of his profession. Consequently, he moved his family from Keppel Street in London out to a farm he owned in Harrow, but he did not know enough about farming to make the land pay, and finally was forced to let out the farm. He moved into a cottage in the grounds and dedicated the rest of his life to compiling an ecclesiastical dictionary which nobody wanted.

In an attempt to provide for her family, Fanny took all her children, except Anthony, to America, but her efforts to set up in business there were a failure, and it was only on her return, three years later, that she finally made some money, with the publication of her successful *Domestic Manners of the Americans*. In the meantime Anthony had been sent to school at Harrow and Winchester, and left very much to his own devices. William Gregory wrote of the young Anthony: 'He was not only slovenly in person and dress, but his work was equally dirty. He gave no signs of promise whatsoever, was always in the lowest part of the form and was regarded by masters and boys as an incorrigible dunce.' He left school in 1834 and through friends of his mother obtained a clerkship in the General Post Office in London. Since his mother had now

moved to Bruges, he lived on his own in dreary lodgings in
Marylebone. Within the next two years a brother and sister
died of consumption, and his father fell victim to mercury
poisoning, because of his addiction to the drug Calomel.

Anthony must have felt further isolated by his mother's
increased closeness to her eldest son, Tom, and his sister's
marriage and removal to Cumberland. But his life, although
to some extent lonely and poverty-stricken, was not without
amusement. He enjoyed walking weekends in the country,
and one feels that experiences such as those enjoyed by
Charley Tudor in *The Three Clerks* were probably based on
the activities of the clerks at the Post Office. Of his work,
however, he writes: 'I hated the office. I hated my work. More
than all I hated my idleness.' He finally found a release from
the drudgery and boredom of clerical work in 1841, when he
was accepted as a post office surveyor's clerk at Banagher, in
King's County, Ireland.

'This', remarked Trollope of his Irish posting, 'was the first
good fortune of my life.' He started to make a success of his
job as inspector and investigator of the local postal service, in
spite of, or perhaps because of, his brusque manner; he
developed a taste for hunting and mixing with the Irish
gentry; he married, and his English wife, Rose, bore him two
sons. Most importantly, he started writing. The first four
pieces of work published were not best-sellers, by any means,
but two, *The Macdermots of Ballycloran* (1847) and *The Kellys
and the O'Kellys* (1848), received some critical acclaim and
showed the author's potential.

Trollope's first successful novel, *The Warden* (1855), was
not finished until he was once again in Ireland, having
completed an assignment in the South West of England
reorganizing the postal system. It was while there, that he
conceived the idea of Barsetshire. In 1857 *Barchester Towers*
was published, and Trollope's reputation was further established with the appearance of *The Three Clerks* a year later.
1858 also saw the publication of *Doctor Thorne* and the
completion of *The Bertrams* (published 1859). Thenceforth
Trollope's output was considerable – two or three books
appearing every year until 1883. He wrote well over forty
novels, various collections of short stories, travel books, a

translation of Caesar's Commentaries, a life of Cicero, an appreciation of Thackeray, and an autobiography.

Trollope's approach to his art was extremely disciplined. He would write a set number of pages before breakfast every day, no matter where he was. *Lady Anna* (1874), for example, was written on a voyage out to Australia. Of his technique he said he went to work 'just like a shoemaker on a shoe, only taking care to make honest stitches.' But another admission reveals that, in spite of his disciplined approach, he was totally involved in his characters: 'I have wandered alone among the woods and rocks, crying at their grief, laughing at their absurdities and thoroughly enjoying their joy.'

The Post Office was indirectly responsible for Trollope's first travel book, because after a successful mission to Egypt in 1858, he was sent to review the postal services of the Caribbean Islands and Central America. This voyage gave rise to *The West Indies and the Spanish Main*, an immediately successful travelogue. Trollope later wrote about the other continents he visited, producing *North America* in 1862, *Australia and New Zealand* in 1873, when he travelled out for the marriage of his farming son, and *South Africa* in 1878.

It was during the sixties that Trollope's most famous works appeared: *Framley Parsonage* (1861), *Orley Farm* (1862), *The Small House at Allington* (1864) *The Last Chronicle of Barset* (1867). After his trip to the Caribbean, he had been appointed Surveyor of the Eastern District of England, and he had bought a house in Waltham cross. His new proximity to London allowed him to mix with the literati of England for the first time. He very soon became a popular member of the Garrick Club, the Athenaeum, and the Cosmopolitan, and he must have been stimulated by his new cultural environment. He admired and became friends with both Thackeray and George Eliot (at whose house he met many famous writers of the day including Turgenev). He was also a close friend of John Everett Millais, who illustrated *Framley Parsonage*, *Orley Farm*, and other novels. He visited his brother and mother in Italy several times, and there he met the Brownings and also a young American, Kate Field, whom he saw irregularly and with whom he corresponded until his death.

When he was fifty-two, in 1867, Trollope resigned from the Post Office and relied on his literary output for finance. He became editor of the new *St. Paul's Magazine*, but he did not enjoy the work and gave it up after three years. During that time he had political aspirations, as is reflected in the writing of the Palliser novels, but his attempt to stand as Parliamentary candidate for Beverley in 1868 was a failure.

Earlier in that same year, he had been in America, and had written *The Vicar of Bulhampton* while in New York. He thought that the story, which was about a prostitute, might be found distasteful, and therefore included an explanatory preface, but *The Times* commented: '. . . the general safeness of the story will make Bulhampton Vicarage welcome to all well-regulated families.' On the other hand, *Lady Anna*, written six years later caused considerable disturbance. The *Saturday Review* warned their readers against it, so that they 'may not betray into reading what will probably leave a disagreeable impression'. Many people, however, did read the novel, and some wrote to Trollope expressing their objections. Apparently the idea of an Earl's daughter honourably marrying a tailor was too extreme a notion for the class-bound Victorian society.

In 1870 Trollope sold Waltham House and moved into London, to Montagu Square. He gave up hunting, but kept his horses and often rode in London. During the seventies he wrote prolifically and travelled widely. His fame was past its peak, but in 1873 he was featured in the popular weekly, *Vanity Fair*, with a cartoon and text, which included: '. . . He is a correct painter of the small things of our small modern English life . . . His manners are a little rough, as is his voice, but he is nevertheless extremely popular among his personal friends . . .' The character outline is complemented and extended by J.R. Lowell's description: '. . . Anthony Trollope, a big red-faced rather underbred Englishman of the bald-with-spectacles type . . . A good roaring fellow who deafened me'; and by G.A. Sala's: 'Crusty, quarrelsome, wrongheaded, prejudiced, obstinate, kind-hearted and thoroughly honest old Tony Tollope.'

All his life Trollope was subject to depression because of what Escott, his biographer, explains as an 'almost feminine sensibility to the opinions of others, a self-consciousness altogether abnormal in a sensible and practical man of the world, as well as a strong love of approbation, whether from stranger or friend.'

By the end of the decade, Trollope was a familiar figure at literary gatherings in London, and in the country. He was a guest both at Lord Carnarvon's home at Highclere, Hampshire, and at Waddesdon Manor, the home of Baron Rothschild. But his health was declining and in 1880 he moved from London to the more salubrious area of the South Downs. He bought The Grange at South Harting in Hampshire, and there he wrote his last novels. These reflected his pessimistic outlook, and two of them concentrated on problems of growing older: *Mr. Scarborough's Family* and *An Old Man's Love*, the first a study of eccentricity, and the second a story of an older man's love for a younger woman. In 1882 he started his final novel, *The Landleaguers*, which was, like his first novel, set in Ireland. He made two trips to Ireland during that year to collect material which probably contributed to a rapid deterioration in his health and in the October of that year he moved up to London for the Winter. He suffered a stroke in November, and died five weeks later on 6 December 1882. He was buried in Kensal Green Cemetery. 'He was removed in a lusty majority, and before decay had begun to cripple his indefatigable industry or dull the brightness of his versatile fancy' (from his obituary in *The Times*).

SHEILA MICHELL

QUEENSLAND

CHAPTER I

EARLY HISTORY AND PRESENT STATE OF THE COLONY

Queensland calls itself the biggest of the English colonies. South Australia, however, may dispute the question with her, as her territories run through from the southern to the northern coast. The Queenslanders boast that Queensland is larger than England, Ireland, Scotland, France, Belgium, Holland, and Denmark, added together. There is room enough therefore for all the energies of all its possible future inhabitants for many years to come. It now contains 120,000 inhabitants, – and is therefore, – in point of population, inferior to many a second-rate English or American city. But it owes a public debt of four million pounds, and spends a public revenue of about £800,000 a year, or nearly £7 a head. Justice is administered and property protected at the rate of £1 per head for every inhabitant of the colony. At the same rate in the British Isles the administration of justice would cost over thirty millions! To a poor Englishman who has all his life heard English taxation complained of as an incubus which no nation can long bear, these amounts seem to threaten instant ruin; but in a young colony they are not much feared, and at least a moiety of the politicians of Queensland seem to think that the welfare of the community is chiefly impeded by a niggardly parsimony which is afraid of a good lively debt, and is not sufficiently awake to the advantages which accrue from a plentiful scattering of public money. In speaking of the taxation of the colony, it must be remembered that a portion of the public revenue arises from the sale of public lands, and is not therefore felt as a direct impost by the people. But the amount so brought annually to the public credit is not nearly as large as I had expected. The average for the last ten years has been £170,000 per annum. This leaves the amount to be collected from taxes £630,000 per annum, or about £5 5s. per head.

Queensland was separated from New South Wales in 1859, as had been Victoria in 1850, and the name was given to the new colony by her Majesty. The question of separation had been mooted for the last nine or ten years, and with it the other question, – hardly less important than separation itself, – whether the new colony should or should not receive convicts. All the world knows that Queensland as a separate colony has never taken convicts, nor were convicts sent to its districts since 1850. In that year the last ship-load of English ruffians was landed on her shores. But the question was one open to much discussion. In the old days, Moreton Bay, – as the district was called in which Brisbane, the present capital of Queensland, is situated, – was a penal settlement dependent on the Government of New South Wales. It was so named by Captain Cook in 1770. Though it kept its name, it seems to have attracted no notice till 1823–24 and '25. A penal settlement for doubly dyed ruffians was then founded at Moreton Bay, where Brisbane now stands, and many of the public works, and not a little of the cultivation of the lands round Brisbane, are due to the forced labour of these unfortunates. When the great question was being mooted within the would-be new colony, its whole population did not exceed 15,000 souls. Among the pastoral aspirants, – squatters as my readers must learn to call them, – the want of labour was the one great difficulty of these days. The squatter, alone, was not afraid of the convict. The freeman, whose lot it would be to work alongside of him should he come, and the shopkeepers, and the small nascent agriculturists, did not wish for him. It was therefore decided that the colony should never take convicts, and it has never taken them. What became of those who had been sent thither up to that date, it is hard to say. They have been so thoroughly absorbed, that one hears little or nothing about them in Queensland, – much less than is heard in New South Wales. It may occasionally happen that a gentleman who has been unfortunate in his youth forces his way up to some place of note, in the legislature or elsewhere, and then a whisper is heard abroad that the gentleman came to the colony in the old-fashioned way. Otherwise, one hears but little of convicts in Queensland.

Before Queensland became a separate colony, the only great commercial interest of the country was pastoral, – including the breeding, rearing, and shearing of sheep, and the care of cattle. The country had been taken up by squatters in large masses up to the line of the tropics, and even within the line. In 1858, just before separation was effected, the first gold rush was made to Canoona, which is just on the line. Since that there have been gold rushes in various parts of the colony, and new rushes are still made from time to time. Having said so much, we will now take Queensland as an established colony, and make no further reference to its ancient history. I have already spoken of its dimensions. I trust to spare my readers many references to maps, as I wish to write of men and their manners and welfare, rather than of rivers and boundaries, and such references are always troublesome; but one slight glimpse of the maps furnished of each of the colonies may be beneficial. It will be seen that Queensland is bisected by the tropic of Capricorn; I have therefore called it semi-tropical. In the way of fruit it produces grapes, oranges, and pineapples, but not apples, gooseberries, or currants. Wheat has been produced, but not so as to pay the grower of it. Oats are grown, but are cut green or half ripe and made into hay. Cotton is grown in the southern parts of the settled districts, but only in small patches. It has not as yet become one of the staples of the country, nor do I think it ever will. Sugar is produced largely, and will probably become the great rival of the wool trade. Cattle do well in most of the various districts, but the distance from the necessary markets makes the trade precarious. Gold-rushing is of all pursuits, – here as in all gold-producing countries, – the most alluring and the most precarious. There is a considerable trade in timber, especially from the rivers on which the town of Maryborough stands. And vineyards have been made, the owners of which make wine, and think that in a little time they will make good wine. I have drunk fairly good wine made in Australia, but none made in Queensland. If on this head any wine-growing Queensland squatter should accuse me of falsehood, – remembering the assenting smile with which I have seemed to acknowledge that his vintage was excellent, – let him reflect how impossible it is for the guest to repudiate the praises with which the host speaks of his own cellar. All the world over it is allowed to the giver to praise his own wine, – a privilege of which Australians avail themselves;

but it is not allowed to the receiver to deny the justness of such encomium, except under circumstances of peculiar intimacy. Here, in these pages, truth must prevail; and I am bound to say that Queensland wine was not to my taste. I am delighted to acknowledge that their pineapples were perfect.

By the last land act of the colony, – that of 1868, – to which I must often refer, Queensland was divided into settled and unsettled districts. The former consists of the whole seacoast line, varying in breadth from about two hundred to about twenty miles. The unsettled districts stretch back over vast distances, from the 152nd to the 138th meridian of longitude. Within the narrow line of the settled districts are all the towns which can be called towns, the best of the sheep stations, most of the gold mines, all the navigable rivers, – which, as is the case throughout Australia, are few and but poorly gifted, – and, as a matter of course, the great bulk of the population. In the unsettled districts pastoral pursuits, – that is the wool trade and the cattle trade, – progress, but do so slowly. That great difficulty of immigration, – which in Queensland has been especially great, – prevents that speedy filling up of the back country which has been the making of the American Western States.

It may be as well to say a few words here about Queensland immigration. The colony, from the first, has been quite alive to the expediency, – it may almost be said the necessity, – of bidding high for Englishmen, Scotchmen, and Irishmen, and has been tempted to bid too high. There have been various acts passed by the legislature of the colony with the object of inducing persons to come out and occupy land in Queensland on terms profitable to themselves; passages have been paid for them and land allotted on certain terms; and to those who would pay for their own passages, lands have been allotted on other terms, more seductive of course. Endeavour has been made to make the 'land orders', – the orders under which the land was to be given up to the immigrants, – not transferable; so that the man with his family whose passage had been paid out of the colony's revenue, or the other comer who had paid for his own passage with the object of obtaining the fuller grant of land, should be a bona-fide beneficent Queensland immigrant, and not simply a traveller passing through the colony, availing himself of the liberality of the colony with the view of going on elsewhere, – and, in fact, robbing the colony by selling his land orders. But these not transferable land orders granted under the Immigration Act of 1864 were sold, and the poorer class of immigrants who had come out with free passages did pass on to other lands. Emigrants from home did come to Queensland with the express view of leaving it, after they had used its liberality. In 1869, there came from the British Isles to Queensland 1,635 souls, – 1,635 souls over and above the comparatively small number who had returned home. And in that year 2,272 souls left Queensland for the other Australian colonies, – 2,272 souls over and above the number that came into Queensland from the other Australian colonies. So that not only did Queensland lose in that year all its immigrants from England, but sent also 637 emigrants to the other Australian colonies. Now this was by no means what Queensland meant when she made her liberal overtures to the would-be emigrant from our own islands; nor is it the way in which any young colony can prosper. It was simply a wasting of her funds. She therefore passed another immigration law in 1869, – which is now in force, – the express intention of which is to compel those who take land orders in Queensland to live on the land so bestowed, and also to compel those who accept assisted passages or free passages to work out within the colony the money which has been expended on them. Great dissatisfaction already prevails because they who have recently brought out themselves and families under the recent act cannot sell their land orders nor avail themselves of the land without residence. They have thought that the old plan of transferring non-transferable orders would still be practicable. There is ground for hope therefore that the colony will no longer be defrauded in that direction. But I fear much success will not attend the giving of free or assisted passages. They who accept them bind themselves to repay the government within a stated time £8 for assisted or £16 for free passages, – and when such payments have been made, orders for land are given to them. But there is nothing to prevent such persons from re-emigrating; and it seems clear that it is their practice to do so.

That such practice should be general must probably be taken as evidence that the colony among colonies is not popular. It implies that Queensland had found it necessary to offer higher bounties than have sufficed with the other colonies, – or these re-emigrating immigrants would not trouble themselves to come to Queensland in the first instance; and it implies also that when she has got her dearly purchased immigrants she cannot keep them. This no doubt is so at the present period of her career. One cause of this will probably not be permanent, – the greatly superior success namely of the New Zealand gold-diggings. What number of men go from Queensland to New Zealand cannot be told, as the route is via Sydney, and these gold-seekers are therefore counted among those who depart to the other Australian colonies; but that the number has been great there is no doubt. The next cause may probably be found in the heat of the climate, and must be permanent. Setting aside for the present the allurements of gold, I think that wheat-growing countries offer the greatest inducements to the class of men who generally emigrate from our own islands. In Queensland the bounties offered to immigrants are bestowed chiefly with the view of creating a class of small farmers, – men who shall select small portions of the Crown lands, by means of land orders or by gradual purchase, and who shall become freeholders and thus permanently wedded to the colony. But a small farmer must have a convenient market for his produce before he can thrive, and must be able to produce what that market demands. The world wants wheat, but the Queensland farmer cannot produce it. Queensland produces wool and meat, and sugar, but these things as articles of trade are generally beyond the reach of the small farmer. Indian corn, or maize, is grown on these small farms, and oaten hay, and something is done in the manufacture of butter. But the markets for these things are bad. The farmer with his Indian corn is generally forced to take other goods for his produce, – tea, or clothes, or perhaps rum. Wheat he could no doubt sell for money. Such being the case, the prospect to the small farmers is not good, and they who manage things in the colony not unnaturally find a difficulty in establishing permanent agriculturists on their soil.

The term 'free-selecters' used above is one with which the traveller soon finds himself very intimately acquainted in the Australian colonies, and if he be fortunate enough to become hand and glove with the squatters, he always hears it as a term of reproach. The normal squatter hates the 'free-selecter' almost as thoroughly as the English country gentleman hates the poacher. In explaining the condition of the Queensland free-selecter, it is necessary to state that a considerable portion of a squatter's run within the settled districts is always open to be selected by any human being above twenty-one years of age. You, oh reader ignorant of your privilege, may go at once and select no less than 10,280 acres on the run of any Queensland squatter within the line of settled districts who has so much as yet unselected, and unprotected by the present laws from immediate selection. You may take not less than 210 nor more than 640 acres of agricultural land at 15s. an acre; also, if you please, not less than 80 or more than 2,560 of first-class pastoral land at 10s. an acre, – and also, if you are so minded, not less than 80 or more than 7,680 acres of second-class pastoral land at 10s. an acre; and for these purchases you need only pay a tenth of the price the first year, and so on for ten years, when the whole estate will be your own. Or, if you be more humble, – and are not a married woman, – you may free-select a nice little farm of 80 acres of agricultural land, or 160 of pastoral, on still easier terms. This you do under the homestead clause, – but as to this you are bound down to residence. This you have at 9d. an acre per annum for agricultural land, or 6d. for pastoral, and if at the end of five years you shall have lived on it continually, and have either fenced it in or cultivated the tenth of it, it is yours for ever with an indefeasible title-deed without further payment. Now 80 acres out of a squatter's run is nothing. Even 10,280 acres out of a large run is not much. But one squatter may be subject to many free-selecters; and when the free-selecter makes his selection with the express object of stealing the squatter's cattle, – as the squatter often believes to be the case, – the squatter of course omits to love his neighbour as himself.

It must be understood that from this order of things arises a very different condition of feeling with regard to land from that to which we are subject at home. With us the owner of the land, the freeholder, is the big man, and he who holds by lease is the little man. In the Australian colonies the squatter who holds his run by lease from the Crown, and who only purchases in order to keep others from purchasing, and who is half ruined by being compelled thus to become the owner of the soil, is the big man; whereas the freeholder, who has free-selected his holding, is the little man. But he is in no degree dependent on the squatter, and their interests are altogether at variance.

There has, however, latterly arisen a point of junction between the classes which does to a certain degree bring them together. The squatter, when he washes and shears his sheep, – during the period, that is, of his harvest, – requires a great deal of temporary labour. Now the free-selecters cannot live on their farms, and are consequently glad to hire themselves out during three or four months of the year as washers and shearers. For this work they receive high wages, – and rations, which enable them to take their earnings home with them. It is always for the advantage both of the employed and of employers that they should think well of each other, and hence some kindly feeling does spring up tending to allay the irritation as to cattle-stealing on the one side, and the anger produced by contempt and perhaps by false accusation on the other. The squatter's money is necessary to the free-selecter, and the free selecter's labour is necessary to the squatter, and in this way the two classes amalgamate.

In this great question between the squatter and the free-selecter of land, – for with its different ramifications in regard to immigration, agricultural produce, and pastoral success, it is the greatest of all questions in Australian life, – it is almost impossible for the normal traveller not to sympathize with the squatter. The normal traveller comes out with introductions to the gentlemen of the colony, and the gentlemen of the colony are squatters. The squatters' houses are open to him. They introduce the traveller to their clubs. They lend their horses and buggies. Their wives and daughters are pretty and agreeable. They excercise all the duties of hospitality with a free hand. They get up kangeroo hunts and make picnics. It is always pleasant to sympathize with an aristocracy when an aristocracy will open its arms to you. We remember republican Mrs. Beecher Stowe with her sunny memories of duchesses. But the traveller ought to sympathize with the free-selecter, – always premising that the man keeps his hands from picking and stealing his neighbour's cattle. He, we may say, is the man for whom colonial life and colonial prosperity is especially intended and without whom no colony can rise to national importance. The pastoral squatter occupying tens of thousands of acres and producing wool that has made Australia what she now is, has done great things for the infancy of the country. But in all discussions on this question it must be remembered that he has no right to the permanent occupation of the land on which his flocks wander. Even though he may have purchased the use of his present run and purchased it for a high price, the land is not his. It belongs to the people of the colony; and should be sold or leased or retained as may be best for the public advantage. The squatter's run, in ordinary colonial language, has been taken up by some original squatter who has driven his sheep or his cattle on it when it knew no other occupant than the black man. In the very early days of squatting some attempts were made to connect this occupation with possession; but this was at once refused by the Crown, which peremptorily and most properly asserted its own rights. When independent government was conceded to the Australian colonies, these rights became the right of the people, and squatters held their runs and knew that they held their runs simply as tenants under the government which acted as agent for the people. Nor have these tenants been in possession of leases running over any long term of years. The rents which they pay are at any rate in Queensland, hardly more than nominal, and no fixity of tenure has ever been accorded to them. In Queensland, by the land act of 1868, every squatter's run was divided into two moieties, of which one moiety was at once made open to free-selection till 1878, – unless a further land act giving further power of free selection should be passed before that time. When the law of 1868 was passed it was perfectly understood that no tenure even for the ten years was given to the squatters of the moieties which were then left to them. The lands were public lands and not their lands. The area open to squatters in Queensland is so vast, and genuine free-selecters unfortunately are so few in number and so limited in means, that there need be no fear that the squatter will be banished from the face of the colony. Of his own condition I shall speak in a further chapter; but in the mean time it should be understood that the encouragement of the free-selecter, – of the genuine free-selecter who intends to cultivate and reside upon the land, – is and should be the first aim of colonial government. A race of men, who will people the earth at the rate, say of a soul to fifty acres, must be more important to a young community than an aristocracy which hardly employs one man permanently for every ten thousand acres. Population is the thing required, and, above all, an agricultural population. But agriculturists, especially on a small scale, do not love a land that does not produce wheat. Hence the difficulty, – but on this account our warmer sympathies should be given to those who make the attempt, and every possible effort should be made to induce such men to settle upon the land.

CHAPTER II

THE NORTHERN TERRITORY

On my first arrival at Brisbane I spent but a few days there, and then hurried up north to Rockhampton, again endeavouring to anticipate the heat. Brisbane is a commodious town, very prettily situated on the Brisbane River, with 12,000 inhabitants, with courts of justice, houses of parliament, a governor's residence, public gardens, and all the requirements of a capital for a fine and independent colony. It must be understood that the voyaging of Australia is chiefly done by steamboat, and on this occasion I went on by steamboat from Brisbane to Rockhampton. On our route we stopped at Maryborough and Gladstone. Of Maryborough I will speak in reference to the return journey. Of Gladstone I will say a few words now. It is a seaport in the so-called Port Curtis district, and a prettier spot or more melancholy town than Gladstone one could hardly find in any country, new or old. It received its name, of course, from our own statesman, and is said to have been peculiarly favoured by him. It has been spoken of as the future capital of Queensland, and there are many in Queensland, – including the present premier of the colony, – who think that it should be selected, as was Ottawa in Canada, because it has the double advantage of a somewhat central position – on the coast, – and of possessing nothing to offend the jealousies either of Brisbane to the south, or Rockhampton to the north. Other apparent fitnesses for a capital it has none, – except that of a fine harbour. Though it has been essentially fostered by the affections of certain politicians, that first primary necessity of a city, population, has refused to cleave to it. The busy part of the town, consisting of a little wharf, two or three stores, and a custom-house, stands about a quarter of a mile up a small creek just broad enough to allow the steamboats to be turned in it. The creek opens into a magnificent harbour, – magnificent in scenery certainly, and equally so, I should imagine, for the use of ships lying at anchor; but for vessels to lie against the shore, the little muddy creek at present affords the only useful spot. But a fine harbour and beautiful scenery will not make a city, – or even help to make one, unless people can find on its shores the means of earning their bread. Gladstone is land-locked by mountains, and has no back country to support it. There is nothing there to produce trade, or to induce people to choose the place as a domicile favourable to their hopes in life.

When at Rockhampton I was at once initiated into the great question of 'Separation', Rockhampton is a town lying exactly on the line of the tropic of Capricorn, some miles up the Fitzroy River, with about seven thousand inhabitants, which considers itself to be the second town of the colony, and thinks a good deal of itself. It has been seized with the ambition to become a capital, and therefore hates Brisbane. It is so hot that people going from it to an evil place are said to send back to earth for their blankets, finding that evil place to be too chilly for them after the home they have left. But the Rockhampton-ites are energetic, as become the aspirants to metropolitan honours. They do, in truth, do those things which are necessary for the well-being of a community. They have a hospital, – and an excellent hospital it is; also a jail, not so excellent; a good hotel, – or, as I was assured, one or two good hotels; wide streets; a grand post-office, – they ought to keep it open for the accommodation of the public after six o'clock in the evening, and no doubt would do so if they knew that here in England post-offices are not closed at the earliest before nine. They have excellent shops, a good quay, and they have a railway. Perhaps the railway is the crowning glory of Rockhampton.

I must say a word of the Rockhampton railway, and it certainly will not be a word in praise. I have my regrets, for I was carried over it free of charge, and was accompanied by the gentleman who manages it, and who made himself very pleasant on the occasion. Nevertheless I can say nothing good of the Rockhampton railway. It was made as a job, and now that it is made it is not only useless but infinitely worse than useless. It would be a great saving to the colony if it could be shut up and abandoned. I asked in my innocence whether, independent of the cost of making, it supported itself, – whether it paid for its own working. I was told that it about paid for the grease used upon it. Now the cause and meaning of the Rockhampton railway may be described as follows: Queensland, a colony vast in extent, as has been described, was at first populated in her southern districts, those which were contiguous to New South Wales, from which she had succeeded in separating herself. But even at the time of her separation, a small and scattered few had driven their cattle up to the hotter northern lands. Then there were gold rushes, and boiling-down establishments, – some explanation of which shall be given presently; and so the town of Rockhampton was formed, while the population and prosperity of Queensland was as yet in her southern borders, – round Brisbane, and the towns of Ipswich, Warwick, and Toowoomba, and on the Darling Downs. It was then deemed expedient that there should be a railway in the South, – not running out of Brisbane, which has easy water communication with Ipswich; but from Ipswich to the other towns above named, and so across the Darling Downs, where are the grand sheep-walks of that country. It must be understood that railways in Australia, with one or two exceptions, have been made by government, – as hitherto have all roads, river clearances, and the like. The government makes the railway and works it, taking and expending the money, and doing all by the hands of official servants. That it should be so is to me distressing. Whether or no the practice is necessary shall not be discussed now, but at any rate such is the fact. But the government can only make its railway when the legislature has sanctioned the making of it, and the borrowing of the money for the purpose. When the making of the Darling Down railway was mooted, – by which undoubtedly the produce of a very fine district would be brought down to the sea, and the people of various towns would be brought within easy reach of the metropolis, – no very strong objection seems to have been raised to the scheme. It was not much debated whether or no the young colony could or could not bear the weight of the borrowed millions. But this was debated, and made very clear in debate, – that if the southern division of the colony had its railway, then also must the northern. The southern population were ten times greater than the northern no doubt. Well, – then let the southern railway be ten times greater than the northern. But if the Darling Downs people were to have their railway, then should Rockhampton have its railway. On no other terms would any northern member dare to vote the appropriation of the money. Unless this were done, Rockhampton, which is not a meek place nor forbearing in its nature, would make such a row that the colony should split to pieces with it. It had to be done, and hence there are thirty miles of a railway that barely pays for its own grease. It goes out thirty miles to three public-houses in the forest which call themselves Westwood; but it does not get the traffic incident to these thirty miles, because for so short a distance it is not worth the while of waggoners, who take down wool and bring back stores, to unload their burden. The squatters can communicate with Rockhampton cheaper by the old way than by using thirty miles of railroad.

And yet we can hardly blame Rockhampton. I fancy that had I been a Rockhamptonite I should have been eager for my railway. Why should Rockhampton submit to a debt, and pay taxes, in order that the wool of Darling Downs should get to market at a cheaper rate than the wool from their own districts? That question of levying taxes and spending public money for other purposes than those of direct government, including the defence and protection of the nation, is very seducing and very dangerous. There has been a hankering among statesmen at home after government railways, and an idea that a patriarchal government would do better for the country than competing companies. There is still, I believe, a desire with some politicians to buy up the railways at any rate in Ireland. When a government can make ever so much a year by monopolizing telegraphs, it may seem to be very well, – but when a government has to lose ever so much a year by distributing railways, it is surely very bad. The Rockhampton and Westwood railway is the very pathos of such attempts.

And this brings me to the great subject of Separation, which I found to be in every man's mouth at Rockhampton. Separation nowadays in Queensland means the division of that colony into two colonies, as in old days it meant the division of New South Wales into two or more colonies. Though Queensland is hardly in her teens, she is already held by the people of her northern districts to be ready for further division. Let there be Queensland and – Albertland some wish to call the would-be future colony. Why should taxes levied in the north go to make roads round Brisbane? Why should northern legislators travel four, five, six, and seven hundred miles to a southern town built on the very borders of New South Wales? Why should we northerners, with our unlimited area, our high ambition, with a great future looming upon us in gold and sugar, be sacrificed to Brisbane and the Darling Downs? Brisbane is hated at Rockhampton, but I think that the Darling Downs are more odious. It must be remembered always that the Darling Downs squatters are the aristocrats of Queensland, and are about as much in favour at Rockhampton as a marquis is at Manchester. We have, say these northern men, ten, fifteen, or twenty thousand inhabitants, – according as the line may be drawn. Let us have a governor of our own, – and above all, the privileges of legislation. We are old enough to go alone, and go alone we will. The sweat of our brow shall no longer go to Brisbane.

But where shall the line be drawn? Just south of Rockhampton say the Rockhamptonites, so that the new colony, the finest that will bear the flag of England, may have this well-built, elegantly organized, and populous town for its capital, – a town with real streets and hotels, with a grand post-office and a railroad. What more can a colony desire? But in that case Rockhampton also would be at the extremity, and the people north of that, – ay, five hundred miles to the north of it, as any man may see by looking at the map, – would have to send the sweat of their brows to that city. The coming golden era of sugar and northern gold is destined to bless a region nearer to the sun even than Rockhampton. Let Cape Palmerston be the point, and Bowen or Townsville the new capital. And so the matter is debated. With this question of course is mixed up that other question of moving the capital from Brisbane to Gladstone, – by which some southern politicians think that the difficulty may be tided over, and separation avoided for a time. Brisbane is certainly very much in a corner.

As to the intrinsic merits of the case, one is tempted to say, – on this as on almost all political questions connected with the colonies, – that the more men can divert their minds from such questions to their own individual interests, the better for them. There must be politicians among young colonists, and there must be houses of legislation, but the less there is of ambition in that direction, the quicker will fortunes be made and families established. The future sugar-grower of Port Mackay will not be so much injured by sending taxes to Brisbane as by having to devote his time to some nearer little parliament, whether in Rockhampton or Townsville. Parliaments, with their debates and all that volubility of words which Mr. Carlyle hates with such genuine vigour, are dear to my heart. Parliaments are to me the very salt of the earth. But, at the first glance, one is driven to doubt the expediency of a fresh parliament for ten thousand people, – the population of a one-membered borough at home, – when that ten thousand has so little of which to complain as have at present the inhabitants of Northern Queensland.

An Englishman cannot be a month in Australia without finding himself driven to speculate, – almost driven to come to some conclusion as to the future destinies of the colonies. At present they are loyal to England with an expressive and almost violent loyalty of which we hear and see little at home. There may be causes of quarrel on this or that subject of custom duties and postal subsidies. One colony may expostulate with a Secretary of State at home in language a little less respectful than another, in accordance with the temperament of the minister of the moment. But the feeling of the people is one of affectionate adherence to England, with some slight anger caused by a growing idea that England is becoming indifferent. The withdrawal of our troops, especially from New Zealand, has probably done more than anything else to produce an apprehension which is certainly unnecessary and, to my thinking, irrational. But the love of the colonies for England, and the Queen, and English government, – what may best probably be described as the adherence of the colonies to the mother country, – cannot be doubted. An Australian of the present day does not like to be told of the future independence of Australia. I think that I met no instance in which the proposition on my part was met with an unqualified assent. And yet it can hardly be doubted that the independence of Australia will come in due time. But other things must come first. Before that day shall arrive the bone and sinews of the colonies must be of colonial produce. The leading men must not only have grown up into life without the still-exciting feeling that England is their veritable 'home'. And I venture to express an opinion that another great change must have come first, as to the coming of which there is at present certainly no sign. The colonies will join themselves together in some Australian provinces, and will learn the political strength and commercial advantage of combined action. But there are difficulties in the way of such a union, which existed indeed in reference to the Canadas, Nova Scotia, and New Brunswick, but which make themselves felt with much greater violence in Australia. Nova Scotia and New Brunswick were hardly strong enough to persist in their jealous fears of a stronger sister, and the two Canadas had already become one before the Dominion was framed. The Australian colonies are very jealous of each other, and in their present moods are by no means ready to unite. Victoria claims supremacy, New South Wales disputes it, and Queensland looks to a future in which she shall become as large as either. South Queensland, thus ambitious, by no means desires internal separation; – but in all probability separation not only in Queensland, but further separation in New South Wales and in South Australia, will come before the federal union which will precede absolute independence. As Maine and New Hampshire were allowed to become States in the early days of American independence, as Kentucky was separated from Virginia, and Tennessee from North Carolina, so will Albertland, – by that or another name, – be divided from Queensland, the Riverinan districts from New South Wales, and some great northern province from South Australia. Whether Victoria will ever submit to division I will not venture to prophesy, – but even that may come. And thus a union of States will be formed infinitely stronger in its interests that can be any one of the colonies as they now exist.

On my way up to Rockhampton, at Maryborough, and again at Rockhampton, and at other places in the colonies, I went through the unsavoury duty of inspecting various meat-preserving establishments, to which is, as a matter of course, attached the still more distressing occupation of boiling down tallow. I should not like to meat-preserve or boil down myself, though I am assured that no more healthy employment can be found. The boiling down is an old trade in Australia, and has followed naturally on the growth of wool. Something has to be done with the dead sheep, and tallow can at any rate be exported. The sheep used to be boiled down without any reference to meat, and as they were of course bought at a proportionate price the boiling-down trade was not a bad one. That of preserving meat and sending it over to Europe is more speculative, and will be infinitely more important if it can be carried on successfully. With mutton at 10*d*. a pound in England and 2*d*. a pound in Australia there seems to be a large margin for expense and profit, if only the thing can be done so as to make the meat popular in England. If there be one thing that England wants and cannot get, – or at any rate has not yet gotten, – it is cheap animal food for her working classes.

Before I left England I bought some Australian preserved meat as an experiment, and for that I then paid 6*d*. a pound. It was sweet and by no means unpalatable, but was utterly tasteless as meat. Whether it did or did not contain the nutritive qualities of meat I am unable to say. Servants in my house would not eat it, – because, no doubt, they could get better. With such of the working classes as can afford themselves meat occasionally or in small quantities, – as to whom a saving in the cost of meat would be a matter of greatest consequence, – I could never find that it was in favour. As the preserved meats are without bone, they may, at the price above named, be regarded as being less than half the cost of first-class English meat. But I think that by most English workman half a pound of English fresh meat would be regarded with more favour than the whole pound of Australian tinned meat. The tinned meats are cooked and only require to be reheated. That they may be sent in better condition in regard to flavour as experience is gained, – sent with less cooking, for at present they are always overcooked, – is probable. Whether they can be sent cheaper is more open to doubt.

But meat is not only preserved. There is another operation by which beef or mutton is converted into essence, and this trade seems to thrive well. The essence is sold at 5s. a pound, and I was assured that it was sold as quickly as made. By means of this operation the traveller may carry an entire sheep, or all the nutritive part of his sheep, done up in a small parcel, in his coat pocket. On board ship, in hospitals, and for commissariat purposes, this essence, – which I presume owes its origin to Liebig, – is invaluable. For purposes of soup I declare it to be most excellent. I was once induced by a liberal manufacturer to put as much into my mouth as I could extract by thrusting my thumb into a can of it, and I felt as though I were pervaded by meatiness for many hours. I believe in the tallow. I believe in the essence. But I shall not believe in the cooked preserved meats, till growing science and increased experience shall have lessened the expense and raised the merit of the article.

CHAPTER III

GOLD

From Rockhampton I returned to Maryborough by steamboat, and from thence made my way back to Brisbane by coach, in order that I might see Gympie, famous for its gold. I found Maryborough to be an active little town with a good deal of business in the way of meat-preserving, timber-sawing, and sugar-making. Of Queensland sugar-growing I shall say a few words before I have done with the colony, as also of the Islanders, Polynesians, or Canakers, who are now much employed in Queensland, and whose services are specially needed among the sugar canes. At present I will pursue my journey on to Gympie.

I had been very much advised against the coach. I was told that the road, and the vehicle, and the horses, and the driving were so rough as to be unfit for a man of my age and antecedents. Our anxious friend implored me not to undertake it with an anxiety which could hardly have been stronger had I been his grandfather. I was, however, obstinate, and can now declare that I enjoyed the drive most thoroughly. It lasted three days, and took me through some magnificent scenery. Woodland country in Australia, – and it must be remembered that the lands occupied are mostly woodland, – is either bush or scrub. Woods which are open, and passable, – passable at any rate for men on horseback, – are called bush. When the undergrowth becomes thick and matted so as to be impregnable without an axe, it is scrub. In Queensland the scrubs are filled with tropical plants, – long vine tendrils, palms, and the parasite fig-tree, – and when a way has been cut through them the effect for a time is very lovely. The fault of all Australian scenery is its monotony. The eye after awhile becomes fatigued with a landscape which at first charmed with its park-like aspect. One never gets out of the trees, and then it

22

rarely happens that water lends its aid to improve the view. As a rule it must be acknowledged that a land of forests is not a land of beauty. Some experience in travelling is needed before this can be acknowledged, as every lover of nature is a lover of trees. But unceasing trees, trees which continue around you from six in the morning till six at night, become a bore, and the traveller begins to remember with regret the open charms of some cultivated plain. I had to acknowledge this monotony before I reached Brisbane, – but I acknowledged also the great beauty of the scrubs, and found some breaks in the mountains which were very grand.

Now for Gympie and its gold. Gympie in its early days was a great rush, – which means that when first the tidings were spread about through the colonies that gold was found at Gympie, the sudden flocking of miners to the place was very great. In those days, some ten years ago, when a new rush came out, the difficulty of supplying the men was excessive, and everything was consequently very dear. The rushes were made to spots in the middle of the forest, to which there were no roads, and to which carriage therefore was very difficult. In addition to this, men half intoxicated with the profusion of gold, which is both the cause and consequence of a new rush, are determined to have, not comforts, for they are unattainable, but luxuries which can be carried. A pair of sheets will be out of the question, but champagne may be had. In this way a singular mode of life seems to have established itself, – and the more singular in this, that the champagne element does not seem to have interfered with work. The miners when they are mining do not drink. Men drink at the gold-fields who are about to mine, or who have mined, or who are having a 'spell', – what we would call a short holiday. But they do not drink at their work, – will frequently work from Monday to Saturday, drinking nothing but tea, – having a fixed and wholesome opinion that work and play should be kept separate. And it may be well to remark here that Australian miners are almost invariably courteous and civil. A drunken man is never agreeable; but even a drunken miner is rarely quarrelsome. They do not steal, and are rough rather than rowdy. It seemed to me that very little care was taken, or was necessary, in the preservation of gold, the men trusting each

other with great freedom. There are quarrels about claims for
land, – and a claim is sometimes unjustly 'jumped'. The
jumping of a claim consists in taking possession of the land
and works of absent miners, who are presumed by their
absence to have deserted their claims. But such bickerings
rarely lead to personal violence. The miners do not fight and
knock each other about. They make constant appeals to the
government officer, – the police magistrate, or, above him, to
the gold commissioner of the district, – and they not unfrequently go to law. They do not punch each other's heads.

At the beginning of a rush the work consists, I think always,
in alluvial washing. Some lucky man or set of men, – three or
four together, probably, – 'prospecting' about the country,
come upon gold. This they are bound to declare to the
government, and it is now thoroughly understood by miners
that it is for their interest to declare it. The 'prospecter' is then
rewarded by being allowed to take up two or three men's
ground, as the case may be. And every miner is allowed to
take up a certain fixed share of ground on the sole condition
that it has not already been taken up by any other miner, and
that gold has been found in the neighbourhood. But the
'prospecter' has the double advantage of choosing the ground
where gold has certainly been found, and of having more
ground than any of his neighbours. And this prospecting may
go on from one side of a hill to another, or from one patch of
ground to another. The original 'prospecter' of Gympie had a
large pecuniary reward besides his double claim ; but at
Gympie there have been many 'prospecters', whose shafts, as
a rule, are placed in the middle of others bearing the same
name, belonging to men who have followed the prospecter.
Thus there will be Smithfield 'prospecting claim', and the
Smithfield Number One, north, and Number Two and
Three, north; and on the other side the Smithfield Numbers
One, Two, and Three, south.

But before there were any shafts Gympie was great with
surface-washing. The auriferous earth was dug up out of
gullies, creeks, and holes, and was then washed out by cradles.
The gold cradle has been so often described as to make it
hardly worth the reader's while to have the description
repeated to him. Puddling for gold I will attempt to explain

when I come to the New South Wales gold-fields. At Gympie, when I was there, the search for gold had taken the phase of regular mining in rock reefs. Shafts are sunk to the necessary depth, – say, perhaps, two hundred feet, – and the auriferous rock or quartz is drawn up in buckets by whins or wheels worked by horses. This rock is taken to a quartz-crushing machine, – which consists of fifteen or twenty stampers, which are worked by steam. The stone is thrown under the stampers, and is crushed by them almost to powder in a stream of water. The water carries the atoms through wire gauges on to a sloping bed, which is covered with flannel spread with quicksilver. And there are troughs filled with quicksilver across the beds. The quicksilver collects the gold, which is afterwards separated from it in a retort. So the gold is got out of a quartz-reef; but I have been assured that as much as twenty-five per cent. of the gold escapes with the refuse or is carried down by the water in the shape of minutely thin, floating gold-leaf. That there is gold in the refuse, or tailing as it is called, is known; but the reworking of it had not as yet been found to be a paying business when I was at Gympie.

An ounce of gold to a ton of raised quartz will, as a rule, pay very well. Of course this calculation cannot be taken to be applicable to all reefs, as the expense will be very various in different mines. At the New Zealand prospect shaft, down which I was taken, they were then getting six ounces of gold to the ton of stone, – so that the shareholders were prospering greatly. These mines or shafts are generally held by small companies of perhaps four or five each. Very little capital is required for the commencement of the work, – just enough to put up a little woodwork, buy a horse or two, and keep the men going, – who are the shareholders themselves, – till they find gold or give up the claim as worthless. A miner while at this work will live on 12s. a week, and the shareholding miner will probably be in partnership with another man who is earning miner's wages at some other claim. These wages run from £2 10s. to £3 a week. The two men therefore will live out of the sum earned by the one, and have a residue to throw into the expenses of their joint speculation.

I was astonished at the small amount of machinery used in comparison with the largeness of the proceeds. Indeed there was none except that applied to the perfectly distinct operation of crushing. The crushing is done by a distinct company, and the charge made at Gympie when I was there was 12s.6d. for a ton of quartz. The water is pumped up by horses, and not pumped by steam. The quartz is dragged up by horses. No company of miners crushes for itself. All seemed to be in a little way, although in some few instances the profits were very large. Different reasons for this were given; but the real reason was the precarious nature of the work, making it inexpedient for the miner to risk a large outlay on operations the productiveness of which may be brought to an end on any day. If it were not for this, the various little bands of men would no doubt club together, so as to acquire space for machinery, – for the claims as at present divided are not large enough to permit the erection of buildings for steam power, – and the heavy work of lifting and pumping could be done with a very great decrease of expense. But the gold found in any shaft may come to an end any day, – and then the money invested would be lost.

I have spoken of a happy family of miners, – of men who were getting six ounces of gold to every ton of quartz, and were realising, perhaps, £10 a day per man. They were a rough, civil, sober, hardworking lot, – four or five as I think, who were employing some four or five others, experienced miners, at £3 a week each. Among such a company it is impossible to recognise the social rank of each. There are what we call 'gentlemen', and what we call 'workmen'. But they dress very much alike, work very much alike, and live very much alike. The ordinary miner who came perhaps from Cornwall or Northumberland, and whose father was a miner before him, gets a lift in the world, – as regards manners and habits as well as position. The 'gentleman', even though in the matter of gold he be a lucky gentleman, gets a corresponding fall. He loses his gentility, his love of cleanliness, his ease of words, his grace of bearing, his preference for good company, and his social exigencies. There are some who will say that these things lost constitute a gain, – and that as long as the man is honest and diligent, earning his bread by high energy and running a chance of making a fortune, he is in every way doing better for himself than by thinking of his tub of cold water, his dress coat and trousers, his last new novel, and his next pretty girl. I cannot agree with these. Idle gentility doubtless is despicable. Idle, penniless, indebted gentility, gentility that will not work but is not ashamed to borrow, gentility that sports itself at clubs on the generosity of toiling fathers, widowed mothers, and good-natured uncles and aunts, is as low a phase of life as any that can be met. From that the rise to the position of a working miner is very great indeed. But gentility itself, – the combination of soft words, soft manners, and soft hands with manly bearing, and high courage, and intellectual pursuits, – is a possession in itself so valuable, and if once laid aside so difficult to be regained, that it should never be dropped without a struggle. I should be sorry to see a man I loved working in a gold-mine, sorry to see him successful in a gold-mine, – doubly sorry to see him unsuccessful, which has been the lot of by far the majority of enterprising gentlemen who have sought fortune on the Australian gold-fields.

I have spoken of a happy family, – but most of the mining families at Gympie were not so blessed. There were, perhaps, fifty or sixty reefing claims at Gympie, in which mining was actually in progress when I was there, but I did not hear of above ten in which gold was being found to give more than average wages, and I heard of many from which no gold was forthcoming. This claim had been abandoned, – that other was about worked out, – a third had been a mere flash in the pan, – at a fourth they had not got deep enough, and did not know that they ever would or could go deep enough, though they were still working hard with no returns, – at a fifth the gold would not pay the expenses. The stranger is of course taken to see the more successful ventures, and the thick streaks of gold which are shown him among the pet lumps of rock, kept by the miners in huge boxes instead of being thrown out among the unguarded heaps of quartz, produce a strange fascination. Where is the man who would not like to have a chest three times as big as a coffin full of such noble stones? But the traveller who desires to understand Gympie or any other digging, should endeavour to see the failures also. It is by no means every little wooden shanty near the mouth of a shaft that has such a box so filled. The unfortunate ones are not far to seek, – and they are very unfortunate though almost invariably brave. It seems to be an understood thing among Australian gold-diggers that a man is not to be querulous or downhearted in his plaints. They are free enough in speaking either of their good or bad fortune, – will own either to the one fact of £10 a day, or to the other that they have not earned a brass farthing for the last three weeks, – but they neither whine nor exult. They are gamblers who know how to bear the fortunes of the table.

Probably the class of miners which as a class does best is that of experienced men who work for wages. A good man, who has come out of England as a miner, or has learned his trade in California or the colonies, can generally earn £2 10s. or £3 a week. For this he must work underground nine or ten hours a day. But he can live very cheaply, – for 12s. or 15s. a week, – and yet, as far as bread and meat and tea are concerned, can live plenteously. To such a man two or three hundred pounds is a fortune, and he may earn his fortune very quickly. In ten years' time a man intent upon his object, and able to resist temptation, might return with £1,000. But unfortunately this is not the object on which they are intent, and they do not resist temptation. They all want to work for themselves, and generally, as I have said before, put their savings into other mines, – or rather live on their 12s. a week, in order that they may speculate with the money they save. The miner who works for himself and runs the hazard of the work is regarded as a higher being than he who contents himself with wages. Men will tell you that the real miner always 'goes on his own hook'. This feeling and the remoter chance of great wealth stand in the way of that permanent success which the working miner might otherwise enjoy.

And probably the class of miners which as a class does worst is that composed of young gentlemen who go to the diggings, led away, as they fancy, by a spirit of adventure, but more generally, perhaps, by a dislike of homely work at home. An office-stool for six or eight hours a day is disagreeable to them, or the profession of the law requires too constant a strain, or they are sick of attending lectures, or they have neglected the hospitals, – and so they go away to the diggings. They soon become as dirty as genuine diggers, but they do not quickly learn anything but the dirt. They strive to work, but they cannot work alongside of experienced miners, and consequently they go to the wall. They are treated with no contempt, for all men at the diggings are free and equal. As there is no gentility, such men are not subject to any reproach or ill-usage on that score. The miner does not expect that any airs will be assumed, and takes it for granted that the young man will not sin in that direction. Our 'gentleman', therefore, is kindly treated; but, nevertheless, he goes to the wall, and becomes little better than the servant, or mining hodsman, of some miner who knows his work. Perhaps he has a little money, and makes things equal with a partner in this way; but they will not long be equal, – for his money will go quicker than his experience will come. On one gold-field I found one young man whom I had known at home, who had been at school with my sons, and had frequented my house. I saw him in front of his little tent, which he occupied in partnership with an experienced working miner, eating a beefsteak out of his frying-pan with his clasp-knife. The occupation was not an alluring one, but it was the one happy moment of his day. He was occupied with his companion on a claim, and his work consisted in trundling a rough windlass, by which dirt was drawn up out of a hole. They had found no gold as yet, and did not seem to expect to find it. He had no friend near him but his mining friend, – or mate, as he called him. I could not but think what would happen to him if illness came, or if his mate should find him too far removed from mining capability. He had been softly nurtured, well educated, and was a handsome fellow to boot; and there he was eating a nauseous lump of beef out of a greasy frying-pan with his pocket-knife, just in front of the contiguous blankets stretched on the ground, which constituted the beds of himself and his companion. It may be that he will strike gold and make a fortune. I hope so with all my heart. But my strong and repeated advice to all young English gentlemen is to resort to any homely mode of earning their bread in preference to that of seeking gold in Australia.

I do not believe that gold-seeking in Australia has been remunerative to any class of men as a class. The gold found is sold to the mint or to the banks at prices varying from £3 10s.

to £4 2s. an ounce. £3 15s. the ounce may perhaps be taken as an average price. I have been assured by those whose profession it has been to look into the matter that all the gold in Australia has been raised at an expense of not less than £5 the ounce. For myself, I can only say that I fully believe the statement. The calculation is one that cannot be made with such accuracy as to afford statistics in the matter. It is impossible to say at what price gold has been raised. If all the capital expended could be known, expended not only in work, but in bringing gold-seekers into the country, – still it would be impossible to estimate the value in wages of the time and work which have been consumed. This, however, is clear, that if a man could have earned £5 whilst he has been getting an ounce of gold to be sold for £3 15s., he has raised that gold at £5 the ounce, and has thus lost £1 5s. by the venture. And if, as was the case in the early days of gold-digging, his living during his gold work cost him 10s. more than would have done his living at other employment, then he raised his gold at £5 10s. the ounce, and lost £1 15s. by the venture. All rates of wages and cost of living were so thrown out of gear throughout the colonies by the early gold rushes, that no exact calculation can be made. Shearers demanded and got £10 a hundred for shearing sheep, whereas the present price may be about 17s. 6d. a hundred. £1 a day was by no means extravagant wages for a groom. Everything for a while was on the same footing, because every man was taught to believe that he had only to rush to the gold-fields to pick up a fortune. But the men who picked up fortunes are very rare. One never meets them. But the men who just failed during this time to pick up fortunes one meets at every corner. 'Ah,' says one, 'if I had gone away from such and such a rush when I had that £7,000.' 'I might have walked off with £12,000 after the first three months at Ballaarat,' says a second. 'I had £15,000 at one time out of Ophir,' says a third. 'Gympie was Gympie when I was rolling up £2,000 a month,' says a fourth. Of course a question is asked as to what has become of these grand sums. The answer is always the same, though probably not always strictly true. The fortunes already made have been lost in pursuit of greater fortunes. It is not admitted that the money has been spent in useless, new-fangled luxuries; but that much has been so spent is certain. The Phoenix who has made his fortune at the diggings, and kept it, is a bird hardly to be found on Australian ground.

Gympie as a town was a marvellous place, and to my eyes very interesting, though at the same time very ugly. Its population was said to consist of about six thousand souls, but I found throughout the country that no statement of the population of a gold-field could be taken as accurate. The men go and come so quickly that the changes cannot be computed. It consists of a long street stretching more than a mile, – up and down hill, – without a single house in it that looked as though it had been built to last ten years. And probably no house had been built with any such ambition, although Gympie is now more than ten years old. The main street contains stores, banks, public-houses, a place of worship or two, and a few eating-houses. They are framed of wood, one storey high, generally built in the first place as sheds with a gable end to the street, on to which, for the sake of importance, a rickety wooden facade has been attached. The houses of the miners, which are seldom more than huts, are scattered over the surrounding little hills, here and there, as the convenience of the men in regard to the different mining places has prompted the builders. All around are to be seen the holes and shallow excavations made by the original diggers, and scattered among them the bigger heaps which have been made by the sinking of deep shafts. When a mine is being worked there is a rough wooden windlass over it, and at a short distance the circular track of the unfortunate horse who, by his rotary motion, pulls the buckets up with the quartz, and lets them down with the miners. Throughout all there stands the stunted stumps of decapitated trees, giving the place a look of almost unearthly desolation. At a distance beyond the mine-shafts are to be seen the great forests which stretch away on every side over almost unlimited distance. If at any place one is tempted to quote the 'aurum irrepertum et sic melius situm', it is at such a place as Gympie.

There is a hospital, and there are schools, which are well attended, and, as I have before said, various places of worship. I put up at an inn kept by a captain, which I found to be fairly comfortable, and by no means expensive. There were a crowd of men there, all more or less concerned in the search of gold, with whom I found myself to be quite intimate before the second night was over; and from whom, – as from everybody at Gympie, – I received much civility, and many invitations to drink brandy and water.

CHAPTER IV

SQUATTERS AND THEIR TROUBLES

Undoubtedly the staple of Australian wealth is wool, and the growers and buyers and sellers of Australian wool are the chief men of the colonies. In Queensland, when I was there, six out of the seven ministers of the Crown were squatters, men owning runs for sheep or cattle. The cattle are reared chiefly for home consumption. The wool is all exported. As wool goes up or down in the London markets, so does the prosperity of Australia vacillate. Any panic in commercial matters of Europe which brings down the price of wool, – as panics have done most cruelly, – half ruins the colonies. Sheep sink in value from 10s. and 7s. 6d. a head to 4s. to 2s. Squatters' runs become valueless and unsaleable, and the smaller squatters, who are almost invariably in debt to the merchants, have to vanish. Then, when trade becomes steady again and wool rises, sheep again resume their former value, and the rich men who during the panic have taken up almost deserted sheep-walks become richer and richer.

The great drawback to the squatter's prosperity is to be found in the fact that a large proportion of them commence a great business with very insufficient capital. A man with £5,000 undertakes to pay £30,000 for a run, and finds himself enabled to enter in upon the possession of perhaps forty thousand sheep and the head station or house which has been built. To all outward appearance he is the owner. He manages everything. He employs and pays the various hands. He puts up fences and erects washpools. He buys and sells flocks. He makes great bales of wool, which he sends to Sydney, to Melbourne, or to London, as he pleases. Any rise in the price of wool is his good fortune, any fall is his calamity. But still he is little more than the manager for others. He has probably bought his run from a bank or from a merchant's house which has held a mortgage on it before, and the mortgage is continued. He has simply paid away the £5,000 to make the security of the mortgage commercially safe. At home when we speak of mortgaged property we allude as a rule to some real estate in land or houses. The squatter's real estate is generally very small, – and, as I shall explain presently, the smaller the better. The property mortgaged consists of the squatter's sheep, – and of his precarious right to feed his flocks on certain large tracts of land, which are the property of the public, and which are for the most part open to purchase. He is not therefore in reality left to himself in the management of his business, as would be a landowner in England who had mortgaged the land which he either farmed himself or let to a tenant. In such case the security of the mortgage would rest on the land, and the farmer would conduct his farming operations without let or hindrance. It is far otherwise with the squatter. The security he has given rests on his wool, and the price of his wool therefore must pass through the hands of the merchant to whom the debt is due. Nor can he lessen his stock of sheep without accounting to the merchant for the price of the sheep sold. The merchant is of course bound to see that the security on which his money has been advanced is not impaired. Consequently the whole produce of the run goes into the merchant's hands. When the wool is sent off, – say direct to London, – an estimated sum on account of its value is placed to the squatter's credit. When the wool has been sold the balance is also placed to his credit. But the money does not come into his hands. The same rule prevails very generally in regard to sheep sold. Consequently the squatter's produce all goes from him, and he is driven to draw upon the merchant for the money necessary to maintain his station, to pay his wages, and to live. It would appear at first sight as though the squatter could lose nothing by such an arrangement. As soon as the merchant receives the money for the wool, the squatter ceases to be charged with interest for so much. And when a sum is advanced to him, he again pays interest for so much, – according to the terms which may exist between him and the merchant. The rate of interest may be eight, nine, or ten per cent, according to the value of the original security. But in addition to this the merchant adds a commission of two and a half per cent. on every new advance, – so that the squatter in giving up his produce pays off a debt bearing say eight per cent interest, and in drawing money to defray his expenses incurs fresh debt at say ten and a half per cent. interest. If things go well with him, he may no doubt free himself even at this rate. If he can sell his wool and sheep every year for £6,000, and carry on his station for £3,000, he will gradually, – but very slowly, – lessen his debt in spite of the interest which he pays. And he will live and the merchant will probably not disturb him. If everything should go well with him, – if his ewes be prolific, if diseases do not decimate his flock, if neither droughts nor floods oppress him, if wool maintain its price, if he cling to his work and be able to deny himself the recreation of long absences from his station, he may succeed in working himself free. But against a man so circumstanced the chances are very strong. Sheep are subject to diseases. Lambing is not always prosperous. Drought and floods do prevail in Australia. And the price of wool vacillates wonderfully, – very wonderfully to the eyes of a non-commercial man who observes that whatever happens in the world men still wear coats and trousers. And when these misfortunes come they fall altogether on the squatter who has begun by owning only one-sixth of the property, and not at all on the merchant who has owned the other five-sixths. At such periods, – when misfortune comes, – the squatter's debt begins to swell instead of dwindle. The produce will not pay for the expenses and the ever-running interest. The thousands down in the book begin to augment, and the merchant begins to see that he must secure himself. Then the station passes into other hands, – into the hands probably of some huge station-owner, who, having commenced life as a shepherd or a drover, has now stations of his own all over the colonies, and money to advance on all such properties, – and our friend with his £5,000 vanishes away, or becomes perhaps the manager with a fixed salary of the very sheep which he used to consider his own.

For a squatter of the true commercial kind not to owe money to his merchant or his banker is an unusual circumstance, – unless he be one who has stuck to his work till he is able to lend instead of borrow. The normal, and I may almost say the proper, condition of a squatter is indebtedness to some amount. The business of squatting would be very restricted, country life in Australia very different from what it is, the amount of wool produced for the benefit of the world woefully diminished, and the extension of enterprise over new lands altogether checked, if no capital were to be invested in the pursuit of squatting except that owned by the squatters themselves. No doubt this, the greatest interest of Australia, has been created and fostered by the combination of squatters and merchants. If the squatter commencing business can do so owing no more than half the value of his run he will probably do well, and in time pay off his debt. If the man with £5,000 will content himself with 12,000 sheep instead of 40,000 and will borrow another £5,000 instead of £25,000, he will find that there is something like a fair partnership between himself and the merchant, and that gradually his partner will be unnecessary to him. His partner, while the partnership lasts, will be getting at least ten per cent. for his money, but in such a condition of things the squatter will get twenty per cent. for his money. No doubt there will still be risks, from which the town partner will be comparatively free, – but unless there come heavy misfortunes indeed these risks will not break the squatter's back if his burden be no heavier than that above described.

The amount of debt in some stations is enormous, and the total interest paid, including bank charges, commission, and what not, frequently amounts to twenty per cent. When this state of things arises, the nominal squatter enjoys a certain security arising from the ambitious importance of his indebtedness, – due even to his own absolute insolvency. Were the merchant to sell him up and get rid of him, more than half the debt must be written off as absolutely bad. In such cases it may be better to maintain the squatter, on condition that he will work at the station. The squatter is maintained, – and lives like other squatters a jolly life. The rate at which his house is kept will depend rather on the number of the sheep to be shorn than on his own income. He has no income, but the station is maintained, and among the expenses of the station are his wife's dresses and his own brandy and water.

I don't know that there can be a much happier life than that of a squatter, if the man be fairly prosperous, and have natural aptitudes for country occupations. He should be able to ride and

to shoot, – and to sit in a buggy all day without inconvenience. He should be social, – for he must entertain often
and be entertained by other squatters; but he must be indifferent to society, for he will live away from towns and be
often alone with his family. He must be able to command
men, and must do so in a frank and easy fashion, – not
arrogating to himself any great superiority, but with full
power to let those around him know that he is master. He
must prefer plenty to luxury, and be content to have things
about him a little rough. He must be able to brave troubles,–
for a squatter has many troubles. Sheep will go amiss. Lambs
will die. Shearers will sometimes drink. And the bullocks with
the most needed supplies will not always arrive as soon as they
are expected. And, above all things, the squatter should like
mutton. In squatters' houses plenty always prevails, but that
plenty often depends upon the sheep-fold. If a man have these
gifts, and be young and energetic when he begins the work, he
will not have chosen badly in becoming a squatter. The sense
of ownership and mastery, the conviction that he is the head
and chief of what is going on around; the absence of any
necessity of asking leave or submitting to others, – these
things in themselves add a charm to life. The squatter owes
obedience to none, and allegiance only to the merchant, – who
asks no questions so long as the debt be reduced or not
increased. He gets up when he pleases and goes to bed when
he likes. Though he should not own an acre of the land around
him, he may do what he pleases with with all that he sees. He
may put up fences and knock them down. He probably lives
in the middle of a forest, – his life is always called life in the
bush, – and he may cut down any tree that he fancies. He has
always horses to ride, and a buggy to sit in, and birds to shoot
at, and kangaroos to ride after. He goes where he likes, and
nobody questions him. There is probably no one so big as
himself within twenty miles of him, and he is proud with the
conviction that he knows how to wash sheep better than any
squatter in the colony. But the joy that mostly endears his life
to him is the joy that he need not dress for dinner.

Queensland is divided into settled and unsettled districts, of
which the settled districts include only a very small portion as
compared with the immense area of the whole colony. It

comprises the coast line running back in some places hardly more than twenty miles, and in others, in which the space is broadest, hardly more than two hundred. The laws in regard to the tenure of land within these so-called settled and unsettled districts is different, – the chief difference consisting in this, that half of every run within the settled districts is open to purchase by any selecters after the fashion described in a previous chapter. In the unsettled districts no such privilege was granted by the law of 1868, because no such privilege would have been of use. No intending agriculturist, purposing to fix his family and to live on a portion of land for which money must be paid, would dream for some years to come of fixing his abode and sowing his seed beyond the line as marked by government. Nor would the survey of such lands have availed anything. There the squatters reign supreme, – more supremely even than the squatter nearer to civilisation. But the very distance of his station makes his existence less important to the colony than that of his nearer brother. His enterprise is not so great, though his courage and perseverance may be quite equal. The Darling Downs are within the line of the settled districts, and beyond them I did not go.

It must be understood, therefore, that the run of the Darling Downs squatter is open to sale, and that he has been terribly injured in his otherwise prosperous career by the law of 1868, which devoted half of his run to free-selection. But the free-selecter who has most injured the Darling Downs squatter is the squatter himself, and for this reason I said that the less land the squatter owned himself, the better. The land selected on the Darling Downs district greatly exceeds in area that purchased in any other, but the squatters have themselves made the selections. They have thought themselves compelled to become purchasers of land on their own runs to the full extent given them by the law, not because they wanted to possess the land in fee, but in order that others might not come near them and disturb them. Anything to them was better than a free-selecting cattle-stealer at their gates. They have, therefore, purchased land by tens of thousands of acres. In this way a vast extent of country has fallen into the hands of the squatters, so as to become veritably their own, if the due installments are paid to the Crown as they become due. If a squatting firm, – for the large stations are generally held by firms, or by two or three of a family together, – should have thus purchased, say 40,000 acres of even the lower class of pastoral land, – land to be purchased within ten years at 6d. an acre in each year, – £1,000 a year would have to be paid to the Crown for those ten years. But this payment would in no degree increase the squatter's means. He would enjoy no power of producing wealth from the land which was not his to the same extent before. His sheep would still run there as his sheep have hitherto run. But the squatter in but few cases was prepared to make these payments out of his own pocket. He was in partnership with the merchant, and the merchant would make the payment. But the matter was of no great concern to the merchant himself. He was not to be even part purchaser. He pays the money annually, but charges the account with his eight, ten, or twelve per cent. according to his agreement, and so the squatter's debt is increased from year to year without any increase to the squatter's means. It may be imagined, therefore, how odious must be the free-selecter to the squatter, although of all free-selecters he is himself by far the most extensive.

I had heard much of all this before I went to the Darling Downs, and I was prepared to hear the question discussed. I cannot but think that it would have been better to welcome the free-selecter, – to have him come and select if he would, – and to have endured him. In 1878, even if no new law should do so before, the half of each run not now open to selection will be in the same category, and the same play must be played again. The more I have seen on the subject, and the more I have heard, the more certain I feel that pastoral pursuits in Queensland will not bear the expense of purchased land. The very system of squatting is based on the idea that the land shall be free, – free with the exception of some annual fee paid to the Crown for license to pasture. The buying up of lands for agricultural purposes has progressed, and must progress slowly, and the squatters feel secure in the fact that large purchases could not be remunerative to anybody. No free-selecter, selecting for the purpose of living on the agricultural produce of his land, could buy any great number of acres. Gradually, but very slowly, men of this class would spread themselves over the settled districts, – and it was the wise intention of the colonial legislature that they should be encouraged to do so. Gradually, but very slowly, the squatter would be driven back from the neighbourhood of rising townships into the vast pastoral areas further back from the coast line. But these men, the aristocracy of the country, were impatient of such treatment, and too proud to endure such neighbours; and therefore they have bought the land themselves. They argue that, as the climate is unsuitable for agricultural pursuits, – as wheat cannot be made to grow in these regions with any permanent success, – the free-selecting farmer cannot live on his farm by honest labour, and that he will therefore live dishonestly. The squatter declares that the normal free-selecter makes his small purchase in order that he may be enabled to steal cattle with impunity, and live after that fashion. He will make any effort, – almost any sacrifice, – to keep the normal free-selecter from his paddocks.

Undoubtedly, the crime of cattle-stealing, – of cattle-stealing and sheep-stealing and horse stealing, – is one of the greatest curses of the Australian colonies. The pastures are so extensive, and therefore so little capable of being easily watched, that the thefts can always be made without difficulty. Every animal is branded, and the brands are all registered. One never sees even an unbranded horse in Australia, unless it be a wild animal in the woods. But the brands are altered, or else the carcasses are carried away while the skins are left. And there is undoubtedly a feeling in the pastoral districts of Australia, among the class of men who labour on the land, that the squatter is fair game for such depredations. We all know the difficulty which is felt in Ireland as to getting evidence against the perpetrators of agrarian violence. There is the same difficulty in these colonies with reference to the cattle-stealer. He has with him much of the sympathy of all men of his own class, – and there are many who do not dare to give evidence against him. The law is severe, but it is too often inoperative.

Very much that the squatter alleges against the free-selecter is true. In arguing the question, as I have done with many a squatter, I always took the part of the free-selecter, expressing a strong opinion that he was the very man whom the colony should be most anxious to encourage, and urging that if here and there a free-selecter should become a thief, the law should be made to deal with him, – but not the least did I feel that the gentleman with whom I might be conversing knew very well where his own shoe pinched him. A peculiar crime has grown up in Australia, – and is attended by one of the worst circumstances which can accompany crime. It has assumed a quasi-respectability among the class of men who are tempted to commit it. It is like smuggling, or illicit distillation, or sedition, or the seduction of women. There is little or no shame attached to it among those with whom the cattle-stealers live. It is regarded as fair war by the small agriculturist against the ascendant squatter. A man may be a cattle-dealer, and yet in his way a decent fellow. I was once standing by, over a kangaroo which we had hunted, and which a free-selecter who had made one in the hunt was skinning. There were two or three others also by. The man was a good sportsman, but I had been told that he liked other people's meat. 'You have heard of the cattle-stealers, sir,' he said, looking up at me; 'this is the way they do it by moonlight, I'm told.' He skinned the kangaroo with great skill and quickness, and I was sure that he was no novice at the business. He knew well enough that by what he did and what he said he was owning himself to have been a cattle-stealer, but he was not a bit ashamed of it.

Nevertheless, I think the free-selecter should be welcomed as a farmer, – although it may often be necessary to punish him, or even but to try to punish him as a cattle-stealer. The more general he becomes, the less necessary it will be for the squatters to depend for their work on the nomad tribe of wandering men which infest the pastoral districts. The squatter's work is of such a nature that he requires very few hands during, perhaps, eight or nine months of the year, and a great many during the other three or four. From the commencement of the washing of his sheep to the packing of the last bale of wool, all is hurry, scurry, and eager business on the station. During those three or four months men are earning from him very high wages, and it is indispensable to him that he should have a large amount of skilled labour. Through the other eight or nine months, their men vanish from the station, and have to live elsewhere, either on their savings or on other labour, – or by a species of beggary which is common in the colonies and the weight of which falls altogether on the squatters. Now the free-selecter, who is also a shearer, has a home to go to, and other pursuits of his own. This temporary work suits his needs, and enables him to live on his bit of land without stealing cattle. And then the free-selecter will come whether he be welcomed or not. As he is a necessity, it must surely be wise to make the best of him.

The nomad tribe of pastoral labourers, – of men who profess to be shepherds, boundary-riders, sheep-washers, shearers, and the like, – form altogether one of the strangest institutions ever known in a land, and one which to my eyes is more degrading and more injurious even than that other institution of sheep-stealing. It is common to all the Australian colonies, and has arisen from the general feeling of hospitality which is always engendered in a new country by the lack of sufficient accommodation for travellers. In the pastoral districts it is understood that when hospitality is demanded from a squatter it shall be given. At small stations there are two classes of welcome. The labouring man, with his 'swag' over his back, – the 'swag' being his luggage, comprising probably all the property he has in the world, – is sent to the 'hut'. There is a hut at every station, fitted up with bunks, in which the workmen sleep. Here the wanderer is allowed to stretch his blanket for the night, – and on all such occasions two meals are allowed to him. He has meat and flour in the morning, and meat and flour in the evening. Then he passes on his way. If the traveller be of another description, – a squatter himself, an overseer journeying from one station to another, a man who on any pretence claims to be akin to gentlehood, – he is taken into the squatter's house, and sits at the squatter's table, and has tea as well as bread and meat, – and brandy and water, if brandy and water be the family beverage. On large stations, at which the overseer has a separate residence, travellers of this superior class are relegated to his house, and the great squatter hears nothing about it, – except that he defrays the cost of the entertainment. In this way a wide hospitality is exercised, which has become proverbial; which, when thus described, has an Arcadian charm about it which is quite refreshing to the imagination, – but which has led to a terrible evil under which the squatter groans with all but acknowledged impotence.

This evil concerns only the first-named class of wanderer. I have heard no squatter complain of the burden of entertaining men who are travelling from one part of the colonies to another on legitimate business. A certain allowance is made for the expense, and the practice is recognised as being convenient to all parties. But it has come to be very far from convenient as regards the so-called workman with his 'swag'. By many men it has been found to be a way of living which enables them to spend in rapid debauch the money earned by the labour of a few months, and to exist in idleness during the remainder of the year. By many others it has been adopted as the practice of the entire twelvemonth. The expense thus entailed upon stations has become incredibly great. One gentleman told me that such men cost him £300 a year. I heard of a squatter's establishment in Victoria at which £1,000 a year was expended in this involuntary entertainment of vagabond strangers. And the evil by no means ends here. A mode of life is afforded to recusant labourers which enables men to refuse work at fair terms, and to rebel against their masters when their work or their wages are not to their liking. They know that the squatters of the colonies do not dare to refuse them food and shelter.

Such men, when they appear, generally ask for work. They not unfrequently come on horseback, and always bring their luggage, – a blanket, a tin pot, and some small personalities wrapped up in the blanket. The squatter, or more probably the overseer, knows very well from the man's aspect that he does not mean to work. Sometimes he is asked to chop wood before he has his supper, but as a rule it is understood that such a demand will not be efficacious for any good purpose. It is better to let him have his lump of meat and his flour, with use of a bunk, – and then pass on to the next squatter. But the lump of meat, and the flour, and the use of the bunk he must have.

But why must he have them? The overseer could refuse the accustomed liberality, and the man with some growling would pass on and 'camp out' with an empty stomach under some log. Or why, at any rate, should not the food be refused till it have been first earned by sufficient work? 'There be the logs, my friend. Reduce them to convenient firewood, – as may be done by three hours' work, – and you shall be fed. Dark is it? Then you should come earlier and earn your victuals. But victuals without earning you shall not have.' The squatter who did so would be at once known; his sheep would be slaughtered; his fences would be burned; and his horses would be houghed. The vagabond wayfarers are too numerous and too strong, and are able to obtain by terrorism that which hospitality no longer bestows. A squatter with his fences burned would be a ruined man.

The social injury which I have endeavoured to describe is worse even to the pastoral labourer himself than to the squatter. The squatter can live and bear it, – though the burden is grievous to him. Meat is cheap, – and if the station be small the calls on him are comparatively few. But the men themselves who practise this life are reduced almost to savagery. They become at last no better than the blacks. They wander about in desolate solitude, idle, worthless, and wretched. The idleness has been the charm, – but we all know how infinite is the misery which that charm produces.

I have attempted to describe some of the great troubles under which squatters labour, – namely debt, free-selecters, and vagabonds. But they have also many others. Drought, floods, foot-rot among their flocks, wild dogs, – or dingoes, – which prey upon their lambs and flurry their sheep, grass-seed which injures the wool, and works its way through the skins of the lambs, utterly destroying the poor little bleaters, grass that is overgrown and rank, grass that won't grow, poisonous grass, too much grass, no grass, – and then that worst of all miseries, panic in the wool trade. But these are not social in their nature, and I will not venture to give any opinion of the best way of meeting them. As to the debt, – I am clear on this point, that a moderate station with a moderate debt, is better than a big station with a big debt. As to the free-selecter, – I believe it will be the wisest course to welcome him and make the best of him. As to the vagabond labourer who won't labour, I do not doubt that all squatters will agree with me in saying that he should be abolished altogether.

CHAPTER V

DARLING DOWNS

When I was in Brisbane in the beginning of August I was told by one of the great squatters of the district which I intended to visit that if I would come up about the second week in September I should see the Downs in all their glory, – vast expanses of verdant plain, waving with grass, and greener than fields in England in the month of May. In regard to date I obeyed my friend to the letter, leaving Brisbane on the 4th of September, and returning to it on the 21st. But, alas, my friend had made his promise without remembering how fickle on such occasions are the winds which bring, or the winds which withhold, rain from the Australian plains. Rain was due, and my friend had counted on genial showers. But not a drop had fallen. When I was in the neighbourhood of Rockhampton, sheep and cattle were dying from want of water and want of grass. I was told then that not a drop had fallen for six months. Not a drop had fallen when I started to the Downs, and not a drop had fallen when I left them. I saw the plains, but I saw them either black with fire, – for it is the custom there to burn off the old dry withered grass which the sheep will not eat, in order that the young shoots may have room to spring, – either black with fire or brown with droughts. The roots stood apart, stiff, rough, and unappetizing to any sheep, – showing the bare black soil between the intervals, showing here and there broad fissures, thirsty, gaping, and ugly. It seemed to me to be a miracle that any sheep could live so pastured. The name of 'Darling Downs' is given to this district because it differs from the great majority of the area occupied by Australian squatters in this, – that the land is open instead of being covered by wood. It consists of vast level plains more like the prairies of Illinois than any other region I have seen, – though very much less in extent than the prairies. Even on the Darling Downs one gets almost beyond the sight of trees; whereas the squatter generally lives 'in the bush', as the phrase goes, and pastures his sheep among thick woodlands.

I went by coach to the town of Ipswich, and stayed there a day, seeing with due diligence all the institutions of the place. There was a handsome school for the sons of men of the better class, towards the expense of which £1,000 per annum is defrayed from the general taxes of the country. Then there was the post-office, and a public room for the purposes of amusement and instruction which did not seem to be much used, two or three mercantile establishments, and the usual assortment of rectangular streets which no doubt is convenient, but which seems to forbid any new town to be picturesque. But the great glory of Ipswich is the fact that it returns three members of parliament. It has a population of about five thousand persons. Rockhampton with about the same number returns one member. This appeared to be another argument for separation. But I was assured that as Brisbane had four members, – or in reality five, for its suburb of Fortitude Valley returns a member, – it was indispensable that Ipswich should have at least three. The two favoured towns, with a joint population of eighteen thousand, return exactly a quarter of the members sent to parliament by the entire colony, with a population of one hundred and twenty thousand. This also seemed to tend the same way.

From Ipswich I rode across Cunningham Gap, through the range of hills which runs down the whole eastern coast of Australia, dividing the narrow eastern strip of the continent from the wide plains of the interior, staying a night at a station on each foot of the mountains. I am inclined to think that this was the prettiest scenery that I saw in Queensland. The two houses were beautifully situated, and the ride between them was magnificent. In going over the gap itself we were obliged to dismount and climb; but the climbing was by no means Alpine in its nature, – as will be understood when I say that we drove our horses before us. Any one who may visit Queensland as a tourist should certainly pass through Cunningham Gap.

I was hardly yet upon the Downs, and at these stations under the mountains did not find things all black and brown as I did when I reached the plains, but even here there was a cry for rain, and a feeling that unless rain came soon squatting affairs would begin to 'look blue'.

Thence I went to the little town of Warwick, which in that part of the world is held to be the perfection of a town. 'You will think Warwick very pretty,' everybody said to me. I did not think Warwick at all pretty. It is unfinished, parallel-ogrammic, and monotonous; and the mountains are just too far from it to give any attraction, – as is also the sluggish Condamine River. It is not so rugged as are many of the towns. And, though here as in other colonial towns the houses are intermittent and every other lot apparently vacant, there has been an eye to decency. But when I am told that such a place is pretty, I do not know what the speaker means. That it should be clean is creditable; that it should be progressive is satisfactory, – but that it should be ugly is a necessity of its condition. I found Warwick to be clean, and I believe it to be prosperous, – and, which was very much to my purpose, I found in it an excellent inn, kept by one Budgen. And I found there Chang, the great Chinese giant, about to show himself at 2s. a head on the evening of my arrival. But I had not come from London to Warwick to see Chang, and I neglected an opportunity which, perhaps, may never occur to me again.

From Warwick I got by railway to the first of the great Darling Down stations, which I visited, and from thence went on across country from one to another till I had visited some six or seven of those which are the largest and the most renowned. It is not my purpose to give any description of each, as I could hardly do so without personal references, which are always distasteful when hospitality has been given and taken. To say that Mr. Smith's house is well-built or his wife agreeable is almost as great a sin as to declare that Mr. Jones's wine was bad or his daughter ugly. At all these houses I found a plentiful easy life, full of material comfort, informal, abundant, careless, and most unlike life in England. There were two great faults, namely these, – that a man was expected to eat two dinners every day, and that no credence could be given when any hour was named for any future event. Breakfast at eight would simply mean to the stranger, after some short experience, that the meal would be ready some time after nine. A start promised for ten is thought to be made very punctually if effected at eleven. As regards the evening meal, the second dinner, there is no pretence of any solicitude as to time. There is nothing to be done after it, and therefore what can it matter? This second dinner differs from the first only in this, – that there is always tea on the table. There is often tea also in the middle of the day. But the generous liver need on that account have no fear at all that he will be debarred from other beverages. In the squatter's house there is always brandy and water within reach, and the teapot, after breakfast, is generally flanked by the decanter. The products of the colonies are always dear to the colonial mind, and sometimes praise is expected for colonial wine which a prejudiced old Englishman feels that he can hardly give. I have also been frowned upon by bright eyes because I could not eat stewed wallabi. Now the wallabi is a little kangaroo, and to my taste is not nice to eat even when stewed to the utmost with wine and spices.

It was a very pleasant life that I led at these stations. I like tobacco and brandy and water, with an easy-chair out on a verandah, and my slippers on my feet. And I like men who are energetic and stand up for themselves and their own properties. I like having horses to ride and kangaroos to hunt, and sheep became quite a fascination to me as a subject of conversation. And I liked that roaming from one house to another, – with a perfect conviction that five minutes would make me intimate with the next batch of strangers. Men in these Colonies are never ashamed of their poverty; nor are they often proud of their wealth. In all country life in Australia there is an absence of any ostentation or striving after effect, – which is delightful. Such as their life is, the squatters share it with you, giving you, as is fitting for a stranger, the best they have to give. Upon the Darling Downs the stations are large and the accommodation plentiful; but I have been on many sheep-runs which were not so well found, – at which bed-rooms were scarce, and things altogether were less well arranged. But there is never any shame as to the inferiority, never any pretence at superiority. What there is, is at your service. If there be not a whole bedroom for you, there is half a bedroom. If there be not wine, there is brandy or rum, – if no other meat, there is at least mutton. If the house be full, some young man can turn out and go to the barracks, or sleep on the verandah. If all the young men have been turned out the old men can follow them. It is a rule of life on a sheep-run that the station is never so full that an other guest need be turned away.

These houses, – stations as they are called, – are built after a very simple and appropriate fashion. There is not often any upper storey. Every room is on the ground floor. There is always a verandah, running the length of the house, and not unfrequently continued round the ends. The rooms all open out upon the verandah, and generally have no communication with each other. The kitchen is invariably a separate building, usually attached to the house by a covered way. When first building his residence the squatter probably has had need for but small accommodation, and has constructed his house with perhaps three rooms. Children have come, and guests, and increased demands, and increased house-room has been wanted. Another little house has therefore been joined on to the first, and then perhaps a third added. I have seen an establishment consisting of seven such little houses. Many hours are passed in the verandah, in which old people sit in easy-chairs and young men lie about, seeming to find the boards soft enough for luxurious ease. Attached to the station there is always a second home called the barracks, or the cottage, in which the young men have their rooms. There are frequently one or two such young men attached to a sheep-station, either learning their business or earning salaries as superintendents. According to the terms of intimacy existing, or to the arrangements made, these men live with the squatter's family or have a separate table of their own. They live a life of plenty, freedom, and hard work, but one which is not surrounded by the comforts which young men require at home. Two or three share the same room, and the washing apparatus is chiefly supplied by the neighbouring creek. Tubs are scarce among them, but bathing is almost a rule of life. They are up and generally on horseback by daylight, and spend their time in riding about after sheep. The general idyllic idea of Arcadian shepherd-life, which teaches us to believe that Tityrus lies under a beech-tree most of his hours, playing on his reed and 'spooning' Phyllis, is very unlike the truth in Australian pastures. Corin is nearer the mark when he tells Touchstone of his greasy hands. It is a life, even for the upper shepherd of gentle birth and sufficient means, of unremitting labour amidst dust and grease, amidst fleeces and carcasses. The working squatter, or the squatter's working assistant, must be a man capable of ignoring the delicacies of a soft way of living. He must endure clouds of dust, and be not averse to touch tar and oil, wool, and skins. He should be able to catch a sheep and handle him almost as a nurse does a baby. He should learn to kill a sheep, and wash a sheep, and shear a sheep. He should tell a sheep's age by his mouth, – almost by his look. He should know his breeding, and the quality of his wool. He should be able to muster sheep, – collect them in together from the vast pastures on which they feed, and above all he should be able to count them. He must be handy with horses, – doing anything which has to be done for himself. He must catch his own horse, – for the horses live on grass, turned out in paddocks, – and saddle him. The animal probably is never shod, never groomed, and is ignorant of corn. And the young man must be able to sit his horse, – which perhaps is more than most young men could do in England, – for it may be that the sportive beast will buck with the young man, jumping up into the air with his head between his legs, giving his rider as he does so such a blow by the contraction of his loins as will make any but an Australian young man sore all over for a week, even if he be not made sore for a much longer time by being sent far over the brute's head. This young man on a station must have many accomplishments, much knowledge, great capability; and in return for these things he gets his rations, and perhaps £100 per annum, perhaps £50, and perhaps nothing. But he lives a free, pleasant life in the open air. He has the scolding of many men, which is always pleasant; and nobody scolds him, which is pleasanter. He has plenty and no care about it. He is never driven to calculate whether he can afford himself a dinner, – as is often done by young men at home who have dress coats to wear and polished leather boots for happy occasions. He has always a horse to ride, or two or three, if he needs them. His salary is small, but he has nothing to buy, – except moleskin trousers and flannel shirts. He lives in the open air, has a good digestion, and sleeps the sleep of the just. After a time he probably works himself up into some partnership, – and has always before him the hope that the day will come in which he too will be a master squatter.

A sheep has to be born, and washed, and shorn, – the three great operations of a squatter's life consisting in the lambing, washing, and shearing of his flocks. On the Darling Downs in Queensland the lambs are dropped in August and September. Washing commences in September, and the shearing is over not much before Christmas. I was astonished to find that the practice in regard to washing and shearing varied very much at different stations, and that very strong opinions were held by the advocates of this or that system, – so that the science of getting the wool off the sheep's back in the best condition must be regarded as being even yet in its infancy. Many declare that sheep should not be washed at all, and that the wool should be shorn 'in the grease'. My opinion will not, I fear, be valued much by the great Queensland squatters, but, such as it is, it goes with the non-washers. Presuming that my own outside garniture required to be cleansed, I should not like to have it done on my back, – and if I knew that it was to be taken off immediately after the operation, I should think that to be an additional reason for deferring the washing process. There are various modes of washing, – but on the stations which I saw on the Darling Downs the sheep were all 'spouted'. I will endeavour to explain to the ordinary non-pastoral reader this system of spouting, premising that perhaps some 200,000 sheep have to undergo the process on one station, and at the same set of spouts.

But before we get to the spouting there is preliminary washing to be undergone, and as to that also there are fierce contests. Shall this preliminary washing be performed with warm or with cold water? And then again there is, so to say, an ante-preliminary washing in vogue, which some call 'raining'. If I remember rightly sheep were 'rained on' in Queensland only at those stations in which warm water was in demand. The sheep by thirties and forties were driven into long narrow pens, over which pipes were supported, pierced with holes from end to end. Into these pipes water is forced by a steam-engine, and pours itself right and left, in the guise of

rain, over the sheep below. In this way the wool is gently
saturated with moisture, and then the sheep are driven out of
the pens into long open tanks filled with water, just luke-
warm. Here they are soaked for a few minutes, – and this
practice is matter for fierce debate among squatters. I have
heard a squatter declare with vehement gesture that he hoped
every squatter would be ruined who was mad enough to use
warm water at his washpool. I have heard others declare with
equal vehemence that no wool could be really clean which had
not been subjected to the process. For myself, I am dead
against washing altogether; but if sheep are to be washed then
I am dead against warm water. The sheep becomes cold after it
and chill during the three or four days necessary for drying,
and in that condition of the animal the yolk which is necessary
to the excellence of the wool does not rise, and the fleece when
taken off, though cleaner than it would otherwise have been,
is less rich in its quality and less strong in its fibre.

But whether out of tanks with warm water or tanks with
cold water, the sheep are passed on, one by one, into the hands
of the men at the spouts. At one washpool I saw fourteen
spouts at work, with two men at each spout. These twenty-
eight men are quite amphibious for the time, standing up to
their middles in a race of running water. But this race is not a
natural stream. High over their heads are huge iron cisterns
which are continually filled by a steam pump, and which
empty themselves by spouts from the bottom, through which
the water comes with great force, – a force which can of
course be moderated by the weight of water thrown in. The
water is kept at a certain height according to the force wanted,
and falls with the required weight, in obedience to the law of
gravitation, on a board between the two rough water-spirits
below. Now the tanks, of which I have spoken, are high
above the water-spirits, and the sheep are brought out from
them on to a small intermediate pen or platform, from which
they are dropped one by one down a steep inclined trap, – each
sheep by a separate trap, – into the very hands of the washers.
The fall may be about twelve or fifteen feet. Then the animal
undergoes the real work of washing, – the bad quarter of an
hour of his life. He is turned backwards and forwards under
the spout with great violence, – for great violence is necessary,

– till the fury of the water shall have driven the dirt from his fleece. The bad quarter of an hour lasts, at some washpools, half a minute, – at others as long as a minute and a half; and I think I am justified in saying that the sheep does not like it. He goes out of the spouter's hands, not into the water, but on to steep boards, arranged so as to give him every facility for travelling up to the pen which is to receive him. But I have seen sheep so weak with what they have endured as to be unable to raise themselves on to their feet. Indeed at some washpools such was the normal condition of the sheep when they came from the spouts. It is impossible that there should not be rough handling. That, and the weight of the water together, prostrates them. This is so much the case that no squatter dares to wash his rams, – the pride of his flock, – for fear of injuring them. But, as a rule, sheep are washed in Queensland, and this is the fashion of their washing.

In Queensland the washpool, as at present arranged, is the squatter's great hobby, and next to it is his wool-shed. They are generally at some distance from each other, – perhaps seven or eight miles, – for the sheep must have time to dry, and it is well that they should travel a little over the pastures, feeding as they go, as being less likely to become again dirty with their own dust, as they would do if they were left together in large numbers. They are mustered and kept apart with infinite care, as ewes with their lambs must not be shorn with hoggetts, or hoggetts with old wethers. And there are sheep of different breeding and various qualities of wool which must not be mixed. In different flocks the sheep make their way from the washpool to the wool-shed, and then are shorn on about the fourth day. It is essentially necessary that they should be dry, so that rain during the double process is very detrimental to the squatter.

The wool shed is a large building open on every side, with a high-pitched roof, – all made of wood and very rough. The sheep are driven in either at one end or both, or at three sides, according to the size of the station and the number of sheep to be shorn. They are then assorted into pens, from which the shearers take them on to the board; – two, three, or four shearers selecting their sheep from each pen. The floor, on which the shearers absolutely work, is called 'the board'. I have seen as few as four or five shearing together, and I have seen as many as seventy-six. I have watched a shearer take the wool off his sheep in five minutes, and I have seen a man occupied nearly fifteen in the same operation. As they are paid by the score or by the hundred, and not by the day, the great object is to shear as many as possible. I have known a man to shear ninety-five in a day. I have heard of a man shearing one hundred and twenty. From sixty to seventy may be taken as a fair day's work. But as rapidity of work is so greatly to her workman's interest, and as too rapid a hand either leaves the wool on the sheep's back or else cuts skin and fleece together, there is often a diversity of opinion between the squatter and the shearer. 'Shear as quick as you can,' says the squatter, who is very anxious to get his work out of hand, – 'but let me have all my wool, – and let it not be cut mincemeat fashion, but with its full length of staple, – and above all do not mutilate and mangle my poor sheep.' But the poor sheep are mutilated and mangled by many a sore wound, and from side to side about the shed the visitor hears the sound of 'Tar'. When a sheep has been wounded the shearer calls for tar, and a boy with a tar-pot rushes up and daubs the gory wound. Each shearer has an outside pen of his own to which the sheep when shorn is demitted, and so the tally is kept.

The shearer does nothing but shear. When one sheep has left his hand he seizes at once another, being very careful to select that which will be easiest shorn. The fleece, when once separated from the animal's back, is no longer a care to him. Some subordinate picks it up and makes away with it, when folded, to the sorter's table. The sorter is a man of mark, and should be a man of skill, who gives himself airs and looks grand. It is his business to allot the wool to its proper sphere, – combing or clothing, first combing or second combing, first clothing or second clothing, broken wool, greasy, ram's-wool, hoggett's-wool, lamb's-wool, and the like. He stands immovable, and does his work with a touch, while ministers surround him, unfolding and folding, and carrying the assorted fleeces to their proper bins. But I am told that in England very little is thought of this primary sorting, and that all the wools are re-sorted as they are scoured. The squatter, however, says that unless he sorted his wool in his own shed he could not realise a good price for a good article.

Then when the wool is sorted it is pressed. Every wool-shed has its press, in which the bales are made into the shape that is familiar to the English eye. The average bale contains about 400 lb., and these are sent away on bullock-drags, – waggons with ten, twelve, or fourteen bullocks, down over bush roads, hundreds of miles, to the seaport at which they are shipped. It is a moot question whether the squatter should sell in the colony or in London. If prices be low, he had better probably send his produce home. If they be high, he had better take the ball at the hop, and realise his money in the colony.

I have said something before of the men employed at these stations. The ordinary hands, – those kept during the whole year, – are not many, and of them I may speak again in what words I shall have to say on the smaller stations in New South Wales. But the great work of the year on a large run with 200,000 sheep, or perhaps even a larger number, – the work of washing and shearing, – demands a crowd of workmen. I found considerably above a hundred employed by one master. That which strikes an Englishman most forcibly with regard to these men is, that the squatter is called upon to feed them all. Rations are given out for them in certain measured quantities. These rations vary somewhat, but in Queensland they were generally as follows. For each man per week:–

Meat	.	.	.	.	.	.	.	14lb.
Flour	.	.	.	.	.	.	.	8lb.
Sugar	.	.	.	.	.	.	.	2lb.
Tea	.	.	.	.	.	.	.	¼lb.

For the ordinary work of the year the squatter gives the rations as part of the allotted wages. Shearers, however, are charged for all that is furnished to them. The squatters provide everything that the men may require, – except drink, of which it is expected that there shall be literally none used while the shearing is in progress. The squatter keeps in his store tobacco, currants, pickles, jam, boots, shirts, moleskin trou-sers, shears, coffee, – and various condiments. These are supplied to the men at prices fixed by the squatter, – and so fixed as generally to leave some little profit. Were it not so, there would be a certain loss. But under this system the squatter becomes a shopkeeper, with a monopoly of supply to certain persons, – and no doubt unfairly high prices may sometimes be charged.

For shearing on the Darling Downs the usual rate is 3s.4d. a score. If a man shear seventy sheep, which is no extraordinary number, he will earn 11s.8d. a day. But it may be that the shearing will be stopped by wet weather, and then he must remain idle. He is bound by a contract, very strongly worded in the employer's favour, to remain till the shearing be done, – and is very much at the mercy of the squatter. He can be dismissed at a word if the squatter or his superintendent disapprove of his style of shearing, and is subject to certain fines. Rules are fixed up on the shed which he must obey, – and if he rebel, he is sent at once from the shed. I have told in a previous chapter how one poor man revenged himself by means of his poetical genius. It is not often, however, that differences arise. The squatter is very anxious to have his sheep shorn, and remembers the old proverb which tells him that the — he knows is better than the — he don't know. I was surprised to find what bad shearing was endured, – bad shearing induced not by want of skill or idleness, but by the rapidity which task-work is sure to produce. The sheep were cut horribly, – as I thought, – and but little was said.

The shearers find their own cook, and pay him 2s.6d. a week each. So that, with fifty, sixty, or seventy shearers, the cook would seem to have a good place. But with such a number there must be assistant cooks, – found by the master cook; and the men are both particular and impatient. They want hot coffee very early, hot meat for breakfast, messes with vegetables for dinner, hot meat for supper; – and are imperative as to hot plum-buns with their tea. Plums and currants seem to be essential to shearing.

Drink is the great crime; – but I am bound to say that, as far as my observation goes, shearers are not great criminals while at their work. It is expected that they shall drink nothing from the beginning to the end of shearing. Any man known to bring spirits to the station is at once dismissed, – and a man who wanders away to some distant public-house, even when his work for the day is done, is supposed to disobey orders. In England we give men beer at their work, and make no inquiry as to their doings after the close of their labour, – being contented that they shall come to their work sober enough to perform it. On sheep-stations, at shearing time, to drink is not only to sin, – but to commit the one sin that cannot be forgiven. If they do drink, they drink spirits. Beer has not as yet become the beverage of the country – nor wine, as I trust it will do before long.

The washers receive wages at different rates at different stations. I may perhaps say that 3s.9d. a day is the average payment for men out of the water, and 4s.9d. for men in the water. These men have, in addition to this, the rations above named, without payment. I believe that the man's food, – the food that is given to him free, – costs the squatter about 5s.6d. a week, so that a washer will earn about £1 14s. a week. The washer's food is cooked for him by the squatter.

The men are provided with huts or barracks in which they sleep. These are fitted up with bunks, – but each man brings his own blankets. A shearer will often take away from £25 to £30 as his wages after shearing, and a washer as much as £15. But then, alas, comes the time for drinking!

I spent a very pleasant time on the Darling Downs, – perhaps the more so because the rigid rule which prevailed in the wool-shed and at the washpool in regard to alcohol was not held to be imperative at the squatters' houses. I could hardly understand how a hospitable gentleman could press me to fill my glass again, – as hospitable gentlemen did do very often, – while he dilated on the wickedness of a shearer who should venture to think of a glass of rum. I took it all in good part, and preached no sermons on that subject. I had some very good kangaroo hunting, – and was surprised to find how well horses could carry me which went out every day, eat nothing but grass, and had no shoes on their feet.

CHAPTER VI

SUGAR, LABOUR FROM THE SOUTH SEA ISLANDS

Wool is no doubt the staple produce of Queensland, as it is of the other colonies; but in Queensland, next to wool, sugar has lately become the most important article. It has been found that much of the soil is fitted for the growth of the sugar-cane, and that in many districts the climate is equally favourable. The best sugar district is about Port Mackay, north of Rockhampton, which I did not visit. But the growth of the cane, which is a purely agricultural employment, has hitherto, all the world over, been joined with the two manufacturing trades of making sugar and distilling rum. In Cuba, in British Guiana, in the West Indies, and, I believe, also in the Mauritius, sugar and rum are always made by the planter. At first it seemed to be necessary that this should be done also in Queensland, and therefore the growth of cane was impeded by the necessity of a large capital, – or of a crushing debt. Gradually the old idea on this subject is vanishing, and small men, – free-selecters and others, – are growing cane for sale to the owners of the mills. Their future success or failure is a question altogether of labour, – and it is one which is now trembling in uncertainty. Queensland at present is supplying itself with labour from the South Sea Islands, and the men employed are called Polynesians, or Canakers, or Islanders; but it may be a question whether Queensland will be allowed to do so long. The philanthropists are hard at work to hinder them, – working as they always do with the best intentions, working as they so often do in much ignorance.

I may as well go into the question of South Sea Island labour at once, – premising, if I may be allowed to do so, that some years since I ventured to express an opinion, exactly similar to that I now entertain, in reference to the employment of Coolie labour for the growth of sugar in Demerara and Trinidad, –

which colonies I found on the road to renewed success through the instrumentality of a body of imported workmen, who were treated with uniform kindness and care. Then as now there was a fear in England that these foreigners in a new country would become slaves under new bonds, and that a state of things would be produced, – less horrible indeed than the slavery of the negroes who were brought into the West Indies by the Spaniards, but equally unjust and equally opposed to the rights and interests of the men concerned. And it was alleged then that benevolence and good intention on the part of those who might first institute such an immigration of foreign labourers, would not suffice to protect a crowd of poor ignorant strangers from the natural greed of the employer, – who would carry on his operations far from strict control, far from the eyes of England, altogether out of sight of Exeter Hall. Is it not incumbent on philanthropy in the present age to see that no new form of serfdom be introduced, – at any rate on soil owned by the British Crown, – and to guard with all the eyes of Argus any approaches to the abomination of slavery? That is the argument from the philanthropical side, stated, I trust, fairly, – and that argument I do not pretend to combat. Let us have no slavery, in God's name. Be careful. Guard the approaches. Defend the defenceless. Protect the poor ignorant dusky foreigner from the possible rapacity of the sugar-planter. But, in doing this, know at any rate what you are doing, and be not led away by a rampant enthusiasm to do evil to all parties. Remember the bear who knocked out his friend's brains with the brickbat when he strove to save him from the fly. An ill-conducted enthusiasm may not only debar Queensland from the labour which she requires, but debar also these poor savages from their best and nearest civilisation. Let philanthropists at any rate look into the matter somewhat closely before they make heavy charges against the Queensland government and the Queensland sugar-growers because they employ Islanders in the colony. If they be in earnest let them send over someone who may learn the truth for them, – some agent or messenger capable of finding out the truth and of telling them without prejudice what are the real facts of this trade.

When I was in Queensland I saw that the attention of the House of Commons at home was drawn to the matter, and that our own Colonial Secretary, if not frightened, was at any rate not quite assured on the subject. It is hard enough for a Colonial Secretary to get accurate information as to facts in a self-governing colony. He applies to the governor, and the governor applies to the executive officers, – and the executive officers in the colony are the very men of whose management or mismanagement in such an affair as this the philanthropists at home stand especially in dread. But I observe that the Queensland prime minister, in concluding a report on the subject to the acting-governor of Queensland, on the 12th of April, 1871, makes to the home government the very suggestion which I have made to the philanthropists. 'So much misapprehension,' he says, 'exists in England with reference to the introduction of these Islanders, that I would suggest to your Excellency the desirability of making such representations to the Secretary of State for the Colonies as would lead to the appointment by the Imperial government of a commission to examine into and report upon the whole subject.' This was written in consequence of a representation made to the Colonial Office at home, by certain gentlemen of whom I intend to speak in no mocking sense when I call them philanthropists, – and was grounded on reports made either to them or in the public press by two gentlemen at Brisbane adverse to the system of Polynesian labour.

I will now describe 'the state of things', as clearly as I can, and will explain what I believe to be the cause of opposition to it in the colony. These Polynesians are brought into Queensland in vessels under government superintendence, and in conformity with an act of the Queensland parliament passed with the view of protecting them from the rapacity of merchants and the possible evil of kidnapping by British or colonial captains. There is also attached to every such vessel a government agent. The act of parliament was in full force when the representation was made to which I have alluded; but the appointment of a government agent was since introduced, – introduced for aught I know in consequence of the representation. The act, dated March 8th, 1868, is long, and will hardly bear quotation; but all the clauses are arranged so as to protect the Polynesian labourer, – to protect him specially in his act of emigration from home, – and to insure that justice shall be done to him on his arrival in Queensland. His clothes and diet aboard ship are prescribed, his clothes and diet during his sojourn with his master are fixed, and the means of return at the end of three years' work in the colony, without cost to himself, are insured to him. He is to have:–

DIET

Beef or mutton	1 lb. daily.
Bread or flour	1 lb. "
Molasses or sugar	5 oz. "
Vegetables	2 lb. "
or rice 4 oz., or maize meal 8 oz.	
Tobacco	1 ½ oz. weekly.
Salt	2 oz. "
Soap	4 oz. "

CLOTHING

Shirts	2 yearly
Trousers	2 "
Hat	1 "
Blankets (a pair)	1 "

And he is to be provided with residence and medical attendance. He can be transferred from one employer to another, but not without the sanction of the government. He cannot be moved out of the colony till the expiration of the three years without his own consent and that of the governor. He cannot be punished otherwise than by appeal to a magisterial bench, – in which case he would be dealt with as would be any other person accused of breaking the law. At the end of the three years he receives wages at the rate of £6 per annum, – or £18 in all. This must be paid to him in money, and this he invariably lays out in the purchase of articles which he takes back with him to the islands, – tools, calico, cloth, small pieces of furniture, boxes, ornaments, and the like. In considering the amount of money-wages the master will bear in mind that the man has been fed, housed, and clothed, and that the wages represent his savings.

I have seen these men working under various masters and at various employments. No doubt their importance to Queensland mainly attaches to the growth and manufacture of sugar; but they are also engaged in wharves, about the towns, in meat-preserving establishments, in some instances as shepherds, and occasionally as domestic servants. I have told how I was rowed up the river Mary by a crew of these islanders. They are always clean, and bright, and pleasant to be seen. They work well, but they know their own position and importance. I never saw one ill used. I never heard of any such ill-usage. The question to my mind is whether they are not fostered too closely, – wrapped up too warmly in the lamb-swool of government protection. Their dietary is one which an English rural labourer may well envy, – as he might also, if he knew it, the general immunity from the crushing cares of toil which these young savages enjoy.

But I am unaware that any serious complaint has been made either by the English philanthropists or by their informants, the colonists, as to the treatment which these men receive in Queensland. The charge is that they are kidnapped, – taken on board the vessels from the islands surreptitiously, – and that they are ill treated on the journey; that the horrors of the middle passage, – as we used to call it when we spoke of the sufferings of the poor Africans, – are in some sort repeated. As regards the immigration into Queensland I believe the charge to be substantially without foundation. The vessels are worked under government surveillance, and every vessel employed in the trade is now accompanied by a government agent. The rule to this effect, which was subsequently added to the law as to the treatment of the men passed in 1868, is no doubt a salutary safeguard. I could not, however, learn that previous to this latter order islanders had been kidnapped for Queensland, though accusations to that effect are rife. The English philanthropists add to their memorial a postscript containing a statement from a gentleman at Melbourne that islanders have been kidnapped and taken to Fiji. I believe that this has been done, – but as neither the islands from which the Polynesian emigrants are brought, nor the Fiji Islands, are as yet even under British protectorate, neither Great Britain nor her colonies can be held to be responsible for the evil.

No doubt the entire colony of Queensland is not in favour of Polynesian labour. But the opposition to it which exists did not spring from the causes which are at work with the English philanthropists. With them the sole object is to prevent a possible return to some form of slavery, and the ill-usage of a certain number of their fellow men. No one charges them with other motives, or believes them to be actuated by other than the purest feelings. But the motives and feelings which have produced the opposition to which they have adhered are other than theirs. Protection of white labour is the cause of that opposition. In Queensland, as elsewhere throughout the world, the political questions which most strongly stir the minds of men are those which refer to the joint employment of labour and capital. The white man in Queensland who can now earn 15s. or 20s. a week and his food would like to earn 25s. or 30s. – in which desire all the world will sympathize with him. And he believes that his desire may be best accomplished by preventing the use of cheaper labour than his own. In this belief, and in the efforts to which it gives rise, the world will not sympathize with him. The belief is as erroneous as the efforts are vicious. It is in some sort a repetition of the infantine political economy which many years ago induced rural labourers in England to destroy thrashing machines and burn out the farmers who used them. It is not necessary for me now to adduce arguments to show that the greater the products of the colony the more general will be the aggregate prosperity of the colonists. The white labourer in Queensland, who is not a good political economist, does believe that cheaper labour than his own is injurious to himself, and therefore desires to keep the Polynesians away. He does not understand that the very business in which he is allowed to earn 4s. or 4s.6d. a day would not exist, – could not be carried on, – without another class of labour at the rate of 2s. or 1s.6d. a day. He therefore becomes quite as zealous in the cause as the philanthropist at home; but he in his zeal hates the shining Polynesian, whom he sees, with a warmth greater even than that which the philanthropist throws into his love for his unseen man and brother. There are a pair of hands, and a supple body, and a willing spirit, and a ready brain, to be had for 2s. a day, – underselling the white man's labour after a fashion most nefarious to the white labourer's imagination! How can this crushing evil be avoided? Are there no means by

which good labour at 2s. a day may be made impossible, – a
thing not to be obtained in the colony of Queensland? Then
the white labourer, with indistinct intelligence on the subject,
hears something of his philanthropical friends at Exeter Hall,
and begins to find that there may be common cause between
them. White labour in the colony may be protected from
Exeter Hall, though Exeter Hall itself has no such intention.
The white labourer soon finds a go-between, – soon comes
into communication with some gentleman, anxious for his
vote, who can make statements to the philanthropists at
home.

It may be taken for granted that the sole object in England
on the part of those who object to the emigration of
Polynesians to Queensland is to save the islanders from
suffering and oppression. It is said of these islanders that as
they cannot understand English, – and as they speak various
languages among themselves, in regard to which it is impossible for us to send interpreters who shall understand them all,
– therefore they cannot understand the contracts made with
them. That they understand the verbal niceties of these
contracts no one can imagine. Their contracts to them are very
much the same as are our legal documents to most of us at
home. We sign them, however, because, from various
concurrent causes, we believe them to be conducive to our
advantage, – not because we understand them. We trust the
person who asks for our signature; and, though we know that
there is sometimes deceit and consequent misfortune, we
believe that the chances are in our favour. Experience has
taught us to trust. These islanders are in precisely the same
condition. Those who go to Queensland for three years are
sent back to their islands with their hands full, in good health,
and with reports of a life far better than that which Providence
has given them at home. It is on the reports of these men that
new contracts are now made, – and it is by the experience thus
gained that they who have served for one term of three years
are induced to return for another term.

Though the white man be jealous of cheap labour from the
islands, hoeing canes within the tropics is not an employment
which he likes for himself, and the best sugar ground of
Queensland is north of the tropical line. Much sugar is grown

south of the line, in the Maryborough district for instance, and in East Moreton, – and sugar is grown also in certain districts in New South Wales. But if Australian sugar ever compete in the markets of the world with sugar from Demerara, Cuba, and Mauritius, it will be produced in North Queensland. Both soil and climate are propitious, and the district, though hot, is healthy. The best land in the best localities is already becoming scarce and dear, – for sugar can never be profitably grown without easy means of transit from the cane-fields to the mill, and of sugar from the mill to the seaport. The trade must be carried on along the coast and river banks, and up creeks, wide, and constant enough in their running to admit of some rough mode of water carriage. I believe that it is already becoming difficult to procure land fitly situated. But the failure or success of the business will, I think, depend altogether on the manner in which the question of labour shall be settled. If the South Sea Islanders be expelled, it is possible that Chinese or Indian coolies may take their place. The exodus of the Chinese is probably as yet hardly more than commenced. But without imported labour I doubt whether Queensland sugar can be grown.

I found the cost to the sugar-planter of these Polynesians to be about £75 per head for the whole term of three years, – which was divided as follows:–

Journey out and back (which is always paid for by the employer of the man)	£15
Average cost of getting the man up to the station	3
Wages for three years	18
Rations(3s.9d. a week, say for three years)	30
Blankets, clothes, &c	6
For lost time by illness, &c.(say)	3
	£75

This amounts to nearly 10s. a week for the entire time. The average wages of a white man on a plantation may be taken at about 25s. a week, including rations. I was told by more than one sugar-grower that two islanders were worth three white men among the canes.

As yet the produce of the colony about supplies the colony. Some sugar is exported to New South Wales. Some sugar is imported from the Mauritius, – the exports and imports being about equal. The retail price is from 3 ½d. to 4 ½d. a pound according to quality. Should the trade go on and flourish it must be made prosperous by supplying markets beyond the bounds of Queensland, and to the Englishman who has not studied the colonies it would appear natural that the desired market should be found in New South Wales, Victoria, and South Australia. The Englishman who has not studied the colonies can hardly bring himself to understand that Australia is not one whole, – that there is as much difficulty in commercial communication between Brisbane and Melbourne as there is between Liverpool and New York, – infinitely more than in that between London and Havre. These colonies lay duties on each other at diverse rates. Tasmania charges 6s. a cwt. on imported raw sugar, Victoria 3s. a cwt. New South Wales 5s., New Zealand 1d. a lb. or 9s. 4d. a cwt. So that sugar from Queensland has no preference in the other colonies over sugar from the Mauritius. Nor under the existing state of the British law as it affects the colonies could such preference be given. New South Wales, for instance, may decide for herself whether she will admit sugar free, or whether she will raise a custom duty upon its import; but she cannot take Queensland sugar free and refuse to take sugar free from other sugar-growing countries. As the colonies at present stand in reference to each other, – with the existing feeling of jealousy, and occasionally almost of hostility, – with a condition of things in which a minister in one colony speaks in his parliament of another as a 'friendly colony', in the spirit in which our ministers at home call this or that nation a 'friendly country', or an 'allied country', laying stress on the alliance, when we know that we are on the brink of war with that country, – with these mutual rivalries and almost antipathies, this British law, tending as it does to the separation of Australian interests, has no very strong immediate effect. The colonies are determined to be separate. Australia is a term that finds no response in the patriotic feeling of any Australian. They are Victorians, or Queenslanders, or men of New South Wales; and each is not at present unwilling to have the pleasure of taxing the other. But this will come to an end sooner or later. The name of Australia will be dearer if not greater to Australian ears than the name of Great Britain, and then the produce of the land will pass free throughout the land.

CHAPTER VII

GOVERNMENT

The system of government is very nearly the same in all the Australian colonies, though the system of politics in vogue may vary considerably. Protection at the present moment is rife in Victoria, but is not in favour in Queensland. In Queensland the interests of the squatters prevail: but in Victoria the squatters are not in the ascendant. In Queensland the ministers and people generally are inclined to be submissive to the Colonial Office at home, with an inclination to hang upon English advice, and to maintain English influences. In Victoria, on the other hand, the Colonial Office in Downing Street is not highly respected, and the politicians of the day are inclined to think that they can best 'paddle their own canoe'. These are political differences, depending on the leading men of the hour, and on the chance circumstances of the colony at the moment. But the forms of legislative and executive administration are nearly identical, – as much so, I think, as they are in the different States of the American Union.

Kings, Lords, and Commons prevail in the colonies as they do at home, – with some variations. The governor enacts the office of king, but he does so with a political responsibility which does not attach to the throne with us. At home the royal veto has become obsolete. The sovereign and the ministry of the day must necessarily be in accord. If the ministers differ from parliament on any matter of moment, they go out of office, and another set of men comes in, supported by majorities. By such a system there can be no need of a veto, – as the parliament which submits its bills to the crown controls the ministers which advise the crown. But in a colony, – even in a colony with representative institutions, – the working is different. The colonial ministers no doubt advise the governor in council; but he is subject to instructions from home. And the legislative powers of the colonies are limited in certain directions. No law is to be passed contrary to the spirit of the laws of England. The governor, therefore, does exercise a temporary veto not unfrequently, – submitting the matter home for decision. In Queensland not long since the ministers of the day proposed a law by which paper money would have become inconvertible, and would have been substituted for gold as the legal tender of the country. The governor refused his acquiescence, and was supported by the Colonial Office at home. In this way the colonies are preserved from crude legislation, which would be the certain and natural result of inexperience in statecraft. In saying this I by no means intend to cast a slur on colonial ministers, or to imply that inefficient men have been chosen for high offices. I certainly make no such charge in regard to Queensland. But it cannot be expected that a colony with a population of 120,000 souls should be able to produce a ministry skilled at all points in questions of government and finance. Among such a population the minister chosen will usually be a gentleman intent on his own profession, – whatever that may be; whose education and chances in life have made him a lawyer, a merchant, or a squatter. Such a man finds himself suddenly in parliament, and almost as suddenly a minister of state, – a colonial secretary or prime minister, – or perhaps a colonial treasurer or chancellor of the exchequer, – backed by a majority in parliament, and enabled therefore, as far as the colonial parliament is concerned, to carry his own measures. His inexperience is brought face to face with the inexperience of a small chamber, – just as the experience of a very large minister with us is encounteredf by the experience of a very large chamber. Though the interests of the colony are comparatively small, – because the numbers are small, – the benefits or injuries which may be the result of good or bad legislation will be as great to the few, as they are to the many in crowded communities. It is by no means wonderful that it should appear expedient to six or seven gentlemen in Queensland that inconvertible paper should be the safest circulating medium for the colonists; but it would be highly prejudicial to the colony that such a question should be left to the unassisted wisdom of these six or seven gentlemen, – and perhaps altogether ruinous. It may be that each of these six or seven should be superior in all good gifts, in eloquence, patriotism, and natural sense, to any secretary of state at home. It is by no means to be supposed that a minister of state in England must be superior to a minister in Queensland, because the one is an Englishman and the other a colonist. But the concrete wisdom of thirty million people is greater than that of a hundred and twenty thousand, and the experience of ages of legislation is needed to control the newness and rawness of a parliament that has existed but for a few years.

This probably is the strongest existing reason for maintaining the present dependent condition of the Australian colonies. There are other reasons, all strong against immediate change; – the possible need of protection in case of attack, which protection we should give with more heartiness and certainty to a colony than to an ally, – the absence of any Australian feeling between the colonies of a nature strong enough to bind them into one whole, – the doubt that would be felt both at home and in the colonies as to the form of government to be selected; the general dislike to a republic and the difficulties which stand in the way of the establishment of a monarchy, – all these objections are valid against the idea of immediate independence which is not without its supporters in England. But strongest among them all is the necessary inexperience of colonial statesmen. The need for guidance and control is that of the youth who is no longer a boy but is not quite a man. He may be better educated than his father, of a higher intellect, of finer aspirations, giving promise of almost Darwinian improvement in his descent, – but he cannot be trusted to go quite alone till he has been taught by experience that paper, without gold to back it, will not long supply his necessities, – till he shall have learned that and other worldly lessons which will not come simply from high intellect and fine aspirations.

The governor, with his instructions from home, and his power of reserving new laws till they shall have been submitted to the judgement of the minister at home, enacts the part of the king. He is assisted by an executive council of which he is the president, and which consists of his ministers. The premier is the vice-president, and has, I think, always in

Queensland filled the office of colonial secretary. This council is the counterpart of our cabinet. The position of the Colonial Governor is different from that of the sovereign in this, – that he is supposed to be consulted as to the measures which are introduced, and that the Constitution does not require him to be in accord with his ministers. Should he differ from them as to a bill which they have succeeded in passing, he has the power of referring the matter to the Home Government.

In Queensland there are, as a rule, six executive ministers. During my visit to the colony there was a seventh member of the cabinet, who held, however, no office and received no salary. Of these six the Constitution requires that only one shall be in the upper chamber, – or legislative council. The other five are supposed to find seats for themselves in the lower house, or legislative assembly, – though there is nothing in the Constitution to make this imperative. There is a colonial secretary, – who seems to combine all duties which do not naturally fall to the lot of his brethren, – a colonial treasurer; a chancellor of the exchequer; a minister for works and gold-fields; a minister for lands; a postmaster-general; and an attorney-general. These gentlemen exercise the patronage of the colony among them, and are much belied if they do not regard that duty as being equal in importance to any that is confided to them. Patronage is indeed one of the greatest curses of the colonies. The public is never a very good paymaster. In no country are fortunes to be made in the public service, – unless such be done by the ministers of a despot. But there is always a craving for official salaries, – even though these salaries be hardly sufficient to give bread and meat. In the United States the public servants are among the most needy of the citizens. In Washington the clerks attached to the public offices can barely exist on their pay. But in the United States the demand for office is so great that expectant presidents are required to come to terms as to the manipulation of patronage before they are assured of the support of their parties. I regret to say that the same greed for public place is growing up in the colonies, – even in a colony so new as Queensland. A minister must make sure of his seat, and constituents demand their share of the plunder, – as they do also not unfrequently elsewhere.

Our House of Lords is represented in the colonies by the
legislative council which consists of twenty-one members.
These are nominated by the governor for life, the governor
being of course subject in this matter to the advice of his
ministers. The nomination therefore practically rests with the
premier. With us at home there is a very general feeling that
the power and influence of the House of Lords is on the wane
in regard to political action. Our Lords can of course throw
out bills, and they do throw out bills very often. But we have
taught ourselves to believe that they should not throw out any
bill as to which the country shows itself to be in earnest above
three or four times at the furthest. They are presumed to be
compressible after a certain amount of resistance, and are
supposed to be allowed to hold their position by reason of
their compressibility. The legislative council in an Australian
parliament is intended to be endowed with similar privileges
and similar feebleness. Their sittings are short and uninteresting, but the chamber in which they are held is imposing and
comfortable. The copy of the home institution is very faithful,
– with the exception of course of the hereditary element. As
the members hold their seats for life, many of them are of
course old, and as the age of the colony advances they will
become older. Nothing can be more respectable and well-
behaved than an Australian legislative council, and I believe
that among legislative councils none is better behaved than
that of Queensland. But the feebleness is there. It is at any rate
supposed to be there. When you are told that a gentleman has
been nominated to the upper house, it is intended that you
should understand that he has been laid honourably on the
shelf. It is, however, competent to him to come down from
the shelf and again to enter upon the arena of true political
action, – a privilege which is altogether denied to members of
the upper house with us.

The arena for political action is the legislative assembly, in
which ministers with their friends sit on the right of the
Speaker, and the opposition on the left, with a great table
between them, and benches below the gangway, – just as we
have it at home. When I was in Queensland the House
consisted of thirty-two members, but it was then in contemplation to add twelve to the number. I had no opportunity of

being present at a debate, as a general election was going on while I was in the colony, and the new House had not as yet sat when I left it. A majority of six was prepared to support the government, – which had, I was informed, dissolved the House with a majority of one. I read some past debates and was not astonished to find that considerable latitude was allowed in the use of vehement language. Such is always the case in a small chamber, in which the united common sense of the whole is not sufficiently extended to repress the temporary folly of one or two. Since I left Queensland a most discreditable scene has taken place in the House, – of such a nature that its repetition would be most injurious to the colony. One honourable member, in the heat of the debate and after dinner, plucked another honourable member by the beard, – and then ran away. It is fair, however, to add that he was driven to resign his seat, and was not re-elected. The proceedings have, however, as a rule, been orderly in Queensland, and creditable to the colony. Men have been got together anxious for the welfare of the colony, – who have acted with greater legislative discretion than a just expectation could have hoped to obtain from so small a population thinly spread over so immense an area. There must always be danger that a parliament selected from a few scattered inhabitants will fail in achieving the work of its constituencies or in gaining the respect of the world at large; and the smaller the number, the greater will be the danger. At first there were but twenty-six members in the Queensland Assembly. There is nothing in the corporate strength of such a chamber to control the energy of the would-be orator; it has no tradition of its own by which to regulate its practice; it feels itself to be but a little copy of a great institution, and is half ashamed of its own pretensions. It may so easily become rowdy, while decorum is so difficult! It is felt that the majesty with which our parliament at home is invested should be copied, but that it can hardly be copied without absurdity! Queensland began her self-government with about 20,000 souls, – and it must be admitted that there was danger. But the Queensland Assembly has not been distinguished for rowdiness among colonial parliaments, and has held up its head, and done its work, and attained that respect without which a parliament must be worthless.

In Queensland the system which regulates a man's capacity to vote for a member of the legislative assembly is certainly not democratic. Every man aged twenty-one can vote, provided that he is possessed of one of the following qualifications, – which qualification, however, must appertain to the district or town in regard to which the vote is to be given. He must have resided for six months. He must then possess some one of the following positions:–

Own a freehold, worth £100 above incumbrances.

Occupy a tenement worth £10 per annum.

Hold a lease of £10 per annum, of which three years are still to run, or of which three years have already run.

Hold a pastoral licence.

Enjoy a salary of £100 per annum.

Pay £40 per annum for board and lodging.

Or pay £10 for lodging only.

By this law the nomad tribes of wandering labourers, – or of wandering beggars, as many of them are more properly described, – are excluded from the registers.

It cannot be said that this young colony has shown any tendency to run headlong into the tempting dangers of democracy. It would appear that the prevailing feelings of the people lie altogether in the other direction. As I have said, I fear more than once before, the squatters are the aristocracy of the country, and I found that a cabinet with seven members contained six squatters. The general election which took place while I was there supported this ministry by a majority of six in a House of thirty-two members, giving nineteen on one side to thirteen on the other. This would be equal to a majority of one hundred and twenty in a House of six hundred and forty, – a result which would with us be taken as showing the sense of the country very plainly. At home, in England, we are inclined to regard the institutions of our Australian colonies as being essentially democratic, – as showing almost republican propensities. In this, I think, we are mistaken, – certainly as regards Queensland. Among the working population outside the towns political feeling is not strong in any direction. Men care little about politics, – not connecting this or that set of ministers with the one important subject of wages. In some districts a certain amount of zeal has been aroused against cheap labour, – and here and there an election may have been turned by the feeling of white men in that direction. The opposition to squatters comes of course from the towns, and chiefly from the metropolis. But it cannot be described as being strong or enthusiastic, and is chiefly due to the ambition of men who, sitting on the left hand of the Speaker, are filled with a natural desire to sit on the right. I am inclined to report as my opinion that politics in Queensland are very quiet, whereas the loyalty to the Crown is very strong.

Nothing strikes a visitor to the colony more forcibly than the desire to hold government place. I myself would certainly not have expected that this would be so among a young population, eager for independence, to whose energy un-limited acres are open, and among whom it cannot be said that the professions and pursuits of commerce are over-crowded. The government pay is not excessively liberal, and the positions when gained do not seem to be very enviable. Four or five hundred a year is a paradise of government promotion, to which but very few can hope to attain. But the thing when seen from a distance allures by its uncertainty, – and I fear also by a conviction that the 'government stroke' may be a light stroke of work. In colonial parlance the government stroke is that light and easy mode of labour, – perhaps that semblance of labour, – which no other master will endure, though government is forced to put up with it. With us the govern-ment stroke has happily taken quite another phase. It is to be hoped that it may gradually be made to do so in the colonies. That the longing for government employment, with the cringing and threats and back-door interest necessary to obtain it, should be made to cease also, is more perhaps than can be at once expected.

CHAPTER VIII

LABOUR

In the preceding pages I have already spoken of the rates of wages in Queensland, but the condition of the labourer cannot be judged simply from the wages he may earn. In Queensland they are high, – so high as to be very tempting to the would-be English emigrant; but the emigrant should learn more than the current rate of wages before he resolves that he will attempt to make himself happy in a new country. As our colonies are chiefly serviceable to us and to the world as offering fields in which labour may make men prosperous and happy, it is essential that something should be known on this matter. After all, democratic institutions, form of government, ballot, responsible ministers, and the like, are but fleabites on the great body of the people. They are talked about, and seen, and known, – and are apt subjects for enthusiastic conversation; but when one gets half an inch below the surface, one finds that questions of politics are but of little interest. It is not the political shoe which pinches, – at any rate in the colonies. How much can a man earn, and with what smallest amount of labour, – and what privileges may a man enjoy when he is earning it? And with what smallest amount of capital can a man settle himself on the soil and live, so that he shall be his own master and owe no obedience to any one? And if a man shall venture so to settle himself and be independent with some smallest imaginable capital, – £2 10s., we will say, as the first payment on forty acres of selected agricultural land, and £7 10s. to build a hut with, &c., – what probability is there that he may be able to live honestly and pay further annual instalments? And if not honestly, – then must he starve, or will any other way be open to him? And, in living, what will be the nature of his life? The labourer here at home has certainly a hard time. His lines have not fallen to him in pleasant places. The farmer's labourer, the carter, ploughman, or hedger and ditcher, with 11s. a week and a wife and four children, must often wonder at the inequality of things, and, if he be imaginative, be tempted into strange thoughts as to God's doings. He has as yet been able to defend his labour by no trade's union, to influence the farmer by no fear of a strike in the parish, and has been powerless to demand more than sufficient bread to keep body and soul together. He is only now making the attempt, urged to do so by the eloquence of outside friends. He is not imaginative, and is too apt to bear his fardel patiently. He hears nothing of Queensland or other colonies, – unless by some special chance in his favour, – and knows no better than to have his body and soul kept together for him. An author would do something useful who could get at him, at him and at his boys as they rise in the world, and tell them what would really befall them if, through friends, or by colonial bounty, or State aid, or by personal industry, they, – or any one of them, – could manage to be landed on the shores of Queensland.

I take it that plenty to eat is, all the world over, the first desire of man and woman. When a man has plenty to eat as a matter of course, – when his food comes to him as does the air which he breathes, – he is apt to think that his own first desires are of a sublimer nature; but any accident in the supplies for twenty-four hours will teach the truth on this subject to the most high-minded. I can imagine that a leg of mutton looms as large to an Essex delver and is as glorious a future, as a seat in parliament to a young barrister. There are legs of mutton, if only it might be possible to get at one! Let the delver get to Queensland and he will at any rate have legs of mutton. Meat three times a day is the normal condition of the Queensland labourer. In the colony mutton may be worth twopence per pound; but of the price the labourer takes no heed. He is provided as a matter of course with rations, – fourteen pounds of meat a week is the ordinary allowance for a labourer in Queensland, – and, as regards food for himself, he is called upon to take no thought of the morrow, any more than if he were a babe. Fourteen pounds of meat, eight pounds of flour, two pounds of sugar, and a quarter of a pound of tea are allotted to him weekly. This in England would cost, at the lowest price, something over 12s. a week, – more than the labourer can earn altogether, – and this labourer in Queensland enjoys as a matter of course before he comes to the question of wages.

I may, however, as well declare at once that the all but divine happiness of such a state of existence, – as it will appear to the delver at home, seems very soon to lose its brilliance in the eyes of the man when he is in Queensland. He has hardly eaten a few hundred pounds of colonial mutton, has not been on rations six months, before he has forgotten entirely that he was ever short of supply in the matter of animal food. The Irishman who has come from the unchanging perpetuity of potatoes to a plethora of meat, teaches himself to believe within twelve months that he never sat down to dinner at home without a beefsteak or a roast fowl. I came to a little dispute once with a working man at Rockhampton. 'If you knew what it was,' he said, 'to have to eat mutton three times a day, day after day, week after week, month after month, you would not come here and tell us that we ought to be contented with our condition.' Looking at the matter in his light, I see that he has some justice on his side. I told him, jeering at him ill-naturedly, that if he would give up one meal a day, he would lessen his sorrow by at least a third, – but I saw that I was not regarded as having the best of the argument. I would wish therefore that the would-be emigrating English labourer should understand that when he gets his meat in plenty it will not be to him a blessing so unalloyed as he now thinks it. Alas, is it not the same with all blessings? What is there for which we toil and sigh, which when gained does not become to us like mutton served thrice daily? The seat in parliament, the beautiful young wife, even accumulated wealth, all pall upon us; and we exclaim, as did my labouring friend at Rockhampton, – 'If you too had to eat this mutton three times a day you would not think your condition so blessed.'

But there is the blessing, – such as it is. The man who works in Queensland is at any rate sufficiently fed. The man who works at home is too often very insufficiently fed. I am of opinion that the English labourer looking at the question from his point of view will make light of the Rockhampton objection which, nevertheless, I have felt it to be my duty to lay before him. The next question is this, – will the immigrating labourer arriving at Queensland find himself sure of labour to suit him? Is it fairly certain that he will fall into one of these places, with all the flour and mutton and sugar and tea? It is at any rate all but certain that he will have no such success unless he be a man who can really work. The old, the idle, the reckless, and the soft-handed will only come to worse grief in a colony than the grief which they will leave behind them. I am speaking now of intending emigrants who purpose to reach the colony without money in their pockets, – and while so speaking I will say at once that the chances in any Australian colony are very bad both for men and women who go thither with some vague idea of earning bread by their education or their wits. The would-be government clerk, the would-be governess, the would-be schoolmaster, lawyer, storekeeper, or the like, has no more probable opening to him in an Australian town than he has in London or in Liverpool. Such a one may possibly prosper in Brisbane or elsewhere; but the would-be government clerk will probably find himself after some months of hardship a shepherd in the bush, – a condition than which nothing in humanity short of starvation can be more wretched; and the would-be governess will find herself vainly striving to fulfil the duties of a nursery-maid, should she even succeed in getting food and shelter with such intention.

But the young man with sinews and horny hands, – the man who is young enough to adapt himself to new labour, – will certainly find occupation. He is worth his rations, and high wages beyond his rations. On that subject of wages he will probably find himself contesting points with employers of labour. Cheap labour, or at any rate labour as cheap as possible, is in Queensland as much regarded as elsewhere. The various industrial enterprises of the country are dependent on it. In that matter of sugar it has been already stated that canes can hardly be grown successfully with white labour. In timber-sawing, meat-preserving, in the working of gold-reefs, at sheep-washing and sheep-shearing, the rate of wages to be paid is all-important; and no doubt an effort is continually being made to reduce them. But I rarely found that a white man's labour could be had for less than 15s. a week in addition to his rations. At meat-preserving and sugar establishments men earn from 15s. to 20s. a week. Washers at sheep-stations earn about 4s. a day. Shearers will earn, according to their skill and strength, from 7s. to 14s. a day, paying, however, for their own rations. These two last employments are only to be had during the last four months of the year. Shepherds on a sheep-run are paid from £30 to £40 per annum, and their rations, – but the life is a life of absolute solitude and of almost continued inaction, and ends very frequently in madness or drunkenness. In various cases I have found that these men have taken up strong Calvinistic ideas in religion, – teaching themselves in their solitary wanderings to believe that they will assuredly be damned. They live in huts by themselves, going out in the morning with their flocks, bringing them back in the evening to the enclosure or yard by which the hut is surrounded. But this miserable occupation is becoming less and less common daily, as the squatters perceive that they can fence in their paddocks at less expense than they can maintain shepherds, – and that by such a system sheep can feed both day and night. On fenced runs men called boundary-riders are employed in lieu of shepherds, and the boundary-rider will receive probably £45 per annum and his rations. He will also have the use of a horse. The wages of mechanics do not seem to be much higher than those in England, – not so, at least, in proportion to the difference found in rural or semi-rural employment. Carpenters and masons in small towns earn from 6s. to 7s.6d. a day, – without rations, – the lower being the more common rate of the two. Gardeners and grooms, when men get employment in such occupations, receive about 20s. a week and rations. Maid-servants in the towns are paid 10s. a week, – being hired almost invariably for the short term, and not, as with us, by the month.

If we may take 17s.6d. as the average money wages of a labouring man, he will receive in the year something over £45, besides his food. It must be understood also that in most of the occupations specified shelter is afforded, – a place, that is, in which to cook, to sleep, and to eat. The man brings his own blankets, but he has a bunk on which he can lie, and the use of a hut. If, therefore, a man be unmarried and really careful, he can very quickly save enough money to enable himself to start as a buyer of land. I now presume myself to be addressing some young English labourer; and the young English labourer is doubtless certain that, when the circumstances described become his own, he will be prudent. I hope he may. There is no reason whatever why he should not. Those among whom he works will respect and even like him the better for it, – and those for whom he works will of course do so. He will have every facility for saving his money, which will be paid to him in comparatively large sums, by cheques. Perhaps he will do so. I am bound to tell him that I have my doubts about it. I shall very much respect him if he does; but, judging from the habits of others of his class, and from the experience of those who know the colony, I think that he will take his cheque to a public-house, give it to the publican, get drunk, and remain so till the publican tells him that the cheque has been consumed. The publican will probably let him eat and drink for a fortnight, and will then turn him out penniless, to begin again. He will begin again, and repeat the same folly time after time, till he will teach himself to think that it is the normal condition of his life.

A Queensland gentleman told me the story of a certain shearer who had shorn for him year after year, and had always gone through the same process of 'knocking down his cheque', as the work is technically called. He liked the man, and on one occasion remonstrated with him as he handed him the paper, explaining to him the madness of the proceeding. Would he not on that occasion be content to get drunk only on a portion of his money, and put the remainder into a savings-bank? No; the man said that when he had earned his money he liked to feel that he could do what he pleased with it. So he took his cheque, – and started for the nearest town. On the following day he returned, – to the astonishment of his employer, who knew that the knocking down of so substantial a cheque should have occupied perhaps three weeks, – and told his story. Having a little silver in his pocket, and having thought much of what had been said to him, he had 'planted' his cheque when he found himself near the town. In the language of the colonies, to plant a thing is to hide it. He had planted his cheque, and gone on to the publican with his silver. To set to work to get drunk was a matter of course. He did get drunk, – but the publican seemed to have had some doubt as to the propriety of supplying him freely. Why had not the man brought out his cheque in the usual manly way at once, instead of paying with loose silver for a few 'nobblers' for himself and the company? The publican put him to bed drunk, – stretching him out on some bunk or board in the customary hospitable manner; but he had his suspicions. Could it be that his old friend should have no cheque after shearing? It behoved him, at any rate, to know. The knocking down of an imaginary cheque would be dreadful to the publican. So the publican stripped him and examined all his clothing, looked into his boots, and felt well through the possible secrets of every garment. The man, though drunk and drugged, was not so drunk or drugged but what he knew and understood the proceeding. He had not paid enough for a sufficient amount of drugs and liquor to make him absolutely senseless. The cheque had been securely planted, and nothing was found. On the next morning he was turned out ignominiously by the justly indignant owner of the house; but in the tree by the roadside he found his cheque, and returned with it to the station a wiser and a better man.

And yet I do not say that the Queensland labourers are drunkards. I call a man a drunkard who is habitually drunk, – not him who gets drunk once or twice a year, though the drunkenness on those special occasions be ever so vigorous. These men at their work are almost invariably sober. The sheds or establishments at which they are employed are often far from any place at which drink can be bought, and from their employers they can get none. During their work they are not allowed to drink. In this respect they are under a restraint quite unintelligible to the ordinary English labourer. For weeks and weeks they go on, drinking nothing but tea. The pint of beer which is the Englishman's heaven is an unknown institution in the colonies. This sobriety, whether enforced or voluntary, during the period of employment has become so much a thing of course, that it is expected and is matter of no complaint. They smoke much tobacco, drink much tea, eat much mutton, – and work very hard. Then comes the short holiday, in which they knock down their cheques and live like brutes.

It must be allowed that the nature of the lives which these men live offers some excuse for their folly. During these periods of work they herd together like sailors on board a ship. Their home is at the wool-shed, or on the station, or somewhere about the establishment. They are, as it were, always subject to discipline, as are sailors and schoolboys, – and, like sailors and schoolboys, when they shake off their discipline they are 'wild for a spree.' There is no other spree open to the man but such as the publican can give him. He finds himself with a large sum of money in his hand, – which is all his own, and he is determined to have whatever enjoyment he can obtain. He has been debarred from liquor perhaps, for months, during which he has felt himself to be little better than a slave. Now he is free. For what has he toiled with unremitting labour and rigid enforced sobriety if he may not enjoy his freedom? So he knocks down his cheque; and then he begins again.

Of course there are varieties in the life. The man may have a wife who will restrain him, or a wife whom he will neglect, or a wife who can help in knocking down cheques. The married men generally do best, and are restrained, caring for their wives and children. When a man has obtained for himself a fixed home, – perhaps a homestead with a bit of land, – he returns thither instead of to a wonted drinking-shop. But the evil which I have described is so general, as to make it necessary that the would-be emigrant should know the temptations which he will encounter. We are often told in England that drink is the bane of the Australian colonies, – and as we know well the constancy of the habit with those of our own population who are given to beer or gin, – the bi-weekly or perhaps nightly attendance at the liquor-shop, – we are induced to believe that the same vice prevails in the same form but with aggravated force in Australia. Speaking, not of the towns, but of the country, I think that this is not the case. Australian drunkenness is not of the English type. It is more reckless, more extravagant, more riotous, – to the imagination of the man infinitely more magnificent, – but it is less enduring, and is certainly upon the whole less debasing.

The man, even if he have no wife, need not make himself a fool and a beast. The young would-be emigrant whom I am addressing will, at any rate, resolve that he will never knock down his cheque. He has my best wishes with him in that resolution, and my assurance that if he will keep it, he will certainly save money. He is to earn wages at the rate of £45 per annum over and above his food, and, if he be unmarried, he will be at no expense for house-rent or fuel while he is employed. He must clothe himself and furnish himself with a pair of blankets. The rest of his money he may save. In three years, provided he be gifted with that power of abstaining from drink altogether which my young friend intends to exercise, he will find himself the owner of £75 or £80, even after he have maintained himself for some weeks in each year, during which he may probably have been looking for fresh employment. What shall he do with his £75 so that he may be a happy and prosperous man?

Nothing but a strong conviction on my part that I shall never again be in Australia, never again meet those friendly squatters at whose tables I have sat, whose hospitality I have enjoyed, with whom I have discussed these matters, and whose hatred of the free-selecter I understand and appreciate, emboldens me to tell this young man that his best opening in colonial life is to buy a bit of land. I live in the hope that at home I may yet meet many a squatter whom I have known in the colonies; – but I shall meet them one at a time, and may hope to be able to endure any attack that may be made on me. 'And you, – after all that you have seen,' – the squatter would say, – 'after all that we have told you, after the pains we have been at to give you colonial experience and make you know the truth, – you recommend this young man to buy land, to become a farmer on soil which will produce no farmer's crop, to place himself where he must necessarily hate and be hated, to become a cattle-stealer in order that he may live, and to bring up his children to be cattle-stealers after his example! You understand the colonies! You are ignorant of the colonies as are all Englishmen, – those who stay at home equally with those who come out here for awhile and then go back crammed with folly and falsehood by interested persons.'

There is something admirable, or at least enviable, in the rock-fast conviction of men, the leading principles of whose lives have been formed by the combined strength of education, custom, and interest. It is so with the Australian squatter, who does not feel more sure that he himself will be injured by the operation of the free-selecter than that the free-selecter himself will be ruined by it. The squatter produces wool, and knows that wool is the staple produce of the colonies. To his thinking, success in wool means Australian greatness, and any drawback on that success, Australian misfortune. Any laws which may interfere with his pastoral and almost patriarchal views of life seem to him to emanate from democracy and the devil. He gets into parliament himself, – going up to Brisbane, if he be a Queenslander, at great personal inconvenience, feeling but little personal ambition as to his seat, – only that he may check the making of such laws. He knows that there must and will be land-laws in his colony, having the same melancholy certainty in the success of democracy and the devil as that which pervades the mind of an English Tory. He will even frame the land-law himself, – the very land-law which is to give power to the free-selecter, – as the Tory in England has framed laws for extended suffrage and the like. The English Tory when he is among his friends does not scruple to declare his hatred for the work of his own hands. In parliament it is necessary to be conciliatory, ready to yield, and almost submissive – but in private life every one knows of course that these changes are the work of democracy and the devil. It is really the same with the Australian Tory, as with his cousin at home. There must be land-laws, and the law must throw open the squatter's run to the rapacity of the free-selecter; – but not the less is the free-selecter an abomination and a curse. Personally, I love a squatter. I like to hear his grievances and to sympathize with them. I can make myself at home with him; – and can talk to him of his sheep more comfortably than I can to a miner of his gold, or a merchant of his dealings. But on principle I take the part of the free-selecter. When the young man shall have got together his £75, my advice to him is to lay it out in the purchase of land; – a small part of it in purchase, so that the remainder may be applied to building and improvement.

As to the cattle-stealing, – at any rate it is not a necessity. That cattle-stealing and sheep-stealing are common practices, is undoubtedly true; – and the squatter is generally the victim, while the free-selecter is as generally the thief. The herds and flocks are so large, and are so far removed from inspection, that such theft is easy. A beast is slain on the run, and skinned, and, if the skin be taken away or hidden, or burned, is hardly missed. A great deal is done in cattle-stealing, but I look on the assertion that free-selecters are as a rule cattle-stealers as monstrous. And it is monstrous also to suggest that a man should not purchase a tract of land, lest he should become a cattle-stealer under stress of circumstances.

In that assertion that the free-selecting farmer can grow nothing for which he can find a ready market, there is more reliable truth. In speaking of Queensland it must be acknowledged that the free-selecter finds it difficult to get ready money for the fruits of his labour. Wheat he cannot produce. It will fail twice with him for once that it will thrive. The alteration of wet weather and dry weather are not sufficiently certain, and the periods of drought or flood are too long for the growth of wheat. I do not know that sugar and wheat have ever thriven in close neighbourhood with each other. He can grow maize, or Indian corn as we call it; and as horses in Queensland, when corn-fed at all, are fed upon maize, there is a sale for it; but the farmer selling it will probably find himself driven to truck it for tea, sugar, or other stores. In the neighbourhood of Ipswich, some five-and-twenty miles from Brisbane, the farmer may grow cotton, – for which there is a ready sale. But in truth for the present the Queensland free-selecter, if he follow my advice, will not attempt to earn his bread by selling the produce of his land. He will not at any rate regard that as the sole means or mainstay of his existence. He will build himself a house and will gradually clear and fence his land. He will keep a few cows and poultry, and will supply himself and his family from his own farm. Then during a period of the year he will work for wages, – and will bring his cheque home with him when the work is done.

In five years or in ten, according to the mode of selection which the intending purchaser may adopt, he will be a freeholder, – but during these five or ten years he will have all the fixity of tenure in his land which belongs to a freehold. He will have learned before he makes his selection the manner in which this is to be done, and will have learned much also of the nature of the land to be selected. The system under which he will select is fully explained in an appendix to this volume, in which an extract is given from a Digest of the Queensland Crown Lands Alienation Act of 1868. It will show the intending purchaser that two modes of purchase are open to him, under one of which he may purchase as small a farm as forty acres, or as large a tract of land as 10,880 acres. For the forty acres he will have to pay 15s. an acre, but will have ten years in which to pay it, – so that he will be called upon for no more than £3 per annum, and at the end of ten years the land will be his own, if he have complied with the required conditions as to improvements. But the man whom I am now addressing will probably choose the other system, – and will buy what is called a homestead. In making this purchase he will find personal residence to be enjoined, – but personal residence will be his intention. By this system he can buy forty acres, or any number of acres not exceeding eighty, of so-called agricultural land. And for this he must pay 9d. an acre for five years, – 3s.9d. an acre altogether, – and then the land will be his own, to do with as he pleases.

The terms certainly do not seem to be hard. If the ambitious would-be freeholder desire to become master of the full amount allowed, – the eighty acres of agricultural land, – he will have to pay but £3 per annum as rent in advance, and will have to pay that only for five years! It is very alluring to the would-be freeholder. Let him not, however, suppose that because the land which he will buy is described as 'agricultural', that he will find hedges and ditches, furrows and headlands, and the like. The land will be land just as nature has produced it, but it will be land which on survey shall be declared to be fit for agricultural purposes.

There is perhaps no feeling stronger in the mind of man than the desire to own a morsel of land. In England efforts which have been made to enable the working man to become the owner even of the house in which he lives have hardly as yet met with much success. In the first place the price of land is too high, and in the second place the earnings of the working man are too low. In many cases in which the thing has been tried the creation of parliamentary voters has been the real object, and the possession of the freehold in the hands of the inhabitant has been no more than nominal. In England if a working man become a freeholder, he can hardly be free on his freehold. He cannot possess himself of the absolute property unencumbered by debt. If he feel the passion strong he must indulge it on some new-found soil, where the old forest still stands, where a man's work is as yet worth more than many acres. I do not know that he can do it anywhere on much better terms than in Queensland; – but he must understand that the land is cheap because the struggle required to make it useful is severe.

The labourer who can live and save his money, who can refrain from knocking down his cheque, may no doubt in Queensland become the real lord of all around him and dwell on his own land in actual independence. As far as I have seen the lives of such men, they never want for food, – are never without abundance of food. Meat and tea and bread they always have in their houses. The houses themselves are often rough, – sheds at first made of bark till the free-selecter can with his own hands put up some stronger and more endurable edifice; but they are never so squalid as are many of our cottages at home. For a labouring man, such as I have described, life in Queensland is infinitely better than life at home. It is sometimes very rough, and must sometimes be very solitary. And Queensland is very hot. But there is plenty to eat and drink; – work is well remunerated; – and the working man, if he can refrain from drink, may hold his own in Queensland, and may enjoy as much independence as is given to any man in this world.

SOUTH AUSTRALIA

CHAPTER I

EARLY HISTORY

South Australia has a peculiar history of its own, differing very much from those of the other Australian colonies, though similar in some degree to that of New Zealand, which was founded after South Australia, and with aspirations of the same nature. New South Wales was taken up by Great Britain as a convict depôt, and grew as such till the free inhabitants who had followed and surrounded the convicts became numerous and strong enough to declare that they would have no more such neighbours sent among them. Van Diemen's Land, which is now Tasmania, and Moreton Bay, which is now Queensland, were occupied as convict dependencies to the parent establishment. Moreton Bay was still part of New South Wales when New South Wales refused to be any longer regarded as an English prison, and Van Diemen's Land did for herself that which New South Wales had done before. Even Port Phillip, which is now Victoria, was first occupied by convicts sent thither from the parent colony, – though it is right to say that the convict system never took root there, and that the attempt never reached fulfilment. On the same principle New South Wales sent an offshoot convict depot to King George's Sound, which is now a part of Western Australia, – an unhappy colony which, in its sore distress, was destined to save itself from utter destruction by delivering itself to the custody of compelled immigrants, who could be made to come thither and work when others would not come. In this way all the now existing Australian colonies, except South Australia, have either owed their origin to convicts, or have been at one period of their existence fostered by convict labour; but South Australia has never been blessed – or cursed – with the custody of a single British exile.

In 1829, when Australian exploration was yet young, Captain Sturt, who had already travelled westwards from Sydney till he found and named the Darling River, and had done much towards investigating the difficult problem of the central Australian waters, received a commission from the government of New South Wales to make his way across to the Murrumbidgee River, and to discover by following its course what became of it. It was then believed by many, and among others by Captain Sturt himself, that the great waters of the continent, which had been reached but of which the estuaries were not known, ran into some huge central lake or internal sea. With the view of proving or of disproving this surmise, Captain Sturt with a few companions started on his journey, carrying with him a boat in detached pieces, in which he proposed to solve the mystery of the river. For, it must be understood, none of those maritime explorers who had surveyed, or partially surveyed, the eastern southern or western coasts of the continent had discovered any river mouth by which it was supposed that these waters could escape to the sea. Sturt was very zealous and ambitious to make for himself a great name among Australian explorers, – as he has done. In his account of a subsequent journey, – made into the interior after he had found that the river did not conduct him thither,— he thus describes his own feelings – 'Let any man lay the map of Australia before him and regard the blank upon its surface, and then let me ask if it would not be an honourable achievement to be the first to place foot upon its centre.' This he did, subsequently, in 1845; but in 1829–1830 he and his companions made their way down the Murrumbidgee till that large river joined a still greater stream, which he first called the Murray. The upper part of this river had been crossed by Hovell and Hume in 1826, and had then been called the Hume. But the name given by Sturt is the one by which it will hereafter be known. He followed it till it was joined by another large river, which he rightly presumed to be that Darling which he had himself discovered on a former journey. Still going on he came to the 'Great Bend' which the Murray makes. Hitherto the course of the wanderers down the Murrumbidgee and down the Murray had been nearly due west. From the Bend the Murray runs south, and from henceforth it waters a territory which is now a part of the province or colony of South Australia.

Sturt, when he had progressed for a while southwards, must have begun to perceive that that surmise as to a great inland sea was incorrect. For the waters both of the Murrumbidgee and the Darling he had so far accounted, and he was now taking with him down to the Southern Ocean the confluence of the three rivers. It is not my purpose in this book to describe the explorations of Australia, and I will not therefore stop to dwell upon the dangers which Sturt encountered. But it should be remembered that he was forced to carry with him all the provisions for his party, that he had no guide except the course of the waters which he was bound to follow, and that as he went he was accompanied along the banks by tribes of black natives, who, if not absolutely hostile, were astonished, suspicious, and irascible. Why they did not surround and destroy him and his little party we can hardly conceive. As far as we yet know, no white man had been there before, and yet it appears from Sturt's account that the natives frequently evinced no astonishment whatever at firearms, looking on while birds were shot, and not even condescending to admire the precision with which they were killed.

He went on southwards till he entered a big lake, – now called Lake Alexandrina. There are indeed a succession of lakes or inland waters here, of which Lakes Alexandrina and Albert are very shallow, rarely having as much as six feet of water, which is fresh or very nearly fresh, – and the Coorong River, which is salt, and, although as much within the mouth as are the lakes, must be regarded as an inlet of the sea. Of Lake Albert and the Coorong River, Sturt appears to have seen nothing, but he did make his way with extreme difficulty through the tortuous, narrow, and shallow opening of the river which takes the waters of the lake down to the sea in Encounter Bay, – and then perceived that for purposes of seaborne navigation the great river of which he had followed the course must always be useless. 'Thus,' he says, 'were our fears of the impracticability and inutility of the chain of communication between the lake and the ocean confirmed.'

Having so far succeeded, and so far failed, he was called upon to decide what he would do next. He could see to the westward ranges of hills, which he rightly conceived to be those which Captain Flinders had described after surveying the coasts of Gulf St. Vincent and Spencer's Gulf. Flinders had called these hills Mount Lofty, and Sturt could perceive, – at any rate could surmise, – that there was a fertile, happy land lying between him and them. But he had not got the means nor had his men the strength to go across the country. He could not take his little whale-boat out to sea, nor could he venture to remain on the shores of Encounter Bay till assistance should come to him from seawards. He had flour and tea left, and birds and kangaroo might be killed on the river banks. So he resolved to go back again up the river, and thus with infinite labour he returned by the Murray and Murrumbidgee, and made his way to Sydney.

The results of this journey were twofold. Though Sturt did not discover the land in which the colony of South Australia was first founded, and on which the city of Adelaide now stands, the history of his journey and the account which had previously been given by Captain Flinders, led to the survey of the land between the two gulfs and the Murray River. There stands a hill, about twenty miles from Adelaide, called Mount Barker; in honour of Captain Barker, who was killed by the blacks while employed on this work. The land was found to be good, and fit for agriculture; not sandy, as is so large a proportion of the continent, nor heavily timbered, as is a larger portion of it. The survey was made immediately on the receipt of Sturt's account, and the operations which were commenced with a view of planting the colony, were no doubt primarily due to him. And he solved the great question as to the Australian waters, proving, what all Australia now knows, to its infinite loss, that the River Murray, – the only considerable outflow of Australian waters, with which we are as yet acquainted, – makes its way into the sea by a mouth which is not suited for navigation. There is already much traffic on the Murray, and no doubt that traffic will increase; – but there is very little traffic indeed from the Murray to the seaports, even on the Australian coast, and it is not probable that the little will be extended. It is yet possible that on the north or north-western coast navigable rivers may be found. Just now men who have visited the northern shore are beginning to tell us that the Roper River and the Victoria River may by certain processes of blasting and dredging become serviceable, not only for inland but also for maritime navigation. But hitherto Australia has had no river into which great ships can make their way, as they do on the open rivers of America, of Europe, and of Asia. The narrowness and shallowness, – or, as I may perhaps call it, the meanness, – of the mouth of the Murray is one of the great natural disadvantages under which Australia labours.

Tidings of the land between the Murray and the Gulfs came home, and then a company formed itself with the object of 'planting' a colony, as British settlements were formerly planted in North America. The plan to be followed was that which came to be known as the Wakefield system, the theory of which required that the land should be sold in small quantities, at a 'sufficient price,' so that the purchasers should settle on their own lands, and hold no more land than they would be able to occupy beneficially for themselves and the colony at large. This theory of occupation was to be adopted in distinct opposition to that under which large grants of land had been made in Western Australia, – the territorial estates so granted having been far too extensive in area for beneficial occupation.

In establishing new homes for the crowded population of old lands it has been found almost impossible to follow out to any perfect success the theories of philanthropists. The greed of individuals on one side, and obstinacy and ambition on other sides, have marred these embryo Utopias in the prospect of which the brains of good men have revelled. Machinery, if the means and skill be sufficient, can be made to do its proposed work in exact conformity with the intentions of the projectors; but men are less reliable. They are, however, more powerful, each being the owner of a new energy; and though the Utopian philanthropist may be disappointed, – even to a broken heart, – the very greed and obstinacy of his followers will often lead to greater results than would have been achieved by a strict compliance with the rules of a leader, however wise, however humane, however disinterested he may have been. The scheme proposed for the colonization of South Australia was not carried out in strictness; but the colony is strong and healthy, and it may be doubted whether it would now be stronger or healthier had a closer compliance with the intentions of the founders been effected.

In 1834 an Act was passed for founding the colony of South Australia. Under this Act it was specially provided that the proceeds of the land should be devoted to immigration. This, however, was no necessary part of Mr. Gibbon Wakefield's plan. In his evidence given subsequently before a committee of the House of Commons in 1836, he thus speaks of his own scheme: 'The object of the price is not to create an immigration fund. You may employ the fund in that way if you please, but the object of the price is to create circumstances in the colony which would render it, instead of a barbarous country, an extension of the old country, with all the good, but without the evils of the old society. There is no relation, – it is easy to see one which is of no consequence, but I can see no proper relation, – between the price required for land and immigration.' He repeats the same opinion in his book, called 'A View of the Art of Colonization'. This is written in the form of letters, and in Letter 55 he says: 'So completely is the production of revenue a mere incident of the price of the land, that the price ought to be imposed, if it ought to be imposed under any circumstances, even though the purchase-money were thrown away.' Again in the same letter he continues, speaking of the money which would arise from the sale of land: 'It is an unappropriated fund which the state or government may dispose of as it pleases without injustice to anybody. If the fund were applied to paying off the public debt of the empire nobody could complain of injustice, because every colony as a whole, and the buyers of land in particular, would still enjoy the intended and expected benefits of sufficient price upon new land. If the fund were thrown into the sea as it arrived, there would still be no injustice, and no reason against producing the fund in that way.' This is a very strong way of putting it; but Mr. Wakefield meant to assert that the consideration of the use to which the fund arising from the sale of land might be applied, was no part of his plan. Let others decide as to that. He had seen that the grants of vast areas of land to men who had taken themselves out with a certain amount of capital and a certain number of fellow-emigrants, had not produced colonial success. There was the terrible example of Western Australia before him. The land was not occupied, and was not tilled. Each new-comer thought that he should have a share of the land, rather than that he should perform a share of the labour. I would not, however, have it supposed that I am an admirer generally either of Mr. Wakefield's system of colonization, as given in his book, or of his practice as carried out in New Zealand. He was right in maintaining that all land should be sold for a price so high as to prevent, at any rate for a time, the formation of large private estates in the hands of individuals, who would be powerless to use such estates when possessed. In almost all beyond that, – as in regard to his idea that English society, under the presidency of some great English magistrate, should be taken out to the young colony 'with all the good, but without the evil,' – he is I think Utopian. Of his own doings as a colonizer I shall have to speak again in reference to New Zealand.

Mr. Wakefield's plan was by no means adopted as a whole by the Act of 1834, in conformity with which the new colony was to be founded. In 1831 an attempt had been made to obtain a charter for forming a company, by which the new colony was to be planted in strict acccordance with Mr. Wakefield's principle. But this scheme broke down, and in 1834 the Act was passed. Under this Act it was provided that the land should be sold in small blocks, – no doubt at a 'sufficient price', – and that the money so realised should be applied to immigration. What the 'sufficient price' should be Mr. Wakefield had never stated. Indeed it would then have been impossible, and is still equally impossible, that any price should be fixed as the value of a commodity, whose value varies in accordance with climate, position, and soil.

The impossibility of fixing a price for land, and yet the apparent necessity of doing so, has been the greatest difficulty felt in arranging the various schemes of Australian colonization. At first sight it may seem easy enough. Let the land be put up to auction, and let the purchaser fix the price. But when the work was commenced it was necessary to get new settlers on to the land, who knew nothing of its relative value, who could not tell whether they could afford to give 5s. or £5 an acre for it and then live upon it. These new-comers required to be instructed in all things, and in nothing more than as to the proper outlay of their small capitals. And the system of auction, when it did come to prevail in the sale of crown lands, was found to produce the grossest abuses, – I think I may say the vilest fraud. Men constituted themselves as land agents with the express purpose of exacting black mail from those who were really desirous of purchasing. 'I will be your agent,' such a one would say to the would-be purchaser. 'I will buy the land for you, at a commission of a shilling an acre. You can buy it for yourself, you say. Then I shall bid against you.' This system has prevailed to such an extent that the agency business has become an Australian profession, and men who did not want an acre of land have made fortunes by exacting tribute from those who were in earnest. As a rule, 20s. an acre has been the normal price fixed in these colonies generally, – though from that there have been various deviations. In South Australia proper, – that is in South Australia exclusive of the northern territory, – the Crown has never alienated an acre for less than 20s. an acre. Mr. Wakefield seems to have considered that 40s. an acre should have been demanded from the early settlers in the new colony, – but he would fix no sum, always adhering to his term of a 'sufficient price.'

The Act required that the money produced by the sale of lands should be employed in bringing immigrants into the country; but this requirement has not been fulfilled. A public debt was soon accumulated, and the colony decided that the proceeds of the land should be divided into three parts, – that a third should go to immigration, a third to the public works, and a third to the repayment of the public debt. But this arrangement has again gone to the wall, and the money produced is now so much revenue, and is like other revenue at the disposal of the House of Assembly. But the Act of 1834 enjoined also that no convicts should ever be sent to South Australia, and this enactment has never been infringed. It also decreed that, as soon as the population of the new colony should have reached 50,000 a constitution, with representative government, should be granted to it. This, too, was carried out with sufficient accuracy. At the close of 1849 the population was 52,904 and in 1850 the British Parliament conferred on the colonists the power of returning elected members to serve in the Legislative Council.

I should hardly interest my readers, if I were to dilate upon all the success and all the failures which the promoters of the South

Australian plan encountered. But it is well that they should understand that there was a plan, and that the work was not done from hand to mouth, – that South Australia did not progress accidentally, and drift into free institutions, as was the case with other Australian colonies. There was much both of success and of failure; but it may be said that the attempt was made in a true spirit of philanthropy, and that the result has been satisfactory if not at first triumphant. Mr. Wakefield, Mr. Hutt, – now Sir William Hutt, – Colonel Torrens, and Mr. Angas were chief among those to whom the colony is indebted for its foundation. The first vessels sent out were dispatched by the South Australian Company, of which Mr. Angas was the chairman. They arrived in 1836, but the new-comers knew nothing of the promised land before them. At the bottom of Gulf St. Vincent, lying off a toe of the land, as Sicily lies off from Italy, is Kangaroo Island. It is barren, covered with thick scrub, and deficient in water. No more unfortunate choice could have been made by young settlers. But here the first attempts were made, and here still linger a few descendants of the first pioneers, who live in primitive simplicity together. They have a town called Kingscote, on Nepean Bay. Mr. Sinnet, in his account of the colony, says that he was there in 1860–61, and that then there were about half-a-dozen houses, chiefly occupied by the descendants and connections of one old gentleman. Such was the fate of the earliest settlement formed by the South Australian Company.

But Nepean Bay was soon relinquished as the future home of the would-be happy colonists. Later in 1836 Colonel Light arrived, sent out as the surveyor-general by the government at home, and Captain Hindmarsh as the first governor of the new colony. There was still much difficulty before a site for the new town was chosen, and apparently much quarrelling. Adelaide, which was to be the earthly paradise of perfected human nature, was founded amidst loud recrimination and a sad display of bitter feeling; – but the site was chosen, and was chosen well, and the town was founded. Captain Hindmarsh, however, was recalled in 1838, as having failed his mission, and Colonel Light died in 1839. Captain Hindmarsh was replaced by Colonel Gawler, who went to work with great energy in making roads and bridges, – and running the colony

into debt over and above the funds on which it was
empowered to draw. The colony was insolvent, and they who
had advanced cash on bills drawn by the governor were for a
while without their money. It seemed as though the great
attempt would end in failure. The colony, with a revenue of
only £30,000, had attained an annual expenditure of £150,000
and a public debt of £300,000.* Such was the condition of
South Australia when Captain (now Sir George) Grey
succeeded Colonel Gawler. Under his influence the expenditure was checked, and money was lent by the British
Parliament. From that time forward the colony flourished.
The debt was repaid, and Elysian happiness was initiated.

The real prosperity of South Australia commenced with the
discovery of copper at the Burra mines in 1845. As I shall say
something of the great wealth which has accrued to the colony
from her copper in a following chapter, I will only remark
here that as gold produced the success of Victoria, so did
copper that of South Australia. But the gold in the former was
very nearly ruinous to the success of the latter. In 1851 began
the rush of diggers to the Victoria gold-fields, and so great
was the attraction that for a time it seemed that the whole male
population of South Australia was about to desert its home. I
will again quote Mr. Sinnett: 'Shipload after shipload of male
emigrants continued to leave the port during many consec-
utive months, while thousands more walked or drove their
teams overland; the little-trodden overland route becoming
the scene of traffic, – the principal camping-places being every
night lighted up by the numerous camp-fires of parties of
travellers. At the same time that the men went, the money
went with them. The banks were drained of coin, and trade
partially ceased. Scores of shops were closed, because the
tradesmen had followed their customers to the diggings. The
streets seemed to contain nothing but women; and strong
feelings were entertained that no harvest would be sown, and
that, allured by the more glittering attractions of the gold
colony, the small landed proprietors, who formed so important a section of our society, would permanently remain away,
selling their land here for whatever trifle it would fetch.' This

* I take these figures from Mr. Sinnett's work.

is a strongly drawn picture of the state of all Australian society at the time. There was one general rush to the gold-fields, and men for a time taught themselves to believe that no pursuit other than the pursuit of gold was worthy of a man's energies. South Australia had no gold-fields, and therefore the current of emigration was all away from her. For a time the gloom was great. But the runagates soon found that everything was not bright in the rich land, – and they returned to their homesteads, many of them with gold in their hands. Though there was great terror in the colony when the exodus was taking place, the opinion is now general that South Australia gained more in wealth than it lost by the discovery of the Victorian gold.

South Australia is at present possessed of a representative government, – as are all the other Australian colonies, except Western Australia. But during the early years of her existence she, as well as the others, was subject to government from our Colonial Office at home. There was from the first a feeling averse to this, which no doubt greatly assisted in producing the troubles by which the early governors were afflicted. They who had been instrumental in founding the colony were hearty Liberals, attached to religious freedom, altogether averse to Established Churches, and anxious for self-rule. For men coming out in such a spirit, but coming out nevertheless with the aid and furtherance of the home government, there were of course trials and crosses. They desired to rule themselves, – as the Pilgrim Fathers had done in Massachusetts. But the office in Downing Street would not relinquish its authority to colonists who might be visionary, and were certainly ambitious. On the other hand, men who were disposed to devote their time and fortunes to a system of philosophical colonisation were apt to feel that their scheme should not be made subject to the interference which a convict colony might probably require. There were troubles, and those two first governors, Captain Hindmarsh and Colonel Gawler, had hot work on their hands. Colonel Robe, who in 1845 succeeded Captain Grey as governor, and who as a military man felt that he was governing the colony on behalf of the Crown rather than on that of the colonists, gave great offence, – especially by providing state endowment for religion, a point as to which the founders of the colony had been particularly sensitive. But a good time was coming. When 50,000 inhabitants had settled themselves on the land, then would those inhabitants be entitled to govern themselves; and then any governor who might be sent to them from the old country would be no more than that appanage of royalty which serves as a binding link between the parent country and its offspring. Then they would make laws for themselves; then they would not have State endowment for clergymen more than for doctors or lawyers; then would their Elysium have truly been initiated.

The work of governing the colony had indeed been commenced with some little attempt at double government. There was a board of South Australian Commissioners in London, and when Captain Hindmarsh came out as governor, there was appointed a certain member of this Board to act as resident commissioner in Adelaide, and to report direct to the commissioners at home. Colonel Gawler and his successor, Captain Grey, held, however, the joint offices of governor and resident commissioner, – so that very little came of the arrangement as a check upon the power of Downing Street. In 1842 the office of resident commissioner was altogether abolished, and the Act of Parliament by which this was done provided for the appointment of a Legislative Council of eight, the whole of which, however, was to be nominated by the Crown. In 1850, – when the requisite population had been achieved, the colonists were allowed to elect two-thirds of the Legislative council, the number of councillors being raised from eight to twenty-four. But this did not long satisfy the cravings of the people for self-government. In other Australian colonies, – especially in the neighbouring colony of Victoria, – demands for free constitutions were being made at the same time; and what colony could have a better right to be free than South Australia, established, as she had been, on philosophical and philanthropical principles?

The Council gave way to the people, and the governor gave way to the Council; but they did not at first give way enough. In 1853 they passed a bill, – subject to confirmation at home, – creating two houses of parliament, of which the Lower House, – to be called the House of Assembly, – should be elective. The members were to be elected for three years, subject of course to dissolution by the governor. But the members of the Legislative Council, to consist of twelve members, were to be appointed for life by the governor. It should be remembered by all who desire to study the form of government and legislative arrangement in these colonies, that members of the Upper House are nominated by the Crown, – and therefore, in fact, by the minister of the day, – in New South Wales and Queensland, but are elected by the people in Victoria and South Australia. In 1853, however, when the Council in South Australia was sitting, with the view of framing a new constitution for the colonies, the question was still unsettled as to any of these colonies. Queensland had not commenced her career. In New South Wales it had been decided that the existing Legislative Council should pass a constitution, but that it should be one under which the future Upper House of the colony should be nominated by the Crown; and an Act to this effect was passed accordingly on 21st December, 1853. No doubt the proposed action of the sister colony was well known and well discussed in Adelaide, the party of the government feeling that a constitution which was supposed to suit New South Wales might well suit South Australia; and the colonists themselves feeling that, however willing the old-fashioned people of New South Wales might be to subject themselves after the old-fashioned way to government nominations, such a legislative arrangement was by no means compatible with the theory of self-rule, under which they had come out to the new country. A petition against the bill was sent home, – a petition praying that the assent of the Crown, for which it had as a matter of course been reserved, might not be given to it. The petition was supposed to represent the feeling of the colony, and the bill was therefore sent back for reconsideration. The Legislative Council was dissolved, and a new Council elected, and nominated, – with sixteen elected and eight nominated members. This Council was obedient to the will of the people, and passed the constitution which is now in force. The new Legislative Council was to be elective, and not nominated; and the governor was to be without the power of dissolving it. It was to consist of eighteen members, six of whom should retire every four years, – so that when the arrangement came to be in full force, as it is now, every member would have a seat for twelve years. The elections were to be made by the country at large. At each election any man possessed of the franchise of the Upper House would vote for any six candidates he pleased, and the six having the majority of votes would come in as returned by the entire colony. When speaking in a future chapter of the acting legislature of the colony, I will give my reasons for disapproving of this form of election. It was adopted, and, having the general approval of the colony, was confirmed by the Crown at home, and is now the law of the land. The second chamber was to consist, and still does consist, of thirty-six members, to be elected for three years each. An elector for the Council must possess a £50 freehold, or a leasehold of £20 per annum, or occupy a dwelling-house valued at £25 per annum. Manhood suffrage prevails in reference to electors for the Lower Chamber, it being simply requisite that the elector's name should have been six months on the roll, and that he shall be twenty-one. A member of the Council must be thirty-four years old, born a subject or naturalised, and a resident in the colony for three years. The qualification of a member for the Legislative Assembly is the same as that for an elector.

This constitution was proclaimed in the colony in October, 1856, and the first parliament elected under it commenced its work on April 22, 1857. Thus constitutional government and self-rule were established in South Australia. With such a parliament responsible ministers were, as a matter of course, a part of the system, and on 24th of October, 1856, five gentlemen undertook the government of the colony as chief secretary, attorney-general, treasurer, commissioner of crown lands and immigration, and commissioner of public works. From that day to the period of my visit to the colony, – April, 1872, – there had been no less than twenty-four sets of ministers; but the cabinet remained the same, with the five officers whom I have named.

CHAPTER II

ADELAIDE

Adelaide is a pleasant, prosperous town, standing on a fertile plain, about seven miles from the sea, with a line of hills called the Mount Lofty Range, forming a background to it. On 31st December, 1871, the city proper contained 27,208 inhabitants, and the suburbs, so called, contained 34,474, making a total of 61,682 persons either living in the metropolis, or so closely in its neighbourhood as to show that they are concerned in the social and commercial activity of the city. On the same date the entire population of the colony was 189,018. Adelaide alone, therefore, contains very nearly a third of the life of the whole community of South Australia. This proportion of urban to rural population, – or I may perhaps better say of metropolitan to non-metropolitan, – is very much in excess of that which generally prevails in other parts of the world.

The same result has come of the immigration to the other great Australian colonies, though not quite to the same extent. The population of Melbourne and its suburbs up to the beginning of 1872 was 206,000, and that of the colony was 755,000. The population of Sydney and its suburbs was 136,000, and that of New South Wales 500,000. In each case the population of the one city with its suburbs is between a third and a fourth of that of the entire colony, and in each case the proportion of urban to rural population is unusually high.

It may, perhaps, be taken as a rule, – though a rule with very wide exceptions, – that the produce of a country comes from the industry of those who live out of the metropolis, and that they who live in the metropolis exercise their energies, and make or mar their fortunes, in the management of that produce. Politicians, lawyers, merchants, government offic-ials, and even retail dealers, with the concourse of people who are got together with the object of providing for them, form a community which can hardly be said to be, itself, productive, though it gives to the products of a country very much of the value which they possess, and which they would not possess without such metropolitan arrangement. I do not know that any political economist has as yet cared to inquire what proportion of the population of a community should be metropolitan – so that the affairs of the community might be ordered in the very best manner. Nor could such inquiry be made with any exact result, as the circumstances of countries and of towns vary very greatly; but the proportions of population as shown in the Australian cities above named cannot be taken as showing a healthy state of things. It goes towards proving that what we may perhaps call the pioneer immigration into these colonies has been checked, – a fact of which we have much other proof. The men who are here, and the men who come afresh, prefer the city, and eschew a life of agricultural labour. The nomadic race of miners will rush after tidings of gold, and will form communities of their own; but the fields of Australia, the vast territories of the continent which we would fain see bearing crops of wheat and Indian maize, as do the vast prairies of the central States of America, do not entice the population. It will be said, and said truly, that if a people can find a living in a city, with all their wants supplied to them by caterers near at hand, why should such a people encounter the hardships of the backwoods, – or bush, as it is called in Australia? Why should not a man stay in town, if he can live in town? We all feel that, as regards any individual man, the argument is good; – but we feel at the same time that cities without country to feed them cannot be long continued; and that a community with extensive means of management, and sparse powers of production, is like a human body without arms or legs. What is the use of the best stomach which nature ever gave to a man without the means of filling it?

It seems to be the case that immigrants coming to the colony stick too closely to the towns, – and are unwilling to encounter the rough chances of agricultural or pastoral life, as long as any means of living is open to them in the cities. The evil, if it be an evil, must cure itself as rural wages advance in proportion to city wages. In the meantime, it is worthy of remark, – and of speculation as to the causes of the fact, – that the city populations of Australia are excessive. As the excess in Adelaide is greater than elsewhere, I have raised the point while speaking of the capital of South Australia.

Perhaps no city, not even Philadelphia, has been laid out with a stronger purpose of regularity and order than has been shown in the founding and construction of Adelaide. Adelaide proper, as distinguished from North Adelaide, – which has been allowed to deviate somewhat from the good manner of the parent city, – stands in exact conformity with the points of the compass. The streets all run north and south, or east and west. There are five squares, – or open spaces so designated, – one in the centre, and the other four at certain fixed intervals. At the extremities of the town, on the northern, southern, eastern, and western sides there are four terraces. That, however, on the eastern side has been allowed to take a devious course, as the city to the south is longer than it is at the north. But there is a precise regularity even in this irregularity. This terrace on the map of the town takes the form of a flight of steps, for nothing so irregular as a sloping or diagonal line has been permitted in the arrangement of the streets. To me the Quaker-like simplicity of such urban construction never renders easy any practical conception of the topography. I find it quite as easy to lose my way in Philadelphia or Adelaide as I do in the old parts of Paris, or in the meandering lanes of such a city as Norwich. I forget which is north and which west, and what set of streets run at right angles to what other set. I never was able to find my way about Adelaide. But for a man with a compass in his pocket, a clear calculating brain, and a good memory, the thing must be very easy. The northern half of the town is the West End. About midway on the Northern Terrace is Government House, and opposite to it is the Adelaide Club. The Houses of Parliament are close, on the same terrace. King William Street, the High Street of the town, runs at right angles from the North Terrace to Victoria Square, which is the centre of the city. Here, in King William Street, is congregated the magnificence of Adelaide, – comprising the Town Hall, the Public Offices, the Post Office, and various banks, and many of the most money-making shops.

The one building in Adelaide on which the town most prides itself, – and of which at the same time the colony is half ashamed because of the expense, – is the Post Office. I was gratified by finding that the colonies generally were disposed to be splendid in their post-offices rather than in any other buildings, – for surely there is no other public building so useful. At Brisbane, when I was there, they were building a fine post-office, At Sydney they had nearly completed a magnificent post-office, of which I have spoken in its proper place. At Melbourne I found a very large post-office indeed, – though, as I thought, one not very convenient to the public. And here at Adelaide the Post Office is the grandest edifice in the town. It is really a beautiful building, with a large centre hall, such as we had in London as long as we could afford ourselves the luxury. We have built up our hall, compelled by exigiencies of space and money, – compelled as I think by a shabby regard to space and money. It will be long before the authorities of Adelaide will be driven to perpetuate a similar architectural meanness, – for surely such a post office will be more than ample for the population for many a year to come. I went over the building, and knowing something of post-offices, I regret to say that the arrangements might have been improved by consultation with English officials. As regarded the building as a building, it is a credit to Adelaide, and would be an ornament to any city in Europe. The government offices are not magnificent, – but are pleasant, commodious, and sufficient. The Town Hall is a fine room, and forms a portion of a very handsome building. In such luxuries as townhalls, large public concert-rooms, public ball-rooms, and the like, the Australian cities greatly beat our own. I do not say that there is any such an edifice on the Australian continent as St. George's Hall at Liverpool, – but then neither is there any town with half the number of inhabitants that Liverpool contains. Adelaide itself has less than 30,000, and I doubt whether there be any town in England with double that number which has such a chamber for public purposes as that of which I am speaking. I am sure there is none with four times the number that has a theatre so pretty, so well constructed, and so fit for its purpose as the Adelaide Theatre. Even little Perth with its 6,000 souls has a grand town-hall. In

almost every municipality, – even in those of the suburbs of
such a town as Adelaide, – halls are erected for public
purposes, for speeches, balls, concerts, and the like. In this
respect our children in Australia take after their cousins in the
United States. In regard to banks also Adelaide flourishes
greatly. I must not name any one in particular, lest it be
thought that I am making return for accommodation given;
but, such was their grandeur, that I felt of them generally that
the banking profits in South Australia must be very great, or
such edifices could not have been erected.

On the farther or southern side of the square are the Law
Courts, as to which I was informed that that intended for the
Supreme Court was not used as intended, being less convenient than an older building opposite to it. I did not go into
either of them.

Adelaide is well provided with churches, – so much so that
this speciality has been noticed ever since its first foundation.
It was peculiarly the idea of those who formed the first
mission to South Australia, that there should be no dominant
Church; – that religious freedom should prevail in the new
colony as it never had prevailed up to that time in any British
settlement; and that the word dissent should have no meaning,
as there should be nothing established from which to disagree.
In spite of all this the Church of England has assumed a certain
ascendancy, partly from the fact that a liberal and worthy
Englishwoman, now Lady Burdett-Coutts, endowed a bishopric at Adelaide; but chiefly from the indubitable fact that
they of the Church of England who have flocked into the
colony have been higher in wealth and intelligence than those
of any other creed. It would be singular indeed had it not been
so, seeing that the country from which they came had for
centuries possessed an established and endowed Church. But
the very fact that the Church of England boasted for itself even
in this colony a kind of ascendancy, and the other fact that the
colony had been founded with the determination that there
should be no ascendancy, have together created great enmity
among the rival sects. While I was in Adelaide a motion was
before parliament, – as to which I heard the debate then in
progress, – for taking away the right of precedency belonging
by royal authority to the present bishop. Both Houses had

passed a bill, with the purpose of taking away from the prelate the almost unmeaning privilege of precedence. It had been reserved by the governor, with undeniable propriety, for the decision of the government at home. The Secretary of State for the Colonies had returned a dispatch, intended to be most conciliatory, stating that the Crown would be happy to consider any proposition made by the colony, but that the legislature of the colony could not be permitted to annul the undoubted prerogative of the Crown to grant honours. But the matter was again argued as though a great injury had been inflicted. It was well understood by all men that in the event of a vacancy in the bishopric no successor would be appointed by the Crown; and that any future bishop, – appointed as he must be by a synod of the Church, – would have conferred on him by his appointment no privilege of walking out of any room before anybody else. But such is the feeling of the colony in regard to religious freedom, and such the feeling especially in the city of Adelaide, that a politician desirous of popularity felt, not without cause, that a stroke of political business might be done in this direction. Of all storms in a teacup, no storm could be more insignificant than this. That the present bishop, who has the good word of everybody, should be allowed to wear to the last the very unimportant honour conferred upon him, would have seemed to be a matter of course. He has, since, resigned the right. It was, however, thought worth while not only to fight the question, but to re-fight it. The matter is worthy of notice only as showing the feeling of the people on the subject. I may here remark that Adelaide has been called especially a city of churches, so strong has been the ambition of various sects to have it seen publicly that their efforts to obtain places of worship worthy of their religion have been as successful as those of their sister sects. The result has tended greatly to the decoration of the town. Amongst them all, the Church of England is, at the present moment, by no means the best represented. A cathedral, however, designed by Butterfield, is now rising as fast as its funds will permit.

All round the city there are reserved lands, of which I may best explain the nature to English readers by calling them parks for the people. These reserves are of various widths in different parts, but are full half a mile wide on an average. They are now being planted, and are devoted to air and recreation. I need hardly explain that they cannot as yet rival the beauty and the shade of our London parks; but that they will do so is already apparent to the eye. And they will have this advantage, – which, indeed, since the growth of the town towards the west belongs also to our London parks, – that they will be in the middle, not on the outside, of an inhabited city. As Adelaide increases in population, these 'reserves' will be in the midst of the inhabitants. But they will have also this additional advantage, – which we in London do not as yet enjoy, in spite of efforts that have been made, – that they will not be a blessing only to one side or to one end of the city. They will run east and west, north and south, and will be within the reach of all Adelaide and her suburbs. There are here also public gardens, – as there are in every metropolis of the Australian colonies. The gardens of Adelaide cannot rival those of Sydney, – which, as far as my experience goes, are unrivalled in beauty anywhere. Nothing that London possesses, nothing that Paris has, nothing that New York has, comes near to them in loveliness. But, as regards Australian cities, those of Adelaide are next to the gardens of Sydney. In Melbourne the gardens are more scientific, but the world at large cares but little for science. In Sydney, the public gardens charm as poetry charms. At Adelaide, they please like a well-told tale. The gardens at Melbourne are as a long sermon from a great divine, – whose theology is unanswerable, but his language tedious.

I have said that the city has a background of hills called the Mount Lofty Range, – so called by Captain Flinders when he made his first survey. The only pretension to landscape beauty which the city possesses is derived from these mountains. It was indeed said many years ago by one much interested in Adelaide, that she was built on a 'pretty stream'. The 'stream' is called the Torrens, after one of the founders of the colony, but I utterly deny the truth of the epithet attached to it. Anything in the guise of a river more ugly than the Torrens it would be impossible to see or to describe. During eleven months of the year it is a dry and ugly channel, – retaining only the sewer-wards property of a river. In this condition I saw it. During the other month it is, I was told, a torrent. But the hills around are very pretty, and afford lovely views and charming sites for villa residences, and soil and climate admirably suited for market gardens. As a consequence of this latter attribute Adelaide is well supplied with vegetables and fruit. By those who can afford to pay the price already demanded for special sites, beautiful nooks for suburban residences may still be obtained.

The city receives its water from an artificial dam constructed about eight miles from it, but the reservoir used when I was there had been deemed insufficient for the growing needs of the town. A larger dam, calculated to hold innumerable gallons, had been just finished as far as the earthworks were concerned, and was waiting to be filled by the winter rains. A tunnel had been made through the hillside for its supply, – so that it might water Adelaide and all her suburbs for generations to come. But generations come so quickly now, that for aught I can tell Adelaide may want a new dam and infinitely increased gallons before one generation has entirely passed away. If it be so, I do not doubt but that the new dam and all the gallons will be forthcoming. While speaking of water, I must acknowledge that during three months of the year water is a matter of vital consideration to the inhabitants of Adelaide. I was not there in December, January, or February; but from the admission of inhabitants, – of Adelaideans not too prone to admit anything against their town, – I learned that it can be very hot during those three months. I liked Adelaide much, – and I liked the Adelaideans; but I must confess to my opinion that it is about the hottest city in Australia south of the tropics. The heat, however, is not excessive for above three months. I arrived in the first week of April, and then the weather was delightful. I was informed that the great heats rarely commence before the second week in December. But when it is hot, it is very hot. Men and women sigh for 95 in the shade, as they, within the tropics, sigh for the temperate zones.

But in all respects such as that of water, – in regard to pavements, gas, and sewers, in regard to hospitals, lunatic asylums, institutions for the poor, and orphanages, – the cities of Australia stand high; and few are entitled to be ranked higher than Adelaide. I had an opportunity of seeing many of these institutions, including the gaol inside the city and the gaol outside; and I saw some of them under the auspices of one who was perhaps better entitled to judge them than any other man in the colony. It seemed to me that they were only short of absolute excellence. When I remembered how small was the population, how short a time had elapsed since the place was a wilderness, how limited the means, how necessarily curtailed were the appliances at the command of what we should call such a handful of men, – and when I remembered also what I have seen in our own workhouses at home, what I have seen in our own gaols, what but a few years since prevailed in many of our own lunatic asylums, – I could not but think that the people of Adelaide had been very active and very beneficent. Of course every new town founded has the advantage of all the experience of every old town founded before it. It is easier for a new country, than for an old country, to get into good ways. No man has visited new countries with his eyes open without learning so much as that. But, not the less, when the observer sees 60,000 people in a new city, with more than all the appliances of humanity belonging to four times the number in old cities, he cannot refrain from bestowing his meed of admiration. I will now finish my remarks about this town with saying that no city in Australia gives one more fixedly the idea that Australian colonisation has been a success, than does the city of Adelaide.

CHAPTER III

LAND

I have said that Adelaide has been called a city of churches. It has also been nicknamed the Farinaceous City. A little gentle ridicule is no doubt intended to be conveyed by the word. The colony by the sister colonies is regarded as one devoted in a special manner to the production of flour. Men who spend their energy in the pursuit of gold consider the growing of wheat to be a poor employment. And again the squatters, or wool-producers of Australia, who are great men, with large flocks, and with acres of land at their command so enormous that they have to be counted, not by acres, but by square miles, look down from a very great height indeed upon the little agriculturists, – small men, who generally live from hand to mouth, – and whose original occupation of their holdings has commonly been supposed to be at variance with the squatters' interests. The agriculturists of Australia generally are free-selecters, men who have bought bits here and bits there off the squatters' runs, and have bought the best bits, – men, too, whose neighbourhood, for reasons explained before, has not been a source of comfort to the squatters generally. In this way agriculture generally, and especially the growing of wheat-crops for sale, has not been regarded in the colonies as it is certainly regarded at home. The farmers of South Australia are usually called 'cockatoos', – a name which prevails also, though less universally, in the other colonies. The word cockatoo in the farinaceous colony has become so common as almost to cease to carry with it the intended sarcasm. A man will tell you of himself that he is a cockatoo, and when doing so will probably feel some justifiable pride in the freehold possession of his acres. But the name has been given as a reproach, and in truth it has been and is deserved. It signifies that the man does not really till his land, but only scratches it as the bird does.

Nevertheless, – and in spite of any gibes conveyed in the words farinaceous, cockatoo, or free-selecter, – South Australia is especially blessed in being the one great wheat-producing province among the Australian colonies. The harvest of 1870–71, – which was, no doubt, specially productive, but is quoted here because it is the last as to which, as I write, I can obtain the statistics, – gave 6,961,164 bushels of wheat, which at 5s. a bushel, the price at which it was sold in Adelaide, produced £1,827,305. In the same year, that is, up to 31st December, 1871, which would take the disposal of the crop above mentioned, – for wheat, it must be remembered, in Australia is garnered in our spring, and not in our autumn, – 104,000 tons of bread-stuff were exported, and sold for £1,253,342. So that the colony consumed not a third of the breadstuffs which it produced. The population of the colony up to 31st December, 1871, was 189,018 persons. So that the value of the foodstuffs exported in that year was something over £6 12s. 6d. a head for every man, woman, and child within it. With such a result, South Australia need not be ashamed of being called farinaceous.

It must not, however, be supposed that the year above quoted shows a fair average. The following table will give the amount of wheat produced, with the area from which it was produced, the average crop per acre, and the value per bushel, together with the amount of breadstuff and grain exported for the year above named, and the four preceding years:–

WHEAT PRODUCED		AREA UNDER WHEAT		AVERAGE CROP PER ACRE		
Year	Bushels	Year	Acres	Year	Bsh.	lb.
1866–7	6,561,451	1866–7	457,628	1866–7	14	20
1867–8	2,579,894	1867–8	550,456	1867–8	4	40
1868–9	5,173,970	1868–9	533,035	1868–9	9	42
1869–70	3,052,320	1869–70	532,135	1869–70	5	45
1870–71	6,961,164	1870–71	604,761	1870–71	11	30

VALUE PER BUSHEL			VALUE OF BREAD-STUFFS AND GRAIN EXPORTED	
Year	s	d	Year	
1866–7	4	5	1867	£1,037,085
1867–8	7	1	1868	568,491
1868–9	5	0	1869	890,343
1869–70	5	3	1870	470,828
1870–71	5	0	1871	1,254,444

In the following year, 1871–72, the decrease of production was very great. There were 692,508 acres under wheat-crops in the colony. The produce was only 3,967,079 bushels, and the average produce per acre 5 bush. 44lbs. What was the amount of wheat exported up to the end of 1872 I am unable to say. In reference to the above table, I must call attention to the fact that the exported articles of which the value is given are not only breadstuffs, but breadstuffs and grain, and the sums named as their value are, therefore, in excess of the real value of the wheat. But the other grain exported is very little. In the year 1871 the total value of the agricultural exports was £1,254,444, whereas the value of the breadstuffs was £1,253,342, leaving the value of all other grain at £1,102. The amount is not sufficient materially to affect the comparison made in the above table. Of this wealth of wheat sent away from South Australia, the other Australasian colonies, including New Zealand, consume the greatest quantity, New South Wales being the best customer. In 1867, when the average produce of the last harvest had exceeded fourteen bushels to the acre, Great Britain was the largest buyer. The price realised was only 4s.5d. a bushel, and it was worth while to send it home; – but, generally, South Australia is the granary of the colonies around her. She sends supplies also, small indeed in amount, to Cape Town, the Mauritius, and New Caledonia, and even to India and the ports of China.

So far I have ventured to say what South Australia does in producing wheat, but I dare not venture to say what she might do. English farmers will not think much of a system of farming which does not produce an average crop of above ten bushels to the acre, – nor will they think much of an average price of 5s.4d. a bushel. The English farmer could hardly pay his rent, and manure and crop his land, and get in his harvest, and take it to market, with a total gross result of £2 13s. 4d. an acre, – more especially as he would only repeat his wheat-crop once in every four years. The answer to this is, of course, that the circumstances of the farmer in the two countries are very different. In South Australia the farmer pays no rent, does not manure his land, pays but little wages either for getting his crop in or out of the land, and grows wheat every year, instead of once in four years. The operations of the two men are distinctly different, and must continue to be different. But it may be well worth while to inquire whether the South Australian farmer might not learn a lesson in his business which would greatly increase his profits.

There can, I think, be no doubt that the cockatooo of South Australia is a very bad farmer, – and that he is so because he has hitherto been able to make a living by bad farming. With reference to the amount of produce, it must be admitted at once that the existing combination of soil and climate in the colony, though it has shown itself to be favourable to the growth of wheat in a country of vast area, is not only unfavourable to heavy crops, but is prohibitory in regard to a high average. Every now and then an average produce of fourteen bushels to the acre may be obtained, as in 1864 and 1867, – and there are districts in the colony in which the produce has on such years exceeded twenty bushels to the acre. But there are, at any rate at present, sources of injury to the wheat crop which make the business of farming very precarious. In one year the red dust will almost destroy the crop, in another year, – as happened during the harvest-time of 1872, – the year last past, – a cloud of locusts will come and eat up wheat and grass throughout the country. That the red rust might be conquered by skill in farming at some future time is probable. And it is not impossible that altered circumstances of soil and climate, produced by population and cultivation, may be unfavourable to the locusts. With the drawbacks as they at present exist, the average produce of wheat must continue to be small. But it might probably be very much higher than it is.

Nearly two-thirds of all the cultivated land of the colony are under wheat every year. In 1870–71 there were 959,000 acres under cultivation in the colony; of these, 200,000 acres were under crops other than wheat; 154,000 were fallow, or laid down with artificial grasses; and 605,000 were under wheat. So that every acre of cultivated land is expected to bear wheat twice in three years. With us the best approved rotation of crops requires the land to give wheat only once in four years. But in fact the expectation and practice of the regular cockatoo farmer demands a crop of wheat every year from his land. The figures above given include, of course, cultivated land of all kinds, – and in all hands. There are agriculturists in South Australia who are endeavouring to give the soil a chance of being permanently productive, and who sow wheat at any rate not more than every other year. There are, too, growers of vines, of potatoes, and hay, – all of whom add their quota to the total of cultivated acres, and deduct materially from the favourable side of the above figures. The ordinary cockatoo knows nothing of the word fallow, and attempts to produce nothing but wheat. Year after year he puts in his seed upon the same acreage, and year after year he takes off his crop. He is the owner of a section of land which may be something between one hundred and two hundred acres, – which is his own, though he has not probably as yet paid for it the entire price. He does his work without any attempt to collect manure, or to give back to the land anything in return for that which he takes from it. He even burns the stubble from his field, finding it to be easier to do so than collect it, that it may rot, and then be ploughed in. He ploughs his land, sows it, and then takes off his crop by a machine called a stripper, which as it passes over the land drags the corn out of the ear, leaving all the straw on the ground; – so that the corn is, as it were, threshed as it is taken off the ground. His labour, therefore, is very small. This last manipulation of the grain, which would be impossible in England, where the climate demands that the grain should become dry before it can be taken from the ear, – is made practicable in South Australia by the great heat prevailing when the wheat is cut. The effect of all this is deleterious both to the man and to the land. The man has but one farming occupation, – that of growing wheat. He ploughs, and reaps, and sells; and ploughs, and reaps, and sells again. He employs his energies on the one occupation, with no diversification of interest, and with nothing to arouse his intelligence. Consequently the South Australian cockatoo is not a pushing or a lively man, – though it should be acknowledged on his behalf that he is orderly, industrious, and self-supporting. But the effect on the land is worse than that on any man, – for the land clearly deteriorates from day to day. No practical farmer will require figures to make him believe that it is so; – but the figures show it. The yield of wheat in South Australia has always been poor, but it has greatly fallen off. In six years, from 1860–61 to 1865–66, it averaged about twelve bushels an acre, and in the six subsequent years it averaged only nine bushels an acre.

The farmer usually owns the land. The system of tenant-farming is by no means unknown in the colony, but it is not popular either with tenant or landlord. The landlord obtains none of those side-wind advantages from his position as owner, – advantages over and above the rent, – which are so valued in the possession and are so dear to the imagination among ourselves. There is neither political power nor political prestige attached to such ownership. It has no peculiar grace of its own as it has with us. The privileges of a squirearchy are quite unknown in the colonies, or, if they exist at all, belong to great graziers and squatters, – or to men who hold large tracts of land in their own hands, and not to those who let their acres. There are game laws, – for the protection of birds in the close season, – but there are no game laws on behalf of the landowner. There is nothing picturesque attaching to the receipt of rural rents, no audit dinners, no dependency grateful alike to the landlord and to the tenant, no feeling that broad acres confer a wide respect. What percentage can a man get for his money if he let land to farmers, and what security will he have for his income? Those are the considerations, and those only, which bear upon the question. As well as I could learn details on the subject, – as to which no accurate information can be obtained because the arrangement is not sufficiently general to produce it, – a landlord may let cleared and enclosed land, worth for sale in the market about £6 an acre, for 10s. an acre; – and he may thus obtain, if he get his rent, something more than nine per cent. for his money. This would do very well as a speculation, if he were sure or nearly sure to get it, as are our landlords at home. But when bad years come the tenants do not pay. It is regarded almost as a matter of course that the payment of agricultural rents is to depend on the season. If the land refuse her increase, why is the loss to fall on the tenant harder than on the owner? The owner, no doubt, has the law on his side; but the tenant understands very well that when the land is barren, the law will be barren also. Unless his rent be remitted in such years, or at least in part remitted, he simply gives up his holding and goes elsewhere, – with his children and his plough, or without his plough if the landlord or other creditor should have seized it. The result is that the landlord is satisfied to remit half the rent in bad years, and the whole rent in very bad years. The further and final result is that the system of letting land to tenant farmers is unpalatable and unprofitable, – and therefore unusual.

The farmer therefore owns the land. He has bought it probably on credit, beginning simply with savings made from two or three years of labour, and owing the price, or the greater part of it, to the government. I will presently say a word as to the system of deferred payments for land which prevails. His homestead is too frequently bare and ugly, without garden or orchard or anything like an English farmyard around it; but it is substantial, and it is his own. The price of the land has probably been something between 20s. and 40s. an acre, – and he calculates that by growing wheat under the existing agricultural circumstances around him, he can live, and bring up his family, and free himself from his debt within ten years. If he be steady and industrious he can do so, – and he does do so. He does not confine his industry to his own farm; but in shearing-time he shears for some large squatter, or he keeps a team of bullocks and brings down wool to the railway station or to the city, or perhaps he takes a month's work at some gold-digging, – for even in South Australia there are gold-fields, though they be not prominent among the resources of the colony. In this way he lives and is independent, and who will dare to find fault with a man who does live, and becomes independent, and makes a property exclusively by his own industry? His life is not picturesque, but he cares nothing for that. His children go to the public school, – at which he pays perhaps 2s. a week for three of them, – and they have plenty to eat and drink. His wife has plenty to eat and drink, and has a decent gown, and material comforts around her. He has plenty to eat and drink, and a decent coat if he cares for it. And he is nobody's servant. Nevertheless he is a very bad farmer, and unless he mend his ways soon the land which he now ploughs will cease to give him the plenty which he desires. It may not improbably come to pass that a considerable portion of the land occupied by farmers for the purpose of growing wheat, will, under the present system, cease altogether to give sufficient increase on the seed to pay even for the labour of ploughing and reaping. In that case it will go back to pastoral purposes and the farmer will remove elsewhere, – as has already happened in certain districts of the colony. But, though the area is immense, the area which will produce wheat is limited; and thus the well-being of South Australia may be much affected, unless a less wasteful use be made of the land.

The laws under which land has been sold in South Australia have been altered frequently, – as has been the case in all the colonies. The free-selecter, of whom I have been speaking, probably bought his land from the Crown at some price varying from 20s. to 40s. an acre, and was allowed four years, – or latterly five years, – to pay the sum, being charged interest at the rate of five per cent. Before entering upon his land he had only to pay one year's interest in advance. He has thus been enabled to buy his land with money produced by the crops he has grown. In other words, he has paid simply a rent for a term of years, and at the end of that term the land has become his own. And this system, though never so far as I am aware clearly expressed in words, seems to have been the ruling policy as to the alienation of agricultural land in all the Australian colonies. If the new settler will come and live upon the land, will till it and fence it, and pay for its use, during a sufficient time to prove that he is in earnest as to the use of it, the land shall be his. The idea of drawing from the land the funds required for government, so that taxation should be unnecessary, which was once dear to the minds of may colonists, has gradually faded away. Great as has been the possession of the land, it has not been a source of wealth available for any such purpose. If only it could be used to

attract serviceable immigrants, if only it could be equitably
distributed among men who would really use it, – not take it
for the purpose of bargaining and gambling with it, – if only it
could be converted into homes for people who would accept
such homes and thus become a nation, the land would then
have done all that it should be expected to do. This seems to
have been the real gist of Mr. Wakefield's scheme, and to this
theory all the land ministers of the various colonies have been
tending; though, as it seems, their progress thitherwards has
for the most part been an unconscious progress. But in this
attempt to bestow the land there has still been the necessity of
exacting Mr. Wakefield's 'sufficient price'. The land, if absolutely given, would be worthless. If it were to be had for
nothing, it would be worth nothing. There must be a price
upon it such as shall in some degree fix its value, and induce
settlers to use with some economy and discretion that which
can only be obtained for a stipulated sum of money. But the
fund so raised has never been a source of wealth to a colony,
and the colonies now cease to look for wealth in that direction.
If the money raised will suffice to pay for surveys, to make
roads, in any way to prepare the land for those who are to
come and take it, all will be done that should be expected. 'For
a term of years you shall pay the colony such a rental as will
enable the colony to make its land serviceable to you; – and
then it shall be yours.' Such, in fact, are the terms offered to
free-selecters.

When I was in South Australia a new land bill was under the
consideration of parliament, – as, indeed, I found new land
bills either just in operation or under consideration wherever I
went in the colonies. The matter has been one which has
required many changes, and as to which no two colonies have
been able to agree. As I think it probable that the bill proposed
to the South Australian parliament will become law, I will
endeavour to explain that instead of referring in detail to the
law existing at this moment; – premising that here, in this
chapter, it is my purpose to refer to the proposed measure
only as far as it relates to the sale of lands to intending farmers,
or free-selecters.

I must first explain that South Australia is a country
peculiarly subject to drought, – more so than are the other

colonies, – and is especially so subject in the interior. This is a
fact so well acknowledged, that all who know the colony are
aware that wheat can only be grown in certain parts of it. In
order that the government might have some guide to tell it
what portions of the land it would be expedient to throw open
to agriculturists, and from what portions it would be expedient to exclude them as being unfit for agricultural purposes, a
line has been drawn. The surveyor-general, Mr. Goyder, has
drawn an arbitrary line across the map of South Australia,
which is now known as Goyder's line of rainfall. It is anything
but a straight line. It runs from a point on the eastern confines
of the colony somewhat south of the city of Adelaide, in a
direction north-west nearly as high as to the top of Spencer's
Gulf. Then with irregular curves it comes south half way
down the Gulf, which it crosses below Moonta and Wallaroo,
and then runs north by east till it loses itself in unknown
deserts. North of this line, or rather beyond it, no farmer
should locate himself. South of this, or within it, he may
expect sufficient rain to produce wheat. Of course Mr.
Goyder gives no guarantee as to precise accuracy, but I found
it to be admitted in the colony that the line had been drawn
with skill and truth. North again of the dry and rainless region
is a tropical country, which is subject to the usual conditions
of tropical latitudes; – but on that Mr. Goyder's line has no
bearing, and of that district I shall not speak in attempting to
describe the agricultural condition of South Australia as now
existing. All land within Goyder's line not hitherto sold, will,
by the proposed law, which is called the 'Waste Land Alienation Act,' be opened to purchase, and on that land would-be
farmers in South Australia are invited to locate themselves.
The lands will be thrown open to selection, and will be
purchasable on a credit of sixteen years, at an interest which is
computed to amount to $3\frac{3}{5}$ per cent. per annum for that term.
The settlement of the price to be paid will be in this wise:– The
Government will fix the upset price of all the areas offered for
sale at what is supposed to be the present maximum value of
the best land in the area, – which, for the sake of illustration,
we may call £2 an acre. I was informed that £2 an acre is in fact
the price at which the majority of the land will probably be
first offered. It will then be in the power of any would-be

purchaser to take it at that price. If there be no such purchaser, the commissioner of lands will, on the part of the government, reduce his demand by 5s. to 35s, and then to 30s., then to 25s., and if necessary to 20s., – at intervals of perhaps a fortnight. Below 20s. an acre the price will not be reduced. According to the nature of the land will be the desire of purchasers to buy it at 40s.; or to wait till it be offered at 30s. or at 20s. It is impossible not to see that even this plan is open to the machinations of 'land agents'; – land sharks, I have heard them sometimes uncourteously called. The land agent, whose special business it is to know who are disposed to buy this or that section of land, will offer to renounce his own intention of buying, we will say at 30s., on receiving 1s. or 1s.6d. an acre on completing the purchase for his victim at 25s. The victim will feel himself obliged to pay the black-mail, as hundreds of victims have done, and the land shark, – I hope he will excuse my discourtesy, – will receive a very large payment, for which he will perform no service whatever.

And the payment of the money is to be arranged in this wise. On making his application for the land, at any fixed price, – say 30s. an acre, – the applicant will pay into the Treasury 10s. per cent. on the whole purchase-money. Presuming the land in question to be 200 acres in extent, the price would be £300, and he would pay down £30 as interest in advance for three years; – and would then be allowed to go in upon the land, and occupy it. He must effect certain improvements, and cultivate a certain portion, and must either live on it himself or by deputy. If he have not done so at the end of three years, he forfeits his £30. If he have done so, he pays another £30, and goes on for another three years. These payments are in place of interest, so that at the end of the six years he will have paid no part of the principal. He may then pay the whole principal, if he has it, and the land will be his; or he may postpone the payment for ten years, paying 2s. each year for each pound of the purchase-money, with interest at the rate of 4 per cent. for the further credit given. The payment for these last ten years would average something under £40 per annum, but would recur yearly. The purchaser of the 200 acres would thus pay £30 as advance rent on entrance; £30 again as advanced rent after three years; a rental of £40 a year annually for ten years further; and then the freehold would be his own.

The selecter may buy under this bill any amount from 1 acre up to 640 acres; – but in cases in which the land lies untowardly for division into exactly 640 acres, he may select as much as 700. If he should attempt to select more, to make applications in other names, or to defraud the land commissioner as land commissioners have been defrauded in all the colonies since the alienation of public lands commenced, terrible is to be the example made of that would-be free-selecter. All the money advanced by him for first payment or payments will be forfeited to the Crown.

The new land bill which I have attempted to describe does not vary very much from that now in operation. Its chief objects are, perhaps, to extend the area of land opened for selection, and to obviate the existing necessity of personal residence. No doubt the proposed terms are somewhat easier than the present to the proposed selecter. I think, however, it is obvious that the terms offered are such as should be attractive to men with small capitals, who are able to work with their own hands. To such I say again, that the South Australian 'cockatoo,' though he be a cockatoo, is an independent man, living on his own freehold in plenty, and knowing no master.

On the other hand, I would not advise farmers to try South Australia with the intention of having their work done for them by paid labourers. Wheat at 5s.4d. a bushel will not pay for labour at the rate of 22s. a week, which may be quoted as about the rate at which rural labour may be obtained. When it is wanted throughout the year, as it would be wanted by any grower of wheat intending to farm his land as land is farmed at home, the labourer is paid about £40 per annum, and also receives his diet, which is worth to the farmer about £18 per annum, making a total of £58 per annum. Twenty-two shillings a week throughout the year amounts to £57 15s. per annum. No doubt the South Australian free-selecter does pay something in wages during his harvest, unless he be specially blessed in the matter of sons who can work; but he pays wages at no other time, and then the demand is higher, – rising probably to 5s. a day, or 4s. with diet. For this expenditure he provides himself by wages earned by himself in the manner I have already explained.

In writing of the agricultural products of South Australia, I should be wrong not to mention the vineyards of the colony. On 31st December, 1871, there were 5,823 acres under vines, which during that year had produced 896,000 gallons of wine, being at the rate of 154 gallons to the acre. I was informed that South Australia produces more wine than any other colony, but have no figures by me which would enable me to test the accuracy of the information. There can be no doubt that the climate is admirably suited for the growth of the grape, but the cultivation of it has not hitherto proved to be remunerative. It seems, indeed, to be retrograding. In the year ended 31st March, 1871, there were 6,127 acres bearing vines. In the subsequent year the number had been reduced to 5,823, – from which it appears that 304 acres of vineyard had been grubbed up.

I cannot say that I liked the South Australian wines. They seemed to me to be heady, and were certainly unpalatable. I came across none that I thought comparable to the Victorian wine of the country made at Yering. I was told that I was prejudiced, and that my taste had been formed on brandied wines suited to the English market. It may be so; – but, if so, the brandied wines suited to the English market not only suit my palate, but do not seem to threaten that a second or third glass will make me tipsy. The South Australian wines had a heaviness about them, – which made me afraid of them even when I would have willingly sacrificed my palate to please a host.

It must, however, be borne in mind that the making of wine is an art which, as far as we know, has not been learned quickly in any country. The perfection to which Spanish, German, and French wines are now brought, has probably come as much from observation and experience as from the peculiarity of the soils or climate. There are many who believe that Italian, Greek, and Hungarian wines will soon rival those of France. If so, the wines of Australia and the United States will probably do the same, when the cultivation and manufacture shall have been long enough in existence for experience and skill to have been created.

In the meantime the one thing desirable in reference to Australian wines, is that the people of the country should drink the produce of the country, not only because it is wholesome, but also because it is cheap. The usual drink now consumed at public-houses is brandy, – so called, – which is a villainous, vitriolic, biting compound of deadly intoxicating qualities, and is sold at 6d. the glass. Though I found the South Australian wine to be 'heady,' – drinking it after the fashion in which wine is drunk, – it is a beverage absolutely innocent in comparison with the spirits which the publicans sell; and it can be sold with profit at 2d. a glass, – the glass being a small, false-bottomed tumbler, about as big as an ordinary claret-glass at home. The wine can be sold by the grower fit for use at 2s.6d. a gallon, and the gallon in the hands of the publican would run to twenty-five 'nobblers' of wine. This would give a profit satisfactory, we may suppose, even to an Australian publican. A nobbler is the proper colonial phrase for a drink at a public-house. It would be very desirable that the men of the country should acquire a taste for drinking their own produce. As men have done so in all vine-growing countries, they will probably do so in South Australia, and when that time shall come the growing of grapes will be profitable.

Already the acreage under vines is very large. It must be remembered that grape-growing, – as is also hop-growing, – is an agricultural pursuit requiring great capital, and that the produce from the acre is very large. A grower with a hundred acres of vines on his hands has probably as great a stake in his vineyard as a farmer with a thousand acres of wheat has in his farm. In South Australia the acreage under vines exceeded that devoted to gardens, orchards, potatoes, lucerne, or artificial

SOUTH AUSTRALIA, YEAR ENDED 31st MARCH, 1871

Total average under cultivation .... 957,482 acres

	Acres		Acres
Wheat	604,400	Permanent artificial grasses	3,712
Barley	22,474	Flax	182
Oats	6,184	Potatoes	3,370
Peas	3,713	Orchards	2,762
Hay	139,807	Gardens	4,330
Wheat, cut green for forage ...	2,598	Vines	6,127
Lucerne	3,441	Other crops	816
		Fallow land	153,566

grasses. I annex a table, showing the number of acres under cultivation in South Australia in the year ended 31st March, 1871, with the number devoted to each class of growth, – premising with reference to the second mention of wheat, that cereals throughout all the colonies are grown for forage for cattle. They are cut green, and made into hay, and then stacked.

The proportion of wheat to that of any other crop grown, – which is so great as to make all the other cereals sink into utter insignificance, – shows very plainly what the South Australian farmer regards as his special business.

CHAPTER IV

WOOL

Whatever interests may for the moment be uppermost in the thoughts and words of Australian legislators and speculators, wool still remains and for many years will remain the staple produce of the country at large. In Victoria, indeed, wool is for the present second to gold. And in South Australia wool is second to wheat. The wheat grown in South Australia during eleven years up to 1871 has fetched an average of £1,283,630 per annum, whereas the wool exported from the colony, – in which is included a small amount exported from south Australian ports but grown in other colonies, – has fetched an average of £987,194 per annum. The wool produced has, in fact, been worth no more than three-fourths of the wheat grown. But the produce of a country which is exported always receives more attention than that which is consumed at home. Who thinks anything of the eggs that are laid around us, or of the butter made? In calculating the wealth of the country, who reckons up the stitching of all the women, or even the ploughing and hedging and ditching of the men? The calico and cutlery and cloth which we export, and the ships which take these things away, are to our eyes the source of our commercial wealth. I remember being told in America that in the year before the war the hay produced in the single State of Maine had been worth more than all the cotton exported from all the cotton states in that year. South Australia is perhaps in a safer condition than any other of the Australian colonies, because she can feed herself. But not the less on this account does she regard wool as the staple of the country. It is the business of Australia to supply fine wools to the world, and South Australia thinks that she performs her part of that business very well. South Australian farmers simply live comfortably and die in obscurity by growing wheat; but South Australian squatters make splendid fortunes or are ruined magnificently by growing wool.

In the last two years things have been going well with the wool-growers; but for some years before that things were not going well, and there was much magnificent ruin. Owing to the drought to which the country is subject, and to the very limited rainfall in the large northern pastoral districts, squatting, – which is always precarious, – is perhaps more precarious in this colony than in others. In 1865 there was a great drought. In 1864 very little rain fell in the districts north of Goyder's line, and in 1865 none fell. When 1866 came many of the South Australian squatters were ruined, – and others were broken-hearted. The records of this time are terrible to hear. It was not so much that sheep were perishing from want of water. The wells did not run dry, and in that district no squatter trusts to surface water for his sheep to drink. But there was not a blade of grass, and the animals were starved. The owners did not know in which direction to stir themselves. Hundreds of thousands of sheep were driven south in order that they might find pasturage as they wandered. It must be understood that a squatter may drive sheep anywhere over unpurchased land, – that is, over land which is simply leased by other squatters from the Crown. But he is bound to give notice of the coming of his flocks, and to move them along at the rate of not less than six miles a day. It has not been an uncommon thing in any of the colonies for small squatters, when short of grass, to have their sheep driven about over hundreds of miles, – say in a wide-spread circle, so that at last they should be brought home again, – in order that thus they might be fed. In ordinary years this is not regarded as a thoroughly honest kind of grazing. It is difficult to prevent the usage, as the owner, though he must give notice of the coming of his sheep, is not bound to explain why they are on the road. They may have been sold and be travelling to the purchaser, or they may have been sent out for sale. But though the practice cannot be stopped, it is known and understood, and the large squatters who are the sufferers are often indignant. But in 1865–66 the larger the flocks were, the more urgent was the necessity which compelled the owner of them to send them forth, lest they should be starved at home. Mob after mob of wretched animals streamed down from the then barren plains, 300 miles north of Adelaide, to the southern districts near the sea and round the lakes, – perishing by the way, or doomed to perish when they got there. Those who started first, – whose owners, either by themselves or their servants, had been the first to see the necessity of going, – were saved. I heard one squatter's overseer tell how he had taken some 10,000 sheep down to the sea-side, and brought them all back again. When I suggested to him, before his tale was at an end, that he had lost many of them, – I had heard more then of what had been lost than of any that were saved, – he answered me with indignant denial. He at that time had been a hero. But there were few such heroes. As the mobs followed, one upon the heels of another, the grass disappeared before them. They were driven hither and thither, till they died; but there was no grass. And it is easy to conceive the sort of welcome which these intruders would receive at such a time, – how the shepherds would be desired to move on, and do their six miles a day whatever might become of them afterwards, how hated they would be, coming with their flocks like locusts upon a country that was bare enough at that time even without such strangers! And the life of those who followed their flocks week after week and month after month could not itself have been very pleasant. Among Australian graziers young men are accustomed to this work. It is no uncommon thing that a flock of sheep, – they call them mobs in Australia, – perhaps four or five thousand strong, should have to travel six hundred miles, either being brought home by a purchaser or taken to some city for sale. There must be necessarily five or six men to accompany them, with seven or eight horses, and probably a cart. They kill their own meat as they go; but they carry their flour and tea, and perhaps a tent. They enter no houses and spend little or no money. They travel on their six miles a day; – and though their work be very tedious, it is endurable as long as each day's work is a portion of a successful commercial operation. But at this terrible time there was no idea of commerce. As they went along, the country was strewed with the bodies of the useless animals, and the only effort was to move on in some district giving still sufficient grass to keep the flock alive. Thousands were slaughtered to reduce the numbers in the scanty herbage, and I heard of one flock-owner who at last adopted the course of drowning a thousand in the sea. In Adelaide a large flock was offered to a merchant, who was also a squatter, at 1s. a head. He offered 6d. for them, and rejoiced afterwards that his bidding was not taken. At that time sheep were simply an encrumbrance. There was imposed on each owner the duty of trying to save his property, but without the hope that he should succeed in doing so. It was a bad time then, in South Australia, for in the same year, – the season of 1865–66, – the wheat crop was also low. But the price of wool was high; – and therefore, though many squatters fell, – they who were already weak on their legs or in debt, – the strong men won their way through, and survived their losses.

After that came a great depression in the price of wool, and the colony was again at a low ebb. In March, 1866, unwashed South Australian wool fetched 1s.2 ½d. a pound. In March, 1869, it fetched 8d. In looking at the difference between these times, the reader must remember that the squatters' liabilities were the same with the low price as they had been with the high. The normal squatter generally owes money to his banker or merchant, for which he pays some rate of interest varying from 8 to 11 per cent., – and not unfrequently a percentage even higher than that. I have endeavoured in the former volume to explain his condition in this respect. With unwashed wool at 1s. 2d. or 1s. 3d. a pound not only will his interest not trouble him, but his debt will diminish apparently without any effort on his own part. But with wool at 8d. his debt, if it be at all heavy, will grow. The sum he realises from his wool will not pay the expenses of his men, keep himself, and pay his interest. After a year or two with such a result the merchant will feel that he is becoming insecure and will foreclose. Then the squatter is no longer a squatter, but takes probably to the care of sheep for some more fortunate man. In March, 1869, 8d. a pound was the price for unwashed or greasy South Australian wool; in 1870 it was 8½d.; in February, 1870, it was again 8d. These had been three bad years, and many men were either ruined or on the brink of ruin; but in July, 1871, it had risen to 11d. a pound; in September, 1871, to 1s. ½d.; and in March, 1872, it was as high as 1s. 2d. and 1s. 3d. Twenty thousand sheep is by no means a large flock. On the contrary a squatter with no more than 20,000 is a small man. But a difference of 6*d.* in the pound on unwashed wool from 20,000 sheep amounts to about £3,000. It will be exactly that sum if each sheep give 6 lbs., which is a high but not excessive average for unwashed wool. The expense of maintaining a run with 20,000 sheep, including the cost of the squatter's own home, may be put at £2,000 per annum, being £100 for every thousand sheep. It will at once be seen how rich the poor man may at once become by such a change in the circumstances of the wool trade. And it will be seen also how speculative and precarious such a business must be. The wool-grower of Australia watches the price-list for England with an intense and natural anxiety. He can do little or nothing to regulate the market. He cannot understand why it is that the fluctuations should be so great. But he obeys the market, too often with an implicit confidence which it does not deserve. When prices are high he increases his flocks, – and with his flocks he increases his debts also. He is almost negligent how much he may owe if wool be high. The temptation is so great that if his credit be good he will almost assuredly increase his flock to the bearing capability of his run. Three years of high prices will, perhaps, make him a rich man. But a fall again, – a speedy fall, – will bring him to the dust. It must be remembered that many of these men are dealing not with 20,000 sheep, but with more than five times that number; sometimes with more than ten times that number. When the large squatter really owns his flocks, – when he owes nothing to his merchant, – then even at the worst of times, with wool even at 8*d.*, he does well; and in that condition, when wool rises he becomes a millionaire. Things, as I write now, are all rose-coloured with the squatters; – but it may well be that before these words are published there shall come a change.

I went about two hundred miles north of Adelaide, so that I might get outside of Goyder's rain-line, and see something of the country in which rain is so scarce. I cannot say that the country is attractive to a visitor. There is very little to gratify the eye, and almost nothing to satisfy the taste. The South Australian free-selecter makes for himself a plentiful and I hope a happy home; – but he does not surround himself; with prettiness or even neatness. The greatest part of our journey, however, was beyond the free-selecter's limits, through a country that was brown, treeless, and absolutely uninteresting. I was frequently told that the run through which I was passing was excellently well adapted for sheep, and that the squatter who owned it was doing well. But I saw no grass and very few sheep. A stranger cannot but remark, throughout the pastoral districts of Australia, how seldom he sees sheep as he travels along. As in this country they do not carry above one sheep to ten acres, and as the animals would hardly be observed if each sheep maintained solitary possession of his own ten-acred domain, the result is not wonderful. But the traveller expects to see sheep and is disappointed. It may be that he will also expect emus and kangaroos, and he will generally be disappointed also in regard to them. Kangaroos I certainly have seen in great numbers, though by no means so often as I expected. An emu running wild I never did see. Tame emus round the houses in towns are very common, and of emus' eggs there is a plethora. On this journey I saw hardly any living animals. We went with four horses, at about six miles an hour, through a brown ugly district, which was bounded, nearly the whole way, by low hills, and on which there is no sign that timber has ever grown there. We put up for the night at the station of a non-resident squatter, in seeking which we lost our way in the dark. For an hour or so, I felt uneasy, thinking that we should have to 'camp out,' without any preparation made for such a picnic; – but at last we were attracted by lights, and a party of us who had gone forth on foot reached the house. We met there a young man who was waiting for a companion, with whom he intended to make his way from the centre of Australia to the western coast. It seemed that his party would be lamentably deficient in means for such an expedition, and that he had hardly the energy for such an undertaking. In this work of Australian exploring men have to carry flour and tea with them, and to be satisfied to live upon flour and tea, – to protect themselves from the blacks, – to run the risk of failing water, – and to be constant, from month to month, without excitement to keep their courage warm. Our new acquaintance seemed to be going because he might as well go as let it alone; – but it may be that under that deportment were hidden all the energies of a Marco Polo, a Columbus, a Sturt, or a Livingstone. We fared sumptuously at the absent squatter's station, and went on our way the next morning.

I had not then seen a salt-bush country, though I subsequently passed through such a region in a part of New South Wales, of which I said a few word in speaking of that colony. Here, in the salt-bush of South Australia, there was not a blade of grass when I visited it. The salt-bush itself is an ugly grey shrub, about two feet high, which seems to possess the power of bringing forth its foliage without moisture. This foliage is impregnated with salt, and both sheep and cattle will feed upon it and thrive. It does not produce wool of the best class, – but it is regarded as being a very safe food for sheep, because it rarely fails. At the period of my visit the country was in want of rain; and I was assured that when the rain, then expected, should fall, the surface of the ground would be covered with grass. I can only say that I never saw a country more bare of grass. But for miles together, – over hundreds of square miles, – the salt-bush spreads itself; and as long as that lives the sheep will not be starved. Sometimes this shrub was diversified by a blue bush, a bush very much the same as the salt-bush in form, though of a dull slate-colour instead of grey. On this the sheep will not feed. There is also a poisonous shrub which the sheep will eat, – as to which there seemed to be an opinion that it was fatal only to travelling sheep, and not to those regularly pastured on the country.

The run which I visited bears about 120,000 sheep, – and they wander over about 1,200,000 acres. For all these sheep, and for all this extent of sheep-run, it is necessary to obtain water by means of wells, sunk to various depths from fifty to one hundred and twenty feet. The water can always be found, – not indeed always at the first attempt, but so surely that no land in that region need be deserted for want of it. The water when procured is invariably more or less brackish; – but the sheep thrive on it and like it. The wells are generally worked by men, sometimes by horses; but on large runs, where capital has been made available, the water is raised by windmills. Such was the case at the place I visited. The water is brought up into large tanks, holding from 30,000 to 60,000 gallons each, and from these tanks is distributed into troughs, made of stone and cement. These are carried out in different directions, perhaps two or three from each tank, and are so arranged that sheep can be watered from either side. If therefore there be three such troughs, the sheep in six different paddocks can be watered from one tank, – the well being so placed as to admit egress to it from various paddocks, all converging on the same centre. In this way 10,000 sheep will be watered at one well. As these paddocks contain perhaps 40 square miles each, or over 25,000 acres, the animals have some distance to travel before they can get a drink. In cold weather they do not require to drink above once in three days; – in moderate weather once in two days; – in very hot weather they will lie near to the troughs and not trouble themselves to go afield in search of food. On the run which I visited there were twenty of these wells, which, with their appurtenances of tanks, and troughs, and windmills, had cost about £500 each; – and there had been about as many failures in the search of water, wells which had been dug but at which no water was found; – and these had not been sunk without considerable expenditure. It may therefore be understood that a man requires some capital before he can set himself up as a grower of wool on a large scale in South Australia.

The state of the meat market in England is already affecting the South Australian squatter very materially, – as also the squatters in the other colonies. I left England in May, 1871, and at that time Australian meats had only begun to make their way in the London markets. In speaking of the Queensland meat-preserving companies as I found them in August and September, 1871, I spoke almost with doubt of the trade; – for there was doubt when I was in Queensland. But when I was in South Australia in April, 1872, the trade was established, and squatters were already calculating that the carcass should not in future be made to give way altogether to the wool. Meat, which is in round figures 10*d.* a pound in London, costs but 2*d.* a pound in South Australia. Then arises the question whether meat can be carried half-way round the globe in a good condition, or whether its nature makes it impossible that good mutton should be imported from Australia as well as good wool. That bad mutton may be imported, – that is, mutton which has been changed from good to bad by processes of cooking and packing previous to exportation, – we have known for some time. That any Australian meat has as yet reached the English market in a state that would enable it to compete with English meat, I do not believe. I feel sure that none has done so. But every mail during the latter months of my sojourn in Australia brought out tidings that the trade was on the increase, – so that when I left the colonies sheep were worth 3s. or 4s. a head more for butchers than they were twelve months earlier, when I arrived at Melbourne. Three shillings a head is certainly not much on a sheep in England, – where the animal at twelve months old may be worth from £3 10s. to £4. But in Australia, where 10s. a head is even now a good price, the difference is very large. When I reached Melbourne in July, 1871, I was told at a meat-preserving company that they could not afford to give more than 6s. a sheep. All that goes home to England is, after all, but a morsel to the markets of that little island; but to this wide continent the preparation of that morsel is most important.

In the district of which I am speaking the sheep are all 'paddocked,' – that is to say, kept in by fences, – so that shepherding is unnecessary. I hope that I have already made clear to my reader the difference between shepherding sheep and paddocking sheep. I found that brush fences had been made at the rate of about £23 a mile. A brush fence, made of loose timber and wood, is not so neat as a wire fence, but it is equally serviceable for sheep; – and when fences have to be made by hundreds of miles, the difference in expenditure is considerable. A wire fence that will keep in sheep and lambs, can hardly be put up for for less than £40 a mile. Five wires would suffice for sheep, but the lamb requires a lower wire to restrain his innocence. Nothing, I think, gives a surer proof of the wealth of the Australian colonies generally, than the immense amount of fencing that has been put up within the last ten years. A run of twenty miles square, or containing 400 square miles, equal to 256,000 acres, is by no means excessive in size, though it is about as big as a small English county. The squatter who intends to paddock his sheep instead of hiring shepherds to go about with them, has to divide his area into perhaps twenty different paddocks. Should he do this, with the smallest possible amount of distance of partitions, he would have to make 240 miles of fencing. At the station which I visited we had come again upon timber, though the country was by no means thickly wooded. But when there is no timber near, the cost of fencing is more than doubled.

It is of course understood that the normal squatter is a tenant of the Crown. In Victoria the great wool-growers now own for the most part their own lands; – and the purchase of pasture lands has become general elsewhere under the pressure of the free-selecter. But the genuine squatter is he who sits upon government land for which he pays a rent to the colony; and in South Australia such is still the condition of the larger wool-growers. Outside of Goyder's range, – which is the South Australian squatter's proper region, the rental varies according to the value of the land and the nature of the pasture. A computation is made of the number of sheep the land should carry, and the squatter is charged 6d. a sheep on the best land, 4d. on the second best, and 2d. on the poorest. If he should keep more sheep than the number computed, he pays at the same rate for the excess. But for the number computed he must pay, even though he should not keep so many. I found that this arrangement gave satisfaction even to the squatters, – a result which has certainly not been common in the Australian colonies generally. On runs within the line of rainfall, this rule as to the rate at which sheep are pastured does not prevail; but such runs have generally been purchased, and are the freehold property of the wool-growers, or are occupied as commonage by the owners of neighbouring freeholds.

I feel it to be impossible to describe with accuracy the effect upon pastoral speculators of a rise in the price of wool amounting to 80 per cent., the whole difference going to profit. My readers may perhaps be able to imagine the present condition of the squatter's mind. 'Non secus in bonis Ab insolenti temperatam Laetitia,' are words which not unfrequently rise to the minds of the observer. It is, however, very much to the advantage of the colony at large that this prosperity should be continued. When wool is low every interest in Australia is depressed. Even mining shares do not go off so readily under the verandahs when the pockets of the squatters are not full of money.

I also visited a large cattle-station in the south of the colony, on the eastern side of the lakes. It belongs to a rich Scotch absentee landowner who sits in our parliament, and I will only say of it that I think I ate the best beef there that ever fell in my way. Like other things beef must have a best and a worst, and I think that the Portalloch beef was the best. I heard that there was beef as good, – perhaps even better, – up at a large cattle station far north; but the information reached me from the owner of the northern station who was with us at Portalloch. As I found his information on all other subjects to be reliable, I am bound to believe him in this. If it be so, he must be the very prince of beef-growers. On the road from Adelaide to the lakes, – on the lake side of of the Mount Lofty hills, – we stayed a night at the little town of Strathalbyn. Afterwards, on my route back to Victoria, which I made by steamer from Port Adelaide to Macdonnel Bay, and thence overland across the border, I stayed also at the little town of Gambier-Town, under Mount Gambier. I mention these places because they were the cleanest, prettiest, pleasantest little towns that I saw during my Australian travels. I would say that they were like well-built thriving English villages of the best class, were it not that they both contained certain appliances and an architectural pretension which hardly belong to villages. When the place in question is dirty, unfinished, and forlorn, – when the attempt at doing something considerable in the way of founding a town seems to have been a failure, – the appearance of this pretension is very disagreeable. But at Strathalbyn and Gambier-Town there had been success, and they had that look about them which makes a stranger sometimes fancy in a new place that it might be well for him to come and abide there to the end. They are both in South Australia. Perhaps I was specially moved to admiration because the inns were good.

The country around Mount Gambier is very pretty, and un-Australian. There are various lakes, – evidently the craters of old volcanoes, – lying high up among hills. And among them and about them the grass is green, and the ferns grow wild, – much to the disgust of the owners of the land, upon whom they have lately come as a new infliction. And the trees stand about in a park-like fashion. The country here was some time since given up to agriculture, and the Gambier-Town people were proud of their wheat. But the grass grows again now, – artificial grass, and a large herd of Lincoln sheep is in fashion, – partly from the increased price of mutton, but chiefly because at this moment the long coarse staple of the Lincoln wool is high priced. The weight of wool given by these sheep is very much greater than that of Merino. Squatters say just at present that the Lincoln sheep pay better than the Merino, where the land will carry the former. I doubt, however, whether this state of things will last.

I was told, when in the neighbourhood, that the farmers from Gambier-Town had gone across the border into Victoria, tempted by the terms on which free-selecters there were allowed to buy land. Many no doubt had done so, settling themselves in the western district of that colony. But when I was again in Victoria, I was told that there was another exodus of farmers commencing, and that men were going back to South Australia under other temptations offered by the south Australian laws. Considering the condition of the population and its sparseness, considering also the great blessing of settled prospects, I could not but feel daily how great was the pity that there should be six different sets of Australian laws for the people of the six colonies. There are in all about 1,700,000 of them, and they agree to be united on no subject.

I will venture here to allude to a matter very far removed indeed from the general scope of this book. Before leaving England a friend of mine had put into my hand a volume of ballads, which had been sent home to him from Australia, called 'Bush Ballads, or Galloping Rhymes.' He told me that the author had been a young Scotch gentleman who had gone out young, but had not done well. He had taken to a sporting life, and had then fallen into a sad melancholy, and had – died. I read the ballads, and was greatly struck by their energy. It was evident that the writer of them had lived out of the literary world, and he had lacked that care and spared himself that labour which criticism and study will produce, and which are necessary to finish work; – but of the man's genius there could be no doubt. There was one called 'Britomarte', which alone entitled him to be called a poet. I found that he had lived in this neighbourhood, near to Mount Gambier, and that he had been well loved by many friends. For a while he was in the

South Australian parliament, but parliamentary work had not suited him. He was given to the riding of racers, – and was prone to write about horses and the race-course. In the literary traces which I found of him in the neighbourhood, there was but scanty allusion to other matters, except to racing, and to the melancholy, thoughtful, solitary, heart-eating life which a bushman lives. His horse had been his companion when he was alone, – and when he got back to the world horses were his delight. They are seldom safe companions for a man prone to excitement. I heard wondrous tales of the courage of his riding. As a steeple-chase rider he was well known in Melbourne; but few seemed to have heard of his as a poet. It is as a poet that I speak of him now. His name was A. L. Gordon.

CHAPTER V

MINERALS

South Australia is a copper colony. Victoria, New South Wales, and Queensland are pre-eminently golden. Tasmania is doing a little business in gold, but by no means enough to give her importance. Western Australia has lead-mines, though as yet she has derived but little wealth from them; she also is waiting for gold, hoping that it may yet turn up. South Australia is undoubtedly auriferous. Not only have specks of gold been found as in Western Australia, but diggers have worked at the trade, and have lived upon it, and the industry is still continued. At a publican's house I saw bottles of gold, which he made it a part of his trade to buy from diggers. At a certain bank in Adelaide I saw a cabinet with drawers half full of gold, which it was a part of the business of the bankers to buy from publicans or other intermediate agents. But this was all digger's gold, not miner's gold, – gold got by little men in little quantities from surface-washing. Of gold mines proper there are none as yet in the colony. That there will be such found and worked up in the northern territory, within the tropics, is now an opinion prevalent in Adelaide. Whether there be ground for such hope I have no evidence on which to form an opinion; but should this be the case, the northern territory will probably become a separate colony. Of this, however, I shall have to speak again in another chapter. Up to the time of my visit to Adelaide gold to the value of three-quarters of a million sterling had as yet been found in South Australia. This, of course, is as nothing to the produce of the three eastern colonies, and therefore South Australia is not hitherto entitled to consider herself as a golden land.

But what she has wanted in gold she has made up in copper. And in some respects the copper has, I think, been better than gold, as affording a more wholesome class of labour. There is

142

less of gambling in the business, – less of gambling even among the shareholders and managing people, and infinitely less temptation to gamble among the workmen. The fact that the metal must be dealt with in large quantities, that vast weights must be moved, and that heavy machinery must be employed, that no man can find enough to support himself for six months by a stroke of luck and carry it away in his waistcoat pocket, gives a sobriety to the employment which the search after gold often lacks. It is quite true that latterly the great discoveries of Australia have needed works as ponderous, shafts as deep, and machinery as costly, as any other description of mining enterprise; but, nevertheless less, the enormous wealth which may be represented by a small quantity has a direct tendency to create a speculative spirit in the minds of all employed. The miner who earns his £2 10s. a week by blasting a quartz reef may work as steadily, and certainly does work as hard, as he who is picking up coal or copper-bearing dirt, but he is conscious all through that it is gold upon which he is working, and his imagination, aroused by the richness of the metal he is seeking, is ever pushing him on to personal speculation; – till the goal before his eyes is not the few hundred pounds which he certainly could save by industry as a miner, but the fortune which he might possibly make by some happy circumstance in his favour as a speculator. The circumstance now and again does occur; but the result is not always happy. There is much less of such incentive to gambling among copper mines; – though it is not altogether absent, for copper mines are also worked upon tribute.

The Kapunda copper-mine is the oldest in the colony, having been discovered in 1843, by two gentlemen engaged in squatting operations. It was considered to be a great day in the colony when the first ore was raised from this mine on January 8, 1844. The Kapunda mines are still worked; but their celebrity was soon eclipsed by the famous Burra Burra mine, and has now been altogether cast into the shade by the mines at Wallaroo and Moonta. I did not visit Kapunda, but I was told that the town itself is prosperous and well ordered.

The Burra Burra copper-mines, if not the next discovered in South Australia, were the next of any magnitude, and were for

some years the great source of South Australian mining
wealth. They have had a much wider fame than those of
Kapunda. They are about ninety miles nearly due north from
Adelaide, and they have the advantage of a railway for the
whole distance. The one great railway of the colony runs from
Adelaide to Kooringa, the name of the town close to which
the Burra Burra mines are situated, with a branch to Kapunda,
of which place I have already spoken. Copper therefore may
be said to have made the existing railways of the colony. The
copper at Burra Burra was first found by a shepherd, named
Pickitt, in 1845. What became of Pickitt I never heard; but two
companies were at once formed for the purchase from the
government of 20,000 acres under special survey. This was the
land in which the copper was known to lie, but its exact
whereabouts was still a mining mystery. Of these two companies one was called the Nobs, as being specially aristocratic;
the others, which were plebeian, were the Snobs. They
combined, as neither could raise sufficient money alone, and
the government could not or would not grant a special survey
under a fixed amount which either separately was unable to
pay. The land was then divided, and the two companies drew
lots. The Snobs got the northern portion and all the copper,
and the Nobs were driven to resell their moiety for pastoral
purposes. Where the copper did lie, it lay absolutely on the
surface. There was as it were a rock of copper, so that deep
sinking was not necessary. During the first six years of the
mine's history 80,000 tons of ore were shipped to England,
giving a profit of nearly half a million sterling. The company
had begun with a capital of only £1,500 over and above the
sum expended on the purchase of the land. Those were the
palmy days of the Burra Burra mines, of which we used to
hear much in England.

In 1851 the miners, attracted by the new gold of the next
colony, rushed away to the Victorian gold-diggings, and the
Burra Burra were almost deserted. But after a time the men
returned, and English miners were got over from Cornwall,
and the success was continued. In 1859, 1,170 persons were
employed there. But gradually the surface copper was worked
out, and the great attraction of other and still richer mines at
Wallaroo and Moonta paled the ineffectual fire of Burra Burra.

For a time the works were almost ceased. When I visited the place in 1872 new operations under a new management had commenced, and many in the colony believed that a complete resuscitation would take place. There were, however, not a great number of hands employed, and the works going on, – which were on a large scale, – seemed to be preparatory to copper production rather than themselves productive. There are three towns adjacent to these mines, Kooringa, which I have already named, Redruth, and Aberdeen. Thrown together they make one broken, meandering, unfinished street, which is by no means tempting to the ordinary traveller. It is hard to say how these things arrange themselves; but the wealth of the great Burra Burra mine certainly has not succeeded in making a great Burra Burra city.

But Wallaroo is now the greatest name in South Australian copper-mines, and Moonta is second to it. Between Gulf St. Vincent and Spencer's Gulf there lies a large outstretching territory, bearing nearly as close a semblance to a man's leg as does Italy, called Yorke's Peninsula. At the top of this, at the part of the leg farthest from the foot, close on the shore of Spencer's Gulf, and therefore on the outside of the leg, is Wallaroo. Here, previous to 1860, a squatter held a station for sheep, which even for that purpose was by no means encouraging. As a spot to be inhabited by men and women nothing could be more dreary or unfortunate. There was no water, and even the wells when dug gave forth water so brackish that it could not be used. The vegetation was stunted and miserable. The ground was sandy and barren. Here, on 17th December, 1859, a shepherd, named Boor, found a piece of copper, and brought the tidings to his master. Within a few months £80,000 had been advanced for working copper-mines by a mercantile firm in Adelaide. The squatter was in the way to become a very rich man, and the shepherd had become a mining hero. In the very next year another shepherd, named Ryan, found another piece of copper at a place called Moonta, about ten miles from Wallaroo, on the same sheep station, – and this was at once worked by the same persons. This other shepherd was also enriched, and the squatter became a millionaire. Perhaps few mines were ever opened in which there has been a quicker, and at the same time a steadier, mercantile progress than in those of Wallaroo and Moonta.

There are five district towns, all created by these mines, standing within ten miles of each other, containing about 17,000 inhabitants; and previous to 1860 there was no house in the district but a wretched cottage, hardly better than a hut. The two townships laid out by government are Kadina, near to the Wallaroo mines, and Moonta, close to those bearing that name. But these mines had the inestimable benefit of being near the sea; – and now there is a third town, called Port Wallaroo, from which the copper is shipped, joined both to Kadina and to Moonta by railway. Port Wallaroo is a thriving harbour, and is perhaps the largest of the five, as here are built the smelting works at which the ore is turned into copper. For a time the ore was sent over to Swansea and was smelted there, – but as the two companies became rich and powerful, smelting works were opened, and the copper is now sent to England in bars. But the miners do not live either at Kadina, at Moonta Town, or at Port Wallaroo. They have built habitations for themselves round the very mouths of the shafts, and in this way two other vast villages have sprung up, called Wallaroo Mines and Moonta Mines. Very singular places they are, – consisting of groups of low cottages, clustering together in streets, one street being added on to another as the need for them arises, not built with any design such as is usual in the towns of new countries, but created by the private enterprise of the inhabitants, – and in fact put up in opposition to the law. The surface is government land leased out specially for mining purposes, and not for building purposes. No one is entitled to build on it. There are the townships, duly laid out in accordance with the law, close by, on which any one may build who desires to live there, purchasing his lot for the purpose in the proper way. But the workman's need to be near his work has been too strong for the law, and these towns, much bigger than the towns of the townships proper, have established themselves.

In no instance is the centralizing tendency of the government in young countries and amidst scanty populations more visible than in their management of new towns; and it never struck me more forcibly than at Wallaroo and Moonta. It is either necessary, or the government thinks that it is necessary, that everything should be arranged for the new-coming inhabitants, and that they should be called upon to manage nothing for themselves. Roads and bridges are made from the taxes. The land is divided out into its sections by the government. Any comer may buy his section at a certain price, and may build his house, – but he must deal with the government officers, and must build his house according to specification. The idea, no doubt, is not only compatible with freedom of action, but is intended to encourage it, and springs from a theory of democratic equality. It is the duty of the government to see that one man does not ride over another, that the smallest and the poorest may have their share of the public wealth of the community, – that as far as possible there shall be no very small men and no very big men. The Utopian politician travels as far as he can away from the despotism of patriarchal rule, but he travels in a circle and comes back to it. The minister, though he be chosen by the people, becomes a despot; and, like other despots, he is forced to rule so that he may please his favourites. The favourites of the minister in a democratic community are they who can support him in parliament; and on their behalf he finds himself too often forced to read the law either this way or that. In these mining townships the land sold for building had been sold with certain protective privileges. They who bought were not only entitled to keep shops, but were encouraged to buy land by the assurance that no shops should be kept by others within a certain distance outside the township. Consequently no miner's wife can buy an ounce of tea, or a yard of ribbon, or a delf cup, without going out of the bigger concourse of people to the lesser to make her purchase; nor can the miner, if he fancies that the prices at Kadina or at Moonta are too high for him, try the question by opening a rival shop for himself in his own immediate locality. In these large mining villages nothing can be bought and nothing sold. In reality the man when he has constructed a house has not even a house to sell. He should have built it in the official town if he desired to avail himself of his property.

The matter is mentioned here chiefly because I thus get an opportunity of alluding to general interference of government in matters which with us are altogether beyond its scope. No doubt such interference is necessary in new communities.

Government must do more when nothing has already been done, than it can do with an old-established nation. It must make roads. It must apportion the land. It must take upon its shoulders for a while the duties which fall afterwards upon local officers. But the tendency is to centralize power, and to put a privilege of interfering into the hands of individuals, which privilege can be and is improperly used for political purposes, and which to an observer from an old country seems to be antagonistic to liberty. I do not know that the miners at Wallaroo and Moonta suffer very much from their restricted rights. I do not think that they know that they suffer at all. But I groaned for them in spirit when I found that not one among them could put up a penn'orth of barley-sugar for sale in his own cottage windows. Such restriction would very quickly create a rebellion in England.

I went down a mine at Wallaroo, finding it always to be a duty to go down a shaft on visiting any mining locality, – and I came up again. But I cannot say that I saw anything when I was down there. The descent was 450 feet, and I felt relieved when I was once more on the surface. I walked below among various levels, and had the whole thing explained to me; – but for no useful purpose whatever. It was very hard work, and I think I should have begged for mercy had any additional level been proposed to me; as it was, I went through it like a man, without complaint, and was simply very much fatigued. As I rose to the air I swore I would never go down another mine, and hitherto I have kept my vow. I found that miners working for simple wages could earn about £1 18s. a week, and that men on tribute would realise something more, – perhaps about £2 5s. The 'tribute' men undoubtedly worked harder, as they were toiling on their own behalf, reaping the advantage of their increased labour. In speaking of the Victorian gold mines, I have endeavoured to explain the system of tribute, – by which the miner is enabled to share both in the profit and in the risk of the speculation. No doubt the result in the raising of copper is the same as in the finding of gold; but the transaction is by no means equally speculative. The man who works for gold on tribute may find none, and be called upon not only to work on, but also to defray expenses. Whereas the miner on tribute in a copper mine goes not go into the affair till it is known that the copper is there. According to the percentage of ore which is extracted, his earnings will be higher or lower; – but his earnings are assured, and, as the result of the arrangement, by working harder than he would otherwise work he simply earns more than he would otherwise earn.

At the Wallaroo mines I found a set of black natives employed on the surface work, at regular wages of 4s. 2d. a day, or 26s. a week. There were about ten of them, and I was told that they had been there for three months, and had been as regular in their attendance as white men. This was the only instance I found in Australia in which I myself came upon any number of these aborigines in regular and voluntary employment. I have seen a man at one station and a woman at another as to whom I have been told that they were regarded as part of the regular establishment, – but it always seemed that their work was of a fitful kind. I learned also that in one or two of the colonies, in Western Australia and in Queensland, they are drilled and used as policemen for the control of their own countrymen; – but such service as this I can hardly regard as steady, regular work. Here the experiment was said to have answered for the period that I have named. I came across one of these men, who was supposed to be a little ill, and therefore not on duty at the moment. He was dressed in a very genteel manner, – with clothes softer and finer than a white miner would wear even when on a holiday. He was very gentle and civil, but not very communicative. He bought clothes with his money, he said, and food, – and the rest he put away. He did not resent the impertinence of my inquiries, but was not quite willing to gratify my curiosity. My desire was to learn whether he had realised the advantage of laying up and permanently possessing property. I doubt whether he had, although he did mutter something as to putting away his wages. He seemed much more willing to talk about the cold in the head under which he had been suffering than of his general condition in life.

At the smelting works of Wallaroo men were earning higher wages than in the mines; – something like an average of £2 10s. a week; – but their hours of labour were longer. The miners work day and night, by shifts of eight hours each. The smelters work also throughout the twenty-four hours, – but they work only in two sets. I should think that twelve hours by a furnace must be worse than eight below ground. The smelters, however, probably do not keep at it during the whole time. The smelters I found had, almost to a man, come from Wales, whereas so many of the miners were Cornish men as to give to Moonta and Wallaroo the air of Cornish towns.

Coal for the smelting is brought from Newcastle, in New South Wales; but the inferior ore is sent to other smelting works at Newcastle, – so that the ships which bring the coal may go back with freights. The copper therefore is sent to the European markets, not only from Port Wallaroo, but also from Newcastle.

When I was in the colony in April, 1872, copper, which in April, 1871, had been worth only £74 per ton, rose to £105, – so that the happy owners of mines in a working condition were revelling in a success not inferior to that of the squatters. Copper and wool were both so high that the fortune of the colony was supposed to be made. I found that there were no less that 70 'reputed' mines in the colony at the close of the year 1870, of which 38 were reported to have been then at work. But sundry even of these 38 were not supposed to be remunerative. Many of the 70 so-called 'reputed' mines are mere mining claims, which are held under government as possible future speculations. Those which are distant from the sea and distant also from railways cannot be worked with a profit, let the ore be ever so rich. The cost of the carriage destroys the wealth of the copper. At present when men talk of the mining wealth of South Australia they allude to Wallaroo and Moonta.

I have said that these places are joined together by a railway, – but they are not joined to any other place by rail. The traveller to Wallaroo is forced to go from Adelaide either by coach or by steamer round the Gulfs. I was taken there by one of the great copper-mining authorities of the colony, and we elected to go by coach, in order that I mights see something of the county. The coach was a mail-coach, with four horses, running regularly on the road every day; – but on our return journey we were absolutely lost in the bush, – coach, coachman, horses, mails, passengers, and all. The man was trying a new track, and took us so far away from the old track that no one knew where we were. At last we found ourselves on the seashore. Of course it will be understood that there was no vestige of a road or path-way. Travellers are often 'bushed' in Australia. They wander off their paths and are lost amidst the forests. In this instance the whole mail-coach was 'bushed' When we came upon the sea, and no one could say what sea it was, I felt that the adventure was almost more than interesting.

CHAPTER VI

THE NORTHERN TERRITORY – TELEGRAPH AND RAILWAY

There are not a few in the colonies who declare that South Australia, as a name for the colony which uses it, is a misnomer. Nearly the whole of Victoria is south of nearly the whole of South Australia. Adelaide is considerably to the north of Melbourne, and but very little to the south of Sydney. Consequently those foolish English people at home are actually making the stupidest mistakes! Letters have been addressed to Melbourne, New South Wales, South Australia. The story is very current, and is often told to show the want of geographical education under which the old country suffers. I have not, however, been able to trace the address to later years, and at any time between 1837 and 1851 the details as given by the letter-writer were only too correct. Melbourne did belong to New South Wales, and certainly was in the most southern district of Australia. But if the name South Australia was bad, or falsely describing the colony, when first given, it is infinitely worse now. Then the proposed confines of the young settlement lay around Spencer Gulf, and Gulf St. Vincent, and Encounter Bay, which armlets of the sea break up into the land from the eastern extremity of the Great Australian Bight, – as the curve in the sea line of the southern coast of the continent is called. The new colonists had settled themselves, or, when the name was chosen, were proposing to settle themselves, at the centre of the south coast, and the name was fair enough. But since those days South Australia has extended herself northwards till she has made good her claim up to a line far north of that which divides Queensland from New South Wales, and now she is supposed to run right through the continent up to the Gulf of Carpentaria and the Indian Ocean, so that she thoroughly divides the vast desert tracts of Western Australia from the three eastern colonies, Queensland, New South Wales, and Victoria. As far as area is concerned, she is at present as much northern as southern. In some of our maps the northern half of these territories is separated by a line from the southern, as though it were a separate colony; – but it has had no name of its own yet given to it; its lands are at the disposition of the government of South Australia; its very few inhabitants are subject to South Australian laws; and it is in fact a part of South Australia. It contains over 500,000 square miles; but, with the exception of one or two very small settlements on the coast, it has no white population. The aborigines who wander through it have been little disturbed, and nothing was known of it till the great enterprise of running a telegraph wire through it from south to north had been conceived and commenced. Now the northern territory has come into fashion, men talk about it in the colonies, and it is becoming necessary that even here in England the fact should be recognised that there is such a land, which will probably before long demand to be instituted as a separate colony.

The telegraph posts and wires by which the Australian colonies are now connected with Great Britain are already an established fact. This line enters the Australia continent from Java, at a point on the northern coast called Port Darwin. At Port Darwin there is a small settlement called Palmerston, around which land had been sold to the extent of 500,000 acreas when I was in the colony, and this has been selected as the landing-place of European news. The colonisation of the northern territory is thus begun, – and there can be little doubt but that a town, and then a settlement, and then a colony, will form themselves.

When the scheme of the telegraph was first put on foot the colony of South Australia undertook to make the entire line across the continent, – the submarine line to Java and the line thence on to Singapore and home to Europe being in other hands. It was an immense undertaking for a community so small in number, and one as to which many doubted the power of the colony to complete it. But it has been completed. I had heard, before I left England in 1871, that an undertaking had been given by the government of South Australia to finish the work by January 1, 1872. This certainly was not done, but very great efforts were made to accomplish it, and the failure was caused by the violence of nature rather than by any want of energy. Unexpected and prolonged rains interfered with the operations and greatly retarded them. The world is used to the breaking of such promises in regard to time, and hardly ever expects that a contractor for a large work shall be punctual within a month or two. The world may well excuse this breach of contract, for surely no contractor ever had a harder job of work on hand. The delay would not be worth mention here, were it not that the leading South Australians of the day, headed by the governor, had been so anxious to show that they could really do all that they had undertaken to perform, and were equally disappointed at their own partial failure.

The distance of the line to be made was about 1,800 miles, and the work had to be done through a country unknown, without water, into which every article needed by the men had to be carried over deserts, across unbridged rivers, through unexplored forests, amidst hostile tribes of savages, – in one of the hottest regions of the world. I speak here of the lack of water, and I have said above that the works were hindered by rain. I hope my gentle readers will not think that I am piling up excuses which obliterate each other. There is room for deviation of temperature in a distance of 1,800 miles, – and Australia generally, though subject specially to drought, is subject to floods also. And the same gentle readers should remember, – when they bethink themselves how easy it is to stick up a few poles in this or another thickly inhabited country, and how small is the operation of erecting a line of telegraph wires as compared with that of constructing a railway or even a road, – how great had hitherto been the difficulty experienced by explorers in simply making their way across the continent, and in carrying provisions for themselves as they journeyed. Burke and Wills perished in the attempt, and the line to be taken was through the very country in which Burke and Wills had been lost. The dangers would of course not be similar. The army of workmen sent to put up the posts and to stretch the wires was accompanied by an army of purveyors. Men could never be without food or without water. But it was necessary that everything should be carried. For the northern portion of the work it was necessary that all stores should be sent round by ships, and then taken up rivers which had not hitherto been surveyed. If the gentle reader will think only of the amount of wire required for 1,800 miles of telegraph communication, and of the circumstances of its carriage, he will, I think, recognise the magnitude of the enterprise.

The colony divided the work, the government undertaking about 800 miles in the centre, which portion of the ground was considered to be most difficult to reach. The remaining distances, consisting of 500 miles in the south and 500 miles in the north, were let out to contractors. The southern part, which was comparatively easy as being accessible from Adelaide, was finished in time, as was also the middle distance which the government had kept in its own hands. But the difficulties at the northern end were so great that they who had undertaken the work failed to accomplish it, and it was at last completed by government, – if I remember rightly, somewhat more than six months after the date fixed. The line did not come into immediate working order, owing to some temporary fault beyond the Australian borders.

The importance of the telegraph to the colonies cannot be overrated, and the anxiety it created can only be understood by those who have watched the avidity with which news from England is received in all her dependencies. Australia had hitherto been dependent on one arrival monthly from England, – and on a very little credited monthly dispatch reaching her shores via New York, San Francisco, and New Zealand. The English monthly mail touches first at King George's Sound, in Western Australia, but thence are no wires into the other colonies. The mail steamer then passes on to Melbourne, while a branch boat takes the mails to Adelaide. As the distance to Adelaide is considerably shorter than to Melbourne, the English news generally reaches that port first, and is thence disseminated to the other colonies. That happens once a month. Then comes, also once a month, the so-called Californian telegrams, not unfrequently giving a somewhat distorted view of English affairs. This is now changed for daily news. We who have daily news, – as do all of us in

England every morning at our breakfast-table, – are some-times apt to regard it as a bore, and tell ourselves that it would be delightful to have a real budget on an occasion after a month of silence. The only way to learn the value of the thing, is to be without it for a time. In the single item of the price of wool in the London market, the Australian telegraph will be of inestimable value to the colonies. When the scheme was first brought forward there was a question whether the line through the Australian continent should be made by the joint efforts of the colonies or by the energy of one. South Australia is justly proud of herself, in that she undertook the work, and has accomplished it.

The telegraph line has certainly been the means of introducing the northern territory into general notice; and now a much larger project has been formed, – which, if it be carried out, will certainly create a new colony on the northern coast. The proposition is to make a railway along the tele-graph line, a railway from Adelaide right across Australia, over the huge desert of the continent, to Port Darwin! Who will travel by it? What will it carry? Whence will the money come? How will it be made to pay? And as it cannot possibly be made to pay, – as far as human sight can see, – what insane philanthropists or speculators will be found able to subscribe the enormous sum of money necessary for such a purpose? These are of course the questions that are asked. The distance to be covered by the new line is very nearly 1,8000 miles, and the money said to be necessary for it is £10,000,000! There are no inhabitants in the county, – at any rate none who would use a railway, and at the distant terminus there is no town, – not as yet a community of 200 white inhabitants.

I soon found that the railway was but a portion of the plan, – and indeed the smaller portion of it. The scheme is as follows: – The parliament of South Australia is to pass a bill authorising the formation of a small preliminary company, which company shall be empowered by the colonial leg-islature to make over no less than two hundred millions of acres in freehold to the shareholders of the proposed railway company. The small company is to give birth to a large company, the residence of which is to be in London, and this large company is to consist of shareholders who will subscribe the money needed for the railway, and take the land as bought by their money. The great object of the promoters, who, when I was in Adelaide, were chiefly gentlemen having seats in the parliament of the colony, was to open up to human uses an immense track of country which is at present useless, and in this way to spread the reputation and increase the prosperity of the colony at large. There can be no doubt that population would follow the railway, as it has always followed railways in the United States. The pastures would be opened to sheep; and contingent advantages are of course anticipated, – such as mineral fields of various kinds. Within 250 miles of the southern end copper exists in large quantities, and the expense of carriage alone suspends its extraction. At the Port Darwin end, on the northern coast, gold has been found, and they who are hopeful declare that a few years will see the richest gold-fields of Australia near the banks of the Victoria and the Roper Rivers. A world of hopes rises to the mind of the sanguine proprietor as the largeness of his scheme endears it more and more to his heart, till he sees the happiness of thousands and the magnificence of himself in the realisation of his project.

That such a railway should be made on the speculation of trade returns is impossible; but if the South Australian parliament be in earnest, and if the colony will give her land, – land which she at present has in such abundance that she cannot use it, – it may be that funds sufficient for commencing the railway will be produced. It is proposed that the land shall be given as the line is made, – so many acres for every mile of railway. The entire territory contiguous to the line is not to be given. The land is to be divided into blocks, of which alternate blocks are to be surrendered, and alternate blocks retained, by the government, so that the new owners of the territory may be constrained as to price and other terms of sale. Of course the company would fail in selling if it charged more than the government, or proposed terms less advantageous than those offered by the government. But there seem to lack two ingredients for the thorough success of such a scheme, – a town at the end, such as was San Francisco when the railway was proposed across the Rocky Mountains from Chicago to that city, and a wheat-growing country for its support, such as

California, – and such as Oregon is, and the Utah territory.

I do not believe that I shall live to see a railway made from Adelaide to Port Darwin, or even that younger men than I will do so. The greatness of many accomplished enterprises is now teaching men to believe that everything is possible; and they who are sanguine are falling into the error, – directly opposite to that of our grandfathers, – of thinking that nothing is too hard to be accomplished. I cannot believe in the expenditure of £10,000,000 on the construction of a railway which is to run through a desert to nowhere. But I do believe in the gold-fields and pastures of Port Darwin, and in the beauties of the Roper and Victoria Rivers; and, hot though the country be, I think that another young colony will found itself on the western shores of the Gulf of Carpentaria.

CHAPTER VII

LEGISLATURE AND GOVERNMENT

With some small variations the scheme as to parliament and executive government is the same in South Australia as in the other colonies. There are king, lords, and commons, – or in other language, Governor, Legislative Council, and House of Assembly. The most remarkable variation is to be found in the mode adopted for getting together the Legislative Council or House of Colonial Lords, – which mode I regard as the worst ever yet invented for summoning a chamber of senators. In England our House of Peers is hereditary, the Crown having the power to add to its number as it pleases, – and thus, at any rate, the country does acquire the services of a body of legislative magnates without any trouble to itself. It is a great thing to be a peer, and the peers as a rule live up to the position which the country assigns them. In the United States the senators of the National Congress are elected from their different States by a complicated machinery which certainly effects its object, by bringing the leading politicians of the day into the Upper House, and by conferring on that House dignity and reputation. In some of our colonies, in New South Wales for instance, and in Queensland, the members of the Upper House are nominated by the Crown, – or rather, in fact, by the responsible ministers of the day, who are account-able for the selections which they make, and who confer the honour on men anxious and for the most part able to take a part in public affairs. As one party becomes stronger than another in the colony, so does the minister of one party have more frequent opportunities of introducing his friends into the Legislative Council than the ministers of the other party, – and the preponderance of public opinion is represented by the Upper as well as the Lower Chamber. In other colonies, as in Victoria and South Australia, the members of the Legislative

Council are elected by the people, – but the manner of doing so is different. In Victoria the whole colony is divided into provinces, and each province periodically elects its members. Even then the interest felt is not very great, as I endeavoured to explain, when speaking of the Victorian legislature, – but their provinces do in some sort identify themselves with their own members; and, though the political feeling in the matter is mild, it exists and has its influence. In South Australia the members of the Upper Chamber are elected by the colony at large, and therefore when elections come round, no political feeling is excited.

This Upper House consists of eighteen members. Every fourth year six members retire, in February, and the votes of the entire colony are taken as to the election of their successors, – so that the members are elected for twelve years. There is a property qualification for voting, – £20 leasehold, £25 household, or £50 freehold. Very slight interest is taken in the elections, – as might be expected from such a scheme. The distances in the colony are enormous, and each district feels that as the election is to be made by the colony at large, its own effect must be very small. When the result of a national election is of extreme importance to parties, – as is the case with the election of a President in the United States, – the country can be awakened to the work; but no political animation can be aroused by the national importance of sending six members to the Upper House. As a consequence men do not vote except in the towns, and do not vote there with any regularity. At the election of 1869, 4,468 votes only were cast, by a body of 15,773 electors. Certain members who have long been in the House keep their seats when the day for their re-election comes round, because no one cares to disturb them; but every now and then some obscure but ambitious and probably absolutely unfit individual puts himself forward, and is elected, to the scandal of the House, – because there has been no interest felt in the matter. The expenditure of a few hundred pounds would almost certainly carry an election, – not because a few hundred pounds have much force in the colony, but because the amount of antagonistic force used is very small. I look upon this as the very worst plan yet adopted for maintaining the existence of a legislative chamber.

The Lower House consists of seventy-two members, who are elected by thirty-six districts, – two members for each district. They sit for three years, – or would do but for dissolutions. Manhood suffrage, with vote by ballot as a matter of course, prevails; but residence for six months is required for an elector – so that the nomad tribe of wandering vagrants who call themselves workmen, but are in truth beggars, is excluded. The competition for seats in the House of Assembly is sufficiently lively to show that a seat is desired, but it is not very keen. At the time of the election for the House of Assembly in 1870, there were 39,647 men in the colony entitled to be electors, but only 17,233 voted.

I found the ballot to be generally popular, – because it tended to make things quiet at elections. Sir James Ferguson, the governor of the colony, – who as a Conservative member for a Scotch county, and as one of the Conservative government at home, cannot have loved the ballot here, in England, – thus expresses his opinion on the subject to the Secretary of State: – 'I am bound to state that the ballot is generally and remarkably popular in the colony. To the people of the colony it appears to give entire satisfaction.' I am bound to report this as the opinion which I found to prevail among almost all classes as to the use of the ballot in Australia. I give my evidence unwillingly, because I myself very much dislike the ballot for English use, and believe that a mistake is made by those who argue that because it suits the colonies, therefore it will suit ourselves. With us the object is secrecy, which I think should not be an object, and which I think also will not be obtained. In the colonies secrecy is not desired, but tranquillity is felt to be a blessing. It is clear that the ballot does assist in producing tranquillity.

But it may be questioned whether even tranquillity at elections is to be regarded as an unmixed blessing. Apathy is certainly not desirable, and it may be that tranquillity will show itself to be akin to apathy. Men are always eager as to that in which they are truly interested, and real human eagerness will produce excitement and noise. Broken heads are bad things, but even broken heads are better than political indifference. They who have framed the Australian constitutions and have selected the modes of election for the legislative chambers of the colonies, have had before their eyes an idea of human political excellence which has

never hitherto prevailed, and never will prevail till that good
time comes which we call the millennium. They have desired
to produce great vitality in the electors without any excitement at the elections. Men are not to rush to the polls, –
certainly not to go thither under stress or fear, or bribery, or
drink; but all men are to walk there in orderly strings, under
the pressure of a high sense of national duty. They are to be
debarred from the interest of personal contest by the ballot and
other means, – but are nevertheless to be constant in voting.
The ballot, and the others means, are successful for the
required ends, – but the people are indifferent as to the results.
It is the boast of Australian politicians that the elections are
quiet. They are often too quiet. If it be the case, as a great man
once said, that any first six men caught walking through
Temple Bar, would make as good members of parliament as
any other six men, the South Australian scheme of voting for
members of the Legislative Council may be good, – but under
no other theory.

  I doubt whether South Australia can boast that its parliament contains its best men. Neither do members of the
government or members of parliament in any of the Australian colonies have that relation to the country at large which
they certainly hold in England. In England the premier is the
head man of his country for the time; and in common
estimation with us, a member of parliament is felt to be a man
who has achieved honourable distinction. It is not so in the
Australian colonies generally, and certainly is not so in South
Australia specially. Prime ministers there have succeeded each
other with wonderful celerity. The first parliament with
responsible government was opened in Adelaide, on April
22nd, 1857, – not yet sixteen years ago as I write, – and since
that date twenty-seven different ministries have been formed.
I found that no less than six of these combinations had been
made by Mr. Ayres, who was the chief secretary or head of
the government when I was in Adelaide, – but even he has
succumbed again. There is, however, always this comfort to
be extracted from such speedy reverses, – that a quick return
of triumph may be expected. When last I heard of the colony
Mr. Ayres was out; but very probably he may be again in
before this is published.

The real work of government is done in South Australia by the Governor in Council with a cabinet of five. Of these one always sits in the Legislative Council, and the other four are supposed to have seats in the House of Assembly. The constitution requires that no minister shall be in office above three months without a seat either in the Upper or in the Lower House.

The debates are fairly well conducted, – at any rate without riot or that personal abuse and continual appeal to the Speaker which I have witnessed elsewhere. There is much useless and quite vapid talking, – members making speeches without even an attempt at a new point or a new argument, to which no one listens, but which are endured with patience. It is understood that when a gentleman has taken the trouble to get a seat, and is willing to sacrifice his time, he should be allowed to air his voice, and to learn by practice to speak with fluency. Mr. Lowe and Mr. Childers have taught colonial legislators the possible results of such lessons; and why should any man throw away a chance? I heard a debate on the great question of cab-lamps, – whether legislation should content itself with requiring simply cabs to be lighted at nights, or whether it should extend the precaution to other vehicles, – on which two-thirds of a full House were eloquent. I heard impassioned eloquence on the question whether the excellent Bishop of Adelaide should be allowed to retain his right of walking out of the room before other people, – a right which, as it came from the Crown, the parliament could not take from him, but which he gracefully abandoned when it gave annoyance to scrupulous politicians. Their minds were much excited on this question. And I heard another debate as to the governor's salary, carried on with much energy. The Lower House, with hot parliamentary zeal expressed in fervid words, decided on cutting off £1,000 a year from the salary of future governors. But the measure of retrenchment, though essentially a money measure, was lost, because no recorder could be found for it in the Upper Chamber.

There was another great debate when I was in the colony, – of which, however, I only heard a small portion, and it gave rise to an incident which I will mention as giving an idea of the feeling displayed towards the House. It was decided, as a new measure, that there should be after-dinner sittings, – and on a certain evening there was an after-dinner sitting. There was a spirited debate, which was conducted with a fair amount of parliamentary animation. One of the leading Adelaide newspapers, giving its history of the affair on the following morning, described the speakers in round terms of having been – unfit for parliamentary work, because they had dined. On the following day one of the gentlemen attacked brought the matter forward on a question of privilege, and there ensued a debate in which it was at any rate shown that the accusation was altogether groundless. But nothing was done. No one seemed seriously to think that the writer of the article, or the editor, proprietor, or printer of the paper, should be punished for the insinuations made. On the next morning the newspaper in question ridiculed the complaining members for having adopted the only meaning of the words of the article which they would bear. I could not but think that had the 'Times' or 'Daily Telegraph' accused the House of Commons of being generally unfit for its duties because it had – dined, that the House of Commons would in some way have made its displeasure felt. But I was anxious to know why such an unwarranted attack should be made by one of the leading newspapers of the colony upon the parliament of the colony, – and I received information on the subject. The newspaper in question had to report the debates, and disliked the trouble and expense of keeping reporter late into the evening.

Few countries can, I think, show a more favourable account of their public financial matters than that exhibited by South Australia. Custom duties are the only taxation to which her people are subject, and the amount paid by them in that shape averages no more than 25s. a head. On the 31st December, 1871, the population was 189,018, and the duties levied in 1871 had amounted to £234,980. The total revenue in that year had been £785,489, and the total expenditure £759,339. But the revenue so stated is made up of various sums, which have no reference whatever to taxation. It includes the gross amounts received from the post-office, from the railways, from the telegraph offices, and from the water-works; – whereas the total of the expenditure includes the expenses of those establishments. The revenue includes also the money carried to the public credit for the sale and lease of lands, which I find estimated for 1872 at £145,000. The public debt amounted to £1,944,600 on the 31st December, 1871, which had been chiefly, – I believe entirely, – expended on public works. One hundred and thirty-three miles of railway had been opened in the country, the working of which in 1871 had cost £88,000, – and which had produced £111,000 by its traffic, thus giving £23,000 as dividends on the cost, and paying about a quarter of the interest on the total of the public debt.

In what I have said it will, I fear, be thought that I have intended to depreciate the parliament of the colony. I have not sought to do so, but I am merely giving my personal impressions of what I heard and saw. Parliaments, like puddings, should be judged by the proof of their results, as shown in the eating. One of the main works of all parliaments is so to adjust the financial affairs of the country entrusted to it, that the people shall not suffer from over-taxation, that the public credit shall be maintained, and that a sufficiency of revenue shall be collected to insure the safety and general well-being of the community. If this be adequately done, a parliament need certainly not be ashamed of its doings. And this is adequately done in South Australia.

WESTERN AUSTRALIA

CHAPTER I

EARLY HISTORY

An ingenious but sarcastic Yankee, when asked what he thought of Western Australia, declared that it was the best country he had even seen to run through an hour-glass. He meant to insinuate that the parts of the colony which he had visited were somewhat sandy. It is sandy. The country round Perth is very sandy. From Freemantle, the seaport, the road up to Perth, the capital lies through sand. From Albany, the seaport at which the mail steamers stop, the distance to Perth is about 260 miles, and the traveller encounters a good deal of sand on the way. The clever Yankee who thought of the hour-glass probably did not go beyond Perth. There is much soil in Western Australia which is not sandy, – which is as good, perhaps, as any land in the Australian colonies; – but it lies in patches, sometimes far distant from each other; and there is very much desert or useless country between. In this is, probably, to be found the chief reason why Western Australia has not progressed as have the other colonies. The distances from settlement to settlement have been so great as to make it almost impossible for settlers to dispose of their produce. This has been the first great difficulty with which Western Australia has had to contend; and to this have been superadded others: the absence of gold, – an evil not so much in itself as in the difference created by the presence of gold in the other colonies, whereby the early settlers in Western Australia were induced to rush away to Adelaide and Melbourne; its remoteness from the populous parts of the Australian continent; the fact that it is not the way from any place to any other place; the denseness and endlessness of its forests; its poisonous shrub, which in many places makes the pasturing of sheep impossible; and the ferocity of the aboriginal tribes when they first encountered their white invaders. These causes have made the progress of Western Australia slow, and have caused the colony to be placed in a category very different from that in which the other colonies are reckoned, and to be looked at from an exceptional point of view.

The other Australian colonies were originally founded on some ground or for some cause special to themselves. New South Wales, which was the first occupied, was selected as a penal settlement for the use of the mother country. Captain Cook had then but lately made himself acquainted with the coast, and had specially recommended Botany Bay to the British Government. Consequently, a young convict world, under the rule of Governor Phillip, was sent to Botany Bay; and finding Botany Bay unsuited for its purposes, the young world settled itself at Port Jackson. From this establishment Van Diemen's Land was an offshoot, first colonised for the same purpose, – that of affording a safe refuge to British criminal exiles. An effort was also made in 1803 to establish a penal settlement near the site on which Melbourne now stands. And indeed the first attempt to set up the British flag on that part of the Australian continent which is now called Western Australia was a step made in the same direction. The governors of Port Jackson, or New South Wales, as it came to be called, having been nearly overwhelmed in their herioc struggles to find food for these convicts fourteen thousand miles away from home, on a land which, as far as they had seen it, was very barren, made a sister settlement, first at Norfolk Island, then in Van Diemen's Land, and thirdly at King George's Sound, – where stands the town of Albany, which place is now the Southern District of Western Australia. A small party of convicts, with Major Lockyer as their governor, were stationed here in 1826, – but the convicts were withdrawn from the place when it was recognised as belonging to the established colony of Western Australia. After this fashion and for this reason, that of affording a home to the transported ruffians of Great Britain, – the first Australian settlements were made. South Australia was colonised by private enterprise. Victoria and Queensland were separated from New South Wales to the south and north as they became sufficiently populous and strong to demand to be allowed to stand alone. But Western Australia arose after another fashion.

She was colonised because she was there, – not because she was wanted for any special purpose, either by the community at large or by any small section of it. We have claimed, and made good our claim, to call all New Holland, hardly by this time known by the name of Australia, as our own. We had done something on the east coast, something in the southern island; some small attempts had been made to utilise the south generally. There were still the west and the north open to us. The northern coast, which even yet we have hardly touched except for telegraphic purposes, was very hot and very unpromising. But there came news to us that on an estuary which had been named the Swan River, running out into the ocean at about the thirty-second parallel of latitude, in a salubrious climate, a commodious settlement might be formed. News to this effect was brought home by Captain Stirling in 1827, and in 1829 the captain, now promoted to the position of Governor Stirling, returned to the Swan River, and founded the colony, – which dates from 1st June of that year. He was preceded, by a few months, by Captain Freemantle in the 'Challenger,' who first hoisted the British flag on the spot on which the town of Freemantle now stands. In the month of August the town of Perth, twelve miles up the Swan River, was founded, and in the following month lands were assigned to the new-comers. In that year twenty ships arrived with settlers, stores, several immigrants, and a few soldiers. I do not know that these were specially high-minded men, flying from the oppressive rule of an old country, as did the Pilgrim Fathers who were landed from the 'Mayflower' on the shores of Massachusetts; – nor that they were gallant, daring spirits, going forth with their lives in their hands, in search either of exceptional wealth or exceptional honour, as has so often been done by the Columbuses and Raleighs of the world. They certainly were not deposited on the shore because they were criminals. They seem to have been a homely crew, who found life at home rather too hard, and who allowed themselves to be persuaded that they could better their condition by a voyage across the world. What was their position, or what might have been their fate had they remained at home, no one now can tell. They certainly did not have light work or an easy time in founding the colony of Western Australia.

Ships continued to come. In 1830 there came thirty-nine ships, with 1,125 passengers, and stores valued at £144,177. I think it right to state that I take my details as to these matters from the early numbers of the 'Western Australian Almanac', which surely among almanacs deserves to be placed in the very highest rank. I may say of all Australian almanacs that they are much better than anything of the kind in England, telling one what one does want to know, and omitting matter which no one would read. Among them all, this 'Western Australian Almanac' should stand high, and will, I hope, show itself to be as charitable as it is good, by pardoning the freedom with which I purloin its information.

Troubles, heavy troubles, soon arose among the young colonists. The heaviest, probably, of these early troubles came from the not unnatural hostility of the natives. All the first years of the colony's existence were saddened by contests with the blacks – by so-called murders on the part of the black men, and so-called executions on the part of their invaders. Looking at these internecine combats from a distance, and by the light of reason, we can hardly regard as murder, – as that horrid crime which we at home call murder, – the armed attempts which these poor people made to retain their property; and though we can justify the retaliations of the white conquerors, – those deeds done in retaliation which they called executions, – we cannot bring ourselves to look upon the sentences of death which they carried out as calm administrations of the law. The poor black wretches understood no pleas that were made against them, – were not alive even to the Christian's privilege of lying in their own defence, and of pleading not guilty. They speared a soldier here and a settler there, ran away with booty, fired houses, and made ravages on women and children, doubtless feeling that they were waging a most righteous war against a most unrighteous and cruel enemy. When caught, they knew that they must suffer. In the old records of the colony, one reads of these things as though all the injuries were inflicted by the blacks and suffered by the whites. Here, at home, all of us believe that we were doing a good deed in opening up these lands to the industry and civilisation of white men. I at any rate so believe. But, if so, we can surely afford to tell the truth about the matter. These

black savages were savage warriors, and not murderers; and
we too, after a fashion, were warriors, very high-handed, and
with great odds in our favour, and not calm administrators of
impartial laws.

I do not say that the black men were ill treated. I think that
in Western Australia, as in the other colonies, great efforts
were made by the leading colonists to treat them well, and, if
possible, so to use the country for the purposes of the
new-comers as not to injure the position of the old possessors.
In this, however, the colonists failed egregiously, and could
not probably have avoided failure by any conduct compatible
with their main object. It was impossible to explain to the
natives that a benevolent race of men had come to live among
them, who were anxious to teach them all good things. Their
kangaroos and fish were driven away, their land was taken
from them, the strangers assumed to be masters, and the black
men did not see the benevolence. The new-comers were
Christians, and were ready enough to teach their religion, if
only the black men would learn it. The black men could not
understand their religion, and did not want it; and, to this day,
remain unimpressed by any of its influences. But the white
men brought rum as well as religion, and the rum was
impressive though the religion was not. It is common to
assert, when we speak of the effect which our colonists have
had on uncivilised races, that we have taught them our vices,
but have neglected to teach them our virtues. The assertion is
altogether incorrect. We have taught them those of our
customs and modes of life which they were qualified to learn.
To sing psalms, and to repeat prayers, we have been able to
teach the young among them. Of any connection between the
praises and prayers and the conduct of their lives, I have seen
no trace. Many arts they have learned from us, the breaking
and training of horses, the use of the gun, the skill and
detective zeal of policemen, – for in Western Australia and in
Queensland the aborigines are used in this capacity, – and
some adroitness in certain crafts, such as those of carpenters
and masons. But we have been altogether unable to teach
them not to be savage. They will not live in houses except by
compulsion. They will not work regularly for wages. They
are not awake to the advantages of accumulated property. In

their best form they are submissive and irresponsible as children, – in their worst form they are savage and irresponsible as beasts of prey.

Two institutions of a philanthropic nature are maintained in this colony for black men and women, or for black children, – or, as I found to be the case at the one which I visited, for half-caste children. One at New Norcia, which I did not see, is in the hands of the Roman Catholics, and was established by Bishop Salvado. There were, according to the census papers, thirty-four adults and twenty-six children at this place. They are associated with and instructed by a large number of monks, and they are made to follow the ceremonies of the Church to which they are attached, and perhaps to understand them as well as do the white proselytes. And there is a Protestant establishment for the teaching of children at Perth, which was first established at Albany, but which has been transplanted to Perth by the present bishop. Here I found twenty-two children, of whom fourteen were half-caste and eight were natives. For each of these the colony paid one shilling a day; – any further expenses incident to the establishment were defrayed by the bishop. The registrar of the colony, in speaking of this establishment in his last annual report, – that for 1870, – says that 'it has gone through a varied history of success and disappointment. Several of the young women trained there have, from their educational attainments and knowledge of music, been sent for, and have gone as teachers at missionary stations in the neighbouring colonies, but it is to be regretted that the numbers now under charge do not exceed fourteen'. He goes on to say that 'the acquirement of a home and property is unknown to the natives of the bush, and it seems essential for the success of any attempt to ameliorate their condition, that this principle should be chiefly promoted and encouraged'. I quite agree with this gentleman as to that which would be chiefly essential; but I must say, at the same time, that I never found an aboriginal Australian in possession of a house of which he was himself the owner or tenant. For the establishment at New Norcia, the colonial government allows £100 a year. I was also informed that £50 per annum was allowed for a school maintained for native children by sisters of mercy. Of this latter school I could find no trace.

It is calculated that in the settled disticts of the colony, there are at present about three thousand aboriginals, including men, women, and children. That the number is decreasing very quickly there is no doubt. Of these three thousand, nearly seven hundred are supposed to be in the service of the settlers of the colony during some portions of the year, – some for a few days at a time, or for a few weeks, – some perhaps for a few months. They cannot be depended upon for continual service. Their doom is to be exterminated; and the sooner that their doom be accomplished, – so that there be no cruelty, – the better will it be for civilisation.

The black men in Western Australia were certainly not treated with exceptional harshness, – were perhaps treated with exceptional kindness, – but they were very troublesome to the new-comers. There was much of spearing on the one side, and much of shooting and hanging on the other. There seem to have been two pertinacious chiefs, or resolute leading natives, named Yagar and Midgegoroo, who gave a great amount of trouble. They carried on the war for four or five years, by no means without success. The records speak of them as horrible savages. They were probably brave patriots, defending their country and their rights. Midgegoroo was at last taken and shot. What was the end of Yagar, or whether he came to an end, no one seems to know.

And there were many other troubles in the young settlement which, as we read the record, make us feel that it was no easy thing to be an early colonist. Food for the new-comers was often wanted. The young crops of wheat, on which so much depended, were destroyed by moths and red rust. There was great lack of any circulating medium. The soil, though good in many places, was good only in patches very distant from each other; and there were no roads, – so that the settler who produced meat in one place could not exchange it for the corn and wheat produced elsewhere. And there was no labour. That of all evils was perhaps the one most difficult to be encountered and overcome. The black man would not work; and the white man who had his block of ground thickly covered with gumtrees and blackboys, – a large resinous shrub common in the country is called by the latter name, – could not clear it and till it and sow it with sufficient rapidity to procure sustenance for himself and family.

It must be remembered in regard to all the Australian colonies that the country, which has proved itself to be exceptionally rich in repaying industrial enterprise, produced almost nothing ready to the hands of the first comers. There were no animals giving meat, no trees giving fruit, no yams, no bread-trees,no cocoa-nuts, no bananas. It was necessary that all should be imported and acclimatized. The quickness with which the country has received the life and products of other countries is marvellous. In some districts of certain Australian colonies, – especially of Victoria and Tasmania, – the English rabbit is already an almost ineradicable pest; in others is the sparrow. The forests are becoming full of the European bee. Wild horses roam in mobs of thousands over the distant sheep and cattle stations. In Western Australia grapes of an enormous size are sold retail at a penny a pound. Mutton through the colonies averaged twopence a pound in 1871. But everything was at first brought from Europe, and at first the struggle for existence was very hard.

This struggle was very hard in the first infant days of Western Australia; and there seems often to have arisen the question whether upon the whole it would not be well that the settlement should be abandoned. In 1832 the troubles were so grievous that the governor, Captain Stirling, went home to represent matters. Could not something be done for the poor strugglers? At the end of this year there were only six hundred acres of land under grain, and the reason given for so slight an advance was the difficulty, or almost impossibility, of procuring seed. In 1834 the governor returned as Sir James Stirling, and the struggle went on. In the same year was taken the first step towards that resolution which has since given the colony its present position and reputation, either for good or for bad as it may be. A petition for convicts from home was got up at King George's Sound, where, as has been before stated, a small convict establishment had been settled in early days by the then governor of New South Wales. In Albany, at King George's Sound, the comforts of convict labour seem already to have been appreciated and regretted. This petition, however, was repudiated by the colony at large. The colonists were in a bad way, – but not yet so bad as that. At this time the system of transportation had already become odious to the

other colonies, – especially to New South Wales. The stain of
the convict element had been felt to be disgraceful, and the
very name was repulsive and injurious. But convicts could be
made to labour, to open out roads and clear timber and build
bridges, and do works without which it is impossible that a
young colony should thrive. And the expense of convicts
would be borne by the imperial revenue. Convict labour, bad
as it might be, meant labour for nothing. The mother country,
which would give but little else, in her desire to rid herself of
her own ruffians, would no doubt give that. It was known
that the mother country was hard pressed in that matter, not
knowing what to do with her convicted ruffianism, and that
she would be only too happy to send a few thousands to the
Swan River. But the colony rejected the petition which was
originated at King George's Sound, and would not as yet
condescend so far.

But things went from bad to worse. In 1838 there was a sad
wail. Ten thousand barrels of oil were taken off the coast, but
not a barrel was taken by an English or colonial vessel. All this
wealth had fallen into the hands of French or American
whalers. And the murders went on, and the hangings. And in
1840 all the wheat was destroyed by a moth. There had indeed
been glimpses of success. In 1832 a Legislative Council first
sat, – nominated of course by the governor; and in the same
year a newspaper was published, – in manuscript. Soon
afterwards a theatrical entertainment was given, and a
printing-press was brought out, and a public clock was set up,
and churches were opened. Struggles were made gallantly.
Mr. Eyre, who was not so successful afterwards when he went
as governor to Jamaica, made his way across the country from
South Australia to King George's Sound, through the most
sterile region of the continent, performing one of those
wonderfully gallant acts by which Australian explorers have
made themselves famous. Fresh acres were brought under
cultivation. In 1843 the white population had risen to nearly
four thousand. But still things were very bad. We are told that
in 1844, from scarcity of money and other causes, the colony
was in a most depressed condition. In 1845 a second petition
for convicts was circulated, – not only at King George's
Sound, but throughout the colony. It did not, however, find

much favour, and was signed by no more than one hundred and four settlers. The struggle still went on, and on the whole very bravely. A literary institute was proposed, if not opened. There was an exhibition of European fruits grown in the colony. There was some success in whaling, instigated no doubt by a feeling of British hatred against those French and Americans who had come with their ships in the early days, and carried off the oil from under the very noses of the colonists. New patches of good land were discovered, – notably in the Toodjay district, about sixty miles from Perth. A subscription of £30 was collected for the poor Irish who were dying at home in want of potatoes. The public revenue in 1849 was £16,000, and the expenditure only £15,800. With £200 in the public chest and no debt, there was clearly a state of public solvency. But still the complaints of the want of labour were very sore, and it is recorded that in 1848 a great number of mechanics and labourers left the colony for South Australia. This was the saddest thing of all, for South Australia was only founded in 1836, whereas Western Australia was seven years her senior.

In 1849 the colony yielded to its fate, and at a public meeting in the capital, with the sheriff in the chair, a deputation was appointed to ask the governor to take steps to make Western Australia a penal settlement. And so the deed was done. Steps were taken which were very quickly successful, and from that time, – or rather from 1st June, 1850, when the first convict arrived, down to 9th January, 1860, when the last convict was put on shore at Freemantle, over 10,000 of these exiles have been sent to a colony which still possesses a population of only 25,000 white persons.

Of this same year, 1849, two other memorable statements are made. It is said that coal was discovered in Western Australia, and that gas admirably fitted for domestic purposes had been extracted from the shrub called the 'blackboy.' I regret to state that neither the gas nor the coal are at present known in the colony. Whether there be coal or not in this part of Australia is still one of the secrets of nature. Search is being made for it now under government auspices, by the process of boring, – not I fear with much promise of success. I am told that geologists say that there is coal, but that it lies very deep in the earth.

From 1850 down to 1868, – and indeed to the present day and for many a day to come, – the history of Western Australia is and will be that of a convict colony. Whether it is well that a young and struggling settlement should be assisted after such a fashion is a question on which they who have studied the subject in regard to Australia differ very much. As regards the colony now under review, I am inclined to think that it could not have been kept alive whithout extraneous aid; and I do not know what other sufficient extraneous aid could have been given to it. It may be well to explain here that the exportation of convicts to Western Australia was discontinued, not in deference to the wishes of the colony itself, nor because the mother country was tired of sending them, – but because the other colonies complained. The convicts when released got away to South Australia and Victoria, – or, at any rate, the Victorians and South Australians so reported; and thus the stain was still continued to the young Eastern world. The other colonies remonstrated, and therefore convicts are no longer sent to the Swan River.

But there are still in Western Australia nearly 2,000 convicts. On 1st January, 1872, there were exactly 1,985, including holders of tickets of leave and of conditional pardons. In addition to these there are the remainder of the 8,000 who have worked out their sentences, – or, in the language of the colony, have become expirees, – and their families. The whole labour market of the colony, as a matter of course, savours of the convict element. No female convicts were sent out to Western Australia, and therefore an influx of women soon became above all things desirable. Women were sent out as emigrants, in respect of whom great complaint is made by the colony against the government at home. It is said that the women were Irish, and were low, and were not calculated to make good mothers for future heroic settlers. It seems to me that this complaint, like many others made in the colonies generally, has been put forward thoughtlessly, if not unjustly. The women in question were sent that they might become the wives of convicts, and could not therefore have been expediently selected from the highest order of the English aristocracy. Another complaint states that the convicts sent there were not convicts of the kind ordered and promised. There was, – so goes the allegation, – a condition made and accepted that the convicts for Western Australia should be convicts of a very peculiar kind, respectable, well-grown, moral, healthy convicts, – who had been perhaps model ploughmen at home, – and men of that class. I have always replied, when the allegation has been made to me, that I should like to see the stipulation in print, or at least in writing. I presume the convicts were sent as they came to hand, – and certainly many of them were not expressly fitted to work on farms at a distance from surveillance. The women, I do not doubt, were something like the men; – and in this way a population not very excellent in its nature was created. But the men worked for nothing.

It is certainly true that the convict element pervades the colony. If you dine out, the probability is that the man who waits upon you was a convict. The rural labourers are ticket-holders, – or expirees who were convicts. Many of the most thriving shopkeepers came out as convicts. There are convict editors of newspapers. A thorough knowledge of the social life of the colony is needed in order to distinguish the free-selecter from him who has been sent out from Great Britain to work out his period of punishment. Men who never were convicts, come under the suspicion of having been so, and men who were convicts are striving to escape from it. The effect is that the convict flavour is over everything, and no doubt many would-be immigrants are debarred from coming to Western Australia by the fear that after a year or two their position would be misconstrued. In this respect a great evil has been done.

But it may be doubted whether the colony would have lived at all without an influx of convicts. They who at last asked for them – so unwillingly, – were clearly of that opinion. There are many in the colony now who express much regret that the settlement should ever have been contaminated by a criminal class, and who profess to believe that nothing but evil has come from the measure. Such regrets are natural, but cannot be taken as indicating any true conception of the difficulties which caused the settlers to ask for convicts. Others declare, and I think with more reason, that the colony could not have lived but for the questionable boon. The parent colony, New South Wales, could not have been founded without convicts. The land was not a land of promise, overflowing with milk and honey. It was a hard land, with much barren soil, often deficient in water, with but few good gifts apparent to the eye of the first comers. The gold was lying hidden and unsuspected among the distant water-courses, and in the bosom of the mountains. The large pastures had to be reached across mountains which were long impervious to explorers. In telling the early tale of New South Wales I have endeavoured to explain how great was the struggle to maintain life on the first settlement; and the struggle was made only because it was necessary to Great Britain that she should find a distant home for her criminal exiles. The convicts were sent; and the attendants on the convicts, with convict assistance, made a new world. The same thing has been done in Western Australia, and the results will at last be the same. As soon as the exiles arrived at the Swan River imperial money fostered and comforted the struggling settlement. Not only was work done by the men who were sent, but for every man sent money was expended. There were imperial officers, comptroller-generals, commissary-generals, commandants, superintendents, surveyors, chaplains, accountants, – all paid from home. And the convicts did work, – not indeed so well or with such result as paid labourers, – but still, after the convict fashion, with considerable effect. If the men individually were bad workmen, yet their number was great. And it was work gratis, – costing the colony nothing. Such roads have been made as the other colonies, – always excepting Tasmania, – do not possess. Public buildings have been erected, and an air of prosperity has been given to the two towns, – Perth and Freemantle, the only towns in the colony, – which could hardly have come to them yet but for this aid. And imperial funds are still spent largely, – though no doubt the money flowing into Western Australia from that source will yearly become less and less. The comptroller-general has gone home, and there is doubt whether there will be another comptroller-general. The comfortable and somewhat imposing house, in which the old comptroller used to live, at Freemantle, – in dignity only second to that of the governor, – has been made a hospital. The numbers are decreasing both of officers and men. The head convict establishment is at Freemantle, and the glory of Freemantle is over. The men are no longer allowed to work on distant roads, because the gangs are expensive when kept at a distant. Everybody is talking of retrenchment. The Home Office is still called upon to pay, but can no longer get rid of a single ruffian in this direction, and of course looks closely to the expenditure. In Western Australia generally much blame is thrust upon the government at home because of its parsimony, and hard things are said of the present Chancellor of the Exchequer, because it is supposed that he has ordered the withdrawal of the gangs from the road. The present Chancellor of the Exchequer is a vigorous man, but I hardly think that his vigour has gone so far as this. The retrenchment has probably sprung from the zeal of officers here, who have felt it to be both their duty and their interest to respond to the general demand for economy expressed by their superiors at home. But still there is money coming, and still there is work done; and it may be that this will last till the colony can exist and prosper without further aid. In this respect great good has been done.

Whether more of good or more of evil has befallen Australia generally from its convicts, is a question which will not be decided to the satisfaction of the English world at large for many a year to come, – though the day for a general decision will come. But this may be said of the system with certain truth, – as it may be of all human institutions, – that now, when the sweets of it have been used and are no longer sweet, the advantages are forgotten and the evils borne in mind. The Bill Sykes physiognomy of a large proportion of the population is to be seen daily throughout Western Australia. And the roads and buildings are also to be seen. But men remember whence Bill Sykes came, and why; but they forget how they got the roads and buildings.

In 1851 the rushes for gold commenced in Victoria and in New South Wales, and before long there came upon Western Australia the conviction that gold was the one thing necessary for its salvation. If gold could only be found, Western Australia would hold up its head with the best of them. Exploring parties were made, and gullies were ransacked, – I will not say altogether in vain, for I have seen small grains of gold which were undoubtedly washed out of Western Australian earth; – but no gold was found to repay the searchers. In 1862 a reward of £5,000 was offered for the discovery of a gold-field that would pay, within a radius of fifty miles of Perth; but no lucky man has claimed the reward. In the same year an offer was made to the colony by Mr. Hargreaves, – one of those who claim to have first discovered gold in Australia, and who possessed the credit of having found it, not by accident, but by search made in consequence of geological comparison instituted by himself between California and Australia. The great Mr. Hargreaves proposed to come to Western Australia and search for a gold-field, on condition that £500 and his expenses were paid to him. The colony at once accepted the proposition. If gold could only be found, what would be £500 and Mr. Hargreave's expenses? Towards the end of the year Mr. Hargreaves came, and started to the north, for the Murchison River. If anywhere, gold might be there. Such seems to have been Mr. Hargreaves's opinion. But in the January following Mr. Hargreaves returned to Perth unsuccessful. The colony, no doubt, paid the stipulated price, – and wept again as it has wept so often. It has since sent, in the same way, for other expensive aids from beyond its own limits, for machinery and skilled science; the machinery and skilled science have come, and the poor colony has paid the bill; – but there have been no results.

From that day to this the craving for gold has continued, – and is still strong as ever. It is the opinion of many that nothing but gold can turn the scale, can bring joy out of despondency, can fill the land with towns, and crowd the streets with men. And there is much truth in the belief. It is not the gold that does it, – the absolute value of the metal which is extracted, – but the vitality to trade, the consumption of things, the life and the stir occasioned by those who, with the reckless energy of gamblers, hurry hither and thither after the very sound of gold. The men come and must live, – and must work for their livelihood, if not in getting gold, then on some other work-field. The one thing wanted is population. Gold, if really found in paying quantities, would be a panacea for all evils in the colony; but, if that be impossible, even tidings of gold, tidings loud enough to gain credit, might turn the scale.

It may easily be conceived that such hopes as these, – hopes which might be gratified any day by an accident, but which could not assure themselves of success by steady industry, – would lead to a state of feeling which I may best describe as the Micawber condition. If only gold would turn up! Gold might turn up any day! But as gold did not turn up, – then would not Providence be so good as to allow something else to turn up? This feeling, than which none can be more pernicious, is likely to befall every population which seeks after hidden and uncertain gains. The gain may come any day, – may come in any quantity, – may turn squalid poverty into wealth in an hour. The splendid transformation has been made over and over again, and may be repeated. Why should it not be repeated here, with me, on my behalf? And, if so, how vain, feeble and contemptible would be a paltry struggle after daily wages? No doubt there was much of the Micawber spirit in the colony, and many waited, thinking that gold would turn up, – or if not gold, pearls, or coal, or copper, or gas made out of blackboys. For there have been promises made by the cruel earth of all these brilliant things.

By the earth or by the water; – for perhaps the promise of pearls has been, of all these promises, the one best performed. In 1861 I find the mention of mother-of-pearl on the northern coast, at Nickol Bay, – far away beyond the limits of the colony which had been explored, but which was geographically a portion of the seacoast of Western Australia. Now there is a settlement at Nickol Bay. At present horses and sheep are reared there; but Nickol Bay is best known for its pearl fishery. This has gradually increased. In 1862 pearl-shell was exported to the value of £250. In 1863, none. In 1864, £5. In 1865, none. In 1866, £7. In 1867, £556. In 1868, £5,554. In 1869, £6,490. In 1870 I have not the amount. In 1871 it arose to £23,895. This enterprise can hardly be regarded as having been carried on by colonial industry, as strangers have come to the coast, and pearl-divers are men of migratory habits, who know little of homes, and are not subject to much patriotic enthusiasm; but they attach themselves for a time to the coast that is nearest to them, and spend upon it some portion of their gains. The fishery on the northern coast of Western Australia, not for pearls, but for pearl-shell, will probably become a properous trade.

The staple of the colony has no doubt been wool, – and it appears to have been the original idea of the wealthier settlers to carry out in Western Australia the system of squatting which had already become successful on the eastern side of the continent. The value of wool exported is more than half that of all the exports of the colony. In 1871 it amounted to £111,06l, – which was shorn from the backs of 671,000 sheep. But these figures cannot be taken as indicating any great success. I could name five stations in Queensland on which more sheep are kept than run through all the pastures of Western Australia. It is common in Western Australia to hear of squatters with 2,000, 3,000, or 4,000 sheep. In the eastern colonies I found it unusual to find less than 10,000 on a single run. I heard of one leviathan squatter in Western Australia, who owned 25,000 sheep. In Queensland, New South Wales, or Victoria, 30,000 is by no means a large number of sheep for a single run, – as the reader of the previous pages will know very well by this time, if he have read attentively. There are various reasons for this comparative smallness of things. The colony has never been popular. It began poorly, and has been since succoured by convicts. It is remote from the other pastoral districts of Australia, and divided from them by a large impassable desert. And there are large districts infested by a poisonous shrub, which is injurious to horses and deadly to cattle if eaten green, but which is absolutely fatal to sheep. The traveller comes on these districts here and there, and some one picks for him a sprig of the plant, – with a caution that, if he eats much of it, it will probably disagree with him. I withstood all temptation in that direction, and ate none. From land wanted for agricultural purposes, the poisonous shrub is easily eradicated; but the cost of doing this over the wide districts required for pastoral purposes would be too great. The baneful localities are known, and the number of sheep poisoned are few; but the fact that so much land should be unserviceable is of course adverse to squatting.

The timber trade has thriven in Western Australia, and at the present moment is so much in request that complaints are made that the available labour of the colony is all taken into the bush, to the great detriment of the farmer. Hitherto the chief export-ation has been of sandal-wood, which in 1871 amounted to £26,926. In 1869 it had risen to £32,998. This goes almost entirely to the east, – to Singapore and China, – and is, I am told, chiefly used there for incense. But the trade in jarrah-wood, which hitherto has been small, will probably soon take the lead.

Tramroads are being laid down in two places, with the view of taking it out from the forests to the seacoast. The wood is very hard, and impervious to the white ants and to water. It is a question whether any wood has come into man's use which is at the same time so durable and so easily worked. It may be that, after all, the hopes of the West Australian Micawbers will be realised in jarrah-wood.

The first object of the first settlers was of course to grow wheat. In any country that will produce a sufficiency of wheat men may live and thrive. Western Australia will produce wheat, and contains many patches of country which, from the nature of the soil, seem to be specially fit for cereal crops. The heat on the western coast is not continuous, nor so intense as it is at the same latitudes in New South Wales and Queensland; but, nevertheless, failure in the wheat crops has been one of the chief sources of misfortune and failure in the colony. One reads constantly of rust and moth, and of the insufficiency of the grain produced, and even of the difficulty of procuring seed. The farming has been thoroughly bad, and very bad it is still.

From the commencement of the settlement up to the present day Western Australia has been a crown colony, or, in other words, has been subject to rule from home instead of ruling itself. A governor has been appointed to it, whose duty it has been to initiate such changes in the laws as have appeared necessary to him, and as have met with the approval of the Secretary of State for the Colonies. He has had a Legislative Council, which was nominated by himself, and therefore subject to him; and, of course, an Executive Council, consisting of paid offices who have done the departmental work for him. Under this scheme of government the colonists themselves had nothing to do with the manner in which they were ruled. The governor was irresponsible to them, but responsible to the government at home. It may be that such a form of rule may be good for an infant community. For an adult colony it cannot be good. How far it has already been altered under the sanction of the present governor, Mr. Weld, I will endeavour to explain in another chapter, and will also speak of the further changes which are in prospect. The absolute power attaching to the governor of a crown colony is already, happily, a thing of the past in Western Australia.

I will also postpone to another chapter such account as I may be able to give of alienation from the Crown of lands of the colony. The manner in which this should be done, and the manner in which it has been and shall be done, have been of all questions the most important to the Australian colonies generally. As a new law on this subject was proclaimed in March, 1872, when I was in the colony, and as the changes made are of vital importance, I will endeavour to explain the present condition of the matter when speaking of the colony as it now is.

And thus Western Australia has struggled on since 1829, having undergone many difficulties; not much heard of in the world; never doomed like Sierra Leone or Guiana; never absolutely ruined as have been some of the West Indian Islands; – but never cropping up in the world, an offspring to be proud of, as are Victoria and Canada.

CHAPTER II

ROTTNEST AND FREEMANTLE

Rottnest is an island some twelve miles distant from Freemantle, and Freemantle is the seaport town nearest to Perth, –
very deficient in its qualification in that respect, as I shall
explain hereafter. The two places are now spoken of together
as containing two convict establishments, – that at Rottnest
for black men or aboriginals, and that at Freemantle for
European and colonial white prisoners. I will speak of
Rottnest first, because it was established for its present
purposes before convicts were sent out from England to
Western Australia.

The island is about four miles long and two miles broad,
and was originally almost covered with brush. The soil is sand
throughout. Here and there through one end of the island
there are five or six small salt lakes. Here black convicts were
confined and made to work very soon after the colony was
first established. In the course of a few years they were taken
to the mainland, in order that they might be employed on the
roads. But they ran away and could not by any amount of
chaining and repression which was compatible with work be
kept from escaping. Then the establishment at Rottnest was
reopened, and has since been maintained as a penal settlement
for black convicts, who have been regularly tried and
condemned in accordance with British law. When I visited
Rottnest there were sixty-five of these aboriginals in the
island, – not a large number, perhaps hardly sufficient to
justify any special mention; but the special mention is made
because it seemed to me that the black men whom I saw in the
prison were very much nearer to a state of civilization and
were upon the whole in a better condition, and indeed
happier, than any whom I encountered in other conditions. Of
course they desired their liberty, though by no means with

that pining desire which creates brooding melancholy; but they were clothed and fed and housed, and constrained to work, – though by no means to work heavily, – and had assumed the look and bearing of human beings. They were not subject, either by night or day, to solitary confinement, – except in cases of outrage and insubordination, and such cases did not often occur. They had a regular dietary, – twelve ounces of meat a day properly cooked, with rice and bread and tea. By their labour wheat was produced from the sand, and barley, and hay. The wheat was thrashed and ground, and of course baked on the island. The only white labour employed was that of six European convicts borrowed from the opposite establishment at Freemantle, to do portions of the work for which black men could not be trained to sufficient skill. These prisoners also made salt from the salt lakes, which is sold on the mainland, and which may be made in such quantity as to pay the expense of the whole establishment. For superintending the salt-works a white man is employed at a salary, – who was himself a convict not long since. I was informed that the produce of the island obtained by the work of the prisoners defrayed the whole expenses of the establishment, except the salaries of the officers. There is a governor, with five warders, and a doctor. There is no chaplain, nor is any attempt made to Christianize these savages. I believe that any such attempt, and that the presence of any chaplain, would be misplaced and useless. I know that for saying this I shall have against me the opinion of many goodmen, – of the very men whose good opinion I should be most proud to win, – but I do not believe in the result of the Christian teaching which these men are able to receive. Nor does it strike me with any special horror that sixty-five savages should be left without this teaching, when I know it to have been the will of God that hundreds of thousands such as they should die without it in their own countries. But here, at Rottnest, the aboriginal convicts do work, and work cheerfully. On Sundays they are allowed to roam at will through the island, and they bring home wallabys, and birds, and fishes. At night they care locked up in cells, never less than three together, and are allowed blankets for bedding. It was the nearest approach that I saw to black adult civilisation, – though made through crimes and violence.

And here I must again express an opinion, that the crime and the violence of these men have altogether a different effect on the mind of the bystander than have the same deeds when done by white men. As we condemn them for much in that they are savages, so must we acquit them of much for the same reason. Our crimes are often their virtues; but we make them subject to our laws, – of which they know little or nothing, – and hang them or lock them up for deeds for which they are not criminal in their own consciences, and for the non-performance of which they would be condemned by their own laws. I was astonished to find how large a proportion of these black prisoners had been convicted of murder; – and that the two who were awaiting their trial were both accused of that crime. But these murders were chiefly tribal retributions. A man in some tribe is murdered, or perhaps simply dies. It is then considered necessary that the next tribe should lose a man, – so that things might be made equal; and some strong young fellow is told off to execute the decision of the elders. Should he refuse to do so, he is knocked about and wounded and ill treated among his own people. But if he perform the deed entrusted to him, he is tracked down by a black policeman, is tried for murder, and has a life-sentence passed against him. When examined as to these occurrences they almost invariably tell the truth; – never endeavouring to screen themselves by any denial of the murder done, or by the absence of sufficient evidence; but appealing to the necessity that was laid upon them. Such an account one of those in prison, who was to be tried, gave to me in the governor's presence, – which was much as follows, though at the time demanding interpretation, which I hope the reader will not need: – 'Him come,' – him being some old chief in the tribe; – 'him say, "Go kill Cracko;"! – Cracko being the destined victim; – 'me nolike; him say, "must;" me no like very much; him hab spear;' – then there was a sign made of the cruel chief wounding his disobedient subject; – 'then me go kill Cracko.' – 'With a tomahawk?' suggests the governor. The prisoner nods assent, and evidently thinks that the whole thing has been made clear and satisfactory. In very many cases the murderer is acquitted, as the judge very properly refuses to take the prisoner's story as a plea of guilty, and demands that the crime shall be proved by evidence. If the evidence be forthcoming the young murderer is sent to Rottnest with a life-sentence, and, – as I think, – enters on a much more blessed phase of existence than he has ever known before.

In the evening it was suggested that the prisoners should 'have a corroboree' for the amusement of the guests, and orders were given accordingly. At that time I had never seen a corroboree, – and was much interested, because it was said that a special tribe from which sixteen or eighteen of these men came were very great in corroborees. A corroboree is a tribal dance in which the men congregate out in the bush, in the front of a fire, and go through various antics with smeared faces and bodies, with spears and sticks, howling, and moving their bodies about in time; – while the gins, and children, and the old people sit round in a circle. I am told that some corroborees are véry interesting. I probably never saw a good one, – as I did not find them to be amusing. This corroboree in the Rottnest prison was the best I saw, – but even in that there was not much to delight. When the order was given, I could not but think of other captives who were desired to sing and make merry in their captivity. Here, however, there was no unwillingness, – and when I proposed that five shillings' worth of tobacco should be divided among the performers, I was assured that the evening would be remembered as a very great occasion in the prison.

I did not find the establishment for white convicts at Freemantle at all as interesting as that at Port Arthur in Tasmania. Port Arthur is in itself very picturesque and beautiful. Freemantle has certainly no natural beauties to recommend it. It is a hot, white, ugly town, with a very large prison, a lunatic asylum, and a hospital for ancient worn-out convicts. No doubt the excitement which one expects to feel in such a place is supposed to be aroused rather by the nature of its inmates and by their treatment, than by any outside accessories; – but the outside accessories of Port Arthur no doubt had a strong effect. And at Port Arthur I met with men who interested me, and with whom I have endeavoured to interest others. At Freemantle there was hardly a man whom it can be worth the reader's while to have introduced to him. Perhaps that stipulation of which I have spoken, that none but respectable convicts should be sent to Western Australia, may have produced the undesirable effect of which I speak. I can call to mind no special individual except a gentleman, whom I remembered to have been tried in England for having got the mate of one of his ships to scuttle the ship out at sea. I saw him walking about with a very placid demeanour, and perhaps his friends may be glad to hear that he was conducting himself in a most exemplary manner. I do not doubt but that he will be editor of a newspaper before long. It was interesting, too, to see tobacco served out to all the European convicts who had not been re-convicted since their arrival. Such men are called probationers, and seem to have considerable privileges, – as though there were much virtue in coming out to the colony and working there gratis, with all expenses paid by the government at home. The poor black fellows only get tobacco on such a very rare holiday occasion as that I have described; but the white men from England, who had scuttled ships and the like, get their weekly supply regularly, – as gentlemen should. I own that I grudged it them.

At Port Arthur I saw men in solitary cells, who had been there long, who would be there long, – who had spent almost their lives either in solitude or under the lash. At Freemantle there were only two or three in the cells, and they only for a day or two each. I rather complained of this to the officer who was showing me the place, giving him to understand that I had expected something more exciting. He had, he said, one locked up for making himself generally objectionable, whom I could see if I liked. But he warned me, that if I did see him, I might find it very difficult to check his eloquence. The cell was opened, and the man came out and made his speech; – or so much of it as we would consent to hear. At last the warder explained to him that his indulgence could not be prolonged, and he was gently put back, and locked up again. I was assured that he would have gone on for hours; – but there was nothing interesting in his speech, whereas the eloquent prison lawyer at Port Arthur delighted me by the malignity and audacity of the charges which he brought against everybody.

The large prison at Freemantle is fitted to hold 850 prisoners. I do not know that so many have ever been confined there. The men, as they have arrived, seem to have been told off into gangs, and the majority of them have been employed at distances from the head-quarters, – chiefly on the construction of roads. When I was in the colony there were still such gangs, some on one road, and some on another; but the system of so employing the men was being brought to a close, because their cost was greater when thus spread about the country than when maintained at one centre establishment. This was declared to be the case, and the allegation was made that the reduction was forced upon the colony by home parisomony. The allegation was made, but did not reach me from official lips, – and I do not believe that they who have the management of the convicts, the governor and comptroller, have ever received orders to put the men to comparatively useless works, in order that the money spent upon them from Great Britain might be lessened. I do not doubt but that general, and perhaps stringent, instructions have been given as to ecconomy. In what branch of the public service have not such instructions been given during the last four or five years? But the zeal which has complied with these instructions by withdrawing the men from the distant and more useful works has probably been colonial, and is, I think, to be lamented. As the colony has had the convicts, it should at any rate get from them all that it can get; – and even though the small extra expense of keeping the men in distant gangs should be borne by the colony itself, the money would be well expended. The matter will probably seem to be insignificant. It is perhaps necessary that a man should visit such a colony as Western Australia before he can realise the need of roads. The distance from Albany to Perth is 258 miles. Perth is the capital of the colony, and Albany is the port from and to which is made the only communication by steamboat with the outside world which the colony possesses. About a third of this road has been properly made. The remaining two-thirds consist of a cleared track through the bushes, with bridges here and there, and occasional attempts at road making. It would be much better that the road should be finished. In the colony there are many excellent roads running out of Perth, without which the colony would be altogether uninhabitable; – and they were all made by convict labour. I mention the two facts in order that I may be excused for dilating upon the subject.

The prison, which, as I have said, can hold 850 inmates, now contains 359 men. Of these 240 are imperial convicts, – convicts who have been sent out from England, and who are now serving under British sentences, or sentences inflicted in the colony within twelve months of the date of their freedom. For all these the expense is paid from home. And there are 119 colonial convicts, – convicts with whom the colony is charged, as being representatives of colonial crime. But even of these about four-fifths came to Western Australia originally as convicts from home. I cannot tell the extent of the charge upon the imperial revenue, – as I did in regard to the establishment in Tasmania, – because at Freemantle the affair is managed on a different basis. At Port Arthur the colony supplies everything, and receives so much a head for the men. At Freemantle the home government does the work for itself in detail, sending out stores from England, and making purchases for itself.

I suggested to the superintendent of the prison that the enormous building through which we were walking would soon become useless. He scouted the idea, and declared, apparently with pride, that the colony would always supply a sufficiency of convicts to keep it going. I suggested that 850 men under sentence would be a great many, – that even half that number would be a very great number, – in a population of 25,000 souls; and the more so, as the enormous distances in the colony made it necessary that other prisons and penitentiaries should be maintained. But he was still hopeful. The population would increase, and with the population crime. It was not likely that a people whose connection with prisons had been so long and so thorough should fail Freemantle at a pinch. I could not agree with him. I do believe that the prison at Freemantle will become all but useless, – as will also that at Port Arthur.

As to the treatment of the men at this establishment, there can be no doubt that it should be held to be free from any charge of harshness. The question is, whether the men be not too well treated. The food is sufficient, and very good. The work is always lighter than that done by free labourers. The utensils and bedding are good. Everything is clean. The punishments are light and infrequent. Flogging still does take place, but very rarely. The men, if they behave well, are allowed more hours of amusement than fall to the lot of freemen; – and have as many means of amusement as most free labourers. It was only half-past five in the evening when I saw the men marshalled at the end of their day's work to receive their tobacco. Why a man who had come from England with a life-sentence against him should receive tobacco, whereas a colonial prisoner sent in for six months should have none, I could not understand.

In the old days, when Norfolk Island was the doubly penal establishment attached to our first penal settlement at Port Jackson, when the managers of these prisons had not yet learned the way to extract work from unwilling convicts without flogging them, penal servitude was no doubt a horrid punishment. Chains and the scourge, darkness and bread and water, were then common. That wretch whom I saw at Tasmania, – who told me that for forty years he had never known a day's freedom, – had been made what he was by the old system. I do not remember that he had ever been a thief, but he had always been a rebel. The manner of the thing is altogether altered now, till one find one's self driven to ask whether punishment so light can be deterrent. As regards our connection with the colonies, the question is not one of much importance, as we shall never send another convict to Australia.

I cannot finish this chapter without giving the copy of a certificate which was handed to me by a policeman at Albany, just as I was about to leave the colony:–

'I hereby certify that the bearer, A. Trollope, about to proceed to Adelaide per A. S. N. Co.'s steamer, is not and never has been a prisoner of the Crown in Western Australia.

(Signed)_____

Resident Magistrate.'

It is perhaps something of a disgrace to Western Australia that the other colonies will not receive a stranger from her shores without a certificate that the visitor has not been a 'lag.' Such a resolution on their part must remind the poor Western Australians grievously of their disgrace. So many have been convicts, that the certificate is demanded from all! But I think that they should not charge a shilling for it, and thus raise a revenue out of their own ill fame. It was not my fault that South Australia demanded the certificate. Considering all the circumstances, I think that they should give the passport, and say nothing about it.

CHAPTER III

PRESENT CONDITION

I learn from a little book, written by Mr. W. H. Knight, and published in Perth, on the history, condition, and prospects of Western Australia, that the colony, 'as defined by her Majesty's Commissioners, includes all that portion of New Holland situated to the westward of the 129th degree of longitude, and extends between the parallels of 13° 44' and 35° south, its greatest length being 1,280 miles from north to south, and its breadth from east to west about 800 miles. The area is about 1,000,000 square miles, or about eight times the size of the United Kingdom of Great Britain and Ireland.' The total population on December 13, 1871, as given in the Blue Book published in 1872, was 25,353. On the 31st March, 1870, the population, as taken by the census, had been 24,785. For a young colony that can thrive by an increasing population, the figures are not promising; and they are the less so, in that the latter number many be probably taken as exact, whereas the former, showing the increase, has been matter of calculation. In such calculations there is always a bias towards the more successful side. With an area so enormous, and a population so small, the value and distribution of the land form together the one all-absorbing question. The new-comers arrive intending to live out of the land, which at any rate is plentiful; – and as newcomers are not plentiful, it is necessary to tempt them with offers of land. In all the Australian colonies the system has been the same, although it has been carried out with various limits and various devices. In the early days of Western Australia very large grants indeed were given on compliance by different individuals with certain stipulations as to the number of emigrants imported and value of stock and goods brought into the colony. The following grants were made: –

To Mr. Thomas Peel . . . . 250,000 acres.
To Colonel Latour 103,000   "
To Sir James Stirling 100,000   "

I need hardly say that the estates thus conferred were very extensive, and such as would together constitute a county in England. The county of Berkshire contains only 481,280 acres. But it has not appeared that grants on this scale have done good to the colony, or to those whom they were made. In neither of the cases above named has any properous settlement been established on the lands granted, nor, as I believe, have the families of the recipients been enriched, or permanently settled in the country. It was soon found that land divided into smaller quantities would more probably produce the energy which was wanted, and other schemes were invented. The grants above named were made under an order issued from the Colonial Office called Circular A, which was in existence prior to the regular settlement of the colony. Circular B was issued in 1829, and entitled settlers to free grants of land at the rate of one acre for every sum of 1s. 6d. invested on the land, – the land to be made over in fee at the end of twenty-one years, if the improvements effected satisfied the government. But this was soon again changed, and Circular C granted land on and from 1st January, 1831, to all settlers, at the rate of an acre for every 3s. invested, and 100 acres for every servant introduced into the colony, limiting the time of improvement to four years. But on the 1st March, 1831, Circular D appeared, doing away with all free grants, – excepting to officers of the army and navy retiring from their profession with the intention of becoming settlers, – and substituting for such free grants the sale of the crown lands at a minimum price of 5s. an acre. In July, 1841, the price of the crown lands was raised to 12s. an acre; and subsequently, in the same year, to 20s. an acre, – which may be called the normal Australian price, though variations have been made upon it in all the Australian colonies; – and, at this rate of 20s. an acre, it was to be sold in blocks of not less than 160 acreas each, with a right of commonage attached to each block. In 1843 another change was made, which, however, did not alter the price, but had reference to the maximum and minimum limits of land which might be purchased. In 1860 the price was again reduced to 10s., and the quantity to 40 acres. Then, in 1864, came further alteration, and other laws were enacted, which were those in operation at the time of my visiting the colony, but which were again changed while I was there. Under the regulations of 1864 lands were classified as town, suburban, country, and mineral. Town and suburban lands, the value of which was of course dependent on the prosperity of the so-called town, and on the nature of the land around it, were saleable by auction, the upset or reserve price being fixed by the governor. Mineral lands, or lands known or supposed to contain minerals, were saleable in lots not less than 80 acres each, at £3 an acre. The ordinary country lands, – land, that is, which might be selected here or there by the immigrant or other intending purchaser, – were again to be sold at 10s. an acre, and in blocks of not less than 40 acres each. It is as to land of this nature, – the ordinary land of the country left open for inspection, – that the emigrant should interest himself. The same law of 1864 also defined the term under which pastoral lands should be let by the Crown in the various districts of the colony, being in one district at the rate of 20s. per 1,000 acres, and in another 10s., – with various other stipulations. But the pastoral squatter's relations with the Crown are of much less interest to him than are those of the free-selecter or purchaser. This last law of 1864, as did all previous land laws in the colony, requires that the purchaser should pay his money down. At first indeed there were free grants under certain stipulations, then 5s. an acre was charged, than 12s., then 20s., than 10s., – but in each case the money was to be paid at once. In this way during the eleven years up to 1869 inclusive, 117,854 acres were alienated in the colony, showing an average of something over 10,000 acres a year. For this the Crown, – or we may more safely say the colony, – received £69,440 – or an average of about £6,300 per annum. The absolute price realised was about 12s. 6d. an acre; but the sale had been very slow, – the injury arising from which was to be found, not in the smallness of the money received, which was and is a question of quite second-rate importance, but in the absence of inducement to immigrants, of which it seemed to be evidence. There is the land, undoubtedly in many districts so fertile as to offer to new-comers the means of living easily upon its bounties, – producing wheat, oats, barley, grapes, potatoes, with ordinary fruits and vegetables in abundance; with a climate preferable to Englishmen to any other Australian climate except that of Tasmania; certainly with many drawbacks, the chief of which is the distance from each other of the districts which are so gifted; – but still a country with all these gifts. How shall men be induced to come to it, and partake of its good things?

I cannot say that the question is asked by the colony at large in any spirit of wide philanthropy, or that it is asked eagerly, as it is, by those in whose hands rests the government of the colony, with any special view to benefit the hungry labourers of England and Ireland. In Western Australia it is simply a question of self-preservation. I do not know that any good can be done by soft words in the matter. The colony has never prospered as yet, and is not prospering at present. I have endeavoured in a previous chapter to show, if not the reason for the fact, at any rate the fact itself. At first a scanty population spread itself over a wise district, and, having no extraneous help to foster it, was on the brink of perishing by its own natural weakness. Then it called for extraneous help, and received it in the guise of convicts. But the very aid was an injury, – which has still to be endured, and, if possible, gradually cured. Convicts do not make a colony popular with intending colonists. Gold makes a colony popular; but gold has not been found in Western Australia. Coal makes any land prosperous; but coal has not been found in Western Australia. Good harbours assist a colony, – and Western Australia has a magnificent harbour at King George's Sound; – but it is 260 miles from the capital, and is divided from the capital by an uninteresting and useless country. The so-called harbour near to the capital, that at Freemantle, is simply a road in which vessels cannot lie safely. Struggling against these evils, the colony has not hitherto prospered; – but the question still arises whether something further may not be done to induce men to settle on its shores and still its lands, and gather its grapes and figs, and make themselves fat with its fatness. There are two things which may yet be tried, say the governors and those who are interested, – which may be tried, perhaps, with some greater confidence than can be placed in the Micawber hope for gold, and coal, and pearls. Let us have representative government, and let us have another land law. The new land law has been passed and proclaimed; and the condition of the government is a state of transit being at present half Crown condition and half representative condition. These at present are the two great panaceas.

As to the land, I have no doubt that the governors are right. I use the word in the plural number, as I neither wish to give to any man the glory which should be another's, or to take from any man the glory that is his, and I am not at all aware how far this gentleman or that is responsible for the new regulations. I will postpone to the next chapter my endeavour to explain the new law, or that part of it which may be important to emigrants, as in this chapter I am desirous of confining myself to the present condition of the colony. The law, though proclaimed when I was there, had not so come into operation that any action had been taken under it. The intermediate step between Crown government and of representative government had already been taken and had produced effects. This step I believe I may safely attribute to Mr. Weld, the present governor of the colony, and my readers will understand that I should not mention his name, did I not thoroughly agree and sympathize with him in his efforts to do away with a fashion of government under which I believe that Englishmen will never prosper.

The other Australian colonies are governed by responsible ministers under irresponsible governors, each with two legislative chambers, of which the larger and more influential is elected and the other is either elected, as in Victoria, or nominated by the leading colonial minister, as in New South Wales. In these larger colonies the kings, lords, and commons to which we are accustomed at home, are repeated, though there is an overriding power in the Secretary of State at home which somewhat clips the wings of these colonial parliaments, and robs them of that omnipotence which is the great attraction of our own Houses. But Western Australia is still a Crown colony. The governor is reponsible, and his advisers, as such, are not so. Legislation takes its initiation with him. He is supposed, in truth, to govern, whereas governors in the other colonies are ornamental vice-sovereigns, whose business it is to superintend society, and to be the medium of communication between the great minister at home and the smaller ministers in the colonies. But in Western Australia at present the governor does not quite govern in the true Crown-Colony fashion. Under the auspices of the present governor, and with the consent of the Secretary of State at home, an intermediate condition of things has been reached which is intended to pave the way to responsible government. There is an executive council, of course, – as there always has been, – consisting of the governor himself and four officers, of whom the colonial secretary is supposed to be the leading spirit. These gentlemen form the governor's cabinet. But there is also a legislative council, – a parliament with one house, – of which six members are nominated by the government and twelve are elected by the different districts of the colony. Of the six nominated members, three, but not more than three, may belong to the executive council, and be paid servants of the Crown. This chamber is nominated and elected for three years. It sat for the first time in November, 1870, and was deposed after a second session early in 1872, in consequence of a change in the adjustment of the right of voting. A re-election was about to take place when I was in the colony. The last session had, I was told, been rather stormy. The next, it was thought, would be less so. As things stand at present, the governor can effect nothing without the House, nor can the House effect anything without the governor. It is not so with us or in the other colonies, – as all who understand parliamentary action are aware. The governor of Western Australia is under no obligation to accede to the wish of the people as expressed by the House; but the House has the power of voting supplies, and can, of course, cause this power to be felt.

Such a confused condition of governing and legislating, – for it is, in truth, a confused condition, – can only be justified by the inexpediency of rushing at once from the secure but repressing depotism of a Crown colony to the unpractical energies of a full-fledged, double-housed parliament, with responsible ministers, who shall go in and out in accordance with the majorities of the day. The feeling of the present governor, and of the minister at home, is, no doubt, in favour of the full-fledged representation system; but in so small a colony, – in a colony with a sparse population, scattered over an immense area, – there must necessarily be great difficulty in finding men fit to be legislators. And they who may, after a while, become fit, have as yet had but slender means of learning how legislation should be conducted. The system, as at present adopted, which will hardly bear strict investigation on its own merits, may probably be found useful in giving the necessary training to the leading men of the colony, and in bringing them by degrees into the ways of discreet legislation. I must confess that in Western Australia one hears of doings in days not far remote which lead one to think that any amount of ignorance in a legislator, that any amount of what I may, perhaps, call rowdyism in a chamber, is better than practically irresponsible power in the hands of a would-be mighty colonial officer, removed from home by half the world's circumference.

I do not wish to be understood to say that I look to responsible representative government as a panacea for all the evils with which Western Australia is afflicted, or that I think that a colony which would perish without that remedy would by that alone be saved from ruin. I have no such belief in any form of government. It is in Western Australia, as elsewhere, by the people and their energy that the people must be made to flourish. But I do think that a people who are empowered to act for themselves in politics, even though their political action should in many instances be unwise, are more likely to be stirred to energy than are a herd of men driven this way or that in matters of policy, according as some men from without may choose to drive them. I am aware that a population of 25,000 is very small to support, very small to need, all the paraphernalia of a double-housed parliament; Queensland, however, had not so many when she commenced the experiment, and with Queensland it has succeeded. I am aware that there is at present great difficulty in getting proper men for the position of legislators in Perth; – perhaps I may go further, and say that as yet these are not to be found in the colony. Men are wanted who can yearly afford to give a portion of their time in the capital for nothing, who shall have trained themselves to think, as legislators, of their country's good, and not of their own special wants, and who shall be possessed of that patient demeanour and forbearing temper such a legislative chamber demands. I doubt whether such men can as yet be found in Western Australia. I know they have not been plentiful in the other colonies. I know that in some of the legislative chambers of Australia rowdy manners are common, and class interests very much in the ascendant. I am well aware that these chambers are not what they should be, – are very short, indeed, of being model legislative chambers. But nevertheless the work is done, – if not in a perfect, still in a wholesome manner, and the colonies are upon the whole raised to energy, vitality, and dignity by the unseen operations of representative government. I believe that the same result would follow in Western Australia, and that the colonists would gradually thrown off that Micawber tone of hoping to which I have alluded, if the duty were imposed upon them of managing for themselves.

I reached the colony from Melbourne at Albany, and I left the colony starting from the same town for Adelaide in South Australia. Albany is a very pretty little town on King George's Sound, – which is, I believe, by far the best harbour on the southern coast of the continent. It is moreover, very picturesque, though not equally so with Port Jackson and the coves round Sydney. In Albany there are a few stores, as shops are always called, a brewery, a depot for coals belonging to the Peninsular and Oriental Company, a church, a clergyman, two or three inns, and two or three government offices. Among the latter I found an old school-fellow of my own, who filled the office of resident magistrate, and in that capacity acted as judge in all matters not affecting life for a district about as big as Great Birtain. His training for these legal duties he had gained by many years' service in the Prussian army, and, I was told, did his work uncommonly well. Albany itself was very pretty, with a free outlook on to a fine harbour, with bluff headlands and picturesque islands. The climate is delightful. The place is healthy. I was assured that the beer brewed there was good. The grapes were certainly good. For a few moments I thought that I also would like to be a president judge at Albany, with unlimited magisterial power over perhaps a thousand people. It is pleasant, wherever one's lot is cast, to be, if not the biggest, at least among the biggest. But I was told that even at Albany there were squabbles and factions, and that the rose-colour of the place did not prevail always. And then, though grapes grew there, and other fruits, and some flowers, I could not find anything else growing. The useless scrub covered the stony hill-tops and close up to the town. The capital was distant 260 miles, and between it and the capital there was nothing. The mails came and went once a month. At each of my visits to Albany the mail excitement was existing. The Tichbourne case was at its highest, and people had much to say. When I was departing, there were two bishops there. I fancy that I saw the best of Albany, and that it would be rather dull between the mails.

I travelled to Perth with a friend, having made a bargain with the mail contractor to take us, – not with the mail, which goes through without stopping in seventy hours, – but by a separate conveyance in four days, so that we might sleep during the nights. This we did, taking our own provisions with us, and campaigning out in the bush under blankets. The camping out was, I think, rather pride on our part, to show the Australians that we Englishmen, – my friend, indeed, was a Scotchman, – could sleep on the ground, sub dio, and do without washing, and eat nastiness out of a box as well as they could. There were police barracks in which we might have got accommodation. At any rate, going and coming we had our way. We lit fires for ourselves, and boiled our tea in billies; and then regaled ourselves with bad brandy and water out of pannikins, cooked bacon and potatoes in a frying-pan, and pretended to think that it was very jolly. My Scotch friend was a young man, and was, perhaps, in earnest. For myself, I must acknowledge that when I got up about five o'clock on a dark wet morning, very damp, with the clothes and boots on which I was destined to wear for the day, with the necessity before me of packing up my wet blankets, and endeavoured, for some minutes in vain, to wake the snoring driver, who had been couched but a few feet from me, I did not feel any ardent desire to throw off for ever the soft luxuries of an effeminate civilisation, in order that I might permanently enjoy the freedom of the bush. But I did it, and it is well to be able to do it.

No man perhaps ever travelled two hundred and sixty miles with less to see. The road goes eternally through wood, – which in Australia is always called bush; and, possibly, sandy desert might be more tedious. But the bush in these parts never develops itself into scenery, never for a moment becomes interesting. There are no mountains, no hills that affect the eye, no vistas through the trees tempting the foot to wander. Once on the journey up, and once on the return, we saw kangaroos, but we saw no other animal; now and again a magpie was heard in the woods, but very rarely. The commonest noise is that of the bull-frog, which is very loud, and altogether unlike the sound of frogs in Europe. It is said that the Dutch under Peter Nuyt, when landing somewhere on these coasts, – were so frightened by the frogs that they ran away. I can believe it, for I have heard frogs at Albany roaring in such a fashion as to make a stranger think that the hills were infested with legions of lions, tigers, bears, and rhinoceroses, and that every lion, tiger, bear and rhinoceros in the country was just about to spring at him. I knew they were only frogs, and yet I did not like it. The bush in Australia generally is singularly destitute of life. One hears much of the snakes, because the snakes are specially deadly; but one sees them seldom, and no precaution in regard to them is taken. Of all animals, the opossum is the commonest. He may be easily taken, as his habits are known, but he never shows himself. In perfect silence the journey through the bush is made, – fifteen miles to some water-hole, where breakfast is eaten; fifteen on to another water-hole, where brandy and water is consumed; fifteen again to more water, and dinner; and then again fifteen, till the place is reached at which the night-fire is made and the blankets are stretched upon the ground. In such a journey, everything depends on one's companion, and in this I was more than ordinarily fortunate. As we were taken by the mail contractor, we had relays of horses along the road.

Perth I found to be a very pretty town, built on a lake of brackish water formed by the Swan River. It contains 6,000 inhabitants, and of course is the residence of the chief people of the colony, – as the governor is there, and the legislative chamber, and the supreme judge, and the bishop. The governor's house is handsome, as is also the town-hall. The churches, – cathedrals I should call them, – both of the Protestants and Roman Catholics, are large and convenient. On my first arrival I stayed at an inn, – which I did not indeed like very much at first; as the people seemed to be too well off to care for strangers; but which in its accommodation was better than can be found in many towns of the same size in England. I must acknowledge, however, that I was much troubled by musquitoes, and did not think the excuse a good one when I was told that a musquito curtain could not be put up because it was Sunday.

I found that crime of a heavy nature was not common in Perth or the districts round it, though so large a portion of the population consisted of men who were or had been convicts. Men were daily committed for bad language, drunkenness, absconding, late hours, and offences of like nature.For men holding tickets-of-leave are subjected to laws, which make it criminal for a man to leave his master's employ, or to be absent from his master's house after certain hours, or to allude in an improper manner in his master's eyes. And for these offences, sentences of punishment are given which seem to be heavy, because it is difficult to bear in mind the difference between free men and prisoners who are allowed partial freedom under certain conditions.

I have heard it said, more than once or twice, in reference not specially to Perth, but to the whole colony, that the ticket-of-leave men are deterred from violence simply by fear, that they are all thieves when they dare to steal, and that the absence of crime is no proof of reformation. The physiognomy, and gait, and general idleness of the men, their habits of drinking when they can get drink, and general low tendencies, are alleged as proof of this. It cannot be supposed that convicts should come out from their prisons industrious, orderly men, fit for self-management. The restraint and discipline to which they have been subject as convicts, independently of their old habits, would prevent this. The Bill Sykes look of which I have spoken, is produced rather by the gaol than by crime. The men are not beautiful to look at. They do spend their money in drink, filling the bars of the public-houses, till the hour comes at which they must retire. But it is much in such a community that they should not return to crimes of violence.

For myself, I must say that I spent my time in Perth very pleasantly. I remember being reminded once of the injustice done to a certain poor community by a traveller who had wandered thither and had received hospital treatment, 'They cannot be so poor,' the traveller had said, 'because they gave me champagne every day.' Doing honour to the stranger, they had broached their last bottles of the generous wine, and though poor, had put their best foot foremost in exercise of genuine hospitality. I was told how cruel this was. 'We were poor,' said my informant, 'but we gave what we had freely, and were then twitted with making false complaints.' I cannot but think of this as I tell my experiences of Perth. I heard very much of the poverty of Western Australia, but I found that people there lived as they do elsewhere. There were carriages and horses, and good dinners, and, if not liveried servants, – a class which is not common in the colonies, – men waiting with white cotton gloves, who in London would be presumed to be greengrocers, but who in Perth were probably 'lags'. They seemed to hand the dishes very well.

Of the other town, Freemantle, I have already spoken. I went also sixty miles up to the west, to Toodjay and Newcastle, which, from the returns showing the acres under cultivation and the produce, I find to be one of the best agricultural districts in the colony. It is surpassed only by the Greenough district. As to the prospects and past experiences of farmers in this and other parts of the colony, I found it very difficult to get information on which I could rely. I came across men who had been farmers, whose report was anything but good, – who said that to farm in Western Australia was simply to break the heart. And I came across others, – notably two old colonists in the Toodjay and Northam districts, – who assured me that they had done very well. In each of these cases the men had had sons capable of working with their own hands and not too proud to work. Hitherto I do not think that there has been scope for farmers who employed much outside labour. The labour has been dear and bad, – and money has been hard to get. There has always been and still is a great effort to pay labourers in produce, – but this cannot be done entirely, and the farmer who hires has drained from him almost all the money that he can earn.

That the farming has been and is atrociously bad, there can be no doubt. Men continue to crop the same ground with the same crops year after year without manuring it, and when the weeds come thicker than the corn, they simply leave it. Machinery has not been introduced. Seed is wasted, and farmers thrash their corn with flails out on the roads after the old Irish fashion. I need hardly say that there is no reason why this should continue to be so. That the land would soon pay for good farming I have no doubt, even though the surplus grain were sent home to England. At present the colony, which should above all things strive to be an agricultural colony, actually imports flour and grain to the amount of about £6,000 per annum.

I have already said that wool is the staple commodity of the country. I doubt much whether it will continue to be so, as the trade of wool-growing does not seem to extend itself in any way at all commensurate with the area of land which it occupies. In 1869, there were 654,054 sheep in Western Australia, and in 1871 the number had increased only to 670,999. In the other wool-growing colonies, it is thought that no squatter can make money on a run with less than 10,000 sheet. In Western Australia, 3,000 or 4,000 are considered to be a fairly large number, and squatters frequently run flocks that do not exceeed 1,500 or 2,000 over enormous tracks of land. In New South Wales and Queensland, few squatters have less than a sheep to three acres. No rule can be laid down, as every run must be considered as a whole, and on most runs there is some land, more or less, which is not fit for use at all. But a squatter with 60,000 acres will generally have grass for 20,000 sheep. In Western Australia, one hears of a sheep to ten acres, and a sheep to twenty acres. The sheep of the Australian colonies amount together, I believe, to about forty millions. In Western Australia, which boasts of being the largest in area of them all, there is not as yet one million. In truth there is very much against the squatter. It is not only that much of the land which is called pastoral bears a poisoned shrub fatal to sheep; – but that, from this and other causes, the distances are so great that a sufficient number of sheep to make the business really remunerative can hardly be kept together.

I found rural wages lower in Western Australia than in the other colonies, – the reason for which is of course to be traced to the nature of the labour market. The squatter, or farmer, expects to get a man who is or was a convict, and the price of the work is arranged accordingly. It averages about 3s. a day without rations, or from 30s. to 40s. a month with rations. I was told that a man's rations cost 10s. a week, – which is much higher than in the other colonies. I do not doubt that the men are charged at this rate. If the man be paid full wages, so that he has to feed himself, he must in most cases get all his supplies from his employer's store, and the employer exacts a large profit. If the employer feeds the man, he calculates the rations supplied at the rate that he would sell them, and fixes his wages accordingly. Thus a man with 40s. a month, with rations, would be supposed to receive 80s. a month, although he would not cost his employer above 68s.

The wages of mechanics are about the same here as in the other colonies: masons, carpenters, and blacksmiths earning about 7s. a day throughout the colony.

There are so-called public schools throughout the colony, supported by government, and free to necessitous persons. They who can pay are made to pay, at rates ranged from 6d. to 1s. a week; but the greater part of the expense of the schools is borne by the colonial revenues. The sum so expended is between £3,000 and £4,000 a year. In 1871, there were 1,730 scholars at these schools, a number which seems to be too small for the population. I find, however, that in the year previous to that, namely, 1870, out of the whole population, there were only 3,945 above the age of five who could neither read nor write.

In Western Australia the State still takes charge of the religion of the people, and pays £3,560 per annum for its ecclesiastical establishment. Of this by far the lion's share goes to the Church of England. There are fourteen so-called chaplains stationed in different districts of the colony, and the theory I believe is, that they are appointed to look after the souls of the convicts. They do, in fact, act as parish clergymen. They receive from the government £200 per annum each, and their income is subsidized to a small degree by the public who attend their churches. Small payments are also made to the Roman Catholic and Wesleyan Churches. But all this will soon be altered. The payments from imperial funds will doubtless be discontinued as the convict establishment dies out, and all ecclesiastical payments will be brought to an end by representative government here, as has been or is being done in the other colonies. I fear that, when it is so, the difficulty of maintaining clergymen in Western Australia will be very great.

CHAPTER IV

FUTURE PROSPECTS

I fear that it will seem that in what I have said I have given a verdict against Western Australia. I have intended rather to show how great may be the difficulties attending the establishment of a young colony, which in its early years finds no special or unexpected aid from remarkable circumstances. The same struggles with equal hardship and similar doubts have no doubt been made before, and nothing has been said of them. The strugglers have lived through and fought their way to prosperity, and but little has been heard of the details of the fight. When the Puritans were landed on the shores of Massachusetts men did not rush about the world and write books. It may probably be that they too, at their first starting, had but few glimpses of the glory of the coming Yankee world. It was perhaps only by hard fighting with adverse circumstances that they could get corn, and labour, and money. But they went on, and the glories of Yankeedom are now patent to the whole earth.

It is to the gold that has been found in Eastern Australia that the eastern colonies have owed their rapid rise and great name; – and in a great measure, the want of reputation under which Western Australia labours is due to the golden achievement of her sisters. She would not have been thought to have done so badly, had not those sisters done so well. This cannot be pleaded as being entirely sufficient to account for the effect, because we know that South Australia has not done much with gold, and South Australia holds up her head. I have not yet spoken of South Australia, but, when doing so, I will endeavour to show how and why she has prospered.

And then, in another way, the gold-diggers of the eastern colonies have been detrimental not only to the reputation, but to the very existence of Western Australia. Men have constantly gone after the gold. It became almost useless to land emigrants on the western shore. Tidings came of this rush and of that rush, and the new-comers disappeared, soon turning up, as new chums again, in the golden land. I have expressed my opinion more than once that the majority of those who have rushed after gold have done themselves but little good; – but they enriched the colony to which their labour was give, and from which they drew their supplies. Gradually this evil of 'rushing' is dying out. The amount of Australian gold produced may go on increasing year by year for many years. They who profess to understand the matter think that it will do so. But the gold will come from quartz-crushing, – from that eating up and digesting of the very bowels of the mountains by heavy machinery, which I have endeavoured to describe elsewhere, – and not by the washing of alluvial soil. It is the latter pursuit which has produced the rushes, whereas the former produces steady industry with a fixed rate of wages. The shifting of labour from colony to colony will, I think, from this cause, become less common than it has been, and agricultural work will hold its own against mining work, – in Australia as in other countries. It is a mining country, and there will be many miners; – but it will not occur to every man that he should be a miner.

In speaking of the future of Western Australia I shall not receive the thanks or sympathies of many of its inhabitants, if I express an opinion that that future is to be independent of gold. The idea is deep-rooted that there should be gold and must be gold, – that Providence cannot have been so unjust as not to have put gold there. Why not in the west as well as in the east? And then the stranger is told of mica, and slate, and quartz, and boulders, – and of the very confident opinion which Mr. Hargreaves expressed. I know nothing of mica, and slate, and quartz, and boulders, – and very little of Mr. Hargreaves. But I know that no gold worthy of the name has been found yet; and that the finding of gold in infinitesimal quantities has been common in many countries. Doubtless gold may turn up in Western Australia, but I trust that the colony will be too wise to wait for it. Should it come, let the favour be accepted from the gods; – but I do not think that men should live expecting it.

In the meantime what other measures may serve to turn the tide, and produce some life and action? The land is good, and if properly tilled will produce all that is necessary for man's life. And the land that will do so, though widely scattered, is abundant. I need hardly say that at home in England there are still among us millions of half-starved people, – half-starved certainly according to the dietary of the poorest even in this poor colony, – to whom the realisation of rural life in Western Australia would seem to be an earthly paradise if it could be understood, – to whom it would be a paradise if it could be reached. I have spoken in anything but flattering terms of the colony and its labourers. I have not depicted the present normal Western Australian carter as a very picturesque fellow. But, bad as he is, he can always get enough to eat and drink, and, if he will behave himself well, can always have a comfortable home.

But they who will come now will not be unpicturesque with the lineaments of the gaol, as he has been, and the more that may come the less probability will there be of mistaken suspicions. Living is cheaper than in England, as meat is 4*d*. instead of 10*d*. a pound, and wages are higher; – for in no agricultural county in England do they rule so high thoughout the year as 18*s*. a week. In the colony 18*s*. a week are the lowest that I have known to be given without rations. And the rural labourer in Western Australia is more independent than in England. How, indeed, could he possibly be less so! He is better clothed, has a better chance of educating his children, and certainly lives a freer and more manly life.

But how shall the rural labourer out of Sussex, Suffolk, Essex, or Cambridgeshire get to Western Australia? If there were no pecuniary difficulty in the journey, – if every labourer were empowered by the Act of Parliament to go to some parish officer and demand to be sent across the ocean, – it is probably that a very large fleet of transport ships would soon be required, and that English farmers would find it difficult to get in their seed. This can never be the case, but something towards it is done. The colonies assist intending immigrants, and the mother country too assists, or, in some cases, pays the entire expense of emigrants. We sent out those ill-born and ill-bred women who were wanted as convicts' wives, – and who, when received, were found to be mere Irish. But it is ill bringing a man out who will not stay when he is brought. If

you, my philanthropical reader, send out some favoured
tenant or parishioner, your object is fairly achieved whether
the man make himself happy in Western Australia or Victoria.
But is is by no means so with the colony, when the colony
pays. When a colony has paid for three or four hundred
immigrants, and finds after a few months that they have all
disappeared, and gone to more fortunate lands, the colony not
unnaturally becomes disgusted. Then it is that the colony feels
that nothing will do but gold. And the mother country is
affected somewhat in the same way, though less bitterly. It is
said now that England hs promised a certain number of free
emigrants to Western Australia, and that she has not kept her
word. But the mother country says that, as regards Western
Australia, it is useless to send her emigrants unless she can
keep them. In speaking of the continuance of the obligation on
the part of England, Lord Granville, in July, 1869, wrote as
follows: – 'It has already been laid down as a condition of that
continuance that the immigration should be wanted, and such
as the colony can provide for; but it is clear from the census
returns that the large proportion of these persons who reach
Western Australia do not remain in it. There is therefore the
strongest prima facie evidence that the immigration is not
wanted.' The men are tempted away; and do the colony, for
whose benefit they were sent, no good by their short sojourn.
Then why send them? Renewed petitions for emigrants,
emigrants to be sent out at the expense of the government,
were made; but the Secretary of State was firm. Nominated
emigrants would remain, – emigrants nominated by friends in
the colony. So pleaded the governor, with an anxiety which
showed that at any rate his heart was in the matter. 'Her
Majesty's Government are fully aware,' he said in 1870, 'that
nominated emigrants are more likely to remain in the colony
than others; but unfortunately they have no evidence before
them that either one or the other class do in fact remain.'

How shall men and women be got who will remain; – who
will come to the place in order that they may live upon the
land, and not simply making it a stepping-stone to some rush
for gold? It can only be done by making the land attractive;
and the great attraction offered by land is ownership. Let a
man understand that he can have land of his own and live upon

it, owing rent to no one to order his coming in and his going out, with no tasks laid on his shoulders by another, that he can be altogether free from the dominion of a master, and you open up to his mental eyes a view of life that is full of attraction. This new home, that is so unlike the home that he is to leave, is indeed far across the waters, in another world, away from the comrades and circumstances of life amidst which he feels that, though wretched, he is secure. He feels that if he go he can never return; and he hears vague, unsatisfactory, even contradictory accounts of the new land. He knows that he is groping his way, and that, should he go, he will at last take a leap in the dark. Even with those among us who have many friends, the nature of whose life has taught us where to look for information, who can not only write but express in writing what we mean, who can not only read but know where to find the books that will teach us that we want to learn, there is felt to be much difficulty when the question arises whether we shall remove ourselves and our household gods to the new home that we call a colony, or whether we shall send a son to push his fortunes in the new country. To digest what we have learned and bring it all together so that we may act upon it safely is no easy task. What must it be to the working man whom some newspaper has reached, or some advertisement to emigrants; and who, in addition to this, has heard the vague surmises of his neighbour? He goes to the parson, or to the squire, or perhaps to his employer, – and is recommended to remain. The adviser hardly dares to say otherwise, and is probably himself impregnated with the patriotic idea that there is no place for an Englishman like England. For members of parliament, and men with £5,000 a year, or with prosperous shops in Cheapside, – for some even whose fortune is less brilliant than that, – England is a very comfortable home. No land can beat it. But for Englishmen in general, that is, for the bulk of the working population of the country, it is I think by no means the best place. A large proportions of our labouring classes cannot even get enough to eat. A still larger proportion are doomed so to work that they can think of nothing but a sufficiency of food. In all the Australian colonies, if a man will work the food comes easily, and he can turn his mind elsewhere. I do not assert that there is no poverty, – no distress. Even in Western Australia the government is obliged to maintain an establishment for paupers. But poverty is not a rule, and a man who will work and can work may be independent.

Success in emigration depends much on the fashion of the thing, and this peculiar exodus, – to Western Australia namely, – is not at present fashionable. If in the course of the next two or three years two or three thousand new-comers were to land upon its shores and stay there, the thing would be done. And the two or three thousand would find plenty and happy homes. But solitary immigrants to the colony feel that they become mixed with the convict population. At the present moment great encouragement has been offered to new-comers, – to men who on arriving with a few pounds in their pockets will be willing to work with their own hands, but who will so work on their own lands.

I do not know how far, in what I have written of the other colonies, I may have been able to make my English reader understand the nature and position of a 'free-selecter'. I found it very difficult to understand myself, or to come to a conclusion whether he should be regarded as the normal British emigrant, – manly, industrious, independent, and courageous, – or a mere sheep-stealer. There was one other alternative, hardly more attractive than the last. He need not be a mere sheep-stealer, though probably he would do a little in that line; but might have free-selected with the first great object of making his presence so unbearable to the squatter on whose run he had perched himself, that the squatter would be obliged to buy him out. I certainly found that the manly, independent, and the couragous free-selecter was not the free-selecter of whom the squatters talked to me in Queensland, New South Wales, and Victoria. The squatters did not carry me with them altogether; but it certainly is the case that free-selectors in these colonies often do steal sheep, and often do make themselves disagreeable. A man desirous of free-selecting, – say in Queensland and New South Wales, for the game has nearly been played out within the smaller and more valuable confines of Victoria, – has the whole world of the colony open to him, and very little to divert his course. He searches and inquires, and, actuated by good or bad motives, settles down on some bit of land which he thinks will grow corn, and where his is sure to be hated by the squatter whom he is invading. The colonial governments offer him every possible encouragement as to money, – land at 15s. an acre, land at 10s. an acre, and especially land with deferred payments, – with payments taking the shape of rent, perhaps 1s. an acre per annum, – the land becoming his own at the end of the term of years, the yearly deferred payments having been taken as the price of it. But the governments have done little or nothing to assist the free-selecter in placing himself. A part of the charm of the thing in the eyes of the free-selecter has been the power of choosing his land. We can understand that there is a pleasure in going well on to the run of some great squatter, pegging out some 40, 80, or 160 acres, and saying, 'By your leave, sir, I mean to have this.' We can understand that there is pleasure in doing it, and great pain in enduring it. My sympathies have been chiefly with the free-selecter, not believing that he is always a sheep-stealer, and feeling that the land should be open to him. Pastoral autocrats with acres by the hundreds of thousands, – acres which are their own, – cannot fill up a country. They are the precursors of population, and, as the population comes, should make way for it. But might it not be arranged that the free-selecters should be invited to come and take up their lands in some manner less objectionable than that which has hitherto prevailed?

When I was in Western Australia new land regulations were issued and proclaimed, having just received the sanction of the Colonial Office at home; and these regulations go a long way towards effecting a remedy for those evils attaching to free-selection which I have attempted to describe, – and they will remedy another evil which, in Western Australia especially, is very detrimental to the selecting farmer. They will bring the agricultural occupiers of the land together. Men are invited to occupy lands chosen for 'special occupation'. By this arrangement the skill and experience of the land officers of the colony will be used on behalf of the selecter, who will not only be enabled to place himself on soil capable of bearing corn, but will find himself surrounded by others, occupied as he is in producing corn. In this way rural communities may be formed which shall not be sheep-stealing communities. The locality having been chosen in the first place, not by the new-comer, but by the government, sheep-stealing will not at any rate have been the object when the choice was made, – nor the idea that a squatter if harassed sufficiently may at last be induced to buy his neighbour out. Communities will be formed, and communities will make markets. I have sometimes thought that free-selecters like to take their land up far away in the bush, at long distances each from another. There is a wild independence in the doing so which charms. But no decision can be more detrimental to the man's material interest. When so located he is driven to consume all that he grows, and then, – unless he steal sheep, – he can consume nothing else. That which is most to be desired by him is that gradually a township should be formed round his homestead.

Immigrants and others are invited by these new regulations to take up land selected for special occupation, and great boons are offered to those who will do so. In the first place the payment of the price of the land is deferred. Hitherto in this colony it has always been necessary that the price of the land should be paid down. The land, as has been explained elsewhere, has been purchased at various prices, ranging from 5s. to 20s. an acre, – but there has been no deferred payment. At last 10s. an acre was the settled price, – and so it remains. The ordinary free-selecter may go where he will beyond the limits of town, suburban, or mineral lands, and, if no purchaser have been before him, may purchase any amount of land in blocks of not less than 40 acres, at 10s. an acre. But when purchasing after this fashion he must pay his money down. If he will take up land selected for special occupation, he need not pay his money down. He need only pay 1s. an acre per annum, such payment being required in advance. He must then fence the whole of his land and till a quarter of it during the ten years over which the payment is deferred, – and if he do thus the land becomes his own.

There are other stipulations which the intending emigrant should understand. The purchaser cannot purchase in this manner less than 100 acres. It is considered that he cannot crop all the land yearly, and that less than 100 acres will not afford a man subsistence. Nor can he take up more than 500 acres. In addition to the use of the land which will be his own at the end of the ten years, and will be in his own hands during the previous occupancy, the selecter will be entitled to run cattle and sheep upon commonages, or neighbouring lands not fitted for agricultural purposes. It is stipulated that the common land shall in no case exceed 200 per cent. of the land fitted for agricultural purposes, – so that the commonage for 2,000 agricultural acres, or acres fit for agriculture, shall not exceed 4,000 acres. It is not stipulated that the commonage shall amount to any fixed number of acres. It is understood, however, that it will suffice, – not of course for the produce of wool, – but for meat and milk.

In writing for the information of future emigrants, it is very difficult to make the exact truth clearly intelligible. The new regulations speak of land fitted for agricultural purposes, and in what I have written above I have spoken of 'agricultural' land. The emigrant who comes out to take up lands selected for special occupation in Western Australia, must not expect that he will find ploughed fields. He will find forest lands, covered more or less thickly with timber, – what all the world in Australia knows as bush, – and it will be his first work to clear that portion of his holding from which he intends to get his first crop. But the land will have been chosen as being fitted, when cleared, for agricultural purposes. The thickness, and what I may call obduracy, of timber is very various. It may be presumed that the land chosen will not be heavily timbered. I was told that the average price of clearing bush in Western Australia was about £4 an acre. A man contracting to do such work would expect to make 25s. a week. If this be so, a man knowing what he was about would clear an acre in three weeks.

But, to my thinking, the best part of the offer made still remains to be told. Any emigrant taking up land in the colony selected for special occupation within six months of his landing, – the time named should I think have been prolonged to at least twelve months, – and who can show that he has fulfilled the above conditions with regard to improvements, is entitled to the value of his passage-money out, provided that passage-money does not exceed £15; and he will have the same allowance made to him for every adult he brings with him, – the money to be credited to him in the payments made for his land. The offer in fact amounts to this, – that thirty acres will be allowed free for every adult whom the immigrant may bring with him to settle on the land, provided that the passage out has cost £15, – which is I presume the usual price of sending an adult to Western Australia. I am also assured, certainly on good authority, that half the allowance will be made for non-adults; but there no proviso in the bill itself to this effect.

The result of all this any intending emigrant can calculate for himself. A man with a wife and one adult and one non-adult child would in fact get his one hundred acres for nothing. If his family were larger, he would get more land; – but he should bear in mind that he has to fence it all and till a quarter of it within ten years, and that in this way a larger acreage may become an increased burden to him rather than an increased property.

Of course I am here addressing those who have in their own hands the means of emigrating. Not only will the £15 a head be wanting in bringing out his family, but also something on which to live when the new country is first reached. But, presuming that a working man with a working family can raise £200, – a very strong presumption I fear, – I do not know that he could do better than establish himself as a farmer in Western Australia.

I believe that Western Australia has no agent at home, as have the other colonies, a part and perhaps the chief part of those whose business it is to facilitate the emigration of those who intend settling themselves in the new colony. Why should we pay an agent to send us emigrants when no emigrants will come to us? That no doubt is the feeling of a desponding Western Australia. And yet the colony has, as I think, with much wisdom offered most alluring terms to emigrants. At present, however, I do not see how these terms are to be made known to persons at home. I say this as an apology for the insertion here of details which cannot, I fear, interest the ordinary reader.

It is admitted on all hands that Western Australia cannot be made to thrive until her population shall be increased by new-comers. Twenty-five thousand people may perhaps live together in comfort within confines which shall be sufficiently extended to afford to all a sufficiency of land, and at the same time compact enough enough to bring them together. But Western Australia is an enormous country, and its scanty population is spread about it by hundreds. The so called settler districts are twelve in number, and the average area of each is more than half as big as England. The average population of each district is only just above 2,000. Let the English reader conceive the ten northern counties of England with 2,000 inhabitants between them! And in saying this I am speaking of the settled districts, – not of the distant regions which are claimed by the colony as belonging to it, and which will remain probably for centuries, perhaps for ever, uninhabited. An influx of population is necessary to Western Australia, not only that there may be enough of men and women to form a community and administer to each other's wants, but that the very nature may be changed of those upon whose industry the colony now depends. In its deep distress it accepted convicts, and was saved, as I think, from utter collapse by doing so. But the salvation effected was not healthy in its nature. I have given the figures over and over again. To make up a population of twenty-five thousand souls, ten thousand male convicts have been sent! Life and property are fairly safe. Work is done. The place is by no means a lawless place. Those who emerge from their sentences reformed are encouraged to prosper. Those who come out unreformed are controlled and kept down. But nevertheless the convict flavour pervades the whole, – to the great detriment of that part of the working population which has always been free. This evil is of course curing itself by degrees. The colony receives no more convicts, and the very birth and growth of its young citizens will gradually obliterate the flavour. But this would be done much more quickly and much more effectually by an influx of new blood. Nothing would tend so much to the improvement of the people as any step that would enable the enfranchised convict to move about among his fellow labourers without being known as a convict. It is so in New South Wales and Tasmania. Intimate intercourse will probably reveal the secrets of a man's past life in any country; and if a man once degraded afterward rise high, his former degradation will be remembered. But in these once convict colonies time is having its effect, and men's minds are not always referring to the matter. It does not affect the rate of wages, nor the character of the work to be done. The once convict does not feel that every one regards him as a convict, and does not therefore work as convicts work. In Western Australia the man who never was a convict will fall into such habits of work, simply because they form the rule of life around him. Nothing but an increasing population will cure this quickly.

But the very fact that it is so, the very injury to which the colony has been subjected in this matter, gives in one respect the surest promise that here a new-comer may find a prosperous home. In England, as all the world knows, residences of all kinds are to be had at a much cheaper rate to the east of London than at the west. The east has all its disadvantages, – which are chiefly of a sentimental or fashionable nature. The man who can despise these may live there in a commodious house, who would be forced to put up with straitened quarters if he allowed himself to follow the fashion. Western Australia is the east side of London. The objections to it, bad as they are, concern chiefly sentiment and fashion. I do not recommend the man who is taking out £20,000 to a colony, with the idea of becoming a great man, to go there; but to him who feels that with £200 or £300 he has but little hope in England, and who would prefer independence and property of his own to the composite luxuries and miseries of a crowded country, I think that Western Australia offers perhaps as good a field for his small capital as any other colony.

I have endeavoured, as I have gone on, to indicate the natural sources of wealth to which the colony has a right to look. To those that I have already named I should add the breeding of horses, for which it seems to be specially adapted. At present the business is limited by the difficulty which the breeders have in disposing of their produce. India is their great market, – together with Batavia and Singapore. But there are no middle traders to take the young horses off the hands of the breeders, – who cannot themselves breed horses, and charter ships, and conduct the sales. This again is one of the evils to which a scanty population is ever subject.

I have no doubt that the exportation of jarrah-wood and of pearl-shell will become large and prosperous trades. The

former will probably be by far the most beneficial to the
colony, as it will be prosecuted by men in the colony, –
whereas the pearl-shell will be sought and taken away by
coasting strangers. It is hard, too, to believe that a country
should be so prolific in grapes as this is without some result. I
will not take upon myself to say that I drank West Australian
wine with delight. I took it with awe and trembling, and in
very small quantities. But we all know that the art of making
wine does not come in a day; – and even should it never be
given to the colony to have its Château This, or Château That,
its 1841, its 1857, or 1865, or the like, – still it may be able to
make raisins against the world.

   Gold of course may turn up even yet. For myself, I look to
corn and fruit, and perhaps oil, – to the natural products
springing from the earth, – as the source of the future comfort
of this enormous territory.

SOME OTHER TITLES
AVAILABLE IN POCKET CLASSICS

*(A full list can be obtained from
Alan Sutton Publishing, 30 Brunswick Road,
Gloucester, GL1 1JJ)*

The West Indies and the Spanish Main

Anthony Trollope

In 1858 Anthony Trollope was selected for the job of reorganising the decrepit postal system in the West Indies. He was in London on November 1st making his preparations and by the 17th was outward bound for the Spanish Main.

The West Indian journey lasted until the following summer and besides the islands included extensive journeys in Central America and British Guiana. He began the book of his travels aboard a trading brig between Kingston, Jamaica and Cien Fuegos on the southern coast of Cuba and from then on the reader is treated to a racily humorous account of his doings in one of the most beautiful regions on earth.

The West Indies and the Spanish Main is full of personal anecdote and all the detail and colour of which Trollope was the master. Long unobtainable, it is sure to delight his many readers.

Lady Anna

Anthony Trollope

Lovel Grange was a small house, the residence of a rich nobleman, lying among the mountains which separate Cumberland from Westmorland, about ten miles from Keswick. To it came Josephine Murray as a beautiful young bride who considered it quite the thing to be the wife of a lord.

She had not lived with the Earl six months before he told her that the marriage was no marriage – she was his mistress. Her unborn child, the Lady Anna, could make no claim to his title. Threats were issued by the Murray family, a duel was fought, but years of suffering were still to come. The stage was set for high drama.

Paris and the Parisians

Fanny Trollope

After the abortive attempt to open and run 'Trollope's Folly', her Cincinnati bazaar, Fanny Trollope returned to England to write *The Domestic Manners of the Americans* which brought overnight fame. But not consolation from her personal misfortunes – this was only achieved by travel and writing.

In 1836 appeared *Paris and the Parisians* which paralleled her earlier book in describing the domestic scene as it was in the French capital of 1835. Fanny was fifty-five with a gift for wit and satire and the ability to amuse some of her readers and infuriate others. With her pen she cut through the many layers of Parisian society to expose every facet of this glittering jewel. From her apartment in the rue de Provence she sallied forth on social and sightseeing expeditions. It was the Paris of Chateaubriand, George Sand and Franz Liszt, and Fanny Trollope brings it all to life.

AUSCHWITZ ET APRÈS I

AUCUN DE NOUS
NE REVIENDRA

OUVRAGES DE CHARLOTTE DELBO

LES BELLES LETTRES, 1961.

LE CONVOI DU 24 JANVIER, 1965.

AUSCHWITZ ET APRÈS

I. AUCUN DE NOUS NE REVIENDRA, 1970.

II. UNE CONNAISSANCE INUTILE, 1970.

III. MESURE DE NOS JOURS, 1971.

chez d'autres éditeurs

LA THÉORIE ET LA PRATIQUE, Anthropos, 1969.

LA SENTENCE, pièce en trois actes, P.-J. Oswald, 1972.

QUI RAPPORTERA CES PAROLES ? tragédie en trois actes, P.-J. Oswald, 1974 (rééd. avec UNE SCÈNE JOUÉE DANS LA MÉMOIRE, HB éditions, 2001).

MARIA LUSITANIA, pièce en trois actes, et LE COUP D'ÉTAT, pièce en cinq actes, P.-J. Oswald, 1975.

LA MÉMOIRE ET LES JOURS, Berg International, 1985.

SPECTRES, MES COMPAGNONS, Maurice Bridel, 1977 ; Berg International, 1995.

CEUX QUI AVAIENT CHOISI, pièce en deux actes, Les Provinciales, 2011.

QUI RAPPORTERA CES PAROLES ? et autres écrits inédits, Fayard, 2013.

CHARLOTTE DELBO

AUSCHWITZ ET APRÈS I

AUCUN DE NOUS
NE REVIENDRA

LES ÉDITIONS DE MINUIT

© 1970/2018 by LES ÉDITIONS DE MINUIT
www.leseditionsdeminuit.fr

ISBN : 978-2-7073-4493-9

Charlotte Delbo

Charlotte Delbo est née en 1913 à Vigneux-sur-Seine (Essonne), de parents immigrés italiens. Après avoir suivi une formation de sténodactylo, elle travaille à Paris comme secrétaire dès l'âge de dix-sept ans. Elle adhère en 1932 au mouvement des Jeunesses communistes. En 1934, elle rencontre Georges Dudach, communiste engagé, très actif au sein du Parti, avec qui elle se marie en 1936. Un an plus tard, elle devient la secrétaire de Louis Jouvet, alors directeur du théâtre de l'Athénée. Celui-ci l'avait convoquée après la lecture d'un article sur le théâtre qu'elle avait écrit pour *Les Cahiers de la Jeunesse*, dont Dudach était le rédacteur en chef.

L'été 1941, Charlotte Delbo accompagne la troupe de l'Athénée lors d'une tournée en Amérique du Sud. Georges Dudach, engagé dans la Résistance intérieure, est resté à Paris. Elle décide de le rejoindre dans la clandestinité, contre l'avis de Jouvet qui la supplie de n'en rien faire. Charlotte regagne Paris et retrouve son mari en novembre 1941. Ils vivent cachés, ne se montrent jamais ensemble. Georges sillonne Paris, rencontre ses contacts, transmet des informations pendant que Charlotte tape à la machine des tracts et des journaux clandestins. Mais la police déploie patiemment ses filets. En février 1942, de nombreux membres de leur réseau de résistants communistes sont pris en filature. Les arrestations se multiplient à la mi-février : Georges et Maï Politzer, Danielle Casanova, Lucien Dorland, Lucienne Langlois, puis André et Germaine Pican, Jacques Decour... De filature en filature, l'étau se resserre. Georges Dudach et Charlotte Delbo sont arrêtés le 2 mars 1942 par les brigades spéciales de la Police française. Delbo est emprisonnée à la Santé, où elle reverra son mari une dernière fois, le 23 mai ; Dudach est fusillé le jour même au Mont-Valérien. Transférée en août au Fort de Romainville, puis à Compiègne, Charlotte Delbo quitte la France pour Auschwitz-Birkenau le 24 janvier 1943, dans un wagon à bestiaux, en compagnie de deux cent vingt-neuf autres femmes, majoritairement engagées comme elle dans la Résistance.

Transférée à Ravensbrück au début de l'année 1944, elle est libérée en avril 1945 après vingt-sept mois de déportation. Sur les deux cent trente femmes du convoi de 1943, elles sont quarante-neuf à rentrer. Quelques mois après son retour, dans une maison de repos en Suisse, elle écrit dans un cahier *Aucun de nous ne reviendra* qui deviendra, vingt-cinq ans plus tard, le premier volume de la trilogie *Auschwitz et après*. À partir de 1947, elle travaille pour l'ONU à Genève. Elle réside douze ans en Suisse avant de regagner Paris, où elle entre au CNRS en 1960, devenant l'assistante du philosophe Henri Lefebvre, qu'elle avait rencontré en 1932. Elle termine sa carrière au CNRS en 1978 et meurt en 1985, âgée de soixante-douze ans.

Auschwitz et après

Charlotte Delbo a gardé pendant vingt ans le manuscrit d'*Aucun de nous ne reviendra*, l'emportant partout avec elle sans pouvoir se décider à le faire publier. C'est l'engagement dans une tout autre cause, la dénonciation de la guerre d'Algérie, qui l'amène à faire paraître son premier livre aux Éditions de Minuit, *Les Belles Lettres*. Révoltée par la guerre coloniale mais ne se sentant pas légitime pour en témoigner directement, elle réunit et présente un ensemble de lettres dans un recueil, se faisant chambre d'écho de l'indignation de ceux qui les ont écrites. Les Éditions de Minuit ont publié *La Question* d'Henri Alleg et une série de témoignages engagés – et plusieurs fois censurés – contre la torture en Algérie. C'est dans cette maison que Charlotte Delbo publiera donc *Les Belles Lettres* en 1961.

Quelques années plus tard, en 1964, Charlotte Delbo apprend par une connaissance du CNRS que Colette Audry recherche des textes écrits par des femmes pour la collection qu'elle dirige aux éditions Gonthier. Elle accepte de leur confier son témoignage de la déportation. Son amie Claudine Riera-Collet propose de le dactylographier pour elle. C'est ainsi qu'*Aucun de nous ne reviendra* paraît pour la première fois en 1965 chez Gonthier. De ce premier témoignage surgit aussitôt un autre livre, né des questions que lui posait son amie pendant la préparation du manuscrit : qui étaient toutes ces femmes, comment s'étaient-elles retrouvées à Auschwitz, quel avait été leur destin ? Charlotte décide de rassembler tout ce qu'elle sait ou peut retrouver sur les deux cent trente femmes. Sur chacune, elle rédige une notice, les notices sont classées par ordre alphabétique. Elle travaille près d'un an à ce livre qu'elle achève en juillet 1965 et porte à Jérôme Lindon aux Éditions de Minuit. *Le Convoi du 24 janvier* paraît en novembre 1965.

Ainsi paraissent en 1965 ses deux premiers livres sur les camps, très différents l'un de l'autre. Tous deux ont une portée universelle : le premier par la sensibilité, l'humanité et la justesse du récit personnel, le second en rapportant le destin de chaque femme d'un point de vue factuel et historique. Si les ventes sont faibles, ces livres recueillent suffisamment d'éloges pour pousser Charlotte Delbo à continuer le récit d'*Aucun de nous ne reviendra*. Le transfert à Ravensbrück en 1944, la libération des camps, le retour, tout cela était absent du premier livre. De plus elle a écrit, au fil des ans, quelques poèmes dont elle va ponctuer son récit : ainsi se constitue le deuxième volume de la trilogie, *Une connaissance inutile*. Les Éditions de Minuit publient le livre en 1970 et rééditent en même temps *Aucun de nous ne reviendra*.

Le troisième volet vient rapidement après : les recherches faites pour le *Convoi*, les camarades survivantes retrouvées, les échanges avec celles-ci et les amitiés renouées avaient donné l'idée à Charlotte d'écrire sur cela aussi : que devient-on *après* Auschwitz ? Dans *Mesure de nos jours*, qui clôt en 1971 la trilogie *Auschwitz et après*, elle fait le portrait de ses camarades rescapées. Chacune à sa façon a construit sa propre stratégie, plus ou moins consciente, pour tenter de vivre alors que rien ne sera jamais plus comme avant, parce qu'on n'en est jamais vraiment *revenu*.

*Aujourd'hui, je ne suis pas sûre que
ce que j'ai écrit soit vrai. Je suis sûre
que c'est véridique.*

Rue de l'arrivée, rue du départ

Il y a les gens qui arrivent. Ils cherchent des yeux dans la foule de ceux qui attendent ceux qui les attendent. Ils les embrassent et ils disent qu'ils sont fatigués du voyage.

Il y a les gens qui partent. Ils disent au revoir à ceux qui ne partent pas et ils embrassent les enfants.

Il y a une rue pour les gens qui arrivent et une rue pour les gens qui partent.

Il y a un café qui s'appelle « À l'arrivée » et un café qui s'appelle « Au départ ».

Il y a des gens qui arrivent et il y a des gens qui partent.

Mais il est une gare où ceux-là qui arrivent sont justement ceux-là qui partent

une gare où ceux qui arrivent ne sont jamais arrivés, où ceux qui sont partis ne sont jamais revenus.

C'est la plus grande gare du monde.

C'est à cette gare qu'ils arrivent, qu'ils viennent de n'importe où.

Ils y arrivent après des jours et après des nuits

ayant traversé des pays entiers

ils y arrivent avec les enfants même les petits qui ne devaient pas être du voyage.

Ils ont emporté les enfants parce qu'on ne se sépare pas des enfants pour ce voyage-là.

Ceux qui en avaient ont emporté de l'or parce qu'ils croyaient que l'or pouvait être utile.

Tous ont emporté ce qu'ils avaient de plus cher parce qu'il ne faut pas laisser ce qui est cher quand on part au loin.

Tous ont emporté leur vie, c'était surtout sa vie qu'il fallait prendre avec soi.

Et quand ils arrivent

ils croient qu'ils sont arrivés

en enfer

possible. Pourtant ils n'y croyaient pas.

Ils ignoraient qu'on prît le train pour l'enfer mais puisqu'ils y sont ils s'arment et se sentent prêts à l'affronter

avec les enfants les femmes les vieux parents avec les souvenirs de famille et les papiers de famille.

Ils ne savent pas qu'à cette gare-là on n'arrive pas.

14

Ils attendent le pire – ils n'attendent pas l'inconcevable.

Et quand on leur crie de se ranger par cinq, hommes d'un côté, femmes et enfants de l'autre, dans une langue qu'ils ne comprennent pas, ils comprennent aux coups de bâton et se rangent par cinq puisqu'ils s'attendent à tout.

Les mères gardent les enfants contre elles – elles tremblaient qu'ils leur fussent enlevés – parce que les enfants ont faim et soif et sont chiffonnés de l'insomnie à travers tant de pays. Enfin on arrive, elles vont pouvoir s'occuper d'eux.

Et quand on leur crie de laisser les paquets, les édredons et les souvenirs sur le quai, ils les laissent parce qu'ils doivent s'attendre à tout et ne veulent s'étonner de rien. Ils disent « on verra bien », ils ont déjà tant vu et ils sont fatigués du voyage.

La gare n'est pas une gare. C'est la fin d'un rail. Ils regardent et ils sont éprouvés par la désolation autour d'eux.

Le matin la brume leur cache les marais.

Le soir les réflecteurs éclairent les barbelés blancs dans une netteté de photographie astrale. Ils croient que c'est là qu'on les mène et ils sont effrayés.

La nuit ils attendent le jour avec les enfants qui pèsent aux bras des mères. Ils attendent et ils se demandent.

Le jour ils n'attendent pas. Les rangs se mettent en marche tout de suite. Les femmes avec les enfants d'abord, ce sont les plus las. Les hommes ensuite. Ils sont aussi las mais ils sont soulagés qu'on fasse passer en premier leurs femmes et leurs enfants.

Car on fait passer en premier les femmes et les enfants.

L'hiver ils sont saisis par le froid. Surtout ceux qui viennent de Candie la neige leur est nouvelle.

L'été le soleil les aveugle au sortir des fourgons obscurs qu'on a verrouillés au départ.

Au départ de France d'Ukraine d'Albanie de Belgique de Slovaquie d'Italie de Hongrie du Péloponnèse de Hollande de Macédoine d'Autriche d'Herzégovine des bords de la mer Noire et des bords de la Baltique des bords de la Méditerranée et des bords de la Vistule.

Ils voudraient savoir où ils sont. Ils ne savent pas que c'est ici le centre de l'Europe. Ils cherchent la plaque de la gare. C'est une gare qui n'a pas de nom.

Une gare qui pour eux n'aura jamais de nom.

Il y en a qui voyagent pour la première fois de leur vie.

Il y en a qui ont voyagé dans tous les pays du monde, des commerçants. Tous les paysages leur étaient familiers mais ils ne reconnaissent pas celui-ci.

Ils regardent. Ils sauront dire plus tard comment c'était.

Tous veulent se rappeler quelle impression ils ont eue et comme ils ont eu le sentiment qu'ils ne reviendraient pas.

C'est un sentiment qu'on peut avoir eu déjà dans sa vie. Ils savent qu'il faut se défier des sentiments.

Il y a ceux qui viennent de Varsovie avec de grands châles et des baluchons noués

il y a ceux qui viennent de Zagreb les femmes avec des mouchoirs sur la tête

il y a ceux qui viennent du Danube avec des tricots faits à la veillée dans des laines multi-colores

il y a ceux qui viennent de Grèce, ils ont emporté des olives noires et du rahat-lokoum

il y a ceux qui viennent de Monte-Carlo

ils étaient au casino

ils sont en frac avec un plastron que le voyage a tout cassé

ils ont des ventres et ils sont chauves

ce sont de gros banquiers qui jouaient à la banque

il y a des mariés qui sortaient de la synagogue avec la mariée en blanc et en voile toute fripée d'avoir couché à même le plancher du wagon

le marié en noir et en tube les gants salis

les parents et les invités, les femmes avec des sacs à perles

qui tous regrettent de n'avoir pu passer à la maison mettre un costume moins fragile.

Le rabbin se tient droit et marche le premier. Il a toujours été un exemple aux autres.

Il y a les fillettes d'un pensionnat avec leurs jupes plissées toutes pareilles, leurs chapeaux à ruban bleu qui flotte. Elles tirent bien leurs chaussettes en descendant. Et elles vont gentiment par cinq comme à la promenade du jeudi, se tenant par la main et ne sachant. Que peut-on faire aux petites filles d'un pensionnat qui sont avec la maîtresse ? La maîtresse leur dit : « Soyons sages, les petites. » Elles n'ont pas envie de n'être pas sages.

Il y a les vieilles gens qui recevaient des nouvelles des enfants en Amérique. Ils ont de l'étranger l'idée que leur en donnaient les cartes postales. Rien ne ressemblait à ce qu'ils voient ici. Les enfants ne le croiront jamais.

Il y a les intellectuels. Ils sont médecins ou architectes, compositeurs ou poètes, ils se distinguent à la démarche et aux lunettes. Eux aussi ont vu beaucoup dans leur vie. Ils ont beaucoup étudié. Certains ont même beaucoup imaginé pour faire des livres et rien de leurs imaginations ne ressemble à ce qu'ils voient ici.

Il y a tous les ouvriers fourreurs des grandes villes et tous les tailleurs pour hommes et pour dames, tous les confectionneurs qui avaient émigré à l'Occident et qui ne reconnaissent pas ici la terre des ancêtres.

Il y a le peuple inépuisable des villes où les hommes occupent chacun son alvéole et ici maintenant cela fait d'interminables rangs et on se demande comment tout cela pouvait tenir dans les alvéoles superposés des villes.

Il y a une mère qui calotte son enfant cinq ans peut-être parce qu'il ne veut pas lui donner la main et qu'elle veut qu'il reste tranquille à côté d'elle. On risque de se perdre on ne doit pas se séparer dans un endroit inconnu et avec tout ce monde. Elle calotte son enfant et nous qui savons ne le lui pardonnons pas. D'ailleurs ce serait la même chose si elle le couvrait de baisers.

Il y a ceux qui avaient voyagé dix-huit jours qui étaient devenus fous et s'étaient entretués dans les wagons et

ceux qui avaient été étouffés pendant le voyage tant ils étaient serrés

évidemment ceux-là ne descendent pas.

Il y a une petite fille qui tient sa poupée sur son cœur, on asphyxie aussi les poupées.

Il y a deux sœurs en manteau blanc qui se promenaient et qui ne sont pas rentrées pour le dîner. Les parents sont encore inquiets.

Par cinq ils prennent la rue de l'arrivée. C'est la rue du départ ils ne savent pas. C'est la rue qu'on ne prend qu'une fois.

Ils marchent bien en ordre – qu'on ne puisse rien leur reprocher.

Ils arrivent à une bâtisse et ils soupirent. Enfin ils sont arrivés.

Et quand on crie aux femmes de se déshabiller elles déshabillent les enfants d'abord en prenant garde de ne pas les réveiller tout à fait. Après des jours et des nuits de voyage ils sont nerveux et grognons

et elles commencent à se déshabiller devant les enfants tant pis

et quand on leur donne à chacune une serviette elles s'inquiètent est-ce que la douche sera chaude parce que les enfants prendraient froid

et quand les hommes par une autre porte entrent dans la salle de douche nus aussi elles cachent les enfants contre elles.

Et peut-être alors tous comprennent-ils.

Et cela ne sert de rien qu'ils comprennent

maintenant puisqu'ils ne peuvent le dire à ceux qui attendent sur le quai

à ceux qui roulent dans les wagons éteints à travers tous les pays pour arriver ici

à ceux qui sont dans des camps et appréhendent le départ parce qu'ils redoutent le climat ou le travail et qu'ils ont peur de laisser leurs biens

à ceux qui se cachent dans les montagnes et dans les bois et qui n'ont plus la patience de se cacher. Arrive que devra ils retourneront chez eux. Pourquoi irait-on les chercher chez eux ils n'ont jamais fait de mal à personne

à ceux qui n'ont pas voulu se cacher parce qu'on ne peut pas tout abandonner

à ceux qui croyaient avoir mis les enfants à l'abri dans un pensionnat catholique où ces demoiselles sont si bonnes.

On habillera un orchestre avec les jupes plissées des fillettes. Le commandant veut qu'on joue des valses viennoises le dimanche matin.

Une chef de block fera des rideaux pour donner à sa fenêtre un air de chambre avec l'étoffe sacrée que le rabbin portait sur lui pour célébrer l'office quoi qu'il lui advînt en quelque lieu qu'il se trouvât.

Une kapo se déguisera avec l'habit et le tube

du marié son amie avec le voile et elles joueront à la noce le soir quand les autres sont couchées mortes de fatigue. Les kapos peuvent s'amuser elles ne sont pas fatiguées le soir.

On distribuera aux Allemandes malades des olives noires et du lokoum mais elles n'aiment pas les olives de Calamata ni les olives en général.

Et tout le jour et toute la nuit

tous les jours et toutes les nuits les cheminées fument avec ce combustible de tous les pays d'Europe

des hommes près des cheminées passent leurs journées à passer les cendres pour retrouver l'or fondu des dents en or. Ils ont tous de l'or dans la bouche ces juifs et ils sont tant que cela fait des tonnes.

Et au printemps des hommes et des femmes répandent les cendres sur les marais asséchés pour la première fois labourés et fertilisent le sol avec du phosphate humain.

Ils ont un sac attaché sur le ventre et ils plongent la main dans la poussière d'os humains qu'ils jettent à la volée en peinant sur les sillons avec le vent qui leur renvoie la poussière au visage et le soir ils sont tout blancs, des rides marquées par la sueur qui a coulé sur la poussière.

Et qu'on ne craigne pas d'en manquer il arrive

des trains et des trains il en arrive tous les jours et toutes les nuits toutes les heures de tous les jours et de toutes les nuits.

C'est la plus grande gare du monde pour les arrivées et les départs.

Il n'y a que ceux qui entrent dans le camp qui sachent ensuite ce qui est arrivé aux autres et qui pleurent de les avoir quittés à la gare parce que ce jour-là l'officier commandait aux plus jeunes de former un rang à part

il faut bien qu'il y en ait pour assécher les marais et y répandre la cendre des autres.

Et ils se disent qu'il aurait mieux valu ne jamais entrer ici et ne jamais savoir.

Vous qui avez pleuré deux mille ans
un qui a agonisé trois jours et trois nuits

quelles larmes aurez-vous
pour ceux qui ont agonisé
beaucoup plus de trois cents nuits et beaucoup
  plus de trois cents journées
combien
pleurerez-vous
ceux-là qui ont agonisé tant d'agonies
et ils étaient innombrables

Ils ne croyaient pas à résurrection dans l'éternité
Et ils savaient que vous ne pleureriez pas.

Ô vous qui savez
saviez-vous que la faim fait briller les yeux que
    la soif les ternit
Ô vous qui savez
saviez-vous qu'on peut voir sa mère morte
et rester sans larmes
Ô vous qui savez
saviez-vous que le matin on veut mourir
que le soir on a peur
Ô vous qui savez
saviez-vous qu'un jour est plus qu'une année
une minute plus qu'une vie
Ô vous qui savez
saviez-vous que les jambes sont plus vulnérables
    que les yeux
les nerfs plus durs que les os
le cœur plus solide que l'acier
Saviez-vous que les pierres du chemin ne pleu-
    rent pas
qu'il n'y a qu'un mot pour l'épouvante
qu'un mot pour l'angoisse

CHARLOTTE DELBO

Saviez-vous que la souffrance n'a pas de limite
l'horreur pas de frontière
Le saviez-vous
Vous qui savez.

Ma mère
c'était des mains un visage
Ils ont mis nos mères nues devant nous

Ici les mères ne sont plus mères à leurs enfants.

Tous étaient marqués au bras d'un numéro in-
   délébile
Tous devaient mourir nus

Le tatouage identifiait les morts et les mortes.

C'était une plaine désolée
au bord d'une ville

La plaine était glacée
et la ville
n'avait pas de nom.

DIALOGUE

« Tu es française ?

– Oui.

– Moi aussi. »

Elle n'a pas d'F sur la poitrine. Une étoile.

« D'où ?

– Paris.

– Il y a longtemps que tu es ici ?

– Cinq semaines.

– Moi, seize jours.

– C'est beaucoup déjà, je sais.

– Cinq semaines... Comment est-ce possible ?

– Tu vois.

– Et tu crois qu'on peut tenir ? »

Elle mendie.

« Il faut essayer.

– Vous, vous pouvez espérer mais nous... »

Elle montre ma jaquette rayée et elle montre son manteau, un manteau trop grand tellement, trop sale tellement, trop en loques tellement.

« Oh, nos chances sont égales, va...

– Pour nous, il n'y a pas d'espoir. »

Et sa main fait un geste et son geste évoque la fumée qui monte.

« Il faut lutter de tout son courage.

– Pourquoi... Pourquoi lutter puisque nous devons toutes... »

Le geste de sa main achève. La fumée qui monte.

« Non. Il faut lutter.

– Comment espérer sortir d'ici. Comment quelqu'un sortira-t-il jamais d'ici. Il vaudrait mieux se jeter dans les barbelés tout de suite. »

Que lui dire ? Elle est petite, chétive. Et je n'ai pas le pouvoir de me persuader moi-même. Tous les arguments sont insensés. Je lutte contre ma raison. On lutte contre toute raison.

La cheminée fume. Le ciel est bas. La fumée traîne sur le camp et pèse et nous enveloppe et c'est l'odeur de la chair qui brûle.

« Regardez. Regardez. »

Nous étions accroupies dans notre soupente, sur les planches qui devaient nous servir de lit, de table, de plancher. Le toit était très bas. On n'y pouvait tenir qu'assis et la tête baissée. Nous étions huit, notre groupe de huit camarades que la mort allait séparer, sur cet étroit carré où nous perchions. La soupe avait été distribuée. Nous avions attendu dehors longtemps pour passer l'une après l'autre devant le bidon qui fumait au visage de la stubhova. La manche droite retroussée, elle plongeait la louche dans le bidon pour servir. Derrière la vapeur de la soupe, elle criait. La buée amollissait sa voix. Elle criait parce qu'il y avait des bousculades ou des bavardages. Mornes, nous attendions, la main engourdie qui tenait la gamelle. Maintenant, la soupe sur les genoux, nous mangions. La soupe était sale, mais elle avait le goût de chaud.

« Regardez, vous avez vu, dans la cour...

– Oh ! » Yvonne P. laisse retomber sa cuiller. Elle n'a plus faim.

Le carreau grillagé donne sur la cour du block 25, une cour fermée de murs. Il y a une porte qui ouvre dans le camp, mais si cette porte s'ouvre quand vous passez, vite vous courez, vous vous sauvez, vous ne cherchez à voir ni la porte ni ce qu'il peut y avoir derrière. Vous vous enfuyez. Nous, par le carreau, nous pouvons voir. Nous ne tournons jamais la tête de ce côté.

« Regardez. Regardez. »

D'abord, on doute de ce qu'on voit. Il faut les distinguer de la neige. Il y en a plein la cour. Nus. Rangés les uns contre les autres. Blancs, d'un blanc qui fait bleuté sur la neige. Les têtes sont rasées, les poils du pubis droits, raides. Les cadavres sont gelés. Blancs avec les ongles marron. Les orteils dressés sont ridicules à vrai dire. D'un ridicule terrible.

Boulevard de Courtais, à Montluçon. J'attendais mon père aux Nouvelles Galeries. C'était l'été, le soleil était chaud sur l'asphalte. Un camion était arrêté, que des hommes déchargeaient. On livrait des mannequins pour la vitrine. Chaque homme prenait dans ses bras un mannequin qu'il déposait à l'entrée du magasin. Les mannequins étaient nus, avec les articulations voyantes. Les hommes les portaient précieusement, les couchaient près du mur, sur le trottoir chaud.

Je regardais. J'étais troublée par la nudité des mannequins. J'avais souvent vu des mannequins dans la vitrine, avec leur robe, leurs souliers et leur perruque, leur bras plié dans un geste maniéré. Je n'avais jamais pensé qu'ils existaient nus, sans cheveux. Je n'avais jamais pensé qu'ils existaient en dehors de la vitrine, de la lumière électrique, de leur geste. Le découvrir me donnait le même malaise que de voir un mort pour la première fois.

Maintenant les mannequins sont couchés dans la neige, baignés dans la clarté d'hiver qui me fait ressouvenir du soleil sur l'asphalte.

Celles qui sont couchées là dans la neige, ce sont nos camarades d'hier. Hier elles étaient debout à l'appel. Elles se tenaient cinq par cinq en rangs, de chaque côté de la Lagerstrasse. Elles partaient au travail, elles se traînaient vers les marais. Hier elles avaient faim. Elles avaient des poux, elles se grattaient. Hier elles avalaient la soupe sale. Elles avaient la diarrhée et on les battait. Hier elles souffraient. Hier elles souhaitaient mourir.

Maintenant elles sont là, cadavres nus dans la neige. Elles sont mortes au block 25. La mort au block 25 n'a pas la sérénité qu'on attend d'elle, même ici.

Un matin, parce qu'elles s'évanouissaient à l'appel, parce qu'elles étaient plus livides que les autres, un SS leur a fait signe. Il a formé d'elles une colonne qui montrait en grossissement toutes les déchéances additionnées, toutes les infirmités qui se perdaient jusque-là dans la masse. Et la colonne, sous la conduite du SS, était poussée vers le block 25.

Il y avait celles qui y allaient seules. Volontairement. Comme au suicide. Elles attendaient qu'un SS vînt en inspection pour que la porte s'ouvrît – et entrer.

Il y avait aussi celles qui ne couraient pas assez vite un jour qu'il fallait courir.

Il y avait encore celles que leurs camarades avaient été obligées d'abandonner à la porte, et qui avaient crié : « Ne me laissez pas. Ne me laissez pas. »

Pendant des jours, elles avaient eu faim et soif, soif surtout. Elles avaient eu froid, couchées presque sans vêtements sur des planches, sans paillasse ni couverture. Enfermées avec des agonisantes et des folles, elles attendaient leur tour d'agonie ou de folie. Le matin, elles sortaient. On les faisait sortir à coups de bâton. Des coups de bâton à des agonisantes et à des folles. Les vivantes devaient traîner les mortes de la nuit dans la cour, parce qu'il fallait compter les mortes aussi. Le SS passait. Il s'amusait à lancer son chien sur elles. On entendait dans tout le camp des hurlements. C'étaient les hurlements de la nuit. Puis le silence. L'appel était fini. C'était le silence du jour. Les vivantes rentraient. Les mortes restaient dans la neige. On les avait déshabillées. Les vêtements serviraient à d'autres.

Tous les deux ou trois jours, les camions venaient prendre les vivantes pour les emporter à la chambre à gaz, les mortes pour les jeter au four crématoire. La folie devait être le dernier espoir de celles qui entraient là. Quelques-unes, que leur entêtement à vivre faisait rusées, échappaient au départ. Elles restaient parfois plusieurs semaines, jamais plus de trois, au block 25. On les voyait aux grillages des fenêtres. Elles suppliaient : « À boire. À boire. » Il y a des spectres qui parlent.

« Regardez. Oh, je vous assure qu'elle a bougé. Celle-là, l'avant-dernière. Sa main... ses doigts se déplient, j'en suis sûre. »

Les doigts se déplient lentement, c'est la neige qui fleurit en une anémone de mer décolorée.

« Ne regardez pas. Pourquoi regardez-vous ? » implore Yvonne P., les yeux agrandis, fixés sur le cadavre qui vit encore.

« Mange ta soupe, dit Cécile. Elles, elles n'ont plus besoin de rien. »

Moi aussi je regarde. Je regarde ce cadavre

qui bouge et qui m'est insensible. Maintenant je suis grande. Je peux regarder des mannequins nus sans avoir peur.

LES HOMMES

Le matin et le soir, sur la route des marais, nous croisions des colonnes d'hommes. Les juifs étaient en civil. Des vêtements délabrés, barbouillés dans le dos d'une croix au minium. Comme les juives. Des vêtements informes qu'ils attachaient autour d'eux. Les autres etaient en rayés. Les uniformes flottaient sur les dos maigres.

Nous les plaignions parce qu'ils devaient marcher au pas. Nous, nous marchions comme nous pouvions. Le kapo, en tête, était gras et botté, chaudement vêtu. Il scandait : Links, Zwei, Drei, Vier. Links. Les hommes suivaient avec peine. Ils étaient chaussés de socques de toile à semelles de bois qui ne tenaient pas aux pieds. Nous nous demandions comment ils pouvaient marcher avec ces socques. Quand il y avait de la neige ou du verglas, ils les prenaient à la main.

Ils avaient la démarche de là-bas. La tête en avant, le cou en avant. La tête et le cou entraînaient le reste du corps. La tête et le cou tiraient les pieds. Dans leurs visages décharnés, les yeux brûlaient, cernés, la pupille noire. Leurs lèvres étaient gonflées, noires ou trop rouges et quand ils les écartaient se voyaient les gencives sanguinolentes.

Ils passaient près de nous. Nous murmurions : « Françaises, Françaises », pour savoir s'il se trouvait de nos compatriotes avec eux. Nous n'en avions pas rencontrés jusqu'alors.

Tout tendus à marcher, ils ne nous regardaient pas. Nous, nous les regardions. Nous les regardions. Nos mains se serraient de pitié. Leur pensée nous poursuivait, et leur démarche, et leurs yeux.

Il y avait parmi nous tant de malades qui ne mangeaient pas que nous avions beaucoup de pain. Nous essayions de tous les arguments pour les convaincre de manger, de surmonter le dégoût que la nourriture leur donnait, de manger pour survivre. Nos paroles ne levaient en elles nulle volonté. Dès l'arrivée, elles avaient renoncé.

Un matin, nous avons emporté du pain sous nos vestes. Pour les hommes. Nous ne rencontrons pas de colonne d'hommes. Nous attendons le soir avec impatience. Au retour, nous entendons leur pas derrière nous. Drei. Vier. Links. Ils marchent plus vite que nous. Nous devons nous ranger pour les laisser passer. Polonais ?

Russes ? Des hommes, pitoyables, saignants de misère comme tous les hommes ici.

Dès qu'ils arrivent à notre hauteur, vite nous sortons notre pain et le leur lançons. Aussitôt, c'est une mêlée. Ils attrapent le pain, se le disputent, se l'arrachent. Ils ont des yeux de loup. Deux roulent dans le fossé avec le pain qui s'échappe.

Nous les regardons se battre et nous pleurons.

Le SS hurle, jette son chien sur eux. La colonne se reforme, reprend sa marche. Links. Zwei. Drei.

Ils n'ont pas tourné la tête vers nous.

L'APPEL

Les SS en pèlerine noire sont passées. Elles
ont compté. On attend encore.

On attend.

Depuis des jours, le jour suivant.

Depuis la veille, le lendemain.

Depuis le milieu de la nuit, aujourd'hui.

On attend.

Le jour s'annonce au ciel.

On attend le jour parce qu'il faut attendre
quelque chose.

On n'attend pas la mort. On s'y attend.

On n'attend rien.

On attend ce qui arrive. La nuit parce qu'elle
succède au jour. Le jour parce qu'il succède à la
nuit.

On attend la fin de l'appel.

La fin de l'appel, c'est un coup de sifflet qui
fait tourner chacune sur soi-même vers la porte.
Les rangs immobiles deviennent les rangs prêts
à se mettre en marche. En marche vers les
marais, vers les briques, vers les fossés.

41

Aujourd'hui nous attendons plus longtemps que d'habitude. Le ciel pâlit plus que d'habitude. Nous attendons.

Quoi ?

Un SS apparaît au bout de la Lagerstrasse, vient vers nous, s'arrête devant nos rangs. Au caducée sur sa casquette, ce doit être le médecin. Il nous considère. Lentement. Il parle. Il ne hurle pas. Il parle. Une question. Personne ne répond. Il appelle : « Dolmetscherine. » Marie-Claude s'avance. Le SS répète sa question et Marie-Claude traduit : « Il demande s'il y en a parmi nous qui ne peuvent pas supporter l'appel. » Le SS nous regarde. Magda, notre blockhova, qui se tient près de lui nous regarde et, se mettant un peu de côté, cligne légèrement des paupières.

En vérité, qui peut supporter l'appel ? Qui peut rester debout immobile des heures ? En pleine nuit. Dans la neige. Sans avoir mangé, sans avoir dormi. Qui peut supporter ce froid pendant des heures ?

Quelques-unes lèvent la main.

Le SS les fait sortir des rangs. Les compte. Trop peu. Doucement, il dit encore une phrase et Marie-Claude traduit encore : « Il demande s'il n'y en a pas d'autres, âgées ou malades, qui trouvent l'appel trop dur le matin. » D'autres mains se lèvent. Alors Magda, vite, pousse Marie-Claude du coude et Marie-Claude, sans changer de ton : « Mais il vaut mieux ne pas le dire. » Les mains qui s'étaient levées s'abaissent. Sauf une. Une petite vieille toute petite qui se hausse sur les pointes, tendant et agitant le bras, aussi haut qu'elle peut tant elle craint qu'on ne la voie pas. Le SS s'éloigne. La petite vieille s'enhardit : « Moi, monsieur. J'ai soixante-sept ans. » Ses voisines lui font : « Chut ! » Elle se fâche. Pourquoi l'empêcherait-on, s'il y a un régime moins rude pour les malades et les vieilles, pourquoi l'empêcherait-on d'en bénéficier ? Désespérée d'avoir été oubliée, elle crie. D'une voix aiguë et vieille comme elle, elle crie : « Moi, monsieur. J'ai soixante-sept ans. » Le SS entend, se retourne : « Komm » et elle se joint au groupe formé tout à l'heure, que le médecin SS escorte au block 25.

Un jour

Elle était accrochée au revers du talus, accrochée des mains et des pieds au revers du talus couvert de neige. Tout son corps était tendu, tendues ses mâchoires, tendu son cou désarticulé en cartilages, tendu ce qui restait de muscle à ses os.

Et ses efforts étaient vains – les efforts de quelqu'un qui tirerait une corde idéale.

Elle était arc-boutée de l'index à l'orteil mais chaque fois qu'elle soulevait une main pour s'agripper plus haut et essayer de gravir le talus, elle retombait. Son corps devenait d'un coup flasque, misérable. Puis elle relevait la tête et on suivait sur son visage le travail mental qui se faisait au-dedans d'elle-même pour réajuster ses membres à l'effort. Ses dents se serraient, son menton s'aiguisait, les côtes se marquaient en cercles sous son vêtement collé, un manteau civil – une juive –, ses chevilles se raidissaient. Elle essayait à nouveau de se hisser à l'autre rive de neige.

44

Chacun de ses gestes était si lent et si mala-
droit, si criant de débilité, qu'on se demandait
comment elle pouvait seulement bouger. En
même temps, on comprenait mal qu'il lui fallût
se donner une peine aussi disproportionnée à
l'entreprise, aussi disproportionnée à ce corps
qui ne devait rien peser.

Maintenant ses mains étaient accrochées à une
croûte de neige durcie, ses pieds sans point
d'appui cherchaient une anfractuosité, un éche-
lon. Ils battaient dans le vide. Ses jambes étaient
entortillées de chiffons. Elles étaient si maigres
que malgré les chiffons elles faisaient penser aux
rames à haricots qu'on accroche aux épouvan-
tails pour figurer des jambes, et qui pendent.
Surtout quand elles battaient dans le vide. Elle
retombait au fond du fossé.

Elle tourne la tête comme pour mesurer le
chemin, regarde vers le haut. On voit grandir
l'égarement dans ses yeux, dans ses mains, dans
son visage convulsé.

« Qu'ont-elles toutes ces femmes à me regarder ainsi ? Pourquoi sont-elles là et pourquoi
sont-elles rangées en lignes serrées, et pourquoi
restent-elles là immobiles ? Elles me regardent
et elles semblent ne pas me voir. Elles ne me
voient pas, elles ne resteraient pas ainsi plan-
tées. Elles m'aideraient à remonter. Pourquoi
ne m'aidez-vous pas, vous qui êtes là si près ?

Aidez-moi. Tirez-moi. Penchez-vous. Tendez la main. Oh, elles ne bougent pas. »

Et la main se tordait vers nous dans un appel désespéré. La main retombe – une étoile mauve fanée sur la neige. Retombée, elle avait perdu de son décharné, elle s'amollissait, redevenait chose vivante et pitoyable. Le coude s'appuie, glisse. Tout le corps s'abat.

Derrière, au-delà des barbelés, la plaine, la neige, la plaine.

Nous étions là toutes, plusieurs milliers, debout dans la neige depuis le matin – c'est ainsi qu'il faut appeler la nuit, puisque le matin était à trois heures de la nuit. L'aube avait éclairé la neige qui jusque-là éclairait la nuit – et le froid s'était accentué.

Immobiles depuis le milieu de la nuit, nous devenions si lourdes à nos jambes que nous enfoncions dans la terre, dans la glace, sans pouvoir rien contre l'engourdissement. Le froid meurtrissait les tempes, les maxillaires, à croire que les os se disloquaient, que le crâne éclatait. Nous avions renoncé à sauter d'un pied sur l'autre, à taper les talons, à frotter nos paumes. C'était une gymnastique épuisante.

Nous restions immobiles. La volonté de lutter et de résister, la vie, s'étaient réfugiées dans une portion rapetissée du corps, juste l'immédiate périphérie du cœur.

Nous étions là immobiles, quelques milliers de femmes de toutes les langues, serrées les unes contre les autres, baissant la tête sous les rafales de neige qui cinglaient.

Nous étions là immobiles, réduites au seul battement de nos cœurs.

Où va-t-elle, celle-ci qui quitte le rang ? Elle marche en infirme ou en aveugle, un aveugle qui regarde. Elle se dirige vers le fossé d'une démarche en bois. Elle est au bord, s'accroupit pour descendre. Elle tombe. Son pied a glissé sur la neige qui s'éboule. Pourquoi veut-elle descendre dans le fossé ? Elle a quitté le rang sans hésiter, sans se cacher de la SS droite dans sa pèlerine noire, droite sur ses bottes noires, qui nous garde. Elle s'en est allée comme si elle était ailleurs, dans une rue où elle changerait de trottoir, ou dans un jardin. D'évoquer un jardin ici peut faire rire. Peut-être une de ces vieilles folles qui font peur aux enfants dans les squares. C'est une femme jeune, une jeune fille presque. Des épaules si frêles.

La voilà au creux du fossé avec ses mains qui grattent, ses pieds qui cherchent, la pesanteur de sa tête qu'elle soulève avec effort. Son visage est maintenant tourné vers nous. Les pommettes sont violettes, accusées, la bouche gonflée, violette noire, les orbites avec de l'ombre au fond. Son visage est celui du désespoir nu.

Longtemps elle lutte contre l'indocilité de ses membres pour se remettre d'aplomb. Elle se débat comme un noyé. Puis elle tend les mains pour se hausser à l'autre rive. Ses mains cherchent prise, ses ongles griffent la neige, tout son corps se tend dans un sursaut. Et elle s'affaisse, épuisée.

Je ne la regarde plus. Je ne veux plus la regarder. Je voudrais changer de place, ne plus voir. Ne plus voir ces trous au fond des orbites, ces trous qui fixent. Que veut-elle faire ? Veut-elle atteindre les barbelés électriques ? Pourquoi nous fixe-t-elle ? N'est-ce pas moi qu'elle désigne ? Moi qu'elle implore ? Je tourne la tête. Regarder ailleurs. Ailleurs.

Ailleurs – devant-nous – c'est la porte du block 25.

Debout, enveloppé dans une couverture, un enfant, un garçonnet. Une tête rasée très petite, un visage où saillent les mâchoires et l'arcade sourcilière. Pieds nus, il sautille sans arrêt, animé d'un mouvement frénétique qui fait penser à celui des sauvages quand ils dansent. Il veut agiter les bras aussi pour se réchauffer. La couverture s'écarte. C'est une femme. Un squelette de femme. Elle est nue. On voit les côtes et les os iliaques. Elle remonte la couverture sur ses épaules, continue à danser. Une danse de mécanique. Un squelette de femme qui danse. Ses pieds sont petits, maigres et nus dans la neige. Il y a des squelettes vivants et qui dansent.

Et maintenant je suis dans un café à écrire cette histoire – car cela devient une histoire.

Une éclaircie. Est-ce l'après-midi ? Nous avons perdu le sentiment du temps. Le ciel apparaît. Très bleu. D'un bleu oublié. Des heures se sont écoulées depuis que j'ai réussi à ne plus regarder la femme dans le fossé. Y est-elle encore ? Elle a atteint le haut du talus – comment a-t-elle pu ? – et elle s'est arrêtée là. Ses mains sont attirées par la neige qui scintille. Elle en prend une poignée qu'elle porte à ses lèvres avec un geste d'une lenteur exaspérante qui doit lui coûter une peine infinie. Elle suce la neige. Nous comprenons pourquoi elle a quitté le rang, cette résolution sur ses traits. Elle voulait de la neige propre pour ses lèvres tuméfiées. Depuis l'aube elle était fascinée par cette neige propre qu'elle voulait atteindre. De ce côté-ci, la neige que nous avons piétinée est noire. Elle suce sa neige mais elle semble n'en avoir plus envie. Cela ne désaltère pas, la neige, quand on a la fièvre. Tous ces efforts pour une poignée de neige qui est à sa bouche une poignée de sel. Sa main retombe, sa nuque ploie. Une tige fragile qui devrait se casser. Son dos s'arrondit, avec les omoplates qui ressortent sous l'étoffe mince du manteau. C'est un manteau jaune, du jaune de notre chien Flac qui était devenu tellement maigre après sa maladie et dont tout le corps s'arrondissait en squelette d'oiseau du muséum au moment qu'il allait mourir. La femme va mourir.

Elle ne nous regarde plus. Elle gît dans la neige, le corps recroquevillé. La colonne vertébrale arquée, Flac va mourir – le premier être que je voyais mourir. Maman, Flac est devant la porte du jardin. Il est tout recroquevillé. Il tremble. André dit qu'il va mourir.

« Il faut que je me relève, que je me relève. Il faut que je marche. Il faut que je lutte encore. Ne m'aideront-elles pas ? Aidez-moi donc vous toutes qui êtes là les bras vides. »

Maman, viens vite, Flac va mourir.

« Je sais pourquoi elles ne m'aident pas. Elles sont mortes. Elles sont mortes. Ah ! elles paraissent vivantes parce qu'elles tiennent debout appuyées les unes aux autres. Elles sont mortes. Moi je ne veux pas mourir. »

Sa main s'agite une fois encore comme un cri – et elle ne crie pas. Dans quelle langue crierait-elle si elle criait ?

Voici une morte qui s'avance vers elle. Mannequin dans le vêtement rayé. En deux pas la morte l'a rejointe, la tire par un bras, la traîne sur notre côté pour qu'elle reprenne sa place dans les rangs. La pèlerine noire de la SS s'est approchée. C'est plutôt un sac jaune sale que la morte traîne vers nous, qui reste là. Des heures. Que pouvons-nous ? Elle va mourir. Flac, vous savez, notre chien jaune qui était si maigre, va mourir. Des heures encore.

Soudain un frémissement parcourt ce tas que fait le manteau jaune dans la boue de neige. La femme essaie de se dresser. Ses mouvements se décomposent dans un ralenti insupportable. Elle s'agenouille, nous regarde. Aucune de nous ne bouge. Elle appuie ses mains au sol – son corps est arqué et maigre comme celui de Flac qui allait mourir. Elle parvient à se mettre debout. Elle titube, cherche où se retenir. C'est le vide. Elle marche. Elle marche dans le vide. Elle est tellement courbée qu'on se demande comment elle ne retombe pas. Non. Elle marche. Elle chancelle mais elle avance. Et les os de sa face portent une volonté qui effraie. Nous la voyons traverser le vide devant nos rangs. Où va-t-elle encore ?

« Pourquoi vous étonnez-vous que je marche ? N'avez-vous pas entendu qu'il m'a appelée, lui, le SS qui est devant la porte avec son chien. Vous n'entendez pas parce que vous êtes mortes. »

La SS en pèlerine noire est partie. Maintenant c'est un SS en vert qui est devant la porte.

La femme s'avance. On croirait qu'elle obéit.

51

Face au SS, elle s'arrête. Son dos est secoué de frissons, son dos arrondi avec les omoplates qui saillent sous le manteau jaune. Le SS tient son chien en laisse. Lui a-t-il donné un ordre, fait un signe ? Le chien bondit sur la femme – sans rugir, sans souffler, sans aboyer. C'est silencieux comme dans un rêve. Le chien bondit sur la femme, lui plante ses crocs dans la gorge. Et nous ne bougeons pas, engluées dans une espèce de visqueux qui nous empêche d'ébaucher même un geste – comme dans un rêve. La femme crie. Un cri arraché. Un seul cri qui déchire l'immobilité de la plaine. Nous ne savons pas si le cri vient d'elle ou de nous, de sa gorge crevée ou de la nôtre. Je sens les crocs du chien à ma gorge. Je crie. Je hurle. Aucun son ne sort de moi. Le silence du rêve.

La plaine. La neige. La plaine.

La femme s'affaisse. Un soubresaut et c'est fini. Quelque chose qui casse net. La tête dans la boue de neige n'est plus qu'un moignon. Les yeux font des plaies sales.

« Toutes ces mortes qui ne me regardent plus. » Maman, Flac est mort. Il a agonisé longtemps. Puis il s'est traîné jusqu'au perron. Il y a eu un râle qui n'a pas pu sortir de sa gorge et il est mort. On aurait dit qu'on l'avait étranglé.

Le SS tire sur la laisse. Le chien se dégage. Il a un peu de sang à la gueule. Le SS sifflote, s'en va.

Devant la porte du block 25, la couverture aux pieds nus, à la tête rasée, n'a pas cessé de sautiller. La nuit vient.

Et nous restons debout dans la neige. Immobiles dans la plaine immobile.

Et maintenant je suis dans un café à écrire ceci.

MARIE

Son père, sa mère, ses frères et ses sœurs ont été gazés à l'arrivée.

Les parents étaient trop vieux, les enfants trop jeunes.

Elle dit : « Elle était belle, ma petite sœur. Vous ne pouvez pas vous représenter comme elle était belle.

Ils n'ont pas dû la regarder.

S'ils l'avaient regardée, ils ne l'auraient pas tuée.

Ils n'auraient pas pu. »

Le lendemain

Depuis la nuit c'était l'appel et maintenant c'est le jour. La nuit était claire et froide, craquante de gel – cette coulée de glace qui coulait des étoiles. Le jour est clair et froid, clair et froid jusqu'à l'intolérable. Sifflet. Les colonnes bougent. Le mouvement ondule jusqu'à nous. Sans savoir, nous avons virevolté. Sans savoir, nous bougeons aussi. Nous avançons. Si engourdies que nous semblons n'être qu'un morceau de froid qui avance d'une pièce. Nos jambes avancent comme si elles n'étaient pas nous. Les premières colonnes franchissent la porte. De chaque côté, les SS avec leurs chiens. Ils sont empaquetés dans des capotes, des passe-montagnes, des cache-nez. Les chiens aussi, dans des manteaux de chiens, avec les deux lettres SS noires sur un rond blanc. Des manteaux faits dans des drapeaux. Les colonnes s'étirent. Il faut se raidir pour franchir la porte, s'espacer. La porte franchie, nous nous resserrons comme font les bêtes mais le froid est si intense que nous ne le sentons plus. Devant nous la plaine étincelle : la mer. Nous suivons. Les rangs traversent la route, marchent droit vers la mer. En silence. Lentement. Où allons-nous ? Nous avançons dans la plaine étincelante. Nous avançons dans la lumière solidifiée par le froid. Les SS crient. Nous ne comprenons pas ce qu'ils crient. Les colonnes s'enfoncent dans la mer, toujours plus loin dans la lumière de glace. Les SS répètent les ordres par-dessus nous. Nous avançons, éblouies par la neige. Et tout à coup nous sommes saisies de peur, de vertige, au bord de cette plaine aveuglante. Que veulent-ils ? Que vont-ils faire de nous ? Ils crient. Ils courent et leurs armes tintent. Que vont-ils faire de nous ?

Alors les colonnes se forment en carrés. Dix par dix, sur dix rangs. Un carré après l'autre. Un damier gris sur la neige étincelante. La dernière colonne. Le dernier carré s'immobilise. Des cris pour que la bordure du damier soit bien nette sur la neige. Les SS gardent les coins. Que veulent-ils faire ? Un officier à cheval passe. Il regarde les carrés parfaits que dessinent quinze mille femmes sur la neige. Il tourne bride, satisfait. Les cris cessent. Les sentinelles commencent à faire les cent pas autour des carrés. Nous reprenons conscience de nous-mêmes, nous respirons toujours. Nous respirons du froid. Au-delà de nous, la plaine.

La neige étincelle dans une lumière réfractée. Il n'y a pas de rayons, seulement de la lumière, une lumière dure et glaciaire où tout s'inscrit en arêtes coupantes. Le ciel est bleu, dur et glaciaire. On pense à des plantes prises dans la glace. Cela doit arriver dans l'Arctique que la glace prenne jusqu'aux végétations sous-marines. Nous sommes prises dans un bloc de glace dure, coupante, aussi transparent qu'un bloc de cristal. Et ce cristal est traversé de lumière, comme si la lumière était prise dans la glace, comme si la glace était lumière. Il nous faut longtemps pour reconnaître que nous pouvons bouger à l'intérieur de ce bloc de glace où nous sommes. Nous remuons nos pieds dans nos souliers, essayons de battre la semelle. Quinze mille femmes tapent du pied et cela ne fait aucun bruit. Le silence est solidifié en froid. La lumière est immobile. Nous sommes dans un milieu où le temps est aboli. Nous ne savons pas si nous sommes, seulement la glace, la lumière, la neige aveuglante, et nous, dans cette glace, dans cette lumière, dans ce silence.

Nous restons immobiles. La matinée s'écoule – du temps en dehors du temps. Et la bordure du damier n'est plus aussi nette. Les rangs se désagrègent. Quelques-unes font des pas, reviennent à leur place. La neige étincelle, immense, sur l'étendue où rien ne fait ombre. Découpés à arêtes vives, les poteaux électriques, les toits des baraques presque enfouis dans la neige, avec les barbelés tracés à la plume. Que veulent-ils faire de nous ?

Le temps s'écoule sans que la lumière change. Elle reste dure, glacée, solide, le ciel aussi bleu, aussi dur. La glace se resserre aux épaules. Elle s'alourdit, nous écrase. Non que nous ayons plus froid, nous devenons de plus en plus inertes, de plus en plus insensibles. Prises dans un bloc de cristal au-delà duquel, loin dans la mémoire, nous voyons les vivants. Viva dit : « Je n'aimerai plus les sports d'hiver. » Bizarre que la neige puisse lui évoquer autre chose qu'un élément mortel, hostile, hors nature, inconnu jusqu'ici.

À nos pieds, une femme s'assoit dans la neige, maladroitement. On se retient de lui dire : « Pas dans la neige, tu vas prendre froid. » C'est encore un réflexe de la mémoire et des notions anciennes. Elle s'assoit dans la neige et s'y creuse une place. Un souvenir de lecture enfantine, les animaux qui font leur couche pour mourir. La femme s'affaire avec des gestes menus et précis, s'allonge. La face dans la neige, elle geint doucement. Ses mains se desserrent. Elle se tait.

Nous avons regardé sans comprendre.

La lumière est toujours immobile, blessante, froide. C'est la lumière d'un astre mort. Et l'immensité glacée, à l'infini éblouissante, est d'une planète morte.

Immobiles dans la glace où nous sommes prises, inertes, insensibles, nous avons perdu tous les sens de la vie. Aucune ne dit : « J'ai faim. J'ai soif. J'ai froid. » Transportées d'un autre monde, nous sommes d'un coup soumises à la respiration d'une autre vie, à la mort vivante, dans la glace, dans la lumière, dans le silence.

Soudain, sur la route qui longe les barbelés, débouche un camion. Il roule dans la neige. Sans bruit. C'est un camion découvert dont on devrait se servir pour transporter des cailloux. Il est chargé de femmes. Elles sont debout, têtes nues. Petites têtes rasées de garçonnets, têtes maigres, serrées les unes contre les autres. Le camion roule en silence avec toutes ces têtes qui s'inscrivent en traits aigus sur le bleu du jour. Un camion silencieux qui glisse le long des barbelés comme un fantôme précis. Une frise de visages sur le ciel.

Les femmes passent près de nous. Elles crient. Elles crient et nous n'entendons rien. Cet air froid et sec devrait être conducteur si nous étions dans le milieu terrestre ordinaire. Elles crient vers nous sans qu'aucun son nous parvienne. Leurs bouches crient, leurs bras tendus vers nous crient, et tout d'elles. Chaque corps est un cri. Autant de torches qui flambent en cris de terreur, de cris qui ont pris corps de femmes. Chacune est un cri matérialisé, un hurlement – qu'on n'entend pas. Le camion roule en silence sur la neige, passe sous un porche, disparaît. Il emporte les cris.

Un autre camion tout pareil au premier, aussi chargé de femmes, qui crient et qu'on n'entend pas, glisse et disparaît à son tour sous le porche. Puis un troisième. Cette fois, c'est nous qui crions, un cri que la glace dans laquelle nous sommes prises ne transmet pas – ou sommes-nous foudroyées là ?

Dans le chargement du camion, des mortes sont mêlées aux vivantes. Les mortes sont nues, entassées. Et les vivantes font des efforts pour éviter le contact des mortes. Mais aux secousses, aux cahots, elles se retiennent à un bras ou à une jambe raides qui passent au-dessus des ridelles. Les vivantes sont contractées de peur. De peur et de répugnance. Elles hurlent. Nous n'entendons rien. Le camion glisse en silence sur la neige.

Nous regardons avec des yeux qui crient, qui ne croient pas.

Chaque visage est écrit avec une telle précision dans la lumière de glace, sur le bleu du ciel, qu'il s'y marque pour l'éternité.

Pour l'éternité, des têtes rasées, pressées les unes contre les autres, qui éclatent de cris, des bouches tordues de cris qu'on n'entend pas, des mains agitées dans un cri muet.

Les hurlements restent écrits sur le bleu du ciel.

C'était le jour où on vidait le block 25. Les condamnées étaient chargées dans les camions qui montaient à la chambre à gaz. Les dernières devaient auparavant charger les cadavres à incinérer, monter à leur tour.

Comme les mortes étaient jetées tout de suite au crématoire, nous nous sommes demandé :

« Celles du dernier camion, les vivantes mélangées aux mortes, est-ce qu'elles passent par la chambre à gaz, ou bien est-ce qu'on déverse directement toute la benne dans le brasier ? »

Elles hurlaient parce qu'elles savaient mais les cordes vocales s'étaient brisées dans leur gorge.

Et nous, nous étions murées dans la glace, dans la lumière, dans le silence.

LE MÊME JOUR

Nous étions statufiées par le froid, sur ce socle de glace qu'étaient nos jambes soudées à la glace du sol. Tous les gestes s'étaient abolis. Se gratter le nez ou souffler dans ses mains relevait du fantastique comme d'un fantôme qui se gratterait le nez ou soufflerait dans ses mains. Quelqu'un dit : « Je crois qu'on nous fait rentrer. » Mais en nous rien ne répond. Nous avions perdu conscience et sensibilité. Nous étions mortes à nous-mêmes. « On nous fait rentrer. Les premiers carrés se mettent en rangs », et l'ordre atteignait tous les carrés. Les rangs se reformaient sur cinq. Les murailles de glace s'élargissaient. Une première colonne gagnait la route.

Nous nous appuyions les unes aux autres pour ne pas tomber. Pourtant, nous ne sentions pas l'effort. Nos corps marchaient en dehors de nous. Possédées, dépossédées. Abstraites. Nous étions insensibles. Nous marchions avec des mouvements rétrécis, juste ce que permettaient

les articulations gelées. Sans parler. On rentre
au camp. Nous n'avions pas prévu d'issue à cette
immobilité qui durait depuis la dernière nuit.

On rentrait. La lumière devenait moins implacable. C'est cela sans doute, le crépuscule. Peut-
être aussi que tout se brouillait à nos yeux et les
barbelés si nets tout à l'heure et la neige étincelante, maintenant tachée de diarrhée. Des flaques sales. La fin de la journée. Des mortes
jonchaient la neige, dans les flaques. Il fallait
quelquefois les enjamber. Elles nous étaient
d'ordinaires obstacles. Il nous était impossible
de ressentir quoi que ce fût encore. Nous marchions. Des automates marchaient. Des statues
de froid marchaient. Des femmes épuisées marchaient.

Nous allions, quand Josée, dans le rang qui
nous précédait, se tournant vers nous, dit :
« Quand vous arriverez à la porte, il faudra courir. Faites passer. » Elle croit que je n'entends
pas et répète : « Il faudra courir. » L'ordre se
transmettait sans éveiller en nous aucune volonté
de l'exécuter, aucune image de nous courant.
Comme si on avait dit : « S'il pleut, ouvrez votre
parapluie. » Aussi saugrenu.

Lorsqu'il se produit une débandade devant
nous, nous savons que nous sommes à la porte.
Toutes se mettent à courir. Elles courent. Les
sabots, les godasses mal assujetties volent de tous

côtés sans qu'elles s'en soucient aucunement. Elles courent. Dans une confusion qui serait du grotesque à une statue de glace, elles courent. Lorsqu'arrive notre tour, lorsque nous arrivons à la porte, nous aussi nous prenons à courir, à courir droit devant nous, décidées sans qu'intervienne notre décision ou notre volonté, à courir jusqu'au bout de notre souffle. Et cela ne nous est plus du tout grotesque. Nous courons. Vers quoi ? Pourquoi ? Nous courons.

Je ne sais pas si j'avais compris qu'il fallait courir parce que, de chaque côté de la porte et le long de la Lagerstrasse, en une double haie, tout ce que le camp comptait de SS en jupes, de prisonnières à brassards ou à blouses de toutes couleurs et de tous grades, tout cela était armé de cannes, de bâtons, de lanières, de ceinturons, de nerfs de bœuf et battait comme au fléau tout ce qui passait entre les deux haies. Éviter un coup de bâton, c'était tomber juste à temps sous une lanière. Les coups pleuvaient sur les têtes, sur les nuques. Et les furies vociféraient : Schneller ! Schneller ! Plus vite, plus vite, en battant du fléau plus vite, toujours plus vite ce grain qui s'écoulait, courait, courait. Je ne sais pas si j'avais compris qu'il fallait courir parce qu'il y allait de la vie. Je courais. Et il ne venait à aucune de ne pas se conformer à l'absurde. Nous courions. Nous courions.

Je ne sais pas si j'ai recomposé, après, toute la scène ou si j'en ai eu tout de suite de moi-même une idée d'ensemble. J'avais pourtant l'impression d'être douée de facultés très aiguës et attentives pour tout voir, tout saisir, tout parer. Je courais.

C'était une course insensée qu'il eût fallu considérer d'un promontoire habituel pour en mesurer tout l'insensé. Il n'était à la portée d'aucune de s'imaginer qu'elle considérait cela de l'extérieur. Nous courions. Schneller. Schneller. Nous courions.

Parvenue au fond du camp et hors d'haleine, j'entends quelqu'un dire : « Au block maintenant. Vite. Rentrez au block. » La première voix humaine qu'on entend au réveil. Je me ressaisis et regarde autour de moi. J'avais perdu mes compagnes. D'autres affluaient à ma suite, se reconnaissaient : « Ah, tu es là ? Et Marie ? Et Gilberte ? »

Je sors de l'hallucination d'où surgissaient les têtes grimaçantes, les têtes de furies congestion-nées, échevelées. Schneller. Schneller. Et la Drexler qui avec la courbe de sa canne croche-tait une de mes voisines. Qui ? Qui était-ce ? Impossible de me souvenir et cependant je voyais son visage, son expression immobilisée net par le col étranglé de derrière, Drexler qui tirait sur la canne, faisant tomber la femme, la jetant de côté. Qui était-ce donc ? Et cette fuite affolée où seul un spectateur du dehors aurait vu la folie, car nous nous étions aussitôt pliées au fantastique et nous avions oublié les réflexes de l'être normal en face de l'extravagant.

« Rentrez au block. Ici. Par ici. » Les premières qui reprennent leurs esprits guident les autres. J'entre dans l'obscurité où les voix me dirigent : « Par ici. Là. Tu y es. Grimpe. » Et je m'accroche aux planches pour grimper sur notre carré.

« Qu'est-ce que tu faisais ? Il ne manquait plus que toi de nous, nous commencions à avoir peur. » Des mains me hissent. « Avec qui étais-tu ? » – « Avec moi, nous étions ensemble », dit Yvonne B. Elle n'avait pas cessé d'être à mon côté, je ne l'avais pas vue.

« Vous avez vu Hélène ?

– Hélène ?

– Oui, elle était par terre, tombée avec Alice Viterbo à qui elle donnait le bras.

– Alice a été prise.

– Hélène voulait l'entraîner, mais Alice ne pouvait plus se relever.

– Alors Hélène l'a laissée. »

Hélène arrivait. « Tu as pu t'échapper ?

– Quelqu'un m'a dégagée et tirée en criant : « Laisse-la. Laisse-la. » Je me suis remise à courir. J'ai dû abandonner Alice. Est-ce qu'on ne peut pas aller la chercher ?

– Non. Il ne faut pas sortir du block. »

Une à une les femmes reviennent. Hébétées. Épuisées. À mesure, nous nous comptons.

« Viva, vous êtes toutes là, votre groupe ?

– Oui. Toutes les huit.

– À côté, vous êtes toutes là ?

– Non. Il manque madame Brabander.

– Qui manque encore ?

– Madame Van der Lee.

– Ici Marie.

– Et grand'mère Yvonne ? »

Nous nommons les âgées, les malades, les faibles.

« Je suis là », répond la voix imperceptible de grand'mère Yvonne.

Nous recomptons. Quatorze manquent.

J'ai vu madame Brabander quand la Drexler l'a arrêtée avec sa canne. Elle a dit à sa fille : « Sauve-toi. Cours. Laisse-moi. »

J'avais couru, couru sans rien voir. J'avais couru, couru sans rien penser, sans savoir qu'il y avait un danger, n'en ayant qu'une notion vague et proche à la fois. Schneller. Schneller. Une fois j'avais regardé ma chaussure, le lacet défait, sans cesser de courir. J'avais couru sans sentir les coups de bâton, de ceinturon qui m'assommaient. Et puis j'avais eu envie de rire.

Ou plutôt non, j'avais vu un double de moi ayant envie de rire. Mon cousin m'affirmait qu'un canard marchait encore le cou tranché. Et ce canard se mettait à courir, à courir, sa tête tombée derrière lui, qu'il ne voyait pas, ce canard courait comme ne court jamais un canard, regardant sa chaussure et se moquant du reste, maintenant, la tête tombée, il ne risquait plus rien.

Nous attendons, espérant encore voir revenir les manquantes. Elles ne reviennent pas. On peut à peine parler d'inquiétude dans notre attente. Nous sommes là dans un naturel second. Et nous pouvons reconstituer.

« Tu comprends, elles ne laissaient passer que les jeunes. Celles qui couraient bien. Toutes les autres ont été prises.

– J'aurais tant voulu entraîner Alice. Je la tenais autant que je pouvais.

– Madame Brabander courait très bien. »

Et une sœur disait à sa sœur : « Si pareille chose arrivait encore, ne t'occupe pas de moi. Sauve-toi. Ne pense qu'à toi. Tu me le promets, n'est-ce pas ? Tu le jures ? »

« Écoute, Hélène, Alice avec sa jambe n'aurait pas résisté de toute façon.

– Ils ont pris beaucoup de Polonaises aussi.

– Avec son visage ridé, elle faisait vieux, madame Brabander. »

Déjà, on parle d'elles au passé.

La petite Brabander, dans sa soupente, a le regard de ceux que rien n'atteindra plus.

Je me demande comment un canard peut courir avec la tête coupée. J'avais les jambes paralysées par le froid.

Qu'est-ce qu'ils vont faire d'elles ?

La chef du block, Magda, une Slovaque, demande le silence et dit quelque chose que Marie-Claude traduit : « Il faut des volontaires. Ce ne sera pas long. Les plus jeunes. » Il paraissait impossible d'obtenir encore le plus petit effort de nos bras, de nos jambes. Pour notre groupe, c'est Cécile qui se lève : « J'y vais », et se chausse. « Il faut y aller, savoir ce qui se passe. »

À son retour, ses dents claquaient. Au sens propre, avec le bruit des castagnettes. Elle était glacée. Et elle pleurait. Nous la frottions pour la réchauffer, pour arrêter ces tremblements qui nous gagnaient et nous l'interrogions comme on interroge un enfant, avec des mots bêtes. « C'était pour ramasser les mortes qui étaient restées dans le champ. Il a fallu les porter devant le block 25. Il y en avait une qui vivait encore, elle suppliait, elle se pendait à nous. Nous voulions l'emporter, quand quelqu'un a crié : « Sauvez-vous, sauvez-vous ! Ne restez pas devant le 25. Taube va arriver et vous y jeter. Sauvez-vous ! » Nos camarades y sont déjà, celles qui ont été prises tout à l'heure. Alors, nous les avons laissées et nous avons couru. La mourante me tenait aux chevilles. »

Toutes les quatorze sont mortes. On a dit qu'Antoinette avait été envoyée aux gaz. Certaines ont tenu très longtemps. Il paraît que madame Van der Lee est devenue folle. La plus longue à mourir a été Alice.

LA JAMBE D'ALICE

Un matin avant l'appel, la petite Simone, qui était allée aux cabinets derrière le block 25, revient toute tremblante : « La jambe d'Alice est là-bas. Venez voir. »

Derrière le block 25, il y avait la morgue, une baraque de planches où l'on entassait les cadavres sortis des révirs. Empilés, ils attendaient le camion qui les emporterait au four crématoire. Les rats les dévoraient. Par l'ouverture sans porte, on pouvait voir l'amoncellement de cadavres nus et les yeux luisants des rats qui apparaissaient et disparaissaient. Quand ils étaient trop, on les empilait dehors.

C'est une meule de cadavres bien rangés comme en une vraie meule dans le clair de lune et la neige, la nuit. Mais nous les regardons sans crainte. Nous savons qu'on atteint là aux limites du supportable et nous nous défendons de céder.

Couchée dans la neige, la jambe d'Alice est

vivante et sensible. Elle a dû se détacher d'Alice morte.

Nous allions exprès voir si elle y était toujours et c'était chaque fois insoutenable. Alice abandonnée qui mourait dans la neige. Alice que nous ne pouvions approcher parce qu'une faiblesse nous clouait là. Alice qui mourait solitaire et n'appelait personne.

Alice était morte depuis des semaines que la jambe artificielle gisait encore sur la neige. Puis il a neigé de nouveau. La jambe a été recouverte. Elle a réapparu dans la boue. Cette jambe dans la boue. La jambe d'Alice – coupée vivante – dans la boue.

Nous l'avons vue longtemps. Un jour elle n'y était plus. Quelqu'un avait dû la prendre pour faire du feu. Une tzigane sûrement, personne autre n'aurait eu le courage.

STÉNIA

Personne ne peut s'endormir ce soir.

Le vent souffle et siffle et gémit. C'est le gémissement qui monte des marais, un sanglot qui gonfle, gonfle et éclate et s'apaise dans un silence de frisson, un autre sanglot qui gonfle, gonfle et éclate et s'éteint.

Personne ne peut s'endormir.

Et dans le silence, entre les sanglots du vent, des râles. Étouffés d'abord, puis distincts, puis forts, si forts que l'oreille qui veut les situer les entend encore quand le vent s'abat.

Personne ne peut s'endormir.

Sténia, la blockhova, ne peut s'endormir. Elle sort de sa chambre, le réduit qui est à l'entrée du block. Sa bougie creuse l'allée obscure entre les cases où nous sommes couchées, étagées. Sténia attend que la tornade se soit abattue, et, dans le silence où les râles s'élèvent, elle crie : « Qui fait du bruit ? Silence ! » Les râles continuent. Sténia crie : « Silence ! » et celle qui agonise n'entend pas. « Silence ! » Les râles emplissent tout le silence entre les vagues de vent, emplissent tout le noir de la nuit.

Sténia élève sa bougie, se dirige vers les râles, identifie celle qui meurt et ordonne qu'on la descende. Les compagnes de la mourante, sous les coups de Sténia, la portent dehors. Elles la couchent le long du mur, aussi doucement que possible, et rentrent se recoucher.

La lumière de Sténia s'éloigne, disparaît. Les rafales de vent et de pluie s'abattent sur la toiture à la fracasser.

Dans la baraque, personne ne peut s'endormir.

Une plaine
couverte de marais
de wagonnets
de cailloux pour les wagonnets
de pelles et de bêches pour les marais
une plaine
couverte d'hommes et de femmes
pour les bêches les wagonnets et les marais
une plaine
de froid et de fièvre
pour des hommes et des femmes
qui luttent
et agonisent

Les marais. La plaine couverte de marais. Les marais à l'infini. La plaine glacée à l'infini.

Nous ne sommes attentives qu'à nos pieds. De marcher en rangs crée une sorte d'obsession. On regarde toujours les pieds qui vont devant soi. Vous avez ces pieds qui avancent, pesamment, avancent devant vous, ces pieds que vous évitez et que vous ne rattrapez jamais, ces pieds qui précèdent toujours les vôtres, toujours, même la nuit dans un cauchemar de piétinement, ces pieds qui vous fascinent à tel point que vous les verriez encore si vous étiez au premier rang, ces pieds qui traînent ou qui butent, qui avancent. Qui avancent avec leur bruit inégal, leur pas déréglé. Et si vous êtes derrière une qui est pieds nus parce qu'on lui a volé ses chaussures, ces pieds qui vont nus dans le verglas ou la boue, ces pieds nus, nus dans la neige, ces pieds torturés que vous voudriez ne plus voir, ces pieds pitoyables que vous craignez de heurter, vous tourmentent jusqu'au malaise. Parfois un sabot quitte un pied, échoue devant vous, vous gêne comme une mouche en été. Vous n'arrêtez pas pour ce sabot que l'autre se baisse pour ramasser. Il faut marcher. Vous marchez. Et vous dépassez la traînarde qui est rejetée hors du rang sur le bas-côté de la route, qui court pour rattraper sa place et ne distingue plus ses compagnes maintenant englouties dans le flot des autres, et du regard cherche leurs pieds, car elle sait les identifier aux godasses. Vous marchez. Vous marchez sur la route lisse comme une patinoire, ou gluante de boue. De boue glaiseuse rouge où les semelles attachent. Vous marchez. Vous marchez vers les marais noyés de brouillard. Vous marchez sans rien voir, les yeux rivés aux pieds qui marchent devant vous. Vous marchez. Vous marchez dans la plaine couverte de marais. Les marais jusqu'à l'horizon. Dans la plaine sans bord, la plaine glacée. Vous marchez.

Nous marchons depuis le jour.

Il y a un moment où le froid tient plus humide aux os, plus cru. Le ciel devient clair. C'est le jour. On dit que c'est le jour.

Nous avions attendu le jour pour partir. Chaque jour nous attendions le jour pour partir. On ne pouvait sortir avant qu'il fît clair, avant que les sentinelles des miradors pussent tirer sur les fuyards. L'idée de fuir ne venait à personne. Il faut être fort pour vouloir s'évader. Il faut savoir compter sur tous ses muscles et sur tous ses sens. Personne ne songeait à fuir.

C'était le jour. Les colonnes se formaient. Nous nous laissions diriger sur n'importe laquelle. Notre seul souci était de n'être pas séparées, aussi nous tenions-nous étroitement l'une à l'autre.

Les colonnes formées, il y avait encore une longue attente. Des milliers de femmes mettent longtemps à sortir, cinq à la fois, comptées au passage. Franchir la porte imprimait un raidissement. Passer sous les yeux de la Drexler, de Taube, sous les yeux de tant de scrutateurs, tous attirés par un col mal fermé, un bouton défait, des mains mal pendantes, un numéro pas assez lisible. Devant la baraque du contrôle, une SS de sa canne touchait la première de chaque rangée et comptait : fünfzehn, zwanzig, jusqu'à cent, jusqu'à deux cents suivant l'importance du commando. Quand celui-ci s'était écoulé, deux SS, qui tenaient chacun un chien en laisse, fermaient la marche. Anneau par anneau, le camp jetait au jour ses entrailles de la nuit.

On tournait à droite ou à gauche. À droite vers les marais. À gauche vers les maisons à démolir, les wagonnets à charger et à pousser. Pendant des semaines, j'ai formé le vœu qu'on tournât à droite parce qu'alors on traversait un ruisseau où je puisais de l'eau pour boire. Pendant des semaines j'ai eu soif. C'était vers les marais que nous allions le plus souvent.

On s'engageait sur la route. La contrainte s'atténuait. On pouvait se donner le bras pour s'aider à marcher, remonter son col, remettre ses mains dans ses manches. La colonne s'étirait sur la route.

Aujourd'hui la route est couverte de gel, polie comme un miroir. On patine sur cette glace. On tombe. La colonne marche. Il y a celles qu'il faut presque porter parce qu'elles ne peuvent plus avancer tant elles ont les jambes enflées. La colonne marche toujours. On atteint un autre tournant, redouté parce que là le vent change. Il souffle en plein visage, coupant, glacé. La proximité des marais se sent au brouillard. On marche dans un brouillard où on ne voit rien. Il n'y a rien à voir. Les marais à l'infini, la plaine noyée de brouillard. La plaine enveloppée d'une ouate glacée.

Nous sommes en route. Attentives seulement aux pieds, nous marchons. Depuis qu'il fait à peine jour, nous marchons.

Nous marchons.

Quand nous ralentissons, les SS en serre-file excitent leurs chiens.

Nous marchons.

Dans la plaine glacée nous marchons.

Au bord du marais, la colonne s'arrête. Chacune des gradées qui commandent le travail compte son lot : Fünfzehn. Zwanzig. Vierzig. Il ne faut pas bouger. Elles comptent encore. Dreissig. Fünfzig. Ne pas bouger. Recomptent. Puis elles nous conduisent à un tas d'outils qui luisent faiblement dans le brouillard. Nous prenons les bêches. Il y a à côté des tragues empilées. Tant pis pour celles qui n'auront pas été assez promptes à se munir d'une bêche.

L'outil à la main, nous descendons dans le marais. Nous nous enfonçons dans le brouillard plus dense du marais. Nous ne voyons rien devant nous. Nous glissons dans des trous, dans des fossés. Les SS hurlent. Assurés sur leurs bottes, ils vont et viennent et font courir. Ils délimitent le carré à travailler. Il faut reprendre à l'entame des bêches de la veille. Sur une ligne dont les extrémités se perdent dans le brouillard, comme autant d'insectes en silhouettes, d'insectes misérables et désarmés, les femmes se mettent en place, se courbent. Tout hurle. Les SS, les anweiserines, les kapos. Il faut planter la bêche dans la glace, attaquer la terre, en tirer des mottes, mettre ces mottes dans la trague que deux posent en bordure du sillon creusé par les bêches. Quand la trague est remplie, elles repartent. Elles marchent douloureusement, les épaules arrachées par la charge. Elles vont vider la trague sur une montagne de mottes qu'elles gravissent en trébuchant, en tombant. Les porteuses font une ronde ininterrompue qui chavire, se rattrape, plie sous le poids, renverse la trague au sommet du tas et revient se placer devant une bêcheuse. Tout au long du parcours, les coups de bâton sur la nuque, les coups de badine sur les tempes, les coups de lanière sur les reins. Les hurlements. Les hurlements. Les hurlements qui hurlent jusqu'aux confins invisibles du marais. Ce ne sont pas les insectes qui hurlent. Les insectes sont muets.

Pour les bêcheuses, les coups viennent de derrière. Elles sont trois furies qui vont et reviennent et frappent tout sur leur passage, sans s'arrêter un instant, criant, criant toujours les mêmes mots, les mêmes injures répétées dans cette langue incompréhensible, frappant à tour de rôle, à tour de bras, de préférence les mêmes, celles qu'elles ont remarquées, celle-ci parce qu'elle est petite et peine trop sur sa bêche, celle-là parce qu'elle est grande et que sa taille les défie, cette autre parce que ses mains saignent d'engelures. Les SS à l'écart ont fait un feu de branches. Ils se chauffent. Leurs chiens se chauffent avec eux. Quand les hurlements atteignent le paroxysme, ils s'en mêlent, hurlent et frappent aussi. Sans savoir. Sans raison. À coups de pied. À coups de poing. Alors il se fait un silence sur le marais, comme si la brume s'épaississait et feutrait le bruit, Puis les hurlements crèvent à nouveau le silence.

Voilà pourquoi nous avons attendu le jour. Nous avons attendu le jour pour commencer la journée.

Quoi est plus près de l'éternité qu'une journée ? Quoi est plus long qu'une journée ? À quoi peut-on savoir qu'elle s'écoule ? Les mottes succèdent aux mottes, le sillon recule, les porteuses continuent leur ronde. Et les hurlements, les hurlements, les hurlements.

Quoi est plus long qu'une journée ? Le temps passe parce que lentement le brouillard se déchire. Les mains se sentent moins gourdes. Le soleil peut-être, loin, vague. Il arrache peu à peu des lambeaux de brouillard. La glace mollit, mollit et fond. Alors les pieds s'enlisent dans la boue, les sabots sont recouverts de vase glacée qui monte jusqu'aux chevilles. On reste immobile dans l'eau bourbeuse, immobile dans l'eau glacée. Pour les porteuses de tragues, le tas de mottes devient plus difficile à gravir, mouillé, glissant.

C'est le jour.

Le marais pâlit d'une clarté nébuleuse et froide avec les rais jaunes du soleil qui percent la brume.

Le marais redevient liquide sous le soleil qui a dissipé maintenant tout le brouillard.

C'est le jour tout à fait.

C'est le jour sur le marais où brillent de grands roseaux dorés.

C'est le jour sur le marais où s'épuisent des insectes aux yeux d'épouvante.

La bêche est de plus en plus lourde.

Les porteuses portent la trague de plus en plus bas.

C'est le jour sur le marais où meurent des insectes à forme humaine.

La trague devient impossible à soulever.

C'est le jour pour jusqu'à la fin du jour.

La faim. La fièvre. La soif.

C'est le jour pour jusqu'au soir.

Les reins sont un bloc de douleur.

C'est le jour pour jusqu'à la nuit.

Les mains glacées, les pieds glacés.

C'est le jour sur le marais où le soleil fait étinceler au loin des formes d'arbres dans leur suaire de givre.

C'est le jour pour toute une éternité.

L'ADIEU

À midi on les avait fait sortir. Au passage, la blockhova leur arrachait leur foulard de tête, leur manteau. Haillons de foulards, haillons de manteaux.

C'était un jour d'hiver sec et froid. Un de ces jours d'hiver où on dit : « Il ferait bon marcher. » Des gens. Ailleurs.

Le sol était couvert de neige durcie.

Dépouillées de leur manteau, beaucoup avaient les bras nus. Elles croisaient les bras et les frictionnaient de leurs mains maigres. Les autres protégeaient leur tête. Aucune n'avait plus d'un centimètre de cheveux, aucune n'était là depuis longtemps. Toutes étaient secouées de tremblements.

La cour était trop petite pour les contenir, mais elles se serraient dans la partie ensoleillée et repoussaient vers l'ombre celles qui agonisaient. Assises dans la neige, elles attendaient. Et à leur regard, on voyait qu'elles ne voyaient rien, rien de ce qui les entourait, rien de la cour, rien des moribondes et des mortes, rien d'elles-mêmes. Elles étaient là, sur la neige, agitées de tremblements qu'elles ne pouvaient réprimer.

Soudain, comme à un signal, elles se mettaient toutes à hurler. Un hurlement qui s'enflait, montait, montait et s'élargissait au-dessus des murs. Ce n'étaient plus que des bouches qui hurlaient, hurlaient au ciel. Un parterre de bouches tordues.

Le hurlement se brisait et dans le silence on entendait les sanglots isolés. Elles s'affaissaient. Abattues, résignées peut-être. Ce n'étaient plus que des yeux creux. Un parterre d'yeux creux.

Bientôt, elles n'en pouvaient plus d'accepter, de se résigner. Un hurlement montait, plus sauvage, montait et se brisait et le silence retombait avec les sanglots et les yeux creux du désespoir.

Dans la bigarrure des haillons et la foule des visages, celles qui ne pleuraient ni ne hurlaient ne tremblaient plus.

Et les hurlements reprenaient.

Rien n'entendait ces appels du bord de l'épouvante. Le monde s'arrêtait loin d'ici. Le monde qui dit : « Il ferait bon marcher. » Seules nos oreilles entendaient et nous n'étions déjà plus des vivants. Nous attendions notre tour.

Un dernier silence dure longtemps. Sont-elles mortes toutes ? Non. Elles sont là. Vaincues et leur conscience refuse encore, refuse, se raidit, veut protester, se débattre. Les hurlements montent à nouveau, montent et enflent et s'élargissent. À nouveau ce ne sont plus que des bouches hurlantes au ciel.

Les silences et les hurlements striaient les heures.

Le soleil se retirait. L'ombre gagnait toute la cour. Il ne restait plus qu'une rangée éclairée de têtes que les derniers rayons du jour accusaient en contours osseux, déformés par les cris.

On entend alors le roulement des camions que les hurlements aussitôt couvrent. Et quand la porte s'ouvre la cour devient trop grande. Toutes se sont levées et se pressent contre le mur opposé et, dans l'espace laissé vide, sur la neige salie, il y a plus de cadavres qu'on n'en avait pu compter.

Deux prisonniers entrent. À leur vue, les hurlements redoublent. C'est le commando du ciel.

Armés de bâtons, ils veulent faire refluer les femmes vers la porte. Elles ne bougent pas. Inertes. Puis elles cèdent. Presque sans qu'ils les bousculent, elles s'approchent.

Le premier camion est arrêté au ras de la porte.

Un prisonnier est debout sur le camion, géant dans une vareuse au col de fourrure relevé, un bonnet d'astrakan sur les oreilles.

(Ceux du commando du ciel ont des privilè-
ges. Ils sont bien vêtus, mangent à leur faim.
Pour trois mois. Le temps écoulé, d'autres les
remplacent qui les expédient, eux. Au ciel. Au
four. Ainsi de trois mois en trois mois. Ce sont
eux qui entretiennent les chambres à gaz et les
cheminées.)

De dos, on voit sur sa vareuse la croix au
minium. Les femmes aussi ont la croix rouge ;
de plus en plus il y a des robes rayées avec,
maintenant.

Les deux autres poussent les femmes vers lui.
Il défait son ceinturon qu'il prend solidement
aux extrémités, le passe sous les bras d'une
femme après l'autre et les charge. Il les lance sur
le plateau du camion. Quand elles reprennent
leurs sens, elles se relèvent. Il y a d'inaltérables
réflexes.

Han. Han. Une autre, une autre. Han. Han.
Une autre.

Il travaille vite, comme un qui sait son travail,
un qui veut faire chaque fois mieux. Le camion
est plein. Pas assez. D'une poussée des reins, il
tasse et tasse puis il continue à charger. Les femmes sont écrasées les unes contre les autres. Elles
ne crient plus, ne tremblent plus.

Quand il ne peut vraiment rien ajouter, il
saute à terre, relève l'arrière, attache les chaînet-
tes. Il donne un dernier coup d'œil à son travail

comme à un travail. À bras le corps, il en attrape encore quelques-unes qu'il jette par-dessus les autres. Les autres les reçoivent sur la tête, sur les épaules. Elles ne crient pas, ne tremblent pas. Le chargement achevé, il monte à côté du chauffeur. Allons ! Le SS met en marche.

Drexler assiste au départ. Les poings aux hanches, elle surveille, en chef qui surveille un travail et qui est content.

Les femmes dans le camion ne crient pas. Trop serrées, elles essaient de dégager les bras ou le torse. Incompréhensible qu'on dégage encore un bras, qu'on veuille encore s'appuyer.

Une tient le buste très en arrière au-dessus des ridelles. Droite. Raidie. Ses yeux étincellent. Elle regarde Drexler avec haine, avec mépris, un mépris qui devrait tuer. Elle n'a pas hurlé avec les autres, son visage n'est creusé que par la maladie.

Le camion démarre. Drexler le suit du regard.

Quand le camion s'éloigne, elle agite la main en adieu et elle rit. Elle rit. Et elle fait longtemps adieu de la main.

C'est la première fois que nous la voyons rire.

Un autre camion s'avance devant la porte du block 25.

Je ne regarde plus.

L'APPEL

Quand il se prolonge, c'est qu'il y a quelque chose. Erreur de compte ou danger. Quelle sorte de danger ? On ne le sait jamais. Un danger.

Un SS s'approche, que nous reconnaissons tout de suite. Le médecin. Aussitôt, les plus fortes se glissent sur le devant, les plus bleues se pincent les joues. Il vient vers nous, nous regarde. Sait-il ce qui nous étreint sous son regard ?

Il passe.

Nous retrouvons notre respiration.

Plus loin, il s'arrête aux rangs des Grecques. Il demande : « Quelles sont les femmes de vingt à trente ans qui ont eu un enfant vivant ? »

Il faut renouveler les cobayes du block d'expériences.

Les Grecques viennent d'arriver.

Nous, nous sommes là depuis trop longtemps. Quelques semaines. Trop maigres ou trop affaiblies pour qu'on nous ouvre le ventre.

La nuit

Les pieuvres nous étreignaient de leurs muscles visqueux et nous ne dégagions un bras que pour être étranglées par un tentacule qui s'enroulait autour du cou, serrait les vertèbres, les serrait à les craquer, les vertèbres, la trachée, l'œsophage, le larynx, le pharynx et tous ces conduits qu'il y a dans le cou, les serrait à les briser. Il fallait libérer la gorge et, pour se délivrer de l'étranglement, céder les bras, les jambes, la taille aux tentacules prenants, envahissants qui se multipliaient sans fin, surgissaient de partout, tant innombrables qu'on était tenté d'abandonner la lutte et cette exténuante vigilance. Les tentacules se déroulaient, déroulaient leur menace. La menace restait un long moment suspendue et nous étions là, hypnotisées, incapables de risquer une esquive en face de la bête qui s'abattait, s'entortillait, collait, broyait. Nous étions près de succomber quand nous avions soudain l'impression de nous éveiller. Ce ne sont pas des pieuvres, c'est la boue. Nous nageons

dans la boue, une boue visqueuse avec les tentacules inépuisables de ses vagues. C'est une mer
de boue dans laquelle nous devons nager, nager
à force, nager à épuisement et nous essouffler à
garder la tête au-dessus des tourbillons de fange.
Nous sommes contractées de dégoût, la boue
entre dans les yeux, dans le nez, dans la bouche,
suffoque et nous battons des bras pour essayer
de reprendre aplomb dans cette boue qui nous
enveloppe de ses bras de pieuvre. Et ce serait
peu de nager dans la boue si nous n'étions obligées de porter des tragues remplies de mottes
de terre, si pesantes que la charge entraîne irré-
médiablement au fond, voilà pourquoi la boue
entre dans la gorge et dans les oreilles, gluante,
glacée. Maintenir cette trague au-dessus de la
tête coûte un effort surhumain et la camarade à
l'avant s'enfonce, disparaît, s'engloutit dans la
boue. Il faut la tirer, la remettre à flot de la boue,
lâcher la trague, impossible de s'en débarrasser,
elle est enchaînée à nos poignets, si solidement,
si serrée que nous coulons toutes deux dans un
corps à corps mortel, liées l'une à l'autre par la
trague d'où les mottes versent, se confondant
avec la boue que nous brassons dans une ultime
tentative pour nous dégager et la trague est
maintenant remplie d'yeux et de dents, d'yeux
qui luisent, de dents qui ricanent et éclairent la
boue comme des madrépores phosphorescents

une eau épaisse, et tous ces yeux et toutes ces dents flamboient et vocifèrent, dardant, mordant, dardant et mordant de toutes parts et hurlant : Schneller, schneller, weiter, weiter, et, quand nous donnons des coups de poing dans ces gueules toutes en dents et en yeux, les poings ne rencontrent que taies molles, éponges pourries. Nous voulons nous sauver, nager hors de cette vase. Le bourbier est plein comme pleine la piscine un midi d'été et nous nous heurtons partout à des masses fuyantes et huileuses qui empêchent toute retraite, et les épaules roulent, se retournent, bousculent d'autres épaules. C'est un enchevêtrement de corps, une mêlée de bras et de jambes et, quand enfin nous croyons atteindre à quelque chose de solide, c'est que nous cognons contre les planches où nous dormons et tout s'évanouit dans l'ombre où bougent cette jambe qui est celle de Lulu, ce bras qui est d'Yvonne, cette tête sur ma poitrine qui m'oppresse, c'est la tête de Viva et, réveillée par la sensation que je suis au bord du vide, au bord du carré, au bord de tomber dans l'allée, je retombe dans un autre cauchemar, car cette grotte d'ombre respirait toute, respirait et soufflait, agitée dans tous ses replis par mille sommeils douloureux et plus de cauchemars. De l'ombre se détache une ombre qui glisse, glisse à terre dans la boue et court vers la porte de la caverne et cette ombre en éveille d'autres qui glissent et courent et trouvent mal leur chemin dans la nuit, tâtent et hésitent, se frôlent, se parlent des paroles sans aucun sens : « Où sont mes chaussures ? C'est toi ? La dysenterie, c'est la troisième fois que je sors. » D'autres ombres reviennent, cherchent leur place des mains, la place de leur tête au toucher d'une tête et de tous les étagements les cauchemars se lèvent, prennent forme dans l'ombre, de tous les étagements montent les plaintes et les gémissements des corps meurtris qui luttent contre la boue, contre les faces d'hyènes hurlantes : Weiter, weiter, car ces hyènes hurlent ces mots-là et il n'y a plus que la ressource de se blottir sur soi-même et essayer de susciter un cauchemar supportable, peut-être celui où l'on rentre à la maison, où l'on revient et où l'on dit : C'est moi, me voilà, je reviens, vous voyez, mais tous les membres de la famille qu'on croyait torturés d'inquiétude se tournent vers le mur, deviennent muets, étrangers d'indifférence. On dit encore : c'est moi, je suis ici, je sais maintenant que c'est vrai, que je ne rêve pas, j'ai si souvent rêvé que je revenais et c'était affreux au réveil, cette fois c'est vrai, c'est vrai puisque je suis dans la cuisine, que je touche l'évier. Tu vois, maman, c'est moi, et le froid de la pierre à évier me tire du sommeil. C'est une brique éboulée de la murette qui

sépare le carré du carré voisin où d'autres larves
dorment et gémissent et rêvent sous les couvertures qui les recouvrent – ce sont des linceuls
qui les recouvrent car elles sont mortes,
aujourd'hui ou demain c'est pareil, elles sont
mortes pour le retour dans la cuisine où leur
mère les attend et nous nous sentons basculer
dans un trou d'ombre, un trou sans fin – c'est
le trou de la nuit ou un autre cauchemar, ou
notre vraie mort, et nous nous débattons furieu-
sement, nous nous débattons. Il faut rentrer,
rentrer à la maison, rentrer pour toucher de nos
mains la pierre à évier et nous luttons contre le
vertige qui nous attire au fond du trou de la nuit
ou de la mort, nous tendons une dernière fois
notre énergie dans un effort désespéré, et nous
nous retenons à la brique, la brique froide que
nous portons contre notre cœur, la brique que
nous avons arrachée à un tas de briques cimen-
tées par la glace, en cassant la glace avec nos
ongles, vite vite les bâtons et les lanières volent
– vite plus vite les ongles saignent – et cette
brique froide contre notre cœur nous la portons
à un autre tas, dans un cortège morne où chacune a une brique sur le cœur, car c'est ainsi
qu'on transporte les briques ici, une brique
après l'autre, du matin au soir, d'un tas de briques à un autre tas de briques, du matin au soir,
et ce n'est pas assez de porter les briques tout

le jour au chantier, nous les portons encore pendant la nuit, car la nuit tout nous poursuit à la
fois, la boue du marais où on s'enlise, les briques
froides qu'il faut porter contre son cœur, les
kapos qui hurlent et les chiens qui eux marchent
sur la boue comme sur la terre ferme et nous
mordent à un signe des yeux flamboyants de
l'ombre et nous avons le souffle chaud et humide
du chien sur le visage et à nos tempes perle la
peur. Et la nuit est plus épuisante que le jour,
peuplée de toux et de râles avec celles qui agonisent solitaires, pressées contre les autres qui
sont aux prises avec la boue, les chiens, les briques et les hurlements, celles que nous trouve-
rons mortes à notre réveil, que nous transporte-
rons dans la boue devant la porte, que nous
laisserons là, roulées dans la couverture où elles
ont rendu la vie. Et chaque morte est aussi légère
et aussi lourde que les ombres de la nuit, légère
tant elle est décharnée et lourde d'une somme
de souffrances que personne ne partagera jamais.

Et quand le sifflet siffle le réveil, ce n'est pas
que la nuit s'achève

car la nuit ne s'achève qu'avec les étoiles qui
se décolorent et le ciel qui se colore,

ce n'est pas que la nuit s'achève

car la nuit ne s'achève qu'avec le jour,

quand le sifflet siffle le réveil il y a tout un

détroit d'éternité à traverser entre la nuit et le jour.

Quand le sifflet siffle le réveil c'est un cauchemar qui se fige, un autre cauchemar qui commence

il n'y a qu'un moment de lucidité entre les deux, celui où nous écoutons les battements de notre cœur en écoutant s'il a la force de battre longtemps encore

longtemps c'est-à-dire des jours parce que notre cœur ne peut compter en semaines ni en mois, nous comptons en jours et chaque jour compte mille agonies et mille éternités.

Le sifflet siffle dans le camp, une voix crie : « Zell Appell » et nous entendons : « C'est l'appel », et une autre voix : « Aufstehen », et ce n'est pas la fin de la nuit

ce n'est pas la fin de la nuit pour celles qui délirent dans les révirs

ce n'est pas la fin de la nuit pour les rats qui attaquent leurs lèvres encore vivantes

ce n'est pas la fin de la nuit pour les étoiles glacées au ciel glacé

ce n'est pas la fin de la nuit

c'est l'heure où des ombres rentrent dans les murs, où d'autres ombres sortent dans la nuit

ce n'est pas la fin de la nuit

c'est la fin de mille nuits et de mille cauchemars.

Jusqu'à cinquante

L'homme s'agenouille. Croise les bras. Baisse la tête. Le kapo s'avance. Il a son bâton. S'approche de l'homme agenouillé et s'assure bien sur ses jambes.

Le SS s'approche avec le chien.

Le kapo lève le bâton qu'il tient des deux mains, assène un coup sur les reins. Eins.

Un autre. Zwei.

Un autre. Drei.

C'est l'homme qui compte. Dans l'intervalle des coups, on l'entend.

Vier.

Fünf. Sa voix faiblit.

Sechs.

Sieben.

Acht. Nous ne l'entendons plus. Mais il compte toujours. Il faut qu'il compte jusqu'à cinquante.

À chaque coup, son corps fléchit un peu plus. Le kapo est grand, il frappe de sa hauteur, de sa force.

À chaque coup, le chien jappe, veut sauter. Sa gueule suit la trajectoire du bâton.

« Weiter », nous crie l'anweiserine parce que nous sommes immobiles sur nos bêches.

« Weiter. » Nos bras sont retombés.

Cet homme qu'on bat avec le bruit d'un tapis qu'on bat.

Il compte toujours. Le SS écoute s'il compte.

C'est interminable, cinquante coups de bâton sur le dos d'un homme.

Nous comptons. Qu'il compte, lui aussi ! Qu'il continue à compter !

Sa tête touche le sol. Chaque coup donne à son corps un sursaut qui le disloque. Chaque coup nous fait sursauter.

C'est interminable, le bruit de cinquante coups de bâton sur le dos d'un homme.

S'il s'arrêtait de compter, les coups s'arrêteraient et recommenceraient de zéro.

C'est interminable et cela résonne, cinquante coups de bâton sur le dos d'un homme.

LA TULIPE

Au loin se dessine une maison. Sous les rafales, elle fait penser à un bateau, en hiver. Un bateau à l'ancre dans un port nordique. Un bateau à l'horizon gris.

Nous allions la tête baissée sous les rafales de neige fondue qui cinglaient au visage, piquaient comme grêle. À chaque rafale, nous redoutions la suivante et courbions davantage la tête. La rafale s'abattait, giflait, lacérait. Une poignée de gros sel lancée à toute violence en pleine figure. Nous avancions, poussant devant nous une falaise de vent et de neige.

Où allions-nous ?

C'était une direction que nous n'avions jamais prise. Nous avions tourné avant le ruisseau. La route en remblai longeait un lac. Un grand lac gelé.

Vers quoi allions-nous ? Que pouvions-nous faire par là ? La question que nous posait l'aube à chaque aube. Quel travail nous attend ? Marais, wagonnets, briques, sable. Nous ne pouvions penser ces mots-là sans que le cœur nous manquât.

Nous marchions. Nous interrogions le paysage. Un lac gelé couleur d'acier. Un paysage qui ne répond pas.

La route s'écarte du lac. Le mur de vent et de neige se déplace de côté. C'est là qu'apparaît la maison. Nous marchons moins durement. Nous allons vers une maison.

Elle est au bord de la route. En briques rouges. La cheminée fume. Qui peut habiter cette maison perdue ? Elle se rapproche. On voit des rideaux blancs. Des rideaux de mousseline. Nous disons « mousseline » avec du doux dans la bouche. Et, devant les rideaux, dans l'entredeux des doubles fenêtres, il y a une tulipe.

Les yeux brillent comme à une apparition. « Vous avez vu ? Vous avez vu ? Une tulipe. » Tous les regards se portent sur la fleur. Ici, dans le désert de glace et de neige, une tulipe. Rose entre deux feuilles pâles. Nous la regardons. Nous oublions la grêle qui cingle. La colonne ralentit. « Weiter », crie le SS. Nos têtes sont encore tournées vers la maison que nous l'avons depuis longtemps dépassée.

Tout le jour nous rêvons à la tulipe. La neige fondue tombait, collait au dos notre veste trempée et raidie. La journée était longue, aussi longue que toutes les journées. Au fond du fossé que nous creusions, la tulipe fleurissait dans sa corolle délicate.

Au retour, bien avant d'arriver à la maison du lac, nos yeux la guettaient. Elle était là, sur le fond des rideaux blancs. Coupe rose entre les feuilles pâles. Et pendant l'appel, à des camarades qui n'étaient pas avec nous, nous disions : « Nous avons vu une tulipe. »

Nous ne sommes plus retournées à ce fossé. D'autres ont dû l'achever. Le matin, au croisement d'où partait la route du lac, nous avions un moment d'espoir.

Quand nous avons appris que c'était la maison du SS qui commandait la pêcherie, nous avons haï notre souvenir et cette tendresse qu'ils n'avaient pas encore séchée en nous.

LE MATIN

Du bord de l'obscurité une voix criait « Aufstehen ». De l'obscurité une voix en écho criait
« Stavache », et il y avait un remuement noir d'où
chacune tirait ses membres. Nous n'avions qu'à
trouver nos chaussures pour sauter en bas. Sur
celles qui ne surgissaient pas assez vite des couvertures, la lanière sifflait et cinglait. La lanière,
à la main de la stubhova debout dans l'allée,
volait jusqu'au troisième étage, volait jusqu'au
milieu des carrés, fouettait les visages, les jambes
endolories de sommeil. Quand tout remuait et
bougeait, quand les couvertures partout se se-
couaient et se pliaient, on entendait un bruit de
métal qui s'entrechoque, la vapeur brouillait le
clignotement de la bougie au centre de l'obscurité, on découvrait les bidons pour servir le thé.
Et celles qui venaient d'entrer s'appuyaient au
mur, la respiration accélérée, aidant leur cœur
de la main sur la poitrine. Elles revenaient des
cuisines qui étaient loin, loin quand on porte un
bidon énorme dont les poignées tranchent les

paumes. Loin dans la neige, dans le verglas ou dans la boue où on avance de trois pas, reculant de deux, avançant et reculant, tombant et se relevant et retombant sous la charge trop lourde à des bras sans force. Lorsqu'elles ont repris haleine, elles disent : « Il fait froid ce matin, plus froid que cette nuit. » Elles disent « ce matin ». Il est pleine nuit, passé trois heures à peine.

Le thé fume en odeur écœurante. Les stubhovas le servent chichement à nos soifs de fièvre. Elles en gardent la plus grande part pour leur toilette. C'est la meilleure utilisation qu'on en puisse faire, certes, et le désir nous vient de nous laver nous aussi dans une bonne eau chaude. Nous ne nous sommes pas lavées depuis notre arrivée, pas même les mains à l'eau froide. Nous prenons le thé dans nos gamelles qui sentent la soupe de la veille. Il n'y a pas d'eau pour les gamelles non plus. Prendre son thé, c'est l'emporter de haute lutte, dans une mêlée de coups de bâton, de coups de coude, de coups de poing, de hurlements. Dévorées par la soif et la fièvre, nous tourbillonnons dans la mêlée. Nous buvons debout, bousculées par celles qui craignent de n'être pas servies et par celles qui veulent sortir, parce qu'elles doivent sortir tout de suite, dès qu'elles sont debout il faut qu'elles sortent tout de suite. Le sifflet siffle le dernier coup. Alles raus.

La porte est ouverte aux étoiles. Chaque matin il n'a jamais fait aussi froid. Chaque matin on a l'impression que si on l'a supporté jusqu'ici, maintenant c'est trop, on ne peut plus. Au seuil des étoiles on hésite, on voudrait reculer. Alors les bâtons, les lanières et les hurlements se déchaînent. Les premières près de la porte sont projetées dans le froid. Du fond du block, sous les bâtons, une poussée projette tout le monde dans le froid.

Dehors, c'est la terre à découvert, des tas de pierres, des tas de terre, autant d'obstacles à contourner, des fossés à éviter, avec le verglas, la boue ou la neige et les excréments de la nuit. Dehors, le froid saisit, saisit jusqu'aux os. Nous sommes transpercées de froid. En lames glacées. Dehors, la nuit est claire de froid. Les ombres de lune sont bleues sur le verglas ou sur la neige.

C'est l'appel. Tous les blocks rendent leurs ombres. Avec des mouvements gourds de froid et de fatigue une foule titube vers la Lagerstrasse. La foule s'ordonne par rangs de cinq dans une confusion de cris et de coups. Il faut longtemps pour que se rangent toutes ces ombres qui perdent pied dans le verglas, dans la boue ou dans la neige, toutes ces ombres qui se cherchent et se rapprochent pour être au vent glacé de moindre prise possible.

Puis le silence s'établit.

Le cou dans les épaules, le thorax rentré, chacune met ses mains sous les bras de celle qui est
devant elle. Au premier rang, elles ne peuvent
le faire, on les relaie. Dos contre poitrine, nous
nous tenons serrées, et tout en établissant ainsi
pour toutes une même circulation, un même
réseau sanguin, nous sommes toutes glacées.
Anéanties par le froid. Les pieds, qui restent
extrémités lointaines et séparées, cessent d'exister. Les godasses étaient encore mouillées de la
neige ou de la boue d'hier, de tous les hiers.
Elles ne sèchent jamais.

Il faudra rester des heures immobiles dans le
froid et dans le vent. Nous ne parlons pas. Les
paroles glacent sur nos lèvres. Le froid frappe
de stupeur tout un peuple de femmes qui restent
debout immobiles. Dans la nuit. Dans le froid.
Dans le vent.

Nous restons debout immobiles et l'admirable
est que nous restions debout. Pourquoi ? Personne ne pense « à quoi bon » ou bien ne le dit
pas. À la limite de nos forces, nous restons
debout.

Je suis debout au milieu de mes camarades et
je pense que si un jour je reviens et si je veux
expliquer cet inexplicable, je dirai : « Je me
disais : il faut que tu tiennes, il faut que tu tiennes debout pendant tout l'appel. Il faut que tu
tiennes aujourd'hui encore. C'est parce que tu

auras tenu aujourd'hui encore que tu reviendras si un jour tu reviens. » Et ce sera faux. Je ne me disais rien. Je ne pensais rien. La volonté de résister était sans doute dans un ressort beaucoup plus enfoui et secret qui s'est brisé depuis, je ne saurais jamais. Et si les mortes avaient exigé de celles qui reviendraient qu'elles rendissent des comptes, elles en seraient incapables. Je ne pensais rien. Je ne regardais rien. Je ne ressentais rien. J'étais un squelette de froid avec le froid qui souffle dans tous ces gouffres que font les côtes à un squelette.

Je suis debout au milieu de mes camarades. Je ne regarde pas les étoiles. Elles sont coupantes de froid. Je ne regarde pas les barbelés éclairés blanc dans la nuit. Ce sont des griffes de froid. Je ne regarde rien. Je vois ma mère avec ce masque de volonté durcie qu'est devenu son visage. Ma mère. Loin. Je ne regarde rien. Je ne pense rien.

Chaque bouffée aspirée est si froide qu'elle met à vif tout le circuit respiratoire. Le froid nous dévêt. La peau cesse d'être cette enveloppe protectrice bien fermée qu'elle est au corps, même au chaud du ventre. Les poumons claquent dans le vent de glace. Du linge sur une corde. Le cœur est rétréci de froid, contracté, contracté à faire mal, et soudain je sens quelque chose qui casse, là, à mon cœur. Mon cœur se décroche de sa poitrine et de tout ce qui l'entoure et le cale en place. Je sens une pierre qui tombe à l'intérieur de moi, tombe d'un coup. C'est mon cœur. Et un merveilleux bien-être m'envahit. Comme on est bien, débarrassé de ce cœur fragile et exigeant. On se détend dans une légèreté qui doit être celle du bonheur. Tout fond en moi, tout prend la fluidité du bonheur. Je m'abandonne et c'est doux de s'abandonner à la mort, plus doux qu'à l'amour et de savoir que c'est fini, fini de souffrir et de lutter, fini de demander l'impossible à ce cœur qui n'en peut plus. Le vertige dure moins qu'un éclair, assez pour toucher un bonheur qu'on ne savait pas exister.

Et quand je reviens à moi, c'est au choc des gifles que m'applique Viva sur les joues, de toute sa force, en serrant la bouche, en détournant les yeux. Viva est forte. Elle ne s'évanouit pas à l'appel. Moi, tous les matins. C'est un moment de bonheur indicible. Viva ne devra jamais le savoir.

Elle dit et dit encore mon nom qui m'arrive lointain du fond du vide – c'est la voix de ma mère que j'entends. La voix se fait dure : « Du cran. Debout. » Et je sens que je tiens après Viva autant que l'enfant après sa mère. Je suis suspendue à elle qui m'a retenue de tomber dans la boue, dans la neige d'où on ne se relève pas.

Et il me faut lutter pour choisir entre cette conscience qui est souffrance et cet abandon qui était bonheur, et je choisis parce que Viva me dit : « Du cran. Debout. » Je ne discute pas son ordre, pourtant j'ai envie de céder une fois, une fois puisque ce sera la seule. C'est si facile de mourir ici. Seulement laisser aller son cœur.

Je reprends possession de moi, je reprends possession de mon corps comme d'un vêtement qu'on endosse froid de mouillé, de mon pouls qui revient et qui bat, de mes lèvres brûlées de froid avec les commissures qui s'arrachent. Je reprends possession de l'angoisse qui m'habite et de mon espoir que je violente.

Viva a quitté sa voix dure et demande : « Tu es mieux ? » et sa voix est si réconfortante de tendresse que je réponds : « Oui, Viva. Je suis mieux. » Ce sont mes lèvres qui répondent en se déchirant un peu davantage aux gerçures de fièvre et de froid.

Je suis au milieu de mes camarades. Je reprends place dans la pauvre commune chaleur que crée notre contact et, puisqu'il faut revenir à soi tout à fait, je reviens à l'appel et je pense : C'est l'appel du matin – quel titre poétique ce serait –, c'est l'appel du matin. Je ne savais plus si c'était le matin ou le soir.

C'est l'appel du matin. Le ciel se colore lentement à l'est. Une gerbe de flammes s'y répand, des flammes glacées, et l'ombre qui noie nos ombres se dissout peu à peu et de ces ombres se modèlent les visages. Tous ces visages sont violacés et livides, s'accentuent en violacé et en livide à proportion de la clarté qui gagne le ciel et on distingue maintenant ceux que la mort a touchés cette nuit, qu'elle enlèvera ce soir. Car la mort se peint sur le visage, s'y plaque implacablement et il n'est pas besoin que nos regards se rencontrent pour que nous comprenions toutes en regardant Suzanne Rose qu'elle va mourir, en regardant Mounette qu'elle va mourir. La mort est marquée à la peau collée aux pommettes, à la peau collée aux orbites, à la peau collée aux maxillaires. Et nous savons qu'il ne servirait de rien à présent d'évoquer leur maison ou leur fils ou leur mère. Il est trop tard. Nous ne pouvons plus rien pour elles.

L'ombre se dissout un peu plus. Les aboiements des chiens se rapprochent. Ce sont les SS qui arrivent. Les blockhovas crient « Silence ! » dans leurs langues impossibles. Le froid mord aux mains qui sortent de sous les bras. Quinze mille femmes se mettent au garde-à-vous.

Les SS passent – grandes dans la pèlerine noire, les bottes, le haut capuchon noir. Elles passent et comptent. Et cela dure longtemps.

Quand elles sont passées, chacune remet ses mains aux creux des aisselles de l'autre, les toux jusque-là contenues s'exhalent et les blockhovas crient « Silence ! » aux toux dans leurs langues impossibles. Il faut attendre encore, attendre le jour.

L'ombre se dissout. Le ciel s'embrase. On voit maintenant passer d'hallucinants cortèges. La petite Rolande demande : « Laissez-moi me mettre au premier rang, je veux voir. » Elle dira plus tard : « J'étais sûre de la reconnaître, elle avait les pieds déformés, j'étais sûre de la reconnaître à ses pieds. » Sa mère était partie au révir quelques jours auparavant. Chaque matin elle guettait pour se rappeler quel jour sa mère serait morte.

Il passe d'hallucinants cortèges. Ce sont les mortes de la nuit qu'on sort des révirs pour les porter à la morgue. Elles sont nues sur un brancard de branches grossièrement assemblées, un brancard trop court. Les jambes – les tibias – pendent avec les pieds au bout, maigres et nus. La tête pend de l'autre côté, osseuse et rasée. Une couverture en loques est jetée au milieu. Quatre prisonnières tiennent chacune une poignée du brancard et c'est vrai qu'on s'en va les pieds devant, c'était toujours dans ce sens-là qu'elles les portaient. Elles marchent péniblement dans la neige ou dans la boue, vont jeter le cadavre sur le tas près du 25, reviennent la civière vide à peine moins lourde et passent de nouveau avec un autre cadavre. C'est tous les jours leur travail de tout le jour.

Je les regarde passer et je me raidis. Tout à l'heure je cédais à la mort. À chaque aube, la tentation. Quand passe la civière, je me raidis. Je veux mourir mais pas passer sur la petite civière. Pas passer sur la petite civière avec les jambes qui pendent et la tête qui pend, nue sous la couverture en loques. Je ne veux pas passer sur la petite civière.

La mort me rassure : je ne le sentirais pas. « Tu n'as pas peur du crématoire, alors pourquoi ? » Qu'elle est fraternelle, la mort. Ceux qui l'ont peinte avec une face hideuse ne l'avaient jamais vue. La répugnance l'emporte. Je ne veux pas passer sur la petite civière.

Alors je sais que toutes celles qui passent passent pour moi, que toutes celles qui meurent meurent pour moi. Je les regarde passer et je dis non. Se laisser glisser dans la mort, ici dans la neige. Laisse-toi glisser. Non, parce qu'il y a la petite civière. Il y a la petite civière. Je ne veux pas passer sur la petite civière.

L'ombre se dissout tout à fait. Il fait plus froid. J'entends mon cœur et je lui parle comme Arnolphe à son cœur. Je lui parle.

Quand viendra le jour où cessera cette commande à un cœur, à des poumons, à des muscles ? Le jour où finira cette solidarité obligée du cerveau, des nerfs, des os et de tous ces organes qu'on a dans le ventre ? Quand viendra le jour où nous ne nous connaîtrons plus, mon cœur et moi ?

Le rouge du ciel s'éteint et tout le ciel blêmit et au loin du ciel blême apparaissent les corbeaux qui fondent noirs sur le camp, en vols épais. Nous attendons la fin de l'appel.

Nous attendons la fin de l'appel pour partir au travail.

WEITER

Les SS aux quatre coins marquaient les limites qu'il ne fallait pas franchir. C'était un grand chantier. Tout s'y trouvait rassemblé de ce qui nous hantait la nuit : cailloux à casser, route à empierrer, sable à extraire, tragues pour transporter cailloux et sable, fossés à creuser, briques à porter d'un tas à l'autre. Réparties dans différentes équipes avec des Polonaises, quand nous nous croisions nous échangions un sourire triste.

Depuis que le soleil brillait, il faisait moins froid. À la pause de midi nous nous étions assises sur des matériaux pour manger. La soupe avalée – il n'y fallait que quelques minutes, le plus long était la distribution, l'attente en rangs devant le bidon –, il nous restait un peu de temps avant de retourner aux cailloux, au sable, à la route, au fossé et aux briques. Nous tuions des poux à l'échancrure de nos robes. C'est là qu'ils se mettent le plus. En tuer, sur la quantité, n'y changeait guère. C'était notre récréation. Morne.

La détente du midi quand nous pouvions nous asseoir parce qu'il faisait beau.

Rassemblées par petits groupes d'amies, nous parlions. Chacune disait sa province, sa maison, invitait les autres à lui faire visite. Vous viendrez, n'est-ce pas ? Vous viendrez. Nous promettions. Que de voyages nous avons faits.

« Weiter. » Le cri rompt le bercement de nos rêves.

« Weiter. » À qui s'adresse-t-il ?

« Weiter. »

Une femme se dirige vers le ruisseau, sa gamelle à la main, sans doute pour la laver. Elle s'arrête, indécise.

« Weiter. » Est-ce à elle ?

« Weiter. » Dans la voix du SS, il y a comme une moquerie.

La femme hésite. Doit-elle vraiment aller plus loin ? N'est-il pas permis de se pencher sur le ruisseau à cet endroit ?

« Weiter », ordonne le SS, plus impérieux.

La femme s'éloigne, s'arrête de nouveau. Debout sur le fond du marais, tout d'elle interroge : « Ici, est-ce permis ? »

« Weiter », hurle le SS.

Alors la femme marche. Elle remonte le cours du ruisseau.

« Weiter. »

Un coup de feu. La femme s'écroule.

Le SS remet l'arme en bandoulière, siffle son chien, va vers la femme. Penché sur elle, il la retourne comme on fait d'un gibier.

Les autres SS de leur place rient.

Elle avait dépassé la limite de vingt pas à peine.

Nous nous comptons. Sommes-nous bien là, toutes ?

Quand le SS a épaulé et visé, la femme marchait dans le soleil.

Elle a été tuée net.

C'était une Polonaise.

Certaines n'ont rien vu et questionnent. Les autres se demandent si elles ont vu et ne disent rien.

LA SOIF

La soif, c'est le récit des explorateurs, vous savez, dans les livres de notre enfance. C'est dans le désert. Ceux qui voient des mirages et marchent vers l'insaisissable oasis. Ils ont soif trois jours. Le chapitre pathétique du livre. À la fin du chapitre, la caravane du ravitaillement arrive, elle s'était égarée sur les pistes brouillées par la tempête. Les explorateurs crèvent les outres, ils boivent. Ils boivent et ils n'ont plus soif. C'est la soif du soleil, du vent chaud. Le désert. Un palmier en filigrane sur le sable roux.

Mais la soif du marais est plus brûlante que celle du désert. La soif du marais dure des semaines. Les outres ne viennent jamais. La raison chancelle. La raison est terrassée par la soif. La raison résiste à tout, elle cède à la soif. Dans le marais, pas de mirage, pas l'espoir d'oasis. De la boue, de la boue. De la boue et pas d'eau.

Il y a la soif du matin et la soif du soir.

Il y a la soif du jour et la soif de la nuit.

Le matin au réveil, les lèvres parlent et aucun

son ne sort des lèvres. L'angoisse s'empare de tout votre être, une angoisse aussi fulgurante que celle du rêve. Est-ce cela, d'être mort ? Les lèvres essaient de parler, la bouche est paralysée. La bouche ne forme pas de paroles quand elle est sèche, qu'elle n'a plus de salive. Et le regard part à la dérive, c'est le regard de la folie. Les autres disent : « Elle est folle, elle est devenue folle pendant la nuit », et elles font appel aux mots qui doivent réveiller la raison. Il faudrait leur expliquer. Les lèvres s'y refusent. Les muscles de la bouche veulent tenter les mouvements de l'articulation et n'articulent pas. Et c'est le désespoir de l'impuissance à leur dire l'angoisse qui m'a étreinte, l'impression d'être morte et de le savoir.

Dès que j'entends leur bruit, je cours aux bidons de tisane. Ce ne sont pas les outres de la caravane. Des litres et des litres de tisane, mais divisés en petites portions, une pour chacune, et toutes boivent encore que j'ai déjà bu. Ma bouche n'est pas même humectée et toujours les paroles se refusent. Les joues collent aux dents, la langue est dure, raide, les mâchoires bloquées, et toujours cette impression d'être morte, d'être morte et de le savoir. Et l'épouvante grandit dans les yeux. Je sens grandir l'épouvante dans mes yeux jusqu'à la démence. Tout sombre, tout échappe. La raison n'exerce plus de contrôle. La soif. Est-ce que je respire ? J'ai soif. Faut-il sortir pour l'appel ? Je me perds dans la foule, je ne sais où je vais. J'ai soif. Fait-il plus froid ou moins froid, je ne le sens pas. J'ai soif, soif à crier. Et le doigt que je passe sur mes gencives éprouve le sec de ma bouche. Ma volonté s'effondre. Reste une idée fixe : boire.

Et si la blockhova m'envoie porter son livre, quand je trouve dans son réduit la bassine de tisane savonneuse dans laquelle elle s'est lavée, mon premier mouvement est d'écarter la mousse sale, de m'agenouiller près de la bassine et d'y boire à la manière d'un chien qui lape d'une langue souple. Je recule. De la tisane de savon où elles ont lavé leurs pieds. Au bord de la déraison, je mesure à quel point la soif me fait perdre le sens.

Je reviens à l'appel. Et à l'idée fixe. Boire. Pourvu que nous prenions la route à droite. Il y a un ruisseau au petit pont. Boire. Mes yeux ne voient rien, rien que le ruisseau, le ruisseau loin, dont tout l'appel me sépare et l'appel est plus long à traverser qu'un sahara. La colonne se forme pour partir. Boire. Je me place à l'extérieur du rang du côté où la berge est le plus accessible.

Le ruisseau. Longtemps avant d'y arriver, je suis prête à bondir comme un animal. Longtemps avant que le ruisseau soit en vue, j'ai ma gamelle à la main. Et quand le ruisseau est là, il faut quitter le rang, courir en avant, descendre sur la berge glissante. Il est quelquefois gelé, vite casser la glace, heureusement le froid diminue, elle n'est pas épaisse, vite casser la glace du rebord de la gamelle, prendre de l'eau et gravir la berge glissante, courir pour regagner ma place, les yeux avides sur l'eau qui verse si je vais trop vite. Le SS accourt. Il crie. Son chien court devant lui, m'atteint presque. Les camarades me happent et le rang m'engloutit. Les yeux avides sur l'eau qui bouge à mon pas je ne vois pas l'inquiétude sur leur visage, l'inquiétude que je leur ai donnée. Mon absence leur a été interminable. Boire. Moi je n'ai pas eu peur. Boire. Comme chaque matin, elles disent que c'est folie de descendre à ce ruisseau avec le SS et son chien derrière moi. Il a fait dévorer une Polonaise l'autre jour. Et puis c'est de l'eau de marais, c'est l'eau qui donne la typhoïde. Non, ce n'est pas de l'eau de marais. Je bois. Rien n'est plus malaisé que boire à une gamelle évasée en marchant. L'eau oscille d'un bord à l'autre, échappe aux lèvres. Je bois. Non, ce n'est pas de l'eau de marais, c'est un ruisseau. Je ne réponds pas parce que je ne peux pas parler encore. Ce n'est pas de l'eau de marais, mais elle a goût de feuilles pourries, et j'ai ce goût dans la bouche aujourd'hui dès que je pense à cette eau, même quand

je n'y pense pas. Je bois. Je bois et je suis mieux.
La salive revient dans ma bouche. Les paroles
reviennent à mes lèvres, mais je ne parle pas. Le
regard revient à mes yeux. La vie revient. Je
retrouve ma respiration, mon cœur. Je sais que
je suis vivante. Je suce lentement ma salive. La
lucidité revient, et le regard – et je vois la petite
Aurore. Elle est malade, épuisée par la fièvre,
les lèvres décolorées, les yeux hagards. Elle a
soif. Elle n'a pas la force de descendre au ruisseau. Et personne ne veut y aller pour elle. Il ne
faut pas qu'elle boive de cette eau malsaine, elle
est malade. Je la vois et je pense : elle pourrait
bien boire de cette eau, puisqu'elle va mourir.
Chaque matin, elle se met près de moi. Elle
espère que je lui laisserai quelques gouttes au
fond de ma gamelle. Pourquoi lui donnerais-je
de mon eau ? Aussi bien elle va mourir. Elle
attend. Ses yeux implorent et je ne la regarde
pas. Je sens sur moi ses yeux de soif, la douleur
à ses yeux quand je remets la gamelle à ma cein-
ture. La vie revient en moi et j'ai honte. Et chaque matin je reste insensible à la supplication de
son regard et de ses lèvres décolorées par la soif,
et chaque matin, j'ai honte après avoir bu.

Ma bouche s'humecte. Je pourrais parler
maintenant. Je ne parle pas. Je voudrais que dure
longtemps cette salive dans ma bouche. Et l'idée
fixe : quand boirai-je encore ? Y aura-t-il de l'eau

là où nous travaillerons ? Il n'y a jamais d'eau.
C'est le marais. Le marais de boue.

Mes camarades me croyaient folle. Lulu me
disait : « Fais attention à toi. Tu sais bien qu'ici
il faut toujours être sur le qui-vive. Tu te feras
tuer. » Je n'entendais pas. Elles ne me quittaient
plus et elles disaient entre elles : « Il faut veiller
sur C., elle est folle. Elle ne voit pas les kapos,
ni les SS, ni les chiens. Elle reste plantée, le regard vague, au lieu de travailler. Elle ne comprend pas quand ils crient, elle va n'importe
où. Ils la tueront. » Elles avaient peur pour moi,
elles avaient peur de me regarder avec ces yeux
fous que j'avais. Elles me croyaient folle et sans
doute l'étais-je. Je ne me suis rien rappelé de
ces semaines-là. Et pendant ces semaines-là qui
étaient les plus dures, tant et tant sont mortes
que j'aimais et je ne me suis pas rappelé que
j'avais appris leur mort.

Les jours où nous prenons l'autre direction, à
l'opposé du ruisseau, je ne sais comment je sup-
porte la déception.

Il y a la soif du matin et la soif du jour.

Depuis le matin, je ne pense qu'à boire.
Quand la soupe de midi est servie, elle est salée,
salée, elle arrache la bouche toute brûlante
d'aphtes. « Mange. Il faut que tu manges. » Tant
étaient mortes déjà qui avaient refusé la nourriture. « Essaie. Elle est assez liquide aujourd'hui.

– Non, elle est salée. » Je rejette la cuillerée que j'ai essayé d'avaler. Rien ne peut passer quand il n'y a pas de salive dans la bouche.

Quelquefois nous allons aux wagonnets. Un chantier de démolition avec des arbustes grêles entre les maisons en ruines. Ils sont couverts de givre. À chaque trague de pierres que je porte au wagonnet, je frôle un arbuste auquel j'arrache une petite branche. Je lèche le givre et cela ne fait pas d'eau dans la bouche. Dès que le SS s'écarte, je cours vers la neige propre, il en reste un morceau comme un drap étendu pour sécher. Je prends une poignée de neige, et la neige ne fait pas d'eau dans la bouche.

Si je passe près de la citerne ouverte à fleur de terre, le vertige me prend, tout tourne dans ma tête. C'est parce que je suis avec Carmen ou Viva que je ne m'y jette pas. Et à chaque passage, elles s'efforcent de faire un détour. Mais je les entraîne, elles me suivent pour ne pas me lâcher et au bord elles me tirent brutalement.

Pendant la pause, les Polonaises se groupent autour de la citerne et puisent de l'eau avec une gamelle attachée à un fil de fer. Le fil de fer est trop court. Celle qui se penche est presque tout engagée dans la citerne, ses camarades la tiennent par les jambes. Elle remonte un peu d'eau trouble au fond de la gamelle et elle boit. Une autre puise à son tour. Je vais vers elles et je leur fais comprendre que j'en voudrais. La gamelle redescend au bout du fil de fer, la Polonaise se penche à tomber, remonte encore une fois un peu d'eau qu'elle me tend en disant : « Kleba ? » Je n'ai pas de pain. Je donne tout mon pain le soir pour avoir du thé. Je réponds que je n'ai pas de pain avec une prière sur les lèvres. Elle renverse la gamelle et l'eau se répand. Je tomberais si Carmen ou Viva n'accourait.

Quand nous sommes au marais, toute la journée je pense au chemin du retour, au ruisseau. Mais le SS se souvient du matin. Dès le tournant d'où on aperçoit le petit pont, il se porte en avant. Il descend dans le ruisseau et y fait patauger son chien. Lorsque nous arrivons, l'eau est bourbeuse et fétide. J'en prendrais bien quand même ; impossible : toutes les anweiserines sont sur les dents.

Il y a la soif du jour et la soif du soir.

Le soir, pendant tout l'appel, je pense à la tisane qu'on va distribuer. Je suis des premières servies. La soif me rend hardie. Je bouscule tout pour passer avant les autres. Je bois et quand j'ai bu j'ai plus soif encore. Cette tisane ne désaltère pas.

J'ai maintenant mon pain à la main, mon morceau de pain et les quelques grammes de margarine qui font le repas du soir. Je les tiens à la main et je les offre de carré en carré à qui voudrait échanger contre sa portion de tisane. Je tremble qu'aucune ne veuille. Il s'en trouve toujours une pour accepter. Tous les soirs j'échange mon pain pour quelques gorgées. Je bois tout de suite et j'ai plus soif encore. Quand je reviens à notre carré, Viva me dit : « Je t'ai gardé mon thé (thé ou tisane, ce n'est ni l'un ni l'autre), ce sera pour avant de t'endormir. » Elle ne peut me faire attendre jusque-là. Je bois et j'ai plus soif encore. Et je pense à l'eau du ruisseau que le chien a gâchée tout à l'heure, dont j'aurais pu avoir une pleine gamelle, et j'ai soif, plus soif encore.

Il y a la soif du soir et la soif de la nuit, la plus atroce. Parce que, la nuit, je bois, je bois et l'eau devient immédiatement sèche et solide dans ma bouche. Et plus je bois, plus ma bouche s'emplit de feuilles pourries qui durcissent.

Ou bien c'est un quartier d'orange. Il crève entre mes dents et c'est bien un quartier d'orange – extraordinaire qu'on trouve des oranges ici –, c'est bien un quartier d'orange, j'ai le goût de l'orange dans la bouche, le jus se répand jusque sous ma langue, touche mon palais, mes gencives, coule dans ma gorge. C'est une orange un peu acide et merveilleusement fraîche. Ce goût d'orange et la sensation du frais qui coule me réveillent. Le réveil est affreux. Pourtant la seconde où la peau de l'orange cède entre mes

dents est si délicieuse que je voudrais provoquer
ce rêve-là. Je le poursuis, je le force. Mais c'est
de nouveau la pâte de feuilles pourries en mor-
tier qui pétrifie. Ma bouche est sèche. Pas amère.
Lorsqu'on sent sa bouche amère, c'est qu'on n'a
pas perdu le goût, c'est qu'on a encore de la
salive dans la bouche.

LA MAISON

Il pleuvait. Un écran de pluie fermait la plaine.

Nous avions marché longtemps. La route n'était que fondrières. Quand nous étions tentées de les contourner, les anweiserines criaient : « En rangs. Gardez les rangs ! » et poussaient dans la boue celles qui hésitaient à cause de leurs godasses. Aucune description ne peut donner idée de ces godasses que nous avions.

Nous étions arrivées à un grand labour. Il fallait enlever les racines de chiendent retournées par la charrue. Courbées, nous arrachions les filaments blanchâtres et les mettions dans notre tablier. Cela faisait froid et mouillé au ventre. Lourd aussi. Au bout du champ, nous vidions notre tablier et prenions un autre sillon. Il pleuvait. Courbées sur les sillons, sillon après sillon. La pluie avait imprégné nos vêtements. Nous étions nues. Un ruisseau glacé se formait entre les omoplates et coulait au creux du dos. Nous n'y faisions plus attention. Seulement, la main qui enlevait le chiendent était morte. Et les mottes collaient de plus en plus aux godasses qui devenaient lourdes, de plus en plus lourdes à retirer du sol. Depuis le matin, il pleuvait.

Les anweiserines s'étaient abritées sous un toit de branchages. Elles criaient de loin. Quand nous étions à l'extrémité du champ, nous ne les entendions plus. Nous nous y attardions un peu. Il fallait de toute façon être courbées sur les sillons, elles nous voyaient. Aussi bien était-il trop douloureux de se redresser.

Nous allions deux par deux. Nous parlions en marchant. Nous parlions du passé et le passé devenait irréel. Nous parlions plus encore de l'avenir et le futur devenait certitude. Nous faisions beaucoup de projets. Nous en faisions sans cesse.

À midi, la pluie avait redoublé. On ne voyait plus le champ transformé en bourbier.

Plus loin, il y avait une maison abandonnée. Cette maison n'était pas pour nous. Déjà le SS sifflait pour que nous reformions les rangs, après la pause. Nous étions résignées à retourner aux racines de chiendent, aux mottes boueuses. Mais la colonne laissait le labour derrière elle. Geneviève dit : « S'ils nous faisaient mettre à l'abri dans la maison... » C'était formuler le vœu que nous faisions toutes. L'exprimer en montrait tout l'irréalisable. Pourtant, nous nous dirigeons vers la maison. Nous en sommes tout près. La colonne s'arrête. Un SS crie que nous allons entrer mais que si nous faisons du bruit, nous sortirons aussitôt. Faut-il y croire ?

Nous entrons dans la maison comme dans une église. C'est une maison de paysans qu'on a commencé à démolir. Ils démolissent toutes les maisons de paysans, suppriment les haies et les clôtures, nivellent les jardins en un vaste domaine. C'est ainsi qu'on liquide la petite culture, ici. Les cultivateurs ont été liquidés d'abord. La maison est marquée d'un « J » à la peinture noire. Des juifs l'habitaient.

Nous entrons dans une odeur de plâtre mouillé. Les parquets et les papiers ont été arrachés. Presque toutes les portes et les fenêtres aussi. Nous nous asseyons par terre sur les gravats. Nous sentons davantage le froid de nos robes et de nos vestes. Les premières se sont assuré des places contre le mur, elles s'appuient. Les autres se serrent partout où elles peuvent.

Nous regardons la maison comme si nous avions oublié et nous retrouvons des mots. « C'est une assez belle pièce. » – « Oui, claire. » – « La table devait être là. » – « Ou le lit. » – « Non, c'est la salle à manger. Voyez le papier. Il y a un lambeau de papier qui pend encore. Moi, je mettrais un divan ici près de la cheminée. » – « Des rideaux rustiques feraient bien. Vous savez, ces toiles de Jouy. »

La maison se pare de tous ses meubles, patinés, confortables, familiers. Elle est achevée qu'on y ajoute des détails. « Il faut une radio près du divan. » – « Ici, ils ont des doubles fenêtres. On peut cultiver des plantes grasses. » – « Tu aimes les plantes grasses ? Je préfère les jacinthes. On met les bulbes dans de l'eau et on a des fleurs avant le printemps. » – « Je n'aime pas l'odeur des jacinthes. »

Les anweiserines se sont installées dans l'autre pièce. Les SS somnolent auprès d'elles. Nous sommes les unes contre les autres. Notre chaleur fait sortir de nos vêtements une buée qui monte vers les trous des fenêtres. La maison devient tiède, habitée. Nous sommes bien. Nous regardons la pluie en souhaitant qu'elle dure jusqu'au soir.

LE SOIR

Au coup de sifflet, il faut poser les outils, les nettoyer, les ranger en un tas bien fait. – Former les rangs. – Se taire. – Ne pas bouger. – Anwei-serines et kapos comptent. Se trompent-elles ? Recomptent. – Hurlent. – Deux en moins. – Se souviennent. Ce sont les deux de l'après-midi. Deux qui s'affaissaient sur leur bêche. Les furies aussitôt se précipitaient, les battaient, les bat-taient. On ne s'habitue pas à voir battre les autres. Les coups n'y faisaient rien. La bêche s'échappait des mains d'où le sang s'était retiré, la vie s'en allait des yeux et les yeux ne priaient pas. Les yeux étaient muets. Les furies s'achar-naient sur les deux femmes qui ne remuaient plus. Si elles ne réagissent plus aux coups, c'est qu'il n'y a plus rien à faire. Qu'on les emporte. Nous les avions portées doucement le long du talus, là où l'herbe est sèche, et nous étions retournées à nos bêches.

Elles manquent maintenant. Toutes ne savent pas, questionnent. Les noms passent de bouche en bouche dans un chuchotement que nulle émotion ne marque. Nous sommes trop fatiguées. Berthe et Anne-Marie sont mortes. Berthe, laquelle ? Berthe de Bordeaux. Elles ont été comptées ce matin à la sortie, elles doivent être comptées au retour. Il faudra les porter. Aucune ne bouge. Involontairement, chacune baisse la tête, voudrait se fondre dans la masse, ne pas être remarquée, ne pas faire signe. Exténuée tellement qu'elle mesure avec effroi ce qu'elle peut encore obtenir de ses jambes. La plupart ne marchent qu'en pesant aux bras des autres. Les anweiserines remontent les rangs, examinent les figures et les pieds. Elles choisiront les plus fortes. Celles qui s'appuient à une moins faible appréhendent que cette dernière soit prise. Comment rentreront-elles si le bras qui les soutient les quitte ? Les anweiserines cherchent les mieux chaussées, les grandes. « Du. Du. Du. », en appellent trois. Alors les autres se désignent. Nous nous détachons et allons vers les mortes. Nous les regardons, embarrassées. Comment les prendre ? Les anweiserines indiquent que chacune doit tenir par un membre. Et vite.

Nous nous penchons sur nos compagnes. Elles ne sont pas encore raidies. Quand nous saisissons les chevilles et les poignets, le corps plie, plie jusqu'à terre et il est impossible de le maintenir haut. Il serait mieux de soulever aux genoux et aux épaules, mais on n'a pas prise. Enfin, nous y parvenons. Nous nous rangeons à la fin de la colonne. On compte encore. Le nombre y est, cette fois. La colonne s'ébranle.

Combien y a-t-il de kilomètres à parcourir ? Nous mesurons les distances à l'effort qu'elles nous coûtent. Elles sont énormes.

La colonne s'est ébranlée.

D'abord, c'est Berthe et Anne-Marie que nous portons. Bientôt ce ne sont plus que des fardeaux trop lourds, qui nous échappent à chaque mouvement. Dès le départ, nous sommes distancées. Nous demandons de faire passer au premier rang qu'on ralentisse. La colonne va toujours aussi vite. La kapo est en tête. Elle a de bonnes chaussures. Elle est pressée.

Les SS nous suivent. Ils traînent leurs bottes puisque nous allons, nous, si lentement. L'anweiserine rit avec eux. Elle leur montre des pas de danse, en faisant des plaisanteries ignobles. Eux s'amusent.

C'est un soir pâle et presque doux. Chez nous, il doit y avoir des bourgeons. Un SS tire un harmonica de sa poche. Il joue et notre détresse devient malaise.

Nous appelons pour qu'on nous relaie. Personne n'entend. Personne ne vient. Personne ne se sent la force de nous remplacer. Nous peinons de plus en plus, courbées, écartelées.

Carmen aperçoit dans le fossé des bouts de planches cassées. Nous posons nos camarades sur la route pour ramasser les planches. Les SS attendent. Le deuxième sort son couteau et écorce la branche qui lui sert de gourdin. L'anweiserine accompagne l'harmonica. Elle chante « J'attendrai ». Leur chanson préférée.

Nous plaçons chaque corps en travers de deux planches dont nous empoignons les extrémités et nous repartons. Carmen dit : « Tu te rappelles, Lulu, quand la mère nous disait : Ne touche pas à ce bois sale. Tu vas te mettre une écharde et tu auras un vilain mal blanc. » Nos mères.

Au début, il semble que cela aille mieux, puis les corps glissent, plient au milieu, tombent. C'est à chaque pas un ajustement qu'il faut faire de ce corps inerte et de ces planches. Les SS soufflent dans l'harmonica à tour de rôle, rient et chantonnent. Ils rient bruyamment, la fille plus bruyamment encore.

La colonne prend de l'avance. Nous fournissons pourtant un effort dont nous ne nous croyions pas capables. Un camion arrive. La colonne s'arrête sur le côté pour faire place. Nous en profitons pour gagner un peu de terrain. Le camion est celui qui ramasse les bidons dans lesquels on a apporté la soupe sur les chantiers, à midi. Il y a des chantiers tout alentour. Loin tout alentour il y a des tas de bêches et de pelles. Le chauffeur freine, parle aux SS. Je suis près de celui à l'harmonica. C'est un gamin. Il paraît dix-sept ans. L'âge de mon plus jeune frère. Je m'adresse à lui : « Ne pourrions-nous pas mettre nos camarades sur ce camion qui rentre au camp ? » Son ricanement nous insulte et il éclate de rire. Il rit, rit et trouve cela d'un drôle ! Il est tout secoué de rire et l'autre l'imite et la fille, qui me donne une gifle en forçant son rire. J'ai honte. Comment peut-on leur demander quelque chose ? Le camion s'éloigne.

Mais en voilà assez. Ils s'avisent que cela a suffisamment duré, cette nonchalance, avec les chiens qui gambadent la laisse molle. Ils rangent l'harmonica, cabrent les chiens et crient : « Schneller jetz ! » Nous nous raidissons. Les chiens sur les talons, il faut maintenant rattraper la colonne.

Il faut. Il faut.

Il faut... Pourquoi faut-il, puisqu'il nous est égal de mourir tout de suite, tuées par les chiens ou les bâtons, là sur la route dans le soir pâle ? Non. Il faut. À cause de leur rire tout à l'heure, peut-être. Il faut.

Nous réussissons à rejoindre la colonne, y touchons presque. Nous supplions qu'on nous relève. Deux viennent. Elles remplacent les deux

plus frêles qui défaillent. Nous changeons de
main sans cesser de marcher. Nous avons les
gueules des chiens aux mollets. Un signe, une
secousse à la laisse, ils mordront. Nous marchons avec ces cadavres qui glissent, que nous
recalons, qui glissent encore. Leurs pieds raclent
la route, la tête renversée presque au sol. Nous
n'en pouvons plus de voir cette tête, avec les
yeux en bas. Berthe. Anne-Marie. De la main
qui ne porte pas, nous la soutenons un moment.
Il faut y renoncer. Abandonner cette tête à qui
nous n'avons pas eu le courage d'abaisser les
paupières.

Nous ne regardons pas, parce que les larmes
coulent sur nos visages, coulent sans que nous
pleurions. Les larmes coulent de fatigue et
d'impuissance. Et nous souffrons dans cette
chair morte comme si elle était vivante. La planche sous les cuisses les écorche, les coupe. Berthe. Anne-Marie.

Pour que les mains ne pendent pas, nous
essayons de les croiser sur la poitrine. Il faudrait
les y maintenir. Les mains pendent et nous battent les jambes au balancement de la marche.

Les SS derrière nous vont au pas militaire. Finie
la promenade, disent-ils. Ils tiennent les laisses
court. Les chiens nous serrent du plus près. Nous
ne nous retournons pas. Nous essayons de ne plus
sentir leur mufle, leur souffle chaud et rapide, de

ne plus entendre leur pas quadruplé, leur pas de chien avec le grattement irritant des griffes sur les cailloux du chemin. De ne plus entendre le martèlement du gourdin contre nous. Il est tout écorcé maintenant, d'un blanc humide.

Nous marchons, tendues. Notre cœur bat, bat à éclater, et nous pensons : mon cœur ne va pas tenir, mon cœur va céder. Il ne cède pas encore, il tient encore. Pour combien de mètres ? Notre angoisse décompose les kilomètres en pas, en mètres, en poteaux électriques, en tournants. Nous nous trompons toujours d'un poteau ou d'un tournant. C'est la plaine, la plaine couverte de marais à perte de vue où il n'y a pas de repères, parfois une touffe de végétation rougie par le gel qui se confond sans cesse avec une autre. Et le désespoir nous écrase.

Mais il faut. Il faut.

On approche. L'approche du camp se sent à l'odeur. Odeur de charogne, odeur de diarrhée qu'enveloppe l'odeur plus épaisse et suffocante du crématoire. Quand nous y sommes, nous ne le sentons pas. En revenant le soir, nous nous demandons comment nous pouvons respirer cette puanteur.

À cet endroit-là, l'endroit où se reconnaît l'odeur, il doit rester deux kilomètres.

Après le petit pont, l'allure s'accélère. Encore un.

Comment nous les avons franchis, je ne sais. Avant l'entrée, notre colonne s'est arrêtée pour laisser le passage à d'autres. Nous avons déposé nos fardeaux. Quand nous avons dû les reprendre, nous avons cru que nous ne pourrions plus.

À la porte, nous nous sommes redressées. Nous avons serré les mâchoires, nous avons regardé haut. C'était un serment que nous nous étions fait, Viva et moi. La tête haute devant Drexler, devant Taube. Nous avions même dit : « La tête haute ou les pieds devant. » Ô Viva.

La SS qui compte au passage interroge de sa canne. « Zwei Französinnen », répond l'anweiserine, dégoûtée.

Nous emportons nos camarades à l'appel. Cela fait deux rangées qui altèrent l'alignement : les quatre porteuses et leur morte couchée devant elles.

Les commandos de juives rentrent à leur tour. Elles en ont deux ce soir. Comme nous. Elles en ont tous les soirs. Elles les ont mises sur des portes enlevées aux maisons qu'elles démolissent, et ont hissé les portes sur leurs épaules. Elles sont défigurées par l'effort. Nous les plaignons. Nous les plaignons jusqu'aux sanglots. Les mortes sont allongées bien à plat, le visage à la face du ciel. Nous pensons : si nous avions eu des portes.

L'appel a été aussi long que d'habitude. À

nous il a semblé plus court. Notre cœur nous emplissait la poitrine et battait fort, fort et cela nous faisait compagnie comme une montre quand on est seul. Et nous écoutions ce cœur qui dominait tout, qui peu à peu, lentement, regagnait son creux, s'y réinstallait, et les coups s'espaçaient, s'espaçaient et s'atténuaient. Et quand nous ne les avons plus entendus qu'à leur rythme accoutumé, nous avons été aussi troublées qu'au bord de la solitude.

À ce moment-là, nos mains ont essuyé nos larmes.

L'appel a duré jusqu'à ce que les réflecteurs éclairent les barbelés, jusqu'à la nuit.

Pendant tout l'appel, nous ne les avons pas regardées.

Un cadavre. L'œil gauche mangé par un rat. L'autre œil ouvert avec sa frange de cils.

Essayez de regarder. Essayez pour voir.

Un homme qui ne peut plus suivre. Le chien le saisit au fondement. L'homme ne s'arrête pas. Il marche avec le chien qui marche derrière lui sur deux pattes, la gueule au fondement de l'homme.

L'homme marche. Il n'a pas poussé un cri. Le sang marque les rayures du pantalon. De l'intérieur, une tache qui s'élargit comme sur du buvard.

L'homme marche avec les crocs du chien dans la chair.

Essayez de regarder. Essayez pour voir.

Une femme que deux tirent par les bras. Une juive. Elle ne veut pas aller au 25. Les deux la traînent. Elle résiste. Ses genoux raclent le sol. Son vêtement tiré aux manches remonte sur le cou. Le pantalon défait – un pantalon d'homme – traîne derrière elle, à l'envers, retenu aux chevilles. Une grenouille dépouillée. Les reins nus, les fesses avec des trous de maigreur sales de sang et de sanie.

Elle hurle. Les genoux s'arrachent sur les cailloux.

Essayez de regarder. Essayez pour voir.

AUSCHWITZ

Cette ville où nous passions
était une ville étrange.
Les femmes portaient des chapeaux
des chapeaux posés sur des cheveux en boucles.
Elles avaient aussi des souliers et des bas
comme à la ville.
Aucun des habitants de cette ville
n'avait de visage
et pour n'en pas faire l'aveu
tous se détournaient à notre passage
même un enfant qui tenait à la main
une boîte à lait aussi haute que ses jambes
en émail violet
et qui s'enfuit en nous voyant.
Nous regardions ces êtres sans visages
et c'était nous qui nous étonnions.
Aussi nous étions déçues
nous espérions voir des fruits et des légumes
    chez les marchands.
Il n'y avait pas non plus de boutiques
seulement des vitrines

où j'aurais bien voulu me reconnaître
dans les rangs qui glissaient sur les vitres.
Je levai un bras
mais toutes voulaient se reconnaître
toutes levaient le bras
et aucune n'a su laquelle elle était.
Il y avait l'heure au cadran de la gare
nous avons été heureuses de la regarder
l'heure était vraie
et allégées d'arriver aux silos de betteraves
où nous allions travailler
de l'autre côté de la ville
que nous avions traversée comme un malaise du
    matin.

LE MANNEQUIN

De l'autre côté de la route, il y a un terrain
où les SS vont dresser les chiens. On les voit s'y
rendre, avec leurs chiens qu'ils tiennent en laisse,
attachés deux par deux. Le SS qui marche en
tête porte un mannequin. C'est une grande poupée de son habillée comme nous. Costume rayé
décoloré, crasseux, aux manches trop longues.
Le SS la tient par un bras. Il laisse traîner les
pieds qui raclent les cailloux. Ils lui ont même
attaché des socques aux pieds.

Ne regarde pas. Ne regarde pas ce mannequin
qui traîne par terre. Ne te regarde pas.

Le dimanche l'appel avait lieu moins tôt. Moins loin de l'aube. Le dimanche, les colonnes ne sortaient pas. On travaillait dans le camp. Le dimanche était le jour le plus redouté de tous.

Ce dimanche-là, il faisait très beau. Le jour s'était levé dans un ciel sans rougeoiements, sans nappes de feu. Le jour s'était levé bleu tout de suite comme un jour de printemps. Le soleil aussi était du printemps. Ne pas penser à la maison, au jardin, à la première sortie de la saison. Ne pas penser. Ne pas penser.

Ici la belle saison différait de la mauvaise en ce qu'il y avait de la poussière au lieu de neige ou de boue, en ce que l'odeur était plus pestilentielle, le paysage plus désolé avec le soleil qu'avec la neige, plus désespéré.

La fin de l'appel siffle. Il faut garder les rangs qui lentement se mettent en marche vers le block 25. Chaque dimanche était différent. Au block 25, pourquoi ? Nous avons peur. Quelqu'un dit : « Le block 25 n'est pas assez grand pour tout le monde. Nous irions directement aux gaz », et nous nous secouons.

Que vont-ils faire ? Nous attendons. Nous attendons longtemps. Jusqu'à ce qu'arrivent des hommes, avec des pelles. Ils se dirigent vers le fossé. Pendant la semaine, le fossé qui isole les barbelés à l'intérieur a été approfondi. Y a-t-il trop de suicides ? Ce sont les coups de feu qu'on entend dans la nuit. Quand une s'approche des barbelés, la sentinelle du mirador tire avant qu'elle y atteigne. Alors, pourquoi le fossé ?

Pourquoi tout ?

Les hommes sont en place, le long du fossé, les pelles en mains.

Les colonnes s'allongent en file indienne. Des milliers de femmes sur une seule file. Une file sans fin. Nous suivons. Que font celles qui nous précèdent ? Nous les voyons passer devant les hommes, tendre leur tablier. Ils y mettent deux pelletées de la terre enlevée au fossé qu'on a creusé. Pourquoi faire, cette terre ? Nous suivons. Elles se mettent à courir. Nous courons. Voilà que les coups de bâton et de lanière s'abattent. On essaie de se protéger le visage, les yeux. Les coups tombent sur la nuque, sur le dos. Schnell. Schnell. Courir.

De chaque côté de la file, kapos et anweiserines hurlent. Schneller. Schneller. Hurlent et frappent.

Nous faisons remplir notre tablier et nous courons.

Nous courons. Il faut garder la file, pas de débandade.

Nous courons.

La porte.

C'est là où les furies sont le plus serré. SS en jupes et en culottes se sont joints à elles. Courir.

La porte franchie, prendre à gauche, s'engager sur une planche mal équilibrée entre les deux rives d'un fossé. Passer sur la planche en courant. Coups de bâton avant et après.

Courir. Vider le tablier à l'endroit qu'indiquent les hurlements.

D'autres avec des râteaux égalisent la terre apportée.

Courir. Longer les barbelés. Ne pas les effleurer, les lampes sont au rouge.

De nouveau franchir la porte pour rentrer. Le passage est étroit. Il faut courir plus vite encore. Tant pis pour celles qui tombent là, elles sont piétinées.

Courir. Schneller. Courir.

Retourner devant les hommes qui remplissent de nouveau le tablier de terre.

Ils doivent faire vite, on les bat. Des pelletées bien pleines, on les bat, on nous bat.

Le tablier rempli, coups de bâton. Schneller.

Courir vers la porte, passer sous les lanières

et les cravaches, courir sur la planche qui bouge et qui plie. Attention à la canne du chef SS qui se tient au débouché de la planche. Vider son tablier sous un râteau, courir, franchir la porte par le passage de plus en plus étroit – les bastonneuses se resserrent au goulet –, courir vers les hommes pour reprendre deux pelletées de terre, courir à la porte, dans un circuit ininterrompu.

Ils veulent faire un jardin à l'entrée du camp.

Ce n'est pas très lourd, deux pelletées de terre. Cela s'alourdit à mesure. Cela s'alourdit et ankylose les bras. Nous nous risquons à mal tenir les coins du tablier pour que la terre coule un peu. Si une furie le voit, elle nous assomme. Nous le faisons pourtant, c'est trop lourd.

Parmi les hommes il y a un Français. Nous rusons et calculons notre course pour que ce soit lui qui nous serve. Nous essayons d'échanger quelques mots. Il parle sans bouger les lèvres, sans lever les yeux, ainsi qu'on apprend à parler en prison. Il faut trois tours pour une phrase.

La ronde ne va plus assez vite. Les furies crient plus fort, battent plus fort. Il se forme des encombrements, parce que des femmes s'affaissent et que leurs camarades les aident à se relever, tandis que les autres, derrière, poussées par les coups, veulent continuer de courir. Et aussi parce que les juives croient qu'elles sont plus battues que nous et viennent se glisser entre nos robes rayées. Elles nous font peine. Elles nous font peine à cause de leur accoutrement. Elles n'ont pas de tablier. On leur a fait mettre leur manteau devant derrière, boutonné dans le dos pour qu'elles prennent la terre dans le bas du manteau qu'elles tiennent à l'ourlet. Elles ont de l'épouvantail et du pingouin, avec les manches à l'envers qui embarrassent les bras. Et celles qui ont un manteau d'homme fendu... Un comique terrifiant.

Elles nous font pitié mais nous ne voulons pas nous séparer. Nous nous protégeons mutuellement. Chacune veut rester près d'une compagne, qui devant une plus faible pour recevoir les coups à sa place, qui derrière une qui ne peut plus courir pour la retenir si elle tombe.

Le Français est arrivé depuis peu. Il est de Charonne. La résistance s'étend en France. Nous affronterions n'importe quoi pour lui parler.

Courir à la porte – schnell – passer – weiter – basculer sur la planche au-dessus du fossé – schneller – vider le tablier – courir – attention aux barbelés – de nouveau la porte il y en a toujours une sur qui on marche c'est là qu'est l'officier avec sa canne maintenant – courir jusqu'aux hommes tendre son tablier – coups de bâton – courir vers la porte. Une course hallucinée.

Nous pensons à nous sauver pour nous cacher dans un block. Impossible, toutes les issues sont gardées par des bâtons. Celles qui tentent de forcer les barrages sont rouées.

Défendu d'aller aux cabinets. Défendu de s'arrêter une minute.

Au début, ralentir est plus pénible que maintenir la course. Au moindre ralentissement, les coups redoublent. Après, nous préférerions être battues et ne pas courir, nos jambes n'obéissent plus. Mais, dès que nous ralentissons, les coups s'abattent si terribles que nous nous remettons à courir.

Des femmes tombent. Les furies les sortent du rang et les traînent à la porte du 25. Taube est là. La confusion augmente. Les juives sont de plus en plus nombreuses entre nous. À chaque tour, notre groupe se défait. Nous réussissons à rester ensemble deux par deux. Ces deux-là ne se quittent pas, elles se tiennent et se tirent l'une l'autre quand au passage de l'entrée elles sont prises dans la panique de celles sur qui on marche et de celles qui ont peur de tomber sur les autres. Une course hallucinée.

Des femmes tombent. La ronde continue. Courir. Courir toujours. Ne pas ralentir. Ne pas s'arrêter. Celles qui tombent, nous ne les regardons pas. Nous nous tenons deux par deux et c'est une attention de toutes les secondes. On ne peut pas s'occuper des autres.

Des femmes tombent. La ronde continue. Schnell. Schnell.

Le parterre s'agrandit. Il faut allonger le circuit.

Courir. Passer sur la planche branlante qui plie de plus en plus – schnell – verser la terre – schnell – la porte – schnell – remplir son tablier – schnell – la porte encore – schnell – la planche. C'est une course hallucinée.

Pour penser à quelque chose, nous comptons les coups. À trente, c'est un tour qui n'a pas été dur. À cinquante, nous ne comptons plus.

Le Français est tenu à l'œil. Un kapo est à son côté. Nous ne pouvons plus nous faire servir par lui. Quelquefois nous échangeons un regard. Entre ses dents, il dit : « Les salauds, les salauds. » Un nouveau. Il a des larmes. Il nous plaint. Pour lui, c'est moins pénible. Il reste en place et il ne fait pas froid.

Nos jambes enflent. Nos traits se crispent. À chaque tour nous sommes plus défaites.

Courir – schnell – la porte – schnell – la planche – schnell – vider la terre – schnell – barbelés – schnell – la porte – schnell – courir – tablier – courir – courir courir courir schnell schnell schnell schnell schnell. C'est une course hallucinée.

Chacune regarde les autres de plus en plus laides, et ne se voit pas.

Près de nous une juive quitte la file. Elle va vers Taube, lui parle. Il ouvre la porte et lui donne une gifle qui l'envoie à terre dans la cour du 25. Elle a abandonné. Quand Taube se retourne, il fait signe à une autre, qu'il jette aussi dans la cour du 25. Nous courons autant que nous pouvons. Qu'il ne croie pas que nous ne pouvons plus courir.

La ronde continue. Le soleil est haut. C'est l'après-midi. La course continue, les coups et les hurlements. À chaque tour, d'autres tombent. Celles qui ont la diarrhée sentent mauvais. Des coulées de diarrhée sèchent sur leurs jambes. Nous tournons toujours. Jusques à quand tournerons-nous ? C'est une course hallucinée que courent des faces hallucinées.

En vidant notre tablier, nous regardons où en est le parterre. Nous le croyions achevé que la couche de terre n'était pas assez haute. Il fallait recommencer.

L'après-midi s'avance. La ronde continue. Les coups. Les hurlements.

Quand Taube a sifflé, quand les furies ont crié : « Au block ! », nous sommes rentrées en nous soutenant les unes les autres. Assises sur nos carrés, nous n'avions pas la force de nous déchausser. Nous n'avions pas la force de parler. Nous nous demandions comment nous avions pu, cette fois encore.

Le lendemain, plusieurs des nôtres entraient au révir. Elles sont sorties sur la civière.

Le ciel était bleu, le soleil retrouvé. C'était un dimanche de mars.

LES HOMMES

Ils attendent devant la baraque. Silencieux. Dans leurs yeux combattent la résignation et la révolte. Il faut que la résignation l'emporte.

Un SS les garde. Il les bouscule. Sans qu'on sache pourquoi, tout à coup il se jette sur eux, crie et frappe. Les hommes restent silencieux, rectifient le rang, mettent les mains au corps. Ils ne prêtent pas attention au SS ni les uns aux autres. Chacun est seul en soi-même.

Il y a parmi eux des garçonnets, tout jeunes, qui ne comprennent pas. Ils observent les hommes et sont gagnés par leur gravité.

Avant d'entrer dans la baraque, ils se déshabillent, plient leurs vêtements qu'ils gardent sur le bras. Ils travaillent le torse nu depuis qu'il fait meilleur. Dévêtus, il semble qu'ils aient un long caleçon blanc qui colle à leurs os.

L'attente est longue. Ils attendent et ils savent.

C'est une nouvelle baraque qui vient d'être aménagée dans l'enceinte de l'infirmerie. Des camions ont livré des appareils laqués et nickelés, un luxe de propreté à peine croyable. On a fait de la baraque une salle de radiographie, diathermie, rayons X.

La première fois que des hommes sont soignés à notre camp. Le camp des hommes est en bas. Il possède un révir, qui est mieux que le nôtre, dit-on. Seulement moins affreux, peut-être. Pourquoi les envoie-t-on ici ? Soigne-t-on les gens ici maintenant ?

Les hommes continuent d'attendre. Silencieux. Le regard lointain et sans couleur.

Un à un, les premiers commencent à sortir. Ils se rhabillent sur le seuil. Leur regard fuit celui des autres qui attendent. Et quand on peut voir leur visage, on comprend.

Comment dire la détresse dans leurs gestes. L'humiliation dans leurs yeux.

Les femmes, c'est à la chirurgie qu'on les stérilise.

Et qu'importe ? Puisque aucun d'eux ne doit revenir. Puisque aucun de nous ne reviendra.

« Oh ! Sally, tu as pensé à ce que je t'ai demandé ? »

Sally court sur la Lagerstrasse. À sa mise, on voit qu'elle travaille aux Effekts. C'est le commando qui trie, inventorie, range tout ce que contiennent les bagages des juifs, les bagages que les arrivants laissent sur le quai. Celles qui travaillent aux Effekts ont de tout.

« Oui, ma chérie, j'y ai pensé, mais il n'y en a pas en ce moment. Il n'est pas arrivé de convoi depuis huit jours. On en attend un cette nuit. De Hongrie. Il était temps, nous n'avions plus rien. Au revoir. À demain. J'aurai ton savon. »

On vient d'installer l'eau dans le camp.

LE COMMANDANT

Deux garçons blonds, les cheveux en barbes d'épis mûrs, jambes nues, torse nu. Deux petits garçons. Onze ans, sept ans. Les deux frères. Tous les deux blonds, yeux bleus, la peau brunie. La nuque plus foncée.

Le plus grand houspille le petit. Le petit est mal disposé. Il grogne et il finit par dire en grognant :

« Non. Non, c'est toujours toi.

– Naturellement. Je suis grand.

– Non. C'est pas juste. C'est jamais moi. »

À regret, puisqu'il faut le décider, l'aîné propose :

« Eh bien, écoute. On va jouer encore une fois comme ça et après on changera. Après, ce sera chacun son tour. Tu veux ? »

Le petit renifle, se détache de mauvais gré du mur où il s'appuie, têtu, les paupières froncées à cause du soleil et rejoint son frère en traînant les pieds. L'autre le secoue : « Tu viens ? On joue ? » et il commence à être celui qu'il veut être. En même temps il surveille si le petit le suit dans le jeu. Le petit attend. Il n'entre pas encore dans le jeu. Il attend que son frère soit prêt.

Le grand se prépare. Il boutonne une veste, sangle un ceinturon, glisse l'épée bien sur le côté, puis assure des deux mains ouvertes la casquette sur sa tête. Doucement, du poignet, il lustre le bord de la casquette, touche la visière bas sur les yeux.

À mesure qu'il se vêt de son personnage, ses traits deviennent durs, et sa bouche. Ses lèvres s'amincissent. Il rejette la tête, les yeux comme gênés par une visière, cambre la taille, met la main gauche à son dos, paume en dehors, de la main droite il ajuste un imaginaire monocle et il regarde autour de lui.

Mais le voilà inquiet. Il s'aperçoit qu'il a oublié quelque chose. Il quitte un instant son personnage pour chercher sa badine. C'est une vraie badine, qui est dans l'herbe – une branche souple dont il se sert d'habitude –, reprend la pose et tape à petits coups de la badine sur ses bottes. Il est prêt. Il se retourne.

Instantanément, le petit entre dans son personnage aussi. Lui y prend moins de soin. Il ne se raidit qu'au premier coup d'œil de son frère et tout de suite s'avance d'un pas, s'immobilise, claque des talons – on n'entend pas le claquement, il est pieds nus –, lève le bras droit, le regard en face, inexpressif. L'autre répond par un salut bref, juste esquissé, supérieur. Le petit abaisse le bras, claque encore des talons et le grand ouvre la marche. Droit, le menton dressé et la bouche de morgue, la badine roulant légèrement entre le pouce et l'index pour tapoter ses mollets nus. Le petit suit à distance. Il marche moins raide. Un simple soldat.

Ils traversent le jardin. C'est un jardin aux gazons carrés, des fleurs à l'alignement en bordure des gazons. Ils traversent le jardin. Le commandant regarde comme on inspecte, de haut. L'ordonnance suit et ne regarde rien, abruti. Le soldat.

Au fond, près d'une haie de rosiers sur tiges, ils s'arrêtent. Le commandant d'abord, l'ordonnance deux pas derrière. Le commandant se met en place, la jambe droite un peu avancée avec le genou un peu plié, une main aux reins, l'autre, qui tient la cravache par le milieu, à la hanche. Il domine les rosiers. Son expression se fait mauvaise et il lance des ordres. Il crie : « Schnell ! Rechts ! Links ! » Sa poitrine se gonfle. « Rechts ! Links ! » Ensuite il intervertit : « Links ! Rechts ! » – de plus en plus vite, de plus en plus fort. « Links ! Rechts ! Links ! Rechts ! Links ! » – plus vite, toujours plus vite.

Bientôt les prisonniers à qui les ordres s'adressent ne peuvent plus suivre. Ils butent sur le sol, perdent le pas. Le commandant est pâle de colère. Avec sa badine il frappe, frappe et frappe. Sans bouger, les épaules toujours droites, les sourcils levés. Il hurle en fureur : « Schnell ! Schneller ! Aber los ! » en frappant à chaque commandement.

Au bout de la colonne, tout à coup, quelque chose qui ne doit pas aller. Il bondit d'une enjambée menaçante pour arriver à point sur son frère qui a aussitôt laissé son rôle d'ordonnance. Il joue maintenant le prisonnier en faute, l'échine voûtée, les jambes qui ne veulent plus soutenir le corps, le visage décomposé, la bouche douloureuse, la bouche de celui qui n'en peut plus. Le commandant change sa cravache de main, serre le poing droit, lui assène un coup en pleine poitrine – un semblant de coup de poing, c'est pour jouer. Le petit chancelle, tourbillonne, s'abat au long du gazon. Le commandant considère le prisonnier qu'il a jeté par terre avec mépris, la salive aux lèvres. Et sa fureur tombe. Il n'a plus que du dégoût. Il lui envoie un coup de botte – un semblant, il est pieds nus et c'est pour jouer. Mais le petit connaît le jeu. Le coup de botte le retourne comme un paquet flasque. Il s'étend, la bouche ouverte, l'œil mort.

Alors le grand, avec un signe de la baguette aux prisonniers invisibles qui l'entourent, ordonne : « Zum Krematorium », et s'éloigne. Raide, satisfait et dégoûté.

Le commandant du camp habite tout près, à l'extérieur des barbelés électriques. Une maison de briques, avec un jardin de rosiers et de gazon, des bégonias aux couleurs brillantes dans des caisses peintes en bleu. Entre la haie de rosiers et les barbelés passe le chemin qui mène au four crématoire. C'est le chemin que suivent les civières sur lesquelles on transporte les morts. Les morts se succèdent tout au long du jour. La cheminée fume tout au long du jour. Les heures déplacent sur le sable des allées et sur les gazons l'ombre de la cheminée.

Les fils du commandant jouent dans le jardin. Ils jouent au cheval, au ballon, ou bien ils jouent au commandant et au prisonnier.

L'APPEL

Il n'en finit pas, ce matin.

Les blockhovas s'agitent, comptent, recomptent. Les SS en pèlerine vont d'un groupe à l'autre, entrent au bureau, en sortent avec des feuilles qu'elles vérifient. Elles vérifient les chiffres de cette comptabilité humaine. L'appel durera jusqu'à ce que les chiffres tombent juste.

Taube arrive. Il prend la direction des recherches. Avec son chien, il part fouiller les blocks. Les blockhovas s'énervent, distribuent coups de poing et de lanière à tort et à travers. Chacune souhaite que ce ne soit pas dans son block qu'il en manque une.

On attend.

Les SS en pèlerine scrutent les chiffres, refont une fois encore les additions humaines.

On attend.

Taube revient. Il a trouvé. Il siffle doucement pour stimuler son chien qui le suit. Le chien traîne une femme qu'il tient à la nuque par la gueule.

Taube conduit son chien jusqu'au groupe du block auquel appartenait la femme. Le compte y est.

Taube donne le coup de sifflet. L'appel est fini.

Quelqu'un dit : « Espérons qu'elle était morte. »

LULU

Depuis le matin nous étions au fond de ce fossé. Nous étions trois. Le commando travaillait plus loin. Les kapos ne poussaient une pointe vers nous que de temps à autre, voir où nous en étions de ce fossé que nous recreusions. Nous pouvions parler. Depuis le matin, nous parlions.

Parler, c'était faire des projets pour le retour parce que croire au retour était une manière de forcer la chance. Celles qui avaient cessé de croire au retour était mortes. Il fallait y croire, y croire malgré tout, contre tout, donner certitude à ce retour, réalité et couleur, en le préparant, en le matérialisant dans tous les détails.

Quelquefois, une qui exprimait la pensée commune interrompait d'un : « Mais comment vous représentez-vous la sortie ? » Nous reprenions conscience. La question tombait dans le silence.

Pour secouer ce silence et l'anxiété qu'il recouvrait, une autre aventurait : « Peut-être qu'un jour nous ne serons pas réveillées pour

164

l'appel. Nous dormirons longtemps. Quand nous nous réveillerons, il fera grand jour et le camp sera tout calme. Celles qui sortiront des baraques les premières s'apercevront que le poste de garde est vide, que les miradors sont vides. Tous les SS se seront enfuis. Quelques heures plus tard, les avant-gardes russes seront là. »

Un autre silence répondait à l'anticipation.

Elle ajoutait : « Auparavant, nous aurons entendu le canon. D'abord loin, puis de plus en plus proche. La bataille de Cracovie. Après la prise de Cracovie, ce sera fini. Vous verrez, les SS se sauveront. »

Plus elle précisait, moins nous y croyions. Et, d'un tacite accord, nous laissions le sujet pour nous relancer dans nos projets, ces projets irréalisables qui avaient la logique qu'ont les propos des insensés.

Depuis le matin nous parlions. Nous étions contentes d'être détachées du commando parce que nous n'entendions pas les cris des kapos. Nous ne recevions pas les coups de bâton qui ponctuent les cris. Le fossé s'approfondissait au long des heures. Nos têtes ne dépassaient plus. La couche de marne atteinte, nous avions les pieds dans l'eau. La boue que nous jetions pardessus nos têtes était blanche. Il ne faisait pas froid – un des premiers jours où il ne fît plus froid. Le soleil nous chauffait aux épaules. Nous étions tranquilles.

Une kapo survient. Elle crie. Elle fait remonter mes deux compagnes et les emmène. Le fossé est presque assez creux, c'est trop de trois pour l'achever. Elles s'en vont et me font au revoir à regret. Elles connaissent l'appréhension qu'a chacune d'être séparée des autres, d'être seule. Pour m'encourager, elles disent : « Dépêche-toi, tu nous rejoindras. »

Je reste seule au fond de ce fossé et je suis prise de désespoir. La présence des autres, leurs paroles faisaient possible le retour. Elles s'en vont et j'ai peur. Je ne crois pas au retour quand je suis seule. Avec elles, puisqu'elles semblent y croire si fort, j'y crois aussi. Dès qu'elles me quittent, j'ai peur. Aucune ne croit plus au retour quand elle est seule.

Me voilà au fond de ce fossé, seule, tellement découragée que je me demande si j'arriverai au bout de la journée. Combien d'heures encore avant le coup de sifflet qui marque la fin du travail, le moment où nous reformons la colonne pour rentrer au camp, en rangs par cinq, nous donnant le bras et parlant, parlant à nous étourdir ?

Me voilà seule. Je ne peux plus penser à rien parce que toutes mes pensées se heurtent à l'angoisse qui nous habite toutes : Comment sor-

tirons-nous d'ici ? Quand sortirons-nous d'ici ?
Je voudrais ne plus penser à rien. Et si cela dure
aucune ne sortira. Celles qui vivent encore se
disent chaque jour que c'est miracle d'avoir tenu
huit semaines. Personne ne peut voir plus d'une
semaine devant soi.

Je suis seule et j'ai peur. J'essaie de m'acharner
à creuser. Le travail n'avance pas. Je m'attaque
à une dernière bosse pour égaliser ce fond, peut-
être la kapo jugera-t-elle que cela suffit. Et je
sens mon dos meurtri, mon dos paralysé dans sa
voussure, mes épaules arrachées par la pelle, mes
bras qui n'ont plus la force de lancer les pelletées
de marne boueuse par-dessus le bord. Je suis là,
seule. J'ai envie de me coucher dans la boue et
d'attendre. D'attendre que la kapo me trouve
morte. Pas si facile de mourir. C'est terrible ce
qu'il faut battre longtemps quelqu'un, à coups
de pelle ou à coups de bâton, avant qu'il meure.

Je creuse encore un peu. J'enlève encore deux
ou trois pelletées. C'est trop dur. Dès qu'on est
seule, on pense : À quoi bon ? Pourquoi faire ?
Pourquoi ne pas renoncer... Autant tout de suite.
Au milieu des autres, on tient.

Je suis seule, avec ma hâte de finir pour rejoindre les camarades et la tentation d'abandonner.
Pourquoi ? Pourquoi dois-je creuser ce fossé ?

« Assez. C'est assez ! » Une voix hurle au-dessus de moi : « Komm, schnell ! » Je m'aide de

la pelle pour grimper. Comme mes bras sont las, ma nuque douloureuse. La kapo court. Il faut la suivre. Elle traverse la route au bord du marais. Le chantier de terrassement. Des femmes comme des fourmis. Les unes apportent du sable à d'autres qui, avec des dames, nivellent le terrain. Un grand espace tout plat, en plein soleil. Des centaines de femmes debout, en une frise d'ombres contre le soleil.

J'arrive à la suite de la kapo qui me donne en même temps une dame et une taloche et m'envoie vers un groupe. Des yeux, je cherche les camarades. Lulu m'appelle : « Viens près de moi, il y a une place », et elle s'écarte un peu pour que je sois à côté d'elle, dans la rangée des femmes qui frappent le sol, tenant à deux mains la dame qu'elles soulèvent et laissent retomber. « Viens ici, face à piler le riz ! » Comment fait-elle, Viva, pour trouver encore la force de lancer cela ? Je ne peux mouvoir mes lèvres même pour une ébauche de sourire. Lulu s'inquiète : « Qu'est-ce que tu as ? Tu es malade ?

– Non, je ne suis pas malade. Je n'en peux plus. Aujourd'hui je n'en peux plus.

– Ce n'est rien. Ça va passer.

– Non, Lulu, ça ne va pas passer. Je te dis que je n'en peux plus. »

Elle n'a rien à répondre. C'est la première fois qu'elle m'entend parler ainsi. Pratique, elle soupèse mon outil. « Ce qu'il est lourd, ton pilon. Prends le mien. Il est plus léger et tu es plus fatiguée que moi avec ce fossé. »

Nous échangeons nos outils. Je commence à marteler le sable moi aussi. Je regarde toutes ces femmes qui font le même geste, de leurs bras de plus en plus faibles pour soulever la masse pesante, les kapos avec leurs bâtons qui vont de l'une à l'autre, et le désespoir m'anéantit. « Comment sortirons-nous jamais d'ici ? »

Lulu me regarde. Elle me sourit. Sa main effleure la mienne pour me réconforter. Et je répète pour qu'elle sache bien que c'est inutile : « Je t'assure qu'aujourd'hui je n'en peux plus. Cette fois, c'est vrai. »

Lulu regarde autour de nous, voit qu'aucune kapo n'est près pour l'instant, me prend le poignet et dit : « Mets-toi derrière moi, qu'on ne te voie pas. Tu pourras pleurer. » Elle parle à voix basse, timidement. Sans doute est-ce justement ce qu'il faut me dire puisque j'obéis à sa poussée gentille. Je laisse retomber mon outil, je reste là appuyée sur le manche et je pleure. Je ne voulais pas pleurer, mais les larmes affleurent, coulent sur mes joues. Je les laisse couler et, quand une larme touche mes lèvres, je sens le salé et je continue de pleurer.

Lulu travaille et guette. Parfois elle se retourne et, de sa manche, doucement, elle essuie

mon visage. Je pleure. Je ne pense plus à rien,
je pleure.

Je ne sais plus pourquoi je pleure lorsque Lulu
me tire : « C'est tout maintenant. Viens travailler. La voilà. » Avec tant de bonté que je n'ai
pas honte d'avoir pleuré. C'est comme si j'avais
pleuré contre la poitrine de ma mère.

L'ORCHESTRE

Il se tenait sur un terre-plein près de la porte.

Celle qui dirigeait avait été célèbre à Vienne. Toutes étaient bonnes musiciennes. Elles avaient subi un examen pour être choisies parmi un grand nombre. Elles devaient le sursis à la musique.

Parce qu'avec la belle saison il avait fallu un orchestre. À moins que ce fût le nouveau commandant. Il aimait la musique. Quand il commandait de jouer pour lui, il faisait distribuer aux musiciennes un demi-pain en supplément. Et quand les arrivants descendaient des wagons pour aller en rangs à la chambre à gaz, il aimait que ce fût au rythme d'une marche gaie.

Elles jouaient le matin lorsque les colonnes partaient. En passant, nous devions prendre le pas. Après, elles jouaient des valses. Des valses qu'on avait entendues ailleurs dans un lointain aboli. Les entendre là était intolérable.

Assises sur des tabourets, elles jouent. Ne regardez pas les doigts de la violoncelliste, ni ses yeux quand elle joue, vous ne pourriez le supporter.

Ne regardez pas les gestes de celle qui dirige. Elle parodie celle qu'elle était dans ce grand café de Vienne où elle dirigeait un orchestre féminin, déjà, et cela se voit, qu'elle pense à ce qu'elle était autrefois.

Toutes portent une jupe plissée bleu marine, un corsage clair, un foulard lavande sur la tête. Elles sont ainsi vêtues pour donner le pas aux autres qui vont aux marais dans des robes avec lesquelles elles dorment, autrement les robes ne sécheraient jamais.

Les colonnes sont parties. L'orchestre reste un moment encore.

Ne regardez pas, n'écoutez pas, surtout s'il joue « La Veuve joyeuse » pendant que, derrière les seconds barbelés, des hommes sortent un à un d'une baraque et que les kapos avec des ceinturons frappent un à un les hommes qui sortent et qui sont nus.

Ne regardez pas l'orchestre qui joue « La Veuve joyeuse ».

N'écoutez pas. Vous n'entendriez que les coups sur le dos des hommes et le bruit métallique que fait la boucle quand le ceinturon vole.

Ne regardez pas les musiciennes qui jouent cependant que des hommes squelettiques et nus sortent sous les coups qui les font chanceler. Ils vont à la désinfection, parce qu'il y a décidément trop de poux dans cette baraque.

Ne regardez pas la violoniste. Elle joue sur un violon qui serait celui de Yehudi si Yehudi n'était au-delà de miles d'océan. C'est le violon de quel Yehudi ?

Ne regardez pas, n'écoutez pas.

Ne pensez pas à tous les Yehudis qui avaient emporté leur violon.

AINSI VOUS CROYIEZ

Ainsi vous croyiez qu'aux lèvres des mourants
  ne montent que des paroles solennelles
parce que le solennel fleurit naturellement au lit
  de la mort
un lit est toujours prêt à l'apparat des funé-
  railles
avec la famille au bord
la sincère douleur l'air de circonstance.

Nues sur les grabats du révir, nos camarades
presque toutes ont dit :
  « Cette fois-ci je vais claboter. »
Elles étaient nues sur les planches nues.
Elles étaient sales et les planches étaient sales
de diarrhée et de pus.
Elles ne savaient pas que c'était leur compli-
quer la tâche, à celles qui survivraient, qui
devraient rapporter aux parents les dernières
paroles. Les parents attendaient le solennel.
Impossible de les décevoir. Le trivial est indigne
au florilège des mots ultimes.

Mais il n'était pas permis d'être faible à soi-même.

Alors elles ont dit : « Je vais claboter » pour ne pas ôter aux autres leur courage

et elles comptaient si peu qu'une seule survécût qu'elles n'ont rien confié qui pût être message.

Le printemps

Toutes ces chairs qui avaient perdu la carnation et la vie de la chair s'étalaient dans la boue séchée en poussière, achevaient au soleil de se flétrir, de se défaire – chairs brunâtres, violacées, grises toutes –, elles se confondaient si bien avec le sol de poussière qu'il fallait faire effort pour distinguer là des femmes, pour distinguer dans ces peaux plissées qui pendaient des seins de femmes – des seins vides.

Ô vous qui leur dites adieu au seuil d'une prison ou au seuil de votre mort au matin terni de longues veillées funèbres, heureux que vous ne puissiez voir ce qu'ils ont fait de vos femmes, de leur poitrine que vous osiez une dernière fois effleurer au seuil de la mort, des seins de femmes si doux toujours, d'une si bouleversante douceur à vous qui partiez mourir – vos femmes.

Il fallait faire effort pour distinguer des visages dans les traits où les prunelles n'éclairaient plus, des visages qui avaient couleur de cendre ou de

terre, taillés dans des souches pourrissantes ou
détachées d'un bas-relief très ancien mais que le
temps n'aurait pu atténuer au saillant des pommettes – un fouillis de têtes – têtes sans cheve-
lure, incroyablement petites – têtes de hiboux à
l'arcade sourcilière disproportionnée – ô tous
ces visages sans regard – têtes et visages, corps
contre des corps à demi couchés dans la boue
séchée en poussière.

D'entre les haillons – auprès de quoi ce que
vous appelez haillons, vous, serait draperies –
d'entre les loques terreuses apparaissaient des
mains – des mains apparaissaient parce qu'elles
bougeaient, parce que les doigts pliaient et se
crispaient, parce qu'ils fourrageaient les haillons, fouillaient les aisselles, et les poux entre les
ongles des pouces craquaient. Du sang faisait
une tache brune sur les ongles qui écrasaient les
poux.

Ce qui restait de vie dans les yeux et dans les
mains vivait encore par ce geste – mais les jambes
dans la poussière – jambes nues suintantes
d'abcès, creusées de plaies – les jambes dans la
poussière étaient inertes comme des pilons de
bois – inertes – pesantes

les têtes penchées tenaient aux cous comme
des têtes de bois – pesantes

et les femmes qui à la chaleur du premier soleil dépouillaient leurs loques pour les épouiller,

découvrant leur cou qui n'était plus que nœuds et cordes, leurs épaules qui étaient clavicules plutôt, leur poitrine où les seins n'empêchaient pas qu'on vît les côtes – cerceaux

toutes ces femmes appuyées les unes aux autres, immobiles dans la boue séchée en poussière, répétaient sans savoir

– elles savaient, vous savez – cela est plus terrible encore

répétaient la scène qu'elles mourraient le lendemain – ou un jour tout proche

car elles mourraient le lendemain ou un jour tout proche

car chacune meurt mille fois sa mort.

Le lendemain ou un jour tout proche, elles seraient cadavres dans la poussière qui succédait à la neige et à la boue de l'hiver. Elles avaient tenu tout l'hiver – dans les marais, dans la boue, dans la neige. Elles ne pouvaient pas aller au-delà du premier soleil.

Le premier soleil de l'année sur la terre nue.

La terre pour la première fois n'était pas l'élément hostile, qui menace chaque pas – si tu tombes, si tu te laisses tomber, tu ne te relèveras pas –

Pour la première fois on pouvait s'asseoir par terre.

La terre, pour la première fois nue, pour la

première fois sèche, cessait d'exercer son atti-
rance de vertige, se laisser glisser par terre – se
laisser glisser dans la mort comme dans la
neige – dans l'oubli – s'abandonner – cesser
de commander à des bras, à des jambes et
à tant de muscles mineurs pour qu'aucun ne
lâche, pour rester debout – pour rester vivant –
glisser – se laisser glisser dans la neige – se
laisser glisser dans la mort à l'étreinte amollie
de neige.

La boue gluante et la neige sale étaient pour
la première fois poussière.

Poussière sèche, tiédie de soleil
il est plus dur de mourir dans la poussière
plus dur de mourir quand il fait soleil.

Le soleil brillait – pâle comme à l'est. Le ciel
était très bleu. Quelque part le printemps chantait.

Le printemps chantait dans ma mémoire –
dans ma mémoire.

Ce chant me surprenait tant que je n'étais pas
sûre de l'entendre. Je croyais l'entendre en rêve.
Et j'essayais de le nier, de ne plus l'entendre, et
je regardais d'un regard désespéré mes compagnes autour de moi. Elles étaient agglutinées là,
au soleil, dans l'espace qui séparait les baraques des barbelés. Les barbelés si blancs dans le
soleil.

Ce dimanche-là.

Un dimanche extraordinaire parce que c'était un dimanche de repos et qu'il était permis de s'asseoir par terre.

Toutes les femmes étaient assises dans la poussière de boue séchée en un troupeau misérable qui faisait penser à des mouches sur un fumier. Sans doute à cause de l'odeur. L'odeur était si dense et si fétide qu'on croyait respirer, non pas dans l'air, mais dans un fluide autre plus épais et visqueux qui enveloppait et isolait cette partie de la terre d'une atmosphère surajoutée où ne pouvaient se mouvoir que des êtres adaptés. Nous.

Puanteur de diarrhée et de charogne. Au-dessus de cette puanteur le ciel était bleu. Et dans ma mémoire le printemps chantait.

Pourquoi seul de tous ces êtres avais-je conservé la mémoire ? Dans ma mémoire le printemps chantait. Pourquoi cette différence ?

Les pousses des saules scintillent argentées dans le soleil – un peuplier plie sous le vent – l'herbe est si verte que les fleurs du printemps brillent de couleurs surprenantes. Le printemps baigne tout d'un air léger, léger, enivrant. Le printemps monte à la tête. Le printemps est cette symphonie qui éclate de toutes parts, qui éclate, qui éclate.

Qui éclate. – Dans ma tête à éclater.

Pourquoi ai-je gardé la mémoire ? Pourquoi cette injustice ?

Et de ma mémoire ne s'éveillent que des images si pauvres que les larmes me viennent de désespoir.

Au printemps, se promener le long des quais et les platanes du Louvre sont de si fine ciselure auprès des marronniers déjà feuillus des Tuileries.

Au printemps, traverser le Luxembourg avant le bureau. Des enfants courent dans les allées, le cartable sous le bras. Des enfants. Penser à des enfants ici.

Au printemps, le merle de l'acacia sous la fenêtre se réveille avant l'aube. Dès avant l'aube il apprend à siffler. Il siffle encore mal. Nous ne sommes qu'au début d'avril.

Pourquoi avoir laissé à moi seulement la mémoire ? Et ma mémoire ne trouve que des clichés. « Mon beau navire, ô ma mémoire »... Où es-tu, ma vraie mémoire ? Où es-tu, ma mémoire terrestre ?

Le ciel était très bleu, d'un bleu si bleu sur les poteaux de ciment blancs et les barbelés blancs aussi, d'un bleu si bleu que le réseau des fils électriques paraissait plus blanc, plus implacable,

ici rien n'est vert

ici rien n'est végétal
ici rien n'est vivant.

Loin au-delà des fils, le printemps voltige, le printemps frissonne, le printemps chante. Dans ma mémoire. Pourquoi ai-je gardé la mémoire ?

Pourquoi avoir gardé le souvenir des rues aux pavés sonores, des fifres du printemps sur les bancs des marchands de légumes au marché, des flèches de soleil sur le parquet blond au réveil, le souvenir des rires et des chapeaux, des cloches dans l'air du soir, des premières blouses et des anémones ?

Ici, le soleil n'est pas du printemps. C'est le soleil de l'éternité, c'est le soleil d'avant la création. Et j'avais gardé la mémoire du soleil qui brille sur la terre des vivants, du soleil sur la terre des blés.

Sous le soleil de l'éternité, la chair cesse de palpiter, les paupières bleuissent, les mains se fanent, les langues gonflent noires, les bouches pourrissent.

Ici, en dehors du temps, sous le soleil d'avant la création, les yeux pâlissent. Les yeux s'éteignent. Les lèvres pâlissent. Les lèvres meurent.

Toutes les paroles sont depuis longtemps flétries

Tous les mots sont depuis longtemps décolorés

Graminée – ombelle – source – une grappe de lilas – l'ondée – toutes les images sont depuis longtemps livides.

Pourquoi ai-je gardé la mémoire ? Je ne puis retrouver le goût de ma salive dans ma bouche au printemps – le goût d'une tige d'herbe qu'on suce. Je ne puis retrouver l'odeur des cheveux où joue le vent, sa main rassurante et sa douceur.

Ma mémoire est plus exsangue qu'une feuille d'automne

Ma mémoire a oublié la rosée

Ma mémoire a perdu sa sève. Ma mémoire a perdu tout son sang.

C'est alors que le cœur doit s'arrêter de battre – s'arrêter de battre – de battre.

C'est pour cela que je ne peux pas m'approcher de celle-ci qui appelle. Ma voisine. Appelle-t-elle ? Pourquoi appelle-t-elle ? Elle a eu tout d'un coup la mort sur son visage, la mort violette aux ailes du nez, la mort au fond des orbites, la mort dans ses doigts qui se tordent et se nouent comme des brindilles que mord la flamme, et elle dit dans une langue inconnue des paroles que je n'entends pas.

Les barbelés sont très blancs sur le ciel bleu.

M'appelait-elle ? Elle est immobile mainte-

nant, la tête retombée dans la poussière souil-
lée.

Loin au-delà des barbelés, le printemps
chante.

Ses yeux se sont vidés
Et nous avons perdu la mémoire.

Aucun de nous ne reviendra.

Aucun de nous n'aurait dû revenir.

CET OUVRAGE A ÉTÉ ACHEVÉ D'IMPRIMER LE
DIX SEPTEMBRE DEUX MILLE VINGT DANS
LES ATELIERS DE NORMANDIE ROTO IM-
PRESSION S.A.S. À LONRAI (61250) (FRANCE)
N° D'ÉDITEUR : 6612
N° D'IMPRIMEUR : 2002956

Dépôt légal : septembre 2020

Jean Echenoz, *Nous trois*.
Jean Echenoz, *Un an*.
Paul Éluard, *Au rendez-vous allemand* suivi de *Poésie et vérité 1942*.
Christian Gailly, *Be-Bop*.
Christian Gailly, *Dernier amour*.
Christian Gailly, *Les Évadés*.
Christian Gailly, *Les Fleurs*.
Christian Gailly, *L'Incident*.
Christian Gailly, *K.622*.
Christian Gailly, *Nuage rouge*.
Christian Gailly, *Un soir au club*.
Anne Godard, *L'Inconsolable*.
Bernard-Marie Koltès, *Une part de ma vie*.
Hélène Lenoir, *L'Entracte*.
Hélène Lenoir, *Son nom d'avant*.
Robert Linhart, *L'Établi*.
Laurent Mauvignier, *Apprendre à finir*.
Laurent Mauvignier, *Autour du monde*.
Laurent Mauvignier, *Continuer*.
Laurent Mauvignier, *Dans la foule*.
Laurent Mauvignier, *Des hommes*.
Laurent Mauvignier, *Loin d'eux*.
Laurent Mauvignier, *Voyage à New Delhi*.
Marie NDiaye, *En famille*.
Marie NDiaye, *Rosie Carpe*.
Marie NDiaye, *La Sorcière*.
Marie NDiaye, *Un temps de saison*.
Christian Oster, *Loin d'Odile*.
Christian Oster, *Mon grand appartement*.
Christian Oster, *Une femme de ménage*.
Robert Pinget, *L'Inquisitoire*.
Robert Pinget, *Monsieur Songe* suivi de *Le Harnais* et *Charrue*.
Yves Ravey, *Enlèvement avec rançon*.
Yves Ravey, *La Fille de mon meilleur ami*.
Yves Ravey, *Un notaire peu ordinaire*.
Yves Ravey, *Trois jours chez ma tante*.
Alain Robbe-Grillet, *Djinn*.
Alain Robbe-Grillet, *Les Gommes*.
Alain Robbe-Grillet, *La Jalousie*.
Alain Robbe-Grillet, *Pour un nouveau roman*.
Alain Robbe-Grillet, *Le Voyeur*.
Jean Rouaud, *Les Champs d'honneur*.
Jean Rouaud, *Des hommes illustres*.
Jean Rouaud, *Pour vos cadeaux*.
Nathalie Sarraute, *Tropismes*.

Eugène Savitzkaya, *Exquise Louise.*
Eugène Savitzkaya, *Marin mon cœur.*
Inge Scholl, *La Rose Blanche.*
Claude Simon, *L'Acacia.*
Claude Simon, *Les Géorgiques.*
Claude Simon, *L'Herbe.*
Claude Simon, *Histoire.*
Claude Simon, *La Route des Flandres.*
Claude Simon, *Le Tramway.*
Claude Simon, *Le Vent.*
Jean-Philippe Toussaint, *L'Appareil-photo.*
Jean-Philippe Toussaint, *Autoportrait (à l'étranger).*
Jean-Philippe Toussaint, *Faire l'amour.*
Jean-Philippe Toussaint, *Fuir.*
Jean-Philippe Toussaint, *La Salle de bain.*
Jean-Philippe Toussaint, *Nue.*
Jean-Philippe Toussaint, *La Télévision.*
Jean-Philippe Toussaint, *L'Urgence et la Patience.*
Jean-Philippe Toussaint, *La Vérité sur Marie.*
Tanguy Viel, *L'Absolue Perfection du crime.*
Tanguy Viel, *Article 353 du code pénal.*
Tanguy Viel, *Cinéma.*
Tanguy Viel, *La Disparition de Jim Sullivan.*
Tanguy Viel, *Insoupçonnable.*
Tanguy Viel, *Paris-Brest.*
Antoine Volodine, *Lisbonne, dernière marge.*
Antoine Volodine, *Le Port intérieur.*
Elie Wiesel, *La Nuit.*
Monique Wittig, *Les Guérillères.*
Monique Wittig, *L'Opoponax.*

What had she just allowed to happen?

She gasped against his lips and he parted from her, still so close their foreheads rested on one another. Her chest rose and fell with her labored breathing, her body heaving with needs she'd never experienced before.

She pushed against him. He dropped his hand and stepped back.

"What, you didn't like it?"

He knew, damn him, that she liked it! "It wasn't appropriate."

He snorted. "Spare me the scandalized rhetoric. There's no harm in a few kisses."

A few kisses? *A few kisses?* The foundations of her life were rocking like pillars in an earthquake, and he'd dismissed what had just happened as "a few kisses."

"We're not inexperienced, you and I." He paused. "Are we?"

She hadn't thought . . . had entirely forgotten the role she played. When he'd taken her in his arms, she'd acted only as herself and made the unforgivable bungle of leaving behind her mask . . .

Other **AVON ROMANCES**

ATTENTION: ORGANIZATIONS AND CORPORATIONS
Most Avon Books paperbacks are available at special quantity discounts for bulk purchases for sales promotions, premiums, or fund-raising. For information, please call or write:

Special Markets Department, HarperCollins Publishers, Inc., 10 East 53rd Street, New York, N.Y. 10022–5299. Telephone: (212) 207–7528. Fax: (212) 207-7222.

REBECCA WADE

AN INNOCENT MISTRESS

FOUR BRIDES FOR FOUR BROTHERS

AVON BOOKS

An Imprint of HarperCollinsPublishers

This is a work of fiction. Names, characters, places, and incidents are products of the author's imagination or are used fictitiously and are not to be construed as real. Any resemblance to actual events, locales, organizations, or persons, living or dead, is entirely coincidental.

AVON BOOKS
An Imprint of HarperCollins*Publishers*
10 East 53rd Street
New York, New York 10022-5299

Copyright © 2001 by Rebecca Wade
ISBN: 0-380-81619-9
www.avonromance.com

All rights reserved. No part of this book may be used or reproduced in any manner whatsoever without written permission, except in the case of brief quotations embodied in critical articles and reviews. For information address Avon Books, an Imprint of HarperCollins Publishers.

First Avon Books paperback printing: September 2001

Avon Trademark Reg. U.S. Pat. Off. and in Other Countries, Marca Registrada, Hecho en U.S.A.
HarperCollins ® is a trademark of HarperCollins Publishers Inc.

Printed in the U.S.A.

10 9 8 7 6 5 4 3 2 1

If you purchased this book without a cover, you should be aware that this book is stolen property. It was reported as "unsold and destroyed" to the publisher, and neither the author nor the publisher has received any payment for this "stripped book."

To Kristen and Carrie, my precious sisters.
This one's yours for a million reasons
but mostly because I can't think of two people
I'd rather share my past and my future with.

Here's to three gray-blonde grannies sitting together
and laughing over things no one else
would find funny.
I cannot wait.

Prologue

Houston, Texas
1878

"Will the defendant please rise."

Jarrod Stone stood, as did his three brothers. Clint and J. T. stood beside him in the first row of the courtroom. Holden stood in front of them at his position at the accused's table. Just like always, Jarrod thought. The four of them against the world, ready to take on all comers.

Heavy on his back, he could feel the attention of those in the courtroom—the crowds who'd come to feast on the details of the trial simply because Holden was his brother. People liked it when bad things happened to the families of rich men. A twitter of anticipation rolled through the space. Jarrod set his jaw against it.

1

"Gentlemen of the jury, what say you in the matter of the State *vs.* Holden Stone?" the judge asked the head juror.

Jarrod's eyes narrowed into a stare that had cowed the most fearsome business magnates in the country as he turned his attention to the head juror. There'd be hell to pay if they found Holden guilty.

For twenty years he'd been the head of this household. As the oldest it was his job, his God-given *right*, to protect the others. If he could have, he'd gladly have shouldered the accusation, the arrest, and the trial on Holden's behalf. For a man like Jarrod, jail time would have been better than being caged in a courtroom, where he could do nothing but watch and wait. His gut churned against the powerlessness of it.

The head juror, a short man with a pockmarked face, pulled taut the paper with Holden's fate, and thus Jarrod's, branded onto it. "We the jury," he cleared his throat, "find the defendant, Holden Stone, guilty of aiding and abetting the crimes of the Lucas gang."

Denial roared within Jarrod. No. *No*! Couldn't any of them see that Holden hadn't done what they accused him of? And yet they dared convict him?

The judge's seat creaked as he turned from the jury box toward Holden. "I sentence you, Holden Stone, to six years in the state penitentiary for your crimes."

The muscles in Jarrod's body braced as if against the lash of a whip on flesh. Six years?

The banging of the gavel ripped across his ears, and then movement and noise trickled through the courtroom. The judge in his flowing black sauntered from his throne, the jurors stirred, the people behind them in row upon row of seats whispered.

Jarrod watched, bile burning the back of his throat, as the bailiff crossed to Holden, gathered his wrists behind his back, and fastened handcuffs to them. His youngest brother hadn't so much as flinched. His profile was hard and expressionless, giving no indication he'd even heard the verdict or the sentence.

Jarrod had seen him do that before—wear indifference like a shield. He wished he didn't still remember the way Holden had looked at their mother's deathbed. A five-year-old in an oversize hat and a too-small shirt struggling hard to pretend that his world wasn't ending. When their mother's chest had stilled, her last labored breath wheezing from her lungs, Holden had lifted his gaze to Jarrod, and Jarrod had read trust in his brother's eyes. That trust had been sacred between them ever since. Inviolate.

The bailiff moved to lead Holden away. Before he could, Jarrod reached out and grabbed his brother's arm. Holden stopped, and their eyes met, as they had all those years before. Oldest brother to youngest.

"I'm going to find him," Jarrod vowed. "I'll get you out."

The bailiff jerked Holden forward, and his brother's arm was wrenched from Jarrod's grasp before Holden could reply. It took mere seconds for them to escort Holden through the back door of the courtroom and out of sight.

J. T. blew out his breath.

"God," Clint said.

Jarrod continued staring at the door, even when it had rested dead in its casing for long moments. He let the crushing reality of what had just happened sink into himself, used its cut to sharpen his resolve. An agent called

Twilight's Ghost was responsible for Holden's arrest. And as the agent responsible, he was also the agent with the power to right the wrong he'd done by accusing an innocent man. Though no one knew the agent's true identity or claimed, even, to have seen the man in the flesh, the people did whisper the name of the man's mistress. Sophia Vanessa LaRue.

At the thought of her, an old remembrance raised its head. A dark-haired girl in a dress of snowy white—he cut off the memory.

Feeling a decade older than when he'd entered the courtroom, Jarrod led his brothers down the center aisle. People made room for them, as people always did. The courtroom doors had been thrown open, and a watery February wind coursed against them, causing Jarrod's greatcoat to billow.

Sophia LaRue was the only lead he had toward finding Twilight's Ghost. So he'd go to her, because no matter how long it took or how much it cost, he *would* locate Twilight's Ghost. And when he did, he'd have both justice for Holden and his own personal revenge against the man.

There was about to be hell to pay.

Chapter 1

Blackhaw Manor
Galveston, Texas
One week later

The agent known by gossips everywhere as Twilight's Ghost swabbed her miniature brush into a pot of lip stain, then dabbed on a nearly invisible quantity of the rosy hue. Sophia Vanessa LaRue rubbed her lips together, scooted back on her dressing-table stool, and peered critically at her reflection in the mirror. Though darkness had fallen, the fringed lamp nearby provided light enough for examinations.

For this evening's dinner party she'd squeezed herself into an old black gown. Mrs. Dewberry had done her best to revive it by stitching dark beading around the V-shaped neckline and replacing the gauzy fabric of the sleeves. Still, Sophia could see worn patches near her waist.

Oh, well. It would have to do. *She* would have to do. Her breath blew out in a stream. She'd rather be dressed tonight in men's clothing, stealing through the streets after the city slept, then waiting and watching for the criminals she caught. That was the part of her job that suited her best. Unfortunately, gathering details on people and events through small talk at dinner parties was also part of her job.

Footsteps sounded in the hall. Sophia watched in the mirror as Maggie swept into the bedroom already wearing her nightgown.

Sophia turned on the stool to face her friend. The too-short length of Maggie's gown, threadbare white cotton dotted with pink roses, exposed her feet. The vulnerability of those lovely, big, pale feet tugged at Sophia's heart. Her Maggie. How was she ever going to keep Blackhaw over both their heads?

"God bless, you look gorgeous," Maggie said, planting her hands on reed-thin hips.

"You think this gown is all right?"

"Yes!"

"You're too kind."

"No, I'm not. I have eyes, that's all. Gorgeous, I tell you." She motioned toward Sophia's face. "I'd just slick on a bit more of that lip stain and here"—she reached toward Sophia's snugly bound hair—"let me just loosen this a bit."

Playfully, Sophia swatted her hand away.

Maggie made another darting attempt, and managed to pull free a wisp near Sophia's ear.

"Maggie," Sophia chided with a smile, glancing in the mirror as she tried to smooth the tendril back into place.

"I swear," Maggie muttered, glaring at her in the mirror, "if I looked even a fourth as beautiful as you do—"

"You're *more* beautiful than I, with that copper hair—"

"I'd wear lower-cut bodices, a helluva lot more lip stain, and all my hair down. You're supposed to be a widow, you know. You can afford to test the boundaries a little."

"I know, I know." She'd heard this refrain countless times before. "I like my hair this way." She patted a miniscule amount of lavender perfume onto her neck and went to the armoire in search of her evening gloves.

"Just came to tell you that Knoxley should be here to fetch you any minute," Maggie said from behind her.

"Thanks."

"And with that, I'm going to bed to imagine all the men I wish I had in my life and don't. Should you happen upon someone devastating to look at and available between here and the front door, don't hesitate to summon me."

"Look around." Sophia found her gloves, swiped up her black reticule, then closed the armoire's doors. "This house is big enough that there might be a man hiding in a cupboard somewhere."

"You don't think I've looked?" Maggie stopped on the room's threshold, halfway out the door. "We've been living here for *years*, girl. There's not a not a single well-endowed man hidden in any corner of this house. I would swear to it before witnesses." Ruefully, she shook her head. "One would think the Secret Service would take better care of their agents."

"One would think," Sophia agreed, smiling.

"Have an enjoyable evening," Maggie said as she vanished.

Sophia had just pressed a folded handkerchief into her reticule when a thunderous knock sounded from below. Clearly, Knoxley had arrived.

Despite the early darkness of a winter's night, the lantern fire from Jarrod's carriage illuminated the round face and rosy cheeks of the housekeeper who'd answered his knock.

"My name's Jarrod Stone. I've come to speak with Mrs. Sophia LaRue."

The woman's chin dimpled with consternation. "I'm sorry, but Mrs. LaRue isn't expecting you, sir."

"I realize that; however, I have a pressing matter to discuss with her and need to see her."

"I'm sorry." The woman shook her curly, gray head. She'd clearly had long years of practice turning away unwanted men. "Mrs. LaRue only visits with those callers who have been previously scheduled."

"Tell her that Jarrod Stone is here—"

Another adamant shake of the head. "No."

Jarrod placed his hand on the door and pushed. He hadn't built his empire by waiting to be listed on some damn schedule.

Incredulity wiped clean the housekeeper's expression for a split second. Then she made a sputtering sound and threw her formidable weight against the door.

Never breaking her gaze, he applied steady pressure in the opposite direction, enough to scoot her back without toppling her. When he'd cleared a large enough opening, he strode into the foyer. "Where is Mrs. LaRue?"

"Well, I never!" the woman huffed, swatting her apron into place.

"Are you going to tell me where she is, or would you rather I search for her?" Jarrod asked, rounding on the woman.

The ornery housekeeper squished her lips together. The fire in her eyes supplied his answer.

"Fine." Jarrod cataloged the rooms emptying off the foyer. He'd search for her. Only a few lamps were lit, and he had to squint against the meager light as he peered into one empty parlor after another.

He'd spent the past week tabling his business interests, moving his household here, and buying up every available scrap of information on Sophia LaRue. Evidently, much had changed for the girl he remembered. When her family lost its fortune and her grandmother died of grief because of it, she'd been farmed off to a Catholic orphanage. She'd been raised by the sisters, married to a man named LaRue, and quickly widowed by the same.

But one thing hadn't changed. She was still living here at Blackhaw Manor. Though he'd seen it countless times from the outside as a boy, this was the first time he'd ever set foot inside the house, an elegant dinosaur of a place with an interior that looked shabbier than he'd expected.

The housekeeper scurried toward the back of the building, yelling for "Father."

Deciding the upper stories held his best bet of finding a bedroom and Sophia LaRue, Jarrod climbed the wide, gracefully curving staircase. He gained the second floor and thew open the first door he came to. Not only was the room unoccupied, it was completely without furniture. He opened the next door and the next and the next. All much the same—vacant rooms with crumbling molding and tattered wallpaper. When he pushed open the fifth door, a woman swirled to face him.

He stopped dead. This was unmistakably her. This was the woman who could and would lead him to Twilight's Ghost.

This was also the girl he recalled from two decades before.

The artful sweep of her brows perfectly complemented the startling color of her eyes, eyes he'd never forgotten. They were the color of expensive coffee in a clear glass container, held to the sunlight. The long, thick eyelashes surrounding them curled outward, giving her gaze a sensual cast, as if she knew all a man could ever want her to know about sex. Those eyes, though, were the only sensual thing about her.

Except for one stray wisp near her ear, her dark brown hair was pulled tightly back into a plain, sophisticated bun at the nape of her neck. Her delicate features reminded him of an ivory cameo. And her posture was practically vibrating with defensiveness, as if she'd bolt for the windows at the slightest provocation. A well-bred, stylish ice princess with the eyes of a siren and a gown that was showing signs of wear. The age of her gown and the state of her house made him wonder whether she loved Twilight's Ghost or whether she might be desperate enough to trade her body to him for the favors he could do her.

The silence between them pulled taut, crackling the air with intensity.

"Mrs. LaRue?"

Sophia stared at the man, the complete stranger, standing in her doorway. Her pulse thrummed hard and fast. No one *ever* barged into her private rooms. Or at least they never had before. Below stairs she could feign wealth. Upstairs the direness of her financial situation was obvious, so all guests were strictly forbidden.

When he'd thrown open her door, she'd plunged her hand into her skirt pocket, through the slit in the bottom, and around the handle of the knife she always wore in her garter. Her grip on the weapon tightened. "And you are?"

"Jarrod Stone."

Her attention streaked over him. Her brain fought to reconcile the man standing before her with all her restless imaginings of the awful children of Adam Stone. "Stone?" she repeated, voice slightly hoarse.

"That's right. Do you know who I am?"

"Yes." Jarrod Stone, the oldest brother, the oil baron. Late at night, she'd pored over reports of his feats on the battlefield. She'd read of the jobs he'd held in boomtowns across West Virginia. She knew the exact date that he himself had struck oil: July 10, 1868. She'd researched the company he'd founded, knew the names of his key associates, and had memorized the acquisitions he'd made. But none of her studies of him had prepared her for the tangible, physical strength of the man in the flesh.

Mother above, she'd envisioned him fat and beady-eyed with a cane and gold rings. She'd not realized he looked like this—that a man that looked like this walked her world at all. He was dressed completely in black, a specter of a man whose mere shadow dwarfed her. His body, hard and unforgiving with the promise of rigidly suppressed power, stood at least six feet tall. He had raven hair, a serious mouth, and a suit that had probably cost half her yearly income.

She imagined him, suddenly, standing with his legs braced apart on the front steps of his marble mansion, ripping thousand-dollar bills to shreds, and feeding them to twin wolves snapping and growling at his feet. Wolves of white with arresting green eyes identical to their master's.

When he stepped into the room, his dark charisma pushed at her, trapping her where she stood and stealing all the air. That, like everything else about him, completely offended her.

"What do you want?" She held her ground despite her instincts, which were all clamoring at her to flee.

"Your help."

"What makes you think I'd lift so much as a finger to help you?"

"Because I'll give you something in return."

She bitterly resented that he'd venture to show his face here, much less have the gall to expect anything from her. They both knew that his father, Adam Stone, had stolen every cent of her family's money. The loss of the fortune she could bear. That Adam Stone had never been caught, never made to pay for what he'd done to her grandmother was what she couldn't abide. Finding him and seeing justice done against him had been the central goal of her life since she'd been eight years old. It was what had initially driven her to seek employment with the Service. It was what had kept her warm in all the cold times, kept her company during all the lonely times, and kept her fighting to keep Blackhaw through all the times when she'd wanted to give up.

From beyond Jarrod, the voices of her alarmed housekeepers merged with thumping sounds as they rushed up the stairs.

"Your protectors are coming to evict me." A sharp smile lifted his lips.

The thought of her motley band of followers attempting to evict Jarrod Stone was laughable. "I'm not in the habit of entertaining men who barge into my private rooms uninvited."

"So I hear. Your housekeeper was so kind as to inform me of your schedule."

Sophia released her hold on the knife just before Mr. and Mrs. Dewberry bustled into the room. Their hectic movement struck a contrast against Jarrod's profound stillness.

"I'm so sorry." Mrs. Dewberry's face pinkened. "I did not issue him permission to enter. In fact, I told him he could not do so. He pushed his way in." She pointed and huffed. "Pushed, he did."

"It's all right," Sophia placated. "Mr. Stone and I have a matter to discuss privately. I'll be down in a moment."

"Certain?" Mrs. Dewberry asked.

"Certain." She'd hear his piece, take from him whatever she could, and get him out of her sight.

Grudgingly, her eyes shooting daggers at Jarrod, Mrs. Dewberry led her husband out. The latch clicked behind the couple, enveloping them in a quiet marred only by the rustling of a breeze-stirred curtain and the rasping of a loose shutter. The tension in the room heightened. For a man who'd sought her out with such fervency, he seemed oddly content to peer at her in silence.

Then, as if he had every right to do so, he started around the room. He scrutinized the simple furnishings, adjusted a book, examined the sampler Maggie had given her last birthday.

"Mr. Stone."

He picked up the candlestick from her bedside table, weighed it idly.

"Mr. Stone," she said more sharply. "Let's cut to the heart of the matter, shall we?"

"I noticed that several of the rooms on this floor are unfurnished," he commented. He eyed the plain white walls, set aside the candlestick. "Why?"

"I can't imagine what business that is of yours."

"None." His gaze honed on her with enough power to slice stone. "I'm asking anyway."

She crossed her arms over her chest and held her silence.

"It must be expensive, trying to keep up a house of this size and age."

She stiffened. How dare he, with all his hundreds of thousands, point out Blackhaw's shortcomings? Love and fierce protectiveness of the place welled in her breast. She and Maggie both worked their hearts out so that they could keep the house on their salaries. It's all she had left from the old days, thanks to his father, and she was both wildly proud of it and painfully aware of all the improvements it needed that she couldn't provide. "I manage."

"Looks like the west wing was damaged in the war."

"I manage."

"And the east wing, what? Hurricane?"

"You have my attention, Mr. Stone." Her voice sounded as tight as she felt. "Why do you need my help?"

He slung his hands into the pockets of his trousers, an action which pushed back the sides of his coat and revealed a snug charcoal gray vest beneath. He came toward her, too close for comfort, and leaned against the edge of her dresser. The pose was deceptively relaxed. She didn't believe it. There was a tenseness beneath his façade that told her his reason for coming here meant a great deal to him.

"Have you ever heard of a Secret Service agent named Twilight's Ghost?" he asked.

Everything inside Sophia went frightfully still. "Yes, I've heard of him." Most people in these parts had. A denial of knowledge from her might arouse his suspicion.

"Do you know him?"

"No."

"Are you sure?"

"Am I sure?" she asked, indignation in her tone. "Yes, I'm sure." For survival's sake she'd become an accomplished actress over the years. So much so, she sometimes forgot which parts of her were real.

"Here's my problem, Sophie—"

"Do not call me that."

"My brother Holden was falsely accused of aiding and abetting the Lucas gang based on a fourteen-year-old arrest warrant. He was found guilty and sentenced to jail."

Falsely accused, her derriere. Her information on Holden had been unambiguous.

"I've learned that Twilight's Ghost was the agent responsible for having Holden brought in and charged. It seems to me that a Secret Service agent would have more pressing matters to concern himself with than fourteen-year-old arrest warrants. My question for you is why Twilight's Ghost would bother with my brother?"

"I've no idea." Though she knew exactly. Two months ago, her friend Oliver, the man who had once been her grandmother's advisor, had crossed paths with Holden Stone at Austin's train station. Holden had treated him with such hostility that he'd warned Sophia about Holden afterward. Oliver had made her promise that should Holden attempt to harass her directly, that she'd inform him so that he could lend her his protection. Holden's belligerent behavior toward Oliver had struck her as suspicious, so she'd gone back over her information on him, then worked to uncover even more about the youngest Stone. When she'd discovered his outstanding arrest warrant, she'd gladly sent officers of the law out after him. Justice was what she did.

"The only reason I can see for Twilight's Ghost to investigate Holden is if he first decided to investigate my father's crimes."

He was exactly right. So right it frightened her.

"And why would the Ghost reopen the case against my father? There's no reason. Unless, of course, someone . . . his mistress, perhaps . . . asked it of him."

She met his gaze, her face void of expression.

"Your family's fortune was stolen twenty years ago," he said. You're the only one who still cares about my father's supposed crime, the only one who'd have asked Twilight's Ghost to find my father, and the only one I know of who has access to Twilight's Ghost."

He was accusing her right to her face. Worse, he was terrifyingly close to the truth.

"So did you?" he asked.

"What?"

"Ask Twilight's Ghost to reopen the case against my father?"

"No."

He extracted his hands from his pockets and braced them next to his hips against the corner of the dresser. Strong man's hands; big, short-nailed, with veins evident beneath the skin. "No?" he asked, one brow cocked with skepticism.

"No."

"You should know that I don't give a damn about my father. The Ghost can search for him, arrest him, hang him for all I care. But when your lover went after my brother for a crime he didn't commit, he went too far. For that I'm going to hunt him down and see that things are set right."

"I fail to see what this has to do with me."

"You're going to help me find Twilight's Ghost."

The fervor in his eyes seared her. He felt that he and his brother had been deeply wronged, she could read that so clearly. Because of it, he wanted more than his brother's release. He wanted revenge against Twilight's Ghost. Against her.

A shiver of foreboding crawled down the back of her neck. Jarrod Stone was a powerful man and his hatred a powerful force.

Needing distance from him, she strode to the nearest of the room's two tall windows. Others had set out to find Twilight's Ghost and failed. There was no reason to think Jarrod Stone would succeed at revealing her identity. So why were her legs quivering? Why had her mouth gone dry?

She pushed aside the heavy curtain and stared at the property below. Every rise and fall of the earth and every tree in the orchard she knew by heart. "You were right," she said at length, "when you said that I have an interest in finding your father. If someone has reopened the case against him, then I'm glad they have. I sincerely hope they hunt him down in the streets and make him pay for what he did." She slanted her body toward him and met his gaze. "But you've come to the wrong place. I don't know anything about either your brother or the agent you're after. I can't help you."

He didn't so much as blink.

"It seems to me that if you want your brother freed, your best option is to cooperate with the Secret Service. Tell them where your father is." It was the subtlest way she could figure to fish for information.

"I don't know where he is. None of us have ever known."

This time, she let her incredulity show.

He shrugged. "We don't."

She made her way to her dressing table, where her gloves and reticule rested. "This conversation is over," she said coolly. "I have an engagement for this evening."

"I'll pay you to help me find the agent," he said.

Typical that he'd throw money at her. It was the only thing men like him understood. "There's no price you could pay me that I'd accept," she answered, not even bothering to look up as she slid her hand into an elbow-length black glove.

"Isn't there?"

"No."

"Name your price."

Her movements slowed as she pressed her second glove into the V between each of her fingertips. If he wanted her to name a price, she would. A price too high for even his rich blood. She paused to consider a fee that would be suitably outrageous.

"Name your price," he said again.

"Five thousand dollars," she replied. For the first time since he'd stormed into her life, she wanted to smile.

"Five thousand dollars," he murmured. He began to walk, slowly, his head canted forward as if deep in thought. He patted his trouser pockets, then his jacket pockets. He whispered the sum again, reached inside his suit jacket, and extracted an enormous stack of money.

Sophia's urge to smile vanished.

He freed the bills from a platinum money clip, counted some out in rapid succession, and placed them on the foot of her bed. Right there on the white quilt the sisters had stitched for her when she was sixteen.

She surveyed the money and him with triple the astonishment she'd experienced when she'd glanced up to see him towering in her doorway. *Mother Mary.* Jarrod Stone had just laid five thousand dollars on her bed. Enough to both pay Blackhaw's taxes and restore it. What sort of man carried that amount of money around with him? What sort was willing to throw so much away?

His gaze swung to her—triumphant. The glitter in his eyes informed her he was pleased with himself. Pleased in that infuriating, cocksure way only men can be pleased.

"Five thousand," he said. "Plus a tip."

"A tip?"

He tested the mattress by pressing down on it a few times, as if his payment for her help came complete with a complimentary tumble beneath the sheets.

Sophia ground her teeth. Smugness had never been one of her favorite characteristics in others. In a Stone it was despicable. She slid her reticule onto her wrist and approached him, scooping up the pile of money. It would be a cold day in hell before she'd take so much as a penny from Jarrod Stone, especially for the service of assisting him track down herself.

She opened his jacket and, holding her breath at his nearness, returned the money to the inside pocket. "I changed my mind." Her gaze flicked to his. "There's no price, not even ten times this much, that could convince me to align myself with you."

The light behind his green eyes turned deadly cold. "Why?"

She stepped away. "Why? Because your father ruined everything in my life I held dear. And because your money can never buy back my trust in anyone with the last name of Stone." She brushed past him, exited her room, and walked swiftly along the upper hallway. The sound of his footsteps followed her down the staircase and through the foyer to the manor's front door. Sophia swung it wide, ridiculously eager for him to be gone.

Jarrod passed over the threshold obediently enough, but turned after just two steps. Beyond him, on the drive, a carriage waited. Black as Satan's chariot, gleaming with its own lanterns as well as reflected light from the house. "I'm going to find Twilight's Ghost," he said, his tone steely sure.

Because she couldn't stand to look at him anymore, to see the fearsome evidence of his determination, she shut

sight the sailing ship whence they'd come. No, she couldn't make it out. Could be any one of several. Which meant she'd bide her time and watch their return trip until she could be sure where they'd gone. Then she'd have to paddle her own tiny vessel out into the harbor, until she was close enough to distinguish the name on the guilty ship's bow. Years ago, she'd learned how easily anonymous ships could be moved between dark and dawn. Rowing out to read their name was the only sure way to identify them.

Then, *then*, she could go home and drink her tea.

An uneventful night, really. Quite boring.

Hell, this waiting is boring.

This was the third night Jarrod had spent here, inside the tiny building holding Blackhaw's tack. So far he'd seen nothing. Realistically, he knew he might have to wait weeks for Twilight's Ghost to show. But God, he hoped not. Inactivity wasn't in his blood.

He stood next to the shack's lone window, leaning against a wall seasoned with the smells of dust, horse, and aging leather. A few more hours and it would be morning, another fruitless night passed, another day arrived. A day he'd pass pacing the floors of the house he'd just bought, ravaged by thoughts of Holden in jail. He'd told Holden he'd find the Ghost and get him out. His youngest brother would be waiting for him to do just that, wondering every day if today would be the day Jarrod kept his promise.

Restless, he stepped across the window to lean against the opposite wall. From here he could observe most of the property's deep rear yard— He straightened. What was that he'd seen? Nothing more than the passing of a darker shade of black against a lighter. Little, but enough to indicate movement. He squinted and angled his head closer to the wall for a wider view.

Again, came the flash of black on black. Relief and anticipation swept through him. Finally, the Ghost had come.

Jarrod watched as a person, a man, moved smoothly through the night toward the tall gate that enclosed Blackhaw's property. When he reached it, the apparition uncovered what looked like a crude rope ladder from beneath a bed of leaves, tossed its end over a spire, and used it to climb up and over. When he reached the inside, he looped the ladder around his shoulder.

Jarrod's unblinking gaze followed his every move. He'd wait for the man to near the back door of the house, which was just yards from the tack shed. Then he'd spring.

But instead of moving toward the back door as Jarrod had expected, Twilight's Ghost veered in the opposite direction and ran along the inside of the fence toward the farthest, most tree-covered corner of the property. Jarrod worked to distinguish the man from the shade cast by branches.

The Ghost paused, then bent and opened a square door that hinged outward from the ground. It appeared to be the entrance to a root cellar. The Ghost looked both ways, then took the first step down into it.

The cellar must provide passage into the house. Swearing under his breath, Jarrod threw open the shack's door and ran toward the cellar, his greatcoat flapping behind him.

Even from a distance, Jarrod saw the Ghost's head come up, the hat brim lifting. In the next instant, the

Ghost leapt from the opening and sprinted in the opposite direction.

Jarrod was already at full speed which enabled him to close on the man as the Ghost weaved through the trees. The rush of Jarrod's breath filled his ears, his chest. He was gaining ... he could almost reach— When the Ghost was forced to slow in preparation to throw his ladder and climb the fence, Jarrod lunged. His fingers sank into the clothing at the man's shoulder.

With a feral growl, the Ghost rounded. Moonlight skated against the blade of a knife as it sheered through the air toward Jarrod's face. Jarrod careened away from its deadly path. The Ghost hesitated for the barest moment before advancing, slashing the knife upward. Jarrod arched back.

With blazingly fast fury, the Ghost struck out at him again and again, air hissing in chorus with his thrusts. Jarrod ducked and swerved out of the way. His heel struck a tree root and he stumbled backward a few steps, reaching into nothingness for a handhold.

When he gained his balance, the Ghost was gone. He spotted the man dropping to the ground on the far side of the fence. Jarrod gritted his teeth into a snarl and pursued, his feet striking hard against dirt. Two houses down, the Ghost darted to the side, then disappeared around the back corner of someone's home. Jarrod charged after him. Cold air whistled against his face, while heat pounded his blood.

On a straight line Jarrod could have easily caught the man, he was certain. But the Ghost kept veering in and out over murky terrain, navigating it with the advantage of familiarity.

The Ghost led him through the back gardens of two

more houses before a towering iron fence stopped him. Jarrod's instincts surged with satisfaction. The man was cornered.

Without the option of continuing forward, his prey wheeled to the right and ran along the face of the fence. Jarrod angled in that direction, hoping to cut him off. Before he could, the Ghost pushed through an opening in the enclosure. Rusty hinges squealed as the gate's door swung inward.

Jarrod shoved his way through. Beyond, tall plants bowed and sighed from geometric plots. He couldn't see the Ghost—no, there he was, zigzagging quick and silent along the cobbled paths. Jarrod followed as fast as he could, his anger building. He should have had him back at Blackhaw, when he'd grabbed the man's coat. He should have god damn *had* him.

Jarrod tripped and cursed as he ran, tripped and cursed, hating the elaborate tile and the fussy stone borders. The Ghost reached the slatted iron fence on the far side of the garden, turned sideways, and stepped a foot between the rungs.

Jarrod's heart contracted violently. With a final burst of speed, he raced toward the Ghost. The man pushed halfway through. Jarrod was almost there, he could almost—he reached out, his fingers closing around cold air in the instant the Ghost slipped through to the other side. The man took several quick steps backward, then paused.

Jarrod faced him through the bars, his chest hitching. The Ghost had trapped him in a cage of flowers and iron and stone. It might as well have been a cage of fire dropped into hell for all Jarrod liked it. He'd been tricked.

His frustration churned, part-disgust, part-outrage. He never lost. Was never outsmarted.

Jarrod wanted to reach through the bars and take a swipe at the Ghost, like some great, rabid beast. As it was, he couldn't stop himself from wrapping his hands around the bars and rattling them.

The Ghost didn't move a muscle.

Jarrod sucked in breath, trying to get a hold of himself. "I need to speak with you," he rasped, "about my brother, Holden Stone."

From beneath the blackness of his hat, Twilight's Ghost regarded him with uncanny stillness. Foe to foe.

"You falsely accused him," Jarrod said.

The Ghost just stared in silence, his facial features a dark void.

"I'm not going to let my brother sit in jail. So free him."

The agent took one deliberate pace backward.

"If you won't help me now, I'll keep searching for you—as long as I have to."

Soundlessly, Twilight's Ghost turned.

"Stop!" Jarrod yelled. But the man refused to heed his order. "Stop!" Impotently, Jarrod again rattled the bars.

Twilight's Ghost melted into the night like a child returning to the fold. Not even the wail of the wind or the crunch of fallen leaves accompanied him, so alone was he.

Jarrod squeezed closed his eyes. The defeat added another weight to the responsibilities he carried on his shoulders. He could feel this newest one, pushing, grinding him down.

Though the knot of disappointment in his gut told him it was impossible, he nonetheless attempted to wedge a shoulder between the rungs of the gate. His arm fit, but no more than that. The metal stopped him firmly at the swell of his chest.

He retraced his steps through the twisting paths of the garden, until he found the gate on the other side. He skirted around the outside of the estate to the place where the Ghost had vanished. Then he combed the property beyond, searching until his eyes ached for sign of a man the color of wind. He found nothing, and still he continued. Walking and walking, a headache pounding against his forehead and temples.

At last, as dawn was just beginning to pinken the eastern sky, he returned to Blackhaw the way he'd come, over the back fence. The cellar door still flopped open, exactly as the Ghost had left it. He could see now that a metal chain had been wound around the inner handle, so that the Ghost might latch it from the inside.

Jarrod descended the steps. Just as he'd expected, a passageway extended underground toward the house. Daybreak's feeble light cut away and he was forced to hunch at the waist and feel his way. The tunnel ended abruptly. Above, light trickled through the crevices of a wooden portal set flush into the floor of the house.

Jarrod reached up and freed the crude inner latch, then tossed the portal open. He stuck his head and shoulders into what appeared to be the kitchen.

With a screech, the housekeeper skittered away from the counter where she'd been kneading bread. A floury hand flew to her breast.

"Good morning," Jarrod said dryly.

"You!"

"Me."

"Well, I *never*!"

"Tell Mrs. LaRue that she and I have much to discuss."

The housekeeper's graying brows crushed dangerously low over her eyes. She reached for a frying pan. "You're not on the schedule."

"No. She's on *my* schedule now."

A half an hour later Jarrod's carriage rocked to a halt in front of his newly acquired house. He tossed open the carriage door before the servant dashing toward him had a chance to, and stalked up the porch stairs. A second servant held the front door wide.

"Get me Collier," Jarrod said as he entered.

"Yes, sir."

One unaccustomed hallway deposited him into another as he made his way to his office.

The day he'd determined that Sophia LaRue was still living in Galveston, he'd sent agents here to purchase a property for his use. They'd informed him that the owners of this estate were not interested in selling, but like everything in life, the property had indeed been for sale for the right price.

Unwilling to sacrifice any more time, he'd simply bought the furniture with the place. It was adequate enough.

He glanced into a parlor as it sailed past—burgundy hues, sophisticated well-crafted pieces. Nothing about this place, from the smallest detail to the largest, elicited within him a single stirring of satisfaction or pride in ownership.

Upon reaching his office, he lowered into his leather desk chair. He swiveled toward the window to gaze out at the morning while he waited for his secretary.

Idly, he drummed his fingers against the well-worn surface of his desk. Wherever he traveled, his chair and desk went with him. He liked the proportions that had been made for him, liked the familiarity of his own utensils resting in places he knew to find them.

Collier arrived moments later wearing navy trousers with sharply pressed creases down the front and a navy waistcoat over a white shirt. His gold cuff links and tie pin gleamed. Every gray hair on his head and mustache had been combed into place. Quite casual for Collier. Their surroundings were obviously having a relaxing effect on the man.

Collier stood, as usual, at the right front corner of his desk.

The joints of Jarrod's chair squeaked as he rocked it slightly, thinking. "I'm going to kidnap Sophia LaRue."

Unruffled, Collier pulled a skinny sheaf of papers from his pocket.

"She lives at Blackhaw Manor," Jarrod said. "At some point today, she's certain to leave her home. As soon as she does, have some of our men bring her here." That Twilight's Ghost had attempted to sneak into her house proved beyond any doubt that she was linked to the agent. He needed her to get to the man and couldn't afford the time it would cost him to woo her politely into helping him.

The tip of Collier's pen scratched across paper.

"She's not to be hurt."

The older man nodded.

"I think she carries a weapon in her pocket. She was reaching for it the night we met."

The pen rasped for a few more moments, then paused awaiting instructions.

"I'm to be notified immediately when she arrives."

"Yes, sir. Restraints might be in order, sir," Collier said.

"Fine. Have them use a soft fabric."

Collier added the remaining details to his pad.

"She has dark hair, dark eyes, ivory complexion. About five feet eight. Beautiful body, beautiful face. Impossible to mistake."

"Yes, sir."

"That's all."

Collier withdrew.

Propping his elbow on the desk's surface, Jarrod rested his fist against his lips and swiveled to gaze out the window again.

His men couldn't bring Sophia here quickly enough for him. The hours between now and her arrival yawned before him, seemingly endless. He'd count every second of them, he knew. There'd be no sleep. No diversions.

It infuriated him that the Ghost had bested him last night and that anger, combined with the urgency he felt to free Holden, accounted for most of his impatience. But not all. There was something about the woman herself that made him hungry to see her. Something that drew him, something that had its roots entrenched decades earlier.

Unwilling to face the memory, Jarrod walked the short length of hall beyond his office, and opened the back door. Maxine was waiting for him, sitting on her mat, just as he'd expected she would be.

"C'mon, girl."

Her tail wagged in answer as she scurried into the house. Side by side they walked toward the library where they'd pass the day until Sophia's arrival.

* * *

That afternoon, Sophia donned her walking hat. It was an enormously wide-brimmed concoction, covered in cream satin, with a spray of elegant brown-speckled feathers at the side. Even after three years of wear, it still looked grand, so long as you didn't look too close.

She tied the hat's thick ribbon beneath her chin, then pulled her brown coat over her plain green skirt and bodice.

Maggie poked her head out of the parlor. "Do you want me to come with you?"

"No, thank you though. If I can't make it the few blocks to Mrs. McBrayer's for luncheon I'm in trouble."

"It's just that what Jarrod Stone said to Mrs. Dewberry this morning sounded . . . worrisome."

Sophia picked up her parasol. "Well, what's he going to do?" She smiled to reassure Maggie. "Nab me off the street?"

Maggie grinned back. "I wish an oil baron would nab *me* off the street," she said as she ducked back into the parlor.

Sophia let herself out and made her way down the long and winding drive to Blackhaw's front entrance. As she walked, she noticed that the handle of her parasol wobbled like it was about to fall off and that the tips of her shoes bore scuff marks. Mentally, she berated the man she'd supposedly married during her time of training at the Secret Service headquarters in Washington. The Service had felt that a dead husband would give her a great deal more freedom to move through society making alliances and collecting information. They'd been right. Still, what kind of a pitiful, sickly, sniveling husband would die without leaving his wife one blessed cent?

As if she'd marry such a nitwit.

She filled her lungs with the bracing air in an effort to flush out the fear that had nagged her since last night's close call with Jarrod Stone. She needed this, the fortification of sunshine and exercise. It would clear her head, help her think, and serve to reassure her that everything was still well with her world. At the street, she exited the protective gates of Blackhaw and turned toward town.

At the end of the second block, a strange shadow slipped across the edge of her peripheral vision. She glanced in its direction, but saw nothing. Her steps slowed. Warning pricked her instincts just as men sprang from their concealed places around her. She went for her knife, but they grabbed her right arm first, pulling it back as if they'd known what she reached for. A man's hand burrowed into her pocket, then farther, to her garter. His crude fingers found her knife and yanked it free.

Fear cinched her chest as they lifted her into the air. She tried to fight, to struggle, but there were five of them—six. Strangers wearing suits that bulged with concealed weapons.

Trees and sun passed in a blinding blur, then she was inside a carriage, stomach down on the floor. Her cheek pressed into the carpet, forcing the brim of her hat back. *My God, what can they want? Are they Stone's men? They have to be. No, not true, they could be acting on the orders of some other enemy.* Her mind was spinning too fast. She couldn't make sense of anything.

She gasped for breath and thrashed her legs. It was no use. In mere moments, they'd bound her wrists, bound her ankles, and locked her inside.

The horses eased into a gallop.

Chapter 3

Finally, the carriage wheels ground to a stop.

The fear hovering at the edge of Sophia's thoughts intensified. She gritted her teeth, fighting it back. Long ago, she'd learned not to court trouble. She dealt with problems at the moment she must and not before.

Her captors, who had the gall to call her ma'am despite binding her like a trussed chicken, lifted her from the carriage and set her on her feet on a crushed-stone drive. One of them knelt to untie the bonds at her ankles.

Her hat had come off, so she squinted through a wash of sunlight. Desperately, she searched her surroundings for clues that would inform her where she'd been taken.

She didn't recognize the mansion or the acreage that surrounded it as far as the eye could see, but as she peered across the circular driveway she *did* recognize the ebony carriage standing in front of the stables, two workers polishing it to a gleaming sheen. It was the same one Jarrod Stone had parked before her front door.

So he *is* behind this. The image of a dark-haired man with an unwavering gaze cut into her mind, replacing her view of the carriage. He was smiling.

Anger flashed through her, obliterating any relief she might have felt that one of the criminals she'd jailed wasn't responsible. Jarrod Accursed Stone had bodily kidnapped her off the street! He was either certifiably insane or completely drunk on his own power.

"My hat, please," she said tightly.

"It will be brought to you."

She dug in her heels when they tried to lead her forward. Somehow, the dignity of a hat seemed important. "My hat."

Unseen hands from behind settled it askew on her head.

She glared at the house as the guards walked her toward the massive double doors. Like all houses in Galveston, the structure was elevated a good five feet off the ground to protect against flooding. In this case, the arched stone base supported a veritable palace.

White pine clapboards ran between enormous windows flanked with black shutters. Eight round columns stood sentinel at the front of the porch, and traveled upward through the second-story balcony before reaching a slate roof marked with soaring chimneys. Recessed behind the home's square front, two wings jutted outward on either side.

The entire effect was as imposing as the man who owned it.

Mahogany front doors pulled silently back at their approach. The men escorted her into the entry room, where her heels clacked against buffed wood. The interior was cool and rife with the scents of pipe tobacco and roasting beef.

The men walked her past a formal parlor, a dining room with a table large enough to sit forty people, and an immense library. Brooding murals of landscapes decorated the walls. Formally garbed servants swarmed everywhere—carrying fresh towels, dusting the mantels, scurrying around distant corners.

Sophia maintained as much of her pride as she could with her wrists bound behind her back and her hat tilting crazily. They led her down a hall, before opening the final door for her. All the hands gripping her released, and seconds later the soft fabric of the bond slipped away.

"Someone will come to fetch you when Mr. Stone is ready to see you," one of the men said.

Without deigning to look at the speaker, she preceded into the room feeling very much like a prisoner entering her cell. The lock tripped closed behind her in the same instant that she came to an abrupt halt.

Her gaze slowly, disbelievingly, cataloged the details of her surroundings. The more she looked, the more shivers streamed over her. Turning degree by degree in a circle, she probed the space for any sign at all that Jarrod Stone hadn't somehow managed to read every desire of her heart.

This suite was nothing like the masculine rooms she'd glimpsed in passing. The walls here had been painted a calm, cool green—the color of moss under mist—her favorite color.

The bed was covered in white, exactly as her beds of

the past twenty years all had been. Matching sheer white draperies hung at the windows, complementing the icing of lace across the top sill. The artwork—she swallowed. The artwork was all by Asher B. Durand, the American artist she admired most. She went to the nearest piece, a mountainous scene framed in tasteful gold. The signature was authentic. A. B. Durand, dated 1845.

Dazed, she waded deeper into the bedroom. Fresh bouquets of her best-loved flowers, wisteria and daffodils, overflowed the tops of both bedside tables, scenting the air.

The books nestled in the top shelf of the bookcase were by Alice and Phoebe Cary. She pulled one free, skimmed the pad of her finger over the binding, then tilted it open. A first edition, of course. Signed by the authors.

"Oh," she whispered.

On the other side of a connecting door, she found a small room entirely dedicated to clothing. Capes lined with dramatic velvets. Fabrics in the sensual, sophisticated colors of black, red, wine, chocolate, plum. Coordinating heeled slippers sat beneath the clothing, and hats to match rested on the ledge above.

She shut the door on the assembly, afraid to find out whether the clothing had been made to fit her.

When Jarrod Stone had come to Blackhaw a few nights ago, she'd flatly rejected his request for help. At that very time, had this room in this house been waiting in silence? It must have been. He had unmistakably furnished this space just for her, a woman he'd yet to meet. For how long had he been planning to imprison her here?

Sophia ran her hands over her forehead, then clasped

her cheeks as she studied her quarters. Within herself, she worked to throw off the astonishment that was dragging at her so she could revolve this situation clearly in her mind. First, she needed to know exactly what she was up against.

She crossed to one of the windows that faced the property's front drive and fingered back a wedge of curtain. Beyond, she saw guards. Two stood sentinel at the porch steps. One was positioned just twenty or so yards in front of her bedroom. Frustration mounting, she walked to a window facing the other direction, outward from the end of the wing. Three more guards—she recognized some of them from her abduction—were chatting near the stables, and one was lying on a patch of grass directly facing her. He removed a hand from behind his head and lifted it in greeting.

She dropped the curtain with a growl. Ire and a suffocating trapped feeling goaded her as she searched the interior of the space. She rifled through every drawer and nook, pulled the cushions from the furniture, and scooted under the bed looking for anything small enough to use to pick the lock or sharp enough to use as a weapon. She found neither. It was almost as if Jarrod had already combed the space for the same.

After pushing up her sleeves, she got down on her hands and knees and pulled high the corners of the bedroom's two carpets, checking for a hatch leading to the area below the house. There wasn't one. Nor did there appear to be any convenient hidden doors or wall panels masking stairways to freedom.

Disappointment swirled down her. She felt it, physically, tunneling deeper and deeper. Escape was going to be a tough proposition.

Heavyhearted, she moved back to the window facing the front of the property and scoured the drive for some sign of Maggie. When Sophia didn't return to Blackhaw this afternoon, Maggie would come looking for her. Someone, after all, must have seen Jarrod's men abduct her in broad daylight, and even if they hadn't, Maggie would suspect Jarrod first. It was futile to expect her to arrive so soon, though. Really, anytime before midday tomorrow would be impossible because Maggie would need to take news of Sophia's predicament to Simon, their supervisor, before she'd be authorized to act.

Sophia was unsure about how Simon would choose to handle this situation and even less sure about how Jarrod would respond to Maggie when she finally arrived—

A discreet twist of a key followed by a knock sounded at her door.

Sophia answered to find a distinguished silver-haired gentleman standing in the hall.

"I'm Collier Melvin," he said by way of introduction. "Mr. Stone's secretary."

She nodded guardedly.

"I'll take you to him now."

Good. She'd a few choice words to unleash on Jarrod Stone. Mr. Melvin led her on the reverse of the path she'd taken to her room. At the entrance to what she recognized as the dining room, he bowed his chin and gestured her forward.

The instant she entered the room, she spotted Jarrod. His attention riveted on her as quickly, and an electric current snapped between them.

He lounged in a thronelike chair at the head of the acres-long table. She was only vaguely aware of the door closing behind her, leaving her caged alone with the wolf. Though two places had been set, the one to the right of his assumedly hers, no servants waited in the corners here, and only a few of the lamps had been lit. The room was dim, shadowy, dangerous. A perfect place for wolves to circle.

As she approached, Jarrod stood, his napkin dangling from one hand. His suit was as dark as the ones he'd worn both times she'd seen him, his aura of power even more palpable. She halted a few feet from him, so furious that her body was practically quivering with the force of her emotion.

"Are you absolutely insane?" she asked, getting right to the point.

"Insane?" A smile played across those serious lips. "Some would say so."

"You *cannot* snatch people off the street. I—"

"Hungry? I'd like for you to sit with me."

"Sit with you?" She drew herself up, bristling. "This is not a social call. Do me the honor, at least, of acknowledging this situation for what it is."

"What's that?"

"A kidnapping. And may I say, that despite your mind-numbing show of arrogance the other night, I never dreamed you'd stoop this low."

With a resigned sigh, he dropped his napkin on the table, crossed his arms, and regarded her with one brow cocked. His attention moved with infuriating leisure along the neckline of her bodice. "Didn't you like the clothing I bought you?" He lifted his gaze to her eyes. "I'll buy others. Anything you want."

"It's not the clothing. It's the kidnapping I find less than satisfactory."

"Is it the artwork?" His forehead furrowed.

"It's the *kidnapping*, Mr. Stone. Stop being deliberately obtuse. You've committed a criminal act."

"You'd have preferred the artwork of Frederic Church, wouldn't you? I knew I should have gone with Church. The nun gave me both names."

Her heart stopped. "Y-you contacted the nuns?" Her years at St. Mary's Orphanage were a part of her life she kept fiercely private. He'd gone to the sisters, spoken to them about her! He'd rummaged around in her past and emerged with knowledge about her favorite things—knowledge he'd used to create a room for her. Ordinarily, the masks she wore covered and protected her. She wasn't used to someone, especially someone like him, looking at her real self.

Her breath was shaky. She couldn't seem to make it smooth. Her real self wasn't as strong as the parts she played. "That's how you discovered all those things about me?" she asked raggedly.

"Nice women down at the convent orphanage. Very obliging to a generous new benefactor such as myself."

She turned from him, refusing to let him see that his claw had connected with tender flesh. Her teeth bit down on her bottom lip as she moved toward the far end of the table, slow at first, then faster. She focused on her rage, letting it clothe the naked feeling he'd left her with.

Jarrod strode along the opposite side of the table, his gaze scorching her skin.

At the end, she stopped and faced him. He stopped and faced her. The air between them fairly sizzled. "You should know," she said, "that people will be looking for me. You won't get away with this."

"Let them come." She could see his ruthlessness in

the clean line of his jaw, the hewn muscle of his cheeks, the flinty hardness that dwelled behind the green of his eyes. He'd use her weaknesses, exploit her history, anything, to get what he wanted.

"What do you honestly hope to gain by imprisoning me here?" she asked, her voice hollow.

"I saw Twilight's Ghost at your home last night." He waited for her to try to deny it.

She didn't, couldn't.

"You're the only person who can help me get to him, which makes you the only person who can help me free my brother. The least I can do for you in return is furnish you with a place to stay while you assist me."

"When you asked me to assist you in trapping Twilight's Ghost I told you no."

"No wasn't good enough."

How did one reason with a man like this? Widely held social laws like personal freedom didn't seem to apply to him. "You had no right to kidnap me off the street—"

"But I did."

"—And no right to hold me against my will."

"Yet here you are."

"You have no right!"

"What are you going to do about it, Sophie?"

Her mouth worked, but nothing came out. She fisted her hands and rapped her knuckles against the wooden table to punctuate her words. "I find you unforgivably egotistical, greedy, and power-hungry."

"Really? I find you beautiful, smart, and desirable."

She gaped at him with shocked mortification.

He smiled in return. "Here." He pulled a thin, square satin box from within his jacket and skated it across the surface of the table toward her. "There are advantages to becoming my ally."

She scowled. "You cannot really be this daft."

"Maybe I can be." He lifted one shoulder, his towering confidence seemingly impenetrable. "Hopefully you'll like this more than you did the clothing and art."

Lips pursed with irritation, she flipped open the box. Within rested the most stunning bracelet she'd ever seen—a circle of fat round rubies at least two carats each bound together by sinuous strips of gold. It glistened with shooting light, fairy-spun, utterly fantastical, the kind of thing a mythical princess might wear.

Disdainfully, she snapped closed the lid and pushed the bracelet toward him. The box spun back across the shiny surface of the table, bumping softly against his thigh.

"I won't wear your jewelry," she said slowly and clearly, looking him straight in the eye. "I won't eat your food, I won't touch the clothing in my closet, and I won't sleep in the bed you've provided."

"Sophie," he chided, "we both know all this fuss of yours is a game."

"Not to me it isn't."

"You have a service I want, I have the money to pay for it."

"What you fail to understand is that I don't want your money, which means you have absolutely nothing to offer that I desire. I will not help you."

His hands slipped into his pockets, which pushed his jacket to the sides revealing a sapphire blue vest buttoned over his taut stomach. "You're an interesting woman, Sophie."

"Don't *call* me that!"

He chuckled as he walked back toward the head of the table.

"Let me out of here."

"You're free to leave at any time."

"What?"

He settled into his chair and placed his napkin on his lap as if oblivious of her presence.

She edged toward the door. When he didn't make a move to stop her, she ran into the corridor and toward the front of the house. The servant standing in the foyer took one look at her and hastened to open the front door. Sophia bolted through the opening. She was halfway across the porch when two guards stationed at the steps converged to block her way.

"Let me pass," she said, as authoritatively as she could.

"I'm sorry, ma'am, we can't do that."

"Mr. Stone just informed me that I'm free to leave."

"We have other orders."

With a hiss, she marched back to the dining room. Jarrod had been served a bowl of soup in the thirty seconds she'd been gone.

He glanced up at her, blowing indifferently at his spoonful.

"Your guards forbade me from leaving," Sophia stated.

As if he had all the time in the world, he blew at his soup again, then sipped at it with that sinfully handsome mouth.

"Your guards forbade me from leaving," she repeated, louder, refusing to be ignored.

He swallowed his soup, then quietly set aside his spoon. A cleft delved into the skin between his eyebrows. "I can't imagine where they got that idea." He flicked his gaze toward the steaming bowl of soup sitting upon her place setting. "Hungry now?"

Chapter 4

Incorrigible, infuriating, impossible man! Sophia had stormed from Jarrod's presence hours before—it was past nightfall now—and yet she couldn't quit stewing. She'd never imagined that the likes of him existed. High-handed, presumptuous—

A key turned in the lock her door. It was followed by a knock.

Sophia scowled toward the noise, but made no move to rise from the pearl pink sofa where she'd been sitting for some time now, damning Jarrod to hell and struggling to plot her escape. First, she'd glean from one of the servants the exact location of this estate so that should she manage escape, she'd be able to orient herself quickly to evade recapture. Then, though she'd never been much of a flirt, she would try to beguile one of the guards.

After a few beats, the knock came again.

She leaned her head against the sofa's back. She'd already told Jarrod she'd not eat his food, so there wasn't much to discuss.

"Ma'am?" Again, a polite rapping of knuckles against wood.

She sighed and made her way to the door. Jarrod's secretary could simply open the thing if he wished—he had the key. He appeared to be a gentleman, however, and wouldn't invade her chamber unless she forced him to. She accepted what puny privacy the wooden door afforded and spoke through it. "Yes?"

The clearing of a throat. "Dinner is served, ma'am. Mr. Stone sent me to escort you."

"That won't be necessary."

"Ma'am?"

"As I informed Mr. Stone earlier today, I won't be taking meals during my stay here."

She heard the floorboards creak as he adjusted his weight. "Yes, ma'am."

The lock slotted back into place before the sound of his measured footsteps diminished to silence.

She crossed to the window, checking for the hundredth time the positioning of the guards. A fresh shift had taken over from the last, though these men still defended all the same stations.

From the hallway she heard footsteps bearing down on her doorway. This set was entirely different than those belonging to Jarrod's secretary. These were heavier, authoritative, determined and she knew exactly, instinctively, to whom they belonged.

As she swirled to face the door a thrill leapt inside her. An awful little thrill.

She hurried away from the window, visually combing the bedroom for something she could use as a makeshift weapon. Her parasol, maybe. She spotted it leaning against the wall. With a quick lunge, she scooped it up and brandished it like a sword.

Had she gone entirely, fully mad? She exhaled and threw the parasol onto the overstuffed sofa. She couldn't fight off Jarrod Stone with a parasol.

He jammed the key into the lock without finesse.

She smoothed her hands down the front of her green skirts and wished for her knife.

Jarrod didn't even bother to knock. He simply shoved open the door with such force that it banged against the inner wall. His imposing, black-garbed form filled the doorway.

Sophia regarded him with utter disdain, even as his charisma flushed against her like a midnight wind off a tumultuous sea. He stood still on her threshold, just as he had at Blackhaw, and simply stared at her for a long moment.

Her insides quaked. The man was ridiculously good-looking. Hard, without the slightest fuzz of youth about him. And dangerous.

"Evening," Jarrod said.

She returned the greeting with a tense nod. "I'm not surprised to see you've no respect for my personal privacy."

"This is, after all, my house."

Of all the arrogant things. . . . "The decency of a knock would have been appreciated."

"I'll endeavor to remember that next time."

Next time? Just how often was he intending to barge into her room?

He glanced over his shoulder. "You may bring that in."

Two male servants eased into the room carrying a small table.

"There," Jarrod said, pointing to a spot in front of the sofa.

"That won't be needed," Sophia said to the men.

One of them looked hesitantly at Jarrod. "There," he repeated, nodding to the place.

Sophia was forced to scoot out of the way. The instant the table was situated, maids scurried in bearing chairs, flatware, dishes covered in domes, butter, salt and pepper, and a silver vase sprouting two perfect rosebuds.

The efficient whirlwind of staff vanished as quickly as they'd come. Jarrod locked the door behind them, turned, and held up the key. It looked tiny in his hand. "You want to fight me for it?" he asked, challenge and something that couldn't possibly be humor glinting in his eyes.

"Not without my knife."

He smiled a rich man's smile. "Pity." He lofted it into the air, caught it with a swipe, and dropped it into his jacket pocket. He strode to the opposite side of the table, and she found herself facing him, both of them standing behind their place settings, like husband and wife.

"Jewel?" he asked.

"What?"

He pulled a velvet ring box from his inside jacket pocket. "Jewel before dinner?"

"No."

"You don't even want to see it?"

"No," she said firmly, though the curiosity she'd cultivated through a career based on observation and investigation wailed at her decision.

"Very well." He slipped it back into his pocket. "Sit with me?"

"No."

He rounded the small table in two paces, so fast he startled her out of an opportunity to retreat. "I'll stand here next to you, then."

Her skin rushed with heat, a tingling wave of it that rolled up her breasts, chest, face. She averted her gaze to the edge of one immaculately tailored shoulder, but couldn't escape the warmth emanating from his powerful body or the smell of his cologne—bracing and crisp with just a hint of spice. This was disastrously intimate, just the two of them locked inside her bedchamber, and him looking all of a sudden like he'd be more than happy to eat her up with a spoon.

"I'm glad you decided that we should dine in here," Jarrod said. He was so near she could feel the warmth of his breath against her scalp. "It's more private than the dining room."

"I decided nothing of the kind."

He ran his fingers down the curve of her shoulder, then across the delicate flesh at her inner elbow.

Lightning flashed up her arm. She jerked away. "Sitting will be fine."

"Very well." He returned to his side of the table, but didn't lower to his chair until she'd slid into hers.

He was probably the type of man that was aroused by an unwilling woman, she realized with a sick, jumpy feeling in the pit of her stomach. He'd made a profession out of crushing obstacles. Her resistance to him was probably only serving to whet his well-honed instincts to battle and conquer.

She spread the linen napkin onto her lap. He followed suit.

But what else could she do? Acquiescence was out of the question. She couldn't very well hand Twilight's Ghost over to him, and she plain wouldn't free his brother. So she'd simply do the best she could, despite her growing sense that she was in far over her head. Her forte was working alone and isolated. She'd never before been forced to confront an aggressor head-on. She'd no training for this, for being so inescapably close to him. No precedent for Jarrod Stone.

Jarrod gripped the top of the shiny metal domes covering both her plate and his, then raised them at the same time. Steam writhed upward from the plate before her laden with beef, corn, and small potatoes tossed with herbs and seasoning. The succulent aroma caused her mouth to water. Breakfast seemed decades past.

"I decided not to press my luck by trying to force you to eat three courses." Jarrod's words were accompanied by a *clang* as he set aside the domes.

Sophia couldn't recall when she'd last seen such gorgeous food. The beef glistened and dripped with a thin burgundy sauce. Not even Mrs. Akers, the best hostess in Galveston, served food this fresh.

She raised her gaze to Jarrod. Though he sprawled casually in his chair, his eyes belied the ease of the pose. They regarded her like a hawk might a mouse. "Do you have an appetite?" he asked.

She'd vowed not to eat his food. Abstinence in the face of all the niceties he'd offered her was one of the few powers she had. Especially abstinence in the face of food, because while Jarrod was a difficult man, she doubted he was cold-blooded enough to watch a woman starve. Of course, she could be wrong. If he didn't release her by tomorrow, she'd have to find a warmhearted maid willing to bring her food. When the time came for her escape she'd need her strength. "I'm not hungry in the least."

Her stomach chose that exact, inopportune moment to fill the air between them with a hearty growl.

He didn't say anything, just raised one eloquent brow.

Oh, damn him anyway. The injustice of it, all of it, his father's thievery, his kidnapping of her, her renegade stomach, caused a scream to build low in her body and begin to rise.

Jarrod lifted the bottle of red wine, examined the label, then filled their glasses. When he raised his glass, light shot from the crystal and illuminated shades of garnet in the wine. "I propose a toast."

Sophia just glared.

He paused, saw she wouldn't be joining him, and murmured, "To us." After saluting her with his glass, he took a sip. She watched the muscles in his throat work as he swallowed. Even his neck was attractive—tan and masculine. It was foolish, the details she noticed about him, more each time they met. She saw tonight that his forehead was slightly lined by years of tough decisions. His brows were uncompromisingly straight above deeper-set eyes. And his thick, dark hair was messier now than it had been earlier in the day. It looked as if he'd been walking outside and the breeze had rifled through it.

Jarrod set aside his glass and gathered his knife and fork. Instead of digging into the meal, however, he gave her a pointed stare and waited.

"I'm not eating," she said. "I believe I mentioned that earlier."

"What do you hope to gain by not eating?"

"It's a statement of my extreme displeasure."

"I can read displeasure in every inch of you, so you've already made your point. Eat."

"Of all the things you can control, Mr. Stone, or think you can, whether or not I chose to eat is not among them."

"Isn't it?" He leaned toward her, rested his elbows on the table. "I can open your mouth and feed you," he said, gesturing toward her lips with the point of his steak knife.

Uncertainty clutched her chest. "No," she replied, too quickly.

"Very well, then eat."

"I won't—"

"Eat," he growled.

Their gazes and wills locked. The china practically vibrated with the room's tension as all noise in the house faded to silence. Sophia planted her palms on the table, lowered her brows over her eyes, and corralled her nerve. "No," she said into the charged quiet.

"Then you've left me no choice."

Mother Mary, he's going to jab his steak knife against my throat and force-feed me.

Menacingly, he set aside his utensils, reached into his suit jacket, and slid a feather from within. Its wisps stroked along the edge of his lapel as he pulled it free. "You're in trouble now."

Her vision honed on the feather. What could he possibly be intending to do with that?

"Ticklish?" he asked.

"Tick . . ." She couldn't quite form the whole word.

He reached across the table, extending the tip of the

feather toward her face. She swatted it away. It came back again. And again. She batted at it for a few moments before releasing her breath in a huff and folding her hands in her lap. Instead of suffering the indignity of fighting off a feather like a ninny afraid of a fly, she'd simply sit and be impervious.

Jarrod skated the silky feather all over her face while she remained rigid—wordless with frustration. Her subdued scream reached her throat and swirled there, gaining force. He swept the feather across her eyelids, coasted it along the apple of a cheek, ran it back and forth over her lips repeatedly, before jiggling it under her earlobe.

"Eat or I'll continue to submit you to this torture," he said.

"I'm terrified."

The feather danced down her throat then licked along the lowest edge of her neckline, far too near her breasts for comfort. She clamped a hand over the area.

"You don't have much of a sense of humor, do you, Sophie?" he asked.

She shot him a withering look out of the corners of her eyes. "I must have lost it the day your father robbed my grandmother blind."

He pushed from his seat. "That's it." Suddenly he was looming over her, then kneeling before her. Without preamble, he clamped the feather between his teeth and tossed up the hem of her skirt.

Sophia gasped and tried to kick him, but he wrapped a hand around each ankle before her shoe could meet his chin. He yanked her forward. She yelped and had to latch her hands against the seat of her chair or be tumbled onto the floor before him. Aghast, mouth sagging

with shock, she struggled against his hold. How dare—
she couldn't believe— Her brain sputtered simply to
comprehend his audacity.

Easily, he notched one of her calves under his arm and
clamped it there with a power that surprised and dismayed her. Both hands now free, he grasped her remaining foot, then slipped off her shoe and tossed it carelessly
over his shoulder, where it skidded under the bed.

She watched in alarm as he released the feather from
between his teeth. Leisurely, he smoothed the tip of it
along her ultrasensitive arch which was protected by
nothing more substantial than a silk stocking.

Sophia made a desperate grab for the feather.

He jerked it out of her reach and punished her by giving her foot another pull. She was forced to return her
hand to her chair and lock both arms, muscles straining
just to stay seated.

The feather grazed her arch again.

To her horror, a tingling sensation unwound up her
calf and hissed along the flesh behind her knee. She
flinched. Oh, this was awful.

He was watching her face now, gauging her reactions
as he coasted the wretched feather under her toes, then
along the ball of her foot.

She clenched her teeth, trying to disconnect from the
feelings zipping across the bottom of her foot, making
her whole leg quiver. When that failed, she tried curling
in her toes, scrunching closed her eyes.

"Not so immune now, are you?" Jarrod taunted. "And
I didn't even have to remove your stockings."

She imagined her lower body, exposed to his scrutiny,
as his big hands rolled down her stockings, his fingers

rasping against flesh no man had ever seen, let alone touched. . . .

The feather's softness was so light—torturous. It teased its way down her arch, up, down, around her heel, and up. . . . A grin tugged at her mouth. She bit her lower lip, trying to stop it. The feather picked up speed, and the skin on the bottom of her foot roared with sensitivity. "Stop!" she demanded.

"Promise me you'll eat."

The floodgates opened, and she started to laugh.

"Promise," he said.

Her laughter intensified, rocking her shoulders now. She fought to jerk her foot from his hold, but he had her soundly. Moisture fuzzed her vision as she laughed and laughed. She fought harder, wild to take a full breath, to be free of his tormenting tickles. The merciless feather continued.

"Stop!" she gasped.

"Will you eat?"

She rammed her foot toward him, hoping to sock him in the chest. But he took her foot's proximity as an opportunity to blow on it, heightening the sensation.

She screamed with laughter.

"Eat?" he asked.

"P-please," she gulped for air, "stop-p!"

"Eat?"

"Yes!"

Instantly, the feather ceased its torment.

Sophia pulled in a deep lungful of air, sniffed, and groped for composure. "Oh," she murmured and dabbed at the corners of her eyes with the knuckle of her index finger.

Jarrod's face came into focus below her. His eyes sparkled and his lips curved with victory. He eased his hold on her ankle.

This time when she attempted to kick him, she succeeded, her heel connecting soundly with his shoulder. He grunted, but his annoying, cocksure expression didn't lessen as he rose and returned to his chair. Sophia tucked her bare foot under the hem of her dress, snuggling it protectively atop the ridges of her remaining shoe. She couldn't quite meet Jarrod's eyes, so she retrieved her napkin from the floor where it had fallen during her writhing. Another sniff, then she smoothed a wisp of mahogany hair back into place. How did one go about regaining ones dignity after that? She risked a glance across the table.

"Shall we?" He nodded at their food.

"Your behavior just now was appalling." She straightened her posture. "I'm embarrassed for you."

"I'm not at all embarrassed for you. You've got beautiful calves, beautiful feet, beautiful toes."

"I have a lover to tell me so. I hardly need you."

She could tell that her barb had sunk home. His eyes darkened, sobered. All levity between them drained away. Here was another distancing tactic she could use against him—his belief that Twilight's Ghost was her lover. It wasn't much, but at least it returned them to their proper position as adversaries, which was far preferable to him tickling her feet or worse, complimenting her.

"Does he tell you how lovely your face is?" he asked. "How perfect your lips are?"

Her throat thickened. See, this was precisely what she wanted to avoid. She was no expert on seduction, didn't even know how to respond to comments that held as much heat and velvet as his did. Jarrod, she got this impression very strongly, had said these same words to a hundred women. No telling how many he'd manipulated to his will. He was smooth, practiced, accustomed to getting what he wanted, and devilishly good at making a woman wonder what his passion must taste and feel and smell like.

"I'm sure you've seen lovelier faces in your time," she said.

"Maybe." The faraway look in his eye narrowed until she had the impression she was the only woman in the world he'd ever looked at as deeply as he was looking at her now. "Maybe never."

She cleared her throat and concentrated on her food. The sooner she ate it, the sooner she'd be rid of him. With fervor, she sliced off bites of meat and scooped up forkfuls of corn. In between, she primly touched her napkin to her lips and took minute sips of wine—just enough to wash down her food but not nearly enough to fog her senses.

Jarrod ate across from her, more slowly than she did. She was painfully aware of him, of every bite he took, the creaking of his chair, and the way he held his fork.

As soon as she finished, she slanted her utensils across her plate and set her napkin alongside.

Jarrod followed her lead. "Dessert?" he asked, placing the ring box from earlier atop the folds of her napkin.

With a long-suffering sigh, she indulged her curiosity by opening the small box. The black-velvet interior ensconced a diamond ring. In a chest gone still, her heartbeat thumped unnaturally loud. The huge central diamond was cut in a rectangular shape, as were the large diamonds on either side of it, as were the not-small diamonds on either side of them. It was the sort of ring that belonged in a museum behind glass. Like everything about him, it proclaimed how very, very rich he was.

The memory of a gaunt boy with ragged clothing and proud eyes slipped into her mind. Years upon years ago he'd stood on the other side of the fence at Blackhaw, his desperation reaching tendrils across to her as he'd clawed up the food she'd offered. She'd never forgotten him.

Lack of wealth could be far more devastating than the possession of it could ever be good. It was because of the boy who'd come to beg, and the girl she'd been, and so many others in similar situations, that she loathed men of Jarrod Stone's ilk, and detested the way they squandered their money.

The heaviness of his attention grew oppressive.

She flicked a look at him from beneath her lashes. "Don't you think it's a little soon to be proposing marriage?" she asked dryly.

He smiled a wolf's smile. "Take it. It's yours."

She snapped closed the lid. "No. Thank you." Resolutely, she reached across the table and set the box on his napkin. "I've always preferred pineapple cake for dessert. Ask anyone."

"So you don't like rubies, and you don't like diamonds." He lounged against the back of his chair, one knee pointing forward, one splayed to the side. He looked far too much like a man content to pass the remainder of the evening sitting in her bedroom. "What do you like? Tell me, I'll buy it."

"I like freedom, Mr. Stone. It's the only gift from you I'll ever accept."

He studied her as a mathematician might a problem he'd yet to solve.

"Well." She rose from her seat and scooted in her chair. "As enjoyable as this has been, I'd appreciate it if you'd relieve me of your company."

When he didn't move, she gestured impatiently toward the hallway.

He unfolded his frame from the chair. Halfway to the door, he caught sight of her bed. He halted, glanced at her. "Did you mean what you said today, about not sleeping in the bed I've provided for you?"

"Yes."

"I can stay in it with you, if that will make you less afraid of scary beasts."

"Why would I ever trade beasts outside the bed for a beast under the covers with me?"

"There are reasons," he said slowly.

Every fine hair on her body seemed to rise. She wondered what he might look like stark naked, what it might feel like to have him slide that naked body on top of hers, for him to bury his hands in her hair and turn his enormous concentration to the task of ravishing her.

The sound of the key fitting into its hole saved her from her thoughts. She stared at his wide back as he freed the lock. Blessed Mary, she couldn't believe she'd just entertained that little fantasy about him—a Stone without a shred of decency, without even one redeeming quality. That she'd envision coupling with him for even one second. Deplorable.

He pulled the door wide and called for his servants, then looked to her. "I'll be back with breakfast in the morning."

"Back?"

"Until you're willing to eat in the dining room, I'll be bringing the food and the torture to you."

Not likely. He'd bested her once, but she had no intention of allowing him to trap her inside here alone with him again. "There's no need. The dining room will be adequate from now on."

He lifted an indifferent shoulder.

As the servants surged past him and swept the remains of their dinner from the room, his gaze weighed on her. The image of him naked returned to her mind with scorching heat.

Oh, Maggie, she thought, *come for me. Come for me quick.*

Chapter 5

The next morning Jarrod watched from his place at the head of the table as Sophia entered the dining room. She was wearing the same dark green skirt and bodice she'd been wearing the day before, except the cloth was now scarred with crisscrossing wrinkles. She'd slept in her clothes. And from the bleary look in her coffee-colored eyes, she hadn't slept well. Not surprising, considering her determination to spurn the bed.

He set aside his cup and stood as she approached. Last night he'd gotten her to eat. Soon, he'd have her wearing the clothes he'd purchased and sleeping in the bed he'd furnished. She wasn't an impractical woman. In fact, the opposite. He sensed that Sophia was far too practical for her own good.

Jarrod held Sophia's chair, then returned to his place

and assessed her profile in silence. He was a man who recognized rarity when he saw it, a connoisseur of fine things. And Sophia Vanessa LaRue was incredibly fine.

She'd brushed the mass of her dark, shiny hair back into another tight bun. Just one brave strand whispered against the tiny buttons at the back of her neck. He studied the refined slope of her nose, the little groove between nose and upper lip, the delicate line of her chin. Together, they combined to an almost breath-stealing beauty.

Still, what fascinated him about Sophia wasn't her looks—many women with perfect features left him cold. What fascinated him was the contrast between the person she revealed to him—no humor, no flirting, no vices—and the person he suspected she truly was. Despite her guardedness, there was a lushness about her, a richness that reminded him of the liquid chocolate he'd once been served in Spain. However, those qualities lived below the surface, down where the fire was.

Once she'd been convinced to share that fire he could only imagine what it would be like to make love to Sophia. He'd thought about little else for most of last night, except for the times he'd thought about what kind of lover she was to Twilight's Ghost.

Had the man really settled for her beauty alone, when any fool could see there was more? Had he allowed her the remoteness she so clearly preferred? He suspected so. "Are you in love with him?" Jarrod asked.

She scowled at him. "Who?"

"You know who."

"I don't believe that's any—"

"Of my business?"

"That's correct, it's not."

A maid bustled into the room, setting a breakfast of ham, eggs, and buttermilk biscuits before them both. "What can we offer you to drink?" Jarrod asked Sophia. "Coffee? Juice?"

"Plain tea will be fine."

"No sugar or cream?"

"No."

Just plain, brown tea. It was as if she'd purposely cut every indulgence out of her life . . . which was something he could remedy. He'd keep testing her with gifts until he found the one that would provide him with the key to her loyalty.

Once the maid left the room, she set about opening her biscuits with her fork.

He moved the pot of honey, the plum jelly, and the butter next to her.

"I just wanted to make sure you're not one of those women who likes to fancy herself in love," he said. He hoped she was too wise and too battered by life for that kind of foolishness.

Her hands stilled. "I thought this conversation was over."

"No." Jarrod had expected Twilight's Ghost to come for her right away, to attempt to steal her back during the night. He hadn't, which might mean that the Ghost was too stupid to value Sophia or too cowardly to risk himself by fighting for her. If the man left her here without a backward glance, Jarrod wanted to know, for reasons he couldn't fully explain, whether Sophia's heart would be broken.

She eyed him for a long moment. "I'm assuming that you, of course, do not believe in love."

He snorted derisively. "No."

"No?" She canted her head at a thoughtful angle. "What about your brother? I suppose you're going to all this trouble to free him because you have a passing fondness for him."

"That's different. That's family."

Something behind her expression tightened—a very old pain. As quickly as it had opened, the slight window into her heart closed, but not before he understood that she wished she were a part of a family. Of course she did. She'd been orphaned early and widowed early. For the majority of her life she'd had only herself.

An uncharacteristic sense of guilt jabbed him. As far as families went, he'd been far more blessed than she. Not because he was more deserving, or had done anything to earn his brothers but because blind fate had been generous with him and stingy with her.

She busied herself smearing a pat of butter on her biscuit, where it instantly started to melt. "Is the love between a man and a woman so far inferior to that between siblings, to your way of thinking?"

"Absolutely. There's no history there, no blood, or loyalty. To put your happiness in the hands of another without those things is idiocy."

She drizzled honey on her biscuit before sampling it.

He watched her lips move as she chewed. "Not that there aren't a myriad of . . . things . . . a man and woman can't enjoy together."

It amazed him, this talent she had for not meeting his eyes whenever he spoke carnally. Usually people fidgeted when he stared at them and eventually had to glance his way. But she managed to refrain from doing so with an air of extreme disinterest. She likely meant for her feigned boredom to squelch his attention. Instead it dared him to prove to them both how little he bored her.

Maybe that's why he couldn't stop himself from saying sexual things to her. He couldn't resist seeing how she'd react.

Never had he met a woman who needed to be seduced more than she did. Sophia Vanessa LaRue was practically screaming for someone to loosen her up, to strip her naked, to make her laugh and strain with pleasure. Her husband and Twilight's Ghost had both clearly bungled the job.

His gaze drifted to her breasts. She had voluptuous breasts for a woman with such a lithe body. He could only imagine them unbound, the weight of them in his cupped palms. He'd never favored women of skin and bones. He liked his women to be women—with full breasts—and this one was.

"So do you?" he asked, his voice slightly rough.

"Do I what?"

"Love him?"

"Do I love Twilight's Ghost," she murmured, studying her biscuit. "Yes, I believe I do."

His lips twisted. Her admission rankled, made him wonder why he'd forced it from her when he hated her answer. His restless instincts split between shaking sense into her or taking the back of her head in his hand and kissing it into her.

The maid from earlier returned with Sophia's tea. A second maid followed, carrying the coat Jarrod had instructed her to bring.

Sophia eyed the coat, then looked to him. "What's this?"

"Your new winter coat."

"It's the most wondrous thing I've ever seen, ma'am."
The maid carrying it slanted it toward the light so Sophia
could get a better look. "Black velvet with this heavenly
black fur around the neck, trimming the sides all the
way . . . all the way to the floor, around the hem, and
around the cuffs. See?" She extended a sleeve for inspection. A sliver of window had been left open to the winter
and the breeze sliding through it swayed the opulent
ebony fur.

"Oh, and it's beautifully fitted, ma'am. Snug around
the waist and the back. Not that I . . ." she darted a look
in Jarrod's direction, "tried it on."

Sophia's lack of response caused the maid to squirm.
"Truly, it's the finest garment I've ever had the pleasure
of touching."

"Then it's yours," Sophia said.

"Oh, no, ma'am." Her eyes rounded with dismay.

"I insist."

"But I couldn't possibly—"

"Certainly, you could."

"No! I—"

"Take it," Jarrod said to the girl.

She paled, nodded, and hurried from the room followed by her companion.

"Care to tell me why I just bought a fur-lined coat for
a kitchen maid?" Jarrod asked.

"I don't relish wearing an animal around my neck."
She speared a bite of egg. "I like them living."

"I didn't see any animals at Blackhaw."

"We used to have them." She gave him a telling look.
"Once."

It surprised him, how much bitterness she still held

toward his father. Usually people's emotions cooled over time and they grew philosophical about past wrongs. Not she. She was still actively blaming his father—him—for the unforgivable. For stealing not just her money and with it the former grandeur of her home, but far worse. For taking her only relative from her.

Primly, Sophia licked a drip of honey off the side of her lip with a glossy little tongue. He had a fierce urge to toss her onto the nearest sofa, pull up her skirts, and bury himself inside her.

"You're not eating," she commented. It was a criticism.

"Why would I when I can sit here and watch you instead?"

In the quiet that followed the conversational tones of his kitchen staff mingled with the clop of hooves as one of the grooms cantered a horse down the drive.

She stared at him pointedly. "Cease saying things like that to me. You waste your breath."

"I never waste anything."

"You waste everything of importance, my time foremost among them."

A polite knock echoed from the doors leading into the hall. He looked up to see Collier standing on the threshold. "Yes?"

"You've a visitor, sir."

At Jarrod's questioning expression, his secretary motioned almost imperceptibly toward Sophia.

"Will you excuse me?" Jarrod asked.

She nodded, her interest focused on Collier.

He strode the length of the table into the hall, then led Collier partway down the corridor. "Who?"

"A woman named Maggie May. She arrived alone asking to visit with Mrs. LaRue."

"I know who she is." Sophia's friend and companion. He'd anticipated that Miss May would come in search of her.

He peered over his shoulder toward the dining room and caught sight of a portion of Sophia's face—an eye, cheek, ear. She reared out of view swiftly. Interesting. Here, finally, was something the ice princess appeared to care about.

"Fine," Jarrod said. "Ensure she carries no weapons. Instruct the guards to take her into the kitchen so the women there can check through her skirts and undergarments."

"Yes, sir."

"Then escort her to Mrs. LaRue's chambers and report to me."

"Yes, sir."

Jarrod separated from Collier and returned to the dining room. He found Sophia back at her place, her demeanor alert.

"Was the visitor here to see me?" she asked before he'd reached his seat.

"Yes."

"And?"

"And you are, of course, welcome to spend time with her."

She immediately scooted back her chair.

"With one stipulation."

Her retreat halted. Glowering, she waited for him to divulge the bad news.

A man acquainted with the value of a well-placed

pause, he took his time settling into his chair. In no hurry, he sipped his coffee, and buttered two biscuits.

By the look of her, Sophia was near ready to explode with impatience. So much so, he had to bite back a grin. Damn, but he liked to rile her, to see her eyes blaze and her chin go rigid and her lips tighten up as if she'd just sucked the juice from a lemon. He started slicing his ham.

"What's the stipulation?" she asked.

"Don't you want to finish your breakfast?"

"Just tell me," she snapped.

"The stipulation is that you not wear that outfit again." He gestured toward it with his fork tines. "You wore it yesterday, and I'm tired of it. I want to see you in the clothes I purchased for you."

"I don't want to wear your clothes—"

"I realize that. So you have a choice to make." He ate a bite of ham, taking his time with it, tasting the salty juice that ran down his tongue as he studied her. "You can either see Miss May or you can continue wearing that gown."

Her eyes narrowed, then narrowed again. They'd come to another stalemate. She took so long to answer that he worried he'd have to look at her in that green bodice until the reckoning.

"I want to see Miss May," she finally decided.

"Then you shall," Jarrod answered. "Collier will return to escort you in a few minutes."

Her gaze traveled over his face, from his brows to his lips before returning to his eyes. "I won't forgive you for this, you know. For holding me hostage."

He ate a bite of eggs, salted them, then tried another

bite. She was wrong, of course. She'd not only forgive him, she'd thank him in time.

"I'm sure bribery and abduction have been profitable for you in the past, but with me you've miscalculated. I've worked hard to earn the freedom I have. When you took that away from me you took something beyond price. No diamond ring or fur coat is going to make me forget that."

He relished her show of temper. She could be a hellion in bed, he just *knew* it.

Clearly, she was more attached to her independence than most, something that had likely resulted from the years when she'd been forced to rely upon the sisters of St. Mary's for food and shelter. Still, he knew the female heart. Underneath the bluster, every one of them, including hers, ultimately wanted to be protected and cared for. She didn't know that yet. She didn't know a lot of things yet.

Collier returned and Sophia went to him immediately. To her frustration, the silver-haired gentleman waited to escort her, his face raised to Jarrod, ears pricking like those of a well-trained hound. How humiliating, to be made to wait for permission simply to return to her cell.

"You may take her to Miss May," Jarrod said.

Collier inclined his head and she walked ahead of him. When he opened her bedroom door for her, Maggie turned from where she'd been standing near the pink sofa. Sophia hurried forward and they met in the middle with a hug.

"Are you all right?" Maggie whispered.

"Yes." Sophia squeezed, Maggie squeezed back, then they parted. Sophia checked over her shoulder to ensure that Collier was gone and the door closed behind him.

"Actually, I'm a bit frayed. Jarrod Stone is certifiably insane."

"Certifiably," Maggie agreed. "Handsome, though. I glimpsed him in passing when his secretary escorted me here."

"Handsome!" She couldn't believe Maggie would point out any redeeming quality in her arch enemy. "You can't really think so."

"Absolutely, I do. So do you."

"No," Sophia answered, scandalized.

"Oh, *please,* Sophia. He makes your mouth water, and you know it. All that dark brooding power. Had he not made his fortune in oil, the man could live luxuriously well posing as an English lord for fashion plates."

"I doubt it." What was she saying? Of course the man was handsome, any fool could see that. Ordinarily, she had no trouble admitting the truth to Maggie, but about *him* . . . she just couldn't bring herself to. "Come." She grabbed Maggie's hand and drew her toward her dressing room. She didn't trust Jarrod or his minions not to attempt to eavesdrop on their conversation. The dressing room was farthest from the door, windowless, and muffled by all those expensive clothes.

Maggie followed, the loping gait of her tall thin body reminding Sophia, as it always did, of a Great Dane puppy with more height and enthusiasm than grace. Once inside, Sophia struck a match and lit the lamp positioned on the dresser adjacent to the mirror. Maggie closed them in.

"This room," Maggie whispered, looking around with awed curiosity. "Are all these clothes for you?" She ran a hand along a silken sleeve, then glanced up at Sophia quizzically.

"I'm afraid so."

"That's . . ." She looked again at the clothes, then back at Sophia. "That's spooky."

"I know. I told you—certifiable."

"It's also somewhat flattering, Sophia, you have to admit." Maggie started going through the racks, assessing each outfit before moving its hanger to the side. "I swear, men *never* do this kind of thing for me. More's the pity."

"So tell me how you found me."

"I knocked on our neighbors' doors. Though Mrs. Pinson from down the street didn't witness your abduction, she did remember the carriage that had been lying in wait across from her house all day."

"And you recognized her description of the carriage."

She nodded. "It matched exactly the description you'd given me of the carriage Jarrod brought with him to Blackhaw. I already suspected him, so Mrs. Pinson simply provided verification. It then became a matter of discovering where Jarrod had taken you. The gossips at the Tremont Hotel proved as reliable as always, informing me that he'd purchased this property just days ago."

"Where is this property, exactly? The servants have refused to tell me."

"It's the Bowmans' old place. Two miles due east of town."

Sophia visualized her location, seeing it like a map in her mind.

Maggie's exploration halted on a dark plum-colored hat decorated with flounces of plum ribbon. "Mind if I try it on?"

"Of course not."

Maggie shed her simple straw hat, releasing long, glossy strands of copper hair to dangle around her face.

While most considered Maggie's skinny, gawky body to be highly unfashionable, no one could dispute the fact that the woman had stunning hair. Maggie donned the plum hat and made a face at her reflection. "Have you ever seen a color that looks worse with my hair?"

Sophia laughed, embarrassingly grateful to have her here. "No."

Maggie reached for another hat.

Content for the moment to wait, Sophia leaned against the wall at the far end of the room and watched her friend. For the first time since her kidnapping, comfort twined through her. They'd worked together for five years, and during that time Maggie had always done this for her, always helped her take herself less seriously. With Maggie she never felt as solemn, dull, and old as she knew she truly was.

"Put something on, Sophia."

She was about to decline as a matter of course, when she thought better of it. From this point on, she'd committed herself to wearing these clothes. Might as well put something on now, while Maggie was here to tell her she looked nice even if she didn't.

Maggie tried on a brown-velvet hat while Sophia wedged off her practical shoes and pulled out a completely impractical pair of red ones with ribbon rosettes stitched onto the toes. Her stockinged feet slid into a fit that couldn't have been more perfect had she been Cinderella and these slippers made of glass. She wanted to hate the shoes. She truly did. And yet it was hard to hate something so frivolous and lovely.

She divested her own clothing and donned the red bodice and skirt that matched the shoes. Then she peered at herself in the standing oval mirror, unsure how she felt about the stranger peering back. The high, silk-trimmed collar of the bodice curved around the back of her neck before dipping into in a low oval just above the cleft between her breasts. The skirt perfectly skimmed her hips before sweeping a graceful line to the floor.

These garments had been made for her. The fabric precisely fit the width of her shoulders, the swell of her breasts, the circumference of her waist, the length of her legs. This ensemble was both more comfortable and more flattering than any she could ever recall owning. And yet, she felt tainted just by putting it on. As if she were betraying her principles.

"You do know, don't you," Maggie asked, "just how astonishing you look in that."

She turned to her friend. "Thank you, but—"

"Sophia, it's not a crime to enjoy a few items of nice clothing, you know. It's practically a feminine imperative." She jauntily retied the brown-velvet bow beneath her chin. "I say luxuriate in what you can while you can."

Maybe. But if Jarrod thought he was going to win her allegiance with a closet full of clothes, he was drastically mistaken. Sophia perched against the edge of the dresser, her relaxed mood gone, and her worries returned. "Did you speak with Simon about my situation?"

At the mention of their supervisor within the agency, Maggie's face sobered. Her hands drifted away from the hat. "I did."

"And?" Sophia's heart shrank in her chest. "I take it he isn't planning to raid this house and rescue me."

"No."

"Not even an attempt to free me using just a piddling agent or two?"

Maggie shook her head slowly.

In some region of herself, the logical region, Sophia had guessed that to be the case. It still pained her unexpectedly to hear it. After all she'd done for the agency, all the times she risked herself, they weren't coming for her. An aged sense of abandonment pushed at her from the inside. Nowadays she could squelch the feeling for months at a time, but it never fully died. It just waited, waited for a situation like this to remind her that no matter how far she'd come, it still had the power to drag her back. She was still ultimately alone.

"Had it been me, I'd have brought a whole army with me, guns blazing," Maggie said. "You know I would have. But he's more cautious, less enamored than I, I'm guessing, of the idea of surrounding himself with an army of good-looking men." She smiled that acres-wide smile of hers that displayed all her teeth.

Sophia couldn't quite dredge up any levity. She was being left here to fend for herself against Jarrod, that's what Maggie was saying.

Chapter 6

Maggie's smile melted away. "Simon's foremost concern is to safeguard your identity as Twilight's Ghost, Sophia. Imagine if agents descended on this place and stole you away. Jarrod Stone, already a man on the hunt for Twilight's Ghost, is smart enough to realize that the Secret Service would never go to such lengths for an agent's mistress. Then there's the problem of where to take you. If you're returned to Blackhaw, what's to stop Jarrod from abducting you again? If you're not returned to Blackhaw, then he'll be supplied with proof that you're not simply Sophia LaRue, beautiful widow. It's too risky."

"I understand."

Maggie's eyes held concern and regret. She doubtless loathed her task as messenger. "Sophia, the work you do is critical in this part of the country. He's not willing to risk that."

She nodded.

"And seeing as how Jarrod's goal is to win your assistance to his cause, Simon was willing to bet you'd be well cared for during your stay." She motioned toward the rows of clothes. "Looks as if he was correct."

"My orders, then, are to stay here and to wait."

"Yes. Though if I return to find you chained in a drafty dungeon, I'll be compelled to take matters into my own hands." Maggie winked.

Sophia crossed her arms and tried to reconcile herself to the idea of staying here—with him—for any length of time. Despite the mature, rational reactions she'd just fed her friend, the idea screeched against every impulse she had. "Did Simon have any other agency news?"

Maggie slipped off the hat and carefully returned it to its place. "You know that local counterfeiter our office has been keeping an eye out for?"

"Yes."

"Well, Simon informed me that Slocum's Mercantile has finally grown weary of being passed fake bills in return for their goods." She picked up her own straw hat, made a face at it, and dusted it off. "According to Simon the agency was able to confirm that the vast majority of the loss they're taking is due to counterfeit bills from the press of the same person, or group of people we've been after. Slocum's is offering a reward to the agent who uncovers them."

"A reward?" Sophia's interest sparked. "How much?"

"Five hundred dollars."

Blessed Mary, with that much money she could pay the taxes she owed on Blackhaw— Her gaze traveled over the walls enclosing her. Hope fizzled. She couldn't even manage to escape from these rooms. How was she supposed to solve a counterfeiting case? "Did you bring me my knife?"

"No. I was worried Jarrod would have me searched before allowing me to see you, and was right to worry. He did have me searched. I managed to bring you some of your toiletries, but that's all." She twisted up her hair and secured it beneath her straw hat.

Sophia pushed away from the dresser and paced the tiny space, toying with her fingernails as she thought. "We need to figure out a way to get me some sort of a weapon. If not my knife, then a gun, a letter opener, something."

"You don't think he might try to physically assault you. . . ."

Vividly, she remembered Jarrod's strong, expert hands holding her foot. A feather dancing torture across her toes. "He's too rich, too powerful, and far too accustomed to acquiescence. I can't predict how he'll respond when I continue to deny him his wishes."

"How do you suggest I smuggle in a weapon?"

Sophia stopped, and ran her gaze over Maggie's clothing. Her attention halted on the plain hem of her friend's gingham skirt. "What if. . . . What if Mrs. Dewberry sewed my knife into the hem of your coat? The fabric of your coat would be weighty enough to conceal it adequately, don't you think?"

"I think you're brilliant, that's what I think." Maggie shook her head, bemusement and respect in her eyes.

Sophia's mind whirled, rotating the situation from all angles, as she'd learned to do when investigating her cases. "And Oliver. Send Oliver here to visit me." Being out of contact with her grandmother's advisor had made her superstitious that he might have unearthed a vital clue in their search for Adam Stone, yet been unable to reach her. Besides, there was no reason why she couldn't continue her quest while confined here. That included bringing Oliver here, and uncovering whatever it was Jarrod knew about his father's disappearance.

"Okay. I'll bring a knife, and I'll contact Oliver."

"Thanks, Maggie." She'd feel ever so much better the next time she faced Jarrod, knowing she carried a knife in her garter.

"The newest items you've ordered are on their way, sir," Collier said. "They'll be here later tonight."

Jarrod rocked slightly in his office chair. Collier, ever proper, liked to use the word "items" for what they both knew were bribery gifts for their beautiful houseguest. Over the years, he'd purchased numerous such presents for women. He'd just never had so little luck in response to them. "Good. What about the search for Twilight's Ghost?" Not one to pile all his eggs in a single basket, Jarrod had hired a cadre of high-priced detectives to hunt down the agent while he dedicated himself to the same goal by way of Sophia.

"Nothing, I'm afraid, sir. They report that they're traveling paths other detectives have previously trodden with the same results. There's plenty of rumor and speculation, but the people know nothing of Twilight's Ghost, have seen nothing of substance. Our men haven't yet found anyone worthy even of payment in return for information."

Jarrod swiveled his leather chair toward the dark window and stared moodily out.

"They report that the man is aptly named."

"He's not a ghost. He's flesh and blood, and there's at least one person out there other than my Mrs. LaRue who must know something. Have them continue."

"Yes, sir."

Maxine ambled into the room, her nails clicking on the wooden floor. She plopped down, laid her head on his foot, and rolled her eyes up at him dolefully.

He reached into a drawer and tossed her a specially made dog biscuit, which she caught mid air. "What about Sophia's husband?" he asked, watching Maxine chomp.

"Nothing there either."

Jarrod's gaze sharpened as it moved to the older man.

"As yet we've come upon no information of him. Not a church record of their marriage, no land ownership deeds, no mercantile or bank accounts."

"Keep searching. I want to know how long they were married, what he died of, what Sophia's life was like during the time after the orphanage and before her return to Blackhaw."

So far that space of her life was a mystery to him. Not that he had any particular desire to hear about Sophia's husband. He didn't. In fact, he instinctively disliked the man almost as much as he hated Twilight's Ghost. Information was strength, however, and the more he knew about Sophia, the more power he had over her.

"Yes, sir, I'll have our men continue their search for Mr. LaRue."

"Tell them to be quick about it." He pictured Holden sitting on his jail-cell cot, his face lifting slowly until his eyes met Jarrod's. "I'm going to find Twilight's Ghost. I want to do it soon."

"Yes, sir."

Jarrod dismissed Collier with a nod, then strode to the back of the house and let himself out, Maxine at his side. He set off toward no particular destination. At least it was quiet here, and open. He loosened his collar. Occasionally, in the rooms of his life—rooms where he negotiated, presided over meetings, planned the expansion of his holdings—he felt like he couldn't breathe. Sophia, he'd been discovering, had the power to make him feel the same way. But for different reasons. She stole his breath from his chest.

Around him the gently rolling, tree-covered hills were painted with different shades of the sun. Golden in places, darker in places where clouds cast their shadows. He lengthened his stride, letting his mind clear, at last permitting his thoughts go to the place where they'd been wanting to travel for days, ever since discovering that the Ghost's mistress was Sophia Warren, all grown-up.

He had been fifteen, that first day he'd seen her.

He was starving, literally. His stomach eating the rest of him up. Still, he'd never have come to Blackhaw Manor, never have stooped to this, if not for his mother. Thoughts of her caused a dull ache to expand in his chest. Since his father had been away from the house so much, working on an investment he said would make them rich, things had gotten bad. He pushed his mother's thin, white face from his mind, forcing his concentration to the house before him.

For what seemed like an eternity he'd been standing here at the gates of Blackhaw. Plenty long enough to stare at the part of the mansion visible to him—a steep roof with lots of gables, expensive-looking windows, and yellow-brick chimneys. He both hated and craved every inch.

His bitter gaze lowered to the trees filled with fruit, just across the bars from him, out of reach. A black-iron gate separated him from the orchard and from everything and everyone inside as surely as oil from water.

The coarse cloth of his shirt itched his skin and let in too much morning air. He shivered and crossed his arms over his chest—then saw her.

A dark-eyed, dark-haired girl in a lacy white dress, white stockings, white button-up shoes. She stood beneath the branches of a peach tree staring at him.

He stood stock-still, wishing in that moment for death. He'd rather anyone else have seen him—her grandmother, a stableboy, one of the uppity advisors his father complained about. From them, he might have been able to do what he'd come to do. To beg.

But not from her. A mere girl of about eight. A rich princess without a spot of mud on her clothes and shoes. For no good reason, she had everything in the world, and he had nothing. She wore silly bows on her braided hair, a shiny pink sash around her waist. She was the most foolish creature on earth, and he hated her for it, for having so much and flaunting it when his mother was dying and his brothers were weak from hunger.

Worst of all, in her expression he recognized pity.

He didn't need to see himself in the reflection of her eyes to know he looked poor, sick, and dirty. He was. The realization of that, regardless of how many times he'd been forced to face it, never failed to disgust him. Mostly because he *felt* different on the inside. He wasn't this person, wasn't meant for this.

What was left of his pride melted into a nauseating mass, and he thought he'd throw up the watery oatmeal he'd had for breakfast, their last.

Without a word, the girl plucked a peach from the tree. Using her skirt as a basket, she picked more fruit and more. A wide selection, until the fabric bowl couldn't hold any more. She walked to the gate, standing just on the other side, and regarded him with a strange soberness—too old and calm for such a little person.

He'd brought a gunnysack with him. Quiet stretched between them in the instant before he grabbed for the fruit, tossing it into the bag. When he'd taken it all, the girl stepped away, her dainty hands releasing the sides of her skirt. She continued peering at him, brown smudges and dust now streaking the front of her dress.

He ran. Carrying the fruit across his back, he had dashed from her like a thief, feeling as guilty, and as branded as if he were one.

For three weeks, he'd returned to the gates of Blackhaw every day. And every day, she'd met him there, passing sacks of food to him without a single word. Each time he took her scraps. And each time the mixture of shame, gratitude, and relief roiling inside made him feel less human. He remembered vowing to himself that he'd be as good as she someday no matter how long it took.

In the distance, a horse whinnied. Jarrod's attention returned to the present with a start. Bitterness lingered in his mouth, no longer directed at the target of the girl, but merely the circumstances of the time.

He wondered how Sophia would react if she knew it was he she'd fed back then, the son of the man she'd one day blame for losing everything.

Maxine loped beside him. He noticed that she'd found a stick somewhere and was patiently clasping it in her mouth. "Here," he murmured, as he took it from her and threw it. He watched, hardly registering the sight, as she went tearing after it.

For years now, he'd remembered that girl in white without malice. With nothing, in fact, but a vague sense of debt. He owed her for easing his mother's final days with all those sacks of food, and for sensing that while he might be able to accept her charity, he wouldn't have been able to bear her words.

He'd never had the desire to see her again, however, and would have been content to thank her for her kindness in some distant, anonymous way. Then all this had happened with Holden and Twilight's Ghost, and they'd been thrown together. There was nothing distant about his association with her now. And nothing, he was certain, he'd yet done for her that she'd view as an expression of thanks.

He wished he didn't see the little dark-eyed girl when he looked at her, wished he didn't still feel this nagging sense of obligation. Without those things, pressuring her to his will the way he needed to for his brother's sake would have been a hell of a lot easier.

Maxine bounded to him, panting. He threw her stick again and she charged after it.

So what could he do for Sophia that would fulfill this troublesome sense of debt? He could discover then give to her whatever it was she valued—there had to be something. If there's one thing he'd learned in his climb from poverty, it was that every person had a price. Perhaps he should alter his tactics, look for her price in other places. It was only a matter of time until he hit on it. . . .

Unfortunately, time, right now, was a commodity far more valuable than money. Every hour it took him to wring the truth from her was an hour Holden was spending in prison. A fact that set his teeth on edge, that never left his mind.

What else could he do for her? Grimly, he smiled. He could do her the favor of ending her relationship with Twilight's Ghost. He himself was no moral paragon. He'd had mistresses and never thought twice about the illicitness of his relationships. Why should he? They'd been greedy women, he was a man with powerful desires. They'd met each other's needs.

Still, what was acceptable for him wasn't acceptable for her. Their discussion over breakfast had confirmed it—he plain didn't like even the *thought* of Sophia having a sexual relationship with Twilight's Ghost. The girl he remembered, as well as the woman he was coming to know, was too good for it. Too good for Twilight's Ghost.

And since he was currently in a position to break their liaison, he would.

Maxine returned, and he sent her after her stick a third time.

There was one more thing he could do for Sophia, he knew. And this one he didn't like. He looked back at the house, squinted toward her chamber.

He could save her from himself.

When she'd licked that drop of honey off her lip, he'd been surprised by how much he'd wanted her. Painfully so. Still, a tryst with him, just like a tryst with the Ghost, wasn't worthy of her. She deserved better, after what life had dealt her.

So while he'd allow himself to compliment her, maybe to touch her just a bit, he'd not allow himself to go farther than that. He'd keep his hands off her, regardless of the restraint it would cost him, regardless of how much he'd relish a chance at seducing the ice princess and discovering just how passionately she could writhe.

He stalked in the direction opposite the house, Maxine trotting beside him. Having a conscience could be damn annoying. Which was why, he acknowledged, he indulged his own so seldom.

For three whole days Sophia survived by following an established pattern. She slept in the bed he'd furnished, wore the clothes he'd purchased, and kept to her room reading, pacing, or otherwise avoiding him at all times except when they ate. At the moment they were sitting at the dining-room table in silence, having just completed a strained midday meal of chicken.

Over the past days, Jarrod had attempted to give her perfume, a sapphire necklace, embroidered lingerie, and emeralds the size of walnuts to hang from her ears.

Regardless of the troublesome current that snapped between them, a fire that grew a little hotter, a little brighter with every meeting, she'd easily declined all his gifts. She leaned back in her chair, interested to see what he'd try to give her next, but unworried about her ability to resist it.

"Will you accompany me outside?" Jarrod asked.

She lifted her brows. She hadn't felt the outside air on her face since coming here. "Why?" she asked suspiciously.

"Because I'd like to rope you to a tree and ravish you."

Her pulse stuttered. "That's not funny."

"You never think anything's funny," he said with a half smile. He assisted her in scooting back her chair.

"The truth is that while I'd like very much to ravish you, I'll wait for you to ask me first."

"That'll be a long wait."

"How long?"

"Longer than the remaining days of your life." She stood, firming her jaw as she faced him.

"Not if I decided to put my mind to it." He assessed her with frank sexuality and something that looked a bit like regret.

Her belly fluttered, the way it had taken to doing lately when he looked at her that way. That I-can-eat-you-alive way.

"Today, however," he said, "I want you to come outside because I have a surprise for you."

"Another gift?"

"Yes, another gift. Am I so predictable?"

"Indeed."

"Then I'll try harder not to bore you. Shall we?" He stepped aside so she could pass.

She walked along the hallway toward the front of the house, Jarrod following like a charismatic black demon. When a servant drew the door open for her, she crossed the threshold then the porch, her eyes squinting as they worked to adjust to the clear February day—

She came immediately to a dead halt, her chest contracting at the sight before her.

At the bottom of the steps pranced a horse, though to call the animal a horse seemed far too inadequate. This creature looked like something Cinderella would have ridden over cobblestones of gold into a castle made of gilt. The horse was pure white with a tail that flowed to the ground and a cascading mane. Its neck formed a high, graceful arch ending in a delicately intelligent face. The animal's body rippled with muscle, the legs tapered to dainty hooves.

She'd adored horses once. . . . Every fantasy she'd ever had of them came rushing back. She remembered for the first time in months—or was it years—her white pony. The pony had been stout and short, with a tendency to bite and a proclivity for rolling in mud. She'd loved him staunchly despite his shortcomings, spent hours riding him, brushing him, leading him in circles, drawing pictures of him. Until he'd been sold like everything else to pay the debts after Grandmother's funeral.

Tears stung her eyes, shocking her. Oh, heaven, she'd nearly forgotten all about that pony until just now. How could it mean anything to her after all this time? How could simply laying eyes on this horse today cause her to feel so forcefully the dreams and wonder of a child who'd grown up?

She stared, mesmerized, at the glorious white horse, knowing only that she'd discovered a part of herself, a love of hers, that had been lost for a long time. Suddenly, brutally, this particular gift of Jarrod's didn't seem so easy to decline.

Chapter 7

She worked to compose herself before chancing a look at him. He hung back slightly, his gaze steady on her, seeming to drink in every nuance of her expression. Which made her very afraid that he'd seen too much.

He smiled at her. Not the usual sharp smile, but one of genuine warmth.

Oh. Entire swarms of butterflies took flight in her stomach. Hastily, she looked away. She schooled her voice to expose no emotion. "What's this?" she asked, motioning her chin toward the horse.

He came to stand beside her. "As a boy, I remember hearing that Sophia of Blackhaw had a white horse."

She didn't so much as blink.

"And since you told me the other day that you have a

fondness for animals despite not owning any currently, I thought you might like this one."

He said it all very casually and noncommittally. By acting as if it didn't matter to him whether or not she accepted the horse, he was clearly trying to make it easier for her to do just that. To accept.

The groom holding the horse's bridle crooned something to her, and the animal threw her head. Flutters of mane lofted into the air, the color of ice in the sun, breathtakingly beautiful. Longing resonated somewhere low inside Sophia.

She laced her hands together and took a step back. Then another. This was ludicrous. She couldn't take anything from Adam Stone's son. No gift could ever make up for the wrong done her family. And nothing could make her forget that this man who offered this horse was the same man who'd stolen her freedom, who'd grind her to dust if he discovered she was Twilight's Ghost. "I cannot accept." Her voice emerged small and stiff.

"Of course you can."

"No," she countered, suddenly afraid. "No, no I can't."

Jarrod muttered a curse and stopped her withdrawal by grabbing her shoulders from behind. She broke his hold by swerving to fight him off, and came face-to-face with the warm bulk of his chest. Maggie had brought her her knife. She wore it against her thigh, and she could pull it free—no. If she used it against him, he could take it from her. Panicked, she made another bid to retreat, but he caught her before she could and lifted her off the ground.

She went taut with mortification. Her hip was

squished against his flat stomach, and the outside of her—her *breast* was wedged against his chest.

"You want that horse," Jarrod said, his rigid features proclaiming to her that he'd not be swayed. Determinedly, he carried her down the steps to the drive. "And I'm going to see that you have her."

She refused to give him the satisfaction of a struggle, so she averted her face and stared over his shoulder. Unfortunately, the view there was no better. Jarrod's minions, including the dignified Collier Melvin, were all watching the spectacle with avid interest. Heat scalded her cheeks.

"Hold her steady," Jarrod instructed the groom.

Alarm clanged inside her. She didn't want to sit on that horse, to ride her. Just think of all the terribly exquisite things doing so might make her feel or want. Most of all, she couldn't allow Jarrod to give her something so wondrous. There was no room for gratitude in their relationship. No possible way she could allow herself to warm to him even the tiniest bit. "No," Sophia breathed, her throat clogging with dread.

"Yes," he answered, as he hoisted her into the air and set her in the side saddle. She gripped the saddle horn sheerly to keep herself from falling off the animal's far side, tumbling on her head, exposing her stockings and drawers, and granting Jarrod and his men yet more to gawk at.

With all her might she fought not to see the horse beneath her, not to notice how it felt to sit high on her back.

A maid dashed from the house with a cloak, a pair of gloves, and one of Sophia's hats. Jarrod took the cloak from the woman and reached up to sweep it over

Sophia's shoulders. She whisked the garment from him and swatted his hands away. Ire shifted inside her, prickly and red. The gall of him to fuss over her in public, as if he had that right.

The maid stood patiently beside the horse, waiting as Sophia fastened the tie of the black cloak, then tugged on the matching gloves. She even handed up hatpins as Sophia reluctantly secured the hat to her hair. The black-trimmed straw number tilted down over her forehead and folded up in back and like every other item of clothing Jarrod had furnished, it fit faultlessly.

From the stables, a groom ran forward leading what was no doubt Jarrod's horse. The animal was all muscle and ferocity. Jarrod mounted up with a command that made Sophia groan inwardly. She kept hoping he'd be inept at some facet of living. In this case, it would have been nice if he'd proven himself a poor horseman thanks to all his years of chauffeured carriage travel. Instead he nudged his horse into a trot looking for all the world like a man born to the saddle.

Though her lovely white horse strained forward, Sophia kept her in check, limiting her pace to a walk. She was plodding past the stables when Jarrod turned his mount and doubled back to her. "Duchess there can move a little faster, you know."

"No. We'll stay at a walk."

"Why?" His horse scooted to the side with mincing steps, clearly eager to unfurl his long legs and carry Jarrod toward the gulf at a blistering sprint.

"I like this speed."

"Not good enough. Try again."

The last thing she wanted was to admit her real reason for wanting to stay at a safe walk.

"You're an accomplished rider, aren't you?" he asked.

"It's not that." Though she mostly traveled in buggies these days, she had plenty of experience with even the most spirited horses.

"What is it then?" he goaded.

Unable to see any way to avoid it, she stared fixedly at her horse's snowy ears and took a deep breath. "I don't wish to injure her, if you must know." To the answering silence she qualified her statement with, "She has very delicate legs."

He didn't laugh, at least, which eased her feeling of foolishness slightly.

"Do you think I'd buy you an easily injured horse?" he asked, his tone utterly serious.

"Not on purpose." She dared to slide her gaze to his. "But horses like this have fragile bones."

"She may look fragile, but she's actually very sturdy. She's an Arabian, a breed with more endurance than any other on this continent. Not only could she gallop across Galveston with you on her back; give her some water, and she could gallop across Texas."

Sophia still wasn't sure. She pursed her lips. Duchess, as he'd called her, was so very fine. What if she stepped in a hole or tangled her tail on a passing branch or was spooked by an animal while Sophia was riding her? She'd never forgive herself. She'd lived without beautiful things long enough to be nervous around them. This horse deserved to be treated with extreme care.

"I rode her myself last night," Jarrod said.

"You're too heavy for her."

"No, I'm not. Nor would I be too heavy for you."

At her dark expression, he chuckled. "C'mon." His horse lunged ahead a few paces. "Prove to me you can keep up." He cantered forward, shooting challenging glances at her over his shoulder. A groan eased up her throat. She couldn't stand it. Couldn't stand not to fly on the back of a fairy horse just this one time, especially today when the air felt so crisp after days indoors. She prayed a quick prayer, eased her hold on the reins, and let Duchess go.

The horse surged forward, moving beneath her with a heavenly smooth gait that lifted and lowered, lifted and lowered her through the air—fast. Gloriously fast as hooves drummed the earth. Duchess's mane snapped toward her face, then fell rhythmically against her gloved hands.

Sophia's breath caught at the sheer exhilaration of it.

They crested a hill and an unblemished panorama of sea spread across the horizon. The two horses lengthened their strides yet again, and wind flushed against Sophia's cheeks and dried her eyes. A tentative smile tugged at her mouth as Duchess raced through the thin fans of water unfurling upon the sand.

For long, heady minutes they soared. In the face of the view, the salt air, the invigorating motion, her mind cleared. Wiped away were her anxieties about Jarrod, about her crumbling house, about the secrecies of her job, about the masks she must present. Gone.

When they neared the place where the sand ended in an outcropping of rock, Jarrod slowed their pace. They walked the horses, giving them time to cool, before Jarrod guided her up the dune fronting the gulf.

Mild disappointment curled inside Sophia. She'd rather have kept up all that wonderful riding right to the moment they returned to the stables. Not only because she didn't want to stop galloping atop Duchess, but because she was afraid to be with Jarrod out here alone. She peered toward the little foamy caplets on the water. Perhaps if she spurred Duchess forward, she could make a dash for freedom. . . . She was being ridiculous. She wasn't a coward. And him being born to the saddle and all, he'd have caught her in an eyeblink anyway.

He came to stand beside her and extended his arms. She nodded, giving him grudging permission to assist her down. It was that or jump.

He gripped her waist and the sensation of his strong hands cupping her middle caused her heart to pick up speed. She could feel the heat from, the press of, each one of his fingertips. He lifted her from the saddle and set her gently on her feet. The second he did, she moved away.

Jarrod watched the play of emotions on Sophia's face, entranced as always by the sides of her. She walked farther from him. He followed. She moved away. He decided to let her have her distance.

She stood silently, content to watch Duchess nibble dune grass. Though she tried to cant her profile away from him, she couldn't quite shield the amazement behind her eyes. Nor could she take back the smile he'd seen on her earlier. When they'd reached the water of the gulf, the ice princess had actually smiled. With true joy. And it had made him feel like a king.

Clearly, he'd been wrong in thinking that expensive trinkets could soften her. She'd shown him today that her key rested in what she was clearly so unaccustomed to— adventure, spontaneity, enjoyment for the sake of it. It was simple really. He should have realized it when he'd tickled her and her stream of laughter had sounded so rusty. All the wonder of childhood—wonder in small things like riding, even—had been squeezed from her

too early, and whether she knew it or not, she needed it
back. From now on he'd give her something worth more
than money—enjoyment.

Looking at her in this moment, her narrow shoulders
set defensively against all the cares in the world, caused
familiarity to stir inside him. With a rush of recognition
he realized that the vulnerability beneath Sophia's tough
façade reminded him of his mother. She'd used to stand
just like that, with her arms crossed over her chest as if to
hold in whatever strength she had left. God knows, she'd
needed that reserve of personal strength, right up until
the end.

A tenderness that no other woman had roused in him
before or since spread through his chest at the memory.
His mother had been a believer to the last. She'd read to
her sons from the Bible each night before bed, telling
them of things that meant more than heat and food and
shelter. When all the time their circumstances had
screamed how wrong she was. Despite what she'd
preached, he'd realized at the earliest age how fundamental money truly was.

In time, he'd made a hell of a lot of it. For himself, and
for the brothers she'd entrusted to him, and for her. But
she had never seen a penny of it and never would. She,
with her chapped hands, and her wrinkled eyes, and her
ragged clothing would never sleep in a single room of a
single one of his mansions, or eat his chef's food, or wear
the silks or jewels he still, to this day, craved to buy her.

Sophia could, though, a small voice inside himself
said. Sophia who, like his mother, had stared into the
abyss of black, difficult times.

He averted his gaze, suddenly finding it painful to
look at her.

His lungs filled with the bite of the February air as his gaze moved restlessly along the line between sky and sea. Whatever his mother would have thought about the tough decisions he'd made to keep his brothers alive, or his ruthless business tactics, she'd have believed it right that he give whatever he could to the girl who'd had Blackhaw stolen from her. He'd seen that girl in the adult Sophia so clearly today, back at the porch when longing had tightened her features.

Turning, he caught her watching him cautiously.

The usual zing of desire arched between them. Lust. He felt it, heavier every time their eyes met. He had enough experience to know it was the kind of instinctive, primal wanting not easily sated. It would keep them rolling in the sheets, limbs intertwined, covered with sweat, panting, him buried deep inside her for hours. Days. "I want to make love to you," he said bluntly.

Her bottom lip trembled a tiny bit before she masked it with a brittle smile. "Funny, I had the feeling you were trying to reform me from my relationship with Twilight's Ghost."

"I am. You're too good to be any man's mistress, including mine." He buried his hands in his pockets. "That doesn't stop me from wanting you, though."

"As if I'd so much as let you touch me."

"Wouldn't you?" He neared. Their gazes locked for a heated moment before, ever so deliberately, he reached out and slowly ran his thumb down her neck.

She flinched, but she didn't jerk away. Her cloak had parted, and beneath her tight burgundy bodice, her breasts rose and fell rapidly. "Don't like my touching you?" he asked in a low voice. "Or like it too much?"

She presented him with her back and walked to the

edge of the dune overlooking the water. The wind pressed her fashionable skirts against her hips and thighs. God, he loved to see her in the clothes he'd bought her. Their cut and quality suited her, like a velvet backdrop suited a diamond. That particular shade of burgundy highlighted the color that was beginning to bloom on her cheeks. And the dipping front of the hat enhanced her smoky eyes, eyes that danced with more life every day.

"Have you ever been made love to well, Sophia?" He spoke the words in a voice that was rough and quiet both as he advanced on her. He came to stand almost flush behind her, intrigued to discover how she'd respond. "Have you ever been so spent afterward you could do nothing but lie naked and unmoving?"

She swallowed.

"Have you?"

"Yes."

"Have you ever wanted someone so much you were consumed with thoughts of him? So much you couldn't eat or drink or sleep because of it?"

Her breasts rose and fell, rose and fell.

"Have you ever given yourself to a man completely, to the point where there was no shame, only lust?"

"What's your point?" she demanded, her vision focused fixedly forward. "Do you in your arrogance think you can render me to those states?"

"I know I can." He measured the tightness of her jaw with his gaze. "You didn't answer my question. Has anyone else ever done that to you?"

"It's none of. . . ." She shook her head, refusing to waste her words telling him it was none of his business. That reprimand hadn't dissuaded him yet, and Sophia doubted it ever would. Mary, if she could only get a hold of herself. Her body was clamoring with quivery sensations not unlike those caused by fear—only better. An ache, a weighty pressure had settled between her legs, and his words kept stirring it, like air against seething coals.

"Has anyone ever done that to you?" he asked, tone firm with an order to answer him.

"Of course," she lied.

"I don't believe you."

"Then stop asking me questions."

"Give me a truthful answer, and I'll stop." He moved beside her.

She slanted her face away, keeping no more than her profile to him.

"Was Twilight's Ghost a good lover?" he asked. "Is that why you're so set on protecting him from me?"

She felt a muscle jump in her cheek. She didn't answer.

"Just what do you think I'll do when I find him? Kill him in cold blood?"

Again, she didn't reply.

"Do you?" he asked impatiently.

She ground her teeth together.

"Do you?" he demanded.

She whipped her gaze toward him. "Can you honestly tell me you have no plans for revenge against him? At the very least, you'll expose his identity so that he cannot work for the Service, so that every outlaw he's ever placed behind bars will know whom to hunt down and shoot through the heart." A lock of hair skated from beneath her hat, she shoved it out of her eyes. "So to answer your question, no, I don't think you'll kill him in cold blood if I hand him over to you. You won't have to kill him personally. He'll be as good as dead anyway."

"Which would mean your chances of using your lover to find my father are as good as gone. Isn't that what you're really concerned about?"

"No, I'm concerned about the man—"

"Like hell."

Never had she met someone who left her trembling in the face of a churning anger she'd not even known she possessed. People had always allowed her her remoteness. Everyone, but him.

A sense of bitter unfairness beat hard against Jarrod's temples. "You're angry about something that happened twenty years ago, and you're refusing to help me free my brother out of spite." He gestured angrily. "Meanwhile, Holden is sitting in jail, waiting on you."

"That's ludicrous," she hissed. "Your brother's imprisonment is not my fault. He committed a crime, he received his just sentence for it."

"He committed no crime."

She blew out her breath derisively.

"He committed *no crime*, Sophia."

She stuck out that lovely chin, unwilling to budge an inch. God, she could be obstinate. He pushed both hands through his hair, letting the blunt tips of his fingers dig into his scalp. Think, he urged himself. The issue that was holding her back from assisting him was in part the Ghost's ability to find his father, thus that was one of the issues that needed to be undone. The obvious answer occurred to him, but he didn't like it and didn't want to pay its price.

He looked into her storm-dark eyes and read there

that she had no intention of relenting, at least not any-time soon. God *damn* it. He waited a moment more, fighting against the decision, searching her posture and his brain for any hint of an easier way.

The woman looked as if she'd like to spit in his face.

Fine. The hell with it, he'd play his card and deal with the cost of it later. "I'll find my father for you."

Above those curly-lashed eyes of hers, her forehead wrinkled. "What did you just say?"

"You want my father. If you help me free my brother, I'll bring him to you. It's as simple as that."

Her expression held volumes of mistrust. "Why haven't you found him yourself in all these years?"

"First tell me why you want to find him at all."

She seemed to swirl the question around in her mouth. "I can't allow him to just . . . just go free. He has to pay for what he did to my grandmother."

"Your grandmother, or you?"

She blinked at him, clearly taken aback. "My grand-mother was the only relative I had, so what he did to her he did to me."

He glimpsed more of her soul, the woundedness and the pain, in that moment than was wise for his own self-preservation. "Do you think you'll ever be happy carry-ing around so much hatred?"

"Do you think you'll ever be happy so long as you treat people like animals to be captured and caged?"

For the first time in memory, he didn't know what to say.

"Now tell me why you've never gone in search of your father," she said.

"Why would I have? He never bothered to search for us after he left."

His words hung for a beat before she nodded. "I see." Her voice was barely louder than the salty wind.

Memories of his father shifted through his mind. He saw himself being hoisted onto broad shoulders, burying his hands into the short, brown coarseness of his father's hair, laughing. He remembered his father sitting at the table with him, lamplight playing over the books between them as he'd assisted him with his studies. He recalled seeing his father, snoozing in his chair, the newborn Holden asleep on his chest.

Adam Stone had been a man of dreams and schemes that never quite came true, but good to him and his brothers up until the moment he'd abandoned them. Jarrod had loved him once, though he could no longer decide whether that had been because his father had once deserved it or because all boys want to love their fathers until their fathers do the unforgivable. And even then want to love them.

For a long time after his father had left, he'd remained loyal to him, harboring hope that he'd return, making . . . and this he couldn't bear . . . making excuses for him to his brothers.

"Think about my offer," he said carefully. "I have vast resources at my disposal and more money than your Ghost will ever see. I can find my father for you."

"Don't you mean you can find your father for Holden?"

"For Holden, then."

Thoughtfully, she made her way back toward the horses, then stopped a few yards from Duchess. She regarded the horse with fearful reverence, as if concerned that Duchess might vanish if she dared touch her.

"Here." Jarrod took hold of her wrist and pulled off her glove.

"Stop!" She tried to yank her hand back.

Ignoring her protest, he herded her forward with gentle but firm pressure, then guided her bare palm flat onto Duchess's neck. He laid his hand over hers, lacing a few of his fingers between. The horse's coat was warm, but the electricity of his skin against hers was warmer.

He heard her tiny, choked gasp and grinned with male satisfaction. "I want you to feel her," he said against her ear, and pushed her hand up the horse's neck. His own sense of touch rushed with life, recording every detail, texture, temperature of her and of the slightly moist, bristly fur beneath. He watched their joined hands travel up and down.

"Enough." She tried again to jerk her hand away.

Instantly, he curved his fingers down, holding her hostage.

"Please." The word held genuine upset.

He let her go.

They faced each other, both of them breathing a little faster than they had the ability to hide.

"Sh-she's an excellent horse," Sophia said stiffly. "But I cannot accept her."

"Cannot or will not?" Her refusal annoyed the hell out of him. Did she have any idea how little Duchess had cost him in the scheme of his wealth? How many horses finer than she he owned? Stables full. Sophia very well would and could accept one small horse from him.

"Will not," she answered, then ended the conversation by reaching up for the saddle horn and awaiting his assistance in mounting.

When he cupped his hands for her, he'd have sworn she purposely gouged the heel of her shoe into them as he lifted her.

By the time they returned to the stables, Sophia had almost recovered from her dismaying physical reaction to Jarrod. When he'd imprisoned her hand against Duchess, she'd felt almost dizzy from his touch, the pulsing warmth and life of his hand, and the ridges of him she'd felt against her back. His hard abdomen, his firm hips, pressing against her. *I want to make love to you—*

Banish it from your memory, she told herself. But the more she instructed herself to do so, the more blatantly she remembered. Did every woman's body react to the touch of an attractive male that way? Or just her virgin body?

No, no it wasn't as simple as that. Other attractive men—kinder, more decent men—had touched her before, and she'd never felt a thing. How abhorrent that Jarrod Stone should have the ability to make her not only quiver, but quake.

Grooms flowed from the stables to greet them, far more than were necessary. That was one of the hallmarks of life inside Jarrod Stone's castle, she'd noticed. Overabundance. Ridiculous man. She wondered if he had any idea that there were starving people in this world.

She walked beside him to the house, trying to present the image of someone whose backside wasn't quite so tender.

The requisite guards parted for them at the base of the steps, and they climbed to the porch, Jarrod insisting on planting his hand against her lower back for assistance.

The doors swung open from the inside, where Collier was waiting for them in the foyer.

"Yes?" Jarrod asked.

"There's a man here to see Mrs. LaRue, sir."

Jarrod's demeanor turned instantly menacing. Sophia could almost see his predatory instincts flaring to life one by one. "Who is he?" he asked her.

"He's not Twilight's Ghost, if that's what you're hoping."

"Would you tell me if he were?" If she hadn't known better, she'd have attributed his darkened mood to jealousy.

She shook her head. She didn't intend to tell him anything about Twilight's Ghost, ever. Certainly not that Twilight's Ghost had no need to call on her at the mansion because the Ghost was already imprisoned here right under his nose.

Chapter 8

"**W**here is he?" Jarrod asked Collier.

"The library, sir."

He started down the hall, the coat of his black suit jacket swelling behind him. She had to walk double time to keep up. In the doorway of the library he halted, master of the mansion, large and intimidating and ready at the slightest provocation to do battle for his brother's sake.

Sophia came to a halt behind him. From just around his shoulder, she watched Oliver Kinsworthy rise from an ink blue chair. The man who had been her grandmother's attorney and trusted friend looked just as he always had. His head, bald except for the fringe of white-gray hair around the bottom, was as shiny as ever. His snowy eyebrows were thick over smart hazel eyes, his white mustache was bushy. He'd doubtless come from his office, as wrinkles marked his shirt at the inner elbows, and the collar looked as if it had already been tugged at. His customary eyepiece dangled from his dark brown vest pocket, a vest that appeared ready to surrender the fight to contain the round expanse of his belly by bursting its buttons.

"This is Mr. Oliver Kinsworthy," Sophia said by way of introduction. "Attorney-at-law."

Despite the wary glint in his eye, Oliver inclined his head politely.

Jarrod looked to Sophia. "May I have a word with you?"

"If you insist."

"I do."

"Please excuse us for a moment," she said to Oliver.

"Certainly."

Jarrod took hold of her elbow and drew her several yards down the cavernous hallway. He stopped her progress by turning inward on her, trapping her against the wall. "I'm not letting you speak with him in private."

"But with Maggie—"

"Maggie is a woman."

Jarrod could glower more frighteningly than anyone she'd ever met. He was dark to begin with, with that raven hair. But when he glowered he seemed to turn darker, his eyes glowing like emeralds backlit with fire. "No chance I'm letting the two of you retreat to your bedroom in private."

"Am I to understand that you don't approve of my being alone in my bedroom with a man?"

"Not at all."

"A shame you acquired this staggering sense of

morality *after* locking yourself inside there with me the other night."

He placed his hand against the wall, inches above her head. "Sophie," he growled, his tone warning.

"Oh, very well. I'll speak to him in the library."

"No. You'll speak to him in the library with me present."

"Why? After seeing him you can't still seriously believe he might be Twilight's Ghost."

He gave her that insolent half shrug. "No, I've seen the Ghost and I know that's not he. Still, he could be the Ghost's emissary or he could be carrying weapons. I don't trust him with you."

She tried to decide whether it was better to send Oliver away or to speak to him with Jarrod present. Her sense of privacy rebelled at the thought of Jarrod listening in. Yet, what if Oliver had news? And . . . perhaps it wouldn't be so terrible for Jarrod to hear more about the kind of man his father was. Oliver's coming might even present her the opportunity she'd been waiting for to decipher just how much Jarrod was and wasn't telling about Adam Stone. Surely he knew more than he let on.

"Who is he to you, anyway?" Jarrod asked.

"Oliver Kinsworthy was my grandmother's advisor. He assists me in the search for your father."

"That's it?"

"That and we're friends."

When he scowled, she strode past him toward the library, wondering what Jarrod would say if he learned that Oliver was the person indirectly responsible for the investigation she'd launched against Holden. Had Oliver not come to her with concerns about her safety after encountering Holden in Austin, she'd never have rolled up her sleeves, done more digging, and discovered Holden's arrest warrant.

It was one thing for the Stone brothers to bear some defensive animosity toward those at Blackhaw who loathed their father. However, it was something else entirely when Oliver had given her reason to suspect one of them might actually come after her. She'd protected herself the way she always had—by collecting information and then by acting on it.

Ironic that her worst fears had still been confirmed. A Stone brother *had* come after her. Just not the one she'd expected. And not for a reason she'd anticipated.

When she entered the library, Oliver rose again, quickly, and took her hand in both of his. "How are you?" he asked. "Since Maggie came to visit, I've been concerned."

Up this close, Oliver's sweet, jowly face had a ruddy cast, and the few broken blood vessels on his nose were visible. She gave Oliver her gamest smile, as if to say that things like kidnappings at the hands of millionaires occasionally happened in life and must be borne with good cheer. "Thank you for your concern," she said sincerely. "I'm quite well."

"I worried . . ." His words drifted off as Jarrod paced into the room, making frigid the atmosphere.

Sophia walked with Oliver to his chair, then settled herself near him at the end of a brown sofa, which promptly dwarfed her. Clearly, the sofa's large proportions had been made for men to lounge upon while smoking, laughing, and drinking whiskey.

Two of the room's walls, those behind her and Oliver, were covered with bookshelves. The third, behind where

Jarrod took a seat, boasted an intimidating fireplace crowned by an oil painting of a ship tossing on a raging sea of blues and grays. Double doors that Collier was quick to shut dominated the fourth wall. Even the air in this room was very male.

Sophia cleared her throat. "Oliver, I don't believe I introduced the owner of this home to you earlier. This is Mr. Jarrod Stone."

Jarrod dipped his chin.

Strained silence invaded the space.

"Have you learned anything new since we last spoke?" she asked Oliver.

"I'm afraid not."

It had been foolish to hope he had, she supposed, though that didn't stop disappointment from trickling through her. They'd been searching for evidence on Adam Stone's whereabouts for years. In all that time, they'd managed to scrape together only meager information. Still, she'd harbored the hope that Adam Stone would hear of his son's sentencing and attempt to reach him.

"Mrs. LaRue tells me you worked for her grandmother," Jarrod said.

"That's correct. She was one of my clients. I served as her attorney and gave her financial guidance."

"And how did you advise her when my father came to her with his idea of building a boot-making factory?"

Oliver shifted uncomfortably, raised his eyepiece, and regarded Jarrod with faint censure. "I advised her against it, sir. There were no other investors except for the late Mrs. Warren, so she'd have borne all the risk. Your father, to be certain, had no capital to contribute."

"No," Jarrod said.

Tension stole over Sophia's body, compressing the muscles at the back of her neck. Oliver had come at her request and didn't deserve Jarrod's browbeating. "Perhaps, Oliver, if you could recount for Mr. Stone the events leading up to his father's disappearance with Blackhaw's fortune. Mr. Stone has expressed interest in assisting our investigation."

He looked at her for a long moment. "Yes, ah," he softly cleared his throat, "I suppose I could do that."

"Thank you."

He leaned back in his chair and returned his attention to Jarrod. "Mrs. Warren's butler was a friend of your father's and the one who introduced him to Mrs. Warren. The first discussion between them took place, I believe, about three weeks before her money was stolen." Absently, he studied his eyepiece, then set about cleaning it with a cloth he extracted from his trouser pocket. "From the beginning, she was extremely interested in your father's proposition of building a factory."

"Why?" Jarrod's posture, one knee pointed forward, one splayed to the side, made him look both casual and foreboding. "Why so eager to invest in something so risky?"

"When her son and his wife—" He glanced at Sophia. "When Sophia's parents were killed in a boating accident, sole control of the estate reverted to Mrs. Warren. Though she was a woman with a great many sterling qualities, financial experience was not among them. Her husband, and after him her son, had always managed the fortune."

Oliver tucked away the cloth, then rolled the circular eyepiece between brawny, age-speckled fingers. "From the start, the responsibility of managing such a large fortune was a difficult burden for her. She immediately wished to increase her holdings, I presume because she hoped she'd feel less burdened . . . more secure, you know . . . with more money in the bank. Doubling her savings quickly was more important to her than safe and steady growth, which led her to make ill-advised investments despite my recommendations to the contrary. By the time Adam Stone came to her, her holdings were perhaps a fifth of what they had been at the time of her son's death."

"Which heightened the appeal of my father's scheme."

"Quite right. As I said, I counseled her against it—"

"Did you have access to her money?"

The eyepiece ceased its movement.

Sophia's attention cut to Jarrod. "It wasn't Oliver who disappeared the day the fortune did."

"It's all right," Oliver murmured. "I'll answer his question. It's a legitimate one." He took a deep, sighing breath. "From time to time Mrs. Warren asked me to courier a transaction to and from the bank for her to sign. So yes, in that respect, I did have some access to her money."

"Go on."

"In the days leading up to your father's disappearance, Mrs. Warren met with him more and more regularly. I believe they crafted the remainder of your father's business plan and drew up a crude layout for the building. I know they projected astronomical earnings, because Mrs. Warren showed those to me. The night the money was stolen, I went to Mrs. Warren one final time, to try and dissuade her. She wouldn't hear of it, informed me the deal had already been struck."

Sophia twined her hands together in her lap, hoping

that if she concentrated on them hard enough, she could fend off the memories.

"The next day, I visited again, late in the afternoon. Mrs. Warren was frantic, said your father was supposed to have met with her earlier in the day. He was four hours late."

Sophia clenched her hands tighter, and still the remembrances of that day came spiraling back. Her grandmother had been dressed in her finery, like always. The fabric of her skirt had twitched, and all her necklaces had clinked together as she'd grown increasingly agitated. Her voice had turned more shrill, her breath less even. Sophia had sat alone at their polished oak dining table watching her in silence, racked with fear, waiting for everything to be fine again. Believing, in those early hours, that it would be.

"Your father never returned," Oliver stated, his voice holding an edge of accusation.

Jarrod's cheeks and jaw hardened with an emotion she couldn't read.

"It was later," Oliver continued, "that I learned she'd given him nearly all the money in her possession. Later still I discovered that she'd accrued debts throughout the city and the state."

The ominous quiet that followed seemed to Sophia to pronounce the smell of the room—that of cigar smoke mixed with the musty scent of old and brittle paper. She could bear anything but this silence in which her beloved grandmother's foolishness hung between the three of them like a sharp, ugly glass bauble the shade of blood.

She schooled her voice to sound matter of fact as she glanced to Jarrod. "It's our understanding that your father never returned home the night my grandmother gave him the money. Is that correct?"

Slowly, Jarrod nodded. "I knew nothing about the money at the time, but that's correct. That's also the night that my mother packed our things and took my brothers and me from Galveston."

"Your mother didn't say anything to you," Sophia asked, "about why you had to leave?"

"Absolutely nothing. She died just weeks afterward, and she took that with her to the grave."

"What did she say to explain your father's absence?"

"Only that he'd gone and couldn't come home for a while." Jarrod held Sophia's gaze.

"You're telling me you know nothing about what happened that night."

"That's right."

"And afterward. Your father never attempted to contact you? Nothing?"

"Nothing."

Sophia's frustration churned. "You've no idea where he might have gone?"

"None."

Was he telling the truth? Could he really know so little about his own father?

"What about you?" Jarrod asked her. "What have you learned about my father's movements after that night?"

"Very little."

Oliver tucked away his eyepiece. "We've had reports of places he might have passed through. Received correspondence from owners of establishments where he might have spent some of the money. Nothing that has led us to him."

"You do know, don't you, that the money's gone?"

Jarrod asked her. "Even if I can find him for you, your money's been spent long since."

She saw Blackhaw in her mind's eye—wallpaper curling away from browned plaster, bricks that wiggled when touched, and glass that bore spidery cracks. "I realize that." God knows, she could use the money, but her desire to bring Adam Stone to justice had never been about that.

"What happened at Blackhaw," Jarrod asked, "afterward?"

"Nothing." Sophia frowned. "That's the end of the story."

"Not the story I'm interested in."

Oliver used his meaty arms to lever himself from his chair. "Mind if I stretch my back?"

Jarrod gestured his acquiescence with the lifting of fingers.

As she'd seen him do a hundred times, Oliver braced his hands against his lower spine and arched backward. A soft "ah" seeped from his mouth. "Not much to tell after Adam Stone's disappearance."

"Tell me what there is," Jarrod answered.

Oliver straightened, rolled his shoulders once, and ambled to the window nestled amongst the bookshelves. His gaze traced the contours of the land outside as he spoke. "Mrs. Warren took to her bed almost immediately. Sophia here tended her, as we had to let nearly all of the staff go."

Sophia shifted restlessly. This was more than Jarrod needed to know, far more than she wanted him to.

"She didn't wish for her friends or anyone else to come calling," Oliver continued, "and see her in what she regarded as her disgrace."

"What was done about the financial situation?" Jarrod asked.

"At first, I thought that if we sold off all the other properties she owned, that we'd be able to keep Black-haw Manor functioning. When the debts were revealed, however, liquidation became the only alternative."

Sophia's heart was thumping like the beating wings of a caged bird. She'd humiliate herself if she interrupted. But would the humiliation be better or worse than having Jarrod know about the desperation of Blackhaw's last days?

"We sold everything but Blackhaw itself," Oliver said. "The other properties, the horses, the furniture, the jewelry. Mrs. Warren passed away before the end of the selling, and sometimes I think it was a blessing. I'm not sure she could have survived seeing that."

Sophia held herself mercilessly still. At the end, her grandmother had aged a hundred years in just a handful of days. Her sweet, funny, lavish grandma had lain beneath sterile sheets, her body shrunken and her eyes hollow.

Sophia had stared into those eyes, watched as the life had drained from them, knowing as their meager light paled that she was losing the only person she had left. Dying, dying, dying. She'd pleaded with God that her efforts would be enough to somehow keep her grand-mother alive. They had to be, she'd thought then in desperation. Who else was there to love her? To be her family? The old terror belonging to the child she'd been curled around her like tentacles of black fog, even now.

"And Sophia?" Jarrod asked.

"You already know what happened to me," she said sharply.

He stared at her without expression, the green in his eyes seeming to shift.

She lifted her chin a fraction, trying to defend herself physically against the reality of having her most private tragedy paraded in front of him. Him, with all his toughness and splendor. Him, who to this day had the luxury of family and the love of his brothers.

"I took Sophia to St. Mary's Orphanage," Oliver said. "Being a bachelor, I knew I couldn't care appropriately for a young girl, and there was no one else."

She had no reason to experience a curdle of shame in her belly, but it was there. The stigma of the abandoned.

"Of course, the house always belonged to her," Oliver said. "It waited only for her to claim it."

"Not much of a prize, was it?" Jarrod asked as he pushed to his feet.

"How can you say that?" she demanded, on her feet as quickly. "That house is—is a landmark, a treasure."

"Quite," Oliver said placatingly.

Jarrod opened the door, called for a servant. As usual, one was almost instantaneously near at hand. "Fetch Mr. Kinsworthy's coat."

The servant nodded and hurried off.

"What methods are you currently using to search for my father?" Jarrod asked, as they gathered near the doorway to wait.

Oliver pulled at the bottom of his vest to straighten it. "We post requests for information in newspapers across the country, have written countless letters to city and county officers asking them to search their records."

Jarrod nodded.

"Will you be assisting us, Mr. Stone?"

"It depends."

The servant returned and handed Oliver his coat.

"On Sophia."

The next day Maggie and Sophia were sitting together in their customary places on the dressing-room floor. As usual, Maggie had ditched her straw hat in favor of a richly decorated one. She adjusted the position of the current hat, a black confection festooned with all manner of dotted lace, then checked her profile in the mirror. "Have you actually seen any of Jarrod's brothers?"

Idly, Sophia thumbed through the stack of mail Maggie had brought her. A letter from one of the sisters at the orphanage, three social invitations. . . . "No."

"Do you think there's any chance in God's green earth that they resemble him?"

"It's a possibility. Why?" She looked up.

"Why? Because I want them for myself, of course. What are their names again?"

"Clint, J. T., and Holden. Three men I promise you you want nothing to do with. They're a slimy, disreputable bunch."

"Yes, that's right, Sophia. I'm a thirty-two-year-old spinster without breasts, and I can afford to be picky."

"Maggie," Sophia warned.

"I'm just saying"—she lifted a bony shoulder—"perhaps they could use the influence of a virtuous wife." She batted her eyelashes.

Sophia shook her head and returned to the pile of envelopes. Two letters from would-be male suitors, and one letter—her pulse hitched—from the state tax assessor's office. Uneasily, she pulled it free.

"I realize the youngest one's in jail," Maggie said. "But what do the other two do?"

"One's a marshall and one's a bounty hunter," she answered distractedly.

"Well, that doesn't sound too disreputable."

"Bounty hunter?" Sophia repeated skeptically.

"I happen to like a man with some mischief in his head."

"You like all men." Sophia turned the letter from the tax assessor over.

"You think there's any possibility of my meeting these brothers of his? Any way you could request it of Jarrod, maybe promise to hand over Twilight's Ghost if one of his strapping brothers will take me to the altar and make me an honest woman?"

"I don't think so."

"No?"

"No."

Maggie muttered moodily before reaching for another of Jarrod's hats.

The letter felt bad to Sophia. The weight of it in her palm just plain felt bad. She stared down at it, sudden dread clumping in her throat. Maybe if she just stuffed it into one of the shoes— Don't be silly. Had her confinement here turned her into such a milksop?

Irritated with herself, she tore open the letter. She was a woman who moved unafraid through the streets at night, an agent, an adult strong enough to bear the responsibility for the fall of thieves masquerading as important men. She certainly wasn't afraid of letters.

The single sheet of paper crackled when she opened it.

"Mrs. LaRue: We regret to inform you that due to

your failure to pay taxes . . ." The words blurred before her eyes and she had to force herself to continue reading. ". . . either for the year 1876 or the year 1877 on the estate located at 2330 Broadway, Galveston, Texas, the property has been slated for auction at noon on March 10. Unless your tax debt in the amount of $468 is paid prior to that day, the house will be sold, with the proceeds reverting to the state government."

Chapter 9

Sophia lowered the letter and stared sightlessly at the wall, feeling every contraction of her heart. Her lips rolled inward to stop them from shaking. They'd finally done it. They'd actually set an auction date. Nineteen days away. Less than three weeks. *Oh, God.*

During her time at St. Mary's there had been just enough left over from the sale of her family's other belongings for Oliver to pay Blackhaw's taxes. When that money had run out, she'd compensated with every cent of her Service income. It hadn't been enough. Not for a long time now. She'd known for the past two years that they'd come after her eventually, but up until today she'd been able to stall them with correspondence and Oliver's legal maneuvering and the insufficient payments she'd sent.

Blackhaw. Her breath burned her lungs. Her proud old house. In her mind it was a meshing of old and new images. Vast acres of thriving orchards, soaring pale brick turrets reaching toward endless sky, war-ravaged rooms, jagged glass begging to be replaced. Mostly, though, it was just . . . hers. The only thing in the world she truly owned and the only possession she loved. To be honest, it wasn't like a possession at all, but rather like a living being that, though not indestructible, had proven more constant than her family ever had.

"I must say that I took a fancy to that last hat," Maggie was saying. "A bit of the air of the rich, wounded widow about it."

Dazedly, Sophia smoothed the letter with shaky hands, folded it along the crease marks, and returned it to its envelope. Adam Stone was trying to strip the final thing from her twenty years after he'd taken their fortune and with it her grandmother's reason for living and life.

Tears threatened to well in her eyes. She sniffed them angrily back. Well, he couldn't have Blackhaw. She had two and a half weeks, at least, to try her damnedest to raise the money she owed.

"However, I'm not entirely won over by this one," Maggie said to her own reflection. "The deep green shade is lovely, but I find this starchy bow on top entirely suspicious. Makes me look as though I've just stuck my head out the window of a train, what with the ends pointing upward like they are. I'd frighten off Jarrod's brothers were they to see me in this. Don't you agree?"

Their eyes met, and Maggie's expression turned instantly concerned. "What's wrong?"

Wordlessly, Sophia handed over the letter.

Maggie scanned its contents. "Oh, Sophia," she

breathed as she read the last line, then rested the letter on her lap. She looked so bereft that Sophia's brittle emotions teetered. She was tempted to surrender her head to Maggie's shoulder and sob. But if she did that, she very much feared she'd never be able to fight her way back up again. "It just means I'll have to gather the money for Blackhaw's taxes before the auction," she said with more confidence than she felt. "That's all."

"How do you propose to do that?"

She shook her head, indicating that she'd no idea. On a wave of agitation, she pushed to her feet and began pacing the small space.

Maggie, still wearing the green hat, slowly straightened. She leaned into one of the clothing racks, her shoulder against the bar, and watched Sophia's movement. "You could always just ask *him* for the money."

"No," she replied immediately.

"Or you could start accepting his gifts, and I could try to sell them for you. That ruby bracelet was probably worth quite a bit, all on its own."

"No." That she'd so much as ridden Duchess was bad enough. Everything she accepted from Jarrod rendered her in some way beholden to him. That sense of obligation would only deepen if his money were going, no matter how indirectly, toward the saving of her home. "No, I don't want him involved in this whatsoever. There has to be another way."

"Well," Maggie drew out the word begrudgingly, "there is that reward I mentioned the first time I visited you here."

Sophia's pacing ceased. She faced Maggie, remembering in a rush about Slocum's Mercantile and the five-hundred-dollar reward they were offering for the capture of a counterfeiter. An overpowering, instinctive sense of rightness filled her. "That's it." She'd find the counterfeiter and earn the reward in time to keep Blackhaw.

"I agree that it has potential," Maggie said. "Except that our mysterious counterfeiter is out there." She jabbed a thumb over her shoulder. "And I hate to be the one to point this out, but you're in here." Her lips curled into an apologetic frown.

"I can't stay in here anymore, Maggie. Not after this."

"Nor can you leave. Simon gave strict orders that you stay—"

"I know. And before this I agreed that the risks of attempting escape outweighed the benefits. They no longer do." She toyed with the fingernails of her left hand, thinking. "I'll leave only at night, only when I won't be missed. I can investigate the case without Jarrod, or Simon, for that matter, being any the wiser."

"Oh, Sophia," Maggie murmured worriedly. "How about this? How about if I investigate the case for you?"

"Thank you for offering, and I'll need your help. But the fact is that I can't bear to remain trapped here for the next nineteen days doing nothing, knowing that Blackhaw's auction date is drawing closer."

Maggie chewed her bottom lip.

"I just can't, Maggie."

"I have the utmost confidence in your abilities, Sophia. You know I do. But think for a minute. What if Jarrod catches you? Your career will be over. Maybe your life, too. There's no telling what he'll do."

"He's not going to catch me. I wouldn't attempt to do this if I didn't believe that."

Maggie regarded her with a deadly solemn expression on features that usually brimmed with humor.

She understood Maggie's concerns, treasured her for them. "I can't let them take Blackhaw," she said softly.

Maggie exhaled, her shoulders slumping slightly. "I know."

"I already have my knife, so I'll only need you to bring my disguise and some lockpicking equipment."

Maggie nodded.

"Oh, and if you can bring me a sketch of the surrounding acreage, as well as the best course to take from here into town, I'd appreciate it."

"I'll do it."

"It would also help to know the positioning of the guards late at night. I can only see the ones outside my windows. There well may be more at other stations around the house. I need to know where."

"Okay. I'll scout out their positions."

"You can use my spyglass."

"Right."

Sophia's mind raced ahead. She could hunt for her counterfeiter through the night and catch sleep between her obligatory meals with Jarrod during the day. Yes, once Maggie brought her the information she needed and the remainder of her equipment, she'd have all the necessities of escape.

"Where are you going?" Jarrod asked, his voice dark against the night air.

Sophia stumbled. "Going?" She tried to look nonchalant. "I'm following you."

"I'm over here." He raised a hand and waved. His grin glistened in the light from the half-moon.

She fought the urge to smile back. Instead, she crossed her arms and angled her steps after his. She couldn't help but notice, as she trudged along after him, that the cold blackness of the late hour suited Jarrod to perfection. It starkened the male beauty of his face and cloaked his body with a kind of dangerous power that only made his shoulders seem wider and his height higher. The savagery of nature under cover of darkness matched a certain savagery inside Jarrod.

She didn't know why she should be surprised. Was it any wonder that the night loved the man? For all she knew Adam Stone could well be the devil's brother, which would make Jarrod too close of kin to contemplate.

After dinner, when he'd suggested they take this outing, she'd been eager to accept because she'd immediately recognized it as an opportunity. After Maggie's visit that morning, a chance to view the back of the house and learn the lay of the surrounding land was welcome indeed. She'd been *trying* to get a surreptitious look at the various planes of the roof when he'd asked her where she was going just now.

They waded farther from the light of the house. She was leaning into the incline of a hill, when the sound of crunching leaves broke the stillness. She turned to see someone—no some*thing*—hurtling toward her. A black shadow, closing the distance fast. Her heart leapt into her throat, and she instinctively lifted her hands to protect herself as the thing raced toward her, then bounded past. Out of the corner of her eye she saw it skid to a stop next to Jarrod. It was a dog, a big one. Though now that the animal was dancing attendance around Jarrod, she could see that it wasn't a scary one.

"Sorry if Maxine frightened you," Jarrod said.

"Maxine?"

"Yeah. I didn't think to warn you that she might be joining us."

"Oh," she replied lamely, at a loss for words.

The best she could make out, Maxine was a retriever with a long coat.

"What have you brought me?" Jarrod asked the dog as he ruffled her ears. "A stick? Okay, just don't blame me again if you can't find it once I throw it."

The dog seemed to nod as she unclamped her jaws so that he could pull free the small branch she'd brought him. He threw it overhanded and Maxine charged after it.

Sophia could only stare, unsure what she was seeing. "That's *your* dog?" she finally asked.

He smiled wryly at her as Maxine returned to him, panting with glee. He threw her stick again. "After a long day's work of torturing small children and robbing old ladies I sometimes like to play with dogs."

Heat rolled against the insides of her cheeks, because that's exactly what she'd been thinking. Good-hearted dogs didn't love men like Jarrod . . . did they? And men like Jarrod certainly didn't ruffle the ears of sweet retrievers named Maxine.

She recalled the image of him she'd had the first night they'd met—Jarrod standing on the steps of a marble mansion, feeding money to twin wolves. That vision couldn't have been more different than this reality. His dog seemed to prefer sticks to cold, hard cash. "Have you had her a long time?"

"More than ten years."

"Oh?" When he failed to explain, she found she was too curious to let it go. "How did you come by her?"

He shrugged it off. "No particular way."

Maxine trotted back to Jarrod. He murmured something to her that Sophia didn't quite catch, then threw her branch for her again.

Warmth curled unbidden inside Sophia. Warmth, oh God, for *him*. She worked to steel herself against it. Maybe there were some things about Jarrod, like the fact that he owned a dog, that she was better off not knowing. Such things threatened the distance she needed to maintain between them.

Jarrod renewed his climb up the hill and she followed in silence. For the first time she wondered just how closed she'd become during all her years of secrecy. So much so that she hadn't been able to dare, just now, to soften her perception of Jarrod in the smallest way? That she couldn't allow any civility at all between them? Yes, that's exactly right, a part of her heart answered. It was the part that had loved her grandmother too foolishly and remembered too well the ache of abandonment.

Overhead, the tree branches, like black lace against the gray of the sky, receded. A circular copse opened on the hill's plateau, and she saw that a table had been set for two. The linens gleamed ghostly white. The silver flatware caught the starlight. And the pale china cups and bowls seemed to glow with their own luster, like the inside of a shell. Behind the otherworldly table stood a telescope, pointed heavenward.

She felt Jarrod's attention without having to look to confirm it.

"What?" she asked. "No servants?"

"I'm certain you're astonished." He came to a stop at the table and motioned to the steam twisting upward from the central dish and the spout of the coffee urn. "They must have just left. It's still hot."

She stood next to him. The table was even more magical close-up. "What is it?"

"Pineapple cake."

Yes. She could smell it now, the scents of baked butter and vanilla. "You told me once it was your favorite," he said.

"It is."

He gazed down at her—that hot perusal again, this time from so close. What did he see when he looked at her, she wondered? Probably a prudish woman with too-big eyes, wearing a scarlet gown that was clearly too grand for her.

"You feed me too much," she said, because something needed saying.

"Nothing that I do for you is too much. More like not enough."

Her mouth went completely dry. That deadly charm again, charm that slid around her like satin and made her want—just for a moment or a minute—to believe it. She eased away from him before hazarding to meet his gaze. "I'm not sure I understand why you brought me all the way out here for pineapple cake."

"Have you ever seen the stars through a telescope?"

She shook her head.

"Good. I wanted to be the first to show you." He used the silver serving spoon to scoop a huge portion of pineapple cake onto a china plate, which he handed to her. Heat seeped through the plate and her gloves into her hands. He poured steaming coffee—no, tea, she could tell by the scent—into a cup for her before bypassing his own empty place setting in favor of the telescope. He squinted at it as he worked to adjust the instrument's height and settings.

She slid into a chair and set her plate before her. Obviously, Jarrod was too engrossed in his telescope to sit with her which made her feel . . . how? Miffed not to be the center of his attention for one tiny moment? No, certainly not. She took advantage of his preoccupation by furtively eyeing the back of the house and the surrounding property.

Her first bite of cake fairly melted on her tongue. Gloriously rich and hot and sweet. Every bit as good as Mrs. Dewberry's. Each mouthful would doubtless deposit itself either on her breasts or her bottom. But when food tasted this delectable, it was hard to care. Someone had even thought to bring whipping cream. She added a dollop and luxuriated in the dessert as she continued to make mental notes regarding the landscape.

"The telescope's ready for you," Jarrod announced.

She slid her attention to him, her last bite halfway to her mouth.

"You can finish that first," he said.

"No, really, I'm full." The portion he'd given her had been truly huge.

He moved to her and used his fingers to press the fork to her mouth. "Finish," he murmured.

She was forced to open her lips and accept the cake or be poked by the fork.

"Have I ever told you I like women with curves?"

She chewed and swallowed as quickly as possible. "Then I shall endeavor to slim my figure."

He smiled wickedly. "No, you won't." He plucked her napkin from her lap, threw it on the table, and drew her to the telescope.

Sophia licked her lips, hoping there were no crumbs clinging there.

"Take a look," he said.

Stargazing didn't particularly inspire her, but since he'd gone to so much trouble, she felt obliged. Somewhat self-consciously, she eased her eye to the eyepiece.

A myriad of stars shone through the rod of the telescope, so close and unbelievably brilliant that she reared back a bit in surprise. As quickly as she did so, however, she was drawn back by the sight. Magnificent. Stars scattered across the sky like ribbons of crystals. These gems twinkled, some more luminously than others. Blindingly radiant. Awe coasted through her as she raised her hands reverently to cup the near end of the telescope. She'd not imagined . . . never seen anything like this.

"What do you think?" Jarrod asked from nearby.

"I . . . They're lovely."

His satisfied silence answered her.

"Which stars am I looking at?" she asked.

"You're looking at a portion of the Milky Way."

"Do you know anything else about them?"

"I know it's called the Milky Way because to the naked eye it looks like milk spilled across a dark table or a band of mist in the sky. It's only with a telescope that you can tell it's actually made up of thick clouds of individual stars."

"Does it shift around the sky like the constellations do?" She often used the moon's position to approximate the hour during her nighttime vigils, but she knew precious little else about astronomy.

"Yes. Sometimes it's so close to the horizon that it can't be seen."

"What else?"

"The Milky Way is an area with more bright stars than any other. Of the twenty-one first-magnitude stars, six-

teen are in or near the Milky Way. It's only their distance
from the earth that makes them appear small."

She nodded, spurring him on, as she drank in the
sight.

"What you're looking at is the rim of our universe,"
he said simply.

To see this expanded the world as she knew it. As if
someone had pulled a scarf from the heavens she'd been
seeing all these years to reveal an unexpected, astonishing beauty. It was easy to forget, unless you took the
time to look, that such beauty existed in the world.

Foolishly, her eyes teared. It made her feel safe, to
see this evidence of vastness beyond herself and be reminded that everything in God's kingdom was truly in
its place. Stalwart and lasting. Just for a moment, her
awful fears for Blackhaw eased. For years she'd been
operating on the belief that if she stopped controlling
everything in her life, all she held as precious would fall
from her hands and shatter. Maybe . . . maybe there was
a larger order that would catch Blackhaw in its sweeping hand.

"Which star do you want me to name in honor of
you?" Jarrod asked.

At that, she looked to him, blinking a few times to ac-
climate her vision. He stood close, his hands buried in
his pockets, the flaps of his coat pushed back.

"You can't name a star," she said.

"Can't I?"

She wondered how many times in their acquaintance
she'd told him he couldn't do something, and he'd
looked at her with that same fate-challenging confidence, and said, "Can't I?" Too many times. "Haven't
they all already been named?"

"Not yours."

Magic tugged at her, drawing her back to the telescope for another look. This was silly. He couldn't name a star Sophia . . . could he? No, no, surely not. Except that all of a sudden, she deeply, *deeply* wanted a star named after her.

"That one," she whispered, finding a star off on the fringes of the sight. It wasn't the brightest or the biggest, but it pulsed steadily. It was a mysterious little star, a star of perseverance, its heart beating bravely backward and forward through time. It was a star that *survived*.

She heard him move toward her and reluctantly surrendered the telescope to him. "It's the one far up to the right," she explained. When he was quiet, searching, she added, "About three up from the brightest star and then two over. The one that pulses the most."

"I see it."

"Will you ever be able to find it again?" Even as she spoke the words, she couldn't believe she was asking them, less that she cared.

"Yes, my little doubter, I'll be able to find it again." He glanced over at her. "How could I not? Sophia just became my favorite star in the galaxy."

Goose bumps rose on her flesh. A tight part of her, deep inside, unfurled.

"Want to look at a planet?" he asked.

"Yes."

He returned to the telescope, angling it anew. "There." The motion of the instrument stopped. "Saturn." He stepped to the side so she could take his place.

She was struck first by the rings surrounding it. She was struck second by the steadiness of Saturn's light, so different from the stars of the Milky Way. "Tell me what you know."

"Saturn is the sixth planet from the sun," he said, "but second in size. It has eight moons, unless you count all the millions of small moons that form Saturn's rings."

Amazing. Here she was, her feet planted on ground, gazing at an actual planet, seeing it in detail as it winged its way around and around the earth. She tried to memorize it for the future. The next time she found herself waiting away the night alone on the dock or some sandy bluff, she wanted to be able to look up and remember. "So bright."

"Yes, although Venus is the brightest, then Jupiter, then Saturn. Mars varies, though it can blaze as bright as the last two at times."

Sophia hugged the sight of the planet into herself before straightening. He hadn't moved away, was still standing just inches from her.

"How do you know all this astronomy?"

"I look through the telescope often. But everything I've been telling you tonight I just read in a book this afternoon."

Her brows lifted. "Truly?" she asked, unsure whether to believe him.

He shrugged. "I wanted to impress you."

She laughed.

"By God, are you laughing?"

"I laugh when it's merited." Her smile plucked at the edges of her lips.

"It's about time *I* merited it," he murmured, humor creasing his eyes. Then, as naturally as if he'd done it a hundred times before, he kissed her.

Sophia froze. His warm lips were on hers, friendly,

and affectionate. Then gone, before she could comprehend what was happening.

She stood stunned, staring helplessly up at him. Ensnared in disbelief, dismay, and the power of his spell.

Every shred of the previous amusement left his features. His attention roved from her eyes down to her lips and held there with a hunger so concentrated, so forceful, that her woman's center contracted at the sight of it.

Deliberately, as if daring her to stop him, he slanted his mouth against hers. She should have stopped him, could have. Except she didn't because she, God save her, wanted his lips on hers.

Chapter 10

⌒◯◯⌒

He pushed his hands up the back of her neck, burying his fingers in her hair and trapping her head in his palms. His lips parted, parting hers as they did so, and his tongue slid inside. Her senses, already drunk on the taste of pineapple cake and the sight of the stars, wheeled.

He drew at her, demanding, wholly dominating, just as he was in every aspect of his life. And hot. Wet. Overwhelming her with the force of his appetite.

Staggered, plunged far beyond her element, she went pliant in his arms and simply let herself be kissed. He moaned and walked her backward until her hips came up against the side of the table. The silverware clanked against the china, a distant sound compared to the rushing in her ears. He possessed her mouth completely, and she let him. Too stunned to do anything but follow his lead.

Her thighs fit snugly between his. She could feel the muscles of them leaping, scorching through her skirt. Shyly, she swept her hands up his broad back, hardly believing that she was touching him this way. Hardly believing it could feel so good to be desired as a woman. She'd never known until now how much she'd longed for someone to look at her and see what Jarrod—unbelievably—saw in her. My God, he truly did want her. The growl in his throat, the thrust of his tongue, the clasp of her head in his hands communicated his need to her.

He tilted back her head, roughly breaking the kiss and exposing her throat. His mouth moved along the slant of her jaw, then down the cords of her neck. She pushed the back of her head more deeply into his hold, offering him more. He kissed her neck, tonguing her, trailing fire down flesh met instants later by the tingle of wind. She clutched at his shoulders, as she would to an island in a pitching sea of feeling and emotion.

He straightened, leaning into her, then he was kissing her again. The heated friction of his lips, the hitch of his breath—it dimmed her awareness, burned it to nothingness.

He dislodged one hand from her hair, pressed it along the skin of her neck he'd just awakened, then lower across her upper chest. The touch of an expert, firm and knowing. He wasn't . . . wouldn't touch her there, surely—he *would*.

His hand blatantly captured her breast.

She gasped against his lips, and he parted from her, still so close their foreheads rested on one another. Without the kissing, his hand on her breast was even more carnal. Pressing in, then rubbing a thumb over a nipple that peaked to almost painful sensitivity. And still he worked her, weighing, stroking. Unembarrassed.

She . . . No man had ever in her entire life fondled her with such intimacy. It was a kind of drunkenness, to be so ruled, so given over into such skillful hands. To experience the lushness of being a woman desired. A wild kernel of daring inside her pined for it to go on. Trembled for it to, despite that it wasn't right, what she was letting him do.

Jarrod Stone. *Stone*. Years, decades of virtue and principles came howling back. What had she gotten herself into? Her breast, he was touching her breast. No, too far. Too much. All wrong.

She pushed against him.

His head lifted so he could gaze at her as his fingers caressed her breast, sending bald feeling whipping through her.

She shoved him again. This time he dropped his hand and stepped back.

Mother Mary, what did I just allow to happen? Her chest rose and fell with her labored breathing. She looked around her, searching for something familiar to cling to. There was nothing. She was draped against the table, her skirts mashed between her legs, a foreign meadow encircling her, and her body heaving with needs she'd never experienced before. Nothing about this was familiar.

Jarrod took a few more steps back. Shadow slanted across his face so that all she could see—or maybe she was imagining even them—were his eyes. Deadly serious eyes, honed on her unrelentingly.

She scrambled inwardly for composure as she smoothed her skirts back into place.

Jarrod didn't move a muscle.

She righted the silverware and straightened the table-cloth where it had bunched. Still, he didn't move.

Steady, she told herself. Steady. She worked to master her voice before braving speech. "I suppose we can both agree that was a mistake."

"What, you didn't like it?"

He knew, damn him, that she'd liked it. "It wasn't appropriate."

He snorted. "Spare me the scandalized rhetoric. There's no harm in a few kisses."

A few kisses? *A few kisses?* Hysteria gurgled dangerously close to the surface. The foundations of her life were rocking like pillars in an earthquake, and he'd dismiss what had just happened as "a few kisses."

"We're not inexperienced, you and I." He paused. "Are we?"

Everything within her crescendoed to stillness. She hadn't thought . . . had entirely forgotten the role she played. When he'd taken her in his arms, she'd acted only as herself and made the unforgivable bungle of leaving behind her mask. He believed her to be a widow and a mistress.

Alarm iced through her. Already she might have communicated her inexperience too strongly through her response to his kiss, giving him an enormous clue, risking her job, her identity, everything.

Had she actually hoped just minutes ago that a few pretty stars could save Blackhaw? They wouldn't save her house, and they wouldn't save her. This was the real world. You were smart and protected yourself, or you were ruined. Her thoughts whirred, seeking ways to right the situation.

"Christ, who were these men you took to your bed?" he asked. "What in the hell were they doing?"

"They were men with more gentleness than you, that's all." Would he believe that? How naïve had her kisses been?

One black brow rose with disdain. "Is gentleness what you want in your lovers?"

"Yes."

"Like hell it is."

She made a big show of lifting her chin. "Regardless of what it is I value in my lovers, I can assure you that you don't have it. I don't even like you."

"You like me more than you'll admit to yourself."

"I like you not at all."

He stalked toward her, measuring her.

Her knees began to shake. In a show of false bravado, she firmed her jaw and held her ground.

He stopped close, continued to gauge her.

How much of the truth did he see in her? The truth was, she didn't want to like him at all, and didn't in many ways. And yet she'd just discovered that she loved his kisses with blazing fervor. It wasn't sane. It made no sense. Even now, she craved for him to touch her breast again so that she could feel that intense shock of pleasure a second time.

He frowned. "I've never seen a woman that begs to be kissed as much as you do."

"Excuse me?"

"It's in your eyes, the tilt of your chin, those damned lips."

"I never!"

"That's right. You've never been kissed the right way until tonight."

She sputtered, feeling ludicrously spited.

"Fortunately," he continued, "you're staying in my home. And I've time on my hands."

Oh heaven, oh heaven. This is bad. But even worse, was the anticipation straining upward within her like a sprout toward the sun.

"It's only kisses, after all." He smiled like the wolf he was. All his supremely well cut suits couldn't cover the ruggedness beneath any more than a wolf wearing a knitted sweater could hide his true nature. Jarrod's earthy upbringing, his ruggedness and strength showed through his businessman's veneer. The truth was in a hundred things, not the least in the way he'd kissed her and in his response to her protestations.

"A lovely offer, but thank you, no." She set off toward the house before she could say or do something else she'd regret. "I'll not be indulging in kisses with you again."

"Yes, you will," he replied. "And often."

Shaking her head, she quickened her pace.

"Afraid to stay?" he called after her.

"Going to bed," she called back without looking at him. "I trust sleep will prove more stimulating than this asinine conversation."

Jarrod watched her behind sway as she picked up her pace yet again, all but lifting her skirts and sprinting away from him. He followed at a distance, battling the instinct to charge after her, spin her around, and cart her to the nearest mound of shrubs to make love to her.

He smiled bleakly. She was twitchy and agitated

enough already. He doubted she'd react well to him stripping her naked behind a bush. He wanted to, though. He finally had her all tousled and flushed and wrinkled—and she was even more painfully desirable that way than he'd imagined.

This attraction between them had been simmering for days. It wasn't going away. Having her under his roof, her constant nearness only heightened his hunger for what he couldn't have.

He pressed his hands up his face, then raked them through his hair. Damn his conscience. As it pertained to Sophia, it plain angered him. Kisses didn't satisfy the driving need he had for her. Eventually he'd either have to incinerate his qualms about seducing her or find someone nearby who was warm and willing and a hell of a lot less prickly than Sophia LaRue.

He walked faster, his long legs eating the distance between them as they crossed the manicured stretch of lawn ringing the house. He reached the door an instant before she did, intending to open it for her. She pushed his hand away. He put it back. She grabbed the knob, and they wrestled with the door for a moment before she yanked at it forcefully.

"I've got it," she bit out, then swept into the hallway ahead of him.

Collier, who'd been waiting for him in the hallway outside his office, swiveled toward them. His secretary watched Sophia flash past, glanced at Jarrod, then set out after her, fishing for the key to her room as he went.

Jarrod halted, eyeing Sophia's retreating back. An erupting volcano couldn't have put forth more sparks. She was some kind of woman, Sophia, frustrating, vengeful, and at times like this damn endearing. As he watched her storm around the corner, a powerful tenderness expanded through his chest.

Yesterday when Oliver had told him the story of her grandmother's death he'd experienced an almost crushing disgust. She'd sat there listening to it, her expression pale but stoic, her hands twisting tightly together. He'd known that it hurt her to hear it, but he'd wanted to fill in the few pieces of her past he hadn't been able to discover. More, something integral inside him had needed to understand just how bad it had gotten for her, the girl who'd fed him when he'd had nothing.

If his father was responsible for what had happened to her, he'd hunt him down and he'd God damn strangle the bastard. Even Adam Stone's abandonment didn't rile him as much as what his father might have let become of the innocent young girl who'd worn snowy white, not knowing the way that life was about to mar her with grime.

He made his way into his office for his standing meeting with Collier. His leather chair creaked as he lowered his weight into it, then swiveled toward the window that framed the hill they'd just come from.

At first when he'd started kissing her, he thought she'd reserved her tongue from him out of expertise. The tease, taunting him. It had worked. Her hesitancy had only fueled his need to *feel* her respond beneath him. When she'd begun to, his blood had coursed through his body, molten hot. It wasn't until she'd pushed him away and he'd seen how frenzied she was that he wondered whether her initial hesitancy might have been genuine.

He could barely comprehend what blathering idiots her husband and the Ghost and whatever other lovers she'd taken to her bed must have been. Had they ever brought her to her own release, even? He doubted it, suddenly. And wanted, just as suddenly, to be the first to do that to her. To watch her while he did it. He could bring her to that place without compromising her. He could do that with his fingers.

He shifted, heavy with need. The woman had either the worst luck or the worst taste where men were concerned. Imagine her striving to defend Twilight's Ghost from him when the man didn't even know how to bed her properly. It was insulting.

With little more than a rustle of trouser fabric, Collier returned. He took up his usual position at the edge of the desk.

"Have our men learned anything new?" Jarrod asked, turning the chair toward Collier.

Collier extracted his papers from his inner jacket pocket. "One of the detectives has located a source who claims to have information on the identity of Twilight's Ghost—for a fee. Our man was able to arrange a time to meet with him to discuss what he knows."

"Who's the source?"

"A fisherman who works down on the docks."

Jarrod scowled. It wasn't much, but thus far the fisherman was only the third person his detectives had found who claimed to have any knowledge at all about the Secret Service agent. The theories of the first two had both run dry. "Have the detective pay the man whatever fee is necessary."

"Yes, sir."

"Report to me as soon as you hear."

"Of course, sir."

"What of Sophia's husband?"

Collier's attention skimmed lower on the page he

held. "We've been able to ascertain that when Mrs. LaRue left Galveston and the orphanage she was gone for just under one year. We've also confirmed that she spent the majority of that time in Washington. That's where she met and married Mr. LaRue, so that's where we've concentrated our search for information on the man."

"Still no luck?"

"Unfortunately, no."

Jarrod suppressed a growl of impatience. Usually his money bought information faster than this. Far faster. "Put more men on it."

"Yes, sir." Collier jotted a notation.

"Do you have anything else for me?"

"Yes, it's in regards to the household here. Mrs. Hoskins, the housekeeper, has informed me that one of the girls who works in the kitchen is with child."

"Unmarried?"

His secretary nodded solemnly.

"Do we know who the father is?"

"She's loath to say, sir."

He could still see the faces of all the women he'd known in the same predicament. During the days when he'd been fending for his brothers' survival, such women had scrabbled alongside him for jobs and money. "Find out if she has a place of her own in which to live. If not, buy one for her. She can leave work, she can continue, or she can leave for now and return whenever she wishes. Regardless, make her a gift of two thousand dollars."

"Yes, sir." Collier didn't need to write it down. Jarrod had given the same instructions numerous times over the years.

"That's all, sir." The older man inclined his head, his

customary good night salutation, before walking toward the door.

"Collier."

His secretary turned immediately.

Jarrod rested the back of his head against his chair and searched the ceiling. A decision had been nagging at him since yesterday. He shifted his weight forward, resting his forearms on his desk. "There's another matter I want investigated."

Collier leafed to a fresh page.

"Namely, my father. I want him found." Even if Sophia refused until doomsday to give Twilight's Ghost over to him, he'd find his father for her. At the very least his family owed her answers. At most, much more. He'd ascertain exactly how much more.

"Contact Allan Pinkerton again. I'll need more men looking for Sophia's husband and more men for this. If he has to bring operatives over from his Colorado offices, then so be it."

Collier nodded.

"The man in charge of the investigation into my father's whereabouts can contact me directly, and I'll provide him with the information he needs. However, Mrs. LaRue is not to be questioned under any circumstances, despite her connection to my father's disappearance. She's not to know about this." He was a pragmatist. His offer to help her find his father was a powerful bargaining chip. So long as there was a chance it would sway her toward releasing information to him about Twilight's Ghost, then he'd keep a grip on it.

"I understand, sir."

"That's all."

Collier left in as civilized a manner as he'd come, the office door clicking closed behind him.

Jarrod prowled from his chair to the window. What would his brothers say about his search for their father? The days after their father's disappearance had been so grim for them all that they never discussed them or the man himself.

In the darkness beyond the glass, he saw his mother's death. Heard the sound of her thin breath. Remembered the weight of the realization that she was truly going to die. He'd understood, then, that the sole responsibility of caring for his brothers was his. He'd done the only thing he could have done—shouldered the role with blinding determination and howling fear.

Holden's face loomed from behind the image of his mother on her death bed, growing brighter, nearer. Holden as he had been then, wearing his treasured possession—a ragged hat. He hadn't even cried. His small fingers had curled around their mother's hand as he'd stared at her unblinkingly.

Lastly, came Sophia's face. He saw her expression when she'd first looked at Duchess—wanting and afraid to want. A study in vulnerability and strength. Heartbreakingly beautiful.

He gritted his teeth as he threw open his office door and stalked the halls toward the master bedroom. He couldn't serve them all. Every day he was near Sophia, he understood more strongly that she needed time to be won. Years of mistrust had wounded her, and he couldn't damn well blame her for being guarded. But he couldn't afford to wait.

His first loyalty was to his brothers, and in this case to

Holden. That loyalty was in his bones, would go with him to the grave and beyond. He couldn't let himself forget why he'd brought Sophia here, why he was slowly gaining her trust. This growing softness he harbored toward her tempted him at times to believe that she was here for him. She wasn't. She was here so he could save Holden, a cause that must and did come first.

The simple fact was that regardless of her reluctance, her hurt, her loveliness, she *must* tell him about Twilight's Ghost.

Inside his bedroom, a carved wooden bed commanded the space. He fisted his hand in the sumptuous maroon covering and ripped it off with a single swipe. Was it fair for him to sleep in luxury when his brother was lying in a jail cell? It was his fault his brother was still there. *His job* to get his brother out, and he was failing.

With a sneer, he seized a handful of his sheets and wrenched them free.

Maggie grumbled the next afternoon as she unwound a man's shirt from around her waist, where she had hidden it beneath her chemise. She tossed the garment to Sophia, who caught it eagerly.

The fabric of her disguise felt glorious to her—coarse, warm, and familiar. Maggie pitched the trousers to her next, and lastly the hat, which Maggie had apparently wedged against the small of her back, underneath both the trousers and the shirt.

"That's the last." Maggie flicked her skirts back into place with an efficient snap. "There was absolutely no chance of my bringing the shoes."

"No?" Sophia hadn't thought of that.

"No. I considered stuffing them into my bodice, toes

pointed outward like breasts, but decided against it." She planted her long hands on her hips. "I worried your guards might suspect something."

Sophia smiled and hugged her clothes snugly to her. They represented hope. These few garments were her chance at keeping Blackhaw safe.

She deposited her armload onto the top of the dresser. One by one she opened the drawers, then jiggled them free. Already Maggie had given her the lockpicking tools, sketches of the territory around the house, and a map marked with the nighttime positions of the guards.

"How are you going to start your search for the counterfeiter?" Maggie asked.

Sophia stashed her hat against the top back panel of the dresser, then slid the uppermost drawer into place against it. "Well, think aloud with me. What's a counterfeiter going to need to do business?"

"Paper and ink."

"Right, and an artist to design the plates."

"Unless the counterfeiter himself is an artist."

"That's a possibility." She worked to hide the trousers behind the second drawer. "What else?"

"A press."

"Exactly. And space for a press, not to mention space enough or insulation enough to muffle the sounds of the press." She leaned against the dresser. "I thought I'd begin tonight simply by moving through the warehouse district, watching and listening for the sound of counterfeit money being made."

She had little expectation of catching the counterfeiter tonight using that method. He was smart enough to have eluded the Service for some time now. Still, it was how she always operated. She began with the broadest possible investigation, giving the criminals the opportunity to be foolish and make things simple for her. Gradually, she'd tighten the net, winding her way in ever-smaller concentric circles, following clues she'd garnered on the circle before, until she'd finally gathered the net so snug that one person was left trapped and thrashing in it.

She slid the final drawer into the dresser, then brushed her hands together as she straightened to face Maggie.

Maggie hadn't made a move to sample any of her hats. Apparently her friend was far too serious about what she viewed as Sophia's impending peril to do so. "How can I help?" Maggie asked.

"You can search through the ownership and leasing information on all the warehouses in town, then try to verify whether or not each warehouse is being used for legitimate business."

"I'll start today." Clouds shifted behind Maggie's typically bright hazel eyes. "It's not too late, you know, to change your mind about trying to sneak away from here."

"I'm not going to change my mind."

"I'll look into warehouse records, and you can just wait and see what comes of it—"

"I'm not going to change my mind," Sophia repeated gently. "I can escape from here and let myself back in without either Jarrod or Simon finding out." She dearly wished Simon hadn't given her the order to stay put. She understood his reasons. Her disappearance would induce Jarrod's suspicion about her identity. And Jarrod probably could kidnap her from Blackhaw a second time if he so chose. Still, she'd have loved to have the freedom to break free tonight and keep on running. As it was, she'd return and bide her time as Simon had instructed.

Maggie still looked worried.

She went to her friend and hugged her, drawing comfort from the green, lemony smell of her soap. "Thank you for helping me," she murmured.

"Thank me when we're all safely back at Blackhaw, taxes paid."

"Okay," Sophia said. "I'll thank you then." When Maggie went to open the closet door, Sophia stilled her. "I think we'd best agree to some sort of communication in case the worst happens. I don't expect it to," she hurried to say, "but we'd be foolish not to establish a plan now."

Maggie gave a quick nod.

"If Jarrod catches me, he'll likely cut off contact between us. Should you arrive for a visit and be turned away, just glance at my bedroom window on the way out. If I can be, I'll be there. If I'm simply standing, that means he refused you visitation because of a reason other than discovery of my identity. Who knows, he's irritable enough he might turn you away for any reason on any given day. However, if I press my palm to the windowpane, that means he's found me out."

"What should I do then?"

"Wait to tell Simon. Give me a few days, then come back. If at any time you see me in the window and I tug at my hair, that means I want you to notify Simon."

"What if I come to visit you, and you're not at the window?"

Sophia grimaced, the possibility turning her cold. "Then tell Simon everything at once."

Maggie studied her somberly.

"We're not going to have to worry about it, because he's not going to catch me," Sophia reassured her.

"I know. I just want to make certain that *you* know that Jarrod's not stupid."

"He's a little stupid," Sophia replied lightly as she opened the closet door and led Maggie into the bedroom. "He hasn't suspected me yet." She said the words not because she believed Jarrod to be the least bit stupid, but out of a perverse need to disparage him. He hadn't been at breakfast that morning. His absence had only served to torture her with even more thoughts of him than usual.

"Sophia," Maggie whispered, wrapping her hand around her upper arm, stopping her progress. "He is *not* stupid. He's a man and, like all men, suffers from the perspective that Twilight's Ghost must also be a man because no mere woman could succeed at evading him. You give him a clue, though . . . it might only take just one . . . and he'll figure it out."

Sophia was forcefully reminded for the thousandth time of the kiss they'd shared last night. She'd be roasted on a spit before she'd admit to Maggie she'd kissed him. Or that she'd already divulged one small clue.

"He built an oil empire from nothing but dust," Maggie said urgently. "He's *not* stupid."

"Easy." Sophia patted her hand, and tried to smile. "I was only teasing. I know how smart he is. Your warning's been heeded."

Frown brackets enclosed Maggie's mouth as she released her hold, then straightened the fabric of Sophia's sleeve. "Be careful."

"I'm always careful."

They walked together to the door and Sophia knocked twice. As always when Maggie came calling, one of Jarrod's guards had escorted her to Sophia's room, locked them in, then waited in the hall to escort Maggie out. Today, the one who'd brought Maggie answered the knock and led Maggie toward the front of the house, but neither closed nor locked Sophia's door behind him.

Sophia's brow knit. Unsure about her newfound freedom, she stepped into the hallway to watch Maggie vanish around a far corner. Nothing happened. Quiet swished about her, beckoning. She took another few tentative steps—

"Afternoon."

Jarrod. Her heart did a crazy *thump bang.* Wildly clashing emotions all jostled for supremacy as she swung to face him.

He was hard to see, leaning against the wall at the far end of the corridor. Curtains had been closed over the window there, leaving a black niche for him, in all his black, with his black hair and black heart to wait in.

So why was excitement the emotion that won out over all others? It practically stole her breath. "I didn't see you there," she said, stating the obvious. His presence was clearly why the guard had left her unattended.

"No."

"H-how long have you been waiting?"

"A while."

How long was a while, she wondered frantically. What if he'd heard her and Maggie talking? The closet was well insulated, but it wasn't inviolate—

"I couldn't hear you," he commented, answering her thoughts.

Relief surged through her. She sent up a jumbled prayer of thanks.

"How do you two communicate, hand signals?"

"No . . ."

"Written notes passed back and forth?"

She shook her head. Something was altered about him today. He was always blunt, but she sensed a rawness in him. A dissatisfaction prowling for prey.

Perhaps she'd better return to her room. She sidled toward the open door.

"If you flee in there, I'll follow," he said, stilling her in her tracks. "I have a key, remember?"

She smiled crisply. "Then I suppose I'll take my chances out here in the hall."

"Wise decision." He walked toward her, all towering charisma and devastating good looks.

She resisted the urge to fidget.

"I want my kiss," he said.

Her throat tightened convulsively with a mix of fear and thrill. She eased against the wall, instinctively seeking protection. "What kiss?"

"You're in my home. And I've time on my hands." He closed in on her. "Am I the only one who remembers this discussion?"

"Apparently, because I replied to you that I would not be indulging in . . ."

He planted both palms on the wall above her head, caging her.

She tried to swallow down a bean-sized throat. When that failed, she reflexively licked her lips. ". . . kisses with you again."

"Sophie," he chastised. His grin was lopsided, but it wasn't innocent. No, that smile was wicked, and it made her pine for wicked things. As if his hands were bound with shackles, he didn't use them at all. He didn't need to. The evidence of his arousal as he angled his body against hers was plenty communication enough.

She closed her eyes, fighting the shattering inside herself. She couldn't let herself be so easily mastered—

His lips grazed hers. She forced herself to remain immobile.

Then nothing. He was close. Even without vision, she knew because she could feel his breath against the edge of her lips and cheek. He didn't move, and she didn't dare to. Oh, God, his body was so near and so hard. What would he do next? Free her hair? Invade her mouth? Caress breasts that were aching for him?

With a *whoosh* of air, he pushed away.

Without daring even to breathe, she waited.

Nothing. He touched her not at all. She cracked open her eyelids.

He'd retreated a few feet away and was watching her intently. "What?" he asked, raising a brow. "You want more?"

More? She wanted it all. "Hardly."

"Until the next kiss, then."

Somehow she dredged up a scoffing sound. "If you'll excuse me." She turned into her room and shut the door. Though she waited, holding her breath, he didn't follow her in as he'd threatened. Instead, he simply locked the door and left.

Sophia promptly collapsed against the wall adjacent to the door, pressing a hand to her chest. Beneath her skin, she could feel the throbbing of her blood. He'd granted her a reprieve. For all her righteous intentions, it had been *he* who'd granted her a reprieve at the crucial second. If he'd kept kissing her, she'd have kept letting him.

Weak, she berated herself. *Weak!*

With a moan she dropped her hand and gazed at the familiar confines of her room. Tonight, she'd escape this place. Tonight Jarrod would be sound asleep and she'd be gone, besting him secretly in one of the few ways it appeared she had left.

That night, Sophia stood to the side of her window, peering out through the crack between the wall and drawn curtains. The guards were all in their usual positions. Maggie's surveillance had confirmed what she herself had been able to see, that Jarrod had concentrated all his security at the front of the house and at intervals around the perimeter of her room. Fortunately for her.

Her gaze moved past the men, to the last of the servants drifting home. Their silhouettes were murky against the misty darkness, but she could see well enough to count each one, just as she'd done every night since coming here. Thus she knew that twenty-four people left the property late every evening, after the house had been put to rest. The twenty-third and twenty-fourth were disappearing up the drive even now, which meant there was no chance she'd meet them on the service stairs leading to the upper floor, and no possibility she'd dash into them as she made her way across the grounds.

She waited until the last shadow of the last servant had melted to nothingness. Tranquillity shrouded the exterior of the house, except for the muffled conversation of the guards and the orange flare of their cigars against the night.

Time to go.

She'd hung her lace-up shoes around her neck, so it was on soundless socked feet that she moved to her bedroom door. Her hands felt stiff as she extracted her instruments from her trouser pocket. For a moment, she simply stared at them, before taking a fortifying breath and slipping one into the keyhole.

Nervousness hummed deep in her belly. She'd never lost that sense of unease—it hounded her before every nocturnal foray she'd ever made as Twilight's Ghost. It was doubly strong, though, tonight. So strong, it seemed to push up her throat.

Blackhaw. She brought the house to the fore of her mind, saw it as a collage of sights, memories, smells, feelings. *For Blackhaw.* She pursed her lips against the queasiness and focused on her work.

The lock was of the ordinary household variety. Not complicated. With a deft turn of her wrist, the bolt clicked free. The sound of it struck her ears with the force of a gong.

Crouching behind the door, she both listened intently for and prayed against hearing someone approach. It wouldn't do, she thought slightly hysterically, to be caught wearing men's clothing and holding lockpicking instruments in her hands.

No one came.

She gave her room one last glance as she mentally ticked off the items she had with her. Knife, map of the territory, lockpicking tools, shoes. That was it. That was everything she needed.

She ensured that every tendril of her hair was tucked securely into her man's hat before cracking the door open, checking both ways down the corridor, and easing into the hallway.

Chapter 11

Hurriedly, she turned to her door and worked to lock it behind her. She felt wildly exposed, with her back to the hall and her disguise a red flag to anyone who might glance her way in passing. But she couldn't very well leave her door open and risk a guard noticing that fact during a routine check of the hall.

Faster, she urged herself. *Faster . . . There. Done.*

Heart knocking, she ran in the direction opposite the foyer, stopping at the door she'd seen Jarrod's servants exit and enter. It opened easily, revealing a stairway beyond.

You see, it's fine, Sophia. Everything's fine, according to plan.

The unlit staircase, cold and gritty against her feet, passed hastily below her. When she reached the upper story, she again cracked the door a fraction and scanned the area beyond. She'd never been in this region of the house, but as far as she could discern, the servants tidied these rooms for guests that never came. More importantly for her causes, she could cross here to the unguarded side of the house with far less risk of chancing upon someone. She simply had to follow this hallway, then find the room that led to the balcony she'd seen from below last night.

One wall lamp burned, its low flame illuminating the corridor. The closed doors were cast in shadow, the wallpaper tan in color with brown fleur de lis scrawling across it. *Go.* Rolling her lips inward, she slid into the hall and, keeping close to the wall, scampered forward. The mouth of the grand staircase passed by, spilling light over her for an instant before dimness doused her again.

Just this last hallway. It ended in two doors facing outward. That one, on the left, was the one with the balcony, she was sure. Her vision latched onto it, her beacon. Not much farther now—

A man's sneeze ripped through the quiet. Her steps slashed to a halt. It had come from the room just to her left. The clearing of a throat followed, then footsteps.

Sophia threw herself toward the door on her right, wildly hoping no one would be within as she hauled it open. The darkness of the interior swallowed her. She shut her door, keeping the knob twisted open so as not to make a noise, exactly as his door opened. Shaking inside and out, she leaned down to look through the keyhole.

She caught a glimpse of Collier Melvin, Jarrod's secretary, before he walked out of her range.

With her free hand, she crossed herself. Her forehead sagged forward to rest against the wood. That had been close. Much too close to bear considering. She'd thought . . . well, she'd thought Collier resided somewhere below.

Silently, she clunked her forehead against the door. What if Collier had left his room just now in order to fetch her for some excursion Jarrod had planned? No, that was crazed thinking. Collier had never come to fetch her once she'd retired. There was no reason to think he would tonight.

. . . However, it appeared there *was* reason to worry that others might be rooming on this floor. Her nervousness churned harder. Maybe Maggie had been right. This was insanity.

Blackhaw. She closed her eyes, holding tight to the word. It was the only thing on earth, damn it, that was really hers. It had been her grandmother's house, and her parents' house before her, and the house of her childhood. There was no one left to fight for it but her. And so she would. Because it held her heart, and if she gave up her heart without a fight, then there'd be nothing left to live for.

Long after a safe amount of time had passed, she eased from the room. Ears straining for any other human sounds, she dashed down the remainder of the corridor. At its end she checked to make certain that no interior light seeped below the door on the left. None did, so she let herself in.

The curtains were drawn, rendering the room as pitch-black as the last one had been. Ever so slowly, she felt her way across it. Her fingertips finally met the crusty surface of a painting. Her hands traveled the contour of the frame, over wall, over wall. Curtain.

She opened the velvety drapery to reveal just what she'd been hoping for—a balcony. And past that, a freedom that swirled with dollops of fog. The landscape called to her almost audibly, a song of challenge, and bravery, and home. Emotion ached in her chest. She was going to make it.

The double doors opened for her. She caught her breath against the flush of cold as she padded to the edge of the wooden balustrade and looked over. Not a guard in sight.

The only thing that stood before her was one enormous pecan tree, spreading its branches to the balcony. The grizzled tree looked as if it had been there long enough to see stranger things than a shoeless woman dressed in men's clothing. This wasn't the first time either, she'd bet, that someone had used its arms as a ladder to grander things than bedrooms offered.

She swung one leg, then the other, over the balustrade and balanced on the strip of wood on the other side. The nearest branch, gnarled and about as thick around as her waist, swept past her at knee height. She took a bracing breath, then stepped onto it, grabbing a thinner, higher branch for a handhold.

The tree held her firm, steady as time. At home, she utilized her cellar for entrances and exits, but she was no stranger to tree climbing. There had been many times at St. Mary's when trees had served her well. It all came back to her now, the chattering of the wind through the branches, the slight sway, the exhilarating height. Added to that, the sensation of the bark against the bottoms of her feet.

She'd donned as many undergarments as possible beneath the shirt and trousers. Still, the chill riding on the damp air zinged the exposed skin of her face, hands, ankles.

She reached the trunk and began her descent, one careful foothold at a time. Twigs broke beneath her feet, gouging flesh usually better protected. No matter. Blackhaw. She drew even with the lower-story kitchen windows, all darkly vacant at this hour. One more step down. *Blackhaw.*

On the lowest branch, she gathered her balance, then leapt to the ground. As soon as she reached cover, perhaps a hundred yards off, she'd don her shoes. Until then, she'd simply run. She took off at a sprint. This she knew well, the churning of her legs, the pumping of her lungs, the feel of lonely air against her face. She glanced back once, then twice. Saw no one.

I did it, she thought as she charged onward.

A smile began to spread across her lips.

Four days later the weather was in the same gloomy mood it had been in the night of her first escape, Sophia noted. Foggy, secretive, and so petulant that it had decided to mask the sun despite the midmorning hour. She lifted a hand to her plum-colored hat to keep it on her head as Jarrod's sailing boat skimmed across the swells.

Wintry as it was, at least the brisk combination of speed and cold was keeping her awake.

"Are you all right?" Jarrod asked gruffly.

"I'm fine, thank you." She glanced over her shoulder to where he sat, manning the rudder. Since their kiss beneath the stars, his disposition had held a sharp edge. Though she'd been trying to read him, to deduce its cause, she'd yet to succeed.

"Need hot tea?" He motioned his chin toward the picnic basket his staff had packed for them.

Inexplicably, the question caused tenderness toward him to swell inside her. He remembered everything she'd ever said to him—like what she preferred to drink and how she preferred it—and he always asked after her comfort. Already, he'd bundled blankets around her and handed her a muff for her hands. Dangerously heady treatment for a woman like her. She'd had only herself to care about her needs for the past twenty years, and in that time had never cared half as much as he appeared to. "I think I'll have my tea a little later," she answered.

He returned his attention to the sea. For the excursion he'd donned his black greatcoat, but had left his head uncovered. Ruddy color burnished his cheekbones, and the breeze rustled his dark hair, lifting sections of it.

He glanced at her, and caught her staring. The intense awareness that lived and breathed between them sprang to life like kerosene tossed on flames. He studied her face almost harshly, causing her lips to heat.

How many times had she been alone with him like this? Too many. Every time she'd felt stripped of protection, and every time he'd reminded her of a wolf, circling.

Madness. She tried to swallow. For all she really knew about the man, he could toss her onto the boat's deck, strip her naked right there in the open, and force himself on her.

Her stomach rolled at the mental picture that presented, but not with revulsion. To her dismay, it groaned with restless desire.

"Now you," he said.

"Excuse me?" she said, jolted from her thoughts.

"Your turn to sail this boat."

"Oh." She waved a hand. "Thank you, no." She'd grown accustomed to her rowboat, but she knew nothing about steering a vessel with a sail.

"I insist," Jarrod replied.

"No, truly—"

"Fine." With a shrug, he let go of the rudder and moved down the bench seat, positioning himself across from her. He rested his elbows on the boat's edge, stretched out his legs, and crossed them at the ankles. The look he gave her was serious, pointed.

The boat began to list. She peeked up at the sail, heard it creak as it swung. Her side of the boat dipped. She jerked her head around, watching as the deep, foaming water neared. Just then a gust caught the sail, pitching her perilously close to the surface. Water spattered against her face, a shock of cold.

Frantic, she looked to Jarrod. Even tilted upward toward the sky, he hadn't moved a muscle.

A second gust nearly capsized them. With a yelp, Sophia scrambled to the rear and grabbed the rudder. She pulled it to the middle, fighting the current to do so. With a tremendous shudder, the vessel began to right itself. "What do you think you're doing?" she yelled at Jarrod, the wind flinging her words back at her.

"Letting you sail this boat," he answered, supremely unaffected.

"We could've been tossed into the water and drowned!"

"I can swim. I'd have saved you."

"You're insane!"

"Perhaps, but only for you."

Oh! Ridiculous man! Quivering with agitation, she

gripped the handle tighter. When the boat had been leaning so wildly, there'd been no fear in his eyes at all. None. Which made her think he really might have been perfectly content to be flung into the sea. "What were you planning to do? Keep me afloat with one arm while righting the boat with the other?"

"Something like that."

She shook her head, refusing to listen. It unnerved her, his lack of fear. Jarrod Stone was accomplished, cocky, and so damn unafraid. Was there anything, anything, that made his chest as tight as hers was now? That had the ability to ruffle those impeccable black feathers? How badly she wanted to see that happen.

Wavelets slapped, then split against the bow, the sole sound. "I feel it wise to inform you I've no idea how to steer this thing," she said.

"Where do you want to go?"

"Straight toward the dock so that I can disembark."

He muttered something that sounded suspiciously like, "no sense of humor." He met her quelling glance head-on, then narrowed his eyes in a challenge partly sensual, partly playful.

A small degree of her anger ebbed. He was infuriating, but he was also just a tiny bit . . . a *very* tiny bit, irresistible, too. "Just tell me how to maneuver it."

"At the moment the wind is coming at us from the side. See if you can't use the rudder to turn her so that the wind is behind us." He set the sail at a different angle. "Then we'll be sailing before the wind."

She did as he instructed. The sail flapped and filled with wind, tugging their boat forward. Despite herself, she grinned. Who'd have thought she could do that? She was sailing the vessel.

A thick curve of mist slightly to the left caught her attention. She wanted to race to it, suddenly, and plow through to see what was on the other side. "How can I make it go faster?"

"Now the wind is coming from the left side, or beam, so we have to adjust the angle of the sail accordingly."

He did so, and sure enough, the boat picked up speed. Beneath her she could feel the wood slapping against water as the boat drove forward. More wind, then more licked at her cheeks and pulled loose thick strands of her hair. It felt good to let her hair tumble free, to tilt her chin into the air, to rise to a new and exhilarating challenge. It made her feel alive.

The thicket of fog drew nearer until she sent the boat lunging directly through it. Beyond it, there was more. Ribbons of the stuff to follow and to chase.

With Jarrod's help, she raced the boat in two more lines, laughing at times in the face of so much half-frightening speed. Finally, she executed a shaky maneuver that eased them into a slower pace. The whip of air on her face eased, and she was able to relax slightly.

Jarrod sat quietly, leaning against the boat's side, watching her. Her pulse stuttered at his uncompromising male beauty. The weather around him was drizzly and gloomy, but those eyes of his shone. Mossy green, glinting from an inner light.

She smiled at him. Tentatively, slightly self-conscious.

"Holden was always the quietest of the four of us," he said.

Her smile immediately faded.

"And the most reserved," he continued. "He's always

been content to keep his own counsel and his own company."

"Why are you telling me this?"

"Because I want you to see that he's not a bad person."

"I never said he was."

"No, but it's what you believe. I think it's partially what's keeping you from helping me free him."

She sighed heavily, wishing she could stick her head in a storage hamper, cover her ears, anything but sit captive and listen to him talk about his brother.

"There was a time, when he was about thirteen, that he left for two days. Just left." He leaned forward, settling his elbows on his parted knees and interlacing his hands between. "It wasn't unusual for him to go away on his own for short periods, but he'd never been gone overnight before."

Perhaps because banks aren't open for robbing during the night, Sophia wanted to retort. She kept the words locked behind her lips.

"Clint and J. T. and I were getting our things together to go out and search for him, when he came walking back to the house barefoot. Never would tell us where he'd been or what had happened to his shoes. This was at a time when shoes were scarce around our place."

She was reminded of climbing down and up the pecan tree beyond Jarrod's balcony in her socks, the uneven bark digging into the bottoms of her feet. Her skin there was delicate because as poor as she'd been as a child, she'd always, at least, had shoes. Had Jarrod and his brothers been poorer than that? Her research into the brothers had yielded little about the years after they left

Galveston and before they became men. She supposed she'd always imagined them living in relative splendor, thanks to the money their father had stolen from her.

"Weeks later, an old man came to our place wearing Holden's shoes. He was a distant neighbor of ours. Evidently, Holden had heard in town that the man's wife of sixty years was dying. Months before, the old man had sent her to live with a daughter when she'd grown too sick for him both to care for her and work their farm enough to feed her. When his wife's time was near, he had no transportation to go to her, and no money to pay for any. Well, neither did Holden, but he did have shoes to give. Turns out, the old man had walked a hundred miles in Holden's shoes in time to hold his wife's hand at the end. He came back to return the shoes."

Despite herself, emotion gathered in Sophia's throat. Partly, at the simple generosity of what Holden had done. And partly at the thought of being loved like that . . . so much that a husband would walk a hundred miles in borrowed shoes, merely to hold your hand and ensure that his face was the last face you looked upon in this life. . . . That was love. To be loved with such ferocity must be the grandest gift a person could ever receive.

Somewhere above a gull cawed. It swooped overhead, white on gray, its wings beating.

Sophia had to wonder who would be there at the end of her life to hold *her* hand. No one, she feared. She'd made choices, both relational and professional, toward that end. And yet there were times, like now, when she felt her aloneness so completely that an almost inconsolable sadness settled over her.

"When the old man came back to return the shoes," Jarrod continued, "Holden tried to insist he keep them,

but the man wouldn't hear of it. Said his wife would never have countenanced such a thing while alive, so he wasn't about to countenance it in the face of her memory. Holden accepted the shoes, but he never wore them again."

"Why?"

"They'd contoured to the man's feet. Every mile he'd walked was marked on them through dirt and scratches and thin places in the sole."

"That's why Holden threw them away?"

He regarded her for a long, steady moment. "No, that's why he kept them. He still has them to this day."

She blinked at him. A shimmering communication moved back and forth between them. It felt very much like understanding.

"I assume such sentimentality escapes you," she said softly, striving for distance, working to remind herself why she couldn't begin to let herself understand Jarrod Stone.

"Perhaps. But then I've never claimed to be half as noble as any one of my brothers."

There it was, that unflinching loyalty he harbored for his family. She could read it in his stubborn jaw, in the battle-ready cant of his shoulders. At times it submerged, and she was almost able to believe that everything he'd done in relation to her was because of *her*. That he might truly see her as deserving of sumptuous gifts, that he might be pursuing her because he wanted her as a woman. Then it surfaced again, his fierce allegiance to his family, and she was reminded. Jarrod had supplied all of this, from the lovely plum gown she was wearing, to the sailboat she was sitting in, to the picnic basket full of food, for Holden's sake. Not because of her. Holden.

Jealousy clutched at her heart. She wished that Jarrod felt even a small measure of that kind of devotion toward her.

Unable to face him, she looked to the sail and slowly steered the boat into a turn. Would that she could turn from who he was and who she was as easily.

Sorrows sucked at her. Sorrow for what had become of the boy who'd once given away his shoes. Sorrow over deceiving Jarrod. Sorrow because for all that was suspect about Jarrod, his loyalty to his family wasn't. And that one most sterling quality about him was the one she could never honor.

She gritted her teeth and turned the sail more deeply into the wind in order to pick up speed. How dare she grieve for Jarrod's troubles? Ludicrous. It made her angry that she'd even *think* it. The man had stolen her off the street, for the love of God! Did he torture himself with regret over that? Not for a second.

"I've tried to be patient," Jarrod said.

She scowled at him.

"But I need for you to help me free my brother now."

She started to shake her head—

"I'll help you find my father."

"I'd like very much for you to help me find your father," she answered honestly. "But I can't turn Twilight's Ghost over to you. Even for that."

With a growl, he pushed to his feet. He was so tall and broad-shouldered standing like that with his feet braced apart, that he blocked out what little sun there was and cast darkness over her. "If it were just me, Sophia, I'd give you all the time you needed to recover from your love of Twilight's Ghost and to overcome your reserva-

tions about assisting me. Hell, I'd give you anything you wanted." The wind whisked open the flaps of his coat and caused it to billow and snap. "However, the time you're taking is costing my brother."

"It's costing me, too."

"Then relent. Give me the man's name."

What an impossible situation. She could never give him what he wanted, and he would never let her go until she did. "I can't."

"Like hell you can't." He kicked an overturned bucket in front of her, then straddled it. His greatcoat fell behind him, his inner thighs bracketed her outer thighs. "If the Ghost is so worthy of your loyalty, then why hasn't he come for you?"

She opened her mouth to answer, had nothing to say.

"What kind of a sorry excuse for a man is he that he would let me take you the way I did? That he would leave you to fend for yourself?"

She didn't, couldn't answer.

"Tell me," he demanded.

"I can't speak for him," she said.

"Well I can speak for myself, and I'll tell you right now that I'd never have let you go. I'd have come after you."

Distressed, she glanced down at the rudder and attempted to distract herself by tying it down.

"Look at me." He nudged her chin to face him. "Whatever he does for you, I can do more. Whatever he gives to you, I can give you better. You can tell me who he is."

"You're right," she said shakily, her senses overrun with his unrelenting pursuit, his nearness, and with a dangerous longing. "I can tell you. But I won't."

He gazed at her unblinkingly. "Name whatever you want. It's yours."

"There's nothing you can purchase—"

"There's always something. Name it, I'll give it to you, and you'll tell me his identity."

"No—"

"Name it, Sophia, and let's get on with this. You've drawn it out long enough. It's past time you divulge his identity."

"I won't."

"It's time you did."

"I won't."

"You *will*," he snarled.

"I—"

He grasped her chin and kissed her, his lips pressed hard against hers, his tongue plunging into her mouth. Ravenous hunger leapt within her, and she responded with equal force and frustration, weaving her hands into the hair at the back of his head, pulling him toward her. It was angry and hot and unapologetically blunt—a kiss that made her tremble with a tempest of desire unlike anything she'd ever imagined. She heard herself moan, sensed her body arching against his.

He bent his head and removed the glove from his right hand with his teeth. "Tilt your head back," he said.

She did, and his mouth immediately claimed the sensitive skin under her ear. She could feel the chill of his nose, the heat of his mouth even as she was aware of his hand penetrating the blankets and the coat that shielded her. She shivered as his fingers slid to the edge of her bodice's neckline. She knew what was coming and *wanted* it. So very badly.

His hand delved into her bodice and captured her breast. The blissful texture of skin on skin drew a gasp from her. Oh, so good— He pulled the fullness of her breast up, over the edge of her garment. Her nipple hardened almost painfully, abrading against the inside of her woolen coat.

He worked quickly with his free hand, ripping open the buttons of her coat. He took the point of her breast into his mouth greedily and deeply. She watched him— dark hair against pale skin—shamelessly suckling her in broad daylight. She buried her hands more deeply in his hair even as tears misted her eyes. She craved to make him love her just a little, for this to be about more than physical attraction, for this to be as precious for him as it was for her.

He was turning more than just her body to liquid— rushing, melting, flowing. He was capturing her soul. And still he tugged at her—suction and warmth. He swirled his tongue around the point of her breast. Then pulled away.

He glanced up at her, one breast bared between them. His eyes were cloudy, his breath ragged against her wet nipple. The urgent pulling sensation between her legs, and within her heart, heightened. He bent his head, lavishing the same treatment on her other breast. Kissing her, cradling her, sucking her, licking. She shifted on the bench seat, impatient. Needy for something—

His mouth released her. Her fingers stroked from his hair as he straightened on his seat, dropping the sides of her coat over her nakedness. Even so, she *felt* her nakedness beneath her coat so powerfully.

She glanced at his ungloved hand. *Mother above* . . . it had cupped her breast, held her up for his lips to feast on. And it hadn't been enough. She was still practically itching, fidgeting with the need for more.

She lifted her gaze and found him watching her—his lips slightly swollen. He didn't say why he'd stopped, and she was too proud to ask.

As modestly as she could, she slanted away from him and fixed her clothing. When she turned back, Jarrod was still studying her. *Thinking about what had just happened between us*, she wondered? *Or thinking about his brother?*

A thought occurred to her, bringing with it a sick twinge in her belly. "Did you . . ." Her words faded. Over the years she'd grown comfortable in her role as silent observer of others, of life. To speak truthfully about her own emotions was far, far harder. "Did you kiss me just now because you hope to gain my help for your brother?"

"Did that kiss feel contrived?"

She couldn't tell him she didn't have experience enough to know. "I'm not certain."

His gaze penetrated to the deepest regions of her hopes and fears. "Every time I've touched you, Sophia, I've done so to serve only one man. Me."

She licked her lips, hating herself because she yearned to believe him even though she realized how wrong, how impossible, how completely doomed were her feelings toward him.

The fact was that Jarrod would never forgive her if he found out that she was Twilight's Ghost. If he discovered her, he would *never* forgive and he would *never* understand. That made honesty impossible. And how could she hope for any kind of relationship with a man who she must constantly lie to, a man who didn't know her identity at the most basic level? She couldn't.

Sophia cleared her throat and reached to untie the rudder. "I'm taking us home."

Late the next night Jarrod was sitting alone in his office, his suit jacket long forgotten, his shirt untucked and half-unbuttoned, papers spread across the surface of his desk. He shook his head, furious at himself for his lack of concentration. This was the first time in remembrance that he was either too disinterested or too preoccupied to focus on business decisions that needed making.

With a groan, he swiveled his chair toward the window. Almost immediately, a fantasy of Sophia rushed to his mind in luscious detail. Her, naked, kneeling between his legs and taking him into her pink mouth. That tongue. Breasts, swinging free. Heavy. Her hair running over his thighs. He could still smell her—clean and warm with a hint of lavender. He shifted, imagining her there, between his knees, imagining the sensation of her—

Just then he saw something beyond the panes of his window.

A shadow. Running.

Chapter 12

Jarrod rushed out the back door of his house. He
paused, scouring the dark vista of trees and hills for a
hint of what he thought he'd seen. At first, nothing
caught his eye. He shook his head, and ran his gaze over
the landscape again, straining—

There. A streak of tan where all else was deepest gray.
So similar to what he'd seen the night he'd waited behind
Blackhaw for Twilight's Ghost that the skin at the back
of his neck pricked.

He took off at a dead run. Curses swam through his
brain, bitingly fervent. Twilight's Ghost. Here. The man
had been coming to see her, after all. Like a damned thief
in the night, as was his way. Right under the watch of all
the idiot guards he'd hired. Right under his own nose.
Making a fool of him.

Jealousy and rage at his own ignorance shot through him. It spurred him to push his body harder and faster, until he was barely aware of his exertion. His legs pumped, he jumped over tree roots, and ducked under low-hanging branches, but he didn't physically *feel* it. The hunt for the agent would end now. Tonight.

Jarrod crashed into a small meadow, just as the Ghost was on the verge of exiting it. The man's hat turned, and recognition fired the air between them like lightning. For an infinitesimal space of time, the Ghost froze, then dashed into the cover of the trees.

Hatred rolled up Jarrod's throat. He'd never been a man to be bested twice by any foe. And he wouldn't be this time. He sprinted across the meadow. Here, there was no iron fence for the agent to cage him in. It was simply man against man, and he was going to goddamn wrap his hands around the bastard's throat when he caught him.

Shrubs and trees flashed past, scratching at his arms and chest through the thin layer of his shirt. He dodged and swerved, gaining on the Ghost with brute speed. As he'd learned the last time, his prey was agile. For moments at a time, he managed to escape Jarrod's sight. Regardless of the whisperings of the townspeople, though, the man was human not ghost. If Jarrod looked closely enough the telltale quivering of a branch always marked his passing. Jarrod raced after those pathway markers until he spotted him again. And he always did, and every time nearer until he'd closed on the man so much he could hear his footsteps pounding the uneven ground.

Jarrod followed him out from under a stand of trees, only to find a steep slope cutting away beneath his feet. The Ghost was half-slipping, half-running down its face, angling his steps toward the right, where more trees offered shelter.

Jarrod plunged after him, taking the hill far faster than was wise, using his hands to keep himself upright as rocks skittered beneath his feet. This hillside was his best chance so far of overtaking the man. Foliage and thickets gave the Ghost room in which to disappear and evade. This hillside offered no such protection.

He drew closer, so close he could make out the plaid of the man's shirt. The dirtiness of his hat.

The Ghost reached flatter ground and scrambled toward cover.

The rage inside Jarrod whipped him on. He hurtled into the air, landed with jarring force at the bottom of the slope, and charged after the agent. Just feet away from him now. Closing. They sprinted together, pursuer and pursued. Darkness sliced over them as they barreled under the overhang of branches.

Just as the Ghost attempted to dart to the side, Jarrod threw his body forward. He collided with the man, and together they crashed to the earth, air bursting from the Ghost's lungs when they hit.

Jarrod pushed himself up from the jumble of their entwined limbs, grabbed hold of the Ghost's upper arm, and roughly turned the man toward him. As he did so, the Ghost's hat slipped free.

Moonlight poured past Jarrod's shoulder to illuminate eyes the color of fine coffee, a delicate nose, and carved cheekbones flushed with exertion. Rich brown hair spilled everywhere, clinging to her temple, cascading onto the ground, curling around his hand that still rested on her arm.

She was gasping for breath as he was, the air between

them misting with labored exhales. Had he . . . God, had he hurt her? He—he'd tackled her. He'd not known it was her. He'd thought . . .

Dazed and uncomprehending, he stared into her eyes. Their piercingly beautiful depths held alarm, fear, and . . .

Apology.

She . . . *Oh my God.* Realization rushed through him with a howl. A howl that was denial. A denial of a betrayal so scorching it paralyzed him with pain. All this time she'd been laughing at him, outsmarting him, holding the keys to Holden's jail cell in her deceitful little hands. She was Twilight's Ghost.

Sophia recognized the exact moment that Jarrod comprehended her identity. His face went slack with shock, and everything behind his eyes seemed to die an instant, icy death. She wanted to sob, to beat on his chest and demand to know why he'd insisted on this. Why he couldn't let her have her secrets?

She'd never wanted to endure this again, this kind of blistering vulnerability. And yet here she was, a victim to it because she'd truly thought she could make it to freedom tonight like she had those other times. Now everything would be lost. She saw it all flash before her—Blackhaw, her career, Maggie, her very life. Emotion swelled high, hammering her temples, pressing at the backs of her eyes. He'd take them all from her because his loyalty and his love belonged to his brothers. She'd never been the one he cared about.

Jarrod jerked away as if he couldn't bear to touch her. When he gained his feet, he staggered back a few steps.

She watched him, eyes watering. *Oh God, Oh God.*

He simply stared at her, his features as sinfully dark,

unforgiving, and brutally handsome as Satan's. His shirt hung open at the neck, revealing a swath of chest muscles that leapt and quivered with the billow of his lungs.

With effort, she pushed herself to sitting. Whatever happened—she struggled for breath—she'd not cower on the ground before him. She'd not let him have that. She was as wounded as a soldier shot through a hundred times, but if he was going to destroy her, then he'd have to face her first—head-on—so he could see her for everything she was and wasn't.

She knelt on one knee, saw that blood was seeping through the fabric there, then rose to her feet. Nowhere to run. Nowhere to hide. Her nails bit into flesh as she fisted her hands.

"You," he accused, his voice rasping.

"Yes."

"You're Twilight's Ghost."

He already knew the answer, but the rigidity of his expression ordered her to speak the truth aloud. "Yes."

The word hovered, refusing to be swallowed into silence.

"How the hell did you get out of my house?"

"I . . ." Her brain spun.

"Maggie." He answered his own question. "She brought you what you needed." He motioned contemptuously to her clothing. "All of this."

She groped for answers but was damned every way she turned—

"How many times have you escaped?" he demanded.

She hesitated to say.

"How many times?" he yelled.

"Five."

"How'd you do it?"

"The . . ." Her heart was clambering its way out of her chest. To reveal information went against everything she'd ever known. "The pecan tree that brushes the second-story balcony."

"Why? What's important enough to sneak away for?"

She rolled her tongue into her cheek.

"No, tell me. I want to know what actually matters to you."

She simply couldn't tell him about Blackhaw and her staggering debts. If she had to bear one more humiliation in front of him just now, he'd break her. "I needed to work on a case."

"What case?"

"A . . . a counterfeiting case."

"I don't believe you. This has to do with my brother."

"No—"

"Yesterday you let me tell you that story about Holden." He spoke in a tone void of feeling. "When I asked you to help me free him you looked me right in the eye and denied me. You told me you couldn't."

"And then I admitted I wouldn't."

The look in his eyes stole the air from her lungs. Where before they'd been dead and icy, now they blazed with fury. She'd always sensed a capacity for ruthlessness in him, but she'd never fully seen it until now, the face of his true anger.

"You'll help Holden now," he said.

"No, I won't. Your brother is guilty of his crimes, Jarrod."

"You're mistaken."

"I don't think so." At least she prayed she wasn't mistaken. If Holden was innocent, she'd brought all this down upon him and upon herself for nothing. She . . .

she wasn't as sure about it as she had once been—desperately, she scrambled for her courage, gathering what remained of it in shaking hands—but she was sure enough. "The evidence on the subject was clear. A jury agreed with me."

"You were both mistaken," he repeated, his voice lashing her like a whip.

"You couldn't have watched your brother every minute when you were growing up—"

"I didn't need to. I know him."

"How completely can one person ever truly know another?"

"Far better than I ever knew you, apparently." His stare raked derisively over her.

Inwardly, she fought a guilt she didn't deserve to feel.

He stalked to a nearby tree and reached for its branch. His hand tightened, loosened, tightened, loosened around its crumbling bark. "What were the charges you brought against Holden really about, Sophia?"

"About?"

His expression held relentless insight. "Tell me you realize that Holden is worth a hundred of my father. Tell me you didn't punish Holden because of some supposed wrong my father did you twenty years ago."

She wanted to deny it . . . and yet over the past days her own motives for prosecuting Holden had muddied in her mind. When the Stone brothers had been one-dimensional characters in her research, she'd hated every one of them. That was before Jarrod had smiled at her, before he'd let her ride a fairy horse, before he'd touched her in ways that made her writhe. And that was before she'd known that Holden had once gone barefoot so an old man could walk to the bedside of his dying wife.

"Tell me you didn't punish my brother for the sins of the father," Jarrod said.

Shame stung her.

"Tell me you didn't."

She groped for the right words to make him understand. "A few months ago Oliver and Holden exchanged words at Austin's train station. Your brother was threatening toward him, and Oliver feared that Holden might also attempt to threaten me."

"What reason would he have to threaten you?"

"I don't know, revenge? It's no secret that Oliver and I have been searching for your father all these years, that we believe him to be a criminal. The guilt we've attributed to your father has tainted all of you by association."

He pushed away from the tree, leaving the branch vibrating angrily.

"All I knew was that Holden might try to harass me. For protection I educated myself on your brother's past. During my research, I uncovered the fact that Holden was still wanted for aiding and abetting the Lucas gang."

"That charge was fourteen years old. Why go after him for it now?"

"For justice's sake. That's what I do. I put away criminals for the sake of justice."

He snorted contemptuously. "What, were you hoping my father would come riding to my brother's rescue?"

She badly wanted to answer no, except that wasn't the whole truth. "Perhaps, in part."

"You were using my brother as bait."

"Isn't that what you've been using me for?"

His brows slashed downward over narrowed eyes. "I'll be using you for another purpose from now on. I'm taking you back to the house."

She watched him, waiting. If she could only articulate it better, perhaps she could make him understand her motives. . . . His expression was endlessly cold. He'd not be understanding anything she had to say tonight.

Corralling every bit of pride she possessed, she picked up her hat from the dirt and walked in the direction of the house.

I'll be using you for another purpose from now on. What would he do with her? How far would he go to avenge Holden and his own injured trust? Far, came the miserable answer. Men like Jarrod never compromised. They used whatever means necessary to get what they wanted, no matter who they crushed or what the cost. She'd understood that all along, and yet her heart had still insisted on coming to care for him. She was about to be shown just how little he cared for her in return.

The weight of her knife pressed into her hip, where she'd secured it beneath the waist of her trousers. She could . . . Could what? Circle on Jarrod and fight for her freedom? Injure him? If she whisked her knife from its sheath, she had to be willing to cut him with it. Her stomach lurched at the thought.

She tripped over a root, and Jarrod caught her from behind. The heat of his hand and fingers seared through her shirt. He let go and she continued walking, trying not to look at him or think of him and berating herself with every step. Common sense dictated that she use her only remaining weapon against him. So what was stopping her? If he were in her position, he'd certainly not hesitate to attack her with his knife. Their intimacies, and all the little things he'd done for her and said to her surely meant nothing to him.

But to her . . . To her they somehow did. She couldn't

bear to make him bleed, any more than she could bear to slice at an injured animal caught in a rusty trap. A trap she was partially responsible for setting.

As they neared the rear entrance to the house, he took hold of her elbow. She could only pray he didn't intend to march her up to Collier, announce her identity, and instruct the man to spread word of it throughout the state.

Inside, the house slumbered. Lamplight seeped through the open door of Jarrod's office as they passed it, but only guttering candles lit the remainder of the way to her bedroom.

Jarrod tested her door, found it locked the way she'd left it, and dug the key from his pocket. Once he'd freed the bolt, he walked her inside and kicked the door closed.

She tried to pull free of his grip. In answer, he tightened his hold on her and twisted her toward him. Unceremoniously, he began running his hands over her.

She stiffened and again tried to retreat. "What are you—"

He caught her by a handful of her shirt fabric and brought her close. "I'm searching for whatever it is that enables you to leave me."

Alarm leapt inside her. She feared her helplessness without her knife and lockpicking equipment, and she feared her body's reaction to his seeking hands. "No," she said, shoving his chest away.

He brought her immediately back. "Yes."

She struggled against him when he reached into one trouser pocket, then the other. Through the fabric of her inner pocket, she could feel every movement of his fingers against her hip. He easily located the tools she'd used to pick the lock.

"Fine," she said, yet again trying to fight free of him. "You have what you want, so let me go."

"I'm not done."

"Yes, you are."

"No." His eyes burned like emeralds held to the fire. "I'm not."

They locked gazes and wills for a long moment. Then, holding her fast with one hand, he used his other to search the rest of her. His palm pressed up and down the insides and outsides of both legs.

Mercy, this was exactly what she hadn't wanted. To be so near to him, to be forced to bear his touch and feel this treacherous wanting for him. It wound upward within her, sinuous.

His palm moved to her abdomen and found the bulge of the knife.

Her eyes sank briefly closed.

He pulled her shirt from her trousers.

She clamped her shirt back into place. That knife was her sole defense. "I need the knife."

"Why?"

"For protection."

"There's no one here to protect yourself from but me, and I'd rather not feel the point of your blade against my throat." He yanked the shirttail from beneath her hold, exposing a line of bare skin above her trousers. Her belly quivered as he brushed his knuckles against the skin there in order to unfasten the sheath.

"I could have used it against you earlier and didn't," she said.

"Maybe you should have." He pulled it free. Then stroked his hand up her ribs and along an arm.

"There isn't anything else."

"You'll understand if I'm disinclined to trust you." He released her only when he'd finished his examination.

She jerked away, flushed.

He stalked toward the door.

"Jarrod."

He paused, hand on the knob.

"What are you going to do with me?" It cost her dearly to ask the question. Yet if she didn't, she'd torture herself with wonderings. Armed with the truth, she'd at least be able to strategize her response to it.

"It's not so much what I'm going to do," he said as he faced her. "It's you. You're going to free my brother."

"I have the capacity to bring charges against people, but once sentencing has occurred I can't just—"

"You'll do everything in your power to free my brother."

"And if I refuse?"

"I'll expose your identity." No wavering showed on his face, no weakness, no indecision. Only determination, merciless and brutal.

Her heart contracted. "Despite what you think of me, I've done a great deal of good over the years." She fought to keep her voice even. Her emotion could no longer move him, but she prayed her logic might. "I have the capacity to put away criminals who don't deserve to be free—men who've hurt and stolen and cheated law-abiding people. If you expose me, you'll take that capacity away from me."

"You mistake me if you think I care."

Ice flowed through her veins.

"You refuse to help my brother and not only will I expose you, I'll do everything in my power to take your house from you."

"Blackhaw?" she breathed.

"Blackhaw," he confirmed.

Dazed and stunned, she watched him yank open the door. Watched it slam behind him. Heard the savage twist of the key. *Blackhaw.* Just when she thought things couldn't get any worse, they had. Her feet fumbled backward until her spine came up against the wall. Not only did he not care for her, he hated her so much that he'd rip her home from her.

She'd known he'd never forgive her if he found her out. She'd known and she'd been right.

Oh my God, what have I done?

She buried her head in her hands and began to sob.

Chapter 13

Jarrod was seething.

He wrenched open the wooden doors of the library cabinet. Inside, Collier had neatly stacked every gift Jarrod had ordered for Sophia but had not yet given her. Boxes of all shapes, sizes and colors rested within—a virtual treasure trove.

He wrenched off the first lid and uncovered a porcelain figure of a woman, fashioned by an artist in New York. He hoisted it in his palm, felt its weight, then hurled it across the room. It shattered against a bookcase, its pieces raining to the floor in a brittle chorus.

It brought him little satisfaction. He wanted to scream, to ruin things with his bare hands, to watch blood flow from his skin. Something. Some outlet.

One by one, he ripped lids off the boxes and discarded

items onto the floor, looking for something else he could throw. Nothing else was fragile enough. Just like the woman herself. She wasn't damned fragile enough for him to break. Worse, he didn't want her to be. He admired her strength. God, he loathed the predicament he found himself in, hated this situation that would force him either to break her spirit or let his brother sit in jail.

He kicked a topaz necklace out of his way, unable to stand the sight of it. Come morning, he'd order all of this taken away. It only served to remind him of his own gullibility.

He walked to the rolling cart in the corner and pulled a stopper from the bottle of brandy that rested there. Almost as quickly, he replaced the stopper. He didn't want it. Beyond breaking the crystal decanters and glasses, the contents of the cart held no appeal for him. He'd never been a man to crave oblivion. No, he'd always preferred tormenting himself with his mistakes, every faculty intact. Escape was for weaklings. Staring square in the eyes of the facts was far more difficult. It was also what made a man stronger and smarter the next time.

He paced around the room once, then again. Restlessness ate at him. The already-confining walls of the library seemed to close in even farther, sucking away his air. Each time he passed the banked fire, crimson light washed over his boots.

Finally, he lowered onto one of the chairs. His elbows dug into his knees as he buried his hands in his hair and clasped his head. He'd known from the first, God damn him, that Sophia had lied to him about Twilight's Ghost and that he couldn't trust her. Yet he'd let himself do so, never once imagining the truth. Why? Why hadn't he guessed at it?

The business world he moved in was the dominion of men. A woman secret agent? He'd have sooner guessed that dogs could fly. And have sooner guessed it of any other woman than the reserved Sophia LaRue. Which is why, no doubt, she'd gone as long as she had without anyone suspecting her.

What an idiot he was. He screwed closed his eyes.

His stupidity was bad. But what he must now do was worse. He'd told her he'd expose her and that he'd take her house from her. Either option or both would be simplicity itself to execute. They'd require no more from him than a matter of words.

Except . . . The memory of a small girl in a white dress burned the backs of his eyelids. She held out her fruit to him, using her skirt as a basket. The same girl had been deposited at an orphanage just weeks later, with nothing to her name but a suitcase. And years later the same girl had looked through his telescope and smiled with long-lost awe.

Even so, the man he'd been before he'd brought her into his home wouldn't have hesitated to enforce her co-operation in any way necessary. The mere thought of it now, though, made him physically sick. He hated his weakness more than he'd ever hated anything about himself.

He rubbed his hands down his face, then let them drop between his knees. Dully, he gazed at the carpet. He was no stranger to disliking parts of himself. Since the age of fourteen he'd been forced to do things that repulsed him. He'd done them anyway because he'd been willing to exchange a conscience for what had mattered more—first money, then power.

Was he willing to destroy a wounded woman who'd

just begun to put her faith in him? Not for money or power this time—he wouldn't have hurt her for either of those. But for something that mattered far more to him. Was he willing to destroy her for his brother's sake?

At noon the next day, Sophia stared out her window through eyes that felt as if they'd been glazed with sand. An ache beat behind her forehead, a souvenir of the fitful night she'd passed. She'd tossed and turned, her sleep riddled with terrible dreams and more terrible realities.

Just as she'd suspected would happen, Maggie walked down the front steps and back into her line of view, accompanied by a guard. Jarrod had not let Maggie see her. Of course he hadn't after what had transpired last night. She'd anticipated that he wouldn't—no, expected it. So how come watching her friend leave filled her with a crushing sense of loss?

Maggie climbed into her buggy and set the horses into motion. Before she turned them down the drive, she looked directly to where Sophia stood. Very deliberately, Sophia pressed her palm to the windowpane, signaling to her friend that Jarrod had discovered her identity.

Maggie gave a grim nod and steered the buggy toward Blackhaw.

"Oh, Maggie," she murmured, so softly the sound barely reached her own ears. She needed her friend's humor and hope today. The vicious circle of her own thoughts was already driving her mad, and, clearly, that's just what Jarrod had intended. She'd dressed carefully for breakfast this morning, only to have the meal brought to her in her room by stony-faced servants. It seemed her host no longer had any wish to share his meals with her. He'd sentenced her to isolation inside the walls of her silken chamber.

She watched steam misting the cold glass around the outline of her fingers. She could trust Maggie to do what they'd agreed upon, to refrain from reporting the news to Simon, and to return in a few days to try again.

A knock sounded.

She quickly crossed the carpeted space. "Come in."

The lock turned and the door opened to reveal the same two servants who had brought her breakfast. They now carried a tray of what she could only assume was lunch.

Her spirits dipped even lower.

The male servant set the tray of food on the table in front of her pink sofa, while the maid bustled up the remains of Sophia's breakfast tray. Out in the hall, Sophia caught sight of a burly guard. He stood directly opposite her doorway, exactly as he had when they'd brought the food that morning. Evidently Jarrod was taking no chances of another escape.

The maid hurried off, but the man paused near her door, his hands clasped behind his back. "Mr. Stone would like to know whether you've decided yet to assist him, ma'am."

"I . . . I need more time."

He inclined his head and made to back out.

"I would like very much," she met his gaze unwaveringly, "to speak to Mr. Stone in person." Instinctively, she sensed that imploring Jarrod face-to-face was still her best hope of softening him.

"I'm sorry." The man flushed. "Mr. Stone is unable to see you today. His schedule is very busy."

"I see." She swallowed against the burn of his rejection. "If you would be so kind as to communicate my wish of an audience to Mr. Stone, I would appreciate it."

"Certainly, ma'am."

She glimpsed the implacable face of the hallway guard in the instant before the door closed, cutting off her view. She sighed and made her way over to her meal tray. Beneath the dome she found fried chicken, turnips, pickles, and relish. The same beautiful food as always. At least it didn't appear that Jarrod planned to keep her alive on gruel and water.

Listlessly, she replaced the dome. Her appetite had been whittled away.

She pressed her fingertips to the bones surrounding her gritty eyes and started pacing the length of her cell. Should she do as Jarrod demanded and level whatever authority she possessed to the cause of freeing his brother?

She could go to Simon and explain things. Owing to her compromised identity, she'd no idea how he might react. He might simply cut her loose, or he might be willing to contact the governor regarding Holden Stone. It was possible that the Secret Service could exchange favors with the state in order to secure Holden's release. Such deals had been struck before.

Her skirts swished about her ankles when she turned. Could she live with herself if she set a guilty man free for her own selfish reasons? Her heart quailed.

Was her career worth having Holden Stone on her conscience for the rest of her life? Was the potential good she could do in the years to come as a Secret Service agent worth sacrificing her principles now?

She didn't know. Wasn't yet sure.

If she could only see Jarrod. If he'd only allow her another opportunity to explain. . . .

Collier's forehead wrinkled. "Our man in Washington has concluded that Mr. LaRue, Mrs. LaRue's supposed husband, never existed."

"What?" Jarrod searched his secretary's expression with hawklike concentration. The long, lean planes of Collier's face were as impassive as always.

"The detective insists that Sophia Warren did not marry an Arthur LaRue in Washington."

"How did he come to that conclusion?"

"He studied the census information of 1870 and interviewed every LaRue he could in the entire city. Those findings, coupled with his lack of success in locating either birth, marriage, or death records of any kind, led him to believe that Mr. LaRue was invented."

Invented. Of course. Widows enjoyed far more freedom than unmarried women did. With a dead husband, Sophia would be allowed to attend—alone—events and parties she wouldn't be invited to otherwise. She'd have the independence to move throughout the city and beyond unchaperoned and unsuspected.

All last night and all day today he'd thought of nothing, nothing, but Sophia and her true identity. Now the remaining details fell into place.

"As to—"

"If you'll give me just one more moment," Jarrod interrupted. He still wasn't grasping the full import of this. Sophia was, with extreme likelihood, a virgin. The memory of her kisses seared him. The tentativeness of her pink little tongue the first time. The way she'd quivered

when he'd captured her in the hallway outside her room.
The way she'd melted into him when he'd taken her
breast into his mouth.

*Oh my God, untouched. She's innocent—not inno-
cent,* he reminded himself grimly. *Anything but innocent.*
But she *was* physically chaste, and that knowledge only
served to feed the driving, unholy need he harbored for
her. It made him hard, just thinking about being the
only one to claim her. Those delectable legs around his
naked hips, arms around his neck as he sank into the
heat of her.

He slowly shook his head before returning his attention to Collier. The man stood patiently, waiting. "Go
on."

"As to the search for the agent masquerading as Twilight's Ghost—"

"Cancel it."

Collier lowered his ever-present papers a fraction. It
was as close as he'd ever come to questioning whether
he'd heard Jarrod correctly.

"Order every man we have working on the search to
stop immediately," Jarrod confirmed.

"Yes, sir." He jotted down the instructions.

The last thing Jarrod wanted was one of his detectives
stumbling onto Sophia's secret.

"What of the men we have investigating the whereabouts of Adam Stone?" Collier asked.

Jarrod pushed from the chair, startling poor Maxine,
who'd been snoozing with her head on his foot. He
reached into a drawer and tossed her a treat, which she
caught in midair.

Thrusting his hands into his pockets, Jarrod walked to
the window. He sure as hell didn't owe Sophia any fa-

vors. No reason to waste his money on her ridiculous quest for his father. He ought to let her and Oliver scratch for clues the rest of their lives. He *should*, and yet . . . Damn her to hell. More than anything, he wished he could hate her as he wanted to so that he could do what needed doing for Holden. Up until now he hadn't been able to stomach it, so he'd caged her until he could.

"Have them continue the hunt for my father," Jarrod answered. He told himself the decision was justified. Once she'd granted her assistance to freeing Holden it would only be reasonable to offer her some reward.

Liar. He'd always been scrupulously honest with himself, and that's not why he'd done what he'd just done.

He shoved away the stink of his motivation, flat refusing to face it.

Collier continued on, updating him on happenings within his company. His secretary's words fell around him, meaningless.

All he could think of, over and over again, was that Sophia was a virgin.

Three days! Three days she'd been trapped inside these walls. Restlessness had frazzled Sophia's nerves until she could no longer even bear to sit. She knew the grain of every surface in this godforsaken room. Every page of every book had been flipped through, each item of clothing examined in detail, every brushstroke of every painting pondered until her head swam.

She stood in front of the door, staring at the jamb, an all-out hysterical fit of impatience threatening perilously close. Minutes ago, the same employee of Jarrod's had brought in yet another tray of food, arranged precisely as all the other trays had been arranged. Whereas before, she'd only ever made polite inquiries to him about securing a visit with Jarrod, this time she'd informed him that she must have air and exercise lest she lose her mind.

He'd promised to ask Jarrod right away and left in a hurry. It had been approximately three minutes, she'd counted every second, and he'd yet to return.

Hands planted on hips, she drummed her fingers.

If Jarrod wouldn't let her out of this room, she'd have to . . . she'd have to start beating her fists against the door, or break the windows by hurling items of furniture at them. This punishment had gone on long enough.

She picked up the sound of the servant's footsteps returning well before he knocked.

"Come in."

The key turned and he opened the door partway.

"Did you speak with him?" she asked.

"Yes, ma'am. He said that you may take a walk out of doors in the company of"—he licked his lips, obviously harried by the entire situation—"Jonathan." He gestured to the guard towering behind him.

"That will be fine."

"It's a bit chilly. Would you like to get your coat?"

She snatched up the hat, coat, and gloves she'd already piled on the circular table next to the door. "Ready."

He waved her forward, and she set off without a glance at her hulking chaperone. She could hear him though. His heavy, plodding footfalls reminded her that she was a prisoner *thump thump* prisoner. She, who had always been free to roam dark streets. She, who had *always* before been the one to send others to prison.

The corridors passed in a blur.

She reached the main hallway and turned toward the back exit of the house. She was sailing past Jarrod's office when she glanced over. Instantly, her gait slashed to a halt.

Jarrod's gaze collided with hers, trapping her where she stood as surely and powerfully as any force on earth. Stronger.

Her heart bolted straight into her throat. He was standing, leaning over his desk, one hand planted on the papers spread there, Collier at his shoulder. She recognized well the black of his suit, the cut of his short hair, the olive green of his eyes. She'd somehow forgotten, though, just how straight and mean Jarrod's brows could be, how severe his jaw.

All air and noise seemed to suck from the house. He didn't move in the slightest way, just stared at her.

Wordlessly, Collier eased past her into the hall and melted out of sight.

Jarrod's gaze flicked to her bodyguard. "Wait down the hall."

"Yes, sir."

Sophia stepped into his office. If she could order the scattered nonsense of her thoughts, she could try to talk sense into him. This was the chance she'd been waiting for.

He straightened, crossing his arms over his chest. "Close the door."

She pulled it shut behind her, but moved no farther. Her hand remained wrapped around the knob, clenching it. What was wrong with her? She'd been rehearsing this meeting for days. Now that she'd gotten it, she felt stricken by the mere sight of him.

She cleared her throat, drew herself up to her tallest height. "I'd like to take this opportunity to explain to you . . . Well, to explain to you about my work and why keeping my identity secret is so crucial to my safety. I didn't do a very good job of it the other night, and I thought perhaps if I told you—"

"You've explained enough."

"If you'd just allow me to tell you—"

"We've been over all of this. Let yourself out."

Like a match rasping into flame, her anger rushed to life, heating her cheeks. Would it cost him so much to give her two minutes of his time? She let go of the knob and gripped her coat with both hands. *By God, he'll listen to me.* "What you don't seem to comprehend is that I am an officer of the law. A federal official."

His stare would have sent woodland animals racing into their burrows.

"You're committing a crime by holding me here, and I *insist* you let me leave at once."

"You're not in a position to insist on anything."

"Yes, I am. I have the entire Secret Service behind me. They *will* come for me."

"Really? Do they expend so much effort for agents whose covers have been ruined?"

Her pride warred with her own grave doubts on the subject. "What you're doing, tormenting me for your brother's crimes, makes no sense. I did not fabricate the aiding and abetting charge against Holden, I did not write the warrant for his arrest."

"No, but you enforced it."

Her nostrils flared as she dragged in a furious breath. "I am *not* the one in the wrong. Holden did wrong for committing the crime. You are doing wrong by imprisoning me here. But I only acted as the law and my principles dictated—"

He crossed the distance between them, reaching around her for the door. Instead of yanking it open, however, he paused.

The air froze in her lungs.

His attention dropped to her lips and caught there. She thought she saw longing flicker in his expression, then realized in the next moment she'd been wrong. He jerked open the door, his expression endlessly cold.

"The law and your principles sent an innocent man to jail," he said, his tone low. "So you'll pardon me if I've no sympathy for your plight."

"Jarrod—"

"Speak to me again only when you're willing to help."

She turned to leave. He caught her upper arm. "And make it soon. I'm getting damn tired of waiting."

She stared at him, ire blazing so hot inside her she could hardly think. "Not nearly as tired as I am of you," she hissed, and wrenched free her arm. Pulse hammering in her ears and emotions in turmoil, she picked up her skirts and stalked toward the door. Distantly, she heard Jarrod order the guard to follow her.

Outside, frosty wind poured over her. Steel-tipped clouds scudded across a threatening sky, and in the distance thunder boomed. The weather suited her temper as nothing had in all her days of confinement. She lifted her face to it, relishing its austere and dangerous beauty, walking as fast as her legs would carry her. She was too angry to bother donning her coat, hat, or gloves, even when the first brace of rain pelted her face. She simply pressed forward, letting the air sail into all the dark, hot, fearful places inside. Faster and faster she went, until locks of hair whipped around her face. Until rain fell all around her. Faster, unaware of anything save the elements and her own movement.

She'd almost delved beneath the shelter of the trees when the sound of rustling, then running, penetrated her isolated thoughts. Her attention jerked to her surroundings in time to see a group of masked men descend upon her in a blur. One yanked her arms behind her back, spilling her belongings onto the ground. Another confronted her head-on, pressing his black-gloved hand against her lips to smother her screams before they could begin. Terror arced high inside her, immobilizing her muscles, her brain.

They twisted her toward their cohorts, who were fighting with Jonathan, the guard Jarrod had assigned her. Already, they'd stripped his gun from him, and though he battled them, he was outnumbered two to one and they succeeded in wrestling him to the ground. Sophia tried to look away, but the man holding her mouth and chin jerked her face back and refused to let her turn her head.

Through the intensifying rain she watched as one attacker partially straddled Jonathon, then drove punches into his face. The sound of knuckles crashing into cartilage caused her stomach to contort. They'd kill him. "Stop," she croaked against the wet cloth of her captor's gloved hand. "Please, stop."

Heedless of her pleas, they beat him again and again, until they finally knocked him unconscious. That done, they abandoned his prostrate body and closed in on her. They wore the clothes of workingmen as well as bandannas to hide their faces. Different sizes, builds. Shifty eyes, alight with feral intent. Edgy to hurt her, willing and able to.

Her chest wheezed as she fought for breath.

The one who'd clamped his hand over her lips, removed it long enough to pull his arm back and slap her across the face. The crack of sound fired through her brain an instant before the biting pain. Her head snapped to the side. She blinked at the view of the trees, her vision fuzzed with the brutality of his strike and her own panic.

"You listening now?" he asked. His voice was blunt, without feeling or remorse.

She brought her gaze back to him and nodded.

"What?" he asked.

"Yes," she rasped, tasting blood. Rain ran into her eyes, down her chin.

"The one who sent us doesn't want Jarrod Stone snooping into the theft of your grandmother's money or the whereabouts of Adam Stone."

She struggled to swallow. Fought harder to understand. Jarrod had never investigated the theft of her grandmother's money or tried to locate his father. He'd offered that to her, but only in exchange—

"Convince him to cease his search."

Must be some mistake. Frenzied, she looked from one face to the next. She'd been the only one to investigate Adam Stone and Blackhaw's stolen fortune. Who—who could have sent them? What would they do to her?

The man behind her wrenched her arms in their sockets, and she cried out involuntarily.

"Convince him to cease his search," her captor repeated, "or far worse than this will happen to you and to him."

He brought back his hand again. This time she had a second to brace herself.

The force of his slap blinded her. She was released from behind and felt herself spinning and falling, hitting the earth with jarring force. Then an inner blackness descended with dizzying speed, and consciousness cut away.

Chapter 14

Jarrod saw Sophia fall. "No!" he screamed with raw fury as he ran toward the scene he'd first glimpsed out his office window. They'd *struck* her, and he'd been too far away to stop them.

Her attackers stood looking down at her where she'd fallen. When he was yards away, one of the them glanced up and spotted him coming. Jarrod lunged at the man, swinging with his right. The man darted backward, the blow glancing off his jaw. Jarrod sent his left fist barreling forward and this time connected soundly with the man's cheek. His enemy grunted and sprawled into the dirt.

Rabid, Jarrod turned to the others, who came at him as a pack. He fought them wildly, lashing out with bruising force, fueled by a protective rage that hazed his vision red. He threw off one who tried to subdue him from behind, rounding on the man with a snarl only partially human. He drove his punches into him, unsatisfied until the man fell to his knees.

The remaining men backed away. He charged toward them. They retreated. He went after them and they scattered, disappearing into the trees.

Jarrod turned to Sophia, dreading what he would see. She lay in the dirt, her clothing and hair drenched, one side of her face flush against trampled grass. Blood leaked from her lip and melded with the water running in rivulets over her ashen features.

His heart stopped in his chest. He went to one knee beside her. His outstretched hand hovered over her. "Christ." He didn't know where to touch, where he wouldn't hurt her more. He reached toward her shoulders, paused. Withdrew his hand. Both his arms were shaking with a tremor that delved into his chest, straight to his core. Look at her. Look at what he'd let happen to her.

His own guards ran up to him, guns drawn. He'd been unaware of their approach. Barely even remembered yelling for them to be sent as he'd left the house. He glanced around. All of her attackers had fled.

"You there, tend to him." He jutted his chin toward Jonathan, who lay on the ground. "The rest of you go after the others."

They did so at once, spreading out to follow sodden footprints.

Heart breaking, he carefully scooped a hand under Sophia's upper back, another under her knees, and lifted her against his chest. She was surprisingly light, unbearably delicate. And cold. Far too cold. His gaze never leaving her face, he set off for the house.

"Sophia," he said.

Nothing.

"Sophia," he said again, louder.

Her only movement was the slight rising of her chest. His gut twisted with fear.

All his life he'd been the protector of his family. It was what he was, who he was. His clearest identity, and the only one he was proud of. He abhorred that she'd been injured, and even worse, injured on his property under his care. This was all wrong, heinously wrong. The limp weight of her, the angry red mark scarring her beautiful cheek—evidence that he'd failed to guard her as he should have. He wanted to throw his head back and to scream.

If he couldn't make her better . . .

He looked up at the approaching house, desperate for help. Collier ran toward him, hunched against the rain. "Get the housekeeper," Jarrod yelled, fighting to be heard above the rolls of thunder and wind. "I need warm blankets, medicine, bandages. Then go to the stables and send the hands back for one of the guards. He's down."

Collier nodded and loped for the house.

A maid was standing at the back door, holding it open for him when he arrived. Water splashed from Sophia's gown, a steady stream against hardwood as he carried her to her bedroom.

Yet another maid waited there, door open. He passed her without acknowledgment. Sophia's head lolled to the side as he laid her gently on the bed's white coverlet.

He towered over her, afraid to touch her with his

clumsy hands. He watched her chest, willing it to continue lifting with her breath. Between each shallow breath he died a hundred times.

His housekeeper strode into the room accompanied by the smell of baking bread. A wiry woman with a plain horse face and efficient hands, Mrs. Hoskins took in the scene with a glance, then set aside her stack of blankets, medicines, and bandages. "What happened?" she asked, coming to stand beside Sophia across the bed from him.

"She was slapped across the face."

"How many times?"

His mind reeled at the possibility that there might have been more than one. "I only saw the once."

"Any bones broken?"

"I don't think so."

She leaned over Sophia and began running her hands along her limbs. When she pressed work-roughened fingertips to Sophia's bruised cheekbone, Jarrod squeezed closed his eyes for a moment, then looked away.

"Mary," Mrs. Hoskins called.

The girl posted at the door rushed inside. "Ma'am?"

"Fetch my smelling salts."

"Yes, ma'am." She raced away in a hail of footsteps.

"Mrs. LaRue?" his housekeeper said in an authoritative tone. She waited a few beats, then gently shook Sophia's shoulder.

Sophia didn't respond.

"The first order of business is to get her out of these wet things," Mrs. Hoskins said to him.

He didn't budge.

"If you'll excuse us," she said pointedly.

His eyebrows crushed downward. "I'm not leaving her."

"Mr. Stone, I need to undress her—"

"Do it then," he barked. "I'm not leaving." No way in hell he'd abandon Sophia now.

Thin lips pursed tight, Mrs. Hoskins marched into the dressing room and returned moments later with a white nightgown.

Jarrod paced to the fireplace, then knelt to stack more logs onto the grate. Despite his action, he recorded every sound his housekeeper made, counted every second as it passed. How bloody long does it take to change a gown? He didn't trust his housekeeper's ability to care for her, to keep her from slipping away.

"There we are," the woman finally said.

He crossed immediately back to the bed. Sophia was dressed in the gown, bare feet poking beyond its hem and the contours of her body obvious through the single layer of fabric. Her face and hands had been dried, the blood at her lip dabbed away.

Mrs. Hoskins returned from where she'd set aside Sophia's wet clothing and soiled towels. "If you'll lift her for me, I'll sweep aside the bed linens."

Jarrod watched Sophia's face as he gathered her up. Still nothing. A gleaming lock of rich chocolate hair clung damply to the cords of her throat. Jarrod's heart contracted.

In seconds, Mrs. Hoskins had pulled free the saturated quilt, turned down the sheets beneath, and placed a fresh towel across the pillow. Jarrod lowered Sophia, then leaned over to tuck her feet beneath the tightly made sheets. Her flesh was so cold. He took both feet in his big hands and rubbed his palms back and forth, hoping to warm them.

Mrs. Hoskins bound up Sophia's hair in the towel.

When she'd completed that, they both drew the sheets up over her. Mrs. Hoskins opened a dresser drawer, shook out a blanket, and lofted it over her charge. As the blanket settled, so did the quiet. His housekeeper held herself as still as a pillar, assessing Sophia with her gaze.

"What's wrong with her?" Jarrod asked

"The force of the blow simply rendered her unconscious," she answered without looking at him. "We'll have to wait and see whether she's caught a chill from the inclement weather."

"She's not . . . she's not breathing well."

Mrs. Hoskins glanced up and pondered him for a moment. "Once I revive her with the smelling salts, all should be fine."

He wasn't convinced. He knew how fragile life could be. His mother's had gone as easily as smoke disappearing on air. His mother. God where had that thought come from? As suddenly, he realized it had been there ever since he'd seen Sophia fall. There were similarities between the two women. The pattern of strength overlying gentleness, their sadness, their fundamental goodness.

He remembered at once and with perfect clarity how awful it was to care about someone you couldn't help. Everything he was experiencing now, he'd experienced before. The constriction of worry in his chest, the thoughts that spiraled too fast into nightmares, the powerlessness of being the one sentenced to stand alongside and watch. All of it came back to him, each facet of a helplessness lived twice in a lifetime now. Two times too many.

He backed away a couple of steps. He didn't want to do this again. This was why he hadn't married anyone or borne any children. *This* was why.

A light knock sounded at the door, and Mrs. Hoskins bid the person enter. The maid walked hesitantly inside. "I'm sorry, ma'am. I had a bit of trouble locating them." She handed over the smelling salts, a repentant expression on her face.

"I swear no one could find their own backside in this house without my help," Mrs. Hoskins grumbled as she unscrewed the cap. "You may take that pile to the laundry."

The girl hoisted the stack of discarded linens and clothing, then dawdled, seemingly unsure whether she'd be needed for further chores.

"Leave us," Jarrod said.

She skittered out.

Mrs. Hoskins waved the smelling salts beneath Sophia's nose. Sophia failed to react. Jarrod held his breath. Two more passes beneath her nostrils, and at last Sophia moaned and turned her face to the side.

"Mrs. LaRue?" his housekeeper asked.

Frown lines creased Sophia's brow. Her lips pursed.

"Can you hear me?"

Sophia's eyes fluttered open, and she squinted at the wall, blinked, squinted. *Where was she?* she wondered. Her senses were groggy, her memory muddled. This was her bedroom at Jarrod's, but how had she gotten here? She brought her wrist up from under the covers and saw that she was wearing a linen nightdress. She let her lids fall closed for a moment, to rest. Mother above, but one side of her face hurt and her . . . she tested the inside of her bottom lip with her tongue . . . her lip was swollen and sore.

"Mrs. LaRue?" A woman's voice.

Fighting disorientation, Sophia opened her eyes and

looked toward the voice. Instead of a woman, however, the first person she saw was the most masculine man she'd ever met.

Jarrod stood at the foot of the bed, arms braced at his sides, his height and maleness more glaring than ever in the feminine environment. She'd never seen his features so grave or so colorless. And his eyes were lit with a wildness both stark and urgent. Distantly, she recalled thinking once that she'd give much to see Jarrod Stone upset. This was it, she realized. He was upset about something.

She ran her gaze over him and noticed that not only did his dark hair gleam with moisture, but that his shirt was plastered to his chest. He was soaking wet.

In a rush she remembered her fight with Jarrod followed by the slanting rain, the men in bandannas, the way they'd beaten her guard, the warning they'd given her, and the slaps. "Oh," she breathed, wishing she hadn't recalled it. The smothering fear she'd experienced at their hands *whooshed* around her, squeezing her chest.

"Easy," Jarrod said, seemingly able to read her distress on her face.

"The guard? Is he . . ."

"Fine. He's being tended to."

Her shoulders and neck muscles relaxed against the bed. Thank God for that.

"How do you feel?" Jarrod asked, his tone tight.

"Fine."

"Like hell."

Typical that he'd not accept a perfectly good response. "If you must know, I have a terrible headache."

She brought up a hand and gingerly explored her lip, cheek, and jaw. "This whole side of my face is tender, but that's all."

"Any nausea?" the woman asked.

Sophia looked over to find a practical-looking woman wearing an apron over her gray gown. "No."

"I'm the housekeeper here," she said by way of barest explanation. "Any confusion?"

"A little, right when I awoke. That's cleared away now."

"What about your lip?" Jarrod asked.

"My lip?" There had been times, growing up at the orphanage and during her years as Twilight's Ghost when she'd fallen ill, or injured herself. She'd been the one to worry about herself on those occasions, and even then hadn't wasted much energy upon it. It felt strange and warm for someone to care about something as minor as a headache and a tender lip.

"It bled," Jarrod said.

"I believe it simply split open a bit on the inside," Sophia answered. "It'll heal in no time."

Jarrod's housekeeper began moving about the room, shutting the curtains against the stormy afternoon.

"Can you feel your legs?" Jarrod asked.

"Yes."

"Can you move them?" Through the blanket, he took hold of her toes.

Behind his back, Jarrod's housekeeper rolled her eyes and smiled at Sophia. The woman patted her heart with her hand, then pointed from Jarrod to her.

Sophia shook her head slightly, unable to let the woman believe something so false.

"You can't move them?" Jarrod asked tensely.

"I'm sorry, I didn't mean . . ." She wiggled her toes against his hand. "Yes, I can move them."

He blew out a breath and released her.

"I'll be on my way," his housekeeper announced. She stood with hands stiffly inserted in her apron pockets. "It's my advice, Mrs. LaRue, that you stay in bed for the remainder of the day to rest—"

"Oh, that's probably not necessary. I feel—"

"You'll do it," Jarrod said.

A dimple dug into the housekeeper's cheek, hinting at her private amusement. "I'll order the lights kept low here in your chambers and a bath drawn for you this evening. Both should help to relieve your headache. Should you begin to feel nauseous, dizzy, or confused, inform a member of my staff at once, and I shall summon the doctor."

"Thank you."

"You're welcome." She walked in her sensible way to the door and closed it in a sensible way behind her.

Sophia met Jarrod's gaze. He gave her a long, hard look.

She wasn't sure after the hard words they'd exchanged earlier, how to be around him. On the one hand, she wanted to strangle him for today's argument and for the past days of confinement. On the other, he was the one who'd been standing at her bedside when she awoke, worrying over her split lip and asking if she could feel her legs. "Will you at least sit down?" she asked cautiously. "You're making me uncomfortable, towering over me like that."

Obligingly, he pulled up a chair and sat. As usual, he leaned into the seat back slightly, rested his arms along the armrests, and splayed one knee to the side. "Who were those men that attacked you?" he asked.

"I don't know. None of them were familiar."

"What did they want?"

"They said . . ." Since the first day she'd met Jarrod, she'd been concealing the truth from him. Who would have thought honesty would come so haltingly or feel so strange? "They said they wanted you to stop investigating the theft of my grandmother's money as well as your father's whereabouts."

His fingers tightened convulsively around the ends of the armrests. "What?"

"I know. There must be some mistake—"

"They used you to get me to me?" Violence flared in his eyes.

"It appears that way."

He stormed from the chair. Swearing under his breath, he prowled around her room. Finally, he yanked open the curtains covering the far window. Hands jammed in pockets, he stared stonily out, his frustration all the more powerful for its muteness. The thundering sky and water-drizzled window painted his profile in shifting shadows of gray. The only sounds were the pattering of rain and the crackling of the fire.

Sophia winced against the pain as she eased herself into a more upright sitting position. "Do you have any idea why they'd think that you've been investigating my grandmother's fortune and your father's disappearance?"

"Yes."

She laced her hands together in her lap.

"Because I have been."

Her jaw sagged open slightly. He'd been *what*? But she'd thought . . . he'd only search for his father if she helped him with Holden. He'd said he'd never bothered hunting for his father because his father had never bothered hunting for him. Myriad responses swam through her mind. In the end, all she said was, "You didn't tell me."

"No." He faced her. The gloom of the room darkened one half of his face. "I didn't."

"Why not?" But as soon as she asked the question, she knew the answer. He'd hoped to use the leverage of his offer for Holden's sake. "I suppose"—she licked her lips— "the better question is *why*. Why have you been looking for your father?"

"Is it impossible to believe I did it for you?"

Her world tilted. "I don't know. Is it?" Time stretched, each second heavy with meaning.

He shrugged in an effort to belittle what he'd done. Seemingly preoccupied, he crossed to the bookcase and idly picked up a gilt candlestick.

"Jarrod," she said carefully, "I'd appreciate it if you'd tell me why."

He set down the candlestick. "My family owes you answers about what happened." He eyed the Durand painting, then returned to the window to peer out at the storm. "I have the means to provide those for you, so I hired detectives and took action to do so."

It was the most decent thing anyone had ever done for her. That a *Stone* had done it for her, with or without the promise of her reciprocation, caused a lump of gratitude and confusion to clog her throat. Why couldn't Jarrod allow her to loathe him? Just when she thought she might be able to manage it, she uncovered a part of his personality that drew her like a moth to a flame. That he'd launched a search for his father because he'd felt she deserved answers, was a gift beyond words.

"I'm assuming you halted the search when you learned of my identity," she said softly.

He didn't reply.

Oh, she thought, her heart dropping. Even after he'd found out about her and been so angry, he'd carried on his search. Tears burned the backs of her eyes. This arrogant, difficult, stubborn man had acted out of inexpressible kindness toward her.

She thought of all the years she'd spent hunting for Adam Stone, all the pitiful leads she and Oliver had labored to piece together, the countless letters she'd written and telegrams she'd sent only to find disappointment at the end of every one. Did Jarrod have any idea how crucial this was to her? It was like a wound that she walked around with and worked, and slept, and lived with. But all the time, she was bleedingly aware of its presence. Until someone paid for her grandmother's death, she'd never be whole.

With a knuckle, she swept away the trickle of moisture that had spilled over her lashes. "It's no small thing you're doing for me," she said simply. "I thank you."

"It's only money."

"No. It's far more than money to me. It means a great deal." He could shrug off the clothes, the furs, the jewels he'd offered her. But this was much more meaningful to her than those, and she'd not let him demean it.

After a long silent moment, Jarrod picked up the poker and jabbed the fire with it. The blaze snarled and hissed, black-red wood collapsing in on itself.

"This new information puts a fresh perspective on today's attack," Sophia said. "What do you think?"

Again, he prodded the fire. "I think the man who stole your money realized that I was after him and retaliated against you."

She gave a quick nod. "Your father must have come across evidence of your investigation—"

"What proof do you have that my father stole your money?"

She paused, wondering how even his trademark loyalty could withstand twenty years of abandonment and the obvious facts of the case. "My grandmother gave your father the money for their investment, and he was never seen again. That's my proof."

"Other people had access to the money."

"Not that night. She gave it to him. He left with it."

"According to whom?"

"According to my grandmother."

He set the poker aside.

She didn't want to have to hurt him by convincing him of his father's guilt. "Did the men who attacked me today flee?"

"Yes. I sent my guards after them."

"If your guards were able to catch even one of them, perhaps we can get him to divulge where your father is located."

"And how do you propose we 'get' him to divulge the information we want?" The barest hint of humor played about his serious lips.

"Please. You're the one with all the skill for imprisoning people and bending them to your will."

"Not if you're any indication."

She opened her mouth to retort and realized he had a point.

He scowled at her as he came to stand at her bedside. With him so near she could see the way his wet pants clung to his muscular thighs and smell the sea-and-wind scent of his cologne.

"Are there any other things that you've been investigating that I should know about?" she asked. "The knowledge might serve me well the next time I'm surrounded by big-fisted men wearing bandannas."

"My investigations aren't for you to concern yourself with."

So he'd already retreated behind the wall that separated them. Disappointment swirled within her. "I know there hasn't been much truth between us up until now," she said, choosing her words carefully, searching for new ground on which they could form some sort of truce. "Could there be?

"I don't trust twice."

"And I've never trusted at all. I'm willing to try." She took a breath. "What else have you been investigating?

"Your husband, for one. I know you were never married." The shrewd gleam in his eye told her he also knew what went along with that. Her inexperience.

"Oh."

"Now lie down," he said, placing a hand on her shoulder and guiding her back to a lying position. Before he pulled away, he captured her chin between his thumb and forefinger. "You certain you're all right?"

"Yes."

He nodded and walked toward the door. Halfway there, he looked back at her over his shoulder. "Do you think you'll feel well enough to leave your bed tomorrow?"

"Yes. In fact, I can't bear this room anymore. I'd love to leave it."

"Good, because I'm taking you away from here."

"Where?"

"To visit Holden."

Chapter 15

It had been an incredibly long day. But as Sophia caught her first glimpse of the Texas State Penitentiary at Huntsville, she sincerely wished it had been far longer. A gate of brick sandstone reared upward from acres of desolate, windswept Texas plains. Jealously, the gate shielded the inner structures from view. The only building she could see was the one outsiders must pass through to enter the prison. It, too, had been built of sandstone brick and boasted an enormous wooden door that might as well have been the portal into the land of demons for all Sophia cared to enter it.

The bleak chill of the place leaked like smoke through the cracks and invisible seams of the rocking carriage to infect the air within. She drew her chocolate-colored cape around her and huddled into its rich folds.

As if that was going to help an iciness spreading from the inside out.

They'd begun their journey from Galveston early that morning. By gleaming black carriage they'd made their way to Houston. From there they'd taken the train. And now she found herself shut inside another sumptuously appointed carriage, being transported like a carefully tended pearl in a velvet box to a destination she dreaded.

She glanced away from the menacing view. Jarrod sat across from her, his big shoulders swaying slightly with the coach's movement. His attention was riveted on the prison and the endlessly grim set of his lips told her all she needed to know about the direction of his thoughts.

She hunkered even lower into her cape. She hadn't seen Jarrod yesterday after their talk in her bedroom. He'd sent Collier to inform her that his men had been unable to capture any of her attackers. That had been their only communication until this morning, when they'd gathered on the porch for this trip. The smallness of their traveling party had surprised her. She'd expected Jarrod to travel like some foreign maharaja—servants dancing attendance on his every whim and men staggering under the weight of all his suitcases and trunks. Instead he'd brought with them only two attendants, both women, both for her comfort.

Jarrod had spared the maids this awful errand, leaving them a few miles back at the hotel in town. More's the pity. She'd have happily gone without food for days in exchange for a scrap of light conversation just now.

Instead there was only Jarrod, whose demeanor gave her the sense that she was being taken to the prison not as a visitor, but as one to be admitted and never again set free.

Lips pursed, she looked back to the approaching penitentiary. When she'd asked him why he was bringing her here, he'd said he needed to get her away from his Galveston property for her own safety.

While it was certainly true that Adam Stone had located her there and succeeded in harming her, they both knew Jarrod had brought her to Huntsville for a far less protective reason. In fact, in coming here, he wished to strip her emotionally bare. He wanted her to look into his brother's face, see Holden's hatred of her, and feel the full force of what she'd done.

Today was a reckoning.

She hugged her arms across her chest in an effort to warm herself. Always, she'd taken pains to separate her feelings from her work. She did what she did for justice. There was no room in that for personal knowledge about men better seen strictly as criminals. Without a doubt, she'd never wanted to come to know the brother of one of the men she'd arrested. And she'd never, but *never* wished to face any of those men across the bars of their jail cells. In her line of work such things spelled disaster.

Too quickly their carriage pulled to a stop before the building's main entrance. Jarrod exited without hesitation, held the door open for her, and offered his hand without a word. She allowed him to assist her down.

Outside, the wind snatched at her skirts and whistled around her calves. Yesterday's storms had passed, leaving a blustery day in which periods of sheer sun had occasionally penetrated churning clouds of gray. At the moment, all was entirely gray.

With her gloved hand positioned in the crook of Jarrod's elbow, they made their way up the stone steps. *How many men?* she wondered, stealing a glance upward at the building's front. *How many men have I put behind these walls?*

The door was opened from within by a guard. "Mr. Stone?"

"Yes."

The man stepped aside, allowing them to pass. "The warden told us to expect you, sir."

Jarrod nodded as they walked into the simple entry room. A second guard rose to his feet and greeted them with a nod. Both men were middle-aged, both wore denim trousers and work shirts, and both had been chiseled flint hard by years of doing a tough job in the company of tough criminals.

The one who'd let them in now locked them in. Sophia flinched at the sound of the bolt thudding into place. "Right this way," he said, indicating a door that led to what looked like a small visiting room.

Sophia moved toward it, but Jarrod stopped her short. "I'd rather visit my brother in his cell."

The guard frowned.

"I want to see where he lives," Jarrod said.

The guard gestured to her. "Wouldn't be suitable for the lady."

"It would be more suitable for this lady than you know."

"It's not done that way, sir. We've a visiting room—"

"I realize that. I'm willing to pay for the privilege."

Sophia released his arm as he reached beneath his coat for his wallet. "The warden and I have already come to an arrangement, but I'm certain there's more I could do for this establishment." Smoothly, he stacked one bill after another onto the surface of the desk. "Perhaps a refurbishment of your quarters. Better food for the security staff. Newer firearms." He looked up and met the guard's gaze.

By his harsh expression, Sophia could tell the guard didn't care for being blackmailed. She hoped he'd refuse Jarrod outright. Not only because it irritated her to watch Jarrod buy his way into anything he wished, but because facing Holden in the squalor of his cell struck her as a far worse proposition than facing him inside the visiting room.

The guard's attention flicked to the money, held there a long moment, then returned to Jarrod. "Deke, you already fetched Holden Stone from work detail to his cell?" he asked.

"Yes, sir," his coworker answered. "Hour ago."

"Then you can escort these folks to visit him there."

Sophia's mouth drained of moisture.

The one called Deke led them down the hallway, then out into the walled prison yard. Dead grass crunched under the soles of her shoes as they walked toward the central building. It looked like barracks: long, low, and composed of the same brick as the other permanent structures. In the far corners of the yard wooden buildings were grouped in clusters. They held the prison's industry, judging from the smoke winding from the chimneys and the sounds ringing from within.

When they entered the barracks, dimness engulfed them. Sophia's stomach churned at the smells of unwashed bodies, encrusted dirt, and long-held bitterness. Cell upon cell passed by. They all looked the same to her—three brick sides, the front side constructed of steel bars inlaid with a door. Each contained nothing more than two beds, a writing table, and a porcelain bowl. Obviously, the inmates were at work. Holden had been brought here in preparation for Jarrod's visit, or he'd be with them.

Her anxiety mounted until she could feel her shoulders knotting. The sound of their footsteps rang like death knells in her ears, brutally loud.

Deke finally stopped before a cell and jerked his chin toward the occupant. "Here he is."

Feeling sick inside, she turned to see a man push to his feet. Her breath caught in her throat. He was devilishly tall, his hair overlong and unkempt, and his jaw rough with stubble. He wore the thick shoes of a laborer and the black-and-white stripes of a prisoner. His shirt, carelessly unbuttoned halfway down his chest, clung to contours of muscles gleaming with sweat. His sharp gaze moved over her in a single sweeping assessment. His eyes were bright with intelligence and hooded with secrets held.

Where had the boy who'd given away his shoes disappeared to? There was no evidence of him here. Had she banished the last of that boy? Was the loss of any innocence that had managed to survive within him her responsibility to bear?

When he strode toward them, Sophia had to force herself to hold her ground.

On occasion she'd thought of Jarrod as a wolf. The man before her was a fox—scrappier than his brother but with instincts just as deadly. Where Jarrod was smooth, this man was all hard edges. Except for his lips. He had beautifully sculpted lips, which made her wonder just how many girls across how many counties were mourning him.

Holden reached through the bars and briefly shook hands with Jarrod. The men were close in height and resembled one another in the firm angles of brow and nose. However, Holden's hair was shades lighter than Jarrod's, and his eyes hazel instead of green. No two men could have been more different in dress, or in situation.

"I'd like some privacy," Jarrod said to Deke.

The man nodded grudgingly. "I'll wait at the end of the hall."

Once they were alone, uncomfortable quiet fell between them. "Is there anything you need?" Jarrod asked his brother.

"No."

"Have they been giving you enough to eat?"

"Yeah."

Jarrod eyed his brother's living quarters. On his face, usually a face of impervious power, she now read pain. Whatever his faults, Jarrod Stone loved his brothers. Her emotions twisted in sympathy for how terrible this must be for him, to see his brother like this.

"There are two of you who sleep in here?" Jarrod asked.

Holden nodded. "Me and a horse thief from Kansas."

No more than five feet by nine, Holden's cell was far too small to house a man of Holden's size, let alone two. The bed he'd risen from held a flat pillow, neatly made sheets, and a tan blanket. Paper and a few basic writing instruments were stacked on the desk.

When she looked back to Holden she found him gazing directly down at her. Her heartbeat skittered.

"This is Sophia Warren LaRue," Jarrod said. "She's the granddaughter of Mrs. Warren of Blackhaw. She's also the agent known as Twilight's Ghost, the one responsible for your arrest."

Sophia wound her hands into a ball and tried to arm

herself against the condemnation that was sure to be forthcoming. She didn't know if she could take him yelling and cussing at her at this particular low point in her life when everything was already in tatters.

"No." Holden's brow furrowed. "This can't be Twilight's Ghost."

"I wish I was wrong," Jarrod said tersely. "I'm not."

Holden's lips set into a harsh line.

"I brought her here," Jarrod said, "because I want her to hear from you that you're not guilty of aiding and abetting the Lucas gang."

Holden exchanged a long, searching look with his elder brother. "I can't tell her that," he said slowly.

"Why not?"

"Because I did it."

Jarrod's resulting silence was like a clap of thunder. Sophia watched disbelief, then confusion, shift across his features as he grappled to understand.

She wanted to reach out to him, hold his hand or clasp his arm. Something. She would have, if she hadn't been so certain that he'd reject her comfort. So she simply stood next to him quietly, her emotions wrenching at the look on his face. Oh, this was too horrible. To see all Jarrod's beautiful, noble beliefs about Holden shattered before her eyes. Perhaps better than anyone, she knew how fervently Jarrod had believed in his brother, how hard he'd worked to free him, how deep his love and loyalty ran.

"I thought you knew." Holden shook his head, clearly disgusted with himself and the wastedness of his choices. "I thought, on some level, that you knew I'd done it."

"You never told me you had," Jarrod said, his tone dead to emotion.

"No, and I never told you I hadn't. It's not something I'm proud of."

Tendons worked in Jarrod's jaw.

"You wanted to fight the charges with your high-priced lawyers, and I was willing to let you try."

Sophia sensed in Holden both a wildness that pressed close to the surface and a rage that burrowed bone deep.

"But here I am," Holden continued, lifting work-roughened hands to signal his surroundings. "I did it, and I'm paying for it. So you can stop trying to get me off, you can stop trying to collect evidence, you can stop hounding the agent that put me here. It's over. There's nothing you can do and there's nothing I can do and there's nothing she can do."

The creases around Jarrod's eyes deepened, making him look older. He retreated a few steps, leaned his shoulders against the bars of the opposing cage, and rested his head back.

A place inside Sophia ripped open, and tears stung her eyes. How was it that she could hurt this desperately for him? He'd been right in so many ways to fight for his brother. She'd give half her heart to have him care for her even a quarter as much. And yet, in the most fundamental way, he'd been wrong. To learn that in one moment and be told in the next that there was nothing he could do was the worst possible fate for a man like Jarrod.

"I've a question for you," Holden said.

She met his dangerous gaze and saw that he'd directed the question at her. Cautiously, she nodded.

"Why come after me now?" he asked. "I was a ten-year-old kid when I did that crime. The gang asked me to hold their horses and I did it because we needed the nickel they paid me per day." He made a scoffing sound low in his throat.

He'd held their horses? Sophia hadn't known. The warrant had been for aiding and abetting. She'd thought . . . Well, she thought he'd done more than hold their horses for a nickel a day. The tide of self-loathing that washed through her stole her ability to speak.

Jarrod had been right about her that night that he'd caught her in the woods. Whether or not she'd acknowledged it at the time, she'd punished Holden for the sins of his father. She swallowed thickly. The worst of it was that when she'd had Holden arrested, she'd taken grim *satisfaction* from it. From exacting vengeance on a man who'd once held horses for a nickel a day.

She could see now, the evidence was standing on the other side of the bars, that she'd held far too much hatred in her breast. Now look what her hatred had cost Jarrod and his brothers—something she could never repay.

"So why have me arrested now?" Holden asked. "That was fourteen years ago."

This hallway was her courtroom, and Holden her jury of one. "I . . ." Painfully, she cleared her throat. "Oliver Kinsworthy, my grandmother's attorney, told me that you confronted him at the train station in Austin a few months ago. Afterward he was afraid for me, warned me to alert him if you ever tried to contact me. His fears prompted me to research more of your past than I had before. It was then that I uncovered your outstanding warrant."

Holden said nothing.

She fervently wanted to stop there. There was more,

however, and if she wished to have any kind of respect for herself, she must say it aloud to him. Now. She made herself go on. "For all my grand notions of justice, I'm ashamed to say that the warrant wasn't the only reason I hunted you down. I hated your father for what he did to me, and so I hated you." She looked to Jarrod, then back to Holden. "All of you. I had you arrested, partially because I hoped your arrest might chase your father out of hiding. And partially"—she pulled in an aching breath—"out of revenge."

Holden regarded her through weary eyes decades wiser than his age.

"I stand here today very, *very* sorry," Sophia said.

Quiet descended, circling the three of them, twining them together. In the distance, Sophia could hear the *clang* of industry, the buzzing of a fly, and the guard at the end of the hall idly jangling the coins in his pocket.

"Jarrod," Holden said.

It was as if he was watching and hearing what was going on around him in a haze, Jarrod thought. His brain felt sluggish, uncomprehending. Despite all the money he'd worked so hard to accumulate, he couldn't protect Holden from this, which meant that the world as he'd known it for the past twenty years was gone.

"There is one thing you can do for me, if you're willing," Holden said.

Jarrod pushed away from the bars he'd been leaning against and buried his hands in his pockets. "Of course." His youngest brother had never asked a single thing of him. There was nothing Holden could request of him now that he'd refuse.

"I want you to help her discover the truth about our father and the stolen money."

To hell with our god damned father, he wanted to roar. All of this was ultimately his fault. Had Adam Stone been the father he should have been he'd have kept Holden out of trouble. Despite Jarrod's best efforts at raising his brothers, it appeared he'd failed at that.

"I think we've all lived under his shadow long enough," Holden said. He wrapped a hand around the steel bar before him. "I don't have much in here to call my own. I'd like, at least, my good name."

"A name is what you make it," Jarrod answered automatically.

"It's also what you inherit."

For years, all the brothers had gone to great lengths to act as if they didn't give a damn about their father or his abandonment, or the ugly suspicions that followed them all because of what Adam Stone was rumored to have done. But now, with everything bare between him and Holden, Jarrod could see on his brother's face that their father's guilt or innocence meant something to him. Something important.

"If it's what you want, I'll find him, and I'll find out what happened," Jarrod answered.

"It's what I want."

"Then I give you my word."

This is a very bad idea.

Sophia stood in the hotel hallway outside Jarrod's darkened door. She glanced nervously in both directions. The hour was so late that nothing and no one stirred. So late that she, herself, had been lying in her rented bed underneath crisply laundered sheets until just minutes ago. The bed had become a sort of hell during the hours she'd spent staring at the ceiling, tasting her own regret and bristling with awareness of Jarrod in the adjacent room.

He hadn't said a word on their carriage ride back to Huntsville from the prison. He hadn't joined her and the maids for dinner in the hotel restaurant. And though she'd waited hopefully in the drawing room downstairs after their meal, he hadn't appeared to talk with her. She'd allowed him to flog himself privately as long as she could possibly bear, but even she had limits. Silently, she'd slipped from her bed, donned the bodice and skirt she'd worn earlier, and padded into the hallway.

With an agitated movement, she pushed the long fall of her hair over her shoulder. Already, the tie she'd hastily fastened around it was coming loose. She lifted her fist to knock, paused. Flattened her palm to the wood of the door. Glanced at her own room and seriously considered running to it. To do what? Lie immobile the rest of the night, listening to the sound of his feet treading the floorboards and wishing she could say something to him, offer him some meager solace?

Before she could change her mind, she rapped softly on his door.

Silence.

Her eyes sank briefly closed. She knocked again.

"It's open." The words were spoken without inflection. Maybe a good sign. At least he hadn't snapped at her to leave him be.

She let herself in. Though the corridor had been dim, his room was far darker. A single lamp warred against the gloom, shedding a sphere of light over the bedside table and the sapphire blue blanket covering the bed. Jarrod . . . She had to squint to make him out. Jarrod stood at the half-opened window. Gauzy white curtains writhed in the winter wind that coasted though.

Sophia's skin pebbled, though whether from the cold or from the sight of the man she didn't know. Tentatively, she approached him, able to make out more details the closer she drew. He wore just his black trousers and a white shirt. The shirt hung untucked and unbuttoned, rolled up at the sleeves. His hair was tousled, his arms crossed, his feet bare. He was staring at her.

Abruptly she stopped. Now that she'd come, she'd not the slightest idea how to begin to help him, nor why on earth he might wish to let her. She groped for the right words—

"Come to gloat?" he asked.

The accusation stung like lemon dashed into a cut. "What would I have to gloat over?"

"You won." He presented her with his profile as he gazed out the window. "You were right about my brother."

"Do you . . ." She dared a few more steps toward him, coming to stand at the edge of his window. She gripped a handful of the curtain and struggled to read what was behind his eyes. She couldn't. "Do you truly think there was a winner today?"

He held his silence, and she wanted to scream. Surely he didn't see the world that way—everything a competition between adversaries. "I was correct in believing your brother to be guilty," she said haltingly. "But I was entirely wrong in pursuing him the way I did for the reasons I did. I've never in my life felt less like a winner."

He didn't react in any way.

She fisted her hand tighter in the silky cool drapery.

"I'm sure you'll never be able to forgive me for arresting your brother, and maybe you shouldn't. Perhaps I shouldn't forgive you, either, for imprisoning me in your house the way you did—"

His gaze sliced to her and the words died on her lips. There, finally, beneath his dark brows, behind green eyes, she could see emotion burning.

"Was it so terrible?" he asked in a menacing tone.

"Yes."

"Why do you say yes when you mean no?" He dropped his arms to his sides and moved toward her.

She retreated. He was spoiling for trouble tonight, angry and reckless. She'd thought to soothe . . . But no. She'd no business circling with a wolf who knew far better than she how to attack.

"Why do you seal your lips when you want to laugh?" He stalked her. "Why do you hold yourself away from people when you want so badly to let somebody see? What are you afraid of, Sophie?"

She came up against the door and scrambled for a hold on the knob. She'd come here to open him and his heart wide, not to have her own heart flayed open. "I don't know what you're talking about."

"Why do you say that, when you know too well what I'm talking about? Even now, you're readying to flee. You'd rather flee than face an ounce of truth about yourself."

He was far too close to being right. "You think you know me so well?" she asked scathingly.

"I know you better than you know yourself."

"Then I shall be pleased to unburden you of my predictable presence. When we reach Galveston tomorrow, I'll return to Blackhaw."

His chest hitched with the rise and fall of his breath. "You actually think, for one second," he snarled, "that I'm letting you go?"

Her heart thumped loudly in her ears.

She watched him cross to the washstand. For a long moment, he braced his hands against its sides and stared into the water pooled in the porcelain dish. Then he dipped his hands in and cupped water in his palms.

"You've no right to keep me where I don't wish to be."

He let the water fall from his hands into the bowl with a splash, then raked his wet fingers through his hair as he rounded on her. "Right? Right?" he growled. "You think I got where I am today by operating within my rights? I'd still be in the gutter if I had. I don't give a damn about what my rights are or aren't. You should know that by now."

"You've no *reason*, then, to punish me any longer."

"I've every reason."

"Name one!"

"One. I promised Holden I'd find our father, and you're not leaving until we do." He jerked open one side of his shirt.

Sophia's disbelieving gaze sank to his hands.

"Two. You arrested my brother out of vengeance, but I haven't finished having my vengeance on you yet." He ripped free the other side of his shirt and hurled it into the corner. "And three." He came to her, grabbed her hand, and placed it flush against the fly of his pants.

His hardness bulged there, unrelenting.

"Three, I think about you all the time." He was so close that his words rasped against the skin of her lips. He pushed her hand more forcefully against him, moved it up and down over the ridge of him. "I fantasize about you at night. When I'm with you I want to strip you naked, I want to suck you here"—his free hand slid over the point of a breast, then lower toward the juncture between her thighs—"and here."

She shoved him away. "How *dare* you try to intimidate me, to frighten me this way? Are you so desperate to take your anger out on someone? Or are you simply too fearful that I might actually glimpse a fragment of human emotion in you? God!" Needing to lash out at him, she balled her fist and socked him in the shoulder.

He absorbed the blow by taking a half step back.

She pursued, pushing at him again with the heels of her hands. "I'm so sick of you bullying me! Do you hear me?" Another shove. "Sick of it. Sick!"

He extended his hands to subdue her. She slapped them away, then clasped his face and kissed him with all the pent-up rage and heat that her body possessed.

Chapter 16

H e responded immediately, meeting her force with force, their kiss hungry and raw and rough. Yearning for something beyond her reach, Sophia strained into him, dug her fingers into his scalp, feasted ravenously from his mouth.

Jarrod's hands were between them, releasing the buttons down the front of her bodice. They weren't coming free fast enough, so breathlessly she helped him, her fingers fumbling and tripping on the buttons at the bottom.

Night air soared against her skin as Jarrod jerked apart the garment. Because she hadn't bothered with her chemise after divesting her nightgown, she was naked underneath. He pulled her flush against the warmth of his chest.

Sensation spilled from her breasts to the core of her,

pulling at her there. She arched against him once, then again, forcing her soft curves against the textured steel of his body.

He twisted her so that her back fit against the planes of his chest. Then he reached around her with one hand to cup her breast, and with the other he spanned her lower abdomen and pressed her backside against him.

Sophia fought for breath. Oh, the feelings. His lips dipped to her neck and shoulder, and she felt the bite of his teeth. Yes. She let her head fall back. The harshness of this gave glorious vent to her frustrations. She could feel his anger, too. Both of them, butting against each other, lost in needs that had no names.

He bunched a handful of her skirt in his hand. Then took up more and more of the fabric until the hem whisked over her knees, over her thighs. When he discovered she wore no drawers beneath, he groaned and thrust against her from behind.

She almost cried out. Her teeth sank into her swollen bottom lip.

He drew her the few steps backward to the side of his bed, then pulled her against him as he sat, positioning her on his lap. His knees came up beneath her naked ones, and then he spread his legs, opening hers as he did so.

Sophia gasped with anticipation.

His fingers caressed her breasts to aching tightness. While his other hand . . . *Oh, mercy.* His other hand smoothed up her quivering inner thigh to the curls between her legs. Ever so lightly he cupped her there. She writhed against his taut thighs, mindless with the feelings he was strumming from her, greedy in her desire for more.

Deftly, he parted her femininity and the breeze

washed over her most private, most heated place. Her back bowed, and she waited without breathing. He simply held her that way, opened.

He kissed the nape of her neck, lifted and massaged her breasts, but he didn't touch the tight bud between her legs that yearned for it. She shifted restlessly, begging him without words.

"Tell me you want it." His voice was sandpaper-rough against her ear.

She gave a helpless sound of distress.

Still, he wouldn't end her torment, wouldn't give her the pleasure she craved.

"Tell me," he said.

"Yes," she moaned.

His blunt middle finger dipped into her. He didn't go deep. Just lightly in and out, his finger slickened with her own desire. Then up his finger stroked, up, until the pad of it skated across—

Her whole body jerked with the intense shock of pleasure.

Rhythmically, he worked her with nothing but that one finger, circling, probing. The friction of it climbed within her—exquisite agony. Too exquisite. Too much. A frission of fear penetrated her thoughts, then built in tandem with her body's physical ecstasy. Even as she bucked against him, straining toward something she desperately wanted, she realized she was losing control.

She should stop it now. But her body was clenching, like the petals of a flower wrapping inward, gathering all their power for something that would explode them apart. Explode her. She pressed her breast into the hard palm of his hand, rode his hips, opened her thighs wider for him. She'd give in to the call of her instincts for once. She wanted this, God help her, she wanted to *weep* over how badly she wanted this.

Wanted what? Her frenzied brain asked. Him? How much of him? Wanted him to make love to her, plant a baby inside her? There was nothing substantial between them on which to build a relationship. Not enough trust. No promises. No future. Only passion, and tonight, anger.

He lifted her, and then her back was against the sapphire cover, her legs off the bed's edge, and him kneeling between them. No, he couldn't possibly. His face lowered. She pressed her knees together, too modest to contemplate. He moved them gently apart. He couldn't possibly—

He could. At the first touch of his lips against her there she nearly bolted off the bed. *Oh my. Oh my.* She tossed back her head and shut her eyes, consumed by sensation. She'd never imagined such a wicked thing existed. Never imagined feelings so glorious. *Oh my.*

He drew at her, teased, drew at her. Her body clenched tighter. Her hands fisted in the bedcovers, her head thrashed to the side. And still he didn't relent, and she prayed he wouldn't. Let it not end. Let it go on and on and on.

Her body's arousal leapt ahead of her ability to keep pace with it. Leapt again. She tried to grab for breath, to master it—couldn't. And then she was throbbing with a pleasure so overwhelming she cried out. It cascaded over her, rippling, rippling, rippling, until she was left lying slack on the bed, blinking in astonishment.

Have you ever been so spent afterward you could do

nothing but lie naked and unmoving? The question he'd once asked her came back to her now. She'd thought it boastful at the time. She'd been wrong.

What had just . . . happened to her? Maggie had told her about the kind of release a woman could achieve. She'd belittled Maggie's description as overly dramatic at the time. She'd been wrong about that, too.

She was aware of Jarrod standing, of him carefully straightening her skirts.

She pressed her hands to her cheeks and could smell the scent of his hair on her fingers. Her heart twisted with a pain that was tenderness. Could she have come to care about him so much that the mere scent of his hair filled her with affection? No. She couldn't have let herself feel that strongly about him. No.

She clasped closed her bodice with hands that bore his scent and met his hooded gaze. *Yes.* Yes, she could and did feel that strongly about him, she realized with a burgeoning sense of disaster.

The bed frame creaked when he planted a knee on the edge of the mattress. She swung her legs onto the bed and scooted over to allow him space. He stretched the length of his body alongside hers, then pulled the far side of the blanket up and over them, creating what felt to Sophia like a warm cocoon. It scared her, how good it was to lie close to him. To feel as if she belonged.

He propped his head in his hand and gazed down at her. With his other hand he reached out and smoothed a lock of hair to the side of her forehead.

"Jarrod, I . . ." How could she begin to account for what had just occurred between them?

"Do you have any idea how long I've been wanting to do that?" He picked up the softly curling end of another tendril of hair and rubbed it gently between his thumb and middle finger.

She smiled shyly. "A long time?"

"Seems like years."

"But you didn't . . . I mean . . ." She couldn't quite bring herself to talk of his own lack of release out loud.

"It was perfect," he murmured. "It was enough."

He could be so incredibly decent. Memories of all the other times he had been flitted through her mind. She turned onto her side toward him and nestled against the planes of his body, fitting her face against his shoulder. She could stay here forever, breathing him in.

He lifted her chin with his thumb and kissed her slow and gently, the force between them that had been a pounding storm minutes ago flowing now like a summer river. Sensual and languid and adoring. His fingers grazed the underside of her chin as he took his time with her.

The string of kisses traveled over the edge of her lips, to her cheek, to the corner of her eyelid, before he parted from her. "Stay with me," he said.

Had he asked her to dance on hot coals in that moment, she would have. "Stay?" she asked.

"Tonight and with me at my estate when we return. Help me find my father. Not because I'm forcing you but because you want to."

Emotion gathered in her throat. She did want to. But until this moment, she hadn't grasped how dearly she'd longed to be asked instead of ordered.

"Well?" he asked.

"Yes."

"You'll come back with me?"

"Yes."

A slow grin moved across his mouth. "Good." He eyed the path of his knuckle as he trailed it down her jaw, her throat, then all the way down the open seam between the two sides of her bodice.

She shivered. "What would you have done if I'd refused to come willingly?"

His gaze returned to her. "I'd have forced you, of course."

She laughed.

"I'm not ready to let you go yet."

Her amusement eased away. He'd said *yet*.

"As soon as we return, we'll start searching for my father. With you and me both working on it solely—"

She placed a finger over his lips. "Actually, I can't work on it solely just now." Touching him was a wonder. Hesitantly, brazenly, she coasted her finger over his cheek then circled his ear.

"Why?"

She tucked her hand against his chest. "Because I've another case I'm also committed to at the moment."

"The counterfeiting case."

She'd forgotten that he'd made her tell him of it the night he'd chased her down in the woods. "Yes. It's somewhat urgent."

"Why?"

"It just . . . is."

Quiet stretched. Guilt niggled at her for evading the truth. Still, she wasn't about to tell it to Jarrod, not only because she was ashamed of the taxes she'd been unable to pay, but because she'd never risk him thinking that she'd told him about Blackhaw because she wanted his charity. She'd rather lose Blackhaw then have him think that even for a second. No, she'd manage her own problems. As always. "I'll give every spare minute I have to finding your father." It was the most honest thing she could say.

"Do you plan to pursue your counterfeiter as Twilight's Ghost?" he asked.

"I do."

"Not without me."

She raised her brows.

"Have your forgotten what happened last time you left the house?" He stroked his thumb over the area of her lip that had split.

"I've been doing this job unescorted for years."

"And now you'll be doing it with an escort."

"Jarrod . . ."

"Look, you can work on your case all you want. It's just that I'll be working on it with you."

"And the search for your father?"

"I'll call in Clint and J. T. With more of us on it, we'll be able to find him faster."

She thought of all the hours she'd spent moving through the night, cold and alone. It would be like the heat of a fire after years of shivering to have him with her. In fact, it worried her how very much the idea tempted her. Once they located Adam Stone, Jarrod would go and once again she'd be left to walk through the deserted, midnight-dark alleys of her life without him.

"I refuse to let you risk yourself," Jarrod said. "If you were mine, I'd never allow you to do such dangerous work."

Allow her? A bone-deep melancholy overtook her. She dared reach for him one last time, let her hand cup his handsome cheek, her thumb rub beneath one of his eyes. Eyes that were wolfishly intense at the moment, ready to fight if need be to enforce his will. "I guess you needn't worry then," she said quietly, "as I'll never be yours."

Exhausted suddenly, she pushed to sitting. Once she'd fastened a few of the buttons of her bodice, she walked to the door.

She didn't dare look back at him for fear of the pining she'd experience. She opened the door, eased into the corridor, and leaned against it on the outside. Bereft.

I'm not ready to let you go yet. But he would be, one day. Regardless of whatever attraction he harbored toward her, she had no illusions. Jarrod Stone wasn't the kind of man who settled down with one woman. And she wasn't the kind of woman who relished being abandoned.

She'd been left once, standing outside an orphanage with nothing but a valise full of clothes and a heart full of unbearable pain. She'd not risk that again, not for any relationship, and especially not one as fated as hers was with Jarrod. He'd said himself just now that he'd never let her do her work if she were his. Even her job, he'd strip from her if given the chance. The one thing that offered her independence, purpose, and, therefore, protection. The one thing other than Blackhaw she would absolutely never part with.

They were doomed, she and Jarrod. It wasn't like she hadn't know it from the beginning. It was just that it hurt now, with a pain so vicious it stole her breath.

Behind the walls of Huntsville prison, Holden lay on his bunk, peering blindly into the darkness above him. All around he heard the snores and muffled grunts of deep sleep, yet he was starkly awake.

The woman Jarrod had brought with him had been one hell of a beauty, with those dark eyes and that porcelain skin. In a million years he'd never have guessed her to be Twilight's Ghost or imagined that she bore invisible scars inflicted by past pain. Her scars ran deep though, so deep that she still pursued his father after all this time. So deep, that she'd turned her sights on him.

God, I'm so sick of it. Twenty years, and the repercussions of what their father had done still haunted him. He hoped his brother killed their father when he found him. His only regret was that he wouldn't be there to pull the trigger himself.

He pushed a hand beneath his lumpy pillow. Restlessly, he canted his face to the side to stare without seeing at the moonlight that planed against the wall, illuminating the rough crisscross of mortar between bricks.

Memory nagged at him. He frowned, annoyed because it was the same feeling he'd been having for a couple of months. As if something was beneath the surface of his brain grasping toward consciousness, but never quite making it. The harder he tried to remember, the more it retreated behind the fog where most of early childhood had gone. Except that this had retreated even farther. Whatever this was lived behind an iron door, locked away as surely as he was locked away in this hellhole.

With a grunt of frustration, he screwed shut his eyes and tried to see it. It was about his mother, that much he knew. . . .

"Holden," she had said that night. "Get your coat."

"We're leaving?" he asked, looking up from the toy soldiers scattered across the table.

He watched her shake loose her thin hair, then wind it into a tight, new bun. She stared into the chipped mirror that hung near the door as she took pins from her mouth and stuck them in her hair. Her eyes met his in the glass. "We're going out for a few minutes."

Holden looked to his older brothers, who were lounging on the rug at the far side of the room. "I can stay here with them."

"No, Jarrod's not back from his activities yet."

Holden knew what that meant. His oldest brother was either working odd jobs or begging in order to bring home food.

"And Clint and J. T. are old enough to take care of themselves but not old enough to look after you proper. So go and fetch your coat, like I said."

Holden slid off the chair. When he reached the coatrack, he had to strain onto his tiptoes to lift his coat from it. He grimaced as he put it on and secured the buttons. Everybody in town knew Mrs. Martin had given his mother this coat when her Jed had outgrown it. Mother had let it out at the cuffs twice, and it was already too small for him again. More eagerly, he donned the felt hat he'd inherited from J. T. He liked his hat.

Mother gathered up her own coat, one of Jarrod's old ones. "Boys, we'll be back in a few minutes."

Clint and J. T. nodded like they had better things to do.

Outside it was real dark, and the sky was misting. Mother pushed her arms into her coat, then took his hand in her red one and led him along the road. Some women wore gloves. He'd seen them. But his mother never did, and her hands were always red from all the scrubbing she did.

She increased their pace, and he clamped his free

hand onto his hat to keep it from falling off. "Where we going?" he asked.

"To find your father. He was supposed to be home two hours ago." Her mouth went tight. She looked a little scared.

Worry shifted through him. He kept one eye on the road and one on her. He waited for her to look like she usually did, like things would be okay.

She coughed.

His worry deepened.

She coughed again, something she did often lately. It sounded as if she was coughing all the way from her stomach, and something was loose in there. If she got any skinnier or coughed any more, he was afraid she might die.

He tightened his short fingers around hers and looked at his feet. He wasn't the only one who thought so. He'd seen Jarrod's face when she coughed. Jarrod thought she might die, too.

She coughed so hard that her hand jerked in his.

"Where's Pa?" he asked, looking over his shoulder and wishing somebody was here other than just him in case she needed help. The street was empty. Nobody even moved behind windows. The only thing he saw was an old newspaper blowing down the street.

"Your father was going to meet with Mrs. Warren."

"Who's that?"

"The grand lady that lives at Blackhaw Estate."

"The one that's going to make us rich?"

Her eyebrows pinched together. "Maybe."

That's what Pa said, anyway. He said the lady at Blackhaw was going to make them rich soon. "So we going to the big house?"

"Yes."

They turned the corner, and he saw a dark turret in the distance.

"We're going to Blackhaw."

And then . . . And then nothing. The iron door clanged shut, cutting off the rest of the memory. Holden's eyes sprang open, and he saw the wall of his cell, felt the tension that gripped his body.

There was more, god damn it. More that was important. And he couldn't, for the life of him, remember what.

Chapter 17

"Are you sure you want to do this?" Sophia whispered to Jarrod two nights later.

He gazed at her where she stood, poised on the back step of what she'd told him was Galveston's foremost stationers, her lockpicking equipment in her hands.

"Of course I'm sure," he answered.

"Because, as of this moment you're still untainted by . . . less than savory acts such as this. There's still time to preserve your lily-white image."

"You think me untainted?" he asked, somewhat offended.

Her eyes glimmered with humor.

"I'll show you tainted," he grumbled. "In fact, I'm more than willing to pull you down"—he nodded toward the alley dirt—"and taint you right here and now." He was only half joking. He'd be more than happy to sate the hunger for her that prowled within him. Right here would be fine. He could pin her against the door, toss up her skirts, and enter her standing up. God knows he'd waited long enough.

She must have read his thoughts, because her tongue darted over her bottom lip. It made him crazy when she did things like that with her mouth.

"You wouldn't want to taint me in this outfit," she said, her voice slightly throaty.

"Wouldn't I?" He cocked an eyebrow.

Since he was accompanying her tonight on their first foray as Twilight's Ghosts, she'd ditched her man's costume in favor of the rags and soiled cap of a charwoman. Her hair was tucked up and her face smeared with dust and grime. Like he cared. No mud could mar the luster of her coffee-colored eyes, and no tattered clothing could erase his memory of the pale breasts, waist, hips, and buttocks underneath. Damn, but he wanted to take her.

She glanced down at her costume. "As it happens," she said with a smile, "this charwoman has morals." She turned her attention to working her instruments into the lock. "Could you hold this?" she asked, handing him a slim tool.

Obligingly, he took it. On the way here, she'd led him through the gloom faultlessly and fast, and now her slender hands wielded her instruments with expert precision. She was good at her job. If there were records inside this shop detailing an order for the large quantities and kinds of paper and ink needed for counterfeiting, Sophia would find them. Of that he had no doubt.

Still, it didn't sit well with him not to be the one in control of this situation. So far the most he'd done was follow behind her like some hulking, idiot bodyguard. Which, he reminded himself, was exactly what he was tonight.

He didn't like it. And he didn't like this damn fool clothing. Sophia had bid him dress this way because she wanted anyone who happened to spot them to assume them a poverty-stricken couple. He wore denim trousers that had thinned at the inner thighs and had holes in the knees. The trousers, as well as the faded flannel shirt and the dirt-stained Stetson belonged to one of his stable hands. The man had been hard-pressed to come up with such shoddy clothing. Regardless, that he'd managed to at all informed Jarrod he needed to pay the man more.

"Almost there," Sophia murmured. She extended her palm, and he placed the tool he'd been holding in it. "Just one more minute. . . ." Her beautiful lips pursed in concentration.

She'd wanted to make this foray last night, when they'd returned from their trip to Huntsville. But after her attack followed by two days of ceaseless travel, exhaustion had pulled at her shoulders and dulled her eyes. He'd insisted that her counterfeiting investigation could wait one night and sent her to bed. She'd slept today until noon.

Click. "There," she said, wiping her hands on her apron, then stashing her instruments. "It was rusty."

Jarrod followed close behind her as she entered the blackened building. Unease trickled through him as his gaze swept the murky back room. He absolutely *hated* the thought of her doing this kind of thing alone. Who the hell had hired her for this job, anyway, and in doing so allowed her to endanger herself?

She slid past furniture and supplies into the front

room of the shop. He had to squint, just to make her out. "It's damn dark," he said under his breath.

"Your eyes get used to it in time." She crouched behind a long rectangular shape that he guessed to be the sales counter and began sliding open drawers and compartments.

Jarrod stood in the doorway between the front and back rooms, primed for noises, searching the stretch of barren street visible beyond the front windows. "Find anything?" he asked.

"Not yet—" Hinges whined. "Oh . . . wait. Here we are." The scratch of a match sounded. The halo of a flame lit her chin and cheeks as she touched it to the wick of the candle she'd brought. She fished a holder from her skirt pocket, impaled the candle on it, and set both on the floor beside her. Nimbly leaning over the deep drawer she'd opened, she began flipping through its contents.

"Sales receipts?" he asked curtly.

She nodded.

He set his jaw and tried to gauge how much light her candle was putting off. Not much. It was a small flame, mostly concealed by the counter. Yet if someone with an observant eye walked past the storefront, they'd see it. The memory of watching her slapped by her attackers, watching her tumble unconscious to the ground, seared his thoughts.

"Here's something." She pulled a sheet from the stack and angled it toward her candle. "It's a large order. Though not large enough to create the magnitude of counterfeit bills our man has been passing."

"It's a start," he said. "Surely he wouldn't be so foolish as to order all his supplies from one merchant and induce suspicion."

Her gaze flicked to his. "That's exactly what I was thinking." She returned to her task. He saw determination in the set of her lips, stubbornness in the bend of her neck. The woman was tireless. She'd never given up on his father in all these years, and now she was hell-bent on finding her counterfeiter, too. She was a fighter, come one come all.

Affection seized his chest. At times like this, she could look so earnest. There were parts of her that seemed so true and yet other parts of her had deceived him with careless ease. She'd proven to him in the bluntest way imaginable that she couldn't be trusted, and *still* he was tempted to put his faith in her. He, who'd never been a man to be burned twice. He shook his head, irritated with himself and his inability to shrug her off. God knows he'd never had that trouble with women in the past. Now that it was actually important that he distance himself from her for his own sanity, he was realizing that Sophia LaRue had gotten under his skin.

He watched her copy the pertinent information from the receipt onto the paper she'd brought along.

He ground his bootheel into the floor and wished she'd hurry. He itched to take her out of here and back to his house and safety. This whole thing was ridiculous. He had a mind to pay Slocum's one good dollar for every fake one they'd ever received or would ever receive in order to end this case.

He could guess just how favorably she'd respond to that idea.

"That's all for this drawer," she said. The hinges again

protested as she slid it back into its space. "They must keep their older records elsewhere—"

Above them, floorboards creaked.

Sophia's attention jerked to Jarrod. They both listened as a man's footsteps moved heavily across the second-story floor. Damn it! They'd awoken the owner. Jarrod reached her in an instant, wrapped his hand around her upper arm, and propelled her toward the rear door. She reached back for her candle and snuffed it with her fingertips before pocketing it.

Muffled voices drifted from above. More movement.

Jarrod hurried her forward. In seconds, they were outside on the step. Sophia rushed to insert her equipment into the lock.

"Just leave it," he ordered, pulling her forward.

"No." She dug in her heels and shook off his arm. "Ghosts don't leave open doors."

His mind filling with curses, he glanced upward. The entrance to the second-story living quarters consisted of a wooden staircase that led to a platform suspended directly above them. Even as he watched, the upper door swung open and light spilled through the cracks between the boards.

Sophia bolted the lock, looked to him, and nodded. But before he could rush her down the alley, a man sauntered onto the platform above. His shadow obliterated sections of the lines of light, and his weight sent flurries of dust twirling down on them. "Who's there?" he asked.

Sophia clamped a hand over his lips. He peeled it free. She pressed her index finger to her own lips, her dire expression urging him to remain silent.

From above, the deadly sound of a gun being cocked echoed through the night.

That did it. Jarrod pulled free his own gun. He didn't want to hurt anyone for protecting his rightful property, but he was even less willing to let Sophia be injured.

"No," she mouthed to him, her eyes horrified.

"I'm coming down." The man stalked toward the mouth of the stairs.

Jarrod pushed Sophia toward the building's corner. She sprinted for it. He barreled after her, glancing over his shoulder as he ran. Just as he looked back, he saw the man stop halfway down the stairs and raise his gun, aiming at them over the banister.

"Faster," Jarrod yelled.

Sophia vanished around the corner just as an explosion rent the stillness. Jarrod hunched against the expected pain of a bullet plowing through his back. Instead, the bullet collided with the wall near his shoulder, pinging him with shards of brick.

He rounded the building's corner and ran down the narrow canyon of space between the stationer's and the adjacent structure. Sophia waited for him, silhouetted by the opening to the street. He motioned for her go on without him. The obstinate woman waited until he'd reached her, then ran just ahead of him. Quick as a cat, she led him across the street and down the mouth of another alleyway.

He looked back to see the man skid onto the road, then charge after them.

Sophia turned down another alley, then another. He could still hear the shop owner behind them, swearing and running. A few more turns into the maze of back streets and passageways, and the sounds of their pursuer grew fainter. Then fainter still, before disappearing altogether.

Jarrod stashed his gun and followed Sophia who continued at a swift pace. She guided him unerringly, never once hesitating, until finally, behind a building on the edge of town, she slowed. Her chest billowing, she leaned against the wooden edifice and watched him. He propped his shoulders against the wall next to her and fought to control his own breathing.

"I can't believe you almost shot that man," she said.

Annoyance flared inside him. "In case you failed to notice, he didn't appear to have a qualm about shooting us."

"No, but that doesn't make harming him right. He was innocent."

"What would you have had me do, stand there with my thumb up my ass while he shot you?"

At his language, a displeased frown stitched her brow. "No, I'd have had us escape by running just as we did."

"Our escape was damned close, Sophie. His bullet missed my shoulder by about an inch."

Her belligerent expression softened immediately. "I hadn't realized . . . Which shoulder?"

"This one." He hefted his right.

She went to it and gently brushed off the mist of mortar, then examined the cloth for holes. "Did any of the brick shards cut you?"

"No."

She kept inspecting the cloth anyway, just to be sure. Only when completely satisfied did she stroke her hand across his shoulder, sigh, and take a step back. "I think I'll have to leave you at home the next time."

"What?" he bellowed.

She scowled and pointed toward the slumbering building.

"What?" he asked, more softly, but equally as irate. "I'm not at fault for what happened back there."

"No, of course not. I just can't bear to have you on my conscience."

"Me on *your* conscience?" He couldn't damn believe her. "I'm telling you right now, you leave to work on this assignment without me while you're under my roof, and I'll bend you over my knee, pull up your skirts, and spank you."

Her eyes, with their amazing long curly lashes, rounded. "Th-that's not funny."

"No, it sure as hell isn't. I don't like this, Sophie. Any of it. I don't like you working as Twilight's Ghost."

She gazed at him for a long moment. "I never imagined you would," she said at last, a hint of resignation in her voice. "This may come as a surprise to you, Jarrod, but I haven't in the past and won't in the future make my life's choices based upon your preferences."

He set his jaw and glared. Back in Huntsville, he'd told her that if she were his, he'd never allow her to do such work. He'd meant it then. He meant it tenfold now. He wasn't the sort of man that could swallow his objections and stand mutely aside while she slipped from his bed to go catch criminals during the dead of night.

"Your property begins just there, over the second rise," she said coldly, motioning with her chin. "I guess we'd best get going."

"I guess we'd better."

They'd walked less than a few feet when he stilled her by taking hold of her arm. She turned to him, eyes wary.

"Did I make my feelings clear regarding you investigating this case on your own?" he asked. He wanted no ambiguity.

"Perfectly," she answered. Then she yanked her arm from his grasp and walked into the gathering heart of the night. It struck him as he watched her that the darkness knew her and that she knew the darkness. Too well. Inexplicably, the observation saddened him.

It made him want to give her light.

The next afternoon, Maggie and Sophia waited together on the covered front porch of Jarrod's house. They both wore full-length coats, gloves, and scarves to protect against a day that had dawned sunny and clear, but cold.

"This is ridiculous," Sophia grumbled. "There's absolutely no reason why we must greet Jarrod's brothers the instant they dismount their horses."

"I already told you," Maggie answered distractedly. She was searching the distance with such fervor that Sophia feared she'd suffer eye strain. "If I'm not the first woman they see upon arrival, then one of the maids that infest this place might catch their eye first." She straightened the hat she'd borrowed from Sophia's closet, a dark green one with a paler green bow at the back, then squinted. "I can't afford the competition."

"I've told you and told you, Maggie, you don't want these men."

"Yes, I do."

"They're probably insufferable, pigheaded"—she thought of Jarrod's threat to spank her—"*presumptuous* scoundrels just like their older brother."

"They're mischievous, is all." Maggie slid her a threatening look out of the corners of her eyes before returning her attention to the far end of the drive.

Sophia studied her friend, torn between laughing and

tearing out her hair. She'd sent for Maggie the night she'd returned from Huntsville. Since then, since learning that Jarrod's brothers would be coming to assist in the search for Adam Stone, Maggie had become Clint and J. T.'s staunchest supporter. She refused to hear a word against them, these two men whom she'd never so much as set eyes upon. In preparation for their arrival, she'd even moved into Jarrod's home as a guest. Jarrod had allowed it because Sophia had asked it of him. But now Sophia wondered whether she should have asked.

What if one of Jarrod's brothers hurt Maggie? Disappointed her? Men, as a rule, were too stupid to see past her friend's tallness and thinness to the golden beauty beneath. *Especially* handsome men. And if Jarrod and Holden were any indication, Sophia suspected both of these Stone brothers would be equally devastating to look at. "If Jarrod's brothers don't appreciate you, Maggie, it's their loss, their fault—"

"Oh!" Maggie grabbed her hand and squeezed hard. "Look."

At the far end of the drive, two men on horseback rounded the curve into view. Both rode with the graceful mastery of men who'd logged years in the saddle.

The dryness of the dirt beneath the pounding hooves of their mounts caused dust to churn high around them, making them look as if they were cantering straight out of the imaginary place where men of mystical proportions lived. Two rugged cowboys, their hats shading their faces, their coats mantling powerful shoulders. Twin coils of rope slapping their saddles. Gun belts ringing their waists. Heroes, both of them. Strapping, strong, chiseled, and brave. The answer to every girlish fantasy since the beginning of time.

Sophia felt Maggie go marble-still beside her. Caught up herself in an uncharacteristic bit of romanticism, Sophia tightly clasped her friend's hand.

"Oh my God," Maggie breathed as the men drew nearer. "I think I'm going to faint."

"Don't you dare. I'll be left standing here, holding your limp body in my arms. What kind of an impression will that make on them?"

"Maybe they like pliable women."

"I don't think so. In fact, I recall that Jarrod made a *point* of telling me the other day that all his brothers have an aversion to pliable women."

"Oh," Maggie said thinly, then swallowed.

In a wave of seething dust, Jarrod's brothers stopped ten yards away. Imagine, four magnificent men all the progeny of Adam Stone.

Both of Jarrod's brothers regarded them appreciatively, though the one with the blonder hair curling from beneath his Stetson did so with an unmistakably flirtatious gleam in his eye. He also had a brash grin—as if he saw something he liked and hadn't the slightest insecurity that they might not like what they saw in return.

Both men tipped their hats. "Ladies," the blonder one said.

"Gentlemen," Sophia replied. She stole a quick glance at Maggie, whose lips were pale. For the first time in memory, Maggie appeared to be at a loss for words.

"I'm J. T. Stone," the blonder one said, "and this is my brother Clint."

"Pleased to make your acquaintance." Clint dipped his chin.

"The pleasure is ours," Sophia responded politely.

"I'm Sophia LaRue and this is my dear friend Maggie May."

J. T. actually winked at her before both men slid their legs over their horses' backs and dismounted.

Sophia studied them as they set to work releasing the girth straps from their saddle rings. Clint was clean-shaven, with broader features than any of his brothers. With his hip-length brown-canvas coat, trail pants, and serious expression, he looked like what he was—a marshal who took laws and justice every bit as seriously as she did.

J. T., on the other hand, appeared far too fun-loving to do the grim work of a bounty hunter. His molded cheeks held the sandy stubble of a two-day-old beard. His beige duster swirled around boots that were worn at the heels as likely from dancing as from pounding sidewalks in search of criminals.

Neither man appeared to be as hardened or as forbidding as either Jarrod or Holden. Fleetingly, she wondered if that was only because they'd learned to mask it better.

Sophia shot another look at Maggie. This time her friend gave her a reassuring smile, then widened her eyes in an expression that said she was happier than a cat who'd fallen into a vat of cream.

Once they'd given over their reins to the stable hands, the Stone brothers climbed the steps. "So what brings you lovely ladies to Jarrod's house?" J. T. asked, slapping his hands together to clear them of travel grime. His charmer's grin made his long-lashed eyes sparkle. "Can't be his winning personality."

Sophia smiled. "No. We're here for the same reason you are, to assist in the search for Adam Stone."

"I see. Is one of you the heiress of Blackhaw?"

"I am," Sophia answered.

"Jarrod mentioned in his telegram that you'd be helping us."

She nodded. It seemed strange to hear him say it like that. To her way of thinking they were helping *her*, seeing as this particular search had belonged to her for close to twenty years. Not that she gave a fig. If Jarrod and his band of brothers wanted to stride in and take over the hunt, she was more than willing to let them. She could barely imagine what her life might be like—how light she might feel—without the black specter of Adam Stone's freedom hovering over her.

She moved her attention to Maggie, only to find her and Clint gazing at one another with grave interest.

"You doing all right there, darlin'?" J. T. asked Maggie, touching her elbow. "You were looking a little peaked when we rode up."

"When you rode up I was suffering from a powerful case of awe." A smile roved across Maggie's wide mouth. "Has anyone told either of you lately how outlandishly handsome you are?"

Clint regarded her with blank shock. J. T. chuckled richly. "Not lately enough and not often enough."

"Well you are. I swear, you and your brothers could start a carnival act and make buckets of money."

"What, like a freak show?" Clint asked, brows lifted.

"Rather like a 'Miracles of Nature' show. I'd be honored to offer my services as ticket taker for such an endeavor."

Sophia inconspicuously tugged Maggie toward the front door. She was relieved that Maggie had recovered from her bout of acute adoration in such fine form. She just didn't want her to overwhelm the brothers at their first meeting.

In the foyer, the men helped them divest their winter things, patiently handing items to the servants who waited in attendance.

Maggie pulled free the beaded hatpin she'd borrowed from Sophia. "Do you like my hat?" she asked Clint, her eyes a transparent window of affection and hope.

"Very much," he answered.

Sophia tugged off her second glove and handed it to J. T.

"I like your hat, too," Maggie responded.

"Thank you kindly." Somewhat self-consciously, Clint removed his hat and combed a hand through closely cropped brown hair that bore creases from his Stetson.

Footsteps rang in the hallway. Before she even looked, the flutter of anticipation in her breast informed her they belonged to Jarrod. Their eyes met with a bolt of awareness.

Oh, how awful. Jarrod stalked her thoughts whenever she was apart from him. Then when she saw him after a separation, it was always the same lately. This catastrophic lurch of emotion, just from *looking* at him. As always, he wore a beautifully tailored black suit, paired today with a charcoal gray vest.

Jarrod smiled with genuine warmth as he shook hands with his brothers. He was the kind of man who rarely if ever gave his love or trust. But once you'd earned it, she understood instinctively that he'd love and trust you forever.

"I see you've already met Mrs. LaRue and Miss May," Jarrod said to his brothers.

"We have." J. T. rested his hand on Sophia's lower back. "Mrs. LaRue was so kind as to make the introductions."

"Yes." Jarrod's gaze turned ominous as he very deliberately removed J. T.'s hand. "Mrs. LaRue is very kind that way. Shall we?" He placed his own muscular hand at her back and guided her down the hall.

"You're looking well," she murmured to him. "I trust you're no worse off for our little excursion last night."

"No, but I'm a damn sight better dressed." He eyed her darkly. "Listen, you take a liking to my brother, and I'll—"

"Spank me?" she asked, then blinked innocently.

He growled low in his throat. "When did you develop a sense of humor?"

"Since I've been forced to deal with you. It was that or go mad."

He grunted. "Spankings are fine, but there are other punishments I'd rather employ." His attention swept over her lips and throat down to her breasts.

The pulse in her neck fluttered wildly.

A servant held open the door to the dining room for them. The massive table within had been cleared of everything but two bulging files. A small-boned gentleman wearing a dapper suit and sporting a combed mustache stood at the far end, apparently waiting for them. Jarrod introduced him as Mr. Tucker from the Pinkerton National Detective Agency as they all settled into chairs near the head of the table. When Clint held Maggie's for her she responded with a meaningful, "Thank you *so* much."

The door to the dining room burst open and Sophia watched in surprise as Oliver rushed in. "Sorry I'm late," he said. "Had trouble getting away from the office." He made a beeline directly to Sophia, then cushioned her hand between his. "Good to see you, my girl."

She smiled up at him. "I hadn't realized you would be joining us."

"Yes, yes. Your host was so good as to inform me of today's meeting."

"I'm glad." Once she'd made the necessary introductions, Oliver lowered his bulk into a chair across the table with a grateful sigh.

"Go ahead," Jarrod instructed the detective.

Mr. Tucker looked around the circle, took a breath. "As you may be aware, Mr. Stone hired our agency some days ago to begin an inquiry into the whereabouts of Mr. Adam Stone and into the happenings surrounding his disappearance. Particularly, Mr. Stone expressed interest in determining whether Adam Stone stole the Warren family fortune."

Tension coiled within Sophia.

"We've yet to track down Adam Stone," he continued, "as Mr. Stone summoned me here while we were still in the process of gathering information. Mr. Stone has instructed me to share with you all that we've collected to this point." He steepled a hand atop one of the files before him. "This is the documentation we've been able to garner about the possible movements of Adam Stone over the past twenty years." He steepled his other hand on the other file. "At Mr. Stone's request we've also collected information on every person employed at Blackhaw Manor at the time of the robbery. This file contains those records."

Quiet swished about the gathering. Sophia stared at the files, wondering if she dared hope that the clue she needed—just that one clue—could possibly be waiting there for her to find.

"Let's get started," Jarrod said, rising to his feet and flipping open the cover of the nearest file.

"So what's really going on between you and Sophia LaRue?" J. T. asked Jarrod late that night. The three brothers were sitting together in the library, Jarrod staring into the steam from his coffee, the other two nursing whiskeys.

"Jarrod?" J. T. prompted.

Jarrod looked up, discovered them both watching him expectantly. "What was that?"

"Sophia LaRue," J. T. prompted. "Last we knew you suspected her of being the mistress of Twilight's Ghost."

Behind Jarrod's chair a log toppled in the hearth, crackling heartily and causing the firelight to stir. "I discovered that she's not and never was the Ghost's mistress."

"No?" J. T. asked.

"No." It was the truth. After their mother's death there had been times when the harsh realities of what he'd had to do to provide for them would have terrified his brothers. He'd lied to them then because it was kinder. He'd never done so since. He was coming close, though, by withholding information about Sophia.

He leaned into his chair, tasted his coffee. He'd revealed her identity to Holden because Holden deserved to know. But he hesitated to tell anyone else, even Clint and J. T., because her safety hinged on his silence. It was a responsibility he took seriously.

"Without the Ghost's mistress to lead you to him," Clint said, "how close are you to finding him?"

"It doesn't matter anymore."

Both brothers regarded him levelly.

"I went to see Holden earlier this week in Huntsville." Jarrod inhaled slowly, fully. "He told me he's guilty."

Clint frowned, creases etching into the skin around his lips.

J. T. stared at him for a few seconds, then knocked back the rest of his whiskey in one swallow.

"Did you know?" Jarrod asked J. T., who was closest in age to Holden and of them all the one who'd always understood their youngest brother best.

"No, but I suspected."

"God," Clint murmured. "He knew better, even back then, than to aid the Lucas gang."

"I thought so, too," Jarrod answered. "Apparently he held their horses for them for a nickel a day." Jarrod still hadn't accustomed himself to it, to having a brother behind bars that he couldn't help. "When I found out Holden had committed the crime I dropped my search for Twilight's Ghost. Can't very well pursue a man for being right."

Clint nodded.

"I took Sophia with me to see Holden. When he learned that she's been searching for our father all these years, he asked me to help her track him down. Said we'd all lived under his shadow long enough."

His brothers solemn gazes rose to meet his.

"Holden's never asked anything of me until now," Jarrod said. "I'm going to see it done."

"As will I," Clint said.

"And I," J.T. said.

Their words were superfluous. Even before he'd sent the telegram, he'd known they'd come. And he'd known they'd work beside him at all costs until the search was over, the job done, and their brother's only request met.

Holden socked the pillow, rolled onto his side on the cot and flung his bent arm over his eyes. Damn the memories. His lips parted with his breath. He could hear the rasp of his inhales and exhales against the relative stillness. He told himself not to think about it. To clear his head. To sleep. And still his thoughts slid to the night his mother had taken him to Blackhaw.

Even from far away, the house had looked scary to him, like it was haunted. His brothers had told him about dead people that didn't go away. Ghosts. Blackhaw was big and old and expensive. Probably lots of ghosts lived there. He slowed his steps, tugging on his mother's hand.

"Stop that," she said, pulling him forward.

"Mama—"

"Come along, Holden."

Grudgingly, he let her tow him alongside her. With his chin buried in the neck of his jacket, he stared at the house, watching it get closer, wishing he hadn't come. His chest started to tighten. When a dog barked, he jumped and wrapped his arms around his mother's legs. "Let's go back to the house."

"We will, just as soon as we find your father." Gently, she tried to pry his hands free.

He clung tighter. This was bad. He swallowed. They shouldn't have come out tonight. "Please."

She gave the top of his head a sensible kiss. "C'mon now, enough of that. Let's go." She unwrapped his arms from her legs and led him toward Blackhaw's tall fence with the sharp arrows on top.

There were no houses close to here and he wished there were.

"I think I . . ." Mother leaned forward, staring real hard. "I see him."

Relief washed through Holden. He looked up and saw him, too. It was dark on the other side of the fence, but he made out Pa's outline. He was carrying a big case, coming toward them down a pathway with pretty grass on either side. "Pa!" he called out.

His father glanced up. When he spotted them, he left the drive and cut across the grass in their direction. Mother and he hurried to the metal bars.

"What are you doing out at this hour?" Pa asked as he neared.

"Coming for you," Mother answered. "I was worried. You were supposed to be home two hours ago."

"I know. I—" he looked over his shoulder—"I had some important things to do, and time got away from me."

Mother nodded, her face tight. "I'm just glad to see you."

Pa looked down at him. "Hello, son."

"Hello, Pa." Holden smiled. His father was here. Nothing bad could happen to them now. No ghosts could kill them.

"Let's get you home," Pa said. He turned up the collar of his coat and started walking toward the gate.

They walked next to him on the other side of the bars.

Pa looked over his shoulder again. He started walking faster. "Perhaps we should hurry."

"All right," Holden said, and had tried his best to keep up.

Holden waited, patiently in the first seconds, then impatiently as the seconds ticked past and no more of the memory revealed itself. He squeezed his eyes shut. Why did he have this god-awful feeling that despite how fast he'd tried to walk, it hadn't been fast enough?

Chapter 18

Sophia yawned, then widened her eyes at the page before her in an effort to fight off sleep. Since the Stone brothers had arrived yesterday she'd spent nearly every waking minute poring over these Pinkerton documents. They hadn't yet yielded her the clue she sought, but she couldn't shake the feeling that if she just went over them one more time, she'd find the piece of evidence that would lead her to Adam Stone.

She yawned again, so wide that her cheek muscles stretched. Settling into the pale pink sofa and readjusting the tilt of her papers, she tried again to focus on print that kept blurring.

A knock echoed at her door.

"Who is it?" she called as she uncurled herself from sitting and moved across the room.

"A man bent on plundering your virtue."

Her senses rushed to humming life at the sound of Jarrod's voice. All vestiges of tiredness vanished. She stopped on her side of the door, rested a hand to her heart, and smiled with girlish delight. This giddiness that was so unlike her felt surprisingly wonderful. "Bent on plundering my virtue, eh? That doesn't sound very promising,"

"Let me in and find out."

She opened the door to find him leaning one shoulder against the frame. The topmost button of his crisp white shirt was undone, and he held a bottle of red wine in one hand. His smile moved like a trickle of warm honey across his lips. "In the mood for plundering I see."

"Only if it's me plundering your head with a blunt object."

He chuckled. "I miss the days when I held the keys to this room and could enter anytime I wanted."

"Really?" She pulled the key from the inside of the lock and spun it around her finger. "I don't."

He made a grab for it. She gave a short shriek and jerked it out of his reach, before safely pocketing it. As she grinned her victory up at him she thought how nice it was to tease and be teased. She'd never had that kind of ease with a man before. It was cozy somehow.

"Care for hors d'oeuvres?" Jarrod asked.

"Hors d'oeuvres?"

"It's almost suppertime, and I thought you could probably use an appetizer."

"Well . . ." She gestured toward the stack of papers on the sofa.

"You can't seriously prefer reading those documents to spending time with me."

He was absolutely right. "Fine. I'll spend time with you."

"In here," he said to someone in the hallway, motioning with his head.

A servant carried in a tray bearing salmon croquettes, cheese and crackers, plates, linen napkins, and glasses. He arranged the food on the squat table in front of the sofa before scurrying out. Jarrod kicked closed the door behind them.

"We could have had hors d'oeuvres with the others," Sophia said.

"I'm sick of sharing you with them."

Her blood surged. "Oh."

He assessed her, his eyes hot with a look so blatantly suggestive her own body seethed in answer. To protect herself, she put the table between them then sat on the edge of the pink sofa. Distractedly, she moved croquettes and cheese wedges onto her plate until she realized she'd filled the tiny circle of china to overflowing.

Jarrod pulled a chair as near to her as he could manage. He poured wine for them both and handed her her glass. The ridges cut into the stemmed crystal felt hard and cool to the touch. No doubt both the glass and the wine inside it were just as expensive as their owner.

Yes, she thought wryly as she set aside her glass, just what she needed. To impair faculties already dizzy at his nearness with wine. A wise choice indeed.

He leaned into his chair, one leg outstretched toward her.

She compulsively popped cheese into her mouth.

He smiled devilishly, as if he could read her distress and had the audacity to like it. He kicked up the hem of her skirt a bit, then slid his shoe beneath and rubbed its tip idly against her instep. "To you," he said as he raised his wine.

"Thank you," she whispered, knowing she should move her foot and finding herself incapable of doing so. She understood that at some point in the future she'd pay with pain for every smile, every kiss, every flirtatious word between them. And yet right now, in this, the only moment that counted, that payment seemed too distant to matter.

Jarrod sipped his wine.

"I've just been looking back over some of the information Pinkerton collected on your father," she said to fill the quiet. "I've thought and thought, but none of this provides me with a new avenue for investigation."

He resettled his shoulders even deeper into his chair. "My brothers think we should split up and speak personally with all the people who worked at Blackhaw at the time."

"I think your brothers are wasting their time even reading about those employees. I know who stole my grandmother's money."

"They . . ." His forehead furrowed.

She waited for him to finish his sentence.

He narrowed his eyes at the door, then at her bed, then at her. Slowly, he brought a hand in front of his face and flexed it, studying the play of muscles with some confusion.

"Is something wrong?" she asked.

"I . . ." He clamped his fingertips against the bridge of his nose.

"Jarrod?"

"My vision, it's blurry."

"Blurry?" Anxiety pierced her. She returned her plate to the table with a clatter.

"I'm sorry . . . I'm . . ." He shook his head. "Sleepy all of a sudden." He leaned forward to set his glass on the table. He'd almost reached it when he slumped. The base of the glass struck the edge of the table and cracked. Wine spilled onto the carpet as the crystal tumbled to the floor.

She lunged toward Jarrod, caught his shoulders, and pressed him back into his chair before he could fall.

"Sophia," he said hoarsely, searching for her.

"I'm here." What was the matter? Her heart sped, beating fearfully against her ribs.

He looked for her, yet couldn't seem to find her.

"I'm here," she said again, gripping his shoulders.

"Something's wrong," he slurred.

"Yes." She darted a look over her shoulder, ridiculously searching for someone to help. The empty room stared back. She shook him slightly. "Stay awake."

"Sophia?" Blindly, he reached for her.

She grabbed one of his hands, pressed it against her waist. "I'm here."

In the next instant, his head lolled onto the back of the chair, and the hand she held went limp.

"No," she breathed. "No." Terror leaping inside her, she tried to jostle him back to consciousness. Except for his erratic breath, he didn't respond.

She took her hands away, made sure he wasn't going to slide onto the floor without her support, then turned and ran. What if something happened to him? The panicked refrain repeated in her mind again and again, faster and faster.

As she flew past the library she spotted Clint and Maggie within, a pile of papers spread before them. Her gaze locked on Clint as she skidded to a halt. "It's your brother." Her voice sounded wild, even to her.

"My brother?"

"Jarrod. Something's wrong. He's unconscious."

His face paled as he pushed to his feet. "Where is he?"

"I'll show you." She led Clint and Maggie back to her room as quickly as she'd come. Jarrod remained exactly as she'd left him. The sight of him like that caused dread to ball in her stomach. It seemed heinous for a man of his power and strength to be lying so still.

Clint rushed to his brother and tried to rouse him. When that failed he went behind Jarrod's chair and hooked his forearms beneath his brother's arms. "Help me get him to the bed."

Both Sophia and Maggie hurried to assist. Clint cleared the pillows from the bed with a swipe, and they managed to lay Jarrod across the mattress.

"What happened?" Clint asked her as he released buttons on his brother's shirt.

"Jarrod brought food. He seemed fine when he came in, but shortly after we started eating he told me his vision was blurry. Moments later he said he was sleepy. His speech—his speech was slurred. Then he asked for me again and again and I answered him that I was here but he didn't seem able to see me."

"It sounds like poison." Clint moved across the room to stare down at the food and at the wine that was soaking into the carpet like blood.

Maggie came up beside Sophia and gripped her hand.

"Did you eat any of this?" Clint asked curtly.

"Yes."

"Did Jarrod?"

"No. But he did have some of the wine."

"And you didn't."

"No."

Clint lifted the bottle and sniffed its contents. "Did this come to you uncorked?"

Sophia tried to steady herself enough to think calmly, to remember. "I don't recall Jarrod uncorking it, so it must have."

"We need to get a doctor. Fast."

"I'll fetch him," Sophia answered. "I know where his office is."

"I can go," Maggie offered.

"No." She'd go insane if forced to stand here waiting and wringing her hands. "I . . . I need to do this for him." Without pausing to collect coat, hat, or gloves, Sophia fled the room and the sight of Jarrod's lifeless body. As she ran from the house to the stables, her heeled shoes pounded hard against the earth. The dusk's chilling wind whipped at her, flaying her worry higher.

When she reached the mouth of the stables, the one boy working within jumped to attention.

"I need my horse," she said breathlessly.

The boy caught the current of her desperation and worked at breakneck pace to saddle Duchess. Sophia snatched a bridle off a peg. Her fingers shook as she fastened the straps around Duchess's head.

"There," the boy said, taking hold of the reins so that she could mount up.

She hoisted herself into the sidesaddle.

"Wait." He grabbed a blanket from a nearby hay bale and handed it to her. "Here you are, ma'am."

She nodded her thanks and goaded Duchess forward.

The horse, seeming to sense her urgency, stretched her legs into a gallop. They charged along the drive then down the road that led to town. Sophia gave Duchess her head, allowing her to carry her so fast that the ground streaked by beneath her.

Jarrod needed her. He'd never needed her before, and if it was the last thing she did, she was going to bring the doctor to him in the shortest possible time. She prayed she wouldn't be too late.

"Faster," she whispered to Duchess as she leaned over the animal's back. She pulled the snapping blanket around her shoulders, taking what thin protection it provided. "Faster."

By the time the doctor turned his buggy onto Jarrod's property some forty minutes later, darkness had fallen. Sophia sat beside Doc Scoggins as tense and tight as a piano wire. Had she been able to speed their return to Jarrod by running behind the buggy and pushing, she'd have done so. It would have been better than sitting here with her hands clenched in her lap while her imagination tortured her with one horrifying scenario after another.

The instant they pulled up in front of Jarrod's brightly lit house, she jumped down from the vehicle. It took the doctor slightly longer to disembark, then gather his leather satchel. She furtively licked her lips and wished he'd hurry.

J. T. met them halfway up the stairs.

"How's Jarrod?" she asked him.

"Not good," he said, his expression grave.

Sophia wanted to wail. At least . . . at least "not good" meant he was still alive. She strove to console herself with that. "J. T. Stone, this is Dr. Scoggins." The doctor was a youngish man, soft-spoken with bookish spectacles and competent hands.

"What can you tell me about the patient's current condition?" the doctor asked, as J. T. led them into the house and along the central hallway.

"He's not regained consciousness and his breath is choppy," J. T. answered.

Dr. Scoggins frowned, nodded.

J. T. escorted them to Jarrod's bedroom, where they'd moved him in her absence. Clint and Maggie stepped away from the thronelike bed, presenting her with a view of Jarrod. Her emotions caught.

The doctor approached him and set aside his satchel. Silence descended as he pressed his thumb to Jarrod's wrist to measure his pulse.

Sophia stood numbly at the foot of the bed. This couldn't be real. She stared at Jarrod mutely—black hair tousled against the white of his pillows, uncompromising facial features, powerfully corded neck, muscled limbs. All of it too slack. Again, it struck her as fundamentally wrong for a man like him to be robbed of his strength.

"You told me, Mrs. LaRue, that he took just two or three sips of the wine?" the doctor asked.

"That's correct." She'd related everything she knew during their ride.

"And this occurred less than an hour ago."

"Yes."

"Ordinarily for a patient who's ingested a poisonous substance, I'd immediately prescribe water and ipecac. With someone who's unconscious, however"—his lips set in a thin line—"there's a danger of choking on the water, and ipecac is out of the question. Have you tried to rouse him?"

"Again and again," Clint answered.

"Well, perhaps if we administer water in very small amounts with a dropper." He moved to his bag and unbuckled the latch. "If someone would be so good as to fetch me some water."

Maggie rushed from the room.

The doctor positioned a clean cloth on the nightstand and set a dropper upon it before turning to the brothers. "I'll need to test the wine he drank in order to try to determine which poison was used. Only then can I administer the correct anecdote."

"I'll get the wine." J. T. strode out.

"Mrs. LaRue?" the doctor said.

Dazedly, she moved her gaze to him.

"If I may ask for your assistance." He motioned to the dropper. She approached, and he showed her how to position it within Jarrod's mouth so the fluid would dribble down the side of his throat. Maggie returned with a bowl full of water, and Sophia made her first attempt, cradling Jarrod's jaw with one hand, holding the dropper with the other. The unnatural coolness of his skin sent chills down her spine. *Oh, God, let him not die.*

"Good," the doctor said. "That's just fine. Nice and slow." He watched her as he shed his coat and rolled up his shirtsleeves. "Continue just as you are."

When J. T. returned the doctor asked for both brothers' help in testing the wine. All three left for the kitchen.

Maggie neared and softly rubbed Sophia's back.

Sophia had no lighthearted words or optimistic sentiments to voice. She simply kept filling the dropper, slowly trickling water down Jarrod's throat, waiting for him to swallow.

"I'll give you a little privacy," Maggie murmured.

Sophia was only vaguely aware of the door clicking closed.

Without anyone left to see, she let hot moisture slip from her eyes down her cheeks. When next she drew water into the dropper, she tenderly, almost desperately, brushed the fingers of her free hand along his forehead, around an eye, down his cheek. Tears ran under her jaw and into her collar.

This was her fault. Jarrod had never asked for this. The search for Adam Stone had been hers. Never, never his. If someone was out to hurt one of them, and someone clearly was, it should rightfully have been her. She'd committed to the risks of her job, she'd accepted the dangers. She was the one they'd warned not to continue. Her. Not Jarrod. This wasn't his fight. He hadn't wanted it. He was a businessman, for God's sake. All he'd ever truly cared about was freeing his brother.

She couldn't see, suddenly, the telltale rise and fall of his chest. Frantic, she bent an ear to his lips. Air flowed from his lungs. Jerky and shallow, but audible. As she slipped the dropper into his mouth, the prayers she'd learned in the orphanage rose unbidden to her lips and poured forth in a quiet, unbroken stream.

She prayed and prayed and prayed until her world and all the will she possessed narrowed to include nothing but Jarrod, the water, and her urgent petitions to God.

She'd lost track of time during this endless night. Rhythmically, she drew more liquid into the dropper, moved it to Jarrod's mouth. The doctor had come to her and told her that he'd been unable to determine which poison had been used. That was perhaps an hour ago. Perhaps four. He'd been too compassionate to tell her that Jarrod would probably die. He hadn't needed to say the words. She'd read apology and pity in his eyes.

She'd seen that look before, on the face of another doctor twenty years ago. He'd told her then to sit with her grandmother because the end was near, and he didn't think her grandmother would survive the night. Lord, she hadn't wanted to enter that room and sit with her grandmother. She'd been terrified to see her like that. To watch her die. But she'd made herself go in and she'd sat on the edge of her grandmother's bed and she'd held her hand. She'd done it because there was no one else to do it. And because maybe, if she stayed and held her hand tight enough, her grandmother wouldn't go away and abandon her.

Her heart wrung with pain, reminding her how excruciating it was to be left behind, alone.

She gazed at Jarrod, his handsome face lit by the somber light of the bedside lamp. She never should have let herself care for him. She'd been so wary these many years, so independent and self-sufficient. So careful not to give over her dreams into the hands of another. Then Jarrod had stalked into her life, and though she'd tried to hide, he'd not allowed her to. He'd ripped off her shields and forced her to ride on a fairy horse, and shown her stars, and challenged her to sail as fast as the wind. Anything, anything else she could have withstood. But she'd been helpless in the face of his pursuit to unlock the joy she'd buried so deep inside herself she'd forgotten where to find it.

Joy, indeed, she thought bitterly. Look where his efforts to help her had gotten him. He was lying prone and sick unto death. His vast sums of money and his enormous power couldn't help him now.

"Sophia, let me do that," J. T. said, walking up behind her.

They'd all been coming to her for hours, asking to take over this job. Shadows sitting in the room's chairs, drifting in and out of the room's space. The only constant shadow had been Maxine. Jarrod's dog had been guarding him from the edge of his bed for almost as long as Sophia had been tending him. She tried not to look at the retriever because the dog's sad, dark eyes broke her heart.

"No," she said quietly but firmly to J. T..

"Sophia, you can't go on this way. You need your rest."

"I have to stay a little longer."

"You've done enough already."

"No. I'm not finished yet." She couldn't explain to J. T. or even to herself what her heart believed to be true. That maybe . . . maybe if she kept administering tiny amounts of water to Jarrod, if she didn't leave his side, that he wouldn't die.

That belief hadn't saved her grandmother.

But it would save Jarrod, she stubbornly told herself. It had to. And so she'd stay.

Sophia roused groggily as she was lifted. Granite arms. A rich masculine scent. Jarrod. No. They passed into the hall and candlelight played over the planes and hollows of J. T.'s face.

Her senses groped for a hold on reality. She must have fallen asleep at Jarrod's side. A bolt of alarm followed. "I need to go back."

"I'm taking you to bed," J. T. answered without looking down at her.

"No, I promise I won't fall asleep again. I can go longer—"

"Shhh. Enough. You're exhausted, and I'm taking you to bed."

"He needs water. The antidote—"

"Clint's feeding it to him now. I'll feed it to him next."

"He'll be alone."

"We won't leave him alone for a second, I swear it."

He'll die without me there. The certainty swirled about her in a demon rush, like wind beating off vulture's wings.

J. T. laid her on her bed. As softness absorbed her, wakefulness drifted away, though she tried to grasp it back. This was terribly wrong. All wrong. He'd die without her there to keep him alive.

He'd die.

REBECCA WADE

292

She ran into the hallway, so
The house beyond gree
caused the tiny ha
ried chatter
di

Sophia cracked open her eyes. Gradually, the winter sunlight glimmering around the edges of her curtains swirled into focus. It was morning. . . .

Memories of the past night came back to her in a single, violent throb. She pushed herself to sitting. Her hair tumbled around her shoulders in disarray. With a downward glance she discovered that she was still wearing yesterday's wrinkled clothing. She slid her feet over the edge of the bed and her shoes peeked out at her from beneath her hem.

Jarrod. Oh my God, how long have I slept?

She swiveled the little gilt clock atop the bedside table toward her. Eleven o'clock. Eleven o'clock! Dismay rushed through her. So long! When she shouldn't have let herself fall asleep in the first place.

____ her with deathly quiet. It
____ emn quiet of a cathedral, and it
____ airs on her arms to lift. No maids scur-
____ corners, as they usually did. No friendly
____ or the sounds of clanging pots emanated from the
___ ection of the kitchen.

Her feet carried her fast, then faster toward Jarrod's bedroom, her panic mounting with each step. She saw no one. The house had been rendered barren, stripped of its life.

A sob climbed up her chest. *Jarrod.*

She pushed open his door, terrified to discover what waited within. Clint and J. T. were standing with the doctor near the bed. Maxine was still at her post, and Jarrod was still where she'd left him, eyes closed, unmoving. The tops of his bronzed shoulders were bare above the line of the sheet.

Sophia eased to a stop. Heart pounding in her chest like cannon fire, she looked to his brothers.

J. T. met her gaze . . . and smiled. *Smiled.*

A wild little hope twirled to life in her abdomen.

"He regained consciousness near dawn," J. T. said.

"He—he actually spoke?"

"Some. He was delirious, but the doctor said that was to be expected."

The flare of hope rose and expanded, heating every chilled, frightened place inside her. "And now?" she asked hoarsely.

"Now he's sleeping," Dr. Scoggins answered. His shirt looked as scrunched as her own clothing did, and red rimmed his eyes. Despite that, she could clearly read the pride in him, the deep satisfaction of a job well-done.

"Sleeping," she repeated, overwhelmed with a relief that was purest white, when everything for so many hours had been filthiest black. She should have known Jarrod would do battle against the poison and win. He was the most willful, hardheaded man she'd ever met.

"A good sound sleep," Dr. Scoggins commented. "He's strong, and his body fought it off. He's going to be fine."

She didn't have the right words to say. Through a mist of tears she brought up her hands, pressed them to her lips, her cheeks, then overlapped them above her heart. "Thank you, Doctor, for your work."

"You're welcome. Thank you for all you did."

"Yes," Clint said. "Thank you."

J. T. nodded his appreciation.

"It was nothing," she whispered as her gaze returned to Jarrod. Their gratitude made her feel like a fraud. If they knew that this was all her fault, they'd understand just how insignificant her efforts had been in the face of her responsibility. "What happens now?"

"We'll let him sleep as long as his body demands," the doctor answered. "Then I'll prescribe a round of treatments that will keep him in bed for two days. After that, he should be well on his way to recovery."

She smiled tremulously, then took her time memorizing Jarrod's face. The straight eyebrows that could lift with humor or lower with danger. The deep-set eyes. The muscled cheeks, burnished this morning with the beginnings of a beard. The hair as black as a raven's wing. All of it she collected in her memory, packing it lovingly there.

"You can come closer," J. T. said with a wry smile. He beckoned her forward.

"No," she said softly and took a step back. It was well past time that she retreat, not just from this room but from this house. After what had happened, she could no longer deceive herself about that. "Please excuse me," she murmured before letting herself out.

"Sophia," J. T. called from behind her when she was only a few yards down the hallway.

She turned. Clint was standing in the middle of the corridor, his hands in his pockets. J. T. leaned against the doorframe of Jarrod's room. Both stances were so like their older brother.

"Where are you going?" J. T. asked.

"I'm going home."

"Home?"

"I still live at Blackhaw, the home my grandmother left me."

J. T. nodded slowly, seeming to measure her. "I know Jarrod would be glad for you to stay here if you're willing."

"For as long as you like," Clint added.

"Of course," J. T. said, "there are no servants for the time being."

"I noticed that," she said.

"Until we figure out who did this—"

"Your father poisoned Jarrod. He's also the one that sent men to attack me in order to scare us off the search."

"That may be," J. T. said, "but whoever did this must have also had someone on the inside in order to have access to the wine. Until we know which servant that is, we don't want any of them lingering around."

Sophia nodded.

"Luckily, Clint here can clean some. And I'm not awful with a spatula." J. T.'s eyes twinkled persuasively. "It won't be the style to which you're accustomed . . ."

"It's not that," she assured them. "It's kind of you to invite me to stay, but the truth is that I've been away from home too long already."

"What about the case?" Clint asked. "We haven't found my father yet."

A piece, a vital piece inside herself, stilled. Cleared. So it had come to this. The road she'd been doggedly following for twenty years ended here in this hallway. She swallowed. "I'm finished pursuing your father. I'm just . . . just finished. People have been hurt."

J. T. regarded her with frank surprise. "You mean this thing with Jarrod?"

"Yes." That, and other hurts. What she'd done to Holden. What she'd done to herself by gathering bitterness and hatred into her breast and using it as fuel. At some point even a dream of justice could cost too much. It was time to end it.

"I'll tell you right now," J. T. said, "Jarrod's not going to give up the search."

"Neither are we," Clint said.

"Jarrod promised Holden we'd find our father," J. T. explained simply.

"I know," she said. "I wish you the very best of luck. I've told Jarrod as much as I can remember about the circumstances surrounding your father's disappearance, and my friend Oliver Kinsworthy knows as much about the information we've gathered over the past years as I do. I'm sure he'll be willing to assist you."

"But not you," Clint said.

"No," she said quietly. "Not me."

The sound of clicking nails heralded Maxine's arrival in the doorway. The dog sat next to J. T.'s leg and looked up at Sophia with her sweet, graying face.

"Where did Jarrod get Maxine?" Sophia asked. For days, she'd wondered about that and about the poverty Jarrod had eluded to after their mother's death.

"It was years ago," J. T. answered. "How old is Maxine?" he asked Clint.

"At least ten."

"I'd say twelve. Anyway, she belonged to one of Jarrod's employees up until the time Jarrod saw him kick her, then beat her with a rope. Jarrod fired the man and kept the dog."

Sophia had figured as much. She thought of all the hours Maxine had spent last night, keeping watch over a man most of the country believed to be a ruthless brute. A brute who had rescued his dog and raised his brothers. "There's one other thing," she said to Clint and J. T., taking time to select her words. "Just how . . . difficult were the years after your mother's death?"

The grimness of their faces in response to her question told her almost everything she needed to know.

"However poor a person can be and still survive," Clint answered, "that's how poor we were for a while. Looking back, I still don't know how Jarrod managed to scrape together enough food for us every month."

"But he always did," J. T. said. "Somehow, he always did."

Understanding wove among the three of them. Blackhaw's demise had absolved no one. It had marked them all in the years that followed. "Thank you for telling me," she said. Then after a few moments, "I—" She gestured in the direction of her room. "I'd best be going."

The brothers dipped their chins.

Sophia turned and walked away from them, from Jarrod.

This was a glorious day, she told herself, a day of thanksgiving. Jarrod was going to be well. If she felt a twinge of heartsickness to be leaving him and his home, to be pulling out of the chase, to be saying good-bye to his brothers, she refused to credit it. Jarrod was going to be well. That's all that mattered.

Back inside her room, she divested every one of the garments she wore, garments Jarrod had allowed her to borrow. After rustling through the dresser in the closet, she came up with the stockings, drawers, and chemise she'd worn here that first day. Jammed at the rear of the clothing rack she located her bodice and skirt, her brown coat, and her cream-colored hat.

The cut of her own clothing, the coarse scratch of its fabric, felt strange to her. She eyed herself in the mirror as she hastily bound her hair. These were her clothes, the only clothes of her own she'd worn in days, and yet they didn't quite seem to fit. In fact, on the whole, she didn't look like herself to herself anymore. Her hair simply refused to be brushed back as tightly as it used to into a bun. A rosy hue burnished her cheeks, and her eyes shone. During her stay, something fundamental had changed.

Relentlessly, she fought to force her hair back into the old ways. Then she collected the bag containing her few toiletries and scooped up her parasol. She revolved in a circle, taking in the room Jarrod had created especially for her.

Everything in it belonged to him. The artwork, the books, the linens. She glanced down at herself, double-checking the items she wore and carried. She didn't want to take a single thing from Jarrod—not a scarf, not a slip of paper, not a hatpin.

Gathering close her pride, she walked through the door without looking back. *This is a happy day*, she told herself. *Jarrod is well.*

Mrs. Dewberry scurried into Sophia's bedroom at Blackhaw ahead of both Sophia and Maggie. In a flurry over their unexpected return, the housekeeper bustled around the room, throwing open the curtains, cracking the windows, and keeping up a steady stream of chatter Sophia barely heard.

How peculiar to be back in this place where nothing had changed, when so much had changed in her heart. Distractedly, she pulled loose the hat bow beneath her chin.

". . . nice pot of tea. How does that sound?"

Sophia turned to find Mrs. Dewberry watching her expectantly.

"That sounds heavenly. Thank you."

"And some peach pie, I think." Mrs. Dewberry wiped her hands on her skirts and smiled. "It just so happens that I soaked the peaches last night and made up a lovely pie for Mr. Dewberry and me just this morning. Still warm, it is. I'll be back in two shakes of a lamb's tail." When she closed the door behind her, the ensuing quiet contrasted sharply with the conversation that had enlivened the space moments before.

Sophia took a deep breath and lofted her hat onto the white quilt. "It seems as if I ought to have something to unpack after such a long absence."

"I know, that is odd, how thoroughly he provided for you while you were gone," Maggie said, flopping into the room's single armchair. "How is it to be back?"

"Lovely," Sophia answered automatically. This was

home. Sweet, unmistakable home, and there was a kind of comfort in that that even Jarrod Stone with all his thousands could never purchase or bottle. So why did she still feel, despite every logical lecture she'd given herself today, so inexplicably melancholy?

Because in coming home she'd left Jarrod behind.

A desolate kind of hollowness dragged at her, making her wish she could crawl into bed, pull the covers over her head, and simply . . . huddle.

Instead, she went to the nearest window and rested her hand on the side casing. Beneath the pads of her fingers she could feel the ridges that had formed when cracking paint had been coated over with fresh. The texture spoke to her of the years and the heritage of her house. Lovingly, possessively, she rubbed her thumb over the surface.

She'd been raised in this bedroom, had looked out these very panes of glass as a small child. The same drive still snaked its way through rolling orchards. The same black-iron gate with spires on top still stood sentinel at the property's rim. The same squirrels dashed across the same ground and climbed the same trees. Blackhaw. The word—the *place*—resonated with her and always would.

Always, she thought with a pang. She no longer had the promise of always. Blackhaw's auction was set for just four days from now, and unless she could find her counterfeiter, collect her reward, and pay the taxes in time, then Blackhaw would no longer belong to her. Her *always* would end in exactly four days, and she, Maggie, and the Dewberrys would be cast out onto the street. Mother above, how could the time have slipped away from her so quickly? "Do you realize we only have a few days left to solve the counterfeiting case?" she asked, turning toward Maggie.

"Unfortunately, yes," Maggie answered.

"So." Sophia shook out her arms and hands, then restlessly began to pace. "Let's go over what we know about our counterfeiter."

Maggie nodded and propped her long, narrow feet on the footrest with the needlepoint cushion of roses. "Well," she began, ticking off one finger, "on your escapes from Jarrod's house you combed the warehouse district."

"Yes, where I saw and heard exactly nothing of import."

"At your request I examined ownership and leasing information on the warehouses." Maggie ticked off another finger. "All appear to be legitimate businesses."

"Or seemingly legitimate."

"I think investigating the warehouses further is a waste of our time, Sophia. The counterfeiting presses could be anywhere. They could feasibly be hidden in someone's backyard shack."

"Right." She paced onward, toying with the fingernails of one hand.

"Which brings us to your ill-fated trip with Jarrod to the stationer's." Maggie ticked off a third finger. "According to the receipt you found there, a Mr. Silas Clarke had ordered a conspicuously large amount of paper and ink."

"Correct." Though she'd heard it all before, hearing it aloud again helped her order it in her mind.

"Our Mr. Clarke is an artist who sells his work off a cart on Main Street. He works in various mediums, including paper and ink. Soft-spoken man. Tall. Nice enough. Especially good at watercolors."

"And potentially as talented at designing counterfeiting plates. Go on."

"He moved here three years ago. No family relations. Clean criminal record, so far as the Agency knows."

"What else?"

"Nothing else."

Sophia perched on the edge of her bed. None of this was stirring her instincts, none of it was heating her blood the way an investigation usually did when she was getting close. She groaned and kneaded her temples. "Mr. Clarke is still our best lead. Do we know where he lives?"

"No, but we could follow him home from his cart."

"I'll do that today. Could be he's living above his means. Maybe he has a costly carriage sitting out back. Or an expensive hobby we ought to know about."

"Could be." Maggie didn't appear very hopeful. "What'll you do if you spot something suspicious?"

"Search his house."

"And if that yields nothing?"

"Then I'll need an opportunity to find out more about him another way, possibly speak with someone who knows him."

Maggie sat up straighter in her chair. "The masquerade ball."

Sophia combed her memory. "The ones the McBrayers give every year?"

"Yes." Maggie's eyes lit with anticipation. "It's night after next. You received an invitation just like always, and I accepted for you, hoping you'd be home by then.

There'll be roomfuls of people to talk with. No telling what you might uncover about Mr. Clarke through a little careful conversation. Not to mention, you'd get to don a costume."

Donning a costume held very little appeal for her. Still, the plan had merit—

A knock sounded at the door. "Tea, darlings," Mrs. Dewberry called. She proudly carried in two plates bearing enormous wedges of peach pie. The smell of fresh pastry crust wafted in her wake. Mr. Dewberry followed his wife, bearing a tray set for tea.

Maggie sprang from her chair and hurried to pull into position the little walnut table that ordinarily clung to the armchair's side. Their housekeeper clucked as she arranged everything, then straightened, and knitted her dimpled hands together. "Do you need anything else?"

"This is more than enough already," Sophia answered. "Thank you."

"Of course, dear. So glad to have you home." She reached out and patted her cheek. "Dinner's at six," she reminded them as she herded her husband out.

Sophia pulled her dressing-table stool up to the table and started pouring tea, while Maggie rummaged around in the bottom of the armoire. "Here it is," Maggie finally declared. She held aloft a bottle of claret as she rose to her feet. "Not a moment too soon."

"None for me," Sophia said as Maggie returned to the armchair.

"Oh, *please*, Sophia." Maggie rolled her eyes and poured a healthy swig into Sophia's cup. "Ordinarily I let you get away with that, but today is not a day for drinking plain tea." She sloshed a generous amount into her own cup, then added three cubes of sugar. On her pie,

Maggie drizzled a river of cream. Paused, made her river into a delta, then set about stirring her tea. Stirring and stirring and stirring, her gaze straying to the windows.

"You miss Clint," Sophia guessed.

Maggie's attention snapped to her. "Not as much as you're pretending not to miss Jarrod."

Because Sophia couldn't stand to think about Jarrod, much less talk about him, she poured her own cream delta atop her slice of pie and took a bite.

"Yes, I miss Clint," Maggie said after a time, "more, even, than claret and pie can cure, which is terribly depressing." She forked off some pie, swallowed. "Have you ever seen such a gorgeous man?"

"He's very handsome."

"He's divine. Wonderful to look at and quiet. I always did like that combination in a man. There's just something about those quiet ones. Still waters and all that." She pointed her fork at Sophia. "I bet he's very well endowed."

"Maggie!"

"Well, I bet he is."

"Margaret Elizabeth May," Sophia whispered.

"I bet Jarrod is too, for that matter."

Sophia could only gape.

"Of course, you probably already know that." Maggie winked roguishly and chewed another bite of pie.

"We were talking about you and Clint."

"I wish there was a me and Clint. But honestly, Sophia." Her expression cleared of humor. "Let's be frank. It's not as if a woman like me is ever going to win a man like Clint Stone. I may as well slam a rock against my head hoping to make water."

"That's not true, Maggie—"

"Yes it is, you're just too kind to say so." She regarded Sophia soberly. "I don't have any illusions about myself. However, you and Jarrod, now that has real possibility."

"It does not!"

"Why? You certainly can't say he's too ugly or that he won't be able to provide for you."

"No." Sophia frowned. "For one, he loathes my career and has told me he'd never let me do it if I were his."

Maggie's eyes widened. "He actually said if you were 'his'?"

"Yes, and secondly, I think he's far more interested in bedding me than in anything more respectable. Then there's his personality. . . ."

"What's wrong with his personality?"

"Wrong? He's rude, bossy—"

"Protective, smart, assertive, and he makes you laugh. He actually has the power to *make you laugh*, Sophia. He gave you a ride on Cinderella's horse and named a star after you."

She stared at her friend, lips parted to say something when there was nothing to say. Maggie was right, of course. It was silly to keep protesting it aloud. For all his faults, Jarrod had given her the ability to glimpse herself as she might have been without the wounds. For a few hours, he'd allowed her to be free. She heaved a sigh. "I found out today that he adopted his dog after he saw her being beaten."

"And there's the way he looks at you every time you enter a room," Maggie said persuasively.

"He provided for his brothers after their mother died. There was a time when they barely had enough money to eat."

"Oh, and one of the maids told me yesterday that when a member of the kitchen staff found herself in a delicate condition—unmarried, you understand—that he bought her a home to live in, gave her money, and said he'd welcome her to keep working for him."

"Really?" Sophia considered impaling herself on a bedpost and ending her misery.

"And even when you were supposed to be his prisoner he kept giving you all those clothes, the gifts. And he's forever asking after your comfort and worrying over your safety."

"So we've established that he's wonderful." Sophia took in a breath that burned. "It's still hopeless, Maggie."

"Hopeless? I'd sell my eyeballs to receive that kind of treatment from Clint."

She regarded her friend through a haze of pain. It *was* hopeless. To talk about it as if it weren't was not only bitterly painful but a pointless waste of time. She and Jarrod had no future. If only that knowledge had hindered her foolish heart from falling for him so completely.

"All right," Maggie murmured, taking pity on her. "We can try to drown our sorrows in claret if you'd rather not talk." She lifted her cup and waited until Sophia lifted hers. They clinked them together. "Bottoms up."

Sophia took a deep sip, then cradled her cup in both hands. The white walls of this room had always seemed so clean and crisp. Now they looked a bit austere. The green rug patterned with a simple floral motif of flowers and vines was scarred with worn patches she'd never noticed before, and her dressing table bore pockmarks and scratches even Mrs. Dewberry's polishing couldn't erase.

Had she become so spoiled during her time at Jarrod's that her own room looked shabby to her now? No. If Jarrod were here, the surroundings would seem as rich as if they'd been drenched in gold. It wasn't its humbleness that stole the light and life from this place. It was his absence.

Oh, dear. She was in very deep trouble. Hastily, she took another drink.

The great room of the McBrayers' home sparkled not only with sconces of candles and neckfuls of jewels, but with the costumes of their ball guests. Sophia resettled her own spidery mask and smiled politely at a matador and his wife, Venus, as they passed.

Since she'd returned to Blackhaw a day and a half ago, Mrs. Dewberry had outdone herself concocting her black widow disguise. Sophia's ebony mask and her long ebony gloves sparkled with lines of black beads that crisscrossed to form a glittering web. Her onyx princess dress was slim and sleek, cut in one line from shoulder to hem. Around her waist she wore a chain that dipped into a vee in front to suspend a fat fake ruby.

She'd had aspirations of confining her hair into a bun that would call to mind the shape of a spider's body. But since the long dark strands continued to misbehave, she'd settled on arranging it in loose curls at the nape of her neck.

"What a lovely costume, my dear."

Sophia looked up to see Joseph Stewart, an old acquaintance, approach with a smile.

"Why thank you. I very much admire the cleverness of yours." Though one of the largest and most important importers of coffee and liquor in town, he was dressed tonight in the garb of a pirate. A graying, distinguished pirate.

They exchanged pleasantries, then companionably watched the spectacle swirling about them.

"Oh, would you look at this," Sophia said, as if just noticing the painting that hung on the wall nearby. She'd steered dozens of people through this same conversation tonight, though she'd yet to receive a single decent clue about Silas Clarke. Couple that with the fact that his modest apartments had also failed to yield her a clue, and she was beginning to feel desperate.

"Why, yes, indeed." He turned to study the piece, lacing his fingers together behind his back.

"The expression of the young girl is beautifully rendered," Sophia said after a moment. "Don't you agree?"

"Quite, quite."

"I've been considering the acquisition of a few new pieces, myself."

"Have you?" He regarded her with kindly interest.

"Yes and I'm particularly interested in the work of local artists. I thought it might be nice to fill my parlor with Galveston's finest talent."

"What a capital idea."

"Is there anyone here locally you'd recommend?"

"Ah . . . There's Will Doogan, of course," Mr. Stewart said. "Horatio Clem is good. So's Matthew Sage."

"What of Silas Clarke?" she asked smoothly. "Have you had an opportunity to familiarize yourself with his work?"

"Silas Clarke," he repeated, seeming to test the name. "No, no I don't believe I have."

Her hopes dropped.

"Wait." He tilted his head to the side. "Is he the one. . . . I'd stay clear of him, my dear. I heard a rumor about him once."

"A rumor?" For the first time in days, her intuition stirred.

"I hate to spread the things."

"As do I." She waited, knowing he'd be unable to resist sharing the tidbit.

He leaned closer. "I was told some time ago that Mr. Clarke was brought to trial to face criminal charges."

Her pulse picked up speed. "What charges?"

"I'm not sure."

"Was he found guilty?"

"I don't believe so."

That would explain why Maggie had told her he had a clean record. In the eyes of the government, he did.

"If I remember correctly," Mr. Stewart said, "he hired himself capable representation."

"I don't recall hearing a thing about this."

"No, you wouldn't have as the trial wasn't held in Galveston."

"You don't say."

"Again if I remember correctly"—he chuckled wryly and tapped his forehead—"it was held in . . . oh . . . I can't recall. One of the small towns near here along the coast."

She gave an interested murmur. "I shall heed your advice and concentrate my efforts on artists other than Silas Clarke."

"Might be wise."

Inwardly, her thoughts churned. She and Maggie

could split up tomorrow and travel to the courthouses of the surrounding towns.

Vaguely, she noticed that the hum of conversation in the great room had waned. Perhaps if they rifled though enough court records, they could discover just what Mr. Clarke had been accused of. Probably too much to hope that it had been counterfeiting.

The small talk dropped in volume another notch. Brow furrowed, Sophia glanced toward the room's open double doors.

Across the yards her gaze collided with the turbulent green eyes of Jarrod Stone. The stare that bore into her with razor-sharp intensity informed her that the time had come to reckon with the devil.

Chapter 20

*O*h, *my Lord*. Every nerve in Sophia's body sprang to life.

He stood framed in the open doorway, as uncompromising and unapologetic as ever. He'd not bothered with a costume. He wore a plain black tailcoat and narrow black trousers with a band of braid covering the outer seam. His white shirt was snowy against his olive skin, his bow tie impeccably tied. He looked like what he was, a surpassingly handsome, ridiculously rich, absurdly powerful oil baron.

His gaze never veering from her, he strode into the room as if he owned it and cut a path directly toward her. The crowd parted to make way for him, their stares avid.

"Is that Jarrod Stone?" Mr. Stewart asked under his breath.

She couldn't talk, couldn't look away from the spell of Jarrod's eyes, so she simply nodded.

This wasn't the same man she'd left a few days before. That man had been desperately sick. This man betrayed no trace of vulnerability. His gait, his posture, and his expression projected only strength, anger, and a determination so fierce it could have caused cold water to churn into a boil.

Amid a buzz of whispers, he came to a halt before her, towering over her. "Mrs. LaRue."

A shiver coursed down her back, arms, hips. "Mr. Stone."

"May I have a word with you in private?"

It would be better if she didn't. Private meetings with him had almost always ended in disaster for her, both in circumstance and emotion. She shot a look at Mr. Stewart, hoping for assistance from his quarter. Unfortunately, he was too busy studying Jarrod with awed respect to come to her aid.

"Certainly," Sophia said, succeeding at keeping her voice even. "If you'll excuse us, Mr. Stewart—"

Jarrod took her by the arm and dragged her away before she could finish her sentence. His grip, firm and commanding, scalded her sensitized flesh. She glanced down at it and thought how much she'd always liked his hands, the blunt fingers, the veins beneath the skin, the masterful way they touched her.

What an absurd thing to think at a moment like this. She was right this minute on her way to meet her doom, and she was rhapsodizing over Jarrod's hands.

He escorted her from the great room into the hallway and through the first door on their right before releasing her. Sophia walked more deeply into the sitting room, which was furnished in luxurious shades of bronze and ivory. The firelight from the hearth reflected off the silver coffee urn and matching cups that had been assembled on a round table for the guests.

Jarrod shut the door, leaving Sophia brutally aware of their isolation. She turned to face him by slow degrees.

"Take off the mask," he ordered. "I want to see your face."

Her fingers shaking the tiniest bit, she reached up and removed the mask.

He kept his distance, choosing to stand just inside the door. In a gesture now familiar to her, he pushed his coat back so that he could bury his hands in his pockets. "You look surprised to see me."

"I am."

"Did you really think, for one minute, Sophia, that I would simply let you leave?"

"I didn't honestly know what you'd do." She didn't say that she'd lain in bed the last two nights praying that he *wouldn't* let her leave, that he'd do just this, that he'd come for her. Praying those things, yearning for him like a lovestruck girl after a man impossibly out of her reach. Despite everything she knew to be true about their relationship. Despite a maturity she'd cultivated at great cost since the day her grandmother and her illusions had died.

"I lost my mind when I awoke to find you gone." He gazed at her harshly, without trying to soften his statement. "I'd have found you sooner if it hadn't been for that damned doctor you hired."

"He's an excellent doctor—"

"He's an idiot. He got it in his fool head I needed to stay in bed for two days to recover."

"Well, you certainly did—"

"Then my brothers got in their heads that they'd been called upon by God to enforce his orders." He appeared genuinely annoyed, a tower of brooding masculine frustration. "I could have taken one of my brothers, but not both."

"Jarrod," she chided. "Don't be ridiculous—"

"Ridiculous?" He neared, brows lowering into a vee. "I'm ridiculous? What about you? You didn't even take Duchess with you."

"Duchess? No, of course not."

"Why?"

A giggling pair of girls entered the room. Jarrod swung on them, stopping them dead in their tracks. They gasped then skittered backward, tripping over their skirts in their haste to exit.

His attention sliced back to her. "Why didn't you take the horse?"

"Because she doesn't belong to me."

"Like hell she doesn't." His voice rose in volume. "We both know I gave her to you, so what's stopping you? Just try to tell me you don't want her." He motioned angrily toward himself. "Just try to tell me that to my face."

She wouldn't lie to him, so she set her teeth tightly together.

"All of it is yours." He flung out a hand. "The clothes, the art, the jewelry, the damned furs. All of it."

"I can't accept any of those things from you."

"Women always accept the things I buy for them."

He'd compare her to others? "Not this woman."

"Why not you?"

"Because I don't . . ." She'd been about to say because she didn't need his gifts, but that wasn't quite true.

In order to save Blackhaw, she desperately needed the money his gifts could have brought her. "Because I'm independent," she answered in a tone that dared him to find fault. "I take pride in that independence."

"So . . . what, Sophie? You're going to go through your whole life never taking anything from people who want to give to you?"

"And you? Are you going to go through your whole life trying to buy people's loyalty with possessions?"

She drew herself up and matched him glare for glare. By God, if he insisted on doing battle with her, it's a battle he'd get.

On a growl, he stalked away. He went to the fireplace and leaned a hand on the mantel while he stared into the licking flames. Sophia studied the lines of his profile, shoulder, back. He was difficult, confrontational, offensive, and, thank the heavens, he was also gloriously, blissfully *alive*.

Only now, with the physical proof of his strength before her in stunning detail, did she feel able to admit just how terrified she had been that he might die. She could live the rest of her life alone, she'd learned to cope with a solitary existence over the years. But she didn't think she could survive another night like the one she'd endured when he'd lain on death's threshold.

"My brothers told me what you did," he said. "How you rode for the doctor. How you fed me medicine." Their gazes locked. "Thank you."

All the concerns that forever clamored inside of her melted in a silken stream, leaving room for tenderness to come. And come it did, shaking and shuddering.

Because she could see he was waiting for her to accept his thanks, she managed a nod.

"I hate like hell that you had to nurse me." He pushed away from the mantel, though he made no move to come closer. "But I can't be sorry that I was the one who was poisoned and not you."

She wanted to clamp her hands on his cheeks and kiss him. She wanted to curl her fingers into the crisp fabric of his shirt, then tear it off of him. "Did you discover who poisoned the wine?"

"No, but I think we have to assume it was the same person that organized the ambush against you."

"I agree."

He crossed his arms. Her fingertips moved restively over the beading on her spider mask.

"My brothers tell me you've given up your pursuit of my father," he said. "I told them I didn't believe it."

Someone opened the parlor door.

"Out!" Jarrod bellowed.

The door shut rapidly.

"So?" he asked her.

She considered her words carefully. "I could live with the damage my vengeance was doing me on the inside. I understood, when I was attacked, that the risk was worthwhile. But when you were hurt . . ." She licked her lips. "That was unacceptable. The next time someone could be killed."

"Some bastard is out there trying to bully us, and you're going to let him win?" Clearly, Jarrod Stone was not a man who allowed anyone either to bully him or to win against him. Not for many, many years.

"That's exactly what I'm going to do. Revenge isn't worth the risk—"

"What about justice?

"Not even justice is worth the risk. I can't be responsible should harm befall you, or Maggie, or your brothers."

Silence stirred between them.

"I'll find my father, you know." He said the words with such fate-challenging confidence that she doubted whether there was any power on earth that could stop him.

"I hope you do."

"I'll find him for Holden, and I'll find him for you."

She got lost in his eyes, the endless green of them.

"It's the only present I can give you that you might accept." He moved toward her. "Stubborn woman." With a mere flick of his gaze, down and up the length of her body, the air between them turned hot. Pulsing. Heavy with intentions.

"Do you know what I want to do to you right now?" he asked when he was just inches away.

Her own words to Maggie came back to her. *He loathes my career.* She sidestepped, trying to put space between them.

He closed the gap immediately. "I want to strip you naked."

He's far more interested in bedding me than in anything more respectable. She turned from him.

He was there. "I want to lay you on that sofa," he nodded to it, "and spread your legs."

His personality. She veered toward the door, frantic.

He cut off her retreat. "I want to run my hands over your bare skin."

With a mewl of distress that sounded more like a moan of desire, she turned from him, then turned again, until they were engaged in a fated dance, and the room was swirling. He was everywhere she looked. Inescapable. Whispering words that were licking, licking over her.

Her shoulder came up against the wall next to the door, halting her retreat. He trapped her there, leaning his body into hers. He tilted his head to feast on her neck. "I want to enter you. I want to feel how tight you are."

She writhed against him and at her body's telltale movement, he lifted his head.

Muscles strung taut, chest heaving, she met his gaze. In the next instant, he claimed her mouth. Distantly, she was aware of his hands spearing into her hair, clasping her head. She kissed him madly, curling her fingers into his shirt as she had wanted to do moments before. The contact was rough, deep, and starved.

Voices grew nearer and the door opened.

Jarrod dislodged a hand from her hair to slam it closed.

They stared at each other, breath ragged. "That's it," he said, and swung her into his arms. "I'm taking you home."

Her senses reeling, she watched the room blur past. He exited by way of the door at the rear of the parlor, which emptied them into a servants' hallway that ran along the far side of the house.

A trio of maids, trays of empty plates and glasses in their hands, halted in astonishment when they saw them.

"She twisted her ankle," Jarrod said by way of gruff explanation.

The three continued to gawk. Jarrod carried her down the hallway, his powerful strides eating the distance. A frigid curtain of air whisked over them when he kicked open a side door and descended the steps beyond.

Purposefully, he strode toward his carriage, which waited at the front of the house. Gleaming black, just like it had been the night it had waited on Blackhaw's drive, the first night she'd met him. *Satan's chariot,* she'd thought then.

Oh, Mother above. She fisted the collar of his dinner jacket more tightly in her hand. If he was Satan, then she wanted to burn.

Jarrod's driver rushed from his perch to open the door for them. Inside, Jarrod deposited her on the velvet seat, then took the one opposite her. "To Blackhaw," he instructed the driver. The man nodded and hurried to close them in.

Assailed by sudden awkwardness, Sophia righted herself on the seat. The fake ruby around her waist shook as she smoothed her ebony skirts into place. She didn't dare meet his eyes, and yet she knew if she didn't, he'd take it as a sign of weakness. The carriage wheels crunched over brick as they rocked into motion.

She dragged her gaze to his. The kisses they'd just shared hung between them as obvious as the darkness that planed across the hard lines of his cheek and jaw. "You're taking me to Blackhaw?" she asked.

"Yes. It's closer." He reached up and rapped his fist against the ceiling of the vehicle. Immediately, the carriage picked up speed.

She resisted the urge to fuss with her skirts again. What were his intentions, exactly, when they reached Blackhaw? If he dropped her off there, she'd never calm her body from this fever pitch he'd churned it to—

"I'm going to take you to your room, and I'm going to make love to you," he said bluntly. "If you don't want me to, you'd best speak now."

Her mouth went completely dry.

"It's past time we settled this thing between us." He scrutinized her. "Don't you agree?"

She, who never risked anything of her heart, looked him dead in the eye and heard herself say, "I do." And she did, violently, want this. She was sick to death of worrying, of protecting, of fearing a thousand demons. Tonight she wanted more for herself. She wanted to live.

The carriage came to an abrupt stop. Jarrod was outside in a flash, holding the door for her. Slightly unsteady on her feet, she lifted her skirts to step down— He hoisted her in his arms again.

Blackhaw's face rose before her, and then they were through the massive front doorway. His shoes rapped the floor as he stalked toward the staircase.

Mrs. Dewberry rushed out from the door leading to the kitchen.

"She twisted her ankle," Jarrod barked.

The housekeeper's hands flew to cover her heart.

"It's all right," Sophia had time to say to the woman, before Mrs. Dewberry was jerked out of sight.

Jarrod mounted the steps, taking her upward. Upward. His fingers found her hairpins and pulled them free. They went pinging down the stairs. Her hair tumbled from its restraints.

He gained the second story and set her on her feet in front of her door. Before she could so much as get her balance, he was kissing her. She banded her arms around his neck, kissing him back, listening to the growl that mounted in his throat. He walked her backward, grasping at the back of her dress. She felt as much as heard fabric rip. Buttons rained against the floor, rolled. He pushed her up against her doorway. Oh—his tongue. He was laying fierce claim to her with it, possessing everything she had and demanding more.

Blindly, she groped for and found the door handle. When she turned it, they rolled inside. He slammed it shut.

She could drown in these kisses, feed off them for days. More impatient yanking on the back of her bodice. More fabric giving way.

Moon and starlight poured into the room through uncurtained windows, coating the furnishings with ethereal light. That's how this felt. Ethereal. This couldn't be happening and yet she pined for it to be true.

Jarrod's knuckles rasped against her lower back as he freed the last of the buttons, then stripped both her gown and her chemise to her waist.

For a breathless moment, he didn't touch her. Air, still faintly warmed from the fire that smoldered in the hearth, looped around her breasts and curved across her nipples.

When at last he grazed the back of his hand across a breast, her body jerked at the splintering contact. It was already too much, this roar of sensation. He kissed her again, his mouth moving in chorus with the hand upon her breast.

Pressure mounted on the inside of her, toward him, summoned by his touch. It was glorious to feel without thinking. To need and so to take. With a soft cry of impatience, she ripped at his jacket, stripping it from him in the way he'd stripped her. Before she could drop the garment to the ground, he was reaching for the fabric at her waist. He pulled everything, including her drawers, down her legs with a single tug. Then he wedged her shoes from her feet and tossed them aside.

The ruby's chain nipped her skin, cold as the heart of

the gem that nestled just above the vee of her legs. She reached around to unfasten—

"Leave it," he said as he straightened. He lifted her immediately against him, and she spread her legs, wrapping them around his hips. Shocks of pleasure quaked upward from between her legs, where her sensitive folds rubbed against the cloth of his trousers and the ridge beneath.

He set her on the edge of her bed. She kept her ankles locked behind him as he tore off his bow tie and shirt. Her hands extended, reaching out greedily to flatten against his chest. He knelt, his mouth hungrily covering an aching nipple as he ripped open the placket of his trousers.

Her body's cravings were driving her forward, but so were longings held in check for years. Piling one on top the other. Some unformed, some piercing, some old, some she'd never known. She longed for a man, for a husband. To be loved. To be made love to, awoken, stirred, touched intimately like this. Exactly like this, she thought, as she caught sight of his dark head bent to her breast. She longed for *him*.

His mouth lifted to hers, and her eyes sank closed as she lost herself to another drugging kiss.

His fingers found her, down low. Opening, delving inside. She began to move and breathe in time to his motion there. Desire hammered through her and she widened her knees, asking for more. He took his hand from her, used it to guide himself to her opening. She felt the tip of his manhood against her.

She was slick for him where he was rubbing against her, throbbing with emptiness. She pulled away just enough to look at him and found him watching her, reading her face.

She loved him in that moment. Adored everything about him. Found in him a piece of her soul that she'd been looking for, ever looking for, and missing.

"Relax for me," he murmured, his voice whiskey-rough.

She eased her tensed muscles, felt herself open against the hardness of him. He nudged inside, and she moaned. He withdrew, and she squirmed. In and out, just an inch each time. The coil inside of her compressed. Her greedy senses screamed for more, deeper.

His expression grew taut with a concentration that looked like pain. In an inch. Out.

Her breath panted shallowly. Heat misted across her chest, raced in unfurling waves up her body to her face, down her limbs.

Finally, she couldn't bear it anymore. Using her ankles, she pulled his hips toward her. He came forward slowly, gauging her eyes, devouring her with his gaze. Again she pulled him toward her, and this time, with a groan, he answered her by thrusting full inside.

A scream tore from her lips, mostly at the fulfillment of it, partly at the hurt. His powerful body stilled.

"Don't stop," she whispered.

His hands snaked underneath to cup her naked buttocks. He held her steady while he stroked in and out of her, slowly but fully. The pain dissipated in the face of the spiraling, seeking feel of him within her—a part of her. The coil compressed tighter, tighter. She threaded her fingers into the hair at the nape of his neck, and they looked into each other's eyes as he entered her even more deeply. Then faster. The ruby thrummed against her belly, beating in time to their rhythm.

She couldn't think for the blazing intimacy of it. The

surrender was glorious. No masks. *No masks.* Just an honesty that made her want to weep. The physical pleasure escalated so quickly she couldn't regulate it—couldn't control—didn't want to. She could only ride it higher.

Jarrod entered her more thoroughly every time, compressing the coil tighter and tighter. She strained into the feeling, mindless, reaching—and then the coil sprang, and pleasure infused her body in a burst that looked like a shower of white sparks. Her woman's center convulsed with ecstasy around Jarrod.

"Oh," she murmured. This time had been even better than the time before because he'd been within her. "Jarrod." She embraced him to her, chest to chest. His bare skin was warm against her own, slicked with moisture as hers was.

Her moon-brushed world tilted as he laid her back, resting her full across the coolness of white cotton. The ruby fell to the side, its chain leaving a gleaming trail across her waist. Languid and drunk with awe, she studied him as he divested his trousers.

Magnificent in his nakedness, he grazed his chest across the tips of her breasts, then held himself above her with his elbows sinking into the bed on either side of her head. She opened for him and he slid inside her in one sure motion. The friction was different for her this time. Almost a pleasure too sharp to take at first, then . . . then *oh*. She lifted her hands to his face and clasped his cheeks. Their mouths joined, and he kissed her while he made love to her.

Passion rolled over her like the undersides of waves. She was deep underwater, warm water, feeling, feeling. Within her, she felt him grow harder, bigger. She accepted him, asked silently for more, for it all. His breath beat against her lips.

He thrust again and again. She felt her body beginning to slip over the cusp. She tried to hold back just until— He inhaled sharply through his teeth. She clasped him against her and let herself go, both of them trembling with the force of their joining, with the shattering release of it, with the magnitude of what they'd created together here tonight.

He held a portion of his weight off her with his elbows and a knee, but he didn't separate from her, and she didn't want him to. Her sanity drifted back in strips as misty as a cloud. He was kissing her shoulder, she knew that. Kissing it softly, lightly. Let her never forget this, not a minute, not a second of it.

When he moved onto his side facing her, she sighed her disappointment.

A grin curled his lips.

She smiled, too, wonderingly. Unable to get her fill of touching him, she ran her fingertips through the hair above his ear.

"You steal my breath," he whispered.

From nowhere, tears of joy stung her eyes.

"You're the most beautiful thing I've ever seen," he said.

"That's something, coming from you." She rifled the hair at his temple again, though she really wanted to knot her hand in it and never let go. "You've seen so many beautiful things."

"None of them were worth half as much as you."

She stilled. She wanted to take that as a promise. Hungered to read the world into his words. Maybe there was hope for them. Maybe he loved her and would want to marry her. Maybe in the same way that she'd made the mistake of hating too much she'd made the mistake of hoping too little. They understood each other, Jarrod and she, on a fundamental level she'd not fully grasped until now. Their hearts at their most basic recognized one another through the eyes of two people who'd scraped and fought and survived.

He moved away.

"Don't go," she whispered, fear leaping within her.

"I'm not leaving you." He kissed her, then lifted her and repositioned her gently so that he could pull the linens down the bed. That done, he climbed in beside her and covered them both with the blankets. Her head fit just beneath his chin, her chest to his chest and her thighs and calves intertwined with his.

She could hear his heartbeat. Steady and sure. She edged even nearer to him and closed her eyes.

I'm not leaving you, he'd said. She hoped he'd meant forever because tonight she'd done more than live. She'd found heaven.

Disgusted with his inability to sleep, Holden threw aside his prison-issue blanket and swung his legs to the floor. Sitting on the edge of his cot, he rested his elbows on his knees and clasped his head in his hands. The floor below him was thick with grit. Even in the darkness, he could make out the dustballs and dirt that the wind sent lapping over his bare toes.

He screwed shut his eyes and squeezed the sides of his head, wishing he could squeeze out the circle of memories that kept playing out in his mind's eye. It was like being forced to sit in the audience and watch himself trapped in the same terrible play over and over and over.

Worse, for this play aborted before the end, leaving him staring with ever-growing frustration at a blank stage.

He groaned as the performance resumed yet again.

"Let's get you home," Pa had said that night. He turned up the collar of his coat and started toward the gates.

He and mother walked next to him on the other side of the fence.

Pa looked over his shoulder again. Then he started walking faster. "Perhaps we should hurry."

"Okay," Holden said, trying his best to keep up. He glanced through the fence toward the big house, to the place where his father kept looking.

A figure on horseback galloped from the shadows.

Feeling sick, he tried to warn his mother. But all that came out was, "M . . . M . . ." Urgently, he tugged on her hand and pointed.

She saw what he saw and stopped. "Adam."

Pa turned and saw him too. The ball in his neck bobbed. "You two stay here," he said. "I'll run to the gate and let myself out."

"Adam—"

But he was already gone. His jacket spread out behind him like wings as he sprinted along the wall toward the gate. The thick case he carried banged against his leg.

The man on the horse charged down the drive. So fast the horse's hooves sounded like the beating of a drum. Pa might not have time to get out before the ghost got him. "Mama," Holden whimpered.

She drew him away from the fence, beneath the shelter of a tree that had no leaves. He pressed his back against the front of her skirts, and she stacked her hands on his chest, clasping him to her protectively.

Pa had nearly reached the gate. The man galloped toward him on his big horse. *Hurry, Pa.* But just before Pa reached the latch that held together the gate's door, the man on the horse cut in front of him, then came to a stop, blocking Pa from the exit.

Holden's chest hitched. Would the man hurt Pa? His brothers called him a baby when he cried, so he bit his lip and tried to be quiet as tears blurred his eyes.

When the stranger dropped to the ground, Pa retreated.

"She gave you the money, didn't she?" the man asked. "She just told me that she gave you the money."

"That's right."

"Give it over." The man stretched out his hand to Pa.

Pa shook his head and took another step back. He clutched the case with both hands.

"Give it over," the stranger said. It was almost a yell.

"Give it to him," Holden whispered. Why wouldn't Pa just give the man what he wanted? It was only money. Tears slipped down his cheeks.

Pa stood his ground. "I will not. This is Mrs. Warren's money to do with as she pleases. She's entrusted it to me on behalf of our factory as you well know."

"Goddamned factory," the stranger swore. "It's going to fail, and I refuse to stand aside and watch her squander away any more money."

"I believe we can succeed—"

Before Pa could finish talking, the stranger pulled a gun from inside his jacket. Pa froze.

"My God," Mother breathed. She drew him farther back beneath the branches of the tree and tried to turn his face to the side.

But he could still see through the break in her fingers.

"It's finished, Adam," the man said in a calm, scary voice. "Hand the money over."

"Hand it over," Holden sobbed. Why wouldn't he give the man what he wanted? He hated his father, wanted to pound his fists against him.

Pa hesitated, then lunged toward the man.

Holden ripped his face away from the restraint of his mother's hand.

Pa shoved the stranger's arm then punched him in the face. The man stumbled to the side, but came back fast. He hit Pa in the chin, then pushed Pa. Pa gained his balance and rounded on the man, barreled toward him—

Boom. Light flashed from the end of the gun.

Mother's whole body lurched. "No," she gasped.

Pa's chest caved in before he fell backward onto the ground. The man moved to stand over him, looking down.

Pa couldn't really be shot. No, no, no, no. He'd get up and hurt the man. He'd come home with them tonight and eat the food Mother had set aside for him. He'd promised to take him fishing.

But Pa didn't get up. He rolled onto his side, then his back, his knees drawn up toward his middle.

Shocked too senseless to cry and too horrified to move, Holden felt his mother start to shake uncontrollably. Pa moved like a snake with its head cut off. Slower, then slower.

"Pa!" Holden screamed.

"Hush." Mother tried to cover his mouth with her hand.

He fought her off. "Pa!" He couldn't be shot. He'd promised to take him fishing.

The man with the gun looked in their direction.

"Pa," Holden begged. "Pa."

The stranger came toward them.

Mother grabbed his hand and tried to pull him away but he couldn't move. He could only watch the man with the gun as the man broke into a run. Coming closer.

With a wail Mother shoved him behind her and shielded him with her body. Her hands clawed into his shoulders to keep him in place.

Beyond her coat, he saw the man stop on the other side of the fence. He scowled at them, his gun held low in one hand. "Who are you?" he demanded.

"A-Adam's wife and son." Mother's voice broke. She was shaking real bad.

"Pa," Holden sobbed. Tears flowed down his face.

The man's lips pursed. "I regret you had to see that, ma'am."

"Don't hurt us, please," Mother beseeched him. She retreated, shuttling him behind her.

"You tell anyone what you saw tonight—"

"I won't!"

"Listen to me," the stranger ordered.

Mother stopped, her breath ripping against the still night air.

"You tell anyone what you saw here tonight," the man said, real calm like, "and I'll kill your boy. I'll kill all your boys. Do you understand me?"

"Yessir," Mother whispered.

"You wouldn't want that to happen now would you?"

"No, no, no." She was crying, too.

Holden saw her tears dully, listened to their conversation dumbly. The man had shot Pa.

"Leave tonight," the man said. "Never come back and never breathe a word of this."

Mother clasped Holden's hand and pulled him. He knew she wanted him to flee, but he couldn't make his legs work.

"C'mon baby," she said frantically. "We have to go."

He only gazed at her.

Without hesitation, she had swept him up in her thin arms and began to run.

Holden raised his head and stared at the brick wall of his prison cell. He knew the face of the man with the gun. It had aged over the years, gone bald. But it was the same face he'd seen at Austin's train station just months before. It belonged to Oliver Kinsworthy, Blackhaw's attorney. No wonder he'd felt such sick rage when he'd seen him.

Oliver Kinsworthy had killed his father for Blackhaw's fortune. All this time, the truth had been locked inside his own mind. *God damn it, I should have been able to remember it sooner.*

He rushed to his feet. Jarrod and Sophia were searching for a dead man. His brain spun. Sophia had told him that Kinsworthy had informed her of their meeting at the train station, which meant the two were still in contact, which meant that Kinsworthy likely knew of Jarrod and Sophia's renewed search for Blackhaw's missing money.

His gut tightened. Hell, he was responsible for Jarrod's involvement in that search. He'd asked it of him. Just how long could Kinsworthy conceal his guilt? And who was he willing to hurt to do so?

He saw again the flash of fire as Kinsworthy shot down their father. In two strides, Holden reached the front of his cell. "Guard!" he yelled.

Men stirred in the adjacent cells, grumbled.

"Guard!" He yelled again. "Guard!"

Finally, one of his jailers appeared at the end of the hall.

Holden's muscles bunched as he tried to rend the metal bars in his bare hands. "I need to get a message to my brother."

The guard, his hulking build covered with slabs of fat, approached.

"It's important that I get a message—"

The guard rammed a hand through the bars, connecting with Holden's chest and sending him back a few paces. "Shut the hell up, Stone. You know the rules."

Holden's fingers curled into fists. He wanted nothing more than to fight the bastard, was itching for it. "I need to get a message—"

"Well you can't. What do you think this is, the fricking post office?" The guard's glare seethed with contempt. "Now shut the hell up, or me and the boys will have to take you out of here and whup the crap out of you." He walked back in the direction he'd come.

"No!" Holden yelled. He went back to the bars, pressed himself against them. "No!"

Chapter 21

Jarrod recognized the exact instant that Sophia eased her warm body away from his. The gray-pink light of dawn seeped through the open windows, illuminating her beautiful back as she slipped from bed.

Halfway across the rug, a floorboard squealed beneath her. She stopped and looked over her shoulder at him. He quickly closed the eye he'd cracked open.

When he heard her pour water into the washbasin, he watched her surreptitiously again. Damn, he loved her body. Her bottom was round and high and full, a perfect fit for his hands. Her waist nipped inward from her hips in a line too perfect for even the greatest artist to capture on canvas.

As she leaned over the dish to soap her wash towel, he

drank in the profile of her breasts, their rosy nipples taut with cold.

His body stirred. He needed to make love to her again, craved to bury himself inside her and have his release. Last night hadn't been near enough. On the contrary, looking at her now, he felt hungrier for her than he ever had before. Like an addiction.

Water trickled against water as she lifted the soapy towel and cleansed herself. A kind of delicious agony tightened his groin as she ran the cloth from her toes up to her thighs. God, she was so concentrated, his Sophia. She even washed with an expression of focus on her features. When she coasted the cloth between her legs, he nearly groaned.

She stilled, then glanced toward him.

He feigned sleep.

More swishing sounds. He watched as she cleaned her upper body, neck, and face, then wrung out her towel and shivered. When he'd told her she was the most beautiful thing he'd ever seen, it had been a gross understatement. He wished there was a word that did her more justice than "beautiful" did.

His lips curved at the memory of her the first night he'd seen her, here in this room. Her hair tightly bound, her face icy white, her posture iron-straight. And now look at her. All rosy and soft, all color and warmth.

She used her wrist to push a long lock of mahogany hair behind her shoulder, then set about brushing her teeth with dental cream.

He wanted to marry her. He'd never been a man content with half measures. No, when he wanted something, he wanted it wholly. And what he wanted, more than he'd ever wanted the money or the power or the possessions, was her. A day with her, a few more nights wouldn't do. He was selfish enough to covet every day of the rest of her life. To demand the right to call her his. To own her love. He needed time enough to treasure her properly, to give her everything the little girl in white had been robbed of.

She tiptoed across to the armoire and hastily donned undergarments.

Once they were married, he'd keep her naked for days at a time and ban undergarments entirely.

She pulled on stockings, strapped her knife to the outside of her thigh, put on a worn-looking navy blue skirt and bodice, and laced up her shoes. It took her only moments at her dressing table to brush her hair, then weave it into a loose, elaborately twisted style that suited her far better than the buns of old. She stood from the stool in a rush.

He closed his eyes, listening to her move toward him, skirts rustling. He could smell the lavender scent of her soap as she bent over him.

He held himself immobile, despite every instinct. Decades of responsibility had fashioned him into a man who protected. He hadn't protected his mother well enough, and her death had been a searing lesson to him. After her, he'd held tight to those he loved, convinced somewhere inside himself that it was his guardianship that kept them from harm.

If given the chance or the choice, he'd control Sophia's actions because that was simply what he did. What would keep her safe. But if he wanted a future with her, he knew he'd have to make his peace with her career. Her work as Twilight's Ghost meant everything to the woman. She'd proven it to him a thousand times, and if he forced her to choose between it and him, as his inclinations were driving him to, she'd choose it. More than that, though. He didn't want to have to force her to choose. He wanted to give her the ultimate sign of his respect by trusting her to make her own decisions.

He would begin this morning. With letting go.

Lighter than the touch of a dandelion, her fingers slid through his hair. *Don't move,* he told himself. *Let her wake you and ask for your help if she will.* Holding himself torturously still, he waited for her to, hoped she would. Her breath soughed against his forehead before she kissed him softly.

Then, too soon, her caress vanished, and he heard the faint sounds of her retreat.

He had to stop her, he couldn't let her go—

The door whispered open then shut.

He pushed himself to sitting. The blankets pooled at his waist. His heart thudded with loss, with doom. He *must* let her go and do her work as Twilight's Ghost. He understood it rationally. Yet doing nothing went against every fiber of him.

He gritted his teeth. Moved to go after her. Stopped.

"Damn it," he said beneath his breath. *Let her go, man.* He understood the kind of woman she was, how stubbornly independent. She'd left him to go hunt down her counterfeiter, and he had to have enough faith in her to let her do what she did best.

She'd be fine, he assured himself. She hadn't found the criminal yet, and there was no reason to think she would today. It was light out. There'd be people around. She was quick and smart.

She'd be fine.

* * *

"Thank you," Sophia said to the town of Hitchcock's courthouse clerk, and accepted a stack of papers from the gentleman. She made her way to the empty desk against the wall and pulled up a chair.

Her stomach yawned with hunger. She'd skipped breakfast in lieu of traveling from one small town to the next, examining records in hopes of finding information on Silas Clarke, her artist with a penchant for ordering large quantities of paper and ink. The hour was now approaching noon, and she'd yet to find anything on the man.

She sighed as she stripped her dusty gloves from her hands and set them aside. She prayed Maggie was having better luck.

Industriously, she straightened the stack and pulled it in front of her. But instead of paper and print, she saw Jarrod pulling her hips toward him as he entered her. Saw the color that tinted his cheeks, the passion that clouded his eyes.

Heat blossomed in her belly. She fidgeted in the wooden chair, hooked a finger around her neckline, and pulled in a fruitless attempt to give her lungs more air. If she was honest with herself, this was why the day's duties so far had been agony. She'd been hungry and tired countless times before while investigating her cases. But she'd never been so thoroughly haunted by a man. Jarrod had dominated every thought she'd had today. Riding in her buggy, leafing through records—it didn't matter. She saw, knew, tasted, felt nothing but him. She physically ached to return to him, to kiss him again, to hear his voice, to see him look at her with love. . . .

Irritated with herself, she shook her head to clear her

thoughts. She *couldn't* allow her hopes to tumble so far beyond themselves that she'd never be able to catch them back. The truth was that he hadn't necessarily looked at her with love. It could have been lust, and she wouldn't have known the difference. He'd promised her nothing.

Yet again, she straightened her papers and tried to concentrate. This investigation was crucially important. It was Blackhaw's last chance. The auction was set for tomorrow, and if she couldn't claim her reward money before then, she'd lose her home.

One deep breath, and she forced herself to start reading over the court papers. She searched one sheet at a time for the name Silas Clarke. Not him. Not him. Not him.

She was two-thirds of the way through the stack, her imaginings returning to Jarrod, when she saw it. Silas Clarke. Black script on white paper. She leaned forward, her pulse picking up tempo as she scanned the record. He'd been tried more than three years before for the crime of . . . Her vision skimmed past inconsequential information . . . Counterfeiting.

Victory soared inside her. "I've got you," she murmured, nearly overwhelmed with relief, satisfaction, and accomplishment.

She read the sheet over more carefully, taking note of the particulars. Silas Clarke had been found not guilty. Mr. Stewart had said that was due to good representation. She traced her fingernail down the words. His representation had been . . . Oliver Kinsworthy.

She blinked, surprised. Then glad. Oliver would be able to give her information about Silas not listed on this document. She hurried to her feet, enlivened by a second wind of renewed purpose. She'd go straight to Oliver. He'd help her.

* * *

The weather was turning ugly.

From astride his horse, Jarrod peered to the north-west, where a storm brewed. There, the sky was darkest gray, paler gray strips arrowing toward earth. Rain. Here, the air swept past them on curling rushes of moist wind.

He turned up the collar of his greatcoat and frowned at the surrounding territory of winter-swept forest. "You sure about this, J. T?"

"I'm sure we're heading in the right direction. The house should be over this next hill." Expertly, J. T. maneuvered his horse through a minefield of fallen logs. "But I'm not certain we'll learn anything useful when we get there."

"Worth a try, though." Clint commented.

His brothers had spent the last few days working doggedly on the pursuit of their father. They'd begun in the right place to Jarrod's way of thinking, by filling gaps in the information the Pinkertons had compiled. They'd almost finished piecing together the past and present of every person who had served at Blackhaw at the time of the theft. Almost but not quite. Clint and J. T. had discovered a missing section of Oliver Kinsworthy's history. Finding out just what Kinsworthy had been do-ing during those years was what had brought them on this fool's errand.

Jarrod trotted his horse along the bank of a brook, watching the water bump and glide over rocks and think-ing of the water that had flowed over Sophia's body that morning.

He hadn't wanted to do this today. Hadn't wanted to do anything but stay in bed with Sophia making love, eating, sleeping, making love. He sure as hell didn't give a good goddamn about riding for the better part of two hours just to chase down information on Kinsworthy's dull past. But when he'd returned home this morning and found his brothers on the verge of riding out, he'd decided to go with them. Unfortunately, the activity hadn't diverted him as much as he'd hoped. His body was physically here, but his mind was with her. Going over the events of last night, remembering every square inch of her skin, her every gasp, and glance.

He sighed impatiently, shifted in the saddle.

They crested a hill and a house, set about a quarter mile distant, speared into view.

"Jesus," Jarrod said.

"Quite a house, eh?" J. T. murmured.

"What happened to it?"

Clint squinted at the structure. "Time, I'd say."

They directed their horses onto the road that led up to the grand old relic. The structure was enormous, clapboard-sided, with round-topped windows cut into three towering stories. Elaborate balconies marked its sides, while steepled dormers and turrets jutted from the roofline. A mansion by anyone's standards, except it looked like a monument to greed gone bad because the paint had frayed off the clapboards, the decorative wooden carvings had been stripped dull by water and wind, and the turret windows gaped with jagged holes.

The negative intuition that had been with Jarrod since morning unwound itself and spread. "What does this place have to do with Kinsworthy?"

"About five years after Sophia's grandmother's death," Clint said, "the Pinkerton file lost track of his whereabouts for a couple of years. Sophia, actually, was the one who helped us discover where he'd been during that time."

"Sophia?"

Clint nodded. "She supplemented the Pinkerton file on our father with all the letters Kinsworthy ever wrote her concerning their search. A few of his letters to her were dated during the missing time period and marked with this return address."

"He owned this place?"

"No, not according to the locals. This house has always been owned by the family who built it. Name of Dobson."

"We think Kinsworthy worked here," J. T. said.

They pulled their horses to a stop and dismounted before the stairs leading up to the front entrance. "It doesn't even look inhabited," Jarrod said.

"No," Clint agreed, as they climbed the steps, their boots ringing against brittle wood. "It doesn't."

Jarrod knocked. J. T. and Clint swept off their Stetsons while they waited.

At first, he heard absolutely no stirrings of life from within. Then, as if originating in some netherworld instead of from the back of the house, footsteps sounded. Jarrod fully expected a wizened old man with a cane and a passel of cats to open the door.

When the door swung inward, it revealed a woman instead. A fairly young one with a frail body, a simple tan dress, and sparse mousy hair. She regarded them through eyes as round as nickels, apparently flabbergasted to find three men standing on her threshold.

"Miss Dobson?" J. T. asked.

"Yes."

"I'm J. T. Stone, and these are my brothers, Jarrod and Clint."

"Ma'am."

"Ma'am."

She simply stared.

"We've come to talk with you," J. T. said, "about a gentleman that may have been in your family's employ some fifteen years ago. A Mr. Oliver Kinsworthy."

J. T. had gentled both his tone and manner so as not to scare her. He'd always had a way with women, been able to cater to whatever it was they needed. Jarrod, on the other hand, was atrocious with shy women.

"Yes," Miss Dobson answered. "I know Mr. Kinsworthy."

"I realize this is a great imposition," J. T. said, "but may we ask you a few questions regarding him?"

"I . . ." The sinewy muscles in her throat worked. Self-consciously, she fluttered a hand over the back of her head. "I haven't had my hair properly styled in some time."

She's insane, Jarrod thought.

"It looks lovely," J. T. replied smoothly, his grin warm and complimentary.

She stepped jerkily back, and held the door for them. "Come in."

They followed her into a parlor that contained a rug, a sofa, and three chairs. Every other item that had once graced it was gone. No curtains, no paintings, no tables, no plants, no baubles. He was reminded of Blackhaw's second-story rooms, rooms that stood empty except for tattering wallpaper and faded paint.

The woman sat on the edge of the sofa. J. T. chose the sofa's other end, while Jarrod and Clint settled into chairs.

"Can I offer you anything?" the woman asked hesitantly. "There's—" She rose to her feet as if she'd suddenly remembered she had water boiling on the stove.

All three of them stood.

"There's *cheese*," she said, motioning vaguely toward the back of the house.

"That's a very kind offer," J. T. responded, "but, no thank you, ma'am. We couldn't possibly impose on you more than we have."

"No imposition."

"Thank you, but we couldn't possibly."

She nodded, and they all took their seats for the second time. A momentary shift in the clouds caused sunlight to slant across her face. She was even younger than Jarrod had first assumed. He doubted she'd yet to reach twenty-five. So, why had he thought her older at first?

She had old eyes, he realized, studying her. The delicate skin around them was smooth and young. But those eyes. They'd been aged by shame and poverty and broken dreams of grandeur.

His sense of unease deepened.

"In what capacity was Mr. Kinsworthy employed here?" J. T. asked.

"He was my grandfather's advisor and attorney. They, ah, worked together on my family's business interests from the offices here in the house." More vague pointing toward a general region of the residence.

"Your grandfather, you say?"

"That's correct."

"Did you and your family live here with him at the time?"

"Oh. No," she said with a wistful note. "My parents

both contracted polio and passed when I was very young, I'm afraid."

"I'm sorry," J. T. said sincerely.

"It was just Grandfather and me during Mr. Kinsworthy's time."

"How long did he work here?"

"Two years or so. Up until the fortune was stolen and Grandfather died."

Jarrod clenched the armrests of his chair.

She pursed pale lips. "After that, you understand, I hadn't the finances to keep Mr. Kinsworthy on. A pity, that."

"You must have been very young," J. T. said.

"Oh . . . Not quite ten. Mr. Kinsworthy's the one who took me to my great-aunt Clara's to live. We still correspond frequently, Mr. Kinsworthy and I." She smiled softly. "I think the world of him. He's even offered to help me find the man who stole our family's money. It would be nice"—her gaze flitted around the room—"to restore this place a bit."

Jarrod stared at her, aghast. He was looking at the woman Sophia might have become. Twice, Kinsworthy had gained the trust of his elderly patron, twice his patrons were robbed, twice no one was left to question it but a small girl.

My God. Sophia had been wrong about his father's guilt and wrong to trust Oliver Kinsworthy, her lifelong friend. Jarrod rushed to his feet. "I need a word with you in private," he said to his brothers.

"If you'll excuse us for a moment, Miss Dobson," J. T. said.

"Certainly. I just remembered. I've also a bit of boiled

ham." She stood, smiling hesitantly. "If that would interest you."

"I'll be back in one moment," J. T. promised her.

The three exited the foyer and stood together on the porch.

"Sophia trusts Kinsworthy," Jarrod said. "She could be with him now, for all I know. I'm going to Blackhaw. I don't want her anywhere near him." He strode halfway down the stairs. Turned back toward them. "As soon as you can get away, ride to my house. If I can't find her, I'll contact you there."

"We'll be there," Clint said.

"And for God's sake, find out what this woman needs." He jerked his chin toward the house. "Whatever it is, I'll buy it for her."

Jarrod mounted his horse in a single movement. He reined the beast in a tight circle before goading him to gallop down the road. Overhead, the gray-black skies churned. Wind whipped through his hair and streaked beneath the collar of his coat and shirt.

Sophia had gone today to investigate her counterfeiter, not to search for his father. She'd told him herself that she'd sworn off the hunt for Blackhaw's thief, which meant there was no possible reason for her to visit Oliver Kinsworthy before Jarrod could get to her and warn her.

She was safe and he was overreacting.

His dread worsened. He knelt over his horse's back, urging the animal to go faster.

Chapter 22

〜〜∾◯◯∿〜〜

"**O**liver?" Sophia knocked on the front door of his home for the second time, then stamped her feet in an effort to warm herself. Her blood, skin, and bones were freezing after the long ride from Hitchcock's courthouse to Oliver's offices in town, then here when his secretary had informed her he wasn't in. The wind wound its way up her body, penetrating straight through her clothing.

Hoping he might be around back, she clasped closed the neck of her coat and hurried to the rear of the house. For almost as long as she could remember, Oliver had lived on this quarter-acre lot on this quietly tasteful residential street. "Oliver?"

Dead leaves tumbled across her shoes when she gained the back-door stoop. "Oliver?" She knocked rapidly.

No answer.

She knocked again as she tested the knob. It turned easily beneath her hand, hinges creaking as the door slid open. For a split second, she hesitated. Surely he wouldn't mind if she escaped the weather and waited for him inside.

She let herself in, the outside noise cutting away as she closed the door. The tick of a clock welcomed her, as did the warmer temperature, the smell of coffee, and the lamps that had been left burning. It looked as if he'd just stepped out for a brief errand.

Rubbing her arms with her gloved hands, she delved into his home. The atmosphere was masculine and muted, comfortable. The artwork hanging on both sides of the hallway watched her pass as she made her way to the front room. Automatically, she reached out to nudge closed a hallway closet that had been left ajar—

Air gusted through the opening, ruffling her hair.

She stopped. Frowning, she opened the closet door, but instead of a closet she found a staircase that led downward to some sort of basement. Darkness shadowed the ten or so steps, but faint light pooled on the floor below. "Oliver?"

Quiet answered.

She took a second look at the door's knob and noticed it had the capability to lock. How odd to discover stairs behind a locking door that looked very much like a closet door. She hadn't even realized this house contained a basement. Curiosity mounting, she eased down the first few steps, then down the rest of the way.

When she reached the bottom she halted. The flame within the basement's lamp sent light flickering over a space perhaps one half the size of the upper story. A printing press stood like a metallic king in the center of the floor. Containers of ink sat upon shelves. On a wide artist's desk piles of money had been stacked. Reams of paper waited in wooden crates.

A chill that had nothing to do with the climate birthed deep in Sophia's stomach. She eyed her surroundings for long moments without moving, her brain turning slowly, like the rusted wheels of an old mill. After a time, she moved around the space, her dull gaze cataloging what her agent's mind recognized but her loyalty refused to credit. The chill invaded her chest, her limbs, her head. She stopped at the room's far end and stared blankly at a newly created artist's plate of a ten-dollar note.

Oh, Oliver. Her thoughts raced back in time, remembering her friend over all the years. All the times he'd visited her at the orphanage and the countless times they'd met to discuss their hunt for Adam Stone. His smiles. The way his speckled hands cushioned hers.

Impossible to reconcile that man with one who could be guilty of counterfeiting. She couldn't force this puzzle piece into the same mold she'd cast of him in her heart.

"Sophia."

She spun toward the sound of his voice.

Oliver stood halfway down the stairs, holding a brown sack. In many ways he looked so familiar . . . his bald head, the snowy white brows and mustache, the too-tight tweed vest. Yet the expression in his eyes, one of sadness and censure, she'd never seen before.

Painful silence strained the air between them.

Disillusionment and confusion tangled Sophia's emotions. Ridiculously, she wanted to apologize for snooping. Especially, *especially*, because in a distant way she realized that nothing could ever be the same for them again, after this, when she'd very much wanted their relationship to continue forever.

He took the last few stairs, stopped at the bottom, then made no move to come closer. "What are you doing here?"

"I came to ask you . . . a question. I let myself in because of the cold, then found the door to this basement ajar."

He didn't answer, just stood there, watching her. The awkward quiet expanded, slinking its way into the room's farthest corners.

"Why?" she asked softly. "Why are you doing this, Oliver?"

"Why?" He shook his head ruefully and tossed his brown bag onto a countertop. "Because large quantities of money are hard to come by."

"Why would you need large quantities of money? You've this house, a flourishing law practice—"

"Do you really think I'd manufacture money for myself?" The wrinkles around his eyes seemed to deepen with disappointment. "No, it's the Southern Army that needs it."

"The Southern Army?"

"Good men, friends of mine, relatives," he said grimly, "fought and died for the right of the South to secede." His lips pursed. "It's a right we were due then and a right we're due now."

"We lost the war," she said feebly.

"I've supported and believed wholeheartedly in this cause for thirty years. I'm no quitter." His eyes blazed with devotion. "They fought and *died*, Sophia. What kind of man would I be if I refused to do whatever I could for the cause? If I refused to do my part?"

"I don't know."

"I do."

"You're paying them?" she asked, slightly disoriented. "The Southern Army?" None of this fit with the man she knew.

"We're gaining strength, but strength takes money that's quickly drained."

Sophia released a painful breath. His convoluted notions of honor and nobility only made this worse. "Perhaps I'd best go."

Oliver rolled his lips into a resigned frown. "I'm sorry you had to find out about this, Sophia."

"I'm sorry, too."

"You're sorry for my sake, I'd hazard to guess. Whereas I'm sorry for your sake."

A frission of fear mingled with her shock.

"This cause is too important," he said. "I can't have you running to the law and informing them of my situation."

What, he'd try to physically stop her? Hurt her? *Her*? He'd not a violent bone in his body and she . . . she was like a daughter to him. For God's sake, he'd hugged her on the steps of the orphanage when she was eight years old— With a sickening lurch, she wondered suddenly what else he was capable of. He'd carted her off to that orphanage because Adam . . . because someone had stolen all their money.

I've supported and believed wholeheartedly in this cause for thirty years.

Mother Mary. He'd been feeding cash to his cause

since before her birth, and certainly at the time of Blackhaw's demise. She felt dizzy with betrayal and heartsickness and her own naïveté. In her mind Adam Stone had
always been guilty of robbing Blackhaw's fortune.
Largely because of what . . . Oliver had told her over the
years. Oh, heavens, Jarrod. Holden. She moved toward
the staircase. Oliver moved, too, so that his bulk squarely
blocked the mouth of the stairs.

She stared at him, anger swirling to the surface.
"You're not going to let me leave?

"I can't."

"We've been friends for twenty years."

"Sophia," he chided, "the most important thing about
honor is that a person can't allow it to be diluted by anything. Even affection. Surely, you've learned that by
now."

"Let me pass." She stormed toward him.

From within his coat, he quietly pulled free a Smith &
Wesson. The round eye of the barrel sighted on her chest.

Disbelief struck her like a punch to the chest. "You
wouldn't shoot me."

"My dear, for the rights of the Southern people, I'd do
anything on earth."

Her breath turned shallow in the face of her reeling
world. Her dear, kind Oliver was willing to kill her—to
kill her—to keep her quiet. She struggled to think as she
retreated. She slipped her hands into her skirt pockets in
a gesture she hoped looked capitulatory. The fingers of
her right hand gripped the hilt of her knife as her gaze
measured the distance up the stairs to freedom.

Could she attack him? She was an agent who acted
through observation, not confrontation. Could she stab

an old man for believing too fervently in the wrong hope?

Upstairs, a door opened and shut. Oliver looked toward the sound of footsteps progressing down the hallway.

A tall, wiry man filled the doorway. Silas Clarke. She recognized him from the day she'd followed him home. Two others came to stand beside Silas. Men whose eyes she'd seen once before, above the lines of their masks when they'd attacked her outside Jarrod's home. Her heart raced. Like an animal cornered, she instinctively backed up until the base of her spine hit the edge of the artist's desk. No farther to go.

"I found her here," Oliver said to the men.

"Well, we can't have that." Silas led the others into the basement. He studied her for a long moment, then shook his head in disgust. "Perhaps you'd best sit down, Mrs. La Rue."

"No."

"Just take a seat right there." He indicated the artist's chair as he approached her. His cohorts loomed behind him.

"No," she repeated.

They closed in, almost near enough to grab her now—She whipped free her knife. Quick as an eyeblink, Silas made a swipe for it. Sophia reared away from his reach and parried, thrusting the blade toward him. He darted backward. "Get out of my way," she snarled, arcing her blade through the air, fighting to hold the three of them at bay.

The one on the right made a quick move in her direction. She swung toward him, even as he was feinting back. Muscled hands closed over her forearm from the other direction. Silas wrenched the knife from her grip.

Terrified, furious, she threw her elbows, squirmed, and kicked. They were everywhere, hauling her off her feet, subduing her flailing limbs. She cried out and tried to fight them off. No luck. They were overpowering her, stronger. The three forced her into the chair—two holding her feet against its legs, Silas behind, trapping her arms behind the chair's back. "I need twine," he bit out.

Sophia struggled, sweat heating her face and neck, strands of hair falling in front of her face, tangling with her eyelashes.

Oliver collected a length of twine from a drawer filled with supplies and tossed it to Silas, who began to bind her wrists.

"Where are we going to take her?" Silas asked.

"Far," Oliver answered. "I don't need to tell you that my neighbors aren't accustomed to hearing gunshots—"

A resounding knock boomed through the house.

All four men froze.

Sophia gasped for breath, tried to pull free her wrists. Silas responded by looping twine around them two more times. Again, came the knock. Forceful, vibrating with impatience.

"Bennett," Oliver said.

"Yes, sir."

"See who's there."

The man grasping her right foot took hold of her left as well, freeing his partner to dash up the stairs.

She recognized the icy eyes of the man at her feet. He'd been the one to slap her that day in the rain. Fear clawing her, she remembered his mercilessness and power. Wondered which servant he'd convinced to poison Jarrod's wine.

This time, knocking rocked the door at the other end of the house. The back door.

The sounds of a scuffle ensued upstairs. A grunt, the breaking of glass, a heavy thud. The three men in the basement exchanged a look. Oliver readjusted his hold on his gun. "Bennett?" he called loudly.

No reply.

Behind her, Silas let the twine he'd been holding fall to the ground. She heard the rasp of a gun sliding past leather as he unsheathed his weapon. Frantically, she tried to yank free the restraint securing her wrists, but he'd looped it tightly and it held firm.

The door at the top of the stairs crashed open.

Jarrod stood on the threshold with his legs braced apart, the silver of the gun he clasped stark against his black greatcoat. He looked like an avenging angel, mad as hell.

Love and relief billowed within Sophia, tamped immediately when Silas and Oliver clicked back the hammers of their guns. There were three of them and only one of him.

Jarrod's forbidding gaze swept the scene, pausing on her for an instant, before coming to rest on Oliver. "You let her go now, and I won't have to kill any of you," Jarrod said.

Lord above. Sophia's muscles strained against the cords at her wrists.

"You're outnumbered, Stone." Oliver's eyes narrowed.

"I've been outnumbered before by better men than you. Let her go."

Sophia saw Oliver's trigger finger whiten as he exerted pressure. "Jarrod!" she screamed.

Jarrod vaulted over the banister of the stairs, landed on the basement floor, and came up swinging. His punch sent Oliver careening into a wall of shelves.

Both men who'd been guarding her ran toward the fight. Sophia stuck out her foot, tripping Silas. He broke his fall with his hands. His gun spiraled across the floor. When he started to push himself upward, Sophia gripped one of the rungs at the back of the chair and stood, swinging its legs at him. She caught him across the back with enough force that the wood splintered. He sprawled to the ground, spewing curses.

Sophia dropped the chair and ran to his gun, kicking it beneath the printing press lest he try to reclaim it. She worked frantically to jerk free her wrists. Jarrod was viciously fighting the man who'd slapped her unconscious, their blows landing with crunching power. Oliver had recovered enough to hold steady his gun, waiting for a clean shot. Movement from above caught her eye. Bennett had come to, and he hurtled down the stairs to help his cohorts. He drove his shoulder into Jarrod's back, snapping Jarrod's head back with the force of it.

Sophia wailed, remembering too well the way she'd watched Jarrod's guard beaten nearly to death by these same men. With a final heave, the twine stretched open enough for her to pull free her hands. She ran toward Jarrod—

Silas grabbed a handful of her skirt and heaved backward. Her knees slammed against the floor.

"Sophia!" Jarrod yelled.

Their gazes met for a split second. He'd knocked Bennett onto the stairs, and blood was gushing from the man's nose. "Watch out," she gasped, as his other attacker coiled his arm for another punch.

There were too many of them. She scratched her way to standing and dashed to help him. Jarrod was breathing hard, a grimace of rage contorting his features. He sent his fist hurtling again and again.

Sophia curled her hands into the back of someone's shirt and tried to pull him off Jarrod. She was shoved away. Her back banged against the wall and pain flashed up her spine, but she returned quickly, fingernails bared, fighting to haul them off Jarrod.

And then there were more fists. Silas was yanked by helping hands into the air, then thrown against the printing press. She looked up to see J. T. growl as he went after the man. She stumbled backward. Clint was there, too, socking Bennett as he tried to stand. And Maggie at the top of the stairs. The scuffle enlarged, fists flying, grunts rushing from split lips.

Her dazed attention cut to Oliver. He raised his gun, determination in his eyes. He was going to start shooting, not caring anymore whether he hit his own men.

She flew at him, managing to strike his gun arm upward just as he pulled the trigger. The bullet howled into the ceiling. Hissing with rage, Oliver turned the gun on her.

"Don't you dare." The muzzle of Jarrod's pistol pressed unrelentingly against Oliver's temple.

All around her, Sophia sensed stillness where moments before there had been hectic motion.

"Put it down," Jarrod said, "or I swear to God I'll kill you."

A muscle near Oliver's eye ticked.

Sophia didn't move, didn't breathe, just stared at the yawning black hole of the gun pointed at her chest.

"Put it down," Jarrod demanded, nudging his own gun so sharply against Oliver's head that the older man flinched.

Slowly, Oliver lowered his weapon.

Sophia's shoulders slumped with deflated tension.

"You're under arrest," Clint said as he gathered Oliver's arms behind his back and fastened cuffs around his wrists.

Sophia looked to Jarrod. He gazed back at her. Blood trickled from the side of his lip.

Her heart twisted at the sight.

She could see his chest pumping beneath the layers of his coat and suit. One of the men lay at his feet. Silas, too, had been knocked out by J. T., who stood with his arms crossed above his prey. Bennett was writhing in pain near the bottom of the stairs, cradling a broken nose.

Maggie picked her way through the rubble. "Are you all right?"

Sophia pushed a chunk of hair out of her eyes with the back of her hand, then nodded, too weak in the aftermath of her terror to speak. Thank God Jarrod was unharmed, that his brothers had come in time to keep him safe. He'd not be crushed and bloodied because of her.

"We returned to your house to find a prison guard from Huntsville waiting for us," J. T. said to Jarrod.

"Huntsville?" Jarrod asked.

"Yeah. In hopes of a messenger's fee, he'd traveled all the way from the prison with a warning from Holden."

"Which is?" Jarrod asked tensely.

"That this one killed our father." Grimly, he inclined his head toward Oliver.

Jarrod's scowl turned frightening as he leveled it on Oliver.

"Holden was only just able to remember it," J. T. said. "He was there that night at Blackhaw with Mother. He saw Kinsworthy shoot our father."

Sophia swallowed a rise of bile.

Oliver looked toward the wall, his mouth tightly sealed.

"He shot him for the money?" Jarrod asked.

Clint nodded. "Mrs. Warren had entrusted our father with it that night for their investment in the factory. Kinsworthy caught up with him before he even reached the gates of the property, killed him for it, and kept it."

A burning ball formed in Sophia's chest. She'd been the first to believe Adam Stone guilty and the last to believe it untrue.

A dangerous pressure built in the room. A pressure borne from the years of stigma and doubt and bitterness the Stone brothers had endured. Sophia sensed it, pumping through her veins, pumping through the veins of Jarrod and J. T. and Clint.

"We rode to Blackhaw Manor to find you," J. T. said to Jarrod. "You and Sophia weren't there, but Miss May was. She's the one who led us here. How'd you know where to find Sophia?"

"When she wasn't at Blackhaw," Jarrod answered, "I went to Kinsworthy's offices. His secretary told me Sophia had just been in and that she'd likely come here." His jaw tightened into a severe line. "She had."

Maggie cleared her throat. "Perhaps we'd best get these boys to the sheriff."

"If you don't mind," Jarrod said to his brothers, "I'd like a word with Sophia alone."

Her heart skipped a beat.

"Do you need my help getting these men upstairs first?" he asked.

" 'Course not." J. T. slung the limp Silas over one shoulder like he might a sack of potatoes, then helped Maggie pull Bennett to his feet. Clint lifted the third, and urged Oliver ahead of him up the stairs, using the point of his gun.

Once they'd straggled out, she and Jarrod faced each other without distractions or noise. She remembered last night in flashes of detail—the flat plane of his stomach, the feel of his hot chest, the fervent look on his face as he'd made love to her. "Jarrod, I. . . ." How did one begin to express this? "I'm so sorry I believed your father to be guilty. I was wrong."

"You had reason to believe what you did." His solemn tone frightened her. "I don't give a damn about that."

"What is it then?"

He swiped at his lip, looked at the blood on his fingers, and angrily cleared the rest with his thumb. She could see tightness invading his shoulders, almost touch the darkening of his mood. Over their weeks together she'd grown attuned to him, to the way his frustration could rise, as it was rising now, to a jagged ridge.

He swiveled away from her, presenting her with his broad back.

Please let him not be about to tell me he doesn't want me. Maybe she could bear it later. But after the beauty of what they'd shared last night, after Oliver's betrayal, she needed him right now. Desperately.

He stalked a few steps away, turned. "Here's how it is."

She held her ground, praying she wouldn't shame herself if he broke her heart.

"I want you," he said bluntly.

Her heart stuttered. Then swelled—

"But I can't do this. I thought I could, but I can't. I can't let you go to your job knowing that every time I do you could be walking into a bullet or a knife." He dashed a hand through his wind-tousled hair. "That's not the kind of man I am. It's not in me."

She couldn't move.

"So you have a choice. Me or Twilight's Ghost."

She understood why he was asking this of her, she did. But it was too much. Old fears twisted around her. He was asking her to put all her hopes and trust—her very existence—in his hands. To risk everything on him.

What if he abandoned her? Where would she be then? Worse off than living the rest of her life without him? Her body, the very material of her tendons and bones longed for him. And yet . . . how could she risk everything? How could she sacrifice the only security she had?

"You've until noon tomorrow to decide," he said, his voice curt. "I summoned my ship into the port a week ago. I'll wait at the dock for you until then." Unspeakable sorrow grooved into his expression. She glimpsed the pain that lived inside him that he so rarely showed.

Then, far too soon, he turned and walked up the stairs, the back of his greatcoat slapping against his heels. His body filled the hallway door, then was gone. And she was deathly alone.

She wrapped her arms around herself and closed her

eyes against the hurt ravaging her insides. He'd given her until noon tomorrow to think about it. But what was there to think about, really? She'd never been a heedless person. She'd always made the safest choices in the interest of protecting herself.

Yes, but *for him*, a part of her argued. He was worth the risk. He could give her the stars from the sky and sea wind across her face. He had the power to make her young again.

She wiped suddenly cold hands down her forehead, her cheeks, her nose, her lips, struggling to compose herself.

By the time she let herself out the front door of Oliver's home, only Maggie remained. Her friend stood in the cold, waiting for her, the breeze mournfully tossing the hem of her coat.

"Come," Maggie said, approaching her and wrapping a comforting arm about Sophia's shoulders. Gently, she guided her toward the buggy. "We need to send word of this to Simon." She smiled sadly, gave Sophia's shoulders a squeeze. "We've a reward to collect and a house to save from the auction block."

"Yes," Sophia said, though she couldn't help feeling that the most valuable reward God had ever given her had just walked out of her life for good.

Chapter 23

❦

The next day Sophia sat beside Maggie on one of the wooden benches that ran down the center of the bank. Her fingers were laced together in her lap, the pads of her thumbs tapping twice every second. She hadn't taken her attention from the clock mounted upon the wall behind the teller's console in exactly seventeen minutes and thirty-three seconds. It was eleven-ten. *Eleventen.* Getting to be too late.

She parted her lips, closed them, stared at the clock in utter distress. Maggie patted her knee. But instead of soothing her, her friend's sympathy made her want to jump out of her skin. After a sleepless night, she was ill prepared to deal with this right now. If she had to watch another minute tick by without the teller informing her that her reward money had arrived, these good people of

361

Galveston, doing their good transactions, would damn well see her go stark raving mad before their eyes.

Blackhaw's auction was scheduled for noon, just as was Jarrod's promised departure, and her money should have arrived by now. Long before now. Immediately when they'd left Oliver's last night they'd couriered a letter to Simon, informing him that they'd caught the counterfeiter and alerting him to the urgency involved in receiving the money first thing in the morning. It was asking a great deal of the Agency, she knew, to move so speedily on this. Ordinarily the processing and receipt of rewards took days or weeks. But over her years of service, she'd *earned* this one favor.

She watched the minute hand tick downward a notch. Eleven-eleven. Simon had sent word straight back, saying that Slocum's Mercantile must first have the opportunity to verify that the counterfeit money they'd been passed had indeed come from Oliver's basement press. For her, he'd promised to attempt to complete that chore yesterday evening so that Slocum's could issue the reward first thing this morning and so that he could transfer it to her account, here.

She and Maggie had been waiting at the bank's front doors when they'd opened for business this morning. Hours ago. And still, nothing. She'd planned to take the reward money to the tax office straight away, so that they'd have time to cancel the auction entirely. Now she was going to have to rush straight to the auction itself and create a spectacle. That's if the money arrived in time at all.

Did Slocum's Mercantile, did Simon, have any idea how very much Blackhaw meant to her? Did they have the slightest inkling? Could they possibly let her do the work, earn the reward, get this close to saving her only possession, and then allow it to be snatched away? A sob built in her throat.

Eleven-fifteen now. And Jarrod— *Don't think about him.* But she couldn't help herself. Because with each jerk of the clock's minute hand, she felt as if he were being ripped farther from her. There was no choice to make where he was concerned. She'd known that from the minute he'd issued his ultimatum, his lip bloodied from fighting on her behalf. So why had she never felt more desolate in all her life?

If she could only get the reward money and save her house. Then she'd feel better, less barren. Then she'd have something.

Maggie leaned in close. "Yesterday at Oliver's did you see the way Clint felled that Bennett person with a single blow? I swear, I almost expired right then and there. The man is an absolute walking, talking, breathing god. Did you see how he handcuffed Oliver and told him he was under arrest? And then, be still my heart, the way he lifted Bennett over his shoulder as if he weighed nothing and marched Oliver outside? My mouth was so dry with . . . well, *awe* . . . that I didn't dare say a word to him, so when we all arrived outside I just stared at him like some sort of magpie while he loaded up the prisoners. Once Jarrod joined them, Clint tipped his hat to me and said good-bye, and I didn't even manage a gurgle. Have you ever heard of anything so humiliating? Not even a *gurgle*, Sophia."

"I . . ." Maggie's conversation was stringing tighter her nerves. "I'm sorry, Maggie, I just can't think about anything at the moment except the time. Something's wrong."

Maggie pulled in a breath and glanced at the clock. When she saw the time, she pushed to her feet. "I'm going to visit Simon."

"We're not to meet with him at his offices—"

"These circumstances are special. I'll take a careful route and use the back entrance."

"Maggie—"

"I can't let you sit here any longer without information. You stay here in case the money comes in, and I'll go."

Sophia couldn't decide. She glanced from Maggie to the teller.

"I'm going," Maggie said firmly. She pulled on her coat as she rushed toward the double doors.

Sophia thought she'd been desperate before, but Maggie's departure heightened her anxiety by bounds. She started tapping her thumbs three times a second. Eleven-twenty came and went. Eleven-twenty-five. Eleven-thirty.

"Mrs. LaRue?"

Sophia's attention sliced to the teller who'd called her name. The short gentleman with the brown doe's eyes motioned for her to hurry forward.

Too harried to be relieved, almost too harried to be polite, she went to his station and waited while he counted out the bills she was owed. She stashed the small fortune in her reticule, thanked him, then turned and fled. She had just enough time to reach the auction they were conducting at the courthouse.

The day greeted her with a swirl of chilly breeze. She paused on the bank steps just long enough to shove her arms into the sleeves of her coat. Then, clasping her reticule close to her chest, she hurried down the sidewalk.

I want you. Jarrod's words snaked out from the buzzing sounds of the city.

She ducked her head and walked faster.

I can't let you go to your job knowing that every time I do you could be walking into a bullet or a knife. That's not the kind of man I am. It's not in me. His voice tugged at her, insistent, persuasive. She shot a look over her shoulder to where the masts of the great ships pointed into the sky beyond the line of buildings. Her heart lurched.

Biting her bottom lip, she brought her concentration back to the sidewalk passing beneath her feet.

So you have a choice. Me or Twilight's Ghost.

The strips of weathered wood began to slow.

Me or Twilight's Ghost.

Her strides cut to a halt, and she was left staring at a square of unmoving wood.

Who was Twilight's Ghost? Not a real person. Just a mask she sometimes wore. It couldn't keep her warm in bed at night. Couldn't make her laugh. Couldn't cherish her.

The reason she'd been so upset back at the bank, she realized, wasn't because the lateness of her reward money had forced her to face the possibility of losing her house. It was because it had forced her to face the certainty that she could no longer have the house and Jarrod both. And having both was the secret hope she'd buried deep within herself. That understanding came like sunbeams parting the clouds and connecting honeyed fingers with the earth.

It was almost noon, and the advancing hour meant she could have either Blackhaw or Jarrod. Twilight's Ghost or Jarrod. Her old life or Jarrod. She raised her face and peered in the direction of the courthouse, where the auctioneer would be preparing his information, where buyers would be gathering. She blinked. Then with a rippling wave of daring that felt like the rushing of a million bubbles against the inside of her skin, she turned.

And she hurried toward the docks.

Until just now, her decision to cut Jarrod out of her life had seemed palatable. But as soon as she'd started her walk toward the courthouse, actually taken action toward a life without Jarrod, everything had changed. Her choice had become brutally wrong.

She wove through a crowd of people.

Mother above, she was tired of being afraid, cautious, untrusting. She'd needed those mantles once, needed her job to feel secure, and her house to feel safe. She didn't need them anymore. Strips that had bound her for years seemed to unwind from her body and whip away on the crests of the wind. Making her lighter, lighter, lighter.

Her steps increased in speed until she was practically running.

She wanted to love Jarrod and be loved by him, perhaps have children together and share a family. *Family.* The thought resonated down to the very deepest core of herself. Suddenly, she wanted a family with a ferocity that told her she'd wanted it her whole life and wanted it more than anything else on earth.

Getting closer now. The dock was almost in sight. She completed the length of one block, then another, then the last remaining block before reaching the harbor. Thanks to her years of observation from the dock's platform, she knew every supporting pier and plank that composed it. Running amidst and between the stevedores as they unloaded cargo, she scanned faces for a pair of green eyes, for black hair, and straight brows.

She didn't see him. Worry burgeoned, stealing just a fraction of her joy. Her skirts churned around her legs. Anxiously, she lifted a hand to shield her eyes. Where was he? He'd be here. He'd said he would. He'd not leave her.

She found herself at the end of the dock, the wood cutting away to reveal frothing water beneath. Panic rising, she turned in a circle, searching for him.

In the distance, she glimpsed the rear of a sleek ship as it eased out the mouth of the harbor, its sails filling with the gale that would carry it away. Because of its design and newness, it looked very much like the kind of vessel Jarrod would own. Her concern thickened, solidified.

She grabbed the arm of a stevedore as he rose from unloading a sack of salt atop a nearby pile of goods. "Do you have the time, sir?"

"Certainly, miss." He smiled, revealing gaps in his ground-down teeth. He pulled a timepiece from his trouser pocket. "It's twelve-ten."

"So late?" she asked, dismayed.

"No need to trouble yourself there, miss," he said encouragingly. "The day's still young."

"Are you," she licked her lips, "Are you familiar with that ship there?" She gestured to the one that was even now cutting its way into open water.

"Ah, yes'm. It's been in port for two days now. Fine ship, that. Excellent lie in the water."

"Do you happen to know who owns it?"

"You ever heard of an oil baron named Jarrod Stone?"

Every muscle in her body clenched. *Mother Mary, no.* She loved him. No, he couldn't possibly have left her here. She gazed at the ship, his beautiful ship, as it sailed away from her. Sailed beyond her ability to catch it back.

She'd watched dreams die before. But never one that mattered so much and never because of her own stupidity. She'd realized she loved him too late. She couldn't breathe beneath the crush of disappointment.

"Are you all right, miss?"

She nodded mutely.

The man stayed at her side for another few seconds, before finally returning to his tasks.

She remained where she was, staring at Jarrod's ship. Within her mind she saw him, his black hair shining, his piercing green eyes glinting and his lips curved into a smile that promised her she was the only woman in the world.

The tragedy was that she knew for certain now. Now that she'd lost him, she knew that Jarrod Stone had been the right choice to make for her life and for her heart.

Her footsteps sounded as hollow as her insides felt as she approached the courthouse steps. Like an old rag doll, there was nothing left to hold her together except a few fraying threads of stubbornness. She clutched at those and walked doggedly forward.

A trio of gentlemen turned toward her as she neared.

She clasped her reticule full of reward money in both hands. "Did you gentlemen by chance attend the auction of Blackhaw Manor?"

"We did." All three studied her with interest.

"Was it already completed?" she asked, both knowing what they would answer and dreading the hearing of it.

"I'm afraid so, ma'am."

Pain cut at her, surprisingly sharp. She looked away from them for a moment, fighting to retain the last of her composure. She had the money needed to pay Black-haw's taxes. She didn't have the money it would take to buy the house back from its new owner. "Do you happen to know," she asked, her attention returning to the men, "who purchased the estate?"

"I did," one of them answered. He was a tidy gentle-man, with a beautifully cut blue suit and a black bowler.

Her courage wavered and she wanted nothing more than to walk away and shut herself inside her bedroom— where? Her bedroom where? She didn't have a bedroom anymore. "Sir, is there any possibility that you might consider selling Blackhaw to me?"

He shook his head.

"It's been in my family since the time that it was built, and I'd very much like to retain it. If there's even the slightest chance that you might consider an offer, I'm sure that I could come up with a figure that would be palatable. . . ." Her words drifted off. He was still shak-ing his head. Despite the kindness she read in his expres-sion, she also read inflexibility.

"I'm sorry, ma'am," he said. "While I sympathize with your situation, there's absolutely no chance of a sale."

"But I'm willing to pay whatever is necessary." And somehow she would.

"I'm sorry." His eyes filled with apology. "It can't be done."

She simply gazed at him. How was she going to tell this to Maggie and the Dewberrys? How could she ever make this right to them?

She bit her upper lip and inclined her head. Spine erect with brittle, futile pride, she turned on her heel and walked toward Blackhaw. She needed somewhere to go to cry. And she needed to say good-bye.

Sophia turned her key in Blackhaw's lock, then eased inside. For an interminable time, she leaned against the inside of the door and allowed her gaze to travel over the foyer. The sounds of the house coasted around her. The Dewberrys appeared to be out, and Maggie had yet to return, so without people to enliven the space there was just the music that was uniquely Blackhaw's. A dignified, very quiet music. Punctuated by the creak of the shutter on the second floor and the wheeze of the door behind her as it withstood the wind.

Tears moistened her eyes and slipped free. *Oh, God. This is awful.* The pain of losing Jarrod, of losing this house, twisted like a knife in her belly. She walked into the foyer, glanced at the parlor—and froze.

Blood rushed from her head in a dizzying stream, because there, every glorious inch of his magnificent body slouched in a wing chair, was Jarrod. He was staring into the fire apparently lost in thought, his elbow planted on the armrest, his hand supporting his head. The firelight burnished his profile, the muscular hollow of his cheeks, the grave set of his lips.

He was here. Now she was truly crying, but the tears welled from a deep spring of gratitude. Immeasurable, untappable gratitude. He'd not left on his ship for better places and better women. He'd come here. For her. She didn't know whether to fall to her knees or run and throw herself on top of him and cover his handsome face with kisses.

She did neither. With such an enormous storm of love gusting inside her, the best she could manage was his name. "Jarrod," she said shakily.

He looked up at once. When he saw her standing there, he pushed quickly to his feet, staring at her as if he didn't quite believe she was real. It was exactly how she felt about him.

She tried a smile, but it wobbled badly. "Jarrod, I—"

"No," he said softly. "I've got something to say to you first, and I need you to hear me out."

Unsure whether she could string any syllables together right now anyway, she nodded.

"I apologize for giving you that ultimatum yesterday."

She opened her mouth to speak, but he lifted his hand to stop her words before they could come. "I stood alone on that dock today waiting for you and feeling like a damn idiot. I don't blame you for not coming. Why would you? I finally told the ship to sail." He took two steps toward her, stopped. "The truth is . . ." A troubled expression crossed his face. "Well, the truth is that I'll take you any way I can get you, job or not. I don't even care if you only love me a little, because I swear to you, Sophia, that I love you enough for us both."

Her bottom lip dropped open in astonishment.

He reached into the inside pocket of his suit as he approached her, smiling a self-deprecating smile that fisted around her heart. He stopped at her side, ran a knuckle lovingly down her cheek to wipe away her tears, then flipped open a tiny satin box. "Marry me."

A ring box, she realized, as she gaped at the diamonds sparkling up at her. Lots of diamonds. A huge oval one in the center, surrounded by a circlet of round diamonds— all of them set in a sumptuous bed of platinum.

"Are you going to throw this one back in my face the way you did all the others?" he murmured, humor warming his voice.

"This one," she said, looking up at him, "I'll keep."

He grinned at her, and her belly did a slow flip. He lifted her left hand, kissed the heart of her palm, then slid the ring onto her third finger.

"May I speak now?" she asked.

"May I kiss you now?" he countered, his gaze turning hot as it dropped to her lips.

"No." She planted her hand against his chest. If he so much as nibbled on her ear, all sense would be lost and she wouldn't get a chance to set him right and say what needed to be said. "First of all . . ." She placed her hands on his cheeks, wanting to be sure he could see the truth in her eyes. "First of all, I did go to the dock today. And I don't just love you a little. I love you so much that I went to the dock ready and willing to give up everything, *everything*, for you, including Blackhaw."

He took her head in his hands and kissed her. The contact was sensual and adoring. Endlessly soft. She felt as if they were exchanging souls in that kiss, promising and accepting promises for a thousand golden things to come.

He pulled away just inches, so close their foreheads were still touching. "Tell me you didn't give up Blackhaw for me."

"I did," she said, pulling away just enough so that she could look into his eyes. "And as for my career . . . I thought we did pretty well that night we broke into the stationery shop together. Maybe we can work as a team from now on. Or not. It doesn't matter anymore."

"Tell me, Sophia, that you didn't give up Blackhaw for me."

She laced her fingers into the hair at his nape. "I couldn't pay the taxes on it, so the state auctioned it today at noon, and I couldn't be in two places at once."

He groaned and kissed her forehead, the corner of her eye, her cheek, her earlobe. "I cannot *believe* you gave up Blackhaw for me. Especially because"—he kissed her chin—"I've already taken the liberty of redecorating the great room."

"Redecorating?" she asked. His kisses must have muddled her mind because that made no sense.

Holding her hand snugly in his, he pulled her across the foyer and threw open the door to the great room. Beyond, a cheer arose. Sophia gaped at the assembled crowd. The Dewberrys and Collier sat before a makeshift pulpit someone had doubtless stolen from a local sanctuary. Jarrod's brothers stood to the right of the pulpit, clapping. And Maggie stood to the left, clapping and laughing. A minister stood behind the pulpit, robes in place, Bible in hand. Her favorite flowers, wisteria and daffodils, spilled from vases on pedestals. Garlands of white ribbon swagged the windows.

It looked for all the world like a wedding.

"Are you trying to blackmail me again?" she whispered.

"If it'll work." His expression glinted unrepentantly.

"You're incorrigible."

"You're irresistible."

Delight spun in heady circles inside her. "Will you . . . will you just excuse us for one moment?" Sophia asked the occupants of the great room. She pulled Jarrod into the hall, out of earshot and view. "I'd love to marry you here, now," she said sincerely. "Only I worry about the new owner. I've no idea when he'll arrive to claim this place, and I'd hate for him to interrupt us, for anything to spoil our wedding."

"Sophie," he chided. He smiled and seemed to wait for her to comprehend the joke.

"What?"

"Do you honestly think I'd let this place go?" he asked. "Knowing how much it means to you?"

He was so beautiful and he loved her and he smelled good and he was actually *hers* and maybe that was why she was having trouble understanding. "Jarrod, I spoke with the gentleman who purchased Blackhaw—"

"Tidy fellow. Wears good suits. Bowler hat?"

". . . yes."

"He's Collier's assistant. I couldn't very well send Collier could I, and risk him missing our wedding?"

Shock cleared her thoughts with a powerful sweep. "You knew about the auction?"

"Of course. I've excellent sources. I ought to, I pay them well."

"You bought this house?"

"No, you did. I purchased it for you in your name."

She gazed up at him, stunned.

"I've always had a hankering for this old place," he said, taking in their surroundings before focusing on her once more. "Ever since I begged at its gates as a kid and a little girl in a white dress gave me fruit from her trees."

Goose bumps flowed over her body as she looked into the green eyes of a man and saw in them the green eyes of a scrappy boy. A boy who had been desperately hungry and equally proud and equally determined. The memory slotted into place with what she knew of Jarrod and suddenly she could see it, how that boy had become this magnificent man.

"Speechless?" he asked.

She nodded, thoroughly overcome. Who knew a body could hold this much happiness without shooting like a firework into a million points of light?

"It looks as if I finally found the gift to melt the heart of an ice princess."

"No. It was you who melted my heart." She lifted onto her tiptoes to press a kiss to his lips. "Thank you for my house."

"It's nothing compared to what you've given me." He walked her backward, pressing her against the wall and deepening the kiss.

"How long you going to make us wait?" J. T. yelled from inside the great room.

Jarrod pulled back. Grinned at her. "Shall we?"

She laughed and let herself be drawn to the open doorway. Jarrod's brothers straightened to attention when they saw them. Maggie jerked her besotted gaze from Clint to them, then beamed.

"You sure about this?" Jarrod asked, as he tucked her hand in the crook of his arm. "This will make you the first Mrs. Stone."

"I've had seven years experience handling criminals, Mr. Stone. I believe I can manage you and your brothers."

Jarrod laughed and led her down the aisle.

Dear Reader,

If you've enjoyed the Avon romance you've just read, then you won't want to miss next month's selections. As always, there's a wonderful mix of contemporary and historical romance for you to choose from. And I encourage you to try a book you might not regularly read. (For example, Regency historical readers might want to be brave and give a different setting a try!) I promise that *every* Avon romance is terrific.

Let's begin with Rita Award-winning and *USA Today* bestselling writer Lorraine Heath's THE OUTLAW AND THE LADY. Angela Bainbridge has spent her life dreaming of the perfect marriage . . . but she knows that this will never be. So when she's kidnapped by the notorious Lee Raven she's angry and captivated. His powerful kisses leave her breathless, but can she ever reveal the truth about herself?

If you love medieval romances, then don't miss Margaret Moore's THE MAIDEN AND HER KNIGHT. Beautiful Lady Allis nearly swoons when she first sees the tall, tempting knight Sir Connor. She is duty-bound to wed another, someone of wealth and privilege . . . but how can she resist this tantalizing knight?

Blackboard bestselling author Beverly Jenkins is one of the most exciting writers of African-American historical romance, and her newest book, BEFORE THE DAWN, is a love story you will never forget. Leah Barnett can't believe how fate has taken her from genteel Boston to the towering Colorado Rockies . . . and into the arms of angry, ruggedly sexy Ryder Damien.

Readers of contemporary romance should not miss Michelle Jerott's HER BODYGUARD. Michelle's books are hot, hot, hot . . . and here, pert pretty Lili Kavanaugh hires sexy Matt Hawkins as her bodyguard—and soon finds herself wanting more from this tough guy than his protection.

Until next month, happy reading!

Lucia Macro

Lucia Macro
Executive Editor

REL 0901

Avon Romances—
the best in exceptional authors
and unforgettable novels!

MEET ME AT MIDNIGHT   by Suzanne Enoch
0-380-80917-6/ $5.99 US/ $7.99 Can

ALWAYS HER HERO   by Adrienne Dewolfe
0-380-80528-6/ $5.99 US/ $7.99 Can

HIS FORBIDDEN TOUCH   by Linda O'brien
0-380-81343-2/ $5.99 US/ $7.99 Can

A WANTED WOMAN   by Rebecca Wade
0-380-81618-0/ $5.99 US/ $7.99 Can

NIGHT OF FIRE   by Barbara Samuel
0-06-101391-9/ $5.99 US/ $7.99 Can

IMPROPER ADVANCES   by Margaret E. Porter
0-380-80773-4/ $5.99 US/ $7.99 Can

A BELATED BRIDE   by Karen Hawkins
0-380-81525-7/ $5.99 US/ $7.99 Can

THE WICKED ONE   by Danelle Harmon
0-380-80909-5/ $5.99 US/ $7.99 Can

MASTER OF DESIRE   by Kinley MacGregor
0-06-108713-0/ $5.99 US/ $7.99 Can

OUTLAW'S BRIDE   by Maureen McKade
0-380-81566-4/ $5.99 US/ $7.99 Can

THE LAWMAN'S SURRENDER   by Debra Mullins
0-380-80775-0/ $5.99 US/ $7.99 Can

HIS FORBIDDEN KISS   by Margaret Moore
0-380-81335-1/ $5.99 US/ $7.99 Can

Available wherever books are sold or please call 1-800-331-3761
to order.   ROM 0301